OFFICIAL BASEBALL GUIDE for 1981

•

PUBLISHER
C. C. JOHNSON SPINK

EDITORS
**LARRY WIGGE
CARL CLARK
CRAIG CARTER
JOE MARCIN**

•

PUBLISHED BY

The Sporting News

1212 North Lindbergh Boulevard
P. O. Box 56
St. Louis, Missouri 63166

Copyright © 1981
The Sporting News Publishing Company
a Times Mirror company

ISBN 0-89204-071-8
ISSN 0078-3838

51

Directory of Organized Baseball

MAJOR LEAGUES

COMMISSIONER—Bowie K. Kuhn
SECRETARY-TREASURER—Alexander H. Hadden
HEADQUARTERS—75 Rockefeller Plaza
New York, N. Y. 10019
Telephone—586-7400 (area code 212)
Teletype—710-581-4279

EXECUTIVE COUNCIL—Bowie K. Kuhn, Commissioner; Leland S. Mac-Phail, Jr., President of American League; Charles S. Feeney, President of National League; John E. Fetzer, Edmund B. Fitzgerald, Ewing Kauffman and Haywood C. Sullivan, representatives of American League, and Daniel M. Galbreath, Robert L. Howsam, Robert A. Lurie and Peter F. O'Malley, representatives of National League.

EXECUTIVE DIRECTOR OF MARKETING AND BROADCASTING—
C. J. (Tom) Villante
ADMINISTRATOR—William A. Murray
SPECIAL ASSISTANTS TO THE COMMISSIONER—
Joseph L. Reichler, Monte Irvin
DIRECTOR OF INFORMATION—Robert A. Wirz
DIRECTOR OF SECURITY—Horace J. (Harry) Gibbs
CONTROLLER—Donald C. Marr, Jr.
CO-ORDINATOR OF INTER-AMERICAN BASEBALL—Pedro Arias
ASSISTANT TO ADMINISTRATOR—George E. Pfister
ADMINISTRATIVE ASSISTANTS—Harry Simmons, Miguel A. Rodriguez
ASSISTANT COUNSEL—Edwin M. Durso
ASSOCIATE DIRECTOR OF INFORMATION, MEDIA—Charles B. Adams
ASSISTANT DIRECTOR OF INFORMATION, PUBLICATIONS—Vince Nauss
ASSISTANT DIRECTOR OF SECURITY—Art Fuss
OFFICE MANAGER—Mary Ann Burns
BOOKKEEPER—Rita Datz

NATIONAL ASSOCIATION REPRESENTATIVES—John Johnson, President of the National Association, and members of National Association Executive Committee.

NATIONAL ASSOCIATION
OF PROFESSIONAL BASEBALL LEAGUES

PRESIDENT-TREASURER—John H. Johnson
VICE-PRESIDENT—John Moss
ADMINISTRATOR OF ASSOCIATION TRANSACTION—Don Avery
CONSULTANT FOR CLASS A CLUBS—Robert L. Freitas
HEADQUARTERS—201 Bayshore Dr. S.E., P. O. Box A
St. Petersburg, Fla. 33731
Telephone—822-6937 (area code 813)
Teletype—810-863-0361

EXECUTIVE COMMITTEE—John Moss, Chairman, President of the South Atlantic League; Carl Sawatski, President of the Texas League; Harold M. Cooper, President of the International League.

TABLE OF CONTENTS

For Index to Contents See Page 600

(Index to Minor League Cities on Page 601)

ON THE COVER: National League Cy Young Award winner STEVE CARLTON of the Philadelphia Phillies. Carlton fashioned 24-9 record in 1980 and pitched decisive victory over Kansas City Royals in World Series to give Phillies their first World Championship ever.

Photo by Richard Pilling

A jubilant MIKE SCHMIDT, 1980 World Series MVP, leaps into the arms of his celebrating teammates after the Phillies defeated the Royals for their first world championship.

NATIONAL LEAGUE

Including

Club Directories

Club Reviews of 1980 Season

Club Day-by-Day Scores

N. L. Team Pictures

1980 League Leaders

1980 Official N. L. Averages

All-Time N. L. Player Performance Tables

CHARLES S. FEENEY
President of the National League

National League

Organized 1876

CHARLES S. FEENEY
President and Treasurer

JOHN J. McHALE
Vice-President

PHYLLIS B. COLLINS
Secretary

BLAKE CULLEN
Administrator and Public Relations Director

KATY FEENEY
Assistant Public Relations Director

LOUIS H. KREMS
Business Manager

ROSE TROTTA
Computer Manager

JOSEPHINE TROY
Administrative Assistant

Headquarters—1 Rockefeller Plaza, New York, N. Y. 10020

Telephone—582-4213 (area code 212)

UMPIRES—Fred Brocklander, Nick Colosi, Jerry Crawford, Jerry Dale, David Davidson, Robert Engel, Steve Fields, Bruce Froemming, Eric Gregg, Lanny Harris, H. Douglas Harvey, John Kibler, John McSherry, Ed Montague, Andy Olsen, Dave Pallone, Paul Pryor, Frank Pulli, Jim Quick, Lawrence (Dutch) Rennert, Paul Runge, Dick Stello, Terry Tata, Ed Vargo, Harry Wendelstedt, Joe West, Lee Weyer, William G. Williams.

OFFICIAL STATISTICIANS—Elias Sports Bureau, Inc., 500 5th Ave., Suite 2114, New York, N. Y. 10036. Telephone (212) 869-1530.

Players cannot be transferred from one major league club to another after June 15 to the close of the championship season except through regular waiver channels.

WAIVER PRICE, $20,000. Interleague waivers, $20,000, except for selected players and draft-excluded players.

ATLANTA BRAVES

Chairman of the Board—William C. Bartholomay

President—R. E. (Ted) Turner III
Executive Vice-President—Allison Thornwell
Vice-President-General Manager—John Mullen
Vice-President, Player Development—Hank Aaron
Asst. General Manager—Patrick Nugent
Director of Scouting—Paul Snyder
Manager of Broadcast Sales—Wayne Long
Director of Broadcasting—Ernie Johnson
Vice-President & Controller—Charles Sanders
Accountant—Michael Warren
Ticket Distribution Manager—Ed Newman
Director Public Relations, Promotions—Wayne Minshew
Ticket Manager—Kris Krebs
Group Sales Manager—Andre DeLorenzo
Director of Stadium Operations—Joe Shirley
Administrative Assistant—Mary Beth Fay
Manager—Bobby Cox
Club Physician—Dr. David T. Watson
Executive Offices—P. O. Box 4064, Atlanta, Ga. 30302
Telephone—522-7630 (area code 404)

SCOUTS—Mike Arbuckle, Sam Berry, Smokey Burgess, Stu Cann, Joe Caputo, Lou Fitzgerald, Pedro Gonzales, John Groth, Chuck Harmon, Willie Harris, Gene Hassell, Herb Hippauf, Phil Holmes, Burney R. (Dickey) Martin, Bob Mavis, Rance Pless, Charles Silvera, Charles Smith, Tony Stiel, Bob Turzilli, Bob Wadsworth, Wesley Westrum, William R. Wight, Don Williams, H. F. (Red) Wooten.

PARK LOCATION—Atlanta-Fulton County Stadium, on Capitol Avenue at the junction of Interstate Highways 20, 75 and 85.

Seating capacity—52,532

FIELD DIMENSIONS—Home plate to left field at foul line, 330 feet; to center field, 402 feet; to right field at foul line, 330 feet.

CHICAGO CUBS

Chairman of the Executive Committee—William Wrigley

President, Chief Executive Officer & Treasurer—Wm. J. Hagenah, Jr.
Executive Vice-President—Robert D. Kennedy
Assistant to Executive Vice-President—John Cox
Vice-President—Park Operations & Secretary—E. R. Saltwell
Honorary Vice-President—Charles Grimm
Assistant Secretary—Claude Brooks
Assistant Director of Park Operations—Dennis Beyreuther
Chief Accounting Officer—Joseph Kirchen
Director of Player Development—C. V. Davis
Director of Scouting—Vedie Himsl
Traveling Secretary & Statistician—Jim Davidovich
Assistant Traveling Secretary—G. A. Settergren
Home Secretary—Howard Roberts
Director of Information & Marketing—Buck Peden
Community Relations—Ernie Banks
Director of Ticket Services—Jerome Foran
Manager of Group Sales—Ernie Banks
Manager of Group Services—Dave Lamont
Grounds Superintendent—Roy Bogren
Manager—Preston Gomez
Club Physician—Dr. Jacob Suker
Executive Offices—Wrigley Field, N. Clark and Addison Streets,
Chicago, Ill. 60613
Telephone—281-5050 (area code 312)

SCOUTS—Dave Bartosch, William Capps, Frank DeMoss, Walt Dixon, Eugene Handley, Herman Hannah, Bob Hartsfield, John Hennessy, Roy Johnson, Bill Jurges, Robert D. Kennedy, Jr., Eddie Lyons, Julio Navarro, John (Buck) O'Neil, Evo Pusich, Pete Reiser, Reuben Rodriguez, Fred J. Shaffer, George Silvey, Gene Thompson, Joaquin Velilla, Harrison Wickel, H. D. (Rube) Wilson, Pedrin Zorrilla.

PARK LOCATION—Wrigley Field, Addison Street, N. Clark Street, Waveland Avenue and Sheffield Avenue.

Seating capacity—37,241

FIELD DIMENSIONS—Home plate to left field at foul line, 355 feet; to center field, 400 feet; to right field at foul line, 353 feet.

CINCINNATI REDS

Chairmen—James R. Williams, William J. Williams
Vice-Chairman—Robert L. Howsam
President & Chief Executive Officer—Richard Wagner
Vice-President/Marketing—Roger Ruhl
Vice-President/Player Personnel—Sheldon Bender
Vice-President/Scouting—Joe Bowen
Treasurer—James R. Williams
Secretary—Henry W. Hobson Jr.
Business Manager—Don Tecklenburg
Special Assignment Scout—Ray Shore
Assistant General Manager—Woody Woodward
Director of Publicity—Jim Ferguson
Controller—D. L. Porco
Business Coordinator, Player Development—Sal Artiaga
Traveling Secretary—Doug Bureman
Director of Speakers Bureau—Gordy Coleman
Director of Stadium Operations—Doug Duennes
Director of Group Sales—Charlie Taylor
Director of Special Projects—Bob Kruetzkamp
Director of Season Tickets & Customer Relations—Janet Wendel
Director of Publications—John Olberding
Director of Ticket Department—Bill Stewart
Director of Broadcasting—Jim Winters
Manager—John McNamara
Club Physician—Dr. George Ballou
Executive Offices—100 Riverfront Stadium, Cincinnati, O. 45202
Telephone—421-4510 (area code 513)

SCOUTS—Larry Barton, Jr., Gene Bennett, Porter Blinn, David Calaway, Bill Clark, Marty Daily, Larry D'Amato, Reno DeBenedetti, Larry Doughty, Elmer Gray, Edwin Howsam, Chester Montgomery, Ed Roebuck, Johnny Sierra, Neil Summers, Fred Uhlman, George Zuraw.

PARK LOCATION—Riverfront Stadium, downtown Cincinnati, bounded by Second Street to Ohio River and from Walnut Street to Broadway.

Seating capacity—52,392

FIELD DIMENSIONS—Home plate to left field at foul line, 330 feet; to center field, 404 feet; to right field at foul line, 330 feet.

HOUSTON ASTROS

Board of Directors—John J. McMullen, Jack T. Trotter,
T. H. Neyland
President & General Manager—Albert L. Rosen
Administrative Asst. to the President & Traveling Secretary—
Donald Davidson
Assistant General Manager—Anthony G. Siegle
Director of Minor League Operations—William J. Wood
Director of Scouting—Lynwood Stallings
Coordinator of Minor League Instruction—Bob Cluck
Director of Publicity—Edward A. Wade
Assistant Director of Publicity—Rick Rivers
Director of Broadcasting & Promotions—Art Elliott
Promotions, Scoreboard Operations—Paul Darst
Broadcast & Promotions Sales—Hugh Pickett
Director of Ticket Sales—Larry Dierker
Manager, Season Ticket Sales—M. M. "Buddy" Hancken
Manager, Group Sales—Larry Serota
Administrative Asst., Major League Operations—
Sandra Zimmerman
Secretary, Minor League Operations and Scouting—
Brenda Derese
Secretary, Publicity—Beverly Rains
Club Physicians—Drs. Harold H. Brelsford, Hatch Cummings
Director of Physical Conditioning—Dr. A. Eugene Coleman
Public Address Announcer—J. Fred Duckett
Field Manager—Bill Virdon
Executive Offices—Astrodome, P.O. Box 288
Houston, Tex. 77001
Telephone—799-9500 (area code 713)
Teletype—901 991-1740
HOUSTON SPORTS ASSOCIATION, INC.
President & Chief Operating Officer—Robert G. Harter
Vice-President, Administration—E. Michael Crowley
Vice-President, Engineering—W. Gary Keller
Vice-President, Public Relations & Advertising—James H. Weidler
Treasurer—A. Eugene Stoffel
Exec. V.P., Astrodome-Astrohall Stadium Corp.—Jimmie D. Fore
Controller—Adam C. Richards
Financial Analyst—Bill Boyd
Ticket Manager—Charles T. Wall
SCOUTS—Clary Anderson, Stan Benjamin, Paul Florence, Carl Greene,
Stan Hollmig, Gerry Hunsicker, David Lakey, Gordon Lakey, Walter Matthews, John Miller, Tony Pacheco, Paul Weaver, Julio Linares, William Melendez, Domingo Mercedes, Fernando Tatis.
PARK LOCATION—Astrodome, Kirby and Interstate Loop 610
Seating capacity—45,000
FIELD DIMENSIONS—Home plate to left field at foul line, 340 feet; to
center field, 406 feet; to right field at foul line, 340 feet.

LOS ANGELES DODGERS

BOARD OF DIRECTORS

Peter O'Malley, President; Harry M. Bardt, Treasurer;
Roland Seidler, Jr., Secretary; Mrs. Roland (Terry) Seidler

President—Peter O'Malley
Vice-President, Player Personnel—Al Campanis
Vice-President, Public Relations and Promotions—Fred Claire
Vice-President, Minor League Operations—William P. Schweppe
Vice-President, Marketing—Merritt Willey
Special Consultant—Walter Alston
Controller and Assistant Treasurer—Ken Hasemann
Assistant Secretary—Irene Tanji
Director, Advertising, Novelties and Souvenirs—Danny Goodman
Director, Dodgertown—Charles Blaney
Director, Stadium Operations—Bob Smith
Director, Ticket Department—Walter Nash
Director, Stadium Club and Transportation—Bob Schenz
Director, Dodger Network—David Van de Walker
Director, Scouting—Ben Wade
Director, Publicity—Steve Brener
Director, Community Relations—Don Newcombe
Community Relations—Roy Campanella
Director, Ticket Marketing—Barry Stockhamer
Director, Speakers' Bureau—Bill Shumard
Executive Pilot, Dodger 720-B Fan Jet—Captain Lewis G. Carlisle
Administrative Assistant—Ike Ikuhara
Traveling Secretary—Billy DeLury
Auditor—Michael Strange
Manager—Tom Lasorda
Club Physicians—Dr. Frank Jobe, Dr. Robert Woods
Executive Offices—Dodger Stadium, 1000 Elysian Park Avenue,
Los Angeles, Calif. 90012.
Telephone—224-1500 (area code 213)

SCOUTS—Rafael Avila, Boyd Bartley, Bob Bishop, Gib Bodet, Mike
Brito, Paul Duval, Jim Garland, Dennis Haren, Gail Henley, Goldie Holt,
Elvio Jimenez, Tony John, Hank Jones, John Keenan, Ron King, Ed
Liberatore, Carl Lowenstine, Dale McReynolds, Charlie Metro, Tommy
Mixon, John O'Neil, Regie Otero, Medardo Perez, Bill Pleis, Jerry Stephenson, Corito Varona, Guy Wellman.

PARK LOCATION—Dodger Stadium, 1000 Elysian Park Avenue.

Seating capacity—56,000

FIELD DIMENSIONS—Home plate to left field at foul line, 330 feet;
to center field, 395 feet; to right field at foul line, 330 feet.

MONTREAL EXPOS

Board of Directors—Charles R. Bronfman, Lorne C. Webster, John J. McHale, Sydney Maislin, Paul Beaudry, Hugh Hallward, Charlemagne Beaudry, E. Leo Kolber, Melvin W. Griffin, Louis R. Desmarais, Arnold Ludwick, Honorary Treasurer

Chairman of the Board—Charles R. Bronfman
President and Chief Executive Officer—John J. McHale
Vice-President, Player Development—James Fanning
Vice-President, Secretary-Treasurer—Harry J. Renaud
Director of Scouting—Danny Menendez
Administrative Assistant, Player Relations—Gene Kirby
Director, Team Travel—Peter Durso
Head Scout, Canada—Ronald Piche
Publicists—Monique Giroux, Richard Griffin
Director, Business Operations—Gerry Trudeau
Concession Manager—Joseph Boire
Manager, Game Services—Gilles Rochefort
Manager, Marketing & Business Development—Normand Martin
Manager, Special Events & Community Relations—Rodger Brulotte
Manager, Group Business Development—Roger Savard
Manager, Group Sales—Suzanne Lemoignan
Manager—Dick Williams
Club Physician—Dr. Robert Brodrick
Mailing Address—P. O. Box 500, Station M, Montreal, Quebec, Canada H1V 3P2
Telephone—253-3434 (area code 514)

SCOUTS—(special assignment)—Charlie Fox, Carroll (Whitey) Lockman, Ed Lopat; (regular)—Bill Adair, Terry Boyle, Harry Bright, Al Harper, Mercer Harris, Dick Lemay, Walter Millies, John (Red) Murff, Herb Newberry, Bob Oldis, Jack Paepke, Harry Postove, Jack Warner; (Canadian)—Wayne Norton.

PARK LOCATION—Olympic Stadium, 4545 Pierre de Coubertin, Montreal, Quebec, Canada H1V 3N7.

Seating capacity—58,838

FIELD DIMENSIONS—Home plate to left field at foul line, 325 feet; to center field, 404 feet; to right field at foul line, 325.

NEW YORK METS

Chairman of the Board—Nelson Doubleday

Directors—Nelson Doubleday, Fred Wilpon, Walter E. Freese
John W. O'Donnell, Steve O'Neil, John T. Sargent
President & Chief Executive Officer—Fred Wilpon
Executive Vice-President, General Manager & Chief Operating Officer—
J. Frank Cashen
Vice-President-Administration—James Nagourney
Vice-President, Baseball Operations—James Lou Gorman
Vice-President—Alan E. Harazin
Controller—Harold W. O'Shaughnessy
Special Assistant to the General Manager & Team
Travel Director—Arthur Richman
Director of Scouting—Joseph McIlvaine
Ticket Manager—Bob Mandt
Director of Minor League Operations—Chris Kager
Director of Public Relations—Jay Horwitz
Director of Promotions—Joseph Donohue
Stadium Manager—John McCarthy
Stadium Superintendant—Samuel Nelson
Manager—Joe Torre
Club Physican—Dr. James C. Parkes II
Team Trainer—Larry Mayol
Executive Offices—William A. Shea Stadium, Roosevelt
Avenue and 126th Street, Flushing, N. Y. 11368
Telephone—672-2000 (area code 212)

SCOUTS—Ed Charles, Nino Escalera, Joe Frazier, Carmen Fusco,
Roger Jongewaard, Hank Kelly, Buddy Kerr, Dave Madison, Joe Mason,
Harry Minor, Julian Morgan, Roy Partee, Terry Ryan, Marvin Scott, Jim
Terrell, Eddy Toledo, Ollie Vanek, Bob Wellman, Len Zanke.

PARK LOCATION—William A. Shea Stadium, Roosevelt Avenue and
126th Street, Flushing, N. Y. 11368

Ticket Information—672-3000 (area code 212)

Seating capacity—55,300

FIELD DIMENSIONS—Home plate to left field at foul line, 338 feet;
to center field, 410 feet; to right field at foul line, 338 feet.

PHILADELPHIA PHILLIES

Chairman of Board—R. R. M. (Bob) Carpenter, Jr.

President—R. R. M. (Ruly) Carpenter III
Executive Vice-President—William Y. Giles
Vice-President-Director of Player Personnel—Paul Owens
Vice-President-Director of Finance—George F. H. Harrison
Secretary-Treasurer—G. Theodore Harrison
Director of Minor Leagues & Scouting—Jim Baumer
Asst. Director of Minor Leagues and Scouting—Jack Pastore
Administrative Assistant—Keith Carpenter
Director of Sales—David P. Montgomery
Director of Publicity and Public Relations—Larry Shenk
Ticket Manager—Raymond B. Krise
Director of Advertising—Thomas T. Hudson
Director of Promotions—Frank H. Sullivan
Director of Stadium Operations—Patrick J. Cassidy
Traveling Secretary—Eddie Ferenz
Director of Group Sales—Richard Deats
Director of Season Ticket Sales—Ray Krise, Jr.
Executive Secretary, Minor Leagues—William V. Gargano
Assistant Director of Publicity and Public Relations—
Chris Wheeler
Public Relations Assistant-Director of Radio Network—
Dennis Lehman
National Scouting Supervisor—Brandy Davis
Special Scouting Assistant—Hugh Alexander
Manager—Dallas Green
Club Physician—Dr. Phillip Marone
Executive Offices—Philadelphia Veterans Stadium
Mailing Address—P. O. Box 7575, Philadelphia, Pa. 19101
Telephone—463-6000 (area code 215)

SCOUTS—Hugh Alexander, Edward Bockman, George Bradley, Keith Carpenter, George Farson, Doug Gassaway, Charles Gault, Gordon Goldsberry, Bill Harper, Wilbur Johnson, John Jorgensen, Lou Kahn, Dick Lawlor, Anthony Lucadello, Ben Marmo, Gene Martin, Gary Nickels, Tom Oliver, Ken Parker, Bob Reasonover, Scott Reid, Joe Reilly, Tony Roig, Andy Seminick, Billy Tracy, Elmer Valo, Randy Waddill, Don Williams.

PARK LOCATION—Philadelphia Veterans Stadium, Broad Street and Pattison Avenue.

Seating capacity—65,454

FIELD DIMENSIONS—Home plate to left field at foul line, 330 feet; to center field, 408 feet; to right field at foul line, 330 feet.

PITTSBURGH PIRATES

President—Daniel M. Galbreath

Chairman of the Board—John W. Galbreath
Executive Vice-President—Harding Peterson
Vice-President/Administration—Joseph M. O'Toole
Vice-President/Public Relations and Marketing—Jack Schrom
Assistant to the Vice-Presidents—Milt Graff
Director of Publicity—Joseph Safety
Administrative Assistant/Publicity—Sally O'Leary
Publicity Assistant—Tom Bird
Director of Minor League Clubs and Scouting—Murray Cook
Assistant Director of Minor League Clubs and Scouting—
Branch B. Rickey III
Assistant Farm Director—William G. Turner
Assistant Director of Scouting—Jon Neiderer
Director of Sales and Advertising—Olin J. Depolo
Assistant Director of Group and Season Sales—Jack H. Berger
Assistant Director of Group and Season Sales—Steve Greenberg
Director of Promotions—Steve Schanwald
Treasurer/Assistant Secretary—Douglas G. McCormick
Assistant to the Treasurer—Kenneth C. Curcio
Ticket Manager—Richard C. Holland
Manager—Chuck Tanner
Traveling Secretary—Charles Muse
Club Physician—Dr. Joseph Coroso
Executive Offices—Three Rivers Stadium, 600 Stadium Circle
Pittsburgh, Pa. 15212
Telephone—323-5000 (area code 412)

SPECIAL ASSIGNMENT SCOUTS—Gene Baker, Babe Barberis, Joe L. Brown, Pablo Cruz, George Detore, Jerry Gardner, Fred Goodman, Howie Haak, Carlton Keller, Jim Maxwell, Mike Mulleady, Lenny Yochim.

SCOUTING ASSISTANTS—Ossie Alvarez, Ed Bakale, Bud Baurle, Calvin Biron, Willie Bojos, Paul Bordi, Bill Bryan, Dave Buccolo, Joe Buccolo, F. "Kid" Carr, Bill Cayavec, Frank Coimbre, Cecil Cole, Nick Creola, Bob Dawson, Ed Farnum, Charles Fletcher, Jim Frail, Pete Grasso, Fred Hannum, Leroy Hill, Bud Hoff, Myron Hunt, Bob Johnson, Jim Lehman, Jose Luna, Harry Miller, Andy Moynihan, Tom Myers, John Nix, Boyd Odom, Steve Oleschuk, Ed Olivares, Elmo Plaskett, Dick Probola, Ron Rahr, Harold Ray, Doug Robbins, Ken Saybel, George Schmidt, John Sloan, Jesse Smith, Lloyd Sorrells, Les Stewart, Cloy Sykes, Tom Urich, Roy Velasco, Tom Venditelli, Bill White, Bill Wigle, Ed Zeidler, Jack Zilles.

PARK LOCATION—Three Rivers Stadium, 600 Stadium Circle.

Seating capacity—54,499

FIELD DIMENSIONS—Home plate to left field at foul line, 335 feet; to center field, 400 feet; to right field at foul line, 335 feet.

ST. LOUIS CARDINALS

Chairman of the Board, President and Chief Executive Officer—
August A. Busch, Jr.

Vice-President—August A. Busch, III
Vice-President—Fred L. Kuhlmann
Vice-President—Margaret M. Snyder
Secretary and Treasurer—John L. Hayward
Assistant Secretary—Richard Schwartz
Assistant Treasurer—H. F. Suellentrop
General Manager-Manager—Whitey Herzog
Executive Assistant-Baseball—Joe McDonald
Executive Vice-President, Business Affairs—Joe McShane
Senior Vice-President—Stan Musial
Vice-President-Public Relations—Jim Toomey
Executive Assistant-Business—Gary Blase
Traveling Secretary—C. J. Cherre
Director of Player Development—Lee Thomas
Director of Scouting—Fred McAlister
Ticket Director—Mike Bertani
Director of Promotions—Marty Hendin
Director of Sales—Joe Cunningham
Director of Operations, Minor Leagues—Paul Fauks
Assistant Director of Public Relations—Robin Monsky
Club Physician—Dr. Stan London
Executive Offices—Busch Memorial Stadium, 250 Stadium
Plaza, St. Louis, Mo. 63102
Telephone—421-3060 (area code 314)

SCOUTS—Jose Arias, Ted Baker, James Belz, Vern Benson, Cameron Bonifay, Red Brown, Eddie Collins, Walker Cress, Roberto Diaz, Cecil Espy, Angel Figueroa, Gary Gilmore, Ray Goodman, Mark Hammond, George Hasser, Don Hennelly, James Holden, Bob Holmes, Fred Jiminez, Roland Johnson, James Johnston, Earl Jones, Marty Keough, Henry Krause, Thornton Lee, Tom McCormack, Ben McLure, Martin Maier, Virgil Melvin, Mo Mozzali, Carlos Negron, Jerry Oswald, Jim Rivers, Mike Roberts, James Robinson, John Rotman, William Sayles, Larry Schultz, Bart Shelly, John Skurski, Hal Smith, Marvin Stendel, John Tatum, Eddie Taylor, Charles (Tim) Thompson, Charles Thompson, Jr., Bill Warren.

PARK LOCATION—Busch Memorial Stadium, Broadway, Walnut Street, Stadium Plaza and Spruce Street.

Seating capacity—50,100

FIELD DIMENSIONS—Home plate to left field at foul line, 330 feet; to center field, 414 feet; to right field at foul line, 330 feet.

SAN DIEGO PADRES

Owner & Chairman Board of Directors—Ray Kroc
Director—Joan Kroc

President & Director—Ballard Smith
Director of Baseball Operations—Jack McKeon
Director of Business Operations—Elten Schiller
Controller—Roberto Martinez
Director, Minor League Operations—Jim Weigel
Director of Scouting—Bob Fontaine Jr.
Director of Public Relations—Bob Chandler
Director of Communications—Jerry Coleman
Director of Promotions—Andy Strasberg
Director of Group Sales—Tom Mulcahy
Director of Merchandising—John Worcester
Traveling Secretary—John Mattei
Trainer—Dick Dent
Manager—Frank Howard
Club Physician—Scripps Clinic
Executive Offices—P. O. Box 2000, San Diego, Calif. 92120
Telephone—283-4494 (area code 714)

SCOUTS—Supervisors: Ken Bracey, Bill Bryk, Joe Cusick, Cliff Ditto, Denny Galehouse, Dick Hager, Jack Hays, Al Heist, Jim Marshall, Bob Miller, Luis Rosa, Brad Sloan, Ed Stevens, Gary Sutherland, Jim Zerilla; Aquiles Angulo, Jose A. Casino, Billy Castell, Grisha Davida, Bill Earnhart, Tony Garcia, Bud Grainger, Lin Hamilton, John Herbold, Edgar Jewell, Jay Lowers, Clyde McCullough, Bill McKeon, Kelly McKeon, Brian Peterson, Andy Pienovi, Bob Polewski, Bob Stamsos, Bob Warner, Hank Zacharias.

PARK LOCATION—San Diego Stadium, 9949 Friars Road

Seating capacity—51,309

FIELD DIMENSIONS—Home plate to left field at foul line, 330 feet; to center field, 420 feet; to right field at foul line, 330 feet.

SAN FRANCISCO GIANTS

President—Robert A. Lurie

Executive Assistant to the President—Corey Busch
Vice-President, Baseball Operations—H. B. "Spec" Richardson
Vice-President, Business Operations—Pat Gallagher
Director of Scouting and Minor League Operations—
Jack Schwarz
Field Director of Player Development—Tom Haller
Director of Player Personnel—Bob Fontaine
Baseball Consultant—Jerry Donovan
Director of Travel—Frank Bergonzi
Traveling Secretary/Statistician—Ralph Nelson
Director of Publicity—Duffy Jennings
Director of Community and Public Relations—Stu Smith
Ticket Manager—Arthur Schulze
Director of Promotions—Charles S. Feeney Jr.
Marketing Manager—Larry Baer
Speakers Bureau—Joe Orengo
Accouting Manager—Ron Mosher
Director of Stadium Operations—Don Foreman
Director of Season Ticket Sales—Lloyd McGovern
Director of Group Sales—Ben Oakes
Manager—Frank Robinson
Executive Offices—Candlestick Park, San Francisco, Calif. 94124
Telephone—468-3700 (area code 415)

SCOUTS—John D. (Dutch) Anderson, Mark Conkin, Larry DeHaven, Morris A. (Dutch) Deutsch, Hugh East, Robert Folkins, George Genovese, Grady Hatton, Joseph W. Henderson, Carl Hubbell, Richard G. (Richie) Klaus, Harvey Koepf, Jim Lyke, Horacio Martinez, Roger Metzger, Marty Miller, Dennis Mizzi, Edward F. (Eddie) Montague, Hugh Poland, Veto Ramirez, Del Rice, Walter Ripley, Lazaro Ruiz, Hank Sauer (also batting instructor), Larry Shepard, Richard (Dick) Wilson.

PARK LOCATION—Candlestick Point, Bayshore Freeway.

Seating capacity—58,000

FIELD DIMENSIONS—Home plate to left field at foul line, 335 feet; to center field, 410 feet; to right field at foul line, 335 feet.

Down the stretch, TUG McGRAW was the ace out of the bullpen for the Phillies. Here the Philadelphia lefthander jumps for joy after saving sixth and final game of World Series.

EAST DIVISION

Phillies Finally Reached Promised Land

By HAL BODLEY

The Philadelphia Phillies were born in 1883, but not until 1980 did they finally reach the Promised Land.

In one of the most exciting finishes of any baseball season, the Phillies first surged to their fourth National League East Division title in five years by ousting Montreal on the penultimate day of the regular campaign, 6-4, in 11 tense innings in the rain and cold at Olympic Stadium in Montreal.

The Phillies used comeback after comeback to win the Championship Series, shocking Houston in the often bizarre best-of-five showdown. That victory landed them in their first World Series since 1950 and only the second in the franchise's not-so-proud history.

They won the first two World Series games against Kansas City at Veterans Stadium, but when the event moved to Missouri, the Royals quickly pulled even. The Phils, however, staged another of their comebacks in the fifth game and returned home to nail down their first World Championship by taking Game 6, 4-1, behind the outstanding pitching of Cy Young Award winner Steve Carlton and relief hero Tug McGraw. Mike Schmidt, who was named MVP in the Series as well as the N.L. regular season, was the batting hero in the clincher that set off a celebration that lasted for weeks in the Delaware Valley.

The Phillies did it by winning six of their last seven games and 19 of 27 to finish with a 91-71 record, a game ahead of second-place Montreal, which had led the division most of the year.

The Phils were 50-36 after the All-Star break and won 21 of their final 31 road games to finish 42-39 for the season in that department.

But the key might have been their one-run victories, a hint that the relief corps, especially McGraw, did the job down the stretch. The Phils were 12-4 in one-run games after September 1, 32-28 for the season.

The Phils won six of seven extra-inning games after August 11 and nine of their last 11.

After coming off the disabled list on July 19, the 36-year-old McGraw had a 5-1 record, 13 saves and an 0.52 ERA. Overall, he was 5-4 in 57 games and had 20 saves, including five in September and October.

And then there was Carlton, whose 24-9 record and 2.34 ERA earned him his third Cy Young Award. He also led the majors in strikeouts with 286.

Schmidt set a major league record for home runs by a third baseman with 48 and led the league in runs batted in (121), slugging percentage (.624) and total bases (342).

Much of the credit for the Phillies' success had to go to Dallas Green, the career front-office man who took over for Danny Ozark as manager the final month of 1979.

In the beginning, the players did not accept Green's team concept. They snickered when they arrived at spring training and saw signs in the clubhouse bearing his much-publicized "We, not I" theme.

"When are the pompon girls arriving?" asked shortstop Larry Bowa,

PHILADELPHIA PHILLIES—1980

Seated in front—Bush, batboy; Watts, ball boy; Anderson, batboy; Cera, assistant clubhouse manager; Seger, trainer; Cooper, assistant trainer; Bush, clubhouse manager. Front row—Smith, Aviles, Ryan, coach; DeMars, coach; Starrette, coach; Green, manager; Elia, coach; Wine, coach; Amaro, coach; Bowa, Gross. Third row—Ferenz, traveling secretary; Ruthven, G. Vukovich, McGraw, Trillo, Unser, Boone, Maddox, Moreland, Larson, Rose, Luzinski, McBride, Owens, vice-president and director of player personnel. Top row—King, batting practice pitcher; Saucier, Lerch, Reed, Walk, Carlton, LaGrow, Noles, Schmidt, J. Vukovich, Hoefling, stretch and flexibility instructor.

which just about summed up many of the players' reactions to Green's philosophies.

Criticism didn't bother Green. He stuck by his guns. He hurt a few feelings, dented a few egos and returned the Phillies to the highest perch in the N.L. East.

He did it with a blend of multi-talented veterans and hungry, eager youngsters.

He did it with Carlton winning 24 of his 33 decisions, but he also did it with Dick Ruthven coming off 1979 elbow surgery to post a 17-10 record and a 3.55 ERA.

Aside from aces Carlton and Ruthven, Green got big boosts from rookie righthanders Bob Walk and Marty Bystrom. Walk, with the team most of the year, was 11-7. Bystrom, a September call-up, was 5-0 with a 1.50 ERA.

During the winter of 1979, Player Personnel Director Paul Owens and Green searched high and low for bullpen help. They came close to landing Sparky Lyle from the Texas Rangers during the winter meetings, but the deal was snuffed because of a clause in Lyle's contract that guaranteed him a broadcasting job with the Rangers at $50,000 a year for 10 seasons after his retirement as a player.

As irony would have it, the Phils finally landed Lyle in mid-September and he saved a pair of games.

Right fielder Bake McBride, mentioned in the original deal for Lyle, hit .309 and drove in a career-high 87 runs.

On Monday night, September 29, after losing two out of three to the Expos at the Vet to fall out of first place, the Phils wiped out a two-run deficit in the 15th inning and defeated Chicago, 6-5. "That was what got us started to the wire," said Green. "Montreal had already beaten St. Louis and we were looking at a two-run deficit. That, to me, was as important as any victory all year."

The next night, the Phils blew out Chicago, 14-2.

The Phils might not have made it without the brilliant performances from rookies such as Walk and Bystrom, outfielder Lonnie Smith (.339 and 33 stolen bases) and catcher Keith Moreland (.314 in 62 games).

And then there was the steady leadership of Pete Rose. Although his batting average dipped to .282, he was still the catalyst. He led the team in hits with 185 and the league in doubles with 42. He made just five errors and played first base brilliantly.

The low point of the season came on August 10 when the Pittsburgh Pirates swept a doubleheader to drop the Phils six games back with 55 to play. Between games, Green exploded in an emotional tirade. The Phils then won 36 of those 55.

On September 1, when it appeared they were falling back into their old habits, Owens called a team meeting in San Francisco and let the players have it.

He criticized Bowa and center fielder Garry Maddox in front of the team and shouted, "You've been wanting this thing (championship) for yourselves and for every other reason the last five months. I want you to win this thing now for Ruly Carpenter (owner) and me, the guys who put this team together."

The Phils won that day behind Carlton and moved into first place. They didn't hold it for long, but they were on their way.

SCORES OF PHILADELPHIA PHILLIES' 1980 GAMES

APRIL

			Winner	Loser
11-Montreal	W	6-3	Carlton	Rogers
12-Montreal	W	6-2	Ruthven	Lee
13-Montreal	W	4-5*	Sosa	LaGrow
15-At St.L.	L	2-7	Vuckovich	Lerch
16-At St.L.	W	8-3	Carlton	Forsch
18-At Mon.	L	5-7	Sanderson	Ruthven
19-At Mon.	W	13-4	Christenson	Rogers
20-At Mon.	L	6-7	Sosa	McGraw
21-N. York	L	0-3	Burris	Carlton
22-N. York	W	14-8	Saucier	Kobel
23-N. York	L	2-3	Bomback	LaGrow
25-St. Louis	L	1-3	Vuckovich	Lerch
26-St. Louis	W	7-0	Carlton	Fulgham
27-St. Louis	L	1-10	Forsch	Ruthven
30-At N.Y.	L	0-2	Bomback	Lerch

Won 6, Lost 9

MAY

			Winner	Loser
1-At N.Y.	W	2-1	Carlton	Falcone
2-Los Ang.	W	9-5	Reed	Hough
3-Los Ang.	W	7-3	Christenson	Hooton
4-Los Ang.	L	10-12	Beckwith	Noles
5-Atlanta	W	7-1	Carlton	Matula
6-Atlanta	W	10-5	Ruthven	Alexander
9-At Cinn.	L	2-5	Leibrandt	Lerch
10-At Cinn.	L	3-5	Seaver	Carlton
11-At Cinn.	W	7-3	Ruthven	LaCoss
13-At Atl.	L	3-7	Alexander	Lerch
14-At Atl.	W	9-1	Carlton	McWilliams
16-At Hous.	W	3-0	Ruthven	Richard
17-At Hous.	W	4-2	Christenson	Niekro
18-At Hous.	L	0-3	Ryan	Lerch
19-Cinn.	W	6-4	Carlton	Pastore
20-Cinn.	L	6-7	Moskau	Ruthven
21-Cinn.	W	9-8	Reed	Hume
23-Houston	W	3-0	Carlton	Ryan
24-Houston	W	5-4	Saucier	Andujar
25-Houston	W	6-2	Ruthven	Forsch
26-Pitts.	W	7-6	Reed	Tekulve
27-Pitts.	L	2-3§	Romo	Noles
28-Pitts.	W	6-3	Lerch	Robinson
29-Pitts.	L	4-5	Solomon	Ruthven
30-At Chi.	L	7-10	Reuschel	Larson
31-At Chi.	W	7-0	Carlton	Hernandez

Won 17, Lost 9

JUNE

			Winner	Loser
1-At Chi.	L	4-5	Tidrow	Reed
2-At Pitts.	L	3-9	Robinson	Lerch
3-At Pitts.	L	3-4	Jackson	McGraw
4-At Pitts.	W	4-3	Carlton	Candelaria
6-Chicago	W	6-5	Walk	Krukow
7-Chicago	W	5-2	Lerch	Reuschel
8-Chicago	L	0-2	McGlothen	Ruthven
9-S. Fran.	L	1-3	Ripley	Noles
10-S. Fran.	W	4-3	Saucier	Knepper
11-S. Fran.	L	4-7	Whitson	Lerch
13-S. Diego	W	9-6	Ruthven	Jones
14-S. Diego	W	3-1	Carlton	Mura
15-S. Diego	W	8-5	Walk	Wise
16-At L.A.	W	3-2‡	Reed	Sutcliffe
17-At L.A.	W	6-5	Reed	Castillo
18-At S.D.	W	5-1	Carlton	Shirley
19-At S.D.	L	3-4	Kinney	Saucier
20-At S.F.	L	1-5	Ripley	Larson
21-At S.F.	L	3-9	Whitson	Lerch
22-At S.F.	W	4-3	Carlton	Blue
24-Montreal	L	6-7*	Sosa	McGraw
25-Montreal	W	2-1*	Reed	Bahnsen
26-Montreal	L	0-1	Sanderson	Lerch
27-N. York	L	2-3	Pacella	Carlton
28-N. York	L	1-2†	Allen	Reed
28-N. York	L	4-5	Hausman	Saucier
29-N. York	W	5-2	Walk	Zachry
30-At Mon.	W	7-5	Noles	Gullickson

Won 14, Lost 14

JULY

			Winner	Loser
1-At Mon.	W	5-4†	Lerch	Fryman
2-At Mon.	L	1-6	Rogers	Carlton
3-At St.L.	W	2-1	Ruthven	Forsch
3-At St.L.	W	8-1	Walk	Otten
4-At St.L.	L	0-1*	Sykes	Saucier
5-At St.L.	L	1-6	Kaat	Lerch
6-At St.L.	W	8-3	Carlton	Vuckovich
10-Chicago	W	5-3	Ruthven	Krukow
11-Chicago	W	7-2	Walk	McGlothen
12-Pitts.	W	5-4	Saucier	Tekulve
13-Pitts.	L	3-7	Robinson	Espinosa
14-Pitts.	L	11-13	Jackson	Reed
15-At Hous.	L	2-3	Sambito	Ruthven
16-At Hous.	W	4-2	Walk	Forsch
17-At Hous.	W	2-1	Carlton	Niekro
18-At Atl.	W	7-2	Espinosa	Niekro
19-At Atl.	L	2-5	Alexander	Ruthven
19-At Atl.	L	2-7	Boggs	Larson
20-At Atl.	L	2-3	McWilliams	Walk
21-At Cinn.	W	4-5	Leibrandt	Lerch
22-At Cinn.	L	2-3	Soto	Carlton
23-At Cinn.	L	3-7	Berenyi	Espinosa
25-Atlanta	W	5-4‡	Ruthven	Camp
25-Atlanta	L	0-3	Boggs	Larson
26-Atlanta	W	6-3	Walk	Niekro
27-Atlanta	W	17-4	Carlton	Matula
28-Houston	L	2-3*	Sambito	Reed
29-Houston	W	9-6	Saucier	LaCorte
30-Houston	W	6-4	Ruthven	Ryan

Won 15, Lost 14

AUGUST

			Winner	Loser
1-Cinn.	W	3-1	Walk	Leibrandt
2-Cinn.	L	0-2	LaCoss	Carlton
3-Cinn.	W	8-4	Espinosa	Berenyi
6-St. Louis	L	0-14	Sykes	Walk
7-St. Louis	W	3-2	Carlton	Fulgham
8-At Pitts.	L	5-6	Tekulve	McGraw
9-At Pitts.	L	1-4	Candelaria	Espinosa
10-At Pitts.	L	1-7	Bibby	Lerch
10-At Pitts.	L	1-4	Robinson	Larson
11-At Chi.	W	8-5a	Brusstar	Riley
12-At Chi.	L	5-2	Carlton	Krukow
13-At Chi.	L	1-2	Tidrow	Ruthven
14-At N.Y.	W	8-1	Espinosa	Zachry
15-At N.Y.	W	8-0	Christenson	Bomback
16-At N.Y.	W	11-6	Walk	Swan
17-At N.Y.	W	9-4	Carlton	Burris
17-At N.Y.	W	4-1	Lerch	Jackson
19-S. Diego	W	7-4	Ruthven	Shirley
20-S. Diego	L	5-7	Curtis	Espinosa
21-S. Diego	W	9-8z	Saucier	Kinney
22-S. Fran.	L	3-4*	Holland	Carlton
23-S. Fran.	L	2-6	Ripley	Christenson
24-S. Fran.	W	7-1	Ruthven	Knepper
25-Los Ang.	L	4-8	Stanhouse	Noles
26-Los Ang.	L	4-8	Castillo	Walk
27-Los Ang.	W	4-3	Carlton	Howe
29-At S.D.	W	3-2	Christenson	Mura
30-At S.D.	W	6-1	Ruthven	Shirley
30-At S.D.	L	1-5	Curtis	Espinosa
31-At S.D.	L	3-10	Lucas	Walk

Won 16, Lost 14

SEPTEMBER

			Winner	Loser
1-At S.F.	W	6-4	Carlton	Minton
2-At S.F.	W	2-1§	Reed	Holland
3-At S.F.	W	4-3	Ruthven	Ripley
4-At L.A.	W	3-2	Walk	Reuss
5-At L.A.	L	0-1	Sutton	Carlton
6-At L.A.	L	3-7	Welch	Lerch
7-At L.A.	L	0-6	Castillo	Ruthven
8-Pitts.	W	6-2	McGraw	Romo
9-Pitts.	W	5-4x	Brusstar	Lee

SEPTEMBER			Winner	Loser	SEPTEMBER			Winner	Loser
10—At N.Y.	W	5-0	Bystrom	Bomback	25—N. York	W	2-1	Bystrom	Jackson
11—At N.Y.	W	5-1	Ruthven	Burris	26—Montreal	W	2-1	McGraw	Palmer
12—St. Louis	L	4-7	Vuckovich	Walk	27—Montreal	L	3-4	Sanderson	Carlton
12—St. Louis	L	0-5†	Littlefield	Reed	28—Montreal	L	3-8	Rogers	Walk
13—St. Louis	W	2-1	Carlton	Forsch	29—Chicago	W	6-5y	Saucier	Lamp
14—St. Louis	W	8-4	Bystrom	Martinez	30—Chicago	W	14-2	Bystrom	McGlothen
16—At Pitts.	L	2-3	Bibby	Ruthven				Won 19, Lost 10	
17—At Pitts.	W	5-4†	McGraw	Tekulve					
19—At Chi.	L	3-4	Smith	Brusstar	OCTOBER				
20—At Chi.	W	7-3	Bystrom	McGlothen	1—Chicago	W	5-0	Carlton	Lamp
21—At Chi.	W	7-3	Ruthven	Lamp	2—Chicago	W	4-2	Walk	Caudill
22—At St.L.	W	3-2*	Carlton	Seaman	3—At Mon.	W	2-1	Ruthven	Sanderson
23—At St.L.	L	3-6	Olmsted	Walk	4—At Mon.	W	6-4†	McGraw	Bahnsen
24—N. York	W	1-0*	McGraw	Allen	5—At Mon.	L	7-8*	Lea	Brusstar
								Won 4, Lost 1	

*10 innings.   †11 innings.   ‡12 innings.   §13 innings.   x14 innings.   y15 innings.   z17 innings.   a15-inning suspended game, completed August 12.

Schmidt Struck Death Blow for Expos

By IAN MacDONALD

One more win—and 1980 would have been so different! For the second year in a row, the Expos' bid for the National League East Division title fell short on the final weekend.

N.L. MVP Mike Schmidt struck the death blow October 4 when he slammed his 48th home run of the season in the 11th inning to give the Philadelphia Phillies a 6-4 win and the championship. The night before, Schmidt had driven home both runs as the Phillies nipped the Expos, 2-1, to take a one-game lead with two games to play.

It was little solace for the Expos that their 185-137 record over the 1979 and '80 seasons was the N.L.'s best. And it didn't make them feel any better to realize that the teams which nipped them for N.L. East laurels went on to win the World Series.

Still, a 90-72 record was something of which to be proud. In '79, the Expos were surprise challengers. In '80, they started the season as contenders and played that way through the final weekend. Injuries took a heavy toll, whereas the team had escaped that nemesis the year before.

The Expos began somewhat slowly and were 23-20 through June 3 before reeling off 10 wins in a row to move into first place. To that stage, their major difficulty had been a lack of consistency in the bullpen, something that was probably the main reason for their eventually falling one game short.

Veteran Woodie Fryman came through in sensational fashion, but his was the only dependable arm in the bullpen. By the 50th game of the season, the 40-year-old lefthander had appeared in 21 games, winning one and saving eight. In one stretch of 12 appearances, Woodie retired 43 of 45 batters he faced and had a shutout streak of 24⅓ innings. Fryman finished the season with a 7-4 mark, a club-high 17 saves, a career-low 2.25 ERA and a new contract.

Steve Rogers and Scott Sanderson tied for the team lead in victories with identical 16-11 records. Rogers led the league in complete games with 14. Between May 7 and August 6, Sanderson was 11-3 with six complete games and an ERA of 2.14.

Rookie Bill Gullickson was tremendous after a slow start. The 21-year-old diabetic was 10-5 with an ERA of 3.00 and on September 10 he flirted with

MONTREAL EXPOS—1980

Front row—Norman, Fryman, Cisco, coach; Alou, coach; Mullin, coach; Williams, manager; Virgil, coach; Sherry, coach; Rapp, coach; Bernazard, Tamargo, Raines. Second row—Pate, Gullickson, Parrish, Dawson, Lea, Sanderson, Valentine, Bahnsen, Lee, Dues, Wallach, Macha. Third row—Stone, equipment manager; Gauvreau, assistant trainer; Ratzer, Montanez, Rogers, Carter, Sosa, Palmer, Speier, LeFlore, McClain, trainer. Fourth row—Ramos, Mills, Manuel, Office, D'Acquisto, Scott, Cromartie, Briggs, White, Hutton. Seated in front—batboys Albertson and Trubiano.

the one-game strikeout record of Steve Carlton, Tom Seaver and Nolan Ryan when he whiffed 18 Cubs at Olympic Stadium. That was one shy of the record, but still tops by a rookie.

Bill Lee, the club's top winner the previous season, was disabled twice and managed only four wins while the team's rookie star of '79, David Palmer, was 8-6 with a 2.98 ERA. Palmer pitched with pain most of the season and underwent arm surgery afterward.

Injuries were costly elsewhere as well. Third baseman Larry Parrish, the team's outstanding player in '79 with a .307 average and 30 home runs, was hit on the wrist by an Ed Whitson pitch on May 3. Parrish remained in the lineup far too long. Though he did finish fairly well, he didn't come close to his statistics of the year before, winding up at .254 with 15 homers.

Right fielder Ellis Valentine managed to start just 83 games because of a series of injuries. Valentine had his cheek shattered when beaned by St. Louis' Roy Thomas on May 30. Out for 40 days, Valentine came back wielding a big bat but went down on August 20 with a hip injury. Shortly after returning from that mishap, Valentine sprained his wrist while diving for a ball and missed most of the stretch run. Nevertheless, he hit .315 and drove in 67 runs.

Catcher Gary Carter and center fielder Andre Dawson came through with brilliant seasons. Carter won the Rawlings Gold Glove for the first time, was named to THE SPORTING NEWS All-Star team by fellow players and was second to Schmidt in the MVP voting. Carter's 29 homers and 101 RBIs led the club and his 13 game-winning RBIs were second only to Dawson, who hit .308, belted 17 homers, stole 34 bases and had 17 game-winners.

The Expos' 237 stolen bases were surpassed only by San Diego's 239. Left fielder and leadoff man Ron LeFlore led the league with 97 steals. Right behind him, second baseman Rodney Scott pilfered 63. With Dawson batting third, the first three Expos had Manager Dick Williams' green light to steal at any time.

Scott led the league with 24 steals of third, while LeFlore had 15. They sparked the Expos to a club record of 18 double steals.

Even that aspect of the Expos' game was grounded for the final drive as LeFlore suffered a fractured wrist when he crashed into a fence in a futile chase of a foul ball September 11. For the final 22 games, LeFlore was reduced to pinch-running roles.

Outfielders Jerry White and Rowland Office came through handsomely in backup roles, but neither could quite spell the regulars.

One fewer injury or one more dependable reliever—three times during the season the Expos and their workhorse ace Rogers had 7-2 late-inning leads only to have the bullpen blow the game—might have provided that one more win.

SCORES OF MONTREAL EXPOS' 1980 GAMES

APRIL			Winner	Loser
11—At Phila.	L	3-6	Carlton	Rogers
12—At Phila.	L	2-6	Ruthven	Lee
13—At Phila.	W	5-4*	Sosa	LaGrow
15—At N.Y.	W	7-3	Rogers	Swan
16—At N.Y.	L	2-3	Burris	Lee
18—Phila.	W	7-5	Sanderson	Ruthven
19—Phila.	L	4-13	Christenson	Rogers
20—Phila.	W	7-6	Sosa	McGraw
21—Pitts.	L	1-7	Candelaria	Grimsley
22—Pitts.	L	3-5	Bibby	Sanderson
23—Pitts.	W	3-2	Rogers	Blyleven
25—At Atl.	L	7-8†	Bradford	Bahnsen

APRIL			Winner	Loser
26—At Atl.	W	4-3	Grimsley	Niekro
27—At Atl.	L	3-6	McWilliams	Sanderson
29—At Pitts.	L	4-5*	Solomon	Sosa
30—At Pitts.	L	0-5	Bibby	Lee
		Won 6, Lost 10		
MAY				
1—At Pitts.	L	1-2*	Tekulve	Fryman
2—S. Fran.	W	4-3	Bahnsen	Lavelle
3—S. Fran.	L	2-3	Moffitt	Sosa
4—S. Fran.	L	4-8	Montefusco	Rogers
4—S. Fran.	W	6-4	Bahnsen	Moffitt

MAY			Winner	Loser
5—Houston	W	10-1	Palmer	Richard
6—Houston	L	4-8	Niekro	Grimsley
7—Houston	W	3-0	Sanderson	Ryan
9—N. York	L	1-2	Swan	Rogers
10—N. York	W	5-3	Lee	Kobel
13—At Hous.	W	3-2	Palmer	Ryan
14—At Hous.	W	1-0	Sanderson	Forsch
16—Cinn.	W	2-1	Rogers	Seaver
17—Cinn.	W	9-6	Bahnsen	Hume
19—Atl.	W	11-8	Palmer	McWilliams
20—Atl.	L	0-1	Niekro	Sanderson
21—Atl.	W	3-2	Rogers	Garber
23—At Cinn.	W	7-4	Lee	LaCoss
24—At Cinn.	L	0-2	Pastore	Palmer
25—At Cinn.	W	7-4	Sanderson	Leibrandt
26—At Chi.	W	4-0	Rogers	Hernandez
27—At Chi.	L	2-4	Lamp	Lee
28—At Chi.	L	4-8x	Lamp	Murray
30—At St.L.	W	10-4	Sanderson	Kaat
31—At St.L.	L	6-8	Forsch	Rogers
Won 15, Lost 10				

JUNE				
1—At St.L.	W	7-6‡	Bahnsen	Frazier
2—Chicago	W	8-7§	Fryman	McGlothen
3—Chicago	L	2-5	Reuschel	Grimsley
4—Chicago	W	8-1	Rogers	McGlothen
5—Chicago	W	2-0	Sanderson	Lamp
6—St. Louis	W	7-2	Lee	Forsch
7—St. Louis	W	2-1§	Sosa	Otten
8—St. Louis	W	6-4	Rogers	Fulgham
8—St. Louis	W	9-4	Grimsley	Thomas
10—S. Diego	W	8-4	Bahnsen	Rasmussen
11—S. Diego	W	7-6	Sosa	Shirley
12—S. Diego	W	9-1	Lea	Lucas
13—Los Ang.	W	4-3	Rogers	Howe
14—Los Ang.	L	0-8	Hooton	Grimsley
15—Los Ang.	L	0-1	Welch	Gullickson
16—At S.F.	L	1-5	Whitson	Lea
17—At S.F.	W	2-1	Palmer	Blue
18—At L.A.	L	7-8	Hough	Sosa
19—At L.A.	L	3-5*	Castillo	Fryman
20—At S.D.	L	2-4	Mura	Sanderson
21—At S.D.	W	7-4	Lea	Curtis
22—At S.D.	W	2-0	Rogers	Lucas
24—At Phila.	W	7-6*	Sosa	McGraw
25—At Phila.	L	1-2*	Reed	Bahnsen
26—At Phila.	W	1-0	Sanderson	Lerch
27—Pitts.	L	4-6	Romo	Rogers
28—Pitts.	L	3-4	Bibby	Lea
29—Pitts.	W	4-1	Palmer	Solomon
30—Phila.	L	5-7	Noles	Gullickson
Won 18, Lost 11				

JULY				
1—Phila.	L	4-5†	Lerch	Fryman
2—Phila.	W	6-1	Rogers	Carlton
3—At N.Y.	L	2-7	Hausman	Lea
4—At N.Y.	L	5-9	Glynn	Palmer
4—At N.Y.	W	6-5	Fryman	Bomback
5—At N.Y.	L	5-7	Falcone	Sanderson
6—At N.Y.	W	9-4*	Fryman	Reardon
10—St. Louis	W	4-3	Palmer	Littlefield
11—St. Louis	L	3-5	Martinez	Fryman
12—Chicago	W	10-2	Sanderson	Reuschel
12—Chicago	L	6-8	Tidrow	Bahnsen
13—Chicago	W	2-1	Bahnsen	Capilla
15—At Cinn.	L	7-11	Moskau	Palmer
16—At Cinn.	W	6-4	Rogers	Soto
17—At Cinn.	W	6-1	Sanderson	LaCoss
18—At Hous.	W	5-4†	Fryman	Smith
19—At Hous.	L	2-4	Andujar	Lea
19—At Hous.	W	5-2	Gullickson	Pladson
20—At Hous.	L	3-4	Sambito	Norman
21—At Atl.	W	8-6	Sanderson	Matula

JULY			Winner	Loser
22—At Atl.	L	5-7	Niekro	Bahnsen
23—At Atl.	L	5-6	Camp	Gullickson
25—Houston	L	8-9	LaCorte	Sosa
26—Houston	W	2-1‡	Bahnsen	LaCorte
27—Houston	L	3-6	Niekro	Lee
28—Cinn.	L	2-3	Bair	Lea
28—Cinn.	W	5-4	Norman	Soto
29—Cinn.	W	4-1	Gullickson	Berenyi
30—Cinn.	W	2-1	Fryman	Bair
Won 15, Lost 14				

AUGUST				
1—Atlanta	W	4-1	Sanderson	Niekro
2—Atlanta	W	5-1	Norman	Alexander
3—Atlanta	W	6-5	Lea	McWilliams
4—N. York	W	4-3*	Sosa	Allen
4—N. York	L	3-4	Bomback	Lee
5—N. York	W	11-5	Gullickson	Pacella
6—N. York	W	4-1	Sanderson	Jackson
7—N. York	L	1-7	Burris	Norman
8—At Chi.	W	5-2	Lea	Krukow
9—At Chi.	L	1-3	Reuschel	Rogers
9—At Chi.	W	4-3	Sosa	Sutter
10—At Chi.	W	7-3	Gullickson	Lamp
11—At St.L.	L	0-16	Sykes	Sanderson
12—At St.L.	W	4-0	Norman	Fulgham
13—At St.L.	L	5-7	Forsch	Dues
15—At Pitts.	L	3-7	Bibby	Rogers
16—At Pitts.	L	0-5	Blyleven	Sanderson
17—At Pitts.	L	1-5	Rhoden	Norman
17—At Pitts.	W	4-2	Gullickson	Robinson
19—Los Ang.	L	2-3	Stanhouse	Sosa
20—Los Ang.	L	1-5	Reuss	Rogers
21—Los Ang.	L	4-5*	Howe	Bahnsen
22—S. Diego	W	6-2	Norman	Jones
23—S. Diego	W	2-0	Gullickson	Mura
24—S. Diego	W	12-9	Sosa	Fingers
25—S. Fran.	W	3-1	Rogers	Hargesh'mer
27—S. Fran.	L	0-1	Whitson	Sanderson
29—At L.A.	L	4-5	Castillo	D'Acquisto
30—At L.A.	L	3-4	Hooton	Gullickson
31—At L.A.	L	0-2	Reuss	Rogers
31—At L.A.	L	2-7	Sutter	Palmer
Won 15, Lost 16				

SEPTEMBER				
1—At S.D.	W	5-3	Sanderson	Wise
2—At S.D.	W	2-1	Lea	Rasmussen
3—At S.D.	L	3-4	Mura	Norman
4—At S.F.	W	4-0	Gullickson	Hargesh'mer
5—At S.F.	W	8-0	Rogers	Montefusco
6—At S.F.	W	9-0	Sanderson	Whitson
7—At S.F.	L	3-6	Blue	D'Acquisto
9—N. York	W	3-0	Rogers	Zachry
10—Chicago	W	4-2	Gullickson	Reuschel
11—Chicago	W	6-5	Fryman	Martz
12—Pitts.	W	1-0	Sanderson	Rhoden
13—Pitts.	L	0-4	Robinson	Rogers
14—Pitts.	W	4-0	Gullickson	Candelaria
16—At N.Y.	W	5-3†	Sosa	Berenguer
16—At N.Y.	W	4-2	Palmer	Jackson
17—At N.Y.	L	2-5	Miller	Sanderson
19—At St.L.	L	8-9	Kaat	Sosa
20—At St.L.	W	4-1	Lee	Littlefield
21—At St.L.	L	1-4	Rincon	Palmer
22—At Pitts.	L	2-4	Bibby	Sanderson
23—At Pitts.	W	7-1	Rogers	Blyleven
24—At Chi.	W	8-4	Lea	Reuschel
25—At Chi.	L	4-5	McGlothen	Gullickson
26—At Phila.	L	1-2	McGraw	Palmer
27—At Phila.	W	4-3	Sanderson	Carlton
28—At Phila.	W	8-3	Rogers	Walk
29—St. Louis	W	5-2	Fryman	Frazier
30—St. Louis	W	7-2	Gullickson	Forsch
Won 19, Lost 9				

OCTOBER			Winner	Loser	OCTOBER			Winner	Loser
1—St. Louis	W	8-0	Palmer	Rincon	4—Phila.	L	4-6†	McGraw	Bahnsen
3—Phila.	L	1-2	Ruthven	Sanderson	5—Phila.	W	8-7*	Lea	Brusstar
							Won 2, Lost 2		

*10 innings.   †11 innings.   ‡12 innings.   §13 innings.   x14-inning suspended game, completed August 8.

Pirates Lacked '79 Comeback Punch

By CHARLEY FEENEY

The tumble from the top wasn't a mystery. The Pittsburgh Pirates played their way into third place in the National League East in 1980.

It was a team effort, only this time it didn't produce a world championship team. This time the Pirates didn't have the comeback punch. This time they didn't win the big games in September. This time they failed.

The Pirates were 83-79, their lowest number of wins since 1973, when they won 80. Injuries played a part, but winning teams had injuries, too. Injuries are a loser's crutch.

The Pirates tumbled together—like a family. Two of their key starting pitchers finished under .500, and no regular in the batting order improved on his 1979 stats.

Mike Easler and Lee Lacy, who were not regulars in '79, tried to carry the Pirates in '80. As platoon left fielders, the firm of Easler and Lacy was awesome. Easler led the Bucs in batting average (.338) and homers (21). Lacy batted .335 and, in less than 300 at-bats, hit seven homers and drove in 33 runs while stealing 18 bases.

The Bucs' leaders were supposed to be Dave Parker and Willie Stargell. Parker played most of the season with fluid on his left knee. Stargell found out in midseason that he had an arthritic left knee. Together, they collected only 117 RBIs, 59 fewer than in the previous season.

Stargell injured his knee in May and later thought that he had recovered. In July, however, he was placed on the disabled list. When the season ended he had appeared in only 67 games. Stargell, who had hit .281 with 32 homers and 82 RBIs in '79 when he shared the N.L. MVP with St. Louis' Keith Hernandez, fell to .262 with 11 homers and 38 RBIs.

Parker batted under .300 (.295) for the first time since 1974.

"It was unbelievable that so many regulars on one team could have off-seasons," said third baseman Bill Madlock, whose average dipped 21 points to .277.

John Candelaria, who was 14-9 in '79, finished at 11-14. Bert Blyleven slumped from 12-5 to 8-13. Relief ace Kent Tekulve lost his last seven decisions and ended up 8-12 with 21 saves. In his last 19 appearances, Tekulve was tagged for 16 earned runs and saved only two games.

The only consistent starter was Jim Bibby, who won 19 games, lost six and had a 3.33 ERA. Said Manager Chuck Tanner: "It's difficult to win with one pitcher trying to carry the club."

And it's difficult to stay out of long losing streaks. The Pirates lost eight in a row once. Three times they lost six in a row.

The losing streaks came after a deceptive start. Known as a club slow to break from the gate, the Pirates were 11-5 in April and 25-18 at the close of May. Their only winning month after that was July when they used an 18-10

PITTSBURGH PIRATES—1980

Front row—Rooker, Berra, Alexander, Graff, batboy; Nicosia, Garner, Ott, Milner. Second row—Jackson, Foli, Monchak, coach; Skinner, coach; Tanner, manager; Haddix, coach; Lonnett, coach; Madlock, Romo, Sanguillen. Third row—Briles, announcer; Martin, announcer; Frattare, announcer; Easler, D. Robinson, Scurry, Lacy, Muse, traveling secretary; Coroso, team physician; Haak, scout; Bartirome, trainer. Top row—B. Robinson, Moreno, Parker, Hassler, Candelaria, Bibby, Tekulve, Stargell, Solomon.

mark to vault into first place.

The Pirates had a problem with West Division clubs, particularly the Atlanta Braves, who beat them 11 times in 12 meetings. The Bucs were 32-40 against the West and 51-39 against East Division rivals. They were 11-7 against the world champion Philadelphia Phillies and 12-6 against the second-place Montreal Expos.

"We just couldn't get anything going during the last two months of the season," Tanner said. "It wasn't a question of attitude. Our attitude was the same as in 1979—great."

Other than Easler and Lacy, Bibby and Buddy Solomon, who won seven games as a long reliever and spot starter, only center fielder Omar Moreno had anything to brag about. Although his average slipped from .282 to .249, Moreno became the first player in modern history to steal 70 or more bases in three consecutive seasons. Moreno finished with 96 thefts, one less than Montreal's Ron LeFlore.

The few personal achievements didn't make up for the disappointment of finishing lower than second for the first time since '73.

"There is no substitute for winning," a dejected Chuck Tanner said at season's end.

SCORES OF PITTSBURGH PIRATES' 1980 GAMES

APRIL			Winner	Loser
10—At St.L.	L	0-1	Vuckovich	Blyleven
11—At St.L.	W	4-3	Jackson	Hood
12—At St.L	W	7-2	Bibby	Fulgham
13—At St.L.	W	3-0	Rooker	Martinez
14—Chicago	W	5-4‡	Tekulve	Sutter
17—St. Louis	L	9-12	Sykes	Candelaria
18—St. Louis	W	12-10	Jackson	Knowles
19—St. Louis	L	1-2	Fulgham	Roberts
20—St. Louis	W	6-3	Rooker	Vuckovich
21—At Mon.	W	7-1	Candelaria	Grimsley
22—At Mon.	W	5-3	Bibby	Sanderson
23—At Mon.	L	2-3	Rogers	Blyleven
25—At Chi.	L	3-5	Reuschel	Rooker
26—At Chi.	W	9-2	Candelaria	Lamp
29—Montreal	W	5-4‡	Solomon	Sosa
30—Montreal	W	5-0	Bibby	Lee

Won 11, Lost 5

MAY				
1—Montreal	W	2-1‡	Tekulve	Fryman
2—Atlanta	L	1-6	Niekro	Rooker
3—Atlanta	L	1-3‡	Hrabosky	Jackson
4—Atlanta	W	13-4	Bibby	Boggs
6—Los Ang.	W	2-1	Tekulve	Howe
7—Los Ang.	W	7-6	Tekulve	Hough
9—At S.D.	W	4-3	Tekulve	Fingers
10—At S.D.	W	9-5	Robinson	Rasmussen
11—At S.D.	L	0-5	Jones	Candelaria
13—At S.F.	L	0-5	Blue	Blyleven
14—At S.F.	W	3-2	Bibby	Knepper
15—At S.F.	W	3-2x	Romo	Griffin
16—At L.A.	L	6-8	Reuss	Tekulve
17—At L.A.	L	1-3	Sutton	Blyleven
18—At L.A.	L	0-2	Welch	Bibby
21—S. Diego	W	4-3	Romo	Fingers
21—S. Diego	W	3-2	Jackson	Curtis
22—S. Diego	L	4-6	Shirley	Tekulve
23—S. Fran.	W	5-4y	Jackson	Holland
24—S. Fran.	L	9-10a	Griffin	Scurry
25—S. Fran.	L	2-5	Blue	Candelaria
26—At Phila.	L	6-7	Reed	Tekulve
27—At Phila.	W	3-2y	Romo	Noles
28—At Phila.	L	3-6	Lerch	Robinson
29—At Phila.	W	5-4	Solomon	Ruthven

MAY			Winner	Loser
30—N. York	L	1-5*	Zachry	Candelaria
31—N. York	W	5-0	Blyleven	Swan

Won 14, Lost 13

JUNE				
1—N. York	W	13-3	Bibby	Falcone
2—Phila.	W	9-3	Robinson	Lerch
3—Phila.	W	4-3	Jackson	McGraw
4—Phila.	L	3-4	Carlton	Candelaria
6—At N.Y.	L	4-9	Hausman	Blyleven
7—At N.Y.	L	5-6§	Allen	Jackson
8—At N.Y.	L	4-6	Burris	Romo
8—At N.Y.	W	3-0	Solomon	Bomback
10—At Cinn.	W	5-3	Candelaria	Soto
11—At Cinn.	L	2-3	Pastore	Blyleven
12—At Cinn.	W	10-6	Bibby	LaCoss
13—Houston	W	5-3	Solomon	Niekro
14—Houston	L	3-7	Ryan	Robinson
15—Houston	W	4-1	Candelaria	Forsch
16—Cinn.	W	5-3	Blyleven	Pastore
17—Cinn.	L	3-4	Moskau	Romo
18—At Atl.	L	2-3	Garber	Tekulve
18—At Atl.	L	4-5	Camp	Romo
19—At Atl.	L	3-4	Matula	Robinson
20—At Hous.	L	4-6	Forsch	Candelaria
21—At Hous.	L	2-4	Ruhle	Blyleven
22—At Hous.	W	2-1	Bibby	Niekro
23—At St.L.	L	1-6	Kaat	Solomon
24—At St.L.	L	2-3	Sykes	Rhoden
25—At St.L.	L	1-4	Hood	Candelaria
27—At Mon.	W	6-4	Romo	Rogers
28—At Mon.	W	4-3	Bibby	Lea
29—At Mon.	L	1-4	Palmer	Solomon
30—St. Louis	W	5-4	Romo	Hood

Won 13, Lost 16

JULY				
1—St. Louis	W	3-2‡	Jackson	Kaat
2—St. Louis	L	5-7§	Urrea	Scurry
3—Chicago	W	5-3	Bibby	Krukow
4—Chicago	W	6-4	McGlothen	Solomon
4—Chicago	L	1-2	Capilla	Robinson
5—Chicago	W	5-4	Candelaria	Hernandez
6—Chicago	W	5-4b	Bibby	Lamp

JULY			Winner	Loser
10—At N.Y.	L	0-2	Zachry	Candelaria
11—At N.Y.	W	4-2	Blyleven	Swan
12—At Phila.	L	4-5	Saucier	Tekulve
13—At Phila.	W	7-3	Robinson	Espinosa
14—At Phila.	W	13-11	Jackson	Reed
15—S. Fran.	W	5-2	Candelaria	Knepper
16—S. Fran.	W	3-1	Blyleven	Whitson
17—S. Fran.	W	3-2	Tekulve	Holland
18—Los Ang.	W	6-4	Rhoden	Welch
19—Los Ang.	W	7-3	Solomon	Sutcliffe
20—Los Ang.	L	2-4	Hooton	Candelaria
20—Los Ang.	W	8-7	Jackson	Castillo
22—At S.D.	W	4-3	Bibby	Lucas
23—At S.D.	L	2-3	Fingers	Romo
24—At S.D.	W	7-1	Blyleven	Shirley
25—At S.F.	W	5-1	Candelaria	Knepper
26—At S.F.	L	3-4‡	Minton	Jackson
27—At S.F.	W	6-4	Bibby	Bordley
28—At L.A.	W	6-4	Rhoden	Welch
29—At L.A.	L	2-10	Hooton	Blyleven
30—At L.A.	L	0-3	Reuss	Candelaria
			Won 18, Lost 10	

AUGUST			Winner	Loser
1—S. Diego	L	0-1	Mura	Bibby
3—S. Diego	L	2-5	Curtis	Rhoden
3—S. Diego	L	1-4	Shirley	Robinson
5—At Chi.	L	3-11	Reuschel	Candelaria
6—At Chi.	W	9-7	Tekulve	Tidrow
6—At Chi.	W	2-0	Blyleven	Capilla
7—At Chi.	W	11-3	Solomon	Hernandez
8—Phila.	W	6-5	Tekulve	McGraw
9—Phila.	W	4-1	Candelaria	Espinosa
10—Phila.	W	7-1	Bibby	Lerch
10—Phila.	W	4-1	Robinson	Larson
11—N. York	W	2-1†	Solomon	Jackson
12—N. York	L	1-3	Burris	Rhoden
13—N. York	L	3-5	Hausman	Candelaria
15—Montreal	W	7-3	Bibby	Rogers
16—Montreal	W	5-0	Blyleven	Sanderson
17—Montreal	W	5-1	Rhoden	Norman
17—Montreal	L	2-4	Gullickson	Robinson
19—At Hous.	L	2-5	Ryan	Candelaria
20—At Hous.	L	1-5	Ruhle	Bibby
21—At Hous.	L	5-12	Sambito	Blyleven
22—At Cinn.	W	4-2	Robinson	Moskau
23—At Cinn.	W	2-1	Rhoden	Pastore

AUGUST			Winner	Loser
24—At Cinn.	W	5-2	Candelaria	LaCoss
25—Atlanta	L	6-8	Hanna	Bibby
26—Atlanta	L	2-4‡	Garber	Tekulve
27—Atlanta	L	4-7	Matula	Robinson
28—Cinn.	L	0-4	Moskau	Rhoden
29—Cinn.	L	7-8	Soto	Tekulve
30—Cinn.	L	3-5	Seaver	Bibby
31—Cinn.	L	4-5	LaCoss	Blyleven
			Won 14, Lost 17	

SEPTEMBER			Winner	Loser
1—Houston	L	4-10	Smith	Robinson
1—Houston	L	7-5	Rhoden	Pladson
3—Houston	W	10-4	Candelaria	Andujar
5—At Atl.	L	4-7	Camp	Tekulve
6—At Atl.	L	2-3	Niekro	Blyleven
7—At Atl.	L	5-6	Bradford	Tekulve
8—At Phila.	L	2-6	McGraw	Romo
9—At Phila.	L	4-5z	Brusstar	Lee
10—At St.L.	W	7-6	Bibby	Hood
11—At St.L.	W	2-1	Blyleven	Martin
12—At Mon.	L	0-1	Sanderson	Rhoden
13—At Mon.	W	4-0	Robinson	Rogers
14—At Mon.	L	0-4	Gullickson	Candelaria
16—Phila.	W	3-2	Bibby	Ruthven
17—Phila.	L	4-5§	McGraw	Tekulve
19—N. York	W	4-3	Rhoden	Lynch
20—N. York	L	6-9§	Allen	Tekulve
21—N. York	W	9-4	Candelaria	Burris
22—Montreal	W	4-2	Bibby	Sanderson
23—Montreal	L	1-7	Rogers	Blyleven
24—St. Louis	W	6-3	Rhoden	Martin
25—St. Louis	L	2-10	Kaat	Robinson
26—At Chi.	L	8-9	Caudill	Tekulve
27—At Chi.	L	0-2	Martz	Bibby
28—At Chi.	L	2-3	Krukow	Blyleven
29—At N.Y.	W	4-5‡	Reardon	Jackson
30—At N.Y.	L	2-3	Falcone	Robinson
			Won 10, Lost 17	

OCTOBER			Winner	Loser
1—At N.Y.	W	10-5	Bibby	Burris
3—Chicago	W	3-1	Jefferson	Reuschel
4—Chicago	L	0-6	McGlothen	Perez
5—Chicago	W	1-0	Robinson	Capilla
			Won 3, Lost 1	

•5½ innings. †6 innings. ‡10 innings. §11 innings. x12 innings. y13 innings. z14 innings. a15 innings. b20 innings.

Cards Played Manager Roulette in '80

By RICK HUMMEL

If the Cardinals had had as many pitchers as they had managers, they might have done better than their fourth-place station in the National League East.

Counting third-base coach Jack Krol, who directed one loss, the Cardinals had four managers during the season and then hired another (Whitey Herzog again) two weeks after it had ended.

Ken Boyer was the first. He got the axe between games of a doubleheader in Montreal after compiling an 18-33 record, but he really didn't have too much chance what with injuries to front-line pitchers John Fulgham, Silvio Martinez and Mark Littell, second baseman Ken Oberkfell and outfielder Bobby Bonds.

Fulgham, Martinez and Littell had combined for 34 victories and 13 saves the previous season but were to amass only nine victories and two saves in 1980. That statistic, as much as anything, accounted for the Cardinals' finishing 74-88, 12 games behind their clip of the year before.

Only Martinez, who finished 5-10, was able to pitch more than half a season, although he was bothered throughout by a bad elbow and later a bad back. Fulgham, a 10-6 pitcher the year before, struggled with a bad shoulder to 4-6 and Littell missed the last four months after shoulder surgery.

Herzog took over June 9 and the Cardinals played their best baseball of the season under him, going 38-35, before, in mid-August, another bombshell was dropped. General Manager John Claiborne, who had recommended the hiring of Herzog, was dumped, and two weeks later, Herzog himself was named general manager.

At this point, the reins were given to Coach Red Schoendienst, who had managed the Cardinals from 1965-76, and he completed the season. Herzog then assumed the dual role of general manager-manager in October.

The Cardinals had no fewer than six regulars or semi-regulars who hit above .300 and they led the league in batting at .275. Their defense also was exemplary but their pitching finished dead last in ERA (3.93) and saves (27).

At the end of May, an 8-18 month, the Cardinals were already almost hopelessly buried. As is their custom, they had a horrendous trip to the West Coast, which sparked a 10-game losing streak. They finished May 16-28 and 9½ games out of first.

The Cardinals had only two winning months out of six, but those were scant triumphs at 15-14 for June and 14-13 for July.

George Hendrick had the best season of his career with 25 home runs, 109 RBIs and a .302 average. Keith Hernandez, the co-MVP and batting champion from the year before, was second in the batting race at .321, scored 111 runs and drove in 99.

Garry Templeton was headed for his best season, too, but suffered a broken finger and broken thumb in the last two months and was limited to 118 games, in which he hit .319. Templeton led the batting race with Hernandez second until the last weekend when the Cubs' Bill Buckner passed them both.

Catcher Ted Simmons hit .303 with 98 RBIs and part-time outfielder Dane Iorg also hit .303. But Bonds, counted on to provide home run power, hit only five homers and batted just .203 and was plagued much of the season by a wrist injury he suffered in the season's second week. Oberkfell, sidelined for six weeks by a knee injury, had his second straight .300 season, a rarity for second basemen.

The pitching staff, however, had only two men with double-figure win totals, Pete Vuckovich at 12-9 and Bob Forsch, who was signed to a $3.5 million, six-year contract, at 11-10. The tipoff on the staff was that 41-year-old Jim Kaat, who was signed as a free agent after a month of the season had elapsed, was third in victories with eight, tied for second in saves with four and third in complete games with six.

All told, 42 players—including 21 pitchers—couldn't put the Cardinals back together again.

The season was a financial disaster. Claiborne had signed Hernandez to a $3.8 million contract for five years, Templeton to a $4 million contract for six years and was paying Bonds $440,000. In addition, several fringe players were working on long-term lucrative contracts. But attendance dipped 242,000 to 1,385,147. And that's how people get fired in baseball.

ST. LOUIS CARDINALS—1980

In front—Forsch, Hernandez, Simmons, Fulgham, Hendrick. Seated, first row—Gieselmann, trainer; De Sa, Littlefield, Lentine, Osteen, coach; Maxvill, coach; Boyer, manager; Schoendienst, coach; Krol, coach; Ricketts, coach; Carbo, Phillips, Oberkfell, Martinez, Yatkeman, equipment manager. Middle row—Bauman, trainer; Bonds, Kennedy, Frazier, Reitz, Waller, Durham, Calise, Roof, Eduardo, Swisher, Herr, McEnaney, Bruno, Schultz, L. Thomas, traveling secretary. Back row—Templeton, Scott, Seaman, Urrea, R. Thomas, Moore, Littell, Freed, Iorg, Smith, Knowles, Vuckovich, Sykes.

SCORES OF ST. LOUIS CARDINALS' 1980 GAMES

APRIL

Date		Score	Winner	Loser
10-Pitts.	W	1-0	Vuckovich	Blyleven
11-Pitts.	L	3-4	Jackson	Hood
12-Pitts.	L	2-7	Bibby	Fulgham
13-Pitts.	L	0-3	Rooker	Martinez
15-Phila.	W	7-2	Vuckovich	Lerch
16-Phila.	L	3-8	Carlton	Forsch
17-At Pitts.	W	12-9	Sykes	Candelaria
18-At Pitts.	W	10-12	Jackson	Knowles
19-At Pitts.	W	2-1	Fulgham	Roberts
20-At Pitts.	L	3-6	Rooker	Vuckovich
22-At Chi.	L	12-16	Sutter	Littell
23-At Chi.	W	3-1	Martinez	Krukow
25-At Phila.	W	3-1	Vuckovich	Lerch
26-At Phila.	L	0-7	Carlton	Fulgham
27-At Phila.	W	10-1	Forsch	Ruthven
28-Chicago	L	2-4	Hernandez	Sykes
29-Chicago	L	4-6	Capilla	Sykes
30-Chicago	W	8-2	Vuckovich	Lamp

Won 8, Lost 10

MAY

Date		Score	Winner	Loser
2-Houston	W	9-1	Hood	Ryan
3-Houston	L	2-4	Ruhle	Martinez
4-Houston	L	2-4	K. Forsch	Sykes
5-S. Fran.	W	9-5	Vuckovich	Blue
6-S. Fran.	W	10-7	Moore	Knepper
7-S. Fran.	W	12-2	Forsch	Whitson
9-Los Ang.	W	15-7	Borbon	Sutcliffe
10-Los Ang.	L	3-5	Hooton	Vuckovich
11-Los Ang.	L	2-4	Goltz	Forsch
13-At S.D.	L	2-3	Fingers	Kaat
14-At S.D.	W	2-1	Thomas	Lucas
15-At S.D.	L	1-2	Curtis	Vuckovich
16-At S.F.	L	3-4	Holland	Forsch
17-At S.F.	L	2-4	Blue	Sykes
18-At S.F.	L	5-6	Knepper	Hood
19-At L.A.	L	1-5	Hooton	Thomas
20-At L.A.	L	3-4	Reuss	Vuckovich
21-At L.A.	L	3-5	Beckwith	Littell
23-S. Diego	L	0-2	Shirley	Kaat
24-S. Diego	L	4-8	Kinney	Moore
25-S. Diego	L	5-11	Fingers	Thomas
26-N. York	W	8-5	Forsch	Falcone
27-N. York	L	5-9	Bomback	Martinez
28-N. York	L	5-6	Kobel	Frazier
30-Montreal	L	4-10	Sanderson	Kaat
31-Montreal	W	8-6	Forsch	Rogers

Won 8, Lost 18

JUNE

Date		Score	Winner	Loser
1-Montreal	L	6-7§	Bahnsen	Frazier
3-At N.Y.	W	8-1	Fulgham	Burris
4-At N.Y.	L	1-0†	Kaat	Allen
5-At N.Y.	L	1-2	Swan	Frazier
6-At Mon.	L	2-7	Lee	Forsch
7-At Mon.	L	1-2x	Sosa	Otten
8-At Mon.	L	4-6	Rogers	Fulgham
8-At Mon.	L	4-9	Grimsley	Thomas
9-At Atl.	W	8-5†	Littlefield	Bradford
10-At Atl.	L	2-5	Niekro	Sykes
11-At Atl.	W	4-3†	Forsch	Bradford
13-Cinn.	L	2-5	Leibrandt	Vuckovich
14-Cinn.	W	4-3	Littlefield	Soto
15-Cinn.	W	10-9x	Thomas	Moskau
16-Atlanta	L	3-6	Boggs	Forsch
17-Atlanta	W	3-2	Vuckovich	Alexander
18-At Hous.	L	0-3	Niekro	Kaat
19-At Hous.	L	0-2	Ryan	Sykes
20-At Cinn.	W	7-5	Seaman	Hume
21-At Cinn.	L	5-8	Pastore	Littlefield
22-At Cinn.	W	12-2	Vuckovich	LaCoss
23-Pitts.	W	6-1	Kaat	Solomon
24-Pitts.	W	3-2	Sykes	Rhoden
25-Pitts.	W	4-1	Hood	Candelaria
27-At Chi.	W	3-2§	Seaman	Hernandez
28-At Chi.	W	8-6	Littlefield	Sutter
28-At Chi.	L	1-2	Krukow	Otten
29-At Chi.	W	9-7	Urrea	McGlothen
30-At Pitts.	L	4-5	Romo	Hood

Won 15, Lost 14

JULY

Date		Score	Winner	Loser
1-At Pitts.	L	2-3†	Jackson	Kaat
2-At Pitts.	W	7-5‡	Urrea	Scurry
3-Phila.	L	1-2	Ruthven	Forsch
3-Phila.	L	1-8	Walk	Otten
4-Phila.	W	1-0†	Sykes	Saucier
5-Phila.	W	6-1	Kaat	Lerch
6-Phila.	L	3-8	Carlton	Vuckovich
10-At Mon.	L	3-4	Palmer	Littlefield
11-At Mon.	W	5-3	Martinez	Fryman
12-At N.Y.	W	8-6§	Littlefield	Glynn
13-At N.Y.	L	4-7	Falcone	Sykes
13-At N.Y.	L	4-10	Bomback	Otten
15-S. Diego	W	5-3	Forsch	Jones
16-S. Diego	W	3-0	Vuckovich	Lucas
17-S. Diego	W	15-3	Kaat	Wise
18-S. Fran.	L	7-8	Holland	Seaman
19-S. Fran.	L	4-7	Hargesh'mer	Sykes
20-S. Fran.	W	2-1	Forsch	Knepper
21-Los Ang.	W	5-2	Vuckovich	Goltz
22-Los Ang.	W	3-2	Urrea	Sutton
23-Los Ang.	W	7-3	Martinez	Welch
25-At S.D.	W	3-2	Sykes	Kinney
26-At S.D.	L	3-4‡	Kinney	Hood
27-At S.D.	L	2-5	Lucas	Vuckovich
29-At S.F.	L	1-4	Ripley	Martinez
30-At S.F.	W	4-0	Fulgham	Knepper
31-At S.F.	L	4-6	Lavelle	Urrea

Won 14, Lost 13

AUGUST

Date		Score	Winner	Loser
1-At L.A.	L	1-2†	Goltz	Forsch
2-At L.A.	L	2-3	Welch	Vuckovich
3-At L.A.	W	4-1	Martinez	Hooton
6-At Phila.	W	14-0	Sykes	Walk
7-At Phila.	L	2-3	Carlton	Fulgham
8-N. York	L	2-3	Reardon	Littlefield
9-N. York	W	9-6	Urrea	Hausman
10-N. York	L	1-4	Bomback	Martinez
11-Montreal	W	16-0	Sykes	Sanderson
12-Montreal	L	0-4	Norman	Fulgham
13-Montreal	W	7-5	Forsch	Dues
14-Chicago	W	10-9†	Kaat	Riley
15-Chicago	L	4-5	McGlothen	Martinez
16-Chicago	L	4-9	Krukow	Sykes
17-Chicago	L	2-6	Reuschel	Fulgham
18-At Cinn.	W	10-1*	Forsch	Leibrandt
19-At Cinn.	L	2-4	LaCoss	Martinez
20-At Cinn.	L	3-4§	Price	Hood
22-At Atl.	W	7-4	Fulgham	Matula
23-At Atl.	L	2-7	Alexander	Vuckovich
24-At Atl.	L	5-10	Boggs	Martinez
25-Houston	W	3-1	Hood	Ruhle
26-Houston	L	2-7	Niekro	Kaat
27-Houston	W	10-2	Martin	K. Forsch
28-Atlanta	W	11-2	Forsch	Alexander
29-Atlanta	L	3-4	Boggs	Martinez
30-Atlanta	W	5-3	Hood	McWilliams
31-Atlanta	L	2-6	Niekro	Otten

Won 12, Lost 16

SEPTEMBER

Date		Score	Winner	Loser
1-Cinn.	L	1-8	Price	Kaat
2-Cinn.	W	12-4	Forsch	Moskau
3-Cinn.	W	4-3†	Kaat	Hume
5-At Hous.	W	7-5	Seaman	Sambito
6-At Hous.	L	5-9	Niekro	Sykes

SEPTEMBER			Winner	Loser	SEPTEMBER			Winner	Loser
6—At Hous.	L	4-6	Ruhle	Martin	22—Phila.	L	2-3†	Carlton	Seaman
7—At Hous.	W	2-0	Vuckovich	K. Forsch	23—Phila.	W	6-3	Olmsted	Walk
8—Chicago	L	2-6	McGlothen	Forsch	24—At Pitts.	L	3-6	Rhoden	Martin
9—Chicago	W	6-4	Martinez	Capilla	25—At Pitts.	W	10-2	Kaat	Robinson
10—Pitts.	L	6-7	Bibby	Hood	26—At N.Y.	W	5-1	Rincon	Allen
11—Pitts.	L	1-2	Blyleven	Martin	27—At N.Y.	W	4-2	Little	Bomback
12—At Phila.	W	7-4	Vuckovich	Walk	28—At N.Y.	L	0-8	Scott	Olmsted
12—At Phila.	W	5-0†	Littlefield	Reed	29—At Mon.	L	2-5	Fryman	Frazier
13—At Phila.	L	1-2	Carlton	Forsch	30—At Mon.	L	2-7	Gullickson	Forsch
14—At Phila	L	4-8	Bystrom	Martinez					
15—At Chi.	W	5-1	Rincon	Capilla			Won 15, Lost 15		
16—At Chi.	L	5-6	Caudill	Littlefield					
17—At Chi.	W	8-5	Vuckovich	Krukow	OCTOBER				
19—Montreal	W	9-8	Kaat	Sosa	1—At Mon.	L	0-8	Palmer	Rincon
20—Montreal	W	4-5	Lee	Littlefield	3—N. York	W	6-4	Frazier	Jackson
21—Montreal	W	4-1	Rincon	Palmer	4—N. York	L	2-5	Bomback	Little
					5—N. York	W	3-2	Martin	Falcone
							Won 2, Lost 2		

*6½ innings.   †10 innings.   ‡11 innings.   §12 innings.   x13 innings.

Torre's Kids Learned Late-Season Lesson

By JACK LANG

For New York Mets fans, 1980 was the season that almost was. It was a season that Manager Joe Torre constantly referred to as one of peaks and valleys. But it is always the bottom line that counts and no matter how many peaks you reach, when you finish in the valley, that is what people remember most.

Torre and General Manager Frank Cashen would prefer that fans remember the Mets of May 14 to August 13. In that period, the Mets were as good as any team in the league. From a 9-18 record, Torre's kids soared to 56-57. Their record in that period was a relatively sizzling 47-39.

The Mets returned home from a winning road trip August 14 in the best shape they had been in all season. Torre finally had all of his starters primed and ready to go. The Mets were 2½ games out of third place, only 7½ out of first. They were, in the eyes of everyone who saw them, legitimate contenders.

"Joe Torre should be named manager of the year for what he has done with that club," said Pittsburgh Manager Chuck Tanner.

But it was the beginning of the end for the Mets. They dropped five straight games to Philadelphia and won only 11 games the rest of the year while losing 33. They finished in fifth place with a 67-95 record, coming out of the basement after three straight years there. For all concerned, however, it was a dismal finish.

The season began with bright hope and fresh money when Nelson Doubleday and Fred Wilpon paid a record $21.1 million for the franchise in late January. Immediately, they assured the fans they would spend money to revitalize the franchise. They brought in Cashen from the Commissioner's office to serve as general manager. The longtime Baltimore Orioles front-office man was to provide the expertise the Mets' executive suite was missing.

As it developed, Cashen's only solid acquisition during the season was outfielder Claudell Washington, a .275 hitter who hit 10 home runs and drove in 72 runs in 79 games.

But Cashen had said from the start that his first year would be spent mainly as an observer. He would take a look-and-see approach before he moved.

Torre did not have that luxury. With a one-year contract, his job was on the line. But by the end of the year, for a job well done, Torre was rewarded with a surprising two-year contract.

The season began slowly for the Mets. Pat Zachry, the fragile righthander, was left in Florida with a tender elbow. The first month of the season, the Mets went 6-10.

Then, things began to happen. Neil Allen (22 saves) and Jeff Reardon both pitched well out of the bullpen. Mark Bomback proved a tremendous surprise as a rookie righthander. By early August, he had nine wins and was leading the staff. He won only one more game the rest of the way, but his 10 victories led the staff.

Therein lay the Mets' major problem. As Torre said, he expected better work from his starters. Unexpectedly, his top three starters all broke down.

Zachry was on the disabled list at the start of the year and did not start a game until May 18. He finished 6-10, but his 3.00 ERA was the league's sixth best.

Craig Swan, after signing a five-year, $3.15 million contract in spring training, had shoulder problems and was only 5-8 when he went on the shelf in mid-July. He made two aborted comeback attempts in August and then was sidelined for good with a slight tear in the rotator cuff.

Ray Burris, the third starter, broke his thumb bunting in the first week of July and was out for a month.

So, people like Pete Falcone (7-10), Roy Lee Jackson (1-7) and John Pacella (3-4) were starting in place of the top three.

To add to their woes, the Mets lost John Stearns for the season July 26 when he broke a finger catching a foul tip, and on August 19 Gold Glove second baseman Doug Flynn broke his right wrist.

When he had a healthy team, Torre moulded them into a contender despite the absence of a power hitter or big RBI man. The Mets, with 61 homers, had less punch than any other team in the majors. They did not have a .300 hitter or anyone with more RBIs than Lee Mazzilli's 76.

Mazzilli also led the team in homers with 16, and Washington was the only other Met with more than 10. Mets catchers failed to hit for circuit.

Torre tried to compensate with speed. The Mets swiped 158 bases, a club record. Mazzilli stole 41 bases, Frank Taveras 32 and Steve Henderson 23.

That kind of baseball excited fans and attendance at Shea Stadium rose almost 400,000 from the club low of 788,905 in 1979.

SCORES OF NEW YORK METS' 1980 GAMES

APRIL			Winner	Loser	MAY			Winner	Loser
10—Chicago	W	5-2	Swan	Reuschel	1—Phila.	L	1-2	Carlton	Falcone
11—Chicago	L	5-7	Lamp	Burris	2—S.Diego	L	0-1	Wise	Burris
12—Chicago	L	3-6	Krukow	Allen	3—S.Diego	L	1-2	Lucas	Swan
13—Chicago	W	5-0	Falcone	Hernandez	4—S.Diego	L	3-4	Curtis	Reardon
15—Montreal	L	3-7	Rogers	Swan	4—S.Diego	W	6-2	Glynn	Rasmussen
16—Montreal	W	3-2	Burris	Lee	5—Cinn.	W	3-2‡	Reardon	Bair
17—At Chi.	L	1-4	Lamp	Hausman	6—Cinn	L	10-12y	Tomlin	Reardon
19—At Chi.	L	9-12	Tidrow	Allen	7—Cinn.	L	2-3x	Hume	Zachry
20—At Chi.	L	3-6	Reuschel	Kobel	9—At Mon.	W	2-1	Swan	Rogers
21—At Phila.	W	3-0	Burris	Carlton	10—At Mon.	L	3-5	Lee	Kobel
22—At Phila.	L	8-14	Saucier	Kobel	13—At Cinn.	L	4-15	Pastore	Burris
23—At Phila.	W	3-2	Bomback	LaGrow	14—At Cinn.	W	7-6‡	Reardon	Hume
25—At Hous.	L	4-7	Richard	Falcone	16—At Atl.	W	5-3	Falcone	Niekro
26—At Hous.	L	0-6	Niekro	Glynn	18—At Atl.	L	1-2	Matula	Zachry
27—At Hous.	L	3-4x	LaCorte	Allen	18—At Atl.	W	2-1	Allen	Garber
30—Phila.	W	2-0	Bomback	Lerch	20—Houston	L	2-3	Forsch	Swan
			Won 6, Lost 10		21—Houston	W	5-1	Falcone	Richard

NEW YORK METS—1980

Front row—McKenna, trainer; Sisler, coach; Pignatano, coach; Walker, coach; Cottier, coach; Osmundsen, coach; Mayol, trainer. Second row—Cardenal, Swan, Stearns, Flynn, Henderson, Torre, manager; Youngblood, Taveras, Mazzilli, Trevino, Zachry, Allen. Third row—Niss, traveling secretary (retired); Berenguer, Reardon, Morales, Jorgensen, Hodges, Burris, Falcone, Maddox, Kobel, D. Norman, Richman, traveling secretary. Fourth row—H. Norman, equipment manager; Searage, Boisclair, Orosco, Mankowski, Jackson, Pacella, Glynn, Scott, Bomback, Wilson, Hausman, Chapman, Samuels, clubhouse attendant. Top row—Rosado, Andrews, Moreno, Harris, Leary, Brooks, Benton, Holman, Ramirez, Backman, Lynch, Hough, Giles.

MAY			Winner	Loser
22—Houston	L	5-8	Niekro	Kobel
23—Atlanta	W	2-1	Burris	Matula
24—Atlanta	W	5-4‡	Allen	Camp
25—Atlanta	W	3-0	Swan	Niekro
26—At St.L	L	5-8	Forsch	Falcone
27—At St.L.	W	9-5	Bomback	Martinez
28—At St.L.	W	6-5	Kobel	Frazier
30—At Pitts.	W	5-1*	Zachry	Candelaria
31—At Pitts.	L	0-5	Blyleven	Swan
		Won 13, Lost 13		

JUNE				
1—At Pitts.	L	3-13	Bibby	Falcone
3—St. Louis	L	1-8	Fulgham	Burris
4—St. Louis	W	0-1‡	Kaat	Allen
5—St. Louis	W	2-1	Swan	Frazier
6—Pitts.	W	9-4	Hausman	Blyleven
7—Pitts.	W	6-5§	Allen	Jackson
8—Pitts.	W	6-4	Burris	Romo
8—Pitts.	L	0-3	Solomon	Bomback
10—Los Ang.	W	5-4	Hausman	Welch
11—Los Ang.	W	6-2‡	Swan	Sutcliffe
12—Los Ang.	W	6-5	Reardon	Castillo
13—S. Fran.	L	1-3	Blue	Burris
14—S. Fran.	W	7-6	Reardon	Ripley
15—S. Fran.	L	0-3	Knepper	Zachry
16—At S.D.	L	2-3	Fingers	Reardon
17—At S.D.	L	1-2	Fingers	Hausman
18—At S.F.	L	5-8	Montefusco	Burris
19—At S.F.	L	3-4‡	Lavelle	Allen
20—At L.A.	L	3-4	Howe	Zachry
21—At L.A.	L	0-5	Reuss	Swan
22—At L.A.	W	9-6	Bomback	Goltz
24—At Chi.	W	6-5	Bomback	Reuschel
25—At Chi.	W	9-1	Zachry	Krukow
25—At Chi.	L	1-4	McGlothen	Falcone
26—At Chi.	W	4-3	Glynn	Tidrow
27—At Phila.	W	3-2	Pacella	Carlton
28—At Phila.	W	2-1§	Allen	Reed
28—At Phila.	W	5-4	Hausman	Saucier
29—At Phila.	L	2-5	Walk	Zachry
		Won 15, Lost 14		

JULY				
1—Chicago	L	3-4	Lamp	Swan
2—Chicago	W	3-1	Pacella	Reuschel
3—Montreal	W	7-2	Hausman	Lea
4—Montreal	W	9-5	Glynn	Palmer
4—Montreal	L	5-6	Fryman	Bomback
5—Montreal	W	7-5	Falcone	Sanderson
6—Montreal	L	4-9‡	Fryman	Reardon
10—Pitts.	W	2-0	Zachry	Candelaria
11—Pitts.	L	2-4	Blyleven	Swan
12—St. Louis	L	6-8x	Littlefield	Glynn
13—St. Louis	W	7-4	Falcone	Sykes
13—St. Louis	W	10-4	Bomback	Otten
15—At Atl.	W	9-2	Zachry	Alexander
16—At Atl.	W	2-1‡	McWilliams	Swan
17—At Atl.	W	6-0	Pacella	Matula
18—At Cinn.	L	3-5	Soto	Falcone
18—At Cinn.	L	3-8	Berenyi	Bomback
19—At Cinn.	W	13-3	Jackson	Leibrandt
20—At Cinn.	L	3-4	Hume	Reardon
21—At Hous.	L	2-5	LaCorte	Allen
22—At Hous.	L	5-6	Roberge	Glynn
23—At Hous.	W	4-3	Reardon	LaCorte
25—Cinn.	W	2-0	Zachry	Moskau
26—Cinn.	L	1-5	Bonham	Jackson
27—Cinn.	L	4-10	Price	Pacella
28—Atlanta	L	3-6	Alexander	Falcone
29—Atlanta	W	2-1	Bomback	McWilliams
30—Atlanta	W	3-0	Zachry	Boggs
		Won 14, Lost 14		

AUGUST			Winner	Loser
1—Houston	W	5-4	Reardon	Smith
2—Houston	W	5-3	Allen	Niekro
3—Houston	L	2-3‡	Sambito	Reardon
4—At Mon.	L	3-4‡	Sosa	Allen
4—At Mon.	W	4-3	Bomback	Lee
5—At Mon.	L	5-11	Gullickson	Pacella
6—At Mon.	L	1-4	Sanderson	Jackson
7—At Mon.	W	7-1	Burris	Norman
8—At St.L.	W	3-2	Reardon	Littlefield
9—At St.L.	L	6-9	Urrea	Hausman
10—At St.L.	W	4-1	Bomback	Martinez
11—At Pitts.	L	1-2†	Solomon	Jackson
12—At Pitts.	W	3-1	Burris	Rhoden
13—At Pitts.	W	5-3	Hausman	Candelaria
14—Phila.	L	1-8	Espinosa	Zachry
15—Phila.	L	0-8	Christenson	Bomback
16—Phila.	L	6-11	Walk	Swan
17—Phila.	L	4-9	Carlton	Burris
17—Phila.	L	1-4	Lerch	Jackson
19—S. Fran.	L	4-5	Knepper	Reardon
20—S. Fran.	L	1-2	Hargesh'mer	Bomback
21—S. Fran.	W	5-1	Falcone	Blue
22—Los Ang.	W	4-2	Burris	Welch
23—Los Ang.	L	2-4	Goltz	Hausman
24—Los Ang.	L	2-3	Hooton	Zachry
26—S. Diego	L	6-8z	Rasmussen	Falcone
27—S. Diego	L	1-4	Wise	Burris
29—At S.F.	L	0-1	Blue	Zachry
30—At S.F.	W	9-5	Hausman	Ripley
31—At S.F.	L	4-11	Lavelle	Falcone
31—At S.F.	L	4-9	Montefusco	Miller
		Won 11, Lost 20		

SEPTEMBER				
1—At L.A.	L	2-5	Welch	Burris
2—At L.A.	L	5-6	Goltz	Pacella
3—At L.A.	L	0-2	Hooton	Zachry
4—At S.D.	L	2-3	Curtis	Allen
5—At S.D.	L	2-4	Eichelberger	Bomback
6—At S.D.	L	7-8	Wise	Burris
7—At S.D.	L	2-5	Shirley	Pacella
9—At Mon.	L	0-3	Rogers	Zachry
10—Phila.	L	0-5	Bystrom	Bomback
11—Phila.	L	1-5	Ruthven	Burris
12—Chicago	L	5-10y	Smith	Hausman
13—Chicago	W	4-2	Lynch	McGlothen
14—Chicago	W	10-7	Allen	Sutter
16—Montreal	L	3-5§	Sosa	Berenguer
16—Montreal	L	2-4	Palmer	Jackson
17—Montreal	W	5-2	Miller	Sanderson
19—At Pitts.	L	3-4	Rhoden	Lynch
20—At Pitts.	W	9-6§	Allen	Tekulve
21—At Pitts.	L	4-9	Candelaria	Burris
22—At Chi.	L	2-3	Caudill	Miller
23—At Chi.	L	5-6	Krukow	Scott
24—At Phila.	L	0-1‡	McGraw	Allen
25—At Phila.	L	1-2	Bystrom	Jackson
26—St. Louis	L	1-5	Rincon	Allen
27—St. Louis	L	2-4	Little	Bomback
28—St. Louis	W	8-0	Scott	Olmsted
29—Pitts.	W	5-4‡	Reardon	Jackson
30—Pitts.	W	3-2	Falcone	Robinson
		Won 7, Lost 21		

OCTOBER				
1—Pitts.	L	5-10	Bibby	Burris
3—At St.L.	L	4-6	Frazier	Jackson
4—At St.L.	W	5-2	Bomback	Little
5—At St.L.	L	2-3	Martin	Falcone
		Won 1, Lost 3		

*5½ innings. †6 innings. ‡10 innings. §11 innings. x12 innings. y14 innings. z18 innings.

Cubs Plummeted to Division Cellar

By JOE GODDARD

Bill Buckner won the National League batting championship and Bruce Sutter again led in saves, but those were the only highlights for the 1980 Chicago Cubs, who finished with the worst record (64-98) in the league and sixth worst in their 80-year modern history.

Although attendance went over one million for the 13th straight season, it was more than 400,000 behind 1979 as the Cubs lost slugger Dave Kingman and catcher Barry Foote for most of the year.

There were problems everywhere. General Manager Bob Kennedy hired Dodgers Coach Preston Gomez as manager, then fired him July 25 when the team was 38-52 and replaced him with third-base coach Joey Amalfitano, who was 26-46 the rest of the way.

Amalfitano agreed to return as manager in 1981 only after receiving assurances from Owner William Wrigley that he would have a voice in personnel changes.

Chicago starters lost a total of 65½ weeks of playing time due to injuries. Kingman, who led the major leagues in home runs in '79, missed half the season with a jammed right shoulder, suffered early in May against San Diego when he anticipated a home-plate collision and hit the ground awkwardly. He finished with 18 homers and 57 RBIs compared to 48 and 115 the previous season.

Catcher Barry Foote played in only 63 games before yielding to a herniated disc in his back. Outfielder Scot Thompson was out five weeks with a severe concussion. Workhorse pitcher Rick Reuschel missed a few turns with a weary arm.

The season got off to a wild and wet start before the first pitch. Kingman dumped a bucket of ice water on reporter Don Friske of the Arlington Heights (Ill.) Daily Herald during spring training, drawing the disapproval of his teammates. They also felt chagrin when Kingman failed to return from a West Coast trip late in May for the start of a homestand. And his weekly guest column for the Chicago Tribune lasted just two months.

The Cubs had a winning record in only one month, April (9-6). They stayed out of the cellar for a while because St. Louis was off to a worse start, but entered the basement to stay July 21.

Buckner, however, stayed near the top of the batting race most of the second half, winning the title with a .324 average to become the fourth Cubs champion in the last nine years. Bill Madlock led the league in 1975-76 and Billy Williams in 1972.

Buckner had criticized the organization a month earlier for what he perceived to be an indifference toward winning. "I didn't say anything the others weren't thinking," he said. "I just feel the club has gone backward a bit."

Sutter didn't go backward. The '79 Cy Young winner was awarded a $700,000 contract in arbitration just before spring training, then saved 28 games to bring his five-year total to 133.

Fellow relievers Dick Tidrow (6-5) and rookie Lee Smith (2-0) were the only Cubs with winning records. The bullpen was a bright spot, with Willie Hernandez (1-9, 4.42 ERA) the only disappointment. Bill Caudill had a 2.18

ERA, Sutter 2.65, Tidrow 2.79 and Smith 2.86 in 18 games.

"If we got to the bullpen with a lead, we were in good shape," Amalfitano said.

Seldom did the starters last as long as the seventh inning. The staff had only 13 complete games, with Reuschel owning six. His 11-13 record was his worst since 1975, yet his 3.40 ERA was far superior to the others. Lynn McGlothen was 12-14 with a 4.80 ERA, Dennis Lamp 10-14 and 5.19, and Mike Krukow 10-15 and 4.39.

They received little help from the defense, which made as many errors of omission as commission. Third base, where 34 errors were made, was particularly vulnerable. Steve Ontiveros, the incumbent third baseman, lost his job under Gomez and ended up in Japan. His successor, Lenny Randle, hit .276 and stole 19 bases but was an erratic fielder.

The Cubs fell from third in team batting average in '79 to 10th, and their .251 mark represented a drop of 18 points. Part-timer Mike Vail (.298) was the only Cub close to Buckner. Shortstop Ivan DeJesus was considered the steadiest everyday player, leading in runs (78), stolen bases (44) and walks (60).

Jerry Martin led in game-winning RBIs (nine), homers (23) and RBIs (73), but hit .227 and struck out 107 times. He too was critical of management and, like Buckner, hoped to be traded.

One player's comment about the injuries summed up the season. "We have a good bench," he said. "The trouble is, the bench is on the field."

SCORES OF CHICAGO CUBS' 1980 GAMES

APRIL			Winner	Loser
10—At N.Y.	L	2-5	Swan	Reuschel
11—At N.Y.	W	7-5	Lamp	Burris
12—At N.Y.	W	6-3	Krukow	Allen
13—At N.Y.	L	0-5	Falcone	Hernandez
14—At Pitts.	L	4-5*	Tekulve	Sutter
17—N. York	W	4-1	Lamp	Hausman
19—N. York	W	12-9	Tidrow	Allen
20—N. York	W	6-3	Reuschel	Kobel
22—St. Louis	W	16-12	Sutter	Littell
23—St. Louis	L	1-3	Martinez	Krukow
25—Pitts.	W	5-3	Reuschel	Rooker
26—Pitts.	L	2-9	Candelaria	Lamp
28—At St.L.	W	4-2	Hernandez	Sykes
29—At St.L.	W	6-4	Capilla	Sykes
30—At St.L.	L	2-8	Vuckovich	Lamp
			Won 9, Lost 6	
MAY				
2—At Cinn.	W	12-4‡	Sutter	Hume
3—At Cinn.	W	7-1	Krukow	Bonham
4—At Cinn.	L	2-3	Leibrandt	Reuschel
4—At Cinn.	L	4-5	Moskau	Caudill
6—S. Diego	L	0-4	Jones	Hernandez
7—S. Diego	W	7-4	Krukow	Wise
8—S. Diego	L	6-9	Shirley	Sutter
9—S. Fran.	L	3-6	Blue	Lamp
10—S. Fran.	W	15-9	McGlothen	Knepper
11—S. Fran.	L	2-3	Whitson	Krukow
12—At L.A.	L	1-2	Sutton	Reuschel
13—At L.A.	L	2-4	Welch	Lamp
14—At L.A.	W	5-2	McGlothen	Hooton
16—At S.D.	L	0-3	Jones	Krukow
17—At S.D.	W	2-1	Reuschel	Rasmussen
18—At S.D.	L	3-4	Fingers	Sutter
20—At S.F.	L	0-2	Whitson	Krukow
21—At S.F.	L	4-5	Blue	Reuschel
23—L.A.	W	2-0	Lamp	Sutton
24—L.A.	L	2-4	Welch	Krukow
25—L.A.	W	2-1	Sutter	Howe
26—Montreal	L	0-4	Rogers	Hernandez

MAY			Winner	Loser
27—Montreal	W	4-2	Lamp	Lee
28—Montreal	W	8-4b	Lamp	Murray
30—Phila.	W	10-7	Reuschel	Larson
31—Phila.	L	0-7	Carlton	Hernandez
			Won 11, Lost 15	
JUNE				
1—Phila.	W	5-4	Tidrow	Reed
2—At Mon.	L	7-8§	Fryman	McGlothen
3—At Mon.	W	5-2	Reuschel	Grimsley
4—At Mon.	L	1-8	Rogers	McGlothen
5—At Mon.	L	0-2	Sanderson	Lamp
6—At Phila.	L	5-6	Walk	Krukow
7—At Phila.	L	2-5	Lerch	Reuschel
8—At Phila.	W	2-0	McGlothen	Ruthven
9—At Hous.	L	2-6	Forsch	Lamp
10—At Hous.	L	2-5	Ruhle	Krukow
11—At Hous.	L	0-3	Richard	Reuschel
13—Atlanta	L	6-7	Alexander	McGlothen
14—Atlanta	L	10-5	Lamp	Niekro
15—Atlanta	W	4-1	Krukow	Matula
16—Houston	L	1-2	Ruhle	Hernandez
17—Houston	L	1-7	Richard	McGlothen
18—Cinn.	W	7-0	Lamp	Leibrandt
19—Cinn.	W	5-2	Krukow	Hume
20—At Atl.	W	4-2	McGlothen	Boggs
21—At Atl.	L	0-8	Alexander	Hernandez
22—At Atl.	W	3-2	Lamp	Niekro
24—N. York	L	5-6	Bomback	Reuschel
25—N. York	L	1-9	Zachry	Krukow
25—N. York	W	4-1	McGlothen	Falcone
26—N. York	L	3-4	Glynn	Tidrow
27—St. Louis	L	2-3‡	Seaman	Hernandez
28—St. Louis	L	6-8	Littlefield	Sutter
28—St. Louis	W	2-1	Krukow	Otten
29—St. Louis	L	7-9	Urrea	McGlothen
			Won 11, Lost 18	
JULY				
1—At N.Y.	W	4-3	Lamp	Swan

CHICAGO CUBS—1980

Top row—Amalfitano, coach; Biittner, Blackwell, Buckner, Capilla, Caudill, Clines. Second row—DeJesus, Dillard, Figueroa, Foote, Gomez, manager; Hernandez, Johnson. Third row—Kelleher, Kingman, Krukow, Lamp, Macko. Fourth row—Martin, McGlothen, Randle, Reuschel, Roarke, coach. Bottom row—Rojas, coach; Sutter, Thompson, Tidrow, Tyson, Vail, Williams, coach.

JULY			Winner	Loser	AUGUST			Winner	Loser
2—At N.Y.	L	1-3	Pacella	Reuschel	21—At Atl.	L	4-6	Niekro	Krukow
3—At Pitts.	L	3-5	Bibby	Krukow	22—At Hous.	L	2-3‡	LaCorte	Caudill
4—At Pitts.	W	4-2	McGlothen	Solomon	23—At Hous.	L	0-1z	Niekro	Riley
4—At Pitts.	W	2-1	Capilla	Robinson	24—At Hous.	L	1-2	Ryan	Caudill
5—At Pitts.	L	4-5	Candelaria	Hernandez	25—At Cinn.	L	0-2	Seaver	McGlothen
6—At Pitts.	L	4-5a	Bibby	Lamp	26—At Cinn.	W	4-2	Reuschel	Hume
10—At Phila.	L	3-5	Ruthven	Krukow	28—Houston	L	1-4	Andujar	Lamp
11—At Phila.	L	2-7	Walk	McGlothen	29—Houston	L	5-6	Smith	Tidrow
12—At Mon.	L	2-10	Sanderson	Reuschel	30—Houston	L	0-2	Ruhle	McGlothen
12—At Mon.	W	8-6	Tidrow	Bahnsen	31—Houston	W	8-7	Tidrow	LaCorte
13—At Mon.	L	1-2	Bahnsen	Capilla				Won 11, Lost 20	
15—Los Ang.	L	2-6	Hooton	McGlothen					
16—Los Ang.	W	4-1	Reuschel	Reuss	SEPTEMBER				
17—Los Ang.	L	1-3	Sutton	Lamp	1—Atlanta	L	2-5	Matula	Lamp
18—S. Diego	L	1-2	Shirley	Capilla	2—Atlanta	L	5-10	Alexander	Krukow
19—S. Diego	W	8-7	Caudill	Kinney	3—Atlanta	L	3-4	Boggs	McGlothen
20—S. Diego	W	6-0	McGlothen	Jones	5—Cinn.	L	3-5	Seaver	Reuschel
21—S. Fran.	L	0-2c	Lavelle	Caudill	6—Cinn.	W	4-3*	Sutter	Hume
22—S. Fran.	W	3-1	Lamp	Bordley	6—Cinn.	L	1-6	Price	Martz
23—S. Fran.	L	6-14	Ripley	Capilla	7—Cinn.	W	6-4	Sutter	Bair
25—At L.A.	L	6-7	Howe	Sutter	8—At St.L.	W	6-2	McGlothen	Forsch
26—At L.A.	W	5-3	McGlothen	Reuss	9—At St.L.	L	4-6	Martinez	Capilla
27—At L.A.	L	2-3‡	Howe	Caudill	10—At Mon.	L	2-4	Gullickson	Reuschel
28—At S.D.	L	2-4†	Fingers	Riley	11—At Mon.	L	5-6	Fryman	Martz
29—At S.D.	L	1-3	Jones	Capilla	12—At N.Y.	W	10-5x	Smith	Hausman
30—At S.D.	L	2-5	Shirley	Sutter	13—At N.Y.	L	2-4	Lynch	McGlothen
			Won 9, Lost 18		14—At N.Y.	L	7-10	Allen	Sutter
					15—St. Louis	L	1-5	Rincon	Capilla
AUGUST					16—St. Louis	W	6-5	Caudill	Littlefield
1—At S.F.	W	5-3	Reuschel	Bordley	17—St. Louis	L	5-8	Vuckovich	Krukow
2—At S.F.	L	5-8	Griffin	Tidrow	19—Phila.	W	4-3	Smith	Brusstar
3—At S.F.	W	3-2	Krukow	Ripley	20—Phila.	L	3-7	Bystrom	McGlothen
3—At S.F.	W	3-2	Tidrow	Knepper	21—Phila.	L	3-7	Ruthven	Lamp
5—Pitts.	W	11-3	Reuschel	Candelaria	22—N. York	W	3-2	Caudill	Miller
6—Pitts.	L	7-9	Tekulve	Tidrow	23—N. York	W	6-5	Krukow	Scott
6—Pitts.	L	0-2	Blyleven	Capilla	24—Montreal	L	4-8	Lea	Reuschel
7—Pitts.	L	3-11	Solomon	Hernandez	25—Montreal	W	5-4	McGlothen	Gullickson
8—Montreal	L	2-5	Lea	Krukow	26—Pitts.	W	9-8	Caudill	Tekulve
9—Montreal	W	3-1	Reuschel	Rogers	27—Pitts.	W	2-0	Martz	Bibby
9—Montreal	L	3-4	Sosa	Sutter	28—Pitts.	W	3-2	Krukow	Blylven
10—Montreal	L	3-7	Gullickson	Lamp	29—At Phila.	L	5-6y	Saucier	Lamp
11—Phila.	L	5-8d	Brusstar	Riley	30—At Phila.	L	2-14	Bystrom	McGlothen
12—Phila.	L	2-5	Carlton	Krukow				Won 12, Lost 17	
13—Phila.	W	2-1	Tidrow	Ruthven					
14—At St.L.	L	9-10*	Kaat	Riley	OCTOBER				
15—At St.L.	W	5-4	McGlothen	Martinez	1—At Phila.	L	0-5	Carlton	Lamp
16—At St.L.	W	9-4	Krukow	Sykes	2—At Phila.	L	2-4	Walk	Caudill
17—At St.L.	W	6-2	Reuschel	Fulgham	3—At Pitts.	L	1-3	Jefferson	Reuschel
19—At Atl.	L	4-5†	Niekro	Tidrow	4—At Pitts.	W	6-0	McGlothen	Perez
20—At Atl.	L	5-9	McWilliams	McGlothen	5—At Pitts.	L	0-1	Robinson	Capilla
								Won 1, Lost 4	

*10 innings. †11 innings. ‡12 innings. §13 innings. x14 innings. y15 innings. z17 innings. a20 innings. b14-inning suspended game, completed August 8. c15-inning suspended game, completed July 22. d15-inning suspended game, completed August 12.

WEST DIVISION

Trials, Tribulations Tainted Astros' Title

By HARRY SHATTUCK

Amidst the joy and excitement of their first National League West Division championship, the Houston Astros also rode an emotional roller coaster which was filled with sadness and despair.

In their previous 19 years of existence in the N.L., the Astros had exceeded .500-baseball only three times. But in 1980 they put together a 93-70 mark, including a 7-1 victory over the Los Angeles Dodgers in a playoff for the West Division title.

The successes were many for the Astros until they succumbed to the Philadelphia Phillies in five games in the league Championship Series.

However, one wonders just how far the Astros could have gone if they had a healthy J. R. Richard, one of the most dominating pitchers in recent N.L. history. Richard, for the four previous years, had won 74 games. Pitching despite arm, shoulder and back trouble the first half of 1980, he was 10-4. He was the N.L. starter in the All-Star Game at Los Angeles. But, history would show that he would pitch only two more innings for the Astros before being struck down by a stroke.

The unexpected continued even after the season. Despite 93 wins in the regular campaign and two more in the Championship Series, despite coming within one run of reaching the World Series, the Astros found their general manager, Tal Smith, fired by Owner John McMullen two weeks later. Smith was still receiving accolades, including THE SPORTING NEWS Executive of the Year award, for remarkably rebuilding a 97-game loser into a division champion within five years. McMullen would cite only "philosophical differences" with Smith and a belief "that the people of Houston deserve a World Series."

Speculation (conjecture, it turned out) was that Manager Bill Virdon would be the next to go in McMullen's unusual scheme. All Virdon had accomplished was to win nearly every Manager of the Year acclamation, including TSN's. Virdon already had signed a three-year contract through the 1983 season, but Smith had more than a year left on his pact, too.

Smith's dismissal caused McMullen's limited partners to rebel. Out of the power struggle came a three-man executive committee, inclusive of McMullen, that would be responsible for major policy decisions.

Among the individual performances, Cesar Cedeno's was perhaps the most satisfying. Making a stellar comeback from knee and hand injuries, he batted .309, drove in 73 runs and stole 48 bases.

Jose Cruz hit .302, giving him a .301 cumulative average for the past five years. And because the Astros were in the spotlight more than in past seasons, he finally achieved the recognition he had deserved for some time.

Terry Puhl, playing both right and center field, continued to establish himself as one of baseball's young stars. Puhl hit .282, led the Astros with 13 homers and stole 27 bases.

Joe Morgan, signed as a re-entry free agent, started slowly but was the team's offensive catalyst down the stretch. Morgan hit only .243 for the season, but his experience and ability to get on base with walks was a key in the late pennant drive.

Pitching, however, was the Astros' chief weapon. Richard, Joe Niekro (20-12), Nolan Ryan (3.35 ERA) and Ken Forsch (3.20 ERA) formed one of the game's best starting rotations the first half of the season. After Richard was struck down, Vern Ruhle moved into the rotation. Rebounding from back surgery, Ruhle was 12-4 with a 2.38 ERA and pitched three brilliant complete games in the season's final two weeks.

Niekro performed superbly in the final weeks, prevailing in clutch game after clutch game, and recorded his second straight 20-win season with the playoff victory over Los Angeles.

Joe Sambito, Frank LaCorte and rookie Dave Smith provided talent and depth in the bullpen, combining for 23 wins and 38 saves.

The team ERA was a glittering 3.10, best in the majors and especially satisfying because Richard, the league ERA champ in 1979 and leading with

1.89 in '80, started only 17 games.

It was an outstanding season, but the satisfaction given by the organization's first title was tempered by the uncertain status of key players. Cedeno suffered a dislocated ankle in the third game of the Championship Series. Morgan was considering retirement and Richard's prospects for a full recovery were undivinable.

SCORES OF HOUSTON ASTROS' 1980 GAMES

APRIL

			Winner	Loser
10—Los Ang.	W	3-2	Richard	Hooton
11—Los Ang.	W	10-6	Smith	Stanhouse
12—Los Ang.	L	5-6§	Howe	Smith
13—Los Ang.	W	4-2	Forsch	Goltz
14—Atlanta	W	5-4	Sambito	Garber
15—Atlanta	W	6-2	Niekro	McWilliams
17—At L.A.	L	4-6	Reuss	Smith
18—At L.A.	W	7-4	Forsch	Goltz
19—At L.A.	W	2-0	Richard	Welch
20—At L.A.	L	2-4	Reuss	Niekro
21—Cinn.	L	5-6	LaCoss	Ruhle
22—Cinn.	W	8-0	Ryan	Pastore
23—Cinn.	L	2-3‡	Hume	Andujar
25—N. York	W	7-4	Richard	Falcone
26—N. York	W	6-0	Niekro	Glynn
27—N. York	W	4-3‡	LaCorte	Allen
29—At Cinn.	W	3-0	Forsch	Leibrandt
30—At Cinn.	W	5-1	Richard	Seaver

Won 13, Lost 5

MAY

			Winner	Loser
1—At Cinn.	W	9-3	Niekro	LaCoss
2—At St.L.	L	1-9	Hood	Ryan
3—At St.L.	W	4-2	Ruhle	Martinez
4—At St.L.	W	4-2	Forsch	Sykes
5—At Mon.	L	1-10	Palmer	Richard
6—At Mon.	W	8-4	Niekro	Grimsley
7—At Mon.	L	0-3	Sanderson	Ryan
9—At Atl.	L	4-5	McWilliams	Forsch
10—At Atl.	W	3-2†	LaCorte	Garber
11—At Atl.	L	4-7	P. Niekro	J. Niekro
13—Mon.	L	2-3	Palmer	Ryan
14—Mon.	L	0-1	Sanderson	Forsch
16—Phila.	L	0-3	Ruthven	Richard
17—Phila.	L	2-4	Christenson	Niekro
18—Phila.	W	3-0	Ryan	Lerch
20—At N.Y.	W	3-2	Forsch	Swan
21—At N.Y.	L	1-5	Falcone	Richard
22—At N.Y.	W	8-5	Niekro	Kobel
23—At Phila.	L	0-3	Carlton	Ryan
24—At Phila.	L	4-5	Saucier	Andujar
25—At Phila.	L	2-6	Ruthven	Forsch
26—S.D.	W	4-1	Richard	Curtis
27—S.D.	W	4-3	LaCorte	Fingers
28—S.D.	L	1-0	Ryan	Wise
30—At S.F.	L	2-3	Blue	Forsch
31—At S.F.	W	5-0	Richard	Montefusco

Won 12, Lost 14

JUNE

			Winner	Loser
1—At S.F.	L	2-6	Knepper	Niekro
2—At S.D.	L	0-3	Wise	Ryan
3—At S.D.	W	3-2	Ruhle	Jones
4—At S.D.	W	4-3	Forsch	Fingers
6—S. Fran.	W	2-0	Richard	Knepper
7—S. Fran.	W	3-0	Niekro	Whitson
8—S. Fran.	W	5-4	Sambito	Minton
9—Chicago	W	6-2	Forsch	Lamp
10—Chicago	W	5-2	Ruhle	Krukow
11—Chicago	W	3-0	Richard	Reuschel
13—At Pitts.	L	3-5	Solomon	Niekro
14—At Pitts.	W	7-3	Ryan	Robinson
15—At Pitts.	L	1-4	Candelaria	Forsch
16—At Chi.	W	2-1	Ruhle	Hernandez

JUNE

			Winner	Loser
17—At Chi.	W	7-1	Richard	McGlothen
18—St. Louis	W	3-0	Niekro	Kaat
19—St. Louis	W	2-0	Ryan	Sykes
20—Pitts.	W	6-4	Forsch	Candelaria
21—Pitts.	W	4-2	Ruhle	Blyleven
22—Pitts.	L	1-2	Bibby	Niekro
23—Los Ang.	L	0-3	Sutcliffe	Andujar
24—Los Ang.	W	5-4‡	LaCorte	Beckwith
25—Los Ang.	L	2-9	Welch	Forsch
27—Cinn.	W	5-4	Niekro	Pastore
28—Cinn.	L	5-8	Price	Richard
29—Cinn.	W	12-10	LaCorte	Soto
30—At Atl.	L	4-5†	Hrabosky	Sambito

Won 18, Lost 9

JULY

			Winner	Loser
1—At Atl.	L	4-13	Alexander	Niekro
2—At Atl.	L	0-14	P. Niekro	Ruhle
3—At Atl.	L	5-3	Richard	Boggs
4—At Cinn.	L	1-8	Leibrandt	Ryan
5—At Cinn.	L	6-8	Soto	Forsch
5—At Cinn.	L	2-3	LaCoss	Andujar
6—At Cinn.	W	3-2	Niekro	Pastore
10—At L.A.	L	3-4	Howe	Ryan
11—At L.A.	L	2-3	Reuss	Forsch
12—Atlanta	W	9-5	Niekro	McWilliams
13—Atlanta	W	6-5	Sambito	Garber
13—Atlanta	W	6-1	Ruhle	Boggs
14—Atlanta	L	0-2	P. Niekro	Pladson
15—Phila.	W	3-2	Sambito	Ruthven
16—Phila.	L	2-4	Walk	Forsch
17—Phila.	L	1-2	Carlton	Niekro
18—Montreal	L	4-5†	Fryman	Smith
19—Montreal	W	4-2	Andujar	Lea
19—Montreal	L	2-5	Gullickson	Pladson
20—Montreal	W	4-3	Sambito	Norman
21—N. York	W	3-2	LaCorte	Allen
22—N. York	W	6-5	Roberge	Glynn
23—N. York	L	3-4	Reardon	LaCorte
25—At Mon.	W	9-8	LaCorte	Sosa
26—At Mon.	L	1-2‡	Bahnsen	LaCorte
27—At Mon.	W	6-3	Niekro	Lee
28—At Phila.	W	3-2*	Sambito	Reed
29—At Phila.	L	6-9	Saucier	LaCorte
30—At Phila.	L	4-6	Ruthven	Ryan

Won 13, Lost 16

AUGUST

			Winner	Loser
1—At N.Y.	L	4-5	Reardon	Smith
2—At N.Y.	L	3-5	Allen	Niekro
3—At N.Y.	W	3-2*	Sambito	Reardon
4—S. Fran.	W	4-2	Ryan	Hargesh'mer
5—S. Fran.	L	3-9	Lavelle	Pladson
6—S. Fran.	W	1-0	Forsch	Blue
7—S. Diego	L	1-5	Shirley	Niekro
8—S. Diego	L	3-5	Eichelberger	Sambito
9—S. Diego	W	9-5	Smith	D'Acquisto
10—S. Diego	L	2-3	Wise	Sambito
11—At S.F.	L	4-5	Blue	Forsch
12—At S.F.	L	0-2	Ripley	Niekro
13—At S.F.	L	5-6‡	Rowland	Smith
13—At S.D.	W	2-1	Ryan	Curtis
15—At S.D.	W	3-1x	Smith	Rasmussen
17—At S.D.	W	5-0	Forsch	Jones

HOUSTON ASTROS—1980

Seated in front—Tucker, batboy. Front row—Kiger, trainer; Cabell, Cedeno, Niekro, Leppert, coach; Jones, coach; Virdon, manager; Wright, coach; Lillis, coach; Andujar, Sambito, Davidson, traveling secretary. Second row—Coleman, conditioning instructor; Bergman, Walling, Pujols, Ashby, Heep, Ruhle, Puhl, Reynolds, LaCorte, Smith, Ewell, trainer emeritus; Waters, assistant equipment manager; Liborio, equipment manager. Third row—Bochy, Ryan, Cruz, Landestoy, Morgan, Roberge, Pladson, Suba, bullpen coach; Howe, Leonard. Not shown—Richard, Forsch.

AUGUST			Winner	Loser
17—At S.D.	W	9-2	Niekro	Mura
19—Pitts.	W	5-2	Ryan	Candelaria
20—Pitts.	W	5-1	Ruhle	Bibby
21—Pitts.	W	12-5	Sambito	Blyleven
22—Chicago	W	3-2‡	LaCorte	Caudill
23—Chicago	W	1-0§	Niekro	Riley
24—Chicago	W	2-1	Ryan	Caudill
25—At St.L.	L	1-3	Hood	Ruhle
26—At St.L.	W	7-2	Niekro	Kaat
27—At St.L.	L	2-10	Martin	Forsch
28—At Chi.	W	4-1	Andujar	Lamp
29—At Chi.	W	6-5	Smith	Tidrow
30—At Chi.	W	2-0	Ruhle	McGlothen
31—At Chi.	L	7-8	Tidrow	LaCorte
Won 18, Lost 12				
SEPTEMBER				
1—At Pitts.	W	10-4	Smith	Robinson
1—At Pitts.	L	5-7	Rhoden	Pladson
3—At Pitts.	L	4-10	Candelaria	Andujar
5—St. Louis	W	5-7	Seaman	Sambito
6—St. Louis	W	9-5	Niekro	Sykes
6—St. Louis	W	6-4	Ruhle	Martin
7—St. Louis	L	0-2	Vuckovich	Forsch
9—Los Ang.	W	5-4	Smith	Howe
10—Los Ang.	W	6-5‡	Roberge	Sutcliffe
12—S. Fran.	W	5-3	Niekro	Whitson

SEPTEMBER			Winner	Loser
13—S. Fran.	W	3-2	Forsch	Blue
14—S. Fran.	W	6-4	Andujar	Montefusco
15—S. Diego	L	3-6	Shirley	Ryan
16—S. Diego	L	3-4	Curtis	Ruhle
17—At Cinn.	L	0-7	Soto	Niekro
18—At Cinn.	W	10-2	Forsch	Pastore
19—At S.F.	L	3-4	Griffin	Andujar
20—At S.F.	W	3-2	Smith	Lavelle
21—At S.F.	W	5-1	Ruhle	Blue
22—At S.D.	W	4-2	Niekro	Shirley
23—At S.D.	L	4-9	Curtis	Niemann
24—At Atl.	L	2-4	Alexander	Andujar
25—At Atl.	W	4-2	Ryan	Niekro
26—Cinn.	W	2-0	Ruhle	Seaver
27—Cinn.	W	2-0	Niekro	Soto
28—Cinn.	L	5-8	LaCoss	Andujar
30—Atlanta	W	7-3	Ryan	Alexander
Won 16, Lost 11				
OCTOBER				
1—Atlanta	W	5-2	Ruhle	P. Niekro
2—Atlanta	W	3-2	Niekro	McWilliams
3—At L.A.	L	2-3*	Valenzuela	Forsch
4—At L.A.	L	1-2	Reuss	Ryan
5—At L.A.	L	3-4	Howe	LaCorte
6—At L.A.	W	7-1	Niekro	Goltz
Won 3, Lost 3				

*10 innings. †11 innings. ‡12 innings. §17 innings. x20 innings.

Dodgers Came Up One Short Vs. Astros

By GORDON VERRELL

When the season began, there were those who doubted the Los Angeles Dodgers' chances in the National League West inasmuch as there were no fewer than six rookies on their 1980 roster.

The Dodgers got off slowly, trailing by as many as six games the first month. But they won 10 straight to close out April and by mid-May had reached first place in what was to be a lead alternated all season between the Dodgers, Houston and Cincinnati.

At the All-Star break the Dodgers were in a virtual tie with the Astros for first (Houston led by .002), and they did not trail by more than 3½ games the rest of the way.

When they returned home October 3 for their final three games of the season—all against first-place Houston—they trailed by three. But with a dramatic three-game sweep of the Astros, by scores of 3-2 (10 innings), 2-1 and 4-3, the Dodgers forced a one-game playoff for the division title—only to lose, 7-1.

It was the fourth time that the Dodgers, who finished 92-71, had been defeated in a playoff.

The Dodgers spared little expense in their attempt to repair the damage of a year before, when they staggered home in third place, a distant 11½ games out of first, and with a 79-83 record, their poorest in more than a decade. They went heavily into the re-entry draft, obtaining pitchers Dave Goltz (for $3 million) and Don Stanhouse (for $2.1 million).

It was Stanhouse whom the Dodgers figured would provide the answer to their bullpen woes of 1979. But he lasted only a week before a series of nagging ailments forced him onto the disabled list, where he resided for three months, the first of many numbing injuries to key personnel.

With Stanhouse gone, and veteran Terry Forster still recovering from a second elbow operation, the bullpen again was a mish-mash.

Jerry Reuss, who would emerge as the Dodgers' biggest winner—and biggest surprise—provided the early relief. Then rookie Steve Howe, less than a year out of the University of Michigan, stepped in to become Manager Tom Lasorda's long-sought stopper, saving 17 games.

Reggie Smith overcame a '79 season filled with disappointment and discontent to carry the Dodgers through the early months. He was having an MVP kind of season when his right shoulder gave out in mid-August. He was hitting .322 at the time, with 15 homers and 55 RBIs.

Then, in September, shortstop Bill Russell was lost when he was hit by a pitch and broke his right index finger. He had just put together an errorless streak of 47 games when he was injured.

Reuss, after winning three games and saving three the first 4½ weeks, won his first three starts. And in his ninth start, June 27 at San Francisco, he pitched the first no-hitter of his career. Only a first-inning error, by Russell, stood in the path of a perfect game as Reuss retired the final 25 batters.

Reuss, who was only 7-14 in '79, his first year at Los Angeles, finished 18-6, matching his career high in wins, and twice he won six games in a row. Only Steve Carlton's 24 wins for Philadelphia deprived him of the Cy Young Award.

Before declaring himself a free agent at season's end, 35-year-old Don Sutton made the last of his 15 years with the Dodgers a memorable one. He won 13 of 18 decisions and his 2.21 ERA was the lowest in the major leagues.

Besides Smith, the Dodgers' attack was led by Dusty Baker and Steve Garvey. Baker had a big first half (18 homers, 53 RBIs), yet failed to be selected to the All-Star team. He tired in September, his average falling from .303 to .294, and after driving in 21 runs in August, he batted in only 13 the final month to fall three short of his first 100-RBI season.

Garvey, who played in all 163 games (he started 162) to run his iron man streak to 835 games, the sixth longest on record, collected 41 hits in the final month for his third straight 200-hit season and sixth overall. His 200 hits led the N.L.

Both of the Dodgers' expensive free agents were a disappointment. Stanhouse, who returned in late July, saved only seven games and had a 5.04 ERA in only 21 appearances. Goltz, who spent a portion of July in the bullpen, was 7-11 with a 4.32 ERA. He lost five consecutive decisions between May 26 and July 21, and he lost his last four, including the one-game playoff with Houston.

Disheartening, too, was the performance of Rick Sutcliffe, whose 17 wins the year before had earned him N.L. Rookie of the Year honors. He was 3-9 with a 5.56 ERA.

Bob Welch, overcoming a '79 season of 5-6 as well as alcoholism, won nine of his first 12 decisions, but arm troubles hurt him the second half and he wound up 14-9.

Another surprise was 19-year-old Fernando Valenzuela, a portly lefthander from Mexico who arrived in mid-September from the Texas League. He made 10 appearances during the agonizing stretch run and did not allow an earned run in 17⅔ innings, while striking out 16.

The Dodgers attracted more than three million fans for the second time in three years. With 3,249,287, they averaged slightly more than 40,000 fans per home date.

SCORES OF LOS ANGELES DODGERS' 1980 GAMES

APRIL

			Winner	Loser
10—At Hous.	L	2-3	Richard	Hooton
11—At Hous.	L	6-10	Smith	Stanhouse
12—At Hous.	W	6-5x	Howe	Smith
13—At Hous.	L	2-4	Forsch	Goltz
14—At S.D.	L	1-2	Fingers	Castillo
15—At S.D.	L	5-9	Wise	Sutcliffe
16—At S.D.	W	10-4	Hooton	Curtis
17—Houston	W	6-4	Reuss	Smith
18—Houston	L	4-7	Forsch	Goltz
19—Houston	L	0-2	Richard	Welch
20—Houston	W	4-2	Reuss	Niekro
21—S. Fran.	W	4-3	Hooton	Blue
22—S. Fran.	W	6-0	Sutton	Knepper
23—S. Fran.	W	4-0	Goltz	Whitson
24—S. Fran.	W	5-2*	Reuss	Lavelle
25—S. Diego	W	6-3	Castillo	Kinney
26—S. Diego	W	4-3	Beckwith	Fingers
27—S. Diego	W	3-1	Sutton	Curtis
29—At S.F.	W	5-0	Goltz	Montefusco
30—At S.F.	W	4-3	Welch	Minton

Won 13, Lost 7

MAY

			Winner	Loser
2—At Phila.	L	5-9	Reed	Hough
3—At Phila.	L	3-7	Christenson	Hooton
4—At Phila.	W	12-10	Beckwith	Noles
6—At Pitts.	L	1-2	Tekulve	Howe
7—At Pitts.	L	6-7	Tekulve	Hough
9—At St.L.	L	7-15	Borbon	Sutcliffe
10—At St.L.	W	5-3	Hooton	Vuckovich
11—At St.L.	W	4-2	Goltz	Forsch
12—Chi.	W	2-1	Sutton	Reuschel
13—Chi.	W	4-2	Welch	Lamp
14—Chi.	L	2-5	McGlothen	Hooton
16—Pitts.	W	8-6	Reuss	Tekulve
17—Pitts.	W	3-1	Sutton	Blyleven
18—Pitts.	W	2-0	Welch	Bibby
19—St.L.	W	5-1	Hooton	Thomas
20—St.L.	W	4-3	Reuss	Vuckovich
21—St.L.	W	5-3	Beckwith	Littell
23—At Chi.	L	0-2	Lamp	Sutton
24—At Chi.	W	4-2	Welch	Krukow
25—At Chi.	L	1-2	Sutter	Howe
26—At Cinn.	W	4-0	Reuss	Seaver
26—At Cinn.	L	4-5	Moskau	Goltz
27—At Cinn.	L	1-6	LaCoss	Sutton
29—Atlanta	W	3-0	Welch	Niekro
30—Atlanta	W	8-4	Hooton	Matula
31—Atlanta	L	5-6	Boggs	Reuss

Won 15, Lost 11

JUNE

			Winner	Loser
1—Atlanta	L	5-9	Alexander	Goltz
2—Cinn.	W	3-2	Sutcliffe	Bair
3—Cinn.	W	5-1	Welch	Seaver
4—Cinn.	L	4-5	Moskau	Hough
6—At Atl.	W	5-0	Reuss	Niekro
7—At Atl.	L	1-6	Alexander	Goltz
8—At Atl.	W	3-1	Sutton	Boggs
10—At N.Y.	L	4-5	Hausman	Welch
11—At N.Y.	L	2-6*	Swan	Sutcliffe
12—At N.Y.	L	5-6	Reardon	Castillo
13—At Mon.	L	3-4	Rogers	Howe
14—At Mon.	W	8-0	Hooton	Grimsley
15—At Mon.	W	1-0	Welch	Gullickson
16—Phila.	L	2-3‡	Reed	Sutcliffe
17—Phila.	L	5-6	Reed	Castillo
18—Montreal	W	8-7	Hough	Sosa
19—Montreal	W	5-3*	Castillo	Fryman
20—N. York	W	4-3	Howe	Zachry
21—N. York	W	5-0	Reuss	Swan
22—N. York	L	6-9	Bomback	Goltz
23—At Hous.	W	3-0	Sutcliffe	Andujar
24—At Hous.	L	4-5‡	LaCorte	Beckwith

JUNE

			Winner	Loser
25—At Hous.	W	9-2	Welch	Forsch
27—At S.F.	W	8-0	Reuss	Blue
28—At S.F.	L	3-4†	Griffin	Sutcliffe
29—At S.F.	L	3-4	Knepper	Castillo
29—At S.F.	W	3-0	Hooton	Ripley
30—S. Diego	L	3-4	Eichelberger	Welch

Won 11, Lost 14

JULY

			Winner	Loser
1—S. Diego	L	1-4	Mura	Reuss
2—S. Diego	W	10-7	Sutcliffe	Blair
3—S. Diego	W	5-4*	Castillo	Shirley
4—S. Fran.	W	4-0	Sutton	Ripley
5—S. Fran.	W	3-2	Welch	Whitson
6—S. Fran.	L	4-7*	Holland	Howe
10—Houston	W	4-3	Howe	Ryan
11—Houston	W	3-2	Reuss	Forsch
12—At S.D.	L	2-3‡	Rasmussen	Beckwith
13—At S.D.	L	3-4§	Kinney	Beckwith
14—At S.D.	L	3-6	Mura	Sutcliffe
15—At Chi.	W	6-2	Hooton	McGlothen
16—At Chi.	L	1-4	Reuschel	Reuss
17—At Chi.	W	3-1	Sutton	Lamp
18—At Pitts.	L	4-6	Rhoden	Welch
19—At Pitts.	L	3-7	Solomon	Sutcliffe
20—At Pitts.	W	4-2	Hooton	Candelaria
20—At Pitts.	L	7-8	Jackson	Castillo
21—At St.L.	L	2-5	Vuckovich	Goltz
22—At St.L.	L	2-3	Urrea	Sutton
23—At St.L.	L	3-7	Martinez	Welch
25—Chicago	W	7-6	Howe	Sutter
26—Chicago	L	3-5	McGlothen	Reuss
27—Chicago	W	3-2‡	Howe	Caudill
28—Pitts.	L	4-6	Rhoden	Welch
29—Pitts.	W	10-2	Hooton	Blyleven
30—Pitts.	W	3-0	Reuss	Candelaria

Won 13, Lost 14

AUGUST

			Winner	Loser
1—St. Louis	W	2-1*	Goltz	Forsch
2—St. Louis	W	3-2	Welch	Vuckovich
3—St. Louis	L	1-4	Martinez	Hooton
4—At Atl.	W	5-3	Reuss	Boggs
5—At Atl.	L	4-6	Camp	Stanhouse
6—At Atl.	W	6-2	Sutton	Matula
7—At Atl.	L	3-4	Alexander	Welch
8—At Cinn.	L	5-8	Hume	Castillo
9—At Cinn.	W	9-4	Reuss	Seaver
10—At Cinn.	W	7-1	Goltz	Moskau
11—Atlanta	L	2-3	Matula	Sutton
12—Atlanta	L	6-7	Garber	Sutcliffe
13—Atlanta	L	0-2	Boggs	Hooton
15—Cinn.	W	3-1	Reuss	Seaver
16—Cinn.	L	2-3	Hume	Howe
17—Cinn.	L	2-6	Soto	Welch
19—At Mon.	W	3-2	Stanhouse	Sosa
20—At Mon.	W	5-1	Reuss	Rogers
21—At Mon.	W	5-4*	Howe	Bahnsen
22—At N.Y.	L	2-4	Burris	Welch
23—At N.Y.	W	4-2	Goltz	Hausman
24—At N.Y.	W	3-2	Hooton	Zachry
25—At Phila.	W	8-4	Stanhouse	Noles
26—At Phila.	W	8-4	Castillo	Walk
27—At Phila.	L	3-4	Carlton	Howe
29—Montreal	W	5-4	Castillo	D'Acquisto
30—Montreal	W	4-3	Hooton	Gullickson
31—Montreal	W	2-0	Reuss	Rogers
31—Montreal	W	7-2	Sutton	Palmer

Won 18, Lost 11

SEPTEMBER

			Winner	Loser
1—N. York	W	5-2	Welch	Burris
2—N. York	W	6-5	Goltz	Pacella
3—N. York	W	2-0	Hooton	Zachry

LOS ANGELES DODGERS—1980

Front row—Yeager, Howe, Adams, coach; Cresse, coach; Mota, player-coach; Lasorda, manager; Basgall, coach; Ozark, coach; Castillo, Thomas, Hatcher, Guerrero. Second row—Buhler, trainer; DeLury, traveling secretary; Law, Thomasson, Ferguson, Monday, Russell, Smith, Cey, Baker, Johnstone, Lopes, Vike, trainer; Muir, clubhouse man. Third row—Forster, Hooton, Hough, Rau, Welch, Sutcliffe, Reuss, Goltz, Sutton, Beckwith. Seated in front—batboys Garcia, C. Murillo, V. Murillo.

SEPTEMBER			Winner	Loser	SEPTEMBER			Winner	Loser
4—Phila.	L	2-3	Walk	Reuss	24—S. Fran.	W	5-4‡	Castillo	Rowland
5—Phila.	W	1-0	Sutton	Carlton	25—S. Fran.	L	2-3	Whitson	Hooton
6—Phila.	W	7-3	Welch	Lerch	26—At S.D.	L	2-3	Tellmann	Goltz
7—Phila.	W	6-0	Castillo	Ruthven	27—At S.D.	W	6-4	Sutton	Rasmussen
9—At Hous.	L	4-5	Smith	Howe	28—At S.D.	L	5-7	Fingers	Howe
10—At Hous.	L	5-6‡	Roberge	Sutcliffe	30—At S.F.	W	4-3*	Valenzuela	Lavelle
12—At Cinn.	W	5-2	Sutton	LaCoss					
13—At Cinn.	W	3-2	Castillo	Soto		Won 15, Lost 12				
14—At Cinn.	W	3-1	Reuss	Moskau					
15—At Atl.	L	0-9	Boggs	Hooton	OCTOBER				
16—At Atl.	L	1-2	Niekro	Goltz	1—At S.F.	W	8-4	Hooton	Whitson
17—S. Diego	W	2-1	Sutton	Eichelberger	2—At S.F.	L	2-3	Minton	Goltz
18—S. Diego	W	7-3	Welch	Wise	3—Houston	W	3-2*	Valenzuela	Forsch
19—Cinn.	L	7-10	LaCoss	Reuss	4—Houston	W	2-1	Reuss	Ryan
20—Cinn.	L	2-10	Seaver	Hooton	5—Houston	W	4-3	Howe	LaCorte
21—Cinn.	L	2-7†	Hume	Howe	6—Houston	L	1-7	Niekro	Goltz
22—Atlanta	L	2-7	Hanna	Sutton					
23—Atlanta	W	4-2	Welch	Matula		Won 4, Lost 2				

*10 innings. †11 innings. ‡12 innings. §15 innings. x17 innings.

Injured Pitchers Disabled Red Machine

By EARL LAWSON

The fact that the Cincinnati Reds weren't counted out in their bid for a second straight National League West title until the final week of the 1980 season, winding up third behind Houston and Los Angeles, was a tribute to the managerial skills of John McNamara, the willingness of key players to perform with injuries and the club's farm system. The Reds' 89-73 record left them 3½ games behind the Astros.

Injuries to members of the pitching staff were particularly critical. McNamara never was able to establish a consistent rotation, using nine different starters.

Bill Bonham, counted on as one of the starters, was plagued by shoulder problems and pitched only 19 innings. Tom Seaver went on the disabled list for the first time in his career. A sore right shoulder sidelined him for all of July, but he was strong down the stretch. During the last six weeks, Seaver was 6-1 with a 1.64 ERA. Still, the 10 victories he recorded, against eight losses, were the fewest of his 13-year career.

At the same time Seaver was sidelined, the Reds were also without the services of Frank Pastore, who wound up the club's top winner with a 13-7 record in his first full season in the majors. Pastore was disabled almost two months with tendinitis in the middle finger of his pitching hand.

That did, however, give the Reds an opportunity to look at rookie lefthander Joe Price and to see what Mario Soto could do as a starter. Neither disappointed. Price went 7-3 and Soto, who began the season as a middle-inning reliever, was by season's end one of the league's most effective starters. Soto finished with a 10-8 record and a 3.08 ERA, but nine of his victories came after the All-Star break. And, during that span, he picked up four saves and had a 2.29 ERA. What's more, his 182 strikeouts in 190 innings was the league's third highest total.

Another rookie lefthander, Charlie Leibrandt, was 8-4 midway through the season but finished 10-9.

The bullpen was anchored by Tom Hume, who shared the N.L. Fireman of the Year award with San Diego's Rollie Fingers. Hume won nine and lost 10, racked up 25 saves and had a 2.56 ERA.

CINCINNATI REDS—1980

Front row—Seaver, Spilman, Bench, Nixon, coach; Fischer, coach; McNamara, manager; Dunlop, coach; Plaza, coach; Hume, Kennedy, Nolan. Second row—Stowe, equipment manager; Miller, batboy; Bureman, traveling secretary; Moskau, Foster, Bonham, Price, LaCoss, Howell, Leibrandt, Knight, Bair, Feltner, assistant trainer. Third row—Geronimo, Driessen, Griffey, Pastore, Tomlin, Oester, Concepcion, Mejias, Soto, Cruz, Collins, Starr, trainer.

Surprisingly, only two N.L. teams—St. Louis and Philadelphia—scored more runs than the Reds. Surprisingly, because George Foster, one of baseball's top run producers for the past four seasons, struggled through a poor first half. Foster hit 16 homers and knocked in 62 runs after the All-Star Game, but still fell short of the century mark in RBIs (93) for the first time since 1976. His .273 average and 25 homers were below expectations, too.

The other outfielders, Ken Griffey and Dave Collins, had banner seasons. Griffey bounced back from knee surgery with a .294 average and notched career highs in homers (13) and RBIs (85). He stole 23 bases in 24 attempts. Collins topped the club with a .303 average and swiped 79 bases, just one short of Bob Bescher's club record that has stood since 1911.

Third baseman Ray Knight, disdaining injuries, batted .264—a 57-point drop from his '79 level—but hit 39 doubles, 14 homers and drove home 78 runs. Three of his homers were grand slams.

Shortstop Davey Concepcion played with a painful right elbow that required post-season surgery. He fielded his position well and, after a slow start at the plate, batted home 77 runs.

Concepcion had two keystone partners. Junior Kennedy opened at second base and was doing a respectable job when a minor injury to his foot opened the door for Ronnie Oester. The switch-hitting rookie hit .277 and quickly gained recognition for his brilliant fielding and gung-ho attitude.

Johnny Bench worked 100 or more games behind the plate for the 13th straight year, tying a major league record that had been held by Bill Dickey of the Yankees, and broke the home run record for catchers previously held by the Yankees' Yogi Berra. The record-breaking homer, Bench's 314th as a catcher, came off Montreal's David Palmer, July 15.

Joe Nolan, Bench's backup for most of the season, batted .307 in 70 games but wasn't expected to be the man to succeed Bench, who made it clear that this was his last season as a regular catcher.

A wrist that required off-season surgery crimped the style of first baseman Dan Driessen. Nevertheless, he hit .265, stole 19 bases and often was brilliant around the bag.

The Reds' lowest finish since 1971 didn't discourage their fans from putting their money down. For the eighth straight year, more than two million customers showed up at Riverfront Stadium.

SCORES OF CINCINNATI REDS' 1980 GAMES

APRIL			Winner	Loser	MAY			Winner	Loser
9—Atlanta	W	9-0	Pastore	Niekro	1—Houston	L	3-9	Niekro	LaCoss
11—Atlanta	W	6-0*	LaCoss	McWilliams	2—Chicago	L	4-12x	Sutter	Hume
12—Atlanta	W	5-4	Hume	Hrabosky	3—Chicago	L	1-7	Krukow	Bonham
13—Atlanta	W	5-0	Leibrandt	Niekro	4—Chicago	W	3-2	Leibrandt	Reuschel
14—S. Fran.	W	6-5	Tomlin	Lavelle	4—Chicago	W	5-4	Moskau	Caudill
15—S. Fran.	W	8-3	Seaver	Whitson	5—At N.Y.	L	2-3‡	Reardon	Bair
16—S. Fran.	W	5-3	LaCoss	Montefusco	6—At N.Y.	W	12-10z	Tomlin	Reardon
17—At Atl.	W	4-1	Pastore	Niekro	7—At N.Y.	W	3-2x	Hume	Zachry
18—At Atl.	L	0-3	Matula	Leibrandt	9—Phila.	W	5-2	Leibrandt	Lerch
19—At Atl.	W	6-1	Bonham	Alexander	10—Phila.	W	5-3	Seaver	Carlton
20—At Atl.	W	5-3	Tomlin	Bradford	11—Phila.	L	3-7	Ruthven	LaCoss
21—At Hous.	W	6-5	LaCoss	Ruhle	13—N. York	W	15-4	Pastore	Burris
22—At Hous.	L	0-8	Ryan	Pastore	14—N. York	L	6-7‡	Reardon	Hume
23—At Hous.	W	3-2x	Hume	Andujar	16—At Mont.	L	1-2	Rogers	Seaver
25—At S.F.	L	3-4	Minton	Bair	17—At Mont.	L	6-9	Bahnsen	Hume
26—At S.F.	L	1-3	Knepper	LaCoss	19—At Phila.	L	4-6	Carlton	Pastore
27—At S.F.	W	3-1	Pastore	Whitson	20—At Phila.	W	7-6	Moskau	Ruthven
29—Houston	L	0-3	Forsch	Leibrandt	21—At Phila.	L	8-9	Reed	Hume
30—Houston	L	1-5	Richard	Seaver	23—Montreal	L	4-7	Lee	LaCoss
					24—Montreal	W	2-0	Pastore	Palmer
		Won 13, Lost 6							

MAY

Date	W/L	Score	Winner	Loser
25—Montreal	L	4-7	Sanderson	Leibrandt
26—Los Ang.	L	0-4	Reuss	Seaver
26—Los Ang.	W	5-4	Moskau	Goltz
27—Los Ang.	W	6-1	LaCoss	Sutton
29—At S.D.	W	5-3	Pastore	Jones
30—At S.D.	W	5-3	Leibrandt	Mura
31—At S.D.	L	5-7	Shirley	Hume

Won 13, Lost 14

JUNE

Date	W/L	Score	Winner	Loser
1—At S.D.	W	7-6	Burnside	Lucas
2—At L.A.	L	2-3	Sutcliffe	Bair
3—At L.A.	L	1-5	Welch	Seaver
4—At L.A.	W	5-4	Moskau	Hough
6—S. Diego	W	4-2	Pastore	D'Acquisto
7—S. Diego	L	1-6	Lucas	LaCoss
8—S. Diego	W	1-0	Leibrandt	Jones
9—S. Diego	T	6-6a	......	
10—Pitts.	L	3-5	Candelaria	Soto
11—Pitts.	W	3-2	Pastore	Blyleven
12—Pitts.	L	6-10	Bibby	LaCoss
13—At St.L.	W	5-2	Leibrandt	Vuckovich
14—At St.L.	L	3-4	Littlefield	Soto
15—At St.L.	L	9-10y	Thomas	Moskau
16—At Pitts.	L	3-5	Blyleven	Pastore
17—At Pitts.	W	4-3	Moskau	Romo
18—At Chi.	L	0-7	Lamp	Leibrandt
19—At Chi.	L	2-5	Krukow	Hume
20—St. Louis	L	5-7	Seaman	Hume
21—St. Louis	W	8-5	Pastore	Littlefield
22—St. Louis	L	2-12	Vuckovich	LaCoss
24—Atlanta	W	8-2	Leibrandt	McWilliams
25—Atlanta	W	15-3	Seaver	Matula
27—At Hous.	L	4-5	Niekro	Pastore
28—At Hous.	W	8-5	Price	Richard
29—At Hous.	L	10-12	LaCorte	Soto
30—At S.F.	L	4-8	Bordley	Seaver

Won 11, Lost 15

JULY

Date	W/L	Score	Winner	Loser
1—At S.F.	L	1-4	Whitson	Moskau
2—At S.F.	W	6-2	Pastore	Montefusco
3—At S.F.	L	3-4	Knepper	Price
4—Houston	W	8-1	Leibrandt	Ryan
5—Houston	W	8-6	Soto	Forsch
5—Houston	W	3-2	LaCoss	Andujar
6—Houston	L	2-3	Niekro	Pastore
10—At Atl.	W	8-6	Moskau	Niekro
11—At Atl.	W	5-3	Soto	Alexander
12—S. Fran.	L	4-7	Lavelle	Bair
12—S. Fran.	L	7-10	Bordley	LaCoss
13—S. Fran.	L	0-2	Ripley	Price
14—S. Fran.	L	3-5	Hargesh'mer	Leibrandt
15—Montreal	W	11-7	Moskau	Palmer
16—Montreal	L	4-6	Rogers	Soto
17—Montreal	L	1-6	Sanderson	LaCoss
18—N. York	W	5-3	Soto	Falcone
18—N. York	W	8-3	Berenyi	Bomback
19—N. York	L	3-13	Jackson	Leibrandt
20—N. York	W	4-3	Hume	Reardon
21—Phila.	W	5-4	Leibrandt	Lerch
22—Phila.	W	3-2	Soto	Carlton
23—Phila.	W	7-3	Berenyi	Espinosa
25—At N.Y.	L	4-5	Zachry	Moskau
26—At N.Y.	W	5-1	Bonham	Jackson
27—At N.Y.	W	10-4	Price	Pacella
28—At Mon.	W	3-2	Bair	Lea
28—At Mon.	L	4-5	Norman	Soto
29—At Mon.	L	1-4	Gullickson	Berenyi
30—At Mon.	L	1-2	Fryman	Bair

Won 16, Lost 14

AUGUST

Date	W/L	Score	Winner	Loser
1—At Phila.	L	1-3	Walk	Leibrandt
2—At Phila.	W	2-0	LaCoss	Carlton
3—At Phila.	L	4-8	Espinosa	Berenyi
4—S. Diego	W	7-1	Seaver	Jones
4—S. Diego	W	11-2	Soto	Kinney
5—S. Diego	W	9-2	Moskau	Lucas
6—S. Diego	W	4-3	Hume	D'Acquisto
8—Los Ang.	W	8-5	Hume	Castillo
9—Los Ang.	L	4-9	Reuss	Seaver
10—Los Ang.	L	1-7	Goltz	Moskau
11—At S.D.	W	1-0	Leibrandt	Mura
12—At S.D.	W	3-2	Price	Jones
13—At S.D.	W	4-3	Soto	Shirley
15—At L.A.	L	1-3	Reuss	Seaver
16—At L.A.	L	3-2	Hume	Howe
17—At L.A.	W	6-2	Soto	Welch
18—St. Louis	L	1-10†	Forsch	Leibrandt
19—St. Louis	W	4-2	LaCoss	Martinez
20—St. Louis	W	4-3x	Price	Hood
22—Pitts.	L	2-4	Robinson	Moskau
23—Pitts.	L	1-2	Rhoden	Pastore
24—Pitts.	L	2-5	Candelaria	LaCoss
25—Chicago	W	2-0	Seaver	McGlothen
26—Chicago	L	2-4	Reuschel	Hume
28—At Pitts.	W	4-0	Moskau	Rhoden
29—At Pitts.	W	8-7	Soto	Tekulve
30—At Pitts.	L	5-3	Seaver	Bibby
31—At Pitts.	W	5-4	LaCoss	Blyleven

Won 18, Lost 10

SEPTEMBER

Date	W/L	Score	Winner	Loser
1—At St.L.	W	8-1	Price	Kaat
2—At St.L.	L	4-12	Forsch	Moskau
3—At St.L.	L	3-4‡	Kaat	Hume
5—At Chi.	W	5-3	Seaver	Reuschel
6—At Chi.	L	3-4‡	Sutter	Hume
6—At Chi.	W	6-1	Price	Martz
7—At Chi.	L	4-6	Sutter	Bair
8—At Atl.	W	6-1	Pastore	Alexander
9—At Atl.	W	7-1	Soto	Boggs
10—At Atl.	W	3-0	Seaver	McWilliams
12—Los Ang.	L	2-5	Sutton	LaCoss
13—Los Ang.	L	2-3	Castillo	Soto
14—Los Ang.	L	1-3	Reuss	Moskau
15—S. Fran.	W	6-2	Seaver	Knepper
16—S. Fran.	L	1-8	Whitson	Price
17—Houston	W	7-0	Soto	Niekro
18—Houston	L	2-10	Forsch	Pastore
19—At L.A.	W	10-7	LaCoss	Reuss
20—At L.A.	W	10-2	Seaver	Hooton
21—At L.A.	W	7-2§	Hume	Howe
22—At S.F.	L	3-7	Ripley	LaCoss
23—At S.F.	W	2-1	Pastore	Hargesh mer
24—At S.D.	W	7-6‡	Bair	Fingers
25—At S.D.	W	5-3‡	Bair	Kinney
26—At Hous.	L	0-2	Ruhle	Seaver
27—At Hous.	L	0-2	Niekro	Soto
28—At Hous.	W	8-5	LaCoss	Andujar
30—S. Diego	L	2-3	Curtis	Leibrandt

Won 15, Lost 13

OCTOBER

Date	W/L	Score	Winner	Loser
1—S. Diego	W	2-1	Hume	Shirley
3—Atlanta	L	1-4	Boggs	Soto
4—Atlanta	W	3-2	Pastore	Alexander
5—Atlanta	W	1-0	Price	Niekro

Won 3, Lost 1

*6 innings. †6½ innings. ‡10 innings. §11 innings. x12 innings. y13 innings. z14 innings. a10½-inning tie game.

Braves Bumblers Became Respectable

By KEN PICKING

What kind of team would lose 16 of 18 games to Cincinnati and win 11 of 12 from Pittsburgh?

What kind of team would demote one of baseball's top power hitters to the minors and bench its only 1979 All-Star?

What kind of team would stop using a pair of million-dollar relievers and turn to one coming off elbow surgery as its stopper?

What kind of team would take a catcher and make him the center fielder?

What kind? To the surprise of very few Georgians, who have become accustomed to their baseball team's antics the last decade, it was the Atlanta Braves who did all those wild and crazy things and finished 81-80, their best record since 1974. It was the first team owned by Ted Turner that did not finish sixth in the National League West.

"In general, .500 has been our goal, but we always thought we could do better," said Manager Bobby Cox, who never stopped thinking pennant until the Braves were mathematically eliminated. "This season should leave us all wanting more. I would like to explore the free-agent market and see what kind of trades could be made this winter. But I think we now have the personnel to do what Houston did with a few breaks."

Cox began building the best team in his three years at the controls during the December winter meetings, when the Braves acquired first baseman Chris Chambliss from Toronto and starting pitcher Doyle Alexander from Texas. Both not only had productive years, but they brought confidence and maturity to a young, inexperienced team. Chambliss, who hit .282 with 18 homers and 72 RBIs, also lent balance to an attack topheavy with righthanded batters.

Third baseman Bob Horner, the leader of that righthanded brigade, was hurt by the week of inactivity anticipating a players' strike and got off to an .059 start in 10 games. The lack of production so infuriated Turner—who said repeatedly, "All I want is my money's worth"—that the 1978 N.L. Rookie of the Year was optioned to the minors.

After a brief round of legal activity, the Braves finally came to their senses and reinstated Horner to the major league roster. He went on to finish second in the N.L. in homers (35) with 89 RBIs in 124 games. That brought his totals for 334 big league games to 91 homers and 250 RBIs.

Benched at about the same time was outfielder Gary Matthews, the team's only '79 All-Star. Matthews hit only .175 in April, but bounced back to finish at .278 with 19 homers and 75 RBIs.

Dale Murphy was moved to center after Eddie Miller was dispatched to the minors and the 24-year-old former catcher became the Braves' lone representative at the All-Star Game. The 6-5, 215-pounder hit 33 homers, third behind the Phillies' Mike Schmidt and Horner, and drove in 89 runs while hitting a career-high .281.

"For offense and defense, I'd take Murphy over any other center fielder in the league," Cox said.

Biff Pocoroba's forearm injury gave Bruce Benedict the opportunity to return from the Richmond farm club, and the young catcher thoroughly pleased Cox with his overall improvement.

ATLANTA BRAVES—1980

Front row—N. Pursley, batboy; Lassiter, batboy; Sullivan, coach; Boyer, coach; Cox, manager; Aaron, coach; Dews, coach; Murphy. Second row—Holland, assistant equipment manager; Alexander, Asselstine, Gomez, Matthews, Hubbard, Pocoroba, Spikes, Bradford, Hanna, Acree, equipment manager. Third row—D. Pursley, trainer; Camp, Niekro, Nahorodny, Matula, Horner, Boggs, McWilliams, Benedict, Lum, Hrabosky, Cowen, clubhouse man; Garber, Royster, Van Wieren, traveling secretary.

After Glenn Hubbard, another farmhand, replaced Jerry Royster at second base, the Braves went 64-54. Hubbard batted .248, but hit nine homers and had several key hits.

Luis Gomez played some of the best shortstop in the history of the Atlanta franchise, but his .191 average hastened the inevitable move to 21-year-old Rafael Ramirez, a .267 hitter in 50 games.

Phil Niekro needed to reel off a career-high seven straight victories late in the season to make his record 15-18. Alexander, a 17-game winner in '77, almost equaled his career high with a 14-11 season. The big boost for the rotation, however, was Tommy Boggs, who finished 12-9 with three shutouts and a 3.42 ERA.

Rick Matula and Larry McWilliams fought with inconsistency all summer and finished 11-13 and 9-14, respectively.

Cox thought that his bullpen would be his strength, but veterans Gene Garber and Al Hrabosky were never consistent enough to be considered the aces they once were. Garber appeared in 68 games and saved seven, 18 fewer than the season before. Hrabosky, who spent most of the second half experimenting with a forkball, had three saves and four victories in 45 appearances.

The Braves' savior was Rick Camp, who underwent elbow surgery the previous year and was thought to be finished by most in the Atlanta front office. But Cox made him his 10th man on the staff and Camp responded with one of the finest seasons by any reliever in the league. Relying almost exclusively on a savage sinker, Camp appeared in 77 games, a club record, saved 22 and finished 6-4 with a 1.92 ERA.

In a team vote, Camp was named the Braves' MVP for '80.

"We're moving up," Cox said, "but I won't be satisfied until we bring Atlanta the pennant. For two years it looked like we were just spinning our wheels, but now we're in the race to stay."

SCORES OF ATLANTA BRAVES' 1980 GAMES

APRIL			Winner	Loser	MAY			Winner	Loser
9—At Cinn.	L	0-9	Pastore	Niekro	13—Phila.	W	7-3	Alexander	Lerch
11—At Cinn.	L	0-6*	LaCoss	McWilliams	14—Phila.	L	1-9	Carlton	McWilliams
12—At Cinn.	L	4-5	Hume	Hrabosky	16—N. York	L	3-5	Falcone	Niekro
13—At Cinn.	L	0-5	Leibrandt	Niekro	18—N. York	W	2-1	Matula	Zachry
14—At Hous.	L	4-5	Sambito	Garber	18—N. York	L	1-2	Allen	Garber
15—At Hous.	L	2-6	J. Niekro	McWilliams	19—At Mon.	L	8-11	Palmer	McWilliams
17—Cinn.	L	1-4	Pastore	Niekro	20—At Mon.	W	1-0	Niekro	Sanderson
18—Cinn.	W	3-0	Matula	Leibrandt	21—At Mon.	L	2-3	Rogers	Garber
19—Cinn.	L	1-6	Bonham	Alexander	23—At N. Y.	L	1-2	Burris	Matula
20—Cinn.	L	3-5	Tomlin	Bradford	24—At N. Y.	L	4-5†	Allen	Camp
22—S. Diego	W	3-2†	Hrabosky	Shirley	25—At N. Y.	L	0-3	Swan	Niekro
23—S. Diego	W	2-1	Matula	Jones	26—S. Fran.	W	2-1	Boggs	Minton
24—S. Diego	W	8-7	Garber	Fingers	27—S. Fran.	W	6-3	McWilliams	Knepper
25—Montreal	W	8-7‡	Bradford	Bahnsen	28—S. Fran.	W	3-2§	Hrabosky	Lavelle
26—Montreal	L	3-4	Grimsley	Niekro	29—At L.A.	L	0-3	Welch	Niekro
27—Montreal	W	6-3	McWilliams	Sanderson	30—At L.A.	L	4-8	Hooton	Matula
30—At S.D.	L	1-2	Rasmussen	Matula	31—At L.A.	W	6-5	Boggs	Reuss
		Won 6, Lost 11					Won 11, Lost 15		

MAY			Winner	Loser	JUNE			Winner	Loser
1—At S.D.	L	3-4	Shirley	Camp	1—At L.A.	W	9-5	Alexander	Goltz
2—At Pitts.	W	6-1	Niekro	Rooker	2—At S.F.	W	4-2	Niekro	Whitson
3—At Pitts.	W	3-1†	Hrabosky	Jackson	3—At S.F.	L	2-3	Minton	Bradford
4—At Pitts.	L	4-13	Bibby	Boggs	4—At S.F.	W	7-2	Matula	Montefusco
5—At Phila.	L	1-7	Carlton	Matula	6—Los Ang.	L	0-5	Reuss	Niekro
6—At Phila.	L	5-10	Ruthven	Alexander	7—Los Ang.	W	6-1	Alexander	Goltz
9—Houston	W	5-4	McWilliams	Forsch	8—Los Ang.	L	1-3	Sutton	Boggs
10—Houston	L	2-3‡	LaCorte	Garber	9—St. Louis	L	5-8†	Littlefield	Bradford
11—Houston	W	7-4	P. Niekro	J. Niekro	10—St. Louis	W	5-2	Niekro	Sykes

JUNE

			Winner	Loser
11–St. Louis	L	3-4†	Forsch	Bradford
13–At Chi.	W	7-6	Alexander	McGlothen
14–At Chi.	L	5-10	Lamp	Niekro
15–At Chi.	L	1-4	Krukow	Matula
16–At St.L.	W	6-3	Boggs	Forsch
17–At St.L.	L	2-3	Vuckovich	Alexander
18–Pitts.	W	3-2	Garber	Tekulve
18–Pitts.	W	5-4	Camp	Romo
19–Pitts.	W	4-3	Matula	Robinson
20–Chicago	L	2-4	McGlothen	Boggs
21–Chicago	W	8-0	Alexander	Hernandez
22–Chicago	L	2-3	Lamp	Niekro
24–At Cinn.	L	2-8	Leibrandt	McWilliams
25–At Cinn.	L	3-15	Seaver	Matula
27–At S.D.	W	5-3	Camp	Curtis
28–At S.D.	W	5-4	Bradford	Shirley
28–At S.D.	L	2-3	D'Acquisto	Camp
29–At S.D.	W	4-2	McWilliams	Rasmussen
30–Houston	W	5-4‡	Hrabosky	Sambito

Won 15, Lost 13

JULY

			Winner	Loser
1–Houston	W	13-4	Alexander	J. Niekro
2–Houston	W	14-0	Niekro	Ruhle
3–Houston	L	3-5	Richard	Boggs
4–S. Diego	W	9-0	McWilliams	Rasmussen
5–S. Diego	W	3-2	Matula	Fingers
6–S. Diego	W	6-5	Alexander	Shirley
10–Cinn.	L	6-8	Moskau	Niekro
11–Cinn.	L	3-5	Soto	Alexander
12–At Hous.	L	5-9	J. Niekro	McWilliams
13–At Hous.	W	5-6	Sambito	Garber
13–At Hous.	L	1-6	Ruhle	Boggs
14–At Hous.	W	2-0	Niekro	Pladson
15–N. York	L	2-9	Zachry	Alexander
16–N. York	W	5-2	McWilliams	Swan
17–N. York	L	0-6	Pacella	Matula
18–Phila.	L	2-7	Espinosa	Niekro
19–Phila.	W	5-2	Alexander	Ruthven
19–Phila.	W	7-2	Boggs	Larson
20–Phila.	W	3-2	McWilliams	Walk
21–Montreal	L	6-8	Sanderson	Matula
22–Montreal	W	7-5	Niekro	Bahnsen
23–Montreal	W	6-5	Camp	Gullickson
25–At Phila.	L	4-5§	Ruthven	Camp
25–At Phila.	W	3-0	Boggs	Larson
26–At Phila.	L	3-6	Walk	Niekro
27–At Phila.	L	4-17	Carlton	Matula
28–At N.Y.	W	6-3	Alexander	Falcone
29–At N.Y.	L	1-2	Bomback	McWilliams
30–At N.Y.	L	0-3	Zachry	Boggs

Won 14, Lost 15

AUGUST

			Winner	Loser
1–At Mon.	L	1-4	Sanderson	Niekro
2–At Mon.	L	1-5	Norman	Alexander
3–At Mon.	L	5-6	Lea	McWilliams
4–Los Ang.	L	3-5	Reuss	Boggs
5–Los Ang.	W	6-4	Camp	Stanhouse
6–Los Ang.	L	2-6	Sutton	Matula
7–Los Ang.	W	4-3	Alexander	Welch
8–S. Fran.	W	7-3	McWilliams	Minton
9–S. Fran.	L	4-5	Holland	Boggs
10–S. Fran.	W	3-1	Niekro	Hargesh'mer
11–At L.A.	W	3-2	Matula	Sutton
12–At L.A.	W	7-6	Garber	Sutcliffe
13–At L.A.	W	2-0	Boggs	Hooton
14–At S.F.	L	1-5	Hargesh'mer	McWilliams
15–At S.F.	W	8-2x	Garber	Lavelle
16–At S.F.	L	1-2	Blue	Matula
17–At S.F.	W	8-2	Alexander	Ripley
19–Chicago	W	5-4‡	Niekro	Tidrow
20–Chicago	W	9-5	McWilliams	McGlothen
21–Chicago	W	6-4	Niekro	Krukow
22–St. Louis	L	4-7	Fulgham	Matula
23–St. Louis	W	7-2	Alexander	Vuckovich
24–St. Louis	W	10-5	Boggs	Martinez
25–At Pitts.	W	8-6	Hanna	Bibby
26–At Pitts.	W	4-2†	Garber	Tekulve
27–At Pitts.	W	7-4	Matula	Robinson
28–At St.L.	L	2-11	Forsch	Alexander
29–At St.L.	W	4-3	Boggs	Martinez
30–At St.L.	L	3-5	Hood	McWilliams
31–At St.L.	L	6-2	Niekro	Otten

Won 19, Lost 11

SEPTEMBER

			Winner	Loser
1–At Chi.	W	5-2	Matula	Lamp
2–At Chi.	W	10-5	Alexander	Krukow
3–At Chi.	W	4-3	Boggs	McGlothen
5–Pitts.	W	7-4	Camp	Tekulve
6–Pitts.	W	3-2	Niekro	Blyleven
7–Pitts.	W	6-5	Bradford	Tekulve
8–Cinn.	L	1-6	Pastore	Alexander
9–Cinn.	L	1-7	Soto	Boggs
10–Cinn.	L	0-3	Seaver	McWilliams
12–S. Diego	W	6-2	Niekro	Eichelberger
13–S. Diego	W	5-3	Matula	Wise
14–S. Diego	W	4-3	Camp	Lucas
15–Los Ang.	W	9-0	Boggs	Hooton
16–Los Ang.	W	2-1	Niekro	Goltz
17–At S.F.	L	0-2	Blue	McWilliams
18–At S.F.	W	2-1	Matula	Hargesh'mer
19–At S.D.	L	4-7	Mura	Alexander
20–At S.D.	L	2-3‡	Rasmussen	Hrabosky
21–At S.D.	L	1-3	Tellmann	Niekro
22–At L.A.	W	7-2	Hanna	Sutton
23–At L.A.	L	2-4	Welch	Matula
24–Houston	W	4-2	Alexander	Andujar
25–Houston	L	2-4	Ryan	Niekro
26–S. Fran.	W	5-3	Boggs	Blue
27–S. Fran.	L	1-2	Ripley	McWilliams
30–At Hous.	L	3-7	Ryan	Alexander

Won 15, Lost 11

OCTOBER

			Winner	Loser
1–At Hous.	L	2-5	Ruhle	J. Niekro
2–At Hous.	L	2-3	J. Niekro	McWilliams
3–At Cinn.	W	4-1	Boggs	Soto
4–At Cinn.	L	2-3	Pastore	Alexander
5–At Cinn.	L	0-1	Price	Niekro

Won 1, Lost 4

*6 innings.   †10 innings.   ‡11 innings.   §12 innings.   x13 innings.

Bristol Axed After Dissension-Filled Year

By NICK PETERS

You name it and it probably happened to the San Francisco Giants during a dissension-torn, injury-riddled campaign that had virtually everyone on the club harping at the conclusion of a 75-86 season that placed them fifth in the National League West, 17 games behind division-winner Houston.

"It was a good season . . . except for the beginning and the end," mused Manager Dave Bristol, who had no reason to smile when slugger Jack Clark and disappointing second baseman Rennie Stennett blasted his leadership down the stretch.

By season's end, there were several disgruntled players, the dissatisfaction attributed to a lack of communication by Bristol and the inability of Mike Ivie, Bob Knepper, John Montefusco and Stennett to perform up to expectations.

But the domestic problems weren't the chief reason for the Giants' demise—after all, the world champion Philadelphia Phillies weren't a study in harmony either.

The club's trouble spots were a pathetic batting order and woeful fielding. Only the pitching was reasonably sound, the staff's 3.46 ERA ranking fourth in the N.L.

Injuries were a big culprit, too. A total of nine Giants had to be placed on the disabled list. From mid-May until mid-September, the club always had at least one player sidelined, and once as many as five.

The costliest injury was a hunting knife mishap in the off-season. Ivie slashed a tendon in his right little finger. The sensitive first baseman couldn't cope with the long rehabilitation process and the injury also affected his brittle confidence, resulting in a stunning mid-season retirement.

Ivie returned a few weeks later, but never supplied the club with the power needed to take some pressure off Clark. Ivie slumped from .286 in 1979 to .241, his home run total plunged from a career-high 27 to four and his RBI count dipped from 89 to 25.

Injuries also did their part to curtail the effectiveness of pitching aces Vida Blue (14-10) and Ed Whitson (11-13). Montefusco (4-8), once the darling of Giants fans, also was sidelined with ailments and his pride was wounded in a mid-season scuffle with Bristol, one that was precipitated by Bristol's removal of Montefusco in the ninth inning of a game against the Mets in which the Giants were leading, 8-2.

Even Clark could not escape the injury jinx. The club was playing well in mid-August, when Clark was struck on the left hand by a Mark Bomback pitch in New York. A broken bone forced Clark to miss most of the remaining games and the club's fortunes went with him.

How valuable was Clark? When he was struck, the Giants were on an upswing, squaring their record at 60-60, making a move on third place and trailing the first-place Astros by 6½ games. The club proceeded to go 15-26 down the stretch.

After 110 games, Clark had 17 game-winning RBIs. He finished with 18, still good enough to top the N.L. The Giants' right fielder also was runnerup to Mike Schmidt in slugging percentage.

Without Clark, the Giants virtually had no offense, save for a respectable 20 homers and 78 RBIs by Darrell Evans. They were last in the league in batting average (.244) and runs scored (573).

Add to that 159 errors and a 10th-place standing in fielding percentage and you have some idea why the club finished where it did.

Under the circumstances—and not considering his off-field problems with some of his charges—Bristol did a decent job keeping the Giants buoyant for most of the season. Nevertheless, he was fired during the winter meetings and replaced by Frank Robinson.

SAN FRANCISCO GIANTS—1980

First row—Strain, Sadek, Knepper, McMahon, coach; Davenport, coach; Benson, coach; Bristol, manager; Van Ornum, coach; Lefebvre, coach; Holland, Wohlford, Stennett, North. Second row—Liscio, trainer; Archibald, assistant trainer; Ripley, Ivie, Minton, Clark, Lavelle, Metzger, Blue, Murphy, equipment manager; Alioto, assistant equipment manager; Nelson, traveling secretary. Third row—Whitson, Whitfield, Evans, LeMaster, Moffitt, Griffin, Murray, McCovey, Bordley, May, Herndon. Kneeling in front—batboys Stoneham and Mahoma. Not pictured—Montefusco.

How the Giants managed to be over .500 that late in the season in the wake of all their problems was a minor mystery. Most of the credit went to a bullpen of rookie Al Holland (5-3, 1.76 ERA, seven saves), Greg Minton (2.47, 19 saves), Gary Lavelle (nine saves) and Tom Griffin (5-1, 2.75).

There were other bright spots. Willie McCovey, at 41, played only half the season before retiring, but managed to whack home run No. 521 (469 of them as a Giant) at Montreal May 3, thereby tying boyhood hero Ted Williams for eighth on the all-time list.

Evans, who had never hit for a high average, came in at .264 but was productive, as evidenced by 14 game-winning RBIs. Left fielder Terry Whitfield, murder on righthanders, led the club in average at .296.

The Giants' free-agent gambles were a so-so proposition. Stennett suffered through a .244 season and had limited range afield, but Milt May (.260) and Jim Wohlford (.280 and 24 RBIs in 193 at-bats) had decent seasons as the catcher and top utilityman, respectively.

The Giants went 38-34 against the East Division after posting a 27-45 record against the same clubs in 1979. They managed a 6-6 standoff with the Phillies, including a 4-2 victory in a game at Philadelphia which concluded at 3:11 a.m. and consumed, including rain delays, seven hours and 36 minutes.

The high point of the season was a 6-0 streak following the All-Star break. It included a four-game sweep at Cincinnati, the first time that had happened to the Reds in the 11-year history of Riverfront Stadium.

There also was a three-game sweep of the Astros at Candlestick Park, where 1,096,115 paying customers watched the Giants fashion a 44-37 home record. But the club was a dismal 37-52 against West Division rivals, managing to win the season series from only the Reds, 11-7.

"It's been a long season," summed up Blue. "I was on a loser at Oakland in 1977, but at least we had an excuse then—we were young. I've never been on a club with such a bad attitude and so many veterans. It was like a cancer . . . it kept spreading."

SCORES OF SAN FRANCISCO GIANTS' 1980 GAMES

APRIL			Winner	Loser	MAY			Winner	Loser
10—At S.D.	L	4-6	Jones	Knepper	6—At St.L.	L	7-10	Moore	Knepper
11—At S.D.	L	3-5	Fingers	Lavelle	7—At St.L.	L	2-12	Forsch	Whitson
12—At S.D.	L	2-4	Curtis	Montefusco	9—At Chi.	W	6-3	Blue	Lamp
13—At S.D.	W	3-1	Blue	Rasmussen	10—At Chi.	L	9-15	McGlothen	Knepper
14—At Cinn.	L	5-6	Tomlin	Lavelle	11—At Chi.	W	3-0	Whitson	Krukow
15—At Cinn.	L	3-8	Seaver	Whitson	13—Pitts.	W	5-0	Blue	Blyleven
16—At Cinn.	L	3-5	LaCoss	Montefusco	14—Pitts.	L	2-3	Bibby	Knepper
17—S. Diego	W	7-3	Blue	Rasmussen	15—Pitts.	L	2-3‡	Romo	Griffin
18—S. Diego	W	5-2	Knepper	Jones	16—St. Louis	W	4-3	Holland	Forsch
18—S. Diego	L	0-3	Lucas	Whitson	17—St. Louis	W	4-2	Blue	Sykes
20—S. Diego	W	5-1	Montefusco	Wise	18—St. Louis	L	6-5	Knepper	Hood
21—At L.A.	L	3-4	Hooton	Blue	20—Chicago	W	2-0	Whitson	Krukow
22—At L.A.	L	0-6	Sutton	Knepper	21—Chicago	W	4-1	Blue	Reuschel
23—At L.A.	L	0-4	Goltz	Whitson	23—At Pitts.	L	4-5§	Jackson	Holland
24—At L.A.	L	2-5*	Reuss	Lavelle	24—At Pitts.	W	10-9x	Griffin	Scurry
25—Cinn.	W	4-3	Minton	Bair	25—At Pitts.	W	5-2	Blue	Candelaria
26—Cinn.	W	3-1	Knepper	LaCoss	26—At Atl.	L	1-2	Boggs	Minton
27—Cinn.	L	1-3	Pastore	Whitson	27—At Atl.	L	3-6	McWilliams	Knepper
29—Los Ang.	L	0-5	Goltz	Montefusco	28—At Atl.	L	2-3‡	Hrabosky	Lavelle
30—Los Ang.	L	3-4	Welch	Minton	30—Houston	W	3-2	Blue	Forsch
			Won 6, Lost 14		31—Houston	L	0-5	Richard	Montefusco
								Won 13, Lost 13	
MAY									
2—At Mon.	L	3-4	Bahnsen	Lavelle	JUNE				
3—At Mon.	W	3-2	Moffitt	Sosa	1—Houston	W	6-2	Knepper	Niekro
4—At Mon.	W	8-4	Montefusco	Rogers	2—Atlanta	L	2-4	Niekro	Whitson
4—At Mon.	L	4-6	Bahnsen	Moffitt	3—Atlanta	W	3-2	Minton	Bradford
5—At St.L.	L	5-9	Vuckovich	Blue	4—Atlanta	L	2-7	Matula	Montefusco

JUNE

			Winner	Loser
6—At Hous.	L	0-2	Richard	Knepper
7—At Hous.	L	0-3	Niekro	Whitson
8—At Hous.	L	4-5	Sambito	Minton
9—At Phila.	W	3-1	Ripley	Noles
10—At Phila.	L	3-4	Saucier	Knepper
11—At Phila.	W	7-4	Whitson	Lerch
13—At N.Y.	W	3-1	Blue	Burris
14—At N.Y.	L	6-7	Reardon	Ripley
15—At N.Y.	W	3-0	Knepper	Zachry
16—Montreal	W	5-1	Whitson	Lea
17—Montreal	L	1-2	Palmer	Blue
18—N. York	W	8-5	Montefusco	Burris
19—N. York	W	4-3*	Lavelle	Allen
20—Phila.	W	5-1	Ripley	Larson
21—Phila.	W	9-3	Whitson	Lerch
22—Phila.	L	3-4	Carlton	Blue
24—At S.D.	L	3-5	D'Acquisto	Knepper
25—At S.D.	L	3-7	Eichelberger	Ripley
26—At S.D.	W	2-1	Whitson	Mura
27—Los Ang.	L	0-8	Reuss	Blue
28—Los Ang.	W	4-3†	Griffin	Sutcliffe
29—Los Ang.	W	4-3	Knepper	Castillo
29—Los Ang.	L	0-3	Hooton	Ripley
30—Cinn.	W	8-4	Bordley	Seaver

Won 15, Lost 13

JULY

			Winner	Loser
1—Cinn.	W	4-1	Whitson	Moskau
2—Cinn.	L	2-6	Pastore	Montefusco
3—Cinn.	W	4-3	Knepper	Price
4—At L.A.	L	0-4	Sutton	Ripley
5—At L.A.	L	2-3	Welch	Whitson
6—At L.A.	W	7-4*	Holland	Howe
10—S. Diego	W	9-2	Knepper	Jones
11—S. Diego	W	7-3	Whitson	Curtis
12—At Cinn.	W	7-4	Lavelle	Bair
12—At Cinn.	W	10-7	Bordley	LaCoss
13—At Cinn.	W	2-0	Ripley	Price
14—At Cinn.	W	5-3	Hargesh'mer	Leibrandt
15—At Pitts.	L	2-5	Candelaria	Knepper
16—At Pitts.	L	1-3	Blyleven	Whitson
17—At Pitts.	L	2-3	Tekulve	Holland
18—At St.L.	W	8-7	Holland	Seaman
19—At St.L.	W	7-4	Hargesh'mer	Sykes
20—At St.L.	L	1-2	Forsch	Knepper
21—At Chi.	W	2-0y	Lavelle	Caudill
22—At Chi.	L	1-3	Lamp	Bordley
23—At Chi.	W	14-6	Ripley	Capilla
25—Pitts.	L	1-5	Candelaria	Knepper
26—Pitts.	W	4-3*	Minton	Jackson
27—Pitts.	L	4-6	Bibby	Bordley
29—St. Louis	W	4-1	Ripley	Martinez
30—St. Louis	L	0-4	Fulgham	Knepper
31—St. Louis	W	6-4	Lavelle	Urrea

Won 16, Lost 11

AUGUST

			Winner	Loser
1—Chicago	L	3-5	Reuschel	Bordley
2—Chicago	W	8-5	Griffin	Tidrow
3—Chicago	L	2-3	Krukow	Ripley
3—Chicago	L	2-3	Tidrow	Knepper
4—At Hous.	L	2-4	Ryan	Hargesh'mer
5—At Hous.	W	9-3	Lavelle	Pladson

AUGUST

			Winner	Loser
6—At Hous.	L	0-1	Forsch	Blue
8—At Atl.	L	3-7	McWilliams	Minton
9—At Atl.	W	5-4	Holland	Boggs
10—At Atl.	L	1-3	Niekro	Hargesh'mer
11—Houston	W	5-4	Blue	Forsch
12—Houston	W	2-0	Ripley	Niekro
13—Houston	W	6-5‡	Rowland	Smith
14—Atlanta	W	5-1	Hargesh'mer	McWilliams
15—Atlanta	L	2-8§	Garber	Lavelle
16—Atlanta	W	2-1	Blue	Matula
17—Atlanta	L	2-8	Alexander	Ripley
19—At N.Y.	W	5-4	Knepper	Reardon
20—At N.Y.	W	2-1	Hargesh'mer	Bomback
21—At N.Y.	L	1-5	Falcone	Blue
22—At Phila.	W	4-3*	Holland	Carlton
23—At Phila.	W	6-2	Ripley	Christenson
24—At Phila.	L	1-7	Ruthven	Knepper
25—At Mon.	L	1-3	Rogers	Hargesh'mer
27—At Mon.	W	1-0	Whitson	Sanderson
29—N. York	W	1-0	Blue	Zachry
30—N. York	L	5-9	Hausman	Ripley
31—N. York	W	11-4	Lavelle	Falcone
31—N. York	W	9-4	Montefusco	Miller

Won 16, Lost 13

SEPTEMBER

			Winner	Loser
1—Phila.	L	4-6	Carlton	Minton
1—Phila.	L	1-2§	Reed	Holland
3—Phila.	L	3-4	Ruthven	Ripley
4—Montreal	L	0-4	Gullickson	Hargesh'mer
5—Montreal	L	0-8	Rogers	Montefusco
6—Montreal	L	0-9	Sanderson	Whitson
7—Montreal	W	6-3	Blue	D'Acquisto
9—At S.D.	L	5-12	Mura	Ripley
10—At S.D.	L	2-4	Fingers	Minton
12—At Hous.	L	3-5	Niekro	Whitson
13—At Hous.	L	2-3	Forsch	Blue
14—At Hous.	L	4-6	Andujar	Montefusco
15—At Cinn.	L	2-6	Seaver	Knepper
16—At Cinn.	W	8-1	Whitson	Price
17—At Atlanta	W	2-0	Blue	McWilliams
18—At Atlanta	L	1-2	Matula	Hargesh'mer
19—Houston	W	4-3	Griffin	Andujar
20—Houston	L	2-3	Smith	Lavelle
21—Houston	L	1-5	Ruhle	Blue
22—Cinn.	W	7-3	Ripley	LaCoss
23—Cinn.	L	1-2	Pastore	Hargesh'mer
24—At L.A.	L	4-5‡	Castillo	Rowland
25—At L.A.	W	3-2	Whitson	Hooton
26—At Atl.	L	3-5	Boggs	Blue
27—At Atl.	W	2-1	Ripley	McWilliams
30—Los Ang.	L	3-6*	Valenzuela	Lavelle

Won 7, Lost 19

OCTOBER

			Winner	Loser
1—Los Ang.	L	4-8	Hooton	Whitson
2—Los Ang.	W	3-2	Minton	Goltz
3—S. Diego	L	0-12	Mura	Ripley
4—S. Diego	W	4-2	Griffin	Stablein
5—S. Diego	L	3-7	Tellmann	Whitson

Won 2, Lost 3

*10 innings. †11 innings. ‡12 innings. §13 innings. x15 innings. y15-inning suspended game, completed July 22.

Padres Plummeted to Last Place

By PHIL COLLIER

In some regards, the San Diego Padres' 1980 season was more disappointing than any of the 11 that had preceded it.

Although they were gambling that Jerry Coleman, the club's play-by-play announcer for the previous eight years, could succeed in something he had never attempted before—managing—the Padres felt they had reason for high expectations.

Backed by Owner Ray Kroc's millions, General Manager Bob Fontaine had invaded the re-entry draft to sign two veteran pitchers to five-year contracts. Righthander Rick Wise left Cleveland for $2 million and lefthander John Curtis deserted San Francisco for $1.75 million.

Fontaine thought he had shored up San Diego's leaky infield when he traded for two well-known veterans—Montreal second baseman Dave Cash and Detroit third baseman Aurelio Rodriguez.

Fontaine also traded for center fielder Jerry Mumphrey and for a veteran lefthanded hitter, Texas first baseman Willie Montanez, at last giving the Padres someone to hit behind All-Star right fielder Dave Winfield. The Padres also appeared to improve their bench strength when they signed outfielder Von Joshua, a free agent.

"If we don't move up in the standings and become competitive, I'll take the blame," Coleman said as he set out to improve on the 68-93 record the fifth-place Padres had recorded under Roger Craig in 1979.

"I told the front office what I thought we had to have to compete (two pitchers, a center fielder, a second baseman, a third baseman and someone to bat behind Winfield)," Coleman added, "and they got everything I asked for."

Appearances were deceiving. At season's end, the Padres stood at 73-89 and had finished last in the National League West for the first time since Kroc purchased the franchise in 1974.

Home attendance was down alarmingly (from 1,456,967 in 1979 and 1,670,107 in 1978 to 1,139,026), prompting club President Ballard Smith, Kroc's son-in-law, to anticipate a loss in excess of $2 million for the year.

Ownership searched for scapegoats. Fontaine was ousted from his position in early July and eventually was replaced by his assistant, Jack McKeon.

Coleman was dismissed at the end of the season, the victim of public assaults launched by several of his most prominent players. He was replaced by still another newcomer to major league managerial rolls—Milwaukee first-base coach Frank Howard.

Within weeks after Howard took the job, he lost in the re-entry draft his cleanup hitter, Winfield, who accounted for 20 of the Padres' 67 homers.

The Padres' 1980 woes began in March, during spring training, when Smith publicly revealed that Winfield was seeking a 10-year, $13 million contract to replace the four-year, $1.3 million agreement he had reached with San Diego management in 1977. Smith's action had the effect of turning Padres fans against Winfield, who became a season-long target of boos.

Winfield declined in every major department. His average dropped from .308 in '79 to .276. He led the Padres in homers (20) and RBIs (87), but those figures were well behind his 34 homers and league-leading 118 RBIs of the previous season.

The Padres finished last in spite of some exceptional individual performances.

Given a green light, Gene Richards (61 stolen bases), Ozzie Smith (57) and Jerry Mumphrey (52) became the first three National League teammates ever to swipe 50 or more bases in the same season. As as result, the

SAN DIEGO PADRES—1980

Front row—Fingers, Shirley, Jones, Heist, coach; Phillips, coach; Tolan, coach; Coleman, manager; Williams, coach; Estrada, coach; Evans, Flannery, Baker. Second row—R. Peralta, equipment manager; Mattei, traveling secretary; Wise, Cash, Perkins, Kinney, Salazar, Eichelberger, Curtis, Fahey, Dent, trainer; V. Peralta, clubhouse assistant. Back row—Mumphrey, Rasmussen, Armstrong, Mura, Winfield, Lucas, Tenace, Stimac, Dade, Richards. Seated in front—batboys Barnes, Heye, Winter and Hoffer.

Padres led the majors in thefts with 239.

Smith set a major league record for assists by a shortstop (621), breaking the mark Glenn Wright set with Pittsburgh in 1924.

Richards, who batted .301, and Winfield led N.L. outfielders in assists with 20 and 19, respectively. Richards set club records for hits (193), stolen bases (61) and assists by an outfielder.

Veteran righthander Rollie Fingers (11-9 record, 23 saves, 2.80 ERA) shared THE SPORTING NEWS Fireman of the Year title with Cincinnati's Tom Hume.

The Padres also set club records for batting average (.255) and fewest errors (132) and were in the middle of the pack in pitching (3.65), though injuries hampered Randy Jones (5-13) and Curtis (10-8).

The Padres won 34 of their last 66 games after McKeon disposed of Rodriguez, Montanez, Joshua, Kurt Bevacqua, Fred Kendall and John D'Acquisto. Third baseman Luis Salazar (.337 and 11 stolen bases in 44 games), first baseman Randy Bass (.286 with three homers in 19 games) and first baseman-outfielder Broderick Perkins (.370 in 43 games) spurred the late-season respectability drive.

Curtis won his last six decisions, rookie righthander Tom Tellmann came up from Hawaii to win three straight, rookie lefthander Gary Lucas had a 1.46 ERA in his last 25 relief stints and there were some encouraging mound performances by Bob Shirley, Steve Mura and Juan Eichelberger.

Mura was 8-7, Shirley 11-12 with seven saves, and Eichelberger 4-2.

Still, after 12 seasons, the Padres had not come of age.

SCORES OF SAN DIEGO PADRES' 1980 GAMES

APRIL			Winner	Loser
10—S. Fran.	W	6-4	Jones	Knepper
11—S. Fran.	W	5-3	Fingers	Lavelle
12—S. Fran.	W	4-2	Curtis	Montefusco
13—S. Fran.	L	1-3	Blue	Rasmussen
14—Los Ang.	W	2-1	Fingers	Castillo
15—Los Ang.	W	9-5	Wise	Sutcliffe
16—Los Ang.	L	4-10	Hooton	Curtis
17—At S.F.	L	3-7	Blue	Rasmussen
18—At S.F.	L	2-5	Knepper	Jones
19—At S.F.	W	3-0	Lucas	Whitson
20—At S.F.	L	1-5	Montefusco	Wise
22—At Atl.	L	2-3*	Hrabosky	Shirley
23—At Atl.	L	1-2	Matula	Jones
24—At Atl.	L	7-8	Garber	Fingers
25—At L.A.	L	3-6	Castillo	Kinney
26—At L.A.	L	3-4	Beckwith	Fingers
27—At L.A.	L	1-3	Sutton	Curtis
30—Atlanta	W	2-1	Rasmussen	Matula

Won 7, Lost 11

MAY				
1—Atlanta	W	4-3	Shirley	Camp
2—At N.Y.	W	1-0	Wise	Burris
3—At N.Y.	W	2-1	Lucas	Swan
4—At N.Y.	W	4-3	Curtis	Reardon
4—At N.Y.	L	2-6	Glynn	Rasmussen
6—At Chi.	W	4-0	Jones	Hernandez
7—At Chi.	L	4-7	Krukow	Wise
8—At Chi.	W	9-6	Shirley	Sutter
9—Pitts.	L	3-4	Tekulve	Fingers
10—Pitts.	L	5-9	Robinson	Rasmussen
11—Pitts.	W	5-0	Jones	Candelaria
13—St. Louis	W	3-2	Fingers	Kaat
14—St. Louis	L	1-2	Thomas	Lucas
15—St. Louis	W	2-1	Curtis	Vuckovich
16—Chicago	W	3-0	Jones	Krukow
17—Chicago	L	1-2	Reuschel	Rasmussen

MAY			Winner	Loser
18—Chicago	W	4-3	Fingers	Sutter
21—At Pitts.	L	3-4	Romo	Fingers
21—At Pitts.	L	2-3	Jackson	Curtis
22—At Pitts.	W	6-4	Shirley	Tekulve
23—At St.L.	W	2-0	Shirley	Kaat
24—At St.L.	W	8-4	Kinney	Moore
25—At St.L.	W	11-5	Fingers	Thomas
26—At Hous.	L	1-4	Richard	Curtis
27—At Hous.	L	3-4	LaCorte	Fingers
28—At Hous.	L	0-1	Ryan	Wise
29—Cinn.	L	3-5	Pastore	Jones
30—Cinn.	L	3-5	Leibrandt	Mura
31—Cinn.	W	7-5	Shirley	Hume

Won 16, Lost 13

JUNE				
1—Cinn.	L	6-7	Burnside	Lucas
2—Houston	W	3-0	Wise	Ryan
3—Houston	L	2-3	Ruhle	Jones
4—Houston	L	3-4	Forsch	Fingers
6—At Cinn.	L	2-4	Pastore	D'Acquisto
7—At Cinn.	W	6-1	Lucas	LaCoss
8—At Cinn.	L	0-1	Leibrandt	Jones
9—At Cinn.	T	6-6a	....	....
10—At Mon.	L	4-8	Bahnsen	Rasmussen
11—At Mon.	L	6-7	Sosa	Shirley
12—At Mon.	L	1-9	Lea	Lucas
13—At Phila.	L	6-9	Ruthven	Jones
14—At Phila.	L	1-3	Carlton	Mura
15—At Phila.	L	5-8	Walk	Wise
16—N. York	W	3-2	Fingers	Reardon
17—N. York	W	2-1	Fingers	Hausman
18—Phila.	L	1-5	Carlton	Shirley
19—Phila.	W	4-3	Kinney	Saucier
20—Montreal	W	4-2	Mura	Sanderson
21—Montreal	L	4-7	Lea	Curtis
22—Montreal	L	0-2	Rogers	Lucas

JUNE			Winner	Loser
24—S. Fran.	W	5-3	D'Acquisto	Knepper
25—S. Fran.	W	7-3	Eichelberger	Ripley
26—S. Fran.	L	1-2	Whitson	Mura
27—Atlanta	L	3-5	Camp	Curtis
28—Atlanta	W	4-5	Bradford	Shirley
28—Atlanta	W	3-2	D'Acquisto	Camp
29—Atlanta	L	2-4	McWilliams	Rasmussen
30—At L.A.	W	4-3	Eichelberger	Welch
			Won 10, Lost 18	
JULY				
1—At L.A.	W	4-1	Mura	Reuss
2—At L.A.	L	7-10	Sutcliffe	Blair
3—At L.A.	L	4-5*	Castillo	Shirley
4—At Atl.	L	0-9	McWilliams	Rasmussen
5—At Atl.	L	2-3	Matula	Fingers
6—At Atl.	L	5-6	Alexander	Shirley
10—At S.F.	L	2-9	Knepper	Jones
11—At S.F.	L	3-7	Whitson	Curtis
12—Los Ang.	W	3-2‡	Rasmussen	Beckwith
13—Los Ang.	W	4-3§	Kinney	Beckwith
14—Los Ang.	W	6-3	Mura	Sutcliffe
15—At St.L.	L	3-5	Forsch	Jones
16—At St.L.	L	0-3	Vuckovich	Lucas
17—At St.L.	L	3-15	Kaat	Wise
18—At Chi.	W	2-1	Shirley	Capilla
19—At Chi.	L	7-8	Caudill	Kinney
20—At Chi.	L	0-6	McGlothen	Jones
22—Pitts.	L	3-4	Bibby	Lucas
23—Pitts.	W	3-2	Fingers	Romo
24—Pitts.	L	1-7	Blyleven	Shirley
25—St. Louis	L	2-3	Sykes	Kinney
26—St. Louis	W	4-3†	Kinney	Hood
27—St. Louis	L	5-2	Lucas	Vuckovich
28—Chicago	W	4-2†	Fingers	Riley
29—Chicago	W	3-1	Jones	Capilla
30—Chicago	W	5-2	Shirley	Sutter
			Won 11, Lost 15	
AUGUST				
1—At Pitts.	W	1-0	Mura	Bibby
3—At Pitts.	W	5-2	Curtis	Rhoden
3—At Pitts.	W	4-1	Shirley	Robinson
4—At Cinn.	L	1-7	Seaver	Jones
4—At Cinn.	L	2-11	Soto	Kinney
5—At Cinn.	L	2-9	Moskau	Lucas
6—At Cinn.	L	3-4	Hume	D'Acquisto
7—At Hous.	W	5-1	Shirley	Niekro
8—At Hous.	W	5-3	Eichelberger	Sambito
9—At Hous.	L	5-9	Smith	D'Acquisto
10—At Hous.	W	3-2	Wise	Sambito
11—Cinn.	L	0-1	Leibrandt	Mura
12—Cinn.	L	2-3	Price	Jones
13—Cinn.	L	3-4	Soto	Shirley
14—Houston	L	1-2	Ryan	Curtis

AUGUST			Winner	Loser
15—Houston	L	1-3z	Smith	Rasmussen
17—Houston	L	0-5	Forsch	Jones
17—Houston	L	2-9	Niekro	Mura
19—At Phila.	L	4-7	Ruthven	Shirley
20—At Phila.	W	7-5	Curtis	Espinosa
21—At Phila.	L	8-9x	Saucier	Kinney
22—At Mon.	L	2-6	Norman	Jones
23—At Mon.	L	0-2	Gullickson	Mura
24—At Mon.	L	9-12	Sosa	Fingers
26—At N.Y.	W	8-6y	Rasmussen	Falcone
27—At N.Y.	W	4-1	Wise	Burris
29—Phila.	L	2-3	Christenson	Mura
30—Phila.	L	1-6	Ruthven	Shirley
30—Phila.	W	5-1	Curtis	Espinosa
31—Phila.	W	10-3	Lucas	Walk
			Won 11, Lost 19	
SEPTEMBER				
1—Montreal	L	3-5	Sanderson	Wise
2—Montreal	L	1-2	Lea	Rasmussen
3—Montreal	W	4-3	Mura	Norman
4—N. York	W	3-2	Curtis	Allen
5—N. York	W	4-2	Eichelberger	Bomback
6—N. York	W	8-7	Wise	Burris
7—N. York	W	5-2	Shirley	Pacella
9—S. Fran.	W	12-5	Mura	Ripley
10—S. Fran.	W	4-2	Fingers	Minton
12—At Atl.	L	2-6	Niekro	Eichelberger
12—At Atl.	L	3-5	Matula	Wise
14—At Atl.	L	3-4	Camp	Lucas
15—At Hous.	W	6-3	Shirley	Ryan
16—At Hous.	W	4-3	Curtis	Ruhle
17—At L.A.	L	1-2	Sutton	Eichelberger
18—At L.A.	L	3-7	Welch	Wise
19—Atlanta	W	7-4	Mura	Alexander
20—Atlanta	W	3-2†	Rasmussen	Hrabosky
21—Atlanta	W	3-1	Tellmann	Niekro
22—Houston	L	2-4	Niekro	Shirley
23—Houston	W	9-4	Curtis	Niemann
24—Cinn.	L	6-7*	Bair	Fingers
25—Cinn.	L	3-5*	Bair	Kinney
26—Los Ang.	W	3-2	Tellmann	Goltz
27—Los Ang.	L	4-6	Sutton	Rasmussen
28—Los Ang.	W	7-5	Fingers	Howe
30—At Cinn.	W	3-2	Curtis	Leibrandt
			Won 16, Lost 11	
OCTOBER				
1—At Cinn.	L	1-2	Hume	Shirley
3—At S.F.	W	12-0	Mura	Ripley
4—At S.F.	L	2-4	Griffin	Stablein
4—At S.F.	W	7-3	Tellmann	Whitson
			Won 2, Lost 2	

*10 innings. †11 innings. ‡12 innings. §15 innings. x17 innings. y18 innings. z20 innings. a10½-inning tie game.

Baseball's Four-Decade Performers

When Minnie Minoso was activated by the White Sox for the final days of the 1980 season he became only the second player ever to play in the majors in five decades, matching the longevity mark set by Nick Altrock.

Jim Kaat, Willie McCovey and Tim McCarver, who entered the big leagues in 1959, became four-decade players, joining: Altrock (1898-1933), Dan Brouthers (1879-1904), Eddie Collins (1906-30), Kid Gleason (1888-1912), Jim McGuire (1884-1912), Bobo Newsom (1929-53), Jack O'Connor (1887-1910), Jim O'Rourke (1876-1904), John Picus Quinn (1909-33), John B. Ryan (1889-1913), Mickey Vernon (1939-60), Ted Williams (1939-60), Early Wynn (1939-63), Minoso (1949-80).

MIKE SCHMIDT
• PHILLIES •
HOMERS (48)
RUNS BATTED IN (121)
TOTAL BASES (342)

STEVE GARVEY
• DODGERS •
HITS (200)

BILL BUCKNER
• CUBS •
BATTING CHAMPION (.324)

1980 NATIONAL LEAGUE LEADERS

DON SUTTON
• DODGERS •
EARNED-RUN AVERAGE (2.21)

JIM BIBBY
• PIRATES •
WINNING PCT. (.760)

STEVE CARLTON
• PHILLIES •
WINS (24)
INNINGS (304)
STRIKEOUTS (286)

National League Averages for 1980

CHAMPIONSHIP WINNERS IN PREVIOUS YEARS

1876—Chicago ..... .788	1911—New York ..... .647	1946—St. Louis° ..... .628
1877—Boston ..... .646	1912—New York ..... .682	1947—Brooklyn ..... .610
1878—Boston ..... .683	1913—New York ..... .664	1948—Boston ..... .595
1879—Providence ..... .705	1914—Boston ..... .614	1949—Brooklyn ..... .630
1880—Chicago ..... .798	1915—Philadelphia ..... .592	1950—Philadelphia ..... .591
1881—Chicago ..... .667	1916—Brooklyn ..... .610	1951—New York† ..... .624
1882—Chicago ..... .655	1917—New York ..... .636	1952—Brooklyn ..... .627
1883—Boston ..... .643	1918—Chicago ..... .651	1953—Brooklyn ..... .682
1884—Providence ..... .750	1919—Cincinnati ..... .686	1954—New York ..... .630
1885—Chicago ..... .777	1920—Brooklyn ..... .604	1955—Brooklyn ..... .641
1886—Chicago ..... .726	1921—New York ..... .614	1956—Brooklyn ..... .604
1887—Detroit ..... .637	1922—New York ..... .604	1957—Milwaukee ..... .617
1888—New York ..... .641	1923—New York ..... .621	1958—Milwaukee ..... .597
1889—New York ..... .659	1924—New York ..... .608	1959—Los Angeles‡ ..... .564
1890—Brooklyn ..... .667	1925—Pittsburgh ..... .621	1960—Pittsburgh ..... .617
1891—Boston ..... .630	1926—St. Louis ..... .578	1961—Cincinnati ..... .604
1892—Boston ..... .680	1927—Pittsburgh ..... .610	1962—San Francisco§ ..... .624
1893—Boston ..... .662	1928—St. Louis ..... .617	1963—Los Angeles ..... .611
1894—Baltimore ..... .695	1929—Chicago ..... .645	1964—St. Louis ..... .574
1895—Baltimore ..... .669	1930—St. Louis ..... .597	1965—Los Angeles ..... .599
1896—Baltimore ..... .698	1931—St. Louis ..... .656	1966—Los Angeles ..... .586
1897—Boston ..... .705	1932—Chicago ..... .584	1967—St. Louis ..... .627
1898—Boston ..... .685	1933—New York ..... .599	1968—St. Louis ..... .599
1899—Brooklyn ..... .677	1934—St. Louis ..... .621	1969—New York (East)a ..... .617
1900—Brooklyn ..... .603	1935—Chicago ..... .649	1970—Cincinnati (West)b ..... .630
1901—Pittsburgh ..... .647	1936—New York ..... .597	1971—Pittsburgh (East)c ..... .599
1902—Pittsburgh ..... .741	1937—New York ..... .625	1972—Cincinnati (West)b ..... .617
1903—Pittsburgh ..... .650	1938—Chicago ..... .586	1973—New York (East)d ..... .509
1904—New York ..... .693	1939—Cincinnati ..... .630	1974—Los Angeles (West)b ..... .630
1905—New York ..... .686	1940—Cincinnati ..... .654	1975—Cincinnati (West)b ..... .667
1906—Chicago ..... .763	1941—Brooklyn ..... .649	1976—Cincinnati (West)e ..... .630
1907—Chicago ..... .704	1942—St. Louis ..... .688	1977—Los Angeles (West)e .. .605
1908—Chicago ..... .643	1943—St. Louis ..... .682	1978—Los Angeles (West)e .. .586
1909—Pittsburgh ..... .724	1944—St. Louis ..... .682	1979—Pittsburgh (East)d .... .605
1910—Chicago ..... .675	1945—Chicago ..... .636	

°Defeated Brooklyn, two games to none, in playoff for pennant. †Defeated Brooklyn, two games to one, in playoff for pennant. ‡Defeated Milwaukee, two games to none, in playoff for pennant. §Defeated Los Angeles, two games to one, in playoff for pennant. aDefeated Atlanta (West) in Championship Series. bDefeated Pittsburgh (East) in Championship Series. cDefeated San Francisco (West) in Championship Series. dDefeated Cincinnati (West) in Championship Series. eDefeated Philadelphia (East) in Championship Series.

STANDING OF CLUBS AT CLOSE OF SEASON

EAST DIVISION

Club	Phil.	Mon.	Pitt.	St.L.	N.Y.	Chi.	Atl.	Cin.	Hou.	L.A.	S.D.	S.F.	W.	L.	Pct.	G.B.
Philadelphia	..	9	7	9	12	13	7	5	9	6	8	6	91	71	.562	....
Montreal	9	..	6	12	10	12	7	9	7	1	10	7	90	72	.556	1
Pittsburgh	11	12	..	10	8	10	1	6	5	6	6	8	83	79	.512	8
St. Louis	9	6	8	..	9	9	6	7	5	5	5	5	74	88	.457	17
New York	6	8	10	9	..	8	9	4	4	5	1	3	67	95	.414	24
Chicago	5	6	8	9	10	..	4	7	1	5	4	5	64	98	.395	27

WEST DIVISION

Club	Hou.	L.A.	Cin.	Atl.	S.F.	S.D.	Chi.	Mon.	N.Y.	Phil.	Pitt.	St.L.	W.	L.	Pct.	G.B.
Houston	..	9	10	11	11	11	5	8	3	7	7	93	70	.571	....	
Los Angeles	10	..	9	7	13	9	7	11	7	6	6	7	92	71	.564	1
Cincinnati	8	9	..	16	7	15	5	3	8	7	6	5	89	73	.549	3½
Atlanta	7	11	2	..	11	12	8	5	3	5	11	6	81	80	.503	11
San Francisco	7	5	11	6	..	8	7	5	9	6	4	7	75	86	.466	17
San Diego	7	9	3	6	10	..	8	2	11	4	6	7	73	89	.451	19½

NOTE: Standing includes one-game playoff between Houston and Los Angeles.
Tie Game—San Diego at Cincinnati.
Cancelled Game—San Francisco at Atlanta.
Championship Series—Philadelphia defeated Houston, three games to two.

RECORD AT HOME

EAST DIVISION

Club	Mon.	Phil.	Pitt.	St.L.	N.Y.	Chi.	Hou.	L.A.	Atl.	S.D.	Cin.	S.F.	W.	L.	Pct.
Montreal	....	4-5	4-5	8-1	5-3	7-2	3-3	1-5	5-1	6-0	5-1	3-3	51	29	.638
Philadelphia	4-5	....	5-4	4-5	4-5	8-1	5-1	3-3	5-1	5-1	4-2	2-4	49	32	.605
Pittsburgh	7-2	7-2	....	5-4	5-4	6-3	4-2	5-1	1-5	2-4	1-5	4-2	47	34	.580
St. Louis	5-4	4-5	4-5	....	4-5	3-6	3-3	4-2	3-3	3-3	4-2	4-2	41	40	.506
New York	5-5	1-8	6-3	4-5	....	5-4	3-3	4-2	5-1	1-5	2-4	2-4	38	44	.463
Chicago	4-5	4-5	5-4	3-6	6-3	....	1-5	3-3	2-4	3-3	4-2	2-4	37	44	.457

WEST DIVISION

Club	Hou.	L.A.	Atl.	S.D.	Cin.	S.F.	Mon.	Phil.	Pitt.	St.L.	N.Y.	Chi.	W.	L.	Pct.
Houston	....	6-3	8-1	4-5	5-4	8-1	2-4	2-4	5-1	4-2	5-1	6-0	55	26	.679
Los Angeles	7-3	....	3-6	7-2	3-6	7-2	6-0	3-3	5-1	5-1	5-1	4-2	55	27	.671
Atlanta	6-3	5-4	....	9-0	1-8	6-2	4-2	4-2	6-0	3-3	2-4	4-2	50	30	.625
San Diego	2-7	7-2	1-8	....	1-8	7-2	2-4	3-3	2-4	4-2	6-0	5-1	45	36	.556
Cincinnati	4-5	3-6	8-1	7-2	....	4-5	2-4	5-1	1-5	3-3	4-2	3-3	44	37	.543
San Francisco	6-3	3-6	4-5	6-3	6-3	....	2-4	2-4	2-4	5-1	5-1	3-3	44	37	.543

RECORD ABROAD

EAST DIVISION

Club	Phil.	Mon.	Pitt.	St.L.	N.Y.	Chi.	Cin.	Hou.	L.A.	S.F.	Atl.	S.D.	W.	L.	Pct.
Philadelphia	....	5-4	2-7	5-4	8-1	5-4	1-5	4-2	3-3	4-2	2-4	3-3	42	39	.519
Montreal	5-4	....	2-7	4-5	5-5	5-4	4-2	4-2	0-6	4-2	2-4	4-2	39	43	.476
Pittsburgh	4-5	5-4	....	5-4	3-6	4-5	5-1	1-5	1-5	0-6	4-2	3-3	36	45	.444
St. Louis	5-4	1-8	4-5	....	5-4	6-3	3-3	2-4	1-5	1-5	3-3	2-4	33	48	.407
New York	5-4	3-5	4-5	5-4	....	3-6	2-4	1-5	1-5	1-5	4-2	0-6	29	51	.363
Chicago	1-8	2-7	3-6	6-3	4-5	....	3-3	0-6	2-4	3-3	2-4	1-5	27	54	.333

WEST DIVISION

Club	Cin.	Hou.	L.A.	S.F.	Atl.	S.D.	Phil.	Mon.	Pitt.	St.L.	N.Y.	Chi.	W.	L.	Pct.
Cincinnati	....	4-5	6-3	3-6	8-1	8-1	2-4	1-5	5-1	2-4	4-2	2-4	45	36	.556
Houston	5-4	....	3-7	3-6	7-2	1-5	3-3	2-4	3-3	3-3	5-1		38	44	.463
Los Angeles	6-3	3-6	....	6-3	4-5	2-7	3-3	5-1	1-5	2-4	2-4	3-3	37	44	.457
San Francisco	5-4	1-8	2-7	....	2-6	2-7	4-2	3-3	2-4	2-4	4-2	4-2	31	49	.388
Atlanta	1-8	1-8	6-3	5-4	....	3-6	1-5	1-5	5-1	3-3	1-5	4-2	31	50	.383
San Diego	2-7	5-4	2-7	3-6	0-9	....	1-5	0-6	4-2	3-3	5-1	3-3	28	53	.346

SHUTOUT GAMES

Club	L.A.	Hou.	Mon.	Cin.	St.L.	S.D.	Atl.	N.Y.	Phil.	Pitt.	S.F.	Chi.	W.	L.	Pct.
Los Angeles	..	1	3	1	0	0	2	2	2	2	6	0	19	4	.826
Houston	1	..	0	4	2	2	0	1	1	0	4	3	18	11	.621
Montreal	0	2	..	0	2	2	0	1	1	2	3	2	15	10	.600
Cincinnati	0	1	1	..	0	2	5	0	1	1	0	1	12	9	.571
St. Louis	0	1	1	0	..	1	0	1	3	1	1	0	9	8	.529
San Diego	0	1	0	0	1	..	0	1	0	2	2	2	9	9	.500
Atlanta	2	2	1	1	0	1	..	0	1	0	0	1	9	11	.450
New York	0	0	0	1	1	0	3	..	2	1	0	1	9	13	.409
Philadelphia	0	2	0	0	1	0	0	3	..	0	0	2	8	12	.400
Pittsburgh	0	0	3	0	1	0	0	2	0	..	0	2	8	12	.400
San Francisco	0	1	1	1	0	0	1	2	0	1	..	3	10	16	.385
Chicago	1	0	0	1	0	1	0	0	1	2	0	..	6	17	.261

OFFICIAL NATIONAL LEAGUE BATTING AVERAGES

Compiled by Elias Sports Bureau, New York, N. Y.

CLUB BATTING

Club	Pct.	G.	AB.	R.	OR.	H.	TB.	2B.	3B.	HR.	RBI.	SH.	SF.	SB.	CS.	LOB.
St. Louis	.275	162	5608	738	710	1541	2242	300	49	101	688	73	49	117	54	1110
Phila.....	.270	162	5625	728	639	1517	2248	272	54	117	674	77	58	140	62	1131
Pittsb'gh	.266	162	5517	666	646	1469	2142	249	38	116	626	75	56	209	102	1087
Los Ang.	.263	163	5568	663	591	1462	2163	209	24	148	638	96	41	123	72	1173
Cinc'ati.	.262	163	5516	707	670	1445	2130	256	45	113	668	78	54	156	43	1149
Houston	.261	163	5566	637	589	1455	2045	231	67	75	599	89	45	194	74	1200
Montreal	.257	162	5465	694	629	1407	2121	250	61	114	647	76	56	237	82	1116
N. York.	.257	162	5478	611	702	1407	1890	218	41	61	554	73	53	158	99	1125
S. Diego	.255	163	5540	591	654	1410	1892	195	43	67	546	92	38	239	73	1239
Chicago.	.251	162	5619	614	728	1411	2053	251	35	107	578	69	40	93	64	1119
Atlanta .	.250	161	5402	630	660	1352	2054	226	22	144	597	69	33	73	52	1054
S. Fran.	.244	161	5368	573	634	1310	1837	199	44	80	539	100	54	100	58	1116
Totals	.259	973	66272	7852	7852	17186	24817	2856	523	1243	7354	967	577	1839	835	13619

INDIVIDUAL BATTING

(Top Fifteen Qualifiers for Batting Championship—502 or More Plate Appearances)

*Bats lefthanded. †Switch-hitter.

Player and Club	Pct.	G.	AB.	R.	H.	TB.	2B.	3B.	HR.	RBI.	GW.	SH.	SF.	SB.	CS.
Buckner, William, Chi.*	.324	145	578	69	187	264	41	3	10	68	7	0	6	1	2
Hernandez, Keith, St.L.*	.321	159	595	111	191	294	39	8	16	99	13	1	4	14	8
Templeton, Garry, St.L.†	.319	118	504	83	161	210	19	9	4	43	3	1	1	31	15
McBride, Arnold, Phila.*	.309	137	554	68	171	251	33	10	9	87	14	2	6	13	10
Cedeno, Cesar, Hou.	.309	137	499	71	154	232	32	8	10	73	7	1	2	48	15
Dawson, Andre, Mtl.	.308	151	577	96	178	284	41	7	17	87	17	1	10	34	9
Garvey, Steven, L.A.	.304	163	658	78	200	307	27	1	26	106	13	3	4	6	11
Collins, David, Cin.†	.303	144	551	94	167	204	20	4	3	35	6	3	3	79	21
Simmons, Ted, St.L.†	.303	145	495	84	150	250	33	2	21	98	12	0	6	1	0
Hendrick, George, St.L.	.302	150	572	73	173	285	33	2	25	109	11	1	4	6	1
Cruz, Jose, Hou.*	.302	160	612	79	185	261	29	7	11	91	15	0	8	36	11
Richards, Eugene, S.D.*	.301	158	642	91	193	247	26	8	4	41	6	7	0	61	16
Mumphrey, Jerry, S.D.†	.298	160	564	61	168	210	24	3	4	59	7	5	4	52	5
Parker, David, Pitt.*	.295	139	518	71	153	237	31	1	17	79	11	0	5	10	7
Griffey, G. Kenneth, Cin.*	.294	146	544	89	160	247	28	10	13	85	13	3	5	23	1

DEPARTMENTAL LEADERS: G—Garvey, 163; AB—O. Moreno, 676; R—K. Hernandez, 111; H—Garvey, 200; TB—Schmidt, 342; 2B—Rose, 42; 3B—O. Moreno, R. Scott, 13; HR—Schmidt, 48; RBI—Schmidt, 121; GW—Clark, 18; SH—O. Smith, 23; SF—Schmidt, 13; SB—LeFlore, 97; CS—O. Moreno, 33.

(All Players—Listed Alphabetically)

Player and Club	Pct.	G.	AB.	R.	H.	TB.	2B.	3B.	HR.	RBI.	GW.	SH.	SF.	SB.	CS.
Aguayo, Luis, Phila.	.277	20	47	7	13	21	1	2	1	8	1	0	1	1	1
Alexander, Doyle, Atl.	.181	35	83	7	15	18	3	0	0	3	0	3	0	0	0
Alexander, Matthew, Pitt.†	.333	37	3	13	1	2	1	0	0	0	0	0	0	10	3
Allen, Neil, N.Y.	.143	59	14	0	2	2	0	0	0	0	1	0	0	0	0
Almon, William, Mtl.-N.Y.†	.193	66	150	15	29	39	4	3	0	7	1	0	1	2	0
Andujar, Joaquin, Hou.†	.172	35	29	3	5	10	0	1	1	3	0	5	0	0	0
Armstrong, Michael, S.D.	.000	11	3	0	0	0	0	0	0	0	0	0	0	0	0
Ashby, Alan, Hou.†	.256	116	352	30	90	122	19	2	3	48	4	2	5	0	0
Asselstine, Brian, Atl.*	.284	87	218	18	62	86	13	1	3	25	2	2	3	1	3
Auerbach, Frederick, Cin.	.333	24	33	5	11	17	1	1	1	4	0	1	0	0	3
Aviles, Ramon, Phila.	.277	51	101	12	28	40	6	0	2	9	0	2	2	0	0
Backman, Walter, N.Y.†	.323	27	93	12	30	33	1	1	0	9	0	4	1	2	3
Bahnsen, Stanley, Mtl.	.111	57	9	1	1	2	1	0	0	0	0	0	0	0	0
Bair, C. Douglas, Cin.	.000	61	2	0	0	0	0	0	0	0	0	0	0	0	0
Baker, Charles, S.D.	.136	9	22	0	3	4	1	0	0	0	0	0	0	0	0
Baker, Johnnie, L.A.	.294	153	579	80	170	291	26	4	29	97	17	1	12	12	10
Bass, Randy, S.D.*	.286	19	49	5	14	25	0	1	3	8	2	0	0	0	0
Beall, Robert, Pitt.†	.000	3	3	0	0	0	0	0	0	0	0	0	0	0	0
Beckwith, T. Joseph, L.A.*	.000	38	2	0	0	0	0	0	0	0	0	0	0	0	0
Bench, Johnny, Cin.	.250	114	360	52	90	174	12	0	24	68	6	0	4	4	2
Benedict, Bruce, Atl.	.253	120	359	18	91	113	14	1	2	34	5	13	1	3	2
Benton, Alfred, N.Y.	.048	12	21	0	1	1	0	0	0	0	0	0	0	0	0

Player and Club	Pct.	G.	AB.	R.	H.	TB.	2B.	3B.	HR.	RBI.	GW.	SH.	SF.	SB.	CS.
Berenguer, Juan, N.Y.	.000	6	0	0	0	0	0	0	0	0	0	0	0	0	0
Berenyi, Bruce, Cin.	.000	6	7	1	0	0	0	0	0	0	0	4	0	0	0
Bergman, David, Hou.°	.256	90	78	12	20	28	6	1	0	3	0	3	0	1	0
Bernazard, Antonio, Mtl.†	.224	82	183	26	41	65	7	1	5	18	2	1	1	9	2
Berra, Dale, Pitt.	.220	93	245	21	54	84	8	2	6	31	4	4	2	2	0
Bevacqua, Kurt, S.D.-Pitt.	.228	84	114	5	26	35	7	1	0	16	2	1	1	1	1
Bibby, James, Pitt.	.156	35	77	6	12	18	3	0	1	7	0	10	1	0	0
Biittner, Larry, Chi.°	.249	127	273	21	68	87	12	2	1	34	2	0	6	1	3
Blackwell, Timothy, Chi.†	.272	103	320	24	87	126	16	4	5	30	3	2	3	0	1
Blair, Dennis, S.D.	.200	5	5	0	1	1	0	0	0	0	0	0	0	0	0
Blanks, Larvell, Atl.	.204	88	221	23	45	57	6	0	2	12	3	4	2	1	2
Blue, Vida, S.F.°	.074	31	68	3	5	6	1	0	0	1	0	7	1	0	0
Blyleven, Rikalbert, Pitt.	.082	37	61	0	5	6	1	0	0	2	0	9	0	0	0
Bochy, Bruce, Hou.	.182	22	22	0	4	5	1	0	0	0	0	0	0	0	0
Boggs, Thomas, Atl.	.159	32	63	2	10	10	0	0	0	2	0	6	1	0	0
Bomback, Mark, N.Y.	.233	36	43	5	10	13	3	0	0	5	0	5	0	0	0
Bonds, Bobby, St.L.	.203	86	231	37	47	73	5	3	5	24	2	1	3	15	5
Bonham, William, Cin.	.000	4	6	1	0	0	0	0	0	0	0	0	0	0	0
Boone, Robert, Phila.	.229	141	480	34	110	162	23	1	9	55	6	4	2	3	4
Borbon, Pedro, St.L.	.250	10	4	0	1	1	0	0	0	1	0	0	0	0	0
Bordley, William, S.F.°	.167	8	6	0	1	1	0	0	0	0	0	2	0	0	0
Bourjos, Christopher, S.F.	.227	13	22	4	5	9	1	0	1	2	0	0	0	0	0
Bowa, Lawrence, Phila.†	.267	147	540	57	144	174	16	4	2	39	6	7	3	21	6
Bradford, Larry, Atl.	.000	56	3	0	0	0	0	0	0	0	0	0	0	0	0
Breining, Fred, S.F.	.000	5	0	0	0	0	0	0	0	0	0	0	0	0	0
Brooks, Hubert, N.Y.	.309	24	81	8	25	32	2	1	1	10	0	1	0	1	1
Brusstar, Warren, Phila.	.000	26	1	0	0	0	0	0	0	0	0	0	0	0	0
Buckner, William, Chi.°	.324	145	578	69	187	264	41	3	10	68	7	0	6	1	2
Burnside, Sheldon, Cin.	.000	7	1	0	0	0	0	0	0	0	0	0	0	0	0
Burris, B. Ray, N.Y.	.098	29	51	1	5	5	0	0	0	0	0	3	0	0	1
Burroughs, Jeffrey, Atl.	.263	99	278	35	73	126	14	0	13	51	3	1	2	1	1
Bystrom, Martin, Phila.	.071	6	14	1	1	1	0	0	0	1	0	0	0	0	0
Cabell, Enos, Hou.	.276	152	604	69	167	212	23	8	2	55	10	1	5	21	13
Camp, Rick, Atl.	.111	77	9	0	1	2	1	0	0	0	0	4	0	0	0
Candelaria, John, Pitt.°	.195	35	77	5	15	18	3	0	0	7	1	3	1	0	0
Capilla, Douglas, Chi.°	.190	40	21	1	4	6	0	1	0	1	1	1	0	0	0
Carbo, Bernardo, StL-Pit°	.235	21	17	0	4	4	0	0	0	1	0	1	0	0	0
Cardenal, Jose, N.Y.	.167	26	42	4	7	8	1	0	0	4	1	0	1	0	1
Carlton, Steven, Phila.°	.188	38	101	7	19	20	1	0	0	6	0	6	3	0	0
Carter, Gary, Mtl.	.264	154	549	76	145	267	25	5	29	101	13	1	8	3	2
Cash, David, S.D.	.227	130	397	25	90	111	14	2	1	23	2	2	3	6	5
Castillo, Robert, L.A.	.111	62	9	0	1	1	0	0	0	0	0	1	0	0	0
Caudill, William, Chi.	.222	72	9	0	2	3	1	0	0	1	0	1	0	0	0
Cedeno, Cesar, Hou.	.309	137	499	71	154	232	32	8	10	73	7	1	2	48	15
Cey, Ronald, L.A.	.254	157	551	81	140	249	25	0	28	77	12	4	1	2	2
Chambliss, C. Chris., Atl.°	.282	158	602	83	170	265	37	2	18	72	13	2	4	7	3
Christenson, Larry, Phila.	.368	14	19	6	7	10	0	0	1	4	0	3	0	0	0
Clark, Jack, S.F.	.284	127	437	77	124	226	20	8	22	82	18	1	10	2	5
Collins, David, Cin.†	.303	144	551	94	167	204	20	4	3	35	6	3	3	79	21
Combe, Geoffrey, Cin.	.000	4	0	0	0	0	0	0	0	0	0	0	0	0	0
Concepcion, David, Cin.	.260	156	622	72	162	224	31	8	5	77	10	2	6	12	2
Cooper, Gary, Atl.†	.000	21	2	3	0	0	0	0	0	0	0	0	0	2	1
Correll, Victor, Cin.	.421	10	19	1	8	9	1	0	0	3	1	0	0	0	0
Cromartie, Warren, Mont.°	.288	162	597	74	172	257	33	5	14	70	11	4	3	8	8
Cruz, Hector, Cin.	.213	52	75	5	16	25	4	1	1	5	1	0	0	0	0
Cruz, Jose, Hou.°	.302	160	612	79	185	261	29	7	11	91	15	0	8	36	11
Curtis, John, S.D.°	.194	31	62	2	12	13	1	0	0	2	1	5	0	0	0
D'Acquisto, John, SD-Mont	.000	50	8	1	0	0	0	0	0	0	0	2	0	0	0
Dade, L. Paul, S.D.	.189	68	53	17	10	10	0	0	0	3	1	0	0	4	5
Davalillo, Victor, L.A.°	.167	7	6	1	1	1	0	0	0	0	0	0	0	0	0
Davis, Mark, Phila.°	.500	2	2	1	1	1	0	0	0	0	0	0	0	0	0
Dawson, Andre, Mont.	.308	151	577	96	178	284	41	7	17	87	17	1	10	34	9
DeJesus, Ivan, Chi.	.259	157	618	78	160	201	26	3	3	33	4	8	2	44	16
Dernier, Robert, Phila.	.571	10	7	5	4	4	0	0	0	1	0	0	0	3	0
De Sa, Joseph, St.L.°	.273	7	11	0	3	3	0	0	0	0	0	0	0	0	0
Dillard, Stephen, Chi.	.225	100	244	31	55	77	8	1	4	27	4	0	2	2	2
Driessen, David, Cin.°	.265	154	524	81	139	219	36	1	14	74	10	0	9	19	6
Dues, Hal, Mont.	.000	6	3	0	0	0	0	0	0	0	0	0	0	0	0
Durham, Leon, St.L.°	.271	96	303	42	82	129	15	4	8	42	5	3	5	8	5

Player and Club	Pct.	G.	AB.	R.	H.	TB.	2B.	3B.	HR.	RBI.	GW.	SH.	SF.	SB.	CS.
Easler, Michael, Pitt.°	.338	132	393	66	133	229	27	3	21	74	9	0	9	5	9
Eichelberger, Juan, S.D.	.111	15	27	1	3	3	0	0	0	0	0	4	0	1	0
Espinosa, Arnulfo, Phila.	.115	13	26	4	3	4	1	0	0	2	0	3	0	0	0
Evans, Barry, S.D.	.232	73	125	11	29	39	3	2	1	14	0	2	3	1	1
Evans, Darrell, S.F.°	.264	154	556	69	147	230	23	0	20	78	14	6	6	17	5
Fahey, William, S.D.°	.257	93	241	18	62	69	4	0	1	22	1	1	2	2	0
Falcone, Peter, N.Y.°	.146	37	41	2	6	6	0	0	0	3	2	6	0	0	0
Ferguson, Joseph, L.A.	.238	77	172	20	41	75	3	2	9	29	7	1	3	2	2
Figueroa, Jesus, Chi.°	.253	115	198	20	50	58	5	0	1	11	1	2	0	2	1
Fingers, Roland, S.D.	.278	66	18	0	5	8	3	0	0	0	0	1	0	0	0
Fischlin, Michael, Hou.	.000	1	1	0	0	0	0	0	0	0	0	0	0	0	0
Flannery, Timothy, S.D.°	.240	95	292	15	70	82	12	0	0	25	3	4	1	2	2
Flynn, R. Douglas, N.Y.	.255	128	443	46	113	138	9	8	0	24	5	6	3	2	2
Foli, Timothy, Pitt.	.265	127	495	61	131	162	22	0	3	38	7	13	7	11	7
Foote, Barry, Chi.	.238	63	202	16	48	81	13	1	6	28	3	0	1	1	1
Forsch, Kenneth, Hou.	.234	32	77	3	18	21	3	0	0	8	0	6	0	1	0
Forsch, Robert, St.L.	.295	32	78	11	23	37	5	0	3	10	0	9	0	1	0
Forster, Terry, L.A.°	.000	9	0	0	0	0	0	0	0	0	0	0	0	0	0
Foster, George, Cin.	.273	144	528	79	144	250	21	5	25	93	16	0	4	1	0
Frazier, George, St.L.	.000	22	0	0	0	0	0	0	0	0	0	0	0	0	0
Frias, Jesus, L.A.	.222	14	9	1	2	3	1	0	0	0	0	0	0	0	0
Fryman, Woodrow, Mont.	.167	61	12	0	2	2	0	0	0	2	0	2	0	0	0
Fulgham, John, St.L.	.000	16	27	1	0	0	0	0	0	0	0	3	0	0	0
Garber, H. Eugene, Atl.	.500	68	2	0	1	1	0	0	0	1	0	0	0	0	0
Garner, Philip, Pitt.	.259	151	548	62	142	196	27	6	5	58	3	7	7	32	7
Garvey, Steven, L.A.	.304	163	658	78	200	307	27	1	26	106	13	3	4	6	11
Geronimo, Cesar, Cin.°	.255	103	145	16	37	48	5	0	2	9	0	2	1	2	1
Glynn, Edward, N.Y.	.000	38	6	0	0	0	0	0	0	0	0	0	0	0	0
Goltz, David, L.A.	.128	35	47	1	6	6	0	0	0	4	0	7	0	0	0
Gomez, Luis, Atl.	.191	121	278	18	53	59	6	0	0	24	0	2	10	1	4
Gonzalez, Julio, Hou.	.115	40	52	5	6	7	1	0	0	1	0	1	0	1	0
Griffey, G. Kenneth, Cin.°	.294	146	544	89	160	247	28	10	13	85	13	3	5	23	1
Griffin, Thomas, S.F.	.111	44	18	1	2	5	0	0	1	1	0	2	0	0	0
Grimsley, Ross, Mont.°	.222	11	9	1	2	3	1	0	0	0	0	0	0	0	0
Gross, Gregory, Phil.°	.240	127	154	19	37	48	7	2	0	12	2	3	0	1	1
Guerrero, Pedro, L.A.	.322	75	183	27	59	91	9	1	7	31	2	1	3	2	1
Gullickson, William, Mont.	.175	24	40	2	7	8	1	0	0	0	0	10	0	0	0
Halicki, Edward, S.F.	.167	11	6	0	1	1	0	0	0	0	0	0	0	0	0
Hanna, Preston, Atl.	.143	32	14	1	2	4	0	1	0	0	0	0	0	0	0
Hargesheimer, Alan, S.F.	.182	15	22	2	4	5	1	0	0	2	1	1	0	0	0
Harper, Terry, Atl.	.185	21	54	3	10	14	2	1	0	3	1	0	0	2	1
Hassler, Andrew, Pitt.°	.000	6	2	0	0	0	0	0	0	0	0	0	0	0	0
Hatcher, Michael, L.A.	.226	57	84	4	19	24	2	0	1	5	1	4	0	0	2
Hausman, Thomas, N.Y.	.063	55	16	0	1	1	0	0	0	0	0	1	0	0	0
Hayes, William, Chi.	.222	4	9	0	2	3	1	0	0	0	0	0	0	0	0
Heep, Daniel, Hou.°	.276	33	87	6	24	32	8	0	0	6	0	1	0	0	0
Henderson, Kenneth, Chi.†	.195	44	82	7	16	25	3	0	2	9	2	0	0	0	0
Henderson, Stephen, N.Y.	.290	143	513	75	149	206	17	8	8	58	9	3	3	23	12
Hendrick, George, St.L.	.302	150	572	73	173	285	33	2	25	109	11	1	4	6	1
Hernandez, Guillermo, Chi.°	.211	53	19	0	4	5	1	0	0	1	0	1	0	0	0
Hernandez, Keith, St.L.°	.321	159	595	111	191	294	39	8	16	99	13	1	4	14	8
Herndon, Larry, S.F.	.258	139	493	54	127	190	17	11	8	49	2	4	4	8	8
Herr, Thomas, St.L.†	.248	76	222	29	55	77	12	5	0	15	2	1	2	9	2
Hill, Marc, S.F.	.171	17	41	1	7	9	2	0	0	0	0	1	0	0	0
Hodges, Ronald, N.Y.°	.238	36	42	4	10	12	2	0	0	5	2	1	1	1	1
Holland, Alfred, S.F.	.200	54	5	2	1	3	0	1	0	2	0	2	0	0	0
Holman, R. Scott, N.Y.	.000	4	0	0	0	0	0	0	0	0	0	0	0	0	0
Hood, Donald, St.L.°	.200	35	20	3	4	4	0	0	0	1	0	2	0	0	0
Hooton, Burt, L.A.	.063	34	64	4	4	7	0	0	1	6	0	14	0	0	0
Horner, J. Robert, Atl.	.268	124	463	81	124	245	14	1	35	89	5	0	4	3	1
Hough, Charles, L.A.	.500	19	2	0	1	1	0	0	0	1	0	1	0	0	0
Householder, Paul, Cin.†	.244	20	45	3	11	14	1	1	0	7	0	0	0	1	0
Howe, Arthur, Hou.	.283	110	321	34	91	143	12	5	10	46	6	4	4	1	0
Howe, Steven, L.A.°	.091	59	11	1	1	1	0	0	0	0	0	0	0	0	0
Howell, Jay, Cin.	.000	5	0	0	0	0	0	0	0	0	0	0	0	0	0
Hrabosky, Alan, Atl.	.000	45	1	0	0	0	0	0	0	0	0	0	0	0	0
Hubbard, Glenn, Atl.	.248	117	431	55	107	161	21	3	9	43	6	2	5	7	5
Hume, Thomas, Cin.	.188	78	16	2	3	5	2	0	0	4	0	1	0	0	0
Hutton, Thomas, Mont.°	.218	62	55	2	12	14	2	0	0	5	1	2	1	0	0

Player and Club	Pct.	G.	AB.	R.	H.	TB.	2B.	3B.	HR.	RBI.	GW.	SH.	SF.	SB.	CS.
Iorg, Dane, St.L.°	.303	105	251	33	76	110	23	1	3	36	2	0	4	1	1
Isales, Orlando, Phila.	.400	3	5	1	2	4	0	1	0	3	0	0	0	0	0
Ivie, Michael, S.F.	.241	79	286	21	69	99	16	1	4	25	3	0	1	1	2
Jackson, Grant, Pitt.†	.000	61	10	0	0	0	0	0	0	0	0	0	0	0	0
Jackson, Roy, N.Y.	.188	26	16	2	3	5	0	1	0	0	0	0	0	0	1
Jefferson, Jesse, Pitt.	.000	1	1	0	0	0	0	0	0	0	0	1	0	0	0
Johnson, Clifford, Chi.	.235	68	196	28	46	84	8	0	10	34	6	0	1	0	0
Johnstone, John, L.A.°	.307	109	251	31	77	102	15	2	2	20	2	2	0	3	2
Jones, Randall, S.D.	.067	25	45	1	3	3	0	0	0	0	0	7	0	0	0
Jorgensen, Michael, N.Y.°	.255	119	321	43	82	114	11	0	7	43	4	1	0	0	3
Joshua, Von, S.D.°	.238	53	63	8	15	25	2	1	2	7	1	0	0	0	1
Kaat, James, St.L.°	.143	49	35	4	5	9	1	0	1	2	0	4	0	1	0
Kelleher, Michael, Chi.	.146	105	96	12	14	17	1	1	0	4	1	1	1	1	3
Kendall, Fred, S.D.	.292	19	24	2	7	7	0	0	0	2	0	0	0	0	0
Kennedy, Junior, Cin.	.261	104	337	31	88	113	16	3	1	34	3	4	8	3	1
Kennedy, Terrence, St.L.°	.254	84	248	28	63	93	12	3	4	34	3	1	4	0	0
Kingman, David, Chi.	.278	81	255	31	71	133	8	0	18	57	4	0	4	2	2
Kinney, Dennis, S.D.°	.083	50	12	0	1	1	0	0	0	0	0	1	0	0	0
Knepper, Robert, S.F.°	.152	35	66	3	10	13	3	0	0	7	0	9	2	1	0
Knicely, Alan, Hou.	.000	1	1	0	0	0	0	0	0	0	0	0	0	0	0
Knight, C. Ray, Cin.	.264	162	618	71	163	258	39	7	14	78	12	5	4	1	2
Knowles, Darold, St.L.°	.000	2	0	0	0	0	0	0	0	0	0	0	0	0	0
Kobel, Kevin, N.Y.	.000	14	2	0	0	0	0	0	0	0	0	0	0	0	0
Krukow, Michael, Chi.	.246	34	65	5	16	19	0	0	1	6	1	7	0	0	0
LaCorte, Frank, Hou.	.167	55	6	0	1	1	0	0	0	1	0	2	0	0	0
LaCoss, Michael, Cin.	.091	34	55	2	5	6	1	0	0	1	1	6	0	0	0
Lacy, Leondaus, Pitt.	.335	109	278	45	93	142	20	4	7	33	4	2	4	18	9
LaGrow, Lerrin, Phila.	.250	25	4	0	1	1	0	0	0	0	0	0	0	0	0
Lamp, Dennis, Chi.	.098	41	61	3	6	6	0	0	0	1	0	7	0	0	0
Landestoy, Rafael, Hou.†	.247	149	393	42	97	129	13	8	1	27	3	6	1	23	12
Landrum, Terry, St.L.	.247	35	77	6	19	25	2	2	0	7	0	0	1	3	2
Larson, Daniel, Phila.	.154	12	13	0	2	3	1	0	0	0	0	0	0	0	0
Lavelle, Gary, S.F.†	.000	62	11	0	0	0	0	0	0	0	0	3	0	0	0
Law, Rudy, L.A.°	.260	128	388	55	101	117	5	4	1	23	4	3	1	40	13
Law, Vance, Pitt.	.230	25	74	11	17	23	2	2	0	3	1	1	0	2	0
Lea, Charles, Mont.	.081	21	37	1	3	5	0	1	0	1	0	1	0	0	0
Lee, Mark, Pitt.	.000	4	0	0	0	0	0	0	0	0	0	0	0	0	0
Lee, William, Mont.°	.220	25	41	2	9	10	1	0	0	0	0	0	0	0	0
LeFlore, Ronald, Mont.	.257	139	521	95	134	189	21	11	4	39	4	2	1	97	19
Leibrandt, Charles, Cin.	.196	36	56	2	11	13	0	1	0	4	1	4	1	0	0
LeMaster, Johnnie, S.F.	.215	135	405	33	87	124	16	6	3	31	2	7	5	0	1
Lentine, James, St.L.	.100	9	10	1	1	1	0	0	0	1	0	0	0	0	0
Leonard, Jeffrey, Hou.	.213	88	216	29	46	72	7	5	3	20	4	1	2	4	1
Lerch, Randy, Phila.°	.267	34	45	5	12	14	2	0	0	3	0	4	0	0	0
Lezcano, Carlos, Chi.	.205	42	88	15	18	33	4	1	3	12	2	2	1	1	2
Littell, Mark, St.L.°	.000	14	1	0	0	0	0	0	0	0	0	0	0	0	0
Little, D. Jeffery, St.L.	.167	7	6	1	1	1	0	0	0	0	0	0	0	0	0
Littlefield, John, St.L.	.000	52	11	1	0	0	0	0	0	0	0	1	0	0	0
Littlejohn, Dennis, S.F.	.241	13	29	2	7	8	1	0	0	2	0	2	0	0	0
Lopes, David, L.A.	.251	141	553	79	139	190	15	3	10	49	5	9	4	23	7
Loucks, Scott, Hou.	.333	8	3	4	1	1	0	0	0	0	0	0	0	0	0
Loviglio, John, Phila.	.000	16	5	7	0	0	0	0	0	0	0	0	0	0	0
Lucas, Gary, S.D.°	.171	46	35	1	6	6	0	0	0	2	0	7	0	0	0
Lum, Michael, Atl.°	.205	93	83	7	17	20	3	0	0	13	0	1	1	0	0
Luzinski, Gregory, Phila.	.228	106	368	44	84	162	19	1	19	56	8	0	4	3	0
Lyle, Albert, Phila.°	.000	10	0	0	0	0	0	0	0	0	0	0	0	0	0
Lynch, Edward, N.Y.	.333	5	6	0	2	2	0	0	0	0	0	0	0	0	0
Macha, Kenneth, Mont.	.290	49	107	10	31	41	5	1	1	8	1	1	0	0	2
Macko, Steven, Chi.°	.300	6	20	2	6	8	2	0	0	2	0	0	0	0	0
Maddox, Elliott, N.Y.	.246	130	411	35	101	131	16	1	4	34	4	5	4	1	9
Maddox, Garry, Phila.	.259	143	549	59	142	212	31	3	11	73	5	7	9	25	5
Madlock, Bill, Pitt.	.277	137	494	62	137	197	22	4	10	53	8	0	3	16	10
Mahler, Michael, Pitt.†	.000	2	0	0	0	0	0	0	0	0	0	0	0	0	0
Mahler, Richard, Atl.	.000	2	0	0	0	0	0	0	0	0	0	0	0	0	0
Mankowski, Philip, N.Y.°	.167	8	12	1	2	3	1	0	0	1	0	0	0	0	0
Manuel, Jerry, Mtl.†	.000	7	6	0	0	0	0	0	0	0	0	0	0	0	0
Martin, Jerry, Chi.	.227	141	494	57	112	207	22	2	23	73	9	0	6	8	3
Martin, John, St.L.†	.273	9	11	0	3	3	0	0	0	1	0	1	0	0	0
Martinez, Silvio, St.L.	.086	25	35	3	3	3	0	0	0	1	0	3	0	0	0

Player and Club	Pct.	G.	AB.	R.	H.	TB.	2B.	3B.	HR.	RBI.	GW.	SH.	SF.	SB.	CS.
Martz, Randy, Chi.°	.111	6	9	0	1	1	0	0	0	0	0	0	0	0	0
Matthews, Gary, Atl.	.278	155	571	79	159	239	17	3	19	75	13	1	5	11	3
Matula, Richard, Atl.	.105	33	57	0	6	6	0	0	0	0	0	5	0	0	0
May, Milton, S.F.°	.260	111	358	27	93	131	16	2	6	50	7	3	6	0	1
Mazzilli, Lee, N.Y.†	.280	152	578	82	162	249	31	4	16	76	9	0	5	41	15
McBride, Arnold, Phila.°	.309	137	554	68	171	251	33	10	9	87	14	2	6	13	10
McCarver, J. Timothy, Phil.°	.200	6	5	2	1	2	1	0	0	2	0	1	0	0	0
McCormack, Donald, Phila.	1.000	2	1	0	1	1	0	0	0	0	0	0	0	0	0
McCovey, Willie, S.F.°	.204	48	113	8	23	34	8	0	1	16	2	0	3	0	0
McGlothen, Lynn, Chi.	.196	41	51	6	10	14	4	0	0	1	1	8	0	0	0
McGraw, Frank, Phila.	.250	57	8	0	2	2	0	0	0	1	0	3	0	0	0
McWilliams, Larry, Atl.°	.157	30	51	3	8	8	0	0	0	1	0	4	0	0	0
Mejias, Samuel, Cin.	.278	71	108	16	30	40	5	1	1	10	0	2	0	4	2
Metzger, Roger, S.F.†	.074	28	27	5	2	2	0	0	0	0	0	1	0	0	0
Miller, Dyar, N.Y.	.000	31	1	0	0	0	0	0	0	0	0	0	0	0	0
Miller, Edward, Atl.†	.158	11	19	3	3	3	0	0	0	0	0	0	0	1	2
Mills, J. Bradley, Mtl.°	.300	21	60	1	18	19	1	0	0	8	0	0	1	0	1
Milner, Eddie, Cin.°	.000	6	3	1	0	0	0	0	0	0	0	0	0	0	0
Milner, John, Pitt.°	.244	114	238	31	58	88	6	0	8	34	6	1	1	2	2
Minton, Gregory, S.F.†	.125	68	8	0	1	1	0	0	0	1	0	2	0	0	0
Mitchell, Robert, L.A.°	.333	9	3	1	1	1	0	0	0	0	0	0	0	0	0
Moffitt, Randall, S.F.	.000	13	1	0	0	0	0	0	0	0	0	0	0	0	0
Monday, Robert, L.A.°	.268	96	194	35	52	91	7	1	10	25	4	0	0	2	2
Montanez, Guillermo, S.D-Mtl.°	.272	142	500	40	136	174	12	4	6	64	0	6	3	5	
Montefusco, John, S.F.	.033	22	30	1	1	1	0	0	0	0	0	3	0	0	0
Moore, Donnie, St.L.°	.750	11	4	1	3	4	1	0	0	2	0	2	0	0	0
Morales, Julio, N.Y.	.254	94	193	19	49	67	7	1	3	30	5	1	8	2	3
Moreland, B. Keith, Phila.	.314	62	159	13	50	70	8	0	4	29	7	1	3	3	1
Moreno, Jose, N.Y.†	.196	37	46	6	9	19	2	1	2	9	2	1	1	1	0
Moreno, Omar, Pitt.°	.249	162	676	87	168	220	20	13	2	36	6	3	7	96	33
Morgan, Joe, Hou.°	.243	141	461	66	112	172	17	5	11	49	11	3	5	24	6
Moskau, Paul, Cin.	.159	33	44	4	7	8	1	0	0	1	0	8	0	0	0
Mota, Manuel, L.A.	.429	7	7	0	3	3	0	0	0	2	1	0	0	0	0
Mumphrey, Jerry, S.D.†	.298	160	564	61	168	210	24	3	4	59	7	5	4	52	5
Munninghoff, Scott, Phila.	1.000	4	1	1	1	3	0	1	0	0	0	0	0	0	0
Mura, Stephen, S.D.	.137	39	51	3	7	9	2	0	0	8	0	0	0	0	0
Murphy, Dale, Atl.	.281	156	569	98	160	290	27	2	33	89	13	2	2	9	6
Murray, Dale, Mtl.	.000	16	3	0	0	0	0	0	0	0	0	0	0	0	0
Murray, Richard, Mtl.	.216	53	194	19	42	66	8	2	4	24	5	1	0	2	1
Nahorodny, William, Atl.	.242	59	157	14	38	65	12	0	5	18	2	0	0	0	0
Nastu, Philip, S.F.°	.000	6	0	0	0	0	0	0	0	0	0	0	0	0	0
Nicosia, Steven, Pitt.	.216	60	176	16	38	49	8	0	1	22	3	2	3	0	1
Niekro, Joseph, Hou.	.275	37	80	7	22	27	5	0	0	10	1	18	0	0	0
Niekro, Philip, Atl.	.133	40	90	2	12	17	5	0	0	5	0	5	0	0	0
Niemann, Randy, Hou.°	.333	22	6	0	2	2	0	0	0	0	0	0	0	0	0
Nolan, Joseph, Atl.-Cin.°	.307	70	176	16	54	71	8	0	3	26	2	3	6	0	0
Noles, Dickie, Phila.	.308	48	13	1	4	4	0	0	0	2	0	2	0	0	0
Norman, Daniel, N.Y.†	.185	69	92	5	17	26	1	1	2	9	2	0	0	5	0
Norman, Fredie, Mtl.†	.050	48	20	1	1	1	0	0	0	0	0	2	0	0	0
North, William, S.F.†	.251	128	415	73	104	121	12	1	1	19	1	2	1	45	19
Oberkfell, Kenneth, St.L.°	.303	116	422	58	128	176	27	6	3	46	6	9	3	4	4
O'Berry, P. Michael, Chi.	.208	19	48	7	10	11	1	0	0	5	1	2	2	0	0
Oester, Ronald, Cin.†	.277	100	303	40	84	110	16	2	2	20	2	5	0	6	2
Office, Rowland, Mtl.°	.267	116	292	36	78	117	13	4	6	30	5	3	4	3	3
Olmsted, Alan, St.L.	.182	5	11	0	2	2	0	0	0	1	0	0	0	0	0
Ontiveros, Steven, Chi.†	.208	31	77	7	16	22	3	0	1	3	0	1	1	0	0
Ott, N. Edward, Pitt.°	.260	120	392	35	102	140	14	0	8	41	7	4	1	1	6
Otten, James, St.L.	.200	31	5	0	1	1	0	0	0	0	0	0	0	0	0
Pacella, John, N.Y.	.100	32	20	0	2	3	1	0	0	1	0	2	0	0	0
Palmer, David, Mtl.	.200	25	45	3	9	11	2	0	0	3	1	2	0	0	0
Parker, David, Pitt.°	.295	139	518	71	153	237	31	1	17	79	11	0	5	10	7
Parrish, Larry, Mtl.	.254	126	452	55	115	193	27	3	15	72	4	1	8	2	6
Pastore, Frank, Cin.	.156	27	64	0	10	10	0	0	0	5	0	6	0	0	0
Pate, Robert, Mtl.	.256	23	39	3	10	12	2	0	0	1	1	0	1	0	1
Pena, Antonio, Pitt.	.429	8	21	1	9	12	1	1	0	1	0	0	0	0	1
Perconte, John, L.A.°	.235	14	17	2	4	4	0	0	0	2	0	2	0	3	0
Perez, Pascual, Pitt.	.250	2	4	1	1	1	0	0	0	0	0	0	0	0	0
Perkins, Broderick, S.D.°	.370	43	100	18	37	52	9	0	2	14	2	0	0	2	1
Pettini, Joseph, S.F.	.232	63	190	19	44	52	3	1	1	9	0	11	0	5	2

Player and Club	Pct.	G.	AB.	R.	H.	TB.	2B.	3B.	HR.	RBI.	GW.	SH.	SF.	SB.	CS.
Phillips, Michael, St.L.°	.234	63	128	13	30	35	5	0	0	7	1	0	1	0	0
Pladson, Gordon, Hou.	.000	12	10	1	0	0	0	0	0	0	0	0	0	0	0
Pocoroba, Biff, Atl.†	.265	70	83	7	22	32	4	0	2	8	2	1	1	1	0
Price, Joseph, Cin.	.128	24	39	1	5	5	0	0	0	0	0	3	0	0	0
Puhl, Terry, Hou.°	.282	141	535	75	151	224	24	5	13	55	11	6	3	27	11
Pujols, Luis, Hou.	.199	78	221	15	44	52	6	1	0	20	2	1	2	0	0
Raines, Timothy, Mtl.†	.050	15	20	5	1	1	0	0	0	0	0	1	0	5	0
Ramirez, Mario, N.Y.	.208	18	24	2	5	5	0	0	0	0	1	0	0	0	0
Ramirez, Rafael, Atl.	.267	50	165	17	44	58	6	1	2	11	2	3	0	2	1
Ramos, Roberto, Mtl.	.156	13	32	5	5	7	2	0	0	2	1	0	0	0	0
Ramsey, Michael, St.L.†	.262	59	126	11	33	43	8	1	0	8	1	0	0	0	0
Randle, Leonard, Chi.†	.276	130	489	67	135	181	19	6	5	39	3	7	2	19	13
Rasmussen, Eric, S.D.	.095	40	21	0	2	4	2	0	0	0	0	6	0	0	0
Ratzer, Stephen, Mtl.	.000	1	1	0	0	0	0	0	0	0	0	0	0	0	0
Reardon, Jeffrey, N.Y.	.000	61	8	0	0	0	0	0	0	0	0	0	0	0	0
Reed, Ronald, Phila.	.300	55	10	0	3	4	1	0	0	0	0	0	0	0	0
Reitz, Kenneth, St.L.	.270	151	523	39	141	198	33	0	8	58	3	8	5	0	1
Reuschel, Ricky, Chi.	.159	44	82	4	13	18	3	1	0	5	0	10	0	0	0
Reuss, Jerry, L.A.°	.088	37	68	4	6	10	1	0	1	3	0	4	0	0	0
Reynolds, G. Craig, Hou.°	.226	137	381	34	86	116	9	6	3	28	2	13	4	2	1
Rhoden, Richard, Pitt.	.375	20	40	3	15	21	3	0	1	11	0	4	0	0	0
Richard, James, Hou.	.154	17	39	2	6	11	2	0	1	3	0	4	0	0	0
Richards, Eugene, S.D.°	.301	158	642	91	193	247	26	8	4	41	6	7	0	61	16
Riley, George, Chi.°	.000	22	1	0	0	0	0	0	0	0	0	1	0	0	0
Rincon, Andrew, St.L.	.250	4	12	0	3	3	0	0	0	1	0	1	0	0	0
Ripley, Allen, S.F.	.150	23	40	2	6	8	0	1	0	2	0	3	0	0	0
Roberge, Bertrand, Hou.	.000	14	3	0	0	0	0	0	0	0	0	1	0	0	0
Roberts, David, Pitt.°	.000	2	0	0	0	0	0	0	0	0	0	0	0	0	0
Robinson, Don, Pitt.	.333	30	57	4	19	26	4	0	1	8	0	0	0	0	1
Robinson, William, Pitt.	.287	100	272	28	78	126	10	1	12	36	7	3	4	1	4
Rodriguez, Aurelio, S.D.	.200	89	175	7	35	52	7	2	2	13	3	2	1	0	1
Rogers, Stephen, Mtl.	.160	38	81	7	13	13	0	0	0	7	0	15	0	0	0
Romo, Enrique, Pitt.	.455	75	11	2	5	8	0	0	1	4	0	2	0	0	0
Rooker, James, Pitt.	.143	4	7	1	1	4	0	0	1	2	0	1	0	0	0
Rosado, Luis, N.Y.	.000	2	4	0	0	0	0	0	0	0	0	0	0	0	0
Rose, Peter, Phila.†	.282	162	655	95	185	232	42	1	1	64	12	4	4	12	8
Rowland, Michael, S.F.	.000	19	0	0	0	0	0	0	0	0	0	0	0	0	0
Royster, Jeron, Atl.	.242	123	392	42	95	125	17	5	1	20	4	4	1	22	13
Ruhle, Vernon, Hou.	.245	28	49	7	12	15	3	0	0	2	0	4	0	0	0
Ruiz, Manuel, Atl.	.308	25	26	3	8	12	2	1	0	2	1	0	0	0	1
Russell, William, L.A.	.264	130	466	38	123	159	23	2	3	34	3	12	1	13	2
Ruthven, Richard, Phila.	.235	33	68	7	16	23	5	1	0	8	1	12	0	1	1
Ryan, L. Nolan, Hou.	.086	35	70	5	6	9	0	0	1	6	0	5	1	0	1
Sadek, Michael, S.F.	.252	64	151	14	38	47	4	1	1	16	0	4	1	0	0
Salazar, Luis, S.D.	.337	44	169	28	57	78	4	7	1	25	1	3	1	11	2
Sambito, Joseph, Hou.°	.000	64	9	0	0	0	0	0	0	0	0	0	0	0	0
Sanderson, Scott, Mtl.	.078	33	64	3	5	8	3	0	0	1	0	8	0	0	0
Sanguillen, Manuel, Pitt.	.250	47	48	2	12	15	3	0	0	2	0	2	0	3	2
Saucier, Kevin, Phila.	.000	40	8	0	0	0	0	0	0	0	0	0	0	0	0
Schmidt, Michael, Phila.	.286	150	548	104	157	342	25	8	48	121	17	0	13	12	5
Scioscia, Michael, L.A.°	.254	54	134	8	34	44	5	1	1	8	0	5	1	1	0
Scott, Anthony, St.L.†	.251	143	415	51	104	129	19	3	0	28	5	5	4	22	10
Scott, Michael, N.Y.	.111	6	9	0	1	1	0	0	0	1	0	0	0	0	0
Scott, Rodney, Mtl.†	.224	154	567	84	127	166	13	13	0	46	4	11	6	63	13
Scurry, Rodney, Pitt.°	.250	20	4	0	1	1	0	0	0	0	0	0	0	0	0
Seaman, Kim, St.L.°	.000	26	1	0	0	0	0	0	0	0	0	0	0	0	0
Seaver, G. Thomas, Cin.	.130	26	46	5	6	9	3	0	0	3	0	7	0	0	0
Shirley, Robert, S.D.	.033	59	30	3	1	1	0	0	0	1	1	4	0	0	0
Simmons, Ted, St.L.†	.303	145	495	84	150	250	33	2	21	98	12	0	6	1	0
Smith, C. Reginald, L.A.†	.322	92	311	47	100	158	13	0	15	55	7	0	9	5	6
Smith, David, Hou.	.000	57	12	0	0	0	0	0	0	0	0	2	0	0	0
Smith, Keith, St.L.	.129	24	31	3	4	5	1	0	0	2	1	0	0	0	0
Smith, Lee, Chi.	.000	18	0	0	0	0	0	0	0	0	0	0	0	0	0
Smith, Lonnie, Phila.	.339	100	298	69	101	132	14	4	3	20	1	1	2	33	13
Smith, Osborne, S.D.†	.230	158	609	67	140	168	18	5	0	35	5	23	4	57	15
Solomon, Eddie, Pitt.	.219	27	32	3	7	9	2	0	0	1	0	3	0	0	0
Sosa, Elias, Mtl.	.091	67	11	0	1	1	0	0	0	1	0	1	0	0	0
Soto, Mario, Cin.	.043	54	46	3	2	2	0	0	0	0	0	8	0	0	0
Speier, Chris, Mtl.	.265	128	388	35	103	128	14	4	1	32	2	6	1	0	3

Player and Club	Pct.	G.	AB.	R.	H.	TB.	2B.	3B.	HR.	RBI.	GW.	SH.	SF.	SB.	CS.
Spikes, L. Charles, Atl.	.278	41	36	6	10	11	1	0	0	2	0	0	0	0	0
Spilman, W. Harry, Cin.°	.267	65	101	14	27	43	4	0	4	19	1	1	2	0	0
Sprowl, Robert, Hou.°	.000	1	0	0	0	0	0	0	0	0	0	0	0	0	0
Stablein, George, S.D.	.000	4	3	0	0	0	0	0	0	0	0	0	0	0	0
Stanhouse, Donald, L.A.	.000	21	2	0	0	0	0	0	0	0	0	0	0	0	0
Stargell, Wilver, Pitt.°	.262	67	202	28	53	98	10	1	11	38	3	0	1	0	0
Stearns, John, N.Y.	.285	91	319	42	91	118	25	1	0	45	4	2	8	7	3
Stember, Jeffrey, S.F.	.000	1	1	0	0	0	0	0	0	0	0	0	0	0	0
Stennett, Renaldo, S.F.	.244	120	397	34	97	120	13	2	2	37	5	2	2	4	4
Stimac, Craig, S.D.°	.220	20	50	5	11	13	2	0	0	7	2	2	3	0	0
Strain, Joseph, S.F.	.286	77	189	26	54	60	6	0	0	16	0	7	1	1	2
Sularz, Guy, S.F.	.246	25	65	3	16	19	1	1	0	3	0	2	1	1	0
Sutcliffe, Richard, L.A.°	.148	44	27	1	4	4	0	0	0	3	0	3	0	0	0
Sutter, H. Bruce, Chi	.111	60	9	0	1	1	0	0	0	1	0	1	0	0	0
Sutton, Donald, L.A.	.078	32	64	3	5	5	0	0	0	1	0	8	0	0	0
Swan, Craig, N.Y.	.219	21	32	1	7	7	0	0	0	5	0	7	0	0	0
Swisher, Steven, St.L.	.250	18	24	2	6	7	1	0	0	2	0	0	0	0	0
Sykes, Robert, St.L.†	.103	27	39	2	4	4	0	0	0	2	0	3	1	0	0
Tamargo, John, Mtl.†	.275	37	51	4	14	20	3	0	1	13	1	0	1	0	0
Taveras, Franklin, N.Y.	.279	141	562	65	157	184	27	0	0	25	1	10	2	32	18
Tekulve, Kenton, Pitt	.000	78	9	0	0	0	0	0	0	0	0	0	0	0	0
Tellmann, Thomas, S.D.	.125	6	8	0	1	1	0	0	0	1	0	0	0	0	0
Templeton, Garry, St.L.†	.319	118	504	83	161	210	19	9	4	43	3	1	1	31	15
Tenace, F. Gene, S.D.	.222	133	316	46	70	134	11	1	17	50	6	0	4	4	4
Thomas, Derrel, L.A.†	.266	117	297	32	79	106	18	3	1	22	2	7	1	7	9
Thomas, Roy, St.L.	.154	24	13	0	2	2	0	0	0	0	0	0	0	0	0
Thomasson, Gary, L.A.°	.216	80	111	6	24	30	3	0	1	12	1	0	0	0	0
Thompson, V. Scot, Chi°	.212	102	226	26	48	66	10	1	2	13	1	1	1	6	6
Tidrow, Richard, Chi.	.000	84	4	1	0	0	0	0	0	0	0	0	0	0	0
Tomlin, David, Cin°	.000	27	0	0	0	0	0	0	0	0	0	0	0	0	0
Tracy, James, Chi°	.254	42	122	12	31	49	3	3	3	9	1	2	0	2	2
Trevino, Alejandro, N.Y.	.256	106	355	26	91	106	11	2	0	37	5	2	5	0	3
Trillo, J. Manuel, Phila	.292	141	531	68	155	219	25	9	7	43	5	4	3	8	3
Turner, John, S.D.°	.288	85	153	22	44	58	5	0	3	18	0	1	2	8	3
Tyson, Michael, Chi†	.238	123	341	34	81	115	19	3	3	23	1	4	1	1	2
Unser, Delbert, Phila°	.264	96	110	15	29	43	6	4	0	10	2	1	2	0	1
Urrea, John, St.L.	.231	30	13	0	3	3	0	0	0	0	0	2	0	0	0
Vail, Michael, Chi	.298	114	312	30	93	132	17	2	6	47	2	1	0	2	5
Valentine, Ellis, Mtl	.315	86	311	40	98	163	22	2	13	67	12	0	4	5	5
Valenzuela, Fernando, L.A.°	.000	10	1	0	0	0	0	0	0	0	0	0	0	0	0
Venable, W. McKinley, S.F.°	.268	64	138	13	37	42	5	0	0	10	0	1	3	8	2
Virgil, Osvaldo, Phila	.200	1	5	1	1	2	1	0	0	0	0	0	0	0	0
Vuckovich, Peter, St.L.	.183	32	71	4	13	19	6	0	0	7	0	9	0	1	0
Vukovich, George, Phila°	.224	78	58	6	13	16	1	1	0	8	0	0	0	0	0
Vukovich, John, Phila.	.161	49	62	4	10	13	1	1	0	5	0	0	1	0	1
Walk, Robert, Phila	.140	27	50	5	7	8	1	0	0	2	0	7	0	0	0
Wallach, Timothy, Mtl	.182	5	11	1	2	5	0	0	1	2	0	0	0	0	0
Waller, E. Tyrone, St.L.	.083	5	12	3	1	1	0	0	0	0	0	0	0	0	0
Walling, Dennis, Hou°	.299	100	284	30	85	110	6	5	3	29	3	0	2	4	3
Washington, Claudell, N.Y.°	.275	79	284	38	78	132	16	4	10	42	4	0	1	17	5
Weiss, Gary, L.A.°	.000	8	2	0	0	0	0	0	0	0	0	0	0	0	0
Welch, Robert, L.A.	.243	34	70	1	17	20	3	0	0	3	1	5	0	0	0
Werner, Donald, Cin	.172	24	64	2	11	13	2	0	0	5	0	0	1	1	0
White, Jerome, Mtl.°	.262	110	214	22	56	92	9	3	7	23	2	1	3	8	7
Whitfield, Terry, S.F.°	.296	118	321	38	95	127	16	2	4	26	8	4	2	4	2
Whitson, Eddie, S.F.	.091	34	66	2	6	6	0	0	0	4	0	9	0	0	0
Wilson, William, N.Y.†	.248	27	105	16	26	37	5	3	0	4	0	2	0	7	7
Winfield, David, S.D.	.276	162	558	89	154	251	25	6	20	87	10	0	4	23	7
Wise, Richard, S.D.	.138	28	58	1	8	10	2	0	0	4	1	2	0	0	0
Wohlford, James, S.F.	.280	91	193	17	54	71	6	4	1	24	4	0	3	1	4
Woods, Gary, Hou	.377	19	53	8	20	31	5	0	2	15	2	0	0	1	0
Yeager, Stephen, L.A.	.211	96	227	20	48	62	8	0	2	20	4	0	1	2	3
Youngblood, Joel, N.Y.	.276	146	514	58	142	196	26	2	8	69	3	0	9	14	11
Zachry, Patrick, N.Y.	.043	28	46	0	2	2	0	0	0	1	0	5	1	0	0

AWARDED FIRST BASE ON INTERFERENCE: Rose, Phila. 4 (Fahey, T. Kennedy; Scioscia, Trevino); Berra, Pitts. 3 (Blackwell, May, Stearns); Chambliss, Atl. 2 (Trevino, Werner); McCovey, S.F. 2 (Fahey, T. Kennedy); Buckner, Chi. (Tenace); Concepcion, Cin. (Trevino); Fahey, S.D. (Nicosia); Hendrick, St.L. (Pujols); Murphy, Atl. (Ott); Scott, St.L. (Carter); Puhl, Hou. (obstruction by McCovey).

PLAYERS WITH TWO OR MORE CLUBS
(Alphabetically Arranged With Player's First Club on Top)

Player and Club	Pct.	G.	AB.	R.	H.	TB.	2B.	3B.	HR.	RBI.	GW	SH	SF.	Tot. BB.	Int. BB.	HP.	SO.	SB.	CS.	GI. DP.
Almon, Mtl	.263	18	38	2	10	13	1	1	0	3	1	0	1	1	0	0	5	0	0	2
Almon, N.Y.	.170	48	112	13	19	26	3	2	0	4	0	0	0	8	1	0	27	2	0	0
Bevacqua, S.D.	.268	62	71	4	19	27	6	1	0	12	2	1	1	6	0	0	1	1	1	1
Bevacqua, Pitt	.163	22	43	1	7	8	1	0	0	4	0	0	0	6	0	1	7	0	0	2
Carbo, St.L.	.182	14	11	0	2	2	0	0	0	0	0	1	0	1	0	0	0	0	0	0
Carbo, Pitt	.333	7	6	0	2	2	0	0	0	1	0	0	0	1	0	0	1	0	0	0
D'Acquisto, S.D.	.000	9	8	1	0	0	0	0	0	0	0	2	0	1	0	0	4	0	0	0
D'Acquisto, Mtl	.000	11	0	0	0	0	0	0	0	0	0	0	0	0	0	0	0	0	0	0
Montanez, S.D.	.274	128	481	39	132	170	12	4	6	63	5	0	6	36	9	3	52	3	4	9
Montanez, Mtl	.211	14	19	1	4	4	0	0	0	1	0	0	0	3	1	0	3	0	1	0
Nolan, Atl	.273	17	22	2	6	7	1	0	0	2	0	0	2	0	0	0	4	0	0	1
Nolan, Cin	.312	53	154	14	48	64	7	0	3	24	2	3	6	13	0	0	8	0	0	3

EXPLANATION OF ABBREVIATIONS

G—Games Played. AB—At Bats. R—Runs. H—Hits. TB—Total Bases. 2B—Two-Base Hits. 3B—Three-Base Hits. HR—Home Runs. RBI—Runs Batted In. GW—Game-winning RBI. SH—Sacrifice Hits. SF—Sacrifice Flies. SB—Stolen Bases. CS—Caught Stealing. BB—Bases on Balls. IBB—Intentional Bases on Balls. HP—Hit by Pitcher. SO—Strikeouts. Pct.—Percentage. GIDP—Grounded Into Double Plays. Slg. Pct.—Slugging Percentage. OR—Opponents' Runs. LOB—Left on Bases. PO—Putouts. A—Assists. E—Errors. TC—Total Chances. DP—Double Plays. TP—Triple Plays. PB—Passed Balls. G—Games Pitched. GS—Games Started. CG—Complete Games. GF—Games Finished in Relief. ShO—Shutouts. W—Games Won. L—Games Lost. IP—Innings Pitched. BFP—Total Batters Facing Pitcher. ER—Earned Runs. HB—Hit Batsmen. WP—Wild Pitches. Bk—Balks. ERA—Earned-Run Average. Sv—Saves.

OFFICIAL MISCELLANEOUS NATIONAL LEAGUE BATTING RECORDS

CLUB MISCELLANEOUS BATTING RECORDS

Club	Slg. Pct.	G.	Tot. BB.	Int. BB.	HP.	SO.	GIDP.	ShO.
St. Louis	.400	162	451	74	21	781	141	8
Philadelphia	.400	162	472	65	33	708	120	12
Los Angeles	.388	163	492	52	24	846	108	4
Pittsburgh	.388	162	452	85	25	760	107	12
Montreal	.388	162	547	75	20	865	102	10
Cincinnati	.386	163	537	68	23	852	116	9
Atlanta	.380	161	434	49	20	899	124	11
Houston	.367	163	540	73	13	755	96	11
Chicago	.365	162	471	54	18	912	119	17
New York	.345	162	501	63	25	840	126	13
San Francisco	.342	161	509	61	14	840	122	16
San Diego	.342	163	563	70	21	791	113	9
Totals	.374	973	5969	789	257	9849	1394	132

INDIVIDUAL MISCELLANEOUS BATTING RECORDS
(Top Fifteen Qualifiers for Slugging Championship—502 or More Plate Appearances)

Player—Club	Slg. Pct.	Tot. BB.	Int. BB.	HP.	SO.	GI DP.	Player—Club	Slg. Pct.	Tot. BB.	Int. BB.	HP.	SO.	GI DP.
Schmidt, Phila.	.624	89	10	2	119	6	Garvey, L.A.	.467	36	6	3	67	17
Clark, S.F.	.517	74	13	2	52	12	Cedeno, Hou.	.465	66	10	1	72	13
Murphy, Atl.	.510	59	9	1	133	8	Parker, Pitt.	.458	25	5	2	69	8
Simmons, St.L.	.505	59	13	2	45	13	Buckner, Chi.	.457	30	11	0	18	13
Baker, L.A.	.503	43	4	3	66	11	Griffey, Cin.	.454	62	4	1	77	4
Hendrick, St.L.	.498	32	9	4	67	14							
Hernandez, St.L.	.494	86	4	4	73	14	DEPARTMENTAL LEADERS: Tot. BB—Driessen,
Dawson, Mtl.	.492	44	7	6	69	9	Morgan, 93; Int. BB—Cromartie, 24; HP—Dawson,
Carter, Mtl.	.486	58	11	1	78	9	Driessen, Foli, E. Maddox, Luzinski, Rose, 6; SO—
Foster, Cin.	.473	75	14	1	99	14	Murphy, 133; GIDP—Cromartie, Knight, 24.

(All Players—Listed Alphabetically)

Player—Club	Slg. Pct.	Tot. BB.	Int. BB.	HP.	SO.	GI DP.	Player—Club	Slg. Pct.	Tot. BB.	Int. BB.	HP.	SO.	GI DP.
Aguayo, Phila.	.447	2	0	0	3	0	Biittner, Chi.	.319	18	2	2	33	6
Alexander, Atl.	.217	3	0	0	24	1	Blackwell, Chi.	.394	41	6	0	62	5
Alexander, Pitt.	.667	0	0	0	0	0	Blair, S.D.	.200	0	0	0	2	0
Allen, N.Y.	.143	1	0	0	7	0	Blanks, Atl.	.258	16	1	0	27	6
Almon, Mtl.-N.Y.	.260	9	1	0	32	2	Blue, S.F.	.088	3	0	0	34	0
Andujar, Hou.	.345	3	0	0	16	1	Blyleven, Pitt.	.098	0	0	1	27	1
Armstrong, S.D.	.000	0	0	0	3	0	Bochy, Hou.	.227	5	1	1	7	0
Ashby, Hou.	.347	35	12	0	40	11	Boggs, Atl.	.159	0	0	0	22	3
Asselstine, Atl.	.394	11	3	1	37	9	Bomback, N.Y.	.302	3	0	2	15	0
Auerbach, Cin.	.515	3	0	0	5	0	Bonds, St.L.	.316	33	3	2	74	4
Aviles, Phila.	.396	10	2	0	9	3	Bonham, Cin.	.000	1	0	0	1	0
Backman, N.Y.	.355	11	1	1	14	3	Boone, Phila.	.338	48	12	1	41	9
Bahnsen, Mtl.	.222	4	0	0	3	1	Borbon, St.L.	.250	0	0	0	2	0
Bair, Cin.	.000	0	0	0	1	0	Bordley, S.F.	.167	1	0	0	1	0
Baker, S.D.	.182	0	0	0	4	0	Bourjos, S.F.	.409	2	0	0	7	1
Baker, L.A.	.503	43	4	3	66	11	Bowa, Phila.	.322	24	7	3	28	9
Bass, S.D.	.510	7	1	1	7	0	Bradford, Atl.	.000	0	0	0	1	1
Beall, Pitt.	.000	0	0	0	1	0	Breining, S.F.	.000	0	0	0	0	0
Beckwith, L.A.	.000	1	0	0	1	0	Brooks, N.Y.	.395	5	0	2	9	1
Bench, Cin.	.483	41	2	2	64	9	Brusstar, Phila.	.000	0	0	0	1	0
Benedict, Atl.	.315	28	8	1	36	11	Buckner, Chi.	.457	30	11	0	18	13
Benton, N.Y.	.048	2	0	1	4	1	Burnside, Cin.	.000	0	0	0	1	0
Berenguer, N.Y.	.000	0	0	0	0	0	Burris, N.Y.	.098	2	0	0	18	0
Berenyi, Cin.	.000	0	0	0	2	0	Burroughs, Atl.	.453	35	6	2	57	4
Bergman, Hou.	.359	10	2	0	10	1	Bystrom, Phila.	.071	1	0	0	9	0
Bernazard, Mtl.	.355	17	4	0	41	3	Cabell, Hou.	.351	26	6	1	84	13
Berra, Pitt.	.343	16	6	1	52	6	Camp, Atl.	.222	0	0	0	6	0
Bevacqua, S.D.-Pitt.	.307	12	0	1	8	3	Candelaria, Pitt.	.234	4	0	0	14	2
Bibby, Pitt.	.234	6	0	1	32	1	Capilla, Chi.	.286	0	0	0	9	1

Player—Club	Slg. Pct.	Tot. BB.	Int. BB.	HP.	SO.	GI DP.
Carbo, St.L.-Pitt.	.235	2	0	0	1	0
Cardenal, N.Y.	.190	6	0	0	4	3
Carlton, Phila.	.198	1	0	0	21	4
Carter, Mtl.	.486	58	11	1	78	9
Cash, S.D.	.280	35	5	0	21	16
Castillo, L.A.	.111	0	0	0	4	0
Caudill, Chi.	.333	0	0	0	2	1
Cedeno, Hou.	.465	66	11	1	72	13
Cey, L.A.	.452	69	5	5	92	16
Chambliss, Atl.	.440	49	6	4	73	11
Christenson, Phila.	.526	3	0	0	9	0
Clark, S.F.	.517	74	13	2	52	12
Collins, Cin.	.370	53	2	3	68	5
Combe, Cin.	.000	0	0	0	0	0
Concepcion, Cin.	.360	37	2	1	107	20
Cooper, Atl.	.000	0	0	0	1	0
Correll, Cin.	.474	0	0	0	2	0
Cromartie, Mtl.	.430	51	24	2	64	24
Cruz, Cin.	.333	8	1	0	16	1
Cruz, Hou.	.426	60	13	0	66	11
Curtis, S.D.	.210	2	0	0	31	0
D'Acquisto,S.D.-Mtl.	.000	1	0	0	4	0
Dade, S.D.	.189	12	0	0	10	2
Davalillo, L.A.	.167	0	0	0	1	0
Davis, Phila.	.500	0	0	0	3	0
Dawson, Mtl.	.492	44	7	6	69	9
DeJesus, Chi.	.325	60	2	4	81	4
Dernier, Phila.	.571	1	0	0	0	0
De Sa, St.L.	.273	0	0	0	2	1
Dillard, Chi.	.316	20	2	1	54	3
Driessen, Cin.	.418	93	17	6	68	14
Dues, Mtl.	.000	0	0	0	2	0
Durham, St.L.	.426	18	1	1	55	3
Easler, Pitt.	.583	43	6	0	65	7
Eichelberger, S.D.	.111	2	0	0	18	0
Espinosa, Phila.	.154	0	0	0	9	0
Evans, S.D.	.312	17	1	0	21	2
Evans, S.F.	.414	83	6	2	65	12
Fahey, S.D.	.286	21	6	0	16	4
Falcone, N.Y.	.146	2	0	0	12	0
Ferguson, L.A.	.436	38	11	0	46	8
Figueroa, Chi.	.293	14	0	2	16	3
Fingers, S.D.	.444	0	0	0	5	1
Fischlin, Hou.	.000	0	0	0	1	0
Flannery, S.D.	.281	18	4	0	30	5
Flynn, N.Y.	.312	22	14	0	20	15
Foli, Pitt.	.327	19	1	6	23	5
Foote, Chi.	.401	13	2	0	18	7
Forsch, Hou.	.273	1	0	0	33	0
Forsch, St.L.	.474	2	0	0	18	1
Forster, L.A.	.000	0	0	0	0	0
Foster, St.L.	.473	75	14	1	99	14
Frazier, St.L.	.000	0	0	0	0	0
Frias, L.A.	.333	0	0	0	0	1
Fryman, Mtl.	.167	0	0	0	4	0
Fulgham, St.L.	.000	0	0	0	17	0
Garber, Atl.	.500	0	0	0	1	0
Garner, Pitt.	.358	46	12	2	53	12
Garvey, L.A.	.467	36	6	3	67	17
Geronimo, Cin.	.331	14	3	0	24	2
Glynn, N.Y.	.000	0	0	0	2	0
Goltz, L.A.	.128	7	0	0	23	0
Gomez, Atl.	.212	17	2	1	27	9
Gonzalez, Hou.	.135	1	1	0	8	1
Griffey, Cin.	.454	62	4	1	77	4
Griffin, S.F.	.278	0	0	0	7	0
Grimsley, Mtl.	.333	0	0	0	4	0
Gross, Phila.	.312	24	1	1	27	4

Player—Club	Slg. Pct.	Tot. BB.	Int. BB.	HP.	SO.	GI DP.
Guerrero, L.A.	.497	12	3	0	31	2
Gullickson, Mtl.	.200	2	0	0	11	0
Halicki, S.F.	.167	0	0	0	2	0
Hanna, Atl.	.286	0	0	0	3	0
Hargesheimer, S.F.	.227	2	0	0	10	1
Harper, Atl.	.259	6	0	1	5	1
Hassler, Pitt.	.000	0	0	0	1	0
Hatcher, L.A.	.286	2	1	0	12	6
Hausman, N.Y.	.063	0	0	0	7	1
Hayes, Chi.	.333	0	0	0	3	0
Heep, Hou.	.368	8	0	1	9	0
Henderson, Chi.	.305	17	3	0	19	3
Henderson, N.Y.	.402	62	3	3	90	17
Hendrick, St.L.	.498	32	9	4	67	14
Hernandez, Chi.	.263	0	0	0	7	0
Hernandez, St.L.	.494	86	4	4	73	14
Herndon, S.F.	.385	19	1	1	91	10
Herr, St.L.	.347	16	5	1	21	8
Hill, S.F.	.220	1	0	0	7	1
Hodges, N.Y.	.286	10	1	0	13	1
Holland, S.F.	.600	2	0	0	2	0
Holman, N.Y.	.000	0	0	0	0	0
Hood, St.L.	.200	0	0	0	9	0
Hooton, L.A.	.109	3	0	0	15	0
Horner, Atl.	.529	27	3	1	50	16
Hough, L.A.	.500	0	0	0	1	0
Householder, Cin	.311	1	0	0	13	0
Howe, Hou	.445	34	6	1	29	9
Howe, L.A.	.091	0	0	0	3	0
Howell, Cin.	.000	0	0	0	0	0
Hrabosky, Atl	.000	0	0	0	0	0
Hubbard, Atl.	.374	49	2	0	69	7
Hume, Cin	.313	0	0	0	5	0
Hutton, Mtl	.255	4	0	0	10	1
Iorg, St.L.	.438	20	2	0	34	5
Isales, Phila	.800	1	0	0	0	0
Ivie, S.F.	.346	19	2	0	40	7
Jackson, Pitt	.000	0	0	0	7	0
Jackson, N.Y.	.313	0	0	0	4	0
Jefferson, Pitt	.000	0	0	0	1	0
Johnson, Chi.	.429	29	5	1	35	4
Johnstone, L.A.	.406	24	1	2	29	3
Jones, S.D.	.067	2	0	0	15	1
Jorgensen, N.Y.	.355	46	6	0	55	10
Joshua, S.D.	.397	5	1	0	15	2
Kaat, St.L.	.257	2	0	0	13	0
Kelleher, Chi	.177	9	1	0	17	5
Kendall, S.D.	.292	0	0	0	3	0
Kennedy, S.D.	.335	36	6	0	34	5
Kennedy, St.L	.375	28	3	0	34	9
Kingman, Chi.	.522	21	3	0	44	10
Kinney, S.D.	.083	1	0	0	7	0
Knepper, S.F.	.197	2	0	0	21	0
Knicely, Hou	.000	0	0	0	1	0
Knight, Cin	.417	36	9	4	62	24
Knowles, St.L	.000	0	0	0	0	0
Kobel, N.Y.	.000	0	0	0	0	0
Krukow, Chi	.292	2	0	0	12	1
LaCorte, Hou	.167	1	0	0	2	0
LaCoss, Cin	.109	1	0	1	23	0
Lacy, Pitt.	.511	28	3	2	33	3
LaGrow, Phila.	.250	0	0	0	1	0
Lamp, Chi	.098	4	0	0	9	4
Landestoy, Hou	.328	31	2	3	37	5
Landrum, St.L.	.325	6	0	1	17	3
Larson, Phila.	.231	1	0	0	1	0
Lavelle, S.F.	.000	0	0	0	7	0
Law, L.A.	.302	23	1	3	27	2

Player—Club	Slg. Pct.	Tot. BB	Int. BB	HP	SO	GIDP
Law, Pitt	.311	3	0	0	7	2
Lea, Mtl	.135	1	0	0	11	1
Lee, Pitt	.000	1	0	0	0	0
Lee, Mtl	.244	0	0	0	12	0
LeFlore, Mtl	.363	62	1	1	99	4
Leibrandt, Cin	.232	3	0	0	14	0
LeMaster, S.F.	.306	25	5	0	57	7
Lentine, St.L.	.100	0	0	0	2	0
Leonard, Hou	.333	19	2	0	46	8
Lerch, Phila	.311	5	0	0	6	2
Lezcano, Chi	.375	11	0	1	29	3
Littell, St.L.	.000	0	0	0	0	0
Little, St.L.	.167	0	0	0	2	2
Littlefield, S.F.	.000	0	0	0	3	0
Littlejohn, S.F.	.276	7	1	0	7	1
Lopes, L.A.	.344	58	2	1	71	8
Loucks, Hou	.333	0	0	0	2	0
Loviglio, Phila	.000	1	0	0	0	0
Lucas, S.D.	.171	1	0	0	11	0
Lum, Atl	.241	18	3	0	19	3
Luzinski, Phila	.440	60	5	6	100	6
Lyle, Phila	.000	0	0	0	0	0
Lynch, N.Y.	.333	0	0	0	2	0
Macha, Mtl	.383	11	1	1	17	5
Macko, Chi	.400	0	0	0	3	0
Maddox, N.Y.	.319	52	5	6	44	9
Maddox, Phila	.386	18	5	0	52	11
Madlock, Pitt	.399	45	12	4	33	15
Mahler, Pitt	.000	0	0	0	0	0
Mahler, Atl	.000	0	0	0	0	0
Mankowski, N.Y.	.250	2	0	0	4	0
Manuel, Mtl	.000	0	0	0	2	0
Martin, Chi.	.419	38	6	2	107	11
Martin, St.L.	.273	1	0	0	3	0
Martinez, St.L.	.086	2	0	0	19	0
Martz, Chi	.111	0	0	0	5	0
Matthews, Atl	.419	42	2	0	93	16
Matula, Atl	.105	2	0	0	25	0
May, S.F.	.366	25	4	1	40	13
Mazzilli, N.Y.	.431	82	11	3	92	8
McBride, Phila	.453	26	4	5	58	17
McCarver, Phila	.400	1	0	0	0	1
McCormack, Phila	1.000	0	0	0	0	0
McCovey, S.F.	.301	13	2	1	23	3
McGlothen, Chi	.275	4	0	0	8	1
McGraw, Phila	.250	0	0	0	2	0
McWilliams, Atl	.157	5	0	0	24	0
Mejias, Cin	.370	6	0	1	13	1
Metzger, S.F.	.074	3	0	0	2	2
Miller, N.Y.	.000	0	0	0	0	0
Miller, Atl	.158	0	0	0	5	0
Mills, Mtl	.317	5	1	0	6	0
Milner, N.Y.	.000	0	0	0	0	0
Milner, Pitt	.370	52	2	0	29	5
Minton, S.F.	.125	0	0	1	3	0
Mitchell, L.A.	.333	1	0	0	0	0
Moffitt, S.F.	.000	0	0	0	0	0
Monday, L.A.	.469	28	3	1	49	1
Montanez, S.D.-Mtl	.348	39	10	3	55	9
Montefusco, S.F.	.033	0	0	1	12	0
Moore, St.L.	1.000	0	0	0	0	0
Morales, N.Y.	.347	13	2	1	31	2
Moreland, Phila	.440	8	2	0	14	6
Moreno, N.Y.	.413	3	2	0	12	1
Moreno, Pitt.	.325	57	11	2	101	9
Morgan, Hou	.373	93	6	0	47	4
Moskau, Cin	.182	1	0	0	10	0
Mota, L.A.	.429	0	0	0	1	1
Mumphrey, S.D.	.372	49	4	0	90	18
Munninghoff, Phila	3.000	0	0	0	0	0
Mura, S.D.	.176	3	0	0	21	0
Murphy, Atl	.510	59	9	1	133	8
Murray, Mtl	.000	0	0	0	1	0
Murray, S.F.	.340	11	1	0	48	8
Nahorodny, Atl	.414	8	1	2	21	5
Nastu, S.F.	.000	0	0	0	0	0
Nicosia, Pitt	.278	19	5	1	16	6
Niekro, Hou.	.338	4	0	0	15	2
Niekro, Atl	.189	1	0	0	19	2
Niemann, Hou	.333	0	0	0	0	1
Nolan, Atl-Cin	.403	15	0	0	12	4
Noles, Phila	.308	0	0	0	5	0
Norman, N.Y.	.283	6	0	0	14	1
Norman, Mtl	.050	0	0	0	4	0
North, S.F.	.292	81	5	1	78	4
Oberkfell, St.L.	.417	51	8	1	23	11
O'Berry, Chi	.229	5	0	0	13	0
Oester, Cin	.363	26	7	1	44	7
Office, Mtl	.401	36	1	0	39	5
Olmsted, St.L.	.182	0	0	0	3	0
Ontiveros, Chi	.286	14	1	0	17	1
Ott, Pitt	.357	33	8	0	47	9
Otten, St.L.	.200	0	0	0	1	0
Pacella, N.Y.	.150	0	0	0	7	0
Palmer, Mtl.	.244	2	0	0	15	0
Parker, Pitt.	.458	25	5	2	69	8
Parrish, Mtl	.427	36	6	4	80	12
Pastore, Cin	.156	3	0	0	23	2
Pate, Mtl	.308	3	0	0	6	0
Pena, Pitt	.571	0	0	0	4	1
Perconte, L.A.	.235	2	0	0	1	1
Perez, Pitt.	.250	0	0	0	2	0
Perkins, S.D.	.529	11	1	0	10	0
Pettini, S.F.	.274	17	1	0	33	3
Phillips, St.L	.273	9	3	0	17	7
Pladson, Hou	.000	1	0	0	5	0
Pocoroba, Atl.	.386	11	0	0	11	2
Price, Cin.	.128	0	0	0	6	1
Puhl, Hou.	.419	60	3	4	52	3
Pujols, Hou.	.235	13	3	1	29	5
Raines, Mtl.	.050	6	0	0	3	0
Ramirez, N.Y.	.208	1	0	0	7	1
Ramirez, Atl.	.352	2	0	4	33	2
Ramos, Mtl.	.219	5	0	0	5	1
Ramsey, St.L.	.341	3	2	0	17	2
Randle, Chi.	.370	50	2	1	55	13
Rasmussen, S.D.	.190	0	0	0	8	0
Ratzer, Mtl.	.000	0	0	0	0	0
Reardon, N.Y.	.000	1	0	0	6	0
Reed, Phila.	.400	0	0	0	2	0
Reitz, St.L.	.379	22	5	3	44	16
Reuschel, Chi.	.220	1	0	0	23	0
Reuss, L.A.	.147	6	0	0	25	0
Reynolds, Hou.	.304	20	1	0	39	4
Rhoden, Pitt.	.525	1	0	0	2	0
Richard, Hou.	.282	0	0	0	15	0
Richards, S.D.	.385	61	7	2	73	9
Riley, Chi.	.000	0	0	0	0	0
Rincon, St.L.	.250	0	0	0	5	1
Ripley, S.F.	.200	1	0	0	14	1
Roberge, Hou.	.000	0	0	0	2	1
Roberts, Pitt.	.000	0	0	0	0	0
D. Robinson, Pitt.	.456	0	0	0	12	0
W. Robinson, Pitt.	.463	15	2	0	45	9
Rodriguez, S.D.	.297	6	0	0	26	5
Rogers, Mtl.	.160	10	0	0	28	0

Player—Club	Slg. Pct.	Tot. BB.	Int. BB.	HP.	SO.	GI DP.
Romo, Pitt.	.727	2	0	0	2	0
Rooker, Pitt.	.571	0	0	0	2	0
Rosado, N.Y.	.000	0	0	1	1	1
Rose, Phila.	.354	66	5	6	33	13
Rowland, S.F.	.000	0	0	0	0	0
Royster, Atl.	.319	37	1	1	48	6
Ruhle, Hou.	.306	4	0	0	15	2
Ruiz, Atl.	.462	3	0	0	7	0
Russell, L.A.	.341	18	0	3	44	6
Ruthven, Phila.	.338	2	0	0	22	1
Ryan, Hou.	.129	7	0	0	29	0
Sadek, S.F.	.311	27	6	0	18	3
Salazar, S.D.	.462	9	1	1	25	4
Sambito, Hou.	.000	1	0	0	5	0
Sanderson, Mtl.	.125	2	0	0	33	1
Sanguillen, Pitt.	.313	3	2	0	1	1
Saucier, Phila.	.000	0	0	0	4	0
Schmidt, Phila.	.624	89	10	2	119	6
Scioscia, L.A.	.328	12	2	0	9	2
Scott, St.L.	.311	35	9	1	68	8
Scott, N.Y.	.111	2	0	0	5	0
Scott, Mtl.	.293	70	4	1	75	10
Scurry, Pitt.	.250	0	0	0	1	0
Seaman, St.L.	.000	0	0	0	1	0
Seaver, Cin.	.196	7	0	0	17	0
Shirley, S.D.	.033	3	0	0	15	0
Simmons, St.L.	.505	59	13	2	45	13
Smith, L.A.	.508	41	1	1	63	4
Smith, Hou.	.000	0	0	0	4	0
Smith, St.L.	.161	2	1	0	2	2
Smith, Chi.	.000	0	0	0	0	0
Smith, Phila.	.443	26	2	4	48	5
Smith, S.D.	.276	71	1	5	49	9
Solomon, Pitt.	.281	1	0	0	11	1
Sosa, Mtl.	.091	0	0	0	6	0
Soto, Cin.	.043	0	0	0	16	0
Speier, Mtl.	.330	52	18	0	38	10
Spikes, Atl.	.306	3	2	1	18	0
Spilman, Cin.	.426	9	1	1	19	2
Sprowl, Hou.	.000	0	0	0	0	0
Stablein, S.D.	.000	0	0	1	2	0
Stanhouse, L.A.	.000	1	0	0	0	0
Stargell, Pitt.	.485	26	10	2	52	2
Stearns, N.Y.	.370	33	1	1	24	5
Stember, S.F.	.000	0	0	0	1	0
Stennett, S.F.	.302	22	10	2	31	10
Stimac, S.D.	.260	1	0	0	6	0
Strain, S.F.	.317	10	0	0	10	8
Sularz, S.F.	.292	9	1	0	6	2
Sutcliffe, L.A.	.148	2	0	0	5	0
Sutter, Chi.	.111	0	0	0	6	0
Sutton, L.A.	.078	1	0	0	19	4
Swan, N.Y.	.219	4	0	0	13	2
Swisher, St.L.	.292	1	0	0	7	2
Sykes, St.L.	.103	1	0	1	14	1
Tamargo, Mtl.	.392	6	0	0	5	0
Taveras, N.Y.	.327	23	0	1	64	15
Tekulve, Pitt.	.000	1	0	0	7	0
Tellman, S.D.	.125	0	0	0	5	0
Templeton, St.L.	.417	18	6	0	43	13
Tenace, S.D.	.424	92	11	4	63	11
Thomas, L.A.	.357	26	3	1	48	5
Thomas, St.L.	.154	1	0	0	4	0
Thomasson, L.A.	.270	17	3	1	26	3
Thompson, Chi.	.292	28	3	1	31	6
Tidrow, Chi.	.000	0	0	0	1	0
Tomlin, Cin.	.000	1	0	0	0	0
Tracy, Chi.	.402	13	1	0	37	1
Trevino, N.Y.	.299	13	1	1	41	11
Trillo, Phila.	.412	32	8	3	46	16
Turner, S.D.	.379	10	4	2	18	1
Tyson, Chi.	.337	15	3	2	61	5
Unser, Phila.	.391	10	1	0	21	2
Urrea, St.L.	.231	0	0	0	6	0
Vail, Chi.	.423	14	1	1	77	8
Valentine, Mtl.	.524	25	0	3	44	3
Valenzuela, L.A.	.000	0	0	0	1	0
Venable, S.F.	.304	15	0	0	22	3
Virgil, Phila.	.400	0	0	0	1	0
Vuckovich, St.L.	.268	1	0	0	13	1
G. Vukovich, Phila.	.276	6	0	0	9	1
J. Vukovich, Phila.	.210	2	1	1	7	2
Walk, Phila.	.160	4	0	1	20	2
Wallach, Mtl.	.455	1	0	0	5	0
Waller, St.L.	.083	1	0	0	5	0
Walling, Hou.	.387	35	4	0	26	2
Washington, N.Y.	.465	20	5	1	63	5
Weiss, L.A.	.000	0	0	0	0	0
Welch, L.A.	.286	1	0	0	13	0
Werner, Cin.	.203	7	0	1	10	2
White, Mtl.	.430	30	0	1	37	1
Whitfield, S.F.	.396	20	3	1	44	6
Whitson, S.F.	.091	1	0	0	21	1
Wilson, N.Y.	.352	12	0	0	19	0
Winfield, S.D.	.450	79	14	2	83	13
Wise, S.D.	.172	2	0	0	21	0
Wohlford, S.F.	.368	13	0	1	23	3
Woods, Hou.	.585	2	0	0	9	1
Yeager, L.A.	.273	20	6	0	54	7
Youngblood, N.Y.	.381	52	10	2	69	10
Zachry, N.Y.	.043	2	0	0	21	3

Bench's 332 Homers—Best by Catcher

Johnny Bench finished the 1980 season with 356 career homers, with 323 of those coming while he was catching. The 323 total surpassed by 10 the number of homers Yogi Berra had achieved as the previous homer leader for catchers.

Bench, thus joined the all-time home run team by position which in-cludes: 1B—Lou Gehrig, 493; 2B—Rogers Hornsby, 289; 3B—Eddie Mathews, 485; SS—Ernie Banks, 293; OF—Babe Ruth, 692; Hank Aaron, 661; Willie Mays, 643; P—Wes Ferrell, 37. No pinch-hit homers are included, or those hit while playing other positions.

OFFICIAL NATIONAL LEAGUE FIELDING AVERAGES

CLUB FIELDING

Club	Pct.	G.	PO.	A.	E.	TC.	DP.	TP.	PB.
Cincinnati	.983	163	4378	1730	106	6214	144	0	12
St. Louis	.981	162	4341	1959	122	6422	174	0	12
Los Angeles	.981	163	4418	1830	123	6371	149	0	12
San Diego	.980	163	4399	2012	132	6543	157	0	6
Philadelphia	.979	162	4440	1936	136	6512	136	0	8
Pittsburgh	.978	162	4375	1819	137	6331	154	0	6
Houston	.978	163	4448	1784	140	6372	145	0	24
Montreal	.977	162	4370	1784	144	6298	126	1	7
New York	.975	162	4354	1682	154	6190	132	0	2
San Francisco	.975	161	4345	1825	159	6329	124	1	7
Atlanta	.975	161	4284	1950	162	6396	156	0	14
Chicago	.974	162	4437	2030	174	6641	149	0	12
Totals	.978	973	52589	22341	1689	76619	1746	2	122

INDIVIDUAL FIELDING

FIRST BASEMEN

°Throws lefthanded.

Leader—Club	Pct.	G.	PO.	A.	E.	DP.
ROSE, Phila.	.997	162	1427	123	5	113

(Listed Alphabetically)

Player—Club	Pct.	G.	PO.	A.	E.	DP.
Bass, S.D.	.985	15	127	6	2	10
Bergman, Hou.°	.995	59	183	16	1	23
Bevacqua, SD-Pit	1.000	3	20	0	0	0
Biittner, Chi.°	.996	41	250	19	1	14
Bochy, Hou.	.000	1	0	0	0	0
Buckner, Chi.°	.993	94	826	73	6	67
Cabell, Hou.	.000	1	0	0	0	0
Cardenal, N.Y.	1.000	5	18	0	0	1
Chambliss, Atl.	.993	158	1626	101	12	140
Cromartie, Mont.°	.991	158	1457	93	14	104
Davalillo, L.A.°	1.000	1	2	0	0	1
De Sa, St.L.°	1.000	1	2	0	0	0
Driessen, Cin.	.995	151	1349	85	7	115
Durham, St.L.°	.981	8	44	8	1	6
Evans, S.D.	1.000	1	2	0	0	1
Evans, S.F.	.985	14	119	12	2	9
Garvey, L.A.	.996	162	1502	112	6	122
Gross, Phila.°	1.000	1	1	0	0	0
Guerrero, L.A.	1.000	2	14	2	0	1
Heep, Hou.°	.990	22	188	8	2	8
Hernandez, St.L.°	.995	157	1572	115	9	146
Horner, Atl.	1.000	1	2	2	0	0
Howe, Hou.	.986	77	580	49	9	47
Hutton, Mont.°	1.000	7	19	1	0	3
Iorg, St.L.	1.000	5	25	0	0	2
Ivie, S.F.	.993	72	669	32	5	46
Johnson, Chi.	.992	46	468	16	4	34
Jorgensen, N.Y.°	.995	72	511	35	3	32
Joshua, S.D.°	1.000	2	8	1	0	1
Kendall, S.D.	1.000	1	1	0	0	0
Kingman, Chi.	.947	2	16	2	1	0
Leonard, Hou.	.987	11	74	3	1	7

Player—Club	Pct.	G.	PO.	A.	E.	DP.
Lum, Atl.°	1.000	10	39	4	0	1
Macha, Mont.	1.000	2	12	0	0	2
Maddox, N.Y.	1.000	2	12	2	0	1
Madlock, Pitt.	.962	12	73	3	3	7
Mazzilli, N.Y.	.983	92	708	49	13	67
McCarver, Phila.	1.000	2	8	0	0	0
McCovey, S.F.°	.992	27	241	12	2	18
Milner, Pitt.°	.991	70	502	32	5	48
Montanez, SD-Mtl.	.994	128	1214	86	8	105
Murphy, Atl.	1.000	1	10	1	0	0
Murray, S.F.	.987	53	508	35	7	32
Nahorodny, Atl.	1.000	1	6	0	0	0
Perkins, S.D.°	.988	20	149	9	2	14
W. Robinson, Pitt.	.985	49	384	19	6	30
Rosado, N.Y.	1.000	1	11	0	0	1
Rose, Phil.	.997	162	1427	123	5	113
Sanguillen, Pitt.	.956	5	40	3	2	3
Spilman, Cin.	.986	18	132	13	2	11
Stargell, Pitt.°	.992	54	460	33	4	54
Stearns, N.Y.	.993	16	120	18	1	10
Tenace, S.D.	.993	19	125	10	1	9
Thomasson, L.A.°	1.000	1	2	0	0	0
Thompson, Chi.°	1.000	12	49	2	0	6
Tracy, Chi.	1.000	1	6	0	0	1
Unser, Phila.°	1.000	31	67	13	0	7
J. Vukovich, Phila.	.000	1	0	0	0	0
Wallach, Mont.	1.000	1	10	0	0	0
Walling, Hou.	.989	63	505	31	6	46

TRIPLE PLAYS: Cromartie, Mont.; Murray, S.F.

FIRST BASEMEN WITH TWO OR MORE CLUBS

Player—Club	Pct.	G.	PO.	A.	E.	DP.
Bevacqua, S.D.	.000	1	0	0	0	0
Bevacqua, Pitt.	1.000	2	20	0	0	0
Montanez, S.D.	.994	124	1185	84	8	105
Montanez, Mont.	1.000	4	29	2	0	0

SECOND BASEMEN

Leader—Club	Pct.	G.	PO.	A.	E.	DP.
FLYNN, N.Y.	.991	128	283	370	6	70

(Listed Alphabetically)

Player—Club	Pct.	G.	PO.	A.	E.	DP.
Aguayo, Phila.	.962	14	41	35	3	9
Alexander, Pitt.	.000	1	0	0	0	0
Almon, Mont.-N.Y.	.943	19	32	50	5	10
Auerbach, Cin.	1.000	1	1	0	0	0
Aviles, Phila.	.943	15	28	22	3	9
Backman, N.Y.	1.000	20	48	43	0	7
Bernazard, Mont.	.976	39	63	103	4	18
Berra, Pitt.	1.000	4	6	4	0	0
Bevacqua, S.D.	1.000	2	2	1	0	0
Blanks, Atl.	1.000	1	1	0	0	0
Cash, S.D.	.987	123	290	326	8	72
Concepcion, Cin.	.000	1	0	0	0	0
Dade, S.D.	1.000	1	0	1	0	0
Dillard, Chi.	.980	38	64	85	3	13
Evans, S.D.	.987	19	33	42	1	9
Flannery, S.D.	.988	53	115	131	3	31
Flynn, N.Y.	.991	128	283	370	6	70
Garner, Pitt.	.976	151	349	499	21	116
Gonzalez, Hou.	1.000	2	1	0	0	0
Guerrero, L.A.	.949	12	12	25	2	3
Herr, St.L.	.984	58	107	136	4	37
Howe, Hou.	1.000	3	0	4	0	0
Hubbard, Atl.	.978	117	268	405	15	91
Kelleher, Chi.	.974	57	62	87	4	17
Kennedy, Cin.	.988	103	200	303	6	53
Landestoy, Hou.	.991	94	97	134	2	33
Law, Pitt.	.964	11	23	30	2	5
Lopes, L.A.	.980	140	304	416	15	85
Loviglio, Phila.	1.000	1	3	2	0	0
Macko, Chi.	1.000	1	2	1	0	0
Metzger, S.F.	.000	1	0	0	0	0
Moreno, N.Y.	.917	4	8	3	1	2
Morgan, Hou.	.988	130	244	348	7	68
Oberkfell, St.L.	.989	101	223	310	6	62
Oester, Cin.	.980	79	144	194	7	42
Perconte, L.A.	1.000	9	13	18	0	3
Pettini, S.F.	1.000	8	8	13	0	3
Phillips, St.L.	.950	9	13	6	1	0
Raines, Mont.	1.000	7	13	16	0	2
Ramirez, N.Y.	1.000	4	4	4	0	1
Ramsey, St.L.	.960	24	36	59	4	13
Randle, Chi.	.978	17	40	48	2	5
Royster, Atl.	.948	49	108	129	13	30
Ruiz, Atl.	1.000	2	2	1	0	1
Scott, Mont.	.982	129	287	380	12	73
Stennett, S.F.	.973	111	244	293	15	53
Strain, S.F.	.989	42	85	102	2	15
Sularz, S.F.	.975	21	46	69	3	14
Thomas, L.A.	.974	18	28	48	2	13
Trevino, Chi.	1.000	1	1	0	0	0
Trillo, Phila.	.987	140	360	467	11	91
Tyson, Chi.	.968	117	222	329	18	69
J. Vukovich, Phila.	1.000	9	3	2	0	0
Youngblood, N.Y.	.926	6	11	14	2	2

TRIPLE PLAYS: Scott, Mont.; Sularz, S.F.

SECOND BASEMAN WITH TWO OR MORE CLUBS

Player—Club	Pct.	G.	PO.	A.	E.	DP.
Almon, Mont.	.750	1	1	2	1	1
Almon, N.Y.	.952	18	31	48	4	9

SHORTSTOPS

Leader—Club	Pct.	G.	PO.	A.	E.	DP.
FOLI, Pitt.	.981	125	212	402	12	87

(Listed Alphabetically)

Player—Club	Pct.	G.	PO.	A.	E.	DP.
Aguayo, Phila.	1.000	5	3	9	0	1
Almon, Mtl.-N.Y.	.948	34	47	81	7	15
Auerbach, Cin.	1.000	3	3	11	0	1
Aviles, Phila.	.944	29	32	52	5	12
Backman, N.Y.	.963	8	14	12	1	4
Baker, S.D.	.963	8	3	23	1	3
Bernazard, Mtl.	.931	22	19	48	5	7
Berra, Pitt.	.952	45	59	98	8	16
Blanks, Atl.	.947	56	43	100	8	21
Bowa, Phila.	.975	147	225	449	17	70
Concepcion, Cin.	.978	155	265	451	16	98
DeJesus, Chi.	.969	156	229	529	24	99
Dillard, Chi.	1.000	2	3	2	0	0
Evans, S.D.	1.000	4	1	4	0	1
Fischlin, Hou.	1.000	1	1	0	0	0
Flynn, N.Y.	1.000	3	1	4	0	0
Foli, Pitt.	.981	125	212	402	12	87
Frias, L.A.	.933	11	5	9	1	2
Garner, Pitt.	1.000	1	0	1	0	0
Gomez, Atl.	.968	119	135	319	15	55
Gonzalez, Hou.	1.000	16	18	23	0	7
Herr, St.L.	.956	14	17	48	3	10
Howe, Hou.	1.000	5	7	6	0	2
Kelleher, Chi.	1.000	17	12	33	0	4
Landestoy, Hou.	.972	65	87	157	7	34
Law, Pitt.	.970	8	8	24	1	3
LeMaster, S.F.	.957	134	200	372	26	54
Macko, Chi.	1.000	3	7	13	0	4
Manuel, Mtl.	.941	7	5	11	1	0
Metzger, S.F.	.971	13	14	19	1	4
Oester, Cin.	.956	17	16	27	2	4
Pettini, S.F.	.955	42	48	99	7	16
Phillips, St.L.	.971	37	49	117	5	26
Ramirez, N.Y.	1.000	7	9	17	0	5
Ramirez, Atl.	.949	46	63	140	11	25
Ramsey, St.L.	.915	20	25	29	5	6
Reynolds, Hou.	.969	135	162	362	17	59
Rodriguez, S.D.	1.000	2	0	2	0	0
Ruiz, Atl.	1.000	4	2	0	0	0
Russell, L.A.	.968	129	179	387	19	57
Scott, Mtl.	.945	21	52	52	6	15
Smith, S.D.	.974	158	288	621	24	113
Speier, Mtl.	.965	127	187	396	21	62
Strain, S.F.	.000	1	0	0	0	0
Taveras, Hou.	.959	140	237	347	25	63
Templeton, St.L.	.959	115	223	451	29	85
Thomas, L.A.	.946	49	74	119	11	25
J. Vukovich, Phila.	1.000	5	1	1	0	0

TRIPLE PLAY: Pettini, S.F.

SHORTSTOP WITH TWO OR MORE CLUBS

Player—Club	Pct.	G.	PO.	A.	E.	DP.
Almon, Mtl.	.911	12	17	24	4	1
Almon, N.Y.	.967	22	30	57	3	14

THIRD BASEMEN

Leader—Club	Pct.	G.	PO.	A.	E.	DP.
REITZ, St.L.	.979	150	86	293	8	25

(Listed Alphabetically)

Player—Club	Pct.	G.	PO.	A.	E.	DP.
Almon, N.Y.	1.000	9	0	3	0	0
Auerbach, Cin.	.750	3	0	3	1	0
Berra, Pitt.	.968	48	23	69	3	7
Bevacqua, SD-Pit ..	.947	22	6	30	2	2
Blanks, Atl.	.924	43	21	89	9	10
Brooks, N.Y.	.966	23	16	40	2	2
Cabell, Hou.	.927	150	118	250	29	15
Cey, L.A.	.972	157	127	317	13	24
Dade, S.D.	.846	21	5	17	4	1
Dillard, Chi.	.908	51	25	84	11	6
Evans, S.D.	.983	43	16	41	1	2
Evans, S.F.	.946	140	113	328	25	26
Flannery, S.D.	.951	41	25	73	5	3
Gonzalez, Hou.	.917	11	3	8	1	1
Guerrero, L.A.	1.000	3	3	9	0	1
Hatcher, L.A.	.921	18	13	22	3	2
Horner, Atl.	.935	121	78	251	23	20
Howe, Hou.	.974	25	11	27	1	3
Iorg, St.L.	1.000	1	1	0	0	0
Kelleher, Chi.	.850	31	8	9	3	2
Knight, Cin.	.969	162	120	291	13	19
Lacy, Pitt.	1.000	3	2	4	0	0
Landestoy, Hou.	1.000	3	1	4	0	0
Law, Pitt.	.000	1	0	0	0	0
Macha, Mtl.	.910	33	18	43	6	3
Macko, Chi.	1.000	2	2	0	0	0
Maddox, N.Y.	.956	115	96	209	14	18
Madlock, Pitt.	.955	127	86	214	14	18
Mankowski, N.Y.	.571	3	0	4	3	0
Mills, Mtl.	.977	18	19	24	1	3
Moreland, Phila.	.800	4	2	2	1	0

Player—Club	Pct.	G.	PO.	A.	E.	DP.
Moreno, N.Y.	.846	4	3	8	2	1
Oberkfell, St.L.	.971	16	4	30	1	2
Oester, Cin.	.800	3	1	3	1	0
Ontiveros, Chi.	.929	24	13	39	4	1
Parrish, Mtl.	.949	124	106	231	18	15
Pettini, St.L.	.978	18	10	35	1	5
Phillips, St.L.	.727	8	1	7	3	1
Pujols, Hou.	1.000	1	1	0	0	0
Ramirez, N.Y.	.000	3	0	0	0	0
Ramsey, St.L.	1.000	8	1	6	0	0
Randle, Chi.	.929	111	76	225	23	7
Reitz, St.L.	.979	150	86	293	8	25
Rodriguez, S.D.	.965	88	38	128	6	12
Royster, Atl.	1.000	48	15	37	0	1
Ruiz, Atl.	.875	16	5	16	3	0
Salazar, S.D.	.944	42	29	88	7	7
Schmidt, Phila.	.946	149	98	372	27	31
Speier, Mtl.	1.000	1	0	1	0	0
Spilman, Cin.	1.000	1	0	2	0	0
Stearns, N.Y.	1.000	1	0	3	0	1
Stimac, S.D.	.923	2	5	7	1	1
Strain, S.F.	.875	6	3	11	2	1
Sularz, S.F.	1.000	5	4	10	0	0
Thomas, L.A.	1.000	4	1	3	0	0
Trevino, N.Y.	.826	14	6	13	4	2
J. Vukovich, Phila.	.958	34	14	32	2	0
Waller, St.L.	1.000	5	1	2	0	0
Wohlford, S.F.	.500	1	0	1	1	0
Youngblood, N.Y.	.889	21	15	33	6	3

TRIPLE PLAY: Parrish, Mtl.

THIRD BASEMAN WITH TWO OR MORE CLUBS

Player—Club	Pct.	G.	PO.	A.	E.	DP.
Bevacqua, S.D.	.929	13	1	12	1	1
Bevacqua, Pitt.	.958	9	5	18	1	1

OUTFIELDERS

Leader—Club	Pct.	G.	PO.	A.	E.	DP.
SCOTT, St.L.	.997	134	324	5	1	2

(Listed Alphabetically)

Player—Club	Pct.	G.	PO.	A.	E.	DP.
Alexander, Pitt.	1.000	4	6	0	0	0
Asselstine, Atl.	.962	61	102	0	4	0
Baker, L.A.	.991	151	308	5	3	3
Bergman, Hou.°	1.000	5	4	0	0	0
Bevacqua, S.D.	1.000	4	4	0	0	0
Biittner, Chi.°	.983	38	55	4	1	2
Bonds, St.L.	.967	70	114	5	4	2
Bourjos, S.F.°	1.000	6	5	0	0	0
Buckner, Chi.°	.979	50	90	5	2	2
Burroughs, Atl.	.977	73	129	0	3	0
Cardenal, N.Y.	1.000	6	12	1	0	0
Castillo, L.A.	.000	1	0	0	0	0
Cedeno, Hou.	.977	136	338	9	8	3
Clark, S.F.	.967	120	229	7	8	1
Collins, Cin.°	.986	141	337	5	5	1
Cooper, Chi.	1.000	13	5	1	0	0
Cromartie, Mtl.°	1.000	2	2	0	0	0
Cruz, Cin.	.955	29	42	0	2	0
Cruz, Hou.°	.969	158	323	16	11	1
Dade, S.D.	.909	8	9	1	1	0
Dawson, Mtl.	.986	147	410	14	6	3
Dernier, Phila.	1.000	3	9	0	0	0
De Sa, St.L.°	1.000	1	1	0	0	0
Durham, St.L.°	.987	78	136	14	2	2
Easler, Pitt.	.986	119	201	6	3	1
Ferguson, L.A.	.000	1	0	0	1	0
Figueroa, Chi.°	.979	57	89	6	2	2
Foster, Cin.	.997	141	295	6	1	1
Geronimo, Cin.°	1.000	86	110	2	0	1
Griffey, Cin.°	.978	138	266	5	6	3
Gross, Phila.	.973	91	68	5	2	2
Guerrero, L.A.	.987	40	74	1	1	0
Harper, Atl.	.968	18	30	0	1	0
Hatcher, L.A.	1.000	25	18	1	0	0
Henderson, Chi.	.944	22	31	3	2	1
Henderson, N.Y.	.981	136	299	7	6	1
Hendrick, S.F.	.994	149	322	10	2	2
Herndon, S.F.	.959	122	247	8	11	1
Householder, Cin.	1.000	14	16	2	0	0
Hutton, Mtl.°	1.000	4	1	0	0	0
Iorg, St.L.	.991	63	108	2	1	0
Isales, Phila.	1.000	2	3	0	0	0
Johnson, Chi.	.667	3	2	0	1	0
Johnstone, L.A.	.965	61	100	9	4	0
Jorgensen, N.Y.°	.981	31	51	2	1	1
Joshua, St.L.°	1.000	12	18	0	0	0
Kennedy, St.L.	1.000	28	49	1	0	0
Kingman, St.L.	.941	61	103	8	7	0
Lacy, Pitt.	.984	88	173	7	3	1
Landrum, St.L.	.976	29	40	1	1	0

OUTFIELDERS—Continued

Player–Club	Pct.	G.	PO.	A.	E.	DP.
Law, L.A.°	.988	106	233	6	3	3
LeFlore, Mtl.	.957	130	233	14	11	1
Lentine, St.L.	1.000	6	4	0	0	0
Leonard, Hou.	.979	56	87	6	2	0
Lezcano, Chi.	.948	39	70	3	4	0
Loucks, Hou.	1.000	4	1	0	0	0
Lum, Atl.°	1.000	19	19	0	0	0
Luzinski, Phila.	.993	105	137	2	1	0
Macha, Mtl.	.000	1	0	0	0	0
Maddox, N.Y.	1.000	4	3	0	0	0
Maddox, Phila.	.976	143	405	7	10	0
Martin, Chi.	.978	129	262	8	6	0
Matthews, Atl.	.960	143	258	8	11	0
Mazzilli, N.Y.	.994	66	166	4	1	1
Mejias, Cin.	.989	67	89	4	1	1
McBride, Phila.	.990	133	282	6	3	1
Miller, Atl.	1.000	9	6	0	0	0
Milner, Pitt.°	.889	11	8	0	1	0
Mitchell, L.A.°	1.000	8	5	0	0	0
Monday, L.A.°	.969	50	92	1	3	0
Morales, N.Y.	.973	63	107	3	3	1
Moreland, Phila.	1.000	2	3	1	0	0
Moreno, Pitt.°	.990	162	479	15	5	2
Mumphrey, S.D.	.974	153	398	10	11	1
Murphy, Atl.	.985	154	374	14	6	4
Norman, N.Y.	1.000	19	19	1	0	0
North, S.F.	.982	115	313	6	6	1
Office, Mtl.°	.987	97	150	2	2	1
Ott, Pitt.	1.000	3	2	0	0	0
Parker, Pitt.	.965	130	235	14	9	0
Pate, Mtl.	1.000	18	18	0	0	0
Perkins, S.D.°	.909	10	10	0	1	0
Puhl, Hou.	.991	135	311	14	3	3
Raines, Mtl.	1.000	1	2	0	0	0
Randle, Chi.	1.000	6	3	0	0	0
Richards, S.D.°	.979	156	307	21	7	4
W. Robinson, Pitt.	.979	41	43	3	1	0
Royster, Atl.	.935	41	72	0	5	1
Salazar, S.D.	1.000	4	10	0	0	0
Scott, St.L.	.997	134	324	5	1	2
Simmons, St.L.	.889	5	8	0	1	0
Smith, L.A.	.994	84	153	15	1	5
Smith, St.L.	1.000	7	10	0	0	0
Smith, Phila.	.969	82	121	2	4	0
Spikes, Atl.	1.000	7	4	0	0	0
Spilman, Cin.	.000	2	0	0	0	0
Tracy, Chi.	.950	31	38	0	2	0
Thomas, L.A.	.987	52	75	2	1	1
Thomasson, L.A.°	.974	31	36	1	1	0
Thompson, Chi.°	.963	66	100	4	4	2
Turner, Pitt.	1.000	34	44	2	0	1
Unser, Phila.°	1.000	23	49	0	0	0
Vail, Chi.	.963	77	126	5	5	1
Valentine, Mtl.	.970	83	154	6	5	1
Venable, S.F.	1.000	40	61	0	0	0
G. Vukovich, Phila.	.933	28	14	0	1	0
Wallach, Mtl.	1.000	3	2	0	0	0
Walling, Hou.	1.000	19	20	0	0	0
Washington, N.Y.°	.978	70	123	12	3	1
White, Mtl.	.946	84	101	5	6	1
Whitfield, S.F.	.987	95	140	11	2	1
Wilson, N.Y.	.973	26	72	1	2	0
Winfield, S.D.	.987	159	273	20	4	4
Wohlford, S.F.	.989	49	89	2	1	0
Woods, Hou.	1.000	14	19	1	0	0
Youngblood, N.Y.	.984	121	292	18	5	6

CATCHERS

Leader–Club	Pct.	G	PO.	A.	E.	DP.	PB.
CARTER, Mtl	.993	149	822	108	7	8	3

(Listed Alphabetically)

Player–Club	Pct.	G.	PO.	A.	E.	DP.	PB.
Ashby, Hou.	.991	114	608	60	6	10	14
Bench, Cin	.991	105	505	39	5	7	6
Benedict, Atl	.988	120	502	76	7	6	11
Benton, N.Y.	.935	8	27	2	2	0	1
Blackwell, Chi	.982	103	572	93	12	16	5
Bochy, Hou.	1.000	10	19	1	0	0	1
Boone, Phila	.979	138	741	88	18	7	5
Carter, Mtl	.993	149	822	108	7	8	3
Correll, Cin	.919	10	33	1	3	0	1
Fahey, S.D.	.977	85	309	34	8	6	3
Ferguson, L.A.	.982	66	297	23	6	4	3
Foote, Chi	.992	55	317	36	3	5	6
Hayes, Chi.	1.000	3	9	2	0	0	0
Hill, S.F.	.972	14	61	8	2	2	1
Hodges, N.Y.	.982	9	47	9	1	0	0
Johnson, Chi.	1.000	1	1	0	0	0	0
Kendall, S.D.	.938	14	30	0	2	0	0
Kennedy, St.L	.967	41	182	21	7	3	3
Littlejohn, S.F.	.983	10	51	8	1	1	1
Macha, Mtl	1.000	1	1	0	0	0	0
May, S.F.	.986	103	500	59	8	12	3
McCormack, Phila	1.000	2	6	0	0	0	0
Moreland, Phila.	.967	39	183	21	7	7	3
Nahorodny, Atl	.990	54	172	24	2	2	2
Nicosia, Pitt.	.984	58	284	25	5	4	0
Nolan, Atl-Cin	.983	56	271	26	5	7	2
O'Berry, Chi	.982	19	94	16	2	2	1
Ott, Pitt	.983	117	569	73	11	5	6
Pena, Pitt	.952	6	38	2	2	0	0
Pocoroba, Atl	.934	10	56	1	4	0	1
Pujols, Hou	.990	75	348	35	4	5	9
Ramos, Mtl	.964	12	47	7	2	0	1
Sadek, S.F.	.974	59	266	29	8	1	2
Scioscia, L.A.	.992	54	226	26	2	5	2
Simmons, St.L.	.985	129	520	71	9	12	9
Spilman, Cin.	.000	1	0	0	0	0	0
Stearns, N.Y.	.985	74	432	41	7	6	1
Stimac, S.D.	.982	11	46	9	1	1	0
Swisher, St.L	.957	8	21	1	1	0	0
Tamargo, Mtl	.975	12	36	3	1	2	3
Tenace, S.D.	.979	104	415	46	10	7	3
Thomas, L.A.	1.000	5	25	3	0	0	3
Trevino, N.Y.	.977	86	443	63	12	5	0
Virgil, Phila	1.000	1	4	0	0	0	0
Werner, Cin	.962	24	119	6	5	1	3
Yeager, L.A.	.984	95	382	36	7	5	4

CATCHER WITH TWO OR MORE CLUBS

Player–Club	Pct.	G.	PO.	A.	E.	DP.	PB.
Nolan, Atl	1.000	6	20	3	0	1	0
Nolan, Cin	.982	51	251	23	5	6	2

PITCHERS

Leader—Club	Pct.	G.	PO.	A.	E.	DP.
CARLTON, Phila°	1.000	38	2	42	0	1

(Listed Alphabetically)

Player—Club	Pct.	G.	PO.	A.	E.	DP.
Alexander, Atl	.942	35	16	49	4	4
Allen, N.Y.	.933	59	4	10	1	0
Andujar, Hou	.872	35	7	27	5	2
Armstrong, S.D.	.500	11	1	0	1	0
Bahnsen, Mtl	1.000	57	6	12	0	1
Bair, Cin	1.000	61	3	21	0	1
Beckwith, L.A.	.800	38	1	7	2	0
Berenguer, N.Y.	1.000	6	0	2	0	0
Berenyi, Cin	1.000	6	0	3	0	0
Bibby, Pitt	.929	35	9	30	3	1
Blair, S.D.	.000	5	0	0	0	0
Blue, S.F.°	.982	31	14	42	1	4
Blyleven, Pitt	.952	34	10	30	2	2
Boggs, Atl	1.000	32	17	16	0	0
Bomback, N.Y.	.981	36	20	32	1	2
Bonham, Cin	.750	4	0	3	1	0
Borbon, St.L.	.750	10	0	3	1	0
Bordley, S.F.°	1.000	8	2	9	0	0
Bradford, Atl°	1.000	56	3	8	0	0
Breining, S.F.	1.000	5	0	1	0	0
Brusstar, Phila	.900	26	2	7	1	0
Burnside, Cin°	1.000	7	0	4	0	0
Burris, N.Y.	.946	29	13	22	2	1
Bystrom, Phila	1.000	6	4	10	0	1
Camp, Atl	.977	77	9	34	1	2
Candelaria, Pitt°	.958	35	8	38	2	3
Capilla, Chi°	.893	39	6	19	3	0
Carlton, Phila°	1.000	38	2	42	0	1
Castillo, L.A.	.963	61	10	16	1	1
Caudill, Chi	1.000	72	7	11	0	0
Christenson, Phila	.875	14	5	16	3	0
Combe, Cin	1.000	4	0	1	0	0
Curtis, S.D.°	.977	30	5	37	1	2
D'Acquisto, SD-Mt.	1.000	50	1	12	0	1
Davis, Phila°	.000	2	0	0	0	0
Dues, Mtl	1.000	6	0	4	0	0
Eichelberger, S.D.	.800	15	2	10	3	0
Espinosa, Phila	.947	12	8	10	1	0
Falcone, N.Y.°	1.000	37	1	12	0	0
Fingers, S.D.	.952	66	9	11	1	0
Forsch, Hou	.949	32	11	45	3	2
Forsch, St.L.	.965	31	11	44	2	5
Forster, L.A.°	.857	9	2	4	1	0
Frazier, St.L	1.000	22	1	4	0	0
Fryman, Mtl°	.917	61	1	10	1	1
Fulgham, St.L	.947	15	7	11	1	1
Garber, Atl	1.000	68	8	18	0	1
Glynn, N.Y.°	1.000	38	0	12	0	0
Goltz, L.A.	.972	35	11	24	1	1
Griffin, S.F.	1.000	42	6	17	0	1
Grimsley, Mtl°	1.000	11	1	8	0	0
Gullickson, Mtl	.962	24	4	21	1	2
Halicki, S.F.	1.000	11	1	4	0	1
Hanna, Atl	1.000	32	6	8	0	0
Hargesheimer, S.F.	1.000	15	2	10	0	0
Hassler, Pitt°	1.000	6	2	4	0	0
Hausman, N.Y.	.919	55	11	23	3	4
Hernandez, Chi°	1.000	53	12	20	0	2
Holland, S.F.°	.857	54	3	15	3	1
Holman, N.Y.	.000	4	0	0	1	0
Hood, St.L°	.957	33	7	15	1	1
Hooton, L.A.	.925	34	23	26	4	2
Hough, L.A.	1.000	19	0	3	0	0

Player—Club	Pct.	G.	PO.	A.	E.	DP.
Howe, L.A.°	.958	59	3	20	1	0
Howell, Cin	.000	5	0	0	0	0
Hrabosky, Atl°	1.000	45	3	2	0	0
Hume, Cin	1.000	78	9	32	0	3
Hutton, Mtl°	.000	1	0	0	0	0
Jackson, Pitt.°	1.000	61	6	9	0	1
Jackson, S.D.	1.000	24	1	7	0	1
Jefferson, Pitt.	1.000	1	1	1	0	0
Jones, S.D.°	.980	24	12	38	1	0
Kaat, St.L.°	.952	49	4	16	1	1
Kinney, S.D.°	1.000	50	2	13	0	0
Knepper, S.F.°	.945	35	7	45	3	3
Knowles, St.L.°	.000	2	0	0	0	0
Kobel, N.Y.°	1.000	14	0	4	0	0
Krukow, Chi.	.853	34	10	19	5	3
LaCorte, Hou.	.800	55	1	3	1	0
LaCoss, Cin.	.935	34	9	34	3	4
LaGrow, Phila.	1.000	25	1	6	0	0
Lamp, Chi.	.965	41	8	47	2	3
Larson, Phila.	1.000	12	4	4	0	0
Lavelle, S.F.°	1.000	62	3	16	0	0
Lea, Mtl.	1.000	21	4	10	0	0
Lee, Pitt.	1.000	4	2	2	0	0
Lee, Mtl.°	1.000	24	7	19	0	2
Leibrandt, Cin.°	.938	36	10	35	3	3
Lerch, Phila.°	.974	30	8	29	1	1
Littell, St.L.	1.000	14	0	1	0	0
Little, St.L.°	1.000	7	0	1	0	0
Littlefield, St.L.	.933	52	2	12	1	3
Lucas, S.D.°	1.000	46	9	23	0	4
Lyle, Phila.°	.000	10	0	0	0	0
Lynch, N.Y.	1.000	5	1	3	0	1
Mahler, Pitt.°	.000	2	0	0	0	0
Mahler, Atl.	1.000	2	0	1	0	0
Martin, St.L.°	1.000	9	0	5	0	0
Martinez, St.L.	.889	25	4	12	2	2
Martz, Chi.	1.000	6	7	6	0	0
Matula, Atl.	.980	33	20	28	1	5
McGlothen, Chi.	.923	39	3	21	2	0
McGraw, Phila.°	1.000	57	3	15	0	1
McWilliams, Atl.°	.921	30	11	24	3	1
Miller, N.Y.	.667	31	0	4	2	1
Minton, S.F.	.967	68	8	21	1	2
Moffitt, S.F.	1.000	13	0	3	0	1
Montefusco, S.F.	1.000	22	6	9	0	1
Moore, St.L.	.667	11	1	1	1	0
Moskau, Cin.	.917	33	11	22	3	4
Munninghoff, Phil.	1.000	4	2	1	0	0
Mura, St.D.	.972	37	9	26	1	3
Murray, Mtl.	.833	16	4	1	1	0
Nastu, St.L.°	1.000	6	1	2	0	0
Niekro, Hou.	.964	37	17	37	2	2
Niekro, Atl.	.983	40	18	40	1	6
Niemann, Hou.°	1.000	22	4	8	0	0
Noles, Phila.	.900	48	8	10	2	0
Norman, Mtl.	.923	48	1	11	1	0
Olmsted, St.L.°	1.000	5	2	9	0	0
Otten, St.L.	1.000	31	0	11	0	2
Pacella, N.Y.	.938	32	6	9	1	0
Palmer, Mtl.	.946	24	9	26	2	0
Pastore, Cin.	.921	27	10	25	3	1
Perez, Pitt.	1.000	2	1	1	0	0
Pladson, Hou.	.857	12	3	9	2	0
Price, Cin.°	.905	24	3	16	2	1
Rasmussen, S.D.	.920	40	8	15	2	2
Ratzer, Mtl.	1.000	1	1	2	0	0
Reardon, N.Y.	.667	61	1	7	4	0

PITCHERS—Continued

Player—Club	Pct.	G.	PO.	A.	E.	DP.
Reed, Phila.	1.000	55	14	15	0	1
Reuschel, Chi.	.977	38	28	56	2	5
Reuss, L.A.°	.921	37	18	40	5	5
Rhoden, Pitt.	.966	20	6	22	1	1
Richard, Hou.°	1.000	17	6	10	0	1
Riley, Chi.°	.867	22	1	12	2	1
Rincon, St.L.	1.000	4	3	5	0	1
Ripley, S.F.	.933	23	9	19	2	0
Roberge, Hou.	1.000	14	2	5	0	0
Roberts, Pitt.°	.000	2	0	0	0	0
D. Robinson, Pitt.	.947	29	13	23	2	2
Rogers, Mtl.	.951	37	21	37	3	3
Romo, Pitt.	.968	74	10	20	1	1
Rooker, Pitt.°	1.000	4	1	4	0	0
Rowland, S.F.	1.000	19	1	4	0	0
Ruhle, Hou.	.941	28	15	17	2	2
Ruthven, Phila.	.900	33	21	33	6	3
Ryan, Hou.	.889	35	13	27	5	0
Sambito, Hou.°	.909	64	7	13	2	2
Sanderson, Mtl.	.972	33	14	21	1	0
Saucier, Phila.°	.929	40	3	10	1	0
Scott, N.Y.	.750	6	1	5	2	1
Scurry, Pitt.°	1.000	20	2	5	0	0
Seaman, St.L.°	1.000	26	1	3	0	0
Seaver, Cin.	1.000	26	16	26	0	0
Shirley, S.D.°	.975	59	7	32	1	1
Smith, N.Y.	.933	57	3	11	1	0
Smith, Chi.	1.000	18	0	3	0	0
Solomon, Pitt.	.885	26	9	14	3	2

Player—Club	Pct.	G.	PO.	A.	E.	DP.
Sosa, Mtl.	.944	67	4	13	1	0
Soto, Cin.	.925	53	12	25	3	2
Sprowl, Hou.°	.000	1	0	0	0	0
Stablein, S.D.	1.000	4	1	1	0	0
Stanhouse, L.A.	1.000	21	2	7	0	2
Stember, S.F.	.000	1	0	0	0	0
Sutcliffe, L.A.	1.000	42	6	13	0	0
Sutter, Chi.	1.000	60	6	14	0	0
Sutton, L.A.	.961	32	24	25	2	3
Swan, N.Y.	.824	21	4	10	3	0
Sykes, St.L.°	.947	27	4	14	1	2
Tekulve, Pitt.	.958	78	5	18	1	1
Tellmann, S.D.	1.000	6	1	4	0	1
Thomas, St.L.	1.000	24	7	10	0	1
Tidrow, Chi.	.952	84	7	13	1	0
Tomlin, Chi.°	1.000	27	1	7	0	0
Urrea, St.L.	.800	30	2	6	2	0
Valenzuela, L.A.°	1.000	10	0	3	0	1
Vuckovich, St.L.	.978	32	16	28	1	3
Walk, Phila.	.970	27	17	15	1	2
Welch, L.A.	.976	32	15	26	1	3
Whitson, S.F.	.921	34	8	27	3	0
Wise, St.L.	.971	27	11	22	1	0
Zachry, N.Y.	.962	28	5	20	1	1

PITCHER WITH TWO OR MORE CLUBS

Player—Club	Pct.	G.	PO.	A.	E.	DP.
D'Acquisto, S.D.	1.000	39	1	9	0	0
D'Acquisto, Mtl.	1.000	11	0	3	0	1

Situations Wanted: SS Needs Part-Time Job

The San Diego Padres wanted to raise shortstop Ozzie Smith's salary substantially from $72,500, even though the third-year player had only hit .211 in 1979. But Smith said he couldn't get by on that amount.

The slick-fielding shortstop had been troubled with bad investment advice from his first agent and he had debts totaling $64,000 coming due just four months into the 1980 season. He borrowed $21,000 from Ed Gottlieb, his new agent, and he told the Padres he might have to quit baseball and take another job to pay off his debts. He also decided to take out an ad in the San Diego Union for part-time employment as a solution which would permit him to continue to play for the Padres.

His want ad brought quick results. In fact, he got 12 job offers as a result of the ad, which ran 10 days.

One such response came from Joan Kroc, wife of Padres Owner Ray Kroc. Mrs. Kroc figured that her gardener could use some assistance and, after consulting with Luis Torres (the gardener), offered Smith a job worth $4.50 an hour.

Gottlieb reported some mundane offers from brokerages and trading companies, but said that there also were offers for Ozzie to be a nude dancer at $500 a show or a pizza deliveryman at $3.25 an hour.

In the end, Smith accepted a position with a Los Angeles credit-trading company for a guaranteed $500 a week, plus commissions, as a year-round sales representative. He finished 1980 with a .230 average, a Gold Glove and he didn't have to make his living as a nude dancer, gardener or pizza deliveryman.

OFFICIAL NATIONAL LEAGUE PITCHING AVERAGES

CLUB PITCHING

Club	ERA	G	CG	Sv	ShO	IP	H	BFP	R	ER	HR	SH	SF	Tot. BB	Int. BB	SO	WP	Bk.
Houston	3.10	163	31	41	18	1482⅔	1367	6160	589	511	69	64	42	466	26	929	38	8
Los Angeles	3.24	163	24	42	18	1472⅔	1358	6117	591	531	105	75	49	480	48	835	32	15
Philadelphia	3.43	162	25	40	8	1480	1419	6251	634	564	87	78	53	530	83	889	51	23
San Francisco	3.48	162	27	35	10	1448⅓	1446	6177	629	556	92	78	45	492	78	811	25	21
Montreal	3.58	162	33	36	15	1456⅔	1447	6160	646	563	100	83	44	460	42	823	37	6
Pittsburgh	3.65	163	25	43	8	1458⅓	1422	6091	654	580	110	74	46	451	52	837	28	12
San Diego	3.77	161	19	39	9	1466⅓	1474	6214	654	595	97	99	44	536	113	728	39	14
Atlanta	3.85	163	29	37	9	1428	1397	6028	660	598	131	81	44	454	49	696	36	7
Cincinnati	3.85	162	30	37	12	1459⅓	1404	6143	670	624	113	74	38	506	60	833	35	19
New York	3.85	163	17	33	9	1459⅔	1473	6204	702	621	140	96	51	510	77	886	38	13
Chicago	3.89	162	13	27	6	1479	1525	6402	728	639	109	105	66	589	85	923	39	17
St. Louis	3.93	162	34	27	9	1447	1454	6113	710	632	90	61	57	495	76	664	39	17
Totals	3.60	973	307	445	132	17529⅔	17186	74060	7852	7014	1243	967	577	5969	789	9849	443	172

(BFP total includes 18 batsmen awarded first base because of interference or obstruction)

NOTE: Total earned runs for several clubs do not agree with composite total of respective club's pitchers due to provisions of Scoring Rule Section 10.18(i). The following differences are to be noted: Houston pitchers add to 512; Los Angeles 534; New York 626; Philadelphia 567; San Diego 596.

PITCHERS' RECORDS

(Top Fifteen Qualifiers for Earned-Run Leadership—162 or More Innings)

Pitcher and Club	ERA	W	L	Pct.	ShO	G	GS	CG	GF	Sv	IP	H	BFP	R	ER	HR	SH	SF	Tot. BB	Int. BB	SO	WP	Bk.
Sutton, Donald, Los Angeles	2.21	13	5	.722	1	32	31	4	0	0	212	163	833	56	52	20	14	8	47	15	128	2	1
Carlton, Steven, Philadelphia*	2.34	24	9	.727	1	38	38	13	0	0	304	243	1228	87	79	15	14	8	86	2	286	17	1
Reuss, Jerry, Los Angeles*	2.52	18	6	.750	6	37	37	10	0	0	229	193	907	74	64	12	10	5	40	7	111	3	1
Blue, Vida, San Francisco*	2.97	14	10	.583	0	37	37	10	0	0	224	202	914	74	74	14	13	6	61	8	129	3	0
Rogers, Stephen, Montreal	2.98	16	11	.593	1	37	37	14	0	0	281	247	1151	101	93	16	19	4	85	5	147	2	1
Zachry, Patrick, New York	3.00	6	10	.375	3	36	28	7	6	0	165	145	680	72	55	11	10	9	55	7	88	5	0
Soto, Mario, Cincinnati	3.08	10	8	.556	2	53	12	4	34	10	190	126	777	76	65	18	11	8	84	6	182	6	4
Whitson, Eddie, San Francisco	3.10	11	13	.458	0	34	34	6	0	0	212	222	898	72	73	11	10	9	56	7	90	6	1
Sanderson, Scott, Montreal	3.11	16	11	.593	3	33	33	7	0	0	211	206	875	76	73	18	11	5	56	3	125	6	0
Forsch, Kenneth, Houston	3.20	12	13	.480	2	32	32	6	0	0	222	230	926	79	79	15	15	4	41	1	84	0	1
Pastore, Frank, Cincinnati	3.26	13	7	.650	2	27	27	9	0	0	185	161	744	72	67	13	12	10	42	5	110	0	1
Welch, Robert, Los Angeles	3.28	14	9	.609	2	32	23	3	1	0	214	190	889	85	78	15	9	7	79	4	141	5	1
Bibby, James, Pittsburgh	3.28	19	6	.760	1	35	34	4	0	0	238	210	985	95	88	20	6	7	88	3	144	5	1
Ryan, L. Nolan, Houston	3.35	11	10	.524	3	35	35	4	0	0	234	205	982	100	87	10	10	7	98	1	200	10	3
Reuschel, Ricky, Chicago	3.40	11	13	.458	2	38	38	6	0	0	257	281	1094	111	97	13	19	14	76	10	140	3	1

*Throws lefthanded.

DEPARTMENTAL LEADERS: W—Carlton, 24; L—P. Niekro, 18; Pct.—Bibby, .760; G—Tidrow, 84; CG—Rogers, 14; GF—Hume, 62; Sv—Sutter, 28; ShO—Reuss, 6; IP—Carlton, 304; H—Reuschel, 281; BFP—Carlton, 1,228; R—Lamp, 123; ER—Lamp, 117; HR—P. Niekro, 30; SH—Reuschel, Rogers, 19; SF—Reuschel, 14; Tot.BB—Ryan, 98; Int.BB—Tekulve, Tidrow, 16; HB—Griffin, Knepper, Krukow, 8; SO—Carlton, 286; WP—Carlton, 17; BK—Carlton, 7.

(All Pitchers—Listed Alphabetically)

Pitcher and Club	ERA.	W.	L.	Pct.	G.	GS.	CG.	GF.	Sv.	ShO.	IP.	H.	BFP.	R.	ER.	HR.	SH.	SF.	Tot. BB.	Int. BB.	HB.	SO.	WP.	Bk.
Alexander, Doyle, Atlanta	4.19	14	11	.560	35	35	7	0	0	1	232	227	981	120	108	20	7	4	74	5	0	114	3	0
Allen, Neil, New York	3.71	7	10	.412	59	0	0	47	22	0	97	87	407	43	40	7	8	4	40	5	1	79	2	1
Andujar, Joaquin, Houston	3.91	3	8	.273	35	14	0	4	0	0	122	132	529	59	53	8	0	3	43	2	0	75	2	0
Armstrong, Michael, San Diego	5.79	0	0	.000	11	0	0	5	0	0	14	16	67	10	9	1	7	0	13	5	0	14	2	0
Bahnsen, Stanley, Montreal	3.07	7	6	.538	57	0	0	19	4	0	91	80	383	42	31	7	6	4	33	8	0	48	6	0
Bair, C. Douglas, Cincinnati	4.24	3	6	.333	61	0	0	38	6	0	85	91	377	40	40	7	3	3	39	10	2	62	0	0
Beckwith, T. Joseph, Los Angeles	1.95	3	3	.500	38	0	0	16	0	0	60	60	258	17	13	7	4	2	23	4	1	40	5	0
Berenguer, Juan, New York	6.00	0	2	.000	6	6	0	0	0	0	28	34	132	24	24	1	1	1	23	2	0	19	0	3
Berenyi, Bruce, Cincinnati	7.71	0	1	.000	6	6	0	0	0	0	28	30	132	26	24	2	2	0	23	0	0	23	0	2
Bibby, James, Pittsburgh	3.33	19	6	.760	35	34	6	0	0	0	238	202	985	95	88	20	6	3	52	6	0	144	3	0
Blair, Dennis, San Diego	6.43	0	1	.000	10	0	0	6	0	0	14	18	61	11	10	1	4	0	10	5	1	11	3	0
Blue, Vida, San Francisco°	2.97	14	10	.583	31	31	10	0	0	5	224	202	914	79	74	14	13	6	61	6	0	129	1	2
Blyleven, Rikalbert, Pittsburgh	3.82	8	13	.381	34	32	5	1	0	1	217	219	907	102	92	20	13	7	59	5	4	168	1	0
Boggs, Thomas, Atlanta	3.42	12	9	.571	32	25	8	4	0	0	192	191	792	80	73	10	7	5	46	3	0	84	2	0
Bomback, Mark, New York	4.09	10	8	.556	36	25	2	2	0	1	163	191	710	80	74	14	17	6	49	5	0	64	2	1
Bonham, William, Cincinnati	4.74	1	2	.333	4	4	0	0	0	0	19	17	84	10	10	3	1	0	5	0	0	13	0	0
Borbon, Pedro, St. Louis	3.79	2	1	.667	10	0	0	6	0	0	19	21	81	10	8	3	3	0	5	0	1	11	0	0
Bordley, William, San Francisco°	4.65	1	3	.400	8	6	0	0	0	0	31	34	141	21	16	3	5	1	21	8	0	11	0	2
Bradford, Larry, Atlanta°	5.14	2	0	1.000	8	0	0	6	0	0	7	11	30	4	4	3	2	0	8	4	1	32	0	0
Breining, Fred, San Francisco	3.69	0	0	.000	5	1	0	1	0	0	5	7	30	2	2	0	3	0	2	0	0	3	0	0
Brusstar, Warren, Philadelphia	1.80	1	2	.500	26	0	0	12	3	0	39	42	165	16	8	1	5	0	13	2	0	21	0	0
Burnside, Sheldon, Cincinnati°	4.02	0	1	.000	7	0	0	3	0	0	19	19	81	10	9	2	0	0	8	0	0	12	0	0
Burris, B. Ray, New York	4.02	7	13	.350	29	29	5	0	0	0	170	181	726	86	76	20	8	7	54	4	0	83	5	0
Bystrom, Martin, Philadelphia	1.50	5	0	1.000	6	5	2	1	0	2	36	26	142	6	6	3	1	0	9	0	0	21	0	0
Camp, Rick, Atlanta	1.92	6	4	.600	77	0	0	44	22	0	108	96	440	32	23	3	10	4	29	8	2	33	0	2
Candelaria, John, Pittsburgh°	4.02	11	14	.440	35	34	7	0	0	0	233	246	969	114	104	17	14	1	50	5	1	97	2	0
Capilla, Douglas, Chicago°	4.10	2	8	.200	39	11	1	10	6	0	90	92	387	47	41	4	14	5	45	12	2	51	6	0
Carlton, Steven, Philadelphia°	2.34	24	9	.727	38	38	13	0	0	3	304	243	1228	87	79	15	14	8	90	5	1	286	17	0
Castillo, Robert, Los Angeles	2.76	8	6	.571	61	0	0	29	5	0	98	82	395	31	30	10	10	4	45	12	3	60	2	2
Caudill, William, Chicago	2.18	4	6	.400	72	0	0	27	1	0	128	100	528	37	31	10	10	1	59	5	1	112	2	0
Christenson, Larry, Philadelphia	4.01	5	1	.833	14	14	0	0	0	0	74	62	308	35	33	9	0	2	27	4	3	49	0	2
Combe, Geoffrey, Cincinnati	10.29	0	0	.000	5	0	0	2	0	0	7	7	31	8	8	0	1	0	4	1	3	10	0	0
Curtis, John, San Diego°	3.51	10	8	.556	30	27	6	0	0	1	187	184	787	84	73	8	15	5	67	13	0	71	3	0
D'Acquisto, John, S. Diego-Montreal	3.38	2	5	.286	50	0	0	14	2	0	88	81	373	36	33	9	5	4	45	7	0	59	9	1
Davis, Mark, Philadelphia°	2.57	0	0	.000	5	0	0	0	0	0	30	17	30	9	9	2	0	0	5	0	0	5	0	0
Dues, Hal, Montreal	6.75	0	2	.000	6	1	0	1	0	0	12	17	57	9	9	0	6	0	5	2	0	5	0	0
Eichelberger, Juan, San Diego	3.64	4	2	.667	15	12	1	1	0	1	89	73	377	41	36	8	1	2	55	4	0	43	3	0
Espinosa, Arnulfo, Philadelphia	3.79	3	5	.375	13	12	0	0	0	0	76	73	317	38	32	5	12	2	19	1	1	13	2	0
Falcone, Peter, New York°	4.53	7	10	.412	37	23	1	5	0	0	157	163	684	95	79	16	6	6	58	6	0	109	5	1
Fingers, Roland, San Diego	2.80	11	9	.550	66	0	0	46	23	0	103	101	428	35	32	8	8	4	32	13	0	69	0	0
Forsch, Kenneth, Houston	3.20	12	13	.480	32	32	8	0	0	1	222	230	926	90	79	15	9	9	41	7	2	84	0	0
Forsch, Robert, St. Louis	3.77	11	10	.524	31	31	8	0	0	0	215	225	878	102	90	12	8	4	33	4	0	87	1	0
Forster, Terry, Los Angeles°	3.00	1	1	.500	9	0	0	7	1	0	12	10	49	4	4	1	6	0	6	3	0	2	0	0
Frazier, George, St. Louis°	2.74	1	4	.200	22	0	0	10	3	0	23	24	96	10	7	2	2	0	7	6	1	11	0	1
Fryman, Woodrow, Montreal°	2.25	7	4	.636	61	0	0	40	17	0	80	61	331	23	20	1	5	2	30	9	2	59	1	1

Pitcher and Club	ERA	W.	L.	Pct.	G.	GS.	CG.	GF.	Sv.	ShO.	IP.	H.	BFP.	R.	ER.	HR.	SH.	SF.	Tot. BB.	Int. BB.	HB.	SO.	WP.	Bk.
Fulgham, John, St. Louis	3.39	2	3	.400	15	14	4	0	0	0	85	82	338	40	32	7	2	1	32	5	1	48	1	2
Garber, H. Eugene, Atlanta	3.84	5	5	.500	68	0	0	31	7	0	95	95	359	42	35	6	2	2	24	1	0	51	0	0
Glynn, Edward, New York°	4.15	2	3	.400	38	0	0	11	1	0	52	49	228	26	24	5	2	3	23	1	1	26	1	0
Goltz, David, Los Angeles	4.32	7	11	.389	35	27	2	1	0	0	171	198	739	91	82	12	10	7	59	3	3	76	3	1
Griffin, Thomas, San Francisco	2.75	5	1	.833	42	4	0	2	0	0	108	80	447	33	33	6	8	4	49	4	0	91	4	3
Grimsley, Ross, Montreal°	6.37	2	4	.333	11	7	0	0	0	0	41	61	196	33	29	5	4	1	12	1	0	11	1	0
Gullickson, William, Montreal	3.00	10	5	.667	22	19	5	0	0	0	141	127	593	53	47	6	3	4	50	2	1	120	0	0
Halicki, Edward, San Francisco	5.40	9	6	.600	21	19	0	0	0	0	25	63	533	53	15	8	5	1	44	2	1	14	5	0
Hanna, Preston, Atlanta	3.19	6	6	.500	32	13	0	4	0	0	79	82	337	38	28	6	3	4	44	1	0	35	0	2
Hargesheimer, Alan, San Francisco	4.32	1	0	1.000	15	0	0	3	0	0	75	82	325	36	38	3	1	4	32	2	0	45	4	0
Hassler, Andrew, Pittsburgh°	3.75	1	3	.250	6	0	0	0	0	0	12	9	26	6	5	1	4	1	9	8	0	6	0	1
Hausman, Thomas, New York	3.98	6	5	.545	53	4	0	14	0	0	122	125	513	63	54	12	11	4	26	8	2	45	2	3
Hernandez, Guillermo, Chicago°	4.42	1	0	1.000	53	0	0	13	7	0	108	115	473	58	53	8	5	1	45	4	0	75	0	1
Holland, Alfred, San Francisco°	1.76	5	3	.625	54	0	0	31	0	0	82	71	325	21	16	5	5	3	34	4	2	65	5	1
Holman, R. Scott, New York	1.29	0	0	.000	4	0	0	1	0	0	7	6	26	2	1	0	0	0	8	1	2	2	3	1
Hood, Donald, St. Louis°	3.40	4	6	.400	33	0	0	4	1	0	82	90	359	39	31	2	11	4	34	5	1	35	5	2
Hooton, Burt, Los Angeles	3.65	14	8	.636	34	33	1	0	5	0	207	194	858	90	84	22	8	5	64	2	3	118	3	1
Hough, Charles, Los Angeles	5.63	7	5	.583	59	1	0	36	17	0	85	83	554	90	24	4	2	3	21	3	0	25	1	0
Howe, Steven, Los Angeles°	2.65	0	1	.000	45	0	0	25	2	0	32	50	19	33	39	1	7	5	20	5	1	39	0	0
Howell, Jay, Cincinnati	15.00	0	0	.000	1	1	0	0	0	0	3	121	289	5	5	3	0	0	2	0	1	1	0	0
Hrabosky, Alan, Atlanta	3.60	0	2	.000	34	0	0	27	3	0	60	71	299	27	24	9	1	0	31	5	3	31	2	1
Hume, Thomas, Cincinnati	2.56	9	10	.474	78	0	0	62	25	0	137	78	299	44	39	6	6	5	38	14	0	68	3	0
Hutton, Thomas, Montreal°	27.00	0	0	.000	3	0	0	0	0	0	1	7	23	7	3	1	0	0	3	0	0	1	0	0
Jackson, Grant, Pittsburgh°	2.92	4	1	.667	61	0	0	27	4	0	71	71	289	24	23	4	2	3	20	3	3	31	0	0
Jackson, Roy, New York	4.18	1	1	.500	24	8	0	9	1	0	71	78	299	37	33	5	8	4	24	2	0	58	0	0
Jefferson, Jesse, Pittsburgh	1.29	1	5	.125	24	8	0	0	0	0	3	3	23	3	1	1	0	0	2	0	0	4	0	0
Jones, Randall, San Diego°	3.92	5	13	.278	24	24	4	0	0	1	154	165	638	71	67	14	11	4	29	5	1	53	5	0
Kaat, James, St. Louis°	3.81	8	7	.533	49	14	4	6	0	1	130	140	546	61	55	6	8	5	33	11	0	36	0	1
Kinney, Dennis, San Diego°	4.23	1	6	.400	35	6	0	22	4	0	79	79	359	45	39	3	1	1	37	11	1	40	5	1
Knepper, Robert, San Francisco°	4.10	9	16	.360	35	33	5	0	0	2	215	242	943	114	98	15	5	9	61	10	0	103	0	0
Knowles, Darold, St. Louis°	9.00	0	0	.000	14	0	0	3	0	0	24	36	114	8	2	0	9	0	11	8	0	2	2	0
Kobel, Kevin, New York°	7.13	1	1	.500	14	0	0	0	0	0	205	200	884	21	100	13	13	13	80	3	0	130	0	0
Krukow, Michael, Chicago	4.39	10	15	.400	55	34	0	0	0	0	83	61	342	100	117	9	4	5	43	8	1	66	5	2
LaCorte, Frank, Houston	2.82	8	12	.615	55	4	0	44	11	0	169	200	762	117	26	7	7	4	68	8	0	59	8	2
LaCoss, Michael, Cincinnati	4.63	10	12	.455	25	29	4	0	0	0	203	42	101	29	106	9	8	7	82	7	0	23	3	2
LaGrow, Lerrin, Philadelphia	4.15	1	10	.417	47	0	0	28	3	0	39	259	921	22	46	16	2	6	17	6	0	81	10	2
Lamp, Dennis, Chicago	5.13	10	14	.417	12	37	9	0	0	0	203	259	921	123	106	17	17	4	82	7	5	83	3	1
Larson, Daniel, Philadelphia	5.13	3	5	.429	12	1	0	3	0	0	46	46	434	24	43	4	6	8	24	0	0	17	1	1
Lavelle, Gary, San Francisco°	3.42	7	3	.583	67	0	0	28	9	0	104	103	458	43	43	4	4	4	36	3	5	66	0	3
Lea, Charles, Montreal	3.72	0	1	.000	21	12	2	0	0	1	104	103	26	51	43	8	4	1	55	1	0	56	2	1
Lee, Mark, Pittsburgh	4.50	0	0	.000	24	0	0	19	2	0	6	156	522	71	65	5	4	0	22	4	2	2	1	1
Lee, William, Montreal°	4.96	4	10	.400	24	18	2	0	0	0	118	156	522	71	65	13	13	2	54	7	0	34	2	6
Leibrandt, Charles, Cincinnati°	4.24	10	9	.526	36	27	5	0	0	0	150	200	754	84	86	12	12	1	55	5	1	62	7	2
Lerch, Randy, Philadelphia°	5.16	4	14	.222	30	22	0	0	0	0	178	178	664	98	86	15	10	10	55	2	0	57	6	0
Littell, Mark, St. Louis°	9.00	0	1	.000	14	0	0	12	2	0	11	14	52	11	11	0	1	0	9	0	0	7	2	2
Little, D. Jeffery, St. Louis°	3.79	1	2	.500	7	2	0	2	0	0	19	18	81	9	8	0	0	0	7	0	0	17	1	0

Pitcher and Club	ERA.	W.	L.	Pct.	G.	GS.	CG.	GF.	Sv.	ShO.	IP.	H.	BFP.	R.	ER.	HR.	SH.	SF.	Tot. BB.	BB. Int.	HB.	SO.	WP.	Bk.
Littlefield, John, St. Louis	3.14	5	5	.500	52	0	0	31	9	0	66	71	280	31	23	2	1	6	20	9	1	22	1	2
Lucas, Gary, San Diego°	3.24	5	8	.385	46	18	0	14	3	0	150	138	614	59	54	8	12	2	43	14	1	85	6	1
Lyle, Albert, Philadelphia°	1.93	0	0	.000	10	0	0	4	0	0	14	11	59	5	3	0	1	1	5	0	0	6	1	0
Lynch, Edward, New York	5.21	1	0	1.000	6	2	0	1	0	0	19	24	86	12	11	2	0	0	6	0	0	9	0	0
Mahler, Michael, Pittsburgh°	63.00	0	0	.000	1	0	0	0	0	0	1	4	10	7	7	1	0	0	4	0	1	0	0	0
Mahler, Richard, Atlanta	4.29	2	2	.500	9	5	0	1	0	0	42	39	169	20	20	1	0	2	9	0	0	23	3	0
Martin, John, St. Louis°	4.80	2	5	.333	25	20	1	1	0	0	120	127	525	75	64	8	14	4	48	8	1	39	3	0
Martinez, Silvio, St. Louis	2.10	1	2	.333	6	6	0	0	0	0	30	28	130	28	7	1	1	0	14	0	0	5	0	0
Martz, Randy, Chicago	4.58	5	10	.333	33	6	0	3	2	0	177	195	761	105	90	17	8	4	60	7	1	62	3	0
Matula, Richard, Atlanta	4.80	11	13	.458	33	30	2	3	0	0	182	188	804	105	90	24	11	4	64	7	1	119	3	1
McGlothen, Lynn, Chicago	4.94	12	14	.462	39	27	3	2	2	0	170	170	715	97	90	27	7	8	23	6	2	75	1	1
McGraw, Frank, Philadelphia	1.47	5	4	.556	57	0	0	48	20	0	92	62	355	16	15	3	8	10	42	2	7	77	5	1
McWilliams, Larry, Atlanta	1.93	9	14	.391	30	30	3	0	0	0	164	188	715	105	90	27	7	8	39	6	2	28	1	0
Miller, Dyar, New York	2.47	4	6	.400	68	0	0	12	19	0	91	90	377	28	25	4	4	2	34	7	7	42	1	1
Minton, Gregory, San Francisco	4.76	1	1	.500	13	0	0	8	2	0	17	17	69	10	9	1	3	2	6	2	0	10	1	1
Moffitt, Randall, San Francisco	4.38	4	8	.333	11	0	0	5	2	0	113	120	498	61	55	15	11	1	39	0	0	85	0	0
Montefusco, John, San Francisco	4.00	4	7	.563	37	23	3	0	0	0	22	147	630	65	68	13	15	5	41	4	2	10	1	0
Moore, Donnie, St. Louis	6.14	0	1	.000	16	0	0	6	4	0	6	13	31	15	13	2	1	4	5	0	0	94	0	0
Moskau, Paul, Cincinnati	4.50	9	7	.563	37	19	2	3	2	0	169	149	719	74	69	12	15	5	79	3	1	2	3	0
Munninghoff, Scott, Philadelphia	6.00	0	0	.000	6	0	0	0	0	0	6	9	33	23	20	3	2	4	85	0	0	109	0	0
Mura, Stephen, San Diego	3.67	8	12	.400	40	11	0	20	6	0	256	149	1096	119	101	12	14	9	85	1	3	16	3	1
Murray, Dale, Montreal	6.21	6	18	.250	48	0	0	20	9	0	275	137	536	119	111	30	7	5	42	11	2	127	0	1
Nastu, Philip, San Francisco°	4.13	0	1	.000	16	8	0	0	0	0	33	39	147	23	20	5	2	2	42	1	1	176	0	0
Niekro, Joseph, Houston	3.55	20	12	.625	37	36	11	0	0	6	256	268	1096	119	101	12	14	9	79	4	2	18	1	0
Niekro, Philip, Atlanta	3.63	15	18	.455	40	38	23	0	0	1	275	256	1137	119	111	30	9	11	85	6	3	127	2	1
Niemann, Randy, Houston°	5.45	1	4	.200	14	0	0	9	0	0	41	42	175	42	35	8	8	2	22	1	0	18	2	0
Noles, Dickie, Philadelphia	3.89	4	4	.500	48	5	1	0	0	0	81	80	367	42	35	6	2	4	26	1	1	57	1	0
Norman, Fredie, Montreal°	4.13	1	3	.250	31	0	0	20	6	0	98	95	426	45	45	8	2	5	47	4	1	58	0	1
Olmsted, Alan, St. Louis°	2.83	1	1	.500	6	5	0	0	0	0	35	32	147	13	11	3	7	1	14	7	1	14	0	0
Otten, James, St. Louis	5.56	1	1	.500	31	0	0	6	0	0	55	57	255	38	34	11	8	4	26	1	2	38	1	0
Pacella, John, New York	5.14	3	6	.333	32	15	1	0	0	0	84	89	388	51	48	11	9	5	59	4	1	68	1	0
Palmer, David, Montreal	2.98	8	6	.571	24	19	0	0	0	2	130	124	529	51	43	13	8	6	30	2	7	73	1	1
Pastore, Frank, Cincinnati	3.26	13	7	.650	27	27	3	0	0	2	185	161	744	72	67	13	6	5	42	3	3	119	2	0
Perez, Pascual, Pittsburgh	3.75	0	1	.000	44	0	0	29	0	0	12	15	51	6	5	2	1	2	16	0	2	7	1	0
Pladson, Gordon, Houston	4.39	1	3	.250	12	6	0	2	0	0	41	38	175	23	20	3	2	1	16	3	0	13	0	0
Price, Joseph, Cincinnati°	3.57	7	3	.700	24	13	0	0	0	0	111	95	448	44	44	9	9	3	47	6	3	44	0	0
Rasmussen, Eric, San Diego	4.38	4	11	.267	40	14	2	12	3	0	114	130	488	60	54	9	10	14	76	10	2	50	3	0
Ratzer, Stephen, Montreal	11.25	0	0	.000	14	0	0	10	1	0	22	23	95	29	22	5	8	3	33	6	0	17	1	0
Reardon, Jeffrey, New York	2.62	8	7	.615	61	0	0	35	7	0	110	88	475	47	40	13	10	10	40	9	4	101	3	1
Reed, Ronald, Philadelphia	4.05	7	5	.583	55	0	0	29	0	0	96	88	387	45	45	13	4	4	30	4	4	54	0	2
Reuschel, Ricky, Chicago	3.40	11	13	.458	38	38	4	2	0	3	257	281	1094	111	97	19	10	9	40	4	3	111	3	1
Reuss, Jerry, Los Angeles	2.52	18	6	.750	37	37	10	0	0	6	229	193	907	74	64	12	10	3	40	10	10	140	1	3
Rhoden, Richard, Pittsburgh	3.83	7	5	.583	20	19	9	0	0	0	127	133	536	58	54	12	5	4	40	4	0	111	3	1
Richard, James, Houston	1.89	10	4	.714	17	17	10	0	0	4	114	65	438	31	24	2	5	2	40	5	4	70	3	1
Riley, George, Chicago°	5.75	4	1	.800	17	2	0	10	0	0	36	41	166	29	23	2	2	0	20	1	2	119	1	2
Rincon, Andrew, St. Louis	2.61	3	1	.750	4	4	0	0	0	0	31	23	116	9	9	1	2	0	7	0	0	22	2	2

Pitcher and Club	ERA	W	L	Pct.	G	GS	CG	GF	Sv.	ShO	IP	H	BFP	R	ER	HR	SH	SF	Tot. BB	Int. BB	HB	SO	WP	Bk
Ripley, Allen, San Francisco	4.14	9	10	.474	23	20	2	2	0	0	113	119	486	59	52	10	6	5	36	6	2	65	5	3
Roberge, Bertrand, Houston	6.00	2	0	1.000	14	0	0	2	0	0	24	24	106	16	16	2	1	1	10	1	0	16	3	0
Roberts, David, Pittsburgh°	4.50	0	1	.000	2	0	0	0	0	0	4	4	18	2	2	0	0	0	1	0	0	1	0	0
Robinson, Don, Pittsburgh	3.99	7	10	.412	29	24	7	1	0	0	160	157	671	74	71	14	8	7	45	5	2	103	7	0
Rogers, Stephen, Montreal	2.98	16	11	.593	37	37	14	0	0	3	281	247	1155	101	93	16	11	7	85	7	3	147	7	0
Romo, Enrique, Pittsburgh	3.27	5	5	.500	74	0	0	38	11	0	124	117	507	53	45	10	9	2	28	12	0	82	2	2
Rooker, James, Pittsburgh°	3.50	5	2	.714	8	7	0	1	0	0	18	16	75	8	7	0	2	0	8	0	1	8	0	0
Rowland, Michael, San Francisco	2.33	2	1	.667	20	0	0	14	1	0	27	20	109	8	7	1	2	3	12	1	0	8	0	0
Ruhle, Vernon, Houston	2.38	12	4	.750	28	22	6	0	0	2	159	148	638	51	42	7	11	8	29	9	1	55	1	2
Ruthven, Richard, Philadelphia	3.55	17	10	.630	33	33	6	0	0	1	234	241	982	99	88	17	8	5	74	1	3	86	0	0
Ryan, L. Nolan, Houston	3.35	11	10	.524	35	35	4	0	0	2	234	205	982	100	87	10	7	9	98	0	3	200	10	3
Sambito, Joseph, Houston°	2.00	8	4	.667	64	0	0	40	17	0	90	65	354	26	22	8	7	2	22	9	2	75	0	1
Sanderson, Scott, Montreal	3.11	16	11	.593	33	33	7	0	0	3	211	206	875	82	73	18	11	5	56	3	3	125	0	0
Saucier, Kevin, Philadelphia°	3.42	7	3	.700	40	0	0	17	3	0	50	50	207	24	19	1	4	6	25	8	1	13	0	0
Scott, Michael, New York	4.34	1	2	.333	6	6	0	0	0	0	29	40	132	21	14	2	3	1	13	1	0	13	2	0
Scurry, Rodney, Pittsburgh°	2.13	3	2	.600	20	0	0	10	0	0	38	23	153	12	9	1	1	0	28	3	0	25	2	0
Seaman, Kim, St. Louis°	3.38	3	1	.750	26	0	0	8	4	0	24	14	99	10	9	4	2	1	13	5	1	10	4	0
Seaver, G. Thomas, Cincinnati.	3.64	10	8	.556	26	26	5	0	0	1	168	140	692	74	68	24	4	6	59	1	4	101	1	0
Shirley, Robert, San Diego°	3.55	11	12	.478	59	12	0	21	5	0	137	143	585	58	54	12	8	5	32	15	3	67	0	4
Smith, David, Houston	1.92	7	5	.583	57	0	0	32	10	0	103	90	422	24	22	6	2	2	32	4	1	85	0	1
Smith, Lee, Chicago.	2.86	2	0	1.000	18	0	0	6	0	0	22	21	97	14	7	2	0	0	14	5	0	17	0	0
Solomon, Eddie, Pittsburgh.	2.70	7	3	.700	26	12	2	5	0	1	100	104	428	37	30	8	5	4	37	4	1	35	1	1
Sosa, Elias, Montreal	3.06	9	6	.600	67	0	0	43	9	0	94	96	394	44	32	10	7	5	19	10	5	58	4	1
Soto, Mario, Cincinnati	3.08	10	8	.556	53	12	0	22	4	0	190	130	777	72	65	11	3	5	84	0	2	182	5	4
Sprowl, Robert, Houston°	0.00	0	0	.000	4	0	0	1	0	0	5	1	16	0	0	0	0	0	3	0	0	5	0	0
Stablein, George, San Diego	3.00	0	1	.000	4	0	0	1	0	0	12	16	51	5	4	1	1	0	5	0	0	7	1	0
Stanhouse, Donald, Los Angeles	5.04	2	2	.500	21	0	0	12	7	0	25	30	117	14	14	1	2	2	16	3	0	9	1	0
Stember, Jeffrey, San Francisco	0.00	0	0	.000	1	0	0	0	0	0	2	2	14	0	0	0	0	0	3	0	0	0	0	0
Sutcliffe, Richard, Los Angeles	5.56	3	9	.250	42	10	1	19	5	0	110	122	491	73	68	13	2	8	55	3	1	59	4	0
Sutter, H. Bruce, Chicago	2.65	5	8	.385	60	0	0	43	28	0	102	90	423	35	30	8	4	3	34	8	0	76	2	0
Sutton, Donald, Los Angeles	2.21	13	5	.722	32	31	4	0	0	2	212	163	833	56	52	20	10	4	47	5	0	128	1	4
Swan, Craig, New York	3.59	5	9	.357	21	19	4	0	0	1	117	117	520	59	59	12	8	3	30	3	1	79	0	0
Sykes, Robert, St. Louis°	4.64	6	10	.375	27	21	3	1	0	1	126	134	545	67	65	12	6	4	54	16	5	50	2	0
Tekulve, Kenton, Pittsburgh	3.39	8	12	.400	78	0	0	57	21	0	93	96	407	39	35	6	6	0	40	16	1	47	0	1
Tellmann, Thomas, San Diego.	1.64	6	5	.545	44	0	0	20	3	0	22	23	95	9	4	0	3	0	8	0	0	9	0	0
Thomas, Roy, St. Louis	4.75	2	3	.400	24	5	0	8	0	0	55	59	248	32	29	9	0	3	25	0	3	22	3	2
Tidrow, Richard, Chicago	2.79	9	6	.545	36	0	0	38	6	0	116	97	495	44	36	10	5	5	53	9	5	97	0	1
Tomlin, David, Cincinnati°	5.54	4	3	.545	27	0	0	8	3	0	26	38	123	17	16	2	12	2	11	9	0	6	1	1
Urrea, John, St. Louis	3.46	4	1	.800	30	5	0	8	1	0	65	57	287	28	25	8	10	1	41	5	2	36	2	2
Valenzuela, Fernando, Los Angeles°	0.00	2	0	1.000	10	0	0	3	1	0	18	8	66	0	0	0	0	0	5	2	0	16	0	1
Vuckovich, Peter, St. Louis	3.41	12	9	.571	32	30	7	1	0	0	222	203	907	96	84	18	8	5	68	5	2	132	9	2
Walk, Robert, Philadelphia	4.56	11	7	.611	27	27	0	0	0	0	163	163	673	82	77	18	5	7	71	2	1	94	7	1
Welch, Robert, Los Angeles	3.28	14	9	.609	32	32	5	0	0	2	214	190	889	85	73	15	12	9	79	9	6	141	5	5
Whitson, Eddie, San Francisco	3.10	11	13	.458	34	34	6	0	0	0	212	222	898	88	73	14	10	7	56	6	3	90	1	1
Wise, Richard, San Diego	3.68	6	9	.400	27	27	3	0	0	1	154	172	651	63	63	14	7	10	37	7	0	90	2	2
Zachry, Patrick, New York	3.00	6	10	.375	28	26	1	0	0	3	165	145	680	65	55	16	9	4	58	5	1	88	2	2

NOTE—Following pitchers combined to pitch shutout games: Chicago (3)—Lamp and Sutter, Martz and Tidrow, McGlothen and Sutter; Cincinnati (3)—Leibrandt and Hume, Price and Hume, Seaver and Soto; Houston (5)—Andujar, Roberge, Sambito and Niekro, Niekro and Smith, Ryan and Sambito, Ryan and Smith, Los Angeles (4)—Goltz and Castillo, Hooton and Howe, Sutton and Howe, Welch and Howe; Montreal (5)—Sanderson and Fryman 2, Gullickson and D'Acquisto, Norman, Sosa and Fryman, Sanderson and Lee; New York (3)—Burris and Allen, Falcone and Allen, Pacella and Reardon; Philadelphia (3)—Christenson and McGraw 2, Carlton and Noles; Pittsburgh (3)—Blyleven and Jackson, Rooker, Romo and Jackson, Solomon and Tekulve; St. Louis (1)—Olmsted, Kaat and Littlefield; San Diego (5)—Lucas and Fingers, Mura, Shirley and Fingers, Wise, D'Acquisto and Mura, Wise and Rasmussen, Wise and Shirley; San Francisco (4)—Ripley and Holland, Ripley and Lavelle, Whitson and Minton, Minton, Whitson, Holland, Griffin and Lavelle.

PITCHER WITH TWO OR MORE CLUBS
(Alphabetically Arranged With Pitcher's First Club on Top)

Pitcher and Club	ERA.	W.	L.	Pct.	G.	GS.	CG.	GF.	Sv.	ShO	IP.	H.	BFP.	R.	ER.	HR.	SH.	SF.	Tot. BB.	Int. BB.	HB.	SO.	WP.	Bk.
D'Acquisto, San Diego	3.76	2	3	.400	39	0	0	12	1	0	67	67	294	29	28	2	4	5	36	9	1	44	4	0
D'Acquisto, Montreal	2.14	0	2	.000	11	0	0	2	2	0	21	14	79	7	5	0	1	1	9	0	0	15	5	0

1980 N.L. Pitching Against Each Club

ATLANTA—81-80

Pitcher	Chi. W–L	Cin. W–L	Hou. W–L	L.A. W–L	Mtl. W–L	N.Y. W–L	Phil. W–L	Pitt. W–L	St.L. W–L	S.D. W–L	S.F. W–L	Totals W–L
Alexander	3–0	0–4	2–1	3–0	0–1	1–1	2–1	0–0	1–2	1–1	1–0	14–11
Boggs	1–1	1–1	0–2	3–2	0–0	0–1	2–0	0–1	3–0	0–0	2–1	12– 9
Bradford	0–0	0–1	0–0	0–0	1–0	0–0	0–0	1–0	0–2	1–0	0–1	3– 4
Camp	0–0	0–0	0–0	1–0	1–0	0–1	0–1	2–0	0–0	2–2	0–0	6– 4
Garber	0–0	0–0	0–3	1–0	0–1	0–1	0–0	2–0	0–0	1–0	1–0	5– 5
Hanna	0–0	0–0	0–0	1–0	0–0	0–0	1–0	0–0	0–0	0–0	0–0	2– 0
Hrabosky	0–0	0–1	0–1	1–0	0–0	0–0	0–0	0–0	0–0	1–1	1–0	4– 2
Matula	1–1	1–1	0–0	1–3	0–1	1–2	0–2	2–0	0–1	3–1	2–1	11–13
McWilliams	1–0	0–3	1–3	0–0	1–2	1–1	1–1	0–0	0–1	2–0	2–3	9–14
Niekro	2–2	0–5	3–2	1–2	2–2	0–2	0–2	2–0	2–0	1–1	2–0	15–18
Totals	8–4	2–16	7–11	11–7	5–7	3–9	5–7	11–1	6–6	12–6	11–6	81–80

No Decisions: Mahler.

CHICAGO—64-98

Pitcher	Atl. W–L	Cin. W–L	Hou. W–L	L.A. W–L	Mtl. W–L	N.Y. W–L	Phil. W–L	Pitt. W–L	St.L. W–L	S.D. W–L	S.F. W–L	Totals W–L
Capilla	0–0	0–0	0–0	0–0	0–1	0–0	0–0	1–2	1–2	0–2	0–1	2– 8
Caudill	0–0	0–1	0–2	0–1	0–0	1–0	0–1	1–0	1–0	1–0	0–1	4– 6
Hernandez	0–1	0–0	0–1	0–0	0–1	0–1	0–1	0–2	1–1	0–1	0–0	1– 9
Krukow	1–2	2–0	0–1	0–1	0–1	2–1	0–3	1–1	2–2	1–1	1–2	10–15
Lamp	2–1	1–0	0–2	1–2	2–2	3–0	0–3	0–2	0–1	0–0	1–1	10–14
Martz	0–0	0–1	0–0	0–0	0–1	0–0	0–0	1–0	0–0	0–0	0–0	1– 2
McGlothen	1–3	0–1	0–2	2–1	1–2	1–1	1–3	2–0	2–1	1–0	1–0	12–14
Reuschel	0–0	1–2	0–1	1–1	2–3	1–3	1–1	2–1	1–0	1–0	1–1	11–13
Riley	0–0	0–0	0–1	0–0	0–0	0–0	0–0	0–1	0–1	0–1	0–0	0– 4
Smith	0–0	0–0	0–0	0–0	0–0	1–0	1–0	0–0	0–0	0–0	0–0	2– 0
Sutter	0–0	3–0	0–0	1–1	0–1	0–1	0–0	0–1	1–1	0–3	0–0	5– 8
Tidrow	0–1	0–0	1–1	0–0	1–0	1–1	2–0	0–0	0–0	1–0	0–1	6– 5
Totals	4–8	7–5	1–11	5–7	6–12	10–8	5–13	8–10	9–9	4–8	5–7	64–98

No Decisions: None.

CINCINNATI—89-73

Pitcher	Atl. W–L	Chi. W–L	Hou. W–L	L.A. W–L	Mtl. W–L	N.Y. W–L	Phil. W–L	Pitt. W–L	St.L. W–L	S.D.* W–L	S.F. W–L	Totals W–L
Bair	0–0	0–1	0–0	0–1	1–1	0–1	0–0	0–0	0–0	2–0	0–2	3– 6
Berenyi	0–0	0–0	0–0	0–0	0–1	1–0	1–1	0–0	0–0	0–0	0–0	2– 2
Bonham	1–0	0–1	0–0	0–0	0–0	1–0	0–0	0–0	0–0	0–0	0–0	2– 1
Burnside	0–0	0–0	0–0	0–0	0–0	0–0	0–0	0–0	0–0	1–0	0–0	1– 0
Hume	1–0	0–4	1–0	3–0	0–1	2–1	0–1	0–0	0–2	2–1	0–0	9–10
LaCoss	1–0	0–0	3–1	2–1	0–2	0–0	1–1	1–2	1–1	0–1	1–3	10–12
Leibrandt	2–1	1–1	1–1	0–0	0–1	0–1	2–1	0–0	1–1	3–1	0–1	10– 9
Moskau	1–0	1–0	0–0	2–2	1–0	0–1	1–0	2–1	0–2	1–0	0–1	9– 7
Pastore	4–0	0–0	0–4	0–0	1–0	1–0	0–1	1–2	1–0	2–0	3–0	13– 7
Price	1–0	1–0	1–0	0–0	0–0	0–0	0–0	0–0	2–0	1–0	0–3	7– 3
Seaver	2–0	2–0	0–2	1–4	0–1	0–0	1–0	1–0	0–0	1–0	2–1	10– 8
Soto	2–1	0–0	2–2	1–1	0–2	1–0	1–0	1–1	0–1	2–0	0–0	10– 8
Tomlin	1–0	0–0	0–0	0–0	0–0	1–0	0–0	0–0	0–0	0–0	1–0	3– 0
Totals	16–2	5–7	8–10	9–9	3–9	8–4	7–5	6–6	5–7	15–3	7–11	89–73

No Decisions: Combe, Howell.

HOUSTON—93-70

Pitcher	Atl. W—L	Chi. W—L	Cin. W—L	L.A. W—L	Mtl. W—L	N.Y. W—L	Phil. W—L	Pitt. W—L	St.L. W—L	S.D. W—L	S.F. W—L	Totals W—L
Andujar	0—1	1—0	0—3	0—1	1—0	0—0	0—1	0—1	0—0	0—0	1—1	3— 8
Forsch	0—1	1—0	2—1	2—3	0—1	1—0	0—2	1—1	1—2	2—0	2—2	12—13
LaCorte	1—0	1—1	1—0	1—1	1—1	2—1	0—1	0—0	0—0	1—0	0—0	8— 5
Niekro	3—2	1—0	4—1	1—1	2—0	2—1	0—2	0—2	3—0	2—1	2—2	20—12
Niemann	0—0	0—0	0—0	0—0	0—0	0—0	0—0	0—0	0—1	0—0	0—0	0— 1
Pladson	0—1	0—0	0—0	0—0	0—1	0—0	0—1	0—0	0—0	0—0	0—1	0— 4
Richard	1—0	2—0	1—1	2—0	0—1	1—1	0—1	0—0	0—0	1—0	2—0	10— 4
Roberge	0—0	0—0	0—0	1—0	0—0	1—0	0—0	0—0	0—0	0—0	0—0	2— 0
Ruhle	2—1	3—0	1—1	0—0	0—0	0—0	0—0	2—0	2—1	1—1	1—0	12— 4
Ryan	2—0	1—0	1—1	0—2	0—2	0—0	1—2	2—0	1—1	2—2	1—0	11—10
Sambito	2—1	0—0	0—0	0—0	1—0	1—0	2—0	1—0	0—1	0—2	1—0	8— 4
Smith	0—0	1—0	0—0	2—2	0—1	0—1	0—0	1—0	0—0	2—0	1—1	7— 5
Totals	11—7	11—1	10—8	9—10	5—7	8—4	3—9	7—5	7—5	11—7	11—7	93—70

No Decisions: Sprowl.

LOS ANGELES—92-71

Pitcher	Atl. W—L	Chi. W—L	Cin. W—L	Hou. W—L	Mtl. W—L	N.Y. W—L	Phil. W—L	Pitt. W—L	St.L. W—L	S.D. W—L	S.F. W—L	Totals W—L
Beckwith	0—0	0—0	0—0	0—1	0—0	0—0	1—0	0—0	1—0	1—2	0—0	3— 3
Castillo	0—0	0—0	1—1	0—0	2—0	0—1	2—1	0—1	0—0	2—1	1—1	8— 6
Goltz	0—3	0—0	1—1	0—3	0—0	2—1	0—0	0—0	2—1	0—1	2—1	7—11
Hooton	1—2	1—1	0—1	0—1	2—0	2—0	0—1	2—0	2—1	1—0	3—1	14— 8
Hough	0—0	0—0	0—1	0—0	1—0	0—0	0—1	0—1	0—0	0—0	0—0	1— 3
Howe	0—0	2—1	0—2	3—1	1—1	1—0	0—1	0—1	0—0	0—1	0—1	7— 9
Reuss	2—1	0—2	4—1	4—0	2—0	1—0	0—1	2—0	1—0	0—1	2—0	18— 6
Stanhouse	0—1	0—0	0—0	0—1	1—0	0—0	1—0	0—0	0—0	0—0	0—0	2— 2
Sutcliffe	0—1	0—0	1—0	1—1	0—0	0—1	0—1	0—1	0—1	1—2	0—1	3— 9
Sutton	2—2	2—1	1—1	0—0	1—0	0—0	1—0	1—0	0—1	3—0	2—0	13— 5
Valenzuela	0—0	0—0	0—0	1—0	0—0	0—0	0—0	0—0	0—0	0—0	1—0	2— 0
Welch	2—1	2—0	1—1	1—1	1—0	1—2	1—0	1—2	1—1	1—1	2—0	14— 9
Totals	7—11	7—5	9—9	10—9	11—1	7—5	6—6	6—6	7—5	9—9	13—5	92—71

No Decisions: Forster.

MONTREAL—90-72

Pitcher	Atl. W—L	Chi. W—L	Cin. W—L	Hou. W—L	L.A. W—L	N.Y. W—L	Phil. W—L	Pitt. W—L	St.L. W—L	S.D. W—L	S.F. W—L	Totals W—L
Bahnsen	0—2	1—1	1—0	1—0	0—1	0—0	0—2	0—0	1—0	1—0	2—0	7— 6
D'Acquisto	0—0	0—0	0—0	0—0	0—0	0—0	0—0	0—0	0—0	0—0	0—1	0— 2
Dues	0—0	0—0	0—0	0—0	0—0	0—0	0—0	0—0	0—1	0—0	0—0	0— 1
Fryman	0—0	2—0	1—0	1—0	0—0	2—0	0—1	0—1	1—1	0—0	0—0	7— 4
Grimsley	1—0	1—0	0—0	0—1	0—1	0—0	0—0	0—1	1—0	0—0	0—0	2— 4
Gullickson	0—1	2—1	1—0	1—0	0—2	1—0	0—1	2—0	1—0	1—0	1—0	10— 5
Lea	1—0	2—0	0—1	0—1	0—0	0—1	1—0	0—1	0—0	3—0	0—1	7— 5
Lee	0—0	0—1	1—0	0—1	0—0	1—2	0—1	1—0	2—0	0—0	0—0	4— 6
Murray	0—0	0—1	0—0	0—0	0—0	0—0	0—0	0—0	0—0	0—0	0—0	0— 1
Norman	1—0	0—0	1—0	0—0	0—1	0—0	0—0	0—1	1—0	1—1	0—0	4— 4
Palmer	1—0	0—0	0—2	2—0	0—1	1—1	0—1	1—0	2—1	0—0	1—0	8— 6
Rogers	1—0	2—1	2—0	0—0	1—2	2—1	2—2	2—3	1—1	1—0	2—1	16—11
Sanderson	2—2	2—0	2—0	2—0	0—0	1—2	3—1	1—3	1—1	1—1	1—1	16—11
Sosa	0—0	1—0	0—0	0—1	0—2	2—0	3—0	0—1	1—1	1—1	2—0	9— 6
Totals	7—5	12—6	9—3	7—5	1—11	10—8	9—9	6—12	12—6	10—2	7—5	90—72

No Decisions: Hutton, Ratzer.

NEW YORK—67-95

Pitcher	Atl. W–L	Chi. W–L	Cin. W–L	Hou. W–L	L.A. W–L	Mtl. W–L	Phil. W–L	Pitt. W–L	St.L. W–L	S.D. W–L	S.F. W–L	Totals W–L
Allen	2–0	1–2	0–0	1–2	0–0	0–1	1–1	2–0	0–2	0–1	0–1	7–10
Berenguer	0–0	0–0	0–0	0–0	0–0	0–1	0–0	0–0	0–0	0–0	0–0	0– 1
Bomback	1–0	1–0	0–1	0–0	1–0	1–1	2–2	0–1	4–1	0–1	0–1	10– 8
Burris	1–0	0–1	0–1	0–0	1–1	2–0	1–2	2–2	0–1	0–3	0–2	7–13
Falcone	1–1	1–1	0–1	1–1	0–0	1–0	0–1	1–1	1–2	0–1	1–1	7–10
Glynn	0–0	1–0	0–0	0–2	0–0	1–0	0–0	0–0	0–1	1–0	0–0	3– 3
Hausman	0–0	0–2	0–0	0–0	1–1	1–0	1–0	2–0	0–1	0–1	1–0	6– 5
Jackson	0–0	0–0	1–1	0–0	0–0	0–2	0–2	0–1	0–1	0–0	0–0	1– 7
Kobel	0–0	0–1	0–0	0–1	0–0	0–1	0–1	0–0	1–0	0–0	0–0	1– 4
Lynch	0–0	1–0	0–0	0–0	0–0	0–0	0–0	0–1	0–0	0–0	0–0	1– 1
Miller	0–0	0–1	0–0	0–0	0–0	0–0	1–0	0–0	0–0	0–0	0–1	1– 2
Pacella	1–0	1–0	0–1	0–0	0–1	0–1	1–0	0–0	0–0	0–1	0–0	3– 4
Reardon	0–0	0–0	2–2	2–1	1–0	0–1	0–0	1–0	1–0	0–2	1–1	8– 7
Scott	0–0	0–1	0–0	0–0	0–0	0–0	0–0	0–0	1–0	0–0	0–0	1– 1
Swan	1–1	1–1	0–0	0–1	1–1	1–1	0–1	0–2	1–0	0–1	0–0	5– 9
Zachry	2–1	1–0	1–1	0–0	0–3	0–1	0–2	2–0	0–0	0–0	0–2	6–10
Totals	9–3	8–10	4–8	4–8	5–7	8–10	6–12	10–8	9–9	1–11	3–9	67–95

No Decisions: Holman.

PHILADELPHIA—91-71

Pitcher	Atl. W–L	Chi. W–L	Cin. W–L	Hou. W–L	L.A. W–L	Mtl. W–L	N.Y. W–L	Pitt. W–L	St.L. W–L	S.D. W–L	S.F. W–L	Totals W–L
Brusstar	0–0	1–1	0–0	0–0	0–0	0–1	0–0	1–0	0–0	0–0	0–0	2– 2
Bystrom	0–0	2–0	0–0	0–0	0–0	0–0	2–0	0–0	1–0	0–0	0–0	5– 0
Carlton	3–0	3–0	1–3	2–0	1–1	1–2	2–2	1–0	6–0	2–0	2–1	24– 9
Christenson	0–0	0–0	0–0	1–0	1–0	1–0	1–0	0–0	0–0	1–0	0–1	5– 1
Espinosa	1–0	0–0	1–1	0–0	0–0	0–0	1–0	0–2	0–0	0–2	0–0	3– 5
LaGrow	0–0	0–0	0–0	0–0	0–0	0–1	0–1	0–0	0–0	0–0	0–0	0– 2
Larson	0–2	0–1	0–0	0–0	0–0	0–0	0–0	0–1	0–0	0–0	0–1	0– 5
Lerch	0–1	1–0	0–2	0–1	0–1	1–1	1–1	1–2	0–3	0–0	0–2	4–14
McGraw	0–0	0–0	0–0	0–0	0–0	2–2	1–0	2–2	0–0	0–0	0–0	5– 4
Noles	0–0	0–0	0–1	0–0	0–2	1–0	0–0	0–1	0–0	0–0	0–1	1– 4
Reed	0–0	0–1	1–0	0–1	3–0	1–0	0–1	1–1	0–1	0–0	1–0	7– 5
Ruthven	2–1	2–2	1–1	3–1	0–1	2–1	1–0	0–2	1–1	3–0	2–0	17–10
Saucier	0–0	1–0	0–0	2–0	0–0	0–0	1–1	1–0	0–1	1–1	1–0	7– 3
Walk	1–0	3–0	1–0	1–0	1–1	0–1	2–0	0–0	1–3	1–1	0–0	11– 7
Totals	7–5	13–5	5–7	9–3	6–6	9–9	12–6	7–11	9–9	8–4	6–6	91–71

No Decisions: Davis, Lyle, Munninghoff.

PITTSBURGH—83-79

Pitcher	Atl. W–L	Chi. W–L	Cin. W–L	Hou. W–L	L.A. W–L	Mtl. W–L	N.Y. W–L	Phil. W–L	St.L. W–L	S.D. W–L	S.F. W–L	Totals W–L
Bibby	1–1	2–1	1–1	1–1	0–1	5–0	2–0	2–0	2–0	1–1	2–0	19– 6
Blyleven	0–1	1–1	1–2	0–2	0–2	1–2	2–1	0–0	1–1	1–0	1–1	8–13
Candelaria	0–0	2–1	2–0	2–2	0–2	1–1	1–3	1–1	0–2	0–1	2–1	11–14
Jackson	0–1	0–0	0–0	0–0	1–0	0–0	0–2	2–0	3–0	1–0	1–1	8– 4
Jefferson	0–0	1–0	0–0	0–0	0–0	0–0	0–0	0–0	0–0	0–0	0–0	1– 0
Lee	0–0	0–0	0–0	0–0	0–0	0–0	0–0	0–1	0–0	0–0	0–0	0– 1
Perez	0–0	0–1	0–0	0–0	0–0	0–0	0–0	0–0	0–0	0–0	0–0	0– 1
Rhoden	0–0	0–0	1–1	1–0	2–0	1–1	1–1	0–0	1–1	0–1	0–0	7– 5
Roberts	0–0	0–0	0–0	0–0	0–0	0–0	0–0	0–0	0–1	0–0	0–0	0– 1
D. Robinson	0–2	1–1	1–0	0–2	0–0	1–1	0–1	3–1	0–1	1–1	0–0	7–10
Romo	0–1	0–0	0–0	0–0	0–0	1–0	0–1	1–1	1–0	1–1	1–0	5– 5
Rooker	0–1	0–1	0–0	0–0	0–0	0–0	0–0	0–0	2–0	0–0	0–0	2– 2
Scurry	0–0	0–0	0–0	0–0	0–0	0–0	0–0	0–0	0–1	0–0	0–1	0– 2
Solomon	0–0	1–1	0–0	1–0	1–0	1–1	2–0	1–0	1–0	0–1	0–0	7– 3
Tekulve	0–4	2–1	0–1	0–0	2–1	1–0	0–1	1–3	0–0	1–1	1–0	8–12
Totals	1–11	10–8	6–6	5–7	6–6	12–6	8–10	11–7	10–8	6–6	8–4	83–79

No Decisions: Hassler, Mahler.

ST. LOUIS—74-88

Pitcher	Atl. W–L	Chi. W–L	Cin. W–L	Hou. W–L	L.A. W–L	Mtl. W–L	N.Y. W–L	Phil. W–L	Pitt. W–L	S.D. W–L	S.F. W–L	Totals W–L
Borbon	0–0	0–0	0–0	0–0	0–0	0–0	0–0	0–0	0–0	0–0	0–0	1–0
Forsch	2–1	0–1	2–0	0–0	0–2	2–2	1–0	1–3	0–0	1–0	2–1	11–10
Frazier	0–0	0–0	0–0	0–0	0–0	0–2	1–2	0–0	0–0	0–0	0–0	1–4
Fulgham	1–0	0–1	0–0	0–0	0–0	0–2	1–0	0–2	1–1	0–0	1–0	4–6
Hood	1–0	0–0	0–1	2–0	0–0	0–0	0–0	0–0	1–3	0–1	0–1	4–6
Kaat	0–0	1–0	1–1	0–2	0–0	1–1	1–0	1–0	2–1	1–2	0–0	8–7
Knowles	0–0	0–0	0–0	0–0	0–0	0–0	0–0	0–0	0–0	0–0	0–0	0–1
Littell	0–0	0–1	0–0	0–0	0–1	0–0	0–0	0–0	0–0	0–0	0–0	0–2
Little	0–0	0–0	0–0	0–0	0–0	0–0	1–1	0–0	0–0	0–0	0–0	1–1
Littlefield	1–0	1–1	1–1	0–0	0–0	0–2	1–1	1–0	0–0	0–0	0–0	5–5
Martin	0–0	0–0	0–0	1–1	0–0	0–0	1–0	0–0	0–2	0–0	0–0	2–3
Martinez	0–2	2–1	0–1	0–1	2–0	1–0	0–2	0–1	0–1	0–0	0–1	5–10
Moore	0–0	0–0	0–0	0–0	0–0	0–0	0–0	0–0	0–1	1–0		1–1
Olmsted	0–0	0–0	0–0	0–0	0–0	0–0	0–0	1–0	0–0	0–0	0–0	1–1
Otten	0–1	0–1	0–0	0–0	0–0	0–1	0–1	0–1	0–0	0–0	0–0	0–5
Rincon	0–0	1–0	0–0	0–0	0–0	1–1	0–0	0–0	0–0	0–0	0–0	3–1
Seaman	0–0	1–0	1–0	0–0	0–0	0–0	0–0	0–0	0–1	0–0	0–1	3–2
Sykes	0–1	0–3	0–0	0–3	0–0	1–0	0–1	2–0	2–0	1–0	0–2	6–10
Thomas	0–0	0–0	1–0	0–0	0–0	0–1	0–1	0–0	0–0	1–1	0–0	2–3
Urrea	0–0	1–0	0–0	0–0	1–0	0–0	1–0	0–0	1–0	0–0	0–1	4–1
Vuckovich	1–1	2–0	1–1	1–0	1–3	0–0	0–0	3–1	1–1	1–2	1–0	12–9
Totals	6–6	9–9	7–5	5–7	5–7	6–12	9–9	9–9	8–10	5–7	5–7	74–88

No Decisions: None.

SAN DIEGO—73-89

Pitcher	Atl. W–L	Chi. W–L	Cin. W–L	Hou. W–L	L.A. W–L	Mtl. W–L	N.Y. W–L	Phil. W–L	Pitt. W–L	St.L. W–L	S.F. W–L	Totals W–L
Blair	0–0	0–0	0–0	0–0	0–1	0–0	0–0	0–0	0–0	0–0	0–0	0–1
Curtis	0–1	0–0	1–0	2–2	0–2	0–1	2–0	2–0	1–1	1–0	1–1	10–8
D'Acquisto	1–0	0–0	0–2	0–1	0–0	0–0	0–0	0–0	0–0	1–0	0–0	2–3
Eichelberger	0–1	0–0	0–0	1–0	1–1	0–0	1–0	0–0	0–0	0–0	1–0	4–2
Fingers	0–2	2–0	0–1	0–2	2–1	0–1	2–0	0–0	1–2	2–0	2–0	11–9
Jones	0–1	3–1	0–4	0–2	0–0	0–0	0–0	0–1	1–0	0–1	1–2	5–13
Kinney	0–0	0–1	0–2	0–0	1–1	0–0	1–1	0–0	2–1	0–0	0–0	4–6
Lucas	0–1	0–0	1–2	0–0	0–0	0–2	1–0	0–1	0–1	1–2	1–0	5–8
Mura	1–0	0–0	0–2	0–1	2–0	2–1	0–0	0–2	1–0	0–0	2–1	8–7
Rasmussen	2–2	2–1	0–0	0–1	1–1	0–2	1–1	0–0	0–1	0–0	0–2	4–11
Shirley	1–3	3–0	1–2	2–1	0–1	0–1	1–0	0–3	2–1	1–0	0–0	11–12
Stablein	0–0	0–0	0–0	0–0	0–0	0–0	0–0	0–0	0–0	0–0	0–1	0–1
Tellmann	1–0	0–0	0–0	0–0	1–0	0–0	0–0	0–0	0–0	0–0	1–0	3–0
Wise	0–1	0–0	0–0	2–1	1–1	0–0	1–0	3–0	0–1	0–0	0–1	6–8
Totals	6–12	8–4	3–15	7–11	9–9	2–10	11–1	4–8	6–6	7–5	10–8	73–89

No Decisions: Armstrong.

SAN FRANCISCO—75-86

Pitcher	Atl. W–L	Chi. W–L	Cin. W–L	Hou. W–L	L.A. W–L	Mtl. W–L	N.Y. W–L	Phil. W–L	Pitt. W–L	St.L. W–L	S.D. W–L	Totals W–L
Blue	2–1	2–0	0–0	2–3	0–2	1–1	2–1	0–1	2–0	1–1	2–0	14–10
Bordley	0–0	0–2	2–0	0–0	0–0	0–0	0–0	0–1	0–0	0–0	0–0	2–3
Griffin	0–0	1–0	0–0	1–0	1–0	0–0	0–0	0–0	1–1	0–0	1–0	5–1
Hargesheimer	1–2	0–0	1–1	0–1	0–0	0–2	1–0	0–0	0–0	1–0	0–0	5–3
Holland	1–0	0–0	0–0	0–0	1–0	1–0	0–0	0–0	1–0	0–0	0–0	4–6
Knepper	0–1	0–2	2–1	1–1	1–1	0–0	2–0	0–2	0–3	1–3	2–2	9–16
Lavelle	0–2	1–0	1–1	1–1	0–2	0–1	2–0	0–0	0–0	1–0	0–1	6–8
Minton	1–2	0–0	1–0	0–1	1–0	0–0	0–0	0–1	1–0	0–0	0–1	4–6
Moffitt	0–0	0–0	0–0	0–0	0–0	1–1	0–0	0–0	0–0	0–0	0–0	1–1
Montefusco	0–1	0–0	0–2	0–2	0–1	1–1	2–0	0–0	0–0	0–0	1–1	4–8
Ripley	1–1	1–1	2–0	1–0	0–2	0–0	0–2	3–1	0–0	1–0	0–3	9–10
Rowland	0–0	0–0	0–0	1–0	0–1	0–0	0–0	0–0	0–0	0–0	0–0	1–1
Whitson	0–1	2–0	2–2	0–2	1–3	2–1	0–0	2–0	0–1	0–1	2–2	11–13
Totals	6–11	7–5	11–7	7–11	5–13	5–7	9–3	6–6	4–8	7–5	8–10	75–86

No Decisions: Breining, Halicki, Nastu, Stember.

NATIONAL LEAGUE

PENNANT WINNERS

Year	Club	Manager	W.	L.	Pct.	°G.A.
1900	Brooklyn	Edward (Ned) Hanlon	82	54	.603	4½
1901	Pittsburgh	Frederick Clarke	90	49	.647	7½
1902	Pittsburgh	Frederick Clarke	103	36	.741	27½
1903	Pittsburgh	Frederick Clarke	91	49	.650	6½
1904	New York	John McGraw	106	47	.693	13
1905	New York	John McGraw	105	48	.686	9
1906	Chicago	Frank Chance	116	36	.763	20
1907	Chicago	Frank Chance	107	45	.704	17
1908	Chicago	Frank Chance	99	55	.643	1
1909	Pittsburgh	Frederick Clarke	110	42	.724	6½
1910	Chicago	Frank Chance	104	50	.675	13
1911	New York	John McGraw	99	54	.647	7½
1912	New York	John McGraw	103	48	.682	10
1913	New York	John McGraw	101	51	.664	12½
1914	Boston	George Stallings	94	59	.614	10½
1915	Philadelphia	Patrick Moran	90	62	.592	7
1916	Brooklyn	Wilbert Robinson	94	60	.610	2½
1917	New York	John McGraw	98	56	.636	10
1918	Chicago	Fred Mitchell	84	45	.651	10½
1919	Cincinnati	Patrick Moran	96	44	.686	9
1920	Brooklyn	Wilbert Robinson	93	61	.604	7
1921	New York	John McGraw	94	59	.614	4
1922	New York	John McGraw	93	61	.604	7
1923	New York	John McGraw	95	58	.621	4½
1924	New York	John McGraw	93	60	.608	1½
1925	Pittsburgh	William McKechnie	95	58	.621	8½
1926	St. Louis	Rogers Hornsby	89	65	.578	2
1927	Pittsburgh	Owen (Donie) Bush	94	60	.610	1½
1928	St. Louis	William McKechnie	95	59	.617	2
1929	Chicago	Joseph McCarthy	98	54	.645	10½
1930	St. Louis	Charles (Gabby) Street	92	62	.597	2
1931	St. Louis	Charles (Gabby) Street	101	53	.656	13
1932	Chicago	Charles Grimm	90	64	.584	4
1933	New York	William Terry	91	61	.599	5
1934	St. Louis	Frank Frisch	95	58	.621	2
1935	Chicago	Charles Grimm	100	54	.649	4
1936	New York	William Terry	92	62	.597	5
1937	New York	William Terry	95	57	.625	3
1938	Chicago	Charles (Gabby) Hartnett	89	63	.586	2
1939	Cincinnati	William McKechnie	97	57	.630	4½
1940	Cincinnati	William McKechnie	100	53	.654	12
1941	Brooklyn	Leo Durocher	100	54	.649	2½
1942	St. Louis	William Southworth	106	48	.688	2
1943	St. Louis	William Southworth	105	49	.682	18
1944	St. Louis	William Southworth	105	49	.682	14½
1945	Chicago	Charles Grimm	98	56	.636	3
1946	St. Louis†	Edwin Dyer	98	58	.628	2
1947	Brooklyn	Burton Shotton	94	60	.610	5
1948	Boston	William Southworth	91	62	.595	6½
1949	Brooklyn	Burton Shotton	97	57	.630	1
1950	Philadelphia	Edwin Sawyer	91	63	.591	2
1951	New York‡	Leo Durocher	98	59	.624	1
1952	Brooklyn	Charles Dressen	96	57	.627	4½
1953	Brooklyn	Charles Dressen	105	49	.682	13
1954	New York	Leo Durocher	97	57	.630	5
1955	Brooklyn	Walter Alston	98	55	.641	13½
1956	Brooklyn	Walter Alston	93	61	.604	1
1957	Milwaukee	Fred Haney	95	59	.617	8
1958	Milwaukee	Fred Haney	92	62	.597	8
1959	Los Angeles§	Walter Alston	88	68	.564	2

PENNANT WINNERS—Continued

Year	Club	Manager	W.	L.	Pct.	°G.A.
1960—Pittsburgh		Daniel Murtaugh	95	59	.617	7
1961—Cincinnati		Frederick Hutchinson	93	61	.604	4
1962—San Francisco x		Alvin Dark	103	62	.624	1
1963—Los Angeles		Walter Alston	99	63	.611	6
1964—St. Louis		John Keane	93	69	.574	1
1965—Los Angeles		Walter Alston	97	65	.599	2
1966—Los Angeles		Walter Alston	95	67	.586	1½
1967—St. Louis		Albert (Red) Schoendienst	101	60	.627	10½
1968—St. Louis		Albert (Red) Schoendienst	97	65	.599	9
1969—New York (E)°°		Gilbert Hodges	100	62	.617	8
1970—Cincinnati (W)°°		George (Sparky) Anderson	102	60	.630	14½
1971—Pittsburgh (E)°°		Daniel Murtaugh	97	65	.599	7
1972—Cincinnati (W)°°		George (Sparky) Anderson	95	59	.617	10½
1973—New York (E)°°		Lawrence (Yogi) Berra	82	79	.509	1½
1974—Los Angeles (W)°°		Walter Alston	102	60	.630	4
1975—Cincinnati (W)°°		George (Sparky) Anderson	108	54	.667	20
1976—Cincinnati (W)°°		George (Sparky) Anderson	102	60	.630	10
1977—Los Angeles (W)°°		Thomas Lasorda	98	64	.605	10
1978—Los Angeles (W)°°		Thomas Lasorda	95	67	.586	2½
1979—Pittsburgh (E)°°		Charles (Chuck) Tanner	98	64	.605	2
1980—Philadelphia (E)°°		G. Dallas Green	91	71	.562	1

°Games ahead of second-place club. †Defeated Brooklyn, two games to none, in playoff for pennant. ‡Defeated Brooklyn, two games to one, in playoff for pennant. §Defeated Milwaukee, two games to none, in playoff for pennant. xDefeated Los Angeles, two games to one, in playoff for pennant. °°Won Championship Series.

YEARLY FINISHES

Year	Atl.	Chi.	Cin.	Hou.	L.A.	N.Y.	Phil.	Pitt.	St.L.	S.F.
1900	°4	x5	7	....	†1	....	3	2	x5	‡8
1901	°5	6	8	....	†3	....	2	1	4	‡7
1902	°3	5	4	....	†2	....	7	1	6	‡8
1903	°6	3	4	....	†5	....	7	1	8	‡2
1904	°7	2	3	....	†6	....	8	4	5	‡1
1905	°7	3	5	....	†8	....	4	2	6	‡1
1906	°8	1	6	....	†5	....	4	3	7	‡2
1907	°7	1	6	....	†5	....	3	2	8	‡4
1908	°6	1	5	....	†7	....	4	x2	8	x‡2
1909	°8	2	4	....	†6	....	5	1	7	‡3
1910	°8	1	5	....	†6	....	4	3	7	‡2
1911	°8	2	6	....	†7	....	4	3	5	‡1
1912	°8	3	4	....	†7	....	5	2	6	‡1
1913	°5	3	7	....	†6	....	2	4	8	‡1
1914	°1	4	8	....	†5	....	6	7	3	‡2
1915	°2	4	7	....	†3	....	1	5	6	‡8
1916	°3	5	x7	....	†1	....	2	6	x7	‡4
1917	°6	5	4	....	†7	....	2	8	3	‡1
1918	°7	1	3	....	†5	....	6	4	8	‡2
1919	°6	3	1	....	†5	....	8	4	7	‡2
1920	°7	x5	3	....	†1	....	8	4	x5	‡2
1921	°4	7	6	....	†5	....	8	2	3	‡1
1922	°8	5	2	....	†6	....	7	x3	x3	‡1
1923	°7	4	2	....	†6	....	8	3	5	‡1
1924	°8	5	4	....	†2	....	7	3	6	‡1
1925	°5	8	3	....	x†6	....	x6	1	4	‡2
1926	°7	4	2	....	†6	....	8	3	1	‡5
1927	°7	4	5	....	J6	....	8	1	2	‡3
1928	°7	3	5	....	†6	....	8	4	1	‡2
1929	°8	1	7	....	†6	....	5	2	4	‡3
1930	°6	2	7	....	†4	....	8	5	1	‡3
1931	°7	3	8	....	†4	....	6	5	1	‡2
1932	°5	1	8	....	†3	....	4	2	x6	x‡6
1933	°4	3	8	....	†6	....	7	2	5	‡1
1934	°4	3	8	....	†6	....	7	5	1	‡2
1935	°8	1	6	....	†5	....	7	4	2	‡3

YEARLY FINISHES—Continued

Year	Atl.	Chi.	Cin.	Hous.	L.A.	N.Y.	Phil.	Pitt.	St.L.	S.F.
1936	°6	x2	5	....	†7	....	8	4	x2	‡1
1937	°5	2	8	....	†6	....	7	3	4	‡1
1938	°5	1	4	....	†7	....	8	2	6	‡3
1939	°7	4	1	....	†3	....	8	6	2	‡5
1940	°7	5	1	....	†2	....	8	4	3	‡6
1941	°7	6	3	....	†1	....	8	4	2	‡5
1942	°7	6	4	....	†2	....	8	5	1	‡5
1943	°6	5	2	....	†3	....	7	4	1	‡8
1944	°6	4	3	....	†7	....	8	2	1	‡5
1945	°6	1	7	....	†3	....	8	4	2	‡5
1946	°4	3	6	....	†2	....	5	7	1	‡8
1947	°3	6	5	....	†1	....	x7	x7	2	‡4
1948	°1	8	7	....	†3	....	6	4	2	‡5
1949	°4	8	7	....	†1	....	3	6	2	‡5
1950	°4	7	6	....	†2	....	1	8	5	‡3
1951	°4	8	6	....	†2	....	5	7	3	‡1
1952	°7	5	6	....	†1	....	4	8	3	‡2
1953	°2	7	6	....	†1	....	x3	8	x3	‡5
1954	°3	7	5	....	†2	....	4	8	6	‡1
1955	°2	6	5	....	†1	....	4	8	7	‡3
1956	°2	8	3	....	†1	....	5	7	4	‡6
1957	°1	x7	4	....	†3	....	5	x7	2	‡6
1958	°1	x5	4	....	7	....	8	2	x5	3
1959	°2	x5	x5	....	1	....	8	4	7	3
1960	°2	7	6	....	4	....	8	1	3	5
1961	°4	7	1	....	2	....	8	6	5	3
1962	°5	9	3	8	2	10	7	4	6	1
1963	°6	7	5	9	1	10	4	8	2	3
1964	°5	8	x2	9	x6	10	x2	x6	1	4
1965	°5	8	4	9	1	10	6	3	7	2
1966	5	10	7	8	1	9	4	3	6	2
1967	7	3	4	9	8	10	5	6	1	2
1968	5	3	4	10	x7	9	x7	6	1	2

		EAST DIVISION					WEST DIVISION				
Year	Chi.	Mon.	N.Y.	Phila.	Pitt.	St.L.	Atl.	Cin.	Hous.	L.A.	S.D.	S.F.
1969	2	6	1	5	3	4	1	3	5	4	6	2
1970	2	6	3	5	1	4	5	1	4	2	6	3
1971	x3	5	x3	6	1	2	3	x4	x4	2	6	1
1972	2	5	3	6	1	4	4	1	2	3	6	5
1973	5	4	1	6	3	2	5	1	4	2	6	3
1974	6	4	5	3	1	2	3	2	4	1	6	5
1975	x5	x5	x3	2	1	x3	5	1	6	2	4	3
1976	4	6	3	1	2	5	6	1	3	2	5	4
1977	4	5	6	1	2	3	6	2	5	1	4	3
1978	3	4	6	1	2	5	6	2	5	1	4	3
1979	5	2	6	4	1	3	6	1	2	3	5	4
1980	6	2	5	1	3	4	4	3	1	2	6	5

°Record of predecessor Boston (1900-1952) and Milwaukee (1953-1965) clubs; †Brooklyn club; ‡New York Giants. xTied for position.

LEADING BATSMEN

Year Player and Club	G.	AB.	R.	H.	TB.	2B.	3B.	HR.	RBI.	B.A.
1900—John (Honus) Wagner, Pittsburgh	134	528	107	201	302	45	22	4	....	.381
1901—Jesse Burkett, St. Louis	142	597	139	228	313	21	17	10	....	.382
1902—Clarence Beaumont, Pittsburgh	131	544	101	194	227	21	6	0	....	.357
1903—John (Honus) Wagner, Pittsburgh	129	512	97	182	265	30	19	5	....	.355
1904—John (Honus) Wagner, Pittsburgh	132	490	97	171	255	44	14	4	....	.349
1905—J. Bentley Seymour, Cincinnati	149	581	95	219	325	40	21	8	....	.377
1906—John (Honus) Wagner, Pittsburgh	140	516	103	175	237	38	9	2	....	.339
1907—John (Honus) Wagner, Pittsburgh	142	515	98	180	264	38	14	6	91	.350
1908—John (Honus) Wagner, Pittsburgh	151	568	100	201	308	39	19	10	106	.354
1909—John (Honus) Wagner, Pittsburgh	137	495	92	168	242	39	10	5	102	.339

LEADING BATSMEN—Continued

Year Player and Club	G.	AB.	R.	H.	TB.	2B.	3B.	HR.	RBI.	B.A.
1910—Sherwood Magee, Philadelphia	154	519	110	172	263	39	17	6	116	.331
1911—John (Honus) Wagner, Pittsburgh	130	473	87	158	240	23	16	9	108	.334
1912—Henry Zimmerman, Chicago	145	557	95	207	318	41	14	14	98	.372
1913—Jacob Daubert, Brooklyn	139	508	76	178	215	17	7	2	46	.350
1914—Jacob Daubert, Brooklyn	126	474	89	156	205	17	7	6	44	.329
1915—Lawrence Doyle, New York	150	591	86	189	261	40	10	4	68	.320
1916—Harold Chase, Cincinnati	142	542	66	184	249	29	12	4	84	.339
1917—Edd Roush, Cincinnati	136	522	82	178	237	19	14	4	62	.341
1918—Zachariah Wheat, Brooklyn	105	409	39	137	158	15	3	0	48	.335
1919—Edd Roush, Cincinnati	133	504	73	162	216	19	13	3	69	.321
1920—Rogers Hornsby, St. Louis	149	589	96	218	329	44	20	9	94	.370
1921—Rogers Hornsby, St. Louis	154	592	131	235	378	44	18	21	126	.397
1922—Rogers Hornsby, St. Louis	154	623	141	250	450	46	14	42	152	.401
1923—Rogers Hornsby, St. Louis	107	424	89	163	266	32	10	17	83	.384
1924—Rogers Hornsby, St. Louis	143	536	121	227	373	43	14	25	94	.424
1925—Rogers Hornsby, St. Louis	138	504	133	203	381	41	10	39	143	.403
1926—Eugene Hargrave, Cincinnati	105	326	42	115	171	22	8	6	62	.353
1927—Paul Waner, Pittsburgh	155	623	113	237	338	40	17	9	131	.380
1928—Rogers Hornsby, Boston	140	486	99	188	307	42	7	21	94	.387
1929—Frank O'Doul, Philadelphia	154	638	152	254	397	35	6	32	122	.398
1930—William Terry, New York	154	633	139	254	392	39	15	23	129	.401
1931—Chas. (Chick) Hafey, St. Louis	122	450	94	157	256	35	8	16	95	.349
1932—Frank O'Doul, Brooklyn	148	595	120	219	330	32	8	21	90	.368
1933—Charles Klein, Philadelphia	152	606	101	223	365	44	7	28	120	.368
1934—Paul Waner, Pittsburgh	146	599	122	217	323	32	16	14	90	.362
1935—J. Floyd (Arky) Vaughan, Pittsburgh	137	499	108	192	303	34	10	19	99	.385
1936—Paul Waner, Pittsburgh	148	585	107	218	304	53	9	5	94	.373
1937—Joseph Medwick, St. Louis	156	633	111	237	406	56	10	31	154	.374
1938—Ernest Lombardi, Cincinnati	129	489	60	167	256	30	1	19	95	.342
1939—John Mize, St. Louis	153	564	104	197	353	44	14	28	108	.349
1940—Debs Garms, Pittsburgh	103	358	76	127	179	23	7	5	57	.355
1941—Harold (Pete) Reiser, Brooklyn	137	536	117	184	299	39	17	14	76	.343
1942—Ernest Lombardi, Boston	105	309	32	102	149	14	0	11	46	.330
1943—Stanley Musial, St. Louis	157	617	108	220	347	48	20	13	81	.357
1944—Fred (Dixie) Walker, Brooklyn	147	535	77	191	283	37	8	13	91	.357
1945—Philip Cavarretta, Chicago	132	498	94	177	249	34	10	6	97	.355
1946—Stanley Musial, St. Louis	156	624	124	228	366	50	20	16	103	.365
1947—Harry Walker, St. Louis-Phila.	140	513	81	186	250	29	16	1	41	.363
1948—Stanley Musial, St. Louis	155	611	135	230	429	46	18	39	131	.376
1949—Jack Robinson, Brooklyn	156	593	122	203	313	38	12	16	124	.342
1950—Stanley Musial, St. Louis	146	555	105	192	331	41	7	28	109	.346
1951—Stanley Musial, St. Louis	152	578	124	205	355	30	12	32	108	.355
1952—Stanley Musial, St. Louis	154	578	105	194	311	42	6	21	91	.336
1953—Carl Furillo, Brooklyn	132	479	82	165	278	38	6	21	92	.344
1954—Willie Mays, New York	151	565	119	195	377	33	13	41	110	.345
1955—Richie Ashburn, Philadelphia	140	533	91	180	239	32	9	3	42	.338
1956—Henry Aaron, Milwaukee	153	609	106	200	340	34	14	26	92	.328
1957—Stanley Musial, St. Louis	134	502	82	176	307	38	3	29	102	.351
1958—Richie Ashburn, Philadelphia	152	615	98	215	271	24	13	2	33	.350
1959—Henry Aaron, Milwaukee	154	629	116	223	400	46	7	39	123	.355
1960—Richard Groat, Pittsburgh	138	573	85	186	226	26	4	2	50	.325
1961—Roberto Clemente, Pittsburgh	146	572	100	201	320	30	10	23	89	.351
1962—H. Thomas Davis, Los Angeles	163	665	120	230	356	27	9	27	153	.346
1963—H. Thomas Davis, Los Angeles	146	556	69	181	254	19	3	16	88	.326
1964—Roberto Clemente, Pittsburgh	155	622	95	211	301	40	7	12	87	.339
1965—Roberto Clemente, Pittsburgh	152	589	91	194	273	21	14	10	65	.329
1966—Mateo Alou, Pittsburgh	141	535	86	183	225	18	9	2	27	.342
1967—Roberto Clemente, Pittsburgh	147	585	103	209	324	26	10	23	110	.357
1968—Peter Rose, Cincinnati	149	626	94	210	294	42	6	10	49	.335
1969—Peter Rose, Cincinnati	156	627	120	218	321	33	11	16	82	.348
1970—Ricardo Carty, Atlanta	136	478	84	175	279	23	3	25	101	.366
1971—Joseph Torre, St. Louis	161	634	97	230	352	34	8	24	137	.363
1972—Billy L. Williams, Chicago	150	574	95	191	348	34	6	37	122	.333
1973—Peter Rose, Cincinnati	160	680	115	230	297	36	8	5	64	.338
1974—Ralph Garr, Atlanta	143	606	87	214	305	24	17	11	54	.353
1975—Bill Madlock, Chicago	130	514	77	182	246	29	7	7	64	.354

LEADING BATSMEN—Continued

Year	Player and Club	G.	AB.	R.	H.	TB.	2B.	3B.	HR.	RBI.	B.A.
1976—	Bill Madlock, Chicago	142	514	68	174	257	36	1	15	84	.339
1977—	David Parker, Pittsburgh	159	637	107	215	338	44	8	21	88	.338
1978—	David Parker, Pittsburgh	148	581	102	194	340	32	12	30	117	.334
1979—	Keith Hernandez, St. Louis	161	610	116	210	313	48	11	11	105	.344
1980—	William Buckner, Chicago	145	578	69	187	264	41	3	10	68	.324

LEADERS IN RUNS SCORED

Year	Player and Club	Runs
1900—	Roy Thomas, Philadelphia	131
1901—	Jesse Burkett, St. Louis	139
1902—	John (Honus) Wagner, Pittsburgh	105
1903—	Clarence Beaumont, Pittsburgh	137
1904—	George Browne, New York	99
1905—	Michael Donlin, New York	124
1906—	John (Honus) Wagner, Pittsburgh	103
	Frank Chance, Chicago	103
1907—	W. Porter Shannon, New York	104
1908—	Frederick Tenney, New York	101
1909—	Thomas Leach, Pittsburgh	126
1910—	Sherwood Magee, Philadelphia	110
1911—	James Sheckard, Chicago	121
1912—	Robert Bescher, Cincinnati	120
1913—	Thomas Leach, Chicago	99
	Max Carey, Pittsburgh	99
1914—	George Burns, New York	100
1915—	Cliff. (Gavvy) Cravath, Philadelphia	89
1916—	George Burns, New York	105
1917—	George Burns, New York	103
1918—	Henry Groh, Cincinnati	88
1919—	George Burns, New York	86
1920—	George Burns, New York	115
1921—	Rogers Hornsby, St. Louis	131
1922—	Rogers Hornsby, St. Louis	141
1923—	Ross Youngs, New York	121
1924—	Frank Frisch, New York	121
	Rogers Hornsby, St. Louis	121
1925—	Hazen (Kiki) Cuyler, Pittsburgh	144
1926—	Hazen (Kiki) Cuyler, Pittsburgh	113
1927—	Lloyd Waner, Pittsburgh	133
	Rogers Hornsby, New York	133
1928—	Paul Waner, Pittsburgh	142
1929—	Rogers Hornsby, Chicago	156
1930—	Charles (Chuck) Klein, Philadelphia	158
1931—	Terry, New York-Klein, Philadelphia	121
1932—	Charles (Chuck) Klein, Philadelphia	152
1933—	John (Pepper) Martin, St. Louis	122
1934—	Paul Waner, Pittsburgh	122
1935—	August Galan, Chicago	133
1936—	J. Floyd (Arky) Vaughan, Pittsburgh	122
1937—	Joseph Medwick, St. Louis	111
1938—	Melvin Ott, New York	116
1939—	William Werber, Cincinnati	115

Year	Player and Club	Runs
1940—	J. Floyd (Arky) Vaughan, Pittsburgh	113
1941—	Harold (Pete) Reiser, Brooklyn	117
1942—	Melvin Ott, New York	118
1943—	J. Floyd (Arky) Vaughan, Brooklyn	112
1944—	William Nicholson, Chicago	116
1945—	Edward Stanky, Brooklyn	128
1946—	Stanley Musial, St. Louis	124
1947—	John Mize, New York	137
1948—	Stanley Musial, St. Louis	135
1949—	Harold (Pee Wee) Reese, Brooklyn	132
1950—	C. Earl Torgeson, Boston	120
1951—	Musial, St. Louis-Kiner, Pittsburgh	124
1952—	Musial, St. Louis-Hemus, St. Louis	105
1953—	Edwin (Duke) Snider, Brooklyn	132
1954—	Musial, St. Louis-Snider, Brooklyn	120
1955—	Edwin (Duke) Snider, Brooklyn	126
1956—	Frank Robinson, Cincinnati	122
1957—	Henry Aaron, Milwaukee	118
1958—	Willie Mays, San Francisco	121
1959—	Vada Pinson, Cincinnati	131
1960—	William Bruton, Milwaukee	112
1961—	Willie Mays, San Francisco	129
1962—	Frank Robinson, Cincinnati	134
1963—	Henry Aaron, Milwaukee	121
1964—	Richard Allen, Philadelphia	125
1965—	Tommy Harper, Cincinnati	126
1966—	Felipe Alou, Atlanta	122
1967—	Henry Aaron, Atlanta	113
	Louis Brock, St. Louis	113
1968—	Glenn Beckert, Chicago	98
1969—	Bobby Bonds, San Francisco	120
	Peter Rose, Cincinnati	120
1970—	Billy Williams, Chicago	137
1971—	Louis Brock, St. Louis	126
1972—	Joe Morgan, Cincinnati	122
1973—	Bobby Bonds, San Francisco	131
1974—	Peter Rose, Cincinnati	110
1975—	Peter Rose, Cincinnati	112
1976—	Peter Rose, Cincinnati	130
1977—	George Foster, Cincinnati	124
1978—	Ivan DeJesus, Chicago	104
1979—	Keith Hernandez, St. Louis	116
1980—	Keith Hernandez, St. Louis	111

LEADERS IN HITS

Year	Player and Club	Hits
1900—	William Keeler, Brooklyn	208
1901—	Jesse Burkett, St. Louis	228
1902—	Clarence Beaumont, Pittsburgh	194
1903—	Clarence Beaumont, Pittsburgh	209
1904—	Clarence Beaumont, Pittsburgh	185
1905—	J. Bentley Seymour, Cincinnati	219

Year	Player and Club	Hits
1906—	Harry Steinfeldt, Chicago	176
1907—	Clarence Beaumont, Boston	187
1908—	John (Honus) Wagner, Pittsburgh	201
1909—	Lawrence Doyle, New York	172
1910—	John (Honus) Wagner, Pittsburgh	178
	Robert Byrne, Pittsburgh	178

LEADERS IN HITS—Continued

Year	Player and Club	Hits
1911	Roy Miller, Boston	192
1912	Henry Zimmerman, Chicago	207
1913	Cliff. (Gavvy) Cravath, Philadelphia	179
1914	Sherwood Magee, Philadelphia	171
1915	Lawrence Doyle, New York	189
1916	Harold Chase, Cincinnati	184
1917	Henry Groh, Cincinnati	182
1918	Charles Hollocher, Chicago	161
1919	Ivy Olson, Brooklyn	164
1920	Rogers Hornsby, St. Louis	218
1921	Rogers Hornsby, St. Louis	235
1922	Rogers Hornsby, St. Louis	250
1923	Frank Frisch, New York	223
1924	Rogers Hornsby, St. Louis	227
1925	James Bottomley, St. Louis	227
1926	Edward Brown, Boston	201
1927	Paul Waner, Pittsburgh	237
1928	Fred Lindstrom, New York	231
1929	Frank O'Doul, Philadelphia	254
1930	William Terry, New York	254
1931	Lloyd Waner, Pittsburgh	214
1932	Charles Klein, Philadelphia	226
1933	Charles Klein, Philadelphia	223
1934	Paul Waner, Pittsburgh	217
1935	William Herman, Chicago	227
1936	Joseph Medwick, St. Louis	223
1937	Joseph Medwick, St. Louis	237
1938	Frank McCormick, Cincinnati	209
1939	Frank McCormick, Cincinnati	209
1940	Stanley Hack, Chicago	191
	Frank McCormick, Cincinnati	191
1941	Stanley Hack, Chicago	186
1942	Enos Slaughter, St. Louis	188
1943	Stanley Musial, St. Louis	220
1944	Musial, St. Louis-Cavarretta, Chicago	197
1945	Thomas Holmes, Boston	224
1946	Stanley Musial, St. Louis	228
1947	Thomas Holmes, Boston	191
1948	Stanley Musial, St. Louis	230
1949	Stanley Musial, St. Louis	207
1950	Edwin (Duke) Snider, Brooklyn	199
1951	Richie Ashburn, Philadelphia	221
1952	Stanley Musial, St. Louis	194
1953	Richie Ashburn, Philadelphia	205
1954	Donald Mueller, New York	212
1955	Theodore Kluszewski, Cincinnati	192
1956	Henry Aaron, Milwaukee	200
1957	Al (Red) Schoendienst, N.Y.-Mil.	200
1958	Richie Ashburn, Philadelphia	215
1959	Henry Aaron, Milwaukee	223
1960	Willie Mays, San Francisco	190
1961	Vada Pinson, Cincinnati	208
1962	H. Thomas Davis, Los Angeles	230
1963	Vada Pinson, Cincinnati	204
1964	Clemente, Pittsburgh-Flood, St. Louis	211
1965	Peter Rose, Cincinnati	209
1966	Felipe Alou, Atlanta	218
1967	Roberto Clemente, Pittsburgh	209
1968	Felipe Alou, Atlanta	210
	Peter Rose, Cincinnati	210
1969	Mateo Alou, Pittsburgh	231
1970	Peter Rose, Cincinnati	205
	Billy Williams, Chicago	205
1971	Joseph Torre, St. Louis	230
1972	Peter Rose, Cincinnati	198
1973	Peter Rose, Cincinnati	230
1974	Ralph Garr, Atlanta	214
1975	David Cash, Philadelphia	213
1976	Peter Rose, Cincinnati	215
1977	David Parker, Pittsburgh	215
1978	Steven Garvey, Los Angeles	202
1979	Garry Templeton, St. Louis	211
1980	Steven Garvey, Los Angeles	200

ONE-BASE HIT LEADERS

Year	Player and Club	1B.
1900	William H. Keeler, Brooklyn	179
1901	Jesse C. Burkett, St. Louis	180
1902	Clarence H. Beaumont, Pittsburgh	167
1903	Clarence H. Beaumont, Pittsburgh	166
1904	Clarence H. Beaumont, Pittsburgh	158
1905	Michael J. Donlin, New York	162
1906	Miller J. Huggins, Cincinnati	141
	William P. Shannon, St. Louis-NY	141
1907	Clarence H. Beaumont, Pittsburgh	150
1908	Michael J. Donlin, New York	153
1909	Edward L. Grant, Philadelphia	147
1910	Edward L. Grant, Philadelphia	134
1911	Jacob E. Daubert, Brooklyn	146
	Roy O. Miller, Boston	146
1912	William J. Sweeney, Boston	159
1913	Jacob E. Daubert, Brooklyn	152
1914	Beals Becker, Philadelphia	128
1915	Lawrence J. Doyle, New York	135
1916	David A. Robertson, New York	142
1917	Benjamin M. Kauff, New York	141
	Edd J. Roush, Cincinnati	141
1918	Charles J. Hollocher, Chicago	130
1919	Ivan M. Olson, Brooklyn	140
1920	Milton J. Stock, St. Louis	170
1921	Carson L. Bigbee, Pittsburgh	161
1922	Carson L. Bigbee, Pittsburgh	166
1923	Frank F. Frisch, New York	169
1924	Zachariah Wheat, Brooklyn	149
1925	Milton J. Stock, Brooklyn	164
1926	Edward W. Brown, Boston	160
1927	Lloyd J. Waner, Pittsburgh	198
1928	Lloyd J. Waner, Pittsburgh	180
1929	Frank J. O'Doul, Philadelphia	181
	Lloyd J. Waner, Pittsburgh	181
1930	William H. Terry, New York	177
1931	Lloyd J. Waner, Pittsburgh	172
1932	Frank J. O'Doul, Brooklyn	158
1933	Charles P. Fullis, Philadelphia	162
1934	William H. Terry, New York	169
1935	Forrest D. Jensen, Pittsburgh	160
1936	Joseph G. Moore, New York	160
1937	Paul G. Waner, Pittsburgh	178
1938	Frank A. McCormick, Cincinnati	160
1939	John A. Hassett, Boston	162
1940	Burgess U. Whitehead, New York	141
1941	Stanley C. Hack, Chicago	141

ONE-BASE HIT LEADERS—Continued

Year	Player and Club	1B.
1942—	Enos B. Slaughter, St. Louis	127
1943—	Nicholas J. Witek, New York	172
1944—	Philip J. Cavarretta, Chicago	142
1945—	Stanley C. Hack, Chicago	155
1946—	Stanley F. Musial, St. Louis	142
1947—	Thomas F. Holmes, Boston	146
1948—	Stanley A. Rojek, Pittsburgh	150
1949—	Albert F. Schoendienst, St. Louis	160
1950—	Edward S. Waitkus, Philadelphia	143
1951—	Richie Ashburn, Philadelphia	181
1952—	Robert H. Adams, Cincinnati	145
1953—	Richie Ashburn, Philadelphia	169
1954—	Donald F. Mueller, New York	165
1955—	Donald F. Mueller, New York	152
1956—	John E. Temple, Cincinnati	157
1957—	Richie Ashburn, Philadelphia	152
1958—	Richie Ashburn, Philadelphia	176
1959—	Don L. Blasingame, St. Louis	144
1960—	Richard M. Groat, Pittsburgh	154
1961—	Vada E. Pinson, Cincinnati	150
	Maurice M. Wills, Los Angeles	150
1962—	Maurice M. Wills, Los Angeles	179
1963—	Curtis C. Flood, St. Louis	152
1964—	Curtis C. Flood, St. Louis	178
1965—	Maurice M. Wills, Los Angeles	165
1966—	Roland T. Jackson, Houston	160
1967—	Maurice M. Wills, Pittsburgh	162
1968—	Curtis C. Flood, St. Louis	160
1969—	Mateo R. Alou, Pittsburgh	183
1970—	Mateo R. Alou, Pittsburgh	171
1971—	Ralph A. Garr, Atlanta	180
1972—	Louis C. Brock, St. Louis	156
1973—	Peter E. Rose, Cincinnati	181
1974—	David Cash, Philadelphia	167
1975—	David Cash, Philadelphia	166
1976—	Guillermo Montanez, San Fran.-Atl.	164
1977—	Garry Templeton, St. Louis	155
1978—	Lawrence Bowa, Philadelphia	153
1979—	Peter Rose, Philadelphia	159
1980—	Eugene Richards, San Diego	155

TWO-BASE HIT LEADERS

Year	Player and Club	2B.
1900—	John (Honus) Wagner, Pittsburgh	45
1901—	Wagner, Pitts-Beckley, Cinn.	39
1902—	John (Honus) Wagner, Pittsburgh	33
1903—	Clarke, Pit-Mertes, NY-Steinfeldt, Cin	32
1904—	John (Honus) Wagner, Pittsburgh	44
1905—	J. Bentley Seymour, Cincinnati	40
1906—	John (Honus) Wagner, Pittsburgh	38
1907—	John (Honus) Wagner, Pittsburgh	38
1908—	John (Honus) Wagner, Pittsburgh	39
1909—	John (Honus) Wagner, Pittsburgh	39
1910—	Robert Byrne, Pittsburgh	43
1911—	Edward Konetchy, St. Louis	38
1912—	Henry Zimmerman, Chicago	41
1913—	J. Carlisle Smith, Brooklyn	40
1914—	Sherwood Magee, Philadelphia	39
1915—	Lawrence Doyle, New York	40
1916—	O. Albert Niehoff, Philadelphia	42
1917—	Henry Groh, Cincinnati	39
1918—	Henry Groh, Cincinnati	28
1919—	Ross Youngs, New York	31
1920—	Rogers Hornsby, St. Louis	44
1921—	Rogers Hornsby, St. Louis	44
1922—	Rogers Hornsby, St. Louis	46
1923—	Edd Roush, Cincinnati	41
1924—	Rogers Hornsby, St. Louis	43
1925—	James Bottomley, St. Louis	44
1926—	James Bottomley, St. Louis	40
1927—	J. Riggs Stephenson, Chicago	46
1928—	Paul Waner, Pittsburgh	50
1929—	John Frederick, Brooklyn	52
1930—	Charles Klein, Philadelphia	59
1931—	Earl (Sparky) Adams, St. Louis	46
1932—	Paul Waner, Pittsburgh	62
1933—	Charles Klein, Philadelphia	44
1934—	Cuyler, Chicago-Allen, Philadelphia	42
1935—	William Herman, Chicago	57
1936—	Joseph Medwick, St. Louis	64
1937—	Joseph Medwick, St. Louis	56
1938—	Joseph Medwick, St. Louis	47
1939—	Enos Slaughter, St. Louis	52
1940—	Frank McCormick, Cincinnati	44
1941—	Reiser, Brooklyn-Mize, St. Louis	39
1942—	Martin Marion, St. Louis	38
1943—	Stanley Musial, St. Louis	48
1944—	Stanley Musial, St. Louis	51
1945—	Thomas Holmes, Boston	47
1946—	Stanley Musial, St. Louis	50
1947—	Edward Miller, Cincinnati	38
1948—	Stanley Musial, St. Louis	46
1949—	Stanley Musial, St. Louis	41
1950—	Al (Red) Schoendienst, St. Louis	43
1951—	Alvin Dark, New York	41
1952—	Stanley Musial, St. Louis	42
1953—	Stanley Musial, St. Louis	53
1954—	Stanley Musial, St. Louis	41
1955—	Logan, Milwaukee-Aaron, Milwaukee	37
1956—	Henry Aaron, Milwaukee	34
1957—	Donald Hoak, Cincinnati	39
1958—	Orlando Cepeda, San Francisco	38
1959—	Vada Pinson, Cincinnati	47
1960—	Vada Pinson, Cincinnati	37
1961—	Henry Aaron, Milwaukee	39
1962—	Frank Robinson, Cincinnati	51
1963—	Richard Groat, St. Louis	43
1964—	A. Lee Maye, Milwaukee	44
1965—	Henry Aaron, Milwaukee	40
1966—	John Callison, Philadelphia	40
1967—	Daniel Staub, Houston	44
1968—	Louis Brock, St. Louis	46
1969—	Mateo Alou, Pittsburgh	41
1970—	M. Wesley Parker, Los Angeles	47
1971—	Cesar Cedeno, Houston	40
1972—	Cesar Cedeno, Houston	39
	Guillermo Montanez, Philadelphia	39
1973—	Wilver Stargell, Pittsburgh	43
1974—	Peter Rose, Cincinnati	45
1975—	Peter Rose, Cincinnati	47
1976—	Peter Rose, Cincinnati	42
1977—	David Parker, Pittsburgh	44
1978—	Peter Rose, Cincinnati	51
1979—	Keith Hernandez, St. Louis	48
1980—	Peter Rose, Philadelphia	42

THREE-BASE HIT LEADERS

Year	Player and Club	3B.	Year	Player and Club	3B.
1900—	John (Honus) Wagner, Pittsburgh	22	1942—	Enos Slaughter, St. Louis	17
1901—	James Sheckard, Brooklyn	21	1943—	Stanley Musial, St. Louis	20
1902—	Samuel Crawford, Cincinnati	23	1944—	John Barrett, Pittsburgh	19
1903—	John (Honus) Wagner, Pittsburgh	19	1945—	Luis Olmo, Brooklyn	13
1904—	Harry Lumley, Brooklyn	18	1946—	Stanley Musial, St. Louis	20
1905—	J. Bentley Seymour, Cincinnati	21	1947—	Harry Walker, St. Louis-Philadelphia	16
1906—	Clarke, Pittsburgh-Schulte, Chicago	13	1948—	Stanley Musial, St. Louis	18
1907—	Ganzel, Cincinnati-Alperman, Brooklyn	16	1949—	Musial, St. Louis-Slaughter, St. Louis	13
1908—	John (Honus) Wagner, Pittsburgh	19	1950—	Richie Ashburn, Philadelphia	14
1909—	Michael Mitchell, Cincinnati	17	1951—	Musial, St. Louis-Bell, Pittsburgh	12
1910—	Michael Mitchell, Cincinnati	18	1952—	Robert Thomson, New York	14
1911—	Lawrence Doyle, New York	25	1953—	James Gilliam, Brooklyn	17
1912—	John (Chief) Wilson, Pittsburgh	36	1954—	Willie Mays, New York	13
1913—	Victor Saier, Chicago	21	1955—	Mays, New York-Long, Pittsburgh	13
1914—	Max Carey, Pittsburgh	17	1956—	William Bruton, Milwaukee	15
1915—	Thomas Long, St. Louis	25	1957—	Willie Mays, New York	20
1916—	William Hinchman, Pittsburgh	16	1958—	Richie Ashburn, Philadelphia	13
1917—	Rogers Hornsby, St. Louis	17	1959—	Moon, Los Angeles-Neal, Los Angeles	11
1918—	Jacob Daubert, Brooklyn	15	1960—	William Bruton, Milwaukee	13
1919—	Hi Myers, Brooklyn-Southworth, Pitt.	14	1961—	George Altman, Chicago	12
1920—	Henry (Hi) Myers, Brooklyn	22	1962—	Callison, Philadelphia-Virdon, Pitt.	10
1921—	Hornsby, St. Louis-Powell, Boston	18		W. Davis, Wills, Los Angeles	10
1922—	Jacob Daubert, Cincinnati	22	1963—	Vada Pinson, Cincinnati	14
1923—	Carey, Pittsburgh-Traynor, Pittsburgh	19	1964—	Allen, Philadelphia-Santo, Chicago	13
1924—	Edd Roush, Cincinnati	21	1965—	John Callison, Philadelphia	16
1925—	Hazen (Kiki) Cuyler, Pittsburgh	26	1966—	J. Timothy McCarver, St. Louis	13
1926—	Paul Waner, Pittsburgh	22	1967—	Vada Pinson, Cincinnati	13
1927—	Paul Waner, Pittsburgh	17	1968—	Louis Brock, St. Louis	14
1928—	James Bottomley, St. Louis	20	1969—	Roberto Clemente, Pittsburgh	12
1929—	Lloyd Waner, Pittsburgh	20	1970—	William Davis, Los Angeles	16
1930—	Adam Comorosky, Pittsburgh	23	1971—	Joe Morgan, Houston	11
1931—	William Terry, New York	20		Roger Metzger, Houston	11
1932—	Floyd (Babe) Herman, Cincinnati	19	1972—	Lawrence Bowa, Philadelphia	13
1933—	J. Floyd (Arky) Vaughan, Pittsburgh	19	1973—	Roger Metzger, Houston	14
1934—	Joseph Medwick, St. Louis	18	1974—	Ralph Garr, Atlanta	17
1935—	Ival Goodman, Cincinnati	18	1975—	Ralph Garr, Atlanta	11
1936—	Ival Goodman, Cincinnati	14	1976—	David Cash, Philadelphia	12
1937—	J. Floyd (Arky) Vaughan, Pittsburgh	17	1977—	Garry Templeton, St. Louis	18
1938—	John Mize, St. Louis	16	1978—	Garry Templeton, St. Louis	13
1939—	William Herman, Chicago	18	1979—	Garry Templeton, St. Louis	19
1940—	J. Floyd (Arky) Vaughan, Pittsburgh	15	1980—	Omar Moreno, Pittsburgh	13
1941—	Harold (Pete) Reiser, Brooklyn	17		Rodney Scott, Montreal	13

HOME RUN LEADERS

Year	Player and Club	HR.	Year	Player and Club	HR.
1900—	Herman Long, Boston	12	1919—	Cliff. (Gavvy) Cravath, Philadelphia	12
1901—	Samuel Crawford, Cincinnati	16	1920—	Fred (Cy) Williams, Philadelphia	15
1902—	Thomas Leach, Pittsburgh	6	1921—	George Kelly, New York	23
1903—	James Sheckard, Brooklyn	9	1922—	Rogers Hornsby, St. Louis	42
1904—	Harry Lumley, Brooklyn	9	1923—	Fred (Cy) Williams, Philadelphia	41
1905—	Fred Odwell, Cincinnati	9	1924—	Jacques Fournier, Brooklyn	27
1906—	Timothy Jordan, Brooklyn	12	1925—	Rogers Hornsby, St. Louis	39
1907—	David Brain, Boston	10	1926—	Lewis (Hack) Wilson, Chicago	21
1908—	Timothy Jordan, Brooklyn	12	1927—	Wilson, Chicago-Williams, Philadelphia	30
1909—	John (Red) Murray, New York	7	1928—	Wilson, Chicago-Bottomley, St. Louis	31
1910—	Fred Beck, Bos.-F. Schulte, Chi.	10	1929—	Charles Klein, Philadelphia	43
1911—	Frank Schulte, Chicago	21	1930—	Lewis (Hack) Wilson, Chicago	56
1912—	Henry Zimmerman, Chicago	14	1931—	Charles Klein, Philadelphia	31
1913—	Cliff. (Gavvy) Cravath, Philadelphia	19	1932—	Klein, Philadelphia-Ott, New York	38
1914—	Cliff. (Gavvy) Cravath, Philadelphia	19	1933—	Charles Klein, Philadelphia	28
1915—	Cliff. (Gavvy) Cravath, Philadelphia	24	1934—	Collins, St. Louis-Ott, New York	35
1916—	Robertson, New York-Williams, Chi.	12	1935—	Walter Berger, Boston	34
1917—	Robertson, New York-Cravath, Phila.	12	1936—	Melvin Ott, New York	33
1918—	Cliff. (Gavvy) Cravath, Philadelphia	8	1937—	Ott, New York-Medwick, St. Louis	31

HOME RUN LEADERS—Continued

Year Player and Club	HR.	Year Player and Club	HR.
1938— Melvin Ott, New York	36	1960— Ernest Banks, Chicago	41
1939— John Mize, St. Louis	28	1961— Orlando Cepeda, San Francisco	46
1940— John Mize, St. Louis	43	1962— Willie Mays, San Francisco	49
1941— Adolph Camilli, Brooklyn	34	1963— H. Aaron, Milw.-McCovey, San Fran.	44
1942— Melvin Ott, New York	30	1964— Willie Mays, San Francisco	47
1943— William Nicholson, Chicago	29	1965— Willie Mays, San Francisco	52
1944— William Nicholson, Chicago	33	1966— Henry Aaron, Atlanta	44
1945— Thomas Holmes, Boston	28	1967— Henry Aaron, Atlanta	39
1946— Ralph Kiner, Pittsburgh	23	1968— Willie McCovey, San Francisco	36
1947— Kiner, Pittsburgh-Mize, New York	51	1969— Willie McCovey, San Francisco	45
1948— Kiner, Pittsburgh-Mize, New York	40	1970— Johnny Bench, Cincinnati	45
1949— Ralph Kiner, Pittsburgh	54	1971— Wilver Stargell, Pittsburgh	48
1950— Ralph Kiner, Pittsburgh	47	1972— Johnny Bench, Cincinnati	40
1951— Ralph Kiner, Pittsburgh	42	1973— Wilver Stargell, Pittsburgh	44
1952— Kiner, Pittsburgh-Sauer, Chicago	37	1974— Michael Schmidt, Philadelphia	36
1953— Edwin Mathews, Milwaukee	47	1975— Michael Schmidt, Philadelphia	38
1954— Theodore Kluszewski, Cincinnati	49	1976— Michael Schmidt, Philadelphia	38
1955— Willie Mays, New York	51	1977— George Foster, Cincinnati	52
1956— Edwin (Duke) Snider, Brooklyn	43	1978— George Foster, Cincinnati	40
1957— Henry Aaron, Milwaukee	44	1979— David Kingman, Chicago	48
1958— Ernest Banks, Chicago	47	1980— Michael Schmidt, Philadelphia	48
1959— Edwin Mathews, Milwaukee	46		

LEADERS IN TOTAL BASES

Year Player and Club	T.B.	Year Player and Club	T.B.
1900— John (Honus) Wagner, Pittsburgh	302	1940— John Mize, St. Louis	368
Elmer Flick, Philadelphia	302	1941— Harold (Pete) Reiser, Brooklyn	299
1901— Jesse Burkett, St. Louis	314	1942— Enos Slaughter, St. Louis	292
1902— Samuel Crawford, Cincinnati	256	1943— Stanley Musial, St. Louis	347
1903— Clarence Beaumont, Pittsburgh	272	1944— William Nicholson, Chicago	317
1904— John (Honus) Wagner, Pittsburgh	255	1945— Thomas Holmes, Boston	367
1905— J. Bentley Seymour, Cincinnati	325	1946— Stanley Musial, St. Louis	366
1906— John (Honus) Wagner, Pittsburgh	237	1947— Ralph Kiner, Pittsburgh	361
1907— John (Honus) Wagner, Pittsburgh	264	1948— Stanley Musial, St. Louis	429
1908— John (Honus) Wagner, Pittsburgh	308	1949— Stanley Musial, St. Louis	382
1909— John (Honus) Wagner, Pittsburgh	242	1950— Edwin (Duke) Snider, Brooklyn	343
1910— Sherwood Magee, Philadelphia	263	1951— Stanley Musial, St. Louis	355
1911— Frank Schulte, Chicago	308	1952— Stanley Musial, St. Louis	311
1912— Henry Zimmerman, Chicago	318	1953— Edwin (Duke) Snider, Brooklyn	370
1913— Cliff (Gavvy) Cravath, Philadelphia	298	1954— Edwin (Duke) Snider, Brooklyn	378
1914— Sherwood Magee, Philadelphia	277	1955— Willie Mays, New York	382
1915— Cliff (Gavvy) Cravath, Philadelphia	266	1956— Henry Aaron, Milwaukee	340
1916— Zachariah Wheat, Brooklyn	262	1957— Henry Aaron, Milwaukee	369
1917— Rogers Hornsby, St. Louis	253	1958— Ernest Banks, Chicago	379
1918— Charles Hollocher, Chicago	202	1959— Henry Aaron, Milwaukee	400
1919— Henry (Hi) Myers, Brooklyn	223	1960— Henry Aaron, Milwaukee	334
1920— Rogers Hornsby, St. Louis	329	1961— Henry Aaron, Milwaukee	358
1921— Rogers Hornsby, St. Louis	378	1962— Willie Mays, San Francisco	382
1922— Rogers Hornsby, St. Louis	450	1963— Henry Aaron, Milwaukee	370
1923— Frank Frisch, New York	311	1964— Richard Allen, Philadelphia	352
1924— Rogers Hornsby, St. Louis	373	1965— Willie Mays, San Francisco	360
1925— Rogers Hornsby, St. Louis	381	1966— Felipe Alou, Atlanta	355
1926— James Bottomley, St. Louis	305	1967— Henry Aaron, Atlanta	344
1927— Paul Waner, Pittsburgh	338	1968— Billy Williams, Chicago	321
1928— James Bottomley, St. Louis	362	1969— Henry Aaron, Atlanta	332
1929— Rogers Hornsby, Chicago	445	1970— Billy Williams, Chicago	373
1930— Charles Klein, Philadelphia	445	1971— Joseph Torre, St. Louis	352
1931— Charles Klein, Philadelphia	347	1972— Billy Williams, Chicago	348
1932— Charles Klein, Philadelphia	420	1973— Bobby Bonds, San Francisco	341
1933— Charles Klein, Philadelphia	365	1974— Johnny Bench, Cincinnati	315
1934— James (Rip) Collins, St. Louis	369	1975— Gregory Luzinski, Philadelphia	322
1935— Joseph Medwick, St. Louis	365	1976— Michael Schmidt, Philadelphia	306
1936— Joseph Medwick, St. Louis	367	1977— George Foster, Cincinnati	388
1937— Joseph Medwick, St. Louis	406	1978— David Parker, Pittsburgh	340
1938— John Mize, St. Louis	326	1979— David Winfield, San Diego	333
1939— John Mize, St. Louis	353	1980— Michael Schmidt, Philadelphia	342

RUNS BATTED IN LEADERS

Year	Player and Club	RBI
1907	John (Honus) Wagner, Pittsburgh	91
1908	John (Honus) Wagner, Pittsburgh	106
1909	John (Honus) Wagner, Pittsburgh	102
1910	Sherwood Magee, Philadelphia	116
1911	Frank Schulte, Chicago	121
1912	Henry Zimmerman, Chicago	98
1913	Cliff (Gavvy) Cravath, Philadelphia	118
1914	Sherwood Magee, Philadelphia	101
1915	Cliff (Gavvy) Cravath, Philadelphia	118
1916	Harold Chase, Cincinnati	84
1917	Henry Zimmerman, New York	100
1918	Frederick Merkle, Chicago	71
1919	Henry (Hi) Myers, Brooklyn	72
1920	George Kelly, New York	94
	Rogers Hornsby, St. Louis	94
1921	Rogers Hornsby, St. Louis	126
1922	Rogers Hornsby, St. Louis	152
1923	Emil Meusel, New York	125
1924	George Kelly, New York	136
1925	Rogers Hornsby, St. Louis	143
1926	James Bottomley, St. Louis	120
1927	Paul Waner, Pittsburgh	131
1928	James Bottomley, St. Louis	136
1929	Lewis (Hack) Wilson, Chicago	159
1930	Lewis (Hack) Wilson, Chicago	190
1931	Charles Klein, Philadelphia	121
1932	Frank (Don) Hurst, Philadelphia	143
1933	Charles Klein, Philadelphia	120
1934	Melvin Ott, New York	135
1935	Walter Berger, Boston	130
1936	Joseph Medwick, St. Louis	138
1937	Joseph Medwick, St. Louis	154
1938	Joseph Medwick, St. Louis	122
1939	Frank McCormick, Cincinnati	128
1940	John Mize, St. Louis	137
1941	Adolph Camilli, Brooklyn	120
1942	John Mize, New York	110
1943	William Nicholson, Chicago	128
1944	William Nicholson, Chicago	122
1945	Fred (Dixie) Walker, Brooklyn	124
1946	Enos Slaughter, St. Louis	130
1947	John Mize, New York	138
1948	Stanley Musial, St. Louis	131
1949	Ralph Kiner, Pittsburgh	127
1950	Delmer Ennis, Philadelphia	126
1951	Monford Irvin, New York	121
1952	Henry Sauer, Chicago	121
1953	Roy Campanella, Brooklyn	142
1954	Theodore Kluszewski, Cincinnati	141
1955	Edwin (Duke) Snider, Brooklyn	136
1956	Stanley Musial, St. Louis	109
1957	Henry Aaron, Milwaukee	132
1958	Ernest Banks, Chicago	129
1959	Ernest Banks, Chicago	143
1960	Henry Aaron, Milwaukee	126
1961	Orlando Cepeda, San Francisco	142
1962	H. Thomas Davis, Los Angeles	153
1963	Henry Aaron, Milwaukee	130
1964	Kenton Boyer, St. Louis	119
1965	Deron Johnson, Cincinnati	130
1966	Henry Aaron, Atlanta	127
1967	Orlando Cepeda, St. Louis	111
1968	Willie McCovey, San Francisco	105
1969	Willie McCovey, San Francisco	126
1970	Johnny Bench, Cincinnati	148
1971	Joseph Torre, St. Louis	137
1972	Johnny Bench, Cincinnati	125
1973	Wilver Stargell, Pittsburgh	119
1974	Johnny Bench, Cincinnati	129
1975	Gregory Luzinski, Philadelphia	120
1976	George Foster, Cincinnati	121
1977	George Foster, Cincinnati	149
1978	George Foster, Cincinnati	120
1979	David Winfield, San Diego	118
1980	Michael Schmidt, Philadelphia	121

Note—Runs batted in not compiled prior to 1907; officially adopted in 1920.

BATTERS LEADING IN BASES ON BALLS

Year	Player and Club	BB.
1910	Miller Huggins, St. Louis	116
1911	James Sheckard, Chicago	147
1912	James Sheckard, Chicago	122
1913	Robert Bescher, Cincinnati	94
1914	Miller Huggins, St. Louis	105
1915	Cliff. (Gavvy) Cravath, Philadelphia	86
1916	Henry Groh, Cincinnati	84
1917	George Burns, New York	75
1918	Max Carey, Pittsburgh	62
1919	George Burns, New York	82
1920	George Burns, New York	76
1921	George Burns, New York	80
1922	Max Carey, Pittsburgh	80
1923	George Burns, New York	101
1924	Rogers Hornsby, St. Louis	89
1925	Jacques Fournier, Brooklyn	86
1926	Lewis (Hack) Wilson, Chicago	69
1927	Rogers Hornsby, New York	86
1928	Rogers Hornsby, Boston	107
1929	Melvin Ott, New York	113
1930	Lewis (Hack) Wilson, Chicago	105
1931	Melvin Ott, New York	80
1932	Melvin Ott, New York	100
1933	Melvin Ott, New York	75
1934	J. Floyd (Arky) Vaughan, Pittsburgh	94
1935	J. Floyd (Arky) Vaughan, Pittsburgh	97
1936	J. Floyd (Arky) Vaughan, Pittsburgh	118
1937	Melvin Ott, New York	102
1938	Adolph Camilli, Brooklyn	119
1939	Adolph Camilli, Brooklyn	110
1940	Elburt Fletcher, Pittsburgh	119
1941	Elburt Fletcher, Pittsburgh	118
1942	Melvin Ott, New York	109
1943	August Galan, Brooklyn	103
1944	August Galan, Brooklyn	101
1945	Edward Stanky, Brooklyn	148
1946	Edward Stanky, Brooklyn	137
1947	Henry Greenberg, Pittsburgh	104
	Harold (Pee Wee) Reese, Brooklyn	104
1948	Robert Elliott, Boston	131
1949	Ralph Kiner, Pittsburgh	117
1950	Edward Stanky, New York	144
1951	Ralph Kiner, Pittsburgh	137
1952	Ralph Kiner, Pittsburgh	110
1953	Stanley Musial, St. Louis	105
1954	Richie Ashburn, Philadelphia	125

BATTERS LEADING IN BASES ON BALLS—Continued

Year	Player and Club	BB.
1955—	Edwin Mathews, Milwaukee	109
1956—	Edwin (Duke) Snider, Brooklyn	99
1957—	Richie Ashburn, Philadelphia	94
	John Temple, Cincinnati	94
1958—	Richie Ashburn, Philadelphia	97
1959—	James Gilliam, Los Angeles	96
1960—	Richie Ashburn, Chicago	116
1961—	Edwin Mathews, Milwaukee	93
1962—	Edwin Mathews, Milwaukee	101
1963—	Edwin Mathews, Milwaukee	124
1964—	Ronald Santo, Chicago	86
1965—	Joe Morgan, Houston	97
1966—	Ronald Santo, Chicago	95
1967—	Ronald Santo, Chicago	96

Year	Player and Club	BB.
1968—	Ronald Santo, Chicago	96
1969—	James Wynn, Houston	148
1970—	Willie McCovey, San Francisco	137
1971—	Willie Mays, San Francisco	112
1972—	Joe Morgan, Cincinnati	115
1973—	Darrell Evans, Atlanta	124
1974—	Darrell Evans, Atlanta	126
1975—	Joe Morgan, Cincinnati	132
1976—	James Wynn, Atlanta	127
1977—	F. Gene Tenace, San Diego	125
1978—	Jeffrey Burroughs, Atlanta	117
1979—	Michael Schmidt, Philadelphia	120
1980—	Daniel Driessen, Cincinnati	93
	Joe Morgan, Houston	93

Note—Bases on balls not included in batting records in National League prior to 1910.

BATTERS LEADING IN STRIKEOUTS

Year	Player and Club	SO.
1910—	John Hummell, Brooklyn	81
1911—	Robert Coulson, Brooklyn	78
	Robert Bescher, Cincinnati	78
1912—	Edward McDonald, Boston	91
1913—	George Burns, New York	74
1914—	Frederick Merkle, New York	80
1915—	H. Douglas Baird, Pittsburgh	88
1916—	Cliff. (Gavvy) Cravath, Philadelphia	89
1917—	Fred Williams, Chicago	78
1918—	Ross Youngs, New York	49
	George Paskert, Chicago	49
1919—	Raymond Powell, Boston	79
1920—	George Kelly, New York	92
1921—	Raymond Powell, Boston	85
1922—	Frank Parkinson, Philadelphia	93
1923—	George Grantham, Chicago	92
1924—	George Grantham, Chicago	63
1925—	Chas. (Gabby) Hartnett, Chicago	77
1926—	Bernard Friberg, Philadelphia	77
1927—	Lewis (Hack) Wilson, Chicago	70
1928—	Lewis (Hack) Wilson, Chicago	94
1929—	Lewis (Hack) Wilson, Chicago	83
1930—	Lewis (Hack) Wilson, Chicago	84
1931—	H. Nicholas Cullop, Cincinnati	86
1932—	Lewis (Hack) Wilson, Brooklyn	85
1933—	Walter Berger, Boston	77
1934—	Adolph Camilli, Chicago-Philadelphia	94
1935—	Adolph Camilli, Philadelphia	113
1936—	Wilbur Brubaker, Pittsburgh	96
1937—	Vincent DiMaggio, Boston	111
1938—	Vincent DiMaggio, Boston	134
1939—	Adolph Camilli, Brooklyn	107
1940—	Chester Ross, Boston	128
1941—	Adolph Camilli, Brooklyn	115
1942—	Vincent DiMaggio, Pittsburgh	87
1943—	Vincent DiMaggio, Pittsburgh	126
1944—	Vincent DiMaggio, Pittsburgh	83

Year	Player and Club	SO.
1945—	Vincent DiMaggio, Philadelphia	91
1946—	Ralph Kiner, Pittsburgh	109
1947—	William Nicholson, Chicago	83
1948—	Henry Sauer, Cincinnati	85
1949—	Edwin (Duke) Snider, Brooklyn	92
1950—	Roy Smalley, Chicago	114
1951—	Gilbert Hodges, Brooklyn	99
1952—	Edwin Mathews, Boston	115
1953—	Stephen Bilko, St. Louis	125
1954—	Edwin (Duke) Snider, Brooklyn	96
1955—	Walter Post, Cincinnati	102
1956—	Walter Post, Cincinnati	124
1957—	Edwin (Duke) Snider, Brooklyn	104
1958—	Harry Anderson, Philadelphia	95
1959—	Walter Post, Philadelphia	101
1960—	J. Francisco Herrera, Philadelphia	136
1961—	Richard Stuart, Pittsburgh	121
1962—	Kenneth Hubbs, Chicago	129
1963—	Donn Clendenon, Pittsburgh	136
1964—	Richard Allen, Philadelphia	138
1965—	Richard Allen, Philadelphia	150
1966—	Byron Browne, Chicago	143
1967—	James Wynn, Houston	137
1968—	Donn Clendenon, Pittsburgh	163
1969—	Bobby Bonds, San Francisco	187
1970—	Bobby Bonds, San Francisco	189
1971—	Wilver Stargell, Pittsburgh	154
1972—	Lee May, Houston	145
1973—	Bobby Bonds, San Francisco	148
1974—	Michael Schmidt, Philadelphia	138
1975—	Michael Schmidt, Philadelphia	180
1976—	Michael Schmidt, Philadelphia	149
1977—	Gregory Luzinski, Philadelphia	140
1978—	Dale Murphy, Atlanta	145
1979—	David Kingman, Chicago	131
1980—	Dale Murphy, Atlanta	133

Note—Strikeouts not included in batting records in National League prior to 1910.

LEADING BASE STEALERS

Year	Player and Club	SB.
1900—	James Barrett, Cincinnati	46
1901—	John (Honus) Wagner, Pittsburgh	48

Year	Player and Club	SB.
1902—	John (Honus) Wagner, Pittsburgh	43
1903—	Sheckard, Brooklyn-Chance, Chicago	67

LEADING BASE STEALERS—Continued

Year	Player and Club	SB.
1904—	John (Honus) Wagner, Pittsburgh	58
1905—	Maloney, Chicago-Devlin, New York	59
1906—	Frank Chance, Chicago	57
1907—	John (Honus) Wagner, Pittsburgh	61
1908—	John (Honus) Wagner, Pittsburgh	53
1909—	Robert Bescher, Cincinnati	54
1910—	Robert Bescher, Cincinnati	70
1911—	Robert Bescher, Cincinnati	80
1912—	Robert Bescher, Cincinnati	67
1913—	Max Carey, Pittsburgh	61
1914—	George Burns, New York	62
1915—	Max Carey, Pittsburgh	36
1916—	Max Carey, Pittsburgh	63
1917—	Max Carey, Pittsburgh	46
1918—	Max Carey, Pittsburgh	58
1919—	George Burns, New York	40
1920—	Max Carey, Pittsburgh	52
1921—	Frank Frisch, New York	49
1922—	Max Carey, Pittsburgh	51
1923—	Max Carey, Pittsburgh	51
1924—	Max Carey, Pittsburgh	49
1925—	Max Carey, Pittsburgh	46
1926—	Hazen (Kiki) Cuyler, Pittsburgh	35
1927—	Frank Frisch, St. Louis	48
1928—	Hazen (Kiki) Cuyler, Chicago	37
1929—	Hazen (Kiki) Cuyler, Chicago	43
1930—	Hazen (Kiki) Cuyler, Chicago	37
1931—	Frank Frisch, St. Louis	28
1932—	Charles Klein, Philadelphia	20
1933—	John (Pepper) Martin, St. Louis	26
1934—	John (Pepper) Martin, St. Louis	23
1935—	August Galan, Chicago	22
1936—	John (Pepper) Martin, St. Louis	23
1937—	August Galan, Chicago	23
1938—	Stanley Hack, Chicago	16
1939—	Hack, Chicago-Handley, Pittsburgh	17
1940—	Linus Frey, Cincinnati	22
1941—	Daniel Murtaugh, Philadelphia	18
1942—	Harold (Pete) Reiser, Brooklyn	20
1943—	J. Floyd (Arky) Vaughan, Brooklyn	20
1944—	John Barrett, Pittsburgh	28
1945—	Al. (Red) Schoendienst, St. Louis	26
1946—	Harold (Pete) Reiser, Brooklyn	34
1947—	Jack Robinson, Brooklyn	29
1948—	Richie Ashburn, Philadelphia	32
1949—	Jack Robinson, Brooklyn	37
1950—	Samuel Jethroe, Boston	35
1951—	Samuel Jethroe, Boston	35
1952—	Harold (Pee Wee) Reese, Brooklyn	30
1953—	William Bruton, Milwaukee	26
1954—	William Bruton, Milwaukee	34
1955—	William Bruton, Milwaukee	35
1956—	Willie Mays, New York	40
1957—	Willie Mays, New York	38
1958—	Willie Mays, San Francisco	31
1959—	Willie Mays, San Francisco	27
1960—	Maurice Wills, Los Angeles	50
1961—	Maurice Wills, Los Angeles	35
1962—	Maurice Wills, Los Angeles	104
1963—	Maurice Wills, Los Angeles	40
1964—	Maurice Wills, Los Angeles	53
1965—	Maurice Wills, Los Angeles	94
1966—	Louis Brock, St. Louis	74
1967—	Louis Brock, St. Louis	52
1968—	Louis Brock, St. Louis	62
1969—	Louis Brock, St. Louis	53
1970—	Robert Tolan, Cincinnati	57
1971—	Louis Brock, St. Louis	64
1972—	Louis Brock, St. Louis	63
1973—	Louis Brock, St. Louis	70
1974—	Louis Brock, St. Louis	118
1975—	David Lopes, Los Angeles	77
1976—	David Lopes, Los Angeles	63
1977—	Franklin Taveras, Pittsburgh	70
1978—	Omar Moreno, Pittsburgh	71
1979—	Omar Moreno, Pittsburgh	77
1980—	Ronald LeFlore, Montreal	97

SLUGGING LEADERS

Year	Player and Club	Slug. Avg.
1900—	John (Honus) Wagner, Pittsburgh	.572
1901—	James Sheckard, Brooklyn	.536
1902—	John (Honus) Wagner, Pittsburgh	.467
1903—	Fred Clarke, Pittsburgh	.532
1904—	John (Honus) Wagner, Pittsburgh	.520
1905—	J. Bentley Seymour, Cincinnati	.559
1906—	Harry Lumley, Brooklyn	477
1907—	John (Honus) Wagner, Pittsburgh	.513
1908—	John (Honus) Wagner, Pittsburgh	.542
1909—	John (Honus) Wagner, Pittsburgh	.489
1910—	Sherwood Magee, Philadelphia	.507
1911—	Frank Schulte, Chicago	.534
1912—	Henry Zimmerman, Chicago	.571
1913—	Cliff. (Gavvy) Cravath, Philadelphia	.568
1914—	Sherwood Magee, Philadelphia	.501
1915—	Cliff. (Gavvy) Cravath, Philadelphia	.510
1916—	Zachariah Wheat, Brooklyn	.461
1917—	Rogers Hornsby, St. Louis	.484
1918—	Edd Roush, Cincinnati	.455
1919—	Henry (Hi) Myers, Brooklyn	.436
1920—	Rogers Hornsby, St. Louis	.559
1921—	Rogers Hornsby, St. Louis	.659
1922—	Rogers Hornsby, St. Louis	.722
1923—	Rogers Hornsby, St. Louis	.627
1924—	Rogers Hornsby, St. Louis	.696
1925—	Rogers Hornsby, St. Louis	.756
1926—	Fred Williams, Philadelphia	.569
1927—	Charles Hafey, St. Louis	.590
1928—	Rogers Hornsby, Boston	.632
1929—	Rogers Hornsby, Chicago	.679
1930—	Lewis (Hack) Wilson, Chicago	.723
1931—	Charles Klein, Philadelphia	.584
1932—	Charles Klein, Philadelphia	.646
1933—	Charles Klein, Philadelphia	.602
1934—	James (Rip) Collins, St. Louis	.615
1935—	J. Floyd (Arky) Vaughan, Pittsburgh	.607
1936—	Melvin Ott, New York	.588
1937—	Joseph Medwick, St. Louis	.641
1938—	John Mize, St. Louis	.614
1939—	John Mize, St. Louis	.626
1940—	John Mize, St. Louis	.636
1941—	Harold (Pete) Reiser, Brooklyn	.558

SLUGGING LEADERS—Continued

Year	Player and Club	Slug. Avg.
1942	John Mize, New York	.521
1943	Stanley Musial, St. Louis	.562
1944	Stanley Musial, St. Louis	.549
1945	Tommy Holmes, Boston	.577
1946	Stanley Musial, St. Louis	.587
1947	Ralph Kiner, Pittsburgh	.639
1948	Stanley Musial, St. Louis	.702
1949	Ralph Kiner, Pittsburgh	.658
1950	Stanley Musial, St. Louis	.596
1951	Ralph Kiner, Pittsburgh	.627
1952	Stanley Musial, St. Louis	.538
1953	Edwin (Duke) Snider, Brooklyn	.6271
1954	Willie Mays, New York	.667
1955	Willie Mays, New York	.659
1956	Edwin (Duke) Snider, Brooklyn	.598
1957	Willie Mays, New York	.626
1958	Ernest Banks, Chicago	.614
1959	Henry Aaron, Milwaukee	.636
1960	Frank Robinson, Cincinnati	.595
1961	Frank Robinson, Cincinnati	.611
1962	Frank Robinson, Cincinnati	.624
1963	Henry Aaron, Milwaukee	.586
1964	Willie Mays, San Francisco	.607
1965	Willie Mays, San Francisco	.645
1966	Richard Allen, Philadelphia	.632
1967	Henry Aaron, Atlanta	.573
1968	Willie McCovey, San Francisco	.545
1969	Willie McCovey, San Francisco	.656
1970	Willie McCovey, San Francisco	.612
1971	Henry Aaron, Atlanta	.669
1972	Billy Williams, Chicago	.606
1973	Wilver Stargell, Pittsburgh	.646
1974	Michael Schmidt, Philadelphia	.546
1975	David Parker, Pittsburgh	.541
1976	Joe Morgan, Cincinnati	.576
1977	George Foster, Cincinnati	.631
1978	David Parker, Pittsburgh	.585
1979	David Kingman, Chicago	.613
1980	Michael Schmidt, Philadelphia	.624

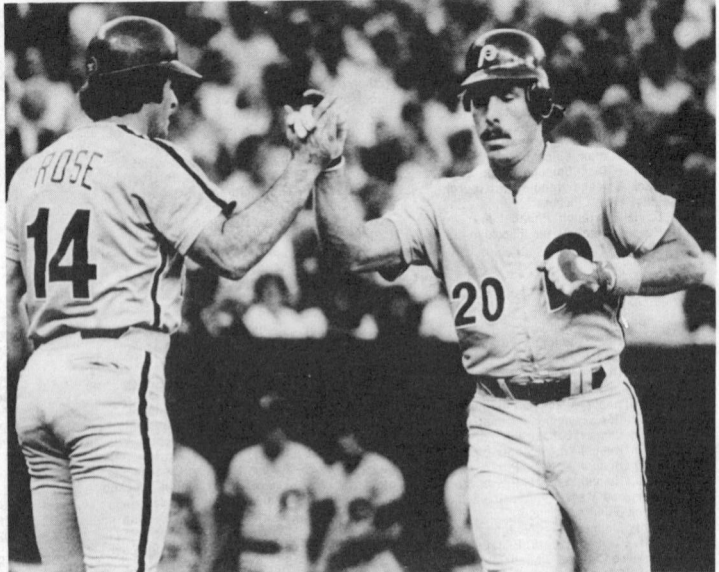

During 1980 season, MIKE SCHMIDT became the all-time Phillies' home run leader when he surpassed Del Ennis' total of 259. Here Schmidt is congratulated by Pete Rose after tying record. Schmidt also won his second N.L. slugging championship in '80.

LEADING PITCHERS IN WINNING PERCENTAGE

(15 OR MORE VICTORIES)

Year	Pitcher	Club	Won	Lost	Pct.
1900—Joseph McGinnity		Brooklyn	29	9	.763
1901—John Chesbro		Pittsburgh	21	9	.700
1902—John Chesbro		Pittsburgh	28	6	.824
1903—Samuel Leever		Pittsburgh	25	7	.781
1904—Joseph McGinnity		New York	35	8	.814
1905—Samuel Leever		Pittsburgh	20	5	.800
1906—Edward Reulbach		Chicago	19	4	.826
1907—Edward Reulbach		Chicago	17	4	.810
1908—Edward Reulbach		Chicago	24	7	.774
1909—Christy Mathewson		New York	25	6	.806
Howard Camnitz		Pittsburgh	25	6	.806
1910—Leonard Cole		Chicago	20	4	.833
1911—Richard (Rube) Marquard		New York	24	7	.774
1912—Claude Hendrix		Pittsburgh	24	9	.727
1913—Albert Humphries		Chicago	16	4	.800
1914—Williams James		Boston	26	7	.788
1915—Grover Alexander		Philadelphia	31	10	.756
1916—Thomas Hughes		Boston	16	3	.842
1917—Ferdinand Schupp		New York	21	7	.750
1918—Claude Hendrix		Chicago	20	7	.741
1919—Walter Ruether		Cincinnati	19	6	.760
1920—Burleigh Grimes		Brooklyn	23	11	.676
1921—William L. Doak		St. Louis	15	6	.714
1922—Peter Donohue		Cincinnati	18	9	.667
1923—Adolfo Luque		Cincinnati	27	8	.771
1924—Emil Yde		Pittsburgh	16	3	.842
1925—William Sherdel		St. Louis	15	6	.714
1926—Ray Kremer		Pittsburgh	20	6	.769
1927—Lawrence Benton		Boston-New York	17	7	.708
1928—Lawrence Benton		New York	25	9	.735
1929—Charles Root		Chicago	19	6	.760
1930—Fred Fitzsimmons		New York	19	7	.731
1931—Paul Derringer		St. Louis	18	8	.692
1932—Lonnie Warneke		Chicago	22	6	.786
1933—Benjamin Cantwell		Boston	20	10	.667
1934—Jerome (Dizzy) Dean		St. Louis	30	7	.811
1935—William Lee		Chicago	20	6	.769
1936—Carl Hubbell		New York	26	6	.813
1937—Carl Hubbell		New York	22	8	.733
1938—William Lee		Chicago	22	9	.710
1939—Paul Derringer		Cincinnati	25	7	.781
1940—Fred Fitzsimmons		Brooklyn	16	2	.889
1941—Elmer Riddle		Cincinnati	19	4	.826
1942—Lawrence French		Brooklyn	15	4	.789
1943—Morton Cooper		St. Louis	21	8	.724
1944—Theodore Wilks		St. Louis	17	4	.810
1945—Harry Breecheen		St. Louis	15	4	.789
1946—Murry Dickson		St. Louis	15	6	.714
1947—Lawrence Jansen		New York	21	5	.808
1948—Harry Brecheen		St. Louis	20	7	.741
1949—Elwin (Preacher) Roe		Brooklyn	15	6	.714
1950—Salvatore Maglie		New York	18	4	.818
1951—Elwin (Preacher) Roe		Brooklyn	22	3	.880
1952—J. Hoyt Wilhelm		New York	15	3	.833
1953—Carl Erskine		Brooklyn	20	6	.769
1954—John Antonelli		New York	21	7	.750
1955—Donald Newcombe		Brooklyn	20	5	.800
1956—Donald Newcombe		Brooklyn	27	7	.794
1957—Robert Buhl		Milwaukee	18	7	.720
1958—Warren E. Spahn		Milwaukee	22	11	.667
S. Lewis Burdette		Milwaukee	20	10	.667
1959—ElRoy Face		Pittsburgh	18	1	.947
1960—Ernest Broglio		St. Louis	21	9	.700
1961—John Podres		Los Angeles	18	5	.783

LEADING PITCHERS IN WINNING PERCENTAGE—Continued

(15 OR MORE VICTORIES)

Year	Pitcher	Club	Won	Lost	Pct.
1962—Robert Purkey		Cincinnati	23	5	.821
1963—Ronald Perranoski		Los Angeles	16	3	.842
1964—Sanford Koufax		Los Angeles	19	5	.792
1965—Sanford Koufax		Los Angeles	26	8	.765
1966—Juan Marichal		San Francisco	25	6	.806
1967—Richard Hughes		St. Louis	16	6	.727
1968—Stephen R. Blass		Pittsburgh	18	6	.750
1969—G. Thomas Seaver		New York	25	7	.781
1970—Robert Gibson		St. Louis	23	7	.767
1971—Donald E. Gullett		Cincinnati	16	6	.727
1972—Gary L. Nolan		Cincinnati	15	5	.750
1973—Thomas E. John		Los Angeles	16	7	.696
1974—John (Andy) Messersmith		Los Angeles	20	6	.769
1975—Donald E. Gullett		Cincinnati	15	4	.789
1976—Steven N. Carlton		Philadelphia	20	7	.741
1977—John R. Candelaria		Pittsburgh	20	5	.800
1978—Gaylord J. Perry		San Diego	21	6	.778
1979—G. Thomas Seaver		Cincinnati	16	6	.727
1980—James Bibby		Pittsburgh	19	6	.760

LEADING PITCHERS—EARNED-RUN AVERAGE

(Based on Ten Complete Games Through 1950, Then 154 Innings Until N. L. Expanded in 1962, When It Became 162 Innings)

Year	Pitcher and Club	G.	IP.	ERA.	Year	Pitcher and Club	G.	IP.	ERA.
1912—Tesreau, New York	36	243	1.96	1947—Spahn, Boston	40	290	2.33
1913—Mathewson, New York	40	306	2.06	1948—Brecheen, St. Louis	33	233	2.24
1914—Doak, St. Louis	36	256	1.72	1949—Koslo, New York	38	212	2.50
1915—Alexander, Philadelphia	49	376	1.22	1950—Hearn, St. Louis-New York	22	134	2.49
1916—Alexander, Philadelphia	48	390	1.55	1951—Nichols, Boston	33	156	2.88
1917—Alexander, Philadelphia	45	388	1.83	1952—Wilhelm, New York	71	159	2.43
1918—Vaughn, Chicago	35	290	1.74	1953—Spahn, Milwaukee	35	266	2.10
1919—Alexander, Chicago	30	235	1.72	1954—Antonelli, New York	39	259	2.29
1920—Alexander, Chicago	46	363	1.91	1955—Friend, Pittsburgh	44	200	2.84
1921—Doak, St. Louis	32	209	2.58	1956—Burdette, Milwaukee	39	256	2.71
1922—Ryan, New York	46	192	3.00	1957—Podres, Brooklyn	31	196	2.66
1923—Luque, Cincinnati	41	322	1.93	1958—Miller, San Francisco	41	182	2.47
1924—Vance, Brooklyn	35	309	2.16	1959—S. Jones, San Francisco	50	271	2.82
1925—Luque, Cincinnati	36	291	2.63	1960—McCormick, San Francisco	40	253	2.70
1926—Kremer, Pittsburgh	37	231	2.61	1961—Spahn, Milwaukee	38	263	3.01
1927—Kremer, Pittsburgh	35	226	2.47	1962—Koufax, Los Angeles	28	184	2.54
1928—Vance, Brooklyn	38	280	2.09	1963—Koufax, Los Angeles	40	311	1.88
1929—Walker, New York	29	178	3.08	1964—Koufax, Los Angeles	29	223	1.74
1930—Vance, Brooklyn	35	259	2.61	1965—Koufax, Los Angeles	43	336	2.04
1931—Walker, New York	37	239	2.26	1966—Koufax, Los Angeles	41	323	1.73
1932—Warneke, Chicago	35	277	2.37	1967—P. Niekro, Atlanta	46	207	1.87
1933—Hubbell, New York	45	309	1.66	1968—Gibson, St. Louis	34	305	1.12
1934—Hubbell, New York	49	313	2.30	1969—Marichal, San Francisco	37	300	2.10
1935—Blanton, Pittsburgh	35	254	2.59	1970—Seaver, New York	37	291	2.81
1936—Hubbell, New York	42	304	2.31	1971—Seaver, New York	36	286	1.76
1937—Turner, Boston	33	257	2.38	1972—Carlton, Philadelphia	41	346	1.98
1938—W. Lee, Chicago	44	291	2.66	1973—Seaver, New York	36	290	2.08
1939—Walters, Cincinnati	39	319	2.29	1974—Capra, Atlanta	39	217	2.28
1940—Walters, Cincinnati	36	305	2.48	1975—Jones, San Diego	37	285	2.24
1941—E. Riddle, Cincinnati	33	217	2.24	1976—Denny, St. Louis	30	207	2.52
1942—M. Cooper, St. Louis	37	279	1.77	1977—Candelaria, Pittsburgh	33	231	2.34
1943—Pollet, St. Louis	16	118	1.75	1978—Swan, New York	29	207	2.43
1944—Heusser, Cincinnati	30	193	2.38	1979—Richard, Houston	38	292	2.71
1945—Borowy, Chicago	15	122	2.14	1980—Sutton, Los Angeles	32	212	2.21
1946—Pollet, St. Louis	40	266	2.10				

STRIKEOUT LEADERS—PITCHING

Year	Pitcher and Club	SO.
1900—	George (Rube) Waddell, Pittsburgh	133
1901—	Frank (Noodles) Hahn, Cincinnati	233
1902—	Victor Willis, Boston	226
1903—	Christopher Mathewson, New York	267
1904—	Christopher Mathewson, New York	212
1905—	Christopher Mathewson, New York	206
1906—	Frederick Beebe, Chicago-St. Louis	171
1907—	Christopher Mathewson, New York	178
1908—	Christopher Mathewson, New York	259
1909—	Orval Overall, Chicago	205
1910—	Christopher Mathewson, New York	190
1911—	Richard (Rube) Marquard, New York	237
1912—	Grover Alexander, Philadelphia	195
1913—	Thomas Seaton, Philadelphia	168
1914—	Grover Alexander, Philadelphia	214
1915—	Grover Alexander, Philadelphia	241
1916—	Grover Alexander, Philadelphia	167
1917—	Grover Alexander, Philadelphia	200
1918—	James (Hippo) Vaughn, Chicago	148
1919—	James (Hippo) Vaughn, Chicago	141
1920—	Grover Alexander, Chicago	173
1921—	Burleigh Grimes, Brooklyn	136
1922—	Arthur (Dazzy) Vance, Brooklyn	134
1923—	Arthur (Dazzy) Vance, Brooklyn	197
1924—	Arthur (Dazzy) Vance, Brooklyn	262
1925—	Arthur (Dazzy) Vance, Brooklyn	221
1926—	Arthur (Dazzy) Vance, Brooklyn	140
1927—	Arthur (Dazzy) Vance, Brooklyn	184
1928—	Arthur (Dazzy) Vance, Brooklyn	200
1929—	Perce (Pat) Malone, Chicago	166
1930—	William Hallahan, St. Louis	177
1931—	William Hallahan, St. Louis	159
1932—	Jerome (Dizzy) Dean, St. Louis	191
1933—	Jerome (Dizzy) Dean, St. Louis	199
1934—	Jerome (Dizzy) Dean, St. Louis	195
1935—	Jerome (Dizzy) Dean, St. Louis	182
1936—	Van Lingle Mungo, Brooklyn	238
1937—	Carl Hubbell, New York	159
1938—	Claiborne Bryant, Chicago	135
1939—	Claude Passeau, Philadelphia-Chicago	137
	William (Bucky) Walters, Cincinnati	137
1940—	W. Kirby Higbe, Philadelphia	137

Year	Pitcher and Club	SO.
1941—	John Vander Meer, Cincinnati	202
1942—	John Vander Meer, Cincinnati	186
1943—	John Vander Meer, Cincinnati	174
1944—	William Voiselle, New York	161
1945—	Elwin (Preacher) Roe, Pittsburgh	148
1946—	John Schmitz, Chicago	135
1947—	Ewell Blackwell, Cincinnati	193
1948—	Harry Brecheen, St. Louis	149
1949—	Warren Spahn, Boston	151
1950—	Warren Spahn, Boston	191
1951—	Warren Spahn, Boston	164
	Donald Newcombe, Brooklyn	164
1952—	Warren Spahn, Boston	183
1953—	Robin Roberts, Philadelphia	198
1954—	Robin Roberts, Philadelphia	185
1955—	Samuel Jones, Chicago	198
1956—	Samuel Jones, Chicago	176
1957—	John Sanford, Philadelphia	188
1958—	Samuel Jones, St. Louis	225
1959—	Donald Drysdale, Los Angeles	242
1960—	Donald Drysdale, Los Angeles	246
1961—	Sanford Koufax, Los Angeles	269
1962—	Donald Drysdale, Los Angeles	232
1963—	Sanford Koufax, Los Angeles	306
1964—	Robert Veale, Pittsburgh	250
1965—	Sanford Koufax, Los Angeles	382
1966—	Sanford Koufax, Los Angeles	317
1967—	James Bunning, Philadelphia	253
1968—	Robert Gibson, St. Louis	268
1969—	Ferguson Jenkins, Chicago	273
1970—	G. Thomas Seaver, New York	283
1971—	G. Thomas Seaver, New York	289
1972—	Steven Carlton, Philadelphia	310
1973—	G. Thomas Seaver, New York	251
1974—	Steven Carlton, Philadelphia	240
1975—	G. Thomas Seaver, New York	243
1976—	G. Thomas Seaver, New York	235
1977—	Philip Niekro, Atlanta	262
1978—	James R. Richard, Houston	303
1979—	James R. Richard, Houston	313
1980—	Steven Carlton, Philadelphia	286

SHUTOUT LEADERS

Year	Pitcher and Club	ShO.
1900—	Clark C. Griffith, Chicago	4
	Frank G. Hahn, Cincinnati	4
	Charles A. Nichols, Boston	4
	Denton T. Young, St. Louis	4
1901—	John D. Chesbro, Pittsburgh	6
	Albert L. Orth, Philadelphia	6
	Victor G. Willis, Boston	6
1902—	John D. Chesbro, Pittsburgh	8
	Christopher Mathewson, New York	8
1903—	Samuel W. Leever, Pittsburgh	7
1904—	Joseph J. McGinnity, New York	9
1905—	Christopher Mathewson, New York	9
1906—	Mordecai P. Brown, Chicago	9
1907—	Orval Overall, Chicago	9
	Christopher Mathewson, New York	9
1908—	Christopher Mathewson, New York	12
1909—	Orval Overall, Chicago	9
1910—	Earl L. Moore, Philadelphia	7

Year	Pitcher and Club	ShO.
1911—	Charles B. Adams, Pittsburgh	7
	Grover C. Alexander, Philadelphia	7
1912—	George N. Rucker, Brooklyn	6
1913—	Grover C. Alexander, Philadelphia	9
1914—	Charles M. Tesreau, New York	8
1915—	Grover C. Alexander, Philadelphia	12
1916—	Grover C. Alexander, Philadelphia	16
1917—	Grover C. Alexander, Philadelphia	8
1918—	George A. Tyler, Chicago	8
	James L. Vaughn, Chicago	8
1919—	Grover C. Alexander, Chicago	9
1920—	Charles B. Adams, Pittsburgh	8
1921—	Grover C. Alexander, Chicago	3
	Philip B. Douglas, New York	3
	Dana Filligim, Boston	3
	Adolph Luque, Cincinnati	3
	Clarence E. Mitchell, Brooklyn	3
	John D. Morrison, Pittsburgh	3

SHUTOUT LEADERS—Continued

Year	Pitcher and Club	ShO.
	Joseph C. Oeschger, Boston	3
	Jesse J. Haines, St. Louis	3
1922—	Arthur C. Vance, Brooklyn	6
1923—	Adolfo Luque, Cincinnati	6
1924—	Jesse L. Barnes, Boston	4
	A. Wilbur Cooper, Pittsburgh	4
	Remy P. Kremer, Pittsburgh	4
	Eppa Rixey, Cincinnati	4
	Allen S. Sothoron, St. Louis	4
	Emil O. Yde, Pittsburgh	4
1925—	Harold G. Carlson, Philadelphia	4
	Adolfo Luque, Cincinnati	4
	Arthur C. Vance, Brooklyn	4
1926—	Peter J. Donohue, Cincinnati	5
1927—	Jesse J. Haines, St. Louis	6
1928—	John F. Blake, Chicago	4
	Burleigh A. Grimes, Pittsburgh	4
	Charles F. Lucas, Cincinnati	4
	Douglas L. McWeeney, Brooklyn	4
	Arthur C. Vance, Brooklyn	4
1929—	Perce L. Malone, Chicago	5
1930—	Charles H. Root, Chicago	4
	Arthur C. Vance, Brooklyn	4
1931—	William H. Walker, New York	6
1932—	Lonnie Warneke, Chicago	4
	Jerome H. Dean, St. Louis	4
	Stephen A. Swetonic, Pittsburgh	4
1933—	Carl O. Hubbell, New York	10
1934—	Jerome H. Dean, St. Louis	7
1935—	Darrell E. Blanton, Pittsburgh	4
	Freddie L. Fitzsimmons, New York	4
	Lawrence H. French, Chicago	4
	Van L. Mungo, Brooklyn	4
	James D. Weaver, Pittsburgh	4
1936—	Darrell E. Blanton, Pittsburgh	4
	James O. Carleton, Chicago	4
	Lawrence H. French, Chicago	4
	William C. Lee, Chicago	4
	Alfred J. Smith, New York	4
	Williams H. Walters, Philadelphia	4
	Lonnie Warneke, Chicago	4
1937—	Louis H. Fette, Boston	5
	Lee T. Grissom, Cincinnati	5
	James R. Turner, Boston	5
1938—	William C. Lee, Chicago	9
1939—	Louis H. Fette, Boston	6
1940—	William L. Lohrman, New York	5
	Manuel L. Salvo, Boston	5
	J. Whitlow Wyatt, Brooklyn	5
1941—	J. Whitlow Wyatt, Brooklyn	7
1942—	Morton C. Cooper, St. Louis	10
1943—	Hiram G. Bithorn, Chicago	7
1944—	Morton C. Cooper, St. Louis	7
1945—	Claude W. Passeau, Chicago	5
1946—	Ewell Blackwell, Cincinnati	6
1947—	Warren E. Spahn, Boston	7
1948—	Harry D. Brecheen, St. Louis	7
1949—	Kenneth A. Heintzelman, Philadelphia	5
	Donald Newcombe, Brooklyn	5

Year	Pitcher and Club	ShO.
	Howard J. Pollet, St. Louis	5
	Kenneth D. Raffensberger, Cincinnati	5
1950—	James T. Hearn, New York	5
	Lawrence A. Jansen, New York	5
	Salvatore A. Maglie, New York	5
	Robin E. Roberts, Philadelphia	5
1951—	Warren E. Spahn, Boston	7
1952—	Salvatore A. Maglie, New York	7
	Ken D. Raffensberger, Cincinnati	7
	Curtis T. Simmons, Philadelphia	7
1953—	Harvey Haddix, St. Louis	6
1954—	John A. Antonelli, New York	6
1955—	Joseph H. Nuxhall, Cincinnati	5
1956—	John A. Antonelli, New York	6
	S. Lewis Burdette, Milwaukee	6
1957—	John L. Podres, Brooklyn	6
1958—	Carlton F. Willey, Milwaukee	4
1959—	John A. Antonelli, San Francisco	4
	Robert R. Buhl, Milwaukee	4
	S. Lewis Burdette, Milwaukee	4
	Roger L. Craig, Los Angeles	4
	Donald S. Drysdale, Los Angeles	4
	Sam Jones, San Francisco	4
	Warren E. Spahn, Milwaukee	4
1960—	John S. Sanford, San Francisco	6
1961—	Joseph R. Jay, Cincinnati	4
	Warren E. Spahn, Milwaukee	4
1962—	Robert B. Friend, Pittsburgh	5
	Robert Gibson, St. Louis	5
1963—	Sanford Koufax, Los Angeles	11
1964—	Sanford Koufax, Los Angeles	7
1965—	Juan A. Marichal, San Francisco	10
1966—	James P. Bunning, Philadelphia	5
	Robert Gibson, St. Louis	5
	Lawrence C. Jackson, Philadelphia	5
	Larry E. Jaster, St. Louis	5
	Sanford Koufax, Los Angeles	5
	James W. Maloney, Cincinnati	5
1967—	James P. Bunning, Philadelphia	6
1968—	Robert Gibson, St. Louis	13
1969—	Juan A. Marichal, San Francisco	8
1970—	Gaylord J. Perry, San Francisco	5
1971—	Stephen R. Blass, Pittsburgh	5
	Alphonso E. Downing, Los Angeles	5
	Robert Gibson, St. Louis	5
	Milton S. Pappas, Chicago	5
1972—	Donald H. Sutton, Los Angeles	9
1973—	John E. Billingham, Cincinnati	7
1974—	Jonathan T. Matlack, New York	7
1975—	John A. Messersmith, Los Angeles	7
1976—	Jonathan T. Matlack, New York	6
	John J. Montefusco, San Francisco	6
1977—	G. Thomas Seaver, N. York-Cincinnati	7
1978—	Robert W. Knepper, San Francisco	6
1979—	G. Thomas Seaver, Cincinnati	5
	Joseph Niekro, Houston	5
	Stephen Rogers, Montreal	5
1980—	Jerry Reuss, Los Angeles	6

PRE-1900 PENNANT WINNERS

Year	Club	Manager	W.	L.	Pct.	Year	Club	Manager	W.	L.	Pct.
1876—Chicago		Albert Spalding	52	14	.788	1888—New York		James Mutrie	84	47	.641
1877—Boston		Harry Wright	31	17	.646	1889—New York		James Mutrie	83	43	.659
1878—Boston		Harry Wright	41	19	.683	1890—Brooklyn		Wm. McGunnigle	86	43	.667
1879—Providence		George Wright	55	23	.705	1891—Boston		Frank Selee	87	51	.630
1880—Chicago		Adrian Anson	67	17	.798	1892—Boston		Frank Selee	102	48	.680
1881—Chicago		Adrian Anson	56	28	.667	1893—Boston		Frank Selee	86	44	.662
1882—Chicago		Adrian Anson	55	29	.655	1894—Baltimore		Edward Hanlon	89	39	.695
1883—Boston		John Morrill	63	35	.643	1895—Baltimore		Edward Hanlon	87	43	.669
1884—Providence		Frank Bancroft	84	28	.750	1896—Baltimore		Edward Hanlon	90	39	.698
1885—Chicago		Adrian Anson	87	25	.777	1897—Boston		Frank Selee	93	39	.705
1886—Chicago		Adrian Anson	90	34	.726	1898—Boston		Frank Selee	102	48	.685
1887—Detroit		Wm. Watkins	79	45	.637	1899—Brooklyn		Edward Hanlon	88	42	.677

PRE-1900 YEARLY FINISHES

Year	Bos.	Bkn.	Chi.	Cin.	N.Y.	Phil.	Pitt.	St.L.	Balt.	Buf.	Clev.
1876	4	....	1	8	6	7	....	3	....	....	....
1877	1	....	5	....	....	....	....	4	....	....	....
1878	1	....	4	2	....	....	....	....	....	....	....
1879	2	....	*3	5	....	....	....	....	....	*3	6
1880	6	....	1	8	....	....	....	....	....	7	3
1881	6	....	1	....	....	....	....	....	....	3	7
1882	*3	....	1	....	....	....	....	....	....	*3	5
1883	1	....	2	....	6	8	....	....	....	5	4
1884	2	....	*4	....	*4	6	....	....	....	3	7
1885	5	....	1	....	2	3	....	8	....	7	....
1886	5	....	1	....	3	4	....	6	....	....	....
1887	5	....	3	....	4	2	6	....	....	....	....
1888	4	....	2	....	1	3	6	....	....	....	....
1889	2	....	3	....	1	4	5	....	....	....	6
1890	5	1	2	4	6	3	8	....	....	....	7
1891	1	6	2	7	3	4	8	....	....	....	5
1892	1	3	7	5	8	4	6	11	12	....	2
1893	1	*6	9	*6	5	4	2	10	8	....	3
1894	3	5	8	10	2	4	7	9	1	....	6
1895	*5	*5	4	8	9	3	7	11	1	....	2
1896	4	*9	5	3	7	8	6	11	1	....	2
1897	1	*6	9	4	3	10	8	12	2	....	5
1898	1	10	4	3	7	6	8	12	2	....	5
1899	2	1	8	6	10	3	7	5	4	....	12

Year	Det.	Hart.	Ind.	K.C.	Lou.	Mil.	Prov.	Syr.	Troy	Wash.	Wor.
1876	...	2	...	....	5	....	....	....	....	....	....
1877	....	3	...	....	2	....	....	....	....	....	....
1878	....	....	5	....	....	6	3	....	....	....	....
1879	....	....	....	....	....	....	1	8	7	....	....
1880	....	....	....	....	....	....	2	....	4	....	5
1881	4	....	....	....	....	....	2	....	5	....	8
1882	6	....	....	....	....	....	2	....	7	....	8
1883	7	....	....	....	....	....	3	....	....	....	....
1884	8	....	....	....	....	....	1	....	....	....	....
1885	6	....	....	....	....	....	4	....	....	....	....
1886	2	....	....	7	....	....	....	....	....	8	....
1887	1	....	8	....	....	....	....	....	....	7	....
1888	5	....	7	....	....	....	....	....	....	8	....
1889	....	....	7	....	....	....	....	....	....	8	....
1890	....	....	....	....	....	....	....	....	....	....	....
1891	....	....	....	....	....	....	....	....	....	....	....
1892	....	....	....	....	9	....	....	....	....	10	....
1893	....	....	....	....	11	....	....	....	....	12	....
1894	....	....	....	....	12	....	....	....	....	11	....
1895	....	....	....	....	12	....	....	....	....	10	....
1896	....	....	....	....	12	....	....	....	....	*9	....
1897	....	....	....	....	11	....	....	....	....	*6	....
1898	....	....	....	....	9	....	....	....	....	11	....
1899	....	....	....	....	9	....	....	....	....	11	....

*Tied for position

PRE-1900 LEADERS

LEADING BATSMEN

Year	Player and Club	G.	H.	Pct.	Year	Player and Club	G.	H.	Pct.
1876	Barnes, Chicago	66	138	.404	1889	Brouthers, Boston	126	181	.373
1877	White, Boston	48	82	.385	1890	Glasscock, New York	124	172	.336
1878	Dalrymple, Milwaukee	60	95	.356	1891	Hamilton, Philadelphia	133	179	.338
1879	Anson, Chicago	49	90	.407	1892	Brouthers, Brooklyn	152	197	.335
1880	Gore, Chicago	75	114	.365		Childs, Cleveland	144	185	.335
1881	Anson, Chicago	84	137	.399	1893	Duffy, Boston	131	203	.378
1882	Brouthers, Buffalo	84	129	.367	1894	Duffy, Boston	124	236	.438
1883	Brouthers, Buffalo	97	156	.371	1895	Burkett, Cleveland	132	235	.423
1884	O'Rourke, Buffalo	104	157	.350	1896	Burkett, Cleveland	133	240	.410
1885	Connor, New York	110	169	.371	1897	Keeler, Baltimore	128	243	.432
1886	Kelly, Chicago	118	175	.388	1898	Keeler, Baltimore	128	214	.379
1887	Anson, Chicago	122	*224	.421	1899	Delahanty, Philadelphia	145	234	.408
1888	Anson, Chicago	134	177	.343					

*Bases on balls counted as hits.

TWO-BASE HIT LEADERS

Year	Player and Club	2B.	Year	Player and Club	2B.
1876	Roscoe Barnes, Chicago	23	1888	James Ryan, Chicago	37
1877	Adrian (Cap) Anson, Chicago	20	1889	John Glasscock, Indianapolis	39
1878	Lewis Brown, Providence	18	1890	Samuel Thompson, Philadelphia	38
1879	Charles Eden, Cleveland	31	1891	Michael Griffin, Brooklyn	36
1880	Fred Dunlap, Cleveland	27	1892	Brouthers, Bkn.-Delahanty, Phil	33
1881	Michael (King) Kelly, Chicago	28	1893	Oliver (Pat) Tebeau, Cleveland	35
1882	Michael (King) Kelly, Chicago	36	1894	Hugh Duffy, Boston	50
1883	Edward Williamson, Chicago	50	1895	Edward Delahanty, Philadelphia	47
1884	Paul Hines, Providence	34	1896	Edward Delahanty, Philadelphia	42
1885	Adrian (Cap) Anson, Chicago	35	1897	Jacob Stenzel, Baltimore	40
1886	Dennis (Dan) Brouthers, Detroit	41	1898	Napoleon Lajoie, Philadelphia	40
1887	Dennis (Dan) Brouthers, Detroit	35	1899	Edward Delahanty, Philadelphia	56

THREE-BASE HIT LEADERS

Year	Player and Club	3B.	Year	Player and Club	3B.
1876	George Hall, Athletics	12	1888	R. Connor, N.Y.-R. Johnson, Bos	17
1877	Brown, Bos.-McVey, Chi.-White, Bos	9	1889	Connor, N.Y.-Fogarty, Ph.-Wilmot, W	17
1878	Thomas York, Providence	9	1890	John McPhee, Cincinnati	25
1879	L. Dickerson, Cin.-M. Kelly, Cin	14	1891	Jacob Beckley, Pittsburgh	20
1880	Harry Stovey, Worcester	14	1892	Dennis (Dan) Brouthers, Brooklyn	20
1881	John Rowe, Buffalo	11	1893	Perry Werden, St. Louis	33
1882	Roger Connor, Troy	17	1894	Henry Reitz, Baltimore	29
1883	Dennis (Dan) Brouthers, Buffalo	17	1895	A. Selbach, Wash.-S. Thompson, Phil	22
1884	William (Buck) Ewing, New York	18	1896	McCreery, Lou.-G. Van Haltren, N.Y.	21
1885	R. Connor, N.Y.-J. O'Rourke, N.Y.	15	1897	Harry Davis, Pittsburgh	28
1886	Roger Connor, New York	19	1898	John Anderson, Bkn.-Wash.	19
1887	Samuel Thompson, Detroit	23	1899	James Williams, Pittsburgh	27

HOME RUN LEADERS

Year	Player and Club	HR.	Year	Player and Club	HR.
1876	George Hall, Athletics	5	1888	Roger Connor, New York	14
1877	George Shaffer, Louisville	3	1889	Samuel Thompson, Philadelphia	20
1878	Paul Hines, Providence	4	1890	T. Burns, Bkn.-M. Tiernan, N.Y.	13
1879	Charles Jones, Boston	9	1891	H. Stovey, Bos.-M. Tiernan, N.Y.	16
1880	J. O'Rourke, Bos.-H. Stovey, Wor	6	1892	James Holliday, Cincinnati	13
1881	Dennis (Dan) Brouthers, Buffalo	8	1893	Edward Delahanty, Philadelphia	19
1882	George Wood, Detroit	7	1894	H. Duffy, Boston-R. Lowe, Boston	18
1883	William (Buck) Ewing, New York	10	1895	William Joyce, Washington	17
1884	Edward Williamson, Chicago	27	1896	Delahanty, Phil.-S. Thompson, Phil	13
1885	Abner Dalrymple, Chicago	11	1897	Napoleon Lajoie, Philadelphia	10
1886	Harding Richardson, Detroit	11	1896	James Collins, Boston	14
1887	R. Connor, N.Y.-T. O'Brien, Wash	17	1899	John (Buck) Freeman, Washington	25

STOLEN BASE LEADERS

Year	Player and Club	SB.
1886	George Andrews, Philadelphia	56
1887	John M. Ward, New York	111
1888	William (Dummy) Hoy, Washington	82
1889	James Fogarty, Philadelphia	99
1890	William Hamilton, Philadelphia	102
1891	William Hamilton, Philadelphia	115
1892	John M. Ward, Brooklyn	94
1893	John M. Ward, New York	72
1894	William Hamilton, Philadelphia	99
1895	William Hamilton, Philadelphia	95
1896	William Lange, Chicago	100
1897	William Lange, Chicago	83
1898	Frederick Clarke, Louisville	66
1899	James Sheckard, Baltimore	78

LEADING PITCHERS IN WINNING PERCENTAGE

(15 OR MORE VICTORIES)

Year	Pitcher and Club	W.	L.	Pct.
1876	Albert Spalding, Chicago	47	13	.783
1877	Thomas Bond, Boston	31	17	.646
1878	Thomas Bond, Boston	40	19	.678
1879	Jom M. Ward, Providence	44	18	.710
1880	Fred Goldsmith, Chicago	22	3	.880
1881	Chas. Radbourn, Providence	25	11	.694
1882	Lawrence Corcoran, Chicago	27	13	.675
1883	James McCormick, Cleveland	27	13	.675
1884	Chas. Radbourn, Providence	60	12	.833
1885	Michael Welch, New York	44	11	.800
1886	John Flynn, Chicago	24	6	.800
1887	Charles Getzein, Detroit	29	13	.690
1888	Timothy Keefe, New York	35	12	.745
1889	John Clarkson, Boston	49	19	.721
1890	Thomas Lovett, Brooklyn	32	11	.744
1891	John Ewing, New York	22	8	.733
1892	Denton (Cy) Young, Cleve.	36	11	.766
1893	Frank Killen, Pittsburgh	34	10	.773
1894	Jouett Meekin, New York	34	9	.791
1895	William Hoffer, Baltimore	30	7	.811
1896	William Hoffer, Baltimore	26	7	.788
1897	Amos Rusie, New York	29	8	.784
1898	Edward Lewis, Boston	25	8	.758
1899	James Hughes, Brooklyn	28	6	.824

MAJOR LEAGUE UMPIRES ASSOCIATION

President—Paul Runge
Vice-President—Jim Evans
Secretary—Bill Williams
Board of Directors—Paul Runge, Jim Evans, John Kibler, Bruce Froemming,
Nick Bremigan, Terry Tata and Don Denkinger
Attorney—Richard G. Phillips

Three Girard Plaza, Suite 2106
Philadelphia, Pa. 19102
Telephone—(215) 568-7368

Major League Baseball Players Association

1370 Avenue of the Americas
Suite 2602
New York, N.Y. 10019
Telephone—(212) 581-8484

Marvin J. Miller—Executive Director
Donald Fehr—General Counsel
Peter Rose—Associate Counsel
Secretarial Staff—Marlene Blake and Nancy Panarella

EXECUTIVE BOARD

Doug DeCinces—American League Representative
Bob Boone—National League Representative
Mark Belanger—Pension Committee
Steve Rogers—Pension Committee
Plus all remaining player representatives

NATIONAL LEAGUE PLAYER REPRESENTATIVES

Phil Niekro—Atlanta Braves
Barry Foote—Chicago Cubs
Bill Bonham—Cincinnati Reds
Joe Niekro—Houston Astros
Jerry Reuss—Los Angeles Dodgers
Steve Rogers—Montreal Expos
John Stearns—New York Mets
Dick Ruthven—Philadelphia Phillies
Phil Garner—Pittsburgh Pirates
Bob Sykes—St. Louis Cardinals
John Curtis—San Diego Padres
Gary Lavelle—San Francisco Giants

AMERICAN LEAGUE PLAYER REPRESENTATIVES

Mark Belanger—Baltimore Orioles
Tom Burgmeier—Boston Red Sox
Don Baylor—California Angels
Lamar Johnson—Chicago White Sox
Wayne Garland—Cleveland Indians
Milt Wilcox—Detroit Tigers
Dan Quisenberry—Kansas City Royals
Buck Martinez—Milwaukee Brewers
Jerry Koosman—Minnesota Twins
Reggie Jackson—New York Yankees
Jeff Newman—Oakland A's
Bruce Bochte—Seattle Mariners
Jon Matlack—Texas Rangers
Al Woods—Toronto Blue Jays

AMERICAN LEAGUE

Including

Club Directories

Club Reviews of 1980 Season

Club Day-by-Day Scores

A.L. Team Pictures

1980 League Leaders

1980 Official A.L. Averages

All-Time A.L. Player Performance Tables

LELAND S. MacPHAIL, JR.
President of the American League

American League

Organized 1900

LELAND S. MacPHAIL, Jr.
President

JOSEPH E. CRONIN
Chairman

CALVIN R. GRIFFITH
Vice-President

ROBERT O. FISHEL
Secretary and
Assistant to the President

DONALD C. MARR, Jr.
Controller

DICK BUTLER
Supervisor of Umpires

ROBERT F. HOLBROOK
Special Assistant

JEANNE BILL, STEPHANIE VARDAVAS
Managers, Waiver & Records Department

PHYLLIS MERHIGE
Assistant Public Relations Director

TESS BASTA, ROBERT GRIM
Administrators

Headquarters—280 Park Avenue, New York, N. Y. 10017

Telephone—682-7000 (area code 212)

ASSISTANT SUPERVISORS OF UMPIRES—Nestor Chylak, Henry Soar, John Stevens.

UMPIRES—Lawrence Barnett, Nicholas Bremigan, Joseph Brinkman, Alan Clark, Terrance Cooney, Derryl Cousins, Donald Denkinger, James Evans, Dale Ford, Richard Garcia, Russell Goetz, William Haller, Ted Hendry, Kenneth Kaiser, Greg Kosc, William Kunkel, George Maloney, Larry McCoy, James McKean, Durwood Merrill, Jerome Neudecker, Stephen Palermo, Dallas Parks, David Phillips, Michael Reilly, John Shulock, Martin Springstead, Vic Voltaggio.

OFFICIAL STATISTICIANS—Sports Information Center, 1776 Heritage Drive, No. Quincy, Mass. 02171. Telephone—(617) 328-4674.

Players cannot be transferred from one major league to another after June 15 to close of the championship season except through regular waiver channels.

WAIVER PRICE, $20,000. Interleague waivers, $20,000, except for selected players and draft-excluded players.

BALTIMORE ORIOLES

Chairman of the Board—Edward Bennett Williams
President—Jerold C. Hoffberger

Executive Vice-President-General Manager—Henry J. Peters
Treasurer—Gerard T. Gabrys
Vice-President for Stadium Operations—Jack Dunn, III
Vice-President for Finance—Joseph P. Hamper, Jr.
Vice-President for Business Affairs—Robert R. Aylward
Public Relations Director—Robert W. Brown
Promotions Director—Walter R. Freeman, Jr.
Traveling Secretary—Philip E. Itzoe
Special Assistant to the General Manager—James J. Russo
Director of Scouting and Player Development—Thomas A. Giordano
Sales Director—Jon Richardson
Ticket Manager—Timothy A. Geraghty
Assistant Scouting and Player Development Director—John J. McCall
Assistant Ticket Manager—Joseph B. Codd
Assistant Public Relations Director—John C. Blake
Assistant Sales & Assistant Promotions Director—Drew M. Sheinman
Washington Area Sales Representative—David Dinerman
Asst. Washington Area Sales Representative—Joseph Felperin
Consultant-President, Oriole Foundation—Herbert E. Armstrong
Manager—Earl S. Weaver
Club Physician—Dr. Leonard Wallenstein
Executive Offices—Memorial Stadium, Baltimore, Md. 21218
Telephone—243-9800 (area code 301)

SCOUTS—Jack Baker, Dick Bowie, Joe Bowman, Dan Cressman, Ray Crone, Joe DeLucca, Jim Driscoll, Tony Franklin, Jim Freitas, Jim Gilbert, Myron Hayworth, Len Johnston, George Lauzerique, Bill Lohr, Frank McGowan, Earl McKenzie, Domenic Napolitano, Lance Nichols, Lamar North, Carlos Pascual, James Pamlayne, Frank Piet, Jim Russo, Jack Sanford, Caesar Sinabaldi, John Stokoe, William Teed, Tommy Thompson, Herman Welsh, Bill Werle.

PARK LOCATION—Memorial Stadium, 33rd Street, Ellerslie Avenue, 36th Street and Ednor Road.

Seating capacity—52,696

FIELD DIMENSIONS—Home plate to left field at foul line, 309 feet; to center field, 410 feet; to right field at foul line, 309 feet.

BOSTON RED SOX

President—Jean R. Yawkey

Executive Vice-President-General Manager—Haywood C. Sullivan
Executive Vice-President, Administration—Edward G. LeRoux, Jr.
Treasurer—James M. Olivier, Jr.
Secretary—Joseph H. LaCour
V. P., Director Player Development—Edward F. Kenney
Director, Scouting—Edward M. Kasko
Traveling Secretary—John J. Rogers
V. P., Director Public Relations—William C. Crowley
Director, Publicity—Richard L. Bresciani
Director, Marketing—James P. Healey
Assistant Publicity Director—John E. McCarthy
Executive Assistant—Joseph F. McDermott
Assistant Treasurer—John J. Reilly
Director, Tickets—Arthur J. Moscato
Superintendent, Grounds & Maintenance—Joseph Mooney
Field Manager—Ralph G. Houk
Club Physicians—Drs. Arthur M. Pappas, William W. Southmayd
Executive Offices—24 Yawkey Way, Boston, Mass. 02215
Telephone—267-9440 (area code 617)

SCOUTS—Milton Bolling, Ray Boone, Wayne Britton, George Digby, Howard (Danny) Doyle, Bill Enos, Larry Flynn, Earl Johnson, Charles Koney, Wilfrid (Lefty) Lefebvre, Don Lenhardt, Tommy McDonald, Felix Maldonado, Frank Malzone, Sam Mele, Ramon Naranjo, Willie Paffen, Edward Scott, Matt Sczesny, Joe Stephenson, Paul Tavares, Larry Thomas, Charlie Wagner.

PARK LOCATION—Fenway Park, Yawkey Way, Lansdowne Street and Ipswich Street.

Seating capacity—33,536

FIELD DIMENSIONS—Home plate to left field at foul line, 315 feet; to center field, 420 feet; right field at foul line, 302 feet; average right field distance, 382 feet.

CALIFORNIA ANGELS

BOARD OF DIRECTORS

Gene Autry, Chairman of the Board; E. J. (Buzzie) Bavasi, Arthur E. Patterson, Walton S. Reid, Forrest Shumway,Clair L. Stout
President—Gene Autry
Executive Vice-President—E. J. (Buzzie) Bavasi
Assistant to the Chairman of the Board—Arthur E. Patterson
Vice-President, Treasurer—Francis X. Leary
Secretary—Clair L. Stout
Assistant Secretary & Treasurer—Michael M. Schreter
Vice-President, Chief Administrative Officer—Mike Port
Administrative Assistant—Rose Anderson
Director of Player Personnel—Gene Mauch
Director Public Relations/Promotions—Tom Seeberg
Asst. Director of Public Relations—Bobby Kargenian
Director Stadium Operations—Jean (Corky) Lippert
Director Scouting—Larry Himes
Asst. Minor League Development—Bill Bavasi
Special Assignments—Bill Rigney, Herman Franks
Director Ticket Department—Carl Gordon
Asst. Ticket Director—Bob Terzes
Traveling Secretary—Ned Bergert
Trainer—Richard Smith
Director Group Sales—Lynn Kirchmann
Film Coordinator/Special Statistics—George Goodale
Manager—Jim Fregosi
Club Physicians—Drs. Robert K. Kerlan, Jules Rasinski,
Lewis Yocum
Executive Offices—Anaheim Stadium, 2000 State College Blvd.,
Anaheim, Calif. 92806
Telephone—937-6700 (area code 714) or 625-1123 (area code 213)

SCOUTS—Edmundo Borrome, Vince Capece, Joe Carpenter, Lloyd Christopher, Lou Cohenour, Pompeyo Davillo, Bob Gardner, Gus Gil, Al Goldis, Harry Hayes, Rick Ingalls, Nick Kamzic, Joe Maddon, Vic Power, Philip Rizzo, Ernie Rudolph, Cobby Saatzer, George Zabala.

PARK LOCATION—Anaheim Stadium, 2000 State College Boulevard.

Seating capacity—65,158

FIELD DIMENSIONS—Home plate to left field at foul line, 333 feet; to center field, 404 feet; to right field at foul line, 333 feet.

CHICAGO WHITE SOX

Chairman of the Board—Jerry M. Reinsdorf

President—Edward M. Einhorn
Vice-President, Administration—Jack M. Gould
Vice-President, General Manager—Roland Hemond
Vice-President, Marketing—H. Russell Potts
Asst. Vice-President, Marketing—Stephen Schanwald
Secretary—Gerald M. Penner
General Counsel—Allan B. Muchin
Director of Promotions—George Koch
Director of Public Relations—Charles A. Shriver
Asst. Director of Public Relations—Kenneth A. Valdiserri
Director of Radio-TV, Special Projects—Laureen Ong Fadil
Director of Minor League Operations—David M. Dombrowski
Traveling Secretary—Glen Rosenbaum
Ticket Manager—Robert K. Devoy
Director of Park Operations—David Schaffer
Groundskeepers—Gene and Roger Bossard
Clubhouse Men—John McNamara and Willie Thompson
Manager—Tony LaRussa
Club Physicians—Drs. Edwin Feldman, William Meltzer, Michael Lewis
and Sid J. Shafer
Co-ordinator of Season Ticket Sales—Millie Johnson
Director of Group Sales—Daniel Cohen
Executive Offices—Comiskey Park, Dan Ryan at 35th Street.
Chicago, Ill. 60616
Telephone—924-1000 (area code 312)

SCOUTS—Special Assignment: Loren Babe, Jerry Krause. Supervisors—Walt Widmayer, Gary Johnson; Bruce Dal Canton, Roger Ferguson, Sam Hairston, Bennie Huffman, Joseph Ingalls, Bart Johnson, Leo Labossiere, Marv Lane, Dario Lodigiani, Terry Logan, Vern McKee, Larry Monroe, Fern Paredes, Silvano Quezada, Duane Shaffer, George Sobek, Stan Zielinski.

PARK LOCATION—Comiskey Park, Dan Ryan at 35th Street, Chicago, Ill. 60616.

Seating capacity—44,492

FIELD DIMENSIONS—Home plate to left field at foul line, 352 feet; to center field, 445 feet; to right field at foul line, 352 feet.

CLEVELAND INDIANS

President & Chief Executive Officer—Gabe Paul

Chairman of the Board—F. J. (Steve) O'Neill
Directors—F. J. O'Neill, C. C. Tippit, Dudley S. Blossom, III,
Alva T. Bonda, Gabe Paul, Phillip Seghi, Bruce Fine, Maurice Stonehill
Secretary-Treasurer—Dudley S. Blossom III
Vice-President & General Manager—Phillip D. Seghi
Vice-President, Player Development & Scouting—Bob Quinn
Vice-President—Bruce Fine
Manager—Dave Garcia
Traveling Secretary—Mike Seghi
Director of Public Relations—Bob DiBiasio
Director of Marketing—Joann Klonowski
Director of Sales—Tom Pulchinski
Director of Stadium Operations—Dan Zerbey
Ticket Director—Jerry Waring
Controller—Art Pease
Community Relations Director—Bob Feller
Special Assignment Scout—Dan Carnevale
Asst. Public Relations Director—Pete Spudich
Minor League Administrator—Joe Pavia
Asst. Farm Director—Phil Thomas
Trainer—Jim Warfield
Club Physicians—Drs. William Wilder, Earl Brightman
Club Dentist—Dr. Marvin Schermer
Club Legal Counsel—Armand D. Arnson
Equipment Manager—Cy Buynak
Groundskeeper—Marshall Bossard
Executive Offices—Cleveland Stadium, Cleveland, Ohio 44114
Telephone—861-1200 (area code 216)

SCOUTS—Dan Carnevale (special assignment scout), Jack Cassini,
Merrill Combs, Al Daniels, Red Gaskill, Leon Hamilton, Luis Isaac, Mark
Just, Bobby Malkmus, Jim Miller, Jack Vallely, Gene Woodling.

PARK LOCATION—Cleveland Stadium, Boudreau Blvd.

Seating capacity—76,685

FIELD DIMENSIONS—Home plate to left field at foul line, 320 feet;
to center field, 400 feet; to right field at foul line, 320 feet.

DETROIT TIGERS

Owner & Chairman of the Board—John E. Fetzer

President & General Manager—James A. Campbell
Vice-President/Finance & Secretary-Treasurer—Alexander C. Callam
Vice-President/Operations—William E. Haase
Vice-President/Baseball—William R. Lajoie
Director of Public Relations—Dan Ewald
Director of Ticket Sales—William H. Willis
Director of Stadium Operations—Ralph E. Snyder
Field Director/Player Development—Walter A. Evers
Scouting Director—David Miller
Administrative Assistant/Minor Leagues—Dan Elve
Traveling Secretary—Bill Brown
Assistant Director of Public Relations—Bob Miller
Asst. Dir. of Public Relations/Special Events—Lew Matlin
Asst. Dir. of Public Relations/Community Affairs—Vince Desmond
Season and Group Ticket Sales—Fred T. Smith
Executive Secretary/Baseball—Alice Sloane
Executive Secretary/Operations—Hazel McLane
Consultants—Richard B. Ferrell, Edward G. Katalinas
Asst. Director of Stadium Operations—Frank Feneck
Manager—Sparky Anderson
Club Physician—Clarence S. Livingood M.D.
Orthopaedic Consultant—Robert A. Teitge M.D.
Executive Offices—Tiger Stadium, Detroit, Mich. 48216
Telephone—962-4000 (area code 313)

SCOUTS—Ray Bellino, Wayne Blackburn, George Bradley, Orlando Pena, William Schudlich, Frank Skaff, Jack Tighe, John Young.

PARK LOCATION—Tiger Stadium, Michigan Avenue, Cochrane Avenue, Kaline Drive and Trumbull Avenue.

Seating capacity—52,687

FIELD DIMENSIONS—Home plate to left field at foul line, 340 feet; to center field, 440 feet; to right field at foul line, 325 feet.

KANSAS CITY ROYALS

BOARD OF DIRECTORS—Joe Burke, William Deramus III, Charles Hughes, Ewing Kauffman, Mrs. Ewing Kauffman, Earl Smith.

President & Chairman of the Board—Ewing Kauffman
Executive Vice-President and General Manager—Joe Burke
Vice-President, Administration—Spencer "Herk" Robinson
Vice-President, Player Personnel—John Schuerholz
Vice-President, Controller—Dale Rohr
Vice-President and Legal Counsel—Phil Koury
Director of Public Relations—Dean Vogelaar
Director of Marketing—Bryan Burns
Traveling Secretary—Bill Beck
Director of Publications—Bruce Carnahan
Director of Minor League Operations—Dick Balderson
Administrative Assistant, Minor League Operations—Dean Taylor
Director of Ticket Operations—Tom Pfannenstiel
Director of Season Ticket Sales—Joe Grigoli
Director of Group Sales—Rush Limbaugh
Manager—Jim Frey
Club Physician—Dr. Paul Meyer
Accountant—Ken Willeke
Director of Event Personnel—Chris Muehlbach
Stadium Engineer—George Humphrey
Stadium Maintenance Coordinator—Bob Frank
Equipment Manager—Al Zych
Groundskeeper—George Toma
Executive Offices—Royals Stadium, Harry S. Truman Sports Complex
Mailing Address—P. O. Box 1969, Kansas City, Mo. 64141
Telephone—921-8000 (area code 816)

SCOUTS—Jose Arcia, Carl Blando, Al Diez, Tom Ferrick, Rosey Gilhousen, Ken Gonzales, Guy Hansen, Al Kubski, Art Lilly, George Noga, Earl Rapp, Rich Schlenker, Jerry Stephens, Red Whitsett, Art Stewart (part time).

PARK LOCATION—Royals Stadium, Harry S. Truman Sports Complex.

Seating capacity—40,628

FIELD DIMENSIONS—Home plate to left field at foul line, 330 feet; to center field, 410 feet; to right field at foul line, 330 feet.

MILWAUKEE BREWERS

President, Chief Executive Officer—Allan H. (Bud) Selig

Chairman of the Board—Edmund B. Fitzgerald
Directors—Edmund B. Fitzgerald, Allan H. Selig, Everett
G. Smith, Roswell N. Stearns
Secretaries—Bernard S. Kubale, Carlton Wilson
Executive Vice-President, General Manager—Harry Dalton
Vice-President, Marketing—Richard Hackett
Vice-President, Administration—Thomas J. Ferguson
Vice-President, Finance—Richard Hoffmann
Vice-President, Stadium Operations—Gabe Paul, Jr.
Assistant General Manager—Walter Shannon
Special Assistants to the General Manager—Dee Fondy,
George Bamberger
Special Assignments Scout—Ray Scarborough
Director of Scouting and Player Development—Ray Poitevint
Administrative Assistant Scouting & Player Development—Bruce Manno
Assistant, Scouting Department—Dan Duquette
Director of Publicity—Tom Skibosh
Assistant Director of Stadium Operations—Jack Hutchinson
Group Sales Director—Tim Trovato
Director of the Speakers Bureau—John Counsell
Asst. Director of Publicity—Mario Ziino
Ticket Office Manager—Alice Boettcher
Director of Speical Events—Mark Paget
Manager—Bob Rodgers
Club Physician—Dr. Paul Jacobs
Superintendent of Grounds & Maintenance—Harry Gill
Executive Offices—Milwaukee Brewers Baseball Club
Milwaukee County Stadium, Milwaukee, Wis. 53214
Telephone—(414) 933-1818

SCOUTS—Scouting supervisors: Julio Blanco-Herrera, Nelson Bur-
brink, Felix Delgado, Tom Gamboa, Roland LeBlanc, Walter Youse. Don
Buford, Ken Califano, Jocko Collins, Gerry Craft, Charles Fitzgerald,
Lippy Lipari, Billy Moffitt, Willie Moore, Johnny Neun, Harry Smith, Milt
Sobel, Sam Suplizio, Paul Tretiak, Jerry Weinstein.

PARK LOCATION—Milwaukee County Stadium, S. 46th St. off Blue-
mound Rd.

Seating capacity—53,192

FIELD DIMENSIONS—Home plate to left field at foul line, 315 feet;
to center field, 402 feet; to right field at foul line, 315 feet.

MINNESOTA TWINS

Chairman of Board, President—Calvin R. Griffith
Vice-President—Mrs. Thelma Griffith Haynes
Executive Vice-President—Clark Griffith
Executive Vice-President—Bruce G. Haynes
Director—H. Gabriel Murphy
Director—Eugene V. Young
Director—Wheelock Whitney
Executive Vice-President—Howard T. Fox, Jr.
Vice-President—William S. Robertson
Vice-President—James K. Robertson
Vice-President-Farm Director—George Brophy
Assistant Farm Director—Jim Rantz
Controller—Jack Alexander
Director of Public Relations—Tom Mee
Director of Sales—Gil Lansdale
Stadium Superintendent—Richard Ericson
Manager—Gene Mauch
Club Physicians—Dr. Leonard J. Michienzi and Dr. Harvey O'Phelan
Executive Offices—Metropolitan Stadium, 8001 Cedar Avenue,
Bloomington, Minn. 55420
Telephone—854-4040 (area code 612)

SCOUTS—Floyd Baker, Zinn Beck, Dave Boswell, Spud Chandler, Edward Dunn, Jesse Flores, Jr., Jesse Flores, Sr., Angelo Giuliani, Tom Hull, Lee Irwin, Hank Izquierdo, William Messmann, Marvin Olson, Spencer (Red) Robbins, Stanley Rogers, Herb Stein.

PARK LOCATION—Metropolitan Stadium, 8001 Cedar Avenue, Bloomington, Minn. 55420.

Seating Capacity—45,919

FIELD DIMENSIONS—Home plate to left field at foul line, 343 feet; to center field, 402 feet; to right field at foul line, 330 feet.

NEW YORK YANKEES

Principal Owner—George M. Steinbrenner III

Limited Partners—Harold Bowman, Michael Burke, Lester Crown, John
Z. DeLorean, Michael Friedman, Marvin Goldklang, Barry Halper,
Harvey Leighton, Daniel McCarthy, Harry Nederlander, Robert
Nederlander, William J. O'Neill, William Rose, Edward
Rosenthal, Jack Satter, Charlotte Witkind.
President—Lou Saban
Executive Vice-President—Cedric Tallis
Vice-President, General Manager—Gene Michael
Manager—Gene Michael
Administrative Vice-President—Eugene J. McHale
Vice-President, General Counsel—Edwin T. Broderick
Vice-President, Baseball Operations—Bill Bergesch
Vice-President—Ed Weaver
Treasurer-Controller—David Weidler
Director of Player Development—Bill Livesey
Director of Scouting—Bobby Hofman
Traveling Secretary—Bill Kane
Administrative Assistant—Gerry Murphy
Director of Media Relations—Larry Wahl
Assistant Director of Media Relations—David Szen
Director of Public Relations—John Fugazy
Stadium Manager—Patrick Kelly
Director of Promotions—Peter Gill
Executive Director of Ticket Operations—Frank Swaine
Ticket Director—Michael Rendine
Assistant Ticket Director—Jim Hodge
Director, Customer Services & Asst. Stadium Manager—Jim Naples
Assistant Director of Player Development—Dale Weeks
Assistant Director of Scouting—Bob Kalaf
Director of Group Sales—Frank McCormick
Director of Speakers Bureau, Publicity Assistant—Joe D'Ambrosio
Director of Accounting—Alan Friedman
Stadium Superintendent—Jimmy Esposito
Director, Yankee Alumni Association—Jim Ogle
Club Physician—Dr. John J. Bonamo
Executive Offices—Yankee Stadium, Bronx, N. Y. 10451
Telephone—293-4300 (area code 212)

SCOUTS—Major League: Harry Craft, Clyde King, Bob Lemon, Birdie Tebbetts; Luis Arroyo, Joe Begani, Jack Bloomfield, Roy Carter, Howard Cassady, Al Cuccinello, Joe DiCarlo, Henry Dotterer, Fred Ferreira, Whitey Ford, Lou Garcia, Jack Gillis, Tom Greenwade, Jim Gruzdis, Roy Hamey, Jim Hegan, Dick Howser, Gary Hughes, John Kennedy, Don Lindeberg, Jack Llewellyn, Jim Naples Sr., Bob Nieman, Frank O'Rourke, Meade Palmer, Gust Poulos, Ray Regalis, Robert Shaw, Russ Sehon, Mickey Vernon, Jerry Walker, Gerald Zimmerman.

PARK LOCATION—Yankee Stadium, E. 161st St. and River Ave., Bronx, N. Y. 10451.

Ticket Information—293-6000 (area code 212)

Seating capacity—57,545

FIELD DIMENSIONS—Home plate to left field at foul line, 312 feet; to center field, 417 feet; to right field at foul line, 310 feet.

OAKLAND A's

President—Roy Eisenhardt

Executive Vice-President—Walter J. Haas
Field Manager-Director of Player Development—Billy Martin
Vice-President, Baseball Administration—Carl A. Finley
Vice-President, Business Operations—Andy Dolich
Director of Scouting and Minor League Personnel—Dick Wiencek
Director, Minor League Operations—Walt Jocketty
Traveling Secretary—Director of Press Relations—Mickey Morabito
Director of Marketing—Roger Moskowitz
Director of Sales—David Rubinstein
Director of Media Relations—Rick Moxley
Director of Broadcast Operations—Bill King
Assistant Director of Broadcast Operations—Wayne Hagin
Ticket Manager—Lorraine Paulus
Executive Assistant—Sharon Jones
Speakers Bureau Coordinator—Dom Valentino
Coordinator Youth Programs—Craig Amerkhanian
Assistant Press Relations—Enzo DeMonte
Director Stadium Operations—Jorge Costa
Assistant Ticket Manager—Shelly Russo
Ticket Office-Administrative Assistant—Julie Delk
Equipment Manager—Frank Ciensczyk
Trainer—Joe Romo
Club Physician—Dr. Thomas E. Richmond
Visiting Clubhouse Manager—Steve Vucinich
Executive Offices—Oakland-Alameda County Coliseum,
Oakland, Calif. 94621
Telephone—638-4900 (area code 415)
PARK LOCATION—Oakland-Alameda County Coliseum, Nimitz
Freeway and Hegenberger Road.

Seating capacity—50,255

FIELD DIMENSIONS—Home plate to left field at foul line, 330 feet;
to center field, 400 feet; to right field at foul line, 330 feet.

SEATTLE MARINERS

Principal Owner—George L. Argyros

Limited Partners—Warren Finley, Stanley Golub, Danny Kaye, Walter
Schoenfeld, Lester M. Smith
President & Chief Executive Officer—Daniel F. O'Brien
Executive Director—Kip Horsburgh
Director of Player Development—Hal Keller
Director of Business Affairs—Jeff Odenwald
Director of Promotions—Jack Carvalho
Director of Team Travel—Lee Pelekoudas
Director of Stadium Operations—Mike Combs
Director of Ticket Services—Lamar Vernon
Dirctor of Public Relations—Randy Adamack
Controller—Ed Waite
Assistant Director, Player Development—Steve Schryver
Assistant Director, Business Affairs—Dan O'Brien III
Assistant Director, Ticket Services—Steve Krause
Vault Manager—Doug Hopkins
Trainer—Gary Nicholson
Club Physicians—Drs. Ernie Burgess, Larry Pedegana,
James Thombold
Club Dentist—Dr. Richard Leshgold
Club Attorney—Irwin Treiger
Home Clubhouse—Henry Genzale
Visiting Clubhouse—Fred Genzale

Executive Offices—P.O. Box 4100
Seattle, Washington 98104
Telephone—628-3555 (area code 206)

SCOUTS—Bill Hallauer, Bob Harrison, Bill Kearns, Jeff Malinoff,
Marty Martinez, Whitey Piurek, Steve Ray, Rip Tutor, Steve Vrablik.

PARK LOCATION—Kingdome, 201 South King Street, Seattle, Washington.

Seating capacity—59,438

FIELD DIMENSIONS—Home plate to left field at foul line, 316 feet;
to center field, 410 feet; to right field at foul line, 316 feet.

TEXAS RANGERS

Chairman of the Board, President, Chief Executive Officer—Eddie Chiles

Vice Chairman, General Counsel, Secretary—Dee J. Kelly
Executive Vice-President, Baseball Operations—Eddie Robinson
Executive Vice-President, Business Operations—Samuel G. Meason
Vice-President—Amon G. Carter Jr.
Vice-President, Marketing—James T. Medick
Directors—Dee J. Kelly, Amon G. Carter Jr., Mack Rankin, William H.
Seay, Charles S. Sharp
Treasurer—Charles F. Wangner
Director of Player Procurement and Development—Joe Klein
Asst. Director of Player Procurement and Development—Tom Grieve
Director of Public Relations—Burton Hawkins
Director of Advertising and Promotions—Dave Fendrick
Director of Ticket Management—Mary Ann Bosher
National Sales Manager—Phil Small
Traveling Secretary—Dan Schimek
Manager—Don Zimmer
Director of Stadium Operations—John L. Welaj
Administrative Assistant and Director
of Speakers Bureau—Bobby Bragan
Administrative Assistants—Wayne Krivsky, Pat Corrales
Physical Fitness Consultant—Dr. Eugene Coleman
Physical Fitness Instructor—Mike Fitzsimmons
Medical Director—Dr. B. J. Mycoskie
Field Superintendent—John Oliveria
Public Address Announcers—Bob Barry, Bill Melton
Executive Offices—Arlington Stadium, P. O. Box 1111,
1500 Copeland Road, Arlington, Tex. 76010
Telephone—273-5222 (area code 817)

SCOUTS—Harley Anderson, Lee Anthony, Lee Ballanfant, Joseph
Branzell, Jackie Brathwaite, Paddy Cottrell, Dick Gernert, Juan Gomez,
Sid Hudson, Pete Kramer, Joseph Lewis, Joseph Marchese.

PARK LOCATION—Arlington Stadium, 1500 Copeland Road, Arlington, Tex.

Seating capacity—41,284

FIELD DIMENSIONS—Home plate to left field at foul line, 330 feet;
to center field, 400 feet; to right field at foul line, 330 feet.

TORONTO BLUE JAYS

DIRECTORS—L. G. Greenwood, N. E. Hardy, J. P. Robarts,
R. Howard Webster, P. N. T. Widdrington
Chairman of the Board—R. Howard Webster
President and Chief Operating Officer—Peter Bavasi
Vice-President, Business Operations—Paul Beeston
Vice-President, Baseball Operations—Pat Gillick
Director, Public Relations—Howard Starkman
Director, Operations—Ken Erskine
Director, Ticket Operations—George Holm
Administrator, Player Personnel—Elliott Wahle
Trainer-Director, Team Travel—Ken Carson
Director, Group Sales—Mike Nash
Manager, Promotions—Bruce Poore
Director, Player Development—Billy Smith
Director, Canadian Scouting—Bob Prentice
Assistant Director, Public Relations—Herb Morell
Assistant Director, Operations—Gord Ash
Assistant Director, Ticket Operations—Len Frejlich
Director, Security—Fred Wootton
Equipment Manager—Jeff Ross
Coordinator, Promotions & Group Services—Sue Palmer
Controller—Sue Sirois
Supervisor, Grounds—Dave Hamilton
Manager—Bobby Mattick
Team Physician—Dr. Ron Taylor
Executive Offices—Exhibition Stadium, Exhibition Place,
Toronto, Ontario
Mailing Address—Box 7777, Adelaide St. P. O., Toronto, Ont. M5C 2K7
Telephone—595-0077 (area code 416)

SCOUTS—Robert Engle, Ric Fleury, Joe Ford, Epy Guerrero, Rich Hacker, Jim Hughes, Al LaMacchia (senior scouting supervisor), Larry Maxie, Wayne Morgan, Herb Raybourn, Paul Ricciarini, Don Welke, Bob Wilbur, Tim Wilken, Dave Yoakum, Bob Zuk (senior scouting supervisor).

PARK LOCATION—Exhibition Stadium on the gounds of Exhibition Place. Entrances to Exhibition Place via Lakeshore Boulevard, Queen Elizabeth Way Highway and Dufferin and Bathurst Streets.

Seating capacity—43,737

FIELD DIMENSIONS—Home plate to left field at foul line, 330 feet; to center field, 400 feet; to right field at foul line, 330 feet.

WILLIE WILSON gives George Brett champagne shampoo after Royals clinched A.L. West title September 19.

WEST DIVISION

Royals Ignored Ghosts to Win A.L. Pennant

By MIKE DeARMOND

It began with a rookie manager ignoring one ghost and ended with a 12-year-old expansion team coming of age by conquering another.

For the first time since midseason of 1975, the Kansas City Royals peeked into the manager's office and found not Whitey Herzog, but a dry wit named Jim Frey, a somewhat glummer, somewhat younger version of George Burns.

And while the comparisons were inevitable between the former manager and the new kid in the clubhouse, Frey stated that it wasn't the ghost of Herzog he was worried about.

"If I was worried about ghosts," the former Orioles coach said, "I'd be worried about more than one. There would be a long line. Whitey Herzog wasn't the only manager the Royals ever had. The only thing I'm worried about is doing a good job."

Frey drove the Royals farther than they had ever been driven before—all the way to the World Series, where they were defeated in six games by the Philadelphia Phillies.

By the All-Star break, Frey and the Royals were looking down at second-place Chicago from an 8½-game advantage. By the final day of August the lead had grown to an insurmountable 20 games over second-place Oakland. Even a September slide didn't make a race of the American League West as Kansas City triumphed over the A's by 14 games, finishing 97-65. Nor did it keep the Royals from setting a club home attendance record of 2,288,714.

George Brett, who finished at .390, flirted with the .400 barrier. Willie Wilson, who finished at .326, led the majors in runs (133) and hits (230) while becoming the first man ever to record 700 at-bats. Wilson stole 79 bases and made 100 hits from each side of the plate.

Dennis Leonard won 20 games for the third time in four seasons. Larry Gura won 18. And young Dan Quisenberry, as fast with the quips as he was with the saves (33), captured the A. L. Fireman of the Year Award.

And yet, this was a difficult year, too. The campaign began with catcher Darrell Porter in an alcohol and drug abuse rehabilitation clinic and center fielder Amos Otis missing the first 39 games because of a ruptured tendon in the little finger of his right hand.

Hal McRae, the team's designated hitter, suffered torn calf muscles May 12 and missed 22 of the next 23 games. Brett, with foot and wrist injuries, missed a total of 45 games. Starting pitchers Rich Gale and Paul Splittorff were sidelined for protracted periods by injuries, too.

The Royals didn't get untracked until the second month of the season and even Brett had initial doubts about the Royals' abilities.

"In spring training we struggled a lot," Brett said. "My brothers (one of whom, Ken, would later join the Royals' pitching staff for the stretch run) said something about coming back (to Kansas City) for the playoffs. And I said, 'I don't think you're going to have to worry about it. We're terrible. We can't do anything right.'

KANSAS CITY ROYALS—1980

First row—Chalk, White, MacKenzie, coach; Martinez, coach; Frey, manager; Schaffer, coach; Connors, coach; G. Brett, Washington, Terrell, Cobb, trainer. Second row—Zych, equipment manager; Torres, Pattin, Barranca, Leonard, Quisenberry, Hurdle, Gura, Aikens, McRae, Mulliniks. Top row—LaCock, Quirk, Eastwick, Wilson, Gale, Christenson, Martin, Splittorff, Wathan, Porter. Seated in front—Stiegler and Harrison, batboys.

"Then, all of a sudden, we starting winning all these ball games," Brett said. "I can't remember any turnaround, but it was like a different team. It was like somebody put a halo over our heads."

Not until June 7 was Frey able to field a starting lineup that included Brett, McRae, Otis and Porter. And then, just when Brett had raised his batting average 90 points to .337 with a 34-for-76 tear, he went down with ligament damage in his foot and missed 26 games.

Upon his return, Brett picked up right where he'd left off. On August 17 in Kansas City, Brett hit in his 29th straight game, a 4-for-4 showing boosting him over .400 for the first time.

The streak ended two days later, at 30, but behind Brett's batting surge and under the scrutiny of the national media, the Royals rolled to 39 games over .500 on August 27 with a 38-12 record in a string of 50 games.

Brett wound up with 118 RBIs in 117 games, the first player to have more RBIs than games played since Walt Dropo's 144 RBIs in 136 games for the Boston Red Sox in 1950.

McRae rebounded from the after-effects of rotator cuff surgery to hit .297.

First baseman Willie Aikens, in his first year after coming over from California, produced 98 RBIs and 20 homers, second only to Brett's 24.

U. L. Washington made people forget Freddie Patek was once the Royals' shortstop.

Frank White, who won a fourth consecutive Gold Glove for his work at second base, went 6-for-11 and won MVP honors in the A. L. playoffs. He finished the year with career highs in hits (148) and RBIs (60).

John Wathan, playing left, right, first and catcher, was the league's most valuable utility man with a .305 average.

And, although it all fell apart in the World Series—Wilson struck out a record 12 times and Brett had to play with hemorrhoids—there was finally the conquest of that other ghost.

In 1-2-3 fashion, the Yankees were vanquished in the playoffs, Brett deciding the final game with a three-run homer off the Yankees' ace reliever Rich Gossage.

It was the most dramatic home run in Royals history, a home run that brought final triumph over a Yankees team that had dealt them playoff defeats in 1976-77-78.

SCORES OF KANSAS CITY ROYALS' 1980 GAMES

APRIL			Winner	Loser
10—Detroit	L	1-5	Morris	Leonard
11—Detroit	W	4-0	Gura	Schatzeder
12—Detroit	W	8-6	Pattin	Underwood
13—Detroit	W	3-2	Splittorff	Rozema
15—At Balt.	L	2-12	Palmer	Leonard
16—At Balt.	L	1-2	Flanagan	Gura
17—At Balt.	L	2-5	Stone	Gale
18—At Det.	W	9-6†	Quisenberry	Lopez
19—At Det.	L	6-8	Morris	Martin
20—At Det.	W	9-6	Martin	Schatzeder
21—Toronto	L	1-7	Stieb	Gale
22—Toronto	W	7-2	Splittorff	Mirabella
23—Toronto	W	7-4	Christenson	McLaughlin
25—Balt.	W	7-0	Gura	Stone
26—Balt.	L	0-4	Flanagan	Gale
27—Balt.	W	3-2	Splittorff	Ford
29—At Tor.	L	1-3	Clancy	Leonard
30—At Tor.	W	3-0	Gura	Jefferson
		Won 10, Lost 8		

MAY			Winner	Loser
2—Boston	L	5-6†	Lockwood	Quisenberry
3—Boston	L	0-7	Rainey	Splittorff
4—Boston	W	5-3	Leonard	Stanley
6—At Chi.	L	0-2	Wortham	Gura
7—At Chi.	W	12-5	Christenson	Kravec
8—At Chi.	L	2-8	Burns	Splittorff
9—At Bos.	W	6-5	Leonard	Stanley
10—At Bos.	W	13-8	Martin	Eckersley
11—At Bos.	L	2-5	Rainey	Gale
12—At N.Y.	W	12-3	Gura	Tiant
13—At N.Y.	W	4-1	Martin	Griffin
14—At N.Y.	L	3-16	Guidry	Leonard
16—Calif.	L	1-11	Kison	Gale
17—Calif.	W	2-1*	Gura	Clear
18—Calif.	W	5-3	Martin	Tanana
19—Oakland	W	6-5†	Quisenberry	Hamilton
20—Oakland	W	1-0	Gale	Norris
21—Oakland	L	2-4§	Lacey	Quisenberry
22—Oakland	W	16-3	Martin	Keough

MAY

Date		Score	Winner	Loser
23—At Calif.	W	13-9	Leonard	Tanana
24—At Calif.	W	6-5*	Quisenberry	Clear
25—At Calif.	W	7-3	Gura	LaRoche
26—At Oak.	L	1-4	Keough	Martin
27—At Oak.	W	4-2	Leonard	Kingman
28—At Oak.	L	3-6	Langford	Gale
30—Chicago	W	9-2	Gura	Wortham
31—Chicago	W	6-4	Martin	Trout

Won 17, Lost 10

JUNE

Date		Score	Winner	Loser
1—Chicago	L	1-6	Burns	Leonard
2—N. York	L	3-5	Guidry	Splittorff
3—N. York	W	6-5*	Quisenberry	Davis
4—N. York	W	9-3	Martin	Tiant
5—At Texas	W	8-0	Leonard	Kern
6—At Texas	W	4-2	Splittorff	Matlack
7—At Texas	W	7-2	Gale	Perry
8—At Texas	W	5-4	Christenson	Babcock
10—At Cleve.	W	8-4	Pattin	Barker
11—At Cleve.	W	5-0	Leonard	Waits
11—At Cleve.	L	5-8	Spillner	Gale
13—At Milw.	W	4-3	Gura	Keeton
14—At Milw.	L	2-5	Travers	Martin
15—At Milw.	W	7-2	Leonard	Haas
16—Texas	L	3-6	Babcock	Quisenberry
17—Texas	W	3-2	Gale	Perry
18—Cleve.	W	10-2	Gura	Denny
19—Cleve.	L	4-5	Barker	Martin
20—Milw.	L	5-10	Haas	Leonard
21—Milw.	L	1-5	Sorensen	Splittorff
22—Milw.	W	7-4	Gale	Caldwell
23—At Minn.	L	1-4	Koosman	Gura
24—At Minn.	L	1-2	Jackson	Quisenberry
24—At Minn.	W	4-2	Martin	Erickson
25—At Minn.	W	4-1	Splittorff	Zahn
27—At Sea.	W	2-1	Gale	Honeycutt
28—At Sea.	W	4-2	Gura	Roberts
29—At Sea.	L	2-7	Abbott	Leonard
30—Minn.	L	3-12	Jackson	Martin

Won 17, Lost 12

JULY

Date		Score	Winner	Loser
1—Minn.	L	1-2	Corbett	Splittorff
2—Minn.	W	4-3*	Quisenberry	Koosman
3—Seattle	L	2-13	Beattie	Gura
4—Seattle	W	5-3	Quisenberry	Roberts
5—Seattle	W	5-4	Twitty	Parrott
6—Seattle	L	3-5	Bannister	Splittorff
10—Detroit	W	3-2	Splittorff	Wilcox
11—Detroit	W	7-3	Leonard	Morris
12—At Balt.	L	1-3	Stone	Martin
13—At Balt.	L	3-7	Gura	Flanagan
14—At Balt.	W	8-4	Splittorff	McGregor
15—At Bos.	W	8-4	Gale	Renko
16—At Bos.	W	5-1	Leonard	Eckersley
17—At Bos.	L	4-12	Tudor	Martin
18—At N.Y.	W	13-1	Gura	May
19—At N.Y.	L	7-13	Bird	Splittorff
20—At N.Y.	W	14-3	Gale	Guidry
21—Chicago	W	2-1	Leonard	Burns
22—Chicago	L	1-6	Trout	Busby
23—Chicago	W	9-2	Gura	Baumgarten
24—Chicago	W	12-4	Splittorff	Wortham
25—N. York	W	6-1	Gale	Tiant
26—N. York	L	4-5	Gossage	Leonard
27—N. York	W	8-0	Gura	John
29—Boston	W	9-8	Quisenberry	Burgmeier
30—Boston	L	1-7	Stanley	Busby
31—Boston	W	13-3	Leonard	Eckersley

Won 18, Lost 9

AUGUST

Date		Score	Winner	Loser
1—At Chi.	W	4-3	Gura	Burns
2—At Chi.	W	8-2	Gale	Trout
3—At Chi.	L	3-5	Dotson	Splittorff
4—At Det.	W	6-5	Quisenberry	Schatzeder
5—At Det.	W	6-3	Leonard	Wilcox
6—At Det.	W	5-4	Gura	Morris
8—At Tor.	W	9-0	Gale	Clancy
8—At Tor.	W	7-4	Pattin	Garvin
9—At Tor.	L	3-4§	Willis	Eastwick
10—At Tor.	W	8-5	Leonard	Jefferson
11—Balt.	L	1-2	D. Martinez	Gura
12—Balt.	W	4-3	Quisenberry	McGregor
13—Balt.	W	6-1	Gale	Palmer
15—Toronto	W	4-3	Leonard	Jefferson
16—Toronto	W	11-5	Gura	Kucek
17—Toronto	W	8-3	Splittorff	Clancy
18—At Texas	W	6-3	Gale	Figueroa
19—At Texas	W	4-3	Twitty	Darwin
20—At Texas	W	5-3‡	Quisenberry	Johnson
21—Cleve.	L	3-4	Waits	Busby
22—Cleve.	L	1-4	Barker	Splittorff
23—Cleve.	W	3-2	Gale	Garland
24—Cleve.	W	7-5	Leonard	Grimsley
25—At Milw.	W	9-3	Gura	Haas
26—At Milw.	W	7-6	Busby	Caldwell
27—At Milw.	W	5-4	Splittorff	Mitchell
28—Texas	L	6-10	Rajsich	Twitty
29—Texas	W	7-3	Leonard	Figueroa
30—Texas	L	5-7†	Johnson	Quisenberry
31—Texas	W	4-3	Quisenberry	Lyle

Won 23, Lost 7

SEPTEMBER

Date		Score	Winner	Loser
1—Milw.	L	1-6	McClure	Gale
3—Milw.	L	1-3*	Sorensen	Leonard
4—Milw.	L	5-9	Castro	Quisenberry
5—At Cleve.	W	2-1	Splittorff	Waits
6—At Cleve.	L	3-8	Barker	Martin
7—At Cleve.	W	6-4	Leonard	Garland
8—At Calif.	L	4-7	Aase	Gura
9—At Calif.	L	3-4	Tanana	Splittorff
10—At Calif.	L	3-8	Aase	Martin
11—At Calif.	W	7-2	Leonard	Ferris
12—At Oak.	L	2-6	Langford	Chamberlain
13—At Oak.	L	2-6	McCatty	Gura
14—At Oak.	W	4-3	Splittorff	Kingman
17—Calif.	W	5-0	Leonard	Botting
17—Calif.	L	4-7	LaRoche	Gura
18—Calif.	W	5-2	Martin	Martinez
19—Oakland	W	13-3	Splittorff	Kingman
20—Oakland	L	0-9	Keough	Jones
21—Oakland	L	3-9	Norris	Leonard
22—At Sea.	L	4-5†	McLaughlin	Quisenberry
23—At Sea.	L	3-9	Beattie	Martin
24—At Sea.	L	2-4	Honeycutt	Splittorff
26—At Minn.	L	0-3	Zahn	Leonard
27—At Minn.	L	3-8	Koosman	Gura
28—At Minn.	L	7-8	Redfern	Gale
30—Seattle	W	7-5§	Quisenberry	Parrott

Won 8, Lost 18

OCTOBER

Date		Score	Winner	Loser
1—Seattle	W	4-1	Pattin	Dressler
2—Seattle	W	6-2	Martin	Bannister
3—Minn.	L	3-5	Koosman	Gura
4—Minn.	W	17-1	Leonard	Erickson
5—Minn.	W	4-0	Splittorff	Jackson

Won 4, Lost 1

*10 innings. †11 innings. ‡12 innings. §14 innings.

Martin-Led A's Were Surprise Contenders

By KIT STIER

Nearly everyone laughed when Billy Martin said he would make the Oakland A's contenders during the 1980 season. Every new manager is prone to making brash statements, especially in spring.

To everyone's surprise, Martin nearly kept his word. That bunch of disorganized misfits that had been in or about the American League West basement for three seasons suddenly found that baseball can be fun.

With much of the same personnel that lost 299 games between 1977 and 1979, Martin went to work. He and his coaching staff taught them about baserunning, pitching, fielding, and how to use their heads. At season's end, the A's had themselves a respectable 83-79 record and were in second place, 14 games behind the Kansas City Royals.

It all began on February 21 when Owner Charlie Finley hired Martin. It was a marriage that couldn't last, they said. Two of baseball's most combustible personalities would certainly clash sooner or later. But Finley let the manager run the club and that satisfied Billy.

Finally, it was Finley who threw in the towel, selling the A's on July 23 to Bay Area locals for $12.7 million. The new owners, members of the family that runs Levi Strauss and Company, a clothing manufacturer, officially took over the A's on November 6. The group included Walter A. Haas, chairman of the board of Levi Strauss; his son, Wally Haas; and son-in-law Roy Eisenhardt, who became the club's president.

The A's jumped off to a 12-8 start in April. Yes, and the A's were 16-5 in April of 1978, when they finished 69-93. But this time the A's played .500 ball in May and began to gather a handful of believers.

The A's began June 2½ games behind the Royals. Then, the roof fell in. Seven wins and 21 losses later they were tied for fourth place and 12 games out.

Martin remained remarkably patient. He kept encouraging the team, with only an occasional outburst, and his patience paid off. The A's were 19-10 in July and climbed back into second place. They split 28 games in August and then won 18 of their last 31.

The team that won only one season series (Seattle) in 1979 had a winning record against every West Division opponent.

The team of no-names developed some talented personalities. From the beginning, it was evident that the A's outfield might develop into one of the best in baseball and it did. Rickey Henderson in left, Dwayne Murphy in center and Tony Armas in right gloved nearly every catchable fly ball and line drive.

And Henderson, in his first full year in the majors, broke Ty Cobb's A. L. stolen base record. The 21-year-old finished with 100 thefts, four more than Cobb had in 1915.

Armas clouted 35 home runs, an astounding figure when you consider that in 293 previous major league games he'd hit only 26.

The cornerstones of the infield, Dave Revering at first and Wayne Gross at third, combined for 29 homers and 123 RBIs. Revering hit .290, Gross .281.

The A's pitching, and particularly the starting pitching, was perhaps the best in baseball. Matt Keough, Rick Langford and Mike Norris enjoyed their

OAKLAND A's—1980

Sitting, front row—Cox, Heath, Henderson, Edwards, Norris. Second row—Picciolo, Klutts, McKay, Boyer, coach; Walls, coach; Martin, manager; Mitterwald, coach; Fowler, coach; Kingman, Essian, Minetto. Third row—Morabito, traveling secretary; Romo, trainer; Jones, Langford, Page, Gross, Revering, Ciensczyk, equipment manager. Top row—Guerrero, Murphy, Keough, Lacey, Beard, Davis, McCatty, Armas, Newman, Gonzalez.

finest seasons. They were a rotation which needed little relief help.

Keough, who had a horrid 2-17 record in '79, rebounded to 16-13 with a 2.92 ERA and was voted the A.L. Comeback Player of the Year.

Norris, who had never won more than five games in a season, blazed to a 5-0 record before finally losing, 1-0, with a four-hitter in 11 innings at Toronto. In the first 60 innings he pitched, Norris gave up just two earned runs. He finished with a 22-9 record and his 2.54 ERA was second to the 2.47 of the Yankees' Rudy May.

Langford (19-12, 3.26) strung together 22 straight complete games, the most in over 30 years. The A's pitched 94 complete games, the most since the Detroit Tigers produced the same number in 1946. Norris, Keough, Langford and Steve McCatty each pitched complete 14-inning games. McCatty was the only loser, a 2-1, six-hit decision against Seattle on August 10.

The A's played aggressively throughout the season. Hardly a day passed when the Martin Gang didn't pull off some kind of surprise. They stole home seven times and completed 14 double steals and one triple steal.

That kind of play began to pay off at the gate. The A's drew 842,259 in 1980, a dramatic increase from the all-time low of 306,763 that turned out at the Oakland Coliseum in 1979.

SCORES OF OAKLAND ATHLETICS' 1980 GAMES

APRIL			Winner	Loser	MAY			Winner	Loser
10—Minn.	L	7-9§	Corbett	McCatty	26—Kan. C.	W	4-1	Keough	Martin
11—Minn.	W	1-0	Keough	Redfern	27—Kan. C.	L	2-4	Leonard	Kingman
12—Minn.	L	0-6	Zahn	Kingman	28—Kan. C.	W	6-3	Langford	Gale
13—Minn.	L	4-1	Norris	Erickson	30—At Texas	W	6-3	McCatty	Perry
14—Seattle	L	1-7	Abbott	McCatty	31—At Texas	W	4-3	Norris	Medich
15—Seattle	W	12-3	McCatty	Parrott			Won 13, Lost 13		
16—Seattle	W	6-1	Keough	Beattie					
18—Calif.	W	6-3	Kingman	Kison	JUNE				
19—Calif.	W	3-1	Norris	Aase	1—At Texas	L	3-7	Darwin	Keough
20—Calif.	W	6-1	Keough	Knapp	2—At Cleve.	L	5-10	Garland	Kingman
20—Calif.	W	8-2	McCatty	Tanana	3—At Cleve.	L	4-6†	Cruz	Langford
21—At Sea.	W	4-2	Jones	Rawley	4—At Cleve.	L	3-5	Spillner	McCatty
22—At Sea.	L	4-5	Honeycutt	Kingman	6—Boston	L	8-14	Rainey	Norris
23—At Sea.	W	5-2	Langford	McLaughlin	7—Boston	W	5-1	Keough	Torrez
25—At Minn.	L	3-10	Koosman	Keough	8—Boston	W	1-6	Burgmeier	Hamilton
26—At Minn.	L	1-5	Redfern	McCatty	9—Balt.	L	2-3	Flanagan	Langford
27—At Minn.	L	11-20	Corbett	Kingman	10—Balt.	W	7-4	McCatty	McGregor
28—At Calif.	W	8-0	Langford	Kison	11—Balt.	W	6-2x	Norris	Stewart
29—At Calif.	W	4-2	Norris	Tanana	13—N. York	W	4-3	Kingman	Guidry
30—At Calif.	L	1-2	Aase	Keough	13—N. York	L	4-6	Davis	Keough
		Won 12, Lost 8			14—N. York	L	1-2	Figueroa	Langford
					15—N. York	L	2-8	Tiant	McCatty
MAY					16—At Bos.	W	11-8	Norris	Rainey
2—Detroit	W	10-6	McCatty	Rozema	17—At Bos.	L	2-6	Torrez	Keough
3—Detroit	W	5-3	Kingman	Morris	18—At Balt.	L	2-3	Flanagan	Jones
4—Detroit	L	0-4	Wilcox	Langford	19—At Balt.	L	3-4	McGregor	Langford
4—Detroit	W	1-0	Norris	Schatzeder	20—At N.Y.	L	7-15	Tiant	McCatty
5—Cleve.	W	5-1	Keough	Denny	21—At N.Y.	L	3-5	John	Norris
6—Cleve.	L	3-4	Barker	McCatty	22—At N.Y.	W	5-2	Keough	Underwood
7—Cleve.	L	1-2	Waits	Kingman	23—Milw.	L	0-8	Cleveland	Kingman
10—Toronto	W	4-3	Langford	Garvin	24—Milw.	L	3-5	Travers	Langford
11—Toronto	W	12-1	Norris	Lemanczyk	25—Milw.	L	2-5	Haas	McCatty
13—At Det.	L	3-4	Morris	Keough	27—Chicago	W	3-1	Norris	Baumgarten
14—At Det.	L	5-6	Lopez	Jones	28—Chicago	L	0-3	Wortham	Keough
16—At Tor.	L	0-1‡	Jefferson	Norris	29—Chicago	L	0-3	Burns	Kingman
17—At Tor.	W	4-2x	Keough	McLaughlin	30—At Milw.	L	2-5	Travers	Langford
18—At Tor.	L	1-12	Mirabella	Langford			Won 7, Lost 21		
19—At K.C.	L	5-6†	Quisenberry	Hamilton					
20—At K.C.	L	0-1	Gale	Norris	JULY				
21—At K.C.	W	4-2x	Lacey	Quisenberry	1—At Milw.	L	3-5	Haas	McCatty
22—At K.C.	L	3-16	Martin	Keough	2—At Milw.	W	5-3†	Norris	McClure
23—Texas	L	1-3	Jenkins	Langford	3—At Milw.	W	7-5	Keough	Caldwell
24—Texas	W	15-7	McCatty	Perry	4—At Chi.	W	2-0	Kingman	Burns
25—Texas	L	3-7	Medich	Norris	5—At Chi.	W	5-0	Langford	Dotson

JULY			Winner	Loser
6—At Chi.	L	0-2	Trout	Norris
6—At Chi.	L	4-5	Farmer	Lacey
10—Calif.	L	1-5	Tanana	Keough
10—Calif.	W	5-4	Langford	Aase
11—Calif.	W	6-2	Kingman	Knapp
12—At Calif.	W	5-4	Norris	Lemanczyk
13—At Calif.	L	4-5x	Montague	Hamilton
14—At Calif.	W	6-4	Langford	Kison
16—Detroit	L	2-7	Weaver	Kingman
17—Detroit	W	5-2	Keough	Morris
18—Cleve.	W	9-1	Norris	Spillner
19—Cleve.	W	3-0	McCatty	Waits
20—Cleve.	W	6-5x	Langford	Cruz
21—Toronto	L	0-1	Stieb	Kingman
22—Toronto	L	2-6	Jefferson	Keough
22—Toronto	W	5-1	Norris	Mirabella
23—Toronto	W	6-2	McCatty	Kucek
25—At Det.	W	5-3	Langford	Robbins
26—At Det.	L	0-7	Schatzeder	Kingman
27—At Det.	L	2-4	Wilcox	Minetto
27—At Det.	W	4-0	Keough	Morris
28—At Tor.	W	5-3*	Norris	Barlow
29—At Tor.	W	6-5§	Lacey	Garvin
30—At Tor.	W	11-1	Langford	Stieb
		Won 19, Lost 10		

AUGUST				
1—At Cleve.	W	2-1	Kingman	Waits
3—At Cleve.	W	11-3	Keough	Garland
3—At Cleve.	L	2-4	Barker	Norris
4—Minn.	W	2-1	McCatty	Zahn
5—Minn.	W	3-2	Langford	Koosman
6—Minn.	W	3-1	Kingman	Erickson
8—Seattle	L	1-2†	Rawley	Keough
9—Seattle	W	2-1	Norris	Honeycutt
10—Seattle	L	1-2x	Heaverlo	McCatty
10—Seattle	W	6-1	Langford	McLaughlin
12—At Minn.	L	2-3	Corbett	Kingman
13—At Minn.	W	6-2	Keough	Arroyo
14—At Minn.	W	2-1‡	Norris	Corbett
15—At Sea.	W	11-3	Langford	Abbott
16—At Sea.	W	8-3	McCatty	McLaughlin
17—At Sea.	L	3-4	Dressler	Kingman
19—Boston	L	5-7	Stanley	Minetto
20—Boston	W	2-1	Norris	Eckersley
21—Boston	L	1-5	Tudor	Langford
22—Balt.	L	2-3	Stewart	McCatty

AUGUST			Winner	Loser
23—Balt.	L	2-4	Stone	Kingman
24—Balt.	L	0-3	Flanagan	Keough
25—N. York	W	9-1	Norris	John
26—N. York	W	3-1	Langford	Tiant
28—At Bos.	L	2-3	Burgmeier	McCatty
29—At Bos.	L	3-6	Torrez	Kingman
30—At Bos.	L	6-7†	Campbell	Lacey
31—At Bos.	L	1-5	Tudor	Norris
		Won 14, Lost 14		

SEPTEMBER				
1—At N.Y.	L	0-5	Underwood	Langford
2—At N.Y.	L	1-6	May	McCatty
3—At N.Y.	L	3-8	John	Kingman
4—At Balt.	W	7-1	Keough	Flanagan
5—At Balt.	L	7-8	Stoddard	Jones
6—At Balt.	W	3-2	Langford	Palmer
7—At Balt.	W	5-2	McCatty	Stone
8—Texas	L	2-6	Butcher	Kingman
9—Texas	W	6-3	Keough	Figueroa
10—Texas	W	3-1	Norris	Matlack
12—Kan. C.	W	9-5	Langford	Chamberlain
13—Kan. C.	W	6-2	McCatty	Gura
14—Kan. C.	L	3-4	Splittorff	Kingman
15—At Texas	L	0-2	Matlack	Keough
16—At Texas	W	4-2‡	Norris	Darwin
17—At Texas	W	6-4	Langford	Butcher
18—At Texas	L	6-10	Darwin	McCatty
19—At K.C.	L	3-13	Splittorff	Kingman
20—At K.C.	W	9-0	Keough	M. Jones
21—At K.C.	W	9-3	Norris	Leonard
23—Chicago	W	6-4	Langford	Proly
24—Chicago	W	7-1	McCatty	Trout
25—Chicago	L	4-6	Proly	Kingman
26—Milw.	L	7-10	Cleveland	Norris
27—Milw.	W	7-4	Langford	Haas
28—Milw.	W	3-2	McCatty	Cleveland
30—At Chi.	W	5-1	Kingman	Trout
		Won 16, Lost 11		

OCTOBER				
1—At Chi.	W	11-3	Norris	Baumgarten
2—At Chi.	L	4-9	Hoffman	Langford
4—At Milw.	W	4-0	Lacey	Haas
5—At Milw.	L	4-5y	Cleveland	Beard
		Won 2, Lost 2		

*7½ innings.　†10 innings.　‡11 innings.　§12 innings.　x14 innings.　y15 innings.

Twins Lost Mauch, Marshall, Cool Million

By PATRICK REUSSE

Finally, Gene Mauch couldn't take it any more. Six weeks shy of completing his fifth season as manager of the Minnesota Twins, Mauch resigned. At the time, the Twins were 54-71, 26½ games out of first place in the American League West and tied for fourth with the Chicago White Sox.

A nine-game losing streak to open August was the catalyst of Mauch's decision. It was, he said, "the capper, the stretch during which I seriously started to think about this. I've had some bad teams—teams that were bad enough to gag a maggot—but even those teams were able to steal some games by executing. This season, we have lost because of a failure to execute."

Johnny Goryl, a longtime manager in the Twins' minor-league system and Mauch's third-base coach for two seasons, was named interim manager.

Under Goryl, the Twins slipped to their lowest point of 1980, 20 games under .500 at 58-78, September 5. But then the Twins rallied to win 19 of their last 25 games, including 12 in a row, the longest winning streak in the major leagues in two seasons.

The Twins were 23-13 under Goryl, rising to third place, 77-84 and 19½ games behind the runaway Kansas City Royals. The team's play improved enough that Twins President Calvin Griffith signed Goryl to manage in 1981.

"I wasn't sure I wanted the job for next season when I first replaced Gene Mauch," Goryl said. "But the players made up my mind for me by playing excellent, enthusiastic baseball."

The players also made up Mauch's mind. He entered the season highly optimistic, particularly after the Twins had an excellent exhibition season, winning 15 of 21 games. The Twins split 20 games in April, but that was the last time they were at .500.

Also departing, though against his will, was Mike Marshall, who had shared A.L. Fireman of the Year honors with Texas' Jim Kern the previous season. Marshall got off to a shaky start, blowing a handful of games in the late innings.

Meanwhile, Marshall was a central figure in the Players Association's preparations for the scheduled May 23 strike, which never came off. Shortly thereafter, on June 6, Marshall was released with a 1-3 record, one save and a 6.19 ERA.

Marshall, whose contract extended through the 1981 season, contended that his release revolved around his union activities, pointing out that he had allowed only one earned run in his last 11 innings. Marshall took his case to the Players Association and it was announced that a grievance would be filed against the Twins, charging them with unfair labor practices.

Mauch turned to Doug Corbett, a 27-year-old rookie, as his late-inning stopper. Drafted from the Cincinnati Reds' organization the previous December for $25,000, Corbett had a sensational season. He finished with an 8-6 record, 23 saves and a 1.99 ERA.

The team's most positive batting achievement came from outfielder Ken Landreaux. He put together a 31-game hitting streak, the season's longest, before being stopped by Baltimore's Scott McGregor in Minnesota on May 31. Landreaux, who hit .281 for the season, batted .392 during the streak, which was the longest in the A.L. since 1949, when Dom DiMaggio hit in 34 straight games for the Boston Red Sox.

The themes of the Twins' season, however, were ineffective starting pitching, a lack of run production (670 compared with 764 in '79), erratic defense in the outfield and, of course, the inevitable injuries.

Shortstop Roy Smalley, who played in every game in '79, missed 28 games because of leg injuries. Landreaux missed more than 30 games with a variety of injuries. After some early success, Pete Redfern dropped out of the starting rotation because of a sore arm and appeared in only 23 games.

Jerry Koosman and Geoff Zahn, the veteran lefthanders who had been the Twins' best starters the previous season, struggled until the final month of the season. Koosman wound up 16-13 with a 4.04 ERA; Zahn was 14-18 with a 4.40 ERA. Although only Oakland's Brian Kingman lost more games, Zahn was second in the A.L. in shutouts, with five.

Only two A.L. teams, Cleveland and Chicago, had fewer homers than Minnesota's 99. The club's top home run hitter was third baseman John Cas-

MINNESOTA TWINS—1980

First row—D. Jackson, Morales, Castino, Kuehl, coach; Zimmerman, coach; Mauch, manager; Randall, coach; Pascual, coach; Goryl, coach; Marshall, Rivera. Middle row—Wiesner, visiting clubhouse man; Adams, Landreaux, Norwood, Cubbage, Sofield, Wynegar, Goodwin, Edwards, R. Jackson, Butera, Dunn, clubhouse man. Top row—Crump, equipment manager; Zahn, Corbett, Powell, Mackanin, Redfern, Verhoeven, Erickson, Koosman, Smalley, Wilfong, Felton, Martin, trainer.

tino with 13. Smalley was next with 12.

Castino, who in his second season was an easy winner in post-season balloting for the club's most valuable player, also led the team in batting average (.302), RBIs (64), runs (67) and hits (165). This from a man who had come to the Twins with a "good field, no hit" reputation. His glovework was often brilliant, but he made 22 errors, several of those at shortstop.

Rob Wilfong was the defensive standout. He committed only three errors in 120 games at second base and his fielding percentage of .9948 set an A.L. record.

The season was a financial disaster. With the Twins' attendance of 769,206 the lowest in the majors and the fourth lowest in the franchise's 20-year history, Griffith said the organizations's losses would be the highest ever, well over $1 million.

SCORES OF MINNESOTA TWINS' 1980 GAMES

APRIL		Winner	Loser	JUNE		Winner	Loser
10–At Oak.	W 9-7§	Corbett	McCatty	3–Boston	W 9-4	Koosman	Billingham
11–At Oak.	L 0-1	Keough	Redfern	6–Toronto	W 5-0	Zahn	Mirabella
12–At Oak.	W 6-0	Zahn	Kingman	7–Toronto	W 3-2	Jackson	Stieb
13–At Oak.	L 1-4	Norris	Erickson	8–Toronto	W 5-1	Erickson	Jefferson
14–At Calif.	W 5-3	Corbett	Clear	8–Toronto	L 4-6x	McLaughlin	Arroyo
15–At Calif.	L 1-3	Tanana	Koosman	10–At Det.	L 3-8	Wilcox	Zahn
16–At Calif.	L 1-2†	Frost	Marshall	11–At Det.	W 9-5	Jackson	Rozema
17–At Sea.	L 3-4	Honeycutt	Zahn	12–At Det.	L 4-8	Underwood	Zahn
18–At Sea.	L 1-3	Bannister	Erickson	13–At Cleve.	L 2-6	Denny	Koosman
18–At Sea.	L 2-3	McLaughlin	Felton	14–At Cleve.	L 2-3	Barker	Erickson
19–At Sea.	W 8-3	Koosman	Abbott	15–At Cleve.	L 5-14	Spillner	Jackson
20–At Sea.	W 4-3	Redfern	Parrott	16–At Tor.	W 4-0	Zahn	Jefferson
22–Calif.	W 8-1	Zahn	Frost	17–At Tor.	W 8-6	Corbett	Mirabella
23–Calif.	L 0-17	Kison	Felton	19–Detroit	W 5-1	Jackson	Schatzeder
25–Oakland	W 10-3	Koosman	Keough	20–Cleve.	L 3-4y	Cruz	Redfern
26–Oakland	W 5-1	Redfern	McCatty	21–Cleve.	W 3-2	Zahn	Garland
27–Oakland	W 20-11	Corbett	Kingman	22–Cleve.	L 6-11	Waits	Redfern
28–Seattle	L 4-6	Honeycutt	Felton	23–Kan. C.	W 4-1	Koosman	Gura
29–Seattle	L 3-5	Rawley	Marshall	24–Kan. C.	W 2-1	Jackson	Quisenberry
30–Seattle	W 10-3	Redfern	Parrott	24–Kan. C.	L 2-4	Martin	Erickson
				25–Kan. C.	L 1-4	Splittorff	Zahn
	Won 10, Lost 10			27–At Texas	L 0-5	Perry	Redfern
				28–At Texas	L 3-11	Comer	Koosman
MAY				29–At Texas	W 5-3	Erickson	Medich
2–N. York	L 6-9	Guidry	Zahn	30–At K.C.	W 12-3	Jackson	Martin
3–N. York	L 3-7	John	Jackson				
4–N. York	L 1-10	Underwood	Koosman		**Won 13, Lost 13**		
5–At Balt.	W 4-2	Redfern	Stone				
6–At Balt.	L 3-10	McGregor	Zahn	**JULY**			
7–At Balt.	L 6-8	Stewart	Marshall	1–At K.C.	W 2-1	Corbett	Splittorff
9–At N.Y.	L 2-5	Guidry	Koosman	2–At K.C.	L 3-4†	Quisenberry	Koosman
10–At N.Y.	W 1-0‡	Jackson	May	3–Texas	W 10-3	Erickson	Comer
11–At N.Y.	L 0-5	John	Zahn	4–Texas	L 3-4§	Darwin	Verhoeven
12–At Bos.	W 4-3	Redfern	Torrez	5–Texas	W 2-1	Zahn	Jenkins
13–At Bos.	L 5-10	Renko	Verhoeven	6–Texas	W 4-1	Arroyo	Matlack
14–At Bos.	L 6-7	Burgmeier	Corbett	10–At Sea.	W 12-4	Koosman	Honeycutt
16–Milw.	W 4-3	Koosman	McClure	11–At Sea.	W 6-3	Jackson	Abbott
17–Milw.	L 11-14	Augustine	Zahn	12–Seattle	W 8-3	Zahn	Bannister
18–Milw.	W 10-4	Redfern	Travers	13–Seattle	W 7-6x	Corbett	Rawley
19–At Chi.	L 0-1	Kravec	Koosman	14–Seattle	L 5-8	Honeycutt	Arroyo
20–At Chi.	L 2-4	Dotson	Jackson	15–At N.Y.	W 5-4	Koosman	Guidry
21–At Chi.	W 3-2	Zahn	Trout	16–At N.Y.	L 1-11	Underwood	Jackson
23–At Milw.	L 0-5	Travers	Redfern	17–At N.Y.	L 3-10	John	Zahn
24–At Milw.	L 0-4	Haas	Koosman	18–At Bos.	L 0-1†	Torrez	Erickson
25–At Milw.	L 2-3	Sorensen	Erickson	19–At Bos.	W 4-0	Arroyo	Ojeda
26–Chicago	L 3-6	Trout	Zahn	20–At Bos.	W 5-4	Corbett	Drago
27–Chicago	L 0-2	Burns	Jackson	21–Balt.	W 8-7†	Verhoeven	T. Martinez
28–Chicago	W 6-4	Marshall	Proly	21–Balt.	L 5-12	Stone	Zahn
29–Chicago	W 5-2	Koosman	Dotson	22–Balt.	L 4-8	Flanagan	Erickson
30–Balt.	L 2-3†	Flanagan	Corbett	23–Balt.	L 7-8	McGregor	Arroyo
31–Balt.	L 1-11	McGregor	Zahn	25–Boston	L 5-7	Rem'swaal	Koosman
				25–Boston	W 6-0	Zahn	Renko
	Won 8, Lost 19			26–Boston	L 1-5	Eckersley	Erickson
				27–Boston	W 5-4	Williams	Torrez
JUNE				28–N. York	L 6-7†	Bird	Verhoeven
2–Boston	L 2-6	Stanley	Redfern				

JULY			Winner	Loser	SEPTEMBER			Winner	Loser
29–N. York	W	3-2	Zahn	Tiant	1–Cleve.	L	2-5	Barker	Williams
30–N. York	W	2-1†	Koosman	Gossage	2–Cleve.	W	5-3	Jackson	Garland
	Won 16, Lost 12				3–Cleve.	L	1-7*	Spillner	Zahn
					5–At Det.	L	0-1	Schatzeder	Erickson
AUGUST					6–At Det.	W	4-0	Koosman	Morris
1–At Balt.	L	2-3	Flanagan	Corbett	7–At Det.	W	3-1	Jackson	Fidrych
2–At Balt.	L	2-9	McGregor	Arroyo	9–Milw.	W	15-2	Williams	Sorensen
3–At Balt.	L	2-7	Palmer	Jackson	10–Milw.	L	1-3	Mitchell	Erickson
4–At Oak.	L	2-11	McCatty	Zahn	12–At Chi.	L	3-5	Burns	Koosman
5–At Oak.	L	2-3	Langford	Koosman	13–At Chi.	W	6-5	Zahn	Trout
6–At Oak.	L	1-3	Kingman	Erickson	14–At Chi.	W	3-2	Arroyo	Baumgarten
7–At Calif.	L	2-4y	Hassler	Williams	17–At Milw.	W	3-2	Koosman	Haas
8–At Calif.	L	5-9	Lemanczyk	Jackson	17–At Milw.	W	6-1	Erickson	Mitchell
9–At Calif.	L	2-8	Tanana	Zahn	18–At Milw.	L	8-9	Flinn	Corbett
10–At Calif.	W	5-2	Koosman	Barr	18–At Milw.	L	0-5	Sorensen	Redfern
12–Oakland	W	3-2	Corbett	Kingman	19–Chicago	W	6-3	Williams	Farmer
13–Oakland	L	2-6	Keough	Arroyo	21–Chicago	W	5-4	Verhoeven	Robinson
14–Oakland	L	1-2‡	Norris	Corbett	21–Chicago	W	6-4	Arroyo	Dotson
15–Calif.	L	4-5	Tanana	Zahn	22–Texas	W	1-0	Koosman	Butcher
17–Calif.	W	8-1	Erickson	Barr	23–Texas	W	8-2	Erickson	Clay
17–Calif.	W	6-5	Koosman	Knapp	24–Texas	W	9-5	Williams	Matlack
18–Calif.	W	8-3	Arroyo	LaRoche	26–Kan. C.	W	3-0	Zahn	Leonard
19–Toronto	L	3-4	Barlow	Corbett	27–Kan. C.	W	8-3	Koosman	Gura
20–Toronto	L	4-10	Todd	Zahn	28–Kan. C.	W	8-7	Redfern	Gale
21–Detroit	W	5-3	Williams	Wilcox		Won 17, Lost 7			
21–Detroit	L	2-4	Morris	Erickson					
22–Detroit	W	6-5x	Arroyo	Rozema					
23–Detroit	L	3-4	Robbins	Jackson	OCTOBER				
24–Detroit	L	2-3	Schatzeder	Zahn	2–At Texas	W	6-3	Zahn	Matlack
25–At Cleve.	L	3-4	Spillner	Arroyo	2–At Texas	W	4-1	Williams	Jenkins
26–At Cleve.	W	5-1	Erickson	Waits	3–At K.C.	W	5-3	Koosman	Gura
27–At Cleve.	L	1-4	Barker	Koosman	4–At K.C.	L	1-17	Leonard	Erickson
28–At Tor.	W	7-5z	Verhoeven	Jefferson	5–At K.C.	L	0-4	Splittorff	Jackson
29–At Tor.	W	5-2	Zahn	Stieb		Won 3, Lost 2			
30–At Tor.	L	2-3	Todd	Verhoeven					
31–At Tor.	L	1-7	Clancy	Koosman					
	Won 10, Lost 21								

*7 innings. †10 innings. ‡11 innings. §12 innings. x13 innings. y15 innings. z15-inning suspended game, completed August 29.

Veteran Relievers Failed Rangers

By RANDY GALLOWAY

They started off playing okay. Then, at midseason, they went bad. And finally, they were just flat awful down the stretch. No, 1980 was not a very good year for the Texas Rangers. In fact, even for a team that has experienced its share of misery and disappointment through the years, the season probably qualified as a new low in the franchise's nine-year history.

"I don't think anybody in baseball would have thought this team would play this poorly," noted Vice-President Eddie Robinson.

The Rangers, who coming out of spring training appeared to be ready to put a solid pennant contender on the field, finished 76-85, in fourth place in the American League West and 20½ games behind first-place Kansas City.

Pat Corrales, who had served longer than any other Rangers manager in history—324 games over two seasons and a day—didn't survive the team's collapse. He was fired after the final game.

Corrales' dismissal caused an uproar among the players as they came to the defense of their manager. However, the front office had an old baseball cliche to fall back on in explaining Corrales' dismissal: it's easier to fire the manager than 25 players.

After all, this was a team that many observers had predicted to win their division in '80. So, what went wrong with the Rangers?

Mainly, it was the pitching. Relief pitching. Jim Kern, who in 1979 shared the A.L. Fireman of the Year honor with Minnesota's Mike Marshall, suddenly couldn't extinguish a campfire. Besides getting knocked around regularly, he had shoulder problems that forced him to the disabled list in June. Later he came down with a neck ailment that sidelined him for the remainder of the season.

Kern had 29 saves and a 13-5 record in '79, but only two saves and a 3-11 record in '80. His strikeouts fell from 136 in 143 innings to 40 in 63 innings.

Sparky Lyle tried to take up the slack, failed, and became a mop-up man until the Rangers unloaded him to Philadelphia in September. Lyle was touched for 97 hits in 81 innings and his 4.67 ERA was the highest of his 13-year career.

However, due to the collapse of Kern and Lyle, there was an opportunity for progress to be made by others in the bullpen, progress that figured to help out in the future. Danny Darwin finished with a 13-4 record and eight saves, and lefthander John Henry Johnson had a 2-2 record and four saves in 33 games. Johnson struck out 44 in 39 innings.

The starting pitching was respectable. Doc Medich won 14 games, Ferguson Jenkins 12 and Jon Matlack 10; their ERAs ranged from 3.68 to 3.93.

Jenkins, who became the fourth pitcher to win 100 games in each major league and the 29th pitcher to win 250 games, might have won more had he not been suspended by Commissioner Bowie Kuhn for most of September. Jenkins was arrested in Toronto August 26 on a charge of possession of narcotics, a misdemeanor, and Kuhn took action against him when he subsequently refused to answer Kuhn's inquiries about the incident.

Two weeks later, arbitrator Raymond Goetz overturned the commissioner's decision, reinstating Jenkins.

With the Kern-Lyle duo sputtering, the Rangers fell out of contention in early June. A pivotal four-game series opened on June 5 against Kansas City at Arlington Stadium. The Royals swept all four games and Texas went from five games out of first to nine games out and never recovered.

There were, however, some outstanding offensive performances. Buddy Bell missed more than 30 games due to various ailments, but ended up with 17 homers, 83 RBIs and a .329 average.

Outfielders Al Oliver and Mickey Rivers posted even better numbers. Oliver hit .319, knocked in a career-high 117 runs and set a club record with 43 doubles among 209 hits. Rivers batted .333, a career high, and set a club record for hits with 210.

Richie Zisk hit .290 and drove in 77 runs, and catcher Jim Sundberg won his fifth straight Gold Glove while hitting a solid .273.

The shortstop position was again one of the club's most painful weaknesses. Nelson Norman was an early washout and was shipped back to the minors a month after the season started. Bud Harrelson, the 36-year-old who was without a team for the first month of the season, ended up handling most of the starting chores.

SCORES OF TEXAS RANGERS' 1980 GAMES

APRIL			Winner	Loser	APRIL			Winner	Loser
10—N. York	W	1-0§	Lyle	Underwood	14—Cleve.	W	7-4	Medich	Waits
11—N. York	W	11-7	Jenkins	Davis	15—Cleve.	W	3-0	Matlack	Owchinko
13—N. York	L	4-9	Tiant	Comer	16—Cleve.	W	8-7	Kern	Cruz
13—N. York	L	2-8	Figueroa	Perry	18—At Bos.	W	6-5	Darwin	Lockwood

TEXAS RANGERS—1980

Front row—Waller, batboy; Norris, Harrelson, Wills, Frias, Putnam, Sample, Cooper, ballboy. Second row—Mycoskie, team physician; Koenig, coach; Brown, coach; Lucchesi, coach; Corrales, manager; Moore, coach; Donnelly, coach; Oliver, Rajsich, Schimek, traveling secretary. Third row—Zeigler, trainer; Comer, Zisk, Staub, Lyle, Ellis, Allard, Ashford, Perry, Macko, clubhouse manager. Top row—Grubb, Medich, Kern, Roberts, Jenkins, Bell, Matlack, Devine, Darwin, Sundberg.

APRIL

Date		Score	Winner	Loser
19—At Bos.	W	8-0	Perry	Eckersley
20—At Bos.	L	5-6‡	Burgmeier	Kern
21—Detroit	W	3-2	Matlack	Wilcox
22—Detroit	L	0-2	Rozema	Jenkins
23—Detroit	L	4-5	Morris	Comer
25—At Cleve.	W	4-1	Darwin	Waits
26—At Cleve.	L	7-8	Cruz	Kern
27—At Cleve.	L	4-7	Barker	Jenkins
29—At Det.	W	10-5*	Comer	Morris
30—At Det.	L	4-5†	Wilcox	Lyle

Won 10, Lost 8

MAY

Date		Score	Winner	Loser
2—Balt.	L	5-7	Flanagan	Kern
3—Balt.	W	3-2	Jenkins	Palmer
4—Balt.	L	5-9	D. Martinez	Comer
5—Boston	W	11-3	Perry	Eckersley
6—Boston	W	7-2	Medich	Hurst
7—Boston	L	4-7‡	Drago	Devine
9—Chicago	W	2-1‡	Kern	Proly
10—Chicago	L	6-10	Farmer	Darwin
11—Chicago	W	5-1	Medich	Wortham
12—At Balt.	W	5-1	Matlack	Ford
13—At Balt.	L	2-4	Stone	Jenkins
14—At Balt.	W	6-3	Perry	Hartzell
16—At N.Y.	L	2-6	John	Medich
17—At N.Y.	L	0-3	Underwood	Matlack
18—At N.Y.	W	5-4†	Lyle	Davis
19—Calif.	L	2-3x	Clear	Kern
20—Calif.	L	4-5*	Martinez	Medich
21—Calif.	L	8-9	Clear	Kern
22—Calif.	W	12-6	Darwin	Aase
23—At Oak.	W	3-1	Jenkins	Langford
24—At Oak.	L	7-15	McCatty	Perry
25—At Oak.	W	7-3	Medich	Norris
26—At Calif.	W	6-5	Devine	Clear
27—At Calif.	L	0-2	Aase	Jenkins
28—At Calif.	L	6-7	Clear	Kern
30—Oakland	L	3-6	McCatty	Perry
31—Oakland	L	3-4	Norris	Medich

Won 12, Lost 15

JUNE

Date		Score	Winner	Loser
1—Oakland	W	7-3	Darwin	Keough
2—At Chi.	T	1-1y	......	......
3—At Chi.	L	4-5	Farmer	Kern
4—At Chi.	W	4-3	Medich	Barrios
4—At Chi.	L	1-5	Dotson	Rajsich
5—Kan. C.	L	0-8	Leonard	Kern
6—Kan. C.	L	2-4	Splittorff	Matlack
7—Kan. C.	L	2-7	Gale	Perry
8—Kan. C.	L	4-5	Christenson	Babcock
10—At Milw.	W	3-1	Jenkins	Haas
11—At Milw.	L	1-7	Sorensen	Matlack
12—At Milw.	L	1-8	Caldwell	Perry
13—At Tor.	W	6-3	Medich	Stieb
14—At Tor.	L	6-7	Buskey	Babcock
15—At Tor.	L	3-5	Clancy	Jenkins
16—At K.C.	W	6-3	Babcock	Quisenberry
17—At K.C.	L	2-3	Gale	Perry
18—Milw.	W	8-1	Medich	Keeton
19—Milw.	L	4-10	Travers	Allard
20—Toronto	W	5-2	Jenkins	Garvin
21—Toronto	W	2-1	Matlack	McLaughlin
22—Toronto	L	5-6†	Garvin	Kern
24—Seattle	W	5-4	Lyle	Rawley
25—Seattle	W	6-1	Jenkins	Parrott
26—Seattle	L	4-8	Bannister	Matlack
27—Minn.	W	5-0	Perry	Redfern
28—Minn.	W	11-3	Comer	Koosman
29—Minn.	L	3-5	Erickson	Medich
30—At Sea.	W	11-5	Jenkins	Parrott

Won 13, Lost 15

JULY

Date		Score	Winner	Loser
1—At Sea.	L	5-6	Rawley	Kern
2—At Sea.	W	6-3	Perry	Honeycutt
3—At Minn.	L	3-10	Erickson	Comer
4—At Minn.	W	4-3§	Darwin	Verhoeven
5—At Minn.	L	1-2	Zahn	Jenkins
6—At Minn.	L	1-4	Arroyo	Matlack
10—N. York	L	5-13	Guidry	Jenkins
11—N. York	W	10-8	Matlack	Underwood
12—Cleve.	L	8-9	Barker	Perry
13—Cleve.	W	12-2	Medich	Spillner
14—Cleve.	W	4-2	Darwin	Waits
15—Chicago	L	1-2	Burns	Jenkins
16—Chicago	W	11-3	Matlack	Dotson
17—Chicago	W	3-2	Darwin	Proly
18—At Balt.	L	7-8	Flanagan	Kern
19—At Balt.	W	11-8†	Darwin	Stewart
20—At Balt.	W	7-1	Jenkins	Palmer
21—At Bos.	W	5-3	Matlack	Eckersley
22—At Bos.	W	4-3	Darwin	Torrez
23—At Bos.	L	5-12	Drago	Johnson
25—At Chi.	W	6-4	Kern	Farmer
26—At Chi.	L	3-4	Hoyt	Jenkins
26—At Chi.	T	1-1y	......	......
27—At Chi.	L	2-3	Trout	Medich
27—At Chi.	W	4-3x	Hough	Proly
29—Balt.	L	3-4	McGregor	Hough
30—Balt.	L	2-3	Palmer	Perry
31—Balt.	W	7-4	Jenkins	Stone

Won 14, Lost 13

AUGUST

Date		Score	Winner	Loser
1—Boston	W	7-5	Medich	Rem'swaal
2—Boston	L	0-1	Ojeda	Figueroa
3—Boston	L	4-6	Torrez	Matlack
4—At N.Y.	L	4-10	Underwood	Perry
5—At N.Y.	W	8-1	Jenkins	John
6—At N.Y.	L	1-2	May	Medich
8—Detroit	L	0-8	Petry	Figueroa
9—Detroit	W	4-3†	Darwin	Lopez
10—Detroit	W	4-2	Perry	Weaver
12—At Cleve.	L	1-2	Waits	Jenkins
13—At Cleve.	L	3-14	Garland	Medich
14—At Cleve.	L	2-7	Barker	Figueroa
15—At Det.	W	6-2	Matlack	Underwood
16—At Det.	W	12-5	Clay	Morris
17—At Det.	W	9-3	Jenkins	Fidrych
17—At Det.	W	12-6	Medich	Wilcox
18—Kan. C.	L	3-6	Gale	Figueroa
19—Kan. C.	L	3-4	Twitty	Darwin
20—Kan. C.	L	3-5§	Quisenberry	Johnson
22—Milw.	W	12-6	Rajsich	Cleveland
22—Milw.	L	3-8	Mitchell	Medich
23—Milw.	W	7-5	Darwin	Augustine
24—Milw.	W	4-3‡	Johnson	Cleveland
25—At Tor.	W	5-1	Clay	Todd
26—At Tor.	W	8-0	Hough	Jefferson
27—At Tor.	L	4-6	Clancy	Medich
28—At K.C.	L	10-6	Rajsich	Twitty
29—At K.C.	L	3-7	Leonard	Figueroa
30—At K.C.	W	7-5‡	Johnson	Quisenberry
31—At K.C.	L	3-4	Quisenberry	Lyle

Won 15, Lost 15

SEPTEMBER

Date		Score	Winner	Loser
1—Toronto	W	9-1	Medich	McLaughlin
2—Toronto	W	3-2	Jenkins	Leal
3—Toronto	L	2-4	Stieb	Figueroa
5—At Milw.	W	6-5	Matlack	Haas
6—At Milw.	L	2-6	Caldwell	Clay
7—At Milw.	W	7-2	Medich	McClure
8—At Oak.	W	6-2	Butcher	Kingman
9—At Oak.	L	3-6	Keough	Figueroa
10—At Oak.	L	1-3	Norris	Matlack
12—At Calif.	L	4-8	Dorsey	Medich
13—At Calif.	L	1-10	Martinez	Butcher
14—At Calif.	L	1-3	Tanana	Clay
15—Oakland	W	2-0	Matlack	Keough

SEPTEMBER			Winner	Loser
16—Oakland	L	2-4‡	Norris	Darwin
17—Oakland	L	4-6	Langford	Butcher
18—Oakland	W	10-6	Darwin	McCatty
19—Calif.	L	2-6	Tanana	Matlack
20—Calif.	L	4-6†	Hassler	Hough
21—Calif.	L	2-9	Barr	Medich
22—At Minn.	L	0-1	Koosman	Butcher
23—At Minn.	L	2-8	Erickson	Clay
24—At Minn.	L	5-9	Williams	Matlack
25—At Sea.	L	6-7‡	Heaverlo	Darwin
26—At Sea.	L	2-7	Abbott	Jenkins

SEPTEMBER			Winner	Loser
27—At Sea.	W	7-3	Medich	Bannister
28—At Sea.	W	4-1	Butcher	Beattie
Won 9, Lost 17				
OCTOBER				
2—Minn.	L	3-6	Zahn	Matlack
2—Minn.	L	1-4	Williams	Jenkins
3—Seattle	W	6-2	Medich	Abbott
4—Seattle	W	11-6	Butcher	Beattie
5—Seattle	W	3-2	Darwin	Parrott
Won 3, Lost 2				

*7 innings.   †10 innings.   ‡11 innings.   §12 innings.   x13 innings.   y6-inning tie game.

Sale Uncertainty Spiced Chisox Woes

By BOB MARKUS

The White Sox made more news off the field than on it in 1980 and had little success either place. The season started well enough when the team broke cleanly from the gate and surged to the top of the American League West under freshman manager Tony LaRussa.

Everything turned around for them on May 23, the day of the settlement of the impending baseball strike. When the day began, the White Sox had a 22-16 record and a half-game lead over the Kansas City Royals. With a strike imminent, it appeared they would stay in first place for quite some time.

Instead, competition was resumed without so much as one day's break in the action and that night the Sox fell out of first place for good when they lost to Seattle. Two more losses in the Kingdome sent them into a tailspin from which they never recovered.

They finished with a 70-90 record, three games worse than in 1979, and had to win eight of their last 10 games to accomplish even that much. The whole last half of the season was played under the cloud of rumors that the club was about to be sold.

The rumors turned out to be all too true, but, alas, the White Sox could no more execute a clean sale of the club in the board room than they could a double play on the field.

American League club owners rejected the sale of the team for $20 million to Edward DeBartolo, an Ohio construction magnate whose family already owned the San Francisco 49ers, Pittsburgh Penguins and three race tracks. Local ownership was desired.

When real estate mogul Jerry Reinsdorf and television executive Eddie Einhorn provided the local ownership and the same $20 million purchase price, the A.L. owners finally approved the sale of the White Sox January 19, 1981.

Back on the field, White Sox President Bill Veeck and Player Personnel Director Roland Hemond were left to ponder how to improve a team that led the league in errors and had not one .300 hitter.

The obvious strength of the team was a young, plentiful pitching staff led by precocious Britt Burns, a 21-year-old lefthander who was the American League's Rookie Pitcher of the Year. Burns posted a 15-13 record and a 2.84 ERA that was third best in the league. Two other rookies, righthanders Richard Dotson and Lamarr Hoyt, had 12-10 and 9-3 records, respectively.

Hoyt was a pleasant surprise, winning seven times as a starting pitcher after getting his first major league start in late July. There were other surprises of a totally different kind, however.

One was lefty Ken Kravec, the nominal ace of the staff and the only veteran starter. For reasons never explained to anyone's satisfaction, least of all his own, Kravec's season was almost a total washout.

A 15-game winner in '79, he won only three in 1980 and had a stratospheric 6.91 ERA. Richard Wortham, who had won 14 in '79, was almost as bad. He picked up only four victories and had a 5.97 ERA.

Another young lefthander, Ross Baumgarten, battled arm problems all year but came up with a solid 3.44 ERA that translated, more often than not, into heartbreak. Baumgarten won his first start of the season, pitched a one-hit shutout over California in July and ended up with a 2-12 record.

The bullpen was well-stocked and solid, led by Ed Farmer, who earned 30 saves, a club record. Mike Proly had a 3.06 ERA (5-10, eight saves) and Dewey Robinson, brought up late in the season, added another dependable arm to the pen.

Elsewhere, the White Sox were shot more full of holes than a target on a rifle range. LaRussa spent all season looking for a leadoff man before finding him in the final month lurking right in the heart of his batting order.

He was center fielder Chet Lemon, who came alive once relieved of RBI responsibility and ended up leading the team in batting with a .292 average.

The only true RBI man the White Sox had was Lamar Johnson, who knocked in 81 (no one else had more than 59) but was a defensive liability at first base, especially when compared with slick-fielding Mike Squires. Squires played regularly over the last six weeks and hit a solid .283.

The team finished the season without a regular third baseman, having gone through four of them—Alan Bannister, Kevin Bell, Greg Pryor, and rookie Fran Mullins—in the course of the season.

Bannister was traded to Cleveland for utilityman Ron Pruitt, Bell hit only .178 after improving briefly upon consulting a hypnotist, Pryor was deemed more valuable as a swing man, and Mullins batted only .194 after his late season call-up.

The Sox were considering moving Jim Morrison, who had 29 errors at second base, to third for 1981. Morrison tied Wayne Nordhagen for the club home run lead with 15 and cracked a career-high 40 doubles to place himself among the more dependable batters.

Todd Cruz, acquired in trade from California, took over at shortstop and displayed a whiplike arm, but finished the year with 28 errors. None of the four catchers who were given a crack at the job took command of the position and catching was considering the prime priority for '81.

SCORES OF CHICAGO WHITE SOX' 1980 GAMES

APRIL			Winner	Loser	APRIL			Winner	Loser
10—Balt.	L	3-5	Palmer	Trout	24—At Bos.	W	9-3	Dotson	Stanley
11—Balt.	W	8-4	Kravec	Flanagan	25—At N.Y.	W	6-0	Trout	Figueroa
12—Balt.	W	8-2	Dotson	Stone	26—At N.Y.	W	8-7§	Farmer	Underwood
13—Balt.	W	5-2	Baumgarten	Stewart	27—At N.Y.	L	0-1	John	Burns
15—N. York	W	4-3y	Wortham	Kaat	29—Boston	L	1-11	Stanley	Baumgarten
16—N. York	L	0-6	John	Kravec	30—Boston	W	2-1	Dotson	Eckersley
17—N. York	W	8-6	Burns	Griffin				**Won 12, Lost 6**	
18—At Balt.	L	2-5	Ford	Dotson					
19—At Balt.	W	5-4§	Farmer	T. Martinez	**MAY**				
20—At Balt.	W	9-6	Wortham	Stewart	1—Boston	L	3-4	Hurst	Trout
21—At Bos.	L	8-9	Lockwood	Scarbery	2—Milw.	L	0-8	Caldwell	Kravec
22—At Bos.	W	2-0	Burns	Torrez	3—Milw.	L	1-4	Haas	Burns
					4—Milw.	L	1-11	Slaton	Baumgarten

CHICAGO WHITE SOX—1980

Seated in front—Cruz, Hoffman, batboys Duffy, O'Leary, Gilliam, McQuery; Proly, Seilheimer. First row—Robinson, Cepeda, batting instructor; Babe, coach; Kusnyer, coach; LaRussa, manager; Schueler, coach; Winkles, coach; Minoso, instructor. Second row—McNamara, equipment manager; Schneider, trainer; Morrison, Pryor, Rosenbaum, traveling secretary; Kimm, Squires, Kraeger, physical fitness coordinator; Thompson, equipment manager. Third row—Bell, Dotson, Wortham, Baines, Kravec, Lemon, Molinaro, Baumgarten, Pruitt. Top row—Hoyt, Barrios, Trout, Burns, Nordhagen, Bosley, R. Johnson, L. Johnson.

MAY

Date		Score	Winner	Loser
5—Milw.	W	11-7	Scarbery	Boitano
6—Kan. C.	W	2-0	Wortham	Gura
7—Kan. C.	L	5-12	Christenson	Kravec
8—Kan. C.	W	8-2	Burns	Splittorff
9—At Texas	L	1-2‡	Kern	Proly
10—At Texas	W	10-6	Farmer	Darwin
11—At Texas	L	1-5	Medich	Wortham
13—At Milw.	W	6-5†	Burns	Cleveland
14—At Milw.	L	1-5	Haas	Proly
15—At Milw.	W	6-4	Dotson	Sorensen
16—Seattle	L	2-4	Beattie	Trout
17—Seattle	W	4-0	Burns	Honeycutt
18—Seattle	W	6-5	Barrios	Dressler
19—Minn.	W	1-0	Kravec	Koosman
20—Minn.	W	4-2	Dotson	Jackson
21—Minn.	L	2-3	Zahn	Trout
23—At Sea.	L	0-8	Honeycutt	Burns
24—At Sea.	L	4-5	Abbott	Kravec
25—At Sea.	L	3-8	Bannister	Scarbery
26—At Minn.	W	6-3	Trout	Zahn
27—At Minn.	W	2-0	Burns	Jackson
28—At Minn.	L	4-6	Marshall	Proly
29—At Minn.	L	2-5	Koosman	Dotson
30—At K.C.	L	2-9	Gura	Wortham
31—At K.C.	L	4-6	Martin	Trout

Won 12, Lost 17

JUNE

Date		Score	Winner	Loser
1—At K.C.	W	6-1	Burns	Leonard
2—Texas	T	1-1*	......	......
3—Texas	W	5-4	Farmer	Kern
4—Texas	L	3-4	Medich	Barrios
4—Texas	W	5-1	Dotson	Rajsich
6—Cleve.	W	8-7	Farmer	Monge
8—Cleve.	L	2-7	Denny	Burns
10—Toronto	L	0-1	Clancy	Baumgarten
11—Toronto	W	7-4	Kravec	Mirabella
13—At Det.	L	4-8	Morris	Trout
14—At Det.	L	0-3	Petry	Burns
16—At Cleve.	L	3-5	Garland	Farmer
17—At Cleve.	W	5-3	Hoyt	Cruz
18—At Tor.	L	4-5	Stieb	Trout
18—At Tor.	L	1-3	Kucek	Dotson
20—Detroit	L	3-5‡	Lopez	Farmer
21—Detroit	L	1-4	Wilcox	Baumgarten
22—Detroit	L	1-7	Rozema	Kravec
22—Detroit	L	4-6	Morris	Wortham
24—At Calif.	W	2-1	Burns	Aase
25—At Calif.	W	5-2	Dotson	Lemanczyk
26—At Calif.	W	5-2	Trout	Tanana
27—At Oak.	L	1-3	Norris	Baumgarten
28—At Oak.	W	3-0	Wortham	Keough
29—At Oak.	W	3-0	Burns	Kingman
30—Calif.	L	6-10	Clear	Farmer

Won 11, Lost 14

JULY

Date		Score	Winner	Loser
1—Calif.	L	2-5	Halicki	Trout
2—Calif.	W	1-0	Baumgarten	Tanana
3—Calif.	L	3-7	Lemanczyk	Wortham
4—Oakland	L	0-2	Kingman	Burns
5—Oakland	L	0-5	Langford	Dotson
6—Oakland	W	2-0	Trout	Norris
6—Oakland	W	5-4	Farmer	Lacey
10—Balt.	L	2-9	McGregor	Burns
11—Balt.	W	5-4	Proly	Palmer
12—N. York	L	0-8	John	Baumgarten
13—N. York	L	1-3	May	Trout
14—N. York	L	5-7	Davis	Farmer
15—At Texas	W	2-1	Burns	Jenkins
16—At Texas	L	3-11	Matlack	Dotson
17—At Texas	L	2-3	Darwin	Proly
18—At Milw.	L	1-5	Haas	Trout
19—At Milw.	W	10-7	Hoyt	McClure
20—At Milw.	L	6-7	Augustine	Proly

JULY

Date		Score	Winner	Loser
21—At K.C.	L	1-2	Leonard	Burns
22—At K.C.	W	6-1	Trout	Busby
23—At K.C.	L	2-9	Gura	Baumgarten
24—At K.C.	L	4-12	Splittorff	Wortham
25—Texas	L	4-6	Kern	Farmer
26—Texas	W	4-3	Hoyt	Jenkins
26—Texas	T	1-1*	......	......
27—Texas	L	3-2	Trout	Medich
27—Texas	L	3-4x	Hough	Proly
29—Milw.	L	1-7	Haas	Dotson
30—Milw.	W	6-5	Hoyt	Sorensen

Won 10, Lost 18

AUGUST

Date		Score	Winner	Loser
1—Kan. C.	L	3-4	Gura	Burns
2—Kan. C.	L	2-8	Gale	Trout
3—Kan. C.	W	5-3	Dotson	Splittorff
5—At Balt.	L	2-8	Stone	Hoyt
6—At Balt.	L	1-4	Flanagan	Burns
7—At Balt.	L	1-2	McGregor	Trout
8—At Bos.	L	1-4	Campbell	Dotson
9—At Bos.	W	5-4	Proly	Renko
10—At Bos.	L	3-4	Eckersley	Hoyt
11—At N.Y.	L	1-3	May	Burns
12—At N.Y.	L	4-8†	Bird	Farmer
13—At N.Y.	W	4-1	Dotson	Guidry
15—Boston	L	5-8	Eckersley	Proly
18—Cleve.	L	2-4	Barker	Burns
18—Cleve.	W	7-2	Trout	Garland
19—Cleve.	L	5-8	Grimsley	Dotson
20—Cleve.	L	0-3	Spillner	Kravec
21—Toronto	L	5-3	Hoyt	Jefferson
22—Toronto	W	2-0	Burns	Clancy
23—Toronto	W	5-1	Dotson	Kucek
24—Toronto	L	3-7	Stieb	Baumgarten
26—Detroit	L	4-5	Lopez	Wortham
27—Detroit	W	3-2y	Proly	Rozema
29—At Cleve.	L	5-6	Monge	Farmer
30—At Cleve.	L	2-6	Spillner	Baumgarten
31—At Cleve.	W	10-8	Hoyt	Cruz
31—At Cleve.	W	8-7	Trout	Grimsley

Won 10, Lost 17

SEPTEMBER

Date		Score	Winner	Loser
1—At Det.	W	11-3	Burns	Morris
2—At Det.	L	2-11	Fidrych	Proly
2—At Det.	L	1-6	Wilcox	Dotson
3—At Det.	L	4-5	Lopez	Wortham
4—At Tor.	L	2-3	Todd	Farmer
5—At Tor.	W	3-0	Hoyt	Clancy
7—At Tor.	L	1-3	McLaughlin	Trout
7—At Tor.	L	6-7	Schrom	Proly
8—Seattle	W	3-2§	Farmer	Heaverlo
9—Seattle	L	1-4	Honeycutt	Baumgarten
10—Seattle	W	4-3	Hoyt	Sarmiento
12—Minn.	W	5-3	Burns	Koosman
13—Minn.	L	5-6	Zahn	Trout
14—Minn.	L	2-3	Arroyo	Baumgarten
15—At Sea.	L	1-12	Dressler	Hoyt
16—At Sea.	W	2-1	Dotson	Abbott
17—At Sea.	L	0-4	Bannister	Burns
18—At Sea.	W	5-4	Proly	Rawley
19—At Minn.	L	3-6	Williams	Farmer
21—At Minn.	L	4-5	Verhoeven	Robinson
21—At Minn.	L	4-6	Arroyo	Dotson
23—At Oak.	L	4-6	Langford	Proly
24—At Oak.	L	1-7	McCatty	Trout
25—At Oak.	W	6-4	Proly	Kingman
26—At Calif.	W	5-4	Robinson	Barr
27—At Calif.	W	6-3	Dotson	Botting
28—At Calif.	W	8-1	Burns	Martinez
30—Oakland	L	1-5	Kingman	Trout

Won 11, Lost 17

OCTOBER			Winner	Loser	OCTOBER			Winner	Loser
1—Oakland	L	3-11	Norris	Baumgarten	4—Calif.	W	4-2	Hoyt	Tanana
2—Oakland	W	9-4	Hoffman	Langford	5—Calif.	W	5-3	Trout	Botting
3—Calif.	W	4-1	Burns	Martinez					

Won 4, Lost 1

*6 innings.   †10 innings.   ‡11 innings.   §12 innings.   x13 innings.   y14 innings.

Angels Endured Riches to Rags Tale

By CARL CLARK

It was a riches to rags tale. Not only did the 1980 California Angels fail to retain their American League West Division title, they failed to retain respectability, falling from 88-74 in 1979 to 65-95 and sixth place, 31 games behind the Kansas City Royals.

They lost early and often, lagging 17 paces behind the leader as early as June 18. Their home record of 30-51, worst in the majors, included 10 consecutive losses in May and eight in a row in June. Nevertheless, their home attendance of 2,297,327 ranked fourth in baseball.

The Angels' pitching was even more abysmally poor than it had been in '79, but injuries to key offensive performers precipitated the club's decline—injuries so pervasive that at one time the salaries of players on the team's disabled list exceeded what three other teams (Seattle, Toronto and the Chicago White Sox) were disbursing to their entire active rosters.

Don Baylor, the A.L. MVP in the Angels' title year, played a month before learning that his miserable start could be blamed on a broken left wrist, incurred in the season's first game. Catcher Brian Downing, who had hit .326 the previous season, broke an ankle in the ninth game. Outfielder Dan Ford, still hobbling on a knee that underwent surgery in the off-season, played only 65 games.

Ford's indifferent attitude about his return to the lineup—he was quoted as saying that with the Angels out of the race there was no urgency to it—nettled General Manager Buzzie Bavasi. "If I was 20 years younger," Bavasi said, "I would punch Ford in the mouth."

Baylor, Ford and Downing had knocked in 315 runs in '79, but drove in only 102 runs in the 185 games they managed to play in '80. Second baseman Bobby Grich dipped from 101 RBIs to 62.

Consequently, the team's run production plummeted from 866 to 698, its batting average from .282 to .265 and its home runs from 164 to 106.

Dave Skaggs, purchased from Baltimore to fill in for Downing, broke an ankle in his third game with the club. Downing's replacements—Skaggs, Tom Donohue, Dan Whitmer and Stan Cliburn—hit .199 with five homers and 36 RBIs. Downing returned in September and finished with 25 RBIs in 30 games.

Aged shortstops were another liability. The position was manned primarily by 35-year-old Freddie Patek and 38-year-old Bert Campaneris. Altogether, 41 errors were made by Angels shortstops.

Much of what firepower Manager Jim Fregosi did have came from Rod Carew, Carney Lansford and Jason Thompson. Carew, in his second year with California, hit .331, two points under his career average but good enough for a club record. Lansford belted 15 homers and had a club-high 80 RBIs. Thompson drove in 90 runs, but 20 of those were before he came to the Angels from Detroit in exchange for outfielder Al Cowens. Dividing the first base and designated hitter positions with Carew, Thompson batted .317 and hit 17 homers in 102 games with the Angels.

The pitching staff was not immune to injury—Bruce Kison and Dave Frost won only three and four games respectively before elbow surgery was prescribed—but its 4.52 ERA was attributable more to lack of ability than lack of health. Oh, there were a few oases, particularly in the bullpen.

Mark Clear won 11 games and saved nine more. Dan Aase spent the last two months in a relief role and went 3-0 with two saves and a 2.08 ERA. Andy Hassler, purchased from Pittsburgh in mid-June, saved 10 games and won five others with a 2.49 ERA.

Rookie Alfredo Martinez, 7-9, pitched well at times and Frank Tanana began to have success with a new style of pitching.

Tanana, robbed of his fastball by arm problems, lost nine of his first 12 decisions and was asked to go to Salt Lake City, the Angels' Triple-A team, to strengthen himself. Tanana refused, saying that his arm and shoulder felt better than they had in 2½ years. "Maybe it would be best if they released me," he said.

A more subtle Tanana won eight of his last 11 decisions. Subtle on the mound, that is. Tanana still was speaking frankly. His postmortem analysis of the Angels' tumble was concise and perspicacious.

"Anytime you're offensive minded in a defensive game," he said, "you're in trouble. Had there been greater emphasis on pitching and defense, the shock of all the injuries wouldn't have been as drastic, we wouldn't have hit bottom in the manner that we hit bottom. But management was lulled to sleep by a year in which seven guys had their greatest offensive years ever and yet the team won only 88 games. It was a freak. We didn't win it on merit, we won it on default."

SCORES OF CALIFORNIA ANGELS' 1980 GAMES

APRIL			Winner	Loser	MAY			Winner	Loser
11—Cleve.	W	10-2	Frost	Spillner	16—At K.C.	W	11-1	Kison	Gale
12—Cleve.	L	1-2	Barker	Kison	17—At K.C.	L	1-2†	Gura	Clear
13—Cleve.	W	8-3	Aase	Denny	18—At K.C.	L	3-5	Martin	Tanana
14—Minn.	L	3-5	Corbett	Clear	19—At Texas	W	3-2§	Clear	Kern
15—Minn.	W	3-1	Tanana	Koosman	20—At Texas	W	5-4*	Martinez	Medich
16—Minn.	W	2-1†	Frost	Marshall	21—At Texas	W	9-8	Clear	Kern
18—At Oak.	L	3-6	Kingman	Kison	22—At Texas	L	6-12	Darwin	Aase
19—At Oak.	L	1-3	Norris	Aase	23—Kan. C.	L	9-13	Leonard	Tanana
20—At Oak.	L	1-6	Keough	Knapp	24—Kan. C.	L	5-6†	Quisenberry	Clear
20—At Oak.	L	2-8	McCatty	Tanana	25—Kan. C.	L	3-7	Gura	LaRoche
22—At Minn.	L	1-8	Zahn	Frost	26—Texas	L	5-6	Devine	Clear
23—At Minn.	W	17-0	Kison	Felton	27—Texas	W	2-0	Aase	Jenkins
25—At Sea.	W	4-3	Aase	Parrott	28—Texas	W	7-6	Clear	Kern
26—At Sea.	W	7-6	LaRoche	Dressler	30—At Det.	L	1-12	Wilcox	Tanana
27—At Sea.	L	3-7	Abbott	Frost	31—At Det.	W	6-1	Kison	Underwood
28—Oakland	L	0-8	Langford	Kison					
29—Oakland	L	2-4	Norris	Tanana			Won 11, Lost 15		
30—Oakland	W	2-1	Aase	Keough					
		Won 8, Lost 10			JUNE				
					2—At Tor.	W	6-3	Frost	Leal
MAY					3—At Tor.	L	6-7‡	McLaughlin	LaRoche
1—Seattle	W	2-1	Montague	Beattie	4—At Tor.	L	2-8	Clancy	Martinez
2—Seattle	W	3-1	Frost	Abbott.	6—Balt.	L	1-6	McGregor	Kison
3—Seattle	L	0-2	Honeycutt	Kison	7—Balt.	L	5-6	Palmer	Frost
4—Seattle	W	4-3	Tanana	Bannister	8—Balt.	L	8-13	Stewart	Knapp
6—Toronto	L	2-3	Lemanczyk	Aase	9—N. York	L	7-8†	Gossage	Lemanczyk
7—Toronto	L	3-7	Stieb	Knapp	10—N. York	W	5-4	Clear	May
8—Toronto	L	0-3	Mirabella	Frost	11—N. York	L	7-9‡	Gossage	Clear
9—Detroit	L	5-6†	Lopez	Montague	12—Boston	L	2-13	Torrez	Frost
10—Detroit	L	1-3	Schatzeder	Tanana	13—Boston	L	0-3	Eckersley	Aase
11—Detroit	L	0-4	Petry	Aase	14—Boston	L	3-7	Stanley	Martinez
14—At Cleve.	W	13-7	Knapp	Spillner	15—Boston	L	5-6	Renko	Tanana
					16—At Balt.	L	2-5	Palmer	Knapp

CALIFORNIA ANGELS—1980

Seated in front—Shishido, equipment manager; Smith, trainer; Thon, Atlas, batboy; ballboys Parillo, Hover; Downing, Bergert, assistant trainer; Reimer, assistant equipment manager. First row—Campaneris, B. Clear, coach; Rettenmund, player-coach; Johnson, coach; Fregosi, manager; Sherry, coach; Knoop, coach; Reese, coach; Patek. Second row—Yocum, orthope-dist; Rasinski, club physician; Donohue, Miller, Carew, Ford, Cliburn, Clark, Seeberg, traveling secretary; Triggs, doctor. Third row—Lansford, Skaggs, Rudi, Martinez, Montague, Barr, LaRoche, Harlow, Baylor. Top row—Thompson, Kison, Knapp, M. Clear, Halicki, Frost, Hassler, Lemanczyk, Aase, Tanana. Not pictured—Grich.

JUNE				Winner	Loser
17—At Balt.	L	3-5		Stone	Frost
18—At N.Y.	L	0-5		Guidry	Aase
19—At N.Y.	L	5-7		May	Lemanczyk
20—At Bos.	W	20-2		Tanana	Renko
21—At Bos.	W	4-2		Knapp	Rainey
22—At Bos.	L	3-6		Torrez	Barr
24—Chicago	L	1-2		Burns	Aase
25—Chicago	L	2-5		Dotson	Lemanczyk
26—Chicago	L	2-5		Trout	Tanana
27—Milw.	W	6-5		Clear	Castro
28—Milw.	L	5-11		Caldwell	Halicki
29—Milw.	L	2-5		Cleveland	Aase
30—At Chi.	W	10-6		Clear	Farmer

Won 6, Lost 21

JULY					
1—At Chi.	W	5-2		Halicki	Trout
2—At Chi.	L	0-1		Baumgarten	Tanana
3—At Chi.	W	7-3		Lemanczyk	Wortham
4—At Milw.	W	2-0		Aase	Cleveland
5—At Milw.	L	3-4		Travers	Knapp
6—At Milw.	W	2-0		Halicki	Haas
10—At Oak.	W	5-1		Tanana	Keough
10—At Oak.	L	4-5		Langford	Aase
11—At Oak.	L	2-6		Kingman	Knapp
12—Oakland	L	4-5		Norris	Lemanczyk
13—Oakland	W	5-4x		Montague	Hamilton
14—Oakland	L	4-6		Langford	Kison
15—Cleve.	W	7-1		Tanana	Denny
16—Cleve.	L	2-6		Garland	Aase
17—Cleve.	L	3-5		Barker	Knapp
18—Toronto	W	6-3		Halicki	Kucek
19—Toronto	L	3-5		Clancy	Montague
20—Toronto	L	3-6†		McLaughlin	Clear
21—Detroit	L	3-14		Wilcox	Aase
22—Detroit	W	6-4		Hassler	Rozema
23—Detroit	L	6-7		Lopez	Clear
25—At Cleve.	L	8-9		Wihtol	Clear
25—At Cleve.	L	2-10		Grimsley	Martinez
26—At Cleve.	L	4-14		Garland	Aase
28—At Det.	W	3-2		Montague	Petry
29—At Det.	W	7-0		Martinez	Robbins
30—At Det.	W	6-5		Clear	Schatzeder
31—At Det.	L	6-15		Wilcox	Aase

Won 12, Lost 16

AUGUST					
1—At Tor.	L	8-9		Garvin	Clear
2—At Tor.	W	5-4		LaRoche	Jefferson
3—At Tor.	L	1-3		Clancy	Martinez
4—Seattle	W	8-3		Hassler	Rawley
5—Seattle	W	5-4		Clear	Heaverlo
6—Seattle	W	8-3		Montague	Dressler
7—Minn.	W	4-2y		Hassler	Williams
8—Minn.	W	9-5		Lemanczyk	Jackson
9—Minn.	W	8-2		Tanana	Zahn
10—Minn.	L	2-5		Koosman	Barr
12—At Sea.	W	9-6		Clear	Heaverlo

AUGUST				Winner	Loser
13—At Sea.	W	10-4†		Hassler	Rawley
14—At Sea.	W	2-1		Martinez	Honeycutt
15—At Minn.	W	5-4		Tanana	Zahn
17—At Minn.	L	1-8		Erickson	Barr
17—At Minn.	L	5-6		Koosman	Knapp
18—At Minn.	L	3-8		Arroyo	LaRoche
19—Balt.	L	2-5		Stone	Martinez
20—Balt.	L	5-6†		Stoddard	Clear
21—Balt.	L	1-7		McGregor	Knapp
22—N. York	W	8-4		Aase	Tiant
23—N. York	L	2-5		May	LaRoche
24—N. York	L	2-4		Davis	Martinez
25—Boston	L	2-4‡		Stanley	Clear
26—Boston	L	1-5		Tudor	Knapp
28—At Balt.	L	8-13		Palmer	LaRoche
29—At Balt.	W	5-0		Martinez	Stone
30—At Balt.	W	12-6		Clear	Flanagan
31—At Balt.	L	0-5		McGregor	Knapp

Won 14, Lost 15

SEPTEMBER					
1—At Bos.	L	3-4		Drago	Frost
2—At Bos.	L	2-10		Renko	Dorsey
3—At Bos.	W	7-2		Martinez	Torrez
4—At N.Y.	L	3-5		Perry	Tanana
5—At N.Y.	L	5-6†		Gossage	Hassler
6—At N.Y.	L	4-7		Underwood	Frost
7—At N.Y.	L	1-4		May	Dorsey
8—Kan. C.	W	7-4		Aase	Gura
9—Kan. C.	W	4-3		Tanana	Splittorff
10—Kan. C.	W	8-3		Aase	Martin
11—Kan. C.	L	2-7		Leonard	Ferris
12—Texas	W	8-4		Dorsey	Medich
13—Texas	W	10-1		Martinez	Butcher
14—Texas	W	3-1		Tanana	Clay
17—At K.C.	L	0-5		Leonard	Botting
17—At K.C.	W	7-4		LaRoche	Gura
18—At K.C.	L	2-5		Martin	Martinez
19—At Texas	W	6-2		Tanana	Matlack
20—At Texas	W	6-4†		Hassler	Hough
21—At Texas	W	9-2		Barr	Medich
22—At Milw.	W	7-3		Clear	McClure
23—At Milw.	W	2-1		Martinez	Caldwell
24—At Milw.	L	0-6		Sorensen	Tanana
26—Chicago	L	4-5		Robinson	Barr
27—Chicago	L	3-6		Dotson	Botting
28—Chicago	L	1-8		Burns	Martinez
29—Milw.	W	6-2		Tanana	Sorensen
30—Milw.	L	2-4		McClure	Ferris

Won 14, Lost 14

OCTOBER					
1—Milw.	L	7-10		Castro	Schuler
3—At Chi.	L	1-4		Burns	Martinez
4—At Chi.	L	2-4		Hoyt	Tanana
5—At Chi.	L	3-5		Trout	Botting

Won 0, Lost 4

*7 innings. †10 innings. ‡11 innings. §13 innings. x14 innings. y15 innings.

Shipwrecked Mariners Summoned Wills

By TRACY RINGOLSBY

As the Seattle Mariners headed into the final days of the 1980 season, there was a feeling of giddiness.

The team with the worst record in baseball had run off six wins in a row, a club record, including a three-game sweep of the American League champion Kansas City Royals.

SEATTLE MARINERS—1980

Front row—Anderson, Meyer, Pinson, coach; Mazeroski, coach; Wills, manager; Stock, coach; Funk, coach; Stein, Cruz, Milbourne. Middle row—Genzale, clubhouse manager; Bannister, Rawley, Heaverlo, L. Cox, Honeycutt, Dressler, McLaughlin, Nicholson, trainer. Top row—Hill, Simpson, Paciorek, L. Roberts, Abbott, Beattie, Bochte, T. Cox, Narron, D. Roberts. Not pictured—Horton, Mendoza, Beniquez.

All of a sudden, it seemed as if the ills which had plagued the Mariners in their fourth year of existence had been put behind them. There was rejoicing in the clubhouse, and even the idea that the Royals were flat in light of their clinching the division title couldn't deter from the excitement.

"Now, they are the Maury Wills Mariners," said Maury Wills, who on August 4 had replaced Darrell Johnson, the original Mariners manager. "Not only are they winning, but they are looking good in winning, too."

So much for euphoria. In the final eight games, the Mariners reaffirmed the worst fears about their ineptitude. The Mariners lost all eight games, and Wills blamed himself.

After the winning streak, he had cut back on the daily meetings and the pre-game workouts. He felt that the Mariners had earned a rest.

"I drove them hard for seven weeks," said Wills, "so I eased up. You can see what happened. Next year, we will go hard for 162 games."

Wills didn't want to see what happened to the Mariners in '80 happen again. They went into the season talking about being contenders, and didn't even do a decent job of putting up a front as pretenders. They finished with a 59-103 record, and their attendance at the Kingdome of 836,204 was the lowest in the majors on a per-date basis and the lowest in the club's history.

It was a season in which Rick Honeycutt began with six straight wins, but finished with a club-record 17 losses, including eight in a row. Honeycutt was suspended for the final five games of the season as well as the first five of 1981 for doctoring baseballs during a game in Kansas City.

It was a season in which Mike Parrott, who was the hub of the Mariners' rotation in '79 when he was 14-12, beat Toronto on opening night, then proceeded to lose an incredible 16 in a row.

It was a season in which Willie Horton, the Mariners' MVP of the previous season, spent two spells on the disabled list and finished with only eight home runs and 36 RBIs.

It was a season in which Julio Cruz, the catalyst of the Mariners' offense, never recovered from a loss in salary arbitration and played in only 119 games, hitting .209 and stealing 45 bases, his lowest total for a full season in the majors.

It was a season in which the Mariners, despite playing in the cozy Kingdome, site of more home runs than any other park in baseball, saw their run production drop from 711 to 610 and saw Tom Paciorek lead the team in homers with 15.

Oh, there was some excitement. There was the winning streak. There was Bruce Bochte hitting .300 for the second straight season. There was the resurrection of Glenn Abbott, who came to spring training on the verge of being released, but won a spot in the rotation and finished with a club-high 12 wins. There was the new running offense the Mariners exhibited under Wills, stealing 64 bases in his 58 games compared with 52 in Johnson's 105 games.

It was a season, however, which the Mariners would generally like to forget.

The low point came in early August. They lost their last nine games under Johnson and then lost their first three under Wills, the most consecutive losses in the club's history.

The big trade of the previous winter also fizzled. The Mariners had sent Ruppert Jones, their starting center fielder in their first three years, to the New York Yankees for pitcher Jim Beattie, catcher Jerry Narron and outfielder Juan Beniquez. The trade showed few positive results.

Beattie had trouble throwing strikes—4.7 walks per nine innings—and winning—a 5-15 record to go with a 4.86 ERA. Narron spent most of the season in the minors, but did get in 48 games with the Mariners, batting .196. And Beniquez, whom the Mariners had counted on to replace Jones, played in only 70 games, spending time on the disabled list and on Wills' blacklist. His insubordination during a road trip in late August and early September earned him a five-day suspension and, when the season ended, Beniquez left the club via free agency.

Even the bright spots in the Mariners' pitching were somewhat adumbrated. Floyd Bannister, who set a record for a Seattle starter with a 3.47 ERA, missed several turns because of a tender elbow. And Shane Rawley, who compiled a 7-7 record with 13 saves and a 3.32 ERA, sat out the final three weeks after suffering a muscle strain in his left shoulder.

All of which added up to make such things as winning seven of the first 10 games and being at the .500 mark as late as June 2 (24-24) seem insignificant in the franchise's gloomiest year.

SCORES OF SEATTLE MARINERS' 1980 GAMES

APRIL

			Winner	Loser
9-Toronto	W	8-6	Parrott	Lemanczyk
11-Toronto	L	7-10†	Moore	Dressler
12-Toronto	W	3-2*	Honeycutt	Garvin
13-Toronto	W	5-1	Bannister	Lemanczyk
14-At Oak.	W	7-1	Abbott	McCatty
15-At Oak.	L	3-12	McCatty	Parrott
16-At Oak.	L	1-6	Keough	Beattie
17-Minn.	W	4-3	Honeycutt	Zahn
18-Minn.	W	3-1	Bannister	Erickson
18-Minn.	W	3-2	McLaughlin	Felton
19-Minn.	L	3-8	Koosman	Abbott
20-Minn.	L	3-4	Redfern	Parrott
21-Oakland	L	2-4	Jones	Rawley
22-Oakland	W	5-4	Honeycutt	Kingman
23-Oakland	L	2-5	Langford	McLaughlin
25-Calif.	L	3-4	Aase	Parrott
26-Calif.	L	6-7	LaRoche	Dressler
27-Calif.	W	7-3	Abbott	Frost
28-At Minn.	W	6-4	Honeycutt	Felton
29-At Minn.	W	5-3	Rawley	Marshall
30-At Minn.	L	3-10	Redfern	Parrott
				Won 11, Lost 10

MAY

			Winner	Loser
1-At Calif.	L	1-2	Montague	Beattie
2-At Calif.	L	1-3	Frost	Abbott
3-At Calif.	W	2-0	Honeycutt	Kison
4-At Calif.	L	3-4	Tanana	Bannister
6-Detroit	L	5-9	Petry	Beattie
7-Detroit	W	7-6*	Heaverlo	Underwood
8-Detroit	W	4-3	Honeycutt	Morris
9-Cleve.	L	1-4	Spillner	Bannister
10-Cleve.	L	3-5	Denny	McLaughlin
11-Cleve.	W	9-4	Beattie	Barker
14-At Tor.	W	7-0	Abbott	Mirabella
15-At Tor.	L	0-1	Clancy	Bannister
16-At Chi.	W	4-2	Beattie	Trout
17-At Chi.	L	0-4	Burns	Honeycutt
18-At Chi.	L	5-6	Barrios	Dressler
19-Milw.	W	4-3‡	Rawley	Castro
20-Milw.	L	5-14	Sorensen	Bannister
21-Milw.	W	6-5	Beattie	Caldwell
23-Chicago	W	8-0	Honeycutt	Burns
24-Chicago	W	5-4	Abbott	Kravec
25-Chicago	W	8-3	Bannister	Scarbery
26-At Milw.	L	1-11	Caldwell	Parrott
27-At Milw.	L	1-4	Keeton	Beattie

MAY

			Winner	Loser
28-At Milw.	L	0-7	Travers	McLaughlin
30-At Cleve.	W	4-3*	Heaverlo	Monge
31-At Cleve.	L	2-5	Spillner	Parrott
				Won 12, Lost 14

JUNE

			Winner	Loser
1-At Cleve.	W	8-7	Heaverlo	Monge
2-At Det.	T	3-3y	....	....
3-At Det.	L	2-4	Lopez	McLaughlin
4-At Det.	L	2-8	Wilcox	Bannister
6-N. York	L	0-3	John	Beattie
7-N. York	L	0-1	Underwood	Honeycutt
8-N. York	W	5-0	Abbott	Guidry
9-Boston	W	8-7§	Heaverlo	Drago
10-Boston	L	2-4	Lockwood	Dressler
11-Boston	L	5-7	Rainey	Beattie
12-Balt.	L	1-4	Stone	Honeycutt
13-Balt.	W	7-6	Abbott	Flanagan
14-Balt.	W	9-8	Roberts	Hartzell
15-Balt.	L	3-9	Stewart	Bannister
16-At N.Y.	L	3-6	John	Beattie
17-At N.Y.	L	2-8	Underwood	Honeycutt
18-At Bos.	L	2-6	Eckersley	Abbott
19-At Bos.	L	0-2	Stanley	Parrott
20-At Balt.	W	3-1	Bannister	Palmer
21-At Balt.	L	0-9	Stone	Roberts
22-At Balt.	W	7-5	Rawley	Stoddard
24-At Tex.	L	4-5	Lyle	Rawley
25-At Tex.	L	1-6	Jenkins	Parrott
26-At Tex.	W	8-4	Bannister	Matlack
27-Kan. C.	L	1-2	Gale	Honeycutt
28-Kan. C.	L	2-4	Gura	Roberts
29-Kan. C.	W	7-2	Abbott	Leonard
30-Texas	L	5-11	Jenkins	Parrott
				Won 9, Lost 18

JULY

			Winner	Loser
1-Texas	W	6-5	Rawley	Kern
2-Texas	L	3-6	Perry	Honeycutt
3-At K.C.	W	13-2	Beattie	Gura
4-At K.C.	L	3-5	Quisenberry	Roberts
5-At K.C.	L	4-5	Twitty	Parrott
6-At K.C.	W	5-3	Bannister	Splittorff
10-Minn.	L	4-12	Koosman	Honeycutt
11-Minn.	L	3-6	Jackson	Abbott
12-At Minn.	L	3-8	Zahn	Bannister
13-At Minn.	L	6-7§	Corbett	Rawley

JULY			Winner	Loser
14—At Minn.	W	8-5	Honeycutt	Arroyo
16—Toronto	L	0-5	Stieb	Abbott
17—Toronto	W	5-3	Rawley	Jefferson
18—Detroit	L	3-5*	Lopez	Beattie
19—Detroit	L	3-5*	Rozema	Honeycutt
20—Detroit	L	2-5	Schatzeder	Parrott
21—Cleve.	W	7-0	Abbott	Garland
22—Cleve.	L	0-4	Barker	Bannister
23—Cleve.	L	6-12†	Cruz	Rawley
25—At Tor.	L	3-5	Clancy	Honeycutt
26—At Tor.	W	7-2	Dressler	Stieb
26—At Tor.	L	5-7	Kucek	Abbott
27—At Tor.	L	0-5	Jefferson	Bannister
28—At Cleve.	L	3-7	Barker	Beattie
29—At Cleve.	L	2-7	Spillner	Honeycutt
30—At Cleve.	L	2-5	Grimsley	Abbott
		Won 7, Lost 19		

AUGUST				
1—At Det.	L	0-1	Morris	Bannister
1—At Det.	L	2-5	Petry	Dressler
2—At Det.	L	3-9	Robbins	Beattie
3—At Det.	L	3-4	Rozema	Honeycutt
4—At Calif.	L	3-8	Hassler	Rawley
5—At Calif.	L	4-5	Clear	Heaverlo
6—At Calif.	L	3-8	Montague	Dressler
8—At Oak.	W	2-1*	Rawley	Keough
9—At Oak.	L	1-2	Norris	Honeycutt
10—At Oak.	W	2-1x	Heaverlo	McCatty
10—At Oak.	L	1-6	Langford	McLaughlin
12—Calif.	L	6-9	Clear	Heaverlo
13—Calif.	L	4-10	Hassler	Rawley
14—Calif.	L	1-2	Martinez	Honeycutt
15—Oakland	L	3-11	Langford	Abbott
16—Oakland	L	3-8	McCatty	McLaughlin
17—Oakland	W	4-3	Dressler	Kingman
19—N. York	L	1-3	Underwood	Honeycutt
20—N. York	L	4-6	John	Abbott
21—N. York	W	6-4	Roberts	Perry
22—Boston	L	0-1	Renko	Beattie
23—Boston	W	3-1	Dressler	Hurst
24—Boston	L	7-10	Campbell	Honeycutt
25—Balt.	W	10-5	Abbott	D. Martinez
26—Balt.	W	2-1	Bannister	McGregor

AUGUST			Winner	Loser
28—At N.Y.	L	5-6	Guidry	Beattie
29—At N.Y.	L	1-5	John	Dressler
30—At N.Y.	L	3-9	Perry	Abbott
31—At N.Y.	W	1-0	Rawley	Guidry
		Won 8, Lost 21		

SEPTEMBER				
1—At Balt.	L	4-5	D. Martinez	Parrott
2—At Balt.	L	4-10	Palmer	Beattie
3—At Balt.	L	1-5	Stone	Dressler
4—At Bos.	W	7-4	Abbott	Eckersley
5—At Bos.	W	4-2	Bannister	Tudor
6—At Bos.	L	1-5	Drago	Parrott
7—At Bos.	W	12-6	McLaughlin	Renko
8—At Chi.	L	2-3‡	Farmer	Heaverlo
9—At Chi.	W	4-1	Honeycutt	Baumgarten
10—At Chi.	L	3-4	Hoyt	Sarmiento
12—Milw.	L	1-7	Haas	Bannister
13—Milw.	L	0-8	Caldwell	Parrott
14—Milw.	L	2-3	McClure	Honeycutt
15—Chicago	W	12-1	Dressler	Hoyt
16—Chicago	L	1-2	Dotson	Abbott
17—Chicago	W	4-0	Bannister	Burns
18—Chicago	L	4-5	Proly	Rawley
19—At Milw.	L	0-4	McClure	Honeycutt
20—At Milw.	L	4-8	LaPoint	Dressler
21—At Milw.	W	7-5	Abbott	Mitchell
22—Kan. C.	W	5-4†	McLaughlin	Quisenberry
23—Kan. C.	W	7-3	Beattie	Martin
24—Kan. C.	W	4-2	Honeycutt	Splittorff
25—Texas	W	7-6†	Heaverlo	Darwin
26—Texas	W	7-2	Abbott	Jenkins
27—Texas	L	3-7	Medich	Bannister
28—Texas	L	1-4	Butcher	Beattie
30—At K.C.	L	5-7x	Quisenberry	Parrott
		Won 12, Lost 16		

OCTOBER				
1—At K.C.	L	1-4	Pattin	Dressler
2—At K.C.	L	2-6	Martin	Bannister
3—At Texas	L	2-6	Medich	Abbott
4—At Texas	L	6-11	Butcher	Beattie
5—At Texas	L	2-3	Darwin	Parrott
		Won 0, Lost 5		

*10 innings. †11 innings. ‡12 innings. §13 innings. x14 innings. y13-inning tie game.

EAST DIVISION

Bottom-Line Boss Blasted Yanks

By PHIL PEPE

The 1980 New York Yankees were the marathon runner who leads the field every step of the way, then trips and falls inches from the finish line.

The Yankees never looked back, almost from start to finish. They pushed to the front of the American League East on May 14 and led every step of the way, fighting off a stern challenge from the Baltimore Orioles, but stumbling in the end, wiped out in three games by the Kansas City Royals in the Championship Series.

For Owner George Steinbrenner, a bottom-line guy, those three days in October erased all the good that had come before; it signaled the necessity to make changes for 1981.

It hardly mattered that the Yankees won 103 games and lost only 59

NEW YORK YANKEES—1980

First row—Dent, Hegan, coach; Berra, coach; Howser, manager; Lau, coach; Ferraro, coach; Williams, coach; Torborg, coach. Second row—Murcer, Underwood, Soderholm, Oates, Jones, Werth, Watson, Cerone. Third row—Bonamo, team doctor; Monahan, trainer; Gamble, Scott, batting practice pitcher; Brown, Tiant, Spencer, Stanley, Piniella, Jackson, Weinberg, trainer; Melvin, batting practice pitcher; Sheehy, equipment manager. Top row—Randolph, Scala, bullpen catcher; Lollar, John, Guidry, Gossage, Davis, Bird, May. Seated in front—Cassidy, Toulon and D'Angelo, batboys.

during the regular season, the best record in baseball, or that they did it with a rookie manager, Dick Howser, only the sixth manager to win 100 games in his first full season. Howser joined Frank Chance, Mickey Cochrane, Ralph Houk, Earl Weaver and Sparky Anderson.

Uncomfortable with conditions imposed by Steinbrenner, Howser resigned as manager in November but remained with the club as a scouting supervisor.

And it hardly mattered that the Yankees set an all-time A. L. home attendance record of 2,627,417, and became the first team in A. L. history to play before more than five million paid customers home and away.

What Steinbrenner wanted were results, and not even the fact that his team, fortified by free agents and excellent trades, won 14 more games than they had in '79 was any consolation.

It was a season sprinkled with outstanding individual achievements.

Reggie Jackson was tied for the league home run championship at 41 by Milwaukee's Ben Oglivie on the final day of the season. Jackson drove in 111 runs and had 17 game-winning RBIs while missing 19 games, and batted .300 for the first time in his career.

Rick Cerone, acquired in an off-season deal with Toronto and playing under the pressure of being hailed as Thurman Munson's replacement behind the plate, posted career highs in average (.277), homers (14) and RBIs (85) and played in 147 games, more than any other member of the Yankees.

Willie Randolph batted a career-high .294, scored 99 runs and walked a league-high 119 times while playing his usual outstanding second base.

Bob Watson, a free-agent acquisition plagued most of the year with a fractured bone in the middle finger of his left hand, led the team in batting at .307, but drove in only 68 runs, less than had been expected.

Bucky Dent led A. L. shortstops in fielding percentage, making only 13 errors.

Tommy John was a 20-game winner for the second straight season, posting a 22-9 record to give him 43 victories in the last two seasons, more than any other pitcher in baseball.

Rich Gossage tied for the major league lead in saves with 33, had a 2.27 ERA and struck out 103 batters in 99 innings. In a stretch of 24 appearances late in the season, the Goose won two games and saved 17. He allowed only two runs and 19 hits in 36⅓ innings and struck out 43 batters.

Rudy May was another pearl plucked from the re-entry pool. Shifted between the starting rotation and the bullpen, May finished with a 15-5 record and his 2.46 ERA was the league's best.

The loss of third baseman Graig Nettles (hepatitis) for all but 89 games, and center fielder Ruppert Jones (stomach surgery, separated shoulder) for all but 83 games was almost too much to overcome. Jones had come from Seattle in a trade to fill the vacancy left by the departure of Mickey Rivers. Jones' defense and power were missed, especially in the playoffs.

It was a great season for the Yankees, for Dick Howser, until those three days in October. "Sure I'm disappointed," the manager said. "Unless you take the whole thing, there's always an empty feeling in your stomach."

All the good that had come before—the crowds, the staving off of Baltimore, the wonderful individual accomplishments—was meaningless, all of it meaningless. The 1980 season was, for the most part, sensational. Only the ending needed to be rewritten.

SCORES OF NEW YORK YANKEES' 1980 GAMES

APRIL			Winner	Loser
10—At Texas	L	0-1‡	Lyle	Underwood
11—At Texas	L	7-11	Jenkins	Davis
13—At Texas	W	9-4	Tiant	Comer
13—At Texas	W	8-2	Figueroa	Perry
15—At Chi.	L	3-4§	Wortham	Kaat
16—At Chi.	W	6-0	John	Kravec
17—At Chi.	L	6-8	Burns	Griffin
18—Milw.	L	2-3	Caldwell	Tiant
19—Milw.	L	1-5	Haas	Figueroa
20—Milw.	W	9-5	Davis	Augustine
21—Balt.	W	3-2	John	Flanagan
22—Balt.	W	5-4	Underwood	Stoddard
23—Balt.	W	6-5	Davis	Palmer
25—Chicago	L	0-6	Trout	Figueroa
26—Chicago	L	7-8‡	Farmer	Underwood
27—Chicago	W	1-0	John	Burns
29—At Balt.	W	4-3	Tiant	McGregor
30—At Balt.	L	4-7	Stone	Underwood
Won 9, Lost 9				
MAY				
2—At Minn.	W	9-6	Guidry	Zahn
3—At Minn.	W	7-3	John	Jackson
4—At Minn.	W	10-1	Underwood	Koosman
6—At Milw.	W	6-5	May	Cleveland
7—At Milw.	W	4-1	John	Travers
9—Minn.	W	2-0	Guidry	Koosman
10—Minn.	L	0-1†	Jackson	May
11—Minn.	W	5-0	John	Zahn
12—Kan. C.	L	3-12	Gura	Tiant
13—Kan. C.	L	1-4	Martin	Griffin
14—Kan. C.	W	16-3	Guidry	Leonard
16—Texas	W	6-2	John	Medich
17—Texas	W	3-0	Underwood	Matlack
18—Texas	L	4-5*	Lyle	Davis
19—At Det.	W	1-0	Guidry	Wilcox
20—At Det.	L	8-12	Hiller	John
21—At Det.	W	9-5†	May	Lopez
22—At Tor.	W	5-1	Griffin	Stieb
23—At Tor.	W	7-3	Guidry	Mirabella
24—At Tor.	W	6-2	Tiant	Clancy
25—At Tor.	L	6-9	Leal	John
26—Detroit	W	13-5	Underwood	Schatzeder
27—Detroit	W	9-6	Griffin	Petry
28—Detroit	L	3-6	Morris	Guidry
30—Toronto	W	6-0	Tiant	Clancy
31—Toronto	W	8-6†	May	McLaughlin
Won 19, Lost 7				
JUNE				
1—Toronto	W	11-7	Underwood	Mirabella
2—At K.C.	W	5-3	Guidry	Splittorff
3—At K.C.	W	5-6*	Quisenberry	Davis
4—At K.C.	L	3-9	Martin	Tiant
6—At Sea.	W	3-0	John	Beattie
7—At Sea.	W	1-0	Underwood	Honeycutt
8—At Sea.	L	0-5	Abbott	Guidry
9—At Calif.	W	8-7*	Gossage	Lemanczyk
10—At Calif.	W	4-5	Clear	May
11—At Calif.	W	9-7†	Gossage	Clear
13—At Oak.	L	3-4	Kingman	Guidry
13—At Oak.	W	6-4	Davis	Keough
14—At Oak.	W	2-1	Figueroa	Langford
15—At Oak.	W	8-2	Tiant	McCatty
16—Seattle	W	6-3	John	Beattie
17—Seattle	W	8-2	Underwood	Honeycutt
18—Calif.	W	5-0	Guidry	Aase
19—Calif.	W	7-5	May	Lemanczyk
20—Oakland	W	15-7	Tiant	McCatty
21—Oakland	W	5-3	John	Norris
22—Oakland	L	2-5	Keough	Underwood
23—Boston	L	2-7	Eckersley	Guidry
24—Boston	W	10-5	May	Tudor
25—Boston	L	3-4*	Burgmeier	John

JUNE			Winner	Loser
27—Cleve.	L	0-2	Waits	May
28—Cleve.	W	11-10	Gossage	Cruz
29—Cleve.	W	7-2	Guidry	Barker
30—At Bos.	W	6-3	John	Stanley
Won 19, Lost 9				
JULY				
1—At Bos.	W	3-2	Figueroa	Eckersley
2—At Bos.	W	6-0	May	Renko
3—At Cleve.	L	0-7	Garland	Underwood
4—At Cleve.	W	11-5	Guidry	Barker
5—At Cleve.	W	3-2	John	Spillner
6—At Cleve.	L	3-5	Waits	Figueroa
10—At Texas	W	13-5	Guidry	Jenkins
11—At Texas	L	8-10	Matlack	Underwood
12—At Chi.	W	8-0	John	Baumgarten
13—At Chi.	W	3-1	May	Trout
14—At Chi.	W	7-6	Davis	Farmer
15—Minn.	L	4-5	Koosman	Guidry
16—Minn.	W	11-1	Underwood	Jackson
17—Minn.	W	10-3	John	Zahn
18—Kan. C.	L	1-13	Gura	May
19—Kan. C.	W	13-7	Bird	Splittorff
20—Kan. C.	L	3-14	Gale	Guidry
21—Milw.	L	4-7	Caldwell	Underwood
22—Milw.	W	3-0	John	Sorensen
22—Milw.	L	1-4	Mitchell	May
23—Milw.	W	4-0	Guidry	Haas
25—At K.C.	L	1-6	Gale	Tiant
26—At K.C.	W	5-4	Gossage	Leonard
27—At K.C.	L	0-8	Gura	John
28—At Minn.	W	7-6*	Bird	Verhoeven
29—At Minn.	L	2-3	Zahn	Tiant
30—At Minn.	L	1-2*	Koosman	Gossage
31—At Milw.	W	7-6†	Gossage	Flinn
Won 16, Lost 12				
AUGUST				
1—At Milw.	W	9-4	Guidry	Travers
2—At Milw.	W	5-3	May	Mitchell
3—At Milw.	L	0-2	Haas	Tiant
4—Texas	W	10-4	Underwood	Perry
5—Texas	L	1-8	Jenkins	John
6—Texas	W	2-1	May	Medich
8—Balt.	L	2-5	Palmer	Guidry
9—Balt.	L	2-4	Stone	Underwood
10—Balt.	L	5-6	Stoddard	John
11—Chicago	W	3-1	May	Burns
12—Chicago	W	8-4*	Bird	Farmer
13—Chicago	L	1-4	Dotson	Guidry
14—At Balt.	L	1-6	Stone	Underwood
15—At Balt.	W	4-3	John	Flanagan
16—At Balt.	W	4-1	Perry	D. Martinez
17—At Balt.	L	0-1	McGregor	Tiant
18—At Balt.	L	5-6	Palmer	Guidry
19—At Sea.	W	3-1	Underwood	Honeycutt
20—At Sea.	W	6-4	John	Abbott
21—At Sea.	L	4-6	Roberts	Perry
22—At Calif.	L	4-8	Aase	Tiant
23—At Calif.	W	5-2	May	LaRoche
24—At Calif.	W	4-2	Davis	Martinez
25—At Oak.	L	1-9	Norris	John
26—At Oak.	L	1-3	Langford	Tiant
28—Seattle	W	6-5	Guidry	Beattie
29—Seattle	W	5-1	John	Dressler
30—Seattle	W	9-3	Perry	Abbott
31—Seattle	L	0-1	Rawley	Guidry
Won 15, Lost 14				
SEPTEMBER				
1—Oakland	W	5-0	Underwood	Langford
2—Oakland	W	6-1	May	McCatty
3—Oakland	W	8-3	John	Kingman
4—Calif.	W	5-3	Perry	Tanana

SEPTEMBER				Winner	Loser
5—Calif.	W	6-5*		Gossage	Hassler
6—Calif.	W	7-4		Underwood	Frost
7—Calif.	W	4-1		May	Dorsey
8—At Tor.	W	7-4		John	Stieb
9—At Tor.	L	4-6		Todd	Perry
10—At Tor.	W	7-6		Davis	Clancy
11—At Bos.	W	8-5*		Davis	Burgmeier
12—At Bos.	W	4-2		May	Torrez
13—At Bos.	W	4-3		John	Eckersley
14—At Bos.	W	5-3		Davis	Eckersley
16—Toronto	W	5-4		Guidry	Clancy
17—Toronto	W	8-7x		Underwood	Kucek
18—Toronto	L	1-2		Leal	John
19—Boston	W	2-1		Tiant	Renko
20—Boston	L	1-4		Eckersley	Perry
21—Boston	W	3-0		Guidry	Tudor

SEPTEMBER				Winner	Loser
22—Cleve.	W	4-3		John	Barker
23—Cleve.	W	5-4		Davis	Stanton
24—Cleve.	W	7-3		Tiant	Owchinko
25—Cleve.	L	0-5		Waits	Perry
26—At Det.	W	7-5		Guidry	Schatzeder
27—At Det.	L	1-5		Morris	John
28—At Det.	L	5-6*		Lopez	Griffin
30—At Cleve.	L	9-12		Monge	Gossage
			Won 21, Lost 7		
OCTOBER					
1—At Cleve.	W	18-7		Perry	Barker
2—Detroit	W	3-2		Guidry	Morris
4—Detroit	W	5-2		May	Weaver
4—Detroit	L	6-7		Tobik	Griffin
5—Detroit	W	2-1		Lollar	Schatzeder
			Won 4, Lost 1		

*10 innings.   †11 innings.   ‡12 innings.   §14 innings.   x13-inning suspended game, completed September 18.

100 Victories Not Enough for Orioles

By KEN NIGRO

The Orioles compiled a stunning 72-32 record after June 14. They were 58-26 after the All-Star break and 52-20 after losing the opener of a double-header on July 21. They won 14 of their last 18 and seven of their last eight to finish 100-62.

Unfortunately for Earl Weaver and his club, the 1980 season began in April, not June. So, because of their sputtering start, the Orioles failed to defend their American League championship. Instead, they finished second in the A.L. East, three games behind the New York Yankees, and had to be content with the fact they were the first team to win 100 games and not finish first since the 1962 Los Angeles Dodgers.

What took the Orioles so long to get their act in gear? One could probably come up with a dozen different reasons, but injuries to pitchers Scott McGregor and Dennis Martinez and that abbreviated players' strike near the end of spring training probably hurt the most.

McGregor, who went on to win 20 games, suffered tendinitis in his left elbow and didn't pitch his first game until April 22—13 days into the season. Martinez came up with a sore right shoulder and was put on the disabled list at the end of spring training. The righthander wasn't much use the first half of the season.

Without two of his starters, Weaver had to juggle his pitching rotation and it cost the Orioles some games.

There were also injuries to John Lowenstein (hip and shoulder bruises) and Gary Roenicke (fractured left wrist) that robbed the Orioles of their left field combination and also stripped Weaver of some of his "deep depth" of 1979.

How much the strike hurt was difficult to measure because all clubs were affected by it to some extent. Some teams stayed together in Florida and worked out during those final days. The Orioles did not.

"There's no doubt in my mind that the players' strike hurt our club a lot," General Manager Hank Peters said. "I like to think that without the strike, we wouldn't have gotten off to the type of start we did."

Still, it was a pretty good year with some fine individual performances.

BALTIMORE ORIOLES—1980

Front row—Tyler, equipment manager; Bumbry, Stewart, Robinson, coach; Miller, coach; Weaver, manager; Ripken, coach; Hendricks, coach; Singleton, Lowenstein, McGregor, Salvon, trainer. Second row—Stoddard, Roenicke, Murray, Belanger, Ayala, Graham, Crowley, Dempsey, May, Kerrigan, Corey, Palmer. Top row—T. Martinez, Ford, Sakata, Flanagan, Dauer, Garcia, DeCinces, Stone, Kelly, D. Martinez. Seated in front—Deaton, batboy.

For one, Cy Young winner Steve Stone blossomed into the major leagues' winningest pitcher, setting a club record with 25 victories. Stone, who had never won more than 15 games in a season, won 14 in a row at one stage.

McGregor won his 20th game on the final day of the season. It marked the sixth time at least two Orioles hurlers had achieved that distinction in the same season and the 13th straight year Baltimore had produced a 20-game winner.

Former Cy Young pitchers Jim Palmer and Mike Flanagan won 16 games apiece.

Tim Stoddard proved a worthy successor to Don Stanhouse in relief and the big righthander set a club record with 26 saves.

On offense, there was center fielder Al Bumbry, the most consistent performer of all the Orioles. Bumbry batted .318, scored 118 runs and set a club record with 205 hits.

The right-left catching duo of Rick Dempsey and Dan Graham gave Weaver tremendous production. The two receivers combined for 24 homers and 94 RBIs.

Ken Singleton was his usual self, batting over .300 (.304) for the third time in six years with the Orioles and driving in more than 100 runs (104) for the second straight season. Singleton's final statistics mirrored the team's performance—he was batting only .236 in mid-June.

And, of course, the Orioles may never have gotten untracked had it not been for a phenomenal year by Eddie Murray. The 24-year-old first baseman finished with career highs of 32 homers and 116 RBIs and was third in the A.L. in total bases. That raised Murray's four-year totals to 111 homers and 398 RBIs.

The highlight of the season had to be the two series with the Yankees on successive weekends in August. The Orioles won six of the eight games between the two teams to move into contention but could never draw even with New York, though they closed the gap from 11 games on July 14 to ½ game on August 28. The five-game series at home against the Yankees drew a record total of 253,636 fans.

"I've got no complaints about 1980," Weaver said. "It was a great year other than that those other clubs couldn't beat the Yankees."

SCORES OF BALTIMORE ORIOLES' 1980 GAMES

APRIL			Winner	Loser	MAY			Winner	Loser
10—At Chi.	W	5-3	Palmer	Trout	2—At Texas	W	7-5	Flanagan	Kern
11—At Chi.	L	4-8	Kravec	Flanagan	3—At Texas	L	2-3	Jenkins	Palmer
12—At Chi.	L	2-8	Dotson	Stone	4—At Texas	W	9-5	D. Martinez	Comer
13—At Chi.	L	2-5	Baumgarten	Stewart	5—Minn.	L	2-4	Redfern	Stone
15—Kan. C.	W	12-2	Palmer	Leonard	6—Minn.	W	10-3	McGregor	Zahn
16—Kan. C.	W	2-1	Flanagan	Gura	7—Minn.	W	8-6	Stewart	Marshall
17—Kan. C.	W	5-2	Stone	Gale	8—At Milw.	L	1-9	Haas	D. Martinez
18—Chicago	W	5-2	Ford	Dotson	9—At Milw.	W	5-2	Stone	Augustine
19—Chicago	L	4-5‡	Farmer	T. Martinez	10—At Milw.	L	3-5	Sorensen	McGregor
20—Chicago	L	6-9	Wortham	Stewart	11—At Milw.	L	4-5	Cleveland	Stewart
21—At N.Y.	L	2-3	John	Flanagan	12—Texas	L	1-5	Matlack	Ford
22—At N.Y.	L	4-5	Underwood	Stoddard	13—Texas	W	4-2	Stone	Jenkins
23—At N.Y.	L	5-6	Davis	Palmer	14—Texas	L	3-6	Perry	Hartzell
25—At K.C.	L	0-7	Gura	Stone	16—At Det.	W	2-1	Flanagan	Petry
26—At K.C.	W	4-0	Flanagan	Gale	18—At Det.	L	4-6	Lopez	Stoddard
27—At K.C.	L	2-3	Splittorff	Ford	19—At Cleve.	W	4-1	Stone	Waits
29—N. York	L	3-4	Tiant	McGregor	20—At Cleve.	L	0-4	Denny	Stewart
30—N. York	W	7-4	Stone	Underwood	20—At Cleve.	W	8-0	Palmer	Owchinko
		Won 7, Lost 11			21—At Cleve.	L	2-4	Barker	Flanagan

MAY

			Winner	Loser
22—Detroit	W	5-1	McGregor	Petry
23—Detroit	W	5-3	Stone	Morris
24—Detroit	W	9-1	Palmer	Wilcox
25—Detroit	L	4-6†	Lopez	T. Martinez
26—Cleve.	W	7-3	McGregor	Barker
27—Cleve.	L	6-7	Cruz	Ford
28—Cleve.	L	6-10	Waits	Palmer
30—At Minn.	W	3-2*	Flanagan	Corbett
31—At Minn.	W	11-1	McGregor	Zahn

Won 15, Lost 13

JUNE

2—Milw.	W	9-8†	T. Martinez	McClure
3—Milw.	L	0-3	Haas	Stewart
4—Milw.	L	2-3	Sorensen	Flanagan
6—At Calif.	W	6-1	McGregor	Kison
7—At Calif.	W	6-5	Palmer	Frost
8—At Calif.	W	13-8	Stewart	Knapp
9—At Oak.	W	3-2	Flanagan	Langford
10—At Oak.	L	4-7	McCatty	McGregor
11—At Oak.	L	2-6x	Norris	Stewart
12—At Sea.	W	4-1	Stone	Honeycutt
13—At Sea.	L	6-7	Abbott	Flanagan
14—At Sea.	W	8-9	Roberts	Hartzell
15—At Sea.	W	9-3	Stewart	Bannister
16—Calif.	W	5-2	Palmer	Knapp
17—Calif.	W	5-3	Stone	Frost
18—Oakland	W	3-2	Flanagan	Jones
19—Oakland	W	4-3	McGregor	Langford
20—Seattle	L	1-3	Bannister	Palmer
21—Seattle	W	9-0	Stone	Roberts
22—Seattle	W	5-7	Rawley	Stoddard
24—Toronto	W	1-0	McGregor	Stieb
25—Toronto	W	6-3	Palmer	Leal
26—Toronto	W	4-1	Stone	Clancy
27—At Bos.	L	2-3	Rainey	Flanagan
28—At Bos.	W	8-4	McGregor	Torrez
30—At Tor.	W	9-7	Stone	Leal

Won 17, Lost 9

JULY

1—At Tor.	W	2-0	Palmer	Clancy
2—At Tor.	W	6-2	Flanagan	Mirabella
3—Boston	L	2-5	Rem'swaal	McGregor
4—Boston	W	10-3	Stone	Torrez
5—Boston	L	0-1	Tudor	Palmer
6—Boston	L	4-6	Eckersley	Flanagan
10—At Chi.	W	9-2	McGregor	Burns
11—At Chi.	L	4-5	Proly	Palmer
12—Kan. C.	W	3-1	Stone	Martin
13—Kan. C.	L	1-5	Gura	Flanagan
14—Kan. C.	L	4-8	Splittorff	McGregor
15—At Milw.	W	7-3	Palmer	Cleveland
16—At Milw.	W	10-4	Stone	Caldwell
17—At Milw.	W	1-0	D. Martinez	Travers
18—Texas	W	8-7	Flanagan	Kern
19—Texas	L	8-11*	Darwin	Stewart
20—Texas	L	1-7	Jenkins	Palmer
21—At Minn.	L	7-8†	Verhoeven	T. Martinez
21—At Minn.	W	12-5	Stone	Zahn
22—At Minn.	W	8-4	Flanagan	Erickson
23—At Minn.	W	8-7	McGregor	Arroyo
25—Milw.	L	0-5	Cleveland	Palmer
26—Milw.	W	4-1	Stone	Caldwell
27—Milw.	W	5-4‡	Stoddard	McClure
29—At Texas	W	4-3	McGregor	Hough
30—At Texas	W	3-2	Palmer	Perry
31—At Texas	L	4-7	Jenkins	Stone

Won 16, Lost 11

AUGUST

			Winner	Loser
1—Minn.	W	3-2	Flanagan	Corbett
2—Minn.	W	9-2	McGregor	Arroyo
3—Minn.	W	7-2	Palmer	Jackson
5—Chicago	W	8-2	Stone	Hoyt
6—Chicago	W	4-1	Flanagan	Burns
7—Chicago	W	2-1	McGregor	Trout
8—At N.Y.	W	5-2	Palmer	Guidry
9—At N.Y.	W	4-2	Stone	Underwood
10—At N.Y.	W	6-5	Stoddard	John
11—At K.C.	W	2-1	D. Martinez	Gura
12—At K.C.	L	3-4	Quisenberry	McGregor
13—At K.C.	L	1-6	Gale	Palmer
14—N. York	W	6-1	Stone	Underwood
15—N. York	L	3-4	John	Flanagan
16—N. York	L	1-4	Perry	D. Martinez
17—N. York	W	1-0	McGregor	Tiant
18—N. York	W	6-5	Palmer	Guidry
19—At Calif.	W	5-2	Stone	A. Martinez
20—At Calif.	W	6-5*	Stoddard	Clear
21—At Calif.	W	7-1	McGregor	Knapp
22—At Oak.	W	3-2	Stewart	McCatty
23—At Oak.	W	4-2	Stone	Kingman
24—At Oak.	W	3-0	Flanagan	Keough
25—At Sea.	L	5-10	Abbott	D. Martinez
26—At Sea.	L	1-2	Bannister	McGregor
28—Calif.	W	13-8	Palmer	LaRoche
29—Calif.	L	0-5	A. Martinez	Stone
30—Calif.	L	6-12	Clear	Flanagan
31—Calif.	W	5-0	McGregor	Knapp

Won 21, Lost 8

SEPTEMBER

1—Seattle	W	5-4	D. Martinez	Parrott
2—Seattle	W	10-4	Palmer	Beattie
3—Seattle	W	5-1	Stone	Dressler
4—Oakland	L	1-7	Keough	Flanagan
5—Oakland	W	8-7	Stoddard	Jones
6—Oakland	L	2-3	Langford	Palmer
7—Oakland	L	2-5	McCatty	Stone
8—At Det.	W	9-2	D. Martinez	Wilcox
8—At Det.	W	8-6	Flanagan	Petry
9—At Det.	W	2-0	McGregor	Schatzeder
10—At Det.	W	8-4	T. Martinez	Morris
11—At Tor.	W	6-1	Stone	Mirabella
12—At Tor.	L	5-7	McLaughlin	Flanagan
13—At Tor.	W	6-4	McGregor	Stieb
14—At Tor.	L	3-4§	Barlow	D. Martinez
16—Detroit	L	3-8	Morris	Stone
17—Detroit	W	9-3	Stewart	Weaver
18—Detroit	W	7-3	McGregor	Wilcox
19—Toronto	W	8-6‡	T. Martinez	Willis
20—Toronto	W	6-1	Stone	Stieb
21—Toronto	W	2-1	Flanagan	Clancy
22—Boston	L	3-5	Drago	McGregor
23—Boston	W	8-6	Stoddard	Stanley
24—Boston	W	12-9	T. Martinez	Torrez
26—At Cleve.	L	4-5	Spillner	Flanagan
27—At Cleve.	L	5-6	Barker	T. Martinez
28—At Cleve.	W	5-3	Palmer	Owchinko
29—At Bos.	W	5-2	D. Martinez	Drago
29—At Bos.	W	4-3	Stone	MacWhorter
30—At Bos.	W	11-6	Flanagan	Renko

Won 21, Lost 9

OCTOBER

1—At Bos.	W	12-8	Stewart	Eckersley
4—Cleve.	W	3-2§	Stewart	Monge
4—Cleve.	L	4-6	Waits	Boddicker
5—Cleve.	W	7-1	McGregor	Barker

Won 3, Lost 1

*10 innings.   †11 innings.   ‡12 innings.   §13 innings.   x14 innings.

Brewers Lost Ground, Despite Super Cooper

By TOM FLAHERTY

The Milwaukee Brewers approached the 1980 season thinking there was nowhere to go but up. Instead, they dropped a notch.

After finishing third in 1978 and second in 1979, the Brewers backtracked, finishing third in the American League East and never making a serious challenge. Their 86-76 record left them 17 games behind the New York Yankees.

The Brewers' problems started before the season began, maybe a sign of things to come. Two weeks before spring training opened, Coach Harvey Kuenn had to have his leg amputated below the knee. A week after the team reported to Sun City, Arizona, Manager George Bamberger suffered a heart attack and was gone from the team until June.

Health was to play a big part in the Brewers' season.

Outfielder Larry Hisle, who missed most of the '79 season with a torn rotator cuff in his right shoulder, reinjured the shoulder in May and had to have surgery. He was out the rest of the season. Pitcher Jim Slaton injured his shoulder in the second week of the season and pitched in only three games.

Second baseman Paul Molitor was leading the league in batting at the time he pulled a muscle in his rib cage in the first week of June and missed six weeks. When he returned to the lineup, he spent a month floundering before finally playing with his old zest in the last month to finish with a .304 batting average and rescue at least a part of his damaged season.

Don Money had an assortment of injuries and the handyman was out of the lineup almost as much as he was in it.

While the injuries had a lot to do with the Brewers' finish, some unhealthy performances from healthy players contributed just as much to the fall.

The pitching, which was spotty all year, took most of the blame, but the Brewers' lineup of sluggers failed again and again to score runs in the late innings.

The Brewers had hoped to improve their bullpen with the addition of rookie Dan Boitano, but he gave up seven home runs and 16 earned runs in 18 innings and was back in the minor leagues by mid-May. The bullpen of Reggie Cleveland, Bob McClure, Bill Castro and John Flinn did a respectable job the first half of the season but managed only eight saves after July 21.

The starters had their problems, too. Moose Haas was the most consistent member of the staff, finishing 16-15 with a 3.11 ERA, but his effectiveness declined in September. Mike Caldwell, the Brewers' biggest winner the previous two seasons, struggled to a 13-11 record and gave up a whopping 29 home runs, including five in one game at Boston.

Lary Sorensen had an up-and-down year in winning 12 and losing 10.

Offensively, the Brewers piled up some impressive individual statistics and continued to score a lot of runs—although not always when they needed them most.

The Brewers led both leagues in home runs (203) and scored 811 runs.

First baseman Cecil Cooper finished second in the league in batting with a .352 average and led both major leagues with 122 RBIs. Left fielder Ben

MILWAUKEE BREWERS—1980

Seated in front—Doman, Rinn, Migliaccio and Watunya, batboys. First row—Ksicinski, visiting clubhouse manager; Howard, coach; McLish, coach; Haney, coach; Bamberger, manager; Rodgers, coach and manager; Kuenn, coach; Hansen, coach; McCormack, clubhouse boy. Second row—Frederico, trainer; Sullivan, equipment manager; Lezcano, McClure, Caldwell, Gantner, Romero, Moore, Rayer, trainer; Ferguson, vice-president. Third row—Mitchell, Oglivie, Keeton, Davis, Thomas, Travers, Hisle, Sorensen, Cleveland, Flinn, Cooper.

Oglivie shared the A.L. home run title with Reggie Jackson (41) and drove in 118 runs while batting .304.

Center fielder Gorman Thomas blasted 38 homers and drove in 105 runs despite batting just .239.

Robin Yount put together his best season, both in the field and at the plate, hitting .293 with 23 homers and 87 RBIs. And the 25-year-old shortstop's 49 doubles topped the majors.

Jim Gantner, who spent most of the season filling in for injured infielders, showed that he could perform as an everyday player, hitting .282, and Charlie Moore, who shared the catching with Buck Martinez, batted .291 in 111 games.

The biggest disappointment was right fielder Sixto Lezcano, who fell from a .321 average to .229.

Despite their problems, the Brewers were in second place most of the first part of the season and headed to New York for a four-game showdown series late in July. The Brewers came out of that with a split, but followed that by losing two of three to the Orioles. The Yankees won three of four in Milwaukee a week later, and the Brewers were never again in the race. After a seven-game losing streak in late August, the Brewers had to struggle to finish third.

Bamberger retired September 7, and Bob (Buck) Rodgers, who had filled in during Bamberger's absence early in the season, was named to replace him.

A new sound was heard at County Stadium during the season—the fans, whose hopes were high after the previous two seasons, started to boo for the first time in the franchise's history. They still turned out, though. Attendance was 1,857,408, down just a bit from the record 1,918,343 of the year before.

SCORES OF MILWAUKEE BREWERS' 1980 GAMES

APRIL			Winner	Loser	MAY			Winner	Loser
10—Boston	W	9-5	Cleveland	Drago	17—At Minn.	W	14-11	Augustine	Zahn
12—Boston	W	18-1	Sorensen	Torrez	18—At Minn.	L	4-10	Redfern	Travers
13—Boston	L	1-3	Stanley	Haas	19—At Sea.	L	3-4‡	Rawley	Castro
16—At Tor.	L	2-11	Stieb	Slaton	20—At Sea.	W	14-5	Sorensen	Bannister
17—At Tor.	L	0-1	Mirabella	Sorensen	21—At Sea.	L	5-6	Beattie	Caldwell
18—At N.Y.	W	3-2	Caldwell	Tiant	23—Minn.	W	5-0	Travers	Redfern
19—At N.Y.	W	5-1	Haas	Figueroa	24—Minn.	W	4-0	Haas	Koosman
20—At N.Y.	L	5-9	Davis	Augustine	25—Minn.	W	3-2	Sorensen	Erickson
21—Cleve.	W	7-5†	McClure	Cruz	26—Seattle	W	11-1	Caldwell	Parrott
22—Cleve.	W	8-4	Caldwell	Barker	27—Seattle	W	4-1	Keeton	Beattie
23—Cleve.	L	3-7	Spillner	Haas	28—Seattle	W	7-0	Travers	McLaughlin
25—Toronto	L	3-5	McLaughlin	Sorensen	29—At Cleve.	L	0-5	Denny	Haas
26—Toronto	L	0-4	Stieb	Caldwell	30—At Bos.	L	3-5	Rainey	Sorensen
27—Toronto	L	2-8	Mirabella	Haas	31—At Bos.	W	19-8	Cleveland	Torrez
29—At Cleve.	W	14-1	Travers	Owchinko					

Won 7, Lost 8   Won 16, Lost 12

MAY					JUNE				
2—At Chi.	W	8-0	Caldwell	Kravec	1—At Bos.	W	8-5	Flinn	Burgmeier
3—At Chi.	W	4-1	Haas	Burns	2—At Balt.	L	8-9†	T. Martinez	McClure
4—At Chi.	W	11-1	Slaton	Baumgarten	3—At Balt.	W	3-0	Haas	Stewart
5—At Chi.	L	7-11	Scarbery	Boitano	4—At Balt.	W	3-2	Sorensen	Flanagan
6—N. York	L	5-6	May	Cleveland	6—Detroit	W	8-4	Caldwell	Underwood
7—N. York	L	4-14	John	Travers	7—Detroit	W	5-3	Keeton	Morris
8—Balt.	W	9-1	Haas	D. Martinez	8—Detroit	L	4-0	Petry	Travers
9—Balt.	L	5-9	Stone	Augustine	10—Texas	L	1-3	Jenkins	Haas
10—Balt.	W	5-3	Sorensen	McGregor	11—Texas	W	7-1	Sorensen	Matlack
11—Balt.	W	8-4	Cleveland	Stewart	12—Texas	W	8-1	Caldwell	Perry
13—Chicago	L	5-6*	Burns	Cleveland	13—Kan. C.	L	3-4	Gura	Keeton
14—Chicago	W	5-1	Haas	Proly	14—Kan. C.	W	5-2	Travers	Martin
15—Chicago	L	4-6	Dotson	Sorensen	15—Kan. C.	L	2-7	Leonard	Haas
16—At Minn.	L	3-4	Koosman	McClure	16—At Det.	L	5-6	Wilcox	Castro

JUNE

Date		Score	Winner	Loser
16—At Det.	W	5-3	Cleveland	Rozema
17—At Det.	L	0-3	Morris	Caldwell
18—At Texas	L	1-8	Medich	Keeton
19—At Texas	W	10-4	Travers	Allard
20—At K.C.	W	10-5	Haas	Leonard
21—At K.C.	W	5-1	Sorensen	Splittorff
22—At K.C.	L	4-7	Gale	Caldwell
23—At Oak.	W	8-0	Cleveland	Kingman
24—At Oak.	W	5-3	Travers	Langford
25—At Oak.	W	5-2	Haas	McCatty
27—At Calif.	L	5-6	Clear	Castro
28—At Calif.	W	11-5	Caldwell	Halicki
29—At Calif.	W	5-2	Cleveland	Aase
30—Oakland	W	5-2	Travers	Langford

Won 18, Lost 10

JULY

Date		Score	Winner	Loser
1—Oakland	W	5-2	Haas	McCatty
2—Oakland	L	3-5*	Norris	McClure
3—Oakland	L	5-7	Keough	Caldwell
4—Calif.	L	0-2	Aase	Cleveland
5—Calif.	W	4-3	Travers	Knapp
6—Calif.	L	0-2	Halicki	Haas
10—Boston	W	2-1	Cleveland	Torrez
10—Boston	L	0-7	Renko	Sorensen
11—Boston	W	7-6	Caldwell	Eckersley
12—At Tor.	W	9-2	Travers	Moore
13—At Tor.	L	1-4	Kucek	Haas
13—At Tor.	W	4-0	Mitchell	McLaughlin
14—At Tor.	W	6-4	Augustine	Clancy
15—Balt.	L	3-7	Palmer	Cleveland
16—Balt.	L	4-10	Stone	Caldwell
17—Balt.	L	0-1	D. Martinez	Travers
18—Chicago	W	5-1	Haas	Trout
19—Chicago	L	7-10	Hoyt	McClure
20—Chicago	W	7-6	Augustine	Proly
21—At N.Y.	W	7-4	Caldwell	Underwood
22—At N.Y.	L	0-3	John	Sorensen
22—At N.Y.	W	4-1	Mitchell	May
23—At N.Y.	L	0-4	Guidry	Haas
25—At Balt.	W	5-0	Cleveland	Palmer
26—At Balt.	L	1-4	Stone	Caldwell
27—At Balt.	L	4-5‡	Stoddard	McClure
29—At Chi.	W	7-1	Haas	Dotson
30—At Chi.	L	5-6	Hoyt	Sorensen
31—N. York	L	6-7†	Gossage	Flinn

Won 13, Lost 16

AUGUST

Date		Score	Winner	Loser
1—N. York	L	4-9	Guidry	Travers
2—N. York	L	3-5	May	Mitchell
3—N. York	W	2-0	Haas	Tiant
4—At Bos.	L	2-7	Renko	Cleveland
5—At Bos.	L	1-3	Eckersley	Caldwell
6—At Bos.	W	9-4	Sorensen	Drago
7—At Bos.	L	3-7	Torrez	Mitchell
8—Cleve.	W	4-1	Travers	Barker
9—Cleve.	W	4-2	Haas	Owchinko
10—Cleve.	W	5-1	Caldwell	Grimsley

AUGUST

Date		Score	Winner	Loser
10—Cleve.	L	4-9	Spillner	Cleveland
12—Toronto	L	1-3	Clancy	Sorensen
12—Toronto	L	4-5	Barlow	Castro
13—Toronto	W	5-4	Travers	McLaughlin
14—Toronto	W	4-2	Haas	Stieb
15—At Cleve.	W	4-1	Caldwell	Grimsley
16—At Cleve.	L	10-5	Augustine	Spillner
17—At Cleve.	W	4-0	Mitchell	Waits
17—At Cleve.	W	11-1	Sorensen	Owchinko
18—Detroit	W	12-5	Travers	Petry
19—Detroit	L	2-6	Schatzeder	Haas
20—Detroit	L	6-8	Ujdur	Caldwell
22—At Texas	L	6-12	Rajsich	Cleveland
22—At Texas	W	8-3	Mitchell	Medich
23—At Texas	L	5-7	Darwin	Augustine
24—At Texas	L	3-4†	Johnson	Cleveland
25—Kan. C.	L	3-9	Gura	Haas
26—Kan. C.	L	6-7	Busby	Caldwell
27—Kan. C.	L	4-5	Splittorff	Mitchell
28—At Det.	L	7-11	Robbins	McClure
29—At Det.	L	2-8	Wilcox	Travers
30—At Det.	W	6-4	Haas	Lopez
31—At Det.	W	11-6	Cleveland	Schatzeder

Won 15, Lost 18

SEPTEMBER

Date		Score	Winner	Loser
1—At K.C.	W	6-1	McClure	Gale
3—At K.C.	W	3-1*	Sorensen	Leonard
4—At K.C.	W	9-5	Castro	Quisenberry
5—Texas	L	5-6	Matlack	Haas
6—Texas	W	6-2	Caldwell	Clay
7—Texas	L	2-7	Medich	McClure
9—At Minn.	L	2-15	Williams	Sorensen
10—At Minn.	W	3-1	Mitchell	Erickson
12—At Sea.	W	7-1	Haas	Bannister
13—At Sea.	W	8-0	Caldwell	Parrott
14—At Sea.	W	3-2	McClure	Honeycutt
17—Minn.	L	2-3	Koosman	Haas
17—Minn.	L	1-6	Erickson	Mitchell
18—Minn.	W	9-8	Flinn	Corbett
18—Minn.	W	5-0	Sorensen	Redfern
19—Seattle	W	4-0	McClure	Honeycutt
20—Seattle	W	8-4	LaPoint	Dressler
21—Seattle	L	5-7	Abbott	Mitchell
22—Calif.	L	3-7	Clear	McClure
23—Calif.	L	1-2	Martinez	Caldwell
24—Calif.	W	6-0	Sorensen	Tanana
26—At Oak.	W	10-7	Cleveland	Norris
27—At Oak.	L	1-7	Langford	Haas
28—At Oak.	L	2-3	McCatty	Cleveland
29—At Calif.	L	2-6	Tanana	Sorensen
30—At Calif.	W	4-2	McClure	Ferris

Won 15, Lost 11

OCTOBER

Date		Score	Winner	Loser
1—At Calif.	W	10-7	Castro	Schuler
4—Oakland	L	0-4	Lacey	Haas
5—Oakland	W	5-4§	Cleveland	Beard

Won 2, Lost 1

*10 innings.   †11 innings.   ‡12 innings.   §15 innings.

Suspect Pitching Staff Slayed Red Sox

By JOE GIULIOTTI

The 1980 season was a disaster for the Boston Red Sox. They went into spring training with a pitching staff that was suspect, but even in their most pessimistic dreams they couldn't have envisioned only one member of the starting rotation winning in double figures.

Along the road to an 83-77 mark and fourth place in the American League East, 19 games behind the New York Yankees, the Red Sox had a losing record at home for the first time in 14 years, hit more home runs on the road than in friendly Fenway Park, suffered some key injuries and lost a manager.

Don Zimmer, who was not the most popular man ever to guide the Red Sox, paid the price for the team's dismal showing when, with five days left in the season, he was fired for the first time in his career.

The play of the team was reflected at the gate where the Red Sox drew 1,956,092. That's a good figure, but it was over 350,000 fewer than the previous year and the lowest attendance since 1976.

The Red Sox struggled to remain a shade over the .500 mark most of the season until a hot streak in August (11 of 12 and 22 of 28) vaulted the club from 13½ games behind into contention.

They had drawn within five games of the Yankees in the lost column when outfielders Fred Lynn and Carl Yastrzemski were lost for the rest of the year with injuries. Lynn fouled a ball off his big toe and broke it August 28; two days later, Yaz suffered a broken rib when he ran into the left-field wall at Fenway making a catch off Oakland's Jim Essian.

It would have taken a miracle for the Red Sox to catch New York even with Lynn and Yastrzemski, but without them they lost 21 of their final 32.

You could talk about the injuries—outfielder Jim Rice was lost for 31 games with a broken wrist, second baseman Jerry Remy was written off for the season when his knee gave out just after the All-Star break, Chuck Rainey was finished on July 3 with an elbow injury after going 8-3 as a starter and Dennis Eckersley, after pitching with a sore arm, missed a month with a back injury—but in the final analysis, it was pitching that killed the Red Sox.

Eckersley was the only starter to win in double figures and his final record was a not very impressive 12-14. Mike Torrez, the No. 2 man in the rotation, was 9-16 with a 5.09 ERA.

Bob Stanley wound up 10-8, but much of his success came in relief after he had failed as a starter. In one stretch of 16 appearances, Stanley won three games, saved 12 others and didn't allow an earned run in 26⅓ innings.

What saved the Red Sox from a sub-.500 year was the relief work of Tom Burgmeier. He carried the club over the first half of the season and, despite suffering tendinitis in the second half, wound up with a 5-4 mark and 24 saves, the most ever by a Red Sox lefthander.

"Without Burgmeier over the first half of the season, who knows where we would have ended?" Zimmer said. "I never saw a team play as badly as we did for the first two months. I wish I knew what the reason was."

There were solid seasons by some old reliables, and great expectations were raised by the performances of some of the younger players.

Carlton Fisk, whose right elbow had put his career in jeopardy in the spring, caught 111 games and batted .289 with 18 homers. Rick Burleson did his usual good job at shortstop and hit a solid .278. First baseman Tony Perez justified the money paid to him in the free-agent market by hitting .275 with 25 homers and 105 RBIs, and Bill Campbell flashed signs of coming back to his 1977 form with a 4-0 mark in 41 innings of work.

Dave Stapleton, called up from Pawtucket on May 30, filled in for Remy at second base and ended with a .321 average to stamp himself as a youngster to watch.

BOSTON RED SOX—1980

Front row—Hobson, Perez, Hriniak, coach; Yost, coach; Pesky, coach; Zimmer, manager; Harper, coach; Podres, coach; Lynn, Fisk, Burleson. Second row—Fitzpatrick, clubhouse man; Orlando, clubhouse man; Remmerswaal, Tudor, Rader, Stapleton, Evans, Hoffman, Hancock, Dwyer, Moss, trainer. Top row—Burgmeier, Lockwood, Stanley, Renko, Torrez, Campbell, Eckersley, Drago. Seated in front—Wood, batboy. Inserts—Yastrzemski, Rice, Rainey.

Rookie Glenn Hoffman replaced the veteran Butch Hobson at third base and hit .285, and rookie lefthander John Tudor went 8-5 after being called up from Pawtucket in late June.

None of that, however, was enough to keep the Red Sox from their worst standing since divisional play began in 1969, or enough to save Zimmer from his first dismissal.

SCORES OF BOSTON RED SOX' 1980 GAMES

			Winner	Loser
APRIL				
10—At Milw.	L	5-9	Cleveland	Drago
12—At Milw.	L	1-18	Sorensen	Torrez
13—At Milw.	W	3-1	Stanley	Haas
14—Detroit	W	3-1	Eckersley	Morris
16—Detroit	W	10-9	Renko	Schatzeder
17—Detroit	W	5-4†	Drago	Lopez
18—Texas	L	5-6	Darwin	Lockwood
19—Texas	L	0-8	Perry	Eckersley
20—Texas	W	6-5†	Burgmeier	Kern
21—Chicago	W	9-8	Lockwood	Scarbery
22—Chicago	L	0-2	Burns	Torrez
24—Chicago	L	3-9	Dotson	Stanley
25—At Det.	L	3-11	Schatzeder	Eckersley
26—At Det.	W	12-7	Hurst	Wilcox
27—At Det.	L	5-8	Rozema	Torrez
29—At Chi.	W	11-1	Stanley	Baumgarten
30—At Chi.	L	1-2	Dotson	Eckersley
		Won 8, Lost 9		
MAY				
1—At Chi.	W	4-3	Hurst	Trout
2—At K.C.	W	6-5†	Lockwood	Quisenberry
3—At K.C.	W	7-0	Rainey	Splittorff
4—At K.C.	L	3-5	Leonard	Stanley
5—At Texas	L	3-11	Perry	Eckersley
6—At Texas	L	2-7	Medich	Hurst
7—At Texas	W	7-4†	Drago	Devine
9—Kan. C.	L	5-6	Leonard	Stanley
10—Kan. C.	L	8-13	Martin	Eckersley
11—Kan. C.	W	5-2	Rainey	Gale
12—Minn.	L	3-4	Redfern	Torrez
13—Minn.	W	10-5	Renko	Verhoeven
14—Minn.	W	7-6	Burgmeier	Corbett
15—At Cleve.	W	6-2	Billingham	Waits
16—At Cleve.	W	2-1	Rainey	Denny
17—At Cleve.	L	3-4*	Stanton	MacWhorter
18—At Cleve.	L	1-3	Spillner	Stanley
19—At Tor.	L	2-7	Clancy	Billingham
20—At Tor.	W	4-3	Rainey	Lemanczyk
21—At Tor.	W	11-2	Torrez	Jefferson
23—Cleve.	W	4-1	Stanley	Spillner
24—Cleve.	L	2-7	Waits	Billingham
25—Cleve.	L	2-3	Denny	Rainey
26—Toronto	L	1-3	Garvin	Drago
27—Toronto	W	5-4	Renko	Buskey
28—Toronto	L	1-4	Stieb	Stanley
30—Milw.	W	5-3	Rainey	Sorensen
31—Milw.	L	8-19	Cleveland	Torrez
		Won 14, Lost 14		
JUNE				
1—Milw.	L	5-8	Flinn	Burgmeier
2—At Minn.	W	6-2	Stanley	Redfern
3—At Minn.	L	4-9	Koosman	Billingham
6—At Oak.	W	14-8	Rainey	Norris
7—At Oak.	L	1-4	Keough	Torrez
8—At Oak.	W	6-1	Burgmeier	Hamilton
9—At Sea.	L	7-8‡	Heaverlo	Drago
10—At Sea.	W	5-4†	Lockwood	Dressler
11—At Sea.	W	7-5	Rainey	Beattie
12—At Calif.	W	13-2	Torrez	Frost
13—At Calif.	W	3-0	Eckersley	Aase
14—At Calif.	W	7-3	Stanley	Martinez
15—At Calif.	W	6-5	Renko	Tanana

			Winner	Loser
JUNE				
16—Oakland	L	8-11	Norris	Rainey
17—Oakland	W	6-2	Torrez	Keough
18—Seattle	W	6-2	Eckersley	Abbott
19—Seattle	W	2-0	Stanley	Parrott
20—Calif.	L	2-20	Tanana	Renko
21—Calif.	L	2-4	Knapp	Rainey
22—Calif.	W	6-3	Torrez	Barr
23—At N.Y.	W	7-2	Eckersley	Guidry
24—At N.Y.	L	5-10	May	Tudor
25—At N.Y.	W	4-3*	Burgmeier	John
27—Balt.	L	3-2	Rainey	Flanagan
28—Balt.	L	4-8	McGregor	Torrez
30—N. York	L	3-6	John	Stanley
		Won 16, Lost 10		
JULY				
1—N. York	L	2-3	Figueroa	Eckersley
2—N. York	L	0-6	May	Renko
3—At Balt.	W	5-2	Rem'swaal	McGregor
4—At Balt.	L	3-10	Stone	Torrez
5—At Balt.	W	1-0	Tudor	Palmer
6—At Balt.	W	6-4	Eckersley	Flanagan
10—At Milw.	L	1-2	Cleveland	Torrez
10—At Milw.	W	7-0	Renko	Sorensen
11—At Milw.	L	6-7	Caldwell	Eckersley
12—Detroit	W	9-3	Tudor	Petry
13—Detroit	W	8-4	Drago	Rozema
14—Detroit	L	4-12	Robbins	Torrez
15—Kan. C.	L	4-8	Gale	Renko
16—Kan. C.	L	1-5	Leonard	Eckersley
17—Kan. C.	W	12-4	Tudor	Martin
18—Minn.	W	1-0*	Torrez	Erickson
19—Minn.	L	0-4	Arroyo	Ojeda
20—Minn.	L	4-5	Corbett	Drago
21—Texas	L	3-5	Matlack	Eckersley
22—Texas	L	3-4	Darwin	Torrez
23—Texas	W	12-5	Drago	Johnson
25—At Minn.	W	7-5	Rem'swaal	Koosman
25—At Minn.	L	0-6	Zahn	Renko
26—At Minn.	W	5-1	Eckersley	Erickson
27—At Minn.	L	4-5	Williams	Torrez
29—At K.C.	L	8-9	Quisenberry	Burgmeier
30—At K.C.	W	7-1	Stanley	Busby
31—At K.C.	L	3-13	Leonard	Eckersley
		Won 12, Lost 16		
AUGUST				
1—At Texas	L	5-7	Medich	Rem'swaal
2—At Texas	W	1-0	Ojeda	Figueroa
3—At Texas	W	6-4	Torrez	Matlack
4—Milw.	W	7-2	Renko	Cleveland
5—Milw.	W	3-1	Eckersley	Caldwell
6—Milw.	L	4-9	Sorensen	Drago
7—Milw.	W	7-3	Torrez	Mitchell
8—Chicago	W	4-1	Campbell	Dotson
9—Chicago	L	4-5	Proly	Renko
10—Chicago	W	4-3	Eckersley	Hoyt
11—At Det.	L	7-8	Lopez	Burgmeier
12—At Det.	W	5-4	Campbell	Fidrych
13—At Det.	L	1-2	Petry	Tudor
14—At Det.	W	3-1	Renko	Schatzeder
15—At Chi.	W	8-5	Eckersley	Proly
18—At Oak.	W	7-5	Stanley	Minetto
20—At Oak.	L	1-2	Norris	Eckersley

AUGUST			Winner	Loser		SEPTEMBER			Winner	Loser
21—At Oak.	W	5-1	Tudor	Langford		14—N. York	L	3-5	Davis	Eckersley
22—At Sea.	W	1-0	Renko	Beattie		16—Cleve.	W	9-5	Tudor	Grimsley
23—At Sea.	L	1-3	Dressler	Hurst		17—Cleve.	L	5-6†	Spillner	Torrez
24—At Sea.	W	10-7	Campbell	Honeycutt		18—Cleve.	W	8-3	Crawford	Garland
25—At Calif.	W	4-2†	Stanley	Clear		19—At N.Y.	L	1-2	Tiant	Renko
26—At Calif.	W	5-1	Tudor	Knapp		20—At N.Y.	W	4-1	Eckersley	Perry
28—Oakland	W	3-2	Burgmeier	McCatty		21—At N.Y.	L	0-3	Guidry	Tudor
29—Oakland	W	6-3	Torrez	Kingman		22—At Balt.	W	5-3	Drago	McGregor
30—Oakland	W	7-6*	Campbell	Lacey		23—At Balt.	L	6-8	Stoddard	Stanley
31—Oakland	W	5-1	Tudor	Norris		24—At Balt.	L	9-12	T. Martinez	Torrez
		Won 20, Lost 7				26—At Tor.	W	3-1	Eckersley	Stieb
						27—At Tor.	W	4-3	Stanley	Clancy
SEPTEMBER						28—At Tor.	W	7-3	Crawford	McLaughlin
1—Calif.	W	4-3	Drago	Frost		29—Balt.	L	2-5	D. Martinez	Drago
2—Calif.	W	10-2	Renko	Dorsey		29—Balt.	L	3-4	Stone	MacWhorter
3—Calif.	L	2-7	Martinez	Torrez		30—Balt.	L	6-11	Flanagan	Renko
4—Seattle	L	4-7	Abbott	Eckersley				Won 12, Lost 17		
5—Seattle	L	2-4	Bannister	Tudor						
6—Seattle	W	5-1	Drago	Parrott		OCTOBER				
7—Seattle	L	6-12	McLaughlin	Renko		1—Balt.	L	8-12	Stewart	Eckersley
8—At Cleve.	W	10-4	Torrez	Spillner		2—Toronto	W	4-1	Tudor	Clancy
9—At Cleve.	W	4-3	Eckersley	Cruz		4—Toronto	L	6-7§	Leal	Stanley
10—At Cleve.	L	4-7	Waits	Tudor		4—Toronto	L	1-3	Mirabella	Drago
11—N. York	L	5-8*	Davis	Burgmeier		5—Toronto	L	1-4	Todd	MacWhorter
12—N. York	L	2-4	May	Renko				Won 1, Lost 4		
13—N. York	L	3-4	John	Torrez						

*10 innings. †11 innings. ‡13 innings. §17 innings.

Tigers Led Majors in Runs—Gave Up More

By TOM GAGE

Sparky Anderson spent the season regretting the breakfast he ate on Opening Day. Not that his eggs and coffee were cold, but that he made the mistake of taking the occasion to predict 90 victories for his Detroit Tigers.

"I don't see why we can't win 90 games," he said. "If our pitching comes through, we'll contend. If not, then we'll disappear. We'll score runs, so the rest depends on pitching."

The manager was wrong with his prediction. The Tigers finished 84-78 and in fifth place, but he was right about the pitching. The Tigers went as far as their 4.25 ERA would take them—which was not very far.

"No club can hope to contend with those kinds of numbers," Anderson said, while admitting that 1980 was his most disappointing season as a major league manager. "It all begins in the arena, out there on the mound, no matter how many runs you score."

Scoring runs was not the Tigers' trouble. They scored 830, the most in the major leagues. Ron LeFlore was traded before the season, and his speed was missed, but the Tigers found other ways to score.

Ricky Peters emerged as the leadoff hitter when Kirk Gibson, the heralded rookie from Michigan State, was sidelined with wrist surgery. Peters took over in center field but his value was at the plate, where he solved the dilemma of replacing LeFlore. Peters hit .291 for the season.

Alan Trammell moved up to the No. 2 spot in the batting order and responded with his most productive season. The shortstop hit .300 and scored 107 runs, easily winning Tiger of the Year honors.

Champ Summers hit .297 and drove in 60 runs, a career high. Richie Hebner, obtained from the New York Mets in an off-season deal, also recorded a career high in RBIs with 82 and hit .290.

Despite several injuries, Steve Kemp drove in 101 runs, only four fewer than in 1979. But all the offense accomplished very little for the Tigers, who haven't finished higher than fourth since 1973. Eighty-four victories was one less than the year before and two less than 1978.

In many ways, it was a turbulent year, ranging from an earthquake which shook the Tiger Stadium stands in late July to two brawls. Al Cowens was suspended for seven games after charging Ed Farmer at the mound in Chicago on June 20. Cowens was retaliating for a Farmer pitch which broke his jaw in 1979 when Cowens played for Kansas City and Farmer pitched for Texas.

Farmer filed criminal charges, preventing Cowens from making the return trip to Chicago in August, but the two shook hands at home plate when the White Sox visited Detroit in September and the charges were dropped.

Cowens was part of the Tigers' biggest swap of the season. The LeFlore deal was the winter blockbuster, but the trading of first baseman Jason Thompson to the California Angels on May 27 was just as significant. The Tigers needed a righthanded hitting outfielder so they dealt Thompson for Cowens, who became a fixture in right field and hit .280 for the rest of the season. Hebner, who had been playing third base, took over at first.

The other brawl involved pitcher Milt Wilcox and George Brett of Kansas City, following two pitches close to Brett's chin. Wilcox hurt a shoulder in the melee and his effectiveness was diminished the final two months of the season.

Jack Morris led the pitching staff with a 16-15 record, but it was hardly the type of season he projected for himself after finishing 17-7 the year before. Wilcox was 13-11 and Dan Schatzeder, whom the Tigers received in return for LeFlore, finished at 11-13. Dan Petry (10-9, 3.93) was the only Detroit starter with an ERA of less than 4.00. Aurelio Lopez was the workhorse of the bullpen again, posting 21 saves along with a 13-6 record, but was inconsistent and finished with a 3.77 ERA.

The Tigers made it clear, however, that they considered the young arms to be their future. Jack Billingham was sold to the Boston Red Sox and John Hiller retired in midseason. Both pitchers were 37 years old.

Mark Fidrych was on hand for another comeback, though. This one was Comeback IV and proved more successful than its predecessors. Fidrych won two games, his first victories in more than two years and offered hope again for 1981.

But most of the accomplishments were at the plate for the Tigers in 1980. Lou Whitaker was the only regular who had an off year with the bat, slipping from .286 to .233.

"We scored more than five runs a game on the average," Sparky noted. "We just have to find a way to keep the other team from scoring six."

SCORES OF DETROIT TIGERS' 1980 GAMES

APRIL			Winner	Loser	APRIL			Winner	Loser
10—At K.C.	W	5-1	Morris	Leonard	19—Kan. C.	W	8-6	Morris	Martin
11—At K.C.	L	0-4	Gura	Schatzeder	20—Kan. C.	L	6-9	Martin	Schatzeder
12—At K.C.	L	6-8	Pattin	Underwood	21—At Texas	L	2-3	Matlack	Wilcox
13—At K.C.	L	2-3	Splittorff	Rozema	22—At Texas	W	2-0	Rozema	Jenkins
14—At Bos.	L	1-3	Eckersley	Morris	23—At Texas	W	5-4	Morris	Comer
16—At Bos.	L	9-10	Renko	Schatzeder	25—Boston	W	11-3	Schatzeder	Eckersley
17—At Bos.	L	4-5‡	Drago	Lopez	26—Boston	L	7-12	Hurst	Wilcox
18—Kan. C.	L	6-9‡	Quisenberry	Lopez	27—Boston	W	8-5	Rozema	Torrez

DETROIT TIGERS—1980

Front row—Kemp, Thompson, G. Brown, coach; Grammas, coach; Craig, coach; Anderson, manager; Consolo, coach; Tracewski, coach; Stegman, Whitaker. Second row—B. Brown, traveling secretary; Schmackel, equipment manager; Hebner, Brookens, Gibson, Corcoran, Trammell, Peters, Behm, trainer; Di Salvo, assistant trainer. Third row—Wockenfuss, Wagner, Lopez, Tobik, Parrish, Schatzeder, Dyer, Summers. Top row—Underwood, Hiller, Morris, Petry, Wilcox, Rozema. Seated in front—Cowart and Nelson, batboys.

APRIL			Winner	Loser
29—Texas	L	5-10*	Comer	Morris
30—Texas	W	5-4†	Wilcox	Lyle
		Won 7, Lost 11		

MAY			Winner	Loser
2—At Oak.	L	6-10	McCatty	Rozema
3—At Oak.	L	3-5	Kingman	Morris
4—At Oak.	W	4-0	Wilcox	Langford
4—At Oak.	L	0-1	Norris	Schatzeder
6—At Sea.	W	9-5	Petry	Beattie
7—At Sea.	L	6-7†	Heaverlo	Underwood
8—At Sea.	L	3-4	Honeycutt	Morris
9—At Calif.	W	6-5†	Lopez	Montague
10—At Calif.	W	6-1	Schatzeder	Tanana
11—At Calif.	W	4-0	Petry	Aase
13—Oakland	W	4-3	Morris	Keough
14—Oakland	W	6-5	Lopez	Jones
16—Balt.	L	1-2	Flanagan	Petry
18—Balt.	W	6-4	Lopez	Stoddard
19—N. York	L	0-1	Guidry	Wilcox
20—N. York	W	12-8	Hiller	John
21—N. York	L	5-9‡	May	Lopez
22—At Balt.	L	1-5	McGregor	Petry
23—At Balt.	L	3-5	Stone	Morris
24—At Balt.	L	1-9	Palmer	Wilcox
25—At Balt.	W	6-4‡	Lopez	T. Martinez
26—At N.Y.	L	5-13	T. Underw'd	Schatzeder
27—At N.Y.	L	6-9	Griffin	Petry
28—At N.Y.	W	6-3	Morris	Guidry
30—Calif.	W	12-1	Wilcox	Tanana
31—Calif.	L	1-6	Kison	Underwood
		Won 12, Lost 14		

JUNE			Winner	Loser
2—Seattle	T	3-3y	....	....
3—Seattle	W	4-2	Lopez	McLaughlin
4—Seattle	W	8-2	Wilcox	Bannister
6—At Milw.	L	4-8	Caldwell	Underwood
7—At Milw.	L	3-5	Keeton	Morris
8—At Milw.	W	9-5	Petry	Travers
10—Minn.	W	8-3	Wilcox	Zahn
11—Minn.	L	5-9	Jackson	Rozema
12—Minn.	W	8-4	Underwood	Zahn
13—Chicago	W	8-4	Morris	Trout
14—Chicago	W	3-0	Petry	Burns
16—Milw.	W	6-5	Wilcox	Castro
16—Milw.	L	3-5	Cleveland	Rozema
17—Milw.	W	3-0	Morris	Caldwell
19—At Minn.	L	1-5	Jackson	Schatzeder
20—At Chi.	W	5-3‡	Lopez	Farmer
21—At Chi.	W	4-1	Wilcox	Baumgarten
22—At Chi.	W	7-1	Rozema	Kravec
22—At Chi.	W	6-4	Morris	Wortham
23—At Cleve.	W	5-4	Schatzeder	Stanton
24—At Cleve.	W	9-4	Weaver	Barker
25—At Cleve.	W	13-3	Wilcox	Spillner
27—At Tor.	W	7-2	Morris	Jefferson
28—At Tor.	W	8-3	Rozema	Kucek
29—At Tor.	L	0-2	Stieb	Petry
30—Cleve.	W	9-4	Schatzeder	Spillner
		Won 19, Lost 6		

JULY				
1—Cleve.	L	7-8	Owchinko	Underwood
2—Cleve.	L	7-6	Morris	Waits
3—Toronto	W	8-5	Underwood	McLaughlin
4—Toronto	W	4-3	Petry	Stieb
5—Toronto	L	3-5	Clancy	Wilcox
6—Toronto	L	7-5	Morris	Garvin
10—At K.C.	L	2-3	Splittorff	Wilcox
11—At K.C.	L	3-7	Leonard	Morris
12—At Bos.	L	3-9	Tudor	Petry
13—At Bos.	L	4-8	Drago	Rozema
14—At Bos.	W	12-4	Robbins	Torrez
16—At Oak.	W	7-2	Weaver	Kingman
17—At Oak.	L	2-5	Keough	Morris

JULY			Winner	Loser
18—At Sea.	W	5-3†	Lopez	Beattie
19—At Sea.	W	5-3†	Rozema	Honeycutt
20—At Sea.	W	5-2	Schatzeder	Parrott
21—At Calif.	W	14-3	Wilcox	Aase
22—At Calif.	L	4-6	Hassler	Rozema
23—At Calif.	L	7-6	Lopez	Clear
25—Oakland	L	3-5	Langford	Robbins
26—Oakland	W	7-0	Schatzeder	Kingman
27—Oakland	W	4-2	Wilcox	Minetto
27—Oakland	L	0-4	Keough	Morris
28—Calif.	L	2-3	Montague	Petry
29—Calif.	L	0-7	Martinez	Robbins
30—Calif.	L	5-6	Clear	Schatzeder
31—Calif.	W	15-6	Wilcox	Aase
		Won 14, Lost 13		

AUGUST			Winner	Loser
1—Seattle	W	1-0	Morris	Bannister
1—Seattle	W	5-2	Petry	Dressler
2—Seattle	W	9-3	Robbins	Beattie
3—Seattle	W	4-3	Rozema	Honeycutt
4—Kan. C.	L	5-6	Quisenberry	Schatzeder
5—Kan. C.	L	3-6	Leonard	Wilcox
6—Kan. C.	L	4-5	Gura	Morris
8—At Texas	W	8-0	Petry	Figueroa
9—At Texas	L	3-4†	Darwin	Lopez
10—At Texas	L	2-4	Perry	Weaver
11—Boston	W	8-7	Lopez	Burgmeier
12—Boston	L	4-5	Campbell	Fidrych
13—Boston	W	2-1	Perry	Tudor
14—Boston	L	1-3	Renko	Schatzeder
15—Texas	L	2-6	Matlack	Underwood
16—Texas	L	5-12	Clay	Morris
17—Texas	L	3-9	Jenkins	Fidrych
17—Texas	L	6-12	Medich	Wilcox
18—At Milw.	L	5-12	Travers	Petry
19—At Milw.	W	6-2	Schatzeder	Haas
20—At Milw.	W	8-6	Ujdur	Caldwell
21—At Minn.	L	3-5	Williams	Wilcox
21—At Minn.	W	4-2	Morris	Erickson
22—At Minn.	L	5-6§	Arroyo	Rozema
23—At Minn.	W	4-3	Robbins	Jackson
24—At Minn.	W	3-2	Schatzeder	Zahn
26—At Chi.	L	5-4	Lopez	Wortham
27—At Chi.	L	2-3x	Proly	Rozema
28—Milw.	W	11-7	Robbins	McClure
29—Milw.	W	8-2	Wilcox	Travers
30—Milw.	L	4-6	Haas	Lopez
31—Milw.	L	6-11	Cleveland	Schatzeder
		Won 15, Lost 17		

SEPTEMBER				
1—Chicago	L	3-11	Burns	Morris
2—Chicago	W	11-2	Fidrych	Proly
2—Chicago	W	6-1	Wilcox	Dotson
3—Chicago	W	5-4	Lopez	Wortham
5—Minn.	W	1-0	Schatzeder	Erickson
6—Minn.	L	0-4	Koosman	Morris
7—Minn.	L	1-3	Jackson	Fidrych
8—Balt.	L	2-9	D. Martinez	Wilcox
8—Balt.	L	6-8	Flanagan	Petry
9—Balt.	L	0-2	McGregor	Schatzeder
10—Balt.	L	4-8	T. Martinez	Morris
12—At Cleve.	W	6-3	Lopez	Barker
13—At Cleve.	W	7-4§	Underwood	Stanton
14—At Cleve.	L	4-5§	Cruz	Lopez
14—At Cleve.	L	0-3	Owchinko	Morris
16—At Balt.	W	8-3	Morris	Stone
17—At Balt.	L	3-9	Stewart	Weaver
18—At Balt.	L	3-7	McGregor	Wilcox
19—Cleve.	W	4-3	Schatzeder	Owchinko
20—Cleve.	W	13-3	Petry	Waits
21—Cleve.	W	13-1	Morris	Spillner
22—Toronto	L	5-6	Garvin	Weaver
23—Toronto	L	7-9	Willis	Rozema
24—Toronto	W	9-8†	Petry	Kucek

SEPTEMBER			Winner	Loser	OCTOBER			Winner	Loser
26—N. York	L	5-7	Guidry	Schatzeder	1—At Tor.	W	11-7	Fidrych	Stieb
27—N. York	W	5-1	Morris	John	2—At N.Y.	L	2-3	Guidry	Morris
28—N. York	W	6-5†	Lopez	Griffin	4—At N.Y.	L	2-5	May	Weaver
29—At Tor.	W	8-2	Weaver	Mirabella	4—At N.Y.	W	7-6	Tobik	Griffin
30—At Tor.	W	5-3	Schatzeder	Todd	5—At N.Y.	L	1-2	Lollar	Schatzeder
			Won 15, Lost 14					**Won 2, Lost 3**	

*7 innings.   †10 innings.   ‡11 innings.   §13 innings.   x14 innings.   y13-inning tie game.

4.68 ERA Doomed Indians

By BOB SUDYK

It wasn't realized at the time, but the Indians' loss to the California Angels in the season opener was a harbinger of 1980 for the Tribe.

There it was, the season in microcosm. John Denny, who was to be the ace of the staff until a midseason injury shelved him for the remainder of the year, became ill and missed his scheduled start. His replacements were battered for 10 runs and 15 hits, three of them home runs. And Joe Charboneau, playing in his first major league game, hammered a line-drive home run in his second at-bat.

Denny suffered a disabling bruised heel while pitching against those same Angels, July 15. Going into the game, he had won six of his previous seven decisions. His loss was the beginning of the end for a club already thin in pitching. The Indians' 4.68 ERA was the worst in the majors.

Charboneau, the most exciting first-year player to join the Indians since Rocky Colavito, copped the American League Rookie of the Year award. He led the team in homers (23) and RBIs (87) and became the first player to homer into the right-field upper deck in remodeled Yankee Stadium.

The Indians had finished a game above .500 in 1979 and optimists were predicting 85 victories in the new season. But a rash of injuries helped keep the Tribe in sixth place for the third straight year in the tough A. L. East Division. Cleveland finished a disappointing 79-81.

Ill fortune preceded the season. The team's leading power hitter, first baseman Andre Thornton, was felled with torn knee ligaments and cartilage in spring training and missed the entire season.

Mike Hargrove moved to first base, opening left field for Charboneau. Hargrove had 12 game-winning RBIs and his .304 average was third on the club behind catcher Ron Hassey's .318 and outfielder Miguel Dilone's .341.

Charboneau himself suffered a painful groin injury which limited him to designated-hitter duty the last two months of the season. He missed 29 games, 13 in September.

The Indians were further hurt by the loss of shortstop Tom Veryzer, who was unavailable for 51 games because of tendinitis in his left shoulder, and the foot ailment that caused outfielder Jorge Orta, a .291 hitter, to miss 31 games.

Other injuries brought the club some talent which it might not have obtained otherwise. In some serendipitous wheeling and dealing, the Indians picked up Dilone and Alan Bannister.

Dilone, who began the season with a .214 average on the major league level, was acquired from the Chicago Cubs to fill in for center fielder Rick Manning, sidelined for three weeks in May with a bruised knee. Dilone did more than fill in. He went on to set a club record with 61 stolen bases and his .341 average was third best in the A. L. Much of the credit for Dilone's improvement went to the tutoring of Alabama-Birmingham University Coach Harry Walker, the former major leaguer who worked with him on bunting and slapping the ball to the opposite field.

When second baseman Duane Kuiper underwent knee surgery in June, the Tribe dealt utilityman Ron Pruitt to the Chicago White Sox for infielder Alan Bannister, who was batting .192. In 81 games with Cleveland, Bannister hit .328.

After Denny's incapacitation, Manager Dave Garcia turned to Len Barker to anchor the starting rotation. Barker obliged, going 19-12 and fanning a league-leading 187 batters in 246 innings. He was 12-5 after the All-Star break.

Dan Spillner won 16 games, but with a 5.29 ERA. Rick Waits won 13 games, but lost 14.

Wayne Garland, still negotiating a comeback from shoulder surgery in 1978, posted only six victories, but was a hero on the best night of the season, a 7-0 victory over the Yankees before 73,096 fans at Municipal Stadium, the largest crowd in baseball in '80. Garland pitched a two-hitter.

The Indians' bullpen wasn't the place to look to for help. Sid Monge and Victor Cruz were 3-5 and 6-7, respectively. Monge saved 14 games, Cruz 12. The previous season Monge had won 12 and saved 19.

The Tribe's hopes for a .500 season, which would have been only their third in 13 years, went down the drain in the final 25 games, all against East Division opponents and the last 12 against New York and Baltimore. With only four regulars in the lineup, the Indians won but nine of the 25.

The Tribe managed to stay at or above the break-even point 75 days of the season. The club's best streak was 17-5, when they moved from six games under on July 21 to six over on August 14.

When the club's physical misfortune was taken into account, the effort was enough to win Garcia a one-year extension on his contract.

SCORES OF CLEVELAND INDIANS' 1980 GAMES

APRIL			Winner	Loser
11—At Calif.	L	2-10	Frost	Spillner
12—At Calif.	W	2-1	Barker	Kison
13—At Calif.	L	3-8	Aase	Denny
14—At Texas	L	4-7	Medich	Waits
15—At Texas	L	0-3	Matlack	Owchinko
16—At Texas	L	7-8	Kern	Cruz
19—Toronto	W	8-1	Waits	Clancy
20—Toronto	L	3-5	Lemanczyk	Denny
21—At Milw.	L	5-7‡	McClure	Cruz
22—At Milw.	L	4-8	Caldwell	Barker
23—At Milw.	W	7-3	Spillner	Haas
25—Texas	L	1-4	Darwin	Waits
26—Texas	W	8-7	Cruz	Kern
27—Texas	W	7-4	Barker	Jenkins
29—Milw.	L	1-14	Travers	Owchinko
		Won 5, Lost 10		

MAY				
1—At Tor.	W	2-1	Denny	Lemanczyk
2—At Tor.	W	6-1	Barker	Stieb
3—At Tor.	L	3-8	Buskey	Waits
4—At Tor.	L	8-9†	Buskey	Monge
4—At Tor.	L	2-7	Jefferson	Owchinko
5—At Oak.	L	1-5	Keough	Denny
6—At Oak.	W	4-3	Barker	McCatty
7—At Oak.	W	2-1	Waits	Kingman
9—At Sea.	W	4-1	Spillner	Bannister
10—At Sea.	W	5-3	Denny	McLaughlin

MAY			Winner	Loser
11—At Sea.	L	4-9	Beattie	Barker
14—Calif.	L	7-13	Knapp	Spillner
15—Boston	L	2-6	Billingham	Waits
16—Boston	L	1-2	Rainey	Denny
17—Boston	W	4-3†	Stanton	MacWhorter
18—Boston	W	3-1	Spillner	Stanley
19—Balt.	L	1-4	Stone	Waits
20—Balt.	W	4-0	Denny	Stewart
20—Balt.	L	0-8	Palmer	Owchinko
21—Balt.	W	4-2	Barker	Flanagan
23—At Bos.	L	1-4	Stanley	Spillner
24—At Bos.	W	7-2	Waits	Billingham
25—At Bos.	W	3-2	Denny	Rainey
26—At Balt.	L	3-7	McGregor	Barker
27—At Balt.	W	7-6	Cruz	Ford
28—At Balt.	W	10-6	Waits	Palmer
29—Milw.	W	5-0	Denny	Haas
30—Sea.	L	3-4†	Heaverlo	Monge
31—Sea.	W	5-2	Spillner	Parrott
		Won 16, Lost 13		

JUNE				
1—Seattle	L	7-8	Heaverlo	Monge
2—Oakland	W	10-5	Garland	Kingman
3—Oakland	W	6-4†	Cruz	Langford
4—Oakland	W	5-3	Spillner	McCatty
6—At Chi.	L	7-8	Farmer	Monge
8—At Chi.	W	7-2	Denny	Burns

CLEVELAND INDIANS—1980

Front row—Warfield, trainer; M. Seghi, traveling secretary; Duncan, coach; Garcia, manager; Nossek, coach; Sommers, coach; Minch, batboy; Buynak, equipment manager; Thornton. Second row—Veryzer, Harrah, Hargrove, Manning, Brohamer, Bannister, Dybzinski, Alston, Diaz, Cruz, Dilone, Orta, Rosello. Top row—Owchinko, Stanton, Alexander, Barker, Garland, Waits, Denny, Charboneau, Spillner, Hassey, Monge, Collins.

JUNE

Date		Score	Winner	Loser
10—Kan. C.	L	4-8	Pattin	Barker
11—Kan. C.	L	0-5	Leonard	Waits
11—Kan. C.	W	8-5	Spillner	Gale
13—Minn.	W	6-2	Denny	Koosman
14—Minn.	W	3-2	Barker	Erickson
15—Minn.	W	14-5	Spillner	Jackson
16—Chicago	W	5-3	Garland	Farmer
17—Chicago	L	3-5	Hoyt	Cruz
18—At K.C.	L	2-10	Gura	Denny
19—At K.C.	W	5-4	Barker	Martin
20—At Minn.	W	4-3y	Cruz	Redfern
21—At Minn.	L	2-3	Zahn	Garland
22—At Minn.	W	11-6	Waits	Redfern
23—Detroit	L	4-5	Schatzeder	Stanton
24—Detroit	L	4-9	Weaver	Barker
25—Detroit	L	3-13	Wilcox	Spillner
27—At N.Y.	W	2-0	Waits	May
28—At N.Y.	L	10-11	Gossage	Cruz
29—At N.Y.	L	2-7	Guidry	Barker
30—At Det.	L	4-9	Schatzeder	Spillner

Won 13, Lost 13

JULY

Date		Score	Winner	Loser
1—At Det.	W	8-7	Owchinko	Underwood
2—At Det.	L	6-7	Morris	Waits
3—N. York	W	7-0	Garland	Underwood
4—N. York	L	5-11	Guidry	Barker
5—N. York	L	2-3	John	Spillner
6—N. York	W	5-3	Waits	Figueroa
10—At Tor.	W	7-3	Denny	Clancy
11—At Tor.	L	3-6	Stieb	Garland
12—At Texas	W	9-8	Barker	Perry
13—At Texas	L	2-12	Medich	Spillner
14—At Texas	L	2-4	Darwin	Waits
15—At Calif.	L	1-7	Tanana	Denny
16—At Calif.	W	6-2	Garland	Aase
17—At Calif.	W	5-3	Barker	Knapp
18—At Oak.	L	1-9	Norris	Spillner
19—At Oak.	L	0-3	McCatty	Waits
20—At Oak.	L	5-6x	Langford	Cruz
21—At Sea.	L	0-7	Abbott	Garland
22—At Sea.	W	4-0	Barker	Bannister
23—At Sea.	W	12-6‡	Cruz	Rawley
25—Calif.	W	9-8	Wihtol	Clear
25—Calif.	L	10-2	Grimsley	Martinez
26—Calif.	W	14-4	Garland	Aase
28—Seattle	W	7-3	Barker	Beattie
29—Seattle	W	7-2	Spillner	Honeycutt
30—Seattle	W	5-2	Grimsley	Abbott

Won 15, Lost 11

AUGUST

Date		Score	Winner	Loser
1—Oakland	L	1-2	Kingman	Waits
3—Oakland	L	3-11	Keough	Garland
3—Oakland	W	4-2	Barker	Norris
4—Toronto	W	11-5	Spillner	Mirabella
5—Toronto	W	8-5	Grimsley	Kucek
6—Toronto	W	5-2	Waits	Jefferson
7—Toronto	W	7-6	Monge	Garvin
8—At Milw.	L	1-4	Travers	Barker
9—At Milw.	L	2-4	Haas	Owchinko
10—At Milw.	L	1-5	Caldwell	Grimsley
10—At Milw.	W	9-4	Spillner	Cleveland
12—Texas	W	2-1	Waits	Jenkins
13—Texas	W	14-3	Garland	Medich
14—Texas	W	7-2	Barker	Figueroa
15—Milw.	L	1-4	Caldwell	Grimsley
16—Milw.	L	5-10	Augustine	Spillner
17—Milw.	L	0-4	Mitchell	Waits
17—Milw.	L	1-11	Sorensen	Owchinko
18—At Chi.	W	4-2	Barker	Burns
18—At Chi.	L	2-7	Trout	Garland
19—At Chi.	W	8-5	Grimsley	Dotson
20—At Chi.	W	3-0	Spillner	Kravec
21—At K.C.	W	4-3	Waits	Busby
22—At K.C.	W	4-1	Barker	Splittorff
23—At K.C.	L	2-3	Gale	Garland
24—At K.C.	L	5-7	Leonard	Grimsley
25—Minn.	W	4-3	Spillner	Arroyo
26—Minn.	L	1-5	Erickson	Waits
27—Minn.	W	4-1	Barker	Koosman
29—Chicago	W	6-5	Monge	Farmer
30—Chicago	W	6-2	Spillner	Baumgarten
31—Chicago	L	8-10	Hoyt	Cruz
31—Chicago	L	7-8	Trout	Grimsley

Won 18, Lost 15

SEPTEMBER

Date		Score	Winner	Loser
1—At Minn.	W	5-2	Barker	Williams
2—At Minn.	L	3-5	Jackson	Garland
3—At Minn.	W	7-1*	Spillner	Zahn
5—Kan. C.	L	1-2	Splittorff	Waits
6—Kan. C.	W	8-3	Barker	Martin
7—Kan. C.	L	4-6	Leonard	Garland
8—Boston	L	4-10	Torrez	Spillner
9—Boston	L	3-4	Eckersley	Cruz
10—Boston	W	7-4	Waits	Tudor
12—Detroit	L	3-6	Lopez	Barker
13—Detroit	L	4-7§	Underwood	Stanton
14—Detroit	W	5-4§	Cruz	Lopez
14—Detroit	W	3-0	Owchinko	Petry
16—At Bos.	L	5-9	Tudor	Grimsley
17—At Bos.	W	6-5‡	Spillner	Torrez
18—At Bos.	L	3-8	Crawford	Garland
19—At Det.	L	3-4	Schatzeder	Owchinko
20—At Det.	L	3-13	Petry	Waits
21—At Det.	L	1-13	Morris	Spillner
22—At N.Y.	L	3-4	John	Barker
23—At N.Y.	L	4-5	Davis	Stanton
24—At N.Y.	L	3-7	Tiant	Owchinko
25—At N.Y.	W	5-0	Waits	Perry
26—Balt.	W	5-4	Spillner	Flanagan
27—Balt.	W	6-5	Barker	T. Martinez
28—Balt.	L	3-5	Palmer	Owchinko
30—N. York	W	12-9	Monge	Gossage

Won 11, Lost 16

OCTOBER

Date		Score	Winner	Loser
1—N. York	L	7-18	Perry	Barker
4—At Balt.	L	2-3§	Stewart	Monge
4—At Balt.	W	6-4	Waits	Boddicker
5—At Balt.	L	1-7	McGregor	Barker

Won 1, Lost 3

*7 innings. †10 innings. ‡11 innings. §13 innings. x14 innings. y15 innings.

Blue Jays Had More Punch in '80

By NEIL MacCARL

The Toronto Blue Jays worked hard in spring training on fundamentals. When the season started, they were not beating themselves. There was a refreshingly different atmosphere in the clubhouse because of relaxed rules

TORONTO BLUE JAYS—1980

Front row—Howell, Iorg, Bailor, Warner, coach; Menke, coach; Mattick, manager; Doerr, coach; Williams, coach; Felske, bullpen coach; Stieb, Garcia. Second row—Silverman, equipment manager; Smyth, assistant trainer; Kucek, Mirabella, Hodgson, Davis, Todd, Schrom, McLaughlin, Leal, Griffin, Bosetti, Carson, trainer and team travel director. Top row—Braun, Whitt, Moseby, Clancy, Jefferson, Mayberry, Barlow, Ault, Cannon, Bonnell, Woods, Garvin, Willis. Not pictured—Ainge, Velez.

concerning dress and hair, and then the Jays discovered how much fun it was twisting tails . . . for a while.

Under 63-year-old rookie manager Bobby Mattick, the 1980 Jays played .500 baseball through June 18, then tumbled to a 67-95 record, the worst in the American League East but the best in the Jays' four-year history. It was the first time they had lost fewer than 102 games.

The Jays' finest hour came early, a May 4 doubleheader sweep of the Cleveland Indians in which Otto Velez hit four home runs and drove in 10 runs. Toronto fans, noted for their reserve, discovered standing ovations for one of their own. It was the first time a member of the Blue Jays hit three homers in a game.

But Disaster was just up ahead. Bob Bailor, a man of many positions, suffered a broken left wrist in an exhibition with the Jays' farm team at Syracuse and outfielder Rick Bosetti was sidelined after June 22 by a broken left forearm.

In August, two more outfielders were struck. Barry Bonnell was beaned in Milwaukee and missed three weeks with a fractured left cheekbone. Al Woods, who had his best season, missed almost a month with a torn right calf muscle.

The final blow was the loss of designated hitter Velez for the final 36 games as the result of his suffering a fractured cheekbone in a car accident.

The injury to Velez helped send the Jays into their worst tailspin of the season, one that reached eight games before the Jays swept the final three games of the season from Boston, winning a season series in Fenway for the first time.

While offense still was a problem, the Jays did set a club record with 126 home runs. First baseman John Mayberry hit 30 of those, also a club record, as were his 82 RBIs. Mayberry hit in 17 consecutive games, which would have been another Toronto record had not shortstop Alfredo Griffin batted safely in 19 straight.

The midfield combination of Griffin and rookie second baseman Damaso Garcia fielded brilliantly and was instrumental in the Jays' turning a club-record 206 double plays. Griffin's average slipped 33 points from its 1979 level to .254, but his 15 triples tied for the league lead. Griffin stole 18 bases but was thrown out 23 times, and he scored only 63 runs, a disappointing total for a leadoff man.

Garcia had a fine .278 average and might improve that with more discipline at the plate—he walked only 12 times.

Woods batted an even .300 and cracked 15 home runs, a personal high. "You are too big and strong to be a singles hitter," Mattick told him in spring training. "We want you to be more aggressive."

Despite his beaning, Bonnell wound up with 13 homers and 56 RBIs, and Velez had 20 homers. Bailor played seven positions, including three mound appearances, but his .236 average was far below the promise of his .310 rookie season of 1977.

Third baseman Roy Howell, in his final season with the Jays before exercising his free agent rights, batted .269 and drove in 57 runs. His 10 game-winning RBIs topped the club.

In Dave Stieb and Jim Clancy, the Jays had two of the finest young pitchers in the league. Stieb, a converted outfielder, was the A.L. Pitcher of the Month in April with a 3-0 start, and he finished 12-15, winning only two of his last 11 decisions. But he tossed four of the Jays' nine shutouts, made the All-Star team, and had a respectable 3.70 ERA.

Clancy, who worked only 64 innings in '79 because of injuries, equaled the team record for wins with a 13-16 slate, and his 3.30 ERA was the best in Jays history.

Early in August after a miserable series in Cleveland, four losses in which Jays pitching gave up 28 walks and 31 runs, the pitching staff was shaken up. Reliever Tom Buskey was released, and lefthanders Balor Moore and Paul Mirabella, the latter winless in almost three months, were sent to the minors.

"We don't do things like other teams," explained Peter Bavasi, the club's president. "We are not going to fire the manager and pat some heads."

Instead, the Jays announced the following day that Mattick and his coaches had been rehired for '81.

Among the pitchers the Jays recalled were Mike Willis, who won two games and saved three with a 1.73 ERA, and Jackson Todd, 5-2.

The Jays finished with 23 saves, 13th in the league but more than twice their '79 total. Jerry Garvin (4-7) led the way with eight and Mike Barlow (3-1) had five.

Joey McLaughlin (6-9) was moved from the bullpen into the starting rotation late in the year and the Jays intended to keep him there.

The Jays' attendance of 1,400,327 was down some 30,000 from the previous season.

SCORES OF TORONTO BLUE JAYS' 1980 GAMES

APRIL			Winner	Loser	MAY			Winner	Loser
9—At Sea.	L	6-8	Parrott	Lemanczyk	23—N. York	L	3-7	Guidry	Mirabella
11—At Sea.	W	10-7†	Moore	Dressler	24—N. York	L	2-6	Tiant	Clancy
12—At Sea.	L	2-3†	Honeycutt	Garvin	25—N. York	W	9-6	Leal	John
13—At Sea.	L	1-5	Bannister	Lemanczyk	26—At Bos.	W	3-1	Garvin	Drago
16—Milw.	W	11-2	Stieb	Slaton	27—At Bos.	L	4-5	Renko	Buskey
17—Milw.	W	1-0	Mirabella	Sorensen	28—At Bos.	W	4-1	Stieb	Stanley
19—At Cleve.	L	1-8	Waits	Clancy	30—At N.Y.	L	0-6	Tiant	Clancy
20—At Cleve.	W	5-3	Lemanczyk	Denny	31—At N.Y.	L	6-8†	May	McLaughlin
21—At K.C.	W	7-1	Stieb	Gale				Won 13, Lost 14	
22—At K.C.	L	2-7	Splittorff	Mirabella	JUNE				
23—At K.C.	L	4-7	Christenson	McLaughlin	1—At N.Y.	L	7-11	Underwood	Mirabella
25—At Milw.	W	5-3	McLaughlin	Sorensen	2—Calif.	L	3-6	Frost	Leal
26—At Milw.	W	4-0	Stieb	Caldwell	3—Calif.	W	7-6†	McLaughlin	LaRoche
27—At Milw.	W	8-2	Mirabella	Haas	4—Calif.	W	8-2	Clancy	Martinez
29—Kan. C.	W	3-1	Clancy	Leonard	6—At Minn.	L	0-5	Zahn	Mirabella
30—Kan. C.	L	0-3	Gura	Jefferson	7—At Minn.	L	2-3	Jackson	Stieb
			Won 9, Lost 7		8—At Minn.	L	1-5	Erickson	Jefferson
					8—At Minn.	W	6-4x	McLaughlin	Arroyo
MAY					10—At Chi.	W	1-0	Clancy	Baumgarten
1—Cleve.	L	1-2	Denny	Lemanczyk	11—At Chi.	L	4-7	Kravec	Mirabella
2—Cleve.	L	1-6	Barker	Stieb	13—Texas	L	3-6	Medich	Stieb
3—Cleve.	W	8-3	Buskey	Waits	14—Texas	W	7-6	Buskey	Babcock
4—Cleve.	W	9-8†	Buskey	Monge	15—Texas	W	5-3	Clancy	Jenkins
5—Cleve.	W	7-2	Jefferson	Owchinko	16—Minn.	L	0-4	Zahn	Jefferson
6—At Calif.	W	3-2	Lemanczyk	Aase	17—Minn.	L	6-8	Corbett	Mirabella
7—At Calif.	W	7-3	Stieb	Knapp	18—Chicago	W	5-4	Stieb	Trout
8—At Calif.	W	9-2	Mirabella	Frost	18—Chicago	W	3-1	Kucek	Dotson
10—At Oak.	L	3-4	Langford	Garvin	20—At Texas	L	2-5	Jenkins	Garvin
11—At Oak.	L	1-12	Norris	Lemanczyk	21—At Texas	L	1-2	Matlack	McLaughlin
14—Seattle	L	0-7	Abbott	Mirabella	22—At Texas	W	6-5†	Garvin	Kern
15—Seattle	W	1-0	Clancy	Bannister	24—At Balt.	L	0-1	McGregor	Stieb
16—Oakland	W	1-0†	Jefferson	Norris	25—At Balt.	L	3-6	Palmer	Leal
17—Oakland	L	2-4y	Keough	McLaughlin	26—At Balt.	L	1-4	Stone	Clancy
18—Oakland	W	12-1	Mirabella	Langford	27—Detroit	L	2-7	Morris	Jefferson
19—Boston	W	7-2	Clancy	Billingham	28—Detroit	L	3-8	Rozema	Kucek
20—Boston	L	3-4	Rainey	Lemanczyk	29—Detroit	W	2-0	Stieb	Petry
21—Boston	L	2-11	Torrez	Jefferson	30—Balt.	L	7-9	Stone	Leal
22—N. York	L	1-5	Griffin	Stieb				Won 10, Lost 17	

JULY			Winner	Loser
1—Balt.	L	0-2	Palmer	Clancy
2—Balt.	L	2-6	Flanagan	Mirabella
3—At Det.	L	5-8	Underwood	McLaughlin
4—At Det.	L	3-4	Petry	Stieb
5—At Det.	W	5-3	Clancy	Wilcox
6—At Det.	L	5-7	Morris	Garvin
10—Cleve.	L	3-7	Denny	Clancy
11—Cleve.	W	6-3	Stieb	Garland
12—Milw.	L	2-9	Travers	Moore
13—Milw.	W	4-1	Kucek	Haas
13—Milw.	L	0-4	Mitchell	McLaughlin
14—Milw.	L	4-6	Augustine	Clancy
16—At Sea.	W	5-0	Stieb	Abbott
17—At Sea.	L	3-5	Rawley	Jefferson
18—At Calif.	L	3-6	Halicki	Kucek
19—At Calif.	W	5-4	Clancy	Montague
20—At Calif.	W	6-3†	McLaughlin	Clear
21—At Oak.	L	1-0	Stieb	Kingman
22—At Oak.	W	6-2	Jefferson	Keough
22—At Oak.	L	1-5	Norris	Mirabella
23—At Oak.	L	2-6	McCatty	Kucek
25—Seattle	W	5-3	Clancy	Honeycutt
26—Seattle	L	2-7	Dressler	Stieb
26—Seattle	W	7-5	Kucek	Abbott
27—Seattle	W	5-0	Jefferson	Bannister
28—Oakland	L	3-5*	Norris	Barlow
29—Oakland	L	5-6§	Lacey	Garvin
30—Oakland	L	1-11	Langford	Stieb
		Won 11, Lost 17		

AUGUST			Winner	Loser
1—Calif.	W	9-8	Garvin	Clear
2—Calif.	L	4-5	LaRoche	Jefferson
3—Calif.	W	3-1	Clancy	Martinez
4—At Cleve.	L	5-11	Spillner	Mirabella
5—At Cleve.	L	5-8	Grimsley	Kucek
6—At Cleve.	L	2-5	Waits	Jefferson
7—At Cleve.	L	6-7	Monge	Garvin
8—Kan. C.	L	0-9	Gale	Clancy
8—Kan. C.	L	4-7	Pattin	Garvin
9—Kan. C.	W	4-3y	Willis	Eastwick
10—Kan. C.	L	5-8	Leonard	Jefferson
12—At Milw.	W	3-1	Clancy	Sorensen
12—At Milw.	W	5-4	Barlow	Castro
13—At Milw.	L	4-5	Travers	McLaughlin
14—At Milw.	L	2-4	Haas	Stieb
15—At K.C.	L	3-4	Leonard	Jefferson
16—At K.C.	L	5-11	Gura	Kucek
17—At K.C.	L	3-8	Splittorff	Clancy
19—At Minn.	W	4-3	Barlow	Corbett
20—At Minn.	W	10-4	Todd	Zahn
21—At Chi.	L	3-5	Hoyt	Jefferson

AUGUST			Winner	Loser
22—At Chi.	L	0-2	Burns	Clancy
23—At Chi.	L	1-5	Dotson	Kucek
24—At Chi.	W	7-3	Stieb	Baumgarten
25—Texas	L	1-5	Clay	Todd
26—Texas	L	0-8	Hough	Jefferson
27—Texas	W	6-4	Clancy	Medich
28—Minn.	L	5-7a	Verhoeven	Jefferson
29—Minn.	L	2-5	Zahn	Stieb
30—Minn.	W	3-2	Todd	Verhoeven
31—Minn.	W	7-1	Clancy	Koosman
		Won 11, Lost 20		

SEPTEMBER			Winner	Loser
1—At Texas	L	1-9	Medich	McLaughlin
2—At Texas	L	2-3	Jenkins	Leal
3—At Texas	W	4-2	Stieb	Figueroa
4—Chicago	W	3-2	Todd	Farmer
5—Chicago	L	0-3	Hoyt	Clancy
7—Chicago	W	3-1	McLaughlin	Trout
7—Chicago	W	7-6	Schrom	Proly
8—N. York	L	4-7	John	Stieb
9—N. York	W	6-4	Todd	Perry
10—N. York	L	6-7	Davis	Clancy
11—Balt.	L	1-6	Stone	Mirabella
12—Balt.	W	7-5	McLaughlin	Flanagan
13—Balt.	L	4-6	McGregor	Stieb
14—Balt.	L	4-3x	Barlow	D. Martinez
16—At N.Y.	L	4-5	Guidry	Clancy
17—At N.Y.	L	7-8b	Underwood	Kucek
18—At N.Y.	W	2-1	Leal	John
19—At Balt.	L	6-8§	T. Martinez	Willis
20—At Balt.	L	1-6	Stone	Stieb
21—At Balt.	L	1-2	Flanagan	Clancy
22—At Det.	W	6-5	Garvin	Weaver
23—At Det.	W	9-7	Willis	Rozema
24—At Det.	L	8-9†	Petry	Kucek
26—Boston	L	1-3	Eckersley	Stieb
27—Boston	L	3-4	Stanley	Clancy
28—Boston	L	3-7	Crawford	McLaughlin
29—Detroit	L	2-8	Weaver	Mirabella
30—Detroit	L	3-5	Schatzeder	Todd
		Won 10, Lost 18		

OCTOBER			Winner	Loser
1—Detroit	L	7-11	Fidrych	Stieb
2—At Bos.	L	1-4	Tudor	Clancy
4—At Bos.	W	7-6z	Leal	Stanley
4—At Bos.	W	3-1	Mirabella	Drago
5—At Bos.	W	4-1	Todd	MacWhorter
		Won 3, Lost 2		

*7½ innings. †10 innings. ‡11 innings. §12 innings. x13 innings. y14 innings. z17 innings. a15-inning suspended game, completed August 29. b13-inning suspended game, completed September 18.

Henderson Set Torrid Base-Stealing Pace

Oakland A's outfielder Rickey Henderson stole 100 bases in 1980 to become only the third player—behind Lou Brock's 118 steals and Maury Wills' 104—to achieve the century mark in steals.

The basepaths were burning everywhere in 1980. Montreal's Ron LeFlore, inserted as a pinch-runner in the final game of the season, had two steals to help him pass Pittsburgh's Omar Moreno 97-96. LeFlore and Rodney Scott of the Expos set a record by two teammates by combining for 160 steals.

Meanwhile, Gene Richards (61), Ozzie Smith (57) and Jerry Mumphrey (52) gave the San Diego Padres three players with more than 50 steals.

GEORGE BRETT
● ROYALS ●
BATTING CHAMPION (.390)
SLUGGING PCT. (.664)

CECIL COOPER
● BREWERS ●
TOTAL BASES (335)
RUNS BATTED IN (122)

WILLIE WILSON
● ROYALS ●
RUNS (133)
HITS (230)

1980 AMERICAN LEAGUE LEADERS

RUDY MAY
● YANKEES ●
EARNED-RUN AVERAGE (2.46)

RICK LANGFORD
● A's ●
COMPLETE GAMES (28)
INNINGS (290)

STEVE STONE
● ORIOLES ●
WINS (25)
WINNING PCT. (.781)

American League Averages for 1980

CHAMPIONSHIP WINNERS IN PREVIOUS YEARS

1900—Chicago° .... .607	1927—New York .... .714	1954—Cleveland.................. .721
1901—Chicago .... .610	1928—New York .... .656	1955—New York .... .623
1902—Philadelphia .... .610	1929—Philadelphia .... .693	1956—New York .... .630
1903—Boston .... .659	1930—Philadelphia .... .662	1957—New York .... .636
1904—Boston .... .617	1931—Philadelphia .... .704	1958—New York .... .597
1905—Philadelphia .... .622	1932—New York .... .695	1959—Chicago .... .610
1906—Chicago .... .616	1933—Washington .... .651	1960—New York .... .630
1907—Detroit .... .613	1934—Detroit .... .656	1961—New York .... .673
1908—Detroit .... .588	1935—Detroit .... .616	1962—New York .... .593
1909—Detroit .... .645	1936—New York .... .667	1963—New York .... .646
1910—Philadelphia .... .680	1937—New York .... .662	1964—New York .... .611
1911—Philadelphia .... .669	1938—New York .... .651	1965—Minnesota .... .630
1912—Boston .... .691	1939—New York .... .702	1966—Baltimore .... .606
1913—Philadelphia .... .627	1940—Detroit .... .584	1967—Boston .... .568
1914—Philadelphia .... .651	1941—New York .... .656	1968—Detroit .... .636
1915—Boston .... .669	1942—New York .... .669	1969—Baltimore (East)‡ .... .673
1916—Boston .... .591	1943—New York .... .636	1970—Baltimore (East)‡ .... .667
1917—Chicago .... .649	1944—St. Louis .... .578	1971—Baltimore (East)§ .... .639
1918—Boston .... .595	1945—Detroit .... .575	1972—Oakland (West)a ...... .600
1919—Chicago .... .629	1946—Boston .... .675	1973—Oakland (West)b ...... .580
1920—Cleveland .... .636	1947—New York .... .630	1974—Oakland (West)b ...... .556
1921—New York .... .641	1948—Cleveland† .... .626	1975—Boston (East)c .... .594
1922—New York .... .610	1949—New York .... .630	1976—New York (East)d ..... .610
1923—New York .... .645	1950—New York .... .636	1977—New York (East)d ..... .617
1924—Washington .... .597	1951—New York .... .636	1978—New York (East)d ..... .613
1925—Washington .... .636	1952—New York .... .617	1979—Baltimore (East)e ..... .642
1926—New York .... .591	1953—New York .... .656	

°Not recognized as major league in 1900. †Defeated Boston in one-game playoff for pennant. ‡Defeated Minnesota (West) in Championship Series. §Defeated Oakland (West) in Championship Series. aDefeated Detroit (East) in Championship Series. bDefeated Baltimore (East) in Championship Series. cDefeated Oakland (West) in Championship Series. dDefeated Kansas City (West) in Championship Series. eDefeated California (West) in Championship Series.

STANDING OF CLUBS AT CLOSE OF SEASON

EAST DIVISION

Club	N.Y.	Balt.	Mil.	Bos.	Det.	Clev.	Tor.	Cal.	Chi.	K.C.	Min.	Oak.	Sea.	Tex.	W.	L.	Pct.	G.B.
New York....	..	6	8	10	8	8	10	10	7	4	8	8	9	7	103	59	.636	....
Baltimore...	7	..	7	8	10	6	11	10	6	6	10	7	6	6	100	62	.617	3
Milwaukee...	5	6	..	7	6	10	5	6	7	6	7	7	9	5	86	76	.531	17
Boston	3	5	6	..	8	7	7	9	6	5	6	9	7	5	83	77	.519	19
Detroit	5	3	7	5	..	10	9	7	10	2	6	6	10	4	84	78	.519	19
Cleveland	5	7	3	6	3	..	8	6	7	5	9	6	8	6	79	81	.494	23
Toronto.......	3	2	8	6	4	5	..	9	7	3	5	4	6	5	67	95	.414	36

WEST DIVISION

Club	K.C.	Oak.	Min.	Tex.	Chi.	Cal.	Sea.	Balt.	Bos.	Clev.	Det.	Mil.	N.Y.	Tor.	W.	L.	Pct.	G.B.
Kansas City..	..	6	5	10	8	8	7	6	7	7	10	6	8	9	97	65	.599	....
Oakland	7	..	7	7	7	10	8	5	3	6	6	5	4	8	83	79	.512	14
Minnesota ...	8	6	..	9	8	6	7	2	6	3	6	5	4	7	77	84	.478	19½
Texas.........	3	6	3	..	7	2	9	6	7	6	8	7	5	7	76	85	.472	20½
Chicago.......	5	6	5	6	..	10	6	6	4	5	2	5	5	5	70	90	.438	26
California	5	3	7	11	3	..	11	2	3	4	5	6	2	3	65	95	.406	31
Seattle........	6	5	6	4	7	2	..	6	5	4	2	3	3	6	59	103	.364	38

Tie Games—Seattle at Detroit and Texas at Chicago (2).
Cancelled Games—Boston at Chicago (2), California at Cleveland (2) and Minnesota at Texas.
- Championship Series—Kansas City defeated New York, three games to none.

RECORD AT HOME

EAST DIVISION

Club	N.Y.	Balt.	Clev.	Det.	Mil.	Bos.	Tor.	K.C.	Oak.	Minn.	Tex.	Chi.	Sea.	Cal.	W.	L.	Pct.
New York		3-3	5-2	5-2	3-4	3-3	5-1	2-4	5-1	4-2	4-2	3-3	5-1	6-0	53	28	.654
Baltimore	4-3	.....	3-3	5-2	3-3	3-4	6-0	4-2	3-3	5-1	2-4	4-2	4-2	4-2	50	31	.617
Cleveland	3-3	4-3	.....	2-5	1-5	3-4	5-1	2-4	4-2	5-1	5-1	3-3	4-2	3-1	44	35	.557
Detroit	3-3	1-5	5-1	.....	4-3	4-3	4-3	1-5	4-2	3-3	1-5	5-1	6-0	2-4	43	38	.531
Milwaukee	1-5	3-4	5-2	3-3	.....	4-2	2-5	1-5	3-3	5-2	3-3	3-3	5-1	2-4	40	42	.488
Boston	0-7	1-5	3-3	5-1	4-3	.....	2-5	2-4	5-1	3-3	2-4	3-3	3-3	3-3	36	45	.444
Toronto	2-5	2-5	4-3	1-5	3-3	1-5	.....	2-4	2-4	2-4	3-3	5-1	4-2	4-2	35	46	.432

WEST DIVISION

Club	K.C.	Oak.	Minn.	Tex.	Chi.	Sea.	Cal.	N.Y.	Balt.	Clev.	Det.	Mil.	Bos.	Tor.	W.	L.	Pct.
Kan. City	.....	4-3	3-3	3-3	5-2	5-2	4-2	4-2	4-2	3-3	5-1	1-5	3-3	5-1	49	32	.605
Oakland	4-2	.....	5-2	3-3	4-3	6-1	3-3	2-4	4-2	4-2	2-4	2-4	4-2	4-6	46	35	.568
Minnesota	5-2	4-2	.....	6-1	5-2	3-3	4-2	2-4	1-5	2-4	3-2	3-3	3-3	4-2	44	36	.550
Texas	0-7	3-4	2-3	.....	4-2	5-1	1-6	3-3	2-4	5-1	3-3	4-2	3-3	4-2	39	41	.488
Chicago	3-3	3-4	3-3	4-3	.....	4-2	4-3	2-4	4-2	2-4	1-5	2-4	1-3	6-1	37	42	.468
Seattle	4-2	2-4	3-4	3-4	5-2	.....	1-5	2-4	4-2	2-4	2-4	2-4	4-2	4-2	36	45	.444
California	3-4	2-4	5-2	5-1	0-6	6-1	.....	2-4	0-6	3-3	1-5	2-4	0-6	1-5	30	51	.370

RECORD ABROAD

EAST DIVISION

Club	Balt.	N.Y.	Bos.	Mil.	Det.	Clev.	Tor.	K.C.	Oak.	Tex.	Cal.	Chi.	Minn.	Sea.	W.	L.	Pct.
Baltimore	.....	3-3	5-1	4-3	5-1	3-4	5-2	2-4	4-2	4-2	6-0	2-4	5-1	2-4	50	31	.617
New York	3-4	.....	7-0	5-1	3-3	3-3	5-2	2-4	3-3	3-3	4-2	4-2	4-2	4-2	50	31	.617
Boston	4-3	3-3	.....	2-4	3-4	4-3	5-1	3-3	2-4	2-3	6-0	3-1	3-3	4-2	47	32	.595
Milwaukee	3-3	4-3	3-4	.....	3-4	5-1	3-3	5-1	4-2	2-4	4-2	2-3	4-2	4-2	46	34	.575
Detroit	2-5	2-5	1-5	3-3	.....	5-2	5-1	1-5	2-4	3-3	5-1	5-1	3-4	4-2	41	40	.506
Cleveland	3-3	2-5	3-3	2-5	1-5	.....	3-4	3-3	2-4	1-5	3-3	4-2	4-2	4-2	35	46	.432
Toronto	0-6	1-5	5-2	5-2	3-4	1-5	.....	1-5	2-4	2-4	5-1	2-4	3-3	2-4	32	49	.395

WEST DIVISION

Club	K.C.	Oak.	Tex.	Cal.	Chi.	Minn.	Sea.	Balt.	N.Y.	Bos.	Mil.	Det.	Clev.	Tor.	W.	L.	Pct.
Kan. City	.....	2-4	7-0	4-3	3-3	2-5	2-4	2-4	4-2	4-2	5-1	5-1	4-2	4-2	48	33	.593
Oakland	3-4	.....	4-3	4-2	4-3	2-4	4-2	3-3	1-5	1-5	3-3	2-4	2-4	4-2	37	44	.457
Texas	3-3	3-3	.....	1-5	3-4	1-6	4-3	4-2	2-4	4-2	3-3	5-1	1-5	3-3	37	44	.457
California	2-4	1-6	6-1	.....	3-4	2-4	5-1	2-4	0-6	3-3	4-2	4-2	1-3	2-4	35	44	.443
Chicago	2-5	3-3	2-4	6-0	.....	2-5	2-5	2-4	3-3	3-3	3-3	1-5	3-3	1-5	33	48	.407
Minnesota	3-3	2-5	3-2	2-5	3-3	.....	4-3	1-5	2-4	3-3	2-5	3-3	1-5	4-2	33	48	.407
Seattle	2-5	3-4	1-5	1-6	2-4	3-3	.....	2-4	1-5	3-3	1-5	0-6	2-4	2-4	23	58	.284

SHUTOUT GAMES

Club	K.C.	Balt.	N.Y.	Bos.	Clev.	Mil.	Chi.	Det.	Tex.	Min.	Tor.	Oak.	Cal.	Sea.	W.	L.	Pct.
Kan. City	..	1	1	0	1	0	0	1	1	1	2	1	1	0	10	5	.667
Baltimore	1	..	1	0	1	1	0	1	0	0	2	1	1	1	10	6	.625
New York	0	0	..	2	0	2	3	1	1	1	1	1	1	2	15	11	.577
Boston	1	1	0	..	0	1	0	0	1	1	0	0	1	2	8	6	.571
Cleveland	0	1	3	0	..	1	1	1	0	0	0	0	0	1	8	6	.571
Milwaukee	0	2	1	0	1	..	1	0	0	3	1	1	1	3	14	11	.560
Chicago	1	0	1	1	0	0	..	0	0	2	2	3	1	1	12	11	.522
Detroit	0	0	0	0	0	1	1	..	2	1	0	2	1	1	9	9	.500
Texas	0	0	1	1	1	0	0	0	..	1	1	1	0	0	6	7	.462
Minnesota	1	0	1	2	0	0	0	1	1	..	2	1	0	0	9	12	.429
Toronto	0	0	0	0	0	2	1	1	0	0	..	2	0	3	9	12	.429
Oakland	1	0	0	0	1	1	2	2	0	1	0	..	1	0	9	13	.409
California	0	1	0	0	0	2	0	1	1	1	0	0	..	0	6	9	.400
Seattle	0	0	2	0	1	0	2	0	0	0	1	0	1	..	7	14	.333

OFFICIAL AMERICAN LEAGUE BATTING AVERAGES

Compiled by Sports Information Center, No. Quincy, Mass.

CLUB BATTING

Club	Pct.	G.	AB.	R.	OR.	H.	TB.	2B.	3B.	HR.	RBI.	SH.	SF.	SB.	CS.	LOB.
Kan. C.	.286	162	5714	809	694	1633	2362	266	59	115	766	34	63	185	43	1209
Texas	.284	163	5690	756	752	1616	2305	263	27	124	720	70	56	91	49	1186
Boston	.283	160	5603	757	767	1588	2443	297	36	162	717	40	50	79	48	1135
Clev.	.277	160	5470	738	807	1517	2085	221	40	89	692	60	74	118	58	1231
Milw.	.275	162	5653	811	682	1555	2534	298	36	203	774	58	51	131	56	1100
Detroit	.273	163	5648	830	757	1543	2310	232	53	143	767	63	55	75	68	1219
Balt.	.273	162	5585	805	640	1523	2307	258	29	156	751	42	46	111	38	1153
N. York	.267	162	5553	820	662	1484	2358	239	34	189	772	51	54	86	36	1178
Minn.	.265	161	5530	670	724	1468	2109	252	46	99	634	92	51	62	46	1098
Calif.	.265	160	5443	698	797	1442	2060	236	32	106	655	71	49	91	63	1113
Oakland	.259	162	5495	686	642	1424	2117	212	35	137	635	99	41	175	82	1076
Chicago	.259	162	5444	587	722	1408	2012	255	38	91	547	67	51	68	54	1078
Tor.	.251	162	5571	624	762	1398	2131	249	53	126	580	63	34	67	72	1083
Seattle	.248	163	5489	610	793	1359	1952	211	35	104	564	106	44	116	62	1095
Totals	.269	1132	77888	10201	10201	20958	31085	3489	553	1844	9574	916	719	1455	775	15954

INDIVIDUAL BATTING

(Top Fifteen Qualifiers for Batting Championship—502 or More Plate Appearances)

°Bats lefthanded. †Switch-hitter.

Player and Club	Pct.	G.	AB.	R.	H.	TB.	2B.	3B.	HR.	RBI.	GW.	SH.	SF.	SB.	CS.
Brett, George, K.C.°	.390	117	449	87	175	298	33	9	24	118	14	0	7	15	6
Cooper, Cecil, Milw.°	.352	153	622	96	219	335	33	4	25	122	11	7	8	17	6
Dilone, Miguel, Clev.†	.341	132	528	82	180	228	30	9	0	40	5	6	2	61	18
Rivers, John, Tex.°	.333	147	630	96	210	275	32	6	7	60	5	6	4	18	7
Carew, Rodney, Calif.°	.331	144	540	74	179	236	34	7	3	59	8	9	3	23	15
Bell, David, Tex.	.329	129	490	76	161	244	24	4	17	83	10	4	0	3	1
Wilson, Willie, K.C.†	.326	161	705	133	230	297	28	15	3	49	4	5	1	79	10
Oliver, Albert, Tex.°	.319	163	656	96	209	315	43	3	19	117	16	1	8	5	7
Bumbry, Alonza, Balt.°	.318	160	645	118	205	279	29	9	9	53	5	9	3	44	11
Watson, Robert, N.Y.	.307	130	469	62	144	214	25	3	13	68	11	1	6	2	1
Wathan, John, K.C.	.305	126	453	57	138	184	14	7	6	58	5	3	1	17	3
Molitor, Paul, Milw.	.304	111	450	81	137	197	29	2	9	37	2	6	5	34	7
Oglivie, Benjamin, Milw.°	.304	156	592	94	180	333	26	2	41	118	12	0	9	11	9
Hargrove, D. Michael, Clev.°	.304	160	589	86	179	238	22	2	11	85	12	2	10	4	2
Singleton, Kenneth, Balt.†	.304	156	583	85	177	283	28	3	24	104	19	0	4	0	2

DEPARTMENTAL LEADERS: G—Oliver, 163; AB—Wilson, 705; R—Wilson, 133; H—Wilson, 230; TB—Cooper, 335; 2B—Yount, 49; 3B—Wilson, Griffin, 15; HR—Oglivie, Re. Jackson, 41; RBI—Cooper, 122; GW—Singleton, 19; SH—Murphy, 22; SF—Lansford, 11; SB—Henderson, 100; CS—Henderson, 26.

(All Players—Listed Alphabetically)

Player and Club	Pct.	G.	AB.	R.	H.	TB.	2B.	3B.	HR.	RBI.	GW.	SH.	SF.	SB.	CS.
Adams, Glenn, Minn.°	.286	99	262	32	75	108	11	2	6	38	5	6	4	2	4
Aikens, Willie, K.C.°	.278	151	543	70	151	235	24	0	20	98	13	0	9	1	0
Ainge, Daniel, Tor.	.243	38	111	11	27	35	6	1	0	4	0	1	0	3	0
Alexander, Gary, Clev.	.225	76	178	22	40	64	7	1	5	31	2	0	3	0	4
Allen, Kim, Sea.	.235	23	51	9	12	15	3	0	0	3	0	2	0	10	3
Allenson, Gary, Bos.	.357	36	70	9	25	31	6	0	0	10	0	1	1	2	2
Alston, Wendell, Clev.°	.222	52	54	11	12	17	1	2	0	9	0	1	2	2	4
Anderson, James, Sea.	.227	116	317	46	72	103	7	0	8	30	2	6	2	2	4
Armas, Antonio, Oak.	.279	158	628	87	175	314	18	8	35	109	11	2	5	5	3
Ashford, Thomas, Tex.	.125	15	32	2	4	4	0	0	0	3	0	0	0	0	0
Ault, Douglas, Tor.	.194	64	144	12	28	44	5	1	3	15	0	0	1	0	1
Ayala, Benigno, Balt.	.265	76	170	28	45	85	8	1	10	33	3	0	2	0	0
Bailor, Robert, Tor.	.236	117	347	44	82	103	14	2	1	16	3	2	1	12	8
Baines, Harold, Chi.°	.255	141	491	55	125	199	23	6	13	49	3	2	5	2	4
Bando, Salvatore, Milw.	.197	78	254	28	50	79	12	1	5	31	5	3	4	5	3
Bannister, Alan, Chi.-Clev.°	.283	126	392	57	111	145	23	4	1	41	4	6	5	14	4
Barranca, German, K.C.°	.000	7	0	3	0	0	0	0	0	0	0	0	0	0	0
Baylor, Donald, Calif.	.250	90	340	39	85	116	12	2	5	51	4	0	5	6	6
Belanger, Mark, Balt.	.228	113	268	37	61	74	7	3	0	22	1	11	0	6	3

Player and Club	Pct.	G.	AB.	R.	H.	TB.	2B.	3B.	HR.	RBI.	GW.	SH.	SF.	SB.	CS.
Bell, David, Tex.	.329	129	490	76	161	244	24	4	17	83	10	4	0	3	1
Bell, Kevin, Chi.	.178	92	191	16	34	46	5	2	1	11	1	2	2	0	0
Beniquez, Juan, Sea.	.228	70	237	26	54	82	10	0	6	21	2	3	1	2	3
Blair, Paul, N.Y.	.000	12	2	0	0	0	0	0	0	0	0	0	0	0	0
Bochte, Bruce, Sea.°	.300	148	520	62	156	237	34	4	13	78	10	4	7	2	3
Bonnell, R. Barry, Tor.	.268	130	463	55	124	193	22	4	13	56	9	3	4	3	4
Bonner, Robert, Balt.	.000	4	4	1	0	0	0	0	0	1	0	0	0	0	0
Borgmann, Glenn, Chi.	.218	32	87	10	19	27	2	0	2	14	2	0	2	0	0
Bosetti, Richard, Tor.	.213	53	188	24	40	61	7	1	4	18	2	1	1	4	6
Bosley, Thaddis, Chi.°	.224	70	147	12	33	41	2	0	2	14	2	4	1	3	2
Bowen, Samuel, Bos.	.154	7	13	0	2	2	0	0	0	0	0	0	0	1	0
Brant, Marshall, N.Y.	.000	3	6	0	0	0	0	0	0	0	0	0	0	0	0
Braun, Stephen, K.C.-Tor.°	.205	51	78	4	16	21	2	0	1	10	3	0	0	0	0
Brett, George, K.C.°	.390	117	449	87	175	298	33	9	24	118	14	0	7	15	6
Brohamer, John, Bos.-Clev.°	.251	74	199	18	50	65	7	1	2	21	2	4	2	0	1
Brookens, Thomas, Det.	.275	151	509	64	140	213	25	9	10	66	9	2	7	13	11
Brouhard, Mark, Milw.	.232	45	125	17	29	50	6	0	5	16	3	0	0	1	0
Brown, Rogers, N.Y.†	.260	137	412	65	107	171	12	5	14	47	5	2	3	27	8
Bumbry, Alonza, Balt.°	.318	160	645	118	205	279	29	9	9	53	5	9	3	44	11
Burleson, Richard, Bos.	.278	155	644	89	179	236	29	2	8	51	6	6	4	12	13
Butera, Salvatore, Minn.	.271	34	85	4	23	24	1	0	0	2	0	1	1	0	0
Campaneris, Dagoberto, Cal.	.252	77	210	32	53	69	8	1	2	18	2	7	2	10	5
Cannon, Joseph, Tor.°	.080	70	50	16	4	4	0	0	0	4	0	0	0	2	2
Cardenal, Jose, K.C.	.340	25	53	8	18	20	2	0	0	5	1	0	3	0	0
Carew, Rodney, Calif.°	.331	144	540	74	179	236	34	7	3	59	8	9	3	23	15
Castillo, E. Manuel, K.C.†	.200	7	10	1	2	2	0	0	0	0	0	0	0	0	0
Castino, John, Minn.	.302	150	546	67	165	235	17	7	13	64	3	21	3	7	5
Cerone, Richard, N.Y.	.277	147	519	70	144	224	30	4	14	85	10	8	10	1	3
Chalk, David, K.C.	.251	69	167	19	42	57	10	1	1	20	1	0	3	1	1
Chappas, Harry, Chi.†	.160	26	50	6	8	10	2	0	0	2	1	1	0	0	2
Charboneau, Joseph, Clev.	.289	131	453	76	131	221	17	2	23	87	8	1	6	2	4
Clark, Robert, Calif.	.230	78	261	26	60	87	10	1	5	23	4	1	0	0	1
Cliburn, Stanley, Calif.	.179	54	56	7	10	18	2	0	2	6	1	0	1	0	0
Concepcion, Onix, K.C.	.133	12	15	1	2	2	0	0	0	2	0	0	0	0	0
Cooper, Cecil, Milw.°	.352	153	622	96	219	335	33	4	25	122	11	7	8	17	6
Corcoran, Timothy, Det.°	.288	84	153	20	44	62	7	1	3	18	0	0	1	0	2
Corey, Mark, Balt.	.278	36	36	7	10	15	2	0	1	2	0	0	0	0	1
Cosey, D. Ray, Oak.°	.111	9	9	0	1	1	0	0	0	0	0	0	0	0	0
Cowens, Alfred, Calif.-Det.	.268	142	522	69	140	184	20	3	6	59	6	7	4	6	8
Cox, Jeffrey, Oak.	.213	59	169	20	36	39	3	0	0	9	2	11	0	8	5
Cox, Larry, Sea.	.202	105	243	18	49	71	6	2	4	20	2	9	0	1	2
Cox, W. Ted, Sea.	.243	83	247	17	60	75	9	0	2	23	2	1	2	0	0
Craig, Rodney, Sea.†	.238	70	240	30	57	83	15	1	3	20	1	5	0	3	6
Crowley, Terrence, Balt.°	.288	92	233	33	67	111	8	0	12	50	7	2	2	0	0
Cruz, Julio, Sea.†	.209	119	422	66	88	109	9	3	2	16	2	13	2	45	7
Cruz, Todd, Calif.-Chi.	.237	108	333	28	79	104	14	1	3	23	3	6	1	2	1
Cubbage, Michael, Minn.°	.246	103	285	29	70	103	9	0	8	42	8	6	3	0	1
Dauer, Richard, Balt.	.284	152	557	71	158	196	32	0	2	63	6	6	6	3	2
Davis, Michael, Oak.°	.211	51	95	11	20	27	2	1	1	8	1	4	1	2	1
Davis, Odie, Tex.	.125	17	8	0	1	1	0	0	0	0	0	0	0	0	0
Davis, Richard, Milw.	.271	106	365	50	99	141	26	2	4	30	4	0	2	3	5
Davis, Robert, Tor.	.216	91	218	18	47	70	11	0	4	19	1	9	0	0	0
Davis, Ronald, N.Y.	.000	53	1	0	0	0	0	0	0	0	0	0	0	0	0
DeCinces, Douglas, Balt.	.249	145	489	64	122	197	23	2	16	64	11	4	4	11	6
Dempsey, J. Richard, Balt.	.262	119	362	51	95	154	26	3	9	40	2	4	1	3	1
Dent, Russell, N.Y.	.262	141	489	57	128	173	26	2	5	52	5	9	5	0	3
Detherage, Robert, K.C.	.308	20	26	2	8	13	2	0	1	7	0	0	1	1	1
Diaz, Baudilio, Clev.	.227	76	207	15	47	71	11	2	3	32	4	5	2	1	0
Dilone, Miguel, Clev.†	.341	132	528	82	180	228	30	9	0	40	5	6	2	61	18
Donohue, Thomas, Calif.	.188	84	218	18	41	53	4	1	2	14	1	3	1	5	1
Downing, Brian, Calif.	.290	30	93	5	27	39	6	0	2	25	4	1	2	0	2
Doyle, Brian, N.Y.°	.173	34	75	8	13	17	1	0	1	5	0	0	0	1	1
Drago, Richard, Bos.	.000	43	1	0	0	0	0	0	0	0	0	0	0	0	0
Dwyer, James, Bos.°	.285	93	260	41	74	114	11	4	9	38	7	1	1	3	2
Dybzinski, Jerome, Clev.	.230	114	248	32	57	73	11	1	1	23	4	14	1	4	1
Dyer, Don, Det.	.185	48	108	11	20	33	1	0	4	11	0	5	0	0	0
Edler, David, Sea.	.225	28	89	12	20	30	1	0	3	9	2	2	0	2	3
Edwards, David, Minn.	.250	81	200	26	50	67	9	1	2	20	3	1	1	2	1
Edwards, Michael, Oak.	.237	46	59	10	14	14	0	0	0	3	0	3	0	1	1

Player and Club	Pct.	G.	AB.	R.	H.	TB.	2B.	3B.	HR.	RBI.	GW.	SH.	SF.	SB.	CS.
Elliott, Randy, Oak.	.128	14	39	4	5	8	3	0	0	1	0	0	0	0	0
Ellis, John, Tex.	.236	73	182	12	43	57	9	1	1	23	2	0	3	3	0
Essian, James, Oak.	.232	87	285	19	66	92	11	0	5	29	4	3	3	1	3
Evans, Dwight, Bos.	.266	148	463	72	123	224	37	5	18	60	3	6	4	3	1
Faedo, Leonardo, Minn.	.250	5	8	1	2	3	1	0	0	0	1	0	0	0	0
Fisk, Carlton, Bos.	.289	131	478	73	138	223	25	3	18	62	5	0	3	11	5
Foley, Marvis, Chi.°	.212	68	137	14	29	46	5	0	4	15	3	1	4	0	0
Ford, Darnell, Calif.	.279	65	226	22	63	95	11	0	7	26	0	1	1	0	1
Frias, Jesus, Tex.	.242	116	227	27	55	62	5	1	0	10	1	12	2	5	1
Gamble, Oscar, N.Y.°	.278	78	194	40	54	110	10	2	14	50	2	0	3	2	0
Gantner, James, Milw.°	.282	132	415	47	117	156	21	3	4	40	5	8	3	11	10
Garcia, Alfonso, Balt.	.199	111	311	27	62	73	8	0	1	27	2	3	2	8	4
Garcia, Damaso, Tor.	.278	140	543	50	151	207	30	7	4	46	4	4	3	13	13
Garr, Ralph, Calif.°	.190	21	42	5	8	9	1	0	0	3	0	0	0	0	0
Gedman, Richard, Bos.°	.208	9	24	2	5	5	0	0	0	1	0	0	0	0	0
Gibson, Kirk, Det.°	.263	51	175	23	46	77	2	1	9	16	1	1	2	4	7
Gonzales, Daniel, Det.°	.143	2	7	1	1	1	0	0	0	0	0	0	0	0	0
Gonzalez, Orlando, Oak.°	.243	25	70	10	17	17	0	0	0	1	0	1	0	0	2
Goodwin, Danny, Minn.°	.200	55	115	12	23	31	5	0	1	11	2	1	1	0	0
Graham, Daniel, Balt.°	.278	86	266	32	74	128	7	1	15	54	5	1	4	0	0
Gray, Gary, Clev.	.148	28	54	4	8	15	1	0	2	4	1	0	0	0	0
Grich, Robert, Calif.	.271	150	498	60	135	203	22	2	14	62	5	5	5	3	7
Griffin, Alfredo, Tor.†	.254	155	653	63	166	228	26	15	2	41	2	10	5	18	23
Gross, Wayne, Oak.°	.281	113	366	45	103	171	20	3	14	61	4	2	6	5	3
Grubb, John, Tex.°	.277	110	274	40	76	117	12	1	9	32	6	2	3	2	3
Guerrero, Mario, Oak.	.239	116	381	32	91	117	16	2	2	23	5	7	6	3	3
Gulden, Bradley, N.Y.°	.333	2	3	1	1	4	0	0	1	2	0	0	0	0	0
Hancock, R. Garry, Bos.°	.287	46	115	9	33	51	6	0	4	19	3	0	2	0	3
Hargrove, D. Michael, Clev.°.	.304	160	589	86	179	238	22	2	11	85	12	2	10	4	2
Harlow, Larry, Calif.	.276	109	301	47	83	116	13	4	4	27	3	4	1	3	2
Harrah, Colbert, Clev.	.267	160	561	100	150	213	22	4	11	72	6	2	7	17	2
Harrelson, Derrel, Tex.†	.272	87	180	26	49	58	6	0	1	9	1	10	0	4	4
Harris, John, Calif.°	.293	19	41	8	12	23	5	0	2	7	0	0	1	0	1
Harris, Victor, Milw.†	.213	34	89	8	19	28	4	1	1	7	1	1	1	4	1
Hart, J. Michael, Tex.†	.250	5	4	1	1	1	0	0	0	0	0	0	0	0	0
Hassey, Ronald, Clev.°	.318	130	390	43	124	174	18	4	8	65	7	1	6	0	2
Hazewood, Drungo, Balt.	.000	6	5	1	0	0	0	0	0	0	0	0	0	0	0
Heath, Michael, Oak.	.243	92	305	27	74	91	10	2	1	33	5	7	1	3	3
Hebner, Richard, Det.°	.290	104	341	48	99	159	10	7	12	82	8	2	5	0	3
Henderson, Rickey, Oak.	.303	158	591	111	179	236	22	4	9	53	4	6	3	100	26
Hill, Marc, Sea.	.229	29	70	8	16	26	2	1	2	9	1	1	0	0	0
Hisle, Larry, Milw.	.283	17	60	16	17	35	0	0	6	16	1	0	1	1	1
Hobson, Clell, Bos.	.228	93	324	35	74	113	6	0	11	39	5	0	3	1	1
Hodgson, Paul, Tor.	.220	20	41	5	9	14	0	1	1	5	0	2	0	0	1
Hoffman, Glenn, Bos.	.285	114	312	37	89	124	15	4	4	42	7	9	4	2	4
Holt, Roger, N.Y.†	.167	2	6	0	1	1	0	0	0	1	0	0	0	0	0
Horton, Willie, Sea.	.221	97	335	32	74	110	10	1	8	36	2	2	4	0	4
Howell, Roy, Tor.°	.269	142	528	51	142	218	28	9	10	57	10	4	5	0	0
Hurdle, Clinton, K.C.°	.294	130	395	50	116	181	31	2	10	60	5	2	5	0	0
Iorg, Garth, Tor.	.248	80	222	24	55	73	10	1	2	14	3	3	0	2	1
Jackson, Reginald, N.Y.°	.300	143	514	94	154	307	22	4	41	111	17	0	2	1	2
Jackson, Ronnie, Minn.	.265	131	396	48	105	155	29	3	5	42	4	4	3	1	8
Johnson, Cliff, Clev	.230	54	174	25	40	63	3	1	6	28	5	0	4	0	1
Johnson, Lamar, Chi	.277	147	541	51	150	221	26	3	13	81	10	1	7	2	3
Johnson, Randall, Chi°	.200	12	20	0	4	4	0	0	0	3	1	0	2	0	0
Johnston, Gregory, Minn°	.185	14	27	3	5	8	3	0	0	1	1	1	0	0	0
Jones, Lynn, Det	.255	30	55	9	14	20	2	2	0	6	0	0	1	1	0
Jones, Ruppert, N.Y.°	.223	83	328	38	73	117	11	3	9	42	5	5	3	18	8
Kelly, D. Patrick, Tor.	.286	3	7	0	2	2	0	0	0	0	0	0	0	0	0
Kelly, H. Patrick, Balt.°	.260	89	200	38	52	73	10	1	3	26	4	0	3	16	2
Kemp, Steven, Det°	.293	135	508	88	149	241	23	3	21	101	10	1	9	5	1
Kimm, Bruce, Chi	.243	100	251	20	61	73	10	1	0	19	0	4	1	1	3
Klutts, Gene, Oak	.269	75	197	20	53	79	14	0	4	21	2	1	1	1	4
Krenchicki, Wayne, Balt°	.143	9	14	1	2	2	0	0	0	0	0	0	0	0	0
Kubski, Gilbert, Calif°	.254	22	63	11	16	19	3	0	0	6	1	0	0	1	1
Kuiper, Duane, Clev°	.282	42	149	10	42	47	5	0	0	9	1	3	1	0	1
Kuntz, Russell, Chi	.226	36	62	5	14	18	4	0	3	10	0	3	1	0	1
LaCock, R. Pierre, K.C.°	.205	114	156	14	32	41	6	0	1	18	3	0	2	1	0
Landreaux, Kenneth, Minn°	.281	129	484	56	136	202	23	11	7	62	9	6	5	8	6

Player and Club	Pct.	G.	AB.	R.	H.	TB.	2B.	3B.	HR.	RBI.	GW.	SH.	SF.	SB.	CS.
Lansford, Carney, Calif	.261	151	602	87	157	235	27	3	15	80	10	7	11	14	5
Lefebvre, Joseph, N.Y.°	.227	74	150	26	34	61	1	1	8	21	2	1	0	0	0
Lemon, Chester, Chi	.292	147	514	76	150	227	32	6	11	51	7	4	3	6	6
Lentine, James, Det	.261	67	161	19	42	55	8	1	1	17	1	4	0	2	1
Lezcano, Sixto, Milw	.229	112	411	51	94	173	19	3	18	55	4	3	4	1	1
Lowenstein, John, Balt°	.311	104	196	38	61	81	8	0	4	27	5	0	3	7	3
Lynn, Fredric, Bos°	.301	110	415	67	125	199	32	3	12	61	7	0	5	12	0
Macha, Michael, Tor	.000	5	8	0	0	0	0	0	0	0	0	0	0	0	0
Mackanin, Peter, Minn	.266	108	319	31	85	115	18	0	4	35	5	7	2	6	2
Manning, Richard, Clev°	.234	140	471	55	110	144	17	4	3	52	2	10	9	12	6
Martinez, John, Milw	.224	76	219	16	49	67	9	0	3	17	0	5	1	1	0
May, Lee, Balt	.243	78	222	20	54	89	10	2	7	31	3	0	2	2	0
Mayberry, John, Tor°	.248	149	501	62	124	237	19	2	30	82	7	3	4	0	0
McKay, David, Oak†	.244	123	295	29	72	93	16	1	1	29	4	11	0	1	1
McRae, Harold, K.C.	.297	124	489	73	145	236	39	5	14	83	8	0	6	10	2
Mendoza, Mario, Sea	.245	114	277	27	68	86	6	3	2	14	1	11	1	3	4
Meyer, Daniel, Sea°	.275	146	531	56	146	216	25	6	11	71	9	4	3	8	4
Milbourne, Lawrence, Sea†	.264	106	258	31	68	86	6	6	0	26	4	15	3	7	6
Miller, Richard, Calif°	.274	129	412	52	113	139	14	3	2	38	2	6	3	7	3
Minoso, Saturnino, Chi	.000	2	2	0	0	0	0	0	0	0	0	0	0	0	0
Molinaro, Robert, Chi°	.291	119	344	48	100	139	16	4	5	36	6	2	5	18	7
Molitor, Paul, Milw	.304	111	450	81	137	197	29	2	9	37	2	6	5	34	7
Money, Donald, Milw	.256	86	289	39	74	144	17	1	17	46	6	6	0	0	0
Moore, Alvin, Chi	.256	45	121	9	31	40	4	1	1	10	1	1	1	0	2
Moore, Charles, Milw	.291	111	320	42	93	116	13	2	2	30	3	8	4	10	5
Mora, Andres, Clev	.111	9	18	0	2	2	0	0	0	0	0	0	0	0	0
Morales, Jose, Minn	.303	97	241	36	73	118	17	2	8	36	5	3	2	0	0
Morrison, James, Chi	.283	162	604	66	171	256	40	6	15	57	4	12	6	9	6
Moseby, Lloyd, Tor°	.229	114	389	44	89	142	24	1	9	46	4	10	2	4	6
Mulliniks, S. Rance, K.C.°	.259	36	54	8	14	17	3	0	0	6	1	0	1	0	0
Mullins, Francis, Chi	.194	21	62	9	12	16	4	0	0	3	0	0	1	0	1
Murcer, Bobby, N.Y.°	.269	100	297	41	80	130	9	1	13	57	10	3	9	2	0
Murphy, Dwayne, Oak°	.274	159	573	86	157	218	18	2	13	68	8	22	3	26	15
Murray, Eddie, Balt†	.300	158	621	100	186	322	36	2	32	116	16	0	6	7	2
Narron, Jerry, Sea°	.196	48	107	7	21	36	3	0	4	18	0	1	2	0	0
Nettles, Graig, N.Y.°	.244	89	324	52	79	141	14	0	16	45	4	0	2	0	0
Newman, Jeffrey, Oak	.233	127	438	37	102	168	19	1	15	56	11	5	5	3	4
Nichols, T. Reid, Bos	.222	12	36	5	8	10	0	1	0	3	0	0	0	0	1
Nordhagen, Wayne, Chi	.277	123	415	45	115	190	22	4	15	59	10	0	2	0	1
Norman, Nelson, Tex†	.219	17	32	4	7	7	0	0	0	1	0	1	0	0	1
Norris, James, Tex°	.247	119	174	23	43	48	5	0	0	16	2	3	5	6	3
Norwood, Willie, Minn	.164	34	73	6	12	17	2	0	1	8	0	0	0	1	1
Oates, Johnny, N.Y.°	.188	39	64	6	12	18	3	0	1	3	1	0	0	1	2
Oglivie, Benjamin, Milw°	.304	156	592	94	180	333	26	2	41	118	12	0	9	11	9
Oliver, Albert, Tex°	.319	163	656	96	209	315	43	3	19	117	16	1	8	5	7
Orta, Jorge, Clev°	.291	129	481	78	140	194	18	3	10	64	9	2	8	6	5
Otis, Amos, K.C.	.251	107	394	56	99	151	16	3	10	53	7	2	10	16	1
Paciorek, Thomas, Sea	.273	126	418	44	114	180	19	1	15	59	4	3	2	3	2
Page, Mitchell, Oak°	.244	110	348	58	85	154	10	4	17	51	5	4	5	14	7
Papi, Stanley, Bos-Det	.237	47	114	12	27	47	3	4	3	17	0	2	1	0	0
Parrish, Lance, Det	.286	144	553	79	158	276	34	6	24	82	2	2	3	6	4
Patek, Fred, Calif	.264	86	273	41	72	107	10	5	5	34	1	8	2	7	6
Perez, Atanasio, Bos	.275	151	585	73	161	273	31	3	25	105	9	0	8	1	0
Peters, Richard, Det†	.291	133	477	79	139	178	19	7	2	42	3	7	2	13	7
Phelps, Kenneth, K.C.°	.000	3	4	0	0	0	0	0	0	0	0	0	0	0	0
Picciolo, Robert, Oak	.240	95	271	32	65	93	9	2	5	18	2	8	0	1	1
Piniella, Louis, N.Y.	.287	116	321	39	92	116	18	0	2	27	2	2	3	0	2
Poff, John, Milw°	.250	19	68	7	17	25	1	2	1	7	0	0	0	0	0
Porter, Darrell, K.C.°	.249	118	418	51	104	143	14	2	7	51	8	0	6	1	1
Powell, Hosken, Minn°	.262	137	485	58	127	172	17	5	6	35	1	3	0	14	3
Pruitt, Ronald, Clev-Chi	.302	56	106	9	32	41	3	0	2	15	0	2	1	0	0
Pryor, Gregory, Chi	.240	122	338	32	81	110	18	4	1	29	6	9	6	2	2
Putnam, Patrick, Tex°	.263	147	410	42	108	167	16	2	13	55	7	3	5	0	2
Quirk, James, K.C.°	.276	62	163	13	45	65	5	0	5	21	4	3	3	3	2
Rader, David, Bos.°	.328	50	137	14	45	65	11	0	3	17	0	0	1	1	1
Ramos, Domingo, Tor.	.125	5	16	0	2	2	0	0	0	0	0	0	0	0	0
Randall, Robert, Minn.	.200	5	15	2	3	4	1	0	0	0	0	0	0	0	0
Randolph, William, N.Y.	.294	138	513	99	151	209	23	7	7	46	5	5	3	30	5
Rayford, Floyd, Balt.	.222	8	18	1	4	4	0	0	0	1	0	0	0	0	0

Player and Club	Pct.	G.	AB.	R.	H.	TB.	2B.	3B.	HR.	RBI.	GW.	SH.	SF.	SB.	CS.
Remy, Gerald, Bos.°	.313	63	230	24	72	83	7	2	0	9	0	7	2	14	6
Rettenmund, Mervin, Calif.	.250	2	4	0	1	1	0	0	0	0	0	0	0	0	0
Revering, David, Oak.°	.290	106	376	48	109	185	21	5	15	62	11	2	2	1	0
Rice, James, Bos.	.294	124	504	81	148	254	22	6	24	86	8	1	3	8	3
Richardt, Michael, Tex.	.225	22	71	2	16	18	2	0	0	8	2	0	0	0	0
Rivera, Jesus, Minn.	.221	44	113	13	25	41	7	0	3	10	1	0	0	0	0
Rivers, John, Tex.°	.333	147	630	96	210	275	32	6	7	60	5	6	4	18	7
Roberts, David, Tex.	.238	101	235	27	56	90	4	0	10	30	1	1	1	0	1
Roberts, Leon, Sea.	.251	119	374	48	94	148	18	3	10	33	5	3	6	8	4
Robinson, Bruce, N.Y.°	.000	4	5	0	0	0	0	0	0	0	0	0	0	0	0
Rodriguez, Aurelio, N.Y.	.220	52	164	14	36	53	6	1	3	14	3	11	0	0	0
Roenicke, Gary, Balt.	.239	118	297	40	71	114	13	0	10	28	4	2	3	2	0
Romero, Edgardo, Milw.	.260	42	104	20	27	37	7	0	1	10	1	2	0	2	0
Rosello, David, Clev.	.248	71	117	16	29	38	3	0	2	12	0	2	3	0	0
Rudi, Joseph, Calif.	.237	104	372	42	88	155	17	1	16	53	6	2	3	1	0
Sakata, Lenn, Balt.	.193	43	83	12	16	26	3	2	1	9	2	0	1	2	1
Sample, William, Tex.	.260	99	204	29	53	75	10	0	4	19	3	4	2	8	5
Seilheimer, Ricky, Chi.°	.212	21	52	4	11	19	3	1	1	3	0	1	0	1	0
Sherrill, Dennis, N.Y.	.250	3	4	0	1	1	0	0	0	0	0	0	0	0	0
Simpson, Joe, Sea.°	.249	129	365	42	91	121	15	3	3	34	3	12	3	17	4
Singleton, Kenneth, Balt.†	.304	156	583	85	177	283	28	3	24	104	19	0	4	0	2
Sizemore, Ted, Bos.	.217	9	23	1	5	6	1	0	0	0	0	0	0	0	0
Skaggs, David, Balt.-Calif.	.197	26	71	7	14	17	0	0	1	9	1	1	1	0	0
Smalley, Roy, Minn.†	.278	133	486	64	135	197	24	1	12	63	12	2	9	3	3
Soderholm, Eric, N.Y.	.287	95	275	38	79	127	13	1	11	35	6	1	0	0	0
Sofield, Richard, Minn.°	.247	131	417	52	103	156	18	4	9	49	6	9	7	4	5
Spencer, James, N.Y.°	.236	97	259	38	61	109	9	0	13	43	6	1	4	1	0
Squires, Michael, Chi.°	.283	131	343	38	97	120	11	3	2	33	3	11	0	8	9
Stanley, Frederick, N.Y.	.209	49	86	13	18	21	3	0	0	5	1	1	0	0	0
Stapleton, David, Bos.	.321	106	449	61	144	208	33	5	7	45	7	5	4	3	2
Staub, Daniel, Tex.°	.300	109	340	42	102	156	23	2	9	55	4	1	6	1	1
Stegman, David, Det.	.177	65	130	12	23	34	5	0	2	9	2	2	1	1	1
Stein, William, Sea.	.268	67	198	16	53	75	5	1	5	27	2	7	3	1	1
Stieb, David, Tor.	.000	36	1	0	0	0	0	0	0	0	0	0	0	0	0
Stinson, G. Robert, Sea.°	.215	48	107	6	23	28	2	0	1	8	0	2	2	0	0
Summers, John, Det.°	.297	120	347	61	103	175	19	1	17	60	4	1	3	4	3
Sundberg, James, Tex.	.273	151	505	59	138	194	24	1	10	63	5	6	5	2	2
Sutherland, Leonardo, Chi°	.258	34	89	9	23	26	3	0	0	5	0	1	1	4	1
Terrell, Jerry, K.C.	.063	23	16	4	1	1	0	0	0	0	0	0	0	0	0
Thomas, J. Gorman, Milw.	.239	162	628	78	150	296	26	3	38	105	13	3	6	8	5
Thompson, Jason, Det-Cal°	.288	138	438	69	126	208	19	0	21	90	7	2	5	2	1
Thon, Richard, Calif.	.255	80	267	32	68	84	12	2	0	15	1	5	2	7	5
Torres, Rosendo, K.C.†	.167	51	72	10	12	12	0	0	0	3	0	0	0	1	3
Trammell, Alan, Det.	.300	146	560	107	168	226	21	5	9	65	9	13	7	12	12
Upshaw, Willie, Tor.°	.213	34	61	10	13	21	3	1	1	5	0	1	0	1	0
Valdez, Julio, Bos.	.263	8	19	4	5	9	1	0	1	4	0	1	0	2	0
Vega, Jesus, Minn.	.167	12	30	3	5	5	0	0	0	4	1	1	0	1	0
Velez, Otoniel, Tor.	.269	104	357	54	96	174	12	3	20	62	7	0	4	0	0
Veryzer, Thomas, Clev.	.271	109	358	28	97	115	12	0	2	28	3	4	3	0	5
Wagner, Mark, Det.	.236	45	72	5	17	18	1	0	0	3	1	2	0	0	1
Walker, Cleotha, Bos.†	.211	19	57	3	12	15	0	0	1	5	2	1	1	3	2
Walton, Daniel, Tex.†	.200	10	10	2	2	2	0	0	0	1	0	0	0	0	0
Walton, Reginald, Sea.	.277	31	83	8	23	35	6	0	2	9	1	0	1	2	2
Ward, Gary, Minn.	.463	13	41	11	19	32	6	2	1	10	0	1	1	0	0
Washington, Claudell, Chi°	.289	32	90	15	26	37	4	2	1	12	2	1	0	4	2
Washington, U.L., K.C.†	.273	153	549	79	150	206	16	11	6	53	7	10	2	20	7
Wathan, John, K.C.	.305	126	453	57	138	184	14	7	6	58	5	3	1	17	3
Watson, Robert, N.Y.	.307	130	469	62	144	214	25	3	13	68	11	1	6	2	1
Werth, Dennis, N.Y.	.308	39	65	15	20	32	3	0	3	12	1	1	0	0	1
Whitaker, Louis, Det.°	.233	145	477	68	111	135	19	1	1	45	7	12	6	8	4
White, Frank, K.C.	.264	154	560	70	148	200	23	4	7	60	11	9	4	19	6
Whitmer, Daniel, Calif.	.241	48	87	8	21	24	3	0	0	7	0	9	2	1	0
Whitt, L. Ernest, Tor.°	.237	106	295	23	70	104	12	2	6	34	3	5	3	1	3
Wilborn, Thaddeaus, N.Y.†	.250	8	8	2	2	2	0	0	0	1	0	0	0	0	0
Wilfong, Robert, Minn.°	.248	131	416	55	103	153	16	5	8	45	6	11	2	10	6
Wills, Elliott, Tex.†	.263	146	578	102	152	208	31	5	5	58	3	15	8	34	9
Wilson, Willie, K.C.†	.326	161	705	133	230	297	28	15	3	49	4	5	1	79	10
Wockenfuss, Johnny, Det.	.274	126	372	56	102	167	13	2	16	65	8	0	1	1	4
Wolfe, Laurence, Bos.	.130	18	23	3	3	7	1	0	1	4	2	0	1	0	0

Player and Club	Pct.	G.	AB.	R.	H.	TB.	2B.	3B.	HR.	RBI.	GW.	SH.	SF.	SB.	CS.
Woods, Alvis, Tor.°	.300	109	373	54	112	179	18	2	15	47	6	5	1	4	5
Wynegar, Harold, Minn.†	.255	146	486	61	124	163	18	3	5	57	4	7	6	3	1
Yastrzemski, Carl, Bos.°	.275	105	364	49	100	168	21	1	15	50	8	1	3	0	2
Yost, Edgar, Milw.	.161	15	31	0	5	5	0	0	0	0	0	0	0	0	0
Yount, Robin, Milw.	.293	143	611	121	179	317	49	10	23	87	9	6	3	20	5
Zisk, Richard, Tex.	.290	135	448	48	130	206	17	1	19	77	6	1	4	0	2

The following pitchers had no plate appearances, primarily because of use of designated hitters; they are listed alphabetically by club with number of games, including pinch-running and defensive appearances, in parentheses:

BALTIMORE—Boddicker, Michael (1); Flanagan, Michael (40); Ford, David (25); Hartzell, Paul (6); Kerrigan, Joseph (1); Martinez, Felix (54); Martinez, J. Dennis (26); McGregor, Scott (37); Palmer, James (37); Stewart, Samuel (33); Stoddard, Timothy (64); Stone, Steven (49).

BOSTON—Aponte, Luis (4); Billingham, John (15—includes 8 with Detroit); Burgmeier, Thomas (62); Campbell, William (23); Crawford, Steve (6); Eckersley, Dennis (30); Hurst, Bruce (12); Lockwood, Claude (24); MacWhorter, Keith (14); Ojeda, Robert (7); Rainey, Charles (16); Remmerswaal, Wilhelmus (14); Renko, Steven (32); Stanley, Robert (52); Torrez, Michael (36); Tudor, John (16).

CALIFORNIA—Aase, Donald (40); Barr, James (24); Botting, Ralph (6); Clear, Mark (58); Dorsey, James (4); Ferris, Robert (5); Frost, David (15); Halicki, Edward (10); Hassler, Andrew (41); Kison, Bruce (13); Knapp, R. Christian (32); LaRoche, David (53); Lemanczyk, David (31—includes 10 with Toronto); Martinez, Alfredo (30); Montague, John (37); Schuler, David (8); Tanana, Frank (32).

CHICAGO—Barrios, Francisco (3); Baumgarten, Ross (24); Burns, R. Britt (34); Contreras, Arnaldo (8); Dotson, Richard (36); Farmer, Edward (64); Hoffman, Guy (23); Hoyt, D. Lamarr (25); Kravec, Kenneth (20); Proly, Michael (62); Robinson, Dewey (15); Scarbery, Randy (24); Trout, Steven (32); Wortham, Richard (41).

CLEVELAND—Barker, Leonard (36); Collins, Donald (4); Cruz, Victor (55); Denny, John (16); Garland, M. Wayne (25); Grimsley, Ross (14); Monge, Isidro (67); Owchinko, Robert (29); Paxton, Michael (4); Spillner, Daniel (34); Stanton, Michael (51); Waits, M. Richard (33); Wihtol, Alexander (17).

DETROIT—Fidrych, Mark (10); Hiller, John (11); Lopez, Aurelio (67); Morris, John (44); Petry, Daniel (27); Robbins, Bruce (15); Rozema, David (42); Schatzeder, Daniel (32); Tobik, David (17); Ujdur, Gerald (9); Underwood, Patrick (49); Weaver, Roger (19); Wilcox, Milton (33).

KANSAS CITY—Brett, Kenneth (8); Busby, Steven (11); Chamberlain, Craig (5); Christenson, Gary (24); Eastwick, Rawlins (14); Gale, Richard (32); Gura, Lawrence (36); Jones, Michael (3); Leonard, Dennis (38); Martin, D. Renie (32); Pattin, Martin (37); Quisenberry, Daniel (75); Splittorff, Paul (34); Twitty, Jeffrey (13).

MILWAUKEE—Augustine, Gerald (39); Boitano, Danny (11); Caldwell, R. Michael (34); Castro, William (56); Cleveland, Reginald (45); Flinn, John (20); Haas, Bryan (33); Holdsworth, Frederick (9); Keeton, Rickey (5); LaPoint, David (5); McClure, Robert (52); Mitchell, Paul (17); Slaton, James (3); Sorensen, Lary (35); Travers, William (29).

MINNESOTA—Arroyo, Fernando (21); Bacsik, Michael (10); Corbett, Douglas (73); Erickson, Roger (33); Felton, Terry (5); Jackson, Darrell (31); Kinnunen, Michael (21); Koosman, Jerry (38); Marshall, Michael (18); Redfern, Peter (23); Verhoeven, John (44); Veselic, Robert (1); Williams, Alberto (18); Zahn, Geoffrey (38).

NEW YORK—Bird, J. Douglas (22); Gossage, Richard (64); Griffin, Michael (13); Guidry, Ronald (37); John, Thomas (36); Kaat, James (14); Lollar, W. Timothy (14); May, Rudolph (41); Perry, Gaylord (24—includes 24 with Texas); Tiant, Luis (25); Underwood, Thomas (38).

OAKLAND—Beard, David (13); Bordi, Richard (1); Camacho, Ernie (5); Hamilton, David (21); Jones, Jeffrey (35); Keough, Matthew (34); Kingman, Brian (32); Lacey, Robert (47); Langford, J. Rick (35); Lysander, Richard (5); McCatty, Steven (33); Minetto, Craig (7); Norris, Michael (33); Souza, K. Mark (5); Wirth, Alan (2).

SEATTLE—Abbott, W. Glenn (31); Anderson, Richard (5); Bannister, Floyd (32); Beattie, James (33); Dressler, Robert (30); Heaverlo, David (60); Honeycutt, Frederick (30); McLaughlin, Byron (45); Parrott, Michael (27); Rawley, Shane (59); Roberts, David (37); Sarmiento, Manuel (9); Wheelock, Gary (1).

TEXAS—Allard, Brian (5); Babcock, Robert (19); Butcher, John (6); Clay, Kenneth (8); Comer, Steven (12); Darwin, Danny (53); Devine, P. Adrian (13); Figueroa, Eduardo (23—includes 15 with New York); Gleaton, Jerry (5); Hough, Charles (16); Jenkins, Ferguson (29); Johnson, John (33); Kainer, Donald (4); Kern, James (38); Lewallyn, Dennis (4); Lyle, Albert (49); Matlack, Jonathan (35); Medich, George (35); Rajsich, David (24).

TORONTO—Barlow, Michael (40); Buskey, Thomas (33); Clancy, James (34); Garvin, T. Jared (61); Jefferson, Jesse (29); Kucek, John (23); Leal, Luis (13); McLaughlin, Joey (55); Mirabella, Paul (33); Moore, Balor (31); Schrom, Kenneth (18); Todd, Jackson (12).

Note—The above game totals for certain Baltimore and Detroit pitchers include times that they were listed in the starting lineup as designated hitter but did not bat, being replaced by a pinch-hitter the first time their position in the batting order came up. While those pitchers were credited with a game on each of those occasions, they were not given credit for any games in the designated-hitting statistics. The pitchers and their number of appearances as ersatz designated hitter follow:

Baltimore—Flanagan 3, F. Martinez 1, J. Dennis Martinez 1, McGregor 1, Palmer 3, Stone 12. Detroit—Fidrych 1, Wilcox 1.

AWARDED FIRST BASE ON INTERFERENCE—Diaz, Clev. (Graham); Graham, Balt. (Gedman); Squires, Chi. (Essian); Stinson, Sea. (Diaz); Wilfong, Minn. (Graham); Wills, Tex. (Graham).

PLAYERS WITH TWO OR MORE CLUBS
(Alphabetically Arranged With Player's First Club on Top)

Player and Club	Pct.	G.	AB.	R.	H.	TB.	2B.	3B.	HR.	RBI.	GW.	SH.	SF.	Tot. BB.	Int. BB.	HP.	SO.	SB.	CS.	GI. DP.
Bannister, Chi	.192	45	130	16	25	31	6	0	0	9	2	3	1	12	5	0	16	5	2	3
Bannister, Clev	.328	81	262	41	86	114	17	4	1	32	2	3	4	28	1	0	25	9	2	6
Braun, K.C.	.043	14	23	0	1	1	0	0	0	1	0	0	0	2	0	0	2	0	0	0
Braun, Tor	.273	37	55	4	15	20	2	0	1	9	3	0	0	8	1	0	5	0	0	2
Brohamer, Bos	.316	21	57	5	18	23	2	0	1	6	1	1	0	4	0	0	3	0	0	2
Brohamer, Clev	.225	53	142	13	32	42	5	1	1	15	1	3	2	14	4	0	6	0	1	5
Cowens, Calif	.227	34	119	11	27	35	5	0	1	17	1	0	0	12	1	1	21	1	2	2
Cowens, Det	.280	108	403	58	113	149	15	3	5	42	5	7	4	37	4	1	40	5	6	6
Cruz, Calif	.275	18	40	5	11	17	3	0	1	5	1	0	0	5	1	0	8	0	0	0
Cruz, Chi	.232	90	293	23	68	87	11	1	2	18	2	6	1	9	0	2	54	2	1	5
Papi, Bos	.000	1	0	0	0	0	0	0	0	0	0	0	0	0	0	0	0	0	0	0
Papi, Det	.237	46	114	12	27	47	3	4	3	17	0	2	1	5	0	0	24	0	0	3
Pruitt, Clev	.306	23	36	1	11	12	1	0	0	4	0	1	1	4	0	0	6	0	0	1
Pruitt, Chi	.300	33	70	8	21	29	2	0	2	11	0	1	0	8	1	0	7	0	0	4
Skaggs, Balt	.200	2	5	0	1	1	0	0	0	0	0	0	0	0	0	0	1	0	0	0
Skaggs, Calif	.197	24	66	7	13	16	0	0	1	9	1	1	1	9	0	0	13	0	0	1
Thompson, Det	.214	36	126	10	27	44	5	0	4	20	2	0	2	13	1	1	26	0	1	4
Thompson, Calif	.317	102	312	59	99	164	14	0	17	70	5	2	3	70	9	0	60	2	0	8

OFFICIAL MISCELLANEOUS AMERICAN LEAGUE BATTING RECORDS

CLUB MISCELLANEOUS BATTING RECORDS

Club	Slg. Pct.	G.	Tot. BB.	Int. BB.	HP.	SO.	GIDP.	ShO.
Milwaukee	.448	162	455	59	25	745	98	11
Boston	.436	160	475	48	32	720	151	6
New York	.425	162	643	58	28	739	136	11
Kansas City	.413	162	508	45	38	709	147	5
Baltimore	.413	162	587	38	21	766	158	6
Detroit	.409	163	645	35	33	844	144	9
Texas	.405	163	480	51	23	589	156	7
Oakland	.385	162	506	49	19	824	124	13
Toronto	.383	162	448	44	33	813	119	12
Minnesota	.381	161	436	40	21	703	151	12
Cleveland	.381	160	617	51	37	625	165	6
California	.378	160	539	38	32	889	141	9
Chicago	.370	162	399	46	39	670	142	11
Seattle	.356	163	483	44	19	727	136	14
Totals	.399	1132	7221	646	400	10363	1968	132

INDIVIDUAL MISCELLANEOUS BATTING RECORDS
(Top Fifteen Qualifiers for Slugging Championship—502 or More Plate Appearances)

Player—Club	Slg. Pct.	Tot. BB.	Int. BB.	HP.	SO.	GI DP.	Player—Club	Slg. Pct.	Tot. BB.	Int. BB.	HP.	SO.	GI DP.
Brett, K.C.	.664	58	16	1	22	11	Parrish, Det.	.499	31	3	3	109	24
Jackson, N.Y.	.597	83	15	2	122	7	Bell, Tex.	.498	40	11	0	39	8
Oglivie, Milw.	.563	54	19	5	71	5	Charboneau, Clev.	.488	49	0	3	70	24
Cooper, Milw.	.539	39	15	2	42	16	Singleton, Balt.	.485	92	1	1	94	19
Yount, Milw.	.519	26	1	6	67	8	Evans, Bos.	.484	64	6	5	98	5
Murray, Balt.	.519	54	10	2	71	18	McRae, K.C.	.483	29	4	8	56	13
Rice, Bos.	.504	30	5	4	87	16	Oliver, Tex.	.480	39	9	5	47	14
Armas, Oak.	.500	29	4	2	128	22							

DEPARTMENTAL LEADERS: Tot. BB—Randolph, 119; Int. BB—Oglivie, 19; HP—Fisk, 13; SO—Thomas, 170; GIDP—Perez, 25.

(All Players—Listed Alphabetically)

Player—Club	Slg. Pct.	Tot. BB.	Int. BB.	HP.	SO.	GI DP.
Adams, Minn.	.412	15	1	0	26	11
Aikens, K.C.	.433	64	3	7	88	23
Ainge, Tor.	.315	2	0	1	29	3
Alexander, Clev	.360	17	1	0	52	9
Allen, Sea	.294	8	2	1	3	1
Allenson, Bos.	.443	13	0	0	11	1
Alston, Clev.	.315	5	2	2	7	1
J. Anderson, Sea.	.325	27	1	3	39	5
Armas, Oak.	.500	29	4	2	128	22
Ashford, Tex.	.125	3	0	0	3	1
Ault, Tor.	.306	14	0	2	23	3
Ayala, Balt.	.500	19	3	0	21	4
Bailor, Tor.	.297	36	3	2	33	5
Baines, Chi.	.405	19	7	1	65	15
Bando, Milw.	.311	29	2	1	35	7
Bannister, Chi-Clev	.370	40	6	0	41	9
Barranca, K.C.	.000	0	0	0	0	0
Baylor, Calif.	.341	24	4	11	32	9
Belanger, Balt.	.276	12	0	0	25	1
Bell, Tex.	.498	40	11	0	39	16
Bell, Chi.	.241	29	1	0	37	3
Beniquez, Sea.	.346	17	0	0	25	10
Blair, N.Y.	.000	0	0	0	0	0
Bochte, Sea.	.456	72	13	0	81	16
Bonnell, Tor.	.417	37	2	2	59	14
Bonner, Balt.	.000	0	0	0	0	0
Borgmann, Chi.	.310	14	0	0	9	1
Bosetti, Tor.	.324	15	1	2	29	2
Bosley, Chi.	.279	10	3	0	27	5
Bowen, Bos.	.154	2	0	0	3	0
Brant, N.Y.	.000	0	0	0	0	0
Braun, K.C.-Tor.	.269	10	1	0	7	2
G. Brett, K.C.	.664	58	16	1	22	11
Brohamer, Bos-Clev	.327	18	4	0	9	7
Brookens, Det.	.418	32	3	1	71	10
Brouhard, Milw.	.400	7	0	1	24	3
Brown, N.Y.	.415	29	4	0	82	8
Bumbry, Balt.	.433	78	8	3	75	9
Burleson, Bos.	.366	62	0	2	51	24
Butera, Minn.	.282	3	0	1	6	4
Campaneris, Calif.	.329	14	0	1	33	4
Cannon, Tor.	.080	0	0	1	14	0
Cardenal, K.C.	.377	5	0	0	5	0
Carew, Calif.	.437	59	7	1	38	15
Castillo, K.C.	.200	0	0	0	0	0
Castino, Minn.	.430	29	1	0	67	15
Cerone, N.Y.	.432	32	2	6	56	14
Chalk, K.C.	.341	18	0	2	27	5
Chappas, Chi.	.200	4	0	1	10	0
Charboneau, Clev.	.488	49	0	3	70	24
Clark, Calif.	.333	11	0	2	42	7
Cliburn, Calif.	.321	3	0	0	9	1
Concepcion, K.C.	.133	0	0	0	1	1
Cooper, Milw.	.539	39	15	2	42	16
Corcoran, Det.	.405	22	2	1	10	4
Corey, Balt.	.417	5	0	0	7	0
Cosey, Oak.	.111	0	0	0	0	0
Cowens, Calif.-Det.	.352	49	5	2	61	8
Cox, Oak.	.231	14	0	0	23	2
L. Cox, Sea.	.292	19	0	0	36	9
T. Cox, Sea.	.304	19	3	0	25	8
Craig, Sea.	.346	17	3	2	35	5
Crowley, Balt.	.476	29	2	0	21	8
Cruz, Sea.	.258	59	0	1	49	6
Cruz, Calif.-Chi.	.312	14	1	2	62	5
Cubbage, Minn.	.361	23	4	1	37	4
Dauer, Balt.	.352	46	1	3	19	22
Davis, Tor.	.321	12	0	1	25	9
Davis, Milw.	.386	11	0	3	43	8
Davis, Oak.	.284	7	0	0	14	2
Davis, Tex.	.125	0	0	0	2	0
Davis, N.Y.	.000	0	0	0	1	0
DeCinces, Balt.	.403	49	5	3	83	20
Dempsey, Balt.	.425	36	1	3	45	11
Dent, N.Y.	.354	48	1	2	37	6
Detherage, K.C.	.500	1	0	0	4	0
Diaz, Clev.	.343	7	3	0	27	12
Dilone, Clev.	.432	28	1	2	45	7
Donohue, Calif.	.243	7	0	1	63	0
Downing, Calif.	.419	12	1	0	12	5
Doyle, N.Y.	.227	6	0	0	7	1
Drago, Bos.	.000	0	0	0	0	0
Dwyer, Bos.	.438	28	5	2	23	4
Dybzinski, Clev.	.294	13	0	2	35	5
Dyer, Det.	.306	13	1	0	34	3
Edler, Sea.	.337	8	1	0	16	3
Edwards, Minn.	.335	12	1	1	51	6
Edwards, Oak.	.237	1	0	0	5	1
Elliott, Oak.	.205	1	0	0	13	1
Ellis, Tex.	.313	14	1	1	23	6
Essian, Oak.	.323	30	0	0	18	14
Evans, Bos.	.484	64	6	5	98	5
Faedo, Minn.	.375	0	0	0	0	0
Fisk, Bos.	.467	36	6	13	62	12
Foley, Chi.	.336	9	3	2	22	0
Ford, Calif.	.420	19	1	2	45	15
Frias, Tex.	.273	4	0	1	23	8
Gamble, N.Y.	.567	28	4	4	21	2
Gantner, Milw.	.376	30	5	1	29	8
Garcia, Tor.	.381	12	2	3	55	14
Garcia, Balt.	.235	24	0	0	57	11
Garr, Calif.	.214	4	2	0	6	0
Gedman, Bos.	.208	0	0	0	5	1
Gibson, Det.	.440	10	0	1	45	0
Gonzales, Det.	.143	0	0	0	1	0
Gonzalez, Oak.	.243	9	0	0	8	0
Goodwin, Minn.	.270	17	0	0	32	4
Graham, Balt.	.481	14	0	0	40	4
Gray, Clev.	.278	3	1	0	13	2
Grich, Calif.	.408	84	2	4	108	16
Griffin, Tor.	.349	24	2	4	58	8
Gross, Oak.	.467	44	9	1	39	2
Grubb, Tex.	.427	42	5	2	35	11
Guerrero, Oak.	.307	19	2	1	32	15
Gulden, N.Y.	1.333	0	0	0	0	0
Hancock, Bos.	.443	3	0	0	11	1
Hargrove, Clev.	.404	111	10	8	36	22
Harlow, Calif.	.385	48	1	1	61	10
Harrah, Clev.	.380	98	3	7	60	16
Harrelson, Tex.	.322	29	0	0	23	3
Harris, Calif.	.561	7	0	0	4	2
Harris, Milw.	.315	12	0	0	13	1
Hart, Tex.	.250	1	0	0	1	0
Hassey, Clev.	.446	49	3	1	51	13
Hazewood, Balt.	.000	0	0	0	4	0
Heath, Oak.	.298	16	2	0	28	7
Hebner, Det.	.466	38	3	2	45	7
Henderson, Oak.	.399	117	7	5	54	6
Hill, Sea.	.371	3	0	0	10	3
Hisle, Milw.	.583	14	2	1	7	1
Hobson, Bos.	.349	25	2	0	69	10
Hodgson, Tor.	.341	3	0	0	12	2
Hoffman, Bos.	.397	19	2	2	41	8
Holt, N.Y.	.167	1	0	0	2	0

Player—Club	Slg. Pct.	Tot. BB.	Int. BB.	HP.	SO.	GI DP.
Horton, Sea.	.328	39	2	4	70	5
Howell, Tor.	.413	50	8	5	92	10
Hurdle, K.C.	.458	34	5	2	61	11
Iorg, Tor.	.329	12	0	0	39	5
Jackson, N.Y.	.597	83	15	2	122	7
R. Jackson, Minn.	.391	28	5	3	41	15
Johnson, Clev.	.362	25	5	0	30	8
L. Johnson, Chi.	.409	47	5	0	53	15
R. Johnson, Chi.	.200	2	0	1	4	0
Johnston, Minn.	.296	2	0	0	4	3
Jones, Det.	.364	10	0	0	5	3
Jones, N.Y.	.357	34	3	3	50	5
Kelly, Balt.	.365	34	0	0	54	4
Kelly, Tor.	.286	0	0	0	4	0
Kemp, Det.	.474	69	3	4	64	24
Kimm, Chi.	.291	17	0	0	26	10
Klutts, Oak.	.401	13	1	0	41	5
Krenchicki, Balt	.143	1	0	0	3	0
Kubski, Calif	.302	6	0	0	10	2
Kuiper, Clev	.315	13	3	0	8	1
Kuntz, Chi	.290	5	0	0	13	2
LaCock, K.C.	.263	17	1	1	10	7
Landreaux, Minn	.417	39	4	2	42	13
Lansford, Calif	.390	50	2	0	93	12
Lefebvre, N.Y.	.407	27	3	0	30	5
Lemon, Chi	.442	71	6	12	56	12
Lentine, Det	.342	28	1	2	30	3
Lezcano, Milw	.421	39	3	3	75	6
Lowenstein, Balt	.413	32	1	0	29	2
Lynn, Bos	.480	58	3	0	39	10
Macha, Tor	.000	0	0	0	1	0
Mackanin, Minn	.361	14	2	0	34	7
Manning, Clev	.306	63	11	2	66	12
Martinez, Milw	.306	12	0	1	33	3
May, Balt	.401	15	1	0	53	11
Mayberry, Tor	.473	77	9	3	80	9
McKay, Oak	.315	10	0	6	57	4
McRae, K.C.	.483	29	4	8	56	13
Mendoza, Sea	.310	16	0	0	42	5
Meyer, Sea	.407	31	4	1	42	11
Milbourne, Sea	.333	19	4	1	13	8
Miller, Calif	.337	48	4	1	71	3
Minoso, Chi	.000	0	0	0	0	0
Molinaro, Chi	.404	26	7	7	29	4
Molitor, Milw	.438	48	4	3	48	9
Money, Milw	.498	40	0	1	36	4
Moore, Chi	.331	7	0	0	11	5
Moore, Milw	.363	24	2	0	28	7
Mora, Clev	.111	0	0	0	0	0
Morales, Minn	.490	22	4	1	19	11
Morrison, Chi	.424	36	2	8	74	19
Moseby, Tor	.365	25	4	4	85	11
Mulliniks, K.C.	.315	7	0	0	10	2
Mullins, Chi	.258	9	0	0	8	3
Murcer, N.Y.	.438	34	2	2	28	9
Murphy, Oak	.380	102	7	2	96	12
Murray, Balt	.519	54	10	2	71	18
Narron, Sea	.336	13	2	0	18	2
Nettles, N.Y.	.435	42	5	1	42	8
Newman, Oak	.384	25	8	1	81	10
Nichols, Bos	.278	3	0	0	8	0
Nordhagen, Chi	.458	10	3	1	45	13
Norman, Tex	.219	1	0	0	1	2
Norris, Tex	.276	23	2	0	16	11
Norwood, Minn	.233	3	0	0	13	3
Oates, N.Y.	.281	2	0	1	3	1
Oglivie, Milw	.563	54	19	5	71	5
Oliver, Tex	.480	39	9	5	47	14
Orta, Clev	.403	71	2	2	44	8
Otis, K.C.	.383	39	0	3	70	9
Paciorek, Sea	.431	17	1	1	67	13
Page, Oak	.443	35	3	1	87	9
Papi, Bos-Det	.412	5	0	0	24	3
Parrish, Det	.499	31	3	3	109	24
Patek, Calif	.392	15	1	1	26	11
Perez, Bos	.467	41	11	1	93	25
Peters, Det	.373	54	2	6	48	17
Phelps, K.C.	.000	0	0	0	2	0
Picciolo, Oak	.343	2	0	0	63	6
Piniella, N.Y.	.361	29	5	0	20	17
Poff, Milw	.368	3	2	0	7	1
Porter, K.C.	.342	69	5	2	50	10
Powell, Minn	.355	32	2	3	46	14
Pruitt, Clev-Chi	.387	12	1	0	13	5
Pryor, Chi	.325	12	0	2	35	10
Putnam, Tex	.407	36	6	0	49	13
Quirk, K.C.	.399	7	2	1	24	7
Rader, Bos	.474	14	1	0	12	4
Ramos, Tor	.125	2	0	0	5	0
Randall, Minn	.267	1	0	0	0	1
Randolph, N.Y.	.407	119	4	2	45	6
Rayford, Balt	.222	0	0	0	5	1
Remy, Bos	.361	10	0	0	14	6
Rettenmund, Calif	.250	1	0	0	1	0
Revering, Oak	.492	32	6	0	37	6
Rice, Bos	.504	30	5	4	87	16
Richardt, Tex	.254	1	0	0	7	1
Rivera, Minn	.363	4	0	0	20	4
Rivers, Tex	.437	20	1	1	34	4
Roberts, Tex	.383	13	2	1	38	5
L. Roberts, Sea	.396	43	1	1	59	12
Robinson, N.Y.	.000	0	0	0	4	0
Rodriguez, N.Y.	.323	7	1	0	35	7
Roenicke, Balt	.384	41	5	6	49	10
Romero, Milw	.356	9	0	0	11	3
Rosello, Clev	.325	9	0	0	19	2
Rudi, Calif	.417	17	2	5	84	10
Sakata, Balt	.313	6	0	0	10	3
Sample, Tex	.368	18	2	6	15	4
Seilheimer, Chi	.365	4	1	0	15	0
Sherrill, N.Y.	.250	0	0	0	1	1
Simpson, Sea	.332	28	3	1	43	6
Singleton, Balt	.485	92	1	1	94	19
Sizemore, Bos	.261	0	0	0	0	1
Skaggs, Balt-Calif	.239	9	0	0	14	1
Smalley, Minn	.405	65	4	2	63	15
Soderholm, N.Y.	.462	27	2	1	25	9
Sofield, Minn	.374	24	2	2	92	3
Spencer, N.Y.	.421	30	2	1	44	7
Squires, Chi	.350	33	1	1	24	6
Stanley, N.Y.	.244	5	0	2	5	0
Stapleton, Bos	.463	13	1	1	32	10
Staub, Tex	.459	39	3	2	18	16
Stegman, Det	.262	14	0	0	23	0
Stein, Sea	.379	16	4	1	25	5
Stieb, Tor	.000	0	0	0	0	0
Stinson, Sea	.262	9	0	1	19	2
Summers, Det	.504	52	6	5	52	10
Sundberg, Tex	.384	64	3	1	67	15
Sutherland, Chi	.292	1	1	0	11	2
Terrell, K.C.	.063	0	0	0	0	0
Thomas, Milw	.471	58	4	2	170	7
Thompson, Det-Calif	.475	83	10	1	86	12
Thon, Calif	.315	10	0	0	28	5
Torres, K.C.	.167	8	0	0	7	1
Trammell, Det	.404	69	2	3	63	10

Player—Club	Slg. Pct.	Tot. BB.	Int. BB.	HP.	SO.	GI DP.	Player—Club	Slg. Pct.	Tot. BB.	Int. BB.	HP.	SO.	GI DP.
Upshaw, Tor	.344	6	1	0	14	0	White, K.C.	.357	19	0	2	69	11
Valdez, Bos	.474	0	0	1	5	0	Whitmer, Calif	.276	4	0	0	21	3
Vega, Minn	.167	3	0	0	7	1	Whitt, Tor	.353	22	0	0	30	11
Velez, Tor	.487	54	8	2	86	8	Wilborn, N.Y.	.250	0	0	0	1	0
Veryzer, Clev	.321	10	1	8	25	11	Wilfong, Minn	.368	34	3	3	61	8
Wagner, Det	.250	7	0	0	11	0	Wills, Tex	.360	51	1	3	71	8
Walker, Bos	.263	6	1	1	10	1	Wilson, K.C.	.421	28	3	6	81	4
Walton, Tex	.200	3	0	0	5	0	Wockenfuss, Det	.449	68	4	3	64	7
Walton, Sea	.422	3	0	1	10	1	Wolfe, Bos	.304	0	0	0	5	1
Ward, Minn	.780	3	1	0	6	0	Woods, Tor	.480	37	3	1	35	4
Washington, Chi	.411	5	0	1	19	5	Wynegar, Minn	.335	63	6	2	36	9
Washington, K.C.	.375	53	0	0	78	13	Yastrzemski, Bos	.462	44	5	0	38	9
Wathan, K.C.	.406	50	6	3	42	19	Yost, Milw	.161	0	0	0	6	1
Watson, N.Y.	.456	48	5	1	56	20	Yount, Milw	.519	26	1	1	67	8
Werth, N.Y.	.492	12	0	0	19	3	Zisk, Tex	.460	39	5	0	72	18
Whitaker, Det	.283	73	0	0	79	9							

OFFICIAL AMERICAN LEAGUE DESIGNATED HITTING

CLUB DESIGNATED HITTING

Club	Pct.	AB.	R.	H.	TB.	2B.	3B.	HR.	RBI.	SH.	SF.	BB.	HP.	SO.	SB.	CS.	GI DP.
California	.310	609	88	189	267	29	2	15	101	1	11	74	7	74	8	11	16
Texas	.301	631	72	190	284	31	3	19	97	2	8	62	1	62	1	5	22
Kansas City	.290	663	89	192	299	42	4	19	119	0	9	52	7	71	10	3	18
Detroit	.285	606	93	173	285	27	2	27	104	5	7	92	5	106	9	5	22
New York	.283	637	94	180	300	25	4	29	91	4	4	74	4	92	1	1	25
Chicago	.273	623	71	170	257	31	7	14	78	5	6	42	4	58	6	4	15
Boston	.273	605	73	165	259	25	3	21	76	2	9	47	3	87	6	2	19
Minnesota	.267	610	79	163	241	33	3	13	80	12	6	55	1	83	3	3	3
Cleveland	.261	616	87	161	250	20	3	21	101	1	10	69	1	112	10	7	32
Seattle	.259	609	70	158	248	29	2	19	71	4	7	61	5	98	4	5	7
Baltimore	.255	631	75	161	271	23	3	27	114	1	5	61	0	122	3	1	22
Milwaukee	.252	640	89	161	251	27	3	19	73	1	5	43	5	83	10	8	14
Oakland	.239	618	81	148	228	17	6	17	70	11	7	57	1	123	17	10	17
Toronto	.229	599	73	137	232	21	4	22	84	1	5	75	1	129	1	0	16
Totals	.270	8697	1134	2348	3672	380	49	282	1259	47	99	864	45	1300	89	65	268

INDIVIDUAL DESIGNATED HITTING
(Listed Alphabetically)

Player and Club	Pct.	G.	AB.	R.	H.	TB.	2B.	3B.	HR.	RBI.	SH.	SF.	BB.	HP.	SO.	SB.	CS.	GI DP.
Adams, Minn.	.280	81	214	29	60	88	11	1	5	33	6	4	14	0	19	1	3	8
Aikens, K.C.	.302	13	53	6	16	23	1	0	2	12	0	0	2	1	9	1	0	1
Ainge, Tor.	.000	2	6	0	0	0	0	0	0	0	0	0	0	0	2	0	0	1
Alexander, Clev.	.217	40	129	15	28	43	6	0	3	17	0	1	15	0	39	0	4	8
Allenson, Bos.	.313	6	16	3	5	5	0	0	0	1	0	0	2	0	4	1	0	0
Alston, Clev.	.000	6	1	0	0	0	0	0	0	0	0	0	0	0	0	0	1	0
J. Anderson, Sea.	.200	5	10	1	2	3	1	0	0	0	1	0	2	0	1	0	0	0
Ault, Tor.	.203	21	64	6	13	18	3	1	0	5	0	0	5	0	10	0	0	1
Ayala, Balt.	.236	41	110	17	26	57	4	0	9	23	0	1	12	0	16	0	0	2
Bailor, Tor.	.000	1	2	1	0	0	0	0	0	0	0	0	0	0	0	1	0	0
Baines, Chi.	.500	1	2	0	1	1	0	0	0	0	0	0	0	0	0	0	0	0
Bando, Milw.	.154	15	52	3	8	9	1	0	0	5	0	0	5	0	10	1	1	2
Baylor, Calif.	.223	36	130	14	29	37	5	0	1	18	0	3	13	4	14	1	4	3
Bell, Chi.	.429	3	7	0	3	4	1	0	0	0	0	0	2	0	1	0	0	0
Beniquez, Sea.	.000	1	1	0	0	0	0	0	0	0	0	0	0	0	1	0	0	0
Bochte, Sea.	.395	11	43	7	17	32	4	1	3	8	0	0	5	0	3	0	0	0
Bonnell, Tor.	.273	3	11	0	3	3	0	0	0	0	0	0	0	0	2	0	0	0
Brant, N.Y.	.000	1	1	0	0	0	0	0	0	0	0	0	0	0	1	0	0	0
Braun, K.C.-Tor.	.171	14	35	2	6	9	0	0	1	5	0	0	5	0	3	0	0	2
Brohamer, Bos.-Cle..	.400	4	10	1	4	7	0	0	0	1	1	0	0	0	1	0	0	0
Brookens, Det.	.000	1	1	0	0	0	0	0	0	0	0	0	0	0	0	0	0	0
Brouhard, Milw.	.203	21	69	11	14	26	3	0	3	7	0	0	4	1	12	0	0	2

Player and Club	Pct.	G.	AB.	R.	H.	TB.	2B.	3B.	HR.	RBI.	SH.	SF.	BB.	HP.	SO.	SB.	CS.	GI DP.
Brown, N.Y.	.000	1	1	1	0	0	0	0	0	0	0	0	0	0	1	0	0	0
Butera, Minn.	.000	2	2	0	0	0	0	0	0	0	0	0	0	0	0	0	0	1
Campaneris, Calif.	1.000	2	1	1	1	1	0	0	0	0	0	0	0	0	0	1	0	0
Cannon, Tor.	.000	1	1	0	0	0	0	0	0	0	0	0	0	0	0	0	0	0
Carew, Calif.	.362	32	127	20	46	59	8	1	1	16	1	2	13	1	5	4	2	2
Castillo, K.C.	.500	2	2	0	1	1	0	0	0	0	0	0	0	0	0	0	0	0
Chalk, K.C.	.273	6	22	3	6	7	1	0	0	3	0	0	3	0	1	0	0	2
Chappas, Chi.	.100	2	10	1	1	1	0	0	0	1	1	0	1	0	1	0	0	0
Charboneau, Clev.	.278	57	209	32	58	105	6	1	13	46	0	3	21	0	29	1	0	15
Cooper, Milw.	.317	11	41	4	13	16	0	0	1	6	0	1	3	0	5	0	0	2
Corcoran, Det.	.125	5	8	0	1	1	0	0	0	0	0	0	2	0	2	0	0	0
Cowens, Calif.-Det.	.500	2	2	1	1	4	0	0	1	3	0	0	0	0	0	0	0	0
Crowley, Balt.	.290	65	207	30	60	99	6	0	11	46	1	2	25	0	20	0	0	6
Cruz, Sea.	.429	3	7	2	3	7	1	0	1	1	1	0	1	0	1	2	0	1
Cubbage, Minn.	.000	1	0	0	0	0	0	0	0	0	0	0	1	0	0	0	0	0
Davis, Milw.	.262	63	233	34	61	89	15	2	3	21	0	1	5	2	27	2	2	4
Davis, Oak.	.071	6	14	1	1	1	0	0	0	0	0	0	2	0	3	1	0	0
Dempsey, Balt.	.000	1	1	0	0	0	0	0	0	0	0	0	0	0	1	0	0	0
Dilone, Clev.	.475	11	40	9	19	24	3	1	0	7	0	1	2	1	1	9	1	0
Downing, Calif.	.357	13	42	2	15	21	3	0	1	14	0	2	5	0	3	0	1	2
Dwyer, Bos.	.538	12	39	8	21	24	3	0	0	4	1	0	2	2	1	1	0	1
Dybzinski, Clev.	.000	2	0	0	0	0	0	0	0	0	0	0	0	0	0	0	0	0
Dyer, Det.	.160	10	25	2	4	10	0	0	2	4	2	0	3	0	7	0	0	0
Edwards, Minn.	.000	3	0	1	0	0	0	0	0	0	0	0	1	0	0	1	0	0
Edwards, Oak.	.111	5	9	3	1	1	0	0	0	0	2	0	1	0	0	0	0	1
Elliott, Clev.	.139	11	36	4	5	8	3	0	0	1	0	0	1	0	11	0	0	1
Ellis, Tex.	.242	20	66	6	16	22	4	1	0	8	0	1	3	0	4	0	0	3
Essian, Oak.	.237	11	38	2	9	10	1	0	0	1	0	0	3	0	4	0	0	2
Evans, Bos.	.333	2	3	0	1	1	0	0	0	0	0	0	1	0	2	0	0	0
Fisk, Bos.	.350	5	20	3	7	12	2	0	1	3	0	0	1	0	3	0	1	0
Ford, Calif.	.276	15	58	5	16	19	3	0	0	5	0	1	7	1	11	0	1	4
Gamble, N.Y.	.250	20	52	8	13	21	2	0	2	10	0	1	4	2	4	0	0	0
Garcia, Tor.	.000	1	4	0	0	0	0	0	0	0	1	0	0	0	0	0	0	0
Garr, Calif.	.241	8	29	4	7	8	1	0	0	2	0	0	2	0	4	0	0	0
Gedman, Bos.	.231	4	13	2	3	3	0	0	0	0	0	0	0	0	3	0	0	1
Gibson, Det.	.000	1	0	0	0	0	0	0	0	0	0	0	0	0	0	0	0	0
Gonzales, Det.	.000	1	2	0	0	0	0	0	0	0	0	0	0	0	1	0	0	0
Gonzales, Oak.	.233	8	30	3	7	7	0	0	0	1	0	1	3	0	3	0	0	0
Goodwin, Minn.	.188	38	80	8	15	18	3	0	0	6	1	0	14	0	27	0	0	2
Graham, Balt.	.000	2	4	0	0	0	0	0	0	0	0	0	1	0	1	0	0	0
Gray, Clev.	.129	9	31	3	4	8	1	0	1	1	0	0	3	0	7	0	0	2
Gross, Oak.	1.000	1	1	0	1	1	0	0	0	1	0	0	0	0	0	0	0	0
Grubb, Tex.	.316	8	19	2	6	10	1	0	1	4	0	0	3	0	2	0	1	0
Hancock, Bos.	.320	12	25	2	8	12	1	0	1	4	0	0	0	0	3	0	0	0
Harlow, Calif.	1.000	1	1	1	1	2	1	0	0	1	0	0	0	0	0	0	0	0
Harrah, Clev.	.167	3	6	0	1	1	0	0	0	0	0	0	1	0	0	0	0	0
Hassey, Clev.	.400	7	5	1	2	2	0	0	0	2	0	0	2	0	1	0	0	0
Heath, Oak.	.267	31	105	10	28	34	2	2	0	12	3	0	6	0	11	1	2	3
Hebner, Det.	.182	5	11	1	2	5	0	0	1	2	0	0	3	0	0	0	0	0
Henderson, Oak.	.333	1	6	0	2	2	0	0	0	0	0	0	1	0	0	1	0	0
Hisle, Milw.	.283	17	60	16	17	35	0	0	6	16	0	1	14	1	7	1	1	1
Hobson, Bos.	.177	36	130	9	23	26	0	0	1	10	0	2	7	0	25	0	0	6
Hodgson, Tor.	.000	3	7	1	0	0	0	0	0	0	0	0	1	0	3	0	0	0
Horton, Sea.	.218	92	330	31	72	105	10	1	7	34	2	4	39	4	68	0	4	5
Howell, Tor.	.143	2	7	1	1	2	1	0	0	1	0	0	0	0	1	0	0	0
Iorg, Tor.	.500	2	2	0	1	2	1	0	0	0	0	0	0	0	0	0	0	0
Jackson, N.Y.	.331	46	169	25	56	101	8	2	11	29	0	0	23	1	39	0	0	3
R. Jackson, Minn.	.000	1	1	0	0	0	0	0	0	0	0	0	0	0	0	0	0	0
Johnson, Clev.	.226	45	168	23	38	55	3	1	4	23	0	3	23	0	30	0	1	7
L. Johnson, Chi.	.277	66	253	25	70	99	11	3	4	39	0	3	19	0	24	1	0	8
R. Johnson, Chi.	.182	4	11	0	2	2	0	0	0	1	0	1	0	1	4	0	0	0
Jones, Det.	.133	6	15	2	2	2	0	0	0	1	0	1	5	0	0	0	0	0
Kelly, Balt.	.205	30	88	8	18	27	4	1	1	14	0	1	9	0	31	1	1	3
Kemp, Det.	.325	46	169	31	55	87	6	1	8	27	1	1	25	3	28	4	1	10
Klutts, Oak.	1.000	1	1	0	1	1	0	0	0	0	0	0	0	0	0	0	0	0
Krenchicki, Balt.	.500	1	2	0	1	1	0	0	0	0	0	0	0	0	0	0	0	0
Landreaux, Minn.	.300	6	20	1	6	10	1	0	1	3	1	0	0	0	2	0	0	0
Lemon, Chi.	.217	6	23	1	5	10	2	0	1	1	0	0	1	0	0	0	0	3

Player and Club	Pct.	G.	AB.	R.	H.	TB.	2B.	3B.	HR.	RBI.	SH.	SF.	BB.	HP.	SO.	SB.	CS.	GI DP.
Lentine, Det.	.438	9	16	1	7	8	1	0	0	2	0	0	7	0	4	0	0	0
Lezcano, Milw	.250	4	16	2	4	9	0	1	1	1	0	0	3	0	3	0	0	1
Lowenstein, Balt	.125	3	8	0	1	2	1	0	0	1	0	0	0	0	3	0	0	0
Mackanin, Minn	.500	5	6	3	3	4	1	0	0	1	0	0	1	0	0	0	0	0
May, Balt	.228	58	184	16	42	69	8	2	5	23	0	1	13	0	46	2	0	10
Mayberry, Tor	.167	8	30	3	5	9	1	0	1	4	0	1	2	0	2	0	0	3
McRae, K.C.	.293	110	450	63	132	215	35	3	14	75	0	6	26	6	50	9	2	13
Meyer, Sea	.387	7	31	10	12	26	2	0	4	8	0	1	1	0	0	0	0	0
Milbourne, Sea	.190	8	21	1	4	4	0	0	0	2	0	0	2	0	1	1	0	0
Molinaro, Chi	.319	47	160	27	51	76	9	2	4	16	2	1	16	2	11	5	4	1
Molitor, Milw	.161	7	31	3	5	5	0	0	0	1	1	1	2	0	7	4	2	0
Money, Milw	.313	14	48	6	15	25	4	0	2	8	0	0	5	1	4	0	0	0
Moore, Chi	.200	2	5	0	1	1	0	0	0	0	0	0	0	0	1	0	0	0
Morales, Minn	.304	86	227	34	69	111	17	2	7	32	3	2	20	1	19	0	0	11
Morris, Det	.000	2	0	0	0	0	0	0	0	0	0	0	0	0	0	0	0	0
Morrison, Chi	.000	1	4	0	0	0	0	0	0	0	0	0	0	0	0	0	0	0
Moseby, Tor	.300	6	20	2	6	11	2	0	1	4	0	0	3	0	4	0	0	1
Murcer, N.Y.	.242	33	120	14	29	41	4	1	2	18	0	3	11	0	15	1	0	7
Murray, Balt	.400	1	5	1	2	5	0	0	1	2	0	0	1	0	1	0	0	0
Narron, Sea	.000	1	1	0	0	0	0	0	0	0	0	0	0	0	0	0	0	0
Newman, Oak	.286	9	21	0	6	7	1	0	0	5	1	2	2	0	4	1	1	1
Nichols, Bos	.000	1	0	0	0	0	0	0	0	0	0	0	0	0	0	0	0	0
Nordhagen, Chi	.250	32	120	15	30	53	7	2	4	16	0	1	3	1	14	0	0	3
Norris, Tex	.000	1	1	0	0	0	0	0	0	0	0	0	0	0	0	0	0	0
Norwood, Minn	.000	9	19	0	0	0	0	0	0	0	0	0	0	0	4	0	0	0
Oglivie, Milw	.294	4	17	1	5	9	1	0	1	4	0	1	0	0	1	0	0	0
Oliver, Tex	.333	4	15	2	5	5	0	0	0	1	0	0	1	0	1	0	0	0
Orta, Clev	.400	7	20	2	8	9	1	0	0	5	0	2	0	0	2	0	0	0
Paciorek, Sea	.315	23	92	11	29	43	5	0	3	10	0	0	6	0	13	0	0	2
Page, Oak	.247	101	340	56	84	153	10	4	17	49	4	5	35	1	84	14	7	9
Parrish, Det	.306	16	62	8	19	31	6	0	2	11	0	1	2	0	15	1	1	5
Perez, Bos	.204	13	54	3	11	16	2	0	1	5	0	1	1	0	8	0	0	2
Peters, Det	.172	11	29	4	5	11	1	1	1	4	2	0	3	0	4	0	0	0
Piniella, N.Y.	.118	7	17	1	2	3	1	0	0	0	0	0	0	0	2	0	0	0
Poff, Milw	.200	7	30	1	6	9	0	0	1	3	0	0	2	0	3	0	0	1
Porter, K.C	.275	34	131	14	36	52	5	1	3	28	0	3	21	0	11	0	1	2
Pruitt, Clev-Chi	.179	9	28	1	5	9	1	0	1	2	2	0	2	0	4	0	0	0
Pryor, Chi	.000	1	1	0	0	0	0	0	0	0	1	0	0	0	0	0	0	0
Putnam, Tex	1.000	1	1	1	1	4	0	0	1	1	0	0	1	0	0	0	0	0
Quirk, K.C	.250	1	4	1	1	1	0	0	0	1	0	0	0	0	0	0	0	0
Rader, Bos	.222	9	27	3	6	14	2	0	2	7	0	1	3	0	3	0	0	0
Ramos, Tor	.000	1	4	0	0	0	0	0	0	0	0	0	0	0	2	0	0	0
Rayford, Balt	1.000	1	1	1	1	1	0	0	0	0	0	0	0	0	0	0	0	0
Rettenmund, Calif	.333	1	3	0	1	1	0	0	0	0	0	0	1	0	1	0	0	0
Revering, Oak	.176	5	17	2	3	3	0	0	0	1	0	0	4	0	2	0	0	0
Rice, Bos	.397	15	58	13	23	44	4	1	5	6	1	0	4	0	7	3	0	2
Richardt, Tex	.333	1	3	0	1	1	0	0	0	0	0	0	0	0	0	0	0	0
Rivera, Minn	.000	1	2	0	0	0	0	0	0	0	0	0	1	0	0	0	0	0
Rivers, Tex	.400	4	15	1	6	6	0	0	0	0	0	0	0	0	0	1	0	0
L. Roberts, Sea	.417	4	12	3	5	9	1	0	1	3	0	1	4	1	3	0	0	0
Rosello, Clev	.000	1	0	1	0	0	0	0	0	0	0	0	0	0	0	0	0	0
Rudi, Calif	.182	3	11	0	2	3	1	0	0	1	0	0	1	1	3	0	0	0
Sakata, Balt	1.000	1	1	0	1	1	0	0	0	0	0	0	0	0	0	0	0	0
Sample, Tex	.143	4	7	0	1	1	0	0	0	0	0	0	0	0	1	0	0	0
Singleton, Balt	.450	5	20	2	9	9	0	0	0	4	0	0	1	0	3	0	0	1
Smalley, Minn	.600	3	5	0	3	3	0	0	0	1	0	0	1	0	1	0	0	0
Soderholm, N.Y.	.305	51	151	24	46	78	6	1	8	22	1	0	18	1	11	0	0	5
Sofield, Minn.	.400	2	5	1	2	2	0	0	0	1	0	0	0	0	3	1	0	0
Spencer, N.Y.	.214	15	28	3	6	9	0	0	1	3	0	0	6	0	4	0	0	3
Stapleton, Bos	.375	3	8	2	3	8	0	1	1	5	0	1	0	0	1	0	0	0
Staub, Tex	.291	57	199	29	58	88	10	1	6	37	1	5	23	1	9	1	1	9
Stegman, Det	.000	2	4	0	0	0	0	0	0	0	0	0	1	0	1	0	0	0
Stein, Sea	.167	5	18	0	3	4	1	0	0	1	0	0	0	0	3	0	0	0
Summers, Det	.302	64	199	38	60	104	11	0	11	38	0	3	36	2	33	3	2	6
Terrell, K.C	.000	1	0	1	0	0	0	0	0	0	0	0	0	0	0	0	0	0
Thomas, Milw	.125	2	8	1	1	2	1	0	0	0	0	0	0	0	2	0	0	0
Thompson, Calif	.351	45	148	34	52	89	4	0	11	36	0	2	31	0	28	2	0	4
Thon, Calif	.310	15	58	6	18	23	3	1	0	5	0	1	1	0	5	1	2	1
Torres, K.C	.000	1	0	1	0	0	0	0	0	0	0	0	0	0	0	0	0	0

Player and Club	Pct.	G.	AB.	R.	H.	TB.	2B.	3B.	HR.	RBI.	SH.	SF.	BB.	HP.	SO.	SB.	CS.	GI DP.
Upshaw, Tor	.161	12	31	3	5	6	1	0	0	2	0	0	4	0	7	1	0	0
Vega, Minn................	.179	9	28	2	5	5	0	0	0	3	1	0	3	0	7	1	0	1
Velez, Tor	.269	97	342	51	92	167	12	3	19	59	0	4	51	1	81	0	0	8
Walker, Bos	.130	7	23	0	3	3	0	0	0	3	0	1	2	1	5	1	0	1
Walton, Tex	.000	1	3	1	0	0	0	0	0	0	0	0	1	0	2	0	0	0
Walton, Sea	.256	11	43	4	11	15	4	0	0	4	0	1	1	0	4	1	1	0
Washington, Chi	.600	2	5	1	3	3	0	0	C	2	0	0	0	0	1	0	0	0
Watson, N.Y	.313	21	83	15	26	42	4	0	4	8	0	0	12	0	9	0	1	6
Werth, N.Y................	.133	8	15	3	2	5	0	0	1	1	0	0	0	0	6	0	0	1
Wockenfuss, Det......	.281	28	64	6	18	26	2	0	2	15	0	1	5	0	11	1	1	1
Wolfe, Bos	.167	4	6	1	1	4	0	0	1	2	0	1	0	0	1	0	0	0
Woods, Tor	.147	13	34	3	5	5	0	0	0	3	1	0	4	0	11	0	0	0
Wynegar, Minn	.000	1	1	0	0	0	0	0	0	0	0	0	0	0	1	0	0	0
Yastrzemski, Bos	.270	49	174	23	47	81	11	1	7	25	0	2	24	0	20	0	1	6
Yount, Milw	.343	9	35	7	12	17	2	0	1	1	0	0	2	0	2	2	2	1
Zisk, Tex	.318	86	302	30	96	147	16	1	11	46	1	2	30	0	43	0	2	10

Game-Winning RBIs by designated hitters, listed alphabetically by club, follow: Baltimore (18)—Ayala 2, Crowley 6, Kelly 3, Lowenstein 1, May 3, Sakata 1, Singleton 2. Boston (11)—Dwyer 1, Hobson 1, Rice 2, Stapleton 1, Walker 1, Wolfe 1, Yastrzemski 4. California (7)—Baylor 3, Carew 1, Cowens 1, Downing 1, Harlow 1. Chicago (13)—L. Johnson 7, Molinaro 3, Nordhagen 3. Cleveland (11)—Charboneau 5, Dilone 1, Johnson 4, Orta 1. Detroit (8)—Kemp 3, Summers 3, Wockenfuss 2. Kansas City (11)—McRae 6, Porter 5. Milwaukee (10)—Brouhard 2, Davis 3, Hisle 1, Money 3, Oglivie 1. Minnesota (13)—Adams 5, Goodwin 2, Mackanin 1, Morales 5. New York (16)—Gamble 1, Jackson 6, Murcer 3, Soderholm 3, Spencer 1. Oakland (11)—Heath 3, Newman 3, Page 5. Seattle (5)—Horton 2, Meyer 1, L. Roberts 1, Walton 1. Texas (9)—Ellis 1, Oliver 1, Staub 2, Zisk 5. Toronto (13)—Braun 1, Howell 1, Mayberry 1, Moseby 1, Velez 7, Woods 2.

REGGIE JACKSON—Picked by players as 1980 All-Star designated hitter.

OFFICIAL AMERICAN LEAGUE FIELDING AVERAGES
CLUB FIELDING

Club	Pct.	G.	PO.	A.	E.	TC.	DP.	TP.	PB.
Baltimore	.985	162	4380	1818	95	6293	178	0	11
Cleveland	.983	160	4284	1713	105	6102	143	0	10
Toronto	.979	162	4398	1939	133	6470	206	0	8
Detroit	.979	163	4402	1787	133	6322	165	1	26
Oakland	.979	162	4415	1631	130	6176	115	0	9
New York	.978	162	4393	1852	138	6383	160	0	16
Kansas City	.978	162	4378	1820	141	6339	150	0	15
California	.978	160	4285	1576	134	5995	144	0	10
Minnesota	.977	161	4353	1996	148	6497	192	0	8
Milwaukee	.977	162	4350	1886	147	6383	189	0	6
Seattle	.977	163	4372	1930	149	6451	189	1	13
Boston	.977	160	4324	1937	149	6410	206	0	6
Texas	.977	163	4355	1818	147	6320	169	0	21
Chicago	.973	162	4306	1923	171	6400	162	1	13
Totals	.978	1132	60995	25626	1920	88541	2368	3	172

INDIVIDUAL FIELDING
FIRST BASEMEN

*Throws lefthanded.

Leader—Club	Pct.	G.	PO.	A.	E.	DP.
COOPER, Milw°	.997	142	1336	106	5	160

(Listed Alphabetically)

Player—Club	Pct.	G.	PO.	A.	E.	DP.
Aikens, K.C.	.990	138	1081	65	12	95
Ault, Tor°	1.000	32	198	20	0	21
Bochte, Sea°	.996	133	1273	98	6	143
Brouhard, Milw	1.000	10	50	4	0	3
Carew, Calif	.994	103	897	57	6	82
Cooper, Milw°	.994	142	1336	106	5	160
Corcoran, Det°	.985	48	249	18	4	32
Cubbage, Minn	.996	72	512	44	2	56
Ellis, Tex	.992	39	240	12	2	22
Gonzalez, Oak°	.990	11	89	8	1	7
Goodwin, Minn	1.000	13	87	6	0	6
Gross, Oak	1.000	10	56	6	0	3
Hargrove, Clev°	.993	160	1391	88	10	128
Harris, Calif°	1.000	10	56	2	0	4
Hebner, Det	.998	61	466	35	1	35
Iorg, Tor	1.000	11	27	4	0	8
R. Jackson, Minn.	.991	119	983	74	10	105
L. Johnson, Chi	.990	80	671	56	7	70
LaCock, K.C.°	.997	86	267	21	1	27
Mayberry, Tor°	.994	136	1243	79	8	138
Money, Milw	.986	14	132	9	2	15
Murray, Balt	.994	154	1369	77	9	158
Newman, Oak	.982	60	446	35	9	28
Norris, N.Y.	1.000	10	23	1	0	1
Paciorek, Sea	.982	36	255	19	5	24
Perez, Bos	.993	137	1301	87	10	150
Putnam, Tex	.992	137	979	80	9	107
Revering, Oak	.989	95	724	67	9	56
Spencer, N.Y.°	.990	75	567	41	6	51
Squires, Chi°	.995	114	904	68	5	79
Staub, Tex	.977	30	243	10	6	27
Thompson, Dt-Ca°	1.000	83	679	51	0	66
Upshaw, Tor°	.983	14	51	7	1	11
Wathan, K.C.	.992	12	112	7	1	14
Watson, N.Y.	.990	104	851	63	9	87
Werth, N.Y.	1.000	12	70	3	0	9
Wockenfuss, Det	.983	52	415	35	8	41
Yastrzemski, Bos	.977	16	160	10	4	19

TRIPLE PLAYS: Bochte, Hebner, Squires.

(Fewer Than Ten Games)

Player—Club	Pct.	G.	PO.	A.	E.	DP.
Bando, Milw	.947	7	16	2	1	2
Brant, N.Y.	1.000	2	9	1	0	2
G. Brett, K.C.	1.000	1	4	0	0	1
Crowley, Balt°	1.000	3	19	5	0	1
Davis, Oak°	.980	7	45	5	1	6
DeCinces, Balt	1.000	1	2	0	0	0
Dempsey, Balt	1.000	2	10	1	0	2
Dwyer, Bos°	.976	9	32	8	1	7
Essian, Oak	1.000	1	6	0	0	0
Fisk, Bos	.889	3	8	0	1	0
Foley, Chi	1.000	3	4	0	0	0
Gray, Clev	1.000	6	14	2	0	1
Grich, Calif.	1.000	3	27	1	0	3
Harlow, Calif°	1.000	1	1	0	0	0
Hassey, Clev	1.000	3	15	0	0	1
R. Johnson, Chi°	.000	1	0	0	0	0
Mackanin, Minn	1.000	4	12	2	0	1
May, Balt	1.000	7	57	3	0	4
Meyer, Sea	1.000	4	27	0	0	4
Moore, Chi	1.000	0	1	0	0	0
Morales, Minn	1.000	2	15	0	0	2
Oliver, Tex°	1.000	1	1	0	0	0
Papi, Det	1.000	1	5	0	0	1
Parrish, Det	.977	5	42	1	1	7
Phelps, K.C.°	1.000	2	14	0	0	2
Poff, Milw°	.958	3	23	0	1	0
Pruitt, Chi	.000	1	0	0	0	0
Quirk, K.C.	1.000	1	3	0	0	0
Roberts, Tex.	1.000	4	4	0	0	0
Rudi, Calif.	1.000	6	24	0	0	4
Simpson, Sea°	.895	3	15	2	2	2
Smalley, Minn	1.000	3	16	2	0	3
Stapleton, Bos	.989	8	84	9	1	11
Stein, Sea	1.000	8	51	4	0	4
Summers, Det	.000	1	0	0	0	0
Terrell, K.C.	1.000	3	18	2	0	0
Thon, Calif	1.000	1	3	0	0	0
Vega, Minn.	1.000	2	1	1	0	0
Velez, Tor	.975	3	36	3	1	2

FIRST BASEMAN WITH TWO OR MORE CLUBS

Player—Club	Pct.	G.	PO.	A.	E.	DP.
Thompson, Det	1.000	36	328	30	0	33
Thompson, Calif	1.000	47	351	21	0	33

SECOND BASEMEN

Leader—Club	Pct.	G.	PO.	A.	E.	DP.
WILFONG, Minn.	.995	120	238	337	3	85

(Listed Alphabetically)

Player—Club	Pct.	G.	PO.	A.	E.	DP.
Allen, Sea	.970	15	23	42	2	8
Bannister, Clev	.968	41	77	106	6	20
Brohamer, Bos-Cl	.981	51	79	125	4	27
Chalk, K.C.	.955	17	33	31	3	7
Cox, Oak	.979	58	107	167	6	28
Cruz, Sea	.983	115	269	355	11	85
Dauer, Balt	.991	137	320	368	6	110
Doyle, N.Y.	.953	20	28	33	3	5
Dybzinski, Clev	.961	29	35	63	4	8
Edwards, Oak	.971	23	19	48	2	7
Gantner, Milw	.988	66	118	203	4	53
Garcia, Balt	.989	27	41	52	1	13
Garcia, Tor	.980	138	316	471	16	112
Grich, Calif	.989	146	326	463	9	101
Iorg, Tor	.988	32	67	104	2	29
Kuiper, Clev	.995	42	87	111	1	28
Mackanin, Minn	.968	71	114	191	10	47
McKay, Oak	.977	62	99	151	6	24
Milbourne, Sea	.976	38	55	111	4	28
Molitor, Milw	.971	91	240	294	16	80
Morrison, Chi	.969	161	422	481	29	117
Mulliniks, K.C.	1.000	14	11	19	0	4
Papi, Det	.973	31	53	55	3	14
Picciolo, Oak	.990	47	87	114	2	19
Randolph, N.Y.	.976	138	361	401	19	97
Remy, Bos	.977	60	109	189	7	30
Richardt, Tex	.978	20	32	55	2	11
Romero, Milw	.984	15	26	34	1	6
Rosello, Clev	.980	43	69	75	3	17
Sakata, Balt	.984	34	55	72	2	18
Stanley, N.Y.	.980	17	21	27	1	8
Stapleton, Bos	.979	94	178	327	11	90
Stein, Sea	.986	14	37	36	1	13
Thon, Calif	.988	21	39	46	1	15
Walker, Bos	.958	11	15	31	2	7
Whitaker, Det	.985	143	340	428	12	93
White, K.C.	.988	153	395	448	10	103

Player—Club	Pct.	G.	PO.	A.	E.	DP.
Wilfong, Minn	.995	120	238	337	3	85
Wills, Tex	.984	144	340	473	13	112

TRIPLE PLAYS: Cruz (Sea.), Morrison, Whitaker.

(Fewer Than Ten Games)

Player—Club	Pct.	G.	PO.	A.	E.	DP.
Ainge, Tor	1.000	1	2	3	0	1
Anderson, Sea	1.000	2	1	1	0	0
Bailor, Tor	.000	1	0	0	0	0
Brookens, Det	1.000	9	13	26	0	10
Campaneris, Calif	.000	1	0	0	0	0
Castillo, K.C.	1.000	1	2	5	0	0
Chappas, Chi	1.000	1	0	2	0	1
Cruz, Calif	.750	1	2	1	1	0
Cubbage, Minn	1.000	1	4	2	0	2
Frias, Tex	.667	2	0	2	1	1
Harrelson, Tex	.833	2	3	2	1	1
Harris, Milw	1.000	1	1	0	0	0
Hoffman, Bos	1.000	2	1	0	0	0
Holt, N.Y.	1.000	2	3	9	0	0
Klutts, Oak	.950	7	9	10	1	2
Krenchicki, Balt	1.000	1	0	1	0	0
Lemon, Chi	1.000	1	0	0	0	0
Money, Milw	1.000	2	3	3	0	2
Newman, Oak	1.000	1	0	0	0	0
Pryor, Chicago	1.000	5	5	11	0	2
Ramos, Tor	1.000	2	2	6	0	1
Randall, Minn	1.000	1	0	1	0	0
Rayford, Balt	.833	1	1	4	1	0
Roberts, Tex	1.000	4	2	0	0	0
Rodriguez, N.Y.	.905	6	7	12	2	4
Sherrill, N.Y.	1.000	1	3	1	0	0
Sizemore, Bos	.927	8	16	22	3	7
Terrell, K.C.	1.000	3	3	4	0	2
Wagner, Det	1.000	6	4	5	0	1

SECOND BASEMAN WITH TWO OR MORE CLUBS

Player—Club	Pct.	G.	PO.	A.	E.	DP.
Brohamer, Bos	1.000	4	2	12	0	0
Brohamer, Clev	.979	47	77	113	4	27

SHORTSTOPS

Leader—Club	Pct.	G.	PO.	A.	E.	DP.
DENT, N.Y.	.982	141	224	489	13	77

(Listed Alphabetically)

Player—Club	Pct.	G.	PO.	A.	E.	DP.
J. Anderson, Sea	.958	65	87	188	12	38
Bailor, Tor	1.000	12	24	29	0	7
Belanger, Balt	.975	109	133	258	10	49
Burleson, Bos	.974	155	301	528	22	147
Campaneris, Calif	.957	64	108	157	12	41
Castino, Minn	.951	18	23	55	4	14
Chappas, Chi	.981	19	18	34	1	9
Cruz, Calif-Chi	.948	102	153	320	26	58
Davis, Tex	.880	13	7	15	3	3
Dent, N.Y.	.982	141	224	489	13	77
Doyle, N.Y.	.965	12	12	43	2	9
Dybzinski, Clev	.971	73	107	198	9	37
Frias, Tex	.947	106	117	167	16	38
Garcia, Balt	.974	96	135	240	10	52
Griffin, Tor	.955	155	295	489	37	126
Guerrero, Oak	.962	116	184	276	18	50
Harrelson, Tex	.952	87	118	220	17	57

Player—Club	Pct.	G.	PO.	A.	E.	DP.
Mackanin, Minn	.949	30	42	88	7	27
McKay, Oak	1.000	10	17	25	0	4
Mendoza, Sea	.959	114	149	290	19	68
Milbourne, Sea	.976	34	45	79	3	21
Molitor, Milw	.938	12	19	41	4	10
Mulliniks, K.C.	.981	18	19	34	1	5
Norman, Tex	.943	17	21	45	4	12
Patek, Calif	.953	81	129	199	16	42
Picciolo, Oak	.977	49	76	94	4	20
Pryor, Chi	.975	76	97	248	9	46
Roberts, Tex	.951	33	19	39	3	8
Romero, Milw	.894	22	33	60	11	14
Smalley, Minn	.975	125	210	446	17	100
Stanley, N.Y.	.923	19	16	44	5	9
Thon, Calif	.928	22	24	66	7	12
Trammell, Det	.980	144	225	412	13	89
Veryzer, Clev	.971	108	169	331	15	59
Wagner, Det	.935	28	39	47	6	7
Washington, K.C.	.957	152	237	467	32	86
Yount, Milw	.961	133	239	455	28	89

TRIPLE PLAY: J. Anderson.

SHORTSTOPS—Continued

(Fewer Than Ten Games)

Player—Club	Pct.	G.	PO.	A.	E.	DP.
Allen, Sea	.000	1	0	0	0	0
Ashford, Tex.	1.000	2	1	1	0	0
Bannister, Clev	1.000	2	0	1	0	1
Bell, Chi	.750	3	1	2	1	1
Bell, Tex	.000	3	0	0	0	0
Bonner, Balt	.889	3	2	6	1	1
Brookens, Det	1.000	1	2	2	0	1
Chalk, K.C.	1.000	1	0	1	0	0
Concepcion, K.C.	.833	6	5	10	3	1
Faedo, Minn.	.818	5	4	5	2	0
Gantner, Milw	1.000	1	0	6	0	2
Harrah, Clev.	1.000	2	1	2	0	1
Hoffman, Bos	.875	5	5	9	2	2
Iorg, Tor	1.000	1	3	3	0	1
Klutts, Oak	.957	8	8	14	1	3
Krenchicki, Balt	1.000	6	9	8	0	2
Morrison, Chi	1.000	1	0	1	0	0
Nettles, N.Y.	1.000	1	1	0	0	0
Papi, Det	1.000	5	4	12	0	3
Ramos, Tor	1.000	2	3	4	0	2
Rosello, Cleve	1.000	3	0	1	0	0
Sakata, Balt	1.000	4	0	1	0	0
Sherrill, N.Y.	1.000	2	2	0	0	0
Valdez, Bos	.935	8	17	26	3	10

SHORTSTOP WITH TWO OR MORE CLUBS

Player—Club	Pct.	G.	PO.	A.	E.	DP.
Cruz, Calif	.860	12	15	22	6	6
Cruz, Chi	.956	90	138	298	20	52

THIRD BASEMEN

Leader—Club	Pct.	G.	PO.	A.	E.	DP.
BELL, Tex	.981	120	125	282	8	26

(Listed Alphabetically)

Player—Club	Pct.	G.	PO.	A.	E.	DP.
J. Anderson, Sea	.906	33	31	65	10	7
Ashford, Tex.	.943	12	9	24	2	1
Bailor, Tor	1.000	11	4	16	0	2
Bando, Milw	.934	57	46	110	11	12
Bannister, Chi-Clev.	.902	20	11	44	6	5
Bell, Chi	.925	83	35	151	15	12
Bell, Tex	.981	120	125	282	8	26
G. Brett, K.C	.955	112	103	256	17	28
Brohamer, Bos	.900	13	10	17	3	3
Brookens, Det	.931	138	112	279	29	27
Castino, Minn	.961	138	105	340	18	34
Chalk, K.C.	.964	33	24	56	3	3
T. Cox, Minn	.945	80	47	142	11	20
Cubbage, Minn	.976	32	29	54	2	6
Dauer, Balt	.970	35	14	50	2	5
DeCinces, Balt.	.960	142	120	340	19	41
Edler, Sea	.965	28	18	64	3	6
Gantner, Milw	.938	69	41	126	11	15
Gross, Oak	.948	99	69	130	11	13
Harrah, Clev	.971	156	120	317	13	27
Hebner, Det	.958	32	19	49	3	10
Hobson, Bos	.910	57	52	109	16	5
Hoffman, Bos	.946	110	72	193	15	17
Howell, Tor	.958	138	105	257	16	24
Iorg, Tor	.983	20	13	44	1	7
Klutts, Oak	.947	62	46	80	7	3
Lansford, Calif	.955	150	151	250	19	29
McKay, Oak	.963	54	39	66	4	5
Money, Milw	.940	55	41	117	10	18
Moore, Chi	.929	34	28	64	7	6
Mullins, Clev	.981	21	15	36	1	7
Nettles, N.Y.	.960	88	58	182	10	18
Papi, Bos.-Det	.905	12	6	13	2	1
Pryor, Chi	.942	41	28	85	7	7
Quirk, K.C	.929	28	21	57	6	2
Roberts, Tex	.930	37	19	47	5	2
Rodriguez, N.Y.	.954	49	26	77	5	5
Rosello, Clev	.957	22	7	15	1	1
Soderholm, N.Y	.952	37	15	65	4	4
Stanley, N.Y	.944	12	2	15	1	1
Stein, Sea	.972	34	31	75	3	4
Thon, Calif	.909	10	4	16	2	1
Wolfe, Bos	1.000	14	3	8	0	2

TRIPLE PLAYS: Brookens, Pryor.

(Fewer Than Ten Games)

Player—Club	Pct.	G.	PO.	A.	E.	DP.
Ainge, Tor	1.000	3	0	6	0	0
Allenson, Bos	1.000	5	1	2	0	1
Braun, Tor	1.000	1	0	1	0	0
Castillo, K.C.	1.000	3	0	3	0	0
Cruz, Calif	.750	4	1	2	1	0
Davis, Tex	.000	1	0	0	0	0
Doyle, N.Y.	1.000	2	0	1	0	0
Dybzinski, Clev	1.000	4	4	2	0	2
Fisk, Bos	.000	3	0	0	0	0
Frias, Tex.	1.000	7	7	13	0	1
Graham, Balt	1.000	9	5	7	0	2
Harris, Milw	1.000	2	0	3	0	0
R. Jackson, Minn	.000	2	0	0	0	0
Macha, Tor	.778	2	2	5	2	1
Mackanin, Minn	.800	3	0	4	1	0
Meyer, Sea	.882	5	3	12	2	1
Milbourne, Sea	.889	6	3	5	1	1
Molitor, Milw	1.000	1	1	1	0	0
Newman, Oak	.000	2	0	0	0	0
Pruitt, Clev-Chi	1.000	5	0	1	0	0
Putnam, Tex	.000	1	0	0	0	0
Randall, Minn.	.909	4	1	9	1	1
Rayford, Balt	.900	4	2	7	1	0
Romero, Milw	1.000	3	1	8	0	0
Stapleton, Bos	1.000	2	1	2	0	0
Wagner, Det	.900	9	0	9	1	0
Werth, N.Y.	.000	1	0	0	0	0

THIRD BASEMEN WITH TWO OR MORE CLUBS

Player—Club	Pct.	G.	PO.	A.	E.	DP.
Bannister, Chi	.893	17	8	42	6	5
Bannister, Clev	1.000	3	3	2	0	0
Papi, Bos	.000	1	0	0	0	0
Papi, Det	.905	11	6	13	2	1
Pruitt, Clev	.000	2	0	0	0	0
Pruitt, Chi	1.000	3	0	1	0	0

OUTFIELDERS

Leader—Club	Pct.	G.	PO.	A.	E.	DP.
ROENICKE, Balt....	1.000	113	197	8	0	1

(Listed Alphabetically)

Player—Club	Pct.	G.	PO.	A.	E.	DP.
Adams, Minn.	.947	12	18	0	1	0
Ainge, Tor.	.986	29	67	3	1	2
Alston, Clev.	.947	26	35	1	2	0
Armas, Oak.	.975	158	374	17	10	2
Ayala, Balt.	1.000	19	20	2	0	1
Bailor, Tor.	.991	98	205	16	2	5
Baines, Chi.°	.963	137	229	6	9	1
Bannister, Chi-Cle ..	.981	63	101	2	2	1
Baylor, Calif.	.969	54	119	4	4	0
Beniquez, Sea.	.957	65	176	3	8	0
Blair, N.Y.	1.000	12	8	0	0	0
Bonnell, Tor.	.973	122	271	15	8	3
Bosetti, Tor.	.985	51	124	4	2	0
Bosley, Chi.°	.958	52	91	1	4	0
Brouhard, Milw.	.964	12	27	0	1	0
Brown, N.Y.	.972	131	303	7	9	0
Bumbry, Balt.	.990	160	488	7	5	1
Cannon, Tor.	.968	33	29	1	1	0
Cardenal, K.C.	.970	23	30	2	1	0
Charboneau, Clev. ..	.963	67	125	6	5	1
Clark, Calif.	.982	77	213	6	4	2
Corcoran, Det.°	.963	18	25	1	1	0
Corey, Balt.	1.000	34	20	0	0	0
Cowens, Cal-Det	.989	137	263	11	3	2
Craig, Sea.	.987	63	155	2	2	1
Davis, Milw.	.971	38	63	3	2	2
Davis, Oak.°	1.000	18	31	2	0	0
Detherage, K.C.	1.000	20	16	0	0	0
Dilone, Clev.	.973	118	249	7	7	2
Dwyer, Bos.°	.975	65	111	7	3	2
Edwards, Minn.	.932	72	144	7	11	1
Evans, Bos.	.982	144	268	11	5	7
Ford, Calif.	.940	45	75	3	5	0
Gamble, N.Y.	1.000	49	65	2	0	1
Gibson, Det.°	.992	49	122	1	1	0
Grubb, Tex.	.952	77	112	6	6	1
Hancock, Bos.°	.963	27	49	3	2	0
Harlow, Calif.°	.976	94	234	11	6	5
Harris, Milw.	.967	31	58	1	2	1
Henderson, Oak.°	.984	157	407	15	7	1
Hodgson, Tor.	1.000	11	19	1	0	0
Hurdle, K.C.	.960	126	233	8	10	1
Iorg, Tor.	1.000	14	12	0	0	0
Jackson, N.Y.°	.962	94	174	3	7	0
R. Jackson, Minn.	1.000	15	17	0	0	0
Johnston, Minn.°	1.000	14	25	0	0	0
Jones, Det.	1.000	17	31	0	0	0
Jones, N.Y.°	.988	82	246	4	3	1
Kelly, Balt.°	1.000	36	48	0	0	0
Kemp, Det.°	.995	85	197	4	1	3
Kubski, Calif.	1.000	20	36	2	0	0
Kuntz, Det.	.979	34	45	2	1	1
LaCock, K.C.°	.978	29	44	1	1	1
Landreaux, Minn.	.976	120	231	8	6	0
Lefebvre, N.Y.	.975	71	75	3	2	1
Lemon, Chi.	.981	139	347	11	7	2
Lentine, Det.	.963	55	98	5	4	0
Lezcano, Milw.	.983	108	228	8	4	4
Lowenstein, Balt.	.992	91	128	3	1	0
Lynn, Bos.°	.994	110	302	11	2	4
Manning, Clev.	.990	139	379	7	4	1
Meyer, Sea.	.961	123	189	10	8	2
Miller, Calif.°	.984	118	299	11	5	3

Player—Club	Pct.	G.	PO.	A.	E.	DP.
Molinaro, Chi.	.957	49	85	3	4	0
Moseby, Tor.	.982	104	208	12	4	1
Murcer, N.Y.	.955	59	82	2	4	0
Murphy, Oak.	.990	158	507	13	5	0
Nordhagen, Chi.	.969	74	120	6	4	1
Norris, Tex.°	1.000	82	73	3	0	0
Norwood, Minn.	1.000	17	42	0	0	0
Oglivie, Milw.°	.978	152	384	18	9	3
Oliver, Tex.°	.973	157	314	9	9	2
Orta, Clev.	.982	120	269	10	5	1
Otis, K.C.	.988	105	310	6	4	1
Paciorek, Sea.	1.000	60	105	3	0	1
Peters, Det.	.977	109	296	1	7	1
Piniella, N.Y.	.971	104	157	8	5	1
Powell, Minn.°	.968	129	265	11	9	1
Pruitt, Clev.-Chi.	1.000	17	29	1	0	1
Rice, Bos.	.988	109	233	10	3	2
Rivera, Minn.	.922	37	58	1	5	1
Rivers, Tex.°	.978	141	342	19	8	4
L. Roberts, Sea.	.984	104	238	6	4	1
Roenicke, Balt.	1.000	113	197	8	0	1
Rudi, Calif.	.991	90	220	5	2	1
Sample, Tex.	.973	72	105	2	3	0
Simpson, Sea.°	.977	119	205	10	5	1
Singleton, Balt.	.984	151	248	3	4	1
Sofield, Minn.	.979	126	267	7	6	0
Staub, Tex.	1.000	14	19	4	0	1
Stegman, Det.	.988	57	82	1	1	0
Summers, Det.	.953	47	60	1	3	0
Sutherland, Chi.°	.943	23	50	0	3	0
Thomas, Milw.	.985	160	455	6	7	1
Torres, K.C.	.973	40	67	4	2	1
Walton, Sea.	.929	17	26	0	2	0
Ward, Minn.	1.000	12	14	0	0	0
Washington, Chi.°	.933	23	41	1	3	1
Wathan, K.C.	.982	35	54	1	1	0
Wilson, K.C.	.988	159	482	9	6	1
Wockenfuss, Det.	1.000	23	37	2	0	1
Woods, Tor.°	.991	88	205	5	2	1
Yastrzemski, Bos.	1.000	39	65	3	0	1
Zisk, Tex.	.980	37	45	3	1	1

TRIPLE PLAY: Baines.

(Fewer Than Ten Games)

Player—Club	Pct.	G.	PO.	A.	E.	DP.
Alexander, Clev.	1.000	2	3	0	0	0
Allen, Sea.	1.000	4	3	0	0	0
Ault, Tor.°	1.000	1	2	0	0	0
Bowen, Bos.	1.000	6	17	1	0	0
Braun, K.C.	1.000	5	2	0	0	0
Burgmeier, Bos.°	.000	1	0	0	0	0
Cruz, Calif.	.000	1	0	0	0	0
Dempsey, Balt.	1.000	6	3	0	0	0
Edwards, Oak.	.000	1	0	0	0	0
Fisk, Bos.	1.000	5	13	0	0	0
Garcia, Balt.	1.000	1	1	0	0	0
Garr, Calif.	.750	2	3	0	1	0
Gonzales, Det.	.750	1	3	0	1	0
Gonzalez, Oak.°	1.000	2	6	0	0	0
Graham, Balt.	.000	1	0	0	0	0
Gray, Clev.	1.000	6	2	0	0	0
Harris, Calif.°	1.000	3	7	1	0	0
Hart, Tex.	1.000	2	1	0	0	0
Hazewood, Balt.	1.000	3	1	0	0	0
Heath, Oak.	1.000	8	24	1	0	0
R. Johnson, Chi.° ..	1.000	1	2	0	0	0
McRae, K.C.	1.000	9	17	0	0	0

OUTFIELDERS—Continued

Player—Club	Pct.	G.	PO.	A.	E.	DP.
Moore, Chi.	1.000	3	2	0	0	0
Mora, Clev.	1.000	3	6	0	0	0
Nichols, Bos.	.962	9	24	1	1	0
Parrish, Det.	1.000	5	8	0	0	0
Picciolo, Oak.	1.000	1	1	0	0	0
Poff, Milw.°	1.000	7	15	0	0	0
Quirk, K.C.	1.000	7	6	0	0	0
Remy, Bos.	.000	1	0	0	0	0
Roberts, Tex.	1.000	5	1	0	0	0
Stapleton, Bos.	1.000	6	6	0	0	0
Stieb, Tor.	.000	1	0	0	0	0
Terrell, K.C.	1.000	7	8	0	0	0
Upshaw, Tor.°	.000	1	0	0	0	0
Werth, N.Y.	.917	8	11	0	1	0
Wilborn, N.Y.	1.000	3	6	1	0	1
Wilfong, Minn.	.889	6	7	1	1	0

OUTFIELDERS WITH TWO OR MORE CLUBS

Player—Club	Pct.	G.	PO.	A.	E.	DP.
Bannister, Chi.	1.000	23	35	0	0	0
Bannister, Clev.	.971	40	66	2	2	1
Cowens, Cal.	.969	30	64	3	0	0
Cowens, Det.	.986	107	199	8	3	2
Pruitt, Clev.	1.000	6	9	1	0	1
Pruitt, Chi.	1.000	11	20	0	0	0

CATCHERS

Leader—Club	Pct.	G.	PO.	A.	E.	DP.	PB.
L. COX, Sea.	.993	104	412	45	3	5	6

(Listed Alphabetically)

Player—Club	Pct.	G.	PO.	A.	E.	DP.	PB.
Alexander, Clev.	.971	13	31	2	1	0	0
Allenson, Bos.	.981	24	99	6	2	0	0
Borgmann, Chi.	1.000	32	134	18	0	1	2
Butera, Minn.	.950	32	106	9	6	0	3
Cerone, N.Y.	.990	147	800	73	9	9	14
Cliburn, Calif.	.971	54	127	9	4	0	0
L. Cox, Sea.	.993	104	412	45	3	5	6
Davis, Tor.	.983	89	317	28	6	6	2
Dempsey, Balt.	.987	112	531	54	8	8	5
Diaz, Clev.	.989	75	317	35	4	4	6
Donohue, Calif.	.986	84	330	29	5	5	3
Downing, Calif.	1.000	16	69	6	0	0	0
Dyer, Det.	.986	37	129	10	2	2	3
Essian, Oak.	.987	68	333	46	5	5	3
Fisk, Bos.	.983	115	522	56	10	8	3
Foley, Chi.	.991	64	216	17	2	3	6
Graham, Balt.	.981	73	328	35	7	3	6
Hassey, Clev.	.993	113	549	52	4	8	4
Heath, Oak.	.986	47	268	19	4	5	3
Hill, Sea.	.991	29	101	10	1	0	0
Kimm, Chi.	.985	98	375	26	6	2	3
Martinez, Milw.	.985	76	293	33	5	3	2
Moore, Milw.	.989	105	319	28	4	3	4
Narron, Sea.	.992	39	115	11	1	0	4
Newman, Oak.	.976	55	229	19	6	0	3
Oates, N.Y.	.991	39	99	10	1	1	1
Parrish, Det.	.990	121	557	66	6	8	17
Porter, K.C.	.978	81	322	37	8	6	12
Quirk, K.C.	.966	15	48	9	2	1	2
Rader, Bos.	.981	34	140	15	3	4	3
Roberts, Tex.	.973	22	93	14	3	1	4
Seilheimer, Chi.	.946	21	62	8	4	2	2
Skaggs, Balt.-Cal.	.971	26	94	6	3	3	1
Stinson, Sea.	.979	45	135	8	3	2	3
Sundberg, Tex.	.993	151	853	76	7	7	17
Wathan, K.C.	.982	77	306	25	6	5	1
Whitmer, Calif.	1.000	48	190	12	0	2	6
Whitt, Tor.	.986	105	436	56	7	11	4
Wockenfuss, Det.	.978	25	123	10	3	2	6
Wynegar, Minn.	.988	142	670	72	9	13	5
Yost, Milw.	1.000	15	41	5	0	0	0

(Fewer Than Ten Games)

Player—Club	Pct.	G.	PO.	A.	E.	DP.	PB.
J. Anderson, Sea.	1.000	1	1	1	0	0	0
Ellis, Tex.	1.000	3	4	0	0	0	0
Gedman, Bos.	.867	2	13	0	2	0	0
Gulden, N.Y.	1.000	2	3	0	0	0	1
Kelly, Tor.	1.000	3	17	0	0	0	2
Macha, Tor.	.000	1	0	0	0	0	0
Morales, Minn.	1.000	2	4	0	0	0	0
Pruitt, Chi.	.833	5	5	0	1	0	0
Robinson, N.Y.	1.000	3	5	0	0	0	0
Squires, Chi.°	1.000	2	1	0	0	0	0
Werth, N.Y.	1.000	1	1	0	0	0	0

CATCHER WITH TWO OR MORE CLUBS

Player—Club	Pct.	G.	PO.	A.	E.	DP.	PB.
Skaggs, Balt.	1.000	2	8	1	0	1	0
Skaggs, Cal.	.968	24	86	5	3	2	1

PITCHERS

Leader—Club	Pct.	G.	PO.	A.	E.	DP.
GURA, K.C.	1.000	36	9	50	0	3

(Listed Alphabetically)

Player—Club	Pct.	G.	PO.	A.	E.	DP.
Aase, Calif.	.889	40	10	22	4	2
Abbott, Sea.	.985	31	25	39	1	1
Arroyo, Minn.	.944	21	9	8	1	0
Augustine, Milw.°	1.000	39	1	13	0	2
Babcock, Tex.	1.000	19	0	3	0	0
Bacsik, Minn.	1.000	10	3	3	0	1
Bannister, Sea.°	1.000	32	12	26	1	2
Barker, Clev.	1.000	36	11	24	0	2
Barlow, Tor.	.917	40	2	9	1	0
Barr, Calif.	.846	24	1	10	2	0
Baumgarten, Chi.°	.973	24	5	31	1	3
Beard, Oak.	1.000	13	0	2	0	0
Beattie, Sea.	1.000	33	10	30	0	1
Billingham, De-Bos	1.000	15	1	5	0	0
Bird, N.Y.	1.000	22	3	10	0	1
Boitano, Milw.	1.000	11	0	3	0	0
Burgmeier, Bos.°	1.000	62	7	27	0	5
Burns, Chi.°	.976	34	6	34	1	0
Busby, K.C.	.900	11	5	4	1	0
Buskey, Tor.	1.000	33	5	10	0	1
Caldwell, Milw.°.	.978	34	8	37	1	5
Campbell, Bos.	1.000	23	3	2	0	0

PITCHERS—Continued

Player—Club	Pct.	G.	PO.	A.	E.	DP.
Castro, Milw.	.880	56	7	15	3	3
Christenson, K.C.°	1.000	24	0	8	0	0
Clancy, Tor.	.961	34	14	35	2	2
Clear, Calif.	1.000	58	3	10	0	0
Cleveland, Milw.	1.000	45	17	16	0	1
Comer, Tex.	.917	12	6	5	1	1
Corbett, Minn.	.978	73	13	31	1	1
Cruz, Clev.	.857	55	1	5	1	1
Darwin, Tex.	1.000	53	7	11	0	1
Davis, N.Y.	.964	53	4	23	1	0
Denny, Clev.	.963	16	8	18	1	2
Devine, Tex.	.833	13	2	3	1	0
Dotson, Chi.	.979	33	13	33	1	0
Drago, Bos.	1.000	43	6	17	0	1
Dressler, Sea.	.927	30	8	30	3	3
Eastwick, K.C.	.900	14	3	6	1	0
Eckersley, Clev.	.919	30	10	24	3	0
Erickson, Minn.	.973	32	8	28	1	4
Farmer, Chi.	1.000	64	5	17	0	4
Figueroa, NY-Tex.	.909	23	13	17	3	4
Flanagan, Balt.°	.980	37	6	42	1	2
Flinn, Milw.	1.000	20	6	3	0	0
Ford, Balt.	1.000	25	4	8	0	0
Frost, Calif.	.900	15	2	7	1	1
Gale, K.C.	.973	32	10	26	1	1
Garland, Clev.	1.000	25	14	16	0	0
Garvin, Tor.°	1.000	61	5	14	0	1
Gossage, N.Y.	.846	64	1	10	2	0
Griffin, N.Y.	.929	13	6	7	1	0
Grimsley, Clev.°	.923	14	1	11	1	0
Guidry, N.Y.°	.963	37	16	36	2	4
Gura, K.C.°	1.000	36	9	50	0	3
Haas, Milw.	.943	33	19	31	3	6
Halicki, Calif.	1.000	10	3	1	0	0
Hamilton, Oak.°	1.000	21	2	3	0	0
Hassler, Calif.°	1.000	41	3	8	0	0
Heaverlo, Sea.	.750	60	7	5	4	0
Hiller, Det.°	.833	11	1	4	1	0
Hoffman, Chi.°	1.000	23	1	1	0	0
Honeycutt, Sea.°	.953	30	9	32	2	1
Hough, Tex.	.900	16	2	7	1	0
Hoyt, Chi.	.929	24	1	12	1	0
Hurst, Bos.°	1.000	12	1	4	0	0
D. Jackson, Minn.°	.941	32	9	23	2	4
Jefferson, Tor.	.935	29	5	24	2	1
Jenkins, Tex.	.959	29	24	23	2	3
John, N.Y.°	.984	36	16	46	1	4
Johnson, Tex.°	1.000	33	0	5	0	0
Jones, Oak.	1.000	35	5	10	0	0
Keough, Oak.	.944	34	23	28	3	2
Kern, Tex.	1.000	38	0	12	0	1
Kingman, Oak.	.906	32	7	22	3	2
Kinnunen, Minn.°	1.000	21	6	3	0	0
Kison, Calif.	.813	13	2	11	3	0
Knapp, Calif.	.941	32	2	14	1	0
Koosman, Minn.°	.941	38	7	41	3	2
Kravec, Chi.°	1.000	20	7	13	0	0
Kucek, Tor.	.733	23	1	10	4	1
LaRoche, Calif.°	.955	52	5	16	1	0
Lacey, Oak.°	1.000	47	3	12	0	0
Langford, Oak.	.986	35	28	45	1	1
Leal, Tor.	.909	13	3	7	1	0
Lemanczyk, Tor-Ca	1.000	31	5	15	0	1
Leonard, K.C.	.980	38	9	41	1	4
Lockwood, Bos.	1.000	24	3	3	0	0
Lollar, N.Y.°	.889	14	1	7	1	1
Lopez, Det.	.941	67	5	11	1	1
Lyle, Tex.°	1.000	49	4	10	0	0
MacWhorter, Bos.	.923	14	5	7	1	1
Marshall, Minn.	1.000	18	4	7	0	0
Martin, K.C.	.875	32	10	18	4	5
Martinez, Calif.	.909	30	3	17	2	0
F. Martinez, Balt.°	1.000	53	5	16	0	3
J.D. Martinez, Balt.	1.000	25	5	16	0	1
Matlack, Tex.°	.882	35	5	25	4	0
May, N.Y.°	.939	41	5	26	2	2
McCatty, Oak.	.975	33	13	26	1	2
McClure, Milw.°	1.000	52	3	9	0	0
McGregor, Balt.°	1.000	36	8	28	0	0
McLaughlin, Tor.	1.000	55	12	15	0	2
McLaughlin, Sea.	.900	45	1	8	1	1
Medich, Tex.	.923	34	9	27	3	3
Mirabella, Tor.°	.967	33	9	20	1	1
Mitchell, Milw.	1.000	17	6	16	0	0
Monge, Clev.°	1.000	67	4	6	0	0
Montague, Calif.	1.000	37	4	13	0	1
Moore, Tor.°	.857	31	2	10	2	1
Morris, Det.	.974	36	31	43	2	2
Norris, Oak.	.963	33	25	52	3	3
Owchinko, Clev.°	.955	29	3	18	1	0
Palmer, Balt.	.962	34	14	37	2	6
Parrott, Sea.	.951	27	11	28	2	2
Pattin, K.C.	.929	37	4	9	1	1
Perry, Tex-N.Y.	.978	34	13	32	1	3
Petry, Det.	.936	27	12	32	3	3
Proly, Chi.	1.000	62	10	29	0	2
Quisenberry, K.C.	.958	75	17	29	2	4
Rainey, Bos.	.875	16	4	10	2	2
Rajsich, Tex.°	1.000	24	0	7	0	1
Rawley, Sea.°	.970	59	4	28	1	3
Redfern, Minn.	.905	23	9	10	2	0
Rem'swaal, Bos.	1.000	14	1	1	0	0
Renko, Bos.	1.000	32	14	17	0	1
Robbins, Det.°	1.000	15	2	9	0	0
Roberts, Sea.°	.900	37	3	6	1	0
Robinson, Chi.	1.000	15	3	4	0	0
Rozema, Det.	.974	42	17	21	1	2
Scarbery, Chi.	1.000	15	2	2	0	0
Schatzeder, Det.°	.903	32	7	21	3	3
Schrom, Tor.	1.000	17	3	6	0	0
Sorensen, Milw.	1.000	35	18	30	0	5
Spillner, Clev.	1.000	34	9	17	0	2
Splittorff, K.C.°	1.000	34	14	30	0	4
Stanley, Bos.	.962	52	9	42	2	8
Stanton, Clev.	1.000	51	4	15	0	2
Stewart, Balt.	.913	33	5	16	2	1
Stieb, Tor.	.987	34	20	58	1	8
Stoddard, Balt.	1.000	64	4	9	0	0
Stone, Balt.	.952	37	14	26	2	1
Tanana, Calif.°	1.000	32	12	24	0	1
Tiant, N.Y.	.944	25	13	21	2	3
Tobik, Det.	1.000	17	4	7	0	1
Todd, Tor.	.920	12	7	16	2	3
Torrez, Bos.	.903	36	20	36	6	4
Travers, Milw.°	.968	29	12	18	1	2
Trout, Chi.°	.964	32	11	42	2	3
Tudor, Bos.°	.967	16	5	24	1	1
Twitty, K.C.°	1.000	13	0	5	0	0
Underwood, Det.°	1.000	49	7	16	0	0
Underwood, N.Y.°	.947	38	10	26	2	2
Verhoeven, Minn.	.875	44	4	17	3	2
Waits, Clev.°	.976	33	10	30	1	0

PITCHERS—Continued

Player–Club	Pct.	G.	PO.	A.	E.	DP.
Weaver, Det.	.895	19	8	9	2	2
Wihtol, Clev.	1.000	17	1	2	0	0
Wilcox, Det.	.926	32	14	36	4	1
Williams, Minn.	.875	18	5	9	2	1
Willis, Tor.°	1.000	20	5	2	0	0
Wortham, Chi.°	.833	41	7	18	5	1
Zahn, Minn.°	.980	38	12	37	1	3

(Fewer Than Ten Games)

Player–Club	Pct.	G.	PO.	A.	E.	DP.
Allard, Tex.	.500	5	0	1	1	0
R. Anderson, Sea.	.000	5	0	0	1	0
Aponte, Bos	1.000	4	0	2	0	0
Bailor, Tor.	.000	3	0	0	0	0
Barrios, Chi.	.600	3	0	3	2	0
Boddicker, Balt.	.000	1	0	0	1	0
Bordi, Oak.	1.000	1	0	0	0	0
Botting, Calif.°	.800	6	1	3	1	0
K. Brett, K.C.°	1.000	8	0	3	0	0
Butcher, Tex.	.875	6	1	6	1	0
Camacho, Oak.	.000	5	0	0	0	0
Chamberlain, K.C.	1.000	5	0	2	0	0
Clay, Tex.	.875	8	3	4	1	0
Collins, Clev.°	1.000	4	0	1	0	0
Contreras, Chi.	.714	8	1	4	2	1
Crawford, Bos.	1.000	6	4	2	0	0
Dorsey, Calif.	1.000	4	1	2	0	0
Felton, Minn.	.667	5	0	2	1	0
Ferris, Calif.	1.000	5	0	3	0	0
Fidrych, Det.	1.000	9	5	9	0	0
Gleaton, Tex.°	1.000	5	1	2	0	0
Hartzell, Balt.	1.000	6	0	1	0	0
Holdsworth, Milw.	1.000	9	0	5	0	0

Player–Club	Pct.	G.	PO.	A.	E.	DP.
Jones, K.C.°	.000	3	0	0	0	0
Kaat, N.Y.°	.800	4	1	3	1	1
Kainer, Tex.	1.000	4	1	9	0	1
Keeton, Milw.	1.000	5	4	3	0	1
Kerrigan, Balt.	1.000	1	0	2	0	0
LaPoint, Milw.°	.000	5	0	0	0	0
Lewallyn, Tex.	1.000	4	0	2	0	0
Lysander, Oak.	1.000	5	2	3	0	0
Minetto, Oak.°	.000	7	0	0	0	0
Ojeda, Bos.°	1.000	7	1	3	0	0
Paxton, Clev.	1.000	4	2	0	0	0
Sarmiento, Sea.	1.000	9	1	0	0	0
Schuler, Calif.°	1.000	8	0	1	0	0
Slaton, Milw.	1.000	3	0	3	0	0
Souza, Oak.°	1.000	5	1	0	0	0
Terrell, K.C.	1.000	1	0	1	0	0
Ujdur, Det.	1.000	9	0	1	0	0
Veselic, Minn.	.000	1	0	0	0	0
Wheelock, Sea.	1.000	1	0	1	0	0
Wirth, Oak.	.000	2	0	0	0	0

PITCHERS WITH TWO OR MORE CLUBS

Player–Club	Pct.	G.	PO.	A.	E.	DP.
Billingham, Det.	1.000	8	0	2	0	0
Billingham, Bos.	1.000	7	1	3	0	0
Figueroa, N.Y.	.933	15	4	10	1	4
Figueroa, Tex.	.889	8	9	7	2	0
Lemanczyk, Tor.	1.000	10	2	11	0	1
Lemanczyk, Cal.	1.000	21	3	4	0	0
Perry, Tex.	.973	24	11	25	1	2
Perry, N.Y.	1.000	10	2	7	0	1

EXPLANATION OF ABBREVIATIONS

G—Games Played. AB—At Bats. R—Runs. H—Hits. TB—Total Bases. 2B—Two-Base Hits. 3B—Three-Base Hits. HR—Home Runs. RBI—Runs Batted In. GW—Game-Winning RBI. SH—Sacrifice Hits. SF—Sacrifice Flies. SB—Stolen Base. CS—Caught Stealing. BB—Bases on Balls. IBB—Intentional Bases on Balls. HP—Hit by Pitcher. SO—Strikeouts. Pct.—Percentage. GIDP—Grounded Into Double Plays. Slg. Pct.—Slugging Percentage. OR—Opponents' Runs. LOB—Left on Bases. PO—Putouts. A—Assists. E—Errors. TC—Total Chances. DP—Double Plays. TP—Triple Plays. PB—Passed Balls. G—Games Pitched. GS—Games Started. CG—Complete Games. GF—Games Finished in Relief. ShO—Shutouts. W—Games Won. L—Games Lost. IP—Innings Pitched. BFP—Total Batters Facing Pitcher. ER—Earned Runs. HB—Hit Batsmen. WP—Wild Pitches. Bk—Balks. ERA—Earned-Run Average. Sv—Saves.

Extra-Inning Games for 1980

AMERICAN LEAGUE				NATIONAL LEAGUE			
Club	W.	L.	Pct.	Club	W.	L.	Pct.
Boston	9	5	.643	St. Louis	11	7	.611
Chicago	6	4	.600	Philadelphia	13	9	.591
Kansas City	8	6	.571	Atlanta	8	6	.571
Toronto	10	8	.556	Houston	9	7	.563
Detroit	9	8	.529	Montreal	11	9	.550
New York	10	9	.526	Cincinnati	7	6	.538
Seattle	9	9	.500	Los Angeles	10	9	.526
Texas	9	9	.500	San Diego	6	6	.500
Baltimore	6	6	.500	San Francisco	8	8	.500
Cleveland	6	6	.500	Pittsburgh	8	10	.444
Oakland	8	9	.471	New York	8	13	.381
Minnesota	7	10	.412	Chicago	4	13	.235
California	6	10	.375				
Milwaukee	3	7	.300				

One-Run Decisions for 1980

AMERICAN LEAGUE				NATIONAL LEAGUE			
Club	W.	L.	Pct.	Club	W.	L.	Pct.
Kansas City	29	12	.707	Cincinnati	32	18	.640
New York	30	20	.600	Houston	33	27	.550
Baltimore	28	23	.549	Montreal	33	27	.550
Cleveland	23	21	.523	Atlanta	31	26	.544
Toronto	23	21	.523	Philadelphia	32	28	.533
Boston	25	23	.521	Pittsburgh	32	29	.525
Minnesota	26	26	.500	San Francisco	27	27	.500
Chicago	25	25	.500	Los Angeles	31	33	.484
Detroit	23	23	.500	San Diego	28	36	.438
California	21	24	.467	New York	26	34	.433
Seattle	22	27	.449	Chicago	21	29	.420
Texas	20	30	.400	St. Louis	18	30	.375
Oakland	16	26	.381				
Milwaukee	12	22	.353				

Five Players Hit for Cycle in '80

Twins outfielder Gary Ward broke into the majors with a bang, hitting for the cycle in only his fourth big league game. Ward opened the first game of a doubleheader September 18 by doubling. He added a single in the third inning, a homer in the fifth and a triple in the seventh. However, Minnesota lost to the Brewers, 9-8. It was the first time in the 27-year history of Milwaukee's County Stadium that any player had achieved a cycle.

Ivan DeJesus of the Cubs was the first of five players in 1980 to hit for the cycle, accomplishing the feat in the first five innings, as Chicago downed the Cardinals, 16-12. Randy Hundley had the last Cubs' cycle against Houston in August of 1966.

Fred Lynn of the Red Sox had his cycle and also drove in four runs in a 10-5 win over the Twins May 13. Pittsburgh's Mike Easler accomplished the feat June 12 in a 10-6 triumph over the Reds. Milwaukee's Charlie Moore waited until October 1 to single in the second, homer in the fourth, triple in the sixth and double in the eighth for a 10-7 victory over the Angels.

OFFICIAL AMERICAN LEAGUE PITCHING AVERAGES

CLUB PITCHING

Club	ERA	G.	CG	Sv.	ShO	IP	H.	BFP.	R.	ER.	HR.	SH.	SF.	Tot. BB.	Int. BB.	HB.	SO.	WP.	Bk.
Oakland	3.46	162	94	13	20	1471⅔	1347	6175	642	566	142	46	47	521	29	31	769	51	8
New York	3.58	162	48	50	15	1464⅓	1433	6143	662	583	102	47	56	507	26	25	845	45	3
Baltimore	3.64	162	42	41	14	1460	1438	6131	640	591	134	51	39	502	33	24	789	43	4
Milwaukee	3.71	162	48	30	14	1450	1496	6202	682	597	137	51	58	507	47	25	575	33	6
Kansas City	3.83	162	37	42	10	1459⅓	1530	6150	694	621	129	63	50	465	47	27	614	35	1
Chicago	3.92	162	37	42	12	1435⅓	1434	6199	722	625	108	65	58	563	49	24	724	48	5
Minnesota	3.93	161	35	30	9	1451	1502	6142	724	634	120	67	55	468	44	39	744	32	12
Texas	4.02	163	39	25	6	1451⅔	1561	6305	752	649	119	65	52	519	32	27	890	58	10
Toronto	4.19	162	39	23	9	1466	1523	6369	762	683	135	55	49	635	57	28	705	41	5
Detroit	4.25	163	40	30	9	1467⅓	1505	6335	757	693	152	92	47	558	72	27	741	52	5
Boston	4.38	160	31	43	8	1441⅓	1557	6192	767	701	129	71	49	481	54	31	696	28	6
Seattle	4.38	163	30	26	7	1457⅓	1565	6330	793	709	159	59	49	540	94	39	703	31	3
California	4.52	160	22	30	6	1428⅓	1548	6256	797	717	141	49	56	529	35	39	725	31	8
Cleveland	4.68	160	35	32	8	1428	1519	6221	807	743	137	51	54	552	37	32	843	59	4
Totals	4.03	1132	549	457	132	20331⅔	20958	87150	10201	9112	1844	916	719	7221	646	400	10363	588	85

(BFP total includes six batsmen awarded first base because of interference or obstruction.)

NOTE—Totals for earned runs for several clubs do not agree with the composite totals for all pitchers due to instances in which provisions of Section 10.18 (i) of the Scoring Rules were applied. The following differences are to be noted: Boston pitchers add to 703; Cleveland, 744; Detroit, 694; Kansas City, 623; Milwaukee, 601; New York, 584; Oakland, 571; Seattle, 710; Texas, 652; Toronto, 684.

PITCHERS' RECORDS

(Top Fifteen Qualifiers for Earned-Run Leadership—162 or More Innings)

Pitcher and Club	ERA	W.	L.	Pct.	G.	GS.	CG.	GF.	Sv.	ShO.	H.	BFP.	R.	ER.	HR.	SH.	SF.	Tot. BB.	Int. BB.	HB.	SO.	WP.	Bk.
May, Rudolph, New York°	2.47	15	5	.750	41	17	4	13	3	1	175	690	56	48	14	9	5	39	2	6	133	9	1
Norris, Michael, Oakland	2.54	22	9	.710	33	33	24	0	0	2	215	1135	88	80	17	18	5	83	2	4	180	9	4
Burns, R. Britt, Chicago°	2.84	15	13	.536	34	32	11	1	0	1	213	970	88	75	15	17	6	63	3	1	133	1	4
Keough, Matthew, Oakland	2.92	16	13	.552	34	32	20	0	0	4	211	1041	94	81	24	12	6	94	3	6	121	13	2
Gura, Lawrence, Kansas City°	2.96	18	10	.643	36	36	16	0	0	3	278	1175	107	93	20	12	4	76	5	5	111	2	0
Haas, Bryan, Milwaukee	3.11	16	15	.516	33	33	14	1	0	2	246	1023	96	87	22	6	12	56	6	6	146	7	1
Stone, Steven, Baltimore	3.23	25	7	.781	37	37	9	0	0	1	224	1048	96	90	25	3	9	101	3	3	149	5	0
Erickson, Roger, Minnesota	3.25	7	13	.350	32	27	11	2	0	2	198	811	83	69	13	9	6	56	6	4	97	1	1
Langford, J. Rick, Oakland	3.26	19	12	.613	34	38	28	0	0	2	276	1075	119	108	28	15	5	56	0	1	102	7	0
Clancy, James, Toronto	3.30	13	16	.448	34	34	15	0	0	4	217	1075	108	92	15	12	12	128	4	4	152	5	1
McGregor, Scott, Baltimore°	3.32	20	8	.714	36	36	16	0	0	2	254	1037	101	93	16	10	9	52	8	2	119	10	0
Stanley, Robert, Boston	3.39	10	8	.556	52	16	5	25	14	0	186	737	75	66	11	15	5	58	5	7	71	3	2
John, Thomas, New York°	3.43	22	9	.710	36	36	16	0	0	6	270	1089	115	101	11	15	8	56	5	8	78	0	0
Bannister, Floyd, Seattle°	3.47	9	13	.409	37	37	8	0	0	0	200	918	96	84	24	15	8	66	5	1	155	5	0
Guidry, Ronald, New York°	3.56	17	10	.630	29	29	15	1	0	3	220	929	97	87	19	12	9	80	1	1	166	5	0

°Throws lefthanded.

DEPARTMENTAL LEADERS: W—Stone, 25; L—Kingman, 20; Pct.—Stone, .781; G—Quisenberry, 75; GS—Langford, 38; GF—Quisenberry, 68; Sv—Quisenberry, Gossage, 33; ShO—John, 6; IP—Langford, 290; H—Flanagan, 278; BFP—Gura, 1175; R—Zahn, 138; ER—Leonard, 118; HR—Leonard, 30; SH—Koosman, 17; SF—Morris, 13; Tot. BB—Clancy, 128; Int. BB—Rawley, 16; HB—Trout, 9; SO—Barker, 187; WP—Barker, 14; Bk—Burns, Norris, 4.

(All Pitchers—Listed Alphabetically)

Pitcher and Club	ERA.	W.	L.	Pct.	G.	GS.	CG.	GF.	Sv.	ShO.	IP.	H.	BFP.	R.	ER.	HR.	SH.	SF.	Tot. BB.	Int. BB.	HB.	SO.	WP.	Bk.
Aase, Donald, California	4.06	8	13	.381	40	21	5	6	2	1	175	193	761	83	79	13	12	9	66	3	1	74	2	1
Abbott, W. Glenn, Seattle	4.10	12	12	.500	31	31	7	0	0	2	215	228	903	110	98	27	10	4	49	4	1	78	1	0
Allard, Brian, Texas	5.79	0	0	.000	5	2	0	0	0	0	14	13	67	13	9	1	1	0	10	1	0	10	1	1
Anderson, Richard, Seattle	3.60	0	0	.000	5	2	0	3	0	0	10	13	46	6	4	0	1	2	8	2	0	7	0	0
Aponte, Luis, Boston	1.29	0	0	.000	6	0	0	4	0	0	7	6	28	1	1	1	0	0	2	0	0	4	0	0
Arroyo, Fernando, Minnesota	4.70	6	6	.500	21	11	1	4	0	0	92	97	396	55	48	7	2	6	32	2	2	27	0	0
Augustine, Gerald, Milwaukee*	4.50	4	3	.571	39	1	0	17	0	0	70	83	321	37	35	5	4	3	36	5	3	22	4	0
Bacsik, Michael, Minnesota	4.70	3	3	.500	19	1	0	8	0	0	23	20	98	13	12	5	1	1	13	2	2	15	0	0
Bailor, Robert, Toronto	4.30	0	0	.000	10	0	0	2	0	0	23	26	104	12	11	1	0	0	11	1	0	9	0	0
Bannister, Floyd, Seattle°	3.47	9	13	.409	32	32	8	0	0	2	218	200	918	96	84	24	8	5	66	6	3	155	8	0
Barker, Leonard, Cleveland	4.17	19	12	.613	36	36	8	0	0	0	246	237	1052	127	114	17	9	9	92	4	3	187	14	1
Barlow, Michael, Toronto	4.09	3	1	.750	40	0	0	19	5	0	55	57	237	29	25	7	4	1	23	5	1	19	1	0
Barr, James, California	5.56	1	3	.250	24	7	0	6	0	0	68	90	311	42	42	12	6	2	21	2	1	22	2	0
Barrios, Francisco, Chicago	5.06	2	2	.500	13	6	0	0	0	0	16	21	75	10	9	2	0	1	8	0	1	12	0	0
Baumgarten, Ross, Chicago°	3.44	2	12	.143	24	23	3	0	0	2	136	127	566	60	52	10	6	5	52	0	4	67	6	2
Beard, David, Oakland	3.38	0	0	.000	13	0	0	3	0	0	16	12	64	6	6	0	1	1	6	0	1	17	0	0
Beattie, James, Seattle	4.86	5	15	.250	30	29	4	0	0	0	187	203	831	115	101	19	11	4	98	1	4	96	3	0
Billingham, John, Detroit-Boston	10.13	1	0	1.000	15	4	1	1	0	0	32	56	166	36	36	7	3	0	18	3	1	12	1	0
Bird, J. Douglas, New York	2.65	3	3	.500	22	1	1	7	1	0	51	47	205	16	15	3	4	0	14	2	0	67	1	0
Boddicker, Michael, Baltimore	6.43	0	1	.000	7	1	0	2	0	0	18	26	85	17	16	1	1	0	5	0	0	4	0	0
Boitano, Danny, Milwaukee	8.00	0	0	.000	11	1	0	3	0	0	18	26	85	17	16	1	1	0	11	0	0	11	1	0
Bordi, Richard, Oakland	4.50	0	3	.000	11	6	0	0	0	0	26	40	130	20	17	6	0	1	13	0	0	12	0	0
Botting, Ralph, California*	5.88	0	0	.000	8	0	0	3	0	0	13	8	54	8	8	0	0	0	5	0	0	10	1	0
Brett, Kenneth, Kansas City*	0.00	0	0	.000	8	0	0	5	0	0	13	8	54	2	0	0	5	0	5	2	0	12	0	0
Burgmeier, Thomas, Boston°	2.00	5	4	.556	62	0	0	39	24	0	99	87	391	30	22	5	6	5	20	6	0	54	1	0
Burns, R. Britt, Chicago°	2.84	15	13	.536	34	32	11	2	0	1	238	213	970	83	75	17	10	5	63	3	4	133	7	0
Busby, Steven, Kansas City	6.21	3	4	.429	11	6	0	2	0	0	42	59	199	30	29	3	2	2	19	0	0	12	1	0
Busby, Thomas, Toronto	4.43	3	1	.750	11	0	0	9	0	0	67	68	279	35	33	11	2	6	26	6	0	34	2	0
Butcher, John, Texas	4.11	1	3	.250	6	6	0	0	0	0	35	34	152	19	16	3	1	0	13	0	0	27	1	0
Caldwell, R. Michael, Milwaukee°	4.04	13	11	.542	34	33	11	1	0	2	225	248	940	112	101	29	12	10	56	4	2	74	3	1
Camacho, Ernie, Oakland	6.75	0	0	.000	5	0	0	1	0	0	12	20	61	10	9	1	0	0	9	0	0	7	0	0
Campbell, William, Boston	4.83	4	6	.400	23	0	0	11	0	0	41	44	180	26	22	2	3	2	22	6	2	17	0	0
Castro, William, Milwaukee	2.79	3	4	.429	56	0	0	36	10	0	84	89	350	35	26	3	4	6	17	4	1	32	3	0
Chamberlain, Craig, Kansas City	7.00	1	2	.333	24	4	0	8	0	0	9	10	43	8	7	0	4	1	10	4	0	16	3	0
Christenson, Gary, Kansas City*	5.23	0	1	.000	34	0	0	8	0	0	31	35	148	23	18	4	2	4	18	4	0	16	2	0
Clancy, James, Toronto	3.30	13	16	.448	34	34	15	0	0	0	251	217	1075	107	92	19	9	9	128	4	5	152	10	0
Clay, Kenneth, Texas	4.60	1	1	.500	8	8	0	0	0	0	43	43	202	24	22	4	1	3	29	2	1	17	3	0
Clear, Mark, California	3.31	11	11	.500	58	0	0	41	9	0	106	82	461	45	39	2	8	1	65	5	2	105	7	0
Cleveland, Reginald, Milwaukee	3.74	11	9	.550	45	13	0	16	4	0	154	150	657	73	64	9	5	5	49	9	5	54	4	0
Collins, Donald, Cleveland*	7.50	2	0	1.000	12	0	0	6	0	0	6	6	33	5	5	0	3	0	7	1	0	9	0	0
Comer, Steven, Texas	7.93	4	4	.333	13	11	0	2	0	0	42	65	205	41	37	5	1	1	22	0	2	9	0	0
Contreras, Arnaldo, Chicago	5.79	2	0	1.000	8	0	0	3	0	0	14	18	65	10	9	2	2	0	7	0	1	8	0	0
Corbett, Douglas, Minnesota*	1.99	8	6	.571	73	0	0	63	23	0	136	102	531	41	30	3	7	2	42	8	2	89	8	0
Crawford, Steve, Boston	3.66	2	0	1.000	6	4	2	1	0	0	32	41	142	14	13	3	2	2	8	2	0	10	3	0

Pitcher and Club	ERA.	W.	L.	Pct.	G.	GS.	CG.	GF.	Sv.	ShO.	IP.	H.	BFP.	R.	ER.	HR.	SH.	SF.	Tot. BB.	Int. BB.	HB.	SO.	WP.	Bk.
Cruz, Victor, Cleveland	3.45	6	7	.462	55	0	0	40	12	0	86	71	355	36	33	10	5	10	27	8	3	88	4	0
Darwin, Danny, Texas	2.62	13	4	.765	53	2	0	35	7	0	110	98	468	50	32	9	10	6	50	8	5	104	5	0
Davis, Ronald, New York	2.95	9	3	.750	53	0	0	29	7	0	131	121	544	50	43	9	10	7	32	3	5	65	4	1
Denny, John, Cleveland	4.38	8	6	.571	16	16	4	0	0	0	109	116	464	54	53	4	0	2	47	3	2	59	5	0
Devine, P. Adrian, Texas	4.82	1	1	.500	13	0	0	3	0	0	28	49	142	22	15	4	1	1	9	1	1	8	1	0
Dorsey, James, California	9.00	0	2	.000	4	4	0	0	0	0	16	25	78	16	16	2	0	0	7	2	0	8	1	0
Dotson, Richard, Chicago	4.27	12	10	.545	33	32	3	0	0	1	198	185	863	105	94	20	7	8	87	2	6	109	6	0
Drago, Richard, Boston	4.13	4	7	.364	40	1	0	18	3	0	133	127	564	61	61	12	5	4	44	7	3	63	3	0
Dressler, Robert, Seattle	3.99	4	10	.286	30	14	0	8	0	0	149	161	624	75	66	14	4	8	33	3	3	50	1	0
Eastwick, Rawlins, Kansas City	5.32	0	2	.000	14	0	0	8	0	0	22	37	114	14	13	2	1	1	14	4	1	18	1	0
Eckersley, Dennis, Boston	4.27	12	14	.462	30	30	8	0	0	0	198	188	818	101	94	25	5	6	44	7	2	121	5	1
Erickson, Roger, Minnesota	3.25	7	13	.350	32	30	7	0	0	2	191	198	811	83	69	13	5	6	56	11	4	97	5	0
Farmer, Edward, Chicago	3.33	7	9	.438	64	0	0	55	30	0	100	92	438	37	37	6	2	5	56	11	6	54	5	0
Felton, Terry, Minnesota	7.00	0	3	.000	5	3	0	0	0	0	18	20	83	18	14	2	0	2	9	1	1	14	0	0
Ferris, Robert, California	6.00	0	0	.000	5	0	0	5	0	0	15	20	74	8	10	1	5	0	9	2	0	4	0	0
Fidrych, Mark, Detroit	5.73	2	3	.400	23	9	0	3	0	0	98	152	215	35	28	12	1	6	36	2	2	16	5	0
Figueroa, Eduardo, New York-Texas	6.52	3	10	.231	17	17	1	0	0	0	98	110	462	58	52	11	10	2	31	3	2	25	1	0
Flanagan, Michael, Baltimore°	4.12	16	13	.552	37	37	12	0	0	2	251	189	1065	121	115	27	3	3	71	2	1	128	1	1
Flinn, John, Milwaukee	3.89	4	1	.667	20	0	0	7	0	0	37	31	164	20	16	3	5	2	23	1	2	15	2	0
Ford, David, Baltimore	4.24	3	1	.750	25	1	0	8	1	0	70	66	281	34	28	11	8	3	21	8	1	22	5	0
Frost, David, California	5.31	4	8	.333	25	15	3	2	0	0	78	97	343	43	46	8	7	1	13	2	2	28	0	0
Gale, Richard, Kansas City	3.91	13	9	.591	32	28	5	0	0	1	192	169	799	90	83	16	8	6	78	2	1	97	5	0
Garland, M. Wayne, Cleveland	4.62	6	9	.400	23	20	4	0	0	1	150	169	657	85	77	18	4	4	48	3	1	55	0	0
Garvin, T. Jared, Toronto	2.28	0	0	.000	61	0	0	24	8	1	83	70	336	23	21	6	0	0	27	0	1	52	0	0
Gleaton, Jerry, Texas*	2.57	0	0	.000	6	0	0	2	0	0	30	30	30	12	12	2	9	12	9	7	1	2	0	0
Gossage, Richard, New York	2.27	6	2	.750	64	0	0	58	33	0	99	74	401	29	25	5	4	4	37	8	5	103	1	0
Griffin, Michael, New York	4.83	2	4	.333	13	11	2	0	0	0	54	64	250	36	29	6	4	9	24	10	5	25	3	0
Grimsley, Ross, Cleveland*	6.72	2	5	.444	13	11	2	1	0	0	75	103	342	63	56	11	12	12	23	6	1	18	3	0
Guidry, Ronald, New York	3.56	17	10	.630	36	29	7	3	0	3	219	215	929	96	87	20	9	9	80	6	6	166	3	0
Gura, Lawrence, Kansas City°	2.96	18	10	.643	36	33	16	0	0	4	283	272	1175	107	93	19	14	12	56	0	5	76	5	1
Haas, Bryan, Milwaukee	3.11	16	15	.516	33	33	14	0	0	1	252	246	1023	96	87	25	3	9	56	0	5	146	5	0
Halicki, Edward, California	4.89	0	0	.000	6	3	0	0	0	0	30	39	153	39	23	6	0	4	28	9	3	16	5	0
Hamilton, David, Oakland*	11.40	0	2	.750	11	0	0	3	0	0	18	44	80	22	38	8	0	0	14	0	2	23	0	0
Hartzell, Paul, Baltimore	4.89	5	3	.833	41	0	0	25	4	0	83	67	354	41	23	9	2	2	37	9	0	5	1	0
Hassler, Andrew, California*	2.49	5	1	.100	60	0	0	38	10	0	79	75	341	25	23	3	14	1	35	8	0	75	0	2
Heaverlo, David, Seattle	3.87	1	1	.667	11	0	0	4	0	0	31	38	140	15	13	3	3	7	12	0	3	42	1	0
Hiller, John, Detroit*	4.35	1	0	1.000	11	0	0	9	0	0	20	24	161	12	15	4	7	2	14	7	1	18	0	0
Hoffman, Guy, Chicago*	2.61	0	0	1.000	6	0	0	0	0	0	20	21	93	12	11	3	8	4	17	2	1	24	0	0
Holdsworth, Frederick, Milwaukee	4.50	10	17	.370	30	30	9	0	0	1	203	221	871	99	89	22	0	1	60	0	0	12	7	0
Honeycutt, Frederick, Seattle	3.95	10	17	.370	30	30	3	0	0	2	203	221	871	99	89	22	2	7	60	9	3	79	4	0
Hough, Charles, Texas	3.98	2	9	.500	16	13	0	0	0	0	61	54	270	30	27	8	11	8	37	0	2	47	8	0
Hoyt, D. Lamar, Chicago	4.58	9	2	.750	24	1	0	7	0	0	112	123	496	66	57	6	4	2	41	7	2	55	4	0
Hurst, Bruce, Boston*	9.00	2	2	.500	12	5	2	2	0	0	31	39	147	33	31	8	0	0	16	2	2	41	3	2
Jackson, Darrell, Minnesota*	3.87	9	9	.500	32	25	7	4	0	2	172	161	724	81	74	15	14	4	69	4	4	90	3	0
Jefferson, Jesse, Toronto	5.46	4	13	.235	30	18	2	4	0	2	122	130	535	81	74	12	5	5	69	2	2	53	5	2
Jenkins, Ferguson, Texas	3.77	12	12	.500	29	29	12	0	0	1	198	190	827	90	83	22	5	5	52	8	4	129	5	0

Pitcher and Club	ERA.	W.	L.	Pct.	G.	GS.	CG.	GF.	Sv.	ShO.	IP.	H.	BFP.	R.	ER.	HR.	SH.	SF.	Tot. BB.	Int. BB.	HB.	SO.	WP.	Bk.
John, Thomas, New York°	3.43	22	9	.710	36	36	16	0	0	6	265	270	1089	115	101	13	15	5	56	4	6	78	5	0
Johnson, John, Texas°	2.31	1	3	.250	33	0	0	13	4	0	39	27	154	12	10	2	5	1	15	2	1	44	2	0
Jones, Jeffrey, Oakland	2.86	1	1	.500	35	0	0	10	5	0	44	32	192	21	14	2	5	1	26	1	3	34	5	0
Jones, Michael, Kansas City°	10.80	0	1	.000	4	3	0	0	0	0	5	8	27	7	6	0	1	0	6	0	0	2	1	0
Kaat, James, New York°	7.20	0	0	.000	4	0	0	0	0	0	5	8	24	5	4	0	1	0	2	0	0	1	0	0
Kainer, Donald, Texas	1.80	0	0	.000	5	0	0	0	0	0	20	22	91	7	4	0	2	0	9	0	1	10	0	0
Keeton, Rickey, Milwaukee	4.82	2	2	.500	5	5	1	0	0	0	28	35	127	15	15	4	1	2	9	0	0	8	0	0
Keough, Matthew, Oakland	2.92	16	13	.552	34	32	20	0	0	2	250	218	1041	94	81	24	12	6	94	5	3	121	3	2
Kern, James, Texas	4.86	3	11	.214	32	0	0	15	2	0	63	65	295	38	34	4	5	0	45	10	2	40	1	0
Kerrigan, Joseph, Baltimore	4.50	0	0	.000	4	0	0	0	0	0	2	3	11	1	1	0	0	0	1	0	0	3	1	0
Kingman, Brian, Oakland	3.84	8	20	.286	32	30	10	0	0	0	211	209	912	105	90	21	10	5	82	1	5	116	5	0
Kinnunen, Michael, Minnesota°	5.04	0	0	.000	21	0	0	2	0	0	25	29	112	18	14	0	5	2	13	0	0	8	0	0
Kison, Bruce, California	4.93	3	6	.333	13	13	2	0	0	0	73	73	321	46	40	11	2	1	32	1	4	28	2	0
Knapp, R. Christian, California	6.15	2	11	.154	38	24	8	0	1	0	117	133	535	83	80	18	9	5	51	1	2	46	2	1
Koosman, Jerry, Minnesota°	4.04	16	13	.552	38	38	9	0	0	0	243	252	1022	119	109	24	17	1	69	5	3	149	5	1
Kravec, Kenneth, Chicago°	6.91	3	6	.333	23	15	2	1	0	0	82	100	394	71	63	13	6	4	44	1	1	37	3	0
Kucek, John, Toronto	6.75	3	8	.273	23	12	0	3	0	0	68	83	325	56	51	7	4	1	41	1	0	35	5	0
LaRoche, David, California°	4.08	3	5	.375	52	0	0	31	7	0	128	122	530	65	58	14	5	5	39	7	0	89	3	0
Lacey, Robert, Oakland°	2.93	3	2	.600	47	1	0	10	1	0	80	82	322	29	26	9	12	3	21	3	0	45	3	0
Langford, J. Rick, Oakland	3.26	19	12	.613	35	33	28	1	0	2	290	276	1166	119	105	29	6	2	64	1	6	102	7	0
LaPoint, David, Milwaukee°	6.00	0	4	.000	13	3	0	1	0	0	15	17	70	12	10	1	5	1	13	0	0	5	0	0
Leal, Luis, Toronto	4.50	3	4	.429	31	10	3	10	0	0	60	72	275	35	30	6	7	5	31	0	3	26	3	0
Lemanczyk, David, Tor-Calif.	4.75	4	9	.308	31	10	0	10	0	0	72	75	300	50	38	12	5	4	42	0	4	29	0	0
Leonard, Dennis, Kansas City	3.79	20	11	.645	38	38	19	0	0	2	280	271	1172	127	118	30	13	8	80	1	5	155	12	0
Lewallyn, Dennis, Texas	7.50	0	1	.000	24	0	0	16	0	0	6	27	27	7	5	1	1	0	5	0	0	2	0	0
Lockwood, Claude, Boston	5.28	3	3	.500	24	0	0	16	2	0	46	61	211	31	27	4	3	4	17	1	1	11	0	0
Lollar, W. Timothy, New York°	3.38	1	0	.750	67	0	0	0	0	0	32	33	144	14	12	1	5	1	25	0	0	13	1	0
Lopez, Aurelio, Detroit	3.77	13	6	.684	49	0	0	59	21	0	124	97	534	56	52	15	3	7	28	7	6	97	6	0
Lyle, Albert, Texas°	4.67	3	2	.600	49	0	0	32	8	0	81	97	353	47	42	7	9	3	28	6	3	43	1	0
Lysander, Richard, Oakland	7.71	0	3	.000	18	2	0	5	0	0	14	24	67	13	12	3	1	0	9	0	1	7	0	0
MacWhorter, Keith, Boston	5.57	0	3	.000	18	5	0	5	0	0	42	46	189	27	26	4	3	4	18	2	2	21	1	0
Marshall, Michael, Minnesota	6.19	1	3	.250	20	0	0	12	0	0	32	42	150	32	22	3	12	2	13	3	1	13	1	0
Martin, D. Renie, Kansas City	4.40	10	10	.500	53	23	3	8	0	0	137	133	599	84	67	18	4	4	70	5	4	68	4	0
Martinez, Alfredo, California°	4.53	7	9	.438	25	23	4	0	0	0	149	150	649	81	75	24	9	5	52	2	2	57	5	0
Martinez, Felix, Baltimore°	3.00	4	4	.500	53	0	0	26	8	0	81	69	329	30	27	5	5	1	34	2	1	68	6	0
Martinez, J. Dennis, Baltimore	3.96	6	4	.600	25	12	2	1	0	0	100	103	428	44	44	17	2	6	48	1	2	42	9	0
Matlack, Jonathon, Texas°	3.68	10	10	.500	35	34	8	1	0	3	235	265	985	111	96	12	9	9	48	6	4	142	5	0
May, Rudolph, New York°	2.47	15	5	.750	25	17	3	0	0	3	175	144	690	56	48	13	6	2	39	8	1	133	9	1
McCatty, Steven, Oakland	3.85	14	14	.500	33	31	11	2	0	0	222	204	960	104	95	27	8	9	99	2	6	114	3	0
McClure, Robert, Milwaukee°	3.07	5	8	.385	52	5	0	15	1	0	91	83	390	47	31	6	10	9	37	8	2	47	7	0
McGregor, Scott, Baltimore°	3.32	20	8	.714	36	36	20	0	0	6	252	254	1037	101	93	26	10	3	50	4	1	71	1	0
McLaughlin, Byron, Seattle	6.82	3	6	.333	45	5	0	23	1	0	91	124	439	74	69	15	10	4	50	5	6	41	4	0
McLaughlin, Joey, Toronto°	4.50	6	9	.400	45	10	0	12	0	0	159	159	600	80	68	16	13	3	53	11	4	70	7	0
Medich, George, Texas	3.93	14	11	.560	34	32	6	0	0	1	204	230	877	104	89	13	8	3	56	4	7	91	4	0
Minetto, Craig, Oakland°	7.88	0	2	.000	7	1	0	2	0	0	8	11	38	7	7	2	0	1	7	0	0	5	1	0
Mirabella, Paul, Toronto°	4.33	3	5	.294	33	22	1	4	0	0	131	151	596	73	63	11	9	5	66	3	0	53	4	0
Mitchell, Paul, Milwaukee°	3.54	5	5	.500	17	11	2	1	0	1	89	92	368	40	35	17	5	3	15	1	1	29	0	0

Pitcher and Club	ERA.	W.	L.	Pct.	G.	GS.	CG.	GF.	Sv.	ShO.	IP.	H.	BFP.	R.	ER.	HR.	SH.	SF.	Tot. BB.	Int. BB.	HB.	SO.	WP.	Bk.
Monge, Isidro, Cleveland*	3.54	3	5	.375	67	0	0	42	14	0	94	80	401	39	37	12	4	5	40	6	3	61	2	1
Montague, John, California	5.11	4	2	.667	31	0	0	18	4	0	74	97	330	47	42	8	4	1	21	1	1	22	1	0
Moore, Balor, Toronto*	5.26	1	1	.500	31	0	0	14	1	0	65	76	290	43	38	6	6	5	31	1	4	22	4	2
Morris, John, Detroit	4.18	16	15	.516	37	36	11	0	0	2	250	252	1074	125	116	20	10	13	83	3	4	112	7	4
Norris, Michael, Oakland	2.54	22	9	.710	33	33	24	0	0	1	284	215	1135	88	80	18	9	3	83	6	2	180	9	0
Ojeda, Robert, Boston*	6.92	1	1	.500	7	7	1	0	0	0	26	39	122	20	20	2	0	1	14	0	0	12	1	0
Owchinko, Robert, Cleveland*	5.29	2	9	.182	29	14	4	9	0	0	114	138	516	71	67	13	11	6	47	0	2	66	9	0
Palmer, James, Baltimore	3.98	16	10	.615	34	33	1	0	0	1	224	238	959	108	99	26	6	7	74	0	1	109	0	0
Parrott, Michael, Seattle	7.28	1	16	.059	27	16	1	1	0	0	94	136	442	83	76	16	6	0	42	9	3	53	4	0
Pattin, Martin, Kansas City	3.64	4	4	.500	37	0	0	8	4	0	89	97	378	39	36	4	1	1	23	7	1	40	0	0
Paxton, Michael, Cleveland	12.38	0	1	.000	4	0	0	2	0	0	8	13	40	11	11	1	0	0	6	1	0	9	0	0
Perry, Gaylord, Tex.-N.Y.	3.67	10	13	.435	34	32	6	1	0	3	206	206	884	107	84	14	9	4	64	1	3	135	0	2
Perry, Daniel, Detroit	3.93	10	9	.526	27	25	0	1	0	0	165	156	716	82	72	9	11	8	83	8	1	88	0	1
Proly, Michael, Chicago	3.06	3	6	.333	62	0	0	21	8	0	147	136	618	67	50	7	8	5	58	1	1	56	0	0
Quisenberry, Daniel, Kansas City	3.09	12	7	.632	75	0	0	68	33	0	128	129	528	47	44	5	8	2	27	15	2	37	0	0
Rainey, Charles, Boston	4.86	8	3	.727	16	13	0	2	0	0	87	83	383	47	47	7	2	4	41	2	1	43	1	3
Rajsich, David, Texas*	6.00	2	1	.667	14	0	0	5	2	0	48	56	221	34	32	7	5	2	22	1	2	35	0	0
Rawley, Shane, Seattle*	3.32	7	7	.500	59	0	0	39	13	0	105	103	484	44	42	11	15	4	63	3	0	68	3	1
Redfern, Peter, Minnesota	4.54	7	7	.500	23	16	2	2	0	1	117	117	455	59	59	17	4	1	33	0	0	73	0	0
Remmerswaal, Wilhelmus, Boston	4.63	2	4	.333	14	3	0	5	0	0	35	39	144	18	18	2	1	1	16	0	0	20	1	0
Renko, Steven, Boston	4.20	9	9	.500	32	23	1	3	0	0	165	180	708	86	77	11	5	4	56	0	0	90	0	1
Robbins, Bruce, Detroit*	6.58	0	1	.000	15	6	0	2	0	0	52	60	241	40	38	2	2	1	28	2	1	23	2	0
Roberts, David, Seattle	4.39	2	3	.400	32	13	0	13	3	0	80	86	355	46	39	11	3	0	27	7	0	47	0	0
Robinson, Dewey, Chicago	3.09	2	2	.500	15	0	0	9	0	0	35	26	141	13	12	3	3	3	16	0	3	28	2	0
Rozema, David, Detroit	3.91	6	4	.600	14	13	0	1	0	1	145	140	620	68	63	11	2	2	49	14	0	49	0	0
Sarmiento, Manuel, Seattle	3.60	1	0	1.000	9	0	0	6	1	0	15	14	63	6	6	1	1	0	6	1	2	18	3	0
Scarbery, Randy, Chicago	4.03	2	3	.400	32	9	2	7	2	0	116	116	505	58	52	13	3	3	19	9	0	15	1	0
Schatzeder, Daniel, Detroit*	4.01	11	13	.458	32	26	9	0	0	2	193	178	794	88	86	23	3	7	58	3	3	94	1	0
Schrom, Kenneth, Toronto	5.23	1	1	.500	3	3	0	0	0	0	31	32	140	18	18	3	1	1	19	0	0	13	1	0
Schuler, David, California*	3.46	0	1	.000	17	0	0	6	1	0	13	13	53	5	5	1	0	0	2	0	1	7	0	0
Slaton, James, Milwaukee	4.50	12	9	.545	35	29	8	3	0	1	196	242	839	103	98	13	7	5	45	6	7	54	3	0
Sorensen, Lary, Milwaukee	3.67	12	11	.593	34	30	10	0	0	0	194	225	865	101	94	17	11	5	74	2	2	100	0	0
Souza, K. Mark, Oakland*	7.71	1	0	1.000	5	0	0	3	1	0	7	9	36	6	6	0	0	0	9	1	0	9	0	0
Spillner, Daniel, Cleveland	5.29	16	11	.593	34	30	7	2	0	0	194	236	861	122	114	23	3	8	74	0	6	100	3	0
Splittorff, Paul, Kansas City*	4.15	14	11	.560	34	33	5	0	0	1	175	236	737	101	94	17	11	6	43	3	1	53	1	0
Stanley, Robert, Boston	3.39	10	8	.556	52	17	5	27	14	0	175	186	737	75	66	9	11	4	52	1	0	74	2	0
Stanton, Michael, Cleveland	5.44	1	3	.250	51	0	2	27	5	0	86	98	385	58	52	5	5	1	60	5	8	25	0	1
Stewart, Samuel, Baltimore	3.55	12	7	.632	51	0	0	14	5	0	119	103	507	51	47	12	12	2	38	8	1	78	2	0
Sieb, David, Toronto	3.70	12	15	.444	34	32	14	0	0	0	243	232	1004	108	100	22	12	2	83	6	0	108	2	0
Stoddard, Timothy, Baltimore	2.51	5	3	.625	34	0	0	25	26	0	86	72	352	27	24	2	12	2	38	1	2	64	0	0
Stone, Steven, Baltimore	3.23	25	7	.781	37	37	9	0	0	0	251	224	1048	103	90	22	8	7	101	3	3	149	0	0
Tanana, Frank, California*	4.15	11	12	.478	32	31	7	1	0	0	204	223	870	107	94	28	6	0	45	3	3	113	4	1
Terrell, Jerry, Kansas City	0.00	0	0	.000	1	0	0	1	0	0	1	1	5	0	0	0	0	0	1	0	0	0	0	0
Tiant, Luis, New York	4.90	8	9	.471	25	25	3	0	0	0	136	139	588	79	74	10	6	7	50	5	3	84	3	0
Tobik, David, Detroit	3.98	1	2	.333	17	1	0	6	0	0	61	61	253	27	27	2	0	1	21	1	1	34	2	0
Todd, Jackson, Toronto	4.02	5	2	.714	12	12	4	0	0	0	85	90	361	40	38	14	2	0	30	1	2	44	4	0

Pitcher and Club	ERA	W.	L.	Pct.	G.	GS.	CG.	GF.	Sv.	ShO.	IP.	H.	BFP.	R.	ER.	HR.	SH.	SF.	Tot. BB.	Int. BB.	HB.	SO.	WP.	Bk.
Torrez, Michael, Boston	5.09	9	16	.360	36	32	6	1	0	1	207	256	918	124	117	18	13	11	75	10	1	97	3	3
Travers, William, Milwaukee°	3.92	12	6	.667	29	25	7	1	0	2	154	147	650	76	67	20	2	4	47	5	6	62	9	0
Trout, Steven, Chicago°	3.69	9	16	.360	32	30	7	1	0	2	200	229	866	102	82	14	14	4	49	8	9	89	9	2
Tudor, John, Boston°	3.03	8	5	.615	16	13	0	2	0	0	92	81	382	35	31	4	4	3	31	1	3	45	4	0
Twitty, Jeffrey, Kansas City°	6.14	1	2	.333	13	0	0	2	0	0	22	33	103	17	15	4	1	1	10	0	1	9	0	0
Ujdur, Gerald, Detroit	7.71	1	0	1.000	9	4	0	2	0	0	21	36	107	20	18	5	1	1	15	0	2	8	1	0
Underwood, Patrick, Detroit°	3.58	3	3	.500	33	7	0	24	5	2	113	121	481	51	45	12	5	1	35	7	1	60	0	2
Underwood, Thomas, New York°	3.66	13	9	.591	38	27	4	5	2	2	187	163	771	85	76	15	9	4	66	6	4	116	2	1
Verhoeven, John, Minnesota	3.96	3	3	.429	44	0	0	13	6	0	100	109	425	53	44	10	7	9	29	2	5	42	3	0
Veselic, Robert, Minnesota	4.50	0	1	.000	4	0	0	0	0	0	4	3	15	2	2	0	1	0	1	0	0	3	0	0
Waits, M. Richard, Cleveland°	4.46	13	14	.481	33	33	9	0	0	2	224	231	955	118	112	18	10	6	82	6	1	109	5	2
Weaver, Roger, Detroit	4.08	4	4	.429	19	6	1	6	0	0	64	56	268	32	29	10	2	4	34	0	1	42	1	1
Wheelock, Gary, Seattle	6.00	0	0	.000	3	1	0	1	0	0	3	5	13	2	2	0	0	0	2	0	0	1	0	0
Wihtol, Alexander, Cleveland	3.60	1	0	1.000	17	0	0	10	1	0	35	35	156	18	14	2	3	2	14	2	0	20	1	0
Wilcox, Milton, Detroit	4.48	13	11	.542	32	31	13	1	0	2	199	201	854	112	99	24	7	7	68	5	6	97	5	0
Williams, Alberto, Minnesota	3.51	6	2	.750	18	9	5	5	0	1	77	73	321	33	30	9	0	0	30	1	0	35	3	0
Willis, Michael, Toronto°	1.73	2	1	.667	20	0	0	9	2	0	26	25	114	6	5	3	0	0	11	4	0	14	1	0
Wirth, Alan, Oakland	4.50	0	2	.000	2	0	0	1	0	0	2	2	9	1	1	0	0	0	1	0	0	0	0	0
Wortham, Richard, Chicago°	5.97	2	4	.364	41	10	0	10	3	0	92	102	430	73	61	14	5	5	58	5	3	45	3	0
Zahn, Geoffrey, Minnesota°	4.40	14	18	.438	38	35	13	0	0	0	233	273	993	138	114	17	11	11	66	3	2	96	3	1

NOTE—Following pitchers combined to pitch shutout games: Baltimore (3)—Palmer and F. Martinez 2, J. Dennis Martinez and F. Martinez; Boston (5)—Eckersley and Drago, Tudor, Stanley and Burgmeier, Renko and Stanley, Ojeda and Stanley, Renko, Burgmeier and Stanley; California (3)—Aase, Hassler and Clear, Halicki and Clear, Martinez and Hassler; Chicago (7)—Burns and Farmer 2, Kravec and Farmer, Cleveland, Cleveland and Cruz; Kansas City (2)—Splittorff, Christenson and Quisenberry, Splittorff and Gale; Milwaukee (2)—Travers and Cleveland, Mitchell and McClure; Minnesota (3)—Koosman and Corbett 2, D. Jackson and Corbett; New York (3)—Tiant and Gossage, Underwood and Gossage, Guidry and Gossage; Oakland (1)—Keough and Lacey; Seattle (4)—Honeycutt and Rawley, Abbott and Rawley, Bannister and Rawley, Bannister and Parrott; Texas (2)—Matlack, Kern and Lyle, Matlack and Johnson.

PITCHERS WITH TWO OR MORE CLUBS
(Alphabetically Arranged With Pitcher's First Club on Top)

Pitcher and Club	ERA	W.	L.	Pct.	G.	GS.	CG.	GF.	Sv.	ShO.	IP.	H.	BFP.	R.	ER.	HR.	SH.	SF.	Tot. BB.	Int. BB.	HB.	SO.	WP.	Bk.
Billingham, Detroit	7.71	0	3	.000	7	1	0	4	0	0	7	11	38	6	6	1	0	1	6	1	0	3	0	0
Billingham, Boston	11.25	1	3	.250	7	4	0	4	0	0	24	45	128	30	30	6	2	3	12	0	4	4	1	0
Figueroa, New York	6.98	3	3	.500	15	9	0	4	1	0	58	90	276	47	45	8	3	0	24	0	2	16	1	0
Figueroa, Texas	5.85	0	7	.000	10	8	0	0	0	0	40	62	186	29	26	9	1	3	22	0	2	9	3	1
Lemanczyk, Toronto	5.44	2	5	.286	10	8	0	0	0	0	43	57	195	29	26	4	4	3	15	2	0	10	1	1
Lemanczyk, California	4.30	2	4	.333	21	2	0	6	0	0	67	81	303	40	32	8	3	2	27	0	2	19	2	1
Perry, Texas	3.43	6	9	.400	24	24	4	0	0	2	155	159	655	74	59	12	6	3	46	3	1	107	4	0
Perry, New York	4.41	4	4	.500	10	8	0	2	0	0	51	65	229	33	25	2	3	4	18	0	0	28	5	0

1980 A.L. Pitching Against Each Club

BALTIMORE—100-62

Pitcher	Bos. W-L	Cal. W-L	Chi. W-L	Clev. W-L	Det. W-L	K.C. W-L	Mil. W-L	Min. W-L	N.Y. W-L	Oak. W-L	Sea. W-L	Tex. W-L	Tor. W-L	Totals W-L
Boddicker	0-0	0-0	0-0	0-1	0-0	0-0	0-0	0-0	0-0	0-0	0-0	0-0	0-0	0- 1
Flanagan	1-2	0-1	1-1	0-2	2-0	2-1	0-1	3-0	0-2	3-1	0-1	2-0	2-1	16-13
Ford	0-0	0-0	1-0	0-1	0-0	0-1	0-0	0-0	0-0	0-0	0-0	0-1	0-0	1- 3
Hartzell........	0-0	0-0	0-0	0-0	0-0	0-0	0-0	0-0	0-0	0-0	0-1	0-1	0-0	0- 2
Martinez, D..	1-0	0-0	0-0	0-0	1-0	1-0	1-1	0-0	0-1	0-0	1-1	1-0	0-1	6- 4
Martinez, T..	1-0	0-0	0-1	0-1	1-1	0-0	1-0	0-1	0-0	0-0	0-0	0-0	1-0	4- 4
McGregor.....	1-2	3-0	2-0	2-0	3-0	0-2	0-1	4-0	1-1	1-1	0-1	1-0	2-0	20- 8
Palmer.........	0-1	3-0	1-1	2-1	1-0	1-1	1-1	1-0	2-1	0-1	1-1	1-2	2-0	16-10
Stewart	1-0	1-0	0-2	1-1	1-0	0-0	0-2	1-0	0-0	1-1	1-0	0-1	0-0	7- 7
Stoddard	1-0	1-0	0-0	0-0	0-1	0-0	1-0	0-0	1-1	1-0	0-1	0-0	0-0	5- 3
Stone	2-0	2-1	1-1	1-0	1-1	2-1	3-0	1-1	3-0	1-1	3-0	1-1	4-0	25- 7
Totals ...	8-5	10-2	6-6	6-7	10-3	6-6	7-6	10-2	7-6	7-5	6-6	6-6	11-2	100-62

No Decisions: Kerrigan.

BOSTON—83-77

Pitcher	Balt. W-L	Cal. W-L	Chi. W-L	Clev. W-L	Det. W-L	K.C. W-L	Mil. W-L	Min. W-L	N.Y. W-L	Oak. W-L	Sea. W-L	Tex. W-L	Tor. W-L	Totals W-L
Billingham....	0-0	0-0	0-0	1-1	0-0	0-0	0-0	0-1	0-0	0-0	0-0	0-0	0-1	1- 3
Burgmeier ...	0-0	0-0	0-0	0-0	0-1	0-1	0-1	1-0	1-1	2-0	0-0	1-0	0-0	5- 4
Campbell	0-0	0-0	1-0	0-0	1-0	0-0	0-0	0-0	0-0	1-0	1-0	0-0	0-0	4- 0
Crawford	0-0	0-0	0-0	1-0	0-0	0-0	0-0	0-0	0-0	0-0	0-0	0-0	1-0	2- 0
Drago	1-1	1-0	0-0	0-0	2-0	0-0	0-2	0-1	0-0	0-0	1-1	2-0	0-2	7- 7
Eckersley	1-1	1-0	2-1	1-0	1-1	0-3	1-1	1-0	2-2	0-1	1-1	0-3	1-0	12-14
Hurst	0-0	0-0	0-0	1-0	1-0	0-0	0-0	0-0	0-0	0-0	0-1	0-1	0-0	2- 2
Lockwood ...	0-0	0-0	1-0	0-0	0-0	1-0	0-0	0-0	0-0	1-0	0-1	0-1	0-0	3- 1
MacWhorter.	0-1	0-0	0-0	0-1	0-0	0-0	0-0	0-0	0-0	0-0	0-0	0-0	0-1	0- 3
Ojeda	0-0	0-0	0-0	0-0	0-0	0-0	0-1	0-0	0-0	0-0	1-0	0-0	0-0	1- 1
Rainey	1-0	0-1	0-0	1-1	0-0	2-0	1-0	0-0	0-0	1-1	1-0	0-0	1-0	8- 3
Rem'rswaal..	1-0	0-0	0-0	0-0	0-0	0-0	0-0	1-0	0-0	0-0	0-1	0-0	0-0	2- 1
Renko	0-1	2-1	0-1	0-0	2-0	0-1	2-0	1-1	0-3	0-0	1-1	0-0	1-0	9- 9
Stanley	0-1	2-0	1-1	1-1	0-0	1-2	1-0	1-0	0-1	1-0	1-0	0-1	1-2	10- 8
Torrez	0-3	2-1	0-1	1-1	0-2	0-0	1-3	1-2	0-1	2-1	0-0	1-1	1-0	9-16
Tudor	1-0	1-0	0-0	1-1	1-1	1-0	0-0	0-0	0-2	2-0	0-1	0-0	1-0	8- 5
Totals ...	5-8	9-3	6-4	7-6	8-5	5-7	6-7	6-6	3-10	9-3	7-5	5-7	7-6	83-77

No Decisions: Aponte.

CALIFORNIA—65-95

Pitcher	Balt. W-L	Bos. W-L	Chi. W-L	Clev. W-L	Det. W-L	K.C. W-L	Mil. W-L	Min. W-L	N.Y. W-L	Oak. W-L	Sea. W-L	Tex. W-L	Tor. W-L	Totals W-L
Aase	0-0	0-0	0-1	1-2	0-3	2-0	1-1	0-0	1-1	1-2	1-0	1-1	0-1	8-13
Barr	0-0	0-1	0-1	0-0	0-0	0-0	0-0	0-2	0-0	0-0	0-0	1-0	0-0	1- 4
Botting	0-0	0-0	0-2	0-0	0-0	0-1	0-0	0-0	0-0	0-0	0-0	0-0	0-0	0- 3
Clear............	1-1	0-1	1-0	0-1	1-1	0-2	2-0	0-1	1-1	0-0	2-0	3-1	0-2	11-11
Dorsey	0-0	0-1	0-0	0-0	0-0	0-0	0-0	0-1	0-0	0-0	1-0	0-0	0-0	1- 2
Ferris...........	0-0	0-0	0-0	0-0	0-0	0-1	0-1	0-0	0-0	0-0	0-0	0-0	0-0	0- 2
Frost	0-2	0-2	0-0	1-0	0-0	0-0	0-0	1-1	0-1	0-0	1-1	0-0	1-1	4- 8
Halicki	0-0	0-0	1-0	0-0	0-0	0-0	1-1	0-0	0-0	0-0	0-0	1-0	0-0	3- 1
Hassler	0-0	0-0	0-0	0-0	1-0	0-0	0-0	1-0	0-0	2-0	1-0	0-0	0-0	5- 1
Kison...........	0-1	0-0	0-0	0-1	1-0	1-0	0-0	1-0	0-0	0-3	0-1	0-0	0-0	3- 6
Knapp..........	0-4	1-1	0-0	1-1	0-0	0-0	0-1	0-1	0-0	0-2	0-0	0-0	0-1	2-11
LaRoche	0-1	0-0	0-0	0-0	0-0	1-1	0-0	0-1	0-1	0-0	1-0	0-0	1-1	3- 5
Lemanczyk ..	0-0	0-0	1-1	0-0	0-0	0-0	0-0	1-0	0-2	0-1	0-0	0-0	0-0	2- 4
Martinez	1-1	1-1	0-2	0-1	1-0	0-1	1-0	0-0	0-1	0-0	1-0	2-0	0-2	7- 9
Montague.....	0-0	0-0	0-0	0-0	1-1	0-0	0-0	0-0	0-0	1-0	2-0	0-0	0-1	4- 2
Schuler	0-0	0-0	0-0	0-0	0-0	0-0	0-1	0-0	0-0	0-0	0-0	0-0	0-0	0- 1
Tanana	0-0	1-1	0-3	1-0	0-2	1-2	1-1	3-0	0-1	1-2	1-0	2-0	0-0	11-12
Totals ...	2-10	3-9	3-10	4-6	5-7	5-8	6-6	7-6	2-10	3-10	11-2	11-2	3-9	65-95

No Decisions: None.

CHICAGO—70-90

Pitcher	Balt. W-L	Bos. W-L	Cal. W-L	Clev. W-L	Det. W-L	K.C. W-L	Mil. W-L	Min. W-L	N.Y. W-L	Oak. W-L	Sea. W-L	Tex. W-L	Tor. W-L	Totals W-L
Barrios	0-0	0-0	0-0	0-0	0-0	0-0	0-0	0-0	0-0	0-0	1-0	0-1	0-0	1- 1
Baumgarten	1-0	0-1	1-0	0-1	0-1	0-1	0-1	0-1	0-1	0-2	0-1	0-0	0-2	2-12
Burns	0-2	1-0	3-0	0-2	1-1	2-2	1-1	2-0	1-2	1-1	1-2	1-0	1-0	15-13
Dotson	1-1	2-1	2-0	0-1	0-1	1-0	1-1	1-2	1-0	0-1	1-0	1-1	1-1	12-10
Farmer	1-0	0-0	0-1	1-2	0-1	0-0	0-0	0-1	1-2	1-0	1-0	2-1	0-1	7- 9
Hoffman	0-0	0-0	0-0	0-0	0-0	0-0	0-0	0-0	0-0	1-0	0-0	0-0	0-0	1- 0
Hoyt	0-1	0-1	1-0	2-0	0-0	0-0	2-0	0-0	0-0	0-0	1-1	1-0	2-0	9- 3
Kravec	1-0	0-0	0-0	0-1	0-1	0-1	0-1	1-0	0-1	0-0	0-1	0-0	1-0	3- 6
Proly	1-0	1-1	0-0	0-0	1-1	0-0	0-2	0-1	0-0	1-1	1-0	0-3	0-1	5-10
Robinson	0-0	0-0	1-0	0-0	0-0	0-0	0-0	0-1	0-0	0-0	0-0	0-0	0-0	1- 1
Scarbery	0-0	0-1	0-0	0-0	0-0	0-0	1-0	0-0	0-0	0-0	0-1	0-0	0-0	1- 2
Trout	0-2	0-1	2-1	2-0	0-1	1-2	0-1	1-2	1-1	1-2	0-1	1-0	0-2	9-16
Wortham	1-0	0-0	0-1	0-0	0-3	1-2	0-0	0-0	1-0	1-0	0-0	0-1	0-0	4- 7
Totals	6-6	4-6	10-3	5-7	2-10	5-8	5-7	5-8	5-7	6-7	6-7	6-7	5-7	70-90

No Decisions: Contreras.

CLEVELAND—79-81

Pitcher	Balt. W-L	Bos. W-L	Cal. W-L	Chi. W-L	Det. W-L	K.C. W-L	Mil. W-L	Min. W-L	N.Y. W-L	Oak. W-L	Sea. W-L	Tex. W-L	Tor. W-L	Totals W-L
Barker	2-2	0-0	2-0	1-0	0-2	3-1	0-2	3-0	0-4	2-0	2-1	3-0	1-0	19-12
Cruz	1-0	0-1	0-0	0-2	1-0	0-0	0-1	1-0	0-1	1-1	1-0	1-1	0-0	6- 7
Denny	1-0	1-1	0-2	1-0	0-0	0-1	1-0	1-0	0-0	0-1	1-0	0-0	2-1	8- 6
Garland	0-0	0-1	2-0	1-1	0-0	0-2	0-0	0-2	1-0	1-1	0-1	1-0	0-1	6- 9
Grimsley	0-0	0-1	1-0	1-1	0-0	0-1	0-2	0-0	0-0	0-0	1-0	0-0	1-0	4- 5
Monge	0-1	0-0	0-0	1-1	0-0	0-0	0-0	0-0	1-0	0-0	0-2	0-0	1-1	3- 5
Owchinko	0-2	0-0	0-0	0-0	2-1	0-0	0-3	0-0	0-1	0-0	0-0	0-1	0-1	2- 9
Spillner	1-0	2-2	0-2	2-0	0-3	1-0	2-1	3-0	0-1	1-1	3-0	0-1	1-0	16-11
Stanton	0-0	1-0	0-0	0-0	0-2	0-0	0-0	0-0	0-1	0-0	0-0	0-0	0-0	1- 3
Waits	2-1	2-1	0-0	0-0	0-2	1-2	0-1	1-1	3-0	1-2	0-0	1-3	2-1	13-14
Wihtol	0-0	0-0	1-0	0-0	0-0	0-0	0-0	0-0	0-0	0-0	0-0	0-0	0-0	1- 0
Totals	7-6	6-7	6-4	7-5	3-10	5-7	3-10	9-3	5-8	6-6	8-4	6-6	8-5	79-81

No Decisions: Collins, Paxton.

DETROIT—84-78

Pitcher	Balt. W-L	Bos. W-L	Cal. W-L	Chi. W-L	Clev. W-L	K.C. W-L	Mil. W-L	Min. W-L	N.Y. W-L	Oak. W-L	Sea. W-L	Tex. W-L	Tor. W-L	Totals W-L
Fidrych	0-0	0-1	0-0	1-0	0-0	0-0	0-0	0-1	0-0	0-0	0-0	0-1	1-0	2- 3
Hiller	0-0	0-0	0-0	0-0	0-0	0-0	0-0	0-0	1-0	0-0	0-0	0-0	0-0	1- 0
Lopez	2-0	1-1	2-0	3-0	1-1	0-1	0-1	0-0	1-1	1-0	2-0	0-1	0-0	13- 6
Morris	1-2	0-1	0-0	2-1	2-0	2-2	1-1	1-1	2-1	1-3	1-1	1-2	2-0	16-15
Petry	0-3	1-1	1-1	1-0	1-1	0-0	1-1	0-0	0-1	0-0	2-0	1-0	2-1	10- 9
Robbins	0-0	1-0	0-0	0-0	0-0	0-0	1-0	1-0	0-0	0-1	1-0	0-0	0-0	4- 2
Rozema	0-0	1-1	0-1	1-1	0-0	0-1	0-1	0-2	0-0	0-1	2-0	1-0	1-1	6- 9
Schatzeder	0-1	1-2	1-1	0-0	3-0	0-3	1-1	2-1	0-3	1-1	1-0	0-0	1-0	11-13
Tobik	0-0	0-0	0-0	0-0	0-0	0-0	0-0	0-0	1-0	0-0	0-0	0-0	0-0	1- 0
Ujdur	0-0	0-0	0-0	0-0	0-0	0-0	1-0	0-0	0-0	0-0	0-0	0-0	0-0	1- 0
Underwood	0-0	0-0	0-1	0-0	1-1	0-1	0-1	1-0	0-0	0-0	0-1	0-1	1-0	3- 6
Weaver	0-1	0-0	0-0	0-0	1-0	0-0	0-0	0-0	0-1	1-0	0-0	0-1	1-1	3- 4
Wilcox	0-3	0-1	3-0	2-0	1-0	0-2	2-0	1-1	0-1	2-0	1-0	1-2	0-1	13-11
Totals	3-10	5-8	7-5	10-2	10-3	2-10	7-6	6-6	5-8	6-6	10-2	4-8	9-4	84-78

No Decisions: Billingham.

KANSAS CITY—97-65

Pitcher	Balt. W-L	Bos. W-L	Cal. W-L	Chi. W-L	Clev. W-L	Det. W-L	Mil. W-L	Min. W-L	N.Y. W-L	Oak. W-L	Sea. W-L	Tex. W-L	Tor. W-L	Totals W-L
Busby	0-0	0-1	0-0	0-1	0-1	0-0	1-0	0-0	0-0	0-0	0-0	0-0	0-0	1-3
Chamberlain	0-0	0-0	0-0	0-0	0-0	0-0	0-0	0-0	0-0	0-1	0-0	0-0	0-0	0-1
Christenson	0-0	0-0	0-0	1-0	0-0	0-0	0-0	0-0	0-0	0-0	0-0	1-0	1-0	3-0
Eastwick	0-0	0-0	0-0	0-0	0-0	0-0	0-0	0-0	0-0	0-0	0-0	0-0	0-1	0-1
Gale	1-2	1-1	0-1	1-0	1-1	0-0	1-1	0-1	2-0	1-1	1-0	3-0	1-1	13-9
Gura	2-2	0-0	2-2	3-1	1-0	2-0	2-0	0-3	3-0	0-0	1-1	0-0	2-0	18-10
Jones	0-0	0-0	0-0	0-0	0-0	0-0	0-0	0-0	0-0	0-1	0-0	0-0	0-0	0-1
Leonard	0-1	4-0	3-0	1-1	3-0	2-1	1-2	1-1	0-2	1-1	0-1	2-0	2-1	20-11
Martin	0-1	1-1	2-1	1-0	0-2	1-1	0-1	1-1	2-0	1-1	1-1	0-0	0-0	10-10
Pattin	0-0	0-0	0-0	0-0	1-0	1-0	0-0	0-0	0-0	0-0	1-0	0-0	1-0	4-0
Quisenberry	1-0	1-1	1-0	0-0	0-0	2-0	1-1	1-1	1-0	1-1	2-1	2-2	0-0	12-7
Splittorff	2-0	0-1	0-1	1-2	1-1	2-0	1-1	2-1	2-2	2-0	0-2	1-0	2-0	14-11
Twitty	0-0	0-0	0-0	0-0	0-0	0-0	0-0	0-0	0-0	0-0	1-0	1-1	0-0	2-1
Totals	6-6	7-5	8-5	8-5	7-5	10-2	6-6	5-8	8-4	6-7	7-6	10-3	9-3	97-65

No Decisions: K. Brett, Terrell.

MILWAUKEE—86-76

Pitcher	Balt. W-L	Bos. W-L	Cal. W-L	Chi. W-L	Clev. W-L	Det. W-L	K.C. W-L	Minn. W-L	N.Y. W-L	Oak. W-L	Sea. W-L	Tex. W-L	Tor. W-L	Totals W-L
Augustine	0-1	0-0	0-0	1-0	1-0	0-0	0-0	1-0	0-1	0-0	0-0	0-1	1-0	4-3
Boitano	0-0	0-0	0-0	0-1	0-0	0-0	0-0	0-0	0-0	0-0	0-0	0-0	0-0	0-1
Caldwell	0-2	1-1	1-1	1-0	3-0	1-2	0-2	0-0	2-0	0-1	2-1	2-0	0-1	13-11
Castro	0-0	0-0	1-1	0-0	0-0	0-1	1-0	0-0	0-0	0-0	0-1	0-0	0-1	2-4
Cleveland	2-1	3-1	1-1	0-1	0-1	2-0	0-0	0-0	0-1	3-1	0-0	0-2	0-0	11-9
Flinn	0-0	1-0	0-0	0-0	0-0	0-0	0-0	1-0	0-0	0-0	0-0	0-0	0-0	2-1
Haas	2-0	0-1	0-1	4-0	1-2	1-1	1-2	1-1	2-1	2-2	1-0	0-2	1-2	16-15
Keeton	0-0	0-0	0-0	0-0	0-0	0-0	1-0	0-1	0-0	0-0	0-1	0-0	1-0	2-2
LaPoint	0-0	0-0	0-0	0-0	0-0	0-0	0-0	0-0	0-0	0-0	0-0	1-0	0-0	1-0
McClure	0-2	0-0	1-1	0-1	1-0	0-1	1-0	0-1	0-0	0-1	2-0	0-1	0-0	5-8
Mitchell	0-0	0-1	0-0	0-0	1-0	0-0	1-1	1-1	0-0	0-1	1-0	1-0	0-0	5-5
Slaton	0-0	0-0	0-0	1-0	0-0	0-0	0-0	0-0	0-0	0-0	0-0	0-0	0-1	1-1
Sorensen	2-0	2-2	1-1	0-2	1-0	0-0	2-0	2-1	0-1	0-0	1-0	1-0	0-3	12-10
Travers	0-1	0-0	1-0	0-0	0-0	2-0	1-2	1-1	0-2	2-0	1-0	1-0	2-0	12-6
Totals	6-7	7-6	6-6	7-5	10-3	6-7	6-6	7-5	5-8	7-5	9-3	5-7	5-8	86-76

No Decisions: Holdsworth.

MINNESOTA—77-84

Pitcher	Balt. W-L	Bos. W-L	Cal. W-L	Chi. W-L	Clev. W-L	Det. W-L	K.C. W-L	Mil. W-L	N.Y. W-L	Oak. W-L	Sea. W-L	Tex. W-L	Tor. W-L	Totals W-L
Arroyo	0-2	1-0	1-0	2-0	0-1	1-0	0-0	0-0	0-0	0-1	0-1	1-0	0-1	6-6
Corbett	0-2	1-1	0-0	0-0	0-0	0-0	1-0	0-1	0-0	3-1	1-0	0-0	1-1	8-6
Erickson	0-1	0-2	1-0	0-0	1-1	0-2	0-2	1-2	0-0	0-2	0-1	3-0	1-0	7-13
Felton	0-0	0-0	0-1	0-0	0-0	0-0	0-0	0-0	0-0	0-0	0-2	0-0	0-0	0-3
Jackson, D.	0-1	0-0	0-1	0-2	1-1	3-1	2-1	0-0	1-2	0-0	1-0	0-0	1-0	9-9
Koosman	0-0	1-1	2-1	1-2	0-2	1-0	3-1	2-1	2-2	1-1	2-0	1-1	0-1	16-13
Marshall	0-1	0-0	0-1	1-0	0-0	0-0	0-0	0-0	0-0	0-0	0-1	0-0	0-0	1-3
Redfern	1-0	1-1	0-0	0-0	0-2	0-0	1-0	1-2	0-0	1-1	2-0	0-1	0-0	7-7
Verhoeven	1-0	0-1	0-0	1-0	0-0	0-0	0-0	0-0	0-1	0-0	0-0	0-1	1-1	3-4
Williams	0-0	1-0	0-1	1-0	0-1	1-0	0-0	1-0	0-0	0-0	0-0	2-0	0-0	6-2
Zahn	0-3	1-1	0-1	2-1	1-1	0-3	1-1	0-1	1-3	1-1	1-1	2-0	3-1	14-18
Totals	2-10	6-6	6-7	8-5	3-9	6-6	8-5	5-7	4-8	6-7	7-6	9-3	7-5	77-84

No Decisions: Bacsik, Kinnunen, Veselic.

NEW YORK—103-59

Pitcher	Balt. W-L	Bos. W-L	Cal. W-L	Chi. W-L	Clev. W-L	Det. W-L	K.C. W-L	Mil. W-L	Min. W-L	Oak. W-L	Sea. W-L	Tex. W-L	Tor. W-L	Totals W-L
Bird	0-0	0-0	0-0	1-0	0-0	0-0	1-0	0-0	1-0	0-0	0-0	0-0	0-0	3- 0
Davis	1-0	2-0	1-0	1-0	1-0	0-0	0-1	1-0	0-0	1-0	0-0	0-2	1-0	9- 3
Figueroa	0-0	1-0	0-0	0-1	0-1	0-0	0-0	0-1	0-0	1-0	0-0	1-0	0-0	3- 3
Gossage	0-0	0-0	3-0	0-0	1-1	0-0	1-0	1-0	0-1	0-0	0-0	0-0	0-0	6- 2
Griffin	0-0	0-0	0-0	0-1	0-0	1-2	0-1	0-0	0-0	0-0	0-0	0-0	1-0	2- 4
Guidry	0-2	1-1	1-0	0-1	2-0	3-1	2-1	2-0	2-1	0-1	1-2	1-0	2-0	17-10
John	2-1	2-1	0-0	3-0	2-0	0-2	0-1	2-0	3-0	2-1	4-0	1-1	1-2	22- 9
Kaat	0-0	0-0	0-0	0-1	0-0	0-0	0-0	0-0	0-0	0-0	0-0	0-0	0-0	0- 1
Lollar	0-0	0-0	0-0	0-0	0-0	1-0	0-0	0-0	0-0	0-0	0-0	0-0	0-0	1- 0
May	0-0	3-0	3-1	2-0	0-0	1-0	2-0	0-1	2-1	0-0	1-0	0-0	1-0	15- 5
Perry	1-0	0-1	1-0	0-0	1-1	0-0	0-0	0-0	0-0	0-0	1-1	0-0	0-1	4- 4
Tiant	1-1	1-0	0-1	0-0	1-0	0-0	0-3	0-2	0-1	2-1	0-0	1-0	2-0	8- 9
Underwood	1-3	0-0	1-0	0-1	0-1	1-0	0-0	0-1	2-0	1-1	3-0	2-2	2-0	13- 9
Totals	6-7	10-3	10-2	7-5	8-5	8-5	4-8	8-5	8-4	8-4	9-3	7-5	10-3	103-59

No Decisions: None.

OAKLAND—83-79

Pitcher	Balt. W-L	Bos. W-L	Cal. W-L	Chi. W-L	Clev. W-L	Det. W-L	K.C. W-L	Mil. W-L	Min. W-L	N.Y. W-L	Sea. W-L	Tex. W-L	Tor. W-L	Totals W-L
Beard	0-0	0-0	0-0	0-0	0-0	0-0	0-0	0-1	0-0	0-0	0-0	0-0	0-0	0- 1
Hamilton	0-0	0-1	0-0	0-0	0-0	0-0	0-1	1-0	0-0	0-0	0-0	0-0	0-0	0- 3
Jones	0-2	0-0	0-0	0-0	0-0	0-1	0-0	0-0	0-0	0-0	1-0	0-0	0-0	1- 3
Keough	1-1	1-1	1-2	0-1	2-0	2-1	2-1	1-0	2-1	1-1	1-1	1-2	1-1	16-13
Kingman	0-1	0-1	2-0	2-2	1-2	1-2	0-3	0-1	1-3	1-1	0-2	0-1	0-1	8-20
Lacey	0-0	0-1	0-0	0-1	0-0	0-0	1-0	1-0	0-0	0-0	0-0	0-0	1-0	3- 2
Langford	1-2	0-1	3-0	2-1	1-1	1-1	2-0	1-2	1-2	1-2	3-0	1-1	2-1	19-12
McCatty	2-1	0-1	1-0	1-0	1-2	1-0	1-0	1-2	1-2	0-3	2-2	2-1	1-0	14-14
Minetto	0-0	0-1	0-0	0-0	0-0	0-1	0-0	0-0	0-0	0-0	0-0	0-0	0-0	0- 2
Norris	1-0	2-2	3-0	2-1	1-1	1-0	1-1	1-1	2-0	1-1	1-0	3-1	3-1	22- 9
Totals	5-7	3-9	10-3	7-6	6-6	6-6	7-6	5-7	7-6	4-8	8-5	7-6	8-4	83-79

No Decisions: Bordi, Camacho, Lysander, Souza, Wirth.

SEATTLE—59-103

Pitcher	Balt. W-L	Bos. W-L	Cal. W-L	Chi. W-L	Clev. W-L	Det. W-L	K.C. W-L	Mil. W-L	Min. W-L	N.Y. W-L	Oak. W-L	Tex. W-L	Tor. W-L	Totals W-L
Abbott	2-0	1-1	1-1	1-1	1-1	0-0	1-0	1-0	0-2	1-2	1-1	1-1	1-2	12-12
Bannister	2-1	1-0	0-1	2-0	0-2	0-2	1-1	0-2	1-1	0-0	0-0	1-1	1-2	9-13
Beattie	0-1	0-2	0-1	1-0	1-1	0-3	2-0	1-1	0-0	0-3	0-1	0-2	0-0	5-15
Dressler	0-1	1-1	0-2	1-1	0-0	0-1	0-1	0-1	0-0	0-1	1-0	0-0	1-1	4-10
Heaverlo	0-0	1-0	0-2	0-1	2-0	1-0	0-0	0-0	0-0	0-0	1-0	1-0	0-0	6- 3
Honeycutt	0-1	0-1	1-1	2-1	0-1	1-2	1-1	0-2	3-1	0-3	1-1	0-1	1-1	10-17
McLaughlin	0-0	1-0	0-0	0-0	0-1	0-1	1-0	0-1	1-0	0-0	0-3	0-0	0-0	3- 6
Parrott	0-1	0-2	0-1	0-1	0-1	0-1	0-2	0-2	0-2	0-0	0-1	0-3	1-0	1-16
Rawley	1-0	0-0	0-2	0-1	0-1	0-0	0-0	1-0	1-1	1-0	1-1	1-1	1-0	7- 7
Roberts, D.	1-1	0-0	0-0	0-0	0-0	0-0	0-2	0-0	0-0	1-0	0-0	0-0	0-0	2- 3
Sarmiento	0-0	0-0	0-0	0-1	0-0	0-0	0-0	0-0	0-0	0-0	0-0	0-0	0-0	0- 1
Totals	6-6	5-7	2-11	7-6	4-8	2-10	6-7	3-9	6-7	3-9	5-8	4-9	6-6	59-103

No Decisions: R. Anderson, Wheelock.

TEXAS—76-85

Pitcher	Balt. W-L	Bos. W-L	Cal. W-L	Chi. W-L	Clev. W-L	Det. W-L	K.C. W-L	Mil. W-L	Min. W-L	N.Y. W-L	Oak. W-L	Sea. W-L	Tor. W-L	Totals W-L
Allard	0-0	0-0	0-0	0-0	0-0	0-0	0-0	0-1	0-0	0-0	0-0	0-0	0-0	0-1
Babcock	0-0	0-0	0-0	0-0	0-0	0-0	1-1	0-0	0-0	0-0	0-0	0-0	0-1	1-2
Butcher	0-0	0-0	0-1	0-0	0-0	0-0	0-0	0-0	0-1	0-0	1-1	2-0	0-0	3-3
Clay	0-0	0-0	0-1	0-0	0-0	1-0	0-0	0-1	0-1	0-0	0-0	0-0	1-0	2-3
Comer	0-1	0-0	0-0	0-0	0-0	1-1	0-0	0-0	1-1	0-1	0-0	0-0	0-0	2-4
Darwin	1-0	2-0	1-0	1-1	2-0	1-0	0-1	1-0	1-0	0-0	2-1	1-1	0-0	13-4
Devine	0-0	0-1	1-0	0-0	0-0	0-0	0-0	0-0	0-0	0-0	0-0	0-0	0-0	1-1
Figueroa	0-0	0-1	0-0	0-0	0-1	0-1	0-2	0-0	0-0	0-0	0-1	0-0	0-1	0-7
Hough	0-1	0-0	0-1	1-0	0-0	0-0	0-0	0-0	0-0	0-0	0-0	0-0	1-0	2-2
Jenkins	3-1	0-0	0-1	0-2	0-2	1-1	0-0	1-0	0-2	2-1	1-0	2-1	2-1	12-12
Johnson	0-0	0-1	0-0	0-0	0-0	0-0	1-1	0-0	0-0	0-0	0-0	0-0	0-0	2-2
Kern	0-2	0-1	0-3	2-1	1-1	0-0	0-0	0-1	0-0	0-0	0-0	0-1	0-1	3-11
Lyle	0-0	0-0	0-0	0-0	0-0	0-1	0-1	0-0	0-0	2-0	0-0	1-0	0-0	3-2
Matlack	1-0	1-1	0-1	1-0	1-0	2-0	0-1	1-1	0-3	1-1	1-1	0-1	1-0	10-10
Medich	0-0	2-0	0-3	2-1	2-1	1-0	0-0	2-1	0-1	0-2	1-1	2-0	2-1	14-11
Perry	1-1	2-0	0-0	0-0	0-1	1-0	0-2	0-1	1-0	0-2	0-2	1-0	0-0	6-9
Rajsich	0-0	0-0	0-0	0-1	0-0	0-0	1-0	1-0	0-0	0-0	0-0	0-0	0-0	2-1
Totals	6-6	7-5	2-11	7-6	6-6	8-4	3-10	7-5	3-9	5-7	6-7	9-4	7-5	76-85

No Decisions: Gleaton, Kainer, Lewallyn.

TORONTO—67-95

Pitcher	Balt. W-L	Bos. W-L	Cal. W-L	Chi. W-L	Clev. W-L	Det. W-L	K.C. W-L	Mil. W-L	Min. W-L	N.Y. W-L	Oak. W-L	Sea. W-L	Tex. W-L	Totals W-L
Barlow	1-0	0-0	0-0	0-0	0-0	0-0	0-0	1-0	1-0	0-0	0-1	0-0	0-0	3-1
Buskey	0-0	0-1	0-0	0-0	2-0	0-0	0-0	0-0	0-0	0-0	0-0	1-0	0-0	3-1
Clancy	0-3	1-2	3-0	1-2	0-2	1-0	1-2	1-1	0-0	0-4	0-0	2-0	2-0	13-16
Garvin	0-0	1-0	1-0	0-0	0-1	1-1	0-1	0-0	0-0	0-0	0-2	0-1	1-1	4-7
Jefferson	0-0	0-1	0-1	0-1	1-1	0-1	0-3	0-0	0-3	0-0	2-0	1-1	0-1	4-13
Kucek	0-0	0-0	0-1	1-1	0-1	0-2	0-1	1-0	0-0	0-1	0-1	1-0	0-0	3-8
Leal	0-2	1-0	0-1	0-0	0-0	0-0	0-0	0-0	0-0	2-0	0-0	0-0	0-1	3-4
Lemanczyk	0-0	0-1	1-0	0-0	1-1	0-0	0-0	0-0	0-0	0-0	0-0	0-2	0-0	2-5
McLaughlin	1-0	0-1	2-0	1-0	0-0	0-1	0-1	1-2	1-0	0-1	0-1	0-0	0-2	6-9
Mirabella	0-2	1-0	1-0	0-1	0-1	0-1	0-1	2-0	0-2	0-2	1-1	0-1	0-0	5-12
Moore	0-0	0-0	0-0	0-0	0-0	0-0	0-0	0-1	0-0	0-0	0-0	1-0	0-0	1-1
Schrom	0-0	0-0	0-0	1-0	0-0	0-0	0-0	0-0	0-0	0-0	0-0	0-0	0-0	1-0
Stieb	0-3	1-1	1-0	2-0	1-1	1-2	1-0	2-1	0-2	0-2	1-1	1-1	1-1	12-15
Todd	0-0	1-0	0-0	1-0	0-0	0-1	0-0	0-0	2-0	1-0	0-0	0-0	0-1	5-2
Willis	0-1	0-0	0-0	0-0	0-0	1-0	1-0	0-0	0-0	0-0	0-0	0-0	0-0	2-1
Totals	2-11	6-7	9-3	7-5	5-8	4-9	3-9	8-5	5-7	3-10	4-8	6-6	5-7	67-95

No Decisions: Bailor.

Four Hurlers Beat Every Club

Even though Bob Welch of the Dodgers finished the 1980 season with only a 14-9 won-lost mark, he was able to notch a victory over each National League club. The Phillies' Steve Carlton defeated each club en route to his 24-9 record, while Baltimore's Steve Stone (25-7) and Oakland's Mike Norris (22-9) achieved the feat against each club in the A.L.

Rick Honeycutt of the Mariners was the only unfortunate pitcher to taste defeat at the hands of each club as part of his 10-17 1980 record.

AMERICAN LEAGUE

PENNANT WINNERS

Year Club	Manager	W.	L.	Pct.	°G.A.
1901—Chicago	Clark Griffith	83	53	.610	4
1902—Philadelphia	Connie Mack	83	53	.610	5
1903—Boston	James Collins	91	47	.659	14½
1904—Boston	James Collins	95	59	.617	1½
1905—Philadelphia	Connie Mack	92	56	.622	2
1906—Chicago	Fielder Jones	93	58	.616	3
1907—Detroit	Hugh Jennings	92	58	.613	1½
1908—Detroit	Hugh Jennings	90	63	.588	½
1909—Detroit	Hugh Jennings	98	54	.645	3½
1910—Philadelphia	Connie Mack	102	48	.680	14½
1911—Philadelphia	Connie Mack	101	50	.669	13½
1912—Boston	Garland Stahl	105	47	.691	14
1913—Philadelphia	Connie Mack	96	57	.627	6½
1914—Philadelphia	Connie Mack	99	53	.651	8½
1915—Boston	William Carrigan	101	50	.669	2½
1916—Boston	William Carrigan	91	63	.591	2
1917—Chicago	Clarence Rowland	100	54	.649	9
1918—Boston	Edward Barrow	75	51	.595	2½
1919—Chicago	William Gleason	88	52	.629	3½
1920—Cleveland	Tristram Speaker	98	56	.636	2
1921—New York	Miller Huggins	98	55	.641	4½
1922—New York	Miller Huggins	94	60	.610	1
1923—New York	Miller Huggins	98	54	.645	16
1924—Washington	Stanley (Bucky) Harris	92	62	.597	2
1925—Washington	Stanley (Bucky) Harris	96	55	.636	8½
1926—New York	Miller Huggins	91	63	.591	3
1927—New York	Miller Huggins	110	44	.714	19
1928—New York	Miller Huggins	101	53	.656	2½
1929—Philadelphia	Connie Mack	104	46	.693	18
1930—Philadelphia	Connie Mack	102	52	.662	8
1931—Philadelphia	Connie Mack	107	45	.704	13½
1932—New York	Joseph McCarthy	107	47	.695	13
1933—Washington	Joseph Cronin	99	53	.651	7
1934—Detroit	Gordon (Mickey) Cochrane	101	53	.656	7
1935—Detroit	Gordon (Mickey) Cochrane	93	58	.616	3
1936—New York	Joseph McCarthy	102	51	.667	19½
1937—New York	Joseph McCarthy	102	52	.662	13
1938—New York	Joseph McCarthy	99	53	.651	9½
1939—New York	Joseph McCarthy	106	45	.702	17
1940—Detroit	Delmer Baker	90	64	.584	1
1941—New York	Joseph McCarthy	101	53	.656	17
1942—New York	Joseph McCarthy	103	51	.669	9
1943—New York	Joseph McCarthy	98	56	.636	13½
1944—St. Louis	J. Luther Sewell	89	65	.578	1
1945—Detroit	Stephen O'Neill	88	65	.575	1½
1946—Boston	Joseph Cronin	104	50	.675	12
1947—New York	Stanley (Bucky) Harris	97	57	.630	12
1948—Cleveland†	Louis Boudreau	97	58	.626	1
1949—New York	Charles (Casey) Stengel	97	57	.630	1
1950—New York	Charles (Casey) Stengel	98	56	.636	3
1951—New York	Charles (Casey) Stengel	98	56	.636	5
1952—New York	Charles (Casey) Stengel	95	59	.617	2
1953—New York	Charles (Casey) Stengel	99	52	.656	8½
1954—Cleveland	Alfonso Lopez	111	43	.721	8
1955—New York	Charles (Casey) Stengel	96	58	.623	3
1956—New York	Charles (Casey) Stengel	97	57	.630	9
1957—New York	Charles (Casey) Stengel	98	56	.636	8
1958—New York	Charles (Casey) Stengel	92	62	.597	10
1959—Chicago	Alfonso Lopez	94	60	.610	5
1960—New York	Charles (Casey) Stengel	97	57	.630	8

PENNANT WINNERS—Continued

Year	Club	Manager	W.	L.	Pct.	°G.A.
1961—New York	Ralph Houk	109	53	.673	8
1962—New York	Ralph Houk	96	66	.593	5
1963—New York	Ralph Houk	104	57	.646	10½
1964—New York	Lawrence (Yogi) Berra	99	63	.611	1
1965—Minnesota	Sabath (Sam) Mele	102	60	.630	7
1966—Baltimore	Henry A. Bauer	97	63	.606	9
1967—Boston	Richard H. Williams	92	70	.568	1
1968—Detroit	E. Mayo Smith	103	59	.636	12
1969—Baltimore (E)°°	Earl S. Weaver	109	53	.673	19
1970—Baltimore (E)°°	Earl S. Weaver	108	54	.667	15
1971—Baltimore (E)°°	Earl S. Weaver	101	57	.639	12
1972—Oakland (W)°°	Richard H. Williams	93	62	.600	5½
1973—Oakland (W)°°	Richard H. Williams	94	68	.580	6
1974—Oakland (W)°°	Alvin Ralph Dark	90	72	.556	5
1975—Boston (E)°°	Darrell D. Johnson	95	65	.594	4½
1976—New York (E)°°	Alfred M. Martin	97	62	.610	10½
1977—New York (E)°°	Alfred M. Martin	100	62	.617	2½
1978—New York (E)†°°	Alfred M. Martin, Robert G. Lemon	100	63	.613	1
1979—Baltimore (E)°°	Earl S. Weaver	102	57	.642	8
1980—Kansas City (W)°°	James G. Frey	97	65	.599	14

°Games ahead of second-place club.   †Defeated Boston in one-game playoff.

°°Won Championship Series.

YEARLY FINISHES

Year	Balt.	Bos.	Calif.	Chi.	Cleve.	Det.	Minn.	N.Y.	Oak.	Wash.
1901	a8	2	....	1	7	3	‡6	z5	†4	....
1902	°2	3	....	4	5	7	‡6	z8	†1	....
1903	°6	1	....	7	3	5	‡8	4	†2	....
1904	°6	1	....	3	4	7	‡8	2	†5	....
1905	°8	4	....	2	5	3	‡7	6	†1	....
1906	°5	8	....	1	3	6	‡7	2	†4	....
1907	°6	7	....	3	4	1	‡8	5	†2	....
1908	°4	5	....	3	2	1	‡7	8	†6	....
1909	°7	3	....	4	6	1	‡8	5	†2	....
1910	°8	4	....	6	5	3	‡7	2	†1	....
1911	°8	5	....	4	3	2	‡7	6	†1	....
1912	°7	1	....	4	5	6	‡2	8	†3	....
1913	°8	4	....	5	3	6	‡2	7	†1	....
1914	°5	2	....	x6	8	4	‡3	x6	†1	....
1915	°6	1	....	3	7	2	‡4	5	†8	....
1916	°5	1	....	2	6	3	‡7	4	†8	....
1917	°7	2	....	1	3	4	‡5	6	†8	....
1918	°5	1	....	6	2	7	‡3	4	†8	....
1919	°5	6	....	1	2	4	‡7	3	†8	....
1920	°4	5	....	2	1	7	‡6	3	†8	....
1921	°3	5	....	7	2	6	‡4	1	†8	....
1922	°2	8	....	5	4	3	‡6	1	†7	....
1923	°5	8	....	7	3	2	‡4	1	†6	....
1924	°4	7	....	8	6	3	‡1	2	†5	....
1925	°3	8	....	5	6	4	‡1	7	†2	....
1926	°7	8	....	5	2	6	‡4	1	†3	....
1927	°7	8	....	5	6	4	‡3	1	†2	....
1928	°3	8	....	5	7	6	‡4	1	†2	....
1929	°4	8	....	7	3	6	‡5	2	†1	....
1930	°6	8	....	7	4	5	‡2	3	†1	....
1931	°5	6	....	8	4	7	‡3	2	†1	....
1932	°6	8	....	7	4	5	‡3	1	†2	....
1933	°8	7	....	6	4	5	‡1	2	†3	....
1934	°6	4	....	8	3	1	‡7	2	†5	....
1935	°7	4	....	5	3	1	‡6	2	†8	....
1936	°7	6	....	3	5	2	‡4	1	†8	....
1937	°8	5	....	3	4	2	‡6	1	†7	....
1938	°7	2	....	6	3	4	‡5	1	†8	....

YEARLY FINISHES—Continued

Year	Balt.	Bos.	Calif.	Chi.	Cleve.	Det.	Minn.	N.Y.	Oak.	Wash.
1939	°8	2	....	4	3	5	†6	1	†7	....
1940	°6	x4	....	x4	2	1	†7	3	†8	....
1941	x°6	2	....	3	x4	x4	x†6	1	†8	....
1942	°3	2	....	6	4	5	†7	1	†8	....
1943	°6	7	....	4	3	5	†2	1	†8	....
1944	°1	4	....	7	x5	2	†8	3	x†5	....
1945	°3	7	....	6	5	1	†2	4	†8	....
1946	°7	1	....	5	6	2	†4	3	†8	....
1947	°8	3	....	6	4	2	†7	1	†5	....
1948	°6	2	....	8	1	5	†7	3	†4	....
1949	°7	2	....	6	3	4	†8	1	†5	....
1950	°7	3	....	6	4	2	†5	1	†8	....
1951	°8	3	....	4	2	5	†7	1	†6	....
1952	°7	6	....	3	2	8	†5	1	†4	....
1953	°8	4	....	3	2	6	†5	1	†7	....
1954	7	4	....	3	1	5	†6	2	†8	....
1955	7	4	....	3	2	5	†8	1	†6	....
1956	6	4	....	3	2	5	†7	1	†8	....
1957	5	3	....	2	6	4	†8	1	†7	....
1958	6	3	....	2	4	5	†8	1	†7	....
1959	6	5	....	1	2	4	†8	3	†7	....
1960	2	7	....	3	4	6	†5	1	†8	....
1961	3	6	§8	4	5	2	7	1	x†9	x9
1962	7	8	§3	5	6	4	2	1	†9	10
1963	4	7	§9	2	x5	x5	3	1	†8	10
1964	3	8	§5	2	x6	4	x6	1	†10	9
1965	3	9	§7	2	5	4	1	6	†10	8
1966	1	9	6	4	5	3	2	10	†7	8
1967	x6	1	5	4	8	x2	x2	9	†10	x6
1968	2	4	x8	x8	3	1	7	5	6	10

	EAST DIVISION						WEST DIVISION					
Year	Balt.	Bos.	Cleve.	Det.	N.Y.	Wash.	Mil.	Calif.	Chi.	K.C.	Mil.	Minn.	Oak.	Tex.
1969	1	3	6	2	5	4	....	3	5	4	y6	1	2	....
1970	1	3	5	4	2	6	....	3	6	x4	x4	3	2	....
1971	1	3	6	2	4	5	....	4	3	3	6	5	1	....
1972	3	2	5	1	4	....	6	5	2	4		3	1	6
1973	1	2	6	3	4	....	5	4	5	2		3	1	6
1974	1	3	4	6	2	....	5	6	4	5		3	1	2
1975	2	1	4	6	3	....	5	6	5	2		4	1	3
1976	2	3	4	5	1	....	6	x4	6	1		3	2	x4

	EAST DIVISION						WEST DIVISION					
Year	Balt.	Bos.	Cleve.	Det.	Mil.	N.Y.	Tor.	Calif.	Chi.	K.C.	Minn.	Oak.	Sea.	Tex.
1977	x2	x2	5	4	6	1	7	5	3	1	4	7	6	2
1978	4	2	6	5	3	1	7	x2	5	1	4	6	7	x2
1979	1	3	6	5	2	4	7	1	5	2	4	7	6	3
1980	2	4	6	5	3	1	7	6	5	1	3	2	7	4

*Record of predecessor St. Louis club. †Predecessor Philadelphia (1901-54), Kansas City (1955-67). ‡Predecessor Washington club. §Known as Los Angeles Angels from 1961 to September 2, 1965. yPredecessor Seattle club. zPredecessor Baltimore club. aPredecessor Milwaukee club. xTied for position.

LEADING BATSMEN

Year	Player and Club	G.	AB.	R.	H.	TB.	2B.	3B.	HR.	RBI.	B.A.
1901—Napoleon Lajoie, Philadelphia	131	543	145	229	345	48	13	14	....	.422
1902—Edward Delahanty, Washington	123	474	103	178	279	41	15	10	....	.376
1903—Napoleon Lajoie, Cleveland	126	488	90	173	260	40	13	7	....	.355
1904—Napoleon Lajoie, Cleveland	140	554	92	211	304	50	14	5	....	.381
1905—Elmer Flick, Cleveland	131	496	71	152	231	29	19	4	....	.306
1906—George Stone, St. Louis	154	581	91	208	288	24	19	6	....	.358
1907—Tyrus Cobb, Detroit	150	605	97	212	286	29	15	5	116	.350
1908—Tyrus Cobb, Detroit	150	581	88	188	276	36	20	4	101	.324
1909—Tyrus Cobb, Detroit	156	573	116	216	296	33	10	9	115	.377

LEADING BATSMEN—Continued

Year　　Player and Club	G.	AB.	R.	H.	TB.	2B.	3B.	HR.	RBI.	B.A.
°1910—Napoleon Lajoie, Cleveland	159	592	94	227	308	53	8	4	76	.383
1911—Tyrus Cobb, Detroit	146	591	147	248	367	47	24	8	144	.420
1912—Tyrus Cobb, Detroit	140	553	119	227	324	30	23	7	90	.410
1913—Tyrus Cobb, Detroit	122	428	70	167	229	18	16	4	65	.390
1914—Tyrus Cobb, Detroit	97	345	69	127	177	22	11	2	57	.368
1915—Tyrus Cobb, Detroit	156	563	114	208	274	31	13	3	95	.369
1916—Tristram Speaker, Cleveland	151	546	102	211	274	41	8	2	83	.386
1917—Tyrus Cobb, Detroit	152	588	107	225	336	44	23	7	108	.383
1918—Tyrus Cobb, Detroit	111	421	83	161	217	19	14	3	64	.382
1919—Tyrus Cobb, Detroit	124	497	92	191	256	36	13	1	69	.384
1920—George Sisler, St. Louis	154	631	137	257	399	49	18	19	122	.407
1921—Harry Heilmann, Detroit	149	602	114	237	365	43	14	19	139	.394
1922—George Sisler, St. Louis	142	586	134	246	348	42	18	8	105	.420
1923—Harry Heilmann, Detroit	144	524	121	211	331	44	11	18	115	.403
1924—George (Babe) Ruth, New York	153	529	143	200	391	39	7	46	121	.378
1925—Harry Heilmann, Detroit	150	573	97	225	326	40	11	13	133	.393
1926—Henry Manush, Detroit	136	498	95	188	281	35	8	14	86	.378
1927—Harry Heilmann, Detroit	141	505	106	201	311	50	9	14	120	.398
1928—Leon (Goose) Goslin, Washington	135	456	80	173	280	36	10	17	102	.379
1929—Lew Fonseca, Cleveland	148	566	97	209	301	44	15	6	103	.369
1930—Aloysius Simmons, Philadelphia	138	554	152	211	392	41	16	36	165	.381
1931—Aloysius Simmons, Philadelphia	128	513	105	200	329	37	13	22	128	.390
1932—Dale Alexander, Detroit-Boston	124	392	58	144	201	27	3	8	60	.367
1933—James Foxx, Philadelphia	149	573	125	204	403	37	9	48	163	.356
1934—H. Louis Gehrig, New York	154	579	128	210	409	40	6	49	165	.363
1935—Chas. (Buddy) Myer, Washington	151	616	115	215	288	36	11	5	100	.349
1936—Lucius Appling, Chicago	138	526	111	204	267	31	7	6	128	.388
1937—Charles Gehringer, Detroit	144	564	133	209	293	40	1	14	96	.371
1938—James Foxx, Boston	149	565	139	197	398	33	9	50	175	.349
1939—Joseph DiMaggio, New York	120	462	108	176	310	32	6	30	126	.381
1940—Joseph DiMaggio, New York	132	508	93	179	318	28	9	31	133	.352
1941—Theodore Williams, Boston	143	456	135	185	335	33	3	37	120	.406
1942—Theodore Williams, Boston	150	522	141	186	338	34	5	36	137	.356
1943—Lucius Appling, Chicago	155	585	63	192	238	33	2	3	80	.328
1944—Louis Boudreau, Cleveland	150	584	91	191	255	45	5	3	67	.327
1945—George Stirnweiss, New York	152	632	107	195	301	32	22	10	64	.309
1946—Jas. (Mickey) Vernon, Washington	148	587	88	207	298	51	8	8	85	.353
1947—Theodore Williams, Boston	156	528	125	181	335	40	9	32	114	.343
1948—Theodore Williams, Boston	137	509	124	188	313	44	3	25	127	.369
1949—George Kell, Detroit	134	522	97	179	244	38	9	3	59	.343
1950—William Goodman, Boston	110	424	91	150	193	25	3	4	68	.354
1951—Ferris Fain, Philadelphia	117	425	63	146	200	30	3	6	57	.344
1952—Ferris Fain, Philadelphia	145	538	82	176	231	43	3	2	59	.327
1953—Jas. (Mickey) Vernon, Washington	152	608	101	205	315	43	11	15	115	.337
1954—Roberto Avila, Cleveland	143	555	112	189	265	27	2	15	67	.341
1955—Albert Kaline, Detroit	152	588	121	200	321	24	8	27	102	.340
1956—Mickey Mantle, New York	150	533	132	188	376	22	5	52	130	.353
1957—Theodore Williams, Boston	132	420	96	163	307	28	1	38	87	.388
1958—Theodore Williams, Boston	129	411	81	135	240	23	2	26	85	.328
1959—Harvey Kuenn, Detroit	139	561	99	198	281	42	7	9	71	.353
1960—James (Pete) Runnels, Boston	143	528	80	169	208	29	2	2	35	.320
1961—Norman Cash, Detroit	159	535	119	193	354	22	8	41	132	.361
1962—James (Pete) Runnels, Boston	152	562	80	183	256	33	5	10	60	.326
1963—Carl Yastrzemski, Boston	151	570	91	183	271	40	3	14	68	.321
1964—Pedro (Tony) Oliva, Minnesota	161	672	109	217	374	43	9	32	94	.323
1965—Pedro (Tony) Oliva, Minnesota	149	576	107	185	283	40	5	16	98	.321
1966—Frank Robinson, Baltimore	155	576	122	182	367	34	2	49	122	.316
1967—Carl Yastrzemski, Boston	161	579	112	189	360	31	4	44	121	.326
1968—Carl Yastrzemski, Boston	157	539	90	162	267	32	2	23	74	.301
1969—Rodney Carew, Minnesota	123	458	79	152	214	30	4	8	56	.332
1970—Alexander Johnson, California	156	614	85	202	282	26	6	14	86	.329
1971—Pedro (Tony) Oliva, Minnesota	126	487	73	164	266	30	3	22	81	.337
1972—Rodney Carew, Minnesota	142	535	61	170	203	21	6	0	51	.318
1973—Rodney Carew, Minnesota	149	580	98	203	273	30	11	6	62	.350
1974—Rodney Carew, Minnesota	153	599	86	218	267	30	5	3	55	.364
1975—Rodney Carew, Minnesota	143	535	89	192	266	24	4	14	80	.359

LEADING BATSMEN—Continued

Year	Player and Club	G.	AB.	R.	H.	TB.	2B.	3B.	HR.	RBI.	B.A.
1976—	George H. Brett, Kansas City	159	645	94	215	298	34	14	7	67	.333
1977—	Rodney Carew, Minnesota	155	616	128	239	351	38	16	14	100	.388
1978—	Rodney Carew, Minnesota	152	564	85	188	249	26	10	5	70	.333
1979—	Fredric Lynn, Boston	147	531	116	177	338	42	1	39	122	.333
1980—	George H. Brett, Kansas City	117	449	87	175	298	33	9	24	118	.390

*League president Ban Johnson declared Ty Cobb batting champion with a .385 average, beating Lajoie's .384. However, subsequent research has led to the revision of Lajoie's average to .383 and Cobb's to .382.

LEADERS IN RUNS SCORED

Year	Player and Club	Runs
1900—	(Not classed as major)	
1901—	Napoleon Lajoie, Philadelphia	145
1902—	David Fultz, Philadelphia	110
1903—	Patrick Dougherty, Boston	108
1904—	Patrick Dougherty, Boston–New York	113
1905—	Harry Davis, Philadelphia	92
1906—	Elmer Flick, Cleveland	98
1907—	Samuel Crawford, Detroit	102
1908—	Matthew McIntyre, Detroit	105
1909—	Tyrus Cobb, Detroit	116
1910—	Tyrus Cobb, Detroit	106
1911—	Tyrus Cobb, Detroit	147
1912—	Edward Collins, Philadelphia	137
1913—	Edward Collins, Philadelphia	125
1914—	Edward Collins, Philadelphia	122
1915—	Tyrus Cobb, Detroit	144
1916—	Tyrus Cobb, Detroit	113
1917—	Owen (Donie) Bush, Detroit	112
1918—	Raymond Chapman, Cleveland	84
1919—	George (Babe) Ruth, Boston	103
1920—	George (Babe) Ruth, New York	158
1921—	George (Babe) Ruth, New York	177
1922—	George Sisler, St. Louis	134
1923—	George (Babe) Ruth, New York	151
1924—	George (Babe) Ruth, New York	143
1925—	John Mostil, Chicago	135
1926—	George (Babe) Ruth, New York	139
1927—	George (Babe) Ruth, New York	158
1928—	George (Babe) Ruth, New York	163
1929—	Charles Gehringer, Detroit	131
1930—	Aloysius Simmons, Philadelphia	152
1931—	H. Louis Gehrig, New York	163
1932—	James Foxx, Philadelphia	151
1933—	H. Louis Gehrig, New York	138
1934—	Charles Gehringer, Detroit	134
1935—	H. Louis Gehrig, New York	125
1936—	H. Louis Gehrig, New York	167
1937—	Joseph DiMaggio, New York	151
1938—	Henry Greenberg, Detroit	144
1939—	Robert (Red) Rolfe, New York	139
1940—	Theodore Williams, Boston	134
1941—	Theodore Williams, Boston	135
1942—	Theodore Williams, Boston	141
1943—	George Case, Washington	102
1944—	George Stirnweiss, New York	125
1945—	George Stirnweiss, New York	107
1946—	Theodore Williams, Boston	142
1947—	Theodore Williams, Boston	125
1948—	Thomas Henrich, New York	138
1949—	Theodore Williams, Boston	150
1950—	Dominic DiMaggio, Boston	131
1951—	Dominic DiMaggio, Boston	113
1952—	Lawrence Doby, Cleveland	104
1953—	Albert Rosen, Cleveland	115
1954—	Mickey Mantle, New York	129
1955—	Alphonse Smith, Cleveland	123
1956—	Mickey Mantle, New York	132
1957—	Mickey Mantle, New York	121
1958—	Mickey Mantle, New York	127
1959—	Edward Yost, Detroit	115
1960—	Mickey Mantle, New York	119
1961—	Mantle, New York–Maris, New York	132
1962—	Albert G. Pearson, Los Angeles	115
1963—	W. Robert Allison, Minnesota	99
1964—	Pedro (Tony) Oliva, Minnesota	109
1965—	Zoilo Versalles, Minnesota	126
1966—	Frank Robinson, Baltimore	122
1967—	Carl Yastrzemski, Boston	112
1968—	Richard McAuliffe, Detroit	95
1969—	Reginald Jackson, Oakland	123
1970—	Carl Yastrzemski, Boston	125
1971—	Donald Buford, Baltimore	99
1972—	Bobby Murcer, New York	102
1973—	Reginald Jackson, Oakland	99
1974—	Carl Yastrzemski, Boston	93
1975—	Fredric Lynn, Boston	103
1976—	Roy White, New York	104
1977—	Rodney Carew, Minnesota	128
1978—	Ronald LeFlore, Detroit	126
1979—	Donald Baylor, California	120
1980—	Willie Wilson, Kansas City	133

LEADERS IN HITS

Year	Player and Club	Hits
1900—	(Not classed as major)	
1901—	Napoleon Lajoie, Philadelphia	229
1902—	Charles Hickman, Cleveland	194
1903—	Patrick Dougherty, Boston	195
1904—	Napoleon Lajoie, Cleveland	211
1905—	George Stone, St. Louis	187
1906—	Napoleon Lajoie, Cleveland	214
1907—	Tyrus Cobb, Detroit	212
1908—	Tyrus Cobb, Detroit	188
1909—	Tyrus Cobb, Detroit	216
1910—	Napoleon Lajoie, Cleveland	227
1911—	Tyrus Cobb, Detroit	248
1912—	Tyrus Cobb, Detroit	227
1913—	Joseph Jackson, Cleveland	197
1914—	Tristram Speaker, Boston	193
1915—	Tyrus Cobb, Detroit	208
1916—	Tristram Speaker, Cleveland	211
1917—	Tyrus Cobb, Detroit	225

LEADERS IN HITS—Continued

Year	Player and Club	Hits
1918—	George Burns, Philadelphia	178
1919—	Cobb, Detroit-Robert Veach, Detroit	191
1920—	George Sisler, St. Louis	257
1921—	Harry Heilmann, Detroit	237
1922—	George Sisler, St. Louis	246
1923—	Charles Jamieson, Cleveland	222
1924—	Edgar (Sam) Rice, Washington	216
1925—	Aloysius Simmons, Philadelphia	253
1926—	George Burns, Cleveland	216
	Edgar (Sam) Rice, Washington	216
1927—	Earle Combs, New York	231
1928—	Henry Manush, St. Louis	241
1929—	Dale Alexander, Detroit	215
	Charles Gehringer, Detroit	215
1930—	U. John Hodapp, Cleveland	225
1931—	H. Louis Gehrig, New York	211
1932—	Aloysius Simmons, Philadelphia	216
1933—	Henry Manush, Washington	221
1934—	Charles Gehringer, Detroit	214
1935—	Joseph Vosmik, Cleveland	216
1936—	H. Earl Averill, Cleveland	232
1937—	Roy (Beau) Bell, New York	218
1938—	Joseph Vosmik, Boston	201
1939—	Robert (Red) Rolfe, New York	213
1940—	Raymond (Rip) Radcliff, St. Louis	200
	W. Barney McCosky, Detroit	200
	Roger (Doc) Cramer, Boston	200
1941—	Cecil Travis, Washington	218
1942—	John Pesky, Boston	205
1943—	Richard Wakefield, Detroit	200
1944—	George Stirnweiss, New York	205
1945—	George Stirnweiss, New York	195
1946—	John Pesky, Boston	208
1947—	John Pesky, Boston	207

Year	Player and Club	Hits
1948—	Robert Dillinger, St. Louis	207
1949—	L. Dale Mitchell, Cleveland	203
1950—	George Kell, Detroit	218
1951—	George Kell, Detroit	191
1952—	J. Nelson Fox, Chicago	192
1953—	Harvey Kuenn, Detroit	209
1954—	Fox, Chicago-Kuenn, Detroit	201
1955—	Albert Kaline, Detroit	200
1956—	Harvey Kuenn, Detroit	196
1957—	J. Nelson Fox, Chicago	196
1958—	J. Nelson Fox, Chicago	187
1959—	Harvey Kuenn, Detroit	198
1960—	Orestes (Minnie) Minoso, Chicago	184
1961—	Norman Cash, Detroit	193
1962—	Robert Richardson, New York	209
1963—	Carl Yastrzemski, Boston	183
1964—	Pedro (Tony) Oliva, Minnesota	217
1965—	Pedro (Tony) Oliva, Minnesota	185
1966—	Pedro (Tony) Oliva, Minnesota	191
1967—	Carl Yastrzemski, Boston	189
1968—	Dagoberto Campaneris, Oakland	177
1969—	Pedro (Tony) Oliva, Minnesota	197
1970—	Pedro (Tony) Oliva, Minnesota	204
1971—	Cesar Tovar, Minnesota	204
1972—	Joseph Rudi, Oakland	181
1973—	Rodney Carew, Minnesota	203
1974—	Rodney Carew, Minnesota	218
1975—	George Brett, Kansas City	195
1976—	George Brett, Kansas City	215
1977—	Rodney Carew, Minnesota	239
1978—	James Rice, Boston	213
1979—	George Brett, Kansas City	212
1980—	Willie Wilson, Kansas City	230

ONE-BASE HIT LEADERS

Year	Player and Club	1B.
1900—	(Not classed as major)	
1901—	Napoleon Lajoie, Philadelphia	154
1902—	Fielder A. Jones, Chicago	148
1903—	Patrick H. Dougherty, Boston	161
1904—	William H. Keeler, New York	164
1905—	William H. Keeler, New York	147
1906—	William H. Keeler, New York	166
1907—	Tyrus R. Cobb, Detroit	163
1908—	Matthew W. McIntyre, Detroit	131
	George R. Stone, St. Louis	131
1909—	Tyrus R. Cobb, Detroit	164
1910—	Napoleon Lajoie, Cleveland	165
1911—	Tyrus R. Cobb, Detroit	169
1912—	Tyrus R. Cobb, Detroit	167
1913—	Edward T. Collins, Philadelphia	145
1914—	John P. McInnis, Philadelphia	160
1915—	Tyrus R. Cobb, Detroit	161
1916—	Tristram Speaker, Cleveland	160
1917—	Tyrus R. Cobb, Detroit	151
	J. Clyde Milan, Washington	151
1918—	George H. Burns, Philadelphia	141
1919—	Edgar C. Rice, Washington	144
1920—	George H. Sisler, St. Louis	171
1921—	John T. Tobin, St. Louis	179
1922—	George Sisler, St. Louis	134
1923—	Charles D. Jamieson, Cleveland	172
1924—	Charles D. Jamieson, Cleveland	168

Year	Player and Club	1B.
1925—	Edgar C. Rice, Washington	182
1926—	Edgar C. Rice, Washington	167
1927—	Earle B. Combs, New York	166
1928—	Henry E. Manush, St. Louis	161
1929—	Earle B. Combs, New York	151
1930—	Edgar C. Rice, Washington	158
1931—	Oscar D. Melillo, St. Louis	142
	Jonathan T. Stone, Detroit	142
1932—	Henry E. Manush, Washington	145
1933—	Henry E. Manush, Washington	167
1934—	Roger M. Cramer, Philadelphia	158
1935—	Roger M. Cramer, Philadelphia	170
1936—	Raymond A. Radcliff, Chicago	161
1937—	John K. Lewis, Washington	162
1938—	Melo B. Almada, Wash.-St. Louis	158
1939—	Roger M. Cramer, Boston	147
1940—	Roger M. Cramer, Boston	160
1941—	Cecil H. Travis, Washington	153
1942—	John M. Pesky, Boston	165
1943—	Roger M. Cramer, Detroit	159
1944—	George H. Stirnweiss, New York	146
1945—	Irvin G. Hall, Philadelphia	139
1946—	John M. Pesky, Boston	159
1947—	John M. Pesky, Boston	172
1948—	L. Dale Mitchell, Cleveland	162
1949—	L. Dale Mitchell, Cleveland	161
1950—	Philip F. Rizzuto, New York	150

ONE-BASE HIT LEADERS—Continued

Year	Player and Club	1B.	Year	Player and Club	1B.
1951	George C. Kell, Detroit	150	1966	Luis E. Aparicio, Baltimore	143
1952	J. Nelson Fox, Chicago	157	1967	Horace M. Clarke, New York	140
1953	Harvey E. Kuenn, Detroit	167	1968	Dagoberto B. Campaneris, Oakland	139
1954	J. Nelson Fox, Chicago	167	1969	Horace M. Clarke, New York	146
1955	J. Nelson Fox, Chicago	157	1970	Alexander Johnson, California	156
1956	J. Nelson Fox, Chicago	158	1971	Cesar L. Tovar, Minnesota	171
1957	J. Nelson Fox, Chicago	155	1972	Rodney C. Carew, Minnesota	143
1958	J. Nelson Fox, Chicago	160	1973	Rodney C. Carew, Minnesota	156
1959	J. Nelson Fox, Chicago	149	1974	Rodney C. Carew, Minnesota	180
1960	J. Nelson Fox, Chicago	139	1975	Thurman Munson, New York	151
1961	Robert C. Richardson, New York	148	1976	George Brett, Kansas City	160
1962	Robert C. Richardson, New York	158	1977	Rodney Carew, Minnesota	171
1963	Albert G. Pearson, Los Angeles	139	1978	Ronald LeFlore, Detroit	153
1964	Robert C. Richardson, New York	148	1979	Willie Wilson, Kansas City	148
1965	Donald A. Buford, Chicago	129	1980	Willie Wilson, Kansas City	184

TWO-BASE HIT LEADERS

Year	Player and Club	2B.	Year	Player and Club	2B.
1900	(Not classed as major)		1943	Richard Wakefield, Detroit	38
1901	Napoleon Lajoie, Philadelphia	48	1944	Louis Boudreau, Cleveland	45
1902	Harry Davis, Philadelphia	43	1945	Wallace Moses, Chicago	35
1903	Ralph Seybold, Philadelphia	43	1946	Jas. (Mickey) Vernon, Washington	51
1904	Napoleon Lajoie, Cleveland	50	1947	Louis Boudreau, Cleveland	45
1905	Harry Davis, Philadelphia	47	1948	Theodore Williams, Boston	44
1906	Napoleon Lajoie, Cleveland	49	1949	Theodore Williams, Boston	39
1907	Harry Davis, Philadelphia	37	1950	George Kell, Detroit	56
1908	Tyrus Cobb, Detroit	36	1951	Kell, Det.-Yost, Wash.-Mele, Wash.	36
1909	Samuel Crawford, Detroit	35	1952	Ferris Fain, Philadelphia	43
1910	Napoleon Lajoie, Cleveland	51	1953	Jas. (Mickey) Vernon, Washington	43
1911	Tyrus Cobb, Detroit	47	1954	Jas. (Mickey) Vernon, Washington	33
1912	Tristram Speaker, Boston	53	1955	Harvey Kuenn, Detroit	38
1913	Joseph Jackson, Cleveland	39	1956	James Piersall, Boston	40
1914	Tristram Speaker, Boston	46	1957	Minoso, Chicago-Gardner, Baltimore	36
1915	Robert Veach, Detroit	40	1958	Harvey Kuenn, Detroit	39
1916	Graney, Cleveland-Speaker, Cleveland	41	1959	Harvey Kuenn, Detroit	42
1917	Tyrus Cobb, Detroit	44	1960	John (Tito) Francona, Cleveland	36
1918	Tristram Speaker, Cleveland	33	1961	Albert Kaline, Detroit	41
1919	Robert Veach, Detroit	45	1962	Floyd Robinson, Chicago	45
1920	Tristram Speaker, Cleveland	50	1963	Carl Yastrzemski, Boston	40
1921	Tristram Speaker, Cleveland	52	1964	Pedro (Tony) Oliva, Minnesota	43
1922	Tristram Speaker, Cleveland	48	1965	Zoilo Versalles, Minnesota	45
1923	Tristram Speaker, Cleveland	59		Carl Yastrzemski, Boston	45
1924	J. Sewell, Cleveland-Heilmann, Detroit	45	1966	Carl Yastrzemski, Boston	39
1925	Martin McManus, St. Louis	44	1967	Pedro (Tony) Oliva, Minnesota	34
1926	George Burns, Cleveland	64	1968	C. Reginald Smith, Boston	37
1927	H. Louis Gehrig, New York	52	1969	Pedro (Tony) Oliva, Minnesota	39
1928	Manush, St. Louis-Gehrig, New York	47	1970	Pedro (Tony) Oliva, Minnesota	36
1929	Manush, St. L.-R. Johnson, Detroit-			Amos Otis, Kansas City	36
	Gehringer, Detroit	45		Cesar Tovar, Minnesota	36
1930	U. John Hodapp, Cleveland	51	1971	C. Reginald Smith, Boston	33
1931	Earl Webb, Boston	67	1972	Louis Piniella, Kansas City	33
1932	Eric McNair, Philadelphia	47	1973	Salvatore Bando, Oakland	32
1933	Joseph Cronin, Washington	45		Pedro Garcia, Milwaukee	32
1934	Henry Greenberg, Detroit	63	1974	Joseph Rudi, Oakland	39
1935	Joseph Vosmik, Cleveland	47	1975	Fredric Lynn, Boston	47
1936	Charles Gehringer, Detroit	60	1976	Amos Otis, Kansas City	40
1937	Roy (Beau) Bell, St. Louis	51	1977	Harold McRae, Kansas City	54
1938	Joseph Cronin, Boston	51	1978	George Brett, Kansas City	45
1939	Robert (Red) Rolfe, New York	46	1979	Chester Lemon, Chicago	44
1940	Henry Greenberg, Detroit	50		Cecil Cooper, Milwaukee	44
1941	Louis Boudreau, Cleveland	45	1980	Robin Yount, Milwaukee	49
1942	Donald Kolloway, Chicago	40			

THREE-BASE HIT LEADERS

Year	Player and Club	3B.
1900—	(Not classed as major)	
1901—	James Williams, Baltimore	22
1902—	James Williams, Baltimore	23
1903—	Samuel Crawford, Detroit	25
1904—	Charles (Chick) Stahl, Boston	22
1905—	Elmer Flick, Cleveland	19
1906—	Elmer Flick, Cleveland	22
1907—	Elmer Flick, Cleveland	18
1908—	Tyrus, Cobb, Detroit	20
1909—	J. Franklin Baker, Philadelphia	19
1910—	Samuel Crawford, Detroit	19
1911—	Tyrus Cobb, Detroit	24
1912—	Joseph Jackson, Cleveland	26
1913—	Samuel Crawford, Detroit	23
1914—	Samuel Crawford, Detroit	26
1915—	Samuel Crawford, Detroit	19
1916—	Joseph Jackson, Chicago	21
1917—	Tyrus Cobb, Detroit	23
1918—	Tyrus Cobb, Detroit	14
1919—	Robert Veach, Detroit	17
1920—	Joseph Jackson, Chicago	20
1921—	Howard Shanks, Washington	19
1922—	George Sisler, St. Louis	18
1923—	Rice, Washington-Goslin, Washington	18
1924—	Walter Pipp, New York	19
1925—	Leon (Goose) Goslin, Washington	20
1926—	H. Louis Gehrig, New York	20
1927—	Earle Combs, New York	23
1928—	Earle Combs, New York	21
1929—	Charles Gehringer, Detroit	19
1930—	Earle Combs, New York	22
1931—	Roy Johnson, Detroit	19
1932—	Joseph Cronin, Washington	18
1933—	Henry Manush, Washington	17
1934—	W. Benjamin Chapman, New York	13
1935—	Joseph Vosmik, Cleveland	20
1936—	Averill, Cleveland-J. DiMaggio, N.Y.	15
	Rolfe, New York	15
1937—	F. Walker, Chicago-Kreevich, Chicago	16
1938—	J. Geoffrey Heath, Cleveland	18
1939—	John (Buddy) Lewis, Washington	16
1940—	Barney McCosky, Detroit	19
1941—	J. Geoffrey Heath, Cleveland	20
1942—	Stanley Spence, Washington	15
1943—	Lindell, New York-Moses, Chicago	12

Year	Player and Club	3B.
1944—	Lindell, N. York-Stirnweiss, N. York	16
1945—	George Stirnweiss, New York	22
1946—	Henry Edwards, Cleveland	16
1947—	Thomas Henrich, New York	13
1948—	Thomas Henrich, New York	14
1949—	L. Dale Mitchell, Cleveland	23
1950—	D. DiMaggio, Doerr, Bos.-Evers, Det.	11
1951—	Orestes (Minnie) Minoso, Clev.-Chi.	14
1952—	Roberto Avila, Cleveland	11
1953—	Manuel (Jim) Rivera, Chicago	16
1954—	Orestes (Minnie) Minoso, Chicago	18
1955—	Mantle, New York-Carey, New York	11
1956—	Minoso, Chicago-Jensen, Boston-	
	Simpson, Kansas City-Lemon, Wash.	11
1957—	McDougald, Bauer, Simpson, New York.	9
1958—	Victor Power, Kansas City-Cleveland	10
1959—	W. Robert Allison, Washington	9
1960—	J. Nelson Fox, Chicago	10
1961—	Jacob Wood, Detroit	14
1962—	Gino Cimoli, Kansas City	15
1963—	Zoilo Versalles, Minnesota	13
1964—	Richard Rollins, Minnesota	10
	Zoilo Versalles, Minnesota	10
1965—	Dagoberto Campaneris, Kansas City	12
	Zoilo Versalles, Minnesota	12
1966—	Robert Knoop, California	11
1967—	Paul L. Blair, Baltimore	12
1968—	James Fregosi, California	13
1969—	Delbert Unser, Washington	8
1970—	Cesar Tovar, Minnesota	13
1971—	Freddie Patek, Kansas City	11
1972—	Carlton Fisk, Boston	9
	Joseph Rudi, Oakland	9
1973—	Alonza Bumbry, Baltimore	11
	Rodney Carew, Minnesota	11
1974—	John (Mickey) Rivers, California	11
1975—	George Brett, Kansas City	13
	John Rivers, California	13
1976—	George Brett, Kansas City	14
1977—	Rodney Carew, Minnesota	16
1978—	James Rice, Boston	15
1979—	George Brett, Kansas City	20
1980—	Alfredo Griffin, Toronto	15
	Willie Wilson, Kansas City	15

HOME RUN LEADERS

Year	Player and Club	HR.
1900—	(Not classed as major)	
1901—	Napoleon Lajoie, Philadelphia	14
1902—	Ralph (Socks) Seybold, Philadelphia	16
1903—	John (Buck) Freeman, Boston	13
1904—	Harry Davis, Philadelphia	10
1905—	Harry Davis, Philadelphia	8
1906—	Harry Davis, Philadelphia	12
1907—	Harry Davis, Philadelphia	8
1908—	Samuel Crawford, Detroit	7
1909—	Tyrus Cobb, Detroit	9
1910—	J. Garland (Jake) Stahl, Boston	10
1911—	J. Franklin Baker, Philadelphia	9
1912—	J. Franklin Baker, Philadelphia	10
	Tristram Speaker, Boston	10
1913—	J. Franklin Baker, Philadelphia	12
1914—	Baker, Philadelphia-Crawford, Detroit	8

Year	Player and Club	HR.
1915—	Robert Roth, Chicago-Cleveland	7
1916—	Walter Pipp, New York	12
1917—	Walter Pipp, New York	9
1918—	Ruth, Boston-Tilly Walker, Phila.	11
1919—	George (Babe) Ruth, Boston	29
1920—	George (Babe) Ruth, New York	54
1921—	George (Babe) Ruth, New York	59
1922—	Kenneth Williams, St. Louis	39
1923—	George (Babe) Ruth, New York	41
1924—	George (Babe) Ruth, New York	46
1925—	Robert Meusel, New York	33
1926—	George (Babe) Ruth, New York	47
1927—	George (Babe) Ruth, New York	60
1928—	George (Babe) Ruth, New York	54
1929—	George (Babe) Ruth, New York	46
1930—	George (Babe) Ruth, New York	49

HOME RUN LEADERS—Continued

Year	Player and Club	HR.
1931—	Ruth, New York-Gehrig, New York	46
1932—	James Foxx, Philadelphia	58
1933—	James Foxx, Philadelphia	48
1934—	H. Louis Gehrig, New York	49
1935—	Foxx, Philadelphia-Greenberg, Detroit	36
1936—	H. Louis Gehrig, New York	49
1937—	Joseph DiMaggio, New York	46
1938—	Henry Greenberg, Detroit	58
1939—	James Foxx, Boston	35
1940—	Henry Greenberg, Detroit	41
1941—	Theodore Williams, Boston	37
1942—	Theodore Williams, Boston	36
1943—	Rudolph York, Detroit	34
1944—	Nicholas Etten, New York	22
1945—	Vernon Stephens, St. Louis	24
1946—	Henry Greenberg, Detroit	44
1947—	Theodore Williams, Boston	32
1948—	Joseph DiMaggio, New York	39
1949—	Theodore Williams, Boston	43
1950—	Albert Rosen, Cleveland	37
1951—	Gus Zernial, Chicago-Philadelphia	33
1952—	Lawrence Doby, Cleveland	32
1953—	Albert Rosen, Cleveland	43
1954—	Lawrence Doby, Cleveland	32
1955—	Mickey Mantle, New York	37
1956—	Mickey Mantle, New York	52
1957—	Roy Sievers, Washington	42
1958—	Mickey Mantle, New York	42
1959—	Colavito, Cleveland-Killebrew, Wash.	42
1960—	Mickey Mantle, New York	40
1961—	Roger Maris, New York	61
1962—	Harmon Killebrew, Minnesota	48
1963—	Harmon Killebrew, Minnesota	45
1964—	Harmon Killebrew, Minnesota	49
1965—	Anthony Conigilaro, Boston	32
1966—	Frank Robinson, Baltimore	49
1967—	Harmon Killebrew, Minnesota	44
	Carl Yastrzemski, Boston	44
1968—	Frank Howard, Washington	44
1969—	Harmon Killebrew, Minnesota	49
1970—	Frank Howard, Washington	44
1971—	William E. Melton, Chicago	33
1972—	Richard Allen, Chicago	37
1973—	Reginald Jackson, Oakland	32
1974—	Richard Allen, Chicago	32
1975—	Reginald Jackson, Oakland	36
	George Scott, Milwaukee	36
1976—	Graig Nettles, New York	32
1977—	James Rice, Boston	39
1978—	James Rice, Boston	46
1979—	J. Gorman Thomas, Milwaukee	45
1980—	Reginald Jackson, New York	41
	Benjamin Oglivie, Milwaukee	41

LEADERS IN TOTAL BASES

Year	Player and Club	T.B.
1900—	(Not classed as major)	
1901—	Napoleon Lajoie, Philadelphia	345
1902—	John (Buck) Freeman, Boston	287
1903—	John (Buck) Freeman, Boston	281
1904—	Napoleon Lajoie, Cleveland	304
1905—	George Stone, St. Louis	260
1906—	George Stone, St. Louis	288
1907—	Tyrus Cobb, Detroit	286
1908—	Tyrus Cobb, Detroit	276
1909—	Tyrus Cobb, Detroit	296
1910—	Napoleon Lajoie, Cleveland	304
1911—	Tyrus Cobb, Detroit	367
1912—	Joseph Jackson, Cleveland	331
1913—	Samuel Crawford, Detroit	298
1914—	Tristram Speaker, Boston	287
1915—	Tyrus Cobb, Detroit	274
1916—	Joseph Jackson, Chicago	293
1917—	Tyrus Cobb, Detroit	336
1918—	George Burns, Philadelphia	236
1919—	George (Babe) Ruth, Boston	284
1920—	George Sisler, St. Louis	399
1921—	George (Babe) Ruth, New York	457
1922—	Kenneth Williams, St. Louis	367
1923—	George (Babe) Ruth, New York	399
1924—	George (Babe) Ruth, New York	391
1925—	Aloysius Simmons, Philadelphia	392
1926—	George (Babe) Ruth, New York	365
1927—	H. Louis Gehrig, New York	447
1928—	George (Babe) Ruth, New York	380
1929—	Aloysius Simmons, Philadelphia	373
1930—	H. Louis Gehrig, New York	419
1931—	H. Louis Gehrig, New York	410
1932—	James Foxx, Philadelphia	438
1933—	James Foxx, Philadelphia	403
1934—	H. Louis Gehrig, New York	409
1935—	Henry Greenberg, Detroit	389
1936—	Harold Trosky, Cleveland	405
1937—	Joseph DiMaggio, New York	418
1938—	James Foxx, Boston	398
1939—	Theodore Williams, Boston	344
1940—	Henry Greenberg, Detroit	384
1941—	Joseph DiMaggio, New York	348
1942—	Theodore Williams, Boston	338
1943—	Rudolph York, Detroit	301
1944—	John Lindell, New York	297
1945—	George Stirnweiss, New York	301
1946—	Theodore Williams, Boston	343
1947—	Theodore Williams, Boston	335
1948—	Joseph DiMaggio, New York	355
1949—	Theodore Williams, Boston	368
1950—	Walter Dropo, Boston	326
1951—	Theodore Williams, Boston	295
1952—	Albert Rosen, Cleveland	297
1953—	Albert Rosen, Cleveland	367
1954—	Orestes (Minnie) Minoso, Chicago	304
1955—	Albert Kaline, Detroit	321
1956—	Mickey Mantle, New York	376
1957—	Roy Sievers, Washington	331
1958—	Mickey Mantle, New York	307
1959—	Rocco Colavito, Cleveland	301
1960—	Mickey Mantle, New York	294
1961—	Roger Maris, New York	366
1962—	Rocco Colavito, Detroit	309
1963—	Richard Stuart, Boston	319
1964—	Pedro (Tony) Oliva, Minnesota	374
1965—	Zoilo Versalles, Minnesota	308
1966—	Frank Robinson, Baltimore	367
1967—	Carl Yastrzemski, Boston	360

LEADERS IN TOTAL BASES—Continued

Year	Player and Club	T.B.	Year	Player and Club	T.B.
1968—	Frank Howard, Washington	330	1974—	Joseph Rudi, Oakland	287
1969—	Frank Howard, Washington	340	1975—	George Scott, Milwaukee	318
1970—	Carl Yastrzemski, Boston	335	1976—	George Brett, Kansas City	298
1971—	C. Reginald Smith, Boston	302	1977—	James Rice, Boston	382
1972—	Bobby Murcer, New York	314	1978—	James Rice, Boston	406
1973—	David L. May, Milwaukee	295	1979—	James Rice, Boston	369
	George Scott, Milwaukee	295	1980—	Cecil Cooper, Milwaukee	335
	Salvatore L. Bando, Oakland	295			

RUNS BATTED IN LEADERS

Note—Runs batted in not compiled prior to 1907; officially adopted in 1920.

Year	Player and Club	RBI	Year	Player and Club	RBI
1907—	Tyrus Cobb, Detroit	116	1945—	Nicholas Etten, New York	111
1908—	Tyrus Cobb, Detroit	101	1946—	Henry Greenberg, Detroit	127
1909—	Tyrus Cobb, Detroit	115	1947—	Theodore Williams, Boston	114
1910—	Samuel Crawford, Detroit	115	1948—	Joseph DiMaggio, New York	155
1911—	Tyrus Cobb, Detroit	144	1949—	Theodore Williams, Boston	159
1912—	J. Franklin Baker, Philadelphia	133		Vernon Stephens, Boston	159
1913—	J. Franklin Baker, Philadelphia	126	1950—	Walter Dropo, Boston	144
1914—	Samuel Crawford, Detroit	112		Vernon Stephens, Boston	144
1915—	Samuel Crawford, Detroit	116	1951—	Gus Zernial, Chicago-Philadelphia	129
1916—	Walter Pipp, New York	99	1952—	Albert Rosen, Cleveland	105
1917—	Robert Veach, Detroit	115	1953—	Albert Rosen, Cleveland	145
1918—	George Burns, Philadelphia	74	1954—	Lawrence Doby, Cleveland	126
	Robert Veach, Detroit	74	1955—	Raymond Boone, Detroit	116
1919—	George (Babe) Ruth, Boston	112		Jack Jensen, Boston	116
1920—	George (Babe) Ruth, New York	137	1956—	Mickey Mantle, New York	130
1921—	George (Babe) Ruth, New York	171	1957—	Roy Sievers, Washington	114
1922—	Kenneth Williams, St. Louis	155	1958—	Jack Jensen, Boston	122
1923—	George (Babe) Ruth, New York	131	1959—	Jack Jensen, Boston	112
1924—	Leon (Goose) Goslin, Washington	129	1960—	Roger Maris, New York	112
1925—	Robert Meusel, New York	138	1961—	Roger Maris, New York	142
1926—	George (Babe) Ruth, New York	145	1962—	Harmon Killebrew, Minnesota	126
1927—	H. Louis Gehrig, New York	175	1963—	Richard Stuart, Boston	118
1928—	George (Babe) Ruth, New York	142	1964—	Brooks Robinson, Baltimore	118
	H. Louis Gehrig, New York	142	1965—	Rocco Colavito, Cleveland	108
1929—	Aloysius Simmons, Philadelphia	157	1966—	Frank Robinson, Baltimore	122
1930—	H. Louis Gehrig, New York	174	1967—	Carl Yastrzemski, Boston	121
1931—	H. Louis Gehrig, New York	184	1968—	Kenneth Harrelson, Boston	109
1932—	James Foxx, Philadelphia	169	1969—	Harmon Killebrew, Minnesota	140
1933—	James Foxx, Philadelphia	163	1970—	Frank Howard, Washington	126
1934—	H. Louis Gehrig, New York	165	1971—	Harmon Killebrew, Minnesota	119
1935—	Henry Greenberg, Detroit	170	1972—	Richard Allen, Chicago	113
1936—	Harold Trosky, Cleveland	162	1973—	Reginald Jackson, Oakland	117
1937—	Henry Greenberg, Detroit	183	1974—	Jeffrey Burroughs, Texas	118
1938—	James Foxx, Boston	175	1975—	George Scott, Milwaukee	109
1939—	Theodore Williams, Boston	145	1976—	Lee May, Baltimore	109
1940—	Henry Greenberg, Detroit	150	1977—	Larry Hisle, Minnesota	119
1941—	Joseph DiMaggio, New York	125	1978—	James Rice, Boston	139
1942—	Theodore Williams, Boston	137	1979—	Donald Baylor, California	139
1943—	Rudolph York, Detroit	118	1980—	Cecil Cooper, Milwaukee	122
1944—	Vernon Stephens, St. Louis	109			

BATTERS LEADING IN BASES ON BALLS

Note—Bases on balls not included in batting records in American League prior to 1913.

Year	Player and Club	BB.	Year	Player and Club	BB.
1913—	Burton Shotton, St. Louis	102	1916—	Burton Shotton, St. Louis	111
1914—	Owen (Donie) Bush, Detroit	112	1917—	John Graney, Cleveland	94
1915—	Edward Collins, Chicago	119	1918—	Raymond Chapman, Cleveland	84

BATTERS LEADING IN BASES ON BALLS —Continued

Note—Bases on balls not included in batting records in American League prior to 1913.

Year	Player and Club	BB.	Year	Player and Club	BB.
1919—	John Graney, Cleveland	105	1950—	Edward Yost, Washington	141
1920—	George (Babe) Ruth, New York	148	1951—	Theodore Williams, Boston	144
1921—	George (Babe) Ruth, New York	144	1952—	Edward Yost, Washington	129
1922—	L. W. (Whitey) Witt, New York	89	1953—	Edward Yost, Washington	123
1923—	George (Babe) Ruth, New York	170	1954—	Theodore Williams, Boston	136
1924—	George (Babe) Ruth, New York	142	1955—	Mickey Mantle, New York	113
1925—	William Kamm, Chicago	90	1956—	Edward Yost, Washington	151
	John Mostil, Chicago	90	1957—	Mickey Mantle, New York	146
1926—	George (Babe) Ruth, New York	144	1958—	Mickey Mantle, New York	129
1927—	George (Babe) Ruth, New York	138	1959—	Edward Yost, Detroit	135
1928—	George (Babe) Ruth, New York	135	1960—	Edward Yost, Detroit	125
1929—	Max Bishop, Philadelphia	128	1961—	Mickey Mantle, New York	126
1930—	George (Babe) Ruth, New York	136	1962—	Mickey Mantle, New York	122
1931—	George (Babe) Ruth, New York	128	1963—	Carl Yastrzemski, Boston	95
1932—	George (Babe) Ruth, New York	130	1964—	Norman Siebern, Baltimore	106
1933—	George (Babe) Ruth, New York	114	1965—	Rocco Colavito, Cleveland	93
1934—	James Foxx, Philadelphia	111	1966—	Harmon Killebrew, Minnesota	103
1935—	H. Louis Gehrig, New York	132	1967—	Harmon Killebrew, Minnesota	131
1936—	H. Louis Gehrig, New York	130	1968—	Carl Yastrzemski, Boston	119
1937—	H. Louis Gehrig, New York	127	1969—	Harmon Killebrew, Minnesota	145
1938—	James Foxx, Boston	119	1970—	Frank Howard, Washington	132
	Henry Greenberg, Detroit	119	1971—	Harmon Killebrew, Minnesota	114
1939—	Harland Clift, St. Louis	111	1972—	Richard Allen, Chicago	99
1940—	Charles Keller, New York	106		Roy White, New York	99
1941—	Theodore Williams, Boston	145	1973—	John Mayberry, Kansas City	122
1942—	Theodore Williams, Boston	145	1974—	F. Gene Tenace, Oakland	110
1943—	Charles Keller, New York	106	1975—	John Mayberry, Kansas City	119
1944—	Nicholas Etten, New York	97	1976—	D. Michael Hargrove, Texas	97
1945—	Roy Cullenbine, Cleveland-Detroit	112	1977—	Colbert (Toby) Harrah, Texas	109
1946—	Theodore Williams, Boston	156	1978—	D. Michael Hargrove, Texas	107
1947—	Theodore Williams, Boston	162	1979—	Darrell Porter, Kansas City	121
1948—	Theodore Williams, Boston	126	1980—	Willie Randolph, New York	119
1949—	Theodore Williams, Boston	162			

BATTERS LEADING IN STRIKEOUTS

Note—Strikeouts not included in batting records in American League prior to 1913.

Year	Player and Club	SO.	Year	Player and Club	SO.
1913—	Daniel Moeller, Washington	106	1936—	James Foxx, Boston	119
1914—	August Williams, St. Louis	120	1937—	Frank Crosetti, New York	105
1915—	John Lavan, St. Louis	83	1938—	Frank Crosetti, New York	97
1916—	Walter Pipp, New York	82	1939—	Hank Greenberg, Detroit	95
1917—	Robert Roth, Cleveland	73	1940—	Samuel Chapman, Philadelphia	96
1918—	George (Babe) Ruth, Boston	58	1941—	James Foxx, Boston	103
1919—	Maurice Shannon, Philadelphia-Boston	70	1942—	Joseph Gordon, New York	95
1920—	Aaron Ward, New York	84	1943—	Chester Laabs, St. Louis	105
1921—	Robert Meusel, New York	88	1944—	J. Patrick Seerey, Cleveland	99
1922—	James Dykes, Philadelphia	98	1945—	J. Patrick Seerey, Cleveland	97
1923—	George (Babe) Ruth, New York	93	1946—	Charles Keller, New York	101
1924—	George (Babe) Ruth, New York	81		J. Patrick Seerey, Cleveland	101
1925—	Martin McManus, St. Louis	69	1947—	Edwin Joost, Philadelphia	110
1926—	Anthony Lazzeri, New York	96	1948—	J. Patrick Seerey, Cleveland-Chicago	102
1927—	George (Babe) Ruth, New York	89	1949—	Richard Kokos, St. Louis	91
1928—	George (Babe) Ruth, New York	87	1950—	Gus Zernial, Chicago	110
1929—	James Foxx, Philadelphia	70	1951—	Gus Zernial, Chicago-Philadelphia	101
1930—	James Foxx, Philadelphia	66	1952—	Lawrence Doby, Cleveland	111
	Edward Morgan, Cleveland	66		Mickey Mantle, New York	111
1931—	James Foxx, Philadelphia	84	1953—	Lawrence Doby, Cleveland	121
1932—	Bruce Campbell, Chicago-St. Louis	104	1954—	Mickey Mantle, New York	107
1933—	James Foxx, Philadelphia	93	1955—	Norbert Zauchin, Boston	105
1934—	Harland Clift, St. Louis	100	1956—	James Lemon, Washington	138
1935—	James Foxx, Philadelphia	99	1957—	James Lemon, Washington	94

BATTERS LEADING IN STRIKEOUTS—Continued

Note—Strikeouts not included in batting records in American League prior to 1913.

Year	Player and Club	SO.
1958—	James Lemon, Washington	120
	Mickey Mantle, New York	120
1959—	Mickey Mantle, New York	126
1960—	Mickey Mantle, New York	125
1961—	Jacob Wood, Detroit	141
1962—	Harmon Killebrew, Minnesota	142
1963—	David Nicholson, Chicago	175
1964—	Nelson Mathews, Kansas City	143
1965—	Zoilo Versalles, Minnesota	122
1966—	George Scott, Boston	152
1967—	Frank Howard, Washington	155
1968—	Reginald Jackson, Oakland	171
1969—	Reginald Jackson, Oakland	142
1970—	Reginald Jackson, Oakland	135
1971—	Reginald Jackson, Oakland	161
1972—	A. Bobby Darwin, Minnesota	145
1973—	A. Bobby Darwin, Minnesota	137
1974—	A. Bobby Darwin, Minnesota	127
1975—	Jeffrey Burroughs, Texas	155
1976—	James Rice, Boston	123
1977—	Clell (Butch) Hobson, Boston	162
1978—	Gary Alexander, Oakland-Cleveland	166
1979—	J. Gorman Thomas, Milwaukee	175
1980—	J. Gorman Thomas, Milwaukee	170

LEADING BASE STEALERS

Year	Player and Club	SB.
1900—	(Not classed as major)	
1901—	Frank Isbell Chicago	48
1902—	Fred (Topsy) Hartsel, Philadelphia	54
1903—	Harry Bay, Cleveland	46
1904—	Elmer Flick, Clev-Harry Bay, Clev.	42
1905—	Daniel Hoffman, Philadelphia	46
1906—	Flick, Cleveland-Anderson, Washington	39
1907—	Tyrus Cobb, Detroit	49
1908—	Patrick Dougherty, Chicago	47
1909—	Tyrus Cobb, Detroit	76
1910—	Edward Collins, Philadelphia	81
1911—	Tyrus Cobb, Detroit	83
1912—	J. Clyde Milan, Washington	88
1913—	J. Clyde Milan, Washington	74
1914—	Frederick Maisel, New York	74
1915—	Tyrus Cobb, Detroit	96
1916—	Tyrus Cobb, Detroit	68
1917—	Tyrus Cobb, Detroit	55
1918—	George Sisler, St. Louis	45
1919—	Edward Collins, Chicago	33
1920—	Edgar (Sam) Rice, Washington	63
1921—	George Sisler, St. Louis	35
1922—	George Sisler, St. Louis	51
1923—	Edward Collins, Chicago	49
1924—	Edward Collins, Chicago	42
1925—	John Mostil, Chicago	43
1926—	John Mostil, Chicago	35
1927—	George Sisler, St. Louis	27
1928—	Charles (Buddy) Myer, Boston	30
1929—	Charles Gehringer, Detroit	27
1930—	Martin McManus, Detroit	23
1931—	W. Benjamin Chapman, New York	61
1932—	W. Benjamin Chapman, New York	38
1933—	W. Benjamin Chapman, New York	27
1934—	William Werber, Boston	40
1935—	William Werber, Boston	29
1936—	Lynford Lary, St. Louis	37
1937—	Werber, Phila-Chapman, Wash-Bos	35
1938—	Frank Crosetti, New York	27
1939—	George Case, Washington	51
1940—	George Case, Washington	35
1941—	George Case, Washington	33
1942—	George Case, Washington	44
1943—	George Case, Washington	61
1944—	George Stirnweiss, New York	55
1945—	George Stirnweiss, New York	33
1946—	George Case, Cleveland	28
1947—	Robert Dillinger, St. Louis	34
1948—	Robert Dillinger, St. Louis	28
1949—	Robert Dillinger, St. Louis	20
1950—	Dominic DiMaggio, Boston	15
1951—	Orestes (Minnie) Minoso, Clev-Chi	31
1952—	Orestes (Minnie) Minoso, Chicago	22
1953—	Orestes (Minnie) Minoso, Chicago	25
1954—	Jack Jensen, Boston	22
1955—	Manuel (Jim) Rivera, Chicago	25
1956—	Luis Aparicio, Chicago	21
1957—	Luis Aparicio, Chicago	28
1958—	Luis Aparicio, Chicago	29
1959—	Luis Aparicio, Chicago	56
1960—	Luis Aparicio, Chicago	51
1961—	Luis Aparicio, Chicago	53
1962—	Luis Aparicio, Chicago	31
1963—	Luis Aparicio, Baltimore	40
1964—	Luis Aparicio, Baltimore	57
1965—	Dagoberto Campaneris, Kansas City	51
1966—	Dagoberto Campaneris, Kansas City	52
1967—	Dagoberto Campaneris, Kansas City	55
1968—	Dagoberto Campaneris, Oakland	62
1969—	Tommy Harper, Seattle	73
1970—	Dagoberto Campaneris, Oakland	42
1971—	Amos Otis, Kansas City	52
1972—	Dagoberto Campaneris, Oakland	52
1973—	Tommy Harper, Boston	54
1974—	William North, Oakland	54
1975—	John Rivers, California	70
1976—	William North, Oakland	75
1977—	Freddie Patek, Kansas City	53
1978—	Ronald LeFlore, Detroit	68
1979—	Willie Wilson, Kansas City	83
1980—	Rickey Henderson, Oakland	100

SLUGGING LEADERS

Year	Player and Club	Slug. Avg.
1900—	(Not classed as major)	
1901—	Napoleon Lajoie, Philadelphia	.630
1902—	Edward Delahanty, Washington	.589
1903—	Napoleon Lajoie, Cleveland	.533
1904—	Napoleon Lajoie, Cleveland	.549
1905—	Elmer Flick, Cleveland	.466
1906—	George Stone, St. Louis	.496
1907—	Tyrus Cobb, Detroit	.473
1908—	Tyrus Cobb, Detroit	.475
1909—	Tyrus Cobb, Detroit	.517
1910—	Tyrus Cobb, Detroit	.554
1911—	Tyrus Cobb, Detroit	.621
1912—	Tyrus Cobb, Detroit	.586
1913—	Joseph Jackson, Cleveland	.551
1914—	Tyrus Cobb, Detroit	.513
1915—	Jacques F. Fournier, Chicago	.491
1916—	Tristram Speaker, Cleveland	.502
1917—	Tyrus Cobb, Detroit	.571
1918—	George (Babe) Ruth, Boston	.555
1919—	George (Babe) Ruth, Boston	.657
1920—	George (Babe) Ruth, New York	.847
1921—	George (Babe) Ruth, New York	.846
1922—	George (Babe) Ruth, New York	.672
1923—	George (Babe) Ruth, New York	.764
1924—	George (Babe) Ruth, New York	.739
1925—	Kenneth Williams, St. Louis	.613
1926—	George (Babe) Ruth, New York	.737
1927—	George (Babe) Ruth, New York	.772
1928—	George (Babe) Ruth, New York	.709
1929—	George (Babe) Ruth, New York	.697
1930—	George (Babe) Ruth, New York	.732
1931—	George (Babe) Ruth, New York	.700
1932—	James Foxx, Philadelphia	.749
1933—	James Foxx, Philadelphia	.703
1934—	H. Louis Gehrig, New York	.706
1935—	James Foxx, Philadelphia	.636
1936—	H. Louis Gehrig, New York	.696
1937—	Joseph DiMaggio, New York	.673
1938—	James Foxx, Boston	.704
1939—	James Foxx, Boston	.694
1940—	Henry Greenberg, Detroit	.670
1941—	Theodore Williams, Boston	.735
1942—	Theodore Williams, Boston	.648
1943—	Rudolph York, Detroit	.527
1944—	Robert Doerr, Boston	.5278
1945—	George Stirnweiss, New York	.476
1946—	Theodore Williams, Boston	.667
1947—	Theodore Williams, Boston	.634
1948—	Theodore Williams, Boston	.615
1949—	Theodore Williams, Boston	.650
1950—	Joseph DiMaggio, New York	.585
1951—	Theodore Williams, Boston	.556
1952—	Lawrence Doby, Cleveland	.541
1953—	Albert Rosen, Cleveland	.613
1954—	Theodore Williams, Boston	.635
1955—	Mickey Mantle, New York	.611
1956—	Mickey Mantle, New York	.705
1957—	Theodore Williams, Boston	.731
1958—	Rocco Colavito, Cleveland	.620
1959—	Albert Kaline, Detroit	.530
1960—	Roger Maris, New York	.581
1961—	Mickey Mantle, New York	.687
1962—	Mickey Mantle, New York	.605
1963—	Harmon Killebrew, Minnesota	.555
1964—	John (Boog) Powell, Baltimore	.606
1965—	Carl Yastrzemski, Boston	.536
1966—	Frank Robinson, Baltimore	.637
1967—	Carl Yastrzemski, Boston	.622
1968—	Frank Howard, Washington	.552
1969—	Reginald Jackson, Oakland	.608
1970—	Carl Yastrzemski, Boston	.592
1971—	Pedro (Tony) Oliva, Minnesota	.546
1972—	Richard Allen, Chicago	.603
1973—	Reginald Jackson, Oakland	.531
1974—	Richard Allen, Chicago	.563
1975—	Fredric Lynn, Boston	.566
1976—	Reginald Jackson, Baltimore	.502
1977—	James Rice, Boston	.593
1978—	James Rice, Boston	.600
1979—	Fredric Lynn, Boston	.637
1980—	George Brett, Kansas City	.664

Game-Winning RBI Introduced to Majors

The RBI that gives a club the lead it never relinquishes: (GAME-WINNING RBI—Rule 10.04 (e) adopted prior to 1980 season).

For trivia buffs, the first game-winning RBI belonged to Cincinnati's George Foster. The Reds' left fielder drilled a first-inning double down the left-field line to start his club off and running toward a 9-0 rout over the Braves April 9.

Later in the day, Ted Cox of the Mariners hit a ground-rule double to score two runs and give Seattle a 4-2 lead—a lead the Mariners never relinquished en route to an 8-6 decision over the Blue Jays.

One of the most unusual game-winning RBIs was achieved by Mets pitcher Pete Falcone, who provided the key blow in New York's eight-run, second-inning outburst. Unfortunately, Falcone couldn't stand prosperity and only lasted 4⅓ innings and did not qualify for the victory, even though the Mets defeated the Pirates, 9-4, June 6.

LEADING PITCHERS IN WINNING PERCENTAGE
(15 OR MORE VICTORIES)

Year	Pitcher	Club	Won	Lost	Pct.
1901—	Clark Griffith	Chicago	24	7	.774
1902—	William Bernhard	Philadelphia-Cleveland	18	5	.783
1903—	Earl Moore	Cleveland	22	7	.759
1904—	John Chesbro	New York	41	12	.774
1905—	Jess Tannehill	Boston	22	9	.710
1906—	Edward Plank	Philadelphia	19	6	.760
1907—	William Donovan	Detroit	25	4	.862
1908—	Edward Walsh	Chicago	40	15	.727
1909—	George Mullin	Detroit	29	8	.784
1910—	Albert (Chief) Bender	Philadelphia	23	5	.821
1911—	Albert (Chief) Bender	Philadelphia	17	5	.773
1912—	Joseph Wood	Boston	34	5	.872
1913—	Walter Johnson	Washington	36	7	.837
1914—	Albert (Chief) Bender	Philadelphia	17	3	.850
1915—	Ernest Shore	Boston	19	8	.704
	George Foster	Boston	19	8	.704
1916—	Edward V. Cicotte	Chicago	15	7	.682
1917—	Ewell (Reb) Russell	Chicago	15	5	.750
1918—	Samuel Jones	Boston	16	5	.762
1919—	Edward V. Cicotte	Chicago	29	7	.806
1920—	James Bagby	Cleveland	31	12	.721
1921—	Carl Mays	New York	27	9	.750
1922—	Leslie (Joe) Bush	New York	26	7	.788
1923—	Herbert Pennock	New York	19	6	.760
1924—	Walter Johnson	Washington	23	7	.767
1925—	Stanley Coveleski	Washington	20	5	.800
1926—	George Uhle	Cleveland	27	11	.711
1927—	Waite Hoyt	New York	22	7	.759
1928—	Alvin Crowder	St. Louis	21	5	.808
1929—	Robert Grove	Philadelphia	20	6	.769
1930—	Robert Grove	Philadelphia	28	5	.848
1931—	Robert Grove	Philadelphia	31	4	.808
1932—	John Allen	New York	17	4	.810
1933—	Robert Grove	Philadelphia	24	8	.750
1934—	Vernon Gomez	New York	26	5	.839
1935—	Elden Auker	Detroit	18	7	.720
1936—	Monte Pearson	New York	19	7	.731
1937—	John Allen	Cleveland	15	1	.938
1938—	Charles (Red) Ruffing	New York	21	7	.750
1939—	Robert Grove	Boston	15	4	.789
1940—	Lynwood (Schoolboy) Rowe	Detroit	16	3	.842
1941—	Vernon Gomez	New York	15	5	.750
1942—	Ernest Bonham	New York	21	5	.808
1943—	Spurgeon (Spud) Chandler	New York	20	4	.833
1944—	Cecil (Tex) Hughson	Boston	18	5	.783
1945—	Harold Newhouser	Detroit	25	9	.735
1946—	David (Boo) Ferriss	Boston	25	6	.806
1947—	Allie Reynolds	New York	19	8	.704
1948—	John Kramer	Boston	18	5	.783
1949—	Ellis Kinder	Boston	23	6	.793
1950—	Victor Raschi	New York	21	8	.724
1951—	Robert Feller	Cleveland	22	8	.733
1952—	Robert Shantz	Philadelphia	24	7	.774
1953—	Edmund Lopat	New York	16	4	.800
1954—	Sandalio Consuegra	Chicago	16	3	.842
1955—	Thomas Byrne	New York	16	5	.762
1956—	Edward (Whitey) Ford	New York	19	6	.760
1957—	Richard Donovan	Chicago	16	6	.727
	Thomas Sturdivant	New York	16	6	.727
1958—	Robert Turley	New York	21	7	.750
1959—	Robert Shaw	Chicago	18	6	.750
1960—	James Perry	Cleveland	18	10	.643
1961—	Edward (Whitey) Ford	New York	25	4	.862
1962—	Raymond Herbert	Chicago	20	9	.690
1963—	Edward (Whitey) Ford	New York	24	7	.774

LEADING PITCHERS IN WINNING
PERCENTAGE—Continued

Year	Pitcher	Club	Won	Lost	Pct.
1964—Wallace Bunker		Baltimore	19	5	.792
1965—James (Mudcat) Grant		Minnesota	21	7	.750
1966—Wilfred (Sonny) Siebert		Cleveland	16	8	.667
1967—Joel Horlen		Chicago	19	7	.731
1968—Dennis McLain		Detroit	31	6	.838
1969—James Palmer		Baltimore	16	4	.800
1970—Miguel (Mike) Cuellar		Baltimore	24	8	.750
1971—David McNally		Baltimore	21	5	.808
1972—James A. Hunter		Oakland	21	7	.750
1973—James A. Hunter		Oakland	21	5	.808
1974—Miguel (Mike) Cuellar		Baltimore	22	10	.688
1975—Michael A. Torrez		Baltimore	20	9	.690
1976—William Campbell		Minnesota	17	5	.773
1977—Paul Splittorff		Kansas City	16	6	.727
1978—Ronald Guidry		New York	25	3	.893
1979—R. Michael Caldwell		Milwaukee	16	6	.727
1980—Steven Stone		Baltimore	25	7	.781

LEADING PITCHERS—EARNED-RUN AVERAGE

(Based on Ten Complete Games Through 1950, Then 154 Innings Until A. L. Expanded in 1961, When It Became 162 Innings)

Year Pitcher and Club	G.	IP.	ERA.	Year Pitcher and Club	G.	IP.	ERA.
1913—Johnson, Washington	48	346	1.14	1947—Chandler, New York	17	128	2.46
1914—Leonard, Boston	35	222	1.01	1948—Bearden, Cleveland	37	230	2.43
1915—Wood, Boston	25	157	1.49	1949—Parnell, Boston	39	295	2.78
1916—Ruth, Boston	44	324	1.75	1950—Wynn, Cleveland	32	214	3.20
1917—Cicotte, Chicago	49	346	1.53	1951—Rogovin, Detroit-Chicago	27	217	2.78
1918—Johnson, Washington	39	325	1.27	1952—Reynolds, New York	35	244	2.07
1919—Johnson, Washington	39	290	1.49	1953—Lopat, New York	25	178	2.43
1920—Shawkey, New York	38	267	2.46	1954—Garcia, Cleveland	45	259	2.64
1921—Faber, Chicago	43	331	2.47	1955—Pierce, Chicago	33	206	1.97
1922—Faber, Chicago	43	353	2.80	1956—Ford, New York	31	226	2.47
1923—S. Coveleski, Cleveland	33	228	2.76	1957—Shantz, New York	30	173	2.45
1924—Johnson, Washington	38	278	2.72	1958—Ford, New York	30	219	2.01
1925—S. Coveleski, Washington	32	241	2.84	1959—Wilhelm, Baltimore	32	226	2.19
1926—Grove, Philadelphia	45	258	2.51	1960—Baumann, Chicago	47	185	2.68
1927—Moore, New York	50	213	2.28	1961—Donovan, Washington	23	169	2.40
1928—Braxton, Washington	38	218	2.52	1962—Aguirre, Detroit	42	216	2.21
1929—Grove, Philadelphia	42	275	2.81	1963—Peters, Chicago	41	243	2.33
1930—Grove, Philadelphia	50	291	2.54	1964—Chance, Los Angeles	46	278	1.65
1931—Grove, Philadelphia	41	289	2.06	1965—McDowell, Cleveland	42	273	2.18
1932—Grove, Philadelphia	44	292	2.84	1966—Peters, Chicago	30	205	1.98
1933—Pearson, Cleveland	19	135	2.33	1967—Horlen, Chicago	35	258	2.06
1934—Gomez, New York	38	282	2.33	1968—Tiant, Cleveland	34	258	1.60
1935—Grove, Boston	35	273	2.70	1969—Bosman, Washington	31	193	2.19
1936—Grove, Boston	35	253	2.81	1970—Segui, Oakland	47	162	2.56
1937—Gomez, New York	34	278	2.33	1971—Blue, Oakland	39	312	1.82
1938—Grove, Boston	24	164	3.07	1972—Tiant, Boston	43	179	1.91
1939—Grove, Boston	23	191	2.54	1973—Palmer, Baltimore	38	296	2.40
1940—Feller, Cleveland	43	320	2.62	1974—Hunter, Oakland	41	318	2.49
1941—T. Lee, Chicago	35	300	2.37	1975—Palmer, Baltimore	39	323	2.09
1942—Lyons, Chicago	20	180	2.10	1976—Fidrych, Detroit	31	250	2.34
1943—Chandler, New York	30	253	1.64	1977—Tanana, California	31	241	2.54
1944—Trout, Detroit	49	352	2.12	1978—Guidry, New York	35	274	1.74
1945—Newhouser, Detroit	40	313	1.81	1979—Guidry, New York	33	236	2.78
1946—Newhouser, Detroit	37	293	1.94	1980—May, New York	41	175	2.47

Note—Wilcy Moore pitched only six complete games—he started 12—in 1927, but was recognized as leader because of 213 innings pitched; Ernie Bonham, New York, had 1.91 ERA and ten complete games in 1940, but appeared in only 12 games and 99 innings, and Bob Feller was recognized as leader.

Note—Earned runs not tabulated in American League prior to 1913.

STRIKEOUT LEADERS—PITCHING

Year	Pitcher and Club	SO.
1900—	(Not classed as major)	
1901—	Denton (Cy) Young, Boston	159
1902—	George (Rube) Waddell, Philadelphia	210
1903—	George (Rube) Waddell, Philadelphia	301
1904—	George (Rube) Waddell, Philadelphia	349
1905—	George (Rube) Waddell, Philadelphia	286
1906—	George (Rube) Waddell, Philadelphia	203
1907—	George (Rube) Waddell, Philadelphia	226
1908—	Edward Walsh, Chicago	269
1909—	Frank Smith, Chicago	177
1910—	Walter Johnson, Washington	313
1911—	Edward Walsh, Chicago	255
1912—	Walter Johnson, Washington	303
1913—	Walter Johnson, Washington	243
1914—	Walter Johnson, Washington	225
1915—	Walter Johnson, Washington	203
1916—	Walter Johnson, Washington	228
1917—	Walter Johnson, Washington	188
1918—	Walter Johnson, Washington	162
1919—	Walter Johnson, Washington	147
1920—	Stanley Coveleski, Cleveland	133
1921—	Walter Johnson, Washington	143
1922—	Urban Shocker, St. Louis	149
1923—	Walter Johnson, Washington	130
1924—	Walter Johnson, Washington	158
1925—	Robert Grove, Philadelphia	116
1926—	Robert Grove, Philadelphia	194
1927—	Robert Grove, Philadelphia	174
1928—	Robert Grove, Philadelphia	183
1929—	Robert Grove, Philadelphia	170
1930—	Robert Grove, Philadelphia	209
1931—	Robert Grove, Philadelphia	175
1932—	Charles (Red) Ruffing, New York	190
1933—	Vernon Gomez, New York	163
1934—	Vernon Gomez, New York	158
1935—	Thomas Bridges, Detroit	163
1936—	Thomas Bridges, Detroit	175
1937—	Vernon Gomez, New York	194
1938—	Robert Feller, Cleveland	240
1939—	Robert Feller, Cleveland	246
1940—	Robert Feller, Cleveland	261

Year	Pitcher and Club	SO.
1941—	Robert Feller, Cleveland	260
1942—	Louis (Bobo) Newsom, Washington	113
	Cecil (Tex) Hughson, Boston	113
1943—	Allie Reynolds, Cleveland	151
1944—	Harold Newhouser, Detroit	187
1945—	Harold Newhouser, Detroit	212
1946—	Robert Feller, Cleveland	348
1947—	Robert Feller, Cleveland	196
1948—	Robert Feller, Cleveland	164
1949—	Virgil Trucks, Detroit	153
1950—	Robert Lemon, Cleveland	170
1951—	Victor Raschi, New York	164
1952—	Allie Reynolds, New York	160
1953—	W. William Pierce, Chicago	186
1954—	Robert Turley, Baltimore	185
1955—	Herbert Score, Cleveland	245
1956—	Herbert Score, Cleveland	263
1957—	Early Wynn, Cleveland	184
1958—	Early Wynn, Chicago	179
1959—	James Bunning, Detroit	201
1960—	James Bunning, Detroit	201
1961—	Camilo Pascual, Minnesota	221
1962—	Camilo Pascual, Minnesota	206
1963—	Camilo Pascual, Minnesota	202
1964—	Alphonso Downing, New York	217
1965—	Samuel McDowell, Cleveland	325
1966—	Samuel McDowell, Cleveland	225
1967—	James Lonborg, Boston	246
1968—	Samuel McDowell, Cleveland	283
1969—	Samuel McDowell, Cleveland	279
1970—	Samuel McDowell, Cleveland	304
1971—	Michael Lolich, Detroit	308
1972—	L. Nolan Ryan, California	329
1973—	L. Nolan Ryan, California	383
1974—	L. Nolan Ryan, California	367
1975—	Frank Tanana, California	269
1976—	L. Nolan Ryan, California	327
1977—	L. Nolan Ryan, California	341
1978—	L. Nolan Ryan, California	260
1979—	L. Nolan Ryan, California	223
1980—	Leonard Barker, Cleveland	187

SHUTOUT LEADERS

Year	Pitcher and Club	ShO.
1900—	(Not classed as major)	
1901—	Clark C. Griffith, Chicago	5
	Denton T. Young, Boston	5
1902—	Adrian Joss, Cleveland	5
1903—	Denton T. Young, Boston	7
1904—	Denton T. Young, Boston	10
1905—	Edward H. Killian, Detroit	8
1906—	Edward A. Walsh, Chicago	10
1907—	Edward S. Plank, Philadelphia	8
1908—	Edward A. Walsh, Chicago	12
1909—	Edward A. Walsh, Chicago	8
1910—	John W. Coombs, Philadelphia	13
1911—	Walter P. Johnson, Washington	6
	Edward S. Plank, Philadelphia	6
1912—	Joseph Wood, Boston	10
1913—	Walter P. Johnson, Washington	12
1914—	Walter P. Johnson, Washington	10
1915—	Walter P. Johnson, Washington	8

Year	Pitcher and Club	ShO.
1916—	George H. Ruth, Boston	9
1917—	Stanley Coveleski, Cleveland	9
1918—	Walter P. Johnson, Washington	8
	Carl W. Mays, Boston	8
1919—	Walter P. Johnson, Washington	7
1920—	Carl W. Mays, New York	6
1921—	Samuel P. Jones, Boston	5
1922—	George E. Uhle, Cleveland	5
1923—	Stanley Coveleski, Cleveland	5
1924—	Walter P. Johnson, Washington	6
1925—	Theodore A. Lyons, Chicago	5
1926—	Edwin L. Wells, Detroit	4
1927—	Horace M. Lisenbee, Washington	4
1928—	Herbert J. Pennock, New York	5
1929—	George F. Blaeholder, St. Louis	4
	Alvin F. Crowder, St. Louis	4
	Samuel D. Gray, St. Louis	4
	Daniel K. MacFayden, Boston	4

SHUTOUT LEADERS—Continued

Year	Pitcher and Club	ShO.
1930—	Clinton H. Brown, Cleveland	3
	George L. Earnshaw, Philadelphia	3
	George W. Pipgras, New York	3
1931—	Robert M. Grove, Philadelphia	4
	Victor G. Sorrell, Detroit	4
1932—	Thomas D. Bridges, Detroit	4
	Robert M. Grove, Philadelphia	4
1933—	Oral C. Hildebrand, Cleveland	6
1934—	Vernon L. Gomez, New York	6
	Melvin L. Harder, Cleveland	6
1935—	Lynwood T. Rowe, Detroit	6
1936—	Robert M. Grove, Boston	6
1937—	Vernon L. Gomez, New York	6
1938—	Vernon L. Gomez, New York	4
1939—	Charles H. Ruffing, New York	5
1940—	Robert W. Feller, Cleveland	4
	Theodore A. Lyons, Chicago	4
	Albert J. Milnar, Cleveland	4
1941—	Robert W. Feller, Cleveland	6
1942—	Ernest E. Bonham, New York	6
1943—	Spurgeon F. Chandler, New York	5
	Paul H. Trout, Detroit	5
1944—	Paul H. Trout, Detroit	7
1945—	Harold Newhouser, Detroit	8
1946—	Robert W. Feller, Cleveland	10
1947—	Robert W. Feller, Cleveland	5
1948—	Robert G. Lemon, Cleveland	10
1949—	Edward M. Garcia, Cleveland	6
	Ellis R. Kinder, Boston	6
	Virgil O. Trucks, Detroit	6
1950—	Arthur J. Houtteman, Detroit	4
1951—	Allie P. Reynolds, New York	7
1952—	Edward M. Garcia, Cleveland	6
	Allie P. Reynolds, New York	6
1953—	Erwin C. Porterfield, Washington	9
1954—	Edward M. Garcia, Cleveland	5
	Virgil O. Trucks, Chicago	5
1955—	William F. Hoeft, Detroit	7
1956—	Herbert J. Score, Cleveland	5

Year	Pitcher and Club	ShO.
1957—	James A. Wilson, Chicago	5
1958—	Edward C. Ford, New York	7
1959—	Camilo A. Pascual, Washington	6
1960—	Edward C. Ford, New York	4
	James E. Perry, Cleveland	4
	Early Wynn, Chicago	4
1961—	Stephen D. Barber, Baltimore	8
	Camilo A. Pascual, Minnesota	8
1962—	Richard E. Donovan, Cleveland	5
	James L. Kaat, Minnesota	5
	Camilo A. Pascual, Minnesota	5
1963—	Raymond E. Herbert, Chicago	7
1964—	W. Dean Chance, Los Angeles	11
1965—	James T. Grant, Minnesota	6
1966—	Thomas E. John, Chicago	5
	Samuel E. McDowell, Cleveland	5
	Luis C. Tiant, Cleveland	5
1967—	Steven L. Hargan, Cleveland	6
	Joel E. Horlen, Chicago	6
	Thomas E. John, Chicago	6
	Michael S. Lolich, Detroit	6
	James E. McGlothlin, California	6
1968—	Luis C. Tiant, Cleveland	9
1969—	Dennis D. McLain, Detroit	9
1970—	Charles T. Dobson, Oakland	5
	James A. Palmer, Baltimore	5
1971—	Vida Blue, Oakland	8
1972—	L. Nolan Ryan, California	9
1973—	Rikalbert Blyleven, Minnesota	9
1974—	Luis C. Tiant, Boston	7
1975—	James A. Palmer, Baltimore	10
1976—	L. Nolan Ryan, California	7
1977—	Frank Tanana, California	7
1978—	Ronald Guidry, New York	9
1979—	L. Nolan Ryan, California	5
	Michael Flanagan, Baltimore	5
	Dennis Leonard, Kansas City	5
1980—	Thomas John, New York	6

Dodgers Have Been Jinxed in Playoffs

By winning their last three games of the 1980 season to force a one-game, pennant-deciding playoff, the Los Angeles Dodgers continued a remarkable quirk in history.

The Dodgers, who lost to the Houston Astros, 7-1, October 6, had been involved in all four previous tie-breaking sequences in the National League and now have lost four of the five they have played.

The most dramatic, of course, occurred in 1951 when Bobby Thomson cracked the "shot heard round the world" to give the Giants a three-run rally in the ninth inning of the third and deciding game. In 1959, the Dodgers beat the Milwaukee Braves in two straight games for their only playoff conquest.

The Dodgers other playoff losses came in 1946 when they lost two straight to the Cardinals and in 1962 when they blew a ninth-inning lead and succumbed to the Giants.

The first A.L. playoff came in 1948 when the Indians defeated the Boston Red Sox. The Sox lost again in a one-game playoff in 1978 to the New York Yankees.

Astros Needed Extra Game to Win N.L. West

By LARRY WIGGE

The odds finally caught up with the Los Angeles Dodgers October 6 when the Houston Astros defeated them 7-1 in a one-game playoff for the National League West Division title.

The Astros took a three-game lead into their final series of the 1980 season, a three-game set in Los Angeles, and the odds of having the Dodgers win all three to force a division playoff must have been mind-boggling. But that's what happened. The Dodgers and Astros finished in a dead heat with 90-72 records.

Righthander Joe Niekro went the distance, limiting the Dodgers to six hits to give him his second straight 20-win season, while balding first baseman Art Howe provided a two-run homer in the third inning and singled home two more runs in the fourth to key the Houston attack.

The Astros took advantage of two Los Angeles errors in the first inning to jump out to a 2-0 lead off Dave Goltz. Dave Lopes booted a leadoff grounder by Terry Puhl and catcher Joe Ferguson dropped a throw by third baseman Mickey Hatcher later in the inning, trying to nail Puhl at the plate on a grounder by Jose Cruz. Cesar Cedeno's grounder accounted for the other run.

Enos Cabell singled before Howe's 10th home run of the season in the third for a 4-0 Houston cushion. The Astros tacked on three more runs in the fourth when Puhl singled and stole second and third. Walks to Cabell and Joe Morgan loaded the bases before Cruz hit a sacrifice fly for one run. After Cedeno walked to reload the bases, Howe singled to center, scoring Cabell and Morgan.

Houston	AB.	R.	H.	RBI.	E.	Los Angeles	AB.	R.	H.	RBI.	E.
Puhl, rf	5	2	1	0	0	Lopes, 2b	4	0	0	0	1
Cabell, 3b	4	2	2	0	1	S. Howe, p	0	0	0	0	0
Bergman, 1b	0	0	0	0	0	Johnstone, rf	4	0	0	0	0
Morgan, 2b	2	1	0	0	0	Baker, lf	4	1	1	0	0
Landestoy, 2b	2	0	0	0	0	Garvey, 1b	4	0	0	0	0
Cruz, lf	4	0	1	1	0	Monday, cf	3	0	1	1	0
Cedeno, cf	4	1	1	1	0	Ferguson, c	4	0	1	0	1
A. Howe, 1b-3b	5	1	3	4	0	Hatcher, 3b	3	0	1	0	0
Ashby, c	4	0	1	0	0	Thomasson, ph	1	0	0	0	0
Reynolds, ss	4	0	3	0	0	Thomas, ss	3	0	2	0	0
Niekro, p	2	0	0	0	0	Goltz, p	0	0	0	0	0
						Law, ph	1	0	0	0	0
						Sutcliffe, p	0	0	0	0	0
						Beckwith, p	0	0	0	0	0
						Castillo, p	0	0	0	0	0
						Davalillo, ph	1	0	0	0	0
						Valenzuela, p	0	0	0	0	0
						Perconte, ph-2b	2	0	0	0	0
Totals	36	7	12	6	1	Totals	34	1	6	1	2

Houston	2	0	2	3	0	0	0	0	0—7
Los Angeles	0	0	0	1	0	0	0	0	0—1

Houston	IP.	H.	R.	ER.	BB.	SO.
Niekro (W. 20-12)	9	6	1	0	2	6

Los Angeles	IP.	H.	R.	ER.	BB.	SO.
Goltz (L. 7-11)	3	8	4	2	0	2
Sutcliffe	⅓	1	3	3	2	0
Beckwith	⅓	1	0	0	1	0
Castillo	1⅓	1	0	0	1	2
Valenzuela	2	1	0	0	0	1
S. Howe	2	0	0	0	0	0

Game-winning RBI—None.

LOB—Houston 9, Los Angeles 8. 2B—Reynolds, Cabell. HR—A. Howe (10). SB—Cabell, Cedeno, Puhl 2. SH—Niekro 2. SF—Cruz. PB—Ashby. T—3:10. A—51,127.

Twelfth Championship Series

Including

A.L. Playoff Review

A.L. Game Box Scores

A.L. Composite Box Scores

N.L. Playoff Review

N.L. Game Box Score

N.L. Composite Box Score

PETE ROSE bowls over Houston catcher Bruce Bochy for winning run in 10th inning of Game 4, giving Phillies victory and setting up fifth and deciding game.

Phillies Prevailed in Playoff Thriller

By LARRY WIGGE

The 1980 National League Championship Series had everything anyone could ever hope for. It had controversy. It had rallies. It had high-drama. It had more rallies. It had heartbreak. Most of all, it had two teams that wouldn't give up.

Not until Garry Maddox cradled that final fly ball by Enos Cabell in the 10th inning of the fifth game October 12 did the Philadelphia Phillies finally gain an edge for an 8-7 victory and a three games to two elimination of the West Division champion Houston Astros.

That Maddox would catch the final out and drive in the winning run with a 10th inning double to center field was poetic justice for the Gold Glove-winning center fielder. It was Maddox who dropped a routine fly ball by Bill Russell which set the stage for the Dodgers to beat the Phillies and capture the 1978 Championship Series. Adding fuel to the fire, there were two fly balls in San Diego in August and another on September 28 against Montreal which caused Garry to be benched for the final seven games of the regular season.

"I can't begin to tell you how I feel right now," said Maddox, whose two-base hit plated the doubling Del Unser to ice a see-saw decision and send the Phillies to the World Series for the first time since 1950. "This pennant is one of the most exciting things to ever happen to me. It has been a long time coming for me, my teammates and the fans of Philadelphia."

The Phillies rebounded from a 1-0 deficit in the first game when Greg Luzinski slammed a two-run homer to left field in the seventh inning and Greg Gross plated Maddox with a pinch-single in the eighth for a 3-1 verdict.

The victory ended a 65-year postseason slump at home. Not since Grover Cleveland Alexander opened the 1915 World Series by defeating the Boston Red Sox had Philadelphia fans seen their team win at home.

The Phils were on the threshold of a second consecutive victory at Veterans Stadium after Steve Carlton and Tug McGraw had collaborated in the opener. However, Bake McBride held up at third base on a single by Lonnie Smith, loading the bases, in a controversial play with the score tied, 3-3, in the ninth inning. Third base coach Lee Elia held up his arms to stop McBride and then motioned feverishly to send McBride when Smith's looper fell safely in right field. Houston reliever Frank LaCorte slammed the door by fanning Manny Trillo and getting Maddox on a foul pop.

The Astros rallied with a four-run outburst in the 10th inning to take a 7-4 decision, sending the series to Houston tied at one game apiece.

Terry Puhl opened the 10th with a single. After a sacrifice by Cabell and an intentional walk to Joe Morgan, Puhl scored on a single by Jose Cruz. Rafael Landestoy, running for Morgan, beat a throw home on a grounder to shortstop Larry Bowa by Cesar Cedeno before Dave Bergman capped the outburst with a two-run triple.

Joe Niekro, Houston's two-time 20-game winner, and injury-plagued Larry Christenson of the Phillies spun zeroes at one another in Game 3. The Phils fired 10 blanks at Niekro while Christenson was shutting out the Astros for six frames and McGraw for three more.

In the 11th, Morgan crashed a leadoff triple and Cruz and Art Howe were walked intentionally, before Dennis Walling's sacrifice fly scored pinch-runner Landestoy and made a winner of Dave Smith for one inning of work.

The victory was costly to the Astros, however, as outfielder Cedeno suffered a compound dislocation of the right ankle when he stepped awkwardly on first base while trying to beat a double-play relay in the sixth inning.

Game 4 abounded in controversy, was protested by both clubs and ended up in a 5-3, 10-inning triumph by the Phillies to tie the series at two games each.

McBride and Trillo started the confusion in the fourth inning with singles off Vern Ruhle. When Maddox stroked a soft liner back to the mound controversy turned to chaos.

Ruhle fielded the ball and threw to first base for an apparent double play. Philadelphia players streamed from the dugout, insisting that Ruhle had trapped the ball. Houston players maintained the ball had been caught. Slow-motion replays from numerous angles were inconclusive.

During the confusion, Houston first baseman Howe strolled over to second base and claimed a triple play.

Plate umpire Doug Harvey, with nearly two decades of National League experience, reset the play after conferring with fellow umpires and meeting with N.L. President Chub Feeney, who was in a first base box seat.

"Maddox hits the ball and steps in front of me," Harvey began. "There are runners out there wondering if it's a catch or a trap. My first reaction is no catch and I put my hands down to signal fair ball in play. But I see the pitcher throw to first as though he's going for the double play.

"So I ask for help and they tell me the pitcher caught the ball, and that's good enough for me."

Inasmuch as time had been called before Howe tagged second base, Harvey disallowed the putout, returned McBride to second and ordered the game to go on. The rhubarb consumed 20 minutes and prompted an official protest by each club before the Phillies were retired without any scoring.

After the Astros had taken a 2-0 lead with single runs in the fourth and fifth, there was another argument in their half of the sixth when Gary Woods was called out for leaving base too soon while attempting to score on a fly ball by Luis Pujols.

The Phillies took a 3-2 lead in the eighth when Gross, pinch-hitting for Carlton, singled and scored on singles by Smith and Pete Rose. Schmidt's infield single scored Smith and Trillo followed with a sacrifice fly.

After the Astros once again tied the score in the ninth on a run-scoring single by Puhl, Rose singled and raced home bowling over catcher Bruce Bochy, when pinch-hitter Luzinski doubled. Trillo also doubled, driving in Luzinski.

Bochy was in the game only because Alan Ashby suffered a rib separation in the West Division playoff with Los Angeles and Pujols was sidelined with an ankle injury when struck by an eighth-inning foul tip.

"I had the advantage over him," Rose pointed out. "He couldn't brace for the throw. I had to charge into him. It was the only way I could reach the plate."

The topsy-turvy fifth game saw the Astros' 5-2 lead evaporate into a 7-5 deficit before they staged a rally in the eighth inning to force extra innings.

"After we came back that way, winning would've been what this season has been all about," said Houston reliever Joe Sambito. "We didn't die when we were behind 7-5. We could've kicked it in then. Something kept telling me we'd pull it out. But we didn't."

Terry Puhl, who was 10-for-19 for a .535 average in the series, capsuled the most exciting Championship Series ever. "Everybody thought we were a team of destiny. They were wrong. The Phillies were a team of destiny in this series."

Unfortunately, someone had to lose.

GAME OF TUESDAY, OCTOBER 7, AT PHILADELPHIA (N)

Houston	AB.	R.	H.	RBI.	PO.	A.		Philadelphia	AB.	R.	H.	RBI.	PO.	A.
Landestoy, 2b	5	0	0	0	1	2		Rose, 1b	4	1	2	0	11	1
Cabell, 3b	4	0	1	0	0	2		McBride, rf	4	0	1	0	2	0
Cruz, lf	3	1	1	0	5	0		Schmidt, 3b	3	0	0	0	0	4
Cedeno, cf	3	0	1	0	1	0		Luzinski, lf	4	1	1	2	0	0
Howe, 1b	4	0	0	0	8	1		Unser, lf	0	0	0	0	1	0
Woods, rf	4	0	2	1	1	0		Trillo, 2b	4	0	0	0	5	8
Pujols, c	3	0	0	0	5	1		Maddox, cf	3	1	1	0	3	0
Bergman, pr	0	0	0	0	0	0		Bowa, ss	2	0	1	0	1	1
Reynolds, ss	2	0	0	0	2	4		Boone, c	3	0	1	0	4	1
Puhl, ph	1	0	0	0	0	0		Carlton, p	2	0	0	0	0	0
Forsch, p	2	0	2	0	1	0		Gross, ph	1	0	1	1	0	0
Leonard, ph	1	0	0	0	0	0		McGraw, p	0	0	0	0	0	0
Totals	32	1	7	1	24	10		Totals	30	3	8	3	27	15

Houston	0	0	1	0	0	0	0	0	0 – 1
Philadelphia	0	0	0	0	2	1	0	x – 3	

Houston	IP.	H.	R.	ER.	BB.	SO.
Forsch (Loser)	8	8	3	3	1	5

Philadelphia	IP.	H.	R.	ER.	BB.	SO.
Carlton (Winner)	7	7	1	1	3	3
McGraw (Save)	2	0	0	0	1	1

Game-winning RBI—Luzinski.

Error—Bowa. Double play—Philadelphia 1. Left on bases—Houston 9, Philadelphia 5. Home run—Luzinski. Stolen bases—McBride, Maddox. Sacrifice hits—Forsch, Bowa. Umpires—Engel, Tata, Froemming, Harvey, Vargo and Crawford. Time—2:35. Attendance—65,277.

GAME OF WEDNESDAY, OCTOBER 8, AT PHILADELPHIA (N)

Houston	AB.	R.	H.	RBI.	PO.	A.		Philadelphia	AB.	R.	H.	RBI.	PO.	A.
Puhl, rf	5	1	3	2	3	0		Rose, 1b	4	0	2	0	14	2
Cabell, 3b	4	0	0	0	0	0		McBride, rf	5	0	1	0	2	0
Morgan, 2b	2	1	1	0	4	0		Schmidt, 3b	6	1	2	0	0	3
Landestoy, pr-2b	0	1	0	0	0	1		Luzinski, lf	4	1	2	1	3	0
Cruz, lf	4	1	2	2	4	0		L. Smith, pr-lf	1	1	1	0	0	0
Cedeno, cf	5	1	1	1	3	0		Trillo, 2b	3	0	1	0	2	7
Howe, 1b	4	0	0	0	5	1		Maddox, cf	5	0	2	2	2	0
Bergman, 1b	1	0	1	2	1	1		Bowa, ss	4	1	2	0	0	4
Ashby, c	5	0	0	0	9	2		Boone, c	4	0	1	0	5	0
Reynolds, ss	3	1	0	0	1	1		Ruthven, p	2	0	0	0	2	0
Ryan, p	1	1	0	0	0	2		Gross, ph	0	0	0	0	0	0
Sambito, p	0	0	0	0	0	0		McGraw, p	0	0	0	0	0	0
D. Smith, p	0	0	0	0	0	0		Unser, ph	1	0	0	0	0	0
Leonard, ph	1	0	0	0	0	0		Reed, p	0	0	0	0	0	0
LaCorte, p	1	0	0	0	0	0		Saucier, p	0	0	0	0	0	0
Andujar, p	0	0	0	0	0	0		G. Vukovich, ph	1	0	0	0	0	0
Totals	36	7	8	7	30	8		Totals	40	4	14	3	30	16

Houston	0	0	1	0	0	0	1	1	0	4 – 7
Philadelphia	0	0	0	2	0	0	0	1	0	1 – 4

Houston	IP.	H.	R.	ER.	BB.	SO.
Ryan	6⅓	8	2	2	1	6
Sambito	⅓	0	0	0	1	1
D. Smith	1⅓	2	1	1	1	2
LaCorte (Winner)	1*	4	1	0	1	1
Andujar (Save)	1	0	0	0	1	0

Philadelphia	IP.	H.	R.	ER.	BB.	SO.
Ruthven	7	3	2	2	5	4
McGraw	1	2	1	1	0	0
Reed (Loser)	1⅓	2	4	4	1	1
Saucier	⅔	1	0	0	1	0

*Pitched to two batters in tenth.

Game-winning RBI—Cruz.

Errors—Schmidt, McBride, Reynolds. Double play—Philadelphia 1. Left on bases—Houston 8, Philadelphia 14. Two-base hits—Schmidt, Luzinski, Puhl, Morgan. Three-base hit—Bergman. Sacrifice hits—Trillo 2, Ryan, Gross, Cabell. Umpires—Tata, Froemming, Harvey, Vargo, Crawford and Engel. Time—3:34. Attendance—65,476.

GAME OF FRIDAY, OCTOBER 10, AT HOUSTON

Philadelphia	AB.	R.	H.	RBI.	PO.	A.	Houston	AB.	R.	H.	RBI.	PO.	A.
Rose, 1b	5	0	1	0	13	0	Puhl, rf-cf	4	0	2	0	5	0
McBride, rf	5	0	1	0	1	0	Cabell, 3b	4	0	2	0	1	4
Schmidt, 3b	5	0	1	0	0	2	Morgan, 2b	4	0	1	0	0	2
Luzinski, lf	5	0	0	0	2	0	Landestoy, pr	0	1	0	0	0	0
Trillo, 2b	5	0	2	0	4	5	Cruz, lf	2	0	1	0	7	0
Maddox, cf	4	0	2	0	6	0	Cedeno, cf	3	0	0	0	1	0
Bowa, ss	3	0	0	0	2	4	Bergman, 1b	1	0	0	0	5	0
Boone, c	4	0	0	0	3	1	Howe, ph	0	0	0	0	0	0
Unser, ph	1	0	0	0	0	0	Walling, 1b-rf	3	0	0	1	5	0
Moreland, c	0	0	0	0	0	1	Pujols, c	3	0	0	0	5	0
Christenson, p	2	0	0	0	0	1	Reynolds, ss	3	0	0	0	3	5
G. Vukovich, ph	1	0	0	0	0	0	Niekro, p	3	0	0	0	1	0
Noles, p	0	0	0	0	0	0	Woods, ph	1	0	0	0	0	0
McGraw, p	1	0	0	0	0	0	Smith, p	0	0	0	0	0	0
Totals	41	0	7	0	31	14	Totals	31	1	6	1	33	11

Philadelphia	0	0	0		0	0	0		0	0	0		0—0
Houston	0	0	0		0	0	0		0	0	1		1—1

One out when winning run scored.

Philadelphia	IP.	H.	R.	ER.	BB.	SO.
Christenson	6	3	0	0	4	2
Noles	1⅓	1	0	0	1	0
McGraw (Loser)	3	2	1	1	3	1

Houston	IP.	H.	R.	ER.	BB.	SO.
Niekro	10	6	0	0	1	2
Smith (Winner)	1	1	0	0	1	2

Game-winning RBI—Walling.

Errors—Christenson, Bergman. Double plays—Philadelphia 2. Left on bases—Philadelphia 11, Houston 10. Two-base hits—Puhl, Trillo, Maddox. Three-base hits—Cruz, Morgan. Stolen bases—Schmidt, Maddox. Sacrifice hits—Reynolds, Cabell. Sacrifice fly—Walling. Hit by pitch—By Niekro (Maddox). Passed ball—Pujols. Umpires—Froemming, Harvey, Vargo, Crawford, Engel and Tata. Time—3:22. Attendance—44,443.

GAME OF SATURDAY, OCTOBER 11, AT HOUSTON

Philadelphia	AB.	R.	H.	RBI.	PO.	A.	Houston	AB.	R.	H.	RBI.	PO.	A.
L. Smith, lf	4	1	2	0	2	1	Puhl, cf	3	0	1	1	2	0
Unser, lf-rf	1	0	0	0	1	0	Cabell, 3b	4	1	1	0	0	2
Rose, 1b	4	2	2	1	6	2	Morgan, 2b	3	0	0	0	1	4
Schmidt, 3b	5	0	2	1	3	5	Woods, rf	2	0	0	0	0	0
McBride, rf	4	0	2	0	3	2	Walling, rf	1	0	0	0	0	0
Luzinski, ph	1	1	1	1	0	0	Leonard, rf	1	0	0	0	2	1
McGraw, p	0	0	0	0	0	0	Howe, 1b	3	0	1	1	12	1
Trillo, 2b	4	0	2	2	3	0	Cruz, lf	3	0	0	0	2	0
Maddox, cf	4	0	0	0	6	0	Pujols, c	3	1	1	0	3	0
Bowa, ss	5	0	1	0	0	0	Bochy, c	1	0	0	0	5	1
Boone, c	4	0	0	0	4	1	Landestoy, ss	3	1	1	1	2	4
Carlton, p	2	0	0	0	0	1	Ruhle, p	3	0	0	0	1	1
Noles, p	0	0	0	0	1	1	D. Smith, p	0	0	0	0	0	0
Saucier, p	0	0	0	0	0	0	Sambito, p	0	0	0	0	0	0
Reed, p	0	0	0	0	1	0							
Gross, ph	1	1	1	0	0	0							
Brusstar, p	1	0	0	0	0	0							
G. Vukovich, lf	0	0	0	0	0	0							
Totals	40	5	13	5	30	13	Totals	30	3	5	3	30	14

Philadelphia	0	0	0		0	0	0		0	3	0		2—5
Houston	0	0	0		1	1	0		0	0	1		0—3

Philadelphia	IP.	H.	R.	ER.	BB.	SO.
Carlton	5⅓	4	2	2	5	3
Noles	1⅓	0	0	0	2	0
Saucier	0*	0	0	0	1	0
Reed	⅓	0	0	0	0	0
Brusstar (Winner)	2	1	1	1	1	0
McGraw (Save)	1	0	0	0	0	1

Houston	IP.	H.	R.	ER.	BB.	SO.
Ruhle	7†	8	3	3	1	3
D. Smith	0‡	1	0	0	0	0
Sambito (Loser)	3	4	2	2	1	5

*Pitched to one batter in seventh.
†Pitched to three batters in eighth.
‡Pitched to one batter in eighth.

Game-winning RBI—Luzinski.
Error—Landestoy. Double plays—Philadelphia 3, Houston 2. Left on bases—Philadelphia 8, Houston 8. Two-base hits—Howe, Cabell, Luzinski, Trillo. Three-base hit—Pujols. Stolen bases—McBride, L. Smith, Landestoy, Woods, Puhl, Bowa. Sacrifice hit—Sambito. Sacrifice flies—Howe, Trillo. Umpires—Harvey, Vargo, Crawford, Engel, Tata and Froemming. Time—3:55. Attendance—44,952.

GAME OF SUNDAY, OCTOBER 12, AT HOUSTON (N)

Philadelphia	AB.	R.	H.	RBI.	PO.	A.
Rose, 1b	3	0	1	1	9	2
McBride, rf	3	0	0	0	3	1
Moreland, ph	1	0	0	1	0	0
Aviles, pr	0	1	0	0	0	0
McGraw, p	0	0	0	0	0	0
G. Vukovich, ph	1	0	0	0	0	0
Ruthven, p	0	0	0	0	0	0
Schmidt, 3b	5	0	0	0	0	3
Luzinski, lf	3	0	1	0	0	0
Smith, pr	0	0	0	0	0	0
Christenson, p	0	0	0	0	0	0
Reed, p	0	0	0	0	0	0
Unser, ph-rf	2	2	2	1	0	0
Trillo, 2b	5	1	3	2	4	5
Maddox, cf	4	1	1	1	6	0
Bowa, ss	5	1	2	0	1	2
Boone, c	3	1	2	0	6	0
Bystrom, p	2	0	0	0	0	0
Brusstar, p	0	0	0	0	0	0
Gross, lf	2	1	1	0	1	0
Totals	39	8	13	8	30	13

Houston	AB.	R.	H.	RBI.	PO.	A.
Puhl, cf	6	3	4	0	3	0
Cabell, 3b	5	0	1	0	0	1
Morgan, 2b	4	0	0	0	4	2
Landestoy, 2b	1	0	1	1	2	1
Cruz, lf	3	1	2	2	1	0
Walling, rf	5	2	1	1	1	0
LaCorte, p	0	0	0	0	0	0
Howe, 1b	4	0	2	1	4	0
Bergman, pr-1b	1	0	0	0	2	1
Pujols, c	1	0	0	0	8	1
Ashby, ph-c	3	0	1	1	2	0
Reynolds, ss	5	1	2	0	2	2
Ryan, p	3	0	0	0	1	1
Sambito, p	0	0	0	0	0	0
Forsch, p	0	0	0	0	0	0
Woods, ph-rf	1	0	0	0	0	0
Heep, ph	1	0	0	0	0	0
Totals	43	7	14	6	30	9

Philadelphia	0	2	0	0	0	0	0	5	0	1—8
Houston	1	0	0	0	0	1	3	2	0	0—7

Philadelphia	IP.	H.	R.	ER.	BB.	SO.
Bystrom	5⅓	7	2	1	2	1
Brusstar	⅔	0	0	0	0	0
Christenson	⅔	2	3	3	1	0
Reed	⅓	1	0	0	0	0
McGraw	1	4	2	2	0	2
Ruthven (Winner)	2	0	0	0	0	0

Houston	IP.	H.	R.	ER.	BB.	SO.
Ryan	7*	8	6	6	2	8
Sambito	⅓	0	0	0	0	0
Forsch	⅔	2	1	1	0	1
LaCorte (Loser)	2	3	1	1	1	1

*Pitched to four batters in eighth.

Game-winning RBI—Maddox.
Errors—Trillo, Luzinski. Double plays—Houston 2. Left on bases—Philadelphia 5, Houston 10. Two-base hits—Cruz, Reynolds, Unser, Maddox. Three-base hits—Howe, Trillo. Stolen base—Puhl. Sacrifice hits—Cabell, Boone. Wild pitch—Christenson. Umpires—Vargo, Crawford, Engel, Tata, Froemming and Harvey. Time—3:38. Attendance—44,802.

PHILADELPHIA PHILLIES' BATTING AND FIELDING AVERAGES

Player—Position	G.	AB.	R.	H.	TB.	2B.	3B.	HR.	RBI.	B.A.	PO.	A.	E.	F.A.
Gross, ph-lf	4	4	2	3	3	0	0	0	1	.750	5	0	0	1.000
L. Smith, pr-lf	3	5	2	3	3	0	0	0	0	.600	2	1	0	1.000
Rose, 1b	5	20	3	8	8	0	0	2	.400	53	7	0	1.000
Unser, lf-ph-rf	5	5	2	2	3	1	0	0	1	.400	2	0	0	1.000
Trillo, 2b	5	21	1	8	12	2	1	0	4	.381	18	25	1	.977
Bowa, ss	5	19	2	6	6	0	0	0	0	.316	4	11	1	.938
Maddox, cf	5	20	2	6	8	2	0	0	3	.300	23	0	0	1.000
Luzinski, lf-ph	5	17	3	5	10	2	0	1	4	.294	5	0	1	.833
McBride, rf	5	21	4	5	5	0	0	0	2	.238	11	3	1	.933
Boone, c	5	18	1	4	4	0	0	0	2	.222	22	3	0	1.000
Schmidt, 3b	5	24	1	5	6	1	0	0	1	.208	3	17	1	.952

PHILADELPHIA PHILLIES' BATTING AND FIELDING AVERAGES—Cont.

Player—Position	G.	AB.	R.	H.	TB.	2B.	3B.	HR.	RBI.	B.A.	PO.	A.	E.	F.A.
Reed, p	3	0	0	0	0	0	0	0	0	.000	1	0	0	1.000
Noles, p	2	0	0	0	0	0	0	0	0	.000	1	2	0	1.000
Saucier, p	2	0	0	0	0	0	0	0	0	.000	0	0	0	.000
Aviles, pr	1	0	1	0	0	0	0	0	0	.000	0	0	0	.000
McGraw, p	5	1	0	0	0	0	0	0	0	.000	0	0	0	.000
Brusstar, p	2	1	0	0	0	0	0	0	0	.000	0	0	0	.000
Moreland, c-ph	2	1	0	0	0	0	0	0	1	.000	0	0	0	.000
Christenson, p	2	2	0	0	0	0	0	0	0	.000	0	1	1	.500
Ruthven, p	2	2	0	0	0	0	0	0	0	.000	2	0	0	1.000
Bystrom, p	1	2	0	0	0	0	0	0	0	.000	0	0	0	.000
G. Vukovich, ph-lf	4	3	0	0	0	0	0	0	0	.000	0	0	0	.000
Carlton, p	2	4	0	0	0	0	0	0	0	.000	0	1	0	1.000
Totals	5	190	20	55	68	8	1	1	19	.290	148	71	6	.973

HOUSTON ASTROS' BATTING AND FIELDING AVERAGES

Player—Position	G.	AB.	R.	H.	TB.	2B.	3B.	HR.	RBI.	B.A.	PO.	A.	E.	F.A.
Forsch, p	2	2	0	2	2	0	0	0	0	1.000	1	0	0	1.000
Puhl, ph-rf-cf	5	19	4	10	12	2	0	0	3	.526	13	0	0	1.000
Cruz, lf	5	15	3	6	9	1	1	0	4	.400	19	0	0	1.000
Bergman, pr-1b	4	3	0	1	3	0	1	0	2	.333	8	2	1	.909
Woods, rf-ph	4	8	0	2	2	0	0	0	1	.250	1	0	0	1.000
Cabell, 3b	5	21	1	5	6	1	0	0	0	.238	1	9	0	1.000
Landestoy, 2b-pr-ss	5	9	3	2	2	0	0	0	2	.222	5	8	1	.929
Howe, 1b-ph	5	15	0	3	6	1	1	0	2	.200	29	3	0	1.000
Cedeno, cf	3	11	1	2	2	0	0	0	1	.182	5	0	0	1.000
Morgan, 2b	4	13	1	2	5	1	1	0	0	.154	9	8	0	1.000
Reynolds, ss	4	13	2	2	3	1	0	0	0	.154	8	12	1	.952
Ashby, c-ph	2	8	0	1	1	0	0	0	1	.125	11	2	0	1.000
Walling, 1b-rf-ph	3	9	2	1	1	0	0	0	2	.111	6	0	0	1.000
Pujols, c	4	10	1	1	3	0	1	0	0	.100	21	2	0	1.000
Sambito, p	3	0	0	0	0	0	0	0	0	.000	0	0	0	.000
D. Smith, p	3	0	0	0	0	0	0	0	0	.000	0	0	0	.000
Andujar, p	1	0	0	0	0	0	0	0	0	.000	0	0	0	.000
LaCorte, p	2	1	0	0	0	0	0	0	0	.000	0	0	0	.000
Bochy, c	1	1	0	0	0	0	0	0	0	.000	5	1	0	1.000
Heep, ph	1	1	0	0	0	0	0	0	0	.000	0	0	0	.000
Leonard, ph-rf	3	3	0	0	0	0	0	0	0	.000	2	1	0	1.000
Niekro, p	1	3	0	0	0	0	0	0	0	.000	1	0	0	1.000
Ruhle, p	1	3	0	0	0	0	0	0	0	.000	1	1	0	1.000
Ryan, p	2	4	1	0	0	0	0	0	0	.000	1	3	0	1.000
Totals	5	172	19	40	57	7	5	0	18	.233	147	52	3	.985

PHILADELPHIA PHILLIES' PITCHING RECORDS

Pitcher	G.	GS.	CG.	IP.	H.	R.	ER.	BB.	SO.	HB.	WP.	W.	L.	Pct.	ERA.
Noles	2	0	0	2⅔	1	0	0	3	0	0	0	0	0	.000	0.00
Saucier	2	0	0	⅔	1	0	0	2	0	0	0	0	0	.000	0.00
Bystrom	1	1	0	5⅓	7	2	1	2	1	0	0	0	0	.000	1.69
Ruthven	2	1	0	9	3	2	2	5	4	0	0	1	0	1.000	2.00
Carlton	2	2	0	12⅓	11	3	3	8	6	0	0	1	0	1.000	2.19
Brusstar	2	0	0	2⅔	1	1	1	1	0	0	0	1	0	1.000	3.38
Christenson	2	1	0	6⅔	5	3	3	5	2	0	1	0	0	.000	4.05
McGraw	5	0	0	8	8	4	4	4	5	0	0	0	1	.000	4.50
Reed	3	0	0	2	3	4	4	1	1	0	0	0	1	.000	18.00
Totals	5	5	0	49⅓	40	19	18	31	19	0	1	3	2	.600	3.28

No shutouts. Saves—McGraw 2.

HOUSTON ASTROS' PITCHING RECORDS

Pitcher	G.	GS.	CG.	IP.	H.	R.	ER.	BB.	SO.	HB.	WP.	W.	L.	Pct.	ERA.
Niekro	1	1	0	10	6	0	0	1	2	1	0	0	0	.000	0.00
Andujar	1	0	0	1	0	0	0	1	0	0	0	0	0	.000	0.00
LaCorte	2	0	0	3	7	2	1	2	2	0	0	1	1	.500	3.00
Ruhle	1	1	0	7	8	3	3	1	3	0	0	0	0	.000	3.86
D. Smith	3	0	0	2⅓	4	1	1	2	4	0	0	1	0	1.000	3.86
Forsch	2	1	1	8⅔	10	4	4	1	6	0	0	0	1	.000	4.15
Sambito	3	0	0	3⅔	4	2	2	2	6	0	0	0	1	.000	4.91
Ryan	2	2	0	13⅓	16	8	8	3	14	0	0	0	0	.000	5.40
Totals	5	5	1	49	55	20	19	13	37	1	0	2	3	.400	3.49

Shutout—Niekro-D. Smith (combined). Save—Andujar.

COMPOSITE SCORE BY INNINGS

Philadelphia	0	2	0	2	0	2	1	9	0	4	0 – 20
Houston	1	0	2	1	1	1	4	3	1	4	1 – 19

Game-winning RBIs—Luzinski 2, Cruz, Walling, Maddox.

Sacrifice hits—Cabell 3, Trillo 2, Forsch, Bowa, Ryan, Gross, Reynolds, Sambito, Boone.

Sacrifice flies—Walling, Howe, Trillo.

Stolen bases—Maddox 2, McBride 2, Puhl 2, Schmidt, L. Smith, Landestoy, Woods, Bowa.

Caught stealing—Rose 2, Maddox, Cabell.

Double plays—Bowa, Trillo and Rose 3; Trillo, Bowa and Rose; Ruhle and Howe; Leonard, Bochy and Morgan; L. Smith and Schmidt; McBride, Boone, Noles and Schmidt; McBride and Rose; Reynolds, Morgan and Howe; Cabell, Morgan and Howe.

Left on bases—Philadelphia 5, 14, 11, 8, 5—43; Houston 9, 8, 10, 8, 10—45.

Hit by pitcher—By Niekro (Maddox).

Passed ball—Pujols.

Balks—None.

Time of games—First game, 2:35; second game, 3:34; third game, 3:22; fourth game, 3:55; fifth game, 3:38.

Attendance—First game, 65,277; second game, 65,476; third game, 44,443; fourth game, 44,952; fifth game, 44,802.

Umpires—Engel, Tata, Froemming, Harvey, Vargo and Crawford.

Official scorers—John Black, Rosenberg (Tex.) Herald-Coaster; Paul Giordano, Bucks County (Pa.) Courier; Ivy McLemore, Houston Post.

Plate umpire DOUG HARVEY and N.L. President CHUB FEENEY discuss disputed fourth inning play in Game 4. Harvey ruled a double play after Garry Maddox' controversial soft liner to Houston pitcher Vern Ruhle.

Kansas City's relief ace DAN QUISENBERRY accepts congratulations from catcher Darrell Porter after saving deciding game in A. L. Championship Series.

Royals Avenged Yankees' Hex for A.L. Title

By LARRY WIGGE

The Kansas City Royals were driven by the idea of beating the New York Yankees. Yes, beating those same Big Apple brutes who had sent the Royals away unhappy with playoff losses in 1976, '77 and '78.

The idea of beating the Yankees was almost haunting to the Royals, even to a player like THE SPORTING NEWS 1980 American League Fireman of the Year Dan Quisenberry, who wasn't with Kansas City during those second-best seasons.

"I thought to myself, 'Hey, you know all the years the Royals had short relief problems and they blew leads—that's how they lost all those playoff games. You're the guy who is supposed to turn all that around this year. What are you walking all these guys for?' " Quisenberry commented before he set down the Yankees to extinguish an eight-inning threat and preserve a 4-2 victory in Game 3, enabling the Royals to sweep the A.L. Championship Series from the Yanks.

"Our fans think we've already won the World Series by beating the Yankees," said George Brett, whose towering three-run homer into the third tier of seats at Yankee Stadium off ace reliever Rich Gossage erased a 2-1 deficit and provided the winning touch to the third game triumph.

Gossage, unhittable for the final eight weeks of the season, entered the contest after Tommy John yielded a two-out double by Willie Wilson. U.L. Washington greeted Gossage by beating out an infield chopper.

The stage was set. As Gossage put it: "It was power versus power."

In one classic swipe of the bat, Brett slayed the giants.

"I thought it was going to go out of the stadium," Brett said of his Ruthian clout.

The Royals didn't begin the series with the glee that climaxed it. In fact, there was doubt in the mind of their starting pitcher Larry Gura after Rick Cerone and Lou Piniella hit back-to-back homers for a 2-0 lead in the second inning of Game 1.

"The whole world was watching I thought," said Gura. "The whole world knows I haven't won a game since August 25. Everything is going bad. If I go bad today . . ."

Well, the 18-game lefty, who lost his last five decisions in 1980, didn't exactly dazzle the Yanks but he did manage to scatter 10 hits and pitch the Royals to a 7-2 verdict and a one-game edge.

Frank White began the Kansas City comeback with a two-out, two-run double in the second and Willie Aikens sent two more runs home with a third-inning single. Brett blasted a homer in the seventh and Wilson doubled in the final two tallies in the eighth.

The Royals put together four straight hits for all their runs in the third inning and shaded the Yanks, 3-2, in Game 2. Darrell Porter and White singled before Wilson cleared the sacks with a triple and Washington completed the outburst with a two-base hit.

The Yankees had an inside-the-park homer by Graig Nettles and a run-scoring double by Willie Randolph for their only runs.

However, the most talked about New York play occurred in the eighth when Randolph was thrown out at the plate attempting to score from first on a two-out double by Bob Watson. Blustery Yankees Owner George Steinbrenner wanted third base coach Mike Ferraro fired. The consensus: when left fielder Wilson overthrew the relay man the runner had to score. Brett, backing up Washington, snared the throw and gunned Randolph out at the plate with a perfect peg.

White, who was voted MVP of the series with his 5-for-11 and several outstanding plays in the field, staked the Royals to a 1-0 lead in Game 3 before the Yanks rallied for two runs in the sixth—one coming off starter Paul Splittorff and the other coming off Quisenberry.

Center stage was set for the Brett-Gossage confrontation.

"We all kept hollering, 'It's going to happen, it's going to happen,' " said White. "We just knew they couldn't keep getting George (0 for his last 7) out like that."

The rest is history.

GAME OF WEDNESDAY, OCTOBER 8, AT KANSAS CITY

New York	AB.	R.	H.	RBI.	PO.	A.	Kansas City	AB.	R.	H.	RBI.	PO.	A.
Randolph, 2b	5	0	2	0	0	5	Wilson, lf	5	0	1	2	2	0
Dent, ss	4	0	2	0	3	3	Washington, ss	4	0	1	0	1	3
Watson, 1b	4	0	2	0	11	2	G. Brett, 3b	3	2	2	1	1	2
Jackson, rf	4	0	0	0	1	0	McRae, dh	3	0	0	0	0	0
Soderholm, dh	4	0	1	0	0	0	Otis, cf	4	2	2	0	5	0
Cerone, c	4	1	1	1	6	1	Wathan, rf	1	0	0	0	4	0
Piniella, lf	3	1	1	1	0	0	Hurdle, rf	0	0	0	0	0	0
Rodriguez, 3b	4	0	1	0	1	2	Aikens, 1b	4	0	1	2	7	0
Brown, cf	4	0	0	0	1	0	LaCock, 1b	0	0	0	0	0	0
Guidry, p	0	0	0	0	0	1	Porter, c	4	1	0	0	5	0
Davis, p	0	0	0	0	0	2	White, 2b	4	1	3	2	2	3
Underwood, p	0	0	0	0	0	1	Gura, p	0	0	0	0	0	1
Totals	36	2	10	2	24	17	Totals	32	7	10	7	27	9

```
New York .......................... 0   2   0     0   0   0     0   0   0 – 2
Kansas City ....................... 0   2   2     0   0   0     1   2   x – 7
```

New York	IP.	H.	R.	ER.	BB.	SO.
Guidry (Loser)	3	5	4	4	4	2
Davis	4	3	1	1	1	3
Underwood	1	2	2	0	0	2
Kansas City	IP.	H.	R.	ER.	BB.	SO.
Gura (Winner)	9	10	2	2	1	4

Game-winning RBI—Aikens.

Error—Watson. Double play—New York 1. Left on bases—New York 9, Kansas City 7. Two-base hits—Randolph, G. Brett, Rodriguez, White, Watson, Otis, Wilson. Home runs—Cerone, Piniella, G. Brett. Stolen bases—Otis, White. Sacrifice hit—Dent. Hit by pitcher—By Davis (McRae). Wild pitch—Guidry. Umpires—Palermo, Brinkman, McCoy, Haller, Kaiser and Maloney. Time—3:00. Attendance—42,598.

GAME OF THURSDAY, OCTOBER 9, AT KANSAS CITY (N)

New York	AB.	R.	H.	RBI.	PO.	A.	Kansas City	AB.	R.	H.	RBI.	PO.	A.
Randolph, 2b	4	0	2	1	1	1	Wilson, lf	3	1	1	2	2	1
Murcer, dh	4	0	0	0	0	0	Washington, ss	3	0	1	1	3	1
Watson, 1b	4	0	1	0	6	2	G. Brett, 3b	4	0	0	0	0	0
Jackson, rf	4	0	2	0	2	0	McRae, dh	3	0	0	0	0	0
Gamble, lf	4	0	0	0	1	0	Otis, cf	4	0	1	0	3	0
Cerone, c	4	0	2	0	4	1	Wathan, rf	3	0	0	0	3	0
Nettles, 3b	4	1	1	1	0	1	Hurdle, rf	0	0	0	0	0	0
Dent, ss	3	0	0	0	3	2	Aikens, 1b	3	0	0	0	7	0
Brown, cf	2	1	0	0	5	0	Porter, c	3	1	1	0	8	1
May, p	0	0	0	0	2	2	White, 2b	3	1	2	0	1	2
							Leonard, p	0	0	0	0	0	0
							Quisenberry, p	0	0	0	0	0	0
Totals	33	2	8	2	24	9	Totals	29	3	6	3	27	8

```
New York .......................... 0   0   0     0   2   0     0   0   0 – 2
Kansas City ....................... 0   0   3     0   0   0     0   0   x – 3
```

New York	IP.	H.	R.	ER.	BB.	SO.
May (Loser)	8	6	3	3	3	4

Kansas City	IP.	H.	R.	ER.	BB.	SO.
Leonard (Winner)	8*	7	2	2	1	8
Quisenberry (Save)	1	1	0	0	0	0

*Pitched to one batter in ninth.

Game-winning RBI—Wilson.

Errors—None. Double play—Kansas City 1. Left on bases—New York 5, Kansas City 5. Two-base hits—Washington, Randolph, Watson. Three-base hit—Wilson. Home run—Nettles. Stolen base—Otis. Umpires—Brinkman, McCoy, Haller, Kaiser, Maloney and Palermo. Time—2:51. Attendance—42,633.

GAME OF FRIDAY, OCTOBER 10, AT NEW YORK (N)

Kansas City	AB.	R.	H.	RBI.	PO.	A.	New York	AB.	R.	H.	RBI.	PO.	A.
Wilson, lf	5	1	2	0	2	0	Randolph, 2b	4	0	1	0	1	3
Washington, ss	4	1	2	0	1	3	Dent, ss	4	0	0	0	3	7
G. Brett, 3b	4	1	1	3	1	2	Watson, 1b	4	0	3	0	11	1
McRae, dh	4	0	2	0	0	0	Jackson, rf	3	1	1	0	2	0
Otis, cf	4	0	1	0	3	0	Soderholm, dh	2	0	0	0	0	0
Aikens, 1b	4	0	3	0	8	1	Gamble, ph-dh	1	1	1	0	0	0
Porter, c	3	0	0	0	4	0	Cerone, c	4	0	1	1	4	2
Hurdle, rf	2	0	0	0	1	0	Piniella, lf	2	0	0	0	4	0
Wathan, ph-rf	2	0	0	0	0	0	Spencer, ph	1	0	0	0	0	0
White, 2b	4	1	1	1	6	5	Lefebvre, lf	0	0	0	0	0	0
Splittorff, p	0	0	0	0	0	1	Rodriguez, 3b	2	0	1	0	1	0
Quisenberry, p	0	0	0	0	1	0	Nettles, ph-3b	2	0	0	0	0	1
							Brown, cf	4	0	0	0	1	0
							John, p	0	0	0	0	0	1
							Gossage, p	0	0	0	0	0	0
							Underwood, p	0	0	0	0	0	1
Totals	36	4	12	4	27	12	Totals	33	2	8	1	27	16

Kansas City	0	0	0		0	1	0		3	0	0 – 4
New York	0	0	0		0	0	2		0	0	0 – 2

Kansas City	IP.	H.	R.	ER.	BB.	SO.
Splittorff	5⅓	5	1	1	2	3
Quisenberry (Winner)	3⅔	3	1	0	2	1

New York	IP.	H.	R.	ER.	BB.	SO.
John	6⅔	8	2	2	1	3
Gossage (Loser)	⅓	3	2	2	0	0
Underwood	2	1	0	0	0	1

Game-winning RBI—G. Brett.

Error—White. Double plays—Kansas City 2, New York 1. Left on bases—Kansas City 6, New York 8. Two-base hits—Watson, Jackson, Wilson. Three-base hit—Watson. Home runs—White, G. Brett. Wild pitch—John. Balk—Splittorff. Umpires—McCoy, Haller, Kaiser, Maloney, Palermo and Brinkman. Time—2:59. Attendance—56,588.

KANSAS CITY ROYALS' BATTING AND FIELDING AVERAGES

Player—Position	G.	AB.	R.	H.	TB.	2B.	3B.	HR.	RBI.	B.A.	PO.	A.	E.	F.A.
White, 2b	3	11	3	6	10	1	0	1	3	.545	9	10	1	.950
Washington, ss	3	11	1	4	5	1	0	0	1	.364	5	7	0	1.000
Aikens, 1b	3	11	0	4	4	0	0	0	0	.364	22	1	0	1.000
Otis, cf	3	12	2	4	5	1	0	0	0	.333	11	0	0	1.000
Wilson, lf	3	13	3	4	8	2	1	0	4	.308	6	1	0	1.000
G. Brett, 3b	3	11	3	3	10	1	0	2	4	.273	2	7	0	1.000
McRae, dh	3	10	0	2	2	0	0	0	0	.200	0	0	0	.000
Porter, c	3	10	2	1	1	0	0	0	0	.100	17	1	0	1.000
Quisenberry, p	2	0	0	0	0	0	0	0	0	.000	0	1	0	1.000
Gura, p	1	0	0	0	0	0	0	0	0	.000	0	0	0	.000
LaCock, 1b	1	0	0	0	0	0	0	0	0	.000	0	0	0	.000
Leonard, p	1	0	0	0	0	0	0	0	0	.000	0	1	0	1.000
Splittorff, p	1	0	0	0	0	0	0	0	0	.000	0	0	0	.000
Hurdle, rf	3	2	0	0	0	0	0	0	0	.000	1	0	0	1.000
Wathan, rf-ph	3	6	1	0	0	0	0	0	0	.000	7	0	0	1.000
Totals	3	97	14	28	45	6	1	3	14	.289	81	29	1	.991

NEW YORK YANKEES' BATTING AND FIELDING AVERAGES

Player—Position	G.	AB.	R.	H.	TB.	2B.	3B.	HR.	RBI.	B.A.	PO.	A.	E.	F.A.
Watson, 1b	3	12	0	6	11	3	1	0	0	.500	28	5	1	.971
Randolph, 2b	3	13	0	5	7	2	0	0	1	.385	2	9	0	1.000
Cerone, c	3	12	1	4	7	0	0	1	2	.333	14	4	0	1.000
Rodriguez, 3b	2	6	0	2	3	1	0	0	0	.333	2	2	0	1.000
Jackson, rf	3	11	3	3	4	1	0	0	0	.273	5	0	0	1.000
Piniella, lf	2	5	1	1	4	0	0	1	1	.200	5	0	0	1.000

NEW YORK YANKEES' BATTING AND FIELDING AVERAGES—Continued

Player—Position	G.	AB.	R.	H.	TB.	2B.	3B.	HR.	RBI.	B.A.	PO.	A.	E.	F.A.
Gamble, lf-ph-dh	2	5	1	1	1	0	0	0	0	.200	1	0	0	1.000
Dent, ss	3	11	0	2	2	0	0	0	0	.182	9	12	0	1.000
Nettles, 3b-ph	2	6	1	1	4	0	0	1	1	.167	0	2	0	1.000
Soderholm, dh	2	6	0	1	1	0	0	0	0	.167	0	0	0	.000
Underwood, p	2	0	0	0	0	0	0	0	0	.000	0	2	0	1.000
Davis, p	1	0	0	0	0	0	0	0	0	.000	0	2	0	1.000
Gossage, p	1	0	0	0	0	0	0	0	0	.000	0	0	0	.000
Guidry, p	1	0	0	0	0	0	0	0	0	.000	0	1	0	1.000
John, p	1	0	0	0	0	0	0	0	0	.000	0	1	0	1.000
Lefebvre, lf	1	0	0	0	0	0	0	0	0	.000	0	0	0	.000
May, p	1	0	0	0	0	0	0	0	0	.000	2	2	0	1.000
Spencer, ph	1	1	0	0	0	0	0	0	0	.000	0	0	0	.000
Murcer, dh	1	4	0	0	0	0	0	0	0	.000	0	0	0	.000
Brown, cf	3	10	1	0	0	0	0	0	0	.000	7	0	0	1.000
Totals	3	102	6	26	44	7	1	3	5	.255	75	42	1	.992

KANSAS CITY ROYALS' PITCHING RECORDS

Pitcher	G.	GS.	CG.	IP.	H.	R.	ER.	BB.	SO.	HB.	WP.	W.	L.	Pct.	ERA.
Quisenberry	2	0	0	4⅔	4	1	0	2	1	0	0	1	0	1.000	0.00
Splittorff	1	1	0	5⅓	5	1	1	2	3	0	0	0	0	.000	1.69
Gura	1	1	1	9	10	2	2	1	4	0	0	1	0	1.000	2.00
Leonard	1	0	8	7	2	2	1	8	0	0	1	0	1.000	2.25
Totals	3	3	1	27	26	6	5	6	16	0	0	3	0	1.000	1.67

No shutouts. Save—Quisenberry.

NEW YORK YANKEES' PITCHING RECORDS

Pitcher	G.	GS.	CG.	IP.	H.	R.	ER.	BB.	SO.	HB.	WP.	W.	L.	Pct.	ERA.
Underwood	2	0	0	3	3	2	0	3	0	0	0	0	0	.000	0.00
Davis	1	0	0	4	3	1	1	3	1	0	0	0	0	.000	2.25
John	1	1	0	6⅔	8	2	2	1	3	0	1	0	0	.000	2.70
May	1	1	1	8	6	3	3	4	0	0	1	0	1	.000	3.38
Guidry	1	1	0	3	5	4	4	4	2	0	1	0	1	.000	12.00
Gossage	1	0	0	⅓	3	2	2	0	0	0	0	0	1	.000	54.00
Totals	3	3	1	25	28	14	12	9	15	1	2	0	3	.000	4.32

No shutouts or saves.

COMPOSITE SCORE BY INNINGS

Kansas City	0	2	5	0	1	0	4	2	0 — 14
New York	0	2	0	0	2	2	0	0	0 — 6

Game-winning RBIs—Aikens, Wilson, G. Brett.
Sacrifice hit—Dent.
Sacrifice flies—None.
Stolen bases—Otis 2, White.
Caught stealing—McRae 3, Washington, Otis.
Double plays—Randolph, Dent and Watson; White, Washington and Aikens; Dent, Randolph and Watson; Splittorff, White and Aikens; Washington and White.
Left on bases—Kansas City 7, 5, 6—18; New York 9, 5, 8—22.
Hit by pitcher—By Davis (McRae).
Passed balls—None.
Balk—Splittorff.
Time of games—First game, 3:00; second game, 2:51; third game, 2:59.
Attendance—First game, 42,598; second game, 42,633; third game, 56,588.
Umpires—Palermo, Brinkman, McCoy, Haller, Kaiser and Maloney.
Official scorers—Red Foley, New York Daily News; Don Pfannenstiel, Independence (Mo.) Examiner.

1980 WORLD SERIES

Including

Review of '80 Series

Official Play-by-Play, Each Game

Official Composite Box Score

**World Series Tables—Attendance, Money,
Results**

World Series

WORLD SERIES CHAMPIONS, 1903-1978

New York, A. L. 22   1923-27-28-32-36-37-38-39-41-43-47-49-50-51-52-53-56-58-
                        61-62-77-78
St. Louis, N. L. 8   1926-31-34-42-44-46-64-67
New York, N. L. 6   1905-21-22-33-54 (Giants). 1969 (Mets)
Philadelphia, A.L. 5   1910-11-13-29-30
Boston, A.L. 5   1903-12-15-16-18
Pittsburgh, N.L. 5   1909-25-60-71-79
Cincinnati, N.L. 4   1919-40-75-76
Los Angeles, N.L. 3   1959-63-65
Detroit, A.L. 3   1935-45-68
Oakland, A.L. 3   1972-73-74
Chicago, A.L. 2   1906-17
Chicago, N. L. 2   1907-08
Cleveland, A. L. 2   1920-48
Baltimore, A.L. 2   1966-70
Boston, N. L. 1   1914
Washington, A.L. 1   1924
Brooklyn, N. L. 1   1955
Milwaukee, N.L. 1   1957
Philadelphia, N.L. 1   1980

American League has won 45, National League 32.

RESULTS OF WORLD SERIES GAMES OF 1980

Game	Where Played	Date	Winner		Winner	Loser	Att.
First	Philadelphia	Oct. 14	Phila'phia	7-6	Walk	Leonard	65,791
Second	Philadelphia	Oct. 15	Phila'phia	6-4	Carlton	Quisenb'ry	65,775
Third	Kansas City	Oct. 17	Kansas City	4-3	Quisenb'ry	McGraw	42,380
Fourth	Kansas City	Oct. 18	Kansas City	5-3	Leonard	Christ'son	42,363
Fifth	Kansas City	Oct. 19	Phila'phia	4-3	McGraw	Quisenb'ry	42,369
Sixth	Philadelphia	Oct. 21	Phila'phia	4-1	Carlton	Gale	65,838

ROSTERS OF ELIGIBLE PLAYERS FOR WORLD SERIES

Philadelphia Phillies—Ramon A. Aviles, Robert R. Boone, Lawrence R. Bowa, Warren S. Brusstar, Martin E. Bystrom, Steven N. Carlton, Larry R. Christenson, Gregory E. Gross, Gregory M. Luzinski, Garry L. Maddox, Arnold R. McBride, Frank E. McGraw, B. Keith Moreland, Dickie R. Noles, Ronald L. Reed, Peter E. Rose, Richard D. Ruthven, Kevin A. Saucier, Michael J. Schmidt, Lonnie Smith, J. Manuel Trillo, Delbert B. Unser, George S. Vukovich, John C. Vukovich, Robert V. Walk; G. Dallas Green, manager; Ruben Amaro, William D. DeMars, Lee C. Elia, Michael J. Ryan, Herman P. Starrette, Robert P. Wine, coaches; Don Seger, Jeff Cooper, trainers.

Kansas City Royals—Willie M. Aikens, George H. Brett, Kenneth A. Brett, Jose D. Cardenal, David L. Chalk, Onix Concepcion, Richard B. Gale, Lawrence C. Gura, Clinton M. Hurdle, R. Pierre LaCock, Dennis P. Leonard, D. Renie Martin, Harold A. McRae, S. Rance Mulliniks, Amos J. Otis, Martin W. Pattin, Darrell F. Porter, James P. Quirk, Daniel R. Quisenberry, Paul W. Splittorff, Jeffrey D. Twitty, U. L. Washington, John D. Wathan, Frank White, Willie J. Wilson; James G. Frey, manager; William J. Connors, H. Gordon MacKenzie, Jose Martinez, Jimmie R. Schaeffer, coaches; Mickey Cobb, trainer.

Phillies Ended 97 Years of Frustration With World Series Win

By LARRY WIGGE

A 1-and-2 fastball from Tug McGraw through the bat of Kansas City's Willie Wilson was the pitch that sent World Series starved Philadelphia fans into ecstasy.

But it wasn't one pitch, or one out, or even one game which finally transformed Phillies fans into their frenzied, fanatical state of being. It was a culmination of 97 years of futility. Frustration which reached proportions greater than those which could be felt by fans of any other major league ball club.

Only twice before in the history of the Phillies, who joined the National League in 1883, had they even reached the World Series and those long-ago squads of 1915 and 1950 were only memories of disappointment. Even more despair was felt after the near-impossible el foldo of the 1964 Phils. And then there were those successive playoff fizzles in 1976, '77 and '78.

As bitter as it was to take being a Phillies fan through those oh so many years and generations of frustrations, defeating the Kansas City Royals four games to two to capture baseball's 77th World Series could be nothing less than rapturous delight to Phillies faithful.

McGraw's final fastball, alluded to earlier, represented a typical 1980 Phillies climax because the lefthanded relief ace—in his ninth post-season appearance—had nothing left, but he still got the job done. Pitching with more determination and guts than energy, he worked out of a bases-loaded, one-out jam in the ninth inning to give the Phils a 4-1 victory over the Royals.

"We never did it the easy way," said Phillies first baseman Pete Rose. "We had to be backed into a corner first."

A 4-0 deficit to 20-game winning righthander Dennis Leonard in the Series opener at Veterans Stadium October 14 was the first obstacle the Phillies faced.

The Phils, who had battled from behind to gain all three of the victories to dispose of the Houston Astros in the N. L. Championship Series, displayed a cocky assuredness in exploding for five runs in their half of the third inning and went on to a 7-6 triumph and one-game edge in the Series.

After Larry Bowa became Philadelphia's first baserunner against Leonard with a single, he promptly stole second. A rather unorthodox maneuver at best, but Phillies' players later said it was a message to the Royals that they were not quitting.

Bob Boone then stroked a run-producing double and he scored after Lonnie Smith singled. The run, which cut Kansas City's advantage to 4-2, actually resulted when Smith slipped rounding first and was caught in a rundown which gave Boone time to score.

The next action was typical Pete Rose.

Spinning his bat into the dirt and veering menacingly toward the mound en route to first base after being plunked in the knee by an off-target Leonard delivery, Rose re-established the Phillies' momentum. Leonard later said he thought Rose could have easily gotten out of the way of that pitch.

Perhaps unnerved by Rose's antics, though, Leonard then walked Mike Schmidt. Bake McBride completed the Phils' message to the Royals when he

MIKE SCHMIDT, who hit safely in all six Series games, singled here to score Phillies' first two runs in third inning of Game 6.

belted a three-run homer over the right-center field fence. Result: a 5-4 Phillies lead.

Meanwhile, by the time Philadelphia's starting pitcher Bob Walk—the first rookie to start a Series opener since Joe Black of the 1952 Brooklyn Dodgers—wore down, the Phils had stretched their advantage to 7-4 on Boone's second RBI double and a bases-loaded sacrifice fly by Garry Maddox.

When Walk permitted a George Brett double and Willie Aikens blasted his second two-run homer of the game to lead off the eighth, the Phillies' margin had evaporated to 7-6 and McGraw was summoned from the bullpen. End story. McGraw allowed just one hit in the final two innings.

A four-run rally by the Phils in the eighth inning and a severe case of hemorrhoids to star third baseman Brett was a ROYAL pain for Kansas City in Game 2.

Brett went 2-for-2 with a walk before he had to remove himself from the game in the sixth inning because of the discomfort. Even without Sir George, the Royals erased a 2-0 deficit with one run in the sixth and—after Phils starter Steve Carlton walked the bases loaded—took a 4-2 lead on Amos Otis' two-run double and John Wathan's sacrifice fly in the seventh.

Royals Manager Jim Frey went to his ace reliever Dan Quisenberry to protect the lead. However, after a perfect seventh-inning performance, the submarining righthander was worked over in the eighth.

Boone walked to initiate the rally. He scored on pinch-hitter Del Unser's long double to left-center. Rose tapped out before McBride sent an AstroTurf chopper over second baseman Frank White. Schmidt then ripped a double that sent McBride home. Keith Moreland plated Schmidt with a single for a 6-4 lead and victory.

Carlton needed ninth-inning relief help from Ron Reed and the backing of four double plays—a record-tying three twin-killings started by Bowa—to earn the win. He made 159 pitches in eight innings.

After a day off for travel to Kansas City and for minor surgery to Brett, the Royals captured a 4-3, 10-inning decision in Game 3.

The Royals had taken one-run leads on three occasions with homers by Brett and Otis in the seventh around a fourth-inning run-producing triple by Aikens. It was the first triple in Aikens' three-year career.

Then, with the heretofore invincible McGraw on the mound in the 10th inning, U. L. Washington singled and Willie Wilson walked. Washington was thrown out at third when White missed a bunt attempt and, after White struck out, Wilson swiped second. Brett was walked intentionally, bringing up the hot-hitting Aikens, who met the challenge by stroking a game-winning single to left-center.

In Game 4, the Phils started Larry Christenson, a righthander who spent most of the season on the disabled list. Insiders didn't have time to second-guess the pitching choice of Manager Dallas Green because Christenson lasted only 1/3 inning—time enough to serve up an RBI triple by Brett, a two-run homer by Aikens and doubles by Hal McRae and Otis for a 4-0 lead.

Aikens put his name in the record books when he unloaded a drive into the Royals' bullpen in right field against Dickie Noles. With two homers in the opener and two more in the fourth game, Aikens became the first player in history to have two multiple-homer games in the same Series.

History will also give attention to a major league knockdown pitch by Noles in the fourth inning of the Royals' 5-3 victory. With a two-strike count on Brett, Noles planted a fastball right under his chin. Brett gazed at Noles while picking himself up from the dirt. Kansas City Manager Frey charged from the dugout. Plate umpire Don Denkinger intercepted the K. C. skipper, who still managed to launch a verbal tirade at Noles and other selected Philadelphia performers.

Game 5 was no different from the four which had preceded it—the game was in the balance in the final time at bat.

For the Phillies, who trailed 3-2 entering their half of the ninth, it was a success. Schmidt singled past Brett at third base. Unser followed with his second pinch-double of the Series, skipping a sizzler by Aikens at first to tie the score. After Moreland sacrificed Unser to third and Maddox tapped out, Trillo whacked a shot up the middle for a 4-3 lead. The outcome was far from over, however.

In the Royals' ninth, White and Aikens walked around a strikeout by

WILLIE AIKENS launched this first-inning homer off Philadelphia's Larry Christenson in Game 4. With another homer later in that contest, Aikens became first player to hit two homers in a game twice in same Series.

Brett. McRae forced pinch-runner Onix Concepcion at second before McGraw gave Otis—who had 11 hits, three homers, seven RBIs and a .550 average to that point in the Series—an unintentional intentional pass to get to Jose Cardenal. Released by the New York Mets late in the season, Cardenal was on the spot and McGraw knew just how to handle him. He fanned Cardenal, giving the Phillies a three games-to-two edge with the Series moving back to Philadelphia.

With a well-rested Carlton on the mound, the Phillies seemed a cinch to win that elusive first World Championship—especially after Schmidt socked an opposite-field single with the bases loaded for two runs in the third. McBride's RBI groundout in the fifth and Boone's run-scoring single in the sixth made the score 4-0.

The Royals touched Carlton for one run in the eighth before he was replaced by the arm-weary McGraw. Kansas City loaded the bases in the ninth, but McGraw fanned Wilson—the 12th time the .326-hitter swung at air in the Series—and the Phillies were the champions.

"Discipline," Bowa said. "It was Dallas' discipline. We didn't have that before. He stood on us for seven days a week, not just two. If we missed batting practice, he let us know about it. If we missed infield practice, he let us know about it. We needed somebody to come in when we were watching a football game on TV and say, 'You're watching a stupid football game and missing batting practice?' . . . He stayed on us. I didn't think veteran players needed that, but I guess we do."

Green's discipline made for great headlines, great feuds with several of the players and even greater satisfaction when it was all over and the Phillies had a championship. It was a salve to soothe 97 years of frustrations.

AT PHILADELPHIA Game 1 OCTOBER 14

Kansas City	AB.	R.	H.	PO.	A.	E.	Philadelphia	AB.	R.	H.	PO.	A.	E.
Wilson, lf	5	0	0	2	1	0	Smith, lf	4	0	2	3	1	0
McRae, dh	3	1	1	0	0	0	Gross, lf	1	0	0	1	0	0
G. Brett, 3b	4	1	1	0	2	0	Rose, 1b	3	1	0	7	2	0
Aikens, 1b	4	2	2	13	0	0	Schmidt, 3b	2	2	1	2	3	0
Porter, c	4	1	3	1	0	0	McBride, rf	4	1	3	3	0	0
Otis, cf	3	0	1	1	0	0	Luzinski, dh	3	0	0	0	0	0
Hurdle, rf	1	0	0	1	0	0	Maddox, cf	3	0	0	2	0	0
aWathan, rf	4	0	1	0	5	0	Trillo, 2b	4	1	1	1	2	0
White, 2b	4	0	0	1	6	0	Bowa, ss	4	1	1	0	3	0
Washington, ss	0	0	0	0	0	1	Boone, c	4	1	3	6	0	0
Leonard, p	0	0	0	0	0	0	Walk, p	0	0	0	2	0	0
Martin, p	0	0	0	0	0	0	McGraw, p	0	0	0	0	0	0
Quisenberry, p	0	0	0	0	0	0							
Totals	34	6	9	24	15	1	Totals	32	7	11	27	11	0

Kansas City	0	2	2	0	0	0	0	2	0	— 6
Philadelphia	0	5	1	1	0	0	0	x	— 7

Kansas City	IP.	H.	R.	ER.	BB.	SO.
Leonard (Loser)	3⅔	6	6	6	1	3
Martin	4	5	1	1	1	1
Quisenberry	⅓	0	0	0	0	0

Philadelphia	IP.	H.	R.	ER.	BB.	SO.
Walk (Winner)	7*	8	6	6	3	3
McGraw (Save)	2	1	0	0	0	2

*Pitched to two batters in eighth.

Bases on balls—Off Leonard 1 (Schmidt), off Martin 1 (Schmidt), off Walk 3 (McRae, Porter 2).

Strikeouts—By Leonard 3 (Schmidt, Luzinski, Maddox), by Martin 1 (Luzinski), by Walk 3 (Wilson, G. Brett, Aikens), by McGraw 2 (Washington, Wilson).

Game-winning RBI—McBride.

aGrounded into double play for Hurdle in eighth. Runs batted in—Aikens 4, Otis 2, McBride 3, Maddox, Boone 2. Two-base hits—Boone 2, G. Brett. Home runs—Otis, Aikens 2, McBride. Stolen bases—Bowa, White. Caught stealing—Smith. Sacrifice fly—Maddox. Hit by pitcher—By Leonard (Rose), by Martin (Luzinski). Wild pitch—Walk. Double play—Bowa, Trillo and Rose. Left on bases—Kansas City 4, Philadelphia 6. Umpires—Wendelstedt (N.L.) plate, Kunkel (A.L.) first base, Pryor (N.L.) second base, Denkinger (A.L.) third base, Rennert (N.L.) left field, Bremigan (A.L.) right field. Time—3:01. Attendance—65,791.

FIRST INNING

Kansas City—Wilson struck out. McRae walked. Brett fouled out to Schmidt. Aikens flied to Maddox. No runs, no hits, no errors, one left.

Philadelphia—Smith grounded to White. Rose grounded to Washington. Schmidt struck out. No runs, no hits, no errors, none left.

SECOND INNING

Kansas City—Porter walked. Otis homered to left, Porter scoring ahead of him. Otis became the 16th man to homer in his first Series at-bat. Hurdle flied to Smith. White flied to McBride. Washington grounded to Rose, who flipped to Walk covering first for the out. Two runs, one hit, no errors, none left.

Philadelphia—McBride grounded to Washington. Luzinski flied to Wilson in deep left. Maddox grounded sharply to Brett. No runs, no hits, no errors, none left.

THIRD INNING

Kansas City—Wilson grounded to Trillo. McRae singled to center. Brett struck out on an inside pitch in the dirt. Aikens belted a homer to right-center, McRae scoring ahead of him. Porter walked. Otis beat out a high chopper to third, Porter advancing to second. Hurdle lined a single to left, but Porter was easily thrown out trying to score, Smith to Boone. Two runs, four hits, no errors, two left.

Philadelphia—Trillo grounded to Washington. Bowa singled to center. With Boone batting, Bowa stole second. Boone cracked a double down the left-field line, Bowa scoring. Smith singled to left, Boone first stopping at third and then scoring when Smith was caught in a rundown and retired, Wilson to Brett to Washington to Aikens. Rose was hit on the right leg by a pitch. Schmidt walked, Rose advancing to second. McBride lined a home run over the right-field fence, Rose and Schmidt scoring ahead of him. Luzinski struck out. Five runs, four hits, no errors, none left.

FOURTH INNING

Kansas City—White grounded to Rose, who tossed to Walk covering first for the out. Washington grounded to Bowa. Wilson grounded to Schmidt. No runs, no hits, no errors, none left.

Philadelphia—Maddox struck out. Trillo bounced a single up the middle. With Bowa batting, Leonard bounced a pickoff throw to first past Aikens for an error, Trillo advancing to second. Bowa bounced to White, Trillo advancing to third. Boone doubled down the right-field line, Trillo scoring. Martin replaced Leonard on the mound for Kansas City. Smith flied to Hurdle. One run, two hits, one error, one left.

FIFTH INNING

Kansas City—McRae flied to McBride on the warning track. Brett flied to Maddox, who made a leaping catch at the wall in right-center. Aikens struck out. No runs, no hits, no errors, none left.

Philadelphia—Rose grounded to Washington. Schmidt walked. McBride laced a single to the left of Brett, Schmidt stopping at second. Luzinski was hit in the back by a pitch, loading the bases. Maddox flied to Wilson, Schmidt tagging and scoring after the catch and the other runners holding their bases. Trillo popped to Aikens. One run, one hit, no errors, two left.

SIXTH INNING

Kansas City—Porter fouled out to Schmidt. Otis flied to McBride. Hurdle grounded to Bowa. No runs, no hits, no errors, none left.

Philadelphia—Bowa fouled out to Porter. Boone grounded to White. Smith beat out a bouncer down the third-base line. With Rose batting, Smith was caught stealing, Porter to Washington. No runs, one hit, no errors, none left.

SEVENTH INNING

Kansas City—White singled up the middle. Washington lined to Smith. With Wilson batting, White stole second. Wilson flied to Smith. McRae grounded to Schmidt. No runs, one hit, no errors, one left.

Philadelphia—Rose grounded to Washington. Schmidt beat out a grounder in the hole between third and short. McBride lined a single to right, Schmidt stopping at second. Luzinski struck out. McBride flied to Otis. No runs, two hits, no errors, two left.

EIGHTH INNING

Kansas City—Gross replaced Smith in left field for Philadelphia. Brett doubled to left-center. With Aikens batting, Brett advanced to third on a wild pitch. Aikens smashed his second home run of the game over the right-field fence, Brett scoring ahead of him. McGraw replaced Walk on the mound for Philadelphia. Porter flied to Gross. Otis singled to left. Wathan batted for Hurdle and grounded into a double play, Bowa to Trillo to Rose. Two runs, three hits, no errors, none left.

Philadelphia—Wathan remained in the game to play right field for Kansas City. Trillo flied to Wathan. Bowa grounded to White. Boone singled to right. Quisenberry replaced Martin on the mound for Kansas City. Gross grounded to Washington. No runs, one hit, no errors, one left.

NINTH INNING

Kansas City—White grounded to Schmidt. Washington was called out on strikes. Wilson struck out. No runs, no hits, no errors, none left.

AT PHILADELPHIA Game 2 OCTOBER 15

Kansas City	AB.	R.	H.	PO.	A.	E.		Philadelphia	AB.	R.	H.	PO.	A.	E.
Wilson, lf	4	1	1	1	0	0		Smith, lf	3	0	0	0	0	0
Washington, ss	4	0	1	0	3	0		aUnser, cf	1	1	1	0	0	0
G. Brett, 3b	2	0	2	2	2	0		Rose, 1b	4	0	0	7	1	0
Chalk, 3b	0	1	0	0	1	0		McBride, rf	3	1	1	2	0	0
cPorter	1	0	0	0	0	0		Schmidt, 3b	4	1	2	1	1	0
McRae, dh	4	1	3	0	0	0		Moreland, dh	4	1	2	0	0	0
Otis, cf	5	1	2	5	0	0		Maddox, cf	3	1	1	1	1	0
Wathan, c	3	0	0	2	0	0		bGross, lf	1	0	0	0	0	0
Aikens, 1b	3	0	1	6	0	0		Trillo, 2b	2	0	0	6	3	1
LaCock, 1b	0	0	0	2	0	0		Bowa, ss	3	0	1	0	6	0
Cardenal, rf	4	0	0	3	0	0		Boone, c	1	1	0	10	1	0
White, 2b	4	0	1	3	3	0		Carlton, p	0	0	0	0	1	0
Gura, p	0	0	0	0	0	0		Reed, p	0	0	0	0	0	0
Quisenberry, p	0	0	0	0	0	0								
Totals	34	4	11	24	9	0		Totals	29	6	8	27	14	1

Kansas City	0	0	0	0	0	1	3	0	0	– 4
Philadelphia	0	0	0	2	0	0	0	4	x	– 6

Kansas City	IP.	H.	R.	ER.	BB.	SO.
Gura	6	4	2	2	2	2
Quisenberry (Loser)	2	4	4	4	1	0

Philadelphia	IP.	H.	R.	ER.	BB.	SO.
Carlton (Winner)	8	10	4	3	6	10
Reed (Save)	1	1	0	0	0	2

Bases on balls—Off Gura 2 (Boone, McBride), off Quisenberry 1 (Boone), off Carlton 6 (Aikens, G. Brett, Wathan, Wilson, Chalk, McRae).

Strikeouts—By Gura 2 (Maddox, Smith), by Carlton 10 (Wilson 3, Cardenal 2, White, Washington 2, McRae, Aikens), by Reed 2 (Porter, Wathan).

Game-winning RBI—Schmidt.

aDoubled in one run for Smith in eighth. bGrounded into double play for Maddox in eighth. cCalled out on strikes for Chalk in ninth. Runs batted in—Otis 2, Wathan, Unser, McBride, Schmidt, Moreland, Trillo, Bowa. Two-base hits—Maddox, Otis, Unser, Schmidt. Stolen bases—Wilson, Chalk. Sacrifice flies—Trillo, Wathan. Wild pitch—Carlton. Double plays—Bowa, Trillo and Rose 3; Washington, White and Aikens; Maddox, Rose and Schmidt; Washington, White and LaCock. Left on bases—Kansas City 11, Philadelphia 3. Umpires—Kunkel (A.L.) plate, Pryor (N.L.) first, Denkinger (A.L.) second, Rennert (N.L.) third, Bremigan (A.L.) left, Wendelstedt (N.L.) right. Time—3:01. Attendance—65,775.

FIRST INNING

Kansas City—Wilson struck out on a pitch in the dirt and was thrown out at first, Boone to Rose. Washington grounded to Bowa. Brett bounced a single up the middle. McRae singled to right, Brett stopping at second. Otis forced McRae, Schmidt to Trillo. No runs, two hits, no errors, two left.

Philadelphia—Smith flied to Otis. Rose flied to Otis. McBride popped to Brett. No runs, no hits, no errors, none left.

SECOND INNING

Kansas City—Wathan popped to Rose. Aikens walked. Cardenal was called out on strikes. White struck out, but the third strike was a wild pitch and he reached first safely, Aikens advancing to second. Wilson struck out. No runs, no hits, no errors, two left.

Philadelphia—Schmidt grounded to Brett. Moreland flied to Wilson. Maddox struck out. No runs, no hits, no errors, none left.

THIRD INNING

Kansas City—Washington was called out on strikes. Brett singled to right. McRae singled to left, Brett stopping at second. Otis grounded into a double play, Bowa to Trillo to Rose. No runs, two hits, no errors, one left.

Philadelphia—Trillo flied to Otis. Bowa fouled out to Brett. Boone flied to Otis. No runs, no hits, no errors, none left.

FOURTH INNING

Kansas City—Wathan flied to McBride. Aikens singled off Carlton's leg into center. Cardenal grounded into a double play, Bowa to Trillo to Rose. No runs, one hit, no errors, none left.

Philadelphia—Smith struck out. Rose flied to Otis. McBride lined to White. No runs, no hits, no errors, none left.

FIFTH INNING

Kansas City—White grounded to Bowa. Wilson struck out. Washington singled up the middle. Brett walked, Washington advancing to second. McRae struck out. No runs, one hit, no errors, two left.

Philadelphia—Schmidt grounded to Brett. Moreland bounced an infield hit to short. Maddox doubled down the left-field line, Moreland stopping at third. Trillo flied to Cardenal, Moreland tagging and scoring after the catch and Maddox advancing to third. Bowa singled to left, Maddox scoring. Boone walked, Bowa advancing to second. Smith flied to Cardenal. Two runs, three hits, no errors, two left.

SIXTH INNING

Kansas City—Otis singled to center. Wathan walked, Otis advancing to second. Aikens hit a high bouncer to Trillo, who threw past Rose for an error, Otis scoring, Wathan advancing to third and Aikens holding first. Cardenal struck out. White grounded into a double play, Bowa to Trillo to Rose. One run, one hit, one error, one left.

Philadelphia—Chalk replaced Brett at third base for Kansas City. Rose flied to Cardenal. McBride walked. Schmidt singled to center, McBride stopping at second. Moreland grounded into a double play, Washington to White to Aikens. No runs, one hit, no errors, one left.

SEVENTH INNING

Kansas City—Wilson walked. Washington sacrificed Wilson to second, Carlton to Trillo covering first for the out. With Chalk batting, Wilson stole third. Chalk walked. With McRae batting, Carlton attempted a pickoff at first, but Chalk stole second with no throw from Rose, who was wary of Wilson at third. McRae walked, loading the bases. Otis doubled down the left-field line, Wilson and Chalk scoring and McRae stopping at third. Wathan flied to Maddox, McRae tagging and scoring after the catch. Rose cut off Maddox' throw to the plate and threw to Schmidt, who tagged out Otis. Three runs, one hit, no errors, none left.

Philadelphia—Quisenberry replaced Gura on the mound for Kansas City. Maddox grounded to Chalk. Trillo grounded to Washington. Bowa grounded to White. No runs, no hits, no errors, none left.

EIGHTH INNING

Kansas City—Aikens struck out. Cardenal flied to McBride, who made a running, backhanded catch on the warning track. White singled to left. Wilson struck a line drive that Rose, with a step to his right and a leap, managed to knock down, White stopping at second on the infield single. Washington struck out. No runs, two hits, no errors, two left.

Philadelphia—LaCock replaced Aikens at first base for Kansas City. Boone walked. Unser batted for Smith and lined a double up the gap in left-center, Boone scoring. Rose grounded to LaCock, who made the play unassisted, Unser advancing to third. McBride singled over the head of a drawn-in White, Unser scoring. Schmidt doubled to the wall in right-center, McBride sliding home with the go-ahead run and Schmidt advancing to third on the throw to the plate. Moreland lined a single to center, Schmidt scoring. Gross batted for Maddox and grounded into a double play, Washington to White to LaCock. Four runs, four hits, no errors, none left.

NINTH INNING

Kansas City—Gross and Unser remained in the game for Philadelphia to play left field and center field, respectively. Reed replaced Carlton on the mound. Porter batted for Chalk and was called out on strikes. McRae bounced a single to center. Otis forced McRae, Bowa to Trillo. Wathan struck out. No runs, one hit, no errors, one left.

AT KANSAS CITY Game 3 OCTOBER 17

Philadelphia	AB.	R.	H.	PO.	A.	E.	Kansas City	AB.	R.	H.	PO.	A.	E.
Smith, lf	4	0	2	0	0	0	Wilson, lf	4	1	0	3	0	0
bGross, lf	0	0	0	0	0	0	White, 2b	5	0	0	4	2	0
Rose, 1b	4	0	1	11	0	0	G. Brett, 3b	4	1	2	0	3	0
Schmidt, 3b	5	1	1	3	3	0	Aikens, 1b	5	1	2	7	1	0
McBride, rf	5	0	2	1	0	0	McRae, dh	4	0	2	0	0	0
Moreland, dh	5	0	1	0	0	0	Otis, cf	4	1	2	9	0	0
Maddox, cf	4	0	1	3	0	0	Hurdle, rf	4	0	2	1	0	0
Trillo, 2b	5	1	2	2	6	0	aConcepcion	0	0	0	0	0	0
Bowa, ss	5	1	3	1	3	0	Cardenal, rf	0	0	0	0	0	0
Boone, c	4	0	1	8	1	0	Porter, c	4	0	0	4	0	0
Ruthven, p	0	0	0	0	0	0	Washington, ss	4	0	1	1	2	0
McGraw, p	0	0	0	0	0	0	Gale, p	0	0	0	0	1	0
							Martin, p	0	0	0	0	0	0
							Quisenberry, p	0	0	0	1	1	0
Totals	41	3	14	29	13	0	Totals	38	4	11	30	10	0

Philadelphia	0	1	0	0	1	0	0	1	0	0 – 3
Kansas City	1	0	0	1	0	0	1	0	0	1 – 4

Two out when winning run scored.

Philadelphia	IP.	H.	R.	ER.	BB.	SO.
Ruthven	9	9	3	3	0	7
McGraw (Loser)	⅔	2	1	1	2	1

Kansas City	IP.	H.	R.	ER.	BB.	SO.
Gale	4⅓	7	2	2	3	3
Martin	3⅓	5	1	1	1	1
Quisenberry (Winner)	2⅓	2	0	0	2	0

Bases on balls—Off McGraw 2 (Wilson, G. Brett), off Gale 3 (Schmidt, Boone, Rose), off Martin 1 (Smith), off Quisenberry 2 (Maddox, Rose).

Strikeouts—By Ruthven 7 (Wilson 2, White 2, Aikens 2, Porter), by McGraw 1 (White), by Gale 3 (Rose, Moreland, McBride), by Martin 1 (Rose).

Game-winning RBI—Aikens.

aRan for Hurdle in ninth. bSacrificed for Smith in tenth. Runs batted in—Smith, Rose, Schmidt, G. Brett, Aikens, McRae, Otis. Two-base hits—Trillo, G. Brett. Three-base hit—Aikens. Home Runs—G. Brett, Schmidt, Otis. Stolen bases—Hurdle, Bowa, Wilson. Caught stealing—Washington. Sacrifice hit—Gross. Double plays—White, Washington and Aikens; Bowa, Trillo and Rose; White unassisted. Left on bases—Philadelphia 15, Kansas City 7. Umpires—Pryor (N.L.) plate, Denkinger (A.L.) first, Rennert (N.L.) second, Bremigan (A.L.) third, Wendelstedt (N.L.) left, Kunkel (A.L.) right. Time—3:19. Attendance—42,380.

FIRST INNING

Philadelphia—Smith singled to right. Rose struck out. Schmidt walked, Smith advancing to second. McBride flied to Wilson, the runners holding. Moreland flied to Otis. No runs, one hit, no errors, two left.

Kansas City—Wilson grounded to Trillo. White grounded to Schmidt. Brett lofted a home run into the right-field stands. Aikens grounded to Trillo. One run, one hit, no errors, none left.

SECOND INNING

Philadelphia—Maddox grounded to Brett. Trillo lined a single off Gale's foot. Bowa singled to right, Trillo stopping at second. Boone walked, loading the bases. Smith lined to Gale, who knocked the ball down and then threw to Aikens for the out, passing up the force at home as Trillo scored, Bowa advanced to third and Boone to second. Rose walked, loading the bases. Schmidt flied to Otis. One run, two hits, no errors, three left.

Kansas City—McRae fouled out to Rose. Otis singled to short. Hurdle forced Otis, Bowa backhanding the ball on his knees in the hole and flipping to Trillo for the out. Porter grounded to Bowa, who tagged second to force Hurdle. No runs, one hit, no errors, one left.

THIRD INNING

Philadelphia—McBride singled to right. Moreland struck out. Maddox forced McBride, Brett to White. Trillo doubled into the right-field corner, Maddox stopping at third. Bowa grounded to Brett. No runs, two hits, no errors, two left.

Kansas City—Washington lined to Maddox. Wilson struck out. White grounded to Schmidt. No runs, no hits, no errors, none left.

FOURTH INNING

Philadelphia—Boone flied to Otis. Smith flied to Otis. Rose grounded to White. No runs, no hits, no errors, none left.

Kansas City—Brett fouled to Schmidt. Aikens hit a looper to short left and when the ball went past a diving Smith into the left-field corner, Aikens went to third with his first triple as a major leaguer. McRae lined a single to right-center, Aikens scoring. With McRae running on the pitch, Otis grounded to Trillo, McRae advancing to second. Hurdle grounded to Trillo. One run, two hits, no errors, one left.

FIFTH INNING

Philadelphia—Schmidt drilled a home run into the left-field bullpen. McBride was called out on strikes. Moreland singled to left. Martin replaced Gale on the mound for Kansas City. Maddox singled to short, Moreland advancing to second. Trillo grounded into a double play, White to Washington to Aikens. One run, three hits, no errors, one left.

Kansas City—Porter grounded to Trillo. Washington flied to Maddox. Wilson struck out. No runs, no hits, no errors, none left.

SIXTH INNING

Philadelphia—Bowa singled to center. Boone flied to Otis. Smith singled to center, Bowa stopping at second. Rose struck out. Schmidt forced Smith, Washington to White. No runs, two hits, no errors, two left.

Kansas City—White struck out. Brett flied to Maddox. Aikens struck out. No runs, no hits, no errors, none left.

SEVENTH INNING

Philadelphia—McBride flied to Otis. Moreland flied to Otis. Maddox flied to Hurdle. No runs, no hits, no errors, none left.

Kansas City—McRae grounded to Schmidt. Otis lined a home run over the 385-foot sign in right-center. Hurdle singled to right. Porter was called out on strikes, Hurdle stealing second on the pitch. Washington fouled out to Schmidt. One run, two hits, no errors, one left.

EIGHTH INNING

Philadelphia—Trillo flied to Wilson. Bowa beat out a bouncer to the left side of the mound. Boone flied to Otis. With Smith batting, Bowa stole second. Smith walked. Rose singled to right-center, Bowa scoring and Smith advancing to third. Quisenberry replaced Martin on the mound for Kansas City. Schmidt flied to Otis. One run, two hits, no errors, two left.

Kansas City—Wilson grounded to Bowa. White struck out. Brett lined a double to right-center. Aikens was called out on strikes. No runs, one hit, no errors, one left.

NINTH INNING

Philadelphia—McBride lined a single to left. Moreland flied to Wilson on the warning track near the left-field line, McBride tagging and advancing to second after the catch. Maddox was walked intentionally. Trillo grounded to Aikens, who flipped to Quisenberry covering first for the out, McBride advancing to third and Maddox to second. Bowa grounded to Quisenberry, who threw on to Aikens for the out. No runs, one hit, no errors, two left.

Kansas City—McRae singled to left. Otis grounded into a double play, Bowa to Trillo to Rose. Hurdle grounded an infield single to short. Concepcion ran for Hurdle. Porter flied to McBride. No runs, two hits, no errors, one left.

TENTH INNING

Philadelphia—Cardenal came in to play right field for Kansas City. Boone singled to center. Gross batted for Smith and sacrificed Boone to second, Aikens fielding the bunt and tagging Gross for the out. Rose was walked intentionally. Schmidt lined to the right of White, who made a lunging catch and then stepped on second to double off Boone. No runs, one hit, no errors, one left.

Kansas City—Gross remained in the game to play left field for Philadelphia and McGraw replaced Ruthven on the mound. Washington bounced sharply past Bowa and into left for a single. Wilson walked, Washington advancing to second. With White attempting a sacrifice, Washington was caught stealing, Boone to Schmidt, who made a fine swipe tag after scrambling back to the bag. White struck out. With Brett batting, Wilson stole second on a 1-1 pitch. Brett was walked intentionally. Aikens lined a single up the gap in left-center, Wilson scoring the winning run. One run, two hits, no errors, two left.

AT KANSAS CITY   Game 4   OCTOBER 18

Philadelphia	AB.	R.	H.	PO.	A.	E.	Kansas City	AB.	R.	H.	PO.	A.	E.
Smith, dh	4	0	0	0	0	0	Wilson, lf	4	1	1	4	0	0
Rose, 1b	4	1	2	8	2	0	White, 2b	5	0	0	2	4	1
McBride, rf	3	0	1	3	0	0	G. Brett, 3b	5	1	1	0	7	0
Schmidt, 3b	3	0	1	2	0	0	Aikens, 1b	3	2	2	13	0	0
Unser, lf	4	0	1	2	0	0	McRae, dh	4	1	2	0	0	0
Maddox, cf	4	2	1	0	6	0	Otis, cf	4	0	2	1	0	0
Trillo, 2b	4	0	2	1	1	0	Hurdle, rf	2	0	1	3	0	0
Bowa, ss	3	0	1	6	0	0	Porter, c	3	0	0	2	1	0
Boone, c	3	0	1	6	0	1	Washington, ss	4	0	1	2	3	1
Christenson, p	0	0	0	1	0	0	Leonard, p	0	0	0	0	0	0
Noles, p	0	0	0	0	0	0	Quisenberry, p	0	0	0	0	0	0
Saucier, p	0	0	0	0	0	0							
Brusstar, p	0	0	0	0	0	0							
Totals	33	3	10	24	9	1	Totals	34	5	10	27	15	2

Philadelphia	0	1	0	0	0	0	1	1	0 – 3
Kansas City	4	1	0	0	0	0	0	0	x – 5

Philadelphia	IP.	H.	R.	ER.	BB.	SO.
Christenson (Loser)	⅓	5	4	4	0	0
Noles	4⅔	5	1	1	2	6
Saucier	⅔	0	0	0	2	0
Brusstar	2⅓	0	0	0	1	0

Royals Manager Jim Frey has to be restrained by plate umpire Don Denkinger after controversial Game 4 duster by Phillies' Dickie Noles. Bottom photo shows K.C. star George Brett scrambling out of the way of Noles fourth inning high and tight delivery.

Kansas City	IP.	H.	R.	ER.	BB.	SO.
Leonard (Winner)	7*	9	3	2	1	2
Quisenberry (Save)	2	1	0	0	0	0

*Pitched to one batter in eighth.

Bases on balls—Off Noles 2 (Hurdle 2), off Saucier 2 (Wilson, Aikens), off Brusstar 1 (Porter), off Leonard 1 (McBride).

Strikeouts—By Noles 6 (Porter 2, Wilson, G. Brett, Aikens, McRae), by Leonard 2 (Schmidt, Unser).

Game-winning RBI—G. Brett.

Runs batted in—Schmidt, Bowa, Boone, G. Brett, Aikens 3, Otis. Two-base hits—McRae 2, Otis, Hurdle, McBride, Trillo, Rose. Three-base hit—G. Brett. Home runs—Aikens 2. Stolen base—Bowa. Caught stealing—McBride. Sacrifice flies—Boone, Schmidt. Wild pitches—Leonard, Saucier. Double play—G. Brett, White and Aikens. Left on bases—Philadelphia 6, Kansas City 10. Umpires—Denkinger (A.L.) plate, Rennert (N.L.) first, Bremigan (A.L.) second, Wendelstedt (N.L.) third, Kunkel (A.L.) left, Pryor (N.L.) right. Time—2:37. Attendance—42,363.

FIRST INNING

Philadelphia—Smith grounded to Brett. Rose grounded a single to the right of White, who made a fine play to get to the ball but then threw past Aikens, Rose advancing to second on the error. McBride flied to Wilson, Rose holding second. Schmidt struck out. No runs, one hit, one error, one left.

Kansas City—Wilson singled to center. With White batting, Christenson attempted a pickoff but his throw went past Rose and down the right-field line, Wilson advancing to third on Christenson's error. White flied to McBride, Wilson holding third. Brett lined a triple down the right-field line, Wilson scoring. Aikens cracked a home run over the right-field fence, Brett scoring ahead of him. McRae lined a hit to center and stretched it into a double. Otis doubled off the wall in right-center, McRae scoring. Noles replaced Christenson on the mound for Philadelphia. Hurdle walked. Porter struck out. Washington beat out a grounder up the middle, loading the bases. Wilson grounded to Rose, who tossed to Noles covering first for the out on a close play. Four runs, six hits, one error, three left.

SECOND INNING

Philadelphia—Unser flied to Wilson. Maddox singled to right. Trillo forced Maddox, White to Washington, and advanced to second when Washington's relay throw to Aikens was errant. Bowa singled to left, Trillo scoring and Bowa advancing to second on Wilson's throw to the plate. Boone grounded to Brett. One run, two hits, one error, one left.

Kansas City—Wilson flied to Maddox. Brett grounded to Trillo. Aikens unloaded a titanic homer into the right-field bullpen. McRae again stretched a hit into a double, this time taking second when McBride was lax in playing his liner to right-center. Otis flied to McBride. One run, two hits, no errors, one left.

THIRD INNING

Philadelphia—Schmidt grounded to Brett. Rose flied to Wilson. McBride walked. With Schmidt batting, McBride was caught stealing, Porter to White. No runs, no hits, no errors, none left.

Kansas City—Hurdle blooped a double down the left-field line. Porter fouled out to Schmidt. Washington grounded to Trillo, Hurdle advancing to third. Wilson struck out. No runs, one hit, no errors, one left.

FOURTH INNING

Philadelphia—Schmidt bunted down the third-base line for a single. Unser flied to Otis. Maddox grounded to Aikens, who tagged him out as they raced for the bag, Schmidt advancing to second. Trillo flied to Hurdle. No runs, one hit, no errors, one left.

Kansas City—White fouled out to Rose. Brett struck out. Aikens struck out. No runs, no hits, no errors, none left.

FIFTH INNING

Philadelphia—Bowa flied to Hurdle. Boone singled to center. Smith grounded into a double play, Brett to White to Aikens. No runs, one hit, no errors, none left.

Kansas City—McRae struck out. Otis singled up the middle. Hurdle walked, Otis advancing to second. Porter struck out. Washington fouled out to Schmidt. No runs, one hit, no errors, two left.

SIXTH INNING

Philadelphia—Rose grounded to Brett. McBride doubled to left-center. Schmidt grounded to Brett, who ranged to his left and threw Schmidt out after first dropping the ball, McBride holding second. With Unser batting, McBride advanced to third on a wild pitch. Unser struck out. No runs, one hit, no errors, one left.

Kansas City—Saucier replaced Noles on the mound for Philadelphia. Wilson walked. White flied to McBride. Brett flied to Unser. With Aikens batting, Wilson advanced to second on a wild pitch. Aikens walked. Brusstar replaced Saucier on the mound for Philadelphia. McRae forced Aikens, Rose to Bowa. No runs, no hits, no errors, two left.

SEVENTH INNING

Philadelphia—Maddox popped to Washington. Trillo doubled to right-center. Bowa slapped a single down the left-field line, Trillo stopping at third. Boone flied to Wilson, who made a running, over-the-shoulder catch on the warning track, Trillo tagging and scoring after the catch and Bowa holding first. With Smith batting, Bowa stole second. Smith grounded to Washington. One run, two hits, no errors, one left.

Kansas City—Otis flied to Maddox. Hurdle grounded to Trillo. Porter walked. Washington grounded to Trillo. No runs, no hits, no errors, one left.

EIGHTH INNING

Philadelphia—Rose doubled to left. Quisenberry replaced Leonard on the mound for Kansas City. McBride grounded to White, Rose advancing to third. Schmidt flied to Hurdle, Rose tagging and scoring after the catch. Unser singled to right. Maddox grounded to Washington. One run, two hits, no errors, one left.

Kansas City—Wilson grounded to Bowa. White grounded to Trillo. Brett grounded to Trillo. No runs, no hits, no errors, none left.

NINTH INNING

Philadelphia—Trillo grounded to Brett. Bowa grounded to White. Boone grounded to Washington. No runs, no hits, no errors, none left.

AT KANSAS CITY   Game 5   OCTOBER 19

Philadelphia	AB.	R.	H.	PO.	A.	E.
Rose, 1b	4	0	0	7	1	0
McBride, rf	4	1	0	2	1	0
Schmidt, 3b	4	2	2	1	1	0
Luzinski, lf	2	0	0	1	0	0
aSmith, lf	0	0	0	0	0	0
cUnser, lf	1	1	1	0	0	0
Moreland, dh	3	0	1	0	0	0
Maddox, cf	4	0	0	2	0	0
Trillo, 2b	4	0	1	3	5	0
Bowa, ss	4	0	1	0	2	0
Boone, c	3	0	1	10	0	0
Bystrom, p	0	0	0	1	1	0
Reed, p	0	0	0	0	0	0
McGraw, p	0	0	0	0	1	0
Totals	33	4	7	27	12	0

Kansas City	AB.	R.	H.	PO.	A.	E.
Wilson, lf	5	0	2	2	0	0
White, 2b	3	0	0	2	6	0
G. Brett, 3b	5	0	1	1	2	1
Aikens, 1b	3	0	1	10	1	1
dConcepcion	0	0	0	0	0	0
McRae, dh	5	0	1	0	0	0
Otis, cf	3	1	2	3	0	0
Hurdle, rf	3	1	1	3	0	0
bCardenal, rf	2	0	0	0	0	0
Porter, c	4	0	2	2	0	0
Washington, ss	3	1	2	2	2	0
Gura, p	0	0	0	2	4	0
Quisenberry, p	0	0	0	0	0	0
Totals	36	3	12	27	15	2

Philadelphia	0	0	0		2	0	0		0	0	2 – 4
Kansas City	0	0	0		0	1	2		0	0	0 – 3

Philadelphia	IP.	H.	R.	ER.	BB.	SO.
Bystrom	5*	10	3	3	1	4
Reed	1	1	0	0	0	0
McGraw (Winner)	3	1	0	0	4	5

Kansas City	IP.	H.	R.	ER.	BB.	SO.
Gura	6⅓	4	2	1	1	2
Quisenberry (Loser)	2⅔	3	2	2	0	0

*Pitched to three batters in sixth.

Bases on balls—Off Bystrom 1 (Aikens), off McGraw 4 (Otis 2, White, Aikens), off Gura 1 (Luzinski).

Strikeouts—By Bystrom 4 (Wilson, Aikens, Otis, Hurdle), by McGraw 5 (G. Brett 2, Aikens, Washington, Cardenal), by Gura 2 (Luzinski, Maddox).

Game-winning RBI—Trillo.

aRan for Luzinski in seventh. bFlied out for Hurdle in seventh. cDoubled in one run for Smith in ninth. dRan for Aikens in ninth. Runs batted in—Schmidt 2, Unser, Trillo, G. Brett, Otis, Washington. Two-base hits—Wilson, McRae, Unser. Home runs—Schmidt, Otis. Stolen base—G. Brett. Sacrifice hits—White, Moreland. Sacrifice fly—Washington. Double plays—White, Aikens and Gura; Gura and Aikens. Left on bases—Philadelphia 4, Kansas City 13. Umpires—Rennert (N.L.) plate, Bremigan (A.L.) first, Wendelstedt (N.L.) second, Kunkel (A.L.) third, Pryor (N.L.) left, Denkinger (A.L.) right. Time—2:51. Attendance—42,369.

FIRST INNING

Philadelphia—Rose bounced to Gura, who threw to Aikens for the out. McBride flied to Otis. Schmidt flied to Wilson. No runs, no hits, no errors, none left.

Kansas City—Wilson struck out. White grounded to Rose, who threw to Bystrom covering first for the out. Brett singled to right. With Aikens batting, Brett stole second. Aikens was called out on strikes. No runs, one hit, no errors, one left.

SECOND INNING

Philadelphia—Luzinski was called out on strikes. Moreland flied to Hurdle. Maddox was called out on strikes. No runs, no hits, no errors, none left.

Kansas City—McRae hit a comebacker that Bystrom deflected to Trillo, who threw to Rose for the out. Otis struck out. Hurdle grounded to Bowa. No runs, no hits, no errors, none left.

THIRD INNING

Philadelphia—Trillo flied to Otis. Bowa singled to center. Boone flied to short right, where White made a running, over-the-head catch, wheeled and doubled Bowa off first, Aikens taking White's throw and relaying it to Gura at the bag for the out. No runs, one hit, no errors, none left.

Kansas City—Porter singled to right. Washington dropped a bunt down the third-base line and had a single when Schmidt had no one to throw to at first, Porter advancing to second. Wilson flied to Maddox, both runners holding. White popped to Trillo. Brett bounced to Trillo. No runs, two hits, no errors, two left.

FOURTH INNING

Philadelphia—Rose hit a line drive headed up the middle until Gura deflected it to White, who threw to Aikens for the out. McBride bounced to Gura but was safe on an error by Aikens, who took Gura's throw while standing off the bag. Schmidt homered to deep right-center, McBride scoring ahead of him. Luzinski grounded to Brett. Moreland popped to Brett. Two runs, one hit, one error, none left.

Kansas City—Aikens singled to center. McRae flied to McBride. Otis singled to left, Aikens stopping at second. Hurdle struck out. Porter lined to Rose. No runs, two hits, no errors, two left.

FIFTH INNING

Philadelphia—Maddox flied to Wilson. Trillo lined to Hurdle. Bowa flied to Otis. No runs, no hits, no errors, none left.

Kansas City—Washington singled to center. Wilson singled to the left of Schmidt, Washington stopping at second. White sacrificed, Schmidt to Trillo covering first, Washington advancing to third and Wilson to second. Brett grounded to Trillo, Washington scoring and Wilson advancing to third. Aikens walked. McRae

DEL UNSER scores winning run in Game 5. Clutch pinch-hitter had doubled home tying run before scoring on Manny Trillo's ninth-inning single. In Game 2, Unser had another run-scoring pinch-double to ignite a four-run eighth-inning rally.

fouled out to McBride, who caught the ball right up against the wall along the foul line in deep right. One run, two hits, no errors, two left.

SIXTH INNING

Philadelphia—Boone singled to right-center. Rose lined to Gura, who threw to Aikens to double off Boone. McBride fouled to Washington. No runs, one hit, no errors, none left.

Kansas City—Otis lashed a home run over the wall in left-center. Hurdle singled to center. Porter lined a single to right, Hurdle advancing to third. Reed replaced Bystrom on the mound for Philadelphia. Washington flied to Luzinski, Hurdle tagging and scoring after the catch and Porter holding first. Wilson doubled off the wall in right, but Porter was thrown out trying to score, McBride to Trillo to Boone. White fouled out to Schmidt. Two runs, four hits, no errors, one left.

SEVENTH INNING

Philadelphia—Schmidt flied to Hurdle. Luzinski walked. Smith ran for Luzinski. Moreland grounded to the right of Washington, whose throw from the hole was not in time to get Smith advancing to second on the single. Quisenberry replaced Gura on the mound for Kansas City. Maddox forced Moreland, Washington to White, Smith advancing to third. Trillo grounded sharply to the right of White, who made a backhand stop and threw to Washington to force Maddox. No runs, one hit, no errors, two left.

Kansas City—Smith remained in the game to play left field for Philadelphia and McGraw replaced Reed on the mound. Brett struck out. Aikens struck out. McRae doubled to left. Otis was walked intentionally. Cardenal batted for Hurdle and flied to Maddox. No runs, one hit, no errors, two left.

EIGHTH INNING

Philadelphia—Cardenal remained in the game to play right field for Kansas City. Bowa grounded to White. Boone grounded to Brett, whose one-hop throw evaded Aikens, Boone advancing to second on Brett's error. Rose grounded to White, Boone advancing to third. McBride grounded to White. No runs, no hits, one error, one left.

Kansas City—Porter grounded to Trillo. Washington struck out. Wilson bounced to McGraw. No runs, no hits, no errors, none left.

NINTH INNING

Philadelphia—Schmidt singled to the left of Brett. Unser batted for Smith and lined a double down the right-field line, Schmidt scoring. Moreland sacrificed Unser to third, Aikens fielding the bunt and tagging out Moreland. Maddox grounded to Brett on the foul line and in front of the bag, Unser holding third. Trillo lined a single off Quisenberry's glove, Unser scoring. Bowa bounced to Washington. Two runs, three hits, no errors, one left.

Kansas City—Unser remained in the game to play left field for Philadelphia. White walked. Brett was called out on strikes. Aikens walked, White advancing to second. Concepcion ran for Aikens. After hitting a long foul into the left-field seats, McRae forced Concepcion, Bowa to Trillo, White advancing to third. Otis walked, loading the bases. Cardenal struck out. No runs, no hits, no errors, three left.

AT PHILADELPHIA Game 6 OCTOBER 21

Kansas City	AB.	R.	H.	PO.	A.	E.	Philadelphia	AB.	R.	H.	PO.	A.	E.
Wilson, lf	4	0	0	3	0	0	Smith, lf	4	2	1	1	0	0
Washington, ss	3	0	1	2	4	0	Gross, lf	0	0	0	0	0	0
G. Brett, 3b	4	0	2	1	1	0	Rose, 1b	4	0	3	9	0	0
McRae, dh	4	0	0	0	0	0	Schmidt, 3b	3	0	1	0	0	0
Otis, cf	3	0	0	2	0	0	McBride, rf	4	0	0	2	0	0
Aikens, 1b	2	0	0	6	0	1	Luzinski, dh	4	0	0	0	0	0
aConcepcion	0	0	0	0	0	0	Maddox, cf	4	0	2	1	0	0
Wathan, c	3	1	2	4	1	0	Trillo, 2b	4	0	0	2	3	0
Cardenal, rf	4	0	2	4	0	0	Bowa, ss	4	1	1	3	3	0
White, 2b	4	0	0	2	1	1	Boone, c	2	1	1	9	1	0
Gale, p	0	0	0	0	0	0	Carlton, p	0	0	0	0	2	0
Martin, p	0	0	0	0	0	0	McGraw, p	0	0	0	0	0	0
Splittorff, p	0	0	0	0	1	0	Totals	33	4	9	27	9	0
Pattin, p	0	0	0	0	0	0							
Quisenberry, p	0	0	0	0	0	0							
Totals	31	1	7	24	8	2							

Kansas City	0	0 0	0	0 0	0	0 1	0 — 1
Philadelphia	0	0 2	0	1 1	0	0 x	— 4

Kansas City	IP.	H.	R.	ER.	BB.	SO.
Gale (Loser)	2	4	2	1	1	1
Martin	2⅓	1	1	1	1	0
Splittorff	1⅔*	4	1	1	0	0
Pattin	1	0	0	0	0	2
Quisenberry	1	0	0	0	0	0

Philadelphia	IP.	H.	R.	ER.	BB.	SO.
Carlton (Winner)	7†	4	1	1	3	7
McGraw (Save)	2	3	0	0	2	2

*Pitched to one batter in seventh.
†Pitched to two batters in eighth.

Bases on balls—Off Gale 1 (Boone), off Martin 1 (Schmidt), off Carlton 3 (Otis, Aikens, Wathan), off McGraw 2 (Wilson, Aikens).

Strikeouts—By Gale 1 (Luzinski), by Pattin 2 (Schmidt, Luzinski), by Carlton 7 (Wilson 2, Washington 2, White, Otis, Aikens), by McGraw 2 (Otis, Wilson).

Game-winning RBI—Schmidt.

aRan for Aikens in ninth. Runs batted in—Washington, Schmidt 2, McBride, Boone. Two-base hits—Maddox, Smith, Bowa. Caught stealing—Rose. Sacrifice fly—Washington. Double plays—Bowa, Trillo and Rose; Bowa and Rose; Splittorff, Washington and Aikens. Left on bases—Kansas City 9, Philadelphia 7. Umpires—Bremigan (A.L.) plate, Wendelstedt (N.L.) first, Kunkel (A.L.) second, Pryor (N.L.) third, Denkinger (A.L.) left, Rennert (N.L.) right. Time—3:00. Attendance—65,838.

FIRST INNING

Kansas City—Wilson was called out on strikes. Washington struck out. Brett grounded to Trillo. No runs, no hits, no errors, none left.

Philadelphia—Smith grounded to White. Rose sent a check-swing single into left field between third and short. Schmidt popped to Washington. McBride lined to Wilson. No runs, one hit, no errors, one left.

SECOND INNING

Kansas City—McRae flied to McBride. Otis walked. Aikens walked, Otis advancing to second. Wathan grounded into a double play, Bowa to Trillo to Rose. No runs, no hits, no errors, one left.

Philadelphia—Luzinski struck out. Maddox doubled to right-center, Otis cutting the ball off on one hop at the track. Trillo flied to Cardenal, Maddox advancing to third after the catch. Bowa fouled out to Wathan in front of the third-base dugout. No runs, one hit, no errors, one left.

THIRD INNING

Kansas City—Cardenal flied to Smith at the edge of the track in left. White struck out. Wilson struck out. No runs, no hits, no errors, none left.

Philadelphia—Boone walked. Smith grounded to the right of White, whose throw to second pulled Washington off the bag, putting runners at first and second on White's error. On a 3-1 pitch, Rose bunted down the third-base line for a single, loading the bases. Schmidt lined a single to right, Boone and Smith scoring and Rose advancing to third. Martin replaced Gale on the mound for Kansas City. McBride fouled out to White, the runners holding. Luzinski lined to Brett. Maddox flied to Cardenal. Two runs, two hits, one error, two left.

FOURTH INNING

Kansas City—Washington singled, Bowa having no play after backhanding the ball in short left. Brett grounded into a double play, Bowa taking the ball coming across the bag and throwing to Rose to complete the twin-killing. McRae grounded to Bowa. No runs, one hit, no errors, none left.

Philadelphia—Trillo flied to Wilson, who made a running catch in short center when Washington had trouble with the high pop. Bowa grounded to Brett. Boone flied to Cardenal, who made the catch running toward the line. No runs, no hits, no errors, none left.

FIFTH INNING

Kansas City—Otis struck out. Aikens was called out on strikes. Wathan grounded a single up the middle. Cardenal popped to Trillo. No runs, one hit, no errors, one left.

Philadelphia—Smith doubled on a grounder through the left side that was eventually cut off by Otis, who backhanded the ball near the track in left-center. Rose flied to Otis, Smith advancing to third after the catch. Schmidt walked. Splittorff replaced Martin on the mound for Kansas City. McBride hit a broken-bat roller that a charging Washington fielded and threw to Aikens for the out, Smith scoring and Schmidt advancing to second. Luzinski grounded to Washington. One run, one hit, no errors, one left.

SIXTH INNING

Kansas City—White popped to Bowa. Wilson bunted to the third base side of the mound, Carlton throwing to Rose for the out. Washington struck out. No runs, no hits, no errors, none left.

Philadelphia—Maddox lined a single to left. Trillo grounded into a double play, Splittorff to Washington to Aikens. Bowa hit a one-hop double against the wall in left. Boone lined a single to center, Bowa scoring. Smith flied to Otis in right-center. One run, three hits, no errors, one left.

SEVENTH INNING

Kansas City—Gross replaced Smith in left field for Philadelphia. Brett grounded a single to right. McRae fouled out to Bowa. Otis flied to McBride, who made the catch one step in front of the wall. Aikens grounded to Carlton, who threw to Rose for the out. No runs, one hit, no errors, one left.

Philadelphia—Rose lined a single off the glove of Brett, who knocked the ball down with a dive to his left. Pattin replaced Splittorff on the mound for Kansas City. With Schmidt batting, Rose was caught stealing, Wathan to White. Schmidt was called out on strikes. McBride grounded to Aikens and reached safely when Aikens' toss to Pattin racing for the bag led the pitcher too far, the ball glancing off his glove for an error on the first baseman. Luzinski struck out. No runs, one hit, one error, one left.

EIGHTH INNING

Kansas City—Wathan walked. Cardenal lined a single to left, Wathan stopping at second. McGraw replaced Carlton on the mound for Philadelphia. White fouled out to Rose. Wilson walked, loading the bases. Washington flied to Maddox, Wathan tagging and scoring after the catch and the other runners holding their bases. Brett beat out a one-hopper that Trillo flagged down moving far to his left, loading the bases. McRae grounded to Trillo. One run, two hits, no errors, three left.

Philadelphia—Quisenberry replaced Pattin on the mound for Kansas City. Maddox fouled out to Wilson. Trillo grounded to Washington. Bowa flied to Cardenal. No runs, no hits, no errors, none left.

NINTH INNING

Kansas City—Otis was called out on strikes. Aikens walked. Concepcion ran for Aikens. Wathan singled to right, Concepcion stopping at second. Cardenal lined a single to center, loading the bases. White lifted a high foul in front of the first-base dugout where Boone positioned himself for the catch—the ball popped out of Boone's mitt, but Rose snatched it for the out. Wilson struck out. No runs, two hits, no errors, three left.

PHILADELPHIA PHILLIES' BATTING AND FIELDING AVERAGES

Player—Position	G.	AB.	R.	H.	TB.	2B.	3B.	HR.	RBI.	BB.	IBB.	SO.	B.A.	PO.	A.	E.	F.A.
Unser, ph-cf-lf	3	6	2	3	5	2	0	0	2	0	0	1	.500	1	0	0	1.000
Boone, c	6	17	3	7	9	2	0	0	4	4	0	0	.412	49	3	0	1.000
Schmidt, 3b	6	21	6	8	15	1	0	2	7	4	0	3	.381	9	8	0	1.000

PHILADELPHIA PHILLIES' BATTING AND FIELDING AVERAGES—Cont.

Player—Position	G.	AB.	R.	H.	TB.	2B.	3B.	HR.	RBI.	BB.	IBB.	SO.	B.A.	PO.	A.	E.	F.A.
Bowa, ss	6	24	3	9	10	1	0	0	2	0	0	0	.375	5	18	0	1.000
Moreland, dh	3	12	1	4	4	0	0	0	1	0	0	1	.333	0	0	0	.000
McBride, rf	6	23	3	7	11	1	0	1	5	2	0	1	.304	13	1	0	1.000
Smith, pr-lf-dh	6	19	2	5	6	1	0	0	1	1	0	1	.263	4	1	0	1.000
Rose, 1b	6	23	2	6	7	1	0	0	1	2	1	2	.261	49	6	0	1.000
Maddox, cf	6	22	1	5	7	2	0	0	1	1	1	3	.227	11	1	0	1.000
Trillo, 2b	6	23	4	5	7	2	0	0	2	0	0	0	.217	14	25	1	.975
Brusstar, p	1	0	0	0	0	0	0	0	0	0	0	0	.000	0	0	0	.000
Bystrom, p	1	0	0	0	0	0	0	0	0	0	0	0	.000	1	1	0	1.000
Carlton, p	2	0	0	0	0	0	0	0	0	0	0	0	.000	0	3	0	1.000
Christenson, p	1	0	0	0	0	0	0	0	0	0	0	0	.000	0	1	0	.000
McGraw, p	4	0	0	0	0	0	0	0	0	0	0	0	.000	0	1	0	1.000
Noles, p	1	0	0	0	0	0	0	0	0	0	0	0	.000	1	0	0	1.000
Reed, p	2	0	0	0	0	0	0	0	0	0	0	0	.000	0	0	0	.000
Ruthven, p	1	0	0	0	0	0	0	0	0	0	0	0	.000	0	0	0	.000
Saucier, p	1	0	0	0	0	0	0	0	0	0	0	0	.000	0	0	0	.000
Walk, p	1	0	0	0	0	0	0	0	0	0	0	0	.000	2	0	0	1.000
Gross, ph-lf	4	2	0	0	0	0	0	0	0	0	0	0	.000	1	0	0	1.000
Luzinski, dh-lf	3	9	0	0	0	0	0	0	0	1	0	5	.000	1	0	0	1.000
Totals	6	201	27	59	81	13	0	3	26	15	2	17	.294	161	68	2	.991

Unser doubled in one run for Smith in eighth inning of second game; doubled in one run for Smith in ninth inning of fifth game.

Gross grounded into double play for Maddox in eighth inning of second game; sacrificed for Smith in 10th inning of third game.

Smith ran for Luzinski in seventh inning of fifth game.

KANSAS CITY ROYALS' BATTING AND FIELDING AVERAGES

Player—Position	G.	AB.	R.	H.	TB.	2B.	3B.	HR.	RBI.	BB.	IBB.	SO.	B.A.	PO.	A.	E.	F.A.
Otis, cf	6	23	4	11	22	2	0	3	7	3	1	3	.478	21	0	0	1.000
Hurdle, rf	4	12	1	5	6	1	0	0	2	0	1	1	.417	8	0	0	1.000
Aikens, 1b	6	20	5	8	22	0	1	4	8	6	0	8	.400	55	2	2	.966
G. Brett, 3b	6	24	3	9	16	2	1	1	3	2	1	4	.375	4	17	1	.955
McRae, dh	6	24	3	9	12	3	0	0	1	2	0	2	.375	0	0	0	.000
Wathan, ph-rf-c	3	7	1	2	2	0	0	0	1	2	0	1	.286	7	1	0	1.000
Washington, ss	6	22	1	6	6	0	0	0	2	0	0	6	.273	8	20	1	.966
Cardenal, ph-rf	4	10	0	2	2	0	0	0	0	0	0	3	.200	7	0	0	1.000
Wilson, lf	6	26	3	4	5	1	0	0	0	4	0	12	.154	15	1	0	1.000
Porter, ph-c	5	14	1	2	2	0	0	0	0	3	0	4	.143	13	2	0	1.000
White, 2b	6	25	0	2	2	0	0	0	1	0	5	0	.080	13	21	2	.944
Chalk, 3b	1	0	1	0	0	0	0	0	1	0	0	0	.000	0	1	0	1.000
Concepcion, pr	3	0	0	0	0	0	0	0	0	0	0	0	.000	0	0	0	.000
Gale, p	2	0	0	0	0	0	0	0	0	0	0	0	.000	0	1	0	1.000
Gura, p	2	0	0	0	0	0	0	0	0	0	0	0	.000	2	4	0	1.000
LaCock, 1b	1	0	0	0	0	0	0	0	0	0	0	0	.000	2	0	0	1.000
Leonard, p	2	0	0	0	0	0	0	0	0	0	0	0	.000	0	1	0	.000
Martin, p	3	0	0	0	0	0	0	0	0	0	0	0	.000	0	0	0	.000
Pattin, p	1	0	0	0	0	0	0	0	0	0	0	0	.000	0	0	0	.000
Quisenberry, p	6	0	0	0	0	0	0	0	0	0	0	0	.000	1	1	0	1.000
Splittorff, p	1	0	0	0	0	0	0	0	0	0	0	0	.000	0	1	0	1.000
Totals	6	207	23	60	97	9	2	8	22	26	2	49	.290	156	72	7	.970

Wathan grounded into double play for Hurdle in eighth inning of first game.

Porter was called out on strikes for Chalk in ninth inning of second game.

Concepcion ran for Hurdle in ninth inning of third game; ran for Aikens in ninth inning of fifth game; ran for Aikens in ninth inning of sixth game.

Cardenal flied out for Hurdle in seventh inning of fifth game.

PHILADELPHIA PHILLIES' PITCHING RECORDS

Pitcher	G.	GS.	CG.	IP.	H.	R.	ER.	HR.	BB.	IBB.	SO.	HB.	WP.	W.	L.	Pct.	ERA.
Brusstar	1	0	0	2⅓	0	0	0	0	1	0	0	0	0	0	0	.000	0.00
Reed	2	0	0	2	2	0	0	0	0	0	2	0	0	0	0	.000	0.00
Saucier	1	0	0	⅔	0	0	0	0	2	0	0	1	0	0	0	.000	0.00
McGraw	4	0	0	7⅔	7	1	1	0	8	2	10	0	0	1	1	.500	1.17
Noles	1	0	0	4⅔	5	1	1	1	2	0	6	0	0	0	0	.000	1.93
Carlton	2	2	0	15	14	5	4	0	9	0	17	0	1	2	0	1.000	2.40
Ruthven	1	1	0	9	9	3	3	2	0	0	7	0	0	0	0	.000	3.00
Bystrom	1	1	0	5	10	3	3	1	1	0	4	0	0	0	0	.000	5.40
Walk	1	1	0	7	8	6	6	3	3	0	3	0	1	1	0	1.000	7.71
Christenson	1	1	0	⅓	5	4	4	1	0	0	0	0	1	0	0	.000	108.00
Totals	6	6	0	53⅔	60	23	22	8	26	2	49	0	3	4	2	.667	3.69

Saves—McGraw 2, Reed. Shutouts—None.

KANSAS CITY ROYALS' PITCHING RECORDS

Pitcher	G.	GS.	CG.	IP.	H.	R.	ER.	HR.	BB.	IBB.	SO.	HB.	WP.	W.	L.	Pct.	ERA.
Pattin	1	0	0	1	0	0	0	0	0	0	2	0	0	0	0	.000	0.00
Gura	2	2	0	12⅓	8	4	3	1	3	0	4	1	0	0	0	.000	2.19
Martin	3	0	0	9⅔	11	3	3	0	3	0	2	1	0	0	0	.000	2.79
Gale	2	2	0	6⅓	11	3	3	1	4	0	4	0	0	0	1	.000	4.26
Quisenberry	6	0	0	10⅓	10	6	6	0	3	2	0	0	0	1	2	.333	5.23
Splittorff	1	0	0	1⅔	4	1	1	0	0	0	0	0	0	0	0	.000	5.40
Leonard	2	2	0	10⅔	15	9	8	1	2	0	5	1	1	1	1	.500	6.75
Totals	6	6	0	52	59	27	24	3	15	2	17	2	1	2	4	.333	4.15

Save—Quisenberry. Shutouts—None.

COMPOSITE SCORE BY INNINGS

Philadelphia	0	2	7	3	5	1	1	6	2	0 – 27
Kansas City	5	3	2	1	1	3	4	3	0	1 – 23

Game-winning RBI—Schmidt 2, McBride, Trillo, Aikens, G. Brett.

Sacrifice hits—Gross, Moreland, Washington, White.

Sacrifice flies—Boone, Maddox, Schmidt, Trillo, Washington 2, Wathan.

Stolen bases—Bowa 3, G. Brett, Chalk, Hurdle, White, Wilson 2.

Caught stealing—McBride, Rose, Smith, Washington.

Double plays—Bowa, Trillo and Rose 6; Maddox, Rose and Schmidt; Bowa and Rose; Washington, White and Aikens; Washington, White and LaCock; White, Washington and Aikens; White unassisted; G. Brett, White and Aikens; White, Aikens and Gura; Gura and Aikens; Splittorff, Washington and Aikens.

Passed balls—None.

Hit by pitcher—By Leonard (Rose), by Martin (Luzinski).

Balks—None.

Bases on balls—Off Carlton 9 (Aikens 2, G. Brett, Wathan 2, Wilson, Otis, Chalk, McRae), off McGraw 8 (Wilson 2, G. Brett, Otis 2, White, Aikens 2), off Walk 3 (McRae, Porter 2), off Noles 2 (Hurdle 2), off Saucier 2 (Wilson, Aikens), off Brusstar 1 (Porter), off Bystrom 1 (Aikens), off Gale 4 (Schmidt, Boone 2, Rose), off Gura 3 (Boone, McBride, Luzinski), off Martin 3 (Schmidt 2, Smith), off Quisenberry 3 (Boone, Maddox, Rose), off Leonard 2 (Schmidt, McBride).

Strikeouts—By Carlton 17 (Wilson 5, Cardenal 2, White 2, Washington 4, McRae, Aikens 2, Otis), by McGraw 10 (Washington 2, Wilson 2, White, G. Brett 2, Aikens, Cardenal, Otis), by Ruthven 7 (Wilson 2, White 2, Aikens 2, Porter), by Noles 6 (Porter 2, Wilson, G. Brett, Aikens, McRae), by Bystrom 4 (Wilson, Aikens, Otis, Hurdle), by Walk 3 (Wilson, G. Brett, Aikens), by Reed 2 (Porter, Wathan), by Leonard 5 (Schmidt 2, Luzinski, Maddox, Unser), by Gura 4 (Maddox 2, Smith, Luzinski), by Gale 4 (Rose, Moreland, McBride, Luzinski), by Martin 2 (Luzinski, Rose), by Pattin 2 (Schmidt, Luzinski).

Left on bases—Philadelphia 41—6, 3, 15, 6, 4, 7; Kansas City 54—4, 11, 7, 10, 13, 9.

Time of games—First game, 3:01; second game, 3:01; third game, 3:19; fourth game, 2:37; fifth game, 2:51; sixth game, 3:00.

Attendance—First game, 65,791; second game, 65,775; third game, 42,380; fourth game, 42,363; fifth game, 42,369; sixth game, 65,838.

Umpires—Wendelstedt (N.L.), Kunkel (A.L.), Pryor (N.L.), Denkinger (A.L.), Rennert (N.L.), Bremigan (A.L.).

Official scorers—Phil Collier, San Diego Union; Bob Kenney, Camden (N.J.) Courier Post; Don Pfannenstiel, Independence (Mo.) Examiner.

Phillies Followed Familiar Script

They could have called the 1980 World Champion Phillies the Come-From-Behind Gang because of their penchant for staging late-inning rallies in their National League Championship Series triumph over the Houston Astros as well as their World Series victory over the Kansas City Royals.

A five-run, third-inning outburst erased a 4-0 hole the Phils had created in Game 1 of the World Series. A four-run rally in the eighth inning of Game 2 canceled out a 4-2 deficit for a 6-4 verdict. Finally, the Phillies 4-3 victory over the Royals in Game 5—spearheaded by a two-run ninth—was the sixth time in post-season competition that Philadelphia had won by coming from behind, including all three victories in the Championship Series.

WORLD SERIES RESULTS

Year–Winner   Loser
1903–Boston A. L., 5 games; Pittsburgh N. L., 3 games.
1904–No Series.
1905–New York N. L., 4 games; Philadelphia A. L., 1 game.
1906–Chicago A. L., 4 games; Chicago N. L., 2 games.
1907–Chicago N. L., 4 games; Detroit A. L., 0 games; 1 tie.
1908–Chicago N. L., 4 games; Detroit A. L., 1 game.
1909–Pittsburgh N. L., 4 games; Detroit A. L., 3 games.
1910–Philadelphia A. L., 4 games; Chicago N. L., 1 game.
1911–Philadelphia A. L., 4 games; New York N. L., 2 games.
1912–Boston A. L., 4 games; New York N. L., 3 games; 1 tie.
1913–Philadelphia A. L., 4 games; New York N. L., 1 game.
1914–Boston N. L., 4 games; Philadelphia A. L., 0 games.
1915–Boston A. L., 4 games; Philadelphia N. L., 1 game.
1916–Boston A. L., 4 games; Brooklyn N. L., 1 game.
1917–Chicago A. L., 4 games; New York N. L., 2 games.
1918–Boston A. L., 4 games; Chicago N. L., 2 games.
1919–Cincinnati N. L., 5 games; Chicago A. L., 3 games.
1920–Cleveland A. L., 5 games; Brooklyn N. L., 2 games.
1921–New York N. L., 5 games; New York A. L., 3 games.
1922–New York N. L., 4 games; New York A. L., 0 games; 1 tie.
1923–New York A. L., 4 games; New York N. L., 2 games.
1924–Washington A. L., 4 games; New York N. L., 3 games.
1925–Pittsburgh N. L., 4 games; Washington A. L., 3 games.
1926–St. Louis N. L., 4 games; New York A. L., 3 games.
1927–New York A. L., 4 games; Pittsburgh N. L., 0 games.
1928–New York A. L., 4 games; St. Louis N. L., 0 games.
1929–Philadelphia A. L., 4 games; Chicago N. L., 1 game.
1930–Philadelphia A. L., 4 games; St. Louis N. L., 2 games.
1931–St. Louis N. L., 4 games; Philadelphia A. L., 3 games.
1932–New York A. L., 4 games; Chicago N. L., 0 games.
1933–New York N. L., 4 games; Washington A. L., 1 game.
1934–St. Louis N. L., 4 games; Detroit A. L., 3 games.
1935–Detroit A. L., 4 games; Chicago N. L., 2 games.
1936–New York A. L., 4 games; New York N. L., 2 games.
1937–New York A. L., 4 games; New York N. L., 1 game.
1938–New York A. L., 4 games; Chicago N. L., 0 games.
1939–New York A. L., 4 games; Cincinnati N. L., 0 games.
1940–Cincinnati N. L., 4 games; Detroit A. L., 3 games.
1941–New York A. L., 4 games; Brooklyn N. L., 1 game.
1942–St. Louis N. L., 4 games; New York A. L., 1 game.
1943–New York A. L., 4 games; St. Louis N. L., 1 game.
1944–St. Louis N. L., 4 games; St. Louis A. L., 2 games.
1945–Detroit A. L., 4 games; Chicago N. L., 3 games.
1946–St. Louis N. L., 4 games; Boston A. L., 3 games.
1947–New York A. L., 4 games; Brooklyn N. L., 3 games.
1948–Cleveland A. L., 4 games; Boston N. L., 2 games.
1949–New York A. L., 4 games; Brooklyn N. L., 1 game.
1950–New York A. L., 4 games; Philadelphia N. L., 0 games.
1951–New York A. L., 4 games; New York N. L., 2 games.
1952–New York A. L., 4 games; Brooklyn N. L., 3 games.
1953–New York A. L., 4 games; Brooklyn N. L., 2 games.
1954–New York N. L., 4 games; Cleveland A. L., 0 games.
1955–Brooklyn N. L., 4 games; New York A. L., 3 games.
1956–New York A. L., 4 games; Brooklyn N. L., 3 games.
1957–Milwaukee N. L., 4 games; New York A. L., 3 games.
1958–New York A. L., 4 games; Milwaukee N. L., 3 games.
1959–Los Angeles N. L., 4 games; Chicago A. L., 2 games.
1960–Pittsburgh N. L., 4 games; New York A. L., 3 games.
1961–New York A. L., 4 games; Cincinnati N. L., 1 game.
1962–New York A. L., 4 games; San Francisco N. L., 3 games.
1963–Los Angeles N. L., 4 games; New York A. L., 0 games.
1964–St. Louis N. L., 4 games; New York A. L., 3 games.
1965–Los Angeles N. L., 4 games; Minnesota A. L., 3 games.
1966–Baltimore A. L., 4 games; Los Angeles N. L., 0 games.
1967–St. Louis N. L., 4 games; Boston A. L., 3 games.
1968–Detroit A. L., 4 games; St. Louis N. L., 3 games.
1969–New York N. L., 4 games; Baltimore A. L., 1 game.
1970–Baltimore A. L., 4 games; Cincinnati N. L., 1 game.
1971–Pittsburgh N. L., 4 games; Baltimore A. L., 3 games.
1972–Oakland A. L., 4 games; Cincinnati N. L., 3 games.
1973–Oakland A. L., 4 games; New York N. L., 3 games.
1974–Oakland A. L., 4 games; Los Angeles N. L., 1 game.
1975–Cincinnati N. L., 4 games; Boston A. L., 3 games.
1976–Cincinnati N. L., 4 games; New York A. L., 0 games.
1977–New York A. L., 4 games, Los Angeles N. L., 2 games.
1978–New York A. L., 4 games, Los Angeles N. L., 2 games.
1979–Pittsburgh N. L., 4 games, Baltimore A. L., 3 games.
1980–Philadelphia N. L., 4 games, Kansas City A. L., 2 games.

WORLD SERIES ATTENDANCE, MONEY

Year	Games	Attendance	Gate Receipts	Players' Tot.	W. Share	L. Share
1903	8	100,429	$ 50,000.00	$ 32,612.00	$ 1,182.00	$ 1,316.25
1905	5	91,723	68,436.81	27,394.20	1,142.00	832.22
1906	6	99,845	106,550.00	33,401.70	1,874.63	439.50
1907	5	78,068	101,728.50	54,933.39	2,142.85	1,945.96
1908	5	62,232	94,975.50	46,114.92	1,317.58	870.00
1909	7	145,295	188,302.50	66,924.90	1,825.22	1,274.76
1910	5	124,222	173,980.00	79,071.93	2,062.79	1,375.16
1911	6	179,851	342,364.50	127,910.61	3,654.58	2,436.39
1912	8	252,037	490,833.00	147,572.28	4,024.68	2,566.47
1913	5	151,000	325,980.00	135,164.16	3,246.36	2,164.22
1914	4	111,009	225,739.00	121,898.94	2,812.28	2,031.65
1915	5	143,351	320,361.50	144,899.55	3,780.25	2,520.17
1916	5	162,859	385,590.50	162,927.45	3,910.26	2,834.82
1917	6	186,654	425,878.00	152,888.58	3,669.32	2,442.21
1918	6	128,483	179,619.00	69,527.70	1,102.51	671.09
1919	8	236,928	722,414.00	260,349.66	5,207.07	3,254.36
1920	7	178,737	564,800.00	214,882.74	4,168.00	2,419.60
1921	8	269,976	900,233.00	292,522.23	5,265.00	3,510.00
1922	5	185,947	605,475.00	247,309.71	4,545.71	2,842.86
1923	6	301,430	1,063,815.00	368,783.04	6,143.49	4,112.88
1924	7	283,665	1,093,104.00	331,092.51	5,959.64	3,820.29
1925	7	282,848	1,182,854.00	339,664.19	5,332.72	3,734.60
1926	7	328,051	1,207,864.00	372,300.51	5,584.51	3,417.75
1927	4	201,705	783,217.00	399,440.67	5,782.24	3,985.47
1928	4	199,072	777,290.00	419,736.60	5,813.20	4,181.30
1929	5	190,490	859,494.00	388,086.66	5,620.57	3,782.01
1930	6	212,619	953,772.00	323,865.00	5,038.07	3,536.68
1931	7	231,567	1,030,723.00	320,303.46	4,467.59	3,023.00
1932	4	191,998	713,377.00	363,822.27	5,231.77	4,244.60
1933	5	163,076	679,365.00	284,665.68	4,256.72	3,019.86
1934	7	281,510	1,031,341.00	327,950.46	5,389.57	3,354.68
1935	6	286,672	1,073,794.00	397,360.24	6,544.76	4,198.53
1936	6	302,924	1,204,399.00	460,002.66	6,430.55	4,655.58
1937	5	238,142	985,994.00	459,629.35	6,471.11	4,489.96
1938	4	200,833	851,166.00	434,094.46	5,728.76	4,674.87
1939	4	183,849	745,329.09	431,117.84	5,541.89	4,193.39
1940	7	281,927	1,222,328.21	404,414.04	5,803.62	3,531.81
1941	5	235,773	1,007,762.00	474,184.54	5,943.31	4,829.40
1942	5	277,101	1,105,249.00	427,579.41	6,192.53	3,351.77
1943	5	277,312	1,105,784.00	488,005.74	6,139.46	4,321.96
1944	6	206,708	906,122.00	309,590.91	4,626.01	2,743.79
1945	7	333,457	1,492,454.00	475,579.04	6,443.34	3,930.22
1946	7	250,071	1,052,900.00	304,141.05	3,742.34	2,140.89
1947	7	389,763	1,781,348.92	493,674.82	5,830.03	4,081.19
1948	6	358,362	1,633,685.56	548,214.99	6,772.07	4,570.73
1949	5	236,716	1,129,627.88	490,855.84	5,626.74	4,272.74
1950	4	196,009	953,669.03	486,371.21	5,737.95	4,081.34
1951	6	341,977	1,633,457.47	560,562.37	6,446.09	4,951.03
1952	7	340,706	1,622,753.01	500,003.28	5,982.65	4,200.64
1953	6	307,350	1,779,269.44	691,341.61	8,280.68	6,178.42
1954	4	251,507	1,566,203.38	881,763.72	11,147.90	6,712.50
1955	7	362,310	2,337,515.34	737,853.59	9,768.21	5,598.58
1956	7	345,903	2,183,254.59	758,561.63	8,714.76	6,934.34
1957	7	394,712	2,475,978.94	709,027.55	8,924.36	5,606.06
1958	7	393,909	2,397,223.03	726,044.55	8,759.10	5,896.08
1959	6	420,784	2,628,809.44	893,301.40	11,231.18	7,257.17
1960	7	349,813	2,230,627.88	682,144.82	8,417.94	5,214.64
1961	5	223,247	1,480,059.95	645,928.28	7,389.13	5,356.37
1962	7	376,864	2,878,891.11	893,281.71	9,882.74	7,291.49
1963	4	247,279	1,995,189.09	1,017,546.43	12,794.00	7,874.32
1964	7	321,807	2,243,187.96	696,520.15	8,622.19	5,309.29
1965	7	364,326	2,975,041.60	885,612.21	10,297.43	6,634.36
1966	4	220,791	2,047,142.46	1,044,042.65	11,683.04	8,189.36
1967	7	304,085	2,350,607.10	705,878.44	8,314.81	5,115.23
1968	7	379,670	3,018,113.40	879,761.08	10,936.66	7,078.71
1969	5	272,378	2,857,782.78	1,142,200.93	*18,338.18	*14,904.21
1970	5	253,183	2,599,170.26	1,098,631.14	*18,215.78	*13,687.59
1971	7	351,091	3,049,803.46	1,032,256.90	*18,164.58	*13,906.46
1972	7	363,149	3,954,542.99	1,142,418.35	*20,705.01	*15,080.25
1973	7	358,289	3,923,968.37	1,144,473.44	*24,617.57	*14,950.18
1974	5	260,004	3,007,194.00	2,045,442.79	*22,219.09	*15,703.97
1975	7	308,272	3,380,579.61	*1,826,264.97	*19,060.46	*13,325.87
1976	4	223,009	2,498,416.53	*2,467,835.98	*26,366.68	*19,935.48
1977	6	337,708	3,978,825.33	*2,778,300.31	*27,758.04	*20,899.05
1978	6	337,304	4,650,164.57	*3,301,933.71	*31,236.99	*25,483.21
1979	7	367,597	4,390,766.14	*2,854,824.33	*28,236.87	*22,113.94
1980	6	324,516	5,131,756.68	*3,915,870.82	*34,693.18	*32,211.95

*Total combined figures for World Series and League Championship Series.
NOTE—Losers' shares in 1903-05-07 and winners' in 1906-07 include club owners' slices which were added to their teams' player pools.

A's Selected Three Players in Draft

By LARRY WIGGE

No clear explanations were given when major league clubs shelled out $475,000 for 19 players in the majors' annual draft of Triple-A players that marked the opening of the 79th winter meetings at Dallas December 8.

In what was to be the most players changing hands in the draft since 1969, a fee of $25,000 was charged for each player taken.

First choice went to the Cubs, based on reverse order of finish in the 1980 standings. They chose catcher Jody Davis from Springfield of the Cardinals' organization. Davis batted .277 at St. Petersburg before slumping to .167 after being promoted to Springfield.

The A's were the most active club in the draft, taking infielder Brian Doyle from the Yankees and righthanders Roy Thomas from the Cardinals and Tom Filer from the Yankees. Another notable selection was outfielder Alan Wiggins by the Padres in the second round from the Dodgers' chain. Wiggins made national headlines by stealing 120 bases—a record in professional baseball history—in 1980 at Lodi of the California League.

Draft choices in order of selection:

FIRST ROUND

Cubs—Catcher Jody Davis from Springfield (American Association) of the Cardinals' organization.

Mets—Righthander Billy Smith from Tucson (Pacific Coast) of the Astros' organization.

Padres—Infielder Mario Ramirez from Tidewater (International) of the Mets' organization.

Blue Jays—Outfielder Jorge Bell from Oklahoma City (American Association) of the Phillies' organization.

Cardinals—Catcher-outfielder Orlando Sanchez from Oklahoma City (American Association) of the Phillies' organization.

White Sox—Pitcher Carlos Arroyo, drafted from Oklahoma City (American Association) of the Phillies' organization.

Giants—Catcher George Bjorkman, drafted from Springfield (American Association) of the Cardinals' organization.

Twins—Righthander Don Cooper, a reliever, drafted from Columbus (International) of the Yankees' organization.

A's—Infielder Brian Doyle, drafted from Columbus (International) of the Yankees' organization.

Tigers—Righthander Larry Rothschild, a starter and reliever drafted from Indianapolis (American Association) of the Reds' organization.

Royals—Righthander James Wright, drafted from Oklahoma City (American Association) of the Phillies' organization.

SECOND ROUND

Padres—Outfielder Alan Wiggins, drafted from Albuquerque (Pacific Coast) of the Dodgers' organization.

Blue Jays—Catcher Dan Whitmer, drafted from Salt Lake City (Pacific Coast) of the Angels' organization.

Cardinals—Outfielder Carlos A. Lopez, drafted from Mexico City Tigers (Mexican).

Twins—Lefthander Jack O'Connor, drafted from Denver (American Association) of the Expos' organization.

A's—Righthander Roy Thomas, a reliever, drafted from Springfield (American Association) of the Cardinals' organization.

Royals—Righthander David Wehrmeister, a reliever, drafted from Columbus (International) of the Yankees' organization.

THIRD ROUND

A's—Righthander Tom Filer, drafted from Columbus (International) of the Yankees' organization.

DELAYED DRAFT

Mariners—Outfielder Gary Gray, drafted from Yucatan (Mexican) of the Indians' organization.

1980 ALL-STAR GAME

Including

Review of '80 Game

Official Box Score

Official Play-by-Play

Results of Previous Games

Cincinnati's KEN GRIFFEY belts fifth-inning home run, while the Yankees' TOMMY JOHN (right) watches flight of ball in dismay. Trailing, 2-0, National Leaguers woke up after Griffey's blast to gain 4-2 decision in All-Star Game July 8 at Dodger Stadium.

N.L. Captured Ninth Straight
All-Star Decision

By LARRY WIGGE

American League Cy Young winner Steve Stone had become the first pitcher since Denny McLain in 1966 to toss three perfect innings, Fred Lynn hit a two-run homer for his third career All-Star Game home run and Tommy John had continued the A.L.'s perfect game until two were out in the fifth inning.

The scene at Dodger Stadium July 8 for the 1980 All-Star Game was unusual because the Americans had lost eight consecutive All-Star encounters and 16 of their last 17 meetings with the Nationals before Ken Griffey of the Cincinnati Reds made a promise to Reggie Smith of the Dodgers.

"I'm going to hit one out," Griffey told Smith moments before he faced the lefthanded offerings of the Yankees' John. "I've always had good success picking up John's pitches. He throws three-quarters and it's easy for me to see the ball."

A fourth-inning replacement for Dave Kingman in left field, Griffey took the confidence of a .422 lifetime hitter against John (when Tommy pitched for the Dodgers) to the plate and turned prophet when he belted a home run over the right-center field fence.

Griffey's homer picked up the rest of the National League squad and they came right back in the sixth inning to score two more runs and take the lead en route to a 4-2 triumph. The victory gave the N.L. a 32-18 edge in All-Star competition with one tie.

After the game, Baltimore's Earl Weaver, manager for the Americans, was second-guessing himself for allowing John to bat for himself in the sixth after he had pitched two innings. "Maybe it was one inning too many," the manager said. "But I thought he was our best bet to get them out."

In the sixth, John retired Bill Russell before Ray Knight of the Reds singled to left. Phil Garner then reached base safely when his shot up the middle went off second baseman Willie Randolph's glove. George Hendrick of the Cardinals followed with a looper to right-center, scoring Knight to tie the score at 2-2 and sending Garner to third.

After Weaver finally removed John, Dave Winfield greeted White Sox relief ace Ed Farmer with a one-hopper toward second which handcuffed Randolph. Garner crossed the plate with the go-ahead tally and Randolph was charged with an error.

"I've seen a lot of short hoppers like that turn into quick double plays," observed the Dodgers' Steve Garvey. "But it's a tough play. It just took an N.L. skip."

The N.L. scored once more in the seventh, with Griffey (who was chosen the game's Most Valuable Player) leading off with a single and Dave Concepcion scoring on a two-out wild pitch by Toronto's Dave Stieb.

Meanwhile, the National League hurlers were mowing down the A.L. after Lynn's fifth-inning round-tripper had rocketed the junior circuit to a 2-0 lead.

Jerry Reuss struck out the side in the sixth inning and was credited with the victory. His strikeouts, along with three by J. R. Richard, four by Bob

Welch and one by Bruce Sutter left the N.L. staff just one short of the record (12).

After Jim Bibby hurled another scoreless frame, Sutter allowed just one hit in his two innings to pick up a save. "It doesn't matter to me whether I get a win, a save or a pat on the back, as long as we win," said Sutter, who was the winning pitcher in the 1978 All-Star contest and again in 1979.

When asked about the N.L.'s superiority in the midsummer classic, Weaver responded: "The only explanation I can give is they end up with more runs."

Indeed they do.

FIRST INNING

Americans—Randolph grounded to Lopes. Carew walked and, with Lynn batting, stole second. Lynn grounded to Lopes, Carew advancing to third. Jackson struck out. No runs, no hits, no errors, one left.

Nationals—Lopes grounded sharply to Nettles. Smith flied to Lynn against the wall. Parker struck out. No runs, no hits, no errors, none left.

SECOND INNING

Americans—Oglivie walked. Fisk struck out. Nettles fouled to Reitz. Dent singled to right on a hit-and-run, Oglivie advancing to third. Stone struck out. No runs, one hit, no errors, two left.

Nationals—Garvey fouled to Fisk. Bench grounded to Dent. Kingman struck out. No runs, no hits, no errors, none left.

THIRD INNING

Americans—Welch came in to pitch for the Nationals. Randolph singled to right and, with Carew batting, was picked off, Welch to Garvey. Carew doubled to left. Lynn struck out. Jackson walked on 3-2 pitch which was wild and rolled to the backstop, Carew advancing to third. Oglivie struck out. No runs, two hits, no errors, two left.

Nationals—Reitz, attempting to avoid a high, inside pitch, rolled weakly to Randolph. Russell flied to Oglivie. Welch struck out. No runs, no hits, no errors, none left.

FOURTH INNING

Americans—Garner, Griffey and Stearns came in to play second base, left field and catcher, respectively, for the Nationals. Fisk struck out. Nettles grounded to Garvey, who made the play unassisted. Dent struck out. No runs, no hits, no errors, none left.

Nationals—John came in to pitch and Yount to play shortstop for the Americans. Yount assumed the ninth spot in the batting order and John the eighth. Garner struck out. Smith grounded to Yount. Parker flied to Lynn. No runs, no hits, no errors, none left.

FIFTH INNING

Americans—Hendrick came in to play center field and Winfield right field for the Nationals. Yount grounded to Russell. Randolph grounded to Russell. Carew singled to right. Lynn, on a two-strike pitch, homered just a few feet inside the foul pole in right, Carew scoring ahead of him. Jackson singled to center. Landreaux ran for Jackson. Oglivie spanked the ball to the right side, but Garvey made a fine stop and beat him to first for the out. Two runs, three hits, no errors, one left.

Nationals—Landreaux remained in the game in right field for the Americans. Cooper, Bumbry, Oliver, Porter and Bell came in to play first base, center field, left field, catcher and third base, respectively. Garvey grounded to Bell. Stearns grounded to Randolph. Griffey homered to right-center. Reitz grounded to Randolph, whose throw to first was in the dirt for an error, but Reitz was out trying to advance when catcher Porter alertly backed up Cooper and threw a strike to Yount at second base. One run, one hit, one error, none left.

SIXTH INNING

Americans—Reuss came in to pitch and Knight to play third base for the Nationals. Knight assumed the ninth spot in the batting order and Reuss the seventh. Porter struck out. Bell struck out. John struck out. No runs, no hits, no errors, none left.

Nationals—Russell bounced to John. Knight singled to left. Garner singled up the middle, Knight stopped at second. Hendrick singled to right-center, Knight scoring and Garner advancing to third. Farmer came in to pitch for the Americans. Winfield hit a tough one-hopper that handcuffed Randolph, Garner scoring and Hendrick stopping at second. Randolph was charged with an error, but Winfield was credited with a run batted in. Hernandez batted for Garvey and lined a single off the glove of Farmer, loading the bases. Rose batted for Stearns and grounded into a double play, Randolph to Yount to Cooper. Two runs, four hits, one error, two left.

SEVENTH INNING

Americans—Hernandez stayed in the game to play first base for the Nationals. Bibby came in to pitch, Carter to catch, and Concepcion to play shortstop. Bibby assumed the fifth spot in the batting order, Concepcion the seventh and Carter the eighth. Yount flied to Winfield. Randolph singled to center. Cooper grounded into a double play, Concepcion to Garner to Hernandez. No runs, one hit, no errors, none left.

Nationals—Stieb came in to pitch and Grich to play second base for the Americans. Stieb assumed the first spot in the batting order and Grich the eighth. Griffey singled to right. Concepcion forced Griffey at second, Grich to Yount. With Carter batting, Concepcion advanced to second on a wild pitch. Carter grounded to Bell, Concepcion holding second. Knight walked and, when the fourth ball escaped Porter, Concepcion advanced to third on the passed ball. With Garner batting, Knight stole second. Then, Concepcion scored and Knight advanced to third on another wild pitch by Stieb. Garner walked. With Hendrick batting, Garner stole second. Hendrick flied to Bumbry. One run, one hit, no errors, two left.

EIGHTH INNING

Americans—Sutter came in to pitch and Murphy to play center field for the Nationals. Sutter assumed the second spot in the batting order and Murphy the fifth. Bumbry grounded to Garner. Landreaux lined out to Winfield, who made a nice running catch along the foul line. Oliver grounded to Garner. No runs, no hits, no errors, none left.

Nationals—Gossage came in to pitch, Parrish to catch, Henderson to play left field and Trammell to play shortstop for the Americans. Gossage assumed the fifth spot in the batting order, Parrish the ninth, Henderson the sixth and Trammell the first. Winfield lined to right, where Landreaux made a diving catch. Hernandez lined a single to left. Murphy grounded to Cooper, who made the play unassisted, Hernandez advancing to second. Griffey flied to Bumbry. No runs, one hit, no errors, one left.

NINTH INNING

Americans—Henderson grounded to Knight. Bell grounded to Concepcion, whose low throw was dug out by Hernandez. Grich walked. Parrish struck out. No runs, no hits, no errors, one left.

AMERICANS	AB.	R.	H.	RBI.	PO.	A.
Randolph (Yankees), 2b.....	4	0	2	0	0	3
Stieb (Blue Jays), p	0	0	0	0	0	0
Trammell (Tigers), ss	0	0	0	0	0	0
Carew (Angels), 1b	2	1	2	0	4	0
Cooper (Brewers), 1b.......	1	0	0	0	6	0
Lynn (Red Sox), cf.........	3	1	1	2	2	0
Bumbry (Orioles), cf	1	0	0	0	2	0
Jackson (Yankees), rf.......	2	0	1	0	0	0
aLandreaux (Twins), rf.....	1	0	0	0	1	0
Oglivie (Brewers), lf.......	2	0	0	0	1	0
Oliver (Rangers), lf.........	1	0	0	0	0	0
Gossage (Yankees), p	0	0	0	0	0	0
Fisk (Red Sox), c	2	0	0	0	5	0
Porter (Royals), c.........	1	0	0	0	1	0
Henderson (A's), lf.........	1	0	0	0	0	0
Nettles (Yankees), 3b	2	0	0	0	0	1
Bell (Rangers), 3b.........	2	0	0	0	0	2
Dent (Yankees), ss.........	2	0	1	0	0	1
John (Yankees), p.........	1	0	0	0	0	1
Farmer (White Sox), p	0	0	0	0	0	0
Grich (Angels), 2b	0	0	0	0	0	1
Stone (Orioles), p.........	1	0	0	0	0	0
Yount (Brewers), ss	2	0	0	0	3	2
Parrish (Tigers), c.........	1	0	0	0	0	0
Totals......................	32	2	7	2	24	12

NATIONALS	AB.	R.	H.	RBI.	PO.	A.
Lopes (Dodgers), 2b...........	1	0	0	0	0	2
Garner (Pirates), 2b...........	2	1	1	0	1	3
Smith (Dodgers), cf	2	0	0	0	0	0
Hendrick (Cardinals), cf	2	0	1	1	0	0
Sutter (Cubs), p	0	0	0	0	0	0
Parker (Pirates), rf	2	0	0	0	0	0
Winfield (Padres), rf.........	2	0	0	1	2	0
Garvey (Dodgers), 1b.........	2	0	0	0	7	0
bHernandez (Cards), 1b	2	0	2	0	5	0
Bench (Reds), c...............	1	0	0	0	5	0
Stearns (Mets), c.............	1	0	0	0	5	0
cRose (Phillies)...............	0	0	0	0	0	0
Bibby (Pirates), p	0	0	0	0	0	0
Murphy (Braves), cf.........	1	0	0	0	0	0
Kingman (Cubs), lf...........	1	0	0	0	0	0
Griffey (Reds), lf.............	3	1	2	1	0	0
Reitz (Cardinals), 3b.........	2	0	0	0	1	0
Reuss (Dodgers), p	0	0	0	0	0	0
Concepcion (Reds), ss.......	1	1	0	0	0	2
Russell (Dodgers), ss	2	0	0	0	0	2
Carter (Expos), c	1	0	0	0	1	0
Richard (Astros), p	0	0	0	0	0	0
Welch (Dodgers), p	1	0	0	0	0	1
Knight (Reds), 3b...........	1	1	1	0	0	1
Totals......................	31	4	7	3	27	11

Americans..	0	0	0		0	2	0		0	0 — 2
Nationals...	0	0	0		0	1	2		1	0 x — 4

Americans	IP.	H.	R.	ER.	BB.	SO.
Stone (Orioles)	3	0	0	0	0	3
John (Yankees)	2⅓	4	3	3	0	1
Farmer (White Sox)	⅔	1	0	0	0	0
Stieb (Blue Jays)	1	1	1	0	2	0
Gossage (Yankees)............	1	1	0	0	0	0

Nationals	IP.	H.	R.	ER.	BB.	SO.
Richard (Astros)	2	1	0	0	2	3
Welch (Dodgers)	3	5	2	2	1	4
Reuss (Dodgers)	1	0	0	0	0	3
Bibby (Pirates)	1	1	0	0	0	0
Sutter (Cubs)	2	0	0	0	1	1

Winning pitcher—Reuss.   Losing pitcher—John.   Save—Sutter.

aRan for Jackson in fifth. bSingled for Garvey in sixth. cGrounded into double play for Stearns in sixth. Errors—Randolph 2. Double plays—Randolph, Yount and Cooper; Concepcion, Garner and Hernandez. Left on bases—Americans 7, Nationals 5. Two-base hit—Carew. Home runs—Lynn, Griffey. Stolen bases—Carew, Knight, Garner. Caught stealing—None. Wild pitches—Welch, Stieb 2. Passed ball—Porter. Bases on balls—Off Stieb 2 (Knight, Garner), off Richard 2 (Carew, Oglivie), off Welch 1 (Jackson), off Sutter 1 (Grich). Strikeouts—By Stone 3 (Parker, Kingman, Welch), by John 1 (Garner), by Richard 3 (Jackson, Fisk, Stone), by Welch 4 (Lynn, Oglivie, Fisk, Dent), by Reuss 3 (Porter, Bell, John), by Sutter 1 (Parrish). Umpires—Kibler (N.L.) plate, Barnett (A.L.) first base, Colosi (N.L.) second base, McKean (A.L.) third base, Dale (N.L.) left field, Garcia (A.L.) right field. Time—2:33. Attendance—56,088. Official scorers—Phil Collier, San Diego Union; Ed Browalski, Polish News; Bob Hunter, Valley News.

RESULTS OF PREVIOUS GAMES

1933—At Comiskey Park, Chicago, July 6. Americans 4, Nationals 2. Managers—Connie Mack, John McGraw. Winning pitcher—Lefty Gomez. Losing pitcher—Bill Hallahan. Attendance—47,595.

1934—At Polo Grounds, New York, July 10. Americans 9, Nationals 7. Managers—Joe Cronin, Bill Terry. Winning pitcher—Mel Harder. Losing pitcher—Van Mungo. Attendance—48,363.

1935—At Municipal Stadium, Cleveland, July 8. Americans 4, Nationals 1. Managers—Mickey Cochrane, Frankie Frisch. Winning pitcher—Lefty Gomez. Losing pitcher—Bill Walker. Attendance—69,831.

1936—At Braves Field, Boston, July 7. Nationals 4, Americans 3. Managers—Charlie Grimm, Joe McCarthy. Winning pitcher—Dizzy Dean. Losing pitcher—Lefty Grove. Attendance—25,556.

1937—At Griffith Stadium, Washington, July 7. Americans 8, Nationals 3. Managers—Joe McCarthy, Bill Terry. Winning pitcher—Lefty Gomez. Losing pitcher—Dizzy Dean. Attendance—31,391.

1938—At Crosley Field, Cincinnati, July 6. Nationals 4, Americans 1. Managers—Bill Terry, Joe McCarthy. Winning pitcher—Johnny Vander Meer. Losing pitcher—Lefty Gomez. Attendance—27,067.

1939—At Yankee Stadium, New York, July 11. Americans 3, Nationals 1. Managers—Joe McCarthy, Gabby Hartnett. Winning pitcher—Tommy Bridges. Losing pitcher—Bill Lee. Attendance—62,892.

1940—At Sportsman's Park, St. Louis, July 9. Nationals 4, Americans 0. Managers—Bill McKechnie, Joe Cronin. Winning pitcher—Paul Derringer. Losing pitcher—Red Ruffing. Attendance—32,373.

1941—At Briggs Stadium, Detroit, July 8. Americans 7, Nationals 5. Managers— Del Baker, Bill McKechnie. Winning pitcher—Ed Smith. Losing pitcher—Claude Passeau. Attendance—54,674.

1942—At Polo Grounds, New York, July 6. Americans 3, Nationals 1. Managers—Joe Cronin, Leo Durocher. Winning pitcher—Spud Chandler. Losing pitcher—Mort Cooper. Attendance—34,178.

1943—At Shibe Park, Philadelphia, July 13 (night game). Americans 5, Nationals 3. Managers—Joe McCarthy, Billy Southworth. Winning pitcher—Dutch Leonard. Losing pitcher—Mort Cooper. Attendance—31,938.

1944—At Forbes Field, Pittsburgh, July 11 (night game). Nationals 7, Americans 1. Managers—Billy Southworth, Joe McCarthy. Winning pitcher—Ken Raffensberger. Losing pitcher—Tex Hughson. Attendance—29,589.

1945—No game played.

1946—At Fenway Park, Boston July 9. Americans 12, Nationals 0. Managers—Steve O'Neill, Charlie Grimm. Winning pitcher—Bob Feller. Losing pitcher—Claude Passeau. Attendance—34,906.

1947—At Wrigley Field, Chicago, July 8. Americans 2, Nationals 1. Managers—Joe Cronin, Eddie Dyer. Winning pitcher—Frank Shea. Losing pitcher—Johnny Sain. Attendance—41,123.

1948—At Sportsman's Park, St. Louis, July 13. Americans 5, Nationals 2. Managers—Bucky Harris, Leo Durocher. Winning pitcher—Vic Raschi. Losing pitcher—Johnny Schmitz. Attendance—34,009.

1949—At Ebbets Field, Brooklyn, July 12. Americans 11, Nationals 7. Managers—Lou Boudreau, Billy Southworth. Winning pitcher—Virgil Trucks. Losing pitcher—Don Newcombe. Attendance—32,577.

1950—At Comiskey Park, Chicago, July 11. Nationals 4, Americans 3 (14 innings). Managers—Burt Shotton, Casey Stengel. Winning pitcher—Ewell Blackwell. Losing pitcher—Ted Gray. Attendance—46,127.

1951—At Briggs Stadium, Detroit, July 10. Nationals 8, Americans 3. Managers—Eddie Sawyer, Casey Stengel. Winning pitcher—Sal Maglie. Losing pitcher—Ed Lopat. Attendance—52,075.

1952—At Shibe Park, Philadelphia, July 8. Nationals 3, Americans 2 (five innings—rain). Managers—Leo Durocher, Casey Stengel. Winning pitcher—Bob Rush. Losing pitcher—Bob Lemon. Attendance—32,785.

1953—At Crosley Field, Cincinnati, July 14. Nationals 5, Americans 1. Managers—Chuck Dressen, Casey Stengel. Winning pitcher—Warren Spahn. Losing pitcher—Allie Reynolds. Attendance—30,846.

1954—At Municipal Stadium, Cleveland July 13. Americans 11, Nationals 9. Managers—Casey Stengel, Walter Alston. Winning pitcher—Dean Stone. Losing pitcher—Gene Conley. Attendance—68,751.

1955—At Milwaukee County Stadium, Milwaukee, July 12. Nationals 6, Americans 5 (12 innings). Managers—Leo Durocher, Al Lopez. Winning pitcher—Gene Conley. Losing pitcher—Frank Sullivan. Attendance—45,643.

1956—At Griffith Stadium, Washington, July 10. Nationals 7, Americans 3. Managers—Walter Alston, Casey Stengel. Winning pitcher—Bob Friend. Losing pitcher—Billy Pierce Attendance—28,843.

1957—At Busch Stadium, St. Louis, July 9. Americans 6, Nationals 5. Managers—Casey Stengel, Walter Alston. Winning pitcher—Jim Bunning. Losing pitcher—Curt Simmons. Attendance—30,693.

1958—At Memorial Stadium, Baltimore, July 8. Americans 4, Nationals 3. Managers—Casey Stengel, Fred Haney. Winning pitcher—Early Wynn. Losing pitcher—Bob Friend. Attendance—48,829.

1959 (first game)—At Forbes Field, Pittsburgh, July 7. Nationals 5, Americans 4. Managers—Fred Haney, Casey Stengel. Winning pitcher—Johnny Antonelli. Losing pitcher—Whitey Ford. Attendance—35,277.

1959 (second game)—At Memorial Coliseum, Los Angeles, August 3. Americans 5, Nationals 3. Managers—Casey Stengel, Fred Haney. Winning pitcher—Jerry Walker. Losing pitcher—Don Drysdale. Attendance—55,105.

1960 (first game)—At Municipal Stadium, Kansas City, July 11. Nationals 5, Americans 3. Managers—Walter Alston, Al Lopez. Winning pitcher—Bob Friend. Losing pitcher—Bill Monbouquette. Attendance—30,619.

1960 (second game)—At Yankee Stadium, New York, July 13. Nationals 6, Americans 0. Managers—Walter Alston, Al Lopez. Winning pitcher—Vern Law. Losing pitcher—Whitey Ford. Attendance—38,362.

1961 (first game)—At Candlestick Park, San Francisco, July 11. Nationals 5, Americans 4 (10 innings). Managers—Danny Murtaugh, Paul Richards. Winning pitcher—Stu Miller. Losing pitcher—Hoyt Wilhelm. Attendance—44,115.

1961 (second game)—At Fenway Park, Boston, July 31. Americans 1, Nationals 1 (nine-inning tie, stopped by rain). Managers—Paul Richards, Danny Murtaugh. Attendance—31,851.

1962 (first game)—At District of Columbia Stadium, Washington, July 10. Nationals 3, Americans 1. Managers—Fred Hutchinson, Ralph Houk. Winning pitcher—Juan Marichal. Losing pitcher—Camilo Pascual. Attendance—45,480.

1962 (second game)—At Wrigley Field, Chicago, July 30. Americans 9, Nationals 4. Managers—Ralph Houk, Fred Hutchinson. Winning pitcher—Ray Herbert. Losing pitcher—Art Mahaffey. Attendance—38,359.

1963—At Municipal Stadium, Cleveland, July 9. Nationals 5, Americans 3. Managers—Alvin Dark, Ralph Houk. Winning pitcher—Larry Jackson. Losing pitcher —Jim Bunning. Attendance—44,160.

1964—At Shea Stadium, New York, July 7. Nationals 7, Americans 4. Managers—Walter Alston, Al Lopez. Winning pitcher—Juan Marichal. Losing pitcher—Dick Radatz. Attendance—50,850.

1965—At Metropolitan Stadium, Bloomington (Minnesota), July 13. Nationals 6, Americans 5. Managers—Gene Mauch, Al Lopez. Winning pitcher—Sandy Koufax. Losing pitcher—Sam McDowell. Attendance—46,706.

1966—At Busch Memorial Stadium, St. Louis, July 12. Nationals 2, Americans 1 (10 innings). Managers—Walter Alston, Sam Mele. Winning pitcher—Gaylord Perry. Losing pitcher—Pete Richert. Attendance—49,936.

1967—At Anaheim Stadium, Anaheim (California), July 11. Nationals 2, Americans 1 (15 innings). Managers—Walter Alston, Hank Bauer. Winning pitcher—Don Drysdale. Losing pitcher—Jim Hunter. Attendance—46,309.

1968—At Astrodome, Houston, July 9 (night). Nationals 1, Americans 0. Managers—Red Schoendienst, Dick Williams. Winning pitcher—Don Drysdale. Losing pitcher—Luis Tiant. Attendance—48,321.

1969—At Robert F. Kennedy Memorial Stadium, Washington, July 23. Nationals 9, Americans 3. Managers—Red Schoendienst, Mayo Smith. Winning pitcher—Steve Carlton. Losing pitcher—Mel Stottlemyre. Attendance—45,259.

1970—At Riverfront Stadium, Cincinnati, July 14 (night). Nationals 5, Americans 4 (12 innings). Managers—Gil Hodges, Earl Weaver. Winning pitcher—Claude Osteen. Losing pitcher—Clyde Wright. Attendance—51,838.

1971—At Tiger Stadium, Detroit, July 13 (night). Americans 6, Nationals 4. Managers—Earl Weaver, George (Sparky) Anderson. Winning pitcher—Vida Blue. Losing pitcher—Dock Ellis. Attendance—53,559.

1972—At Atlanta Stadium, Atlanta, July 25 (night). Nationals 4, Americans 3 (10 innings). Managers—Danny Murtaugh, Earl Weaver. Winning pitcher—Tug McGraw. Losing pitcher—Dave McNally. Attendance—53,107.

1973—At Royals Stadium, Kansas City, July 24 (night). Nationals 7, Americans 1. Managers—George (Sparky) Anderson, Dick Williams. Winning pitcher—Rick Wise. Losing pitcher—Bert Blyleven. Attendance—40,849.

1974—At Three Rivers Stadium, Pittsburgh, July 23 (night). Nationals 7, Americans 2. Managers—Yogi Berra, Dick Williams. Winning pitcher—Ken Brett. Losing pitcher—Luis Tiant. Attendance—50,706.

1975—At Milwaukee County Stadium, Milwaukee, July 15 (night). Nationals 6, Americans 3. Managers—Walter Alston, Alvin Dark. Winning pitcher—Jon Matlack. Losing pitcher—Jim Hunter. Attendance—51,480.

1976—At Veterans Stadium, Philadelphia, July 13 (night). Nationals 7, Americans 1. Managers—George (Sparky) Anderson, Darrell Johnson. Winning pitcher—Randy Jones. Losing pitcher—Mark Fidrych. Attendance—63,974.

1977—At Yankee Stadium, New York, July 19 (night). Nationals 7, Americans 5. Managers—Alfred (Billy) Martin, George (Sparky) Anderson. Winning pitcher—Don Sutton. Losing pitcher—Jim Palmer. Attendance—56,683.

1978—At San Diego Stadium, San Diego, July 11. Nationals 7, Americans 3. Managers—Alfred (Billy) Martin, Thomas Lasorda. Winning pitcher—Bruce Sutter. Losing pitcher—Rich Gossage. Attendance—51,549.

1979—At Kingdome, Seattle, July 17, Nationals 7, Americans 6. Managers—Chuck Tanner, Bob Lemon. Winning pitcher—Bruce Sutter. Losing pitcher—Jim Kern. Attendance—58,905.

Carlton's Six Wins Vs. Cards Best Since '71

Since the Cardinals traded Steve Carlton to the Philadelphia Phillies prior to the 1972 season, the big lefthander has treated his ex-St. Louis mates rudely.

Coming into the 1980 season, Carlton had compiled a 23-8 record vs. the Redbirds. But during the '80 schedule he was even tougher, posting a 6-0 won-lost mark which included a one-hitter April 26 and only eight earned runs in 52 innings for a 1.38 ERA.

It was the first time since Ferguson Jenkins of the Cubs won six games (6-0) against his former Philadelphia teammates in 1971 that any pitcher had accumulated so many victories against one club.

The last time an American League pitcher accomplished the feat was 1968 when Denny McLain of the Tigers was 6-0 against the Twins.

The six defeats were the most the Cardinals had suffered to a single hurler since Warren Spahn was 6-1 vs. St. Louis in 1955.

Lee, Manuel Shined in Orient

For only the third time in Japanese baseball history, an American led the Pacific League in batting as Leron Lee batted .358 with 175 hits in 489 at-bats in 1980. His brother Leon finished second in the league with a .340 average.

In the power department, Charlie Manuel continued to set all sorts of slugging records in Japan. In 1980, he smashed 48 homers with 129 RBIs while batting .325. Over the past four years Charlie has averaged 42 homers, 106 RBIs and .319. He set records for the fastest 100 homers (in 348 games) and fastest 150 homers (in 475 games). Meanwhile, another Yank slugger, Tony Solaita, clubbed 45 homers—more than any other first-year player had ever hit in Japanese baseball.

A list of the 26 Americans in Japan and their 1980 records follows:

Player—Club	G.	AB.	H.	HR.	RBI.	B.A.
Leron Lee, Lotte Orions	127	489	175	33	90	.358
Leon Lee, Lotte Orions	128	486	165	41	116	.340
Carlos May, Nankai Hawks	124	423	138	27	75	.326
Charlie Manuel, Kintetsu Buffaloes	118	459	149	48	129	.325
Steve Ontiveros, Seibu Lions	65	258	81	16	50	.314
Tommy Cruz, Nippon Ham Fighters	127	488	151	26	84	.309
Bobby Marcano, Hankyu Braves	116	445	131	24	85	.294
Felix Millan, Yokohama Taiyo Whales	107	332	95	4	20	.286
Mike Reinbach, Hanshin Tigers	106	348	99	15	44	.284
Roy White, Yomiuri Giants	128	469	133	29	75	.284
Sam Perlozzo, Yakult Swallows	118	473	133	15	43	.281
Bobby Jones, Chunichi Dragons	64	178	50	4	19	.281
Jim Lyttle, Hiroshima Toyo Carp	130	507	142	23	82	.280
Jim Tyrone, Seibu Lions	128	529	146	35	68	.276
Skip James, Yokohama Taiyo Whales	111	368	99	21	57	.269
John Scott, Yakult Swallows	123	449	120	16	69	.267
Mike Dupree, Hiroshima Toyo Carp	127	459	122	10	40	.266
Frank Ortenzio, Nankai Hawks	36	101	26	7	14	.257
Bernie Williams, Hankyu Braves	120	345	87	21	50	.252
Chris Arnold, Kintetsu Buffaloes	91	254	64	11	37	.252
Bruce Boisclair, Hanshin Tigers	80	177	44	8	26	.249
Tony Solaita, Nippon Ham Fighters	125	447	107	45	95	.239
Taylor Duncan, Seibu Lions	64	230	54	14	36	.235
John Sipin, Yomiuri Giants	75	219	49	9	21	.224
Wayne Garrett, Chunichi Dragons	77	189	41	8	22	.217
Dave Hilton, Hanshin Tigers	18	71	14	0	4	.197

GEORGE BRETT
• KANSAS CITY ROYALS •
MAJOR LEAGUE
PLAYER OF THE YEAR

TAL SMITH
• HOUSTON ASTROS •
MAJOR LEAGUE EXECUTIVE

BILL VIRDON
• HOUSTON ASTROS •
MAJOR LEAGUE MANAGER

HAL LANIER
• SPRINGFIELD •
MINOR LEAGUE MANAGER

JIM BURRIS
• DENVER •
MINOR LEAGUE EXECUTIVE
IN CLASS AAA

TIM RAINES
• DENVER •
MINOR LEAGUE PLAYER

FRANCES CORBETT
• CHARLOTTE •
MINOR LEAGUE EXECUTIVE
IN CLASS AA

The Sporting News

NO. **1**

MEN

of

1980

TOM ROMENESKO
• GREENSBORO •
MINOR LEAGUE EXECUTIVE
IN CLASS A

GEORGE BRETT—The Sporting News Man of the Year for 1980. His chase of a .400 average drew national attention.

REVIEW OF 1980

Including

Summation of Year's Activities

MVP Tables, All-Star Teams

Homers by Parks

RAY GREBEY, the chief negotiator for Major League Baseball,
and MARVIN MILLER (shown
below), executive director of
Players' Association, were the
cleanup hitters in the labor-management ball game for 1980.

Labor Strife, Big Salaries Topped '80 News

By CLIFFORD KACHLINE

Like much of mankind, baseball experienced some of the best and some of the worst of times in 1980. It was truly a year of great contrasts. In many ways, developments mirrored the ups and downs on the world's social, political and economic fronts. Even while attaining new heights in popularity and revenue, the game was plagued by serious problems.

The 1970s generally were regarded as baseball's most turbulent decade, but the 1980s got away to an even more tempestuous start. Gamesmanship at the labor-management bargaining table frequently overshadowed the game on the field, and the names of the negotiators and of many player agents became almost as familiar to the public as those of some players. Unrest and upheaval occasionally stole the spotlight from the remarkable performances on the diamond. Despite it all, the industry prospered both in the counting house and in the media as never before.

To most fans, the preseason walkout, strike threats and the possibility of a shutdown made for disturbing moments. It was obvious the huge amounts of money involved had radicalized the relationship between the players and owners—and possibly the public. Some in the media referred to the situation as "the inmates running the asylum." But the off-the-field goings-on failed to detract from such superb on-the-field achievements as George Brett's near-.400 batting average, Steve Carlton's great pitching, Steve Stone's remarkable 25-victory effort and the heroics of the Houston Astros, Kansas City Royals and Philadelphia Phillies in postseason competition.

Stability or Financial Disaster?

"Dugout to dugout, the game happily remains unchanged in our changing world," commented Bill Veeck, owner of the struggling Chicago White Sox, early in the '80 season. "We are an island of stability in an unstable world."

Nevertheless, many major league officials and other observers were concerned about baseball's future. Would there be continued prosperity, they wondered, or was there disaster ahead?

"I am worried about the future of the game. I really am," admitted Commissioner Bowie Kuhn. He said more than half of the 26 major league clubs were losing money. "I have access to the financial figures of the clubs, which I am not at liberty to discuss, but they are not good," he continued. "We have held down ticket prices against the rise in the cost of living index, but how long will we be able to remain 'The Family Game'? If we lose family support because tickets keep going up, there will be no baseball."

Kuhn cited player-management relations as the sport's biggest unsolved bugaboo. "Many other industries seem capable of sitting down at the bargaining table and talking out their differences. Not baseball," he said. "We always seem to go to the wire. We have to improve in that area. I know fans get fed up with threatening labor situations."

A Strike and a Near-Strike

For the sixth time in the last 12 years, it was just such labor strife that dominated spring training. It resulted in cancellation of the last eight days of exhibition games, and only an 11th-hour settlement averted a strike by the Major League Baseball Players Association late in May. Even so, one paramount issue remained unresolved, and in an unusual development, the club owners actually granted the players the right to schedule a walkout in 1981, under certain conditions.

The situation as spring drills began was reminiscent of 1972, when the players struck for 13 days, and also of 1979, when the regular major league umpires remained off the job almost six weeks. This time management and the players were at odds again. The latest four-year Basic Agreement had expired on December 31, 1979. Despite some 20 bargaining sessions covering more than three months, the sides remained far apart when the players reported to the Florida, Arizona and California camps.

The chief negotiators were Ray Grebey, director of the owners' Player Relations Committee for the last two years, and Marvin Miller, executive director of the players' association since 1966. Members of the management committee, in addition to Grebey, were Presidents Lee MacPhail of the American League and Chub Feeney of the National League, Dan Galbreath of Pittsburgh, Bob Howsam of Cincinnati, John McHale of Montreal, Joe Burke of Kansas City, Ed Fitzgerald of Milwaukee and Clark Griffith of Minnesota. Several of them occasionally sat in on the meetings, as did some players. Barry Rona, counsel to Grebey, and Don Fehr, the players' attorney, also participated in most of the sessions.

Owners Propose Salary Scale

The issues creating the widest gulf were the owners' proposals for a wage scale for players with six or fewer seasons in the majors and for more significant compensation for players who opted for free agency. At the same time, the players were seeking a higher minimum salary and a larger contribution to their pension and benefit plan than management offered, a reduction from six years to four in the length of major league service required to gain free agency, and the right to go to salary arbitration after 86 days—half a season—in the majors instead of after two full years and service in at least three seasons.

Under the owners' proposed salary structure, the old minimum of $21,000 was to be replaced by a figure of $25,000 for each of a player's first four years and $30,000 for his fifth and sixth seasons. In addition, players in their first six years in the majors would be subject to maximums and would not be eligible for multi-year contracts. The entire proposal eventually was withdrawn.

Arguments on Free Agent Compensation

Management's bid for what it termed "more equitable" free agency compensation called for the team that lost a "premier" player in the November re-entry draft to receive a major league player from the team signing the free agent. In the past, a club that signed a free agent had to give up only a selection in the amateur draft of high school and college talent to its rival. The owners' proposal stipulated that any free agent selected by seven or more teams (later changed to eight or more) in the re-entry process would be considered a "premier" player if he met certain performance levels. The team signing him could protect 15 or 18 players on its roster, including all those with no-trade contracts, and then the free agent's former team could choose one player from the remainder of the roster.

Miller and the players termed the free agency plan a "regressive move" and contended that the owners were attempting to reduce players' salaries.

Player salaries, of course, had risen dramatically over the last decade and especially since the advent of free agency in 1976. Only 10 players were reported to be earning in excess of $100,000 a year in 1970 and none was collecting more than $150,000. By contrast, many teams had half a dozen in the $150,000-plus salary category in 1980, and most teams had several players earning $300,000 or more.

As an alternative to the owners' free-agency plan, Miller suggested the clubs create a cash fund from which to compensate a team losing a free agent. He stressed that this would help provide the equity the owners claimed they need. The idea was promptly rejected.

Except for Grebey, the owners' chief negotiator, management personnel seldom offered comments on the bargaining except anonymously. A gag rule had been imposed, calling for fines of up to $500,000 for any club official who discussed the negotiations publicly.

Players Authorize 'Strike Actions'

When attempts to hammer out a new labor contract showed little progress after 23 negotiating sessions, the players' militancy began to rise. At a meeting lasting 4½ hours in Tampa on March 4, the Executive Board of the Players' Association voted 27-0 to authorize "strike action" on or about April 1 "if an appropriate agreement is not concluded." This meant baseball could face another shutdown such as the one that wiped out the first 86 games of the 1972 season.

"Don't count on opening the season if a new agreement has not been ratified," Miller notified management. He said he felt the players would be foolish to start the season without a new contract because "the individual player contract is only as good as the Basic Agreement which enforces it."

"This is a move which almost all unions take when they consider it helpful in their negotiations," Grebey countered. "What's he going to strike for? The baseball player, in security and reward, already stands in the top one percent in America," the owners' negotiator continued. "We don't want what we had after the dispute in 1976: everybody hating everybody else."

To support his position that there was no need for a strike, Grebey pointed out that the National Basketball Association was functioning at the time without a player-management contract, that the National Football League once went three seasons without a contract and that baseball was played for a period in 1976 under an expired contract.

967-to-1 Vote for Walkout

The rank-and-file players nevertheless quickly showed support for the decision of their Executive Board. In a voice vote taken by Miller on subsequent visits to the camps of the 26 clubs, the final tally was 967-1 in favor of striking. The lone dissenter was identified as Jerry Terrell, Kansas City player representative. He was said to have voted no because of religious convictions.

The first significant breakthrough occurred on March 18 when both sides revised their bargaining posture. Grebey withdrew the owners' salary-scale proposal, and the players modified some of their proposals and withdrew others.

On March 27, with a threatened strike only a few days away, Grebey asked the Federal Mediation and Conciliation Service to enter the dispute "in an effort to continue the collective bargaining now proceeding and to avoid a work stoppage." The mediator chosen was Kenneth E. Moffett, deputy director of the federal agency and a 20-year veteran in mediation.

Moffett met jointly and separately with the two sides for almost nine hours in Palm Springs, Calif., on March 30, but the sessions produced no movement on the crucial issue of free-agency compensation.

Two days later, convening in Dallas, the 27-member Executive Board of the Players' Association voted unanimously to cancel all remaining spring exhibition games and to go on strike if no Basic Agreement was approved by midnight of Thursday, May 22. The decisions obviously were aimed at the owners' wallets. By wiping out the 92 remaining exhibition games, including a lucrative Freeway Series between the California Angels and Los Angeles Dodgers, the players would be cutting off an immediate source of club income. And a strike on the eve of the Memorial Day weekend, when large crowds normally begin packing the parks, would have greater financial impact than a boycott during the early weeks of the season.

In addition, by opening the season and continuing negotiations until late May, the players would be receiving three paychecks. In many cases, they would earn enough to carry them comfortably through the year. An insurance fund estimated at $1 million built up from bubble gum endorsement money, was available to help the lower-salaried athletes.

May 23 Deadline Established

"The players will open the season as scheduled and hope the owners will negotiate in good faith," Miller announced. "But if no new agreement is reached by midnight of May 22, the players will go on strike on May 23."

He emphasized there were three management proposals "we cannot accept," listing them as: (1) Free-agent compensation in the form of another major league player; (2) Limiting players with fewer than five seasons of experience to one-year contracts, and (3) Salary arbitration geared primarily to years of experience.

The players' decision to halt spring exhibitions effective April 2 led to mass confusion temporarily. The possibility that the owners would retaliate by locking the players out of camp was quickly dispelled when Grebey announced that training camps would remain open for players who wanted to work out. But he added that the owners were cutting off meal money, allowance and hotel funds—a loss of approximately $420 per player for the period. This forced the athletes to fund their own conditioning program during the final week preceding the April 9-10 inaugurals.

Most players remained in training camp and continued regular workouts under their manager and coaches. The San Diego Padres were a notable exception. They voted to depart their Yuma, Ariz., camp, return to San Diego and work out there. While most squads remained intact, some players headed for home on April 2. The New York Mets were the most drastically affected. Only 12 of their 28 players remained in camp.

Gene Autry, owner of the Angels, was especially irate over the players' actions. "Frankly, if I had my way and the other owners would agree with me, I'd close down for the season," he said. It was estimated his club stood to lose at least $400,000 as a result of cancellation of two home games with the Dodgers in the Freeway Series.

To protect themselves in the event of a shutdown, the owners reportedly had assembled a strike fund of approximately $3.5 million by withholding two percent of their 1979 gate receipts and had taken out an estimated $30 million in strike insurance with Lloyds of London. The policy was said to provide for a 14-day "deductible" period, after which each club would receive a total of $1,153,840 if the strike lasted six weeks.

Negotiations Schedule Established

Moffett brought the negotiators together again in New York on April 3 and set up a schedule of seven meetings over the next three weeks. However, following a heated exchange on April 16, it was agreed at management's request to recess the negotiations until May 6.

"Let's face it, this is really a one-issue negotiation," Moffett offered. "The rest is housekeeping." The issue to which he referred, of course, was the owners' demand for better compensation for certain "quality" free agents.

"The owners' demand to turn free agency into a trade is the biggest stumbling block," Miller agreed.

In justifying their insistence on compensation, several executives cited the ratifying statement which accompanied the 1976 Basic Agreement. The statement declared both sides recognized the agreement was "experimental" in nature and that subsequent events might make changes desirable. Miller claimed it was the players, not the owners, who suggested the statement and did so after having agreed to allow free agency only for those with six years of experience instead of insisting on unlimited free agency at the expiration of each contract, as was granted them by arbitrator Peter Seitz and the courts.

On the playing field, meantime, it was business as usual as the major league season opened on April 9-10. But stories about the games and the players' achievements frequently were subordinated to reports of the negotiations.

Players' Salaries Disclosed

Shortly after the season began, management released information on salaries that was designed to support its contention that threats of a strike made no sense. The data, based on opening-day rosters, showed the average salary for a major league player in 1980 was $149,700. The owners claimed this was 23 percent above the $121,900 average of 1979 and a whopping 191 percent over the 1976 average of $51,500. It also pegged the average 1980 pay for the previous winter's crop of free agents at $228,300. Miller disputed some of the figures, claiming the 1979 average was closer to $113,000.

Beginning May 6, the negotiators met on three successive days in New York and began narrowing many issues. But the real hangups continued to be compensation for free agents and the benefit plan.

Debate on Pensions and Benefits

Grebey revealed that the owners had offered to raise their contribution to the pension and benefit plans to a total package of $14 million a year. "This proposal would provide a pension for every player with 60 days in the major leagues. The players are asked to pay nothing," he said.

Seeking to break the stalemate, Miller on May 15 proposed separating the free-agency compensation issue from the other points of contention and putting it on hold. He suggested a study committee representing both sides be appointed to examine the effects and ramifications of the current system. The idea was rejected by Grebey with the comment: "The owners feel now is the time to deal with this issue." In another area, Grebey was more concilia-tory, offering to raise the contribution to the pension plan to $14.4 million. Miller continued to hold out for $16.5 million a year—almost a 100 percent hike over the $8.5 million of the four previous years—on the basis that baseball's latest TV package had risen from around $93 million to about $185 million.

Grebey tried a new approach the next day in a bid to prevent the shut-down. He advised the players' association boss that the owners would guar-antee to maintain all terms and conditions of the expired Basic Agreement, at least up to the start of the next season, if bargaining continued and there was no interruption of play through the '80 World Series. Miller turned down the proposal.

A gloomy forecast was offered by mediator Moffett following another fruitless meeting May 18. "The chances for averting a strike are not good," he said. "There has been no progress and the climate is highly charged."

Countdown to a Settlement

The next day, Commissioner Kuhn moved into the picture. Earlier he had said he would enter the dispute only if a "long and serious strike" loomed, but now he held a series of meetings with the three principals—Grebey, Mil-ler and Moffett. Nonetheless, another negotiating session between the two sides on May 21 produced little progress. "I'm guardedly optimistic," Grebey maintained on leaving the meeting. "This is a tough emotional problem." But Miller declared: "It would take a small miracle to prevent a strike."

With the clock running out, the parties resumed negotiations at the Doral Inn in New York at 11:15 a.m. on May 22. About 90 minutes later, they re-cessed. Shortly after 5 o'clock, they went back into session and broke again an hour later. When they returned around 10 p.m., it still looked as if a stoppage the next day was inevitable.

Fortunately, with Moffett and his counsel, David Vaughn, providing a significant assist, seemingly insurmountable odds were overcome during the next four hours. The first indication of a break came at 2:20 a.m. when Moffett informed the media that progress had been made. A few minutes later, Grebey and the two league presidents left the Doral and went to American League headquarters a few blocks away. There four members of the Player Relations Committee—Galbreath, Howsam, Burke and Griffith—were waiting along with Peter O'Malley and Haywood Sullivan of the Execu-tive Council. Half an hour later, Grebey notified Miller that the deal was acceptable. Shortly before 5 o'clock on Friday morning, May 23, the weary negotiators concluded the seven-hour session by announcing that a new four-year Basic Agreement had been concluded.

Joint Committee to Study Compensation

The key to the settlement was management's last-minute decision to agree to put off the crucial issue of free-agent compensation and create a joint committee to study the matter.

"I feel exhilarated," declared Kuhn following the announcement. "It looked very bleak for a while. Quite honestly, what bothered me most was hearing fans say, 'We want to see baseball played.' I felt the same way. Not only were the clubs concerned, but the players, too. Someone had to figure out how to do this, and in that regard, I can't say enough for Marvin Miller and Ray Grebey. They were determined to find a solution and they did."

Some observers viewed the agreement as more of an armed truce than a peace pact and felt the players gained the most. But Grebey himself termed the settlement "the best deal ever negotiated between players and management."

Ratification by Owners and Players

The 26 club owners or their representatives met at the O'Hare Hilton in Chicago on June 5 and ratified the new Basic Agreement by a 21-5 vote. The dissenting teams were Minnesota, St. Louis, Oakland, San Diego and Cleveland. After the meeting, Dan Galbreath, a member of the policy-setting Player Relations Committee, said: "It's the first time in 15 years that both parties made a genuine commitment to work things out. I look at this as a victory for baseball, not a victory for the players and not for the owners."

Two other owners—Gabe Paul of Cleveland and Calvin Griffith of Minnesota—took a different view. "I think we paid a heavy price for not having a strike," commented Paul. "It is our conviction that we gave up too much on pensions." Griffith, who in the first four years of free agency had lost more than a dozen players, said: "It costs us $1 million to develop a player. We should get something in return (when we lose one to free agency). I don't like the idea that there's still the possibility of a strike hanging over us next season."

The players' association also overwhelmingly ratified both the new agreement and the new player benefit plan at a meeting in Los Angeles the day prior to the July 8 All-Star Game. Excluding the Cincinnati Reds, who had no player representative present, the tally was 619-22 in favor of the Basic Agreement and 749-11 for the pension plan. Although Minnesota had released Mike Marshall, its veteran reliever and outspoken player representative, the Twins were the only team to vote against the agreement in the player poll with 17 negative votes to seven in favor. The Twins also accounted for all 11 nay votes on the pension issue.

Major Points of Basic Agreement

The major points of the new Basic Agreement and pension and benefit plans, which run through March 31, 1984, are as follows:

—The minimum major league player salary shall be $30,000 in 1980, $32,500 in 1981, $33,500 in 1982 and $35,000 in 1983.

—Effective with the 1981 season, any player under major league contract who (1) signed a major league contract for a prior year and (2) has been credited with at least one day of major league service shall be paid—if shipped to the minors—at the rate of $14,000 in 1981 and 1982 and $16,000 in 1983.

—The players' meal money and tip allowances while on the road were increased to $33.50 per day in 1980 and $37.50 per day in 1981, with future increases tied to the rise in the consumer price index.

—Any player with at least two full years of major league service, however accumulated, is eligible for salary arbitration.

—Any player with at least six full years of major league service but who is not eligible for free agency is eligible for salary arbitration. Should his club refuse to consent to arbitration, the player may elect free agency and then negotiate with any club without any restrictions.

—Any player released prior to the start of spring training will receive a termination payment equal to 30 days' salary, the same as a player released during spring training.

—A player on the disabled list may, with his written consent, be sent to the minors for a maximum of 20 days for the purpose of rehabilitation. The time counts as major league service for the player, but the assignment does not count as an option.

—The minimum guarantees for the World Series/League Championship Series players' pool were increased to $720,000 for members of the winning team and $540,000 for the losers in the World Series, $250,000 for each of the LCS losers, $95,000 for each second-place team and $25,000 for each third-place team.

—The second interleague trading period, previously February 15 to March 15, has been extended to midnight of April 1.

—The number of consecutive playing dates permitted for any team has been increased from 19 to 20. In addition, an open date is now mandatory for or following travel from a city in the Pacific time zone to cities in the Eastern time zone except in the case of a holiday.

—The minimums of six years of major league service to qualify for free agency and five years before a player can demand a trade were retained.

—Various health and safety provisions were modified and moving allowances were increased in line with the rise in the consumer price index.

—The clubs agreed to increase their contribution to the players' pension and benefit plans to $15.5 million annually. This permitted boosts in life insurance coverage for active players from the previous $50,000 to $150,000 and in major medical coverage from $100,000 to $250,000. Pensions were increased and expanded to include any player with just one day of major league service instead of the four years previously needed. Examples of the annual pension payments for which major league players now are eligible follow:

Age When Player Begins Collecting.....	———Years in the Major Leagues———				
	1	5	10	15	20
45	$1,260	$ 6,288	$12,576	$14,616	$16,656
50	$1,560	$ 8,940	$17,856	$20,856	$23,844
55	$2,448	$12,264	$24,516	$28,512	$32,496
60	$3,336	$16,668	$33,276	$38,280	$43,260
65	$4,596	$22,992	$45,912	$51,912	$57,888

On the free-agent compensation issue, the two parties signed a Memorandum of Agreement providing for a study committee consisting of two players and two management representatives. The memorandum called for the joint committee to convene no later than August 1 and to present its report to the players' association and Player Relations Committee no later than January 1, 1981. It also provided for subsequent courses of action on the subject.

New Disagreement on Compensation

The uneasy labor peace was interrupted briefly on August 5 when Grebey issued a news release on behalf of management that announced the study group would begin its deliberations two days later and also stated: "It should be kept in mind that the question before the study group is not whether there will be compensation for free agents. . . . That was negotiated and established in the 1976 Basic Agreement and was reaffirmed in the 1980 Agreement, which provides for a new form of compensation."

Miller immediately charged the release was "misleading and provocative." He pointed out that if the study committee was unable to agree on a compromise plan, the owners had a right to announce between February 15-20, 1981, that they intended to put their compensation proposal into effect. Should the players find the plan unsatisfactory, they then could give management notice by March 1—under terms of the memorandum—that they planned to strike, and the strike would have to start no later than June 1, 1981.

Under the owners' free-agent compensation proposal, a club losing a player in the re-entry procedure would be entitled to no compensation if he was selected by three or fewer clubs and to only an amateur draft choice, as in the past, if selected by four to seven teams. For those players chosen by eight to 13 clubs, his former team would receive not only an amateur draft choice but also a player off the signing team's roster provided the free agent met certain performance criteria and was not exercising repeater rights. In the event the player ranked in the upper half of certain performance categories in his league, the signing club could protect 18 players, while the number would be reduced to 15 if the free agent ranked among the upper third.

A report prepared by management's Player Relations Committee indicated that of the 134 free agents involved in the 1978-79-80 re-entry drafts, only 15 met the performance criteria that would have required extra compensation in the form of a major leaguer. Among the 1980 crop, only Dave Winfield, Don Sutton and Darrell Porter would have qualified.

Miller scoffed at those figures. "Do you think they want compensation for three or four players?" he asked. "How can anybody believe that? What they want to do is stymie free agency for the overwhelming majority of players."

Arbitrator Gives Sutter $700,000

Like the situations created by free agency, salary arbitration results produced reverberations that were felt during negotiations on the new Basic Agreement. The bonanza reaped by Bruce Sutter in the 1980 salary hearings doubtless had an impact. The 27-year-old Chicago Cubs pitcher, a Cy Young Award winner the previous season and widely regarded as baseball's best reliever, won the biggest salary ever awarded by an arbitrator.

Sutter was entering the last year of a three-year contract with the Cubs calling for a total of $450,000. The pact contained a proviso allowing for renegotiation prior to the final season. At one point, Sutter disclosed, the Cubs offered him a new five-year contract worth $475,000 per season plus a $100,000 bonus—a total of $2,475,000. He and his agent, Jim Bronner, made a counterproposal, including a request to have most of the money in deferred payments to reduce the tax bite. Subsequently, the Cubs reportedly began lowering their offer, and Sutter asked to go to arbitration.

Shortly before the February 25 hearing, attorney Dick Moss, who represented the players' association, requested a postponement to allow more time to work out an agreement. The Cubs and the owners' Player Relations Committee turned down the request. "Both Sutter's and the Cubs' best inter-

BRUCE SUTTER   JOE SAMBITO

ests would have been served if they could have worked out a long-term agreement," commented Moss.

In submitting for arbitration, Sutter asked for a salary of $700,000 while the Cubs proposed $350,000. Under the rules, the arbiter must choose one figure or the other. Tom Christenson, a New York University law professor, heard the case and decided in the pitcher's favor.

The $700,000 award made Sutter the third highest-paid pitcher in the sport—behind Nolan Ryan and Vida Blue—and caused consternation among major league executives. Dick Wagner, Cincinnati Reds president, said the verdict was "almost like an atom bomb to our industry," adding: "This will have a rippling effect throughout the league. The whole arbitration thing has gotten out of hand."

Athletes Win 15 of 26 Appeals

Altogether, 26 players went to salary arbitration in 1980. Sutter and 14 others were awarded the pay they sought, while 11 had to settle for the club's offer. Charlie Finley, Oakland A's owner, lost all five of his salary appeals. The Detroit Tigers, involved in the salary hearings for the first time, lost each of their three cases.

It marked the second successive year that the athletes won more cases than they lost. The owners had prevailed the first three years. Overall, the results in 92 hearings over five years found the players winning 44, management 48. The salaries presented here were obtained by Murray Chass and published in the New York Times and THE SPORTING NEWS.

The 14 who joined Sutter in gaining the salaries they sought, with the clubs' offer in parentheses, were: Joe Sambito of Houston, $213,000 ($143,000); Steve Kemp of Detroit, $210,000 ($150,000); Geoff Zahn of Minnesota, $200,000 ($130,000); Ray Knight of Cincinnati, $175,000 ($112,500); Dave Collins of Cincinnati, $167,500 ($126,000); Roy Howell of Toronto, $133,000

($110,000); Joaquin Andujar of Houston, $130,000 ($90,000); Alan Trammell of Detroit, $130,000 ($102,000); Lou Whitaker of Detroit, $130,000 ($105,000), and the five Oakland players—Jeff Newman, $150,000 ($85,000); Jim Essian, $125,000 ($100,000); Rick Langford, $115,000 ($82,500); Mitchell Page, $100,000 ($85,000), and Bob Lacey, $75,000 ($55,00).

The 11 who had to settle for the club's offer, with the figure the player requested in parentheses, were: Larry Harlow of California, $50,000 ($75,000); Will McEnaney of St. Louis, $65,000 ($125,000); Billy Smith of Baltimore, $65,000 ($95,000); John Montague of California, $70,000 ($95,000); Don Aase of California, $77,500 ($100,000); Mike Parrott of Seattle, $82,500 ($130,000); Julio Cruz of Seattle, $95,000 ($130,000); Ron Jackson of Minnesota, $115,000 ($150,000); Rodney Scott of Montreal, $125,000 ($185,000); Dave Lemanczyk of Toronto, $130,000 ($175,000), and Ken Kravec.of the Chicago White Sox, $150,000 ($175,000).

Winfield Hits Jackpot

Another milestone also was achieved in the November re-entry draft. Because many of the previous year's free agents had fared poorly on the field in 1980, there was a feeling that financial inducements offered the new crop might be more modest. Several owners who had been burned in the earlier free-agent bidding took a restrained approach, but others ventured into the market with enthusiasm. As a consequence, even though the number of blue-chip performers available was smaller than usual, a fresh group of millionaires was created—and Dave Winfield became baseball's all-time salary champion at $1.3 million-plus per year.

Winfield began his bid to become the game's highest-paid athlete early in the year. During spring training his agent, Al Frohman, notified the San Diego Padres management that Winfield wanted a 10-year pact worth around $13 million. Frohman also laid down other demands, including an agreement that Owner Ray Kroc would not sell the club without Winfield's consent.

Ballard Smith, Padres president, countered by offering a long-term contract calling for an estimated $700,000 annually. Winfield turned it down.

Shortly after the World Series, New York Yankees Owner George Steinbrenner launched an all-out effort to land Winfield. He sought to work out a trade with the Padres. It fell through when the player declined to sign a new San Diego contract.

Winfield subsequently sent letters to a reported 17 clubs advising them not to draft his negotiating rights. He said he wasn't interested in playing for them. "I am determined to sign with a club that clearly will provide the opportunity for me to . . . contribute to the winning of a pennant," he wrote. "A metropolitan area where programs of the Winfield Foundation can be the most productive is a requirement." The Padres' captain-outfielder had formed the David M. Winfield Foundation three years earlier. Its purpose was to aid underprivileged children.

The letters reportedly went to all teams except the Yankees, New York Mets, Los Angeles Dodgers, California Angels, Boston Red Sox, Montreal Expos, Philadelphia Phillies, Atlanta Braves and Houston Astros.

Gabe Paul, Cleveland president, termed the letter a ploy to discourage teams from drafting Winfield and thus guarantee that the Yankees would have a crack at him. Under the re-entry draft setup, the Yankees were scheduled to pick last among the 26 clubs and, according to Paul, Winfield feared

Newest Yankees' millionaire DAVE WINFIELD meets resident moneybags REGGIE JACKSON after former San Diego outfielder came to terms with the Bronx Bombers.

that 13 teams—the maximum allowed—might select him before the Yankees had a chance.

Forty-eight players went the free-agency route in '80. Several others were on the verge of doing so, but reached agreement on long-term contracts at the last minute. Dusty Baker, Los Angeles Dodgers outfielder, was the most notable in that category. The Dodgers beat the deadline of midnight, November 10, with just minutes to spare when they satisfied Baker and his agent, Jerry Kapstein, with the richest contract in the Los Angeles club's history. The five-year, guaranteed contract was said to be worth around $4 million.

48 Free Agents Listed

Thirty of the 48 who opted for free agency were from American League clubs. Four teams—Kansas City, Seattle, Texas and Montreal—had four players each who entered the pool. The complete list of those included in the re-entry process follows:

AMERICAN LEAGUE

Baltimore—Outfielder Pat Kelly, designated hitter Lee May. **Boston**—Outfielder Jim Dwyer, catcher Dave Rader. **Chicago**—Catcher Glenn Borgmann. **Cleveland**—Pitcher Dan Spillner. **Kansas City**—Catcher Darrell Porter, pitcher Marty Pattin, first baseman Pete LaCock, outfielder Jose Cardenal. **Milwaukee**—Pitcher Bill Castro, pitcher Bill Travers, outfielder Vic Harris. **Minnesota**—Pitcher Geoff Zahn, infielder Mike Cubbage, designated hitter Jose Morales. **New York**—Pitcher Gaylord Perry, pitcher Luis Tiant, catcher Johnny Oates. **Oakland**—Catcher Jim Essian. **Seattle**—Catcher Marc Hill, pitcher David A. Roberts, infielder Bill Stein, outfielder Juan Beniquez. **Texas**—Pitcher Ed Figueroa, utilityman David W. Roberts, infielder Bud Harrelson, designated hitter Rusty Staub. **Toronto**—Infielder Roy Howell, outfielder Steve Braun.

NATIONAL LEAGUE

Atlanta—Outfielder Charlie Spikes. **Chicago**—Infielder Lenny Randle, infielder Mick Kelleher, first baseman-outfielder Larry Biittner. **Los Angeles**—Pitcher Don Sutton. **Montreal**—Pitcher Stan Bahnsen, pitcher John D'Acquisto, first baseman Willie Montanez, outfielder Ron LeFlore. **New York**—Pitcher Ray Burris, outfielder Claudell Washington, outfielder Jerry Morales. **Philadelphia**—Pitcher Tug McGraw, outfielder Del Unser. **Pittsburgh**—Pitcher Jesse Jefferson, first baseman-outfielder John Milner. **San Diego**—Outfielder Dave Winfield. **San Francisco**—Catcher Mike Sadek.

Utilitymen Popular in Draft

The fifth annual re-entry draft, held at the Plaza Hotel in New York on November 13, was marked by surprises and an air of mystery. The biggest surprise was that two utilitymen—Dave W. Roberts, a .238 hitter with Texas, and Jim Dwyer, a lifetime .250 hitter—were the most frequently selected. Twelve clubs put in for negotiation rights to Roberts, not counting the Rangers, and Dwyer was chosen by 11 teams.

The biggest eye-opener, however, was the almost total rejection of Tug McGraw and Ron LeFlore. McGraw was passed over by all clubs, possibly because of a suspicion that he wanted to remain with the Philadelphia Phillies. LeFlore, who led the National League with 97 stolen bases, was chosen by only the Chicago White Sox. Altogether, the 26 clubs made only 156 selections, the fewest in the history of the re-entry procedure.

McGraw and 13 others were not selected by any team. They were Borgmann, Braun, Cardenal, Harrelson, Harris, Hill, LaCock, May, Oates, Rader, Dave A. Roberts, Spikes and Tiant. And six who were picked by just one team—Figueroa, Jefferson, Kelleher, Kelly, LeFlore and Jerry Morales—became free under the rules to dicker with any club.

Four teams—Detroit, Kansas City, Minnesota and San Diego—made no selections except for the Padres' request to retain negotiation rights to Winfield.

Although Winfield was rated the prime talent, only 10 of a possible 13 rival clubs chose him. Five that did so—Baltimore, Cleveland, Cincinnati, Pittsburgh and St. Louis—had been notified by the outfielder that he wasn't interested in them. The others selecting Winfield were the two New York entries, the Yankees and Mets; California, Atlanta and Houston.

The fact that two journeymen were picked by more teams than some of the standouts led to speculation that many owners were bargain hunting and no longer willing to shell out the big bucks. But it quickly became obvious there still were big spenders.

The Claudell Washington Bombshell

Less than 24 hours after the draft, Atlanta Braves Owner Ted Turner jolted the sport by signing much-traveled Claudell Washington to a five-year, no-trade contract worth at least $3.5 million according to Atlanta writers. Washington's agent, Tom Baenziger, got his client a signing bonus of $250,000 and a salary of $400,000 for 1981, with annual $50,000 increases to $600,000 in 1987, plus $150,000 a year deferred for five years, a $350,000 interest-free loan and several incentive bonuses. Should Washington qualify for all the bonuses, it was estimated his take for the five years would reach $4,825,000.

Winfield, of course, was the big prize. In his eight years with San Diego, he had compiled a .284 career batting average and 154 home runs. The two New York teams engaged in hot bidding for his services, and the Cleveland Indians' prospective new owners also supposedly made a strong pitch. Winfield finally announced at a press conference in New York on December 15 that he had agreed to a 10-year contract with the Yankees.

Details of the financial arrangements were not made public, but New York writers disclosed they had learned Winfield would be paid $1.3 million in 1981 and receive annual cost of living increases up to 10 percent per year. It was projected that the contract could be worth between $15 and $23 million over the 10-year period.

Winfield's agent claimed another club, presumably Cleveland or the New York Mets, had made a higher offer. He then cited three reasons why the Yankees won out: Yankees tradition, the club's wealth of talent and the Yankees' ability to aid the Winfield Foundation.

Winfield and his foundation still had one bit of unfinished business in San Diego. San Diego writers reported that under terms of his Padres contract, the club had paid him $100,000 above his salary, with the money to be used by the foundation to purchase tickets to Padres games for underprivileged kids. The San Diego management claimed it still had $62,763 coming from this arrangement. Winfield's agent explained that the foundation had experienced difficulty finding children who wanted to attend Padres games.

More Free-Agent Millionaires

Other free agents who received contracts worth $1 million or more in 1980, according to the New York Times' Murray Chass:

—Don Sutton, signed by Houston for four years for $3.5 million, including three years and $2.85 million guaranteed. Signing bonus of $500,000, salaries of $750,000 in 1981 and $700,000 in both 1982 and 1983, plus $500,000 if he plays in 1984 or $200,000 if he doesn't play.

—Darrell Porter, signed by St. Louis for five years for an estimated $3.25

to $3.5 million.

—Ron LeFlore, signed by the Chicago White Sox for four years for between $2 and $2.5 million.

—Dan Spillner, re-signed by Cleveland for five years for $2 million.

—Tug McGraw, re-signed by Philadelphia for four years for $1.5 million, with the first three years guaranteed.

—David W. Roberts, signed by Houston for five years for $1.3 million, including $200,000 in incentive clauses.

—Geoff Zahn, signed by California for three years for $1.25 million.

—John D'Acquisto, signed by California for four years for $1.1 million.

—Rusty Staub, signed by the New York Mets for three years for $1 million.

—Mike Cubbage, signed by the New York Mets for three years for $1 million.

—Jim Essian, signed by the Chicago White Sox for four years for $1 million.

Rich, Long-Term Pacts in Vogue

Players who opted for free agency weren't the only ones cashing in handsomely. Most clubs, though not all, were yielding to contract demands that a few years earlier would have been considered outlandish. It was now a case of offering star players long-term, multimillion-dollar pacts or seeing them become free agents.

Before the players' association was organized, usually only the player, the club owner, general manager and financial officer, the league president and the IRS knew what his salary actually was. In recent years, contract terms of all players have become widely available at both the labor and management level. With most of the leading performers employing agents, the pressure for huge long-term contracts has continued to increase. As a result, the salary plateau for good—though not great—players reached the $500,000 to $600,000 range.

"I don't think any of us is worth the money we're getting," the Dodgers' Dusty Baker said early in the year, "but the owners have created this situation, and we'd be fools not to take advantage of it."

Over the past three years, payrolls of several teams had tripled or quadrupled. All National League teams were said to be around the $4 million level in 1980, while nine of the 14 American League teams reportedly were still under $3 million. The top six clubs in order of payroll reportedly were the Yankees, Pirates, Phillies, Angels, Dodgers and Red Sox.

Fat Contracts for Cardinals, Orioles

Examples of some of the fattest contracts negotiated in 1980, excluding free agents, included the following:

First baseman Keith Hernandez, who earned $75,000 as the National League's co-MVP the previous season, signed a five-year, $3.8 million agreement with the St. Louis Cardinals in February. A few weeks later, the Cardinals gave shortstop Garry Templeton a six-year, $4 million contract, and in September they inked pitcher Bob Forsch to a six-year, $3.5 million pact.

Pitcher Jim Palmer, in the last year of a contract paying $260,000 annually, agreed in midseason to a new contract with the Baltimore Orioles calling for a $250,000 signing bonus, a total of $1.25 million for the 1982-83 seasons and an option at $500,000 for 1984. In December, the Orioles also gave pitcher Scott McGregor a five-year contract worth nearly $2.5 million and first baseman Eddie Murray a five-year pact which might be worth close to $1 million a year, including bonuses and deferrals.

Catcher Jim Sundberg, also in the last year of his contract, accepted a new six-year pact from the Texas Rangers worth more than $3 million.

The New York Mets made pitcher Craig Swan the highest-paid player in their history by signing him to a five-year, $3 million agreement in March. Five months later, the 29-year-old righthander's career was imperiled by a muscle tear in the right shoulder.

Outfielder Garry Maddox agreed on April 14 to a six-year, $4 million guaranteed contract with the Philadelphia Phillies that includes a four-year, no-trade clause and an additional $100,000 a year for eight years in deferred payments.

In July, one of the wire services reported the Kansas City Royals had agreed to a five-year, $5 million extension of third baseman George Brett's contract. Brett, who signed for five years in 1977 for a total of $750,000, denied the report.

Two who landed multi-year million-dollar contracts prior to the season were outfielder Ken Griffey, who signed for two years at $1.4 million with the Cincinnati Reds, and relief ace Kent Tekulve, who accepted a four-year, $2 million agreement with the Pittsburgh Pirates.

Many teams found themselves shelling out heavily for players who failed to make the grade. Early in the season, the Phillies dropped reliever Rawly Eastwick, who had a guaranteed contract through 1982 for $225,000 annually, while the Cardinals released pitcher Darold Knowles, who was collecting $100,000. In June, the California Angels decided to swallow outfielder Ralph Garr's $130,000 salary and release him.

The game's new order was causing other complications for management. Faced with the prospect of losing a player to free agency, a club would try to swap him and get at least something in return. In some instances, clubs had to ante up sizable sums to get players to waive no-trade provisions of their contracts.

No-Trade Buyouts Set Precedent

Two precedent-setting buyouts of no-trade provisos occurred during the annual meetings in December and another took place a few days later. Larue Harcourt, agent for third baseman Ken Reitz and catcher Ted Simmons of the Cardinals, arranged for both to collect handsomely before agreeing to trades. Reitz was given $150,000 to waive his no-trade rights and pave the way for his shift to the Chicago Cubs in the Bruce Sutter deal. The St. Louis and Milwaukee clubs reportedly had to pay Simmons $750,000—on top of his $740,000 annual salary—to get him to switch to the Brewers as part of a six-player trade. A few days later, the New York Mets' acquisition of pitcher Randy Jones was completed when he accepted $200,000 to waive his no-trade provision.

The changing times began taking a toll among ownership. Two clubs were sold and controlling interest in a third changed hands in 1980. The sale of three other teams fell through for varying reasons, but deals involving two of them were consummated early in 1981.

Although some owners were crying the financial blues, the prices

TED SIMMONS

KEN REITZ

fetched by the five clubs that were sold hardly supported claims that baseball was in trouble. The transactions likewise emphasized there still are many wealthy individuals eager to own a major league team.

Mets Sold for $21.1 Million

The first club to be peddled was the New York Mets. A two-months bidding war ended January 24 with the announcement that the team had been purchased by a group headed by the huge New York publishing firm of Doubleday & Co. for $21.1 million. It was by far the highest price ever paid for a baseball team and more than twice the $10 million which George Steinbrenner and his associates shelled out to acquire the New York Yankees seven years earlier. No real estate was involved in either transaction.

Until the sale, the Mets had been owned by the Payson family ever since their debut in 1962. The late Mrs. Joan Payson, founder of the team, paid $1.8 million for the expansion franchise, including 22 players. Observers estimated the club enjoyed operating profits of $30 million over the years. However, after seeing the team finish in the cellar the last three seasons and experiencing annual operating losses as high as $3.8 million, Charles S. Payson, 81-year-old patriarch of the family, decided to unload.

A three-man committee was created to screen the offers. Twenty-one groups and individuals bid for the club, but when bidding passed the $15 million mark, only the Doubleday and Earl E. T. Smith groups remained in the running. Smith, a former ambassador to Cuba, headed a combine from the Allen & Co. brokerage.

The Doubleday firm's winning bid brought a familiar name to the game. Nelson Doubleday Jr., 46-year-old Princeton graduate and head of the publishing firm, is a great-great-nephew of Major General Abner Doubleday, who is credited by some with inventing baseball. Doubleday & Co. acquired 80 percent of the Mets' stock and was joined in the purchase by two partners.

Fred Wilpon, 43, chairman of the board of Sterling Equities of Manhasset, N.Y., a Long Island real estate firm, bought 13½ percent and City Investing Co. purchased a 6½ percent interest.

The new owners changed the corporate name of the club to Doubleday Sports, Inc. Doubleday was named chairman of the board and Wilpon assumed the role of president.

Chiles Takes Over Rangers

Brad Corbett's controversial six-year reign as head of the Texas Rangers ended February 27 when he sold his holdings in the club. Eddie Chiles, 69-year-old Fort Worth oilman, took over as top man after joining with two other stockholders, Fort Worth publisher Amon Carter and attorney Dee Kelly, to buy out Corbett for nearly $4 million.

Corbett had encountered troubles a month earlier during contract negotiations with catcher Jim Sundberg. Corbett agreed to a $5.1 million contract with Sundberg that included $500,000 a season as a player for six years and then a 10-year deal as a radio-TV announcer and promotions man. The Rangers' five-man executive board overruled Corbett, and two weeks later Sundberg accepted a revised pact.

Chiles, who heads a large oil-well servicing outfit, had saved the debt-ridden Texas franchise for Corbett early in 1979 by kicking in $900,000 to acquire a minority interest. At the time, he urged Corbett to "quit running the baseball team like a toy."

In the Rangers' reorganization, Chiles was named board chairman and chief executive officer on April 29. Eddie Robinson was elevated to president and chief operating officer, while Carter was named a vice-president. Chiles also named a new six-man board of directors. It consisted of three from Fort Worth—Chiles, Carter and Kelly—and three Dallas members—Charles Sharp, Mack Rankin, who bought into the club for an estimated $750,000, and Bill Seay, who had resigned a year earlier because of his continuing disagreement with Corbett.

Mavericks Veeck and Finley Sell Out

Two of baseball's most celebrated maverick owners—Bill Veeck and Charlie Finley—announced the sale of their clubs within 24 hours of each other. Both contended they could no longer afford to operate under the sport's inflated player costs.

Veeck disclosed on August 22 that the Chicago White Sox board of directors had agreed to accept an offer of $20 million made by Edward J. DeBartolo Sr., of Youngstown, O. One day later, Finley revealed he was turning the Oakland A's over to officers of Levi Strauss & Co., a giant clothing concern from San Francisco, for $12.7 million. The White Sox deal included Comiskey Park and 30 acres of land valued at almost $7 million. No real estate was involved in the A's sale.

The Oakland transaction was carried out with no problems, but eager as most other American League owners were to see both Finley and Veeck depart, they blocked the White Sox deal for more than four months.

Veeck had been recommending sale of the club for two years. He and his 46 partners purchased 80 percent of the White Sox holdings in December, 1975, for $8 million. Three weeks later, the landmark Messersmith-McNally decision by arbitrator Peter Seitz occurred. "That changed the whole philosophy of operating a club," Veeck emphasized.

DeBartolo, 69-year-old shopping center magnate, said his only partner in the deal for the White Sox would be his daughter, Mrs. Marie Denise York, whose husband John was a physician at Vanderbilt University.

Opposition to DeBartolo

Soon after DeBartolo's offer was accepted, word got out that several American League owners opposed his acquisition of the club. The objections had nothing to do with his finances. After all, he reputedly was worth $500 million and his family-owned corporation was said to control 49 enclosed shopping malls in 15 states as well as several banks and hotels, the Pittsburgh Penguins of the National Hockey League and three thoroughbred race tracks. In addition, his son Edward Jr. owned the San Francisco 49ers of the National Football League.

The opposition to DeBartolo centered around the issues of absentee ownership and his involvement in the three race tracks. A comment he had made earlier about wanting to put major league baseball in New Orleans' Superdome also prompted fears that he might try to move the White Sox. However, Veeck said he had received assurances from DeBartolo that the team would not be moved.

Commissioner Kuhn and Lee MacPhail, American League president, met with DeBartolo at a Pittsburgh airport hotel on September 5 and informed him of the opposition of several A.L. owners, enough to doom approval of his purchase of the White Sox. The Youngstown multimillionaire subsequently offered a $5 million indemnity against any transfer of the club out of Chicago. "If that isn't enough, make it $20 million," he added.

DeBartolo went head-to-head with American League owners for the first time in Chicago on September 17 during a meeting called to act on the Oakland sale. He addressed the group for eight minutes. Because the White Sox shareholders weren't scheduled to vote on his bid until October 15, the league took no action on him.

American League magnates met in Chicago again on October 24 for formal consideration of DeBartolo's bid. With 10 votes needed for approval, he fell two short on a final count of 8-6. Published reports indicated the Baltimore, Boston, Detroit, Kansas City, Milwaukee and Toronto clubs opposed the transaction. "There appears to be a strong feeling to keep local ownership if it is available," MacPhail declared.

When members of the media pointed out that the principal owners of several other teams—notably the Yankees, Pirates, Astros and Padres—lived in other cities, Kuhn responded: "There certainly has been some absentee ownership. But in the main, it has been local. There is no absolute mandatory prohibition against absentee owners, but it is a factor." Kuhn stressed that when clubs were sold to outsiders, it was because there were no viable local owners available. Viable local owners were available in Chicago, he said.

Despite the rebuff, DeBartolo sent a letter to Kuhn and the 14 American League owners on November 28 in which he offered to sell his three race tracks "in the shortest possible time, even it it means a loss," and to spend at least 20 percent of his time in Chicago if those moves would overcome objections.

DeBartolo's efforts proved fruitless. Another vote was taken on December 11 during the winter meetings in Dallas, and this time he was turned down decisively with 11 of the 14 clubs voting nay. Only the Cleveland and Oakland managements joined Veeck in approving.

Reinsdorf and Einhorn Gain Control

Exactly four weeks later—on January 8, 1981—a group headed by one of the original bidders, Jerry Reinsdorf, and television executive Eddie Einhorn bought the White Sox for $20 million. The sale was approved later in the month by the other A.L. owners. Reinsdorf, 44, disclosed he would serve as chairman and run the baseball end of the operations. Einhorn, 45, founded TVS, an independent syndicated sports network, and more recently was executive producer of the CBS "Sports Spectacular." He became president and took charge of the non-baseball phases.

"Doubling my investors' money is one very bright spot in all this," Veeck declared when the White Sox transaction finally was completed.

The sale of the Oakland A's spelled the end of Finley's 20-year ownership. He transferred the club to the Bay Area from Kansas City in 1968 and had come close to peddling it several times in recent years, only to be thwarted by a lease commitment at Oakland-Alameda County Coliseum.

A's Shift to Denver Collapses

As late as mid-February, it appeared the A's might be acquired by Marvin Davis, Denver multimillionaire oil man, and shifted to the Mile High City. Finley had accepted Davis' offer of $12 million, but the deal was contingent upon resolution of the stadium contract. Baseball had offered to buy out the remainder of the A's 20-year park lease for $4 million, with Finley, Davis, San Francisco Giants Owner Bob Lurie and the American League each putting up $1 million. The departure of the A's, of course, would have given the Giants the entire Bay Area to themselves. Oakland Mayor Lionel Wilson proposed using the buyout money to finance $8.5 million in stadium improvements to keep the Oakland Raiders of the National Football League from moving to Los Angeles.

The Denver deal fell through when the Oakland Coliseum board declined to terminate the A's lease.

New Oakland Ownership

The press conference for Finley's August 23 announcement of the sale of the club to Levi Strauss & Co. was held at the Oakland headquarters of Kaiser Aluminum and Chemical Co. Cornell Maier, Kaiser president, was instrumental in bringing the two parties together. The new owners include Walter H. Haas Jr., 64, chairman of Levi Strauss and a great-grandnephew of the firm's founder; his 30-year-old son, Walter J. (Wally) Haas, also a Levi executive, and Roy Eisenhardt, a San Franciso attorney, law professor at the University of California at Berkeley and son-in-law of the elder Haas. Eisenhardt, 41, became president of the A's, the elder Haas, chairman, and Wally Haas, vice-president. The new group took over November 6.

The new owners emphasized they intended to complete the seven years remaining on the Oakland Coliseum lease and added they would then consider extending it for another 20 years. Eisenhardt disclosed the Levi Strauss organization had arranged for a demographic study of the East Bay before purchasing the club. "The big question, of course, is: Can the Bay Area support two teams?" he admitted. "We intend to be successful. We want everyone to catch baseball fever."

In discussing Finley's disposition of the club, A.L. President Lee Mac-Phail commented: "Baseball has lost its No. 1 innovator. The designated hitter, divisional play, night World Series games, colorful uniforms and opening the Series on Saturday were all ideas that Charlie pushed before others did. But Charlie had three big problems. He was an absentee owner who never could tear himself away from the streets of Chicago. He didn't have the organization needed to market his product properly. And more than anything, he was hurt by the new (free agent) system."

Finley himself said the main reason he was leaving baseball was "because I can no longer compete financially. During the time we were winning championships, survival was a battle of wits. We did all right then. But it is no longer a battle of wits, but how much can you have on the hip. I can no longer compete."

Background on Sale of Mariners

The financially distressed Seattle Mariners also were the subject of frequent sale rumors. Early in the year, before bidding for the White Sox, Edward J. DeBartolo Sr., made a pitch for the Mariners. In July, disenchantment with the financial drain caused by the club prompted James A. Walsh, one of the six original owners, to sell his interest to his five partners—Stan Golub, Danny Kaye, Les Smith, Jim Stillwell and Walter Schoenfeld. Sea-First Bank of Seattle was said to hold a $6 million note against the Mariners.

Nelson Skalbania, Canadian millionaire and sports entrepreneur, moved into the picture in August with a reported offer of $12.25 million for the Mariners. Subsequently, his interest seemed to cool, apparently because of an American League rule requiring a buyer to come up with 60 percent of the purchase price as down payment. In the meantime, Skalbania, who owned 50 percent of the Calgary Flames of the National Hockey League, purchased a 49.9 percent interest in the Vancouver team of the Pacific Coast League from Harry Ornest for $1.5 million. The British Columbia government was said to be committed to constructing a 60,000-seat domed stadium in Vancouver by 1982, and Ornest announced he planned to apply for a major league franchise.

Seattle finished the season with an attendance of only 836,204, second lowest in the majors. After attracting 1,338,511 during their first season in 1977, the Mariners had seen their gate dip each year.

New ownership for the club finally surfaced on January 14, 1981, when George Argyros purchased controlling interest for a reported $10.4 million. Joining him in the deal on a limited basis was Warren Finley, his personal attorney. Four of the Mariners' original owners—Golub, Kaye, Schoenfeld and Smith—remained as limited partners. Argyros, 43, has real estate and financial interests in Southern California and Idaho and his company is headquartered in Santa Ana, Calif.

Deal for Indians Falls Through

The Cleveland Indians were on the verge of being peddled before a snag caused the transaction to be called off. On October 30, F. J. (Steve) O'Neill, principal owner, and the club's board of directors approved a sale in principle to a syndicate headed by James Nederlander, New York theater tycoon, and Neil Papiano, Los Angeles attorney. The Nederlander group was to acquire

63 percent of the Tribe stock for $10 million and reportedly was to assume a $2.27 million bank debt as well as 1980 operating losses of close to $2.3 million. Under terms of the transaction, O'Neill, who owned 70 percent, would retain a 10 percent interest and Gabe Paul, president of the Indians, planned to keep seven percent.

Nederlander operates 28 legitimate theaters across the U.S. Papiano had served as Charlie Finley's attorney and helped negotiate the sale of the Oakland team.

O'Neill, 81, was said to have grown weary of the Cleveland club's financial losses, estimated at $2 million each of the last two years. He had acquired the financially troubled Indians in February, 1978, after disposing of his minority holdings in the Yankees.

Negotiations with the Nederlander-Papiano group were abruptly terminated by the Indians' ownership on January 6, 1981. Paul said that certain issues existed "which could not be resolved."

New Brass for Royals, Reds

The Kansas City Royals gained a new minority stockholder. On December 23 Owner Ewing Kauffman announced that Joe Burke, the club's executive vice-president, "has accepted my offer to sell him stock so he can become a minority owner of the Royals." The size of Burke's holdings was not disclosed.

Louis Nippert, principal owner of the Cincinnati Reds, said late in the year that he planned to unload most of his 90 percent interest in the club. Vice-President William J. Williams succeeded Nippert as chairman of the Reds' board of directors.

Another change in minority ownership seemed imminent on the Minnesota Twins. Following the club's mid-November directors' meeting, Gabe Murphy disclosed he wanted to sell his 40 percent interest. Murphy, 77-year-old Washington, D.C., insurance executive, was the Twins' biggest individual stockholder. President Calvin Griffith and his sister, Thelma Griffith Haynes, each owned 26 percent.

'Palace Revolt' in Houston

A "palace revolt" among Houston Astros partners brought about a change. The former partnership was dissolved and replaced by a corporation. The furor erupted on October 27 when John J. McMullen, managing general partner, announced the firing of President-General Manager Tal Smith. Coming just two weeks after the Astros closed the best season in their 19-year history, the decision stunned the media and other Astros partners.

McMullen said "philosophical differences" were the reason for the dismissal. Smith said McMullen's explanation to him was that because of an attendance bonus in Smith's contract, the club could no longer afford him.

McMullen promptly signed Al Rosen to a three-year contract as Astros general manager. Rosen had resigned a few weeks earlier as executive vice-president of Bally Corporation's Park Place casino-hotel in Atlantic City, N.J. He served first as executive vice-president and then president of the Yankees from 1977 until he joined Bally in July, 1979.

Following Smith's ouster, a group of limited partners representing 60 percent of the Astros ownership offered to buy McMullen out. He refused. The insurgents also filed suit to dissolve the partnership and form a corporation. Together with his family and a Montclair, N.J., neighbor, McMullen had controlled 34 percent of the partnership. McMullen himself owned 25 percent. The next biggest stockholder was Dave LeFevre, Wall Street Lawyer, with 10 percent. A group of 20 Houstonians held the remaining 56 percent.

The move to oust McMullen apparently was resolved on November 24 with the appointment of a three-man committee, including McMullen himself, to guide the club. Joining the New York shipbuilder and principal owner on the committee were Jack Trotter, a certified public accountant and two percent owner, and Herb Neyland, a retired millionaire.

When Houston signed free-agent Don Sutton to a hefty contract on December 3, observers saw the move as a signal that McMullen still was running the team. He also had been responsible for the huge outlay to land Nolan Ryan a year earlier.

General Managers Sent Packing

It was a tough year for general managers. Besides Smith, three others were either dismissed or demoted. They were Joe McDonald, Bob Fontaine and John Claiborne. The changes indicated the owners were taking a harder look at the performances of the men responsible for the product on the field.

McDonald became a victim of the Mets' change in ownership. On February 21 the new owners appointed Frank Cashen as executive vice-president and general manager. Cashen, 53, had been an official with the Baltimore Orioles for 10 years before joining Commissioner Kuhn's staff as administrator in February, 1979.

Fontaine, in his third year as San Diego G.M., was fired on July 7. The move signaled a shakeup that saw the disappointing Padres shuffle their playing personnel. Jack McKeon, Fontaine's assistant, and Manager Jerry Coleman shared the duties of general manager briefly until McKeon was named acting G.M. After interviewing nearly a dozen candidates, Padres President Ballard Smith on September 23 appointed McKeon as general manager and director of baseball operations.

Claiborne's 21-month tenure as St. Louis Cardinals general manager ended August 18 when Owner August A. Busch Jr., dismissed him. Busch, impatient for another pennant, said the decision was the result of a "basic disagreement" with Claiborne over the team's progress. On August 26, Whitey Herzog was elevated from field manager to general manager of the Cardinals.

Contrasting sharply with the ouster of the four general managers was the experience of two of their counterparts. Hank Peters received a new four-year contract as executive vice-president and general manager of the Orioles in February, while the Cincinnati Reds handed Dick Wagner, their chief executive, a new five-year pact in December.

New Faces in the Front Office

Several other top-level front-office changes were made prior to the season. They included Bill Murray's departure as vice-president and treasurer of the Mets to join the commissioner's staff as administrator, succeeding Cashen; the resignation of Jim Thomson as vice-president of the Mets and his replacement by James Nagourney, and the appointment of Al Thornwell as executive vice-president of the Braves.

After the season, the Texas Rangers dropped Eddie Robinson's title from president to executive vice-president of baseball operations and Samuel G. Meason was appointed executive vice-president for business affairs. Bob Fontaine, former San Diego general manager, joined the San Francisco Giants as director of player personnel. Late in October, Joe McDonald left the Mets to become executive assistant to Herzog with the Cardinals. Resigning as general manager at Seattle, Lou Gorman then succeeded McDonald as the Mets' vice-president for baseball operations while Arthur Richman was promoted to special assistant to Cashen. Al Harazin, a vice-president with Baltimore, also joined the Mets as vice-president of marketing. And Woody Woodward, former player and the Cincinnati Reds' minor league coordinator, was appointed assistant general manager by the Reds.

Following the sale of the Oakland A's, the new owners announced they would operate without a general manager but gave Manager Billy Martin the additional title of director of player development. They also appointed Andrew Dolich and Carl Finley as vice-presidents of baseball operations and business administration, respectively.

Rookie Skippers Win Races

At the managerial level, the game of the musical chairs continued. Two rookie pilots won division titles, but one of them found himself an ex-manager at year's end. Another field boss, after being elevated to general manager during the season, later decided to return to the dugout.

Six teams boasted new managers when spring training began. The newcomers included four who were making their debuts as big league pilots—Bobby Mattick of Toronto, the second oldest rookie manager ever at 63; Jim Frey of Kansas City, Dick Howser of the New York Yankees and Jerry Coleman of San Diego. The two others were Preston Gomez of the Chicago Cubs and Billy Martin of Oakland.

Finley didn't get around to hiring Martin until February 21, just one day before the A's opened training camp. Billy succeeded Jim Marshall and was given a two-year contract. Fired the previous October by the Yankees, he still had two years remaining on his New York contract at $125,000 annually. Negotiations to settle that pact also figured in the delay in his signing with the A's. The settlement reportedly involved a $150,000 payment by the Yankees. In returning to Oakland, his hometown, Martin became the 18th manager to work for Finley in his 20 years as owner.

Manager George Bamberger of Milwaukee, who had intended to retire at the end of the season, was hospitalized on March 6 after suffering a mild heart attack. Coach Bob (Buck) Rodgers took over as interim pilot. Bamberger underwent five coronary bypasses during an eight-hour operation March 26. Following a 10-week recuperation, during which he shed 23 pounds, he returned to the Brewers' helm on June 6 as planned.

Boyer First to Get the Axe

The season's first managerial casualty was Ken Boyer of St. Louis. General Manager John Claiborne delivered the word to him between games of a Sunday doubleheader in Montreal on June 8. At the same time, Owner August A. Busch, Jr., was holding a press conference in St. Louis to announce the appointment of Whitey Herzog as Boyer's successor. The Cards had suffered 22 losses in their last 27 games. Boyer stayed on with the Cardinals in a special assignments role.

Gomez became the second pilot to walk the plank when the Cubs fired him on July 25. Coach Joey Amalfitano replaced him. "When I took the job in spring training," a bitter Gomez commented, "I noticed the unhappy players, outspoken and complaining about management. I thought to myself, 'Why did I get into this?' But I did the best I could."

Darrell Johnson was next. On August 4 he gave way at Seattle to Maury Wills, who'd almost succeeded Johnson a year earlier. The appointment made Wills the third black manager in major league history, behind Frank Robinson, who led Cleveland in 1975-76-77, and Larry Doby, who piloted the Chicago White Sox part of 1978.

Gene Mauch, the majors' oldest manager in point of service, pulled a surprise on August 24 by quitting as skipper of Minnesota. After watching the Twins bow to Detroit that afternoon, he announced his resignation, effective immediately, in a brief clubhouse meeting with the players. His contract with the Twins ran through 1981 and was said to call for $100,000 annually, but he decided to forfeit the balance. Mauch, 54, had managed in the majors for 21 consecutive seasons. Coach John Goryl was appointed to succeed him.

Herzog Elevated to G.M. Post

The Cardinals on August 29 promoted Herzog to general manager, replacing Claiborne, and named coach Red Schoendienst as interim pilot. "I sure as heck didn't come here (to St. Louis) to be general manager," Herzog said, "but I can do more for the Cardinals as G.M. than as field manager." Two months later, after hiring Joe McDonald as administrative assistant, Herzog announced he would attempt the combined role of manager-general manager in 1981.

Milwaukee also experienced another change in field leadership when Bamberger stepped aside following the Brewers' September 8 game. Although declaring himself completely recovered from his spring siege, the popular 55-year-old decided to retire from managing, and Rodgers took over again. Bamberger was named a special assistant to General Manager Harry Dalton.

Alarmed by a dip in attendance and bowing to fan pressure, the Boston Red Sox dismissed Manager Don Zimmer on October 1. "I don't think we're going to find a better baseball man than Don Zimmer," executive Vice-President Haywood Sullivan told the media after announcing the firing. Coach Johnny Pesky ran the club for the last five games of the season, and on October 27, the Red Sox signed Ralph Houk to a two-year contract as manager. Houk, 61, had been serving as a consultant with the Detroit Tigers since retiring as their pilot in 1978.

The final weekend of the season saw two more managers draw their walking papers. On Saturday night, October 4, the San Diego Padres disclosed that Jerry Coleman would not return. Next day, the Texas Rangers announced the dismissal of Pat Corrales. Coleman, who had interrputed a long career as broadcaster to sign a three-year managerial contract the previous October, was promptly named director of broadcasting and No. 1 announcer by the Padres. Corrales remained with the Rangers as assistant to Vice-President Eddie Robinson.

San Diego filled its managerial vacancy on October 6 with the appointment of Frank Howard, a coach for Milwaukee the past four years. Zimmer accepted a one-year contract on November 12 to become Texas' eighth manager—excluding two interim pilots—in 10 years.

Meanwhile, the manager whose team compiled the year's best won-lost record was left dangling. While Kansas City was singing the praises of its rookie pilot, Jim Frey, for leading the Royals to the pennant, Yankees Owner George Steinbrenner was indicating displeasure with his freshman skipper, Dick Howser. The Yankees had chalked up a 103-59 record, making Howser only the sixth manager ever to attain 100 victories in his first full season, but Steinbrenner became irked when the club lost three straight to Kansas City in the A.L. Championship Series. "There will be changes. You can count on that," the Yankees' head man declared following a 4½-hour meeting of club officials the morning after the final loss to the Royals.

Howser still had two years at $100,000 per season remaining on his Yankees managerial contract. But reports began circulating that he was on the outs with his boss. Shortly after the League Championship Series, Steinbrenner expressed interest in signing Don Zimmer as third base coach to replace Mike Ferraro. The latter had drawn the owner's ire when the Yankees' potential tying run was thrown out at the plate in the second LCS game. Asked by the media about Zimmer, Howser expressed displeasure about not having been consulted. The Yankees owner immediately chastised his manager for speaking out.

Howser Gives Up Yankees Post

More than five weeks of rumors ensued. The melodrama culminated with the November 21 announcement to a select group of New York media that Howser was resigning as manager and that General Manager Gene Michael had accepted a three-year contract to take over on the field. Michael, who had been appointed G.M. a year earlier, turned over his front-office duties to two other Yankees executives, Cedric Tallis and Bill Bergesch.

Although Steinbrenner insisted Howser was not fired, Howser's only response when the media pressed the point was: "I'm not going to comment on that." The 43-year-old ex-manager continued on the Yankees' payroll as scouting supervisor for the southeastern section of the U.S. and said he also would pursue some business ventures.

The world champion Philadelphia Phillies likewise were facing a managerial dilemma. During the season Dallas Green, who switched from farm director to field boss the previous summer, announced that if the club won the World Series he would quit as pilot and return to the front office. However, on November 6, following subtle pressure from Owner Ruly Carpenter and General Manager Paul Owens, Green agreed to stay on as manager under a new one-year contract calling for an estimated $125,000 or more.

The year's final managerial change came when Dave Bristol was fired as San Francisco skipper during the winter meetings in Dallas. Under contract through 1981 and supposedly in line for an extension, Bristol was notified of the decision in a meeting in Owner Bob Lurie's suite on December 9.

Bristol at Odds With Players

A rift that developed between Bristol and his players apparently prompted Lurie's move. On June 18, the manager and pitcher John Montefusco engaged in postgame fisticuffs. Bristol also had verbal clashes with Rennie Stennett and Jack Clark, and during the World Series he angered Lurie by

DAVE BRISTOL   JOHN MONTEFUSCO

referring to Mike Ivie as "a cancer on this club." Ivie had walked out on the Giants for about two weeks in midsummer and left again three days before the season ended.

Five weeks after Bristol's ouster, the Giants appointed Frank Robinson as their manager. He thus became the fourth Baltimore Orioles coach to move up as manager in the last four years, following Billy Hunter, George Bamberger and Jim Frey.

The annual winter meetings at the Loews Anatole Hotel in Dallas produced other excitement. Much of it revolved around a flurry of player swapping. Herzog, the Cardinals' double-duty man, was the focus of the trading activity. He negotiated three deals that sent 13 players to other clubs and brought nine to St. Louis.

Altogether, 18 transactions involving 59 players were consummated during the week-long session. In numerous instances clubs dealt away players who a year hence would be eligible for free agency. One such transaction fell through when outfielder Fred Lynn, whom the Red Sox sought to send to the Dodgers, notified the Los Angeles club that he would sign for only one year and then choose free agency.

Alexander Forces a Trade

Another little-known facet of baseball's new system spawned one trade. Under terms of the 1976 Basic Agreement, a player with five years of major league service who is acquired from another club—and does not sign a new contract with his new team—may demand to be traded at the conclusion of a season even if his contract hasn't expired. Doyle Alexander, Atlanta's 14-game winner, found himself in this position. Obtained from Texas the previous winter, he joined the Braves with three years remaining on his pact at $150,000 annually. When Atlanta declined his request for a $300,000 bonus for "past services" and a renegotiated salary of $500,000 for both 1981 and 1982, he exercised his right by asking to be swapped and was dealt to the Giants.

In other action at the winter meetings, National League owners extended the contract of President Chub Feeney for two years through 1983 at an increase in salary, Commissioner Kuhn revealed the annual budget for the Umpire Development Program, covering partial payroll costs and allowances for minor league arbiters had been increased from $505,000 to $685,000, and the Official Playing Rules Committee amended the designated-hitter rule. The committee also voted approval for the International League to experiment in 1981 with resuming all games that are halted before going 4½ or five innings.

The change in the designated-hitter rule was prompted by a gimmick introduced in 1980 by Earl Weaver, Baltimore manager. To counter the possibility of a pitching change by the opposition before his DH came to bat, Weaver on 21 occasions filled the DH spot on his lineup card with the name of a pitcher who wasn't due to play and then used another player in his place. Under the revised rule, the DH listed in the starting lineup must bat at least once unless the opposing team has changed pitchers before the DH is due.

The National League continued to reject the designated-hitter rule. At a midsummer meeting, four teams—Atlanta, New York, St. Louis and San Diego—supported the idea, while three abstained—Houston, Philadelphia and Pittsburgh—and the five others voted against it.

Kuhn Warns of Financial Disaster

In his annual "state of the sport" address at the December conclave, Commissioner Kuhn said the game "may have a bad case of economic pneumonia." Referring to a study made by the firm of Ernst and Whinney, certified public accountants, Kuhn declared: "There are those who argue that baseball's increased operating revenues are more than adequate to meet the rising costs of our business, particularly player compensation (salaries). This simply is not so. The Ernst and Whinney analysis shows that even before free agency, player salaries were increasing at a more rapid rate than revenues. With the onset of free agency in 1976, this continued. The percent of increase in player compensation has been running nearly double that of operating revenues."

He added the study showed that only 11 major league teams operated in the black in 1979. "What is more disturbing are our forecasts of profit-and-loss prospects for the season ahead," Kuhn continued. "Using conservative but realistic assumptions, our office with the help of Ernst and Whinney projects losses in the five years 1980-84 nearly 10 times greater than the losses in the preceding five years.

"Operating revenues simply will not grow fast enough to keep even close to the vaulting cost of doing business. We are projecting player compensation (salary) by 1984 at $320,000 per player. What is to become of some of our more afflicted franchises and what is to become of ticket prices?"

Kuhn also pointed to the "companion problem" brought about by free agency—"the threat to competitive balance." Declaring that "time and again we hear the comment from our players that they want to play with a winner," he said the blame for that philosophy "lies not with the players, but in the system, and the system needs changes."

Kuhn's comments were termed "absurd" by Marvin Miller, director of the players' association. He said it was "just preposterous to talk about ailing franchises when, in reality, every time a franchise changes hands, there are tremendous capital gains. . . . The price of franchises continues to go up . . . and up . . . and up."

As for concern about free agency destroying competitive balance, Miller's reaction was: "The major leagues have been more competitive since free agency than ever before. More new teams have figured in the championship races—eight different clubs in two years—and three of four division races this year went to the final weekend of the season."

The season was crowned by two remarkable League Championship Series. Many observers rated the five-game Philadelphia-Houston clash the most dramatic LCS ever. The Phillies then provided a fitting climax with their six-game conquest of Kansas City in the World Series.

The campaign also produced its share of remarkable player feats. George Brett's late-season flirtation with a .400 batting average attracted national attention. The Kansas City third baseman eventually had to settle for a .390 average. Teammate Willie Wilson led both majors in hits with 230 and duplicated Garry Templeton's 1979 feat of collecting 100 hits from each side of the plate. Mike Schmidt, Philadelphia third baseman, paced both leagues with 48 homers, but lost RBI honors by one, 122-121, to Milwaukee's Cecil Cooper. Among pitchers, Baltimore's Steve Stone gained the spotlight with a remarkable 25-7 record, while Steve Carlton of the Phillies was right behind at 24-9.

For the first time ever, all teams in one league—the National—topped the million mark in attendance. All but three American League teams also achieved that figure. Both circuits, however, fell short of their all-time turnstile highs set in 1979. The N.L. total of 21,124,084 was down 54,335 from a year earlier, while the American League with 21,890,052 experienced a dip of almost 482,000. The Los Angeles Dodgers again led all clubs at the turnstiles with 3,249,287. The Yankees set an American League record with 2,627,417, and four other teams—Baltimore, Kansas City, Houston and Montreal—likewise broke their attendance records.

J. R. Richard Felled by Stroke

Tragedy struck when J. R. Richard, Houston's brilliant 30-year-old pitcher, suffered a stroke on July 30. He was finished for the season and there were doubts whether he would ever pitch again.

Despite complaining several times of a "dead arm," Richard enjoyed a great first half. At the All-Star break, he owned a 10-4 record and led the league in ERA. Some media members viewed his mysterious arm ailment as a case of malingering or possible drug involvement. On July 26, he entered Houston's Methodist Hospital and during a three-day series of tests, doctors discovered a circulatory problem affecting the flow of blood to his right arm. Four days later, while working out at the Astrodome, he collapsed from a stroke and was rushed back to the hospital. Emergency surgery was performed to remove a blood clot behind his right collarbone which had cut off the flow of blood to the brain and threatened his life.

The ailment left Richard partially paralyzed on the left side and kept him hospitalized until September 12. With his Astros teammates headed for the division title, the big pitcher made his first return visit to the Astrodome on September 27 and received a standing ovation.

On October 12, Richard entered Moffitt Hospital in San Francisco. Vas-

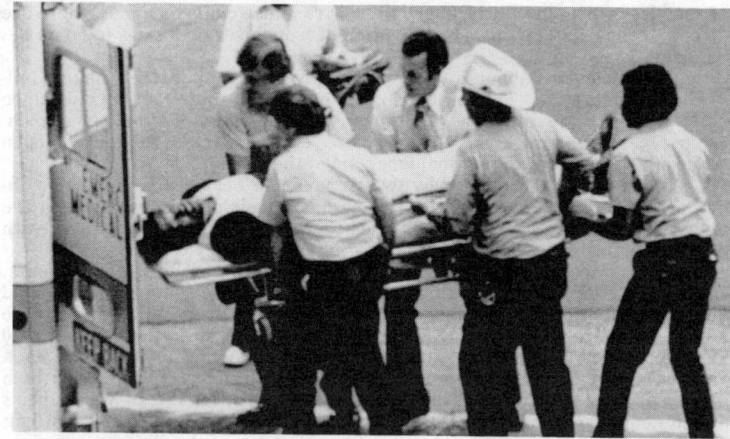

Houston pitcher J.R. RICHARD is lifted into an ambulance after collapsing following a short workout at the Astrodome July 30. Troubled hurler suffered a stroke and had emergency surgery to remove a blood clot behind his right collarbone which threatened his life.

cular surgeons replaced an obstructed artery in his right shoulder during a complex 18-hour operation and rebuilt his damaged vascular system through the use of arterial grafts and Dacron tubing. After the surgery, they expressed hope that he might eventually resume pitching.

Other veterans who experienced physical misfortune were Harvey Kuenn, 49-year-old Milwaukee coach and former infielder; Milwaukee Manager George Bamberger, 55, and third baseman Graig Nettles of the Yankees. Kuenn's right leg was amputated below the knee on February 16 because of blood clots. He rejoined the Brewers late in July. Bamberger suffered a heart attack March 6, underwent bypass surgery and returned June 6. He retired on September 5, but denied that health was a factor. Nettles, after missing six games with what was thought to be the flu, learned on July 31 that he was suffering from infectious hepatitis. The illness kept him out of uniform until October 2.

Several celebrated incidents also marred the season. The first centered on Bob Horner, Atlanta third baseman who a year earlier had been involved in a salary battle that resulted in a landmark arbitration case. Like the Braves, the young slugger got off to a slow start. In the club's first 10 games, of which Atlanta lost nine, Horner made just two hits—both singles—in 34 at-bats, had no RBIs and committed six errors. Following the 10th game, April 30, Owner Ted Turner read the riot act to the team in a clubhouse session and threatened wholesale changes.

Horner Fights Ticket to Minors

The next day the Braves optioned Horner to Richmond (International).

Revealing photo of Pittsburgh's BILL MADLOCK shoving his glove into the face of umpire GERRY CRAWFORD during fifth inning argument May 1. Madlock was suspended for 15 days and fined $5,000 by N.L. President Chub Feeney for the incident.

Manager Bobby Cox and General Manager John Mullen reportedly opposed the move, but were overruled by Turner and his chief aide, Al Thornwell. Horner, in the first season of a three-year, $350,000 annual contract, immediately announced he would not report to Richmond.

The players' association filed a grievance against the Braves, claiming the demotion was "an improper disciplinary action" and violated the no-trade provision of Horner's contract. "If the Braves refuse to return Horner to the roster within 10 days, an arbitration hearing will be held in regard to free agency," Marvin Miller warned.

On April 28, the Braves placed Horner on the disqualified list. Two days later, they reinstated him, and he rejoined his mates in Pittsburgh May 2. The 22-year-old slugger went on to hit .268 with 35 home runs and 89 RBIs in 124 games.

Unhappiness over Manager Chuck Tanner's quick hook prompted pitcher Bert Blyleven to quit the Pittsburgh Pirates April 30. The 29-year-old right-hander, said to be earning $300,000, informed club officials that he would retire unless they traded him. After placing Blyleven on the disqualified list, they reactivated him on May 13 when he consented to rejoin the team.

Another Pirate, third baseman Bill Madlock, became embroiled in a more serious situation. On May 5 National League President Chub Feeney ordered Madlock suspended for 15 days and fined $5,000 for shoving his glove into the face of umpire Gerry Crawford during an argument four days earlier.

Madlock Appeals Penalty

The decision, one of the majors' longest suspensions ever for an on-the-field incident, was promptly appealed by Madlock and the players' association. Under the rules, Madlock was permitted to continue playing pending outcome of the appeal. Feeney held a hearing on May 8, but when more than three weeks passed with no decision, National League umpires announced that, beginning June 6, they would eject Madlock from every game. The threat was removed when Feeney ruled on June 2 that the 15-day suspension would stand.

The players' association then lodged an appeal with Commissioner Kuhn. However, on June 6, Madlock abruptly withdrew the appeal and announced he would accept the punishment. According to a copyrighted story in the Pittsburgh Post-Gazette, Madlock dropped the appeal at Pirates Owner John Galbreath's urging. On the basis of his estimated $250,000 salary, the 15-day absence could have cost Madlock $20,700 in pay, but the Pirates decided not to dock him.

A bench-clearing brawl at Chicago's Comiskey Park on June 20 resulted in the issuance of a warrant for the arrest of Al Cowens, Detroit outfielder, on a charge of assault and battery. After grounding out in the 11th inning, Cowens rushed to the mound and attacked Ed Farmer, White Sox pitcher. The fight was another chapter in a feud that dated back to the previous season when Farmer broke Cowens' jaw with a pitch. Lee MacPhail, American League president, dealt Cowens a seven-game suspension and fine, and Farmer swore out a warrant against the Detroit outfielder. Cowens passed up the Tigers' late-August visit to Chicago to avoid the warrant. When the White Sox visited Detroit on September 1, the two protagonists ended their feud by shaking hands at home plate after carrying the lineup cards to the umpires.

Jenkins Faces Narcotics Charge

Ferguson Jenkins, veteran pitcher with Texas, also became involved in an episode with far-ranging consequences. On August 25, shortly after the Rangers arrived in Toronto, the 36-year-old Canadian native was arrested by police on a narcotics possession charge. Two ounces of marijuana, four grams of cocaine and two grams of hashish, with a value of $500, were found in his luggage at the airport.

Jenkins and his attorney, Ed Greenspan, were summoned to Commissioner Kuhn's office for an August 30 interview. Because of the pending criminal case, the pitcher, on advice of counsel, declined to answer questions relating to possession of illegal drugs. Nine days later, Kuhn sent Jenkins a notice ordering him out of uniform, but adding: "I am asking the Texas club to continue your salary and benefits during your absence, which should make clear that my action is in no sense intended to be punitive."

Following the filing of a grievance, baseball's permanent arbitrator, Professor Raymond Goetz of the University of Kansas law faculty, conducted a hearing in Chicago on September 18. His decision, issued four days later, overruled Kuhn and ordered Jenkins back to active duty immediately. It was believed to be the first time that one of Kuhn's actions had been overturned.

The Jenkins case went to trial in Ontario Provincial Court in Brampton December 18, and Judge Gerald Young found the pitcher guilty of possession of cocaine. Conviction could have carried a maximum penalty of six months in jail and $1,000 fine.

Because of Jenkins' otherwise upstanding record, Judge Young decided to erase the verdict and gave him an absolute discharge.

Several weeks later, following another meeting with Jenkins, Kuhn decided not to take any further disciplinary action. The pitcher agreed to donate $10,000 to a drug-education program and to make public appearances in support of anti-drug efforts.

Welch Reveals Alcoholism

The drug issue was brought into focus early in 1980 by several other cases. The first was the disclosure by Bob Welch, young Los Angeles Dodgers pitcher, that he was an alcoholic and had spent five weeks during the winter at the Meadows in Wickenberg, Ariz., for treatment. Late in the year, Welch appeared in a 20-minute film called "Comebacker" that depicted his drinking problems and how he overcame them.

During spring training, catcher Darrell Porter left the Kansas City Royals March 14 under mysterious circumstances. Subsequently, it was revealed he had entered an alcohol and drug rehabilitation program. After six weeks at the Meadows, Porter rejoined the Royals on April 26.

A copyrighted story in the Trenton (N.J.) Times on July 8 reported that Pennsylvania authorities wanted to question eight members of the Philadelphia Phillies about acquiring amphetamine pills illegally from the physician for the Phils' Reading (Eastern) farm team. The players angrily denied the charges. Following hearings in February, 1981, charges against the physician, Dr. Patrick A. Mazza, and two others named in the case were dropped.

One of the game's veteran stars, Willie McCovey, retired in midseason. The slugging San Francisco first baseman, tied with Ted Williams for ninth place on the all-time home-run list with 521, made his farewell appearance on July 6.

Late in the season three other veterans came out of retirement to make brief appearances. Manny Mota, coach with the Los Angeles Dodgers, marked his return to action with three more pinch-hits to extend his major league record for safeties in pinch-hitting roles to 150. Minnie Minoso, a special coach with the Chicago White Sox, was used twice as a pinch-hitter by the club in September at age 57. The appearances gave Minoso the distinction of being only the second player in major league history to play in five dec-

WILLIE McCOVEY

MANNY MOTA

MINNIE MINOSO

ades, counting 1980 as the start of a new decade. The first was Nick Altrock. Tim McCarver, who had moved up to the Philadelphia Phillies' broadcasting booth, also returned to uniform in September for six pinch-hitting turns and thus joined McCovey and Jim Kaat of St. Louis among those who performed in the majors in four decades.

Schmidt, Brett Named MVPs

Climaxing the great seasons they enjoyed, the third basemen of the World Series rivals—Mike Schmidt and George Brett—were named Most Valuable Player of their respective leagues. The voting, of course, was done between the end of the regular season and the start of the League Championship Series by committees of the Baseball Writers' Association.

Schmidt was a unanimous choice in the National League poll. The Phillies' slugger thus became the first N.L. player to make a sweep since Orlando Cepeda of the 1967 Cardinals. Montreal catcher Gary Carter finished a distant second in the balloting, in which each first-place vote counted for 10 points, with nine for second, eight for third and so on.

A breakdown of the voting in the Most Valuable Player polls follows:

Name	1	2	3	4	5	6	7	8	9	10	Tot.
M. Schmidt	24	–	–	–	–	–	–	–	–	–	336
G. Carter	–	14	4	2	1	3	–	–	–	–	193
J. Cruz	–	7	3	5	4	2	1	2	–	–	166
D. Baker	–	1	4	5	5	3	3	1	1	–	138
S. Carlton	–	1	4	1	9	4	2	–	2	–	134
S. Garvey	–	1	5	5	–	4	4	3	1	–	131
A. Dawson	–	–	1	2	1	2	5	4	–	2	72
G. Hendrick	–	–	2	1	1	–	1	2	2	7	50
B. Horner	–	–	–	1	1	–	3	5	–	2	42
B. McBride	–	–	–	–	1	1	3	1	2	2	32
K. Hernandez	–	–	1	1	–	–	–	1	5	1	29
D. Murphy	–	–	–	–	–	1	1	2	3	2	23
C. Cedeno	–	–	–	–	–	2	–	–	2	–	14
J. Bibby	–	–	–	–	1	–	1	–	–	1	11
B. Buckner	–	–	–	–	–	–	–	2	2	1	11
T. McGraw	–	–	–	–	–	2	–	–	–	–	10
J. Bench	–	–	–	1	–	–	–	–	–	–	7
J. Clark	–	–	–	–	–	–	–	1	1	1	6
J. Niekro	–	–	–	–	–	–	–	–	1	1	3
M. Easler	–	–	–	–	–	–	–	–	1	–	2
J. Reuss	–	–	–	–	–	–	–	–	1	–	2
K. Griffey	–	–	–	–	–	–	–	–	–	1	1
R. LeFlore	–	–	–	–	–	–	–	–	–	1	1
G. Richards	–	–	–	–	–	–	–	–	–	1	1
R. Scott	–	–	–	–	–	–	–	–	–	1	1

Brett was the top pick of 17 of the 28 members of the BBWAA's American League committee, and the Kansas City star finished with 335 points. Reggie Jackson of the Yankees was runnerup with 234 points.

Name	1	2	3	4	5	6	7	8	9	10	Tot.
G. Brett	17	9	2	—	—	—	—	—	—	—	335
R. Jackson	5	5	11	1	1	3	—	1	—	—	234
R. Gossage	4	9	1	5	2	3	1	1	2	—	218
W. Wilson	1	—	5	8	6	3	—	2	1	—	169
C. Cooper	—	3	6	4	2	5	4	1	—	1	160
E. Murray	—	—	—	2	9	3	5	1	—	—	106
R. Cerone	1	1	2	—	1	3	2	2	1	1	77
D. Quisenberry	—	—	1	1	1	2	5	6	3	1½	76½
S. Stone	—	1	—	2	2	—	—	1	7	1	53
R. Henderson	—	—	—	2	1	—	2	3	4	6	51
A. Oliver	—	—	—	1	1	—	—	4	2	2½	31½
T. Armas	—	—	—	1	—	3	1	—	—	3	29
A. Bumbry	—	—	—	1	—	1	2	2	—	1	27
B. Oglivie	—	—	—	—	1	—	2	3	2	—	27
W. Randolph	—	—	—	—	—	1	1	—	—	1	10
M. Norris	—	—	—	—	—	—	1	1	1	1	10
R. Yount	—	—	—	1	—	—	—	—	—	2	8
M. Rivers	—	—	—	—	—	1	—	—	1	—	7
B. Bell	—	—	—	—	—	—	1	—	1	1	7
A. Trammell	—	—	—	—	—	—	1	—	1	—	6
K. Singleton	—	—	—	—	—	—	—	—	1	2	4
T. Perez	—	—	—	—	—	—	—	—	1	—	2
M. Dilone	—	—	—	—	—	—	—	—	—	2	2
F. Lynn	—	—	—	—	—	—	—	—	—	1	1
J. Wathan	—	—	—	—	—	—	—	—	—	1	1

Steve Carlton of the Phillies captured his third Cy Young Award, while Steve Stone of Baltimore gained Cy Young honors in the American League. Twenty-three of the 24 members of the National League committee listed Carlton No. 1 and he finished with 118 points to 55 for runnerup Jerry Reuss of Los Angeles. Stone narrowly edged Oakland's Mike Norris in the A.L. voting, 100 points to 91. Both were accorded first-place votes by 13 of the 28 committee members, but Norris was left off three ballots altogether. Each writer was permitted to vote for three pitchers.

The breakdown of the voting (on a 5-3-1 basis) follows:

American League	1	2	3	Pts.
Steve Stone	13	10	5	100
Mike Norris	13	7	5	91
Goose Gossage	2	7	6½	37½
Tommy John	—	2	8	14
Dan Quisenberry	—	2	1½	7½
Larry Gura	—	—	1	1
Scott McGregor	—	—	1	1

National League	1	2	3	Pts.
Steve Carlton	23	1	0	118
Jerry Reuss	1	15	5	55
Jim Bibby	—	5	13	28
Joe Niekro	—	3	2	11
Tug McGraw	—	—	1	1
Steve Rogers	—	—	1	1
Joe Sambito	—	—	1	1
Mario Soto	—	—	1	1

Joe Charboneau, Cleveland outfielder, and Steve Howe, Los Angeles Dodgers reliever, gained Rookie of the Year honors in the poll of writers.

Charboneau, the top choice of 15 of 28 ballots, polled 103 points to easily outdistance his nearest American League rival, Boston second baseman Dave Stapleton, who received 40 points. Howe edged Montreal pitcher Bill Gullickson, 80 to 53, in the National League.

Deposed Tal Smith Named Top G.M.

The No. 1 Man of the Year designations by THE SPORTING NEWS in the majors went to George Brett, Kansas City third baseman; Bill Virdon, Houston manager, and Tal Smith, deposed Houston president and general manager. Winners of TSN No. 1 Man awards in the minors were: Player of the Year—Tim Raines, second baseman of Denver (American Association); Manager of the Year—Hal Lanier of Springfield (American Association); and Executives of the Year—Jim Burris of Denver (American Association) in Class AAA, Frances Crockett of Charlotte (Southern) in Class AA and Tom Romenesko of Greensboro (South Atlantic) in Class A.

Other award winners chosen by THE SPORTING NEWS included: A.L. Player and Pitcher of the Year—George Brett and Steve Stone, respectively; N.L. Player and Pitcher of the Year—Mike Schmidt and Steve Carlton, respectively; and Rookie Player and Pitcher of the Year—Joe Charboneau of Cleveland and Britt Burns of the Chicago White Sox, respectively, in the American League and Lonnie Smith of the Phillies and Bill Gullickson of Montreal, respectively, in the National League; Fireman of the Year—Tom Hume of Cincinnati and Rollie Fingers of San Diego tied for the honor in the N.L. and Dan Quisenberry won it in the A.L.

The players themselves again chose THE SPORTING NEWS All-Star Teams and named the following:

American League: 1B—Cecil Cooper, Milwaukee; 2B—Willie Randolph, New York; 3B—George Brett, Kansas City; SS—Robin Yount, Milwaukee; LF—Ben Oglivie, Milwaukee; CF—Al Bumbry, Baltimore; RF-DH—Reggie Jackson, New York; C—Rick Cerone, New York; RHP—Steve Stone, Baltimore; LHP—Tommy John, New York.

National League: 1B—Keith Hernandez, St. Louis; 2B—Manny Trillo, Philadelphia; 3B—Mike Schmidt, Philadelphia; SS—Garry Templeton, St. Louis; LF—Dusty Baker, Los Angeles; CF—Cesar Cedeno, Houston; RF—George Hendrick, St. Louis; C—Gary Carter, Montreal; RHP—Jim Bibby, Pittsburgh; LHP—Steve Carlton, Philadelphia.

Gold and Silver Glove Winners

Gold Glove winners for fielding excellence, as chosen by each league's managers and coaches, included: 1B—Cecil Cooper, Milwaukee, in the American League and Keith Hernandez, St. Louis, in the National; 2B—Frank White, Kansas City, and Doug Flynn, New York Mets; 3B—Buddy Bell, Texas, and Mike Schmidt, Philadelphia; SS—Alan Trammell, Detroit, and Ozzie Smith, San Diego; OF—Willie Wilson, Kansas City; Fred Lynn, Boston, and Dwayne Murphy, Oakland, in the American and Garry Maddox, Philadelphia; Andre Dawson, Montreal, and Dave Winfield, San Diego, in the National; C—Jim Sundberg, Texas, and Gary Carter, Montreal; P—Mike Norris, Oakland, and Phil Niekro, Atlanta.

Silver Glove winners for fielding supremacy in the minors were: 1B—Fritzie Connally, Geneva (NYP); 2B—Neil Fiala, Springfield (American Association); 3B—Frederick DeVito, West Haven (Eastern); SS—Mark DeJohn,

Evansville (American Association); OF—Wayne Harer, Columbus (International); Ray Boyer, Pawtucket (International), and Larry Littleton, Tacoma (Pacific Coast); C—Kevin Shannon, Oneonta (NYP); P—Kevin Hickey, Glens Falls (Eastern).

A new award, the Hillerich & Bradsby Silver Slugger for hitting prowess, was introduced and the winners were:

American League: 1B—Cecil Cooper, Milwaukee; 2B—Willie Randolph, New York; 3B—George Brett, Kansas City; SS—Robin Yount, Milwaukee; OF—Ben Oglivie, Milwaukee; Al Oliver, Texas, and Willie Wilson, Kansas City; C—Lance Parrish, Detroit; DH—Reggie Jackson, New York.

National League: 1B—Keith Hernandez, St. Louis; 2B—Manny Trillo, Philadelphia; 3B—Mike Schmidt, Philadelphia; SS—Garry Templeton, St. Louis; OF—Dusty Baker, Los Angeles; Andre Dawson, Montreal, and George Hendrick, St. Louis; C—Ted Simmons, St. Louis; P—Bob Forsch, St. Louis.

Homers by Parks for 1980

NATIONAL LEAGUE

	At Atl.	At Chi.	At Cin.	At Hou.	At L.A.	At Mont.	At N.Y.	At Phil.	At Pitt.	At St.L.	At S.D.	At S.F.	Totals 1980	1979
Atlanta	84	5	5	3	13	0	2	4	5	8	5	10	144	126
Chicago	5	54	5	0	5	8	12	2	7	7	0	2	107	135
Cincinnati	13	2	66	3	6	1	2	1	6	3	7	3	113	132
Houston	11	3	8	26	2	1	8	2	4	1	4	5	75	49
Los Angeles	9	3	7	4	82	5	8	8	5	2	5	10	148	183
Montreal	11	4	7	4	5	51	8	7	1	8	2	6	114	143
New York	4	4	4	0	3	4	35	1	3	1	1	1	61	74
Philadelphia	1	14	6	1	2	9	11	64	5	3	1	0	117	119
Pittsburgh	3	6	7	3	4	5	8	9	63	2	5	1	116	148
St. Louis	9	8	8	1	4	3	11	4	10	41	2	0	101	100
San Diego	6	4	4	1	7	2	4	2	2	3	29	3	67	93
San Francisco	7	9	9	2	7	2	6	4	5	4	1	24	80	125
1980 Totals	163	116	136	48	140	91	115	108	116	83	62	65	1243	....
1979 Totals	153	151	124	46	161	119	88	124	151	113	83	114	....	1427

AT ATLANTA (163): Atlanta (84)—Horner 23, Murphy 17, Chambliss 12, Matthews 9, Burroughs 8, Hubbard 6, Blanks 2, Nahorodny 2, Ramirez 2, Asselstine, Benedict, Pocoroba. Chicago (5)—Buckner 2, Henderson, Johnson, Martin. Cincinnati (13)—Foster 4, Bench 3, Dreissen 2, Knight 2, Concepcion, Griffey. Houston (11)—Puhl 4, Cruz 2, Morgan 2, Ashby, Landestoy, Walling. Los Angeles (9)—Baker 3, Cey 2, Smith 2, Garvey, Monday. Montreal (11)—Parrish 3, Carter 2, Valentine 2, Bernazard, Cromartie, Dawson, Speier. New York (4)—Henderson 2, Mazzilli 2. Philadelphia (1)—Schmidt. Pittsburgh (3)—Berra, Milner, B. Robinson. St. Louis (9)—Hendrick 2, Hernandez 2, Simmons 2, Forsch, Reitz, Templeton. San Diego (6)—Richards 2, Bass, Montanez, Mumphrey, Tenace. San Francisco (7)—Clark 2, Evans, Herndon, Murray, Sadek, Whitfield.

AT CHICAGO (116): Atlanta (5)—Murphy 3, Benedict, Matthews. Chicago (54)—Martin 13, Johnson 6, Kingman 6, Blackwell 4, Foote 4, Buckner 3, DeJesus 3, Lezcano 3, Tracy 3, Tyson 2, Vail 2, Biittner, Dillard, Figueroa, Krukow, Ontiveros. Cincinnati (2)—Bench, Driessen. Houston (6)—Cruz 2, Cabell. Los Angeles (3)—Cey, Lopes, Smith. Montreal (4)—Carter 2, Parrish, Valentine. New York (4)—Maddox 2, Jorgensen, Washington. Philadelphia (14)—Schmidt 8, Boone 2, Aviles, Luzinski, Maddox, McBride. Pittsburgh (6)—Easler 2, Stargell 2, Berra, Madlock. St. Louis (8)—Bonds 2, Durham, Forsch, Hendrick, Hernandez, Reitz, Simmons. San Diego (4)—Cash, Fahey, Richards, Turner. San Francisco (9)—Clark 2, Herndon 2, Evans, North, Pettini, Stennett, Wohlford.

AT CINCINNATI (136): Atlanta (5)—Murphy 3, Burroughs 2. Chicago (5)—Kingman 2, Foote, Martin, Randle. Cincinnati (66)—Foster 14, Driessen 11, Bench 9, Griffey 9, Knight 6, Concepcion 4, Collins 3, Nolan 3, Geronimo 2, Spilman 2, Cruz, Kennedy, Mejias. Houston (8)—Cedeno 3, Morgan 3, Cruz, Richard. Los Angeles (7)—Cey 3, Monday 2, Garvey, Lopes. Montreal (7)—Carter 2, Parrish 2, Valentine 2, Dawson. New York (4)—Mazzilli 2, Henderson, Washington. Philadelphia (6)—Schmidt 2, Boone, Bowa, McBride, Moreland. Pittsburgh (7)—Easler 2, Milner 2, Berra, Garner, Stargell. St. Louis (8)—Kennedy 3, Simmons 3, Hendrick, Hernandez. San Diego (4)—Winfield 2, Tenace, Turner. San Francisco (5)—Clark 3, Evans 3, May 2, LeMaster.

AT HOUSTON (48): Atlanta (3)—Horner 2, Chambliss. Chicago—None. Cincinnati (3)—Foster, Griffey, Knight. Houston (26)—Cruz 4, Puhl 4, Howe 3, Leonard 3, Cedeno 2, Morgan 2, Reynolds 2, Woods 2, Andujar, Ashby, Ryan, Walling. Los Angeles (4)—Baker 2, Smith, Yeager. Montreal (4)—Valentine 2, Bernazard, Carter. New York—None. Philadelphia (1)—Christenson. Pittsburgh (3)—Easler, Milner, Moreno. St. Louis (1)—Durham. San Diego (1)—Montanez. San Francisco (2)—Clark, Whitfield.

AT LOS ANGELES (140): Atlanta (13)—Horner 4, Matthews 3, Murphy 2, Burroughs, Chambliss, Hubbard, Nahorodny. Chicago (5)—Kingman 2, Dillard, Randle, Vail. Cincinnati (6)—Bench 3, Foster, Griffey, Knight. Houston (2)—Howe, Puhl. Los Angeles (82)—Cey 16, Garvey 16, Baker 14, Ferguson 8, Smith 8, Lopes 5, Guerrero 3, Monday 3, Johnstone 2, Russell 2, Hatcher, Hooton, Law, Scioscia, Thomas. Montreal (5)—LeFlore 3, Cromartie, Dawson. New York (3)—Washington 3. Philadelphia (2)—Luzinski, Schmidt. Pittsburgh (4)—Ott 2, Madlock, B. Robinson. St. Louis (4)—Hendrick 2, Hernandez, Simmons. San Diego (7)—Winfield 4, Montanez, Mumphrey, Perkins. San Francisco (7)—Evans 2, Clark, Herndon, May, Murray, Whitfield.

AT MONTREAL (91): Atlanta—None. Chicago (8)—Martin 2, Dillard, Henderson, Johnson, Kingman, Thompson, Vail. Cincinnati (1)—Oester. Houston (1)—Puhl. Los Angeles (5)—Cey, Garvey, Guerrero, Russell, Smith. Montreal (51)—Carter 12, Cromartie 7, Dawson 7, Parrish 6, Office 5, White 5, Valentine 4, Bernazard 2, LeFlore, Macha, Tamargo. New York (4)—Morales 2, Mazzilli, Youngblood. Philadelphia (9)—Schmidt 4, Luzinski 2, Moreland 2, Rose. Pittsburgh (5)—Easler 3, Parker 2. St. Louis (3)—Bonds, Oberkfell, Templeton. San Diego (2)—Tenace, Winfield. San Francisco (2)—LeMaster, McCovey.

AT NEW YORK (115): Atlanta (2)—Matthews, Murphy. Chicago (12)—Kingman 6, Martin 2, Randle 2, Foote, Vail. Cincinnati (2)—Knight, Spilman. Houston (8)—Cedeno 2, Puhl 2, Ashby, Cabell, Morgan, Reynolds. Los Angeles (8)—Baker 5, Garvey 2, Monday. Montreal (8)—Cromartie 3, Parrish 3, Bernazard, Carter. New York (35)—Mazzilli 10, Youngblood 6, Jorgensen 5, Washington 5, Henderson 4, Maddox 2, Morales, Moreno, Norman. Philadelphia (11)—Schmidt 3, Maddox 2, Trillo 2, Aguayo, Boone, McBride, Smith. Pittsburgh (5)—Easler 2, Garner, Parker, B. Robinson, Romo. St. Louis (11)—Durham 2, Hendrick 2, Hernandez 2, Simmons 2, Bonds, Oberkfell, Reitz. San Diego (4)—Winfield 2, Mumphrey, Rodriguez. San Francisco (6)—Evans 3, Ivie, May, Stennett.

AT PHILADELPHIA (108): Atlanta (4)—Asselstine, Horner, Hubbard, Murphy. Chicago (2)—Martin, Vail. Cincinnati (1)—Bench. Houston (1)—Howe, Walling. Los Angeles (8)—Baker 3, Cey 2, Garvey, Reuss, Smith. Montreal (4)—Carter 4, Dawson 2, Valentine. New York (1)—Mazzilli. Philadelphia (64)—Schmidt 25, Luzinski 15, Maddox 6, Boone 5, McBride 4, Trillo 4, Smith 2, Aviles, Bowa, Moreland. Pittsburgh (9)—Lacy 2, Milner 2, Parker 2, Foli, D. Robinson, Stargell. St. Louis (4)—Hendrick 2, Durham, Oberkfell. San Diego (2)—Winfield 2. San Francisco (4)—Clark 2, Griffin, Murray.

AT PITTSBURGH (116): Atlanta (5)—Matthews 2, Chambliss, Horner, Murphy. Chicago (7)—Buckner 3, Johnson 2, Martin, Thompson. Cincinnati (6)—Foster 3, Bench 2, Knight. Houston (4)—Howe 2, Cedeno, Morgan. Los Angeles (5)—Garvey, Guerrero, Monday, Thomasson, Yeager. Montreal (1)—Cromartie. New York (3)—Henderson, Jorgensen, Norman. Philadelphia (5)—Schmidt 2, Maddox, McBride, Trillo. Pittsburgh (63)—Parker 10, Easler 9, Madlock 7, Stargell 7, Ott 6, B. Robinson 6, Lacy 4, Berra 3, Garner 3, Foli 2, Milner 2, Bibby, Moreno, Nicosia, Rhoden. St. Louis (10)—Simmons 3, Hendrick 2, Iorg 2, Hernandez, Reitz, Templeton. San Diego (2)—Joshua, Winfield. San Francisco (5)—Clark 2, Evans 2, Ivie.

AT ST. LOUIS (83): Atlanta (8)—Murphy 3, Burroughs, Chambliss, Matthews, Pocoroba, Royster. Chicago (7)—Buckner 2, Blackwell, Kingman, Martin, Randle, Tyson. Cincinnati (3)—Auerbach, Bench, Spilman. Houston (1)—Cedeno. Los Angeles (2)—Cey, Monday. Montreal (8)—Carter 4, Dawson 2, Valentine, White. New York (1)—Brooks. Philadelphia (3)—Schmidt 2, Maddox. Pittsburgh (2)—B. Robinson, Rooker. St. Louis (41)—Hendrick 13, Hernandez 8, Simmons 8, Durham 3, Reitz 3, Bonds, Forsch, Iorg, Kaat, Kennedy, Templeton. San Diego (3)—Tenace 2, Evans. San Francisco (4)—Clark, Ivie, LeMaster, May.

AT SAN DIEGO (62): Atlanta (5)—Burroughs, Horner, Matthews, Murphy, Nahorodny. Chicago—None. Cincinnati (7)—Bench 4, Foster, Knight, Oester. Houston (4)—Cedeno, Cruz, Morgan, Puhl. Los Angeles (5)—Lopes 2, Garvey, Guerrero, Monday. Montreal (2)—Dawson, Office. New York (1)—Youngblood. Philadelphia (1)—McBride. Pittsburgh (5)—Parker 2, B. Robinson 2, Madlock. St. Louis (2)—Reitz, Simmons. San Diego (29)—Tenace 11, Winfield 7, Montanez 3, Bass 2, Joshua, Mumphrey, Perkins, Richards, Rodriguez, Turner. San Francisco (1)—Herndon.

AT SAN FRANCISCO (65): Atlanta (10)—Horner 3, Chambliss 2, Asselstine, Hubbard, Matthews, Murphy, Nahorodny. Chicago (2)—Dillard, Martin. Cincinnati (3)—Foster, Griffey, Knight. Houston (5)—Howe 3, Cruz, Morgan. Los Angeles (10)—Baker 2, Cey 2, Garvey 2, Ferguson, Guerrero, Lopes, Smith. Montreal (6)—Dawson 2, Carter, Cromartie, Wallach, White. New York (1)—Moreno. Philadelphia—None. Pittsburgh (1)—Lacy. St. Louis—None. San Diego (3)—Salazar, Tenace, Winfield. San Francisco (24)—Clark 8, Evans 8, Herndon 3, Bourjos, Ivie, May, Murray, Whitfield.

AMERICAN LEAGUE

	At Balt.	At Bos.	At Calif.	At Chi.	At Clev.	At Det.	At K.C.	At Milw.	At Minn.	At N.Y.	At Oak.	At Sea.	At Tex.	At Tor.	Totals 1980	1979
Baltimore	75	10	6	4	4	8	2	8	6	7	7	4	9	156	181
Boston	8	79	10	5	4	8	3	6	6	2	6	8	6	11	162	194
California	3	9	49	0	3	9	2	3	4	1	10	6	3	104	164
Chicago	7	3	3	41	2	7	2	7	3	3	2	4	4	3	91	127
Cleveland	5	3	2	1	55	3	2	2	4	1	1	4	1	5	89	138
Detroit	8	5	9	2	2	77	5	8	4	4	4	4	6	143	164
Kansas City	2	5	5	4	5	8	47	8	3	5	4	5	6	4	115	116
Milwaukee	11	7	13	6	13	13	4	90	6	4	11	13	8	4	203	185
Minnesota	4	5	5	2	0	4	4	5	51	2	3	10	1	3	99	112
New York	9	8	6	3	12	10	5	6	7	91	7	6	8	11	189	150
Oakland	7	4	6	5	9	6	7	3	7	5	58	10	4	6	137	108
Seattle	1	2	1	2	3	2	7	2	3	0	3	74	1	3	104	132
Texas	10	8	1	2	2	9	7	4	4	5	3	8	58	3	124	140
Toronto	5	6	9	1	7	8	1	5	4	5	5	10	4	56	126	95
1980 Totals	156	153	125	78	121	172	98	155	114	138	115	173	115	131	1844	
1979 Totals	131	180	126	116	159	175	134	172	128	136	111	182	132	124		2006

AT BALTIMORE (156): Baltimore (75)—Singleton 12, Murray 10, Crowley 8, DeCinces 7, Graham 7, Ayala 6, Bumbry 6, Dempsey 5, Roenicke 4, May 3, Lowenstein 2, Corey, Dauer, Garcia, Kelly, Sakata. Boston (8)—Perez 5, Evans, Rice, Yastrzemski. California (3)—Clark, Ford, Thompson. Chicago (7)—Baines 2, L. Johnson 2, Foley,

Lemon, Morrison. Cleveland (5)—Charboneau 2, Hargrove, Harrah, Hassey. Detroit (8)—Kemp 2, Parrish 2, Wockenfuss 2, Dyer, Trammell. Kansas City (2)—G. Brett, Washington. Milwaukee (11)—Cooper 3, Thomas 3, Molitor 2, Oglivie 2, Money. Minnesota (4)—Adams, Powell, Wilfong, Wynegar. New York (9)—Jackson 3, Gamble 2, Randolph 2, Dent, Soderholm. Oakland (7)—Armas 3, Guerrero, Henderson, Murphy, Newman. Seattle (2)—T. Cox, Paciorek. Texas (10)—Sundberg 4, Zisk 2, Putnam, Rivers, Roberts, Wills. Toronto (5)—Mayberry 2, Braun, Hodgson, Moseby.

AT BOSTON (153): Baltimore (10)—Murray 3, Graham 2, Crowley, Dauer, DeCinces, Dempsey, Singleton. Boston (79)—Fisk 12, Evans 11, Rice 11, Perez 9, Lynn 6, Stapleton 5, Yastrzemski 5, Hancock 4, Hobson 4, Burleson 3, Hoffman 2, Rader 2, Brohamer, Dwyer, Valdez, Walker, Wolfe. California (9)—Parrish 2, Thompson 2, Baylor, Carew, Lansford, Miller. Chicago (3)—Baines, L. Johnson, Nordhagen. Cleveland (3)—Alexander, Charboneau, Johnson. Detroit (5)—Brookens, Cowens, Parrish, Peters, Wockenfuss. Kansas City (4)—McRae 2, Porter 2, Otis. Milwaukee (7)—Yount 2, Bando, Davis, Molitor, Oglivie, Thomas. Minnesota (5)—Castino, Cubbage, Landreaux, Smalley, Sofield. New York (8)—Jackson 3, Dent, Nettles, Rodriguez, Soderholm, Watson. Oakland (4)—Page 2, Armas, Newman. Seattle (1)—Meyer. Texas (8)—Bell 2, Rivers 2, Staub 2, Oliver, Putnam. Toronto (6)—Moseby 2, Bonnell, Mayberry, Upshaw, Woods.

AT CALIFORNIA (125): Baltimore (6)—Ayala, DeCinces, Graham, Lowenstein, Murray, Singleton. Boston (10)—Hobson 3, Yastrzemski 3, Rice 2, Evans, Stapleton. California (49)—Rudi 11, Thompson 9, Lansford 8, Grich 5, Ford 4, Carew 2, Clark 2, Downing 2, Harris 2, Patek 2, Donohue, Harlow, Thompson. Chicago (3)—Lemon, Morrison, Nordhagen. Cleveland (2)—Charboneau, Gray. Detroit (9)—Kemp 3, Parrish 2, Hebner, Stegman, Summers, Thompson. Kansas City (5)—Aikens 2, G. Brett, Hurdle, Otis. Milwaukee (13)—Oglivie 4, Thomas 4, Molitor 2, Gantner, Lezcano, Moore. Minnesota (5)—Smalley 2, Adams, Morales, Powell. New York (6)—Watson 3, Jackson 2, Lefebvre. Oakland (6)—Armas 3, Henderson, Murphy, Revering. Seattle (1)—L. Roberts. Texas (1)—Roberts. Toronto (9)—Mayberry 2, Velez 2, Woods 2, Bonnell, Howell, Moseby.

AT CHICAGO (78): Baltimore (4)—Murray 2, Dempsey, Singleton. Boston (5)—Fisk 2, Perez 2, Rice. California—None. Chicago (41)—Nordhagen 10, L. Johnson 7, Lemon 5, Morrison 5, Baines 3, Bosley 2, Squires 2, Bell, Borgmann, Cruz, Foley, Pruitt, Pryor, Seilheimer. Cleveland (1)—Harrah. Detroit (2)—Parrish, Wockenfuss. Kansas City (4)—Detherage, McRae, Porter, White. Milwaukee (6)—Oglivie 3, Yount 2, Cooper. Minnesota (2)—Castino, Morales. New York (3)—Cerone, Gamble, Jones. Oakland (3)—Henderson 3, Murphy, Picciolo. Seattle (2)—Meyer, Narron. Texas (2)—Putnam, Zisk. Toronto (1)—Garcia.

AT CLEVELAND (121): Baltimore (4)—DeCinces 2, Singleton 2. Boston (4)—Dwyer 2, Perez, Rice. California (3)—Cliburn, Lansford, Skaggs. Chicago (2)—Lemon, Morrison. Cleveland (55)—Charboneau 13, Harrah 7, Hargrove 6, Orta 6, Hassey 5, Johnson 4, Alexander 3, Manning 3, Diaz 2, Rosello 2, Bannister, Dybzinski, Gray, Veryzer. Detroit (2)—Summers 2. Kansas City (5)—Aikens 2, G. Brett, Hurdle, White. Milwaukee (13)—Lezcano 3, Oglivie 3, Bando 2, Davis, Hisle, Molitor, Thomas, Yount. Minnesota—None. New York (12)—Jackson 3, Murcer 2, Brown, Cerone, Gamble, Lefebvre, Rodriguez, Soderholm, Werth. Oakland (9)—Revering 3, Page 2, Armas, Gross, Murphy, Newman. Seattle (3)—L. Cox, Cruz, Paciorek. Texas (2)—Bell, Oliver. Toronto (7)—Ault 3, Velez 2, Bonnell, Whitt.

AT DETROIT (172): Baltimore (8)—DeCinces 2, Murray 2, Bumbry, Crowley, Kelly, Roenicke. Boston (8)—Perez 2, Dwyer, Evans, Hobson, Lynn, Rice, Yastrzemski. California (9)—Baylor 2, Grich 2, Lansford 2, Campaneris, Clark, Donohue. Chicago (2)—Baines, Borgmann, Foley, L. Johnson, Molinaro, Morrison, Nordhagen. Cleveland (3)—Brohamer, Diaz, Veryzer. Detroit (77)—Kemp 15, Hebner 10, Summers 9, Wockenfuss 8, Brookens 7, Parrish 7, Trammell 5, Corcoran 3, Gibson 3, Papi 3, Cowens 2, Dyer 2, Thompson 2, Whitaker. Kansas City (8)—G. Brett 3, Aikens 2, McRae, Porter, Washington, White. Milwaukee (13)—Cooper 4, Lezcano 3, Money 2, Thomas 2, Davis, Martinez. Minnesota (4)—Castino 2, Cubbage, Smalley. New York (10)—Brown 2, Nettles 2, Randolph 2, Soderholm 2, Jones, Piniella. Oakland (6)—Armas 2, Gross 2, Revering 2. Seattle (2)—L. Roberts, Stein. Texas (9)—Oliver 4, Zisk 2, Rivers, Staub, Wills. Toronto (8)—Bonnell 3, Howell 2, Mayberry 2, Whitt.

AT KANSAS CITY (98): Baltimore (2)—DeCinces, Murray. Boston (3)—Burleson, Hobson, Rice. California (2)—Harlow, Lansford. Chicago (2)—L. Johnson, Pruitt. Cleveland (2)—Hassey, Orta. Detroit (5)—Summers 2, Gibson, Parrish, Trammell. Kansas City (47)—G. Brett 13, McRae 6, Aikens 5, Wathan 5, Otis 4, Hurdle 3, Quirk 3, Washington 3, Wilson 2, Chalk, Porter, White. Milwaukee (4)—Money 3, Thomas. Minnesota (4)—Castino 2, Cubbage, Edwards. New York (5)—Jackson 2, Jones, Soderholm, Watson. Oakland (4)—Armas 3, Gross 3, Murphy. Seattle (7)—Bochte 2, Paciorek 2, Anderson, L. Cox, Walton. Texas (7)—Oliver 2, Ellis, Putnam, Rivers, Sample, Zisk. Toronto (1)—Bosetti.

AT MILWAUKEE (155): Baltimore (6)—May 2, DeCinces, Dempsey, Graham, Roenicke. Boston (6)—Lynn 2, Burleson, Fisk, Hobson, Yastrzemski. California (3)—Thompson 2, Rudi. Chicago (7)—Lemon 2, Morrison 2, Baines, Moore, Nordhagen. Cleveland (2)—Charboneau, Hargrove. Detroit (8)—Brookens 2, Parrish 2, Dyer, Gibson, Lentine, Wockenfuss. Kansas City (8)—Aikens 3, Hurdle 2, Otis 2, McRae. Milwaukee (90)—Thomas 18, Oglivie 15, Yount 13, Cooper 12, Money 10, Lezcano 8, Brouhard 3, Bando 2, Hisle 2, Molitor 2, Davis, Gantner, Martinez, Moore, Romero. Minnesota (4)—Adams, Jackson, Ward, Wilfong, Wynegar. New York (6)—Jackson 2, Dent, Gamble, Soderholm, Watson. Oakland (3)—Henderson, Murphy, Picciolo. Seattle (4)—Bochte, Horton. Texas (4)—Oliver, Rivers, Staub, Sundberg. Toronto (5)—Bonnell 2, Mayberry 2, Woods.

AT MINNESOTA (114): Baltimore (8)—Graham 2, May 2, Murray 2, Crowley, Roenicke. Boston (6)—Evans 3, Dwyer, Perez, Yastrzemski. California (4)—Baylor, Cliburn, Ford, Thompson. Chicago (3)—Baines 2, Nordhagen. Cleveland (4)—Charboneau, Hargrove, Hassey, Orta. Detroit (4)—Hebner, Kemp, Parrish, Wockenfuss. Kansas City (3)—G. Brett, McRae, White. Milwaukee (6)—Hisle 2, Oglivie 2, Cooper, Thomas. Minnesota (51)—Castino 7, Smalley 5, Sofield 5, Landreaux 4, Mackanin 4, Powell 4, Adams 3, Cubbage 3, Jackson 3, Morales 3, Wilfong 3, Wynegar 3, Rivera 2, Edwards, Goodwin. New York (7)—Cerone 3, Jackson 2, Soderholm, Spencer. Oakland (7)—Gross 3, McKay, Newman, Picciolo, Revering. Seattle (3)—Beniquez, Meyer, Stein. Texas (4)—Bell 3, Putnam. Toronto (4)—Mayberry 2, Griffin, Velez.

AT NEW YORK (138): Baltimore (6)—Murray 3, Bumbry 2, Dempsey. Boston (2)—Yastrzemski 2. California (1)—Clark, Grich, Harlow, Miller. Chicago (3)—Cruz, Molinaro, Morrison. Cleveland (1)—Charboneau. Detroit (5)—

—Gibson, Parrish, Peters, Stegman, Summers. **Kansas City** (5)—Aikens, G. Brett, Hurdle, Porter, Wilson. **Milwaukee** (4)—Lezcano, Money, Oglivie, Thomas. **Minnesota** (2)—Norwood, Wilfong. **New York** (91)—Jackson 16, Nettles 11, Brown 9, Gamble 8, Spencer 8, Cerone 7, Murcer 7, Jones 5, Lefebvre 4, Soderholm 3, Watson 3, Dent 2, Randolph 2, Doyle, Gulden, Oates, Piniella, Rodriguez, Werth. **Oakland** (5)—Armas 2, Newman, Page, Revering. **Seattle**—None. **Texas** (5)—Zisk 2, Bell, Oliver, Rivers. **Toronto** (5)—Mayberry 4, Howell.

　　AT OAKLAND (115): **Baltimore** (7)—Graham 2, Murray 2, Crowley, Roenicke, Singleton. **Boston** (6)—Perez 2, Rice 2, Hobson, Hoffman. **California** (1)—Baylor. **Chicago** (2)—Foley, L. Johnson. **Cleveland** (1)—Harrah. **Detroit** (4)—Gibson, Parrish, Thompson, Wockenfuss. **Kansas City** (4)—Aikens, LaCock, Washington, Wathan. **Milwaukee** (11)—Brouhard 2, Lezcano 2, Cooper, Gantner, Martinez, Oglivie, Poff, Thomas, Yount. **Minnesota** (3)—Landreaux, Smalley, Sofield. **New York** (7)—Jackson 3, Murcer 2, Brown, Watson. **Oakland** (58)—Armas 17, Page 8, Newman 7, Murphy 5, Essian 4, Gross 3, Henderson 3, Klutts 3, Revering 3, Newman 2, Page 2. **Seattle** (3)—Craig, Meyer, Simpson. **Texas** (3)—Grubb, Oliver, Staub. **Toronto** (5)—Woods 2, Garcia, Howell, Velez.

　　AT SEATTLE (173): **Baltimore** (7)—Ayala 3, Singleton 3, Murray. **Boston** (8)—Lynn 2, Rice 2, Burleson, Fisk, Perez, Stapleton. **California** (10)—Rudi 4, Grich 3, Lansford 2, Campaneris. **Chicago** (1)—Lemon, Molinaro, Morrison, Washington. **Cleveland** (4)—Charboneau 3, Hargrove. **Detroit** (4)—Parrish 2, Gibson, Wockenfuss. **Kansas City** (5)—Aikens 3, G. Brett, White. **Milwaukee** (13)—Oglivie 5, Yount 3, Thomas 2, Gantner, Hisle, Molitor. **Minnesota** (10)—Morales 2, Smalley 2, Wilfong 2, Cubbage, Landreaux, Rivera, Sofield. **New York** (6)—Jackson 2, Watson 2, Brown, Murcer. **Oakland** (10)—Armas 3, Revering 3, Newman 2, Page 2. **Seattle** (74)—Paciorek 11, Bochte 10, L. Roberts 8, Anderson 7, Meyer 7, Beniquez 5, Horton 5, Edler 3, Narron 3, Craig 2, Hill 2, Mendoza 2, Simpson 2, Stein 2, L. Cox, T. Cox, Cruz, Stinson, Walton. **Texas** (8)—Roberts 3, Bell 2, Grubb, Putnam, Sample. **Toronto** (10)—Mayberry 5, Velez 2, Bonnell, Howell, Whitt.

　　AT TEXAS (115): **Baltimore** (4)—Roenicke 2, Kelly, Singleton. **Boston** (6)—Fisk 2, Burleson, Evans, Hoffman, Lynn. **California** (6)—Grich 2, Cowens, Cruz, Ford, Harlow. **Chicago** (4)—Molinaro 2, Baines, Morrison. **Cleveland** (1)—Orta. **Detroit** (4)—Parrish 2, Gibson, Summers. **Kansas City** (6)—G. Brett 2, Aikens, Hurdle, Otis, White. **Milwaukee** (8)—Oglivie 3, Cooper 2, Thomas 2, Harris. **Minnesota** (1)—Cubbage. **New York** (8)—Jackson 3, Spencer 2, Gamble, Nettles, Watson. **Oakland** (4)—Page 2, Klutts, Murphy. **Seattle** (1)—L. Cox. **Texas** (58)—Zisk 11, Bell 8, Oliver 8, Putnam 7, Grubb 6, Roberts 5, Sundberg 5, Staub 3, Sample 2, Wills 2, Harrelson. **Toronto** (4)—Bosetti, Iorg, Moseby, Whitt.

　　AT TORONTO (131): **Baltimore** (9)—Murray 5, Singleton 2, DeCinces, Lowenstein. **Boston** (11)—Dwyer 4, Perez 2, Rice 2, Burleson, Rader, Yastrzemski. **California** (3)—Thompson 2, Grich. **Chicago** (3)—Baines 2, Morrison. **Cleveland** (5)—Alexander, Hargrove, Harrah, Johnson, Orta. **Detroit** (6)—Cowens 2, Trammell 2, Parrish, Summers. **Kansas City** (8)—McRae 2, Quirk 2, Aikens, Hurdle, Otis, Porter. **Milwaukee** (4)—Cooper, Oglivie, Thomas, Yount. **Minnesota** (3)—Jackson, Morales, Sofield. **New York** (11)—Cerone 2, Lefebvre 2, Spencer 2, Jones, Murcer, Nettles, Randolph, Werth. **Oakland** (6)—Gross 2, Essian, Murphy, Newman, Revering. **Seattle** (3)—Horton 2, Stein. **Texas** (3)—Grubb, Staub, Wills. **Toronto** (56)—Velez 12, Mayberry 10, Woods 9, Bonnell 4, Davis 4, Howell 4, Moseby 4, Bosetti 2, Garcia 2, Whitt 2, Bailor, Griffin, Iorg.

Toughest to Strike Out in 1980

(Based on at-bats per strikeout)

AMERICAN LEAGUE		NATIONAL LEAGUE	
Rich Dauer, Baltimore	29.3	Bill Buckner, Chicago	34.2
George Brett, Kansas City	20.4	Doug Flynn, New York	23.7
Mickey Rivers, Texas	18.5	Tim Foli, Pittsburgh	23.5
Mike Hargrove, Cleveland	16.4	Pete Rose, Philadelphia	22.4
Cecil Cooper, Milwaukee	14.8	Ken Oberkfell, St. Louis	21.1

Toughest to Double Up in 1980

(Based on at-bats per GIDP)

AMERICAN LEAGUE		NATIONAL LEAGUE	
Willie Wilson, Kansas City	176.2	Terry Puhl, Houston	178.3
Mickey Rivers, Texas	157.5	Ivan DeJesus, Chicago	154.5
Ben Oglivie, Milwaukee	118.4	Ken Griffey, Cincinnati	136.0
Rickey Henderson, Oak	98.5	Ron LeFlore, Montreal	130.3
Alfredo Griffin, Toronto	93.3	Joe Morgan, Houston	115.3

NO-HITTERS

Including

Review of '80 No-Hitter

Official Box Score

BATTING, PITCHING FEATURES

THE SPORTING NEWS AWARDS

Including

BBWAA Awards

MAJOR LEAGUE FARM SYSTEMS

HALL OF FAME ELECTIONS

Including

Features of Electees

All Hall-of-Famers Listed According to Years Selected

Raising his arm in victory, Dodgers' JERRY REUSS is mobbed by teammates following his no-hitter and near-perfect effort June 26 against the Giants.

Reuss Was Almost Perfect in No-Hitter

By LARRY WIGGE

No matter how much he meant it, Bill Russell's apology could not change the outcome and it couldn't change history.

With two out in the first inning of a game between the Los Angeles Dodgers and San Francisco Giants June 26 at Candlestick Park, shortstop Russell committed a throwing error which allowed Jack Clark to reach first base safely. That error and baserunner was the only thing that kept Dodgers lefthander Jerry Reuss from becoming the ninth man in modern baseball history to hurl a perfect game.

"I just threw a no-hitter," Reuss exclaimed. "What could be a bigger thrill?"

Reuss' lack of disappointment at missing a perfect game was understandable. After all, this was the same Jerry Reuss who had finished the 1979 season with a 7-14 won-lost mark and started the 1980 campaign in the Los Angeles bullpen. The 31-year-old southpaw's last successful season had come in 1976 when he was 14-9 with the Pittsburgh Pirates.

So when he became the author of the majors' only no-hitter in 1980—an 8-0 victory over the Giants—it was just icing on the cake for Reuss.

This new Reuss had just completed his fourth shutout of the season and had extended his scoreless inning streak to 24⅔ en route to an 18-6 record with six shutouts and a 2.52 ERA.

Reuss, who had his sinker working, threw 17 ground ball outs in the game. He struck out only two. The only threat to the no-hitter came in the eighth inning when third baseman Ron Cey made a diving stop of Larry Herndon's hard smash.

"It was one of the most overpowering games I have ever seen," said Giants hitting coach and former Dodgers player Jim Lefebvre. "He was literally breaking the bats in our hands."

Los Angeles	AB.	R.	H.	RBI.	E.
Lopes, 2b	5	2	3	0	0
Law, cf	5	1	3	2	0
Smith, rf	4	1	1	1	0
Guerrero, rf	1	0	0	0	0
Thomas, rf	0	0	0	0	0
Garvey, 1b	5	2	2	1	0
Baker, lf	5	1	1	3	0
Cey, 3b	5	1	2	0	0
Russell, ss	5	0	3	1	1
Yeager, c	4	0	2	0	0
REUSS, p	4	0	0	0	0
Totals	43	8	17	8	1

San Francisco	AB.	R.	H.	RBI.	E.
North, cf	4	0	0	0	0
Evans, 3b	3	0	0	0	0
Clark, rf	2	0	0	0	0
Wohlford, rf	1	0	0	0	0
Murray, 1b	3	0	0	0	0
Herndon, lf	3	0	0	0	1
Strain, 2b	3	0	0	0	0
LeMaster, ss	3	0	0	0	0
Sadek, c	3	0	0	0	1
Blue, p	1	0	0	0	0
Griffin, p	0	0	0	0	0
Whitfield, ph	1	0	0	0	0
Lavelle, p	0	0	0	0	0
Stennett, ph	1	0	0	0	0
Totals	28	0	0	0	2

Los Angeles	1	0	1	0	5	0	1	0	0 – 8
San Francisco	0	0	0	0	0	0	0	0	0 – 0

Los Angeles	IP.	H.	R.	ER.	BB.	SO.
REUSS (W. 9-1)	9	0	0	0	0	2

San Francisco	IP.	H.	R.	ER.	BB.	SO.
Blue (L. 9-5)	4⅔	10	7	6	1	4
Griffin	1⅓	2	0	0	0	0
Lavelle	3	5	1	1	0	0

Game-winning RBI—Law.

LOB—Los Angeles 9, San Francisco 1. 2B—Cey 2, Yeager, Law. 3B—Lopes. HR—Baker (17), Garvey (16). SB—Lopes. T—2:13. A—20,285.

Ryan and Richard Headed Low-Hit List

By CARL CLARK

Although run production in the big leagues fell almost four percent from its 1979 level, major league pitchers were able to limit the opposition to two or fewer hits only 50 times in 1980, the lowest total since the 32 of 1962.

The American League, despite the lack of a hitless game for the third consecutive season, had more low-hit games than the National, which had a no-hitter by Los Angeles' Jerry Reuss. There were eight one-hit games in the A.L., five fewer than the record number spun in '79, and 21 two-hitters. The National League had only four one-hitters and 16 two-hitters. In '79, there were 10 one-hitters in the N.L. and 24 two-hitters.

The Astros, who had the lowest ERA in the majors, led the way in low-hit games. They turned in five, and bullet-throwing righthanders J. R. Richard and Nolan Ryan, with a little help from Joe Sambito, accounted for all of them.

Ryan had the majors' greatest involvement in low-hitters, with a pair of two-hitters and a one-hitter that he shared with Sambito.

In none of those games, however, did Ryan go into the late innings with a chance for a record fifth no-hitter. Garry Templeton broke up his June 19 one-hitter against St. Louis with a third-inning blooper that fell on the left-field line for a double. His first two-hitter, May 28 against San Diego, also was marked by a third-inning double, this time by pitcher Rick Wise. Ozzie Smith added an infield single in the eighth. The Cubs' only hits off Ryan on August 24 were a triple by Larry Biittner in the fifth and an eighth-inning single by Tim Blackwell.

Richard, who pitched only one game after the All-Star break before suffering a stroke, ran his career record against Los Angeles to 15-4 with a pair of dominating efforts in the season's first weeks. In his first start, J. R. struck out 13 Dodgers and gave up only a pair of hits in the seventh of his eight innings of work. Sambito preserved the 3-2 victory. Richard needed no help at Los Angeles, April 19. He struck out 12 and gave up only one hit—a single by Reggie Smith in the fourth inning—in the 2-0 victory.

Bob Welch was the Dodgers' tough-luck loser in the latter game. He allowed only two hits, both in the fourth inning, but the Astros turned them into runs. About six weeks later, May 29, Welch pitched his own one-hitter, a 3-0 shutout of Atlanta in which the Braves' only hit was a single by Larvell Blanks in the fourth inning.

The league's other one-hitter was an historic one. N. L. Cy Young winner Steve Carlton blanked the Cardinals on April 26, 7-0. The only hit was a leadoff single by Ted Simmons in the second inning. It was Carlton's third one-hitter in the last two years and the sixth of his career, breaking the league record that he had shared with Tom Seaver, Jim Maloney, Mordecai Brown, Grover Cleveland Alexander and Don Sutton.

Carlton's last start of the season, against Chicago on October 1, resulted in a two-hitter, with the Cubs not getting their initial hit until Mike Vail's single in the eighth.

Phil Niekro of Atlanta was the only other N. L. pitcher with more than one low-hit effort. The 41-year-old righthander threw a two-hitter at Houston, July 14, and went into the eighth inning of a September 6 two-hitter against the Pirates that was finished off by Gene Garber.

More than half a dozen A. L. staffs turned in three low-hit performances each. Top individuals were Boston's Dennis Eckersley, a one-hitter against Toronto and a two-hitter against Oakland; Ross Baumgarten of the White Sox, a one-hitter against California and a two-hitter against Texas in a game that was stopped by rain after six innings with the score tied, 1-1; Steve Stone of Baltimore, a pair of two-hitters—a complete game against the Yankees and a combined job with Tippy Martinez against California; and the Yankees' Tommy John, two-hitters against Chicago and Seattle.

Bruce Kison of the Angels won only three games before elbow and wrist ailments ended his season in July, but his first A. L. victory was a one-hitter against Minnesota, April 23. The Twins' only hit in the 17-0 keelhauling was a double by Ken Landreaux with one out in the ninth.

It was the first of three times that Minnesota could manage only one hit in a game. Toronto also was held to one hit three times—twice John Mayberry had the hit—and the Blue Jays suffered a trio of two-hitters as well.

Cleveland's Dan Spillner came as close to a no-hitter as Kison. The only hit the White Sox managed off him on August 20 was an opposite-field single by Leo Sutherland with one out in the ninth.

A complete list of one-hit and two-hit games follows:

AMERICAN LEAGUE
One-Hit Games

April 23—Kison, California vs. Minnesota, 17-0—Landreaux, double in ninth.
April 30—Gura, Kansas City vs. Toronto, 3-0—Garcia, double in sixth.
June 6—Zahn, Minnesota vs. Toronto, 5-0—Mayberry, single in seventh.
July 2—Baumgarten, Chicago vs. California, 1-0—Carew, single in seventh.
Aug. 20—Spillner, Cleveland vs. Chicago, 3-0—Sutherland, single in ninth.
Aug. 21—Morris, Detroit vs. Minnesota, 4-2 (second game)—Wilfong, single in first.
Sept. 26—Eckersley, Boston vs. Toronto, 3-1—Mayberry, homer in fifth.
Oct. 5—Splittorff (five innings) and Gale (four innings), Kansas City vs. Minnesota, 4-0—Castino, single in first.

Two-Hit Games

April 16—John, New York vs. Chicago, 6-0—Bannister, single in first; Nordhagen, single in fifth.
May 2—Barker (seven innings) and Stanton (two innings), Cleveland vs. Toronto, 6-1—Garcia, doubles in third and seventh.
May 22—McGregor, Baltimore vs. Detroit, 5-1—Kemp, homer in first; Parrish, double in fourth.
May 23—Jenkins, Texas vs. Oakland, 3-1—Picciolo, double in third; Armas, single in fourth.
June 2—Baumgarten (six innings), Chicago vs. Texas, 1-1 (stopped by rain)—Rivers, double in first and single in sixth.
June 6—John, New York vs. Seattle, 3-0—Horton, single in second; Paciorek, single in fourth.
June 11—Leonard, Kansas City vs. Cleveland, 5-0 (first game)—Dilone, single in first; Harrah, double in second.
July 3—Garland, Cleveland vs. New York, 7-0—Jackson, single in fourth; Lefebvre, single in ninth.
July 6—Halicki (eight and one-third innings) and Clear (two-thirds inning), California vs. Milwaukee, 2-0—Cooper, single in first; Yount, double in ninth.
July 13—May, New York vs. Chicago, 3-1—Lemon, double in seventh; Pruitt, single in seventh.
July 17—Travers, Milwaukee vs. Baltimore, 0-1—DeCinces, homer in second; Garcia, single in fifth.
July 27—Keough (eight and two-thirds innings) and Lacey (one-third inning), Oakland vs. Detroit, 4-0 (second game)—Whitaker, single in fourth; Corcoran, single in eighth.
July 27—Jefferson, Toronto vs. Seattle, 5-0—Simpson, single in fourth; Roberts, single in eighth.
July 30—Langford, Oakland vs. Toronto, 11-1—Griffin, homer in seventh; Ault, single in eighth.
Aug. 14—Stone, Baltimore vs. New York, 6-1—Jackson, homer in second; Dent, single in fifth.
Aug. 19—Stone (seven and one-third innings) and T. Martinez (one and two-thirds innings), Baltimore vs. California, 5-2—Campaneris, single in eighth; Ford, single in eighth.
Aug. 20—Eckersley, Boston vs. Oakland, 1-2—Page, single in seventh; Guerrero, homer in eighth.
Sept. 5—Hoyt, Chicago vs. Toronto, 3-0—Woods, single in second; Iorg, single in sixth.
Sept. 12—Haas, Milwaukee vs. Seattle, 7-1—Bochte, homer in fifth; Milbourne, single in fifth.
Sept. 18—Leal, Toronto vs. New York, 2-1—Jackson, single in fourth; Spencer, single in fourth.
Sept. 24—McCatty, Oakland vs. Chicago, 7-1—Squires, double in third; Molinaro, single in fourth.

NATIONAL LEAGUE
One-Hit Games

April 19—Richard, Houston vs. Los Angeles, 2-0—Smith, single in fourth.
April 26—Carlton, Philadelphia vs. St. Louis, 7-0—Simmons, single in second.
May 29—Welch, Los Angeles vs. Atlanta, 3-0—Blanks, single in fourth.
June 19—Ryan (seven innings) and Sambito (two innings), Houston vs. St. Louis, 2-0—Templeton, double in third.

Two-Hit Games

April 10—Richard (eight innings) and Sambito (one inning), Houston vs. Los Angeles, 3-2—Law, single in seventh; Smith, double in seventh.

April 19—Welch (eight innings) and Howe (one inning), Los Angeles vs. Houston, 0-2—Cedeno, single in fourth; Cruz, single in fourth.

April 30—Bomback, New York vs. Philadelphia, 2-0—Schmidt, single in second; Maddox, single in seventh.

May   2—Burris (eight innings) and Reardon (one inning), New York vs. San Diego, 0-1—Mumphrey, singles in second and seventh.

May 24—Pastore, Cincinnati vs. Montreal, 2-0—Valentine, single in second; Cromartie, single in eighth.

May 28—Ryan, Houston vs. San Diego, 1-0—Wise, double in third; Smith, single in eighth.

June 26—Sanderson, Montreal vs. Philadelphia, 1-0—Rose, single in first; Trillo, single in eighth.

July   2—Pacella (seven and one-third innings) and Allen (one and two-thirds innings), New York vs. Chicago, 3-1—Foote, double in fifth; Tyson, triple in fifth.

July 14—Niekro, Atlanta vs. Houston, 2-0—Richard, double in third; Morgan, single in ninth.

Aug. 16—Blyleven, Pittsburgh vs. Montreal, 5-0—Office, single in seventh; Scott, single in eighth.

Aug. 24—Ryan, Houston vs. Chicago, 2-1—Biittner, triple in fifth; Blackwell, single in eighth.

Aug. 25—Seaver (six and one-third innings) and Soto (two and two-thirds innings), Cincinnati vs. Chicago, 2-0—DeJesus, single in first; Figueroa, single in ninth.

Aug. 27—Whitson (six innings) and Minton (three innings), San Francisco vs. Montreal, 1-0—Parrish, single in fifth; Office, single in seventh.

Sept. 5—Rogers, Montreal vs. San Francisco, 8-0—May, single in second; Whitfield, single in seventh.

Sept. 6—Niekro (seven innings) and Garber (two innings), Atlanta vs. Pittsburgh, 3-2—Milner, homer in second; Easler, single in eighth.

Oct.   1—Carlton, Philadelphia vs. Chicago, 5-0—Vail, single in eighth; Buckner, single in ninth.

STEVE CARLTON—Beat Cardinals April 26 for an N.L. record sixth one-hitter.

Gullickson Set Rookie Strikeout Record

By LARRY WIGGE

He fanned Jerry Martin four times. Tim Blackwell was thrice his victim. In all, Montreal Expos righthander Bill Gullickson fanned the side three times in the first seven innings en route to an 18-strikeout total September 10 in a 4-2 victory over the Cubs, setting a new single-game standard for rookie hurlers.

The 21-year-old fireballer fell just one strikeout short of the all-time record of 19 held by Steve Carlton, Nolan Ryan and Tom Seaver. He far outdistanced the Montreal club record of 14 twice achieved by Bill Stoneman in 1971.

Just one day earlier, Cincinnati sidearmer Mario Soto spun one of the two other 15-or-more strikeout performances in 1980. The righthander struck out the side in the ninth inning at Atlanta to finish with 15 K's and a 7-1 triumph over the Braves. Jerry Koosman of the Twins fanned 15 June 23 in a 4-1 decision over the Royals. It was the second time Koosman had a 15-strikeout game—he once fanned 15 batters in a 10-inning stint while a member of the Mets.

Following is a complete recap of the 15-strikeout games in 1980:

Date	Pitcher—Club—Opp.	Place	IP.	H.	R.	ER.	BB.	SO.	Result
June 23—Koosman, Twins vs. Royals		H	9	10	1	1	2	15	W 4-1
Sept. 9—Soto, Reds vs. Braves		A	9	7	1	1	1	15	W 7-1
Sept. 10—Gullickson, Expos vs. Cubs		H	9	4	2	2	2	18	W 4-2

Steve Carlton of the Phillies raised his career strikeout total to 2,969, making him the leading all-time lefty after passing Mickey Lolich, who was at 2,832. Ryan, with 3,109 strikeouts, became the fourth player in history to surpass the 3,000 level.

Meanwhile, Carlton's 286 strikeouts paced the N.L. while Len Barker of the Indians topped the A.L. with 187. It was the first time since Early Wynn of the White Sox had 179 strikeouts in 1958 that a league leader finished with less than 200 K's.

In a season when there were only 53 10-strikeout games in the majors, Carlton had 11 of them. Bert Blyleven of the Pirates was next with four. Ryan had three 10-strikeout games in '80 to raise his all-time record total to 131—114 of those 10-strikeout performances coming while the fireballing Astros' righthander was with the Angels in the A.L.

The following includes a complete list of 10-strikeout games in 1980 and the number of times achieved:

AMERICAN LEAGUE: Baltimore (1)—Stone. Boston (1)—Tudor. California—None. Chicago—None. Cleveland (3)—Barker 2, Waits. Detroit—None. Kansas City—None. Milwaukee (1)—Haas. Minnesota (1)—Koosman. New York (1)—May. Oakland (2)—Norris 2. Seattle (3)—Bannister 3. Texas (3)—Darwin, Jenkins, Perry. Toronto (2)—Clancy, Jefferson.

NATIONAL LEAGUE: Atlanta (1)—Niekro. Chicago—None. Cincinnati (5)—Soto 3, Pastore, Seaver. Houston (6)—Richard 3, Ryan 3. Los Angeles (1)—Sutton. Montreal (5)—Gullickson 2, Sanderson 2, Palmer. New York (1)—Jackson. Philadelphia (11)—Carlton 11. Pittsburgh (4)—Blyleven 4. St. Louis—None. San Diego—None. San Francisco (1)—Montefusco.

Hume, Fingers and Quisenberry
Were Top Firemen in '80

By LARRY WIGGE

Tom Hume of the Cincinnati Reds and Rollie Fingers of the San Diego Padres tied for THE SPORTING NEWS National League Fireman of the Year Award for 1980 and Dan Quisenberry of the Kansas City Royals captured the American League honors.

Hume pitched the final inning to preserve Cincinnati's 1-0 victory over the Atlanta Braves on the final day of the season to pull into a deadlock with Fingers with 34 points apiece. A point is awarded for each save and each relief win.

Fingers, who won the N.L. Fireman Award in 1977 and 1978, finished with 23 saves and 11 wins, while Hume accounted for his points on 25 saves and nine victories. Bruce Sutter of the Chicago Cubs, the 1979 Fireman winner, came in second with 33 points on 28 saves and five wins.

Quisenberry collected an amazing total of 45 points on 33 saves and 12 victories to finish six points ahead of Rich Gossage of the New York Yankees, who logged 33 saves and six wins. Ed Farmer of the Chicago White Sox, the runaway leader in the first half of the season, finished third with 30 saves and seven wins. Quisenberry became the bulwark of the Kansas City bullpen after posting five saves and three victories in 1979, his rookie season.

It was only the second time a tie had resulted since THE SPORTING NEWS originated the award in 1960. Mike Marshall of the Minnesota Twins and Jim Kern of the Texas Rangers shared the A.L. honors in 1979.

Fingers tied Marshall as the only pitchers to collect three Fireman of the Year trophies.

American League

Pitcher—Club	Saves	Relief Wins	Tot. Pts.	Pitcher—Club	Saves	Relief Wins	Tot. Pts.
Quisenberry, Kansas City	33	12	45	May, New York	3	5	8
Gossage, New York	33	6	39	McLaughlin, Toronto	4	4	8
Farmer, Chicago	30	7	37	Pattin, Kansas City	4	4	8
Lopez, Detroit	21	13	34	Drago, Boston	3	4	7
Corbett, Minnesota	23	8	31	Montague, California	3	4	7
Stoddard, Baltimore	26	5	31	Underwood, Detroit	5	2	7
Burgmeier, Boston	24	5	29	Augustine, Milwaukee	2	4	6
Clear, California	9	11	20	Johnson, Texas	4	2	6
Darwin, Texas	8	12	20	Jones, Oakland	5	1	6
Rawley, Seattle	13	7	20	LaRoche, California	4	2	6
Cruz, Cleveland	12	6	18	Rozema, Detroit	4	2	6
Stanley, Boston	14	4	18	Stanton, Cleveland	5	1	6
Monge, Cleveland	14	3	17	Aase, California	2	3	5
Davis, New York	7	9	16	Kern, Texas	2	3	5
Hassler, California	10	5	15	Lockwood, Boston	2	3	5
T. Martinez, Baltimore	10	4	14	McLaughlin, Seattle	2	3	5
Garvin, Toronto	8	4	12	Willis, Toronto	3	2	5
Proly, Chicago	8	4	12	Campbell, Boston	0	4	4
Lyle, Texas	8	3	11	Christenson, Kansas City	1	3	4
McClure, Milwaukee	10	1	11	Flinn, Milwaukee	2	2	4
Castro, Milwaukee	8	2	10	Rajsich, Texas	2	2	4
Cleveland, Milwaukee	4	6	10	D. Roberts, Seattle	3	1	4
Heaverlo, Seattle	4	6	10	Underwood, New York	2	2	4
Stewart, Baltimore	3	6	9	Bird, New York	1	2	3
Barlow, Toronto	5	3	8	Buskey, Toronto	0	3	3
Lacey, Oakland	6	2	8	Koosman, Minnesota	2	1	3

Pitcher—Club	Saves	Relief Wins	Tot. Pts.	Pitcher—Club	Saves	Relief Wins	Tot. Pts.
Martin, Kansas City	2	1	3	Marshall, Minnesota	1	1	2
Parrott, Seattle	3	0	3	Mitchell, Milwaukee	1	1	2
Redfern, Minnesota	2	1	3	Moore, Toronto	1	1	2
Scarbery, Chicago	2	1	3	Remmerswaal, Boston	0	2	2
Verhoeven, Minnesota	0	3	3	Renko, Boston	0	2	2
Wortham, Chicago	1	2	3	Robbins, Detroit	0	2	2
Arroyo, Minnesota	0	2	2	Schatzeder, Detroit	0	2	2
Guidry, New York	1	1	2	Schrom, Toronto	1	1	2
Hoffman, Chicago	1	1	2	Twitty, Kansas City	0	2	2
Hoyt, Chicago	0	2	2	Weaver, Detroit	0	2	2
Knapp, California	1	1	2	Wihtol, Cleveland	1	1	2
Kucek, Toronto	1	1	2	Williams, Minnesota	1	1	2
Lollar, New York	2	0	2				

One Save—Barr, California; Beard, Oakland; K. Brett, Kansas City; Caldwell, Milwaukee; Figueroa, New York-Texas; Ford, Baltimore; Gale, Kansas City; D. Jackson, Minnesota; LaPoint, Milwaukee; D. Martinez, Baltimore; Matlack, Texas; Minetto, Oakland; Sarmiento, Seattle; Sorensen, Milwaukee.

One Relief Win—Babcock, Texas; Burns, Chicago; Devine, Texas; Hiller, Detroit; Hough, Texas; Langford, Oakland; Leal, Toronto; Lemanczyk, Toronto-California; Owchinko, Cleveland; Perry, Texas-New York; Petry, Detroit; Robinson, Chicago; Spillner, Cleveland; Wilcox, Detroit.

National League

Pitcher—Club	Saves	Relief Wins	Tot. Pts.	Pitcher—Club	Saves	Relief Wins	Tot. Pts.
Hume, Cincinnati	25	9	34	Moskau, Cincinnati	2	4	6
Fingers, San Diego	23	11	34	Noles, Philadelphia	6	0	6
Sutter, Chicago	28	5	33	Reuss, Los Angeles	3	3	6
Allen, New York	22	7	29	Urrea, St. Louis	3	3	6
Tekulve, Pittsburgh	21	8	29	Caudill, Chicago	1	4	5
Camp, Atlanta	22	6	28	D'Acquisto, S.D.–Montreal	3	2	5
McGraw, Philadelphia	20	5	25	Kinney, San Diego	1	4	5
Sambito, Houston	17	8	25	Frazier, St. Louis	3	1	4
Howe, Los Angeles	17	7	24	Glynn, New York	1	3	4
Fryman, Montreal	17	7	24	Lucas, San Diego	3	1	4
Minton, San Francisco	19	4	23	Norman, Montreal	4	0	4
LaCorte, Houston	11	8	19	Rasmussen, San Diego	1	3	4
Sosa, Montreal	9	9	18	Beckwith, Los Angeles	0	3	3
Smith, Houston	10	7	17	Griffin, San Francisco	0	3	3
Jackson, Pittsburgh	9	8	17	LaGrow, Philadelphia	3	0	3
Romo, Pittsburgh	11	5	16	Tomlin, Cincinnati	0	3	3
Reed, Philadelphia	9	7	16	Valenzuela, Los Angeles	1	2	3
Lavelle, San Francisco	9	6	15	Andujar, Houston	2	0	2
Littlefield, St. Louis	6	8	14	Bomback, New York	0	2	2
Reardon, New York	6	8	14	Borbon, St. Louis	1	1	2
Shirley, San Diego	7	6	13	Brusstar, Philadelphia	0	2	2
Castillo, Los Angeles	5	8	13	Falcone, New York	1	1	2
Garber, Atlanta	7	5	12	Goltz, Los Angeles	1	1	2
Holland, San Francisco	7	5	12	Hough, Los Angeles	1	1	2
Tidrow, Chicago	6	6	12	LaCoss, Cincinnati	0	2	2
Bahnsen, Montreal	4	7	11	Littell, St. Louis	2	0	2
Bair, Cincinnati	6	3	9	Lyle, Philadelphia	2	0	2
Soto, Cincinnati	4	5	9	Miller, New York	1	1	2
Stanhouse, Los Angeles	7	2	9	Mura, San Diego	2	0	2
Bradford, Atlanta	4	3	7	Niekro, Atlanta	1	1	2
Hausman, New York	1	6	7	Price, Cincinnati	0	2	2
Hrabosky, Atlanta	3	4	7	Roberge, Houston	0	2	2
Kaat, St. Louis	4	3	7	Smith, Chicago	0	2	2
Saucier, Philadelphia	0	7	7	Solomon, Pittsburgh	0	2	2
Seaman, St. Louis	4	3	7	Tellmann, San Diego	1	1	2
Sutcliffe, Los Angeles	5	2	7				

One Save—Candelaria, Pittsburgh; Hooton, Los Angeles; Jackson, New York; Niemann, Houston; D. Robinson, Pittsburgh; Sutton, Los Angeles; Vuckovich, St. Louis.

One Relief Win—Bibby, Pittsburgh; Burnside, Cincinnati; Capilla, Chicago; Eichelberger, San Diego; Hanna, Atlanta; Hernandez, Chicago; Hood, St. Louis; Kobel, New York; Lamp, Chicago; Lea, Montreal; Lee, Montreal; Leibrandt, Cincinnati; Martin, St. Louis; Martinez, St. Louis; Moffitt, San Francisco; Montefusco, San Francisco; Moore, St. Louis; Niekro, Houston; Ripley, San Francisco; Rowland, San Francisco; Thomas, St. Louis.

Sanderson Twirled Three 1-0 Victories

By CARL CLARK

In 1980, 21 National League games were decided by 1-0 scores, with Montreal's Scott Sanderson being involved in nearly a quarter of them, winning three and losing two. In his first victory, Sanderson worked five innings against Houston, May 14, before being picked up by Woodie Fryman. Sanderson blanked Philadelphia on two singles, June 26, and threw a five-hitter against Pittsburgh September 12.

Rookie lefthander Charlie Leibrandt of Cincinnati was the only other N.L. hurler to win more than one 1-0 game. Leibrandt defeated San Diego by that score twice. A second-inning home run by Dan Driessen was all Leibrandt needed on June 8 when he threw a three-hitter against the Padres. The next time, August 11, Leibrandt needed help from Tom Hume, who pitched the last 2⅔ innings.

Jim Clancy of Toronto and Scott McGregor of Baltimore won two 1-0 games apiece to lead the hurlers of the American League, where 26 games were decided by a 1-0 score. Minnesota's Roger Erickson, Oakland's Mike Norris and Seattle's Floyd Bannister all lost a pair of 1-0 games.

Home runs decided 10 of the majors' 47 minimum-score games.

Boston copped team honors with four 1-0 wins in as many games. Cincinnati and St. Louis were undefeated in three games, and Toronto won five of six. The Mets lost all four of their 1-0 games.

The complete list of 1-0 games, including the winning and losing pitchers and the inning in which the run was scored, follows:

AMERICAN LEAGUE (26)

Date	Winner	Loser	Inning
APRIL—			
10	*Lyle, Tex.	*Underwood, N.Y.	12
11	Keough, Oak.	Redfern, Minn.	9
17	Mirabella, Tor.	Sorensen, Milw.	9
27	John, N.Y.	Burns, Chi.	5
MAY—			
4‡	Norris, Oak.	*Schatzeder, Det.	6
10	*D. Jackson, Minn.	*May, N.Y.	11
15	Clancy, Tor.	Bannister, Sea.	2
16	Jefferson, Tor.	Norris, Oak.	11
19	Guidry, N.Y.	Wilcox, Det.	2
19	*Kravec, Chi.	Koosman, Minn.	3
20	*Gale, K.C.	Norris, Oak.	4
JUNE—			
7	*Underwood, N.Y.	Honeycutt, Sea.	2
10	Clancy, Tor.	Baumgarten, Chi.	2
24	McGregor, Balt.	Stieb, Tor.	1
JULY—			
2	Baumgarten, Chi.	Tanana, Calif.	7
5	*Tudor, Bos.	Palmer, Balt.	2
17	*D. Martinez, Balt.	Travers, Milw.	2
18	Torrez, Bos.	Erickson, Minn.	10
21	Stieb, Tor.	Kingman, Oak.	5
AUGUST—			
1†	Morris, Det.	*Bannister, Sea.	9
2	*Ojeda, Bos.	*Figueroa, Tex.	2
17	McGregor, Balt.	*Tiant, N.Y.	6
22	*Renko, Bos.	Beattie, Sea.	9
31	*Rawley, Sea.	*Guidry, N.Y.	9
SEPTEMBER—			
5	Schatzeder, Det.	Erickson, Minn.	1
22	*Koosman, Minn.	*Butcher, Tex.	1

NATIONAL LEAGUE (21)

Date	Winner	Loser	Inning
APRIL—			
10	Vuckovich, St.L.	*Blyleven, Pitts.	2
MAY—			
2	*Wise, S.D.	*Burris, N.Y.	2
14	*Sanderson, Mont.	*Forsch, Hou.	5
20	Niekro, Atl.	*Sanderson, Mont.	7
28	Ryan, Hou.	*Wise, S.D.	2
JUNE—			
4	Kaat, St.L.	*Allen, N.Y.	10
8	Leibrandt, Cin.	*Jones, S.D.	2
15	Welch, Los Ang.	*Gullickson, Mont.	6
26	Sanderson, Mont.	Lerch, Phila.	5
JULY—			
4	Sykes, St.L.	*Saucier, Phila.	10
AUGUST—			
1	*Mura, S.D.	*Bibby, Pitts.	6
6	Forsch, Hou.	*Blue, San Fran.	6
11	*Leibrandt, Cin.	*Mura, S.D.	7
23	*Niekro, Hou.	Riley, Chi.	17
27	*Whitson, San Fran.	*Sanderson, Mont.	4
29	Blue, San Fran.	Zachry, N.Y.	8
SEPTEMBER—			
5	*Sutton, Los Ang.	*Carlton, Phila.	2
12	Sanderson, Mont.	*Rhoden, Pitts.	2
24	*McGraw, Phila.	*Allen, N.Y.	10
OCTOBER—			
5	*Price, Cin.	Niekro, Atl.	8
5	D. Robinson, Pitts.	*Capilla, Chi.	4

*Did not pitch complete game. †First game of doubleheader. ‡Second game of doubleheader.

Knight Swatted Three Grand Slams

By CARL CLARK

Reds third baseman Ray Knight led the majors in 1980 with three bases-loaded homers. Knight's first one, off the Mets' Ed Glynn May 13, capped the eight-run fifth inning of a 15-4 victory and put Ray in the record book. Knight, who led off the inning with a homer off Mark Bomback, became the 17th major leaguer since 1900 to hit two homers in an inning.

Johnny Bench, one of Knight's Cincinnati teammates, Gary Carter of Montreal and Cliff Johnson of the Chicago Cubs hit two slams apiece. Bench's slams, both of which came against Los Angeles, were the 10th and 11th of his career and lifted him into a tie for the grand slam lead among active players with Willie Stargell and Lee May.

Robin Yount was the only A. L. player to hit a pair of grand slams.

The Brewers struck three bases-loaded blows in their first series of the season, against Boston, and tied a major league record when Cecil Cooper and Don Money connected in the same inning of an 18-1 drubbing April 12. Their last slam, September 26 against Oakland's Mike Norris, was an inside-the-park job by Ben Oglivie.

The complete list of grand slams, with the inning in which each was hit in parentheses follows:

AMERICAN LEAGUE (39)

APRIL—
10 —Lezcano, Milwaukee vs. Drago, Boston .... (9)
12 —Cooper, Milwaukee vs. Torrez, Boston .... (2)
12 —Money, Milwaukee vs. Rainey, Boston .... (2)
13*—Spencer, New York vs. Comer, Texas .... (5)
14 —Orta, Cleveland vs. Medich, Texas .... (1)
14 —Sundberg, Texas vs. Waits, Cleveland .... (1)
19 —Staub, Texas vs. Eckersley, Boston .... (7)
26 —Bonnell, Toronto vs. Caldwell, Milwaukee ..... (9)
26 —Oliver, Texas vs. Denny, Cleveland .... (5)

MAY—
4*—Velez, Toronto vs. Spillner, Cleveland .... (1)
4 —Yount, Milwaukee vs. Wortham, Chicago ...... (8)
14 —Roberts, Texas vs. Hartzell, Baltimore.......... (4)
20 —Hebner, Detroit vs. John, New York .... (10)
26 —Cerone, New York vs. Tobik, Detroit .... (8)
27 —Peters, Detroit vs. Griffin, New York............ (6)

JUNE—
6 —Perez, Boston vs. Camacho, Oakland .... (5)
11 —Armas, Oakland vs. Stewart, Baltimore........ (14)
13†—Jackson, New York vs. Keough, Oakland .... (7)
19 —Morales, Minnesota vs. Schatzeder, Detroit .. (3)
23 —Gantner, Milwaukee vs. Kingman, Oakland. (6)

JULY—
1 —Diaz, Cleveland vs. Weaver, Detroit............. (6)
4 —Murcer, New York vs. Owchinko, Cleveland. (4)
19 —Wills, Texas vs. Stewart, Baltimore............. (10)
20 —Harrah, Cleveland vs. Langford, Oakland ..... (9)
21†—Graham, Baltimore vs. Zahn, Minnesota .... (4)
23 —Charboneau, Cleve. vs. McLaughlin, Seattle. (11)
29 —Grich, California vs. Weaver, Detroit .... (5)

AUGUST—
5 —Crowley, Baltimore vs. Hoyt, Chicago.......... (5)
12 —Jones, New York vs. Farmer, Chicago........... (10)
16 —Yount, Milwaukee vs. Spillner, Cleveland ..... (2)
18 —Thomas, Milwaukee vs. Petry, Detroit .... (6)
28 —Summers, Detroit vs. McClure, Milwaukee..... (6)

SEPTEMBER—
10 —Kelly, Baltimore vs. Rozema, Detroit .... (6)
11 —Watson, New York vs. Stanley, Boston .... (6)

*First game of doubleheader.
†Second game of doubleheader.
‡Completion of suspended game of May 28.

17†—Wilfong, Minnesota vs. Mitchell, Milwaukee (7)
20 —Kemp, Detroit vs. Grimsley, Cleveland .... (4)
26 —Soderholm, N. York vs. Schatzeder, Detroit.. (3)
26 —Oglivie, Milwaukee vs. Norris, Oakland........ (9)
28 —Brett, Kansas City vs. Redfern, Minnesota ... (6)

NATIONAL LEAGUE (28)

APRIL—
19 —Kingman, Chicago vs. Allen, New York .... (8)
22 —Foote, Chicago vs. Littell, St. Louis .... (9)
22 —Schmidt, Phila. vs. Pacella, New York .... (8)

MAY—
4†—Kennedy, Cincinnati vs. Caudill, Chicago..... (6)
13 —Knight, Cincinnati vs. Glynn, New York .... (5)
17 —Evans, San Francisco vs. Sykes, St. Louis .... (5)
25 —Evans, San Diego vs. Borbon, St. Louis........ (9)
26†—Foster, Cincinnati vs. Beckwith, Los Ang..... (5)

JUNE—
1 —Berra, Pittsburgh vs. Bomback, New York... (5)
11 —Jorgensen, New York vs. Sutcliffe, Los Ang.. (10)
18 —Martin, Chicago vs. Bair, Cincinnati........... (7)
25 —Knight, Cincinnati vs. Matula, Atlanta......... (1)
30 —Moreland, Phila. vs. Gullickson, Montreal .... (4)

JULY—
12 —Johnson, Chicago vs. Bahnsen, Montreal ..... (7)
18 —May, San Francisco vs. Seaman, St. Louis..... (9)
21 —Carter, Montreal vs. Matula, Atlanta........... (1)

AUGUST—
8†—Johnson, Chicago vs. Murray, Montreal........ (14)
8 —Bench, Cincinnati vs. Stanhouse, Los Ang.... (8)
14 —Clark, San Fran. vs. McWilliams, Atlanta ..... (3)
17 —Murphy, Atlanta vs. Ripley, San Francisco... (1)
26 —Cedeno, Houston vs. Kaat, St. Louis............ (5)

SEPTEMBER—
6†—Cruz, Houston vs. Martin, St. Louis............. (3)
12*—Durham, St. Louis vs. Brusstar, Phila.......... (5)
17 —Knight, Cincinnati vs. Niekro, Houston .... (4)
19 —Carter, Montreal vs. Forsch, St. Louis......... (7)
19 —Bench, Cincinnati vs. Reuss, Los Angeles..... (2)
25 —Simmons, St. Louis vs. D. Robinson, Pitts. .. (7)

OCTOBER—
1 —Romo, Pittsburgh vs. Jackson, New York ..... (8)

Velez, Oliver Tied Record with HR Binge

By LARRY WIGGE

Belting four homers in a doubleheader had been accomplished only 10 times in the long history of the American League; however, Otto Velez of the Blue Jays and Al Oliver of the Rangers both achieved the feat in 1980.

Velez connected for a grand slam and two-run homer before his solo shot in the 10th inning May 4 gave Toronto its 9-8 victory over the Indians in the first game of a twin-bill. He homered again in the second game, giving the Blue Jays their sweep, 7-2. Oliver clouted one homer in a 9-3 triumph at Detroit August 17 before leading the Rangers to a 12-6 victory in the second game when he added a two-run blast and a pair of solo homers.

Larry Parrish of the Expos had the first three-homer game of the 1980 season when he tied the Braves, 7-7, with a ninth-inning homer April 25. However, his third career three-homer burst came in a losing effort as the homestanding Braves rallied for an 8-7 victory in 11 innings. Johnny Bench also connected for three homers in a game for the third time in his career as he powered the Reds to a 5-3 win May 29 at San Diego.

Fred Patek, who had only five homers the whole season, blasted three with seven RBIs to pace California's 26-hit attack for a 20-2 rout at Boston June 20. The pint-sized shortstop tied a club record with 14 total bases in the game. Claudell Washington, who had been 1-for-17 since being acquired by the Mets, touched off his first three N. L. homers June 22 for a 9-6 victory at Los Angeles. Eddie Murray put the Orioles ahead 3-2 in the 11th inning September 14, but the Blue Jays went on to win the game 4-3 in 13 innings.

It was the second time Washington, Oliver and Murray had connected for three homers in a game in their careers.

A detailed look at the seven three-homer games in 1980:

Date	Player—Opposition	Place	AB.	R.	H.	2B.	3B.	HR.	RBI.	Result
April 25	Parrish, Expos vs. Braves (11 inn.)	A	5	3	3	0	0	3	7	L 7-8
May 4*	Velez, Blue Jays vs. Indians (10 inn.)	H	5	3	3	0	0	3	7	W 9-8
May 29	Bench, Reds vs. Padres	A	4	3	3	0	0	3	4	W 5-3
June 20	Patek, Angels vs. Red Sox	A	6	4	4	1	0	3	7	W 20-2
June 22	Washington, Mets vs. Dodgers	A	5	3	4	0	0	3	5	W 9-6
Aug. 17+	Oliver, Rangers vs. Tigers	A	4	3	3	0	0	3	4	W 12-6
Sept. 14	Murray, Orioles vs. Blue Jays (13 inn.)	A	6	3	4	0	0	3	3	L 3-4

*First game of doubleheader. †Second game of doubleheader.

Mike Schmidt, the major league home run king with 48, also led the majors with five multi-homer games in 1980. Following is a list of each player who hit two or more homers in '80 and the number of times achieved:

AMERICAN LEAGUE: Baltimore (6)—Murray 2, Crowley, Dempsey, Graham, Singleton. Boston (11)—Perez 3, Dwyer 2, Rice 2, Evans, Hobson, Lynn, Stapleton. California (5)—Rudi 2, Grich, Patek, Thompson. Chicago (2)—Baines, Nordhagen. Cleveland (2)—Charboneau, Hargrove. Detroit (9)—Kemp 3, Hebner 2, Parrish 2, Summers, Trammell. Kansas City (4)—Aikens, McRae, Otis, Quirk. Milwaukee (15)—Oglivie 4, Thomas 3, Cooper 2, Lezcano 2, Bando, Hisle, Money, Yount. Minnesota (1)—Morales. New York (6)—Cerone, Jackson, Jones, Lefebvre, Murcer, Watson. Oakland (9)—Armas 3, Page 3, Gross 2, Revering. Seattle (2)—Meyer, Roberts. Texas (8)—Bell 4, Oliver, Putnam, Roberts, Zisk. Toronto (6)—Mayberry 4, Howell, Velez.

NATIONAL LEAGUE: Atlanta (8)—Horner 4, Matthews 3, Murphy. Chicago (7)—Kingman 4, Martin 2, Foote. Cincinnati (3)—Bench, Foster, Knight. Houston (2)—Cruz, Puhl. Los Angeles (5)—Baker 3, Ferguson, Garvey. Montreal (8)—Carter 3, Cromartie, Dawson, LeFlore, Parrish, Valentine. New York (4)—Washington 2, Henderson, Mazzilli. Philadelphia (6)—Schmidt 5, Luzinski. Pittsburgh (9)—Easler 2, Parker 2, Garner, Lacy, Madlock, Ott, Stargell. St. Louis (9)—Hendrick 2, Simmons 2, Durham, Hernandez, Iorg, Kennedy, Reitz. San Diego (2)—Montanez, Tenace. San Francisco (1)—Clark.

Orta Exploded for Six-Hit Salvo

By CARL CLARK

With five singles and a double against Minnesota on June 15, Jorge Orta of the Indians became the first American League player with six hits in a game since Milwaukee's John Briggs in 1973 and the 25th A.L. batter to record six hits in as many at-bats. There were 16 five-hit games in the A.L. and 12 in the National in 1980.

Orta doubled in the fourth inning of Cleveland's 14-5 victory and singled in the first, second, sixth, seventh and eighth innings. Five of those hits came against lefthanded pitching. Orta, a lefthanded batter, had three hits off Darrell Jackson, one off Fernando Arroyo and two off Mike Kinnunen.

George Brett of the Royals, Cesar Cedeno of the Astros and Dave Winfield of the Padres made the five-hit list for the second consecutive season.

Records of all players with five or more hits in a game follow:

Date	Player—Opposition	Place	AB.	R.	H.	2B.	3B.	HR.	RBI.	Result
April 21	Foster, Reds vs. Astros	A	5	1	5	0	0	1	2	W 6-5
April 22	DeJesus, Cubs vs. Cards	H	6	2	5	1	1	1	2	W 16-12
April 27	Hernandez, Cards vs. Phils	A	5	2	5	1	0	0	3	W 10-1
May 10	Oliver, Rangers vs. White Sox	H	5	2	5	1	0	0	2	L 6-10
May 28	Thon, Angels vs. Rangers	H	5	1	5	1	0	0	0	W 7-6
June 1	Soderholm, Yankees vs. Blue Jays	H	5	2	5	0	1	0	2	W 11-7
June 2	Dauer, Orioles vs. Brewers (11 inn.)	H	5	2	5	0	0	0	1	W 9-8
June 2	Meyer, Mariners vs. Tigers (13 inn.)	A	6	2	5	0	1	0	0	T 3-3
June 6	Burleson, Red Sox vs. A's	A	6	3	5	1	1	0	3	W 14-8
June 8†	Dawson, Expos vs. Cards	H	5	3	5	1	0	2	4	W 9-4
June 15	Orta, Indians vs. Twins	H	6	4	6	1	0	0	1	W 14-5
June 24	Cedeno, Astros vs. Dodgers (12 inn.)	H	5	2	5	2	0	0	2	W 5-4
June 25	Baker, Dodgers vs. Astros	A	6	1	5	2	0	0	0	W 9-2
July 2	Winfield, Padres vs. Dodgers	A	5	3	5	0	0	1	4	L 7-10
July 11	Moore, Brewers vs. Red Sox	H	5	3	5	0	0	0	0	W 7-6
July 13	Grich, Angels vs. A's (14 inn.)	H	7	2	5	1	0	1	2	W 5-4
July 14	Smith, Phils vs. Pirates	H	6	3	5	0	0	0	0	L 11-13
July 18	Wilson, Royals vs. Yankees	A	6	4	5	1	0	0	2	W 13-1
July 20†	Lacy, Pirates vs. Dodgers	H	5	3	5	1	1	0	2	W 8-7
July 29	McBride, Phils vs. Astros	H	5	2	5	0	0	3	3	W 9-6
Aug. 1	Bell, Rangers vs. Red Sox	H	5	2	5	0	0	0	2	W 7-5
Aug. 2	McRae, Royals vs. White Sox	A	5	2	5	0	0	0	2	W 8-2
Aug. 15	Montanez, Padres vs. Astros (20 inn.)	H	9	1	5	1	0	0	0	L 3-1
Aug. 20	Brookens, Tigers vs. Brewers	A	5	2	5	0	1	1	2	W 8-6
Aug. 26	G. Brett, Royals vs. Brewers	A	5	2	5	1	0	0	1	W 7-6
Aug. 26	Mumphrey, Padres vs. Mets (18 inn.)	A	9	2	5	2	0	1	2	W 8-6
Sept. 16	Stapleton, Red Sox vs. Indians	H	5	2	5	2	0	0	2	W 9-5
Sept. 29	Trammell, Tigers vs. Blue Jays	A	6	1	5	2	0	0	1	W 8-2
Oct. 4*	Evans, Red Sox vs. Blue Jays (17 inn.)	H	7	2	5	3	0	1	1	L 6 -7

*First game of doubleheader.   †Second game of doubleheader.

The season's most newsworthy hitting streaks were in the A.L. The longest streak, 31 games, belonged to Twins outfielder Ken Landreaux, who hit .392 with two homers and 19 RBIs from April through May 30.

Beginning July 18, Brett mounted a strong challenge to that but came up one game short. Brett hit .467 (57-for-122) in his 30-game streak and had six homers and 42 RBIs. He had seven game-winning RBIs and raised his average from .366 to .404 before he was shackled in three at-bats by Texas' Jon Matlack August 19.

Cecil Cooper, runnerup to Brett in the major league batting race, had three streaks of 15 or more games. The Milwaukee first baseman hit .453 in a 15-game span in August, .424 in 16 games in July and .372 in a 22-game streak that began May 16. Cooper's cumulative totals for those 53 games were a .411

batting average, 10 home runs and 51 RBIs.

The A.L. had five other strings of 20 or more games, and the Rangers' Mickey Rivers had two of them. Rivers hit .424 in his first streak, one of 20 games that began June 17, and .394 in a 24-game tear that started in mid-August.

Two of Rivers' 20-game comrades had a pair of streaks of 15 or more games. Jim Rice of the Red Sox slugged seven homers in a 15-game run in June and in his 21-game streak in September he hit .419 and drove in 24 runs. Al Oliver, also of the Rangers, launched on August 19 a streak that reached 21 games. After Oakland's Mike Norris snapped that, holding him hitless in four trips September 10, Oliver then embarked on a 17-game streak in which he hit .394.

Cleveland's Mike Hargrove hit .381 in a 23-game stretch that had its incipience in mid-April, and yet another member of the Rangers, Buddy Bell, hit .402 and had six homers in a midseason streak that encompassed 21 games.

Rick Burleson of Boston spiced his 16-game burst in June (.419) with a five-hit game and a pair of four-hit games.

In August, Cubs third baseman Lenny Randle put together the N.L.'s longest streak, 21 games, but hit only .337 in that span.

Streaks of 15 or more games were also recorded by these players: 19 games—Andre Dawson, Expos; Alfredo Griffin, Blue Jays; Dave Stapleton, Red Sox; 18 games—Rod Carew, Angels; Warren Cromartie, Expos; Tim Foli, Pirates; Lee Mazzilli, Mets; Robin Yount, Brewers; 17 games—Al Bumbry, Orioles; John Mayberry, Blue Jays; Jorge Orta, Indians; Tony Perez, Red Sox; Champ Summers, Tigers; 16 games—Dusty Baker, Dodgers; Mike Easler, Pirates; Dan Ford, Angels; Eddie Murray, Orioles; 15 games—Dave Collins, Reds; Miguel Dilone, Indians; Dave Lopes, Dodgers; Jerry Mumphrey, Padres; Dave Parker, Pirates; Bump Wills, Rangers.

Rivers and Willie Wilson of Kansas City led the majors in games with four or more hits. They had seven apiece.

The complete list of players with four or more hits in one game follows:

AMERICAN LEAGUE: Baltimore (13)—Murray 4, Dauer 3, Bumbry 2, Singleton 2, Graham, Roenicke. Boston (16)—Burleson 4, Evans 2, Lynn 2, Remy 2, Stapleton 2, Fisk, Hoffman, Perez, Rader. California (16)—Grich 3, Lansford 3, Patek 2, Baylor, Clark, Ford, Harlow, Miller, Rudi, Thompson, Thon. Chicago (10)—L. Johnson 2, Lemon 2, Morrison 2, Baines, Chappas, Molinaro, Nordhagen. Cleveland (8)—Dilone 2, Harrah 2, Bannister, Hargrove, Manning, Orta. Detroit (13)—Brookens 2, Cowens 2, Parrish 2, Peters 2, Trammell 2, Corcoran, Kemp, Summers. Kansas City (25)—Wilson 7, G. Brett 5, Wathan 5, McRae 2, Porter 2, Washington 2, Otis, Quirk. Milwaukee (14)—Cooper 4, Molitor 3, Moore 2, Oglivie 2, Thomas 2, Lezcano. Minnesota (18)—Castino 5, Landreaux 4, R. Jackson 2, Ward 2, Mackanin, Morales, Powell, Smalley, Wilfong. New York (10)—Randolph 2, Watson 2, Brown, Cerone, Dent, Jackson, Piniella, Soderholm. Oakland (9)—Armas 2, Henderson 2, Revering 2, Guerrero, Murphy, Newman. Seattle (9)—Meyer 2, Stein 2, Bochte, Craig, Cruz, Horton, Paciorek. Texas (21)—Rivers 7, Oliver 5, Bell 3, Sundberg 2, Wills 2, Putnam, Staub. Toronto (9)—Woods 2, Howell 2, Mayberry, Moseby, Velez, Whitt.

NATIONAL LEAGUE: Atlanta (12)—Matthews 4, Royster 3, Chambliss 2, Benedict, Murphy, Ramirez. Chicago (11)—DeJesus 3, Buckner 2, Vail 2, Biittner, Foote, Randle, Tracy. Cincinnati (17)—Foster 3, Griffey 3, Collins 2, Kennedy 2, Knight 2, Auerbach, Bench, Concepcion, Geronimo, Oester. Houston (12)—Cedeno 4, Howe 2, Landestoy 2, Puhl 2, Cabell, Walling. Los Angeles (10)—Baker 3, Garvey 3, Law, Lopes, Scioscia, Smith. Montreal (14)—Cromartie 4, Dawson 4, Carter 3, Almon, LeFlore, Parrish. New York (15)—Taveras 5, Washington 3, Mazzilli 2, Almon, Backman, Henderson, Wilson, Youngblood. Philadelphia (13)—Schmidt 4, McBride 3, Smith 3, Rose 2, Maddox. Pittsburgh (11)—Foli 2, Lacy 2, Moreno 2, B. Robinson 2, Easler, Parker, Stargell. St. Louis (22)—Templeton 5, Iorg 4, Hernandez 3, Simmons 3, Hendrick 2, Oberkfell 2, Landrum, Ramsey, Scott. San Diego (9)—Richards 3, Montanez 2, Mumphrey 2, Stimac, Winfield. San Francisco (10)—Clark 3, Pettini 2, Ivie, May, Stennett, Whitfield, Wohlford.

Dodgers Reactivated Pinch-Hit Ace Mota

Manny Mota extended his major league record to 150 career pinch-hits when he went 3-for-7 with two RBIs, one a game-winner, after being activated from the coaching ranks to help the Dodgers in their 1980 pennant chase.

Mota's Los Angeles teammate Pedro Guerrero led the N.L. with a .647 pinch-hitting aveage, while Detroit's Richie Hebner headed the A.L. with .545.

Jeff Burroughs of the Braves and Cliff Johnson (Indians and Cubs) each had three pinch-homers in '80. Johnson became the majors' active leader with 15 pinch-homers, just three short of the all-time mark set by Pittsburgh's Jerry Lynch.

NATIONAL LEAGUE PINCH-HITTING
(Compiled by Elias Sports Bureau)

Club Pinch-Hitting

Club	AB.	H.	HR.	RBI.	Pct.	Club	AB.	H.	HR.	RBI.	Pct.
Pittsburgh	173	48	2	20	.2775	San Francisco	259	62	3	37	.239
Los Angeles	231	64	3	34	.2771	Chicago	299	71	3	40	.237
Philadelphia	174	48	0	25	.276	Cincinnati	164	36	4	16	.220
Montreal	186	47	4	29	.253	St. Louis	201	44	1	21	.219
Atlanta	233	58	6	33	.249	Houston	189	32	4	17	.169
San Diego	261	63	5	36	.241	New York	238	40	4	33	.168
						Totals	2608	613	39	341	.235

Individual Pinch-Hitting
(10 or More At-Bats)

Player–Club	AB.	H.	HR.	RBI.	Pct.	Player–Club	AB.	H.	HR.	RBI.	Pct.
Guerrero, Los Angeles	17	11	1	7	.647	Geronimo, Cincinnati	21	5	0	0	.238
Youngblood, New York	13	7	0	5	.538	Carbo, St.L.-Pittsburgh	17	4	0	1	.235
Flannery, San Diego	12	5	0	2	.417	Hutton, Montreal	43	10	0	3	.233
Moreland, Philadelphia	17	7	0	6	.412	Joshua, San Diego	39	9	1	5	.231
Kingman, Chicago	15	6	0	4	.400	Morales, New York	31	7	0	6	.226
May, San Francisco	15	6	0	6	.400	Monday, Los Angeles	36	8	1	4	.222
Burroughs, Atlanta	24	9	3	15	.375	White, Montreal	29	6	1	5	.207
Office, Montreal	17	6	1	4	.353	Biittner, Chicago	54	11	1	12	.204
Venable, San Francisco	26	9	0	4	.346	Simmons, St. Louis	15	3	1	3	.200
Perkins, San Diego	12	4	0	2	.333	Whitfield, San Francisco	25	5	0	5	.200
Ramsey, St. Louis	18	6	0	3	.333	Hatcher, Los Angeles	21	4	0	0	.190
Sanguillen, Pittsburgh	37	12	0	1	.324	Walling, Houston	21	4	1	4	.190
Spikes, Atlanta	31	10	0	2	.323	Bernazard, Montreal	22	4	1	3	.182
Unser, Philadelphia	38	12	0	6	.316	Dillard, Chicago	11	2	0	1	.182
Figueroa, Chicago	54	17	0	3	.315	Fahey, San Diego	11	2	0	2	.182
Durham, St. Louis	16	5	0	1	.313	Hodges, New York	22	4	0	5	.182
Lacy, Pittsburgh	16	5	0	2	.313	Macha, Montreal	11	2	0	0	.182
B. Robinson, Pittsburgh	16	5	0	0	.313	Maddox, New York	11	2	0	0	.182
Easler, Pittsburgh	13	4	2	5	.308	Martin, Chicago	11	2	0	1	.182
Tamargo, Montreal	23	7	1	5	.304	Tracy, Chicago	11	2	0	0	.182
Oester, Cincinnati	10	3	0	1	.300	Auerbach, Cincinnati	17	3	1	1	.176
Bevacqua, S.D.-Pitts.	57	17	0	12	.298	Smith, St. Louis	17	3	0	2	.176
Spilman, Cincinnati	41	12	2	10	.293	Norman, New York	47	8	2	2	.170
Herndon, San Francisco	21	6	1	6	.286	Bergman, Houston	24	4	0	1	.167
Thompson, Chicago	21	6	0	1	.286	McCovey, San Francisco	18	3	0	3	.167
Pocoroba, Atlanta	53	15	2	6	.283	Henderson, Chicago	19	3	1	3	.158
Turner, San Diego	47	13	1	7	.277	Bench, Cincinnati	13	2	1	3	.154
Montanez, S.D.-Mont.	11	3	0	1	.273	Kennedy, St. Louis	13	2	0	3	.154
Stargell, Pittsburgh	11	3	0	0	.273	Moreno, New York	26	4	1	2	.154
Johnstone, Los Angeles	41	11	0	3	.268	Ferguson, Los Angeles	14	2	1	5	.143
Strain, San Francisco	30	8	0	0	.267	Asselstine, Atlanta	22	3	0	1	.136
Vail, Chicago	45	12	0	11	.267	Bonds, St. Louis	15	2	0	0	.133
Iorg, St. Louis	38	10	0	6	.263	Johnson, Chicago	17	2	1	1	.118
North, San Francisco	19	5	0	0	.263	Tenace, San Diego	17	2	1	2	.118
Gross, Philadelphia	39	10	0	5	.256	Landestoy, Houston	26	3	1	1	.115
Law, Los Angeles	16	4	0	0	.250	Blanks, Atlanta	10	1	0	0	.100
Leonard, Houston	24	6	1	4	.250	Jorgensen, New York	20	2	0	4	.100
Morgan, Houston	16	4	0	3	.250	Dade, San Diego	11	1	0	2	.091
Nolan, Atl.-Cincinnati	12	3	0	1	.250	Evans, San Diego	11	1	0	0	.091
Trevino, New York	12	3	0	2	.250	Stennett, San Francisco	13	1	0	0	.077
Wohlford, San Francisco	48	12	0	8	.250	Howe, Houston	28	2	1	2	.071
Thomasson, Los Angeles	45	11	0	9	.244	Cruz, Cincinnati	22	1	0	0	.045
G. Vukovich, Phila.	45	11	0	5	.244	Gonzalez, Houston	11	0	0	0	.000
Milner, Pittsburgh	33	8	0	3	.242	Cardenal, New York	15	0	0	1	.000
Lum, Atlanta	50	12	0	4	.240						

AMERICAN LEAGUE PINCH-HITTING
(Compiled by Sports Information Center)

Club Pinch-Hitting

Club	AB.	H.	HR.	RBI.	Pct.	Club	AB.	H.	HR.	RBI.	Pct.
Baltimore	183	54	6	40	.295	Kansas City	98	25	1	17	.255
Texas	193	55	7	43	.285	Detroit	141	35	5	25	.248
California	117	33	2	27	.282	Cleveland	123	30	6	33	.244
Toronto	100	28	3	15	.280	Milwaukee	62	15	0	9	.242
Minnesota	205	56	4	40	.273	Oakland	117	26	3	12	.222
Chicago	170	45	4	34	.265	Seattle	147	27	4	19	.184
New York	137	35	6	39	.255	Boston	79	14	2	17	.177
						Totals	1872	478	53	370	.255

Individual Pinch-Hitting
(10 or More At-Bats)

Player—Club	AB.	H.	HR.	RBI.	Pct.	Player—Club	AB.	H.	HR.	RBI.	Pct.
Hebner, Detroit	11	6	2	6	.545	Ellis, Texas	15	4	0	3	.267
Roenicke, Baltimore	12	6	0	2	.500	Grubb, Texas	28	7	1	4	.250
Putnam, Texas	18	8	2	5	.444	Pruitt, Clev-Chi	20	5	0	5	.250
LaCock, Kansas City	12	5	0	1	.417	Nordhagen, Chicago	21	5	0	6	.238
Lowenstein, Baltimore	12	5	0	6	.417	Gamble, New York	17	4	1	8	.235
Newman, Oakland	12	5	0	2	.417	Wockenfuss, Detroit	17	4	1	6	.235
May, Baltimore	27	11	0	5	.407	Gross, Oakland	13	3	1	4	.231
Miller, California	10	4	0	2	.400	Peters, Detroit	13	3	0	0	.231
Sutherland, Chicago	10	4	0	0	.400	Sample, Texas	23	5	0	3	.217
Bosley, Chicago	27	10	0	7	.370	Narron, Seattle	14	3	1	5	.214
Carew, California	11	4	0	1	.364	Baines, Chicago	10	2	0	3	.200
Revering, Oakland	11	4	1	1	.364	Brohamer, Bos-Clev	15	3	0	1	.200
Spencer, New York	22	8	1	6	.364	Woods, Toronto	10	2	0	0	.200
Morales, Minnesota	36	13	2	9	.361	R. Jackson, Minnesota	21	4	1	5	.190
Ault, Toronto	14	5	1	2	.357	Corcoran, Detroit	16	3	0	0	.188
Wilfong, Minnesota	14	5	0	1	.357	Davis, Oakland	22	4	0	1	.182
Molinaro, Chicago	20	7	1	5	.350	Dwyer, Boston	11	2	0	2	.182
Harlow, California	12	4	0	4	.333	Ayala, Baltimore	28	5	2	9	.179
Hassey, Cleveland	18	6	0	4	.333	Meyer, Seattle	17	3	0	0	.176
Mackanin, Minnesota	15	5	0	1	.333	Hancock, Boston	12	2	0	2	.167
Squires, Chicago	15	5	0	3	.333	Piniella, New York	24	4	0	7	.167
Staub, Texas	15	5	2	7	.333	L. Roberts, Seattle	12	2	0	1	.167
Watson, New York	12	4	0	4	.333	Milbourne, Seattle	19	3	0	1	.158
Murcer, New York	22	7	0	3	.318	Zisk, Texas	19	3	1	6	.158
Roberts, Texas	13	4	1	2	.308	Thon, California	13	2	0	0	.154
Sofield, Minnesota	13	4	0	2	.308	Chalk, Kansas City	14	2	0	3	.143
Alexander, Cleveland	23	7	2	10	.304	Paciorek, Seattle	14	2	0	4	.143
Wathan, Kansas City	10	3	0	1	.300	Powell, Minnesota	14	2	0	0	.143
Crowley, Baltimore	37	11	1	6	.297	Adams, Minnesota	16	2	0	3	.125
Moore, Milwaukee	27	8	0	0	.296	Page, Oakland	19	2	0	2	.105
Norris, Texas	31	9	0	7	.290	Simpson, Seattle	11	1	0	1	.091
Braun, KC-Tor	35	10	0	6	.286	Stein, Seattle	11	1	0	0	.091
Thompson, Det-Calif	14	4	1	9	.286	Gray, Cleveland	12	1	1	2	.083
Kelly, Baltimore	29	8	2	7	.276	Quirk, Kansas City	12	1	0	0	.083
Goodwin, Minnesota	22	6	0	5	.273	Stinson, Seattle	12	1	0	0	.083
Soderholm, New York	11	3	1	4	.273	Bannister, Chi-Clev	13	0	0	0	.000
Summers, Detroit	26	7	1	5	.269						

PINCH-HOMERS FOR 1980

AMERICAN LEAGUE: Baltimore (6)—Ayala 2, Kelly 2, Crowley, Sakata. Boston (2)—Stapleton, Wolfe. California (2)—Cowens, Thompson. Chicago (4)—Foley, L. Johnson, Molinaro, Pryor. Cleveland (6)—Alexander 2, Johnson 2, Charboneau, Gray. Detroit (5)—Hebner 2, Parrish, Summers, Wockenfuss. Kansas City (1)—G. Brett. Milwaukee (0). Minnesota (4)—Morales 2, Edwards, R. Jackson. New York (6)—Gamble, Lefebvre, Nettles, Soderholm, Spencer, Werth. Oakland (3)—Gross, Klutts, Revering. Seattle (4)—Anderson, Horton, Narron, Walton. Texas (7)—Putnam 2, Staub 2, Grubb, Roberts, Zisk. Toronto (3)—Ault, Davis, Howell.

NATIONAL LEAGUE: Atlanta (6)—Burroughs 3, Pocoroba 2, Matthews. Chicago (3)—Biittner, Henderson, Johnson. Cincinnati (4)—Spilman 2, Auerbach, Bench. Houston (4)—Howe, Landestoy, Leonard, Walling. Los Angeles (3)—Ferguson, Guerrero, Monday. Montreal (4)—Bernazard, Office, Tamargo, White. New York (4)—Norman 2, Henderson, Moreno. Philadelphia (0). Pittsburgh (2)—Easler 2. St. Louis (1)—Simmons. San Diego (5)—Joshua, Mumphrey, Tenace, Turner, Winfield. San Francisco (3)—Bourjos, Evans, Herndon.

Roberts, Dwyer Upstaged Winfield in Re-Entry Draft

By LARRY WIGGE

If you combined the 1980 home run and runs batted in totals of Dave W. Roberts and Jim Dwyer, you would still come up short of the marks compiled by slugging outfielder Dave Winfield. But both Roberts and Dwyer commanded more attention than Winfield in baseball's fifth annual re-entry draft November 13.

Roberts, a catcher-infielder for the Rangers, was the first player chosen (by the Cubs) and the most-sought-after player in the draft. The Rangers retained rights to Roberts and 12 other clubs put in their claim for the .240 career hitter, once a first-round draft choice by the Padres. Dwyer was claimed by 11 clubs in addition to the Red Sox, for whom he hit .285 in '80.

In the end, however, Winfield won out when he signed a $13 million contract for 10 years with the Yankees. A stipulation in the pact, which made Winfield the highest-paid player ever, calls for up to a 10 percent cost of living increase, which over the 10-year period is estimated to increase the worth of the agreement to over $20 million.

The Yanks, always prominent in the free-agent proceedings, had failed to land former Dodgers pitcher Don Sutton (who agreed to terms with the Astros) before signing Winfield.

In addition to Winfield and Sutton, Roberts signed with the Astros and Dwyer switched to the Orioles. Darrell Porter left Kansas City in favor of the Cardinals and Claudell Washington became the first free-agent to sign when he inked a lucrative agreement with the Braves. Gaylord Perry also agreed to terms with the Braves. Ron LeFlore, who led the N. L. with 97 stolen bases in '80, signed with the White Sox—the only club which selected the fleet outfielder in the draft. The White Sox also signed catcher Jim Essian.

The Mets laid claim to Rusty Staub, Mike Cubbage and Dave A. Roberts. Pat Kelly bolted to the Indians, Lee May went to the Royals, Roy Howell to the Brewers, Bill Stein to the Rangers, Jose Morales to the Orioles and Bill Travers, Geoff Zahn, John D'Acquisto and Juan Beniquez to the Angels. The Reds signed Larry Biittner, Cincinnati's first endeavor into the free-agent market. Ray Burris signed with the Expos and Bill Castro went to the Yanks.

Re-signing with their 1980 clubs were: Stan Bahnsen and Willie Montanez with the Expos, Tug McGraw and Del Unser with the Phillies, John Milner with the Pirates and Dan Spillner with the Indians.

Following is a list of 48 free-agent players and the teams which selected them in the re-entry draft. The number in parentheses after each player's name indicates the number of clubs which picked him. The number after each club indicates the round in which the player was chosen. Capital letters indicate the player's former club chose to retain negotiating rights:

STAN BAHNSEN (5): Phillies (3), Braves (5), Angels (11), Rangers (11), EXPOS.
JUAN BENIQUEZ (4): Orioles (6), Indians (8), White Sox (9), Angels (10).
LARRY BIITTNER (3): Reds (2), Pirates (5), Giants (8).
GLENN BORGMANN (0): Not selected.
STEVE BRAUN (0): Not selected.
RAY BURRIS (4): Expos (2), Rangers (7), Mariners (9), METS.
JOSE CARDENAL (0): Not selected.
BILL CASTRO (7): A's (2), Expos (3), Rangers (6), Mariners (7), Yankees (9),

Mets (12), BREWERS.

MIKE CUBBAGE (6): Mariners (4), Orioles (4), Brewers (6), Mets (7), White Sox (7), TWINS.

JOHN D'ACQUISTO (8): Brewers (2), Mets (4), Angels (4), Indians (5), Phillies (5), Yankees (5), Giants (5), EXPOS.

JIM DWYER (12): Phillies (1), Orioles (3), Giants (4), Expos (4), White Sox (5), Rangers (5), Brewers (5), Mets (6), Yankees (6), Indians (9), Pirates (12), RED SOX.

JIM ESSIAN (7): Mariners (1), Giants (2), Blue Jays (3), White Sox (3), Rangers (3), Brewers (7), A's.

ED FIGUEROA (1): Brewers (10).

BUD HARRELSON (0): Not selected.

VIC HARRIS (0): Not selected.

MARC HILL (0): Not selected.

ROY HOWELL (6): A's (3), Brewers (3), White Sox (4), Indians (6), Orioles (8), Yankees (10).

JESSE JEFFERSON (1): Mariners (10).

MICK KELLEHER (1): Rangers (8).

PAT KELLY (1): Indians (10).

PETE LaCOCK (0): Not selected.

RON LeFLORE (1): White Sox (11).

LEE MAY (0): Not selected.

TUG McGRAW (0): Not selected.

JOHN MILNER (3): Orioles (7), Mets (10), PIRATES.

WILLIE MONTANEZ (3): Pirates (7), Rangers (9), EXPOS.

JERRY MORALES (1): Orioles (9).

JOSE MORALES (7): Red Sox (1), Dodgers (3), Mets (5), Orioles (5), Pirates (6), Mariners (11), TWINS.

JOHNNY OATES (0): Not selected.

MARTY PATTIN (3): A's (5), Mariners (8), Angels (9).

GAYLORD PERRY (3): Braves (4), Pirates (9), YANKEES.

DARRELL PORTER (9): Blue Jays (1), White Sox (1), A's (1), Cardinals (2), Angels (3), Pirates (4), Brewers (4), Astros (4), ROYALS.

DAVE RADER (0): Not selected.

LENNY RANDLE (3): Mariners (3), Giants (5), White Sox (6).

DAVE A. ROBERTS (0): Not selected.

DAVE W. ROBERTS (13): Cubs (1), Mariners (2), Blue Jays (2), White Sox (2), Phillies (2), Dodgers (2), Astros (2), Orioles (2), Giants (3), Yankees (4), Angels (8), Brewers (8), RANGERS.

MIKE SADEK (3): White Sox (13), Rangers (13), GIANTS.

CHARLIE SPIKES (0): Not selected.

DAN SPILLNER (5): Mariners (5), Angels (6), Rangers (10), White Sox (15), INDIANS.

RUSTY STAUB (8): Astros (6), Indians (7), Yankees (7), Mets (8), White Sox (8), Pirates (8), Mariners (12), RANGERS.

BILL STEIN (4): White Sox (10), Rangers (12), Angels (13), MARINERS.

DON SUTTON (10): Angels (1), Indians (1), Expos (1), Brewers (1), Mets (2), Rangers (2), Braves (2), Pirates (2), Yankees (2), Astros (3).

LUIS TIANT (0): Not selected.

BILL TRAVERS (8): Angels (2), Mets (3), Indians (3), Rangers (4), A's (4), Astros (5), Mariners (6), BREWERS.

DEL UNSER (5): Red Sox (2), Giants (6), Brewers (9), Pirates (10), PHILLIES.

CLAUDELL WASHINGTON (6): Giants (1), Dodgers (1), Braves (3), Pirates (3), Yankees (4), METS.

DAVE WINFIELD (11): Mets (1), Cardinals (1), Braves (1), Pirates (1), Reds (1), Astros (1), Orioles (1), Yankees (1), Indians (2), Angels (5), PADRES.

GEOFF ZAHN (6): Rangers (1), Indians (4), Phillies (4), Angels (7), Yankees (8), TWINS.

The Sporting News AWARDS

THE SPORTING NEWS MVP AWARDS

AMERICAN LEAGUE

Year	Player	Club	Points
1929	Al Simmons, Philadelphia, of		40
1930	Joseph Cronin, Washington, ss		52
1931	H. Louis Gehrig, New York, 1b		40
1932	James Foxx, Philadelphia, 1b		56
1933	James Foxx, Philadelphia, 1b		49
1934	H. Louis Gehrig, New York, 1b		51
1935	Henry Greenberg, Detroit, 1b		64
1936	H. Louis Gehrig, New York, 1b		55
1937	Charles Gehringer, Detroit, 2b		78
1938	James Foxx, Boston, 1b		305
1939	Joseph DiMaggio, N. York, of		280
1940	Henry Greenberg, Detroit, of		292
1941	Joseph DiMaggio, N. York, of		291
1942	Joseph Gordon, New York, 2b		270
1943	Spurgeon Chandler, N. Y., p		246
1944	Robert Doerr, Boston, 2b		
1945	Edward J. Mayo, Detroit, 2b		

NATIONAL LEAGUE

Player	Club	Points
No selection		
William Terry, New York, 1b		47
Charles Klein, Philadelphia, of		40
Charles Klein, Philadelphia, of		46
Carl Hubbell, New York, p		64
Jerome Dean, St. Louis, p		57
J. Floyd Vaughan, Pitts., ss		42
Carl Hubbell, New York, p		61
Joseph Medwick, St. Louis, of		70
Ernest Lombardi, Cincinnati, c		229
William Walters, Cincinnati, p		303
Frank McCormick, Cinn., 1b		274
Adolph Camilli, Brooklyn, 1b		300
Morton Cooper, St. Louis, p		263
Stanley Musial, St. Louis, of		267
Martin Marion, St. Louis, ss		
Thomas Holmes, Boston, of		

THE SPORTING NEWS PLAYER, PITCHER OF YEAR

	AMERICAN LEAGUE		NATIONAL LEAGUE
1948	Louis Boudreau, Cleveland, ss	1948	Stanley Musial, St. Louis, of-1b
	Robert Lemon, Cleveland, p		John Sain, Boston, p
1949	Theodore Williams, Boston, of	1949	Enos Slaughter, St. Louis, of
	Ellis Kinder, Boston, p		Howard Pollet, St. Louis, p
1950	Philip Rizzuto, New York, ss	1950	Ralph Kiner, Pittsburgh, of
	Robert Lemon, Cleveland, p		C. James Konstanty, Phila., p
1951	Ferris Fain, Philadelphia, 1b	1951	Stanley Musial, St. Louis, of
	Robert Feller, Cleveland, p		Elwin Roe, Brooklyn, p
1952	Luscious Easter, Cleveland, 1b	1952	Henry Sauer, Chicago, of
	Robert Shantz, Philadelphia, p		Robin Roberts, Philadelphia, p
1953	Albert Rosen, Cleveland, 3b	1953	Roy Campanella, Brooklyn, c
	Erv (Bob) Porterfield, Wash., p		Warren Spahn, Milwaukee, p
1954	Roberto Avila, Cleveland, 2b	1954	Willie Mays, New York, of
	Robert Lemon, Cleveland, p		John Antonelli, New York, p
1955	Albert Kaline, Detroit, of	1955	Edwin Snider, Brooklyn, of
	Edward Ford, New York, p		Robin Roberts, Philadelphia, p
1956	Mickey Mantle, New York, of	1956	Henry Aaron, Milwaukee, of
	W. William Pierce, Chicago, p		Donald Newcombe, Brooklyn, p
1957	Theodore Williams, Boston, of	1957	Stanley Musial, St. Louis, 1b
	W. William Pierce, Chicago, p		Warren Spahn, Milwaukee, p
1958	Jack Jensen, Boston, of	1958	Ernest Banks, Chicago, ss
	Robert Turley, New York, p		Warren Spahn, Milwaukee, p
1959	J. Nelson Fox, Chicago, 2b	1959	Ernest Banks, Chicago, ss
	Early Wynn, Chicago, p		Samuel Jones, San Francisco, p
1960	Roger Maris, New York, of	1960	Richard Groat, Pittsburgh, ss
	Charles Estrada, Baltimore, p		Vernon Law, Pittsburgh, p
1961	Roger Maris, New York, of	1961	Frank Robinson, Cincinnati, of
	Edward Ford, New York, p		Warren Spahn, Milwaukee, p
1962	Mickey Mantle, New York, of	1962	Maurice Wills, Los Angeles, ss
	Richard Donovan, Cleveland, p		Donald Drysdale, Los Angeles, p
1963	Albert Kaline, Detroit, of	1963	Henry Aaron, Milwaukee, of
	Edward Ford, New York, p		Sanford Koufax, Los Angeles, p
1964	Brooks Robinson, Baltimore, 3b	1964	Kenton Boyer, St. Louis, 3b
	Dean Chance, Los Angeles, p		Sanford Koufax, Los Angeles, p

PLAYER, PITCHER OF YEAR—Continued

AMERICAN LEAGUE	NATIONAL LEAGUE
1965—Pedro (Tony) Oliva, Minn., of James Grant, Minnesota, p	1965—Willie Mays, San Francisco, of Sanford Koufax, Los Angeles, p
1966—Frank Robinson, Baltimore, of James Kaat, Minnesota, p	1966—Roberto Clemente, Pittsburgh, of Sanford Koufax, Los Angeles, p
1967—Carl Yastrzemski, Boston, of Jim Lonborg, Boston, p	1967—Orlando Cepeda, St. Louis, 1b Mike McCormick, San Fran., p
1968—Ken Harrelson, Boston, of Denny McLain, Detroit, p	1968—Pete Rose, Cincinnati, of Bob Gibson, St. Louis, p
1969—Harmon Killebrew, Minn., 1b-3b Denny McLain, Detroit, p	1969—Willie McCovey, San Fran., 1b Tom Seaver, New York, p
1970—Harmon Killebrew, Minn., 3b Sam McDowell, Cleveland, p	1970—Johnny Bench, Cin., c Bob Gibson, St. Louis, p
1971—Pedro (Tony) Oliva, Minn., of Vida Blue, Oakland, p	1971—Joe Torre, St. Louis, 3b Ferguson Jenkins, Chicago, p
1972—Richie Allen, Chicago, 1b Wilbur Wood, Chicago, p	1972—Billy Williams, Chicago, of Steve Carlton, Philadelphia, p
1973—Reggie Jackson, Oakland, of Jim Palmer, Baltimore, p	1973—Bobby Bonds, San Francisco, of Ron Bryant, San Francisco, p
1974—Jeff Burroughs, Texas, of Jim Hunter, Oakland, p	1974—Lou Brock, St. Louis, of Mike Marshall, Los Angeles, p
1975—Fred Lynn, Boston, of Jim Palmer, Baltimore, p	1975—Joe Morgan, Cincinnati, 2b Tom Seaver, New York, p
1976—Thurman Munson, New York, c Jim Palmer, Baltimore, p	1976—George Foster, Cincinnati, of Randy Jones, San Diego, p
1977—Rod Carew, Minnesota, 1b Nolan Ryan, California, p	1977—George Foster, Cincinnati, of Steve Carlton, Philadelphia, p
1978—Jim Rice, Boston, of Ron Guidry, New York, p	1978—Dave Parker, Pittsburgh, of Vida Blue, San Francisco, p
1979—Don Baylor, California, of Mike Flanagan, Baltimore, p	1979—Keith Hernandez, St. Louis, 1b Joe Niekro, Houston, p
1980—George Brett, Kansas City, 3b Steve Stone, Baltimore, p	1980—Mike Schmidt, Philadelphia, 3b Steve Carlton, Philadelphia, p

FIREMAN (Relief Pitcher) OF THE YEAR

Year	Player Club	Player Club
1960—Mike Fornieles, Boston		Lindy McDaniel, St. Louis
1961—Luis Arroyo, New York		Stu Miller, San Francisco
1962—Dick Radatz, Boston		Roy Face, Pittsburgh
1963—Stu Miller, Baltimore		Lindy McDaniel, Chicago
1964—Dick Radatz, Boston		Al McBean, Pittsburgh
1965—Eddie Fisher, Chicago		Ted Abernathy, Chicago
1966—Jack Aker, Kansas City		Phil Regan, Los Angeles
1967—Minnie Rojas, California		Ted Abernathy, Cincinnati
1968—Wilbur Wood, Chicago		Phil Regan, L.A.-Chicago
1969—Ron Perranoski, Minnesota		Wayne Granger, Cincinnati
1970—Ron Perranoski, Minnesota		Wayne Granger, Cincinnati
1971—Ken Sanders, Milwaukee		Dave Giusti, Pittsburgh
1972—Sparky Lyle, New York		Clay Carroll, Cincinnati
1973—John Hiller, Detroit		Mike Marshall, Montreal
1974—Terry Forster, Chicago		Mike Marshall, Los Angeles
1975—Rich Gossage, Chicago		Al Hrabosky, St. Louis
1976—Bill Campbell, Minnesota		Rawly Eastwick, Cincinnati
1977—Bill Campbell, Boston		Rollie Fingers, San Diego
1978—Rich Gossage, New York		Rollie Fingers, San Diego
1979—Mike Marshall, Minnesota Jim Kern, Texas		Bruce Sutter, Chicago
1980—Dan Quisenberry, Kansas City		Rollie Fingers, San Diego Tom Hume, Cincinnati

THE SPORTING NEWS ROOKIE AWARDS

1946—Combined selection—Delmer Ennis, Philadelphia, N. L., of
1947—Combined selection—Jack Robinson, Brooklyn, 1b
1948—Combined selection—Richie Ashburn, Philadelphia, N. L., of

	AMERICAN LEAGUE		NATIONAL LEAGUE	
Year	Player	Club	Player	Club
1949—	Roy Sievers, St. Louis, of		Donald Newcombe, Brooklyn, p	
1950—	Combined selection—Edward Ford, New York, A. L., p			
1951—	Orestes Minoso, Chicago, of		Willie Mays, New York, of	
1952—	Clinton Courtney, St. Louis, c		Joseph Black, Brooklyn, p	
1953—	Harvey Kuenn, Detroit, ss		James Gilliam, Brooklyn, 2b	
1954—	Robert Grim, New York, p		Wallace Moon, St. Louis, of	
1955—	Herbert Score, Cleveland, p		William Virdon, St. Louis, of	
1956—	Luis Aparicio, Chicago, ss		Frank Robinson, Cincinnati, of	
1957—	Anthony Kubek, New York, inf-of		Edward Bouchee, Philadelphia, 1b	
	(No pitcher named)		Jack Sanford, Philadelphia, p	
1958—	Albert Pearson, Washington, of		Orlando Cepeda, San Francisco, 1b	
	Ryne Duren, New York, p		Carlton Willey, Milwaukee, p	
1959—	W. Robert Allison, Washington, of		Willie McCovey, San Francisco, 1b	
1960—	Ronald Hansen, Baltimore, ss		Frank Howard, Los Angeles, of	
1961—	Richard Howser, Kansas City, ss		Billy Williams, Chicago, of	
	Donald Schwall, Boston, p		Kenneth Hunt, Cincinnati, p	
1962—	Thomas Tresh, New York, of-ss		Kenneth Hubbs, Chicago, 2b	
1963—	Peter Ward, Chicago, 3b		Peter Rose, Cincinnati, 2b	
	Gary Peters, Chicago, p		Raymond Culp, Philadelphia, p	
1964—	Pedro (Tony) Oliva, Minn., of		Richard Allen, Philadelphia, 3b	
	Wallace Bunker, Baltimore, p		William McCool, Cincinnati, p	
1965—	Curtis Blefary, Baltimore, of		Joseph Morgan, Houston, 2b	
	Marcelino Lopez, California, p		Frank Linzy, San Francisco, p	
1966—	Tommie Agee, Chicago, of		Tommy Helms, Cincinnati, 3b	
	James Nash, Kansas City, p		Donald Sutton, Los Angeles, p	
1967—	Rod Carew, Minnesota, 2b		Lee May, Cincinnati, 1b	
	Tom Phoebus, Baltimore, p		Dick Hughes, St. Louis, p	
1968—	Del Unser, Washington, of		Johnny Bench, Cincinnati, c	
	Stan Bahnsen, New York, p		Jerry Koosman, New York, p	
1969—	Carlos May, Chicago, of		Coco Laboy, Montreal, 3b	
	Mike Nagy, Boston, p		Tom Griffin, Houston, p	
1970—	Roy Foster, Cleveland, of		Bernie Carbo, Cincinnati, of	
	Bert Blyleven, Minnesota, p		Carl Morton, Montreal, p	
1971—	Chris Chambliss, Cleveland, 1b		Earl Williams, Atlanta, c	
	Bill Parsons, Milwaukee, p		Reggie Cleveland, St. Louis, p	
1972—	Carlton Fisk, Boston, c		Dave Rader, San Francisco, c	
	Dick Tidrow, Cleveland, p		Jon Matlack, New York, p	
1973—	Al Bumbry, Baltimore, of		Gary Matthews, San Fran., of	
	Steve Busby, Kansas City, p		Steve Rogers, Montreal, p	
1974—	Mike Hargrove, Texas, 1b		Greg Gross, Houston, of	
	Frank Tanana, California, p		John D'Acquisto, San Francisco, p	
1975—	Fred Lynn, Boston, of		Gary Carter, Montreal, of-c	
	Dennis Eckersley, Cleveland, p		John Montefusco, San Francisco, p	
1976—	Butch Wynegar, Minnesota, c		Larry Herndon, San Francisco, of	
	Mark Fidrych, Detroit, p		Butch Metzger, San Diego, p	
1977—	Mitchell Page, Oakland, of		Andre Dawson, Montreal, of	
	Dave Rozema, Detroit, p		Bob Owchinko, San Diego, p	
1978—	Paul Molitor, Milwaukee, 2b		Bob Horner, Atlanta, 3b	
	Rich Gale, Kansas City, p		Don Robinson, Pittsburgh, p	
1979—	Pat Putnam, Texas, 1b		Jeff Leonard, Houston, of	
	Mark Clear, California, p		Rick Sutcliffe, Los Angeles, p	
1980—	Joe Charboneau, Cleveland, of		Lonnie Smith, Philadelphia, of	
	Britt Burns, Chicago, p		Bill Gullickson, Montreal, p	

MAJOR LEAGUE EXECUTIVE

Year	Executive	Club	Year	Executive	Club
1936	Branch Rickey, St. Louis NL		1959	E. J. (Buzzie) Bavasi, L.A. NL	
1937	Edward Barrow, New York AL		1960	George Weiss, New York AL	
1938	Warren Giles, Cincinnati NL		1961	Dan Topping, New York AL	
1939	Larry MacPhail, Brooklyn NL		1962	Fred Haney, Los Angeles AL	
1940	W. O. Briggs, Sr., Detroit AL		1963	Vaughan (Bing) Devine, St.L.NL	
1941	Edward Barrow, New York AL		1964	Vaughan (Bing) Devine, St.L.NL	
1942	Branch Rickey, St. Louis NL		1965	Calvin Griffith, Minnesota AL	
1943	Clark Griffith, Washington AL		1966	Lee MacPhail, Commissioner's Office	
1944	Wm. O. DeWitt, St. Louis AL				
1945	Philip K. Wrigley, Chicago NL		1967	Dick O'Connell, Boston AL	
1946	Thomas A. Yawkey, Boston AL		1968	James Campbell, Detroit AL	
1947	Branch Rickey, Brooklyn NL		1969	John Murphy, New York NL	
1948	Bill Veeck, Cleveland AL		1970	Harry Dalton, Baltimore AL	
1949	Robt. Carpenter, Phila'phia NL		1971	Cedric Tallis, Kansas City AL	
1950	George Weiss, New York AL		1972	Roland Hemond, Chicago AL	
1951	George Weiss, New York AL		1973	Bob Howsam, Cincinnati NL	
1952	George Weiss, New York AL		1974	Gabe Paul, New York AL	
1953	Louis Perini, Milwaukee NL		1975	Dick O'Connell, Boston AL	
1954	Horace Stoneham, N. York NL		1976	Joe Burke, Kansas City AL	
1955	Walter O'Malley, Brooklyn NL		1977	Bill Veeck, Chicago AL	
1956	Gabe Paul, Cincinnati NL		1978	Spec Richardson, San Fran. NL	
1957	Frank Lane, St. Louis NL		1979	Hank Peters, Baltimore AL	
1958	Joe L. Brown, Pittsburgh NL		1980	Tal Smith, Houston NL	

MAJOR LEAGUE MANAGER

Year	Manager	Club	Year	Manager	Club
1936	Joe McCarthy, New York AL		1959	Walter Alston, Los Angeles NL	
1937	Bill McKechnie, Boston NL		1960	Danny Murtaugh, Pitts. NL	
1938	Joe McCarthy, New York AL		1961	Ralph Houk, New York AL	
1939	Leo Durocher, Brooklyn NL		1962	Bill Rigney, Los Angeles AL	
1940	Bill McKechnie, Cincinnati NL		1963	Walter Alston, Los Angeles NL	
1941	Billy Southworth, St. Louis NL		1964	Johnny Keane, St. Louis NL	
1942	Billy Southworth, St. Louis NL		1965	Sam Mele, Minnesota AL	
1943	Joe McCarthy, New York AL		1966	Hank Bauer, Baltimore AL	
1944	Luke Sewell, St. Louis AL		1967	Dick Williams, Boston AL	
1945	Ossie Bluege, Washington AL		1968	Mayo Smith, Detroit AL	
1946	Eddie Dyer, St. Louis NL		1969	Gil Hodges, New York NL	
1947	Bucky Harris, New York AL		1970	Danny Murtaugh, Pittsb'gh NL	
1948	Bill Meyer, Pittsburgh NL		1971	Charlie Fox, San Francisco NL	
1949	Casey Stengel, New York AL		1972	Chuck Tanner, Chicago AL	
1950	Red Rolfe, Detroit AL		1973	Gene Mauch, Montreal NL	
1951	Leo Durocher, New York NL		1974	Bill Virdon, New York AL	
1952	Eddie Stanky, St. Louis NL		1975	Darrell Johnson, Boston AL	
1953	Casey Stengel, New York AL		1976	Danny Ozark, Philadelphia NL	
1954	Leo Durocher, New York NL		1977	Earl Weaver, Baltimore AL	
1955	Walter Alston, Brooklyn NL		1978	George Bamberger, Milw'kee AL	
1956	Birdie Tebbetts, Cincinnati NL		1979	Earl Weaver, Baltimore AL	
1957	Fred Hutchinson, St. Louis NL		1980	Bill Virdon, Houston NL	
1958	Casey Stengel, New York AL				

MAJOR LEAGUE PLAYER

Year	Player	Club	Year	Player	Club
1936	Carl Hubbell, New York NL		1939	Joe DiMaggio, New York AL	
1937	Johnny Allen, Cleveland AL		1940	Bob Feller, Cleveland AL	
1938	Johnny Vander Meer, Cinn. NL		1941	Ted Williams, Boston AL	

MAJOR LEAGUE PLAYER—Continued

Year	Player	Club
1942—	Ted Williams, Boston AL
1943—	Spud Chandler, New York AL
1944—	Marty Marion, St. Louis NL
1945—	Hal Newhouser, Detroit AL
1946—	Stan Musial, St. Louis NL
1947—	Ted Williams, Boston AL
1948—	Lou Boudreau, Cleveland AL
1949—	Ted Williams, Boston AL
1950—	Phil Rizzuto, New York AL
1951—	Stan Musial, St. Louis NL
1952—	Robin Roberts, Philadelphia NL
1953—	Al Rosen, Cleveland AL
1954—	Willie Mays, New York NL
1955—	Duke Snider, Brooklyn NL
1956—	Mickey Mantle, New York AL
1957—	Ted Williams, Boston AL
1958—	Bob Turley, New York AL
1959—	Early Wynn, Chicago AL
1960—	Bill Mazeroski, Pittsburgh NL
1961—	Roger Maris, New York AL
1962—	Maury Wills, Los Angeles NL
	Don Drysdale, Los Angeles NL
1963—	Sandy Koufax, Los Angeles NL
1964—	Ken Boyer, St. Louis NL
1965—	Sandy Koufax, Los Angeles NL
1966—	Frank Robinson, Baltimore AL
1967—	Carl Yastrzemski, Boston AL
1968—	Denny McLain, Detroit AL
1969—	Willie McCovey, San Fran. NL
1970—	Johnny Bench, Cin. NL
1971—	Joe Torre, St. Louis NL
1972—	Billy Williams, Chicago NL
1973—	Reggie Jackson, Oakland AL
1974—	Lou Brock, St. Louis NL
1975—	Joe Morgan, Cincinnati NL
1976—	Joe Morgan, Cincinnati NL
1977—	Rod Carew, Minnesota AL
1978—	Ron Guidry, New York AL
1979—	Willie Stargell, Pittsburgh NL
1980—	George Brett, Kansas City AL

MINOR LEAGUE EXECUTIVE (HIGHER CLASSIFICATIONS)
(Restricted to Class AAA Starting in 1963)

Year	Executive	Club
1936—	Earl Mann, Atlanta, Southern
1937—	Robt. LaMotte, Savannah, Sally
1938—	Louis McKenna, St. Paul, A.A.
1939—	Bruce Dudley, Louisville, A.A.
1940—	Roy Hamey, Kansas City, A.A.
1941—	Emil Sick, Seattle, PCL
1942—	Bill Veeck, Milwaukee, A.A.
1943—	Clar. Rowland, Los Angeles, PCL
1944—	William Mulligan, Seattle, PCL
1945—	Bruce Dudley, Louisville, A.A.
1946—	Earl Mann, Atlanta, Southern
1947—	Wm. Purnhage, Waterloo, I.I.I.
1948—	Ed. Glennon, Bir'ham, Southern
1949—	Ted Sullivan, Indianapolis, A.A.
1950—	Cl. (Brick) Laws, Oakland, PCL
1951—	Robert Howsam, Denver, West.
1952—	Jack Cooke, Toronto, Int.
1953—	Richard Burnett, Dallas, Texas
1954—	Edward Stumpf, Indpls., A.A.
1955—	Dewey Soriano, Seattle, PCL
1956—	Robert Howsam, Denver, A.A.
1957—	John Stiglmeier, Buffalo, Int.
1958—	Ed. Glennon, Bir'ham, Southern
1959—	Ed. Leishman, Salt Lake, PCL
1960—	Ray Winder, Little Rock, Sou.
1961—	Elten Schiller, Omaha, A.A.
1962—	Geo. Sisler, Jr., Rochester, Int.
1963—	Lewis Matlin, Hawaii, PCL
1964—	Ed. Leishman, San Diego, PCL
1965—	Harold Cooper, Columbus, Int.
1966—	John Quinn, Jr., Hawaii, PCL
1967—	Hillman Lyons, Richmond, Int.
1968—	Gabe Paul, Jr., Tulsa, PCL
1969—	Bill Gardner, Louisville, Int.
1970—	Dick King, Wichita, A.A.
1971—	Carl Steinfeldt, Jr., Roch'ter, Int.
1972—	Don Labbruzzo, Evansville, A.A.
1973—	Merle Miller, Tucson, PCL
1974—	John Carbray, Sacramento, PCL
1975—	Stan Naccarato, Tacoma, PCL
1976—	Art Teece, Salt Lake City, PCL
1977—	George Sisler, Jr., Col'bus, Int.
1978—	Willie Sanchez, Albu'que, PCL
1979—	George Sisler, Jr., Col'bus, Int.
1980—	Jim Burris, Denver, A.A.

MINOR LEAGUE EXECUTIVE (LOWER CLASSIFICATIONS)
(Separate Awards for Class AA and Class A Started in 1963)

Year	Executive	Club
1950—	H. Cooper, Hutch'son, West. A.
1951—	O. W. (Bill) Hayes, T'ple, B.S.
1952—	Hillman Lyons, Danville, MOV
1953—	Carl Roth, Peoria, III
1954—	James Meaghan, Cedar R., III
1955—	John Petrakis, Dubuque, MOV
1956—	Marvin Milkes, Fresno, Calif.
1957—	Richard Wagner, L'coln, West.

MINOR LEAGUE EXECUTIVE (LOWER CLASSIFICATIONS)
(Continued)

Year	Executive	Club
1958	Gerald Waring, Macon, Sally
1959	Clay Dennis, Des Moines, III
1960	Hubert Kittle, Yakima, Northw.
1961	David Steele, Fresno, California
1962	John Quinn, Jr., S. Jose, Calif.
1963	Hugh Finnerty, Tulsa, Texas
	Ben Jewell, M. Valley. Pioneer
1964	Glynn West, B'ham, Southern
	Jas. Bayens, Rock Hill, W. Car.
1965	Dick Butler, Dallas-Ft.W., Tex.
	Ken. Blackman, Quad C., Midw.
1966	Tom Fleming, Evansville, South.
	Cappy Harada, Lodi, California
1967	Robt. Quinn, Reading, East.
	Pat Williams, Spar'burg, W. C.
1968	Phil Howser, Charlotte, South.
	Merle Miller, Burlington, Midw.
1969	Charlie Blaney, Albuq., Tex.
	Bill Gorman, Visalia, Calif.
1970	Carl Sawatski, Arkansas, Tex.
	Bob Williams, Bakersfield, Calif.

Year	Executive	Club
1971	Miles Wolff, Savannah, Dixie A.
	Ed Holtz, Appleton, Midwest
1972	John Begzos, S. Antonio, Texas
	Bob Piccinini, Modesto, Calif.
1973	Dick Kravitz, Jacksonville, Sou.
	Fritz Colschen, Clinton, Midw.
1974	Jim Paul, El Paso, Texas
	Bing Russell, Portland, N'west
1975	Jim Paul, El Paso, Texas
	Cordy Jensen, Eugene, N'west
1976	Woodrow Reid, Chat'ooga, Sou.
	Don Buchheister, Ced. Rap., Mid.
1977	Jim Paul, El Paso, Texas
	Harry Pells, Quad Cities, Midw.
1978	Larry Schmittou, Nashville, Sou.
	Dave Hersh, Appleton, Midw.
1979	Bill Rigney Jr., Midland, Tex.
	Tom Romenesko, Greensboro, W.C.
1980	Frances Crockett, C'lotte, Sou.
	Tom Romenesko, G'sboro, Sally

MINOR LEAGUE MANAGER

Year	Manager	Club
1936	Al Sothoron, Milwaukee, A.A.
1937	Jake Flowers, Salis'y, East. Sh.
1938	Paul Richards, Atlanta, South.
1939	Bill Meyer, Kansas City, A.A.
1940	Larry Gilbert, Nashville, South.
1941	Burt Shotton, Columbus, A.A.
1942	Eddie Dyer, Columbus, A.A.
1943	Nick Cullop, Columbus, A.A.
1944	Al Thomas, Baltimore, Int.
1945	Lefty O'Doul, San Fran., PCL
1946	Clay Hopper, Montreal, Int.
1947	Nick Cullop, Milwaukee, A.A.
1948	Casey Stengel, Oakland, PCL
1949	Fred Haney, Hollywood, PCL
1950	Rollie Hemsley, Columbus, A.A.
1951	Charlie Grimm, Milw., A.A.
1952	Luke Appling, Memphis, South.
1953	Bobby Bragan, Hollywood, PCL
1954	Kerby Farrell, Indpls., A.A.
1955	Bill Rigney, Minneapolis, A.A.
1956	Kerby Farrell, Indpls., A.A.
1957	Ben Geraghty, Wichita, A.A.
1958	Cal Ermer, Birmingham, South.

Year	Manager	Club
1959	Pete Reiser, Victoria, Texas
1960	Mel McGaha, Toronto, Int.
1961	Kerby Farrell, Buffalo, Int.
1962	Ben Geraghty, Jackson'le, Int.
1963	Rollie Hemsley, Indpls., Int.
1964	Harry Walker, Jacks'vle., Int.
1965	Grady Hatton, Okla. City, PCL
1966	Bob Lemon, Seattle, PCL
1967	Bob Skinner, San Diego, PCL
1968	Jack Tighe, Toledo, Int.
1969	Clyde McCullough, Tide., Int.
1970	Tom Lasorda, Spokane, PCL
1971	Del Rice, Salt Lake City, PCL
1972	Hank Bauer, Tidewater, Int.
1973	Joe Morgan, Charleston, Int.
1974	Joe Altobelli, Rochester, Int.
1975	Joe Frazier, Tidewater, Int.
1976	Vern Rapp, Denver, A.A.
1977	Tommy Thompson, Arkan., Tex.
1978	Les Moss, Evansville, A.A.
1979	Vern Benson, Syracuse, Int.
1980	Hal Lanier, Springfield, A.A.

MINOR LEAGUE PLAYER

Year	Player	Club
1936	Jn. Vander Meer, Durham, Pied.
1937	Charlie Keller, Newark, Int.
1938	Fred Hutchinson, Seattle, PCL
1939	Lou Novikoff, Tulsa-Los A'les.
1940	Phil Rizzuto, Kansas City, A.A.
1941	John Lindell, Newark, Int.
1942	Dick Barrett, Seattle, PCL
1943	Chet Covington, Scranton, East.
1944	Rip Collins, Albany, Eastern
1945	Gil Coan, Chattanooga, South.
1946	Sibby Sisti, Indianapolis, A.A.
1947	Hank Sauer, Syracuse, Int.
1948	Gene Woodling, S. F., PCL
1949	Orie Arntzen, Albany, Eastern
1950	Frank Saucier, San Ant'o, Tex.
1951	Gene Conley, Hartford, Eastern
1952	Bill Skowron, Kans. City, A.A.
1953	Gene Conley, Toledo, A.A.
1954	Herb Score, Indianapolis, A.A.
1955	John Murff, Dallas, Texas
1956	Steve Bilko, Los Angeles, PCL
1957	Norm Siebern, Denver, A.A.
1958	Jim O'Toole, Nashville, South.
1959	Frank Howard, Victoria-Spok.

Year	Player	Club
1960	Willie Davis, Spokane, PCL
1961	Howie Koplitz, Bir'ham, South.
1962	Bob Bailey, Columbus, Int.
1963	Don Buford, Indianapolis, Int.
1964	Mel Stottlemyre, Richm'd., Int.
1965	Joe Foy, Toronto, International
1966	Mike Epstein, Rochester, Int.
1967	Johnny Bench, Buffalo, Int.
1968	Merv Rettenmund, Roch'ter, Int.
1969	Danny Walton, Okla. City, A.A.
1970	Don Baylor, Rochester, Int.
1971	Bobby Grich, Rochester, Int.
1972	Tom Paciorek, Albuq'que, PCL
1973	Steve Ontiveros, Phoenix, PCL
1974	Jim Rice, Pawtucket, Int.
1975	Hector Cruz, Tulsa, A.A.
1976	Pat Putnam, Asheville, W. Car.
1977	Ken Landreaux, S.L.C., PCL-El Paso, Tex.
1978	Champ Summers, Indi'polis, A.A.
1979	Mark Bomback, Vancouver, PCL
1980	Tim Raines, Denver, A.A.

Baseball Writers' Association Awards
Most Valuable Player Citations

CHALMERS AWARD

AMERICAN LEAGUE

Year	Player	Club	Points
1911	Tyrus Cobb, Detroit, of	64
1912	Tristram Speaker, Boston, of	59
1913	Walter Johnson, Washington, p	54
1914	Edward Collins, Phila., 2b	63

NATIONAL LEAGUE

Player	Club	Points
Frank Schulte, Chicago, of	29
Lawrence Doyle, N. Y., 2b	48
Jacob Daubert, Brooklyn, 1b	50
John Evers, Boston, 2b	50

LEAGUE AWARDS

AMERICAN LEAGUE

Year	Player	Club	Points
1922	George Sisler, St. Louis, 1b	59
1923	George Ruth, New York, of	64
1924	Walter Johnson, Washington, p	55
1925	Roger Peckinpaugh, Wash., ss	45
1926	George Burns, Cleveland, 1b	63
1927	H. Louis Gehrig, New York, 1b	56
1928	Gordon Cochrane, Phila., c	53
1929	No selection		

NATIONAL LEAGUE

Player	Club	Points
No selection		
No selection		
Arthur Vance, Brooklyn, p	74
Rogers Hornsby, St. Louis, 2b	73
Robert O'Farrell, St. Louis, c	79
Paul Waner, Pittsburgh, of	72
James Bottomley, St. Louis, 1b	76
Rogers Hornsby, Chicago, 2b	60

BASEBALL WRITERS' ASSOCIATION MVP AWARDS

	AMERICAN LEAGUE		NATIONAL LEAGUE		
Year	Player Club	Points	Player	Club	Points
1931	Robert Grove, Philadelphia, p	78	Frank Frisch, St. Louis, 2b		65
1932	James Foxx, Philadelphia, 1b	75	Charles Klein, Phila., of		78
1933	James Foxx, Philadelphia, 1b	74	Carl Hubbell, New York, p		77
1934	Gordon Cochrane, Detroit, c	67	Jerome Dean, St. Louis, p		78
1935	Henry Greenberg, Detroit, 1b	*80	Charles Hartnett, Chicago, c		75
1936	H. Louis Gehrig, New York, 1b	73	Carl Hubbell, New York, p		60
1937	Charles Gehringer, Detroit, 2b	78	Joseph Medwick, St. Louis, of		70
1938	James Foxx, Boston, 1b	305	Ernest Lombardi, Cincinnati, c		229
1939	Joseph DiMaggio, N. York, of	280	William Walters, Cincinnati, p		303
1940	Henry Greenberg, Detroit, of	292	Frank McCormick, Cinn., 1b		274
1941	Joseph DiMaggio, N. York, of	291	Adolph Camilli, Brooklyn, 1b		300
1942	Joseph Gordon, New York, 2b	270	Morton Cooper, St. Louis, p		263
1943	Spurgeon Chandler, N. Y., p	246	Stanley Musial, St. Louis, of		267
1944	Harold Newhouser, Detroit, p	236	Martin Marion, St. Louis, ss		190
1945	Harold Newhouser, Detroit, p	236	Philip Cavarretta, Chicago, 1b		279
1946	Theodore Williams, Boston, of	224	Stanley Musial, St. Louis, 1b		319
1947	Joseph DiMaggio, N. York, of	202	Robert Elliott, Boston, 3b		205
1948	Louis Boudreau, Cleveland, ss	324	Stanley Musial, St. Louis, of		303
1949	Theodore Williams, Boston, of	272	Jack Robinson, Brooklyn, 2b		264
1950	Philip Rizzuto, New York, ss	284	C. James Konstanty, Phila., p		286
1951	Lawrence Berra, New York, c	184	Roy Campanella, Brooklyn, c		243
1952	Robert Shantz, Phila., p	280	Henry Sauer, Chicago, of		226
1953	Albert Rosen, Cleveland, 3b	*336	Roy Campanella, Brooklyn, c		297
1954	Lawrence Berra, New York, c	230	Willie Mays, New York, of		283
1955	Lawrence Berra, New York, c	218	Roy Campanella, Brooklyn, c		226
1956	Mickey Mantle, N. Y., of	*336	Donald Newcombe, Brkn., p		223
1957	Mickey Mantle, New York, of	233	Henry Aaron, Milwaukee, of		239
1958	Jack Jensen, Boston, of	233	Ernest Banks, Chicago, ss		283
1959	J. Nelson Fox, Chicago, 2b	295	Ernest Banks, Chicago, ss		232½
1960	Roger Maris, New York, of	225	Richard Groat, Pittsburgh, ss		276
1961	Roger Maris, New York, of	202	Frank Robinson, Cincinnati, of		219
1962	Mickey Mantle, New York, of	234	Maurice Wills, Los Angeles, ss		209
1963	Elston Howard, New York, c	248	Sanford Koufax, Los Angeles, p		237
1964	Brooks Robinson, Balti., 3b	269	Kenton Boyer, St. Louis, 3b		243
1965	Zoilo Versalles, Minn., ss	275	Willie Mays, San Francisco, of		224
1966	Frank Robinson, Balti., of	*280	Roberto Clemente, Pitts., of		218
1967	Carl Yastrzemski, Boston, of	275	Orlando Cepeda, St. Louis, 1b		*280
1968	Dennis McLain, Detroit, p	*280	Robert Gibson, St. Louis, p		242
1969	Harmon Killebrew, Minn., 1-3b	294	Willie McCovey, San Fran., 1b		265
1970	John (Boog) Powell, Balti., 1b	234	Johnny Bench, Cincinnati, c		326
1971	Vida Blue, Oakland, p	268	Joseph Torre, St. Louis, 3b		318
1972	Richie Allen, Chicago, 1b	321	Johnny Bench, Cincinnati, c		263
1973	Reggie Jackson, Oak., of	*336	Pete Rose, Cincinnati, of		274
1974	Jeff Burroughs, Texas, of	248	Steve Garvey, Los Angeles, 1b		270
1975	Fred Lynn, Boston, of	326	Joe Morgan, Cincinnati, 2b		321½
1976	Thurman Munson, N. Y., c	304	Joe Morgan, Cincinnati, 2b		311
1977	Rod Carew, Minn., 1b	273	George Foster, Cincinnati, of		291
1978	Jim Rice, Boston, of	352	Dave Parker, Pittsburgh, of		320
1979	Don Baylor, California, of	347	Willie Stargell, Pittsburgh, 1b		216
			Keith Hernandez, St. Louis, 1b		216
1980	George Brett, Kansas City, 3b	335	Mike Schmidt, Philadelphia, 3b		*336

*Unanimous selection.

BASEBALL WRITERS' ASSOCIATION ROOKIE AWARDS

1947—Combined selection—Jack Robinson, Brooklyn, 1b.
1948—Combined selection—Alvin Dark, Boston, N. L., ss.

AMERICAN LEAGUE			NATIONAL LEAGUE		
Year	Player Club	Votes	Player Club		Votes
1949	Roy Sievers, St. Louis, of	10	Donald Newcombe, Brkn, p		21
1950	Walter Dropo, Boston, 1b	15	Samuel Jethroe, Boston, of		11
1951	Gilbert McDougald, N. Y., 3b	13	Willie Mays, New York, of		18
1952	Harry Byrd, Philadelphia, p	9	Joseph Black, Brooklyn, p		19
1953	Harvey Kuenn, Detroit, ss	23	James Gilliam, Brooklyn, 2b		11
1954	Robert Grim, New York, p	15	Wallace Moon, St. Louis, of		17
1955	Herbert Score, Cleveland, p	8	William Virdon, St. Louis, of		15
1956	Luis Aparicio, Chicago, ss	22	Frank Robinson, Cincinnati, of	*24
1957	Anthony Kubek, N. Y., inf-of	23	John Sanford, Philadelphia, p		16
1958	Albert Pearson, Washington, of.	14	Orlando Cepeda, S. Fran., 1b	*†21
1959	W. Robert Allison, Wash., of.	18	Willie McCovey, San Fran., 1b	*24
1960	Ronald Hansen, Baltimore, ss	22	Frank Howard, Los Angeles, of..	12
1961	Donald Schwall, Boston, p	7	Billy Williams, Chicago, of		10
1962	Thomas Tresh, New York, of-ss.	13	Kenneth Hubbs, Chicago, 2b		19
1963	Gary Peters, Chicago, p	10	Peter Rose, Cincinnati, 2b		17
1964	Pedro (Tony) Oliva, Minn., of	19	Richard Allen, Philadelphia, 3b	18
1965	Curtis Blefary, Baltimore, of	12	James Lefebvre, Los Ang., 2b		13
1966	Tommie Agee, Chicago, of	16	Tommy Helms, Cincinnati, 3b		12
1967	Rod Carew, Minnesota, 2b	19	Tom Seaver, New York, p		11
1968	Stan Bahnsen, New York, p	17	Johnny Bench, Cincinnati, c	10½
1969	Lou Piniella, Kansas City, of	9	Ted Sizemore, Los Angeles, 2b	14
1970	Thurman Munson, N. Y., c	23	Carl Morton, Montreal, p		11
1971	Chris Chambliss, Cleveland, 1b..	11	Earl Williams, Atlanta, c		18
1972	Carlton Fisk, Boston, c	*24	Jon Matlack, New York, p		19
1973	Al Bumbry, Baltimore, of	13½	Gary Matthews, San Fran., of	11
1974	Mike Hargrove, Texas, 1b	16½	Bake McBride, St. Louis, of		16
1975	Fred Lynn, Boston, of	23	John Montefusco, San Fran., p	12
1976	Mark Fidrych, Detroit, p	22	Butch Metzger, San Diego, p		11
			Pat Zachry, Cincinnati, p		11
1977	Eddie Murray, Balt., dh-1b	12½	Andre Dawson, Montreal, of	10
1978	Lou Whitaker, Detroit, 2b	21	Bob Horner, Atlanta, 3b		12½
1979	John Castino, Minn., 3b	7	Rick Sutcliffe, L.A., p		20
	Alfredo Griffin, Tor., ss	7			
1980	Joe Charboneau, Clev., of	103	Steve Howe, L.A., p		80

*Unanimous selection. †Three writers did not vote.

CY YOUNG MEMORIAL AWARD

Year	Pitcher Club	Votes				
1956	Donald Newcombe, Brkn	10	1971	A. L.	Vida Blue, Oakland	†98
1957	Warren Spahn, Milwaukee..	15		N. L.	Fergy Jenkins, Chi	†97
1958	Robert Turley, N. Y., A. L.	5	1972	A. L.	Gaylord Perry, Cleve.	†64
1959	Early Wynn, Chicago, A.L.	13		N. L.	Steve Carlton, Phil..*†120
1960	Vernon Law, Pittsburgh	8	1973	A. L.	Jim Palmer, Balt.	†88
1961	Edward Ford, N. Y., A. L.	9		N. L.	Tom Seaver, N. Y.	†71
1962	Don Drysdale, L.A., N.L.	14	1974	A. L.	Jim Hunter, Oakland..†90
1963	Sanford Koufax, L.A., N.L.	*20		N. L.	Mike Marshall, L. A...†96
1964	Dean Chance, L. A., A. L.	17	1975	A. L.	Jim Palmer, Balt.	†98
1965	Sanford Koufax, L.A., N.L.	*20		N. L.	Tom Seaver, N. Y.	†98
1966	Sanford Koufax, L.A., N.L.	*20	1976	A. L.	Jim Palmer, Balt.	†108
1967	A. L.	Jim Lonborg, Boston..	18		N. L.	Randy Jones, S. D.	†96
	N. L.	M. McCormick, S. F.	18	1977	A. L.	Sparky Lyle, N.Y.	†56½
1968	A. L.	Dennis McLain, Det.	*20		N. L.	Steve Carlton, Phil	†104
	N. L.	Bob Gibson, St. L.	*20	1978	A. L.	Ron Guidry, N.Y.	*†140
1969	A. L.	Dennis McLain, Det.	10		N. L.	Gaylord Perry, S.D...†116
		Mike Cuellar, Balt.	10	1979	A. L.	Mike Flanagan, Balt.	†136
	N. L.	Tom Seaver, N. Y.	23		N. L.	Bruce Sutter, Chi.	†72
1970	A. L.	Jim Perry, Minn.	†55	1980	A. L.	Steve Stone, Balt.	100
	N. L.	Bob Gibson, St. L.	†118		N. L.	Steve Carlton, Phil	118

*Unanimous selection. †Point system used.

BOB GIBSON—1980 Hall of Fame inductee.

Gibson Voted Into Hall of Fame

By LARRY WIGGE

His sometimes short treatment of the press made little difference when Bob Gibson's name was placed on the Hall of Fame ballot for the first time. Gibson became only the 11th player exclusive of the original five to be elected to Cooperstown in his first year of eligibility.

Gibson, a fireballing righthander who won 251 games in a career which spanned 17 years with the St. Louis Cardinals, received 337 votes out of a possible 401 cast by 10-year members of the Baseball Writers' Association of America.

With 75 percent of the vote required for election, Gibson was the only one of the 39 candidates on the ballot to gain the 301 votes necessary for election. He was followed by Don Drysdale with 243 votes, Gil Hodges with 241, Harmon Killebrew with 239, Hoyt Wilhelm with 238 and Juan Marichal with 233. Killebrew and Marichal, like Gibson, were on the ballot for the first time.

Johnny Mize, who had 359 career home runs and a .312 lifetime average with the Cardinals, Giants and Yankees from 1936 through 1953, and Rube Foster, who founded the Negro National League in 1920, were selected to the Hall in a vote by the Committee on Veterans.

Gibson will long be remembered for his no-nonsense approach to pitching. He won the Cy Young Award in 1968 and 1970, led the National League in shutouts with 13 in 1968 and authored a no-hitter on August 14, 1971, against the Pirates.

He said the '68 season, in which he went 22-9 with a magnificent 1.12 ERA, ranked as his most significant achievement in the game. During that season, he won 15 games in a row and ran off a 47-inning scoreless streak. In addition to the Cy Young Award, he was also the N. L. MVP that season. He is the only pitcher to have twice won the seventh game of a World Series. And were if not for a lost fly ball in 1968, he would have extended that mark to three Series-clinching victories.

Gibson, who retired in 1975, finished his career with a 251-174 record and a 2.91 ERA. His 3,117 strikeouts made him one of only four pitchers to surpass the 3,000-plateau. He won 20 games in a season five times. He could hit and field as well, clubbing 24 homers and winning nine Gold Glove Awards.

Always at his best when money was on the line, Gibson sported an excellent 7-2 World Series record. In addition to his previously mentioned Series heroics, Bob fanned a record 17 Detroit Tigers in the opening game of the 1968 Series.

The complete Hall of Fame voting follows: Bob Gibson 337, Don Drysdale 243, Gil Hodges 241, Harmon Killebrew 239, Hoyt Wilhelm 238, Juan Marichal 233, Nelson Fox 168, Red Schoendienst 166, Jim Bunning 164, Maury Wills 163, Richie Ashburn 142, Roger Maris 94, Harvey Kuenn 93, Elston Howard 83, Orlando Cepeda 77, Thurman Munson 62, Ted Kluszewski 56, Luis Aparicio 48, Lew Burdette 48, Bill Mazeroski 38, Don Larsen 33, El Roy Face 23, Vada Pinson 18, Jim Perry 6, Dave McNally 5, Claude Osteen 2, Glenn Beckert 1, Gates Brown 1, Leo Cardenas 1, Lindy McDaniel 1, Jim Northrup 1, Sonny Siebert 1.

Following is a complete list of those enshrined in the Hall of Fame prior to 1981 with the vote by which each enrollee was elected:

1936—Tyrus Cobb (222), John (Honus) Wagner (215), George (Babe) Ruth (215), Christy Mathewson (205), Walter Johnson (189), named by

Baseball Writers Association of America. Total ballots cast, 226.

1937—Napoleon Lajoie (168), Tristram Speaker (165), Denton (Cy) Young (153), named by the BBWAA. Total ballots cast, 201. George Wright, Morgan G. Bulkeley, Byron Bancroft Johnson, John J. McGraw, Cornelius McGillicuddy (Connie Mack), named by Centennial Commission.

1938—Grover C. Alexander (212), named by BBWAA. Total ballots, 262. Henry Chadwick, Alexander J. Cartwright, named by Centennial Commission.

1939—George Sisler (235), Edward Collins (213), William Keeler (207), Louis Gehrig, named by BBWAA. (Gehrig by special election after retirement from game was announced). Total ballots cast, 274. Albert G. Spalding, Adrian C. Anson, Charles A. Comiskey, William (Buck) Ewing, Charles Radbourn, William A. (Candy) Cummings, named by committee of old-time players and writers.

1942—Rogers Hornsby (182), named by BBWAA. Total ballots cast, 233.

1944—Judge Kenesaw M. Landis, named by committee on old timers.

1945—Hugh Duffy, Jimmy Collins, Hugh Jennings, Ed Delahanty, Fred Clarke, Mike Kelly, Wilbert Robinson, Jim O'Rourke, Dennis (Dan) Brouthers and Roger Bresnahan, named by committee on old-timers.

1946—Jesse Burkett, Frank Chance, Jack Chesbro, Johnny Evers, Clark Griffith, Tom McCarthy, Joe McGinnity, Eddie Plank, Joe Tinker, Rube Waddell and Ed Walsh, named by committee on old timers.

1947—Carl Hubbell (140), Frank Frisch (136), Gordon (Mickey) Cochrane (128) and Robert (Lefty) Grove (123), named by BBWAA. Total ballots, 161.

1948—Herbert J. Pennock (94) and Harold (Pie) Traynor (93), named by BBWAA. Total ballots cast, 121.

1949—Charles Gehringer (159), named by BBWAA in runoff election. Total ballots cast, 187. Charles (Kid) Nichols and Mordecai (Three-Finger) Brown, named by committee on old-timers.

1951—Mel Ott (197) and Jimmie Foxx (179), named by BBWAA. Total ballots cast, 226.

1952—Harry Heilmann (203) and Paul Waner (195), named by BBWAA. Total ballots cast, 234.

1953—Jerome (Dizzy) Dean (209) and Al Simmons (199), named by BBWAA. Total ballots cast, 264. Charles Albert (Chief) Bender, Roderick (Bobby) Wallace, William Klem, Tom Connolly, Edward G. Barrow and William Henry (Harry) Wright, named by the new Committee on Veterans.

1954—Walter (Rabbit) Maranville (209), William Dickey (202) and William Terry (195), named by BBWAA. Total ballots cast, 252.

1955—Joe DiMaggio (223), Ted Lyons (217), Arthur (Dazzy) Vance (205) and Charles (Gabby) Hartnett (195), named by BBWAA. Total ballots cast, 251. J. Franklin (Home Run) Baker and Ray Schalk, named by Committee on Veterans.

1956—Hank Greenberg (164) and Joe Cronin (152), named by BBWAA. Total ballots cast, 193.

1957—Joseph V. McCarthy and Sam Crawford, named by Committee on Veterans.

1959—Zachariah (Zack) Wheat, named by Committee on Veterans.

1961—Max Carey and William Hamilton, named by Committee on Veterans.

1962—Bob Feller (150) and Jackie Robinson (124), named by BBWAA. Total ballots cast, 160. Bill McKechnie and Edd Roush, named by Committee on Veterans.

1963—Eppa Rixey, Edgar (Sam) Rice, Elmer Flick and John Clarkson, named by Committee on Veterans.

1964—Luke Appling (189), named by BBWAA in runoff election. Total ballots cast, 225. Urban (Red) Faber, Burleigh Grimes, Tim Keefe, Heinie Manush, Miller Huggins and John Montgomery Ward, named by Committee on Veterans.

1965—James (Pud) Galvin, named by Committee on Veterans.

1966—Ted Williams (282), named by BBWAA. Total ballots cast, 302. Casey Stengel, named by Committee on Veterans.

1967—Charles (Red) Ruffing (266), named by BBWAA in runoff election. Total ballots cast, 306. Branch Rickey and Lloyd Waner, named by Committee on Veterans.

1968—Joseph (Ducky) Medwick (240), named by BBWAA. Total ballots cast, 283. Leon (Goose) Goslin and Hazen (Kiki) Cuyler, named by Committee on Veterans.

1969—Stan (The Man) Musial (317) and Roy Campanella (270), named by BBWAA. Total ballots cast, 340. Stan Coveleski and Waite Hoyt, named by Committee on Veterans.

1970—Lou Boudreau (232), named by BBWAA. Total ballots cast, 300. Earle Combs, Jesse Haines and Ford Frick, named by Committee on Veterans.

1971—Chick Hafey, Rube Marquard, Joe Kelley, Dave Bancroft, Harry Hooper, Jake Beckley and George Weiss, named by Committee on Veterans. Satchel Paige, named by Special Committee on Negro Leagues.

1972—Sandy Koufax (344), Yogi Berra (339) and Early Wynn (301), named by BBWAA. Total ballots cast, 396. Lefty Gomez, Will Harridge and Ross Youngs, named by Committee on Veterans. Josh Gibson and Walter (Buck) Leonard, named by Special Committee on Negro Leagues.

1973—Warren Spahn (316), named by BBWAA. Total ballots cast, 380. Roberto Clemente (393), in special election by BBWAA in which 424 ballots were cast. Billy Evans, George Kelly and Mickey Welch, named by Committee on Veterans. Monte Irvin, named by Special Committee on Negro Leagues.

1974—Mickey Mantle (322) and Whitey Ford (284), named by BBWAA. Total ballots cast, 365. Jim Bottomley, Sam Thompson and Jocko Conlan, named by Committee on Veterans. James (Cool Papa) Bell, named by Special Committee on Negro Leagues.

1975—Ralph Kiner (273), named by BBWAA. Total ballots cast, 362. Earl Averill, Bucky Harris and Billy Herman, named by Committee on Veterans. William (Judy) Johnson, named by Special Committee on Negro Leagues.

1976—Robin Roberts (337) and Bob Lemon (305), named by BBWAA. Total ballots cast, 388. Roger Connor, Cal Hubbard and Fred Lindstrom, named by Committee on Veterans. Oscar Charleston, named by Special Committee on Negro Leagues.

1977—Ernie Banks (321), named by BBWAA. Total ballots cast, 383. Joe Sewell, Al Lopez and Amos Rusie, named by Committee on Veterans. Martin Dihigo and John Henry Lloyd, named by Special Committee on Negro Leagues.

1978—Eddie Mathews (301), named by BBWAA. Total ballots cast, 379. Larry MacPhail and Addie Joss, named by Committee on Veterans.

1979—Willie Mays (409), named by BBWAA. Total ballots cast, 432. Hack Wilson and Warren Giles, named by Committee on Veterans.

1980—Al Kaline (340) and Duke Snider (333), named by BBWAA. Total ballots cast, 385. Chuck Klein and Tom Yawkey, named by Committee on Veterans.

Major League Attendance for 1980

NATIONAL LEAGUE			AMERICAN LEAGUE		
	Home	Away		Home	Away
Atlanta	1,048,411	1,566,569	Baltimore	1,797,438	1,608,616
Chicago	1,206,776	1,691,378	Boston	1,956,092	1,807,603
Cincinnati	2,022,450	1,876,775	California	2,297,327	1,399,826
Houston	2,278,217	1,838,719	Chicago	1,200,365	1,393,850
Los Angeles	3,249,287	2,063,206	Cleveland	1,033,827	1,430,960
Montreal	2,208,175	1,616,068	Detroit	1,785,293	1,446,946
New York	1,192,073	1,546,278	Kansas City	2,288,714	1,624,562
Philadelphia	2,651,650	1,766,359	Milwaukee	1,857,408	1,599,024
Pittsburgh	1,646,757	2,197,247	Minnesota	769,206	1,363,019
St. Louis	1,385,147	1,623,520	New York	2,627,417	2,460,645
San Diego	1,139,026	1,608,660	Oakland	842,259	1,573,068
San Francisco	1,096,115	1,729,305	Seattle	836,204	1,396,912
N.L. 1980 Total—21,124,084			Texas	1,198,175	1,499,612
			Toronto	1,400,327	1,285,409
			A.L. 1980 Total—21,890,052		

BEST MAJOR LEAGUE ATTENDANCE MARKS

1.	Los Angeles	3,347,845	1978	14.	Los Angeles	2,617,029	1966
2.	Los Angeles	3,249,287	1980	15.	Philadelphia	2,583,389	1978
3.	Los Angeles	2,955,087	1977	16.	Los Angeles	2,553,577	1965
4.	Los Angeles	2,860,954	1979	17.	Los Angeles	2,539,349	1975
5.	Philadelphia	2,775,011	1979	18.	Los Angeles	2,538,602	1963
6.	Los Angeles	2,755,184	1962	19.	N.Y. Yankees	2,537,765	1979
7.	Philadelphia	2,700,070	1977	20.	Cincinnati	2,532,497	1978
8.	New York Mets	2,697,479	1970	21.	California	2,523,575	1979
9.	Philadelphia	2,651,650	1980	22.	Cincinnati	2,519,670	1977
10.	Los Angeles	2,634,474	1974	23.	Philadelphia	2,480,150	1976
11.	Cincinnati	2,629,708	1976	24.	Los Angeles	2,386,301	1976
12.	N.Y. Yankees	2,627,417	1980	25.	N.Y. Yankees	2,373,901	1948
13.	Cleveland	2,620,627	1948				

NECROLOGY

MAJOR LEAGUE DEALS

MAJOR LEAGUE HOTELS

MINOR LEAGUE PRESIDENTS

Hall of Famer RUBE MARQUARD died in 1980.

Marquard, Elston Howard Died in 1980

By CARL CLARK

Hall of Fame pitcher Rube Marquard, who won 201 National League games, headed the list of baseball personalities who died in 1980. The 90-year-old lefthander succumbed to cancer June 1 at his home in Baltimore, Md.

Marquard's pursuit of a career in baseball resulted in severed ties with his father, the chief engineer of the city of Cleveland, who bade his son goodbye by saying, "When you cross that threshold, don't come back. I don't ever want to see you again."

Eventually, Rube's success won his father's approval. After Marquard had won 51 games in two minor league seasons, the New York Giants purchased his contract for a record $11,000. That, however, only intensified the ridicule that was to come his way. A 9-17 record in his first two full seasons with New York (1909-10) caused him to be dubbed "The $11,000 Lemon."

Vindication was quick to come, though, as Marquard pitched the Giants to pennants the next three seasons, winning 73 games and losing only 28. In 1911, he won 24 games and struck out a league-leading 237 batters. Rube kicked off the 1912 season with 19 straight wins, still the record for most consecutive victories in a season. That fall he accounted for two of the Giants' three victories over the Boston Red Sox in the World Series.

Marquard pitched for the Giants until September of 1915 when Manager John McGraw, angered by reports that Rube was entertaining offers from the Federal League, sold him to Brooklyn, against whom Marquard had pitched a no-hitter earlier that season. He remained with the Dodgers through 1920, pitched for Cincinnati in 1921 and the Boston Braves from 1922-25.

Rube, whose nickname came from comparisons with Philadelphia Athletics pitcher Rube Waddell, later worked as a mutuels clerk at racetracks in Florida and Maryland and was elected to the Hall of Fame in 1971 by the Veterans Committee.

Death also claimed Elston Howard, the first black to play for the New York Yankees and win the American League MVP, and Emmett Ashford, the major leagues' first black umpire.

Howard, one of the game's finest gentlemen, played for New York from 1955-67 and for the Red Sox in 1967-68. Because the Yankees had Yogi Berra behind the plate, Howard spent his first three seasons in the outfield. When an aging Berra could no longer handle the catching chores, Howard capitalized on his chance, batting .348 in 1961 with 21 homers. Two years later, he was named A.L. MVP after hitting .287 with 28 homers and 85 RBIs.

Ellie played in 10 World Series and five All-Star Games and was the catcher on THE SPORTING NEWS' A.L. All-Star team in 1961-63-64. He coached for the Yankees from 1969 until a heart ailment forced him into the front office ten years later. The same condition led to his death in New York City December 14. He was 51.

Said Yankees Manager Casey Stengel in 1958: "Every time a fellow comes up to me with a list of names he's willing to deal, he also has a list of Yankees he must have—and Elston Howard is at the top of the list. Well, he ain't gonna go anywhere. He's worth more than any other player in the league in a trade. I'd have to get a whole ball club for him—and then I'm not sure I need some of the junk the others have instead of him.''

Ashford began umpiring professionally in 1951, but it wasn't until 1966—18 years after Jackie Robinson had smashed the color barrier for players—that he broke into the American League. Some said the flamboyant Ashford spent 15 years in the minors only because he was black; others said his color was the only reason he was given a chance in the majors.

A recurrent criticism was that he wasn't firm enough. "He takes too much guff from everybody," one player said. "I just wish I could run into him away from the field. I'd tell him to kick guys out—kick me out—but get tough.''

Commissioner Kuhn, in whose office Ashford worked as a public relations assistant after his 1970 retirement, took a different view. "As the first black umpire in the major leagues," he said, "his magnanimous nature was sternly tested, but he was unshaken.''

Ashford, 65, died at Marina del Rey, Calif., March 1, five months before the passing of 70-year-old Bill McKinley, an A.L. umpire from 1946-65, at Mount Pleasant, Pa. McKinley, who called 25 World Series games and three All-Star Games, worked 3,578 contests, 2,200 of those consecutively.

A trio of prominent journalists were taken in 1980—Fred Lieb, the 92-year-old dean of baseball writers and reporter at every World Series from 1911-58; Oscar Kahan, the 71-year-old assistant managing editor of THE SPORTING NEWS; and Jack Murphy, 57, sports editor and columnist of the San Diego Union who played an important part in bringing major league baseball and football to his city.

Other notable players who died included Hughie Critz, second baseman for Cincinnati and the New York Giants from 1930-35; Ed Head, who pitched a no-hitter for Brooklyn in 1946; Joe Page, Yankees relief ace in the late 1940s; Bob Porterfield, THE SPORTING NEWS A.L. Pitcher of the Year in 1953; Rosy Ryan, winner of 33 games and two World Series contests for the Giants in 1922-23; Bob Shawkey, four times a 20-game winner for the Yankees and the A.L. ERA champion in 1920; and Ernie Shore, author for the 1917 Red Sox of a perfect game that is disputed to this day.

An alphabetical listing of baseball deaths in 1980 follows:

John T. (Red) Adams, 79, president of Rochester (International) in the 1960s, at Brighton, N.Y., February 13.

Emmett L. Ashford, 65, the major leagues' first black umpire, of a heart attack, at Marina del Rey, Calif., March 1; umpired in the American League from 1966-70 and in the Pacific Coast League from 1954-65; worked in the 1967 All-Star Game and the 1970 World Series; after his retirement he served as a public relations representative for Commissioner Kuhn.

Everett Duane (Eppie) Barnes, 79, first baseman in four games for Pittsburgh in 1923-24, at Mineola, N.Y., November 17; later served as athletic director and baseball coach at Colgate University; member of the U.S. Olympic Committee and president of the NCAA's executive committee.

Clyde Lee (Pooch) Barnhart, 83, outfielder for Pittsburgh from 1920-28, at Hagerstown, Md., January 21; a third baseman in his first few seasons, he was a .295 lifetime hitter; his son, Vic, played in 74 games for Pittsburgh, mostly at shortstop, from 1944-46.

Emil Bossard, 88, patriarch of baseball's foremost groundskeeping family, at Cleveland, O., May 6; field manicurist for the Indians from 1935 until the 1970s, he is credited with developing spun glass tarpaulins and protective screens for batting practice; sons Marshall and Harold followed him as Cleveland groundskeepers, son Gene works for the Chicago White Sox, and grandson Brian is a recent addition to the Cleveland staff.

Edgar Dudley (Dud) Brannon, 82, first baseman in 30 games for the 1927 Philadelphia Athletics, at Sun City, Ariz., February 4.

Jim Britt, 70, the voice of both the Boston Red Sox and Boston Braves for 10 years in the 1940s and 1950s, at Monterrey, Calif., December 28; handled seven All-Star Games and five World Series.

Jesse J. Brown Jr., 66, pitcher in the Negro National League during the 1940s and 1950s for the New York Black Yankees, the Baltimore Elite Giants and the Newark Eagles, at Wellesley, Mass., May 25.

Eloy (Buck) Canel, 74, broadcaster of New York Yankees games and World Series games in Spanish to Latin American countries, at New York, N.Y., April 7.

Curtis Hancock Coleman, 93, third baseman in 12 games for the 1912 New York Highlanders (Yankees), at Newport, Ore., July 1.

Allen Howard (Red) Conkwright, 82, pitcher in five games for Detroit in 1920, at Houston, Tex., October 27.

Jerome Patrick Conway, 78, pitcher in one game for the 1920 Washington Senators, at Holyoke, Mass., April 16.

Walter Anderson Craddock, 48, pitcher for the Kansas City Athletics in 1955-56 and 1958, at Parma Heights, O., July 6; back problems voided what promise the lefthander had and he finished his 29-game major league career with an 0-7 record.

Hugh Melville (Hughie) Critz, 79, second baseman for Cincinnati from 1924-30 and the New York Giants from 1930-35, at Greenwood, Miss., January 10; little Hughie, 5-8 and 147 pounds, hit .268 in 1,478 games; despite his size, he never drew more than 40 bases on balls in any season yet scored more than 90 runs four times; scouted for Giants in 1936-37; president of Greenwood (Cotton States) in 1938-39.

William Elmer (Bill) Crouch, 70, pitcher for Brooklyn in 1939, the Philadelphia Phillies in 1941 and the St. Louis Cardinals in 1941 and 1945, at Howell, Mich., December 26; appeared in 50 games and had an 8-5 record; he was baseball coach at Eastern Michigan University from 1947-69; son of William Henry Crouch, who pitched in one game for the 1910 St. Louis Browns.

Frank Donald (Dingle) Croucher, 65, shortstop for Detroit from 1939-41 and Washington in 1942, of a heart attack, at Houston, Tex., May 21; in 1941, the only season he was a regular, he hit .254, three points above his career average.

Charleton Ross (Chauncey) DeVault, 69, president of the Appalachian League from 1947 until his death, at Bristol, Tenn., February 2; at the 1979 winter meetings in Toronto, the National Association presented him with the George Trautman Award for outstanding service to baseball.

Raymond Joseph (Lefty) Dobens, 73, pitcher in 11 games with no decisions for the 1929 Boston Red Sox, at Stuart, Fla., April 21; scouted for Cincinnati from 1954-58.

William James (Bill) Dunlap, 71, outfielder in 26 games for the Boston Braves in 1929-30, at Reading, Pa., November 29; he had 12 hits in 29 at-bats in 1929 but only two in 29 at-bats the next season.

Foster Hamilton (Eddie) Edwards, 76, pitcher for the Boston Braves from 1925-28 and for the New York Yankees in 1930, at Orleans, Mass., January 4; primarily a reliever, he was 6-9 in 56 games.

Welton Claude (Rube) Ehrhardt, 85, pitcher for Brooklyn from 1924-28 and Cincinnati in 1929, at Chicago Heights, Ill., April 27; he was 22-34 in 193 games.

Herman Adam Fink, 69, pitcher for the Philadelphia Athletics from 1935-37, August 24; won and lost 20 in 67 appearances.

Leslie Harvey (Les) Fleming, 64, first baseman and outfielder for Detroit in 1939, Cleveland in 1941-42 and 1945-47 and Pittsburgh in 1949, at Cleveland, Tex., March 5; a .277 hitter in 434 games, he hit .292 with 14 homers and 82 RBIs in 1942, the only season he was a starter.

Percival Edmund Wentworth (Wenty) Ford, 33, pitcher in four games for the 1973 Atlanta Braves, killed in an auto accident, at Nassau, Bahamas, July 8.

Sidney Allen (Pudge) Gautreaux, 67, pinch-hitter and occasional catcher for the Brooklyn Dodgers in 1936-37, at Morgan City, La., April 19; in 1936 he rapped out 16 pinch-hits in 55 at-bats.

Robert Norton (Speed) Geary, 88, pitcher for the Philadelphia Athletics in 1918-19 and Cincinnati in 1921, at Cincinnati, O., January 3; in 35 games he was 4-9.

Jonah John Goldman, 73, shortstop for Cleveland in 1928 and 1930-31, at Palm Beach, Fla., August 17; he batted .224 in 148 games.

Robert Earl Grace, 73, National League catcher for eight seasons, at Phoenix, Ariz., December 22; played for Chicago in 1929 and 1931, Pittsburgh from 1931-35 and Philadelphia in 1936-37; a backup for most of his career, he hit .263 in 627 games.

Robert Julius (Bob) Habenicht, 54, pitcher for the St. Louis Cardinals in 1951 and the St. Louis Browns in 1953, at Richmond, Va., December 24; he had no decisions in four games.

Arvel Odell (Bad News) Hale, 71, second baseman and third baseman for Cleveland in 1931 and from 1933-40 and for the Boston Red Sox and New York Giants in 1941, June 9, at El Dorado, Ark.; a .289 lifetime hitter, he batted over .300 four times, including a career-high .316 in 1936; most productive years were 1934-36—during that time, he scored 288 runs, drove in 289 and belted 131 doubles and 43 homers.

Edward Marvin (Ed) Head, 62, pitcher for Brooklyn in 1940, 1942-44 and again in 1946, at Bastrop, La., January 31; pitched a no-hitter against the Boston Braves in 1946, but arm troubles soon forced him out of baseball; 27-23 in 118 games with an ERA of 3.48; managed in several minor league cities and scouted for the Houston Colt 45s from 1962-64.

Albert Bartel (Duke) Hermann, 78, infielder in 32 games for the Boston Braves in 1923-24, at Lewes, Del., August 20; a graduate of Colgate University, he studied law before entering New Jersey politics; eventually became executive director of the Republican National Committee from 1949-52 and 1957-61.

Urban John (Johnny) Hodapp, 74, infielder for Cleveland from 1925-32, the Chicago White Sox in 1932 and the Boston Red Sox in 1933, at Cincinnati, O., June 14; he had a lifetime batting average of .311 but was a regular for only two seasons; as a second baseman in 1930 he hit .354, drove in 121 runs and led the American League in hits (225) and doubles (51).

Kenneth Sylvester (Kenny) Hogan, 77, outfielder in one game for Cincinnati in 1921 and in three games for Cleveland in 1923-24, at Cleveland, O., January 2.

Robert Nelson (Bob) Hooper, 57, pitcher for the Philadelphia Athletics from 1950-52, Cleveland in 1953-54 and Cincinnati in 1955, at New Brunswick, N.J., March 17; in 194 games, 137 of those as a reliever, he was 40-41; managed in the minors from 1957-60 and scouted for the New York Mets in 1963.

Elston Gene (Ellie) Howard, 51, stalwart catcher for the New York Yankees from 1955-67 and the Boston Red Sox in 1967-68 and the first black to win the American League MVP award, of heart failure, at New York, N.Y., December 14; the International League MVP at Toronto in 1954, he became the first black to play with the Yankees when he broke in as Yogi Berra's second; in his first three seasons, he actually saw more time as an outfielder; it wasn't until 1961 that he got the opportunity to catch full time—he made the most of it, hitting .348 that year with 21 homers and winning the first of his two Gold Gloves; in 1963, he batted .287 with 28 homers and 85 RBIs and was named A.L. MVP; a .274 lifetime hitter, he played in 10 World Series and is one of 16 players to hit a home run in his first Series at-bat; played in five All-Star Games and in 1961-63-64 was the catcher on THE SPORTING NEWS' A.L. All-Star team; coached for the Yankees from 1969 into the 1979 season when heart problems forced him from the field into a front-office position.

Wilbert William (Bill) Hubbell, 83, National League pitcher for seven years whose craftiness led to a change in the intentional walk rule, at Lakewood, Colo., August 3; pitched for New York in 1919-20, Philadelphia from 1920-24 and spent his last season, 1925, with the Phillies and Brooklyn; while with Philadelphia, he twice walked a batter by throwing to first base four times—N.L. President John Heydler threatened a fine for making a travesty of the game, and the rules were later amended to prohibit the tactic.

Clarence Eugene (Hooks) Iott, 60, pitcher for the St. Louis Browns in 1941 and the Browns and New York Giants in 1947, of a heart attack, at St. Petersburg, Fla., August 17; a sensational strikeout artist in the minors, he was 3-9 in 26 major league appearances.

Norman (Jelly) Jackson, 67, shortstop in the Negro National League from 1934-45 for the Cleveland Red Sox and Homestead Grays, at Washington, D.C., February 13.

Anthony Robert (Tony) Jacobs, 55, pitcher in one game for the 1948 Chicago Cubs and in one game for the 1955 St. Louis Cardinals, at Nashville, Tenn., December 21.

Vic Johnson, 78, Boston cartoonist whose work frequently appeared in THE SPORTING NEWS, at Boston, Mass., May 4.

Dale Eldon (Nubs) Jones, 61, pitcher in two games for the 1941 Philadelphia Phillies and a major league scout for 33 years, at Orlando, Fla., November 8; scouted for the Phillies from 1948-70 and Los Angeles from 1971 until his death.

John Paul (Johnny) Jones, 85, pitcher with a 1-0 record in two games for the 1919 New York Giants and the same mark in three games for the 1920 Boston Braves, at Ruston, La., June 5.

Arndt Ludwig (Art) Jorgens, 74, backup catcher behind Bill Dickey for the New York Yankees from 1929-39, at Wilmette, Ill., March 1; the Norway native appeared in only 306 games but collected five World Series checks without ever playing in a Series game; his brother Orville pitched for the Philadelphia Phillies from 1935-37.

Oscar Kahan, 71, assistant managing editor of THE SPORTING NEWS and a member of the staff for 32 years, at St. Louis, Mo., December 21; before coming to TSN, he worked as a reporter for the St. Louis Star-Times and for the Associated Press in New York and Kansas City; his considerable writing and editing skills were put to use in the development of coverage of the minor leagues and baseball's annual winter meetings; he also edited TSN's annual American Legion Junior Baseball section and in 1967 was honored by the Legion for 10 years of service to their program.

William E. Kay, 56, part owner and director of the Tucson Toros (Pacific Coast), at Tucson, Ariz., December 27.

James William (Jimmie) Keenan, 91, pitcher for the Philadelphia Phillies in 1920-21, at Seminole, Fla., June 5; he was 1-2 in 16 games.

John Fitzgerald (Jack) Kelich, 68, scout for the Chicago White Sox from 1956-72, at San Diego, Calif., August 17.

Arthur Ray (Bill) Kimball, 69, scout for the Chicago Cubs from 1948-50, the New York Giants from 1951-56 and the Chicago White Sox from 1957 until his death, at North Platte, Neb., February 2.

Robert Kingsley, 65, government cartographer with an engineering background, the accuracy of whose projections on how many home runs would be hit in various major league parks caused executives to consult him on the probable effect of proposed changes in stadium dimensions, at Rockville, Md., December 22; among the variables he considered were wind currents, temperature, humidity, air density and minor deviations in gravity.

Stanley Harold (Betz) Klopp, 69, pitcher for the 1944 Boston Braves, at Robesonia, Pa., March 11; in 24 games, all as a reliever, he was 1-2.

Wallace Luther (Lou) Knerr, 58, pitcher for the Philadelphia Athletics in 1945-46 and Washington in 1947, at Denver, Pa., March 23; he was the American League's losingest pitcher in 1946 when he had a 3-16 record en route to a career worksheet of 8-27 with a 5.04 ERA.

Frank J. (Hank) Lamanna, 61, pitcher and outfielder for the Boston Braves from 1940-42, at Syracuse, N.Y., September 1; played in 62 games, 45 of them as a pitcher, and hit .256 and had a 6-5 record with a 5.24 ERA.

Harry B. Latina Sr., 84, retired designer of baseball gloves for the Rawlings Sporting Goods Company, at Belleville, Ill., July 12; before joining Rawlings in 1922, he was a minor league infielder and pitcher for six years; played key role in rules specifications of glove sizes.

Clifford Walker Lee, 84, outfielder and first baseman for eight big league seasons, at Denver, Colo., August 25; started his career with Pittsburgh in 1919-20, played for the Philadelphia Phillies from 1921-24, for Cincinnati in 1924, and finished up with Cleveland in 1925-26; a versatile player who also caught in 52 games, he hit .300 in 521 games and in 1922 batted .322 with 17 homers and 77 RBIs.

Frederick G. (Fred) Lieb, 92, longtime baseball writer, at Houston, Tex., June 3; began writing for Baseball Magazine in 1909 on an on-and-off basis before becoming a regular for the old New York Press in 1911; covered every World Series from 1911-58, many for THE SPORTING NEWS, and saw more than 30 All-Star Games; wrote nine books on baseball and two on metaphysics; although he covered the Giants and Dodgers for most of his career, he was assigned occasionally to the Yankees; it was during one of his stints with the Yankees that he made one of baseball's most controversial scoring decisions—Howard Ehmke of Boston, who had pitched a no-hitter in his previous start, set the Yanks down on one hit, a scratch single by Whitey Witt in the first inning: despite being urged to make an ex post facto reversal, Lieb refused to change his call to an error.

Francis Patrick (Frank) Loftus, 80, pitcher in one game for Washington in 1926, at Belchertown, Mass., October 27.

Richard William (Rube) Marquard, 90, Hall of Fame pitcher, of cancer, at Baltimore, Md., June 1; pitched the New York Giants to three consecutive pennants, 1911-13, winning 73 games—including a record 19 in a row to begin the 1912 season; the tall lefthander from Cleveland went into baseball against his father's wishes, a defiance that created a 10-year breach between them; led the National League in strikeouts in 1911 with 237; pitched an opening game no-hitter against the Dodgers in 1915, and won two World Series games against five losses; late in the 1915 season, he was traded to Brooklyn, for whom he pitched for five seasons before spending the 1921 season with Cincinnati; in 1922 he joined the Boston Braves and wound up his 201-177 career with them in 1925; managed at Providence (Eastern) in 1926 and at Jacksonville (Southeastern) in 1929-30 and umpired in the Eastern League in 1931.

Frank J. Marasco, 86, retired sports cartoonist for the Milwaukee Sentinel and secretary-treasurer of the Milwaukee Baseball Writers for 17 years, at Milwaukee, Wisc., January 8.

Roy DeVerne (Rube) Marshall, 89, pitcher for the Philadelphia Phillies from 1912-14 and for Buffalo's Federal League team in 1915, at Dover, O., June 11; he was 5-9 in the National League and 3-1 in the Federal.

Herschel Ray Martin, 71, outfielder for the Philadelphia Phillies from 1937-40 and the New York Yankees in 1944-45, at Cuba, Mo., November 17; a .285 lifetime hitter, a .302 mark in 1944 was his best effort; scouted for the Phillies in 1955-56, the Chicago Cubs in 1958 and the New York Mets from 1961-79.

John Christopher (Jack) Martin, 93, shortstop for the New York Yankees in 1912 and the Boston Braves and Philadelphia Phillies in 1914, at the Bronx, N.Y., July 4; he hit .237 in 185 games.

James McGrath, 46, member of the board of directors of the New York Mets, of cancer, at New York, N.Y., September 22.

William F. (Bill) McKinley, 70, American League umpire from 1946-65, of a heart attack, at Mt. Pleasant, Pa., August 1; worked 3,578 games, including 2,200 in a row; called 25 World Series games and three All-Star Games; he was behind the plate in the A.L.'s longest game—New York's 9-7 victory over Detroit in 22 innings June 24, 1962, that lasted seven hours.

Dale Miller, 85, national commissioner of the American Legion Junior Baseball program from 1947-52 and business manager and secretary for Indianapolis (American Association) from 1930-41, at New Albany, Ind., October 28; he also served as a college basketball referee for 22 years and as president of the Florida-International League.

Edward Carre (Eddie) Morgan, 75, first baseman and outfielder for Cleveland from 1928-33 and first baseman for the 1934 Boston Red Sox, at New Orleans, La., April 9; a .313 lifetime hitter, he smashed 26 homers and knocked in 136 runs in 1930 while batting .349.

Joseph Allen Muir, 57, pitcher for Pittsburgh in 1951-52, of a kidney ailment, at Baltimore, Md., June 25; he was 2-5 in 21 games.

Gregory Thomas (Greg) Mulleavy, 72, shortstop for the Chicago White Sox in 1930 and 1932 and for the Boston Red Sox in 1933, at Arcadia, Calif., February 1; managed in minors and coached for the Brooklyn and Los Angeles Dodgers from 1957-60 and 1962-64;

scouted for the Dodgers in 1961 and from 1965 until his death.

Jack Murphy, 57, sports editor and columnist for the San Diego Union, of cancer, at San Diego, Calif., September 24; civic leaders credited him with playing a major role in bringing major league baseball and football to San Diego; after his death, the home of the Padres and NFL Chargers was renamed San Diego-Jack Murphy Stadium.

Andrew James (Andy) O'Connor, 96, pitcher and loser in one game for the 1908 New York Highlanders (Yankees), at Norwood, Mass., September 26.

Ernest Gayhart (Ernie) Ovitz, 94, pitcher in one game for the 1911 Chicago Cubs, at Green Bay, Wisc., September 11.

Don W. Padgett, 67, catcher and outfielder for four National League teams, at High Point, N.C., December 9; played for St. Louis from 1937-41, Brooklyn and Boston in 1946 and Philadelphia in 1947-48; compiled a .288 career batting average and almost won the batting title in 1939—that year he hit .399 but played in only 92 games, eight fewer than was needed to qualify.

Joseph Francis (Joe) Page, 62, lefthanded relief specialist for the New York Yankees from 1944-50 and Pittsburgh in 1954, at Latrobe, Pa., April 21; started 42 games in his first three seasons before switching to the bullpen, leading the A. L. in games pitched with 55 in 1948 and 60 in 1949; recorded a 14-8 mark in 1947 with a 2.48 ERA and in 1949 was 13-8 with a 2.59 ERA; his lifetime record was 57-49.

Charles Edward Pechous, 83, third baseman in 35 games for the Chicago Cubs in 1916-17 and in 18 games for Chicago's 1915 Federal League entry, at Kenosha, Wisc., September 13.

Charles Andrew (Cap) Peterson, 37, outfielder and occasional infielder for San Francisco from 1962-66, Washington in 1967-68 and Cleveland in 1969, at Tacoma, Wash., May 16; played 536 games and hit .230 with 19 homers and 122 RBIs.

Erwin Coolidge (Bob) Porterfield, 55, THE SPORTING NEWS American League Pitcher of the Year in 1953, of cancer, at Charlotte, N.C., April 28; except for that banner year, when he threw nine shutouts and accounted for 22 of the Washington Senators' 76 victories, the injury-plagued righthander was largely ineffective, winding up a 12-year career with an 87-97 record; pitched for the New York Yankees from 1948-51, Washington from 1951-55, the Boston Red Sox from 1956-58, Pittsburgh in 1958-59 and the Chicago Cubs in 1959.

Melvin Adolphus (Mel) Preibisch, 64, outfielder in 16 games for the Boston Braves in 1940-41 and scout for the Chicago White Sox from 1948 until his death, at Sealy, Tex., April 12.

Gerald Edward (Jerry) Priddy, 60, American League second baseman for 11 seasons, of a heart attack, at North Hollywood, Calif., March 3; played for New York in 1941-42, Washington in 1943 and 1946-47, St. Louis in 1948-49 and Detroit from 1950-53; perhaps the best season for the .265 hitter was 1948 when he hit .296, scored 96 runs and had 40 doubles and 79 RBIs.

Arthur August (Art) Reinholz, 76, third baseman in two games for the 1928 Cleveland Indians, at New Port Richey, Fla., December 29.

Joe Roman, a scout for Philadelphia from 1975-78, at Cherry Hill, N.J., December 13.

John Houston (Jack) Rothrock, 74, outfielder and all-round handyman for the Boston Red Sox from 1925-32, the Chicago White Sox in 1932, the St. Louis Cardinals in 1934-35 and the Philadelphia Athletics in 1937, at San Bernardino, Calif., February 2; in 1928 he played every position and it is believed that he was the first major leaguer to do so; the .276 lifetime hitter was the right fielder for St. Louis' world champions in 1934.

Harvey Holmes Russell, 89, catcher and .241 hitter for Baltimore of the Federal League in 1914-15, at Alexandria, Va., January 8.

Wilfred Patrick Dolan (Rosy) Ryan, 82, pitcher for four major league teams in 10 seasons, of cancer, at Scottsdale, Ariz., December 10; best years were for the New York Giants, for whom he pitched from 1919-24, accumulating 48 of his 51 big league wins and 36 of his 47 losses; appeared in three World Series (1922-24) and won both his decisions; first National League pitcher to hit a home run in Series (1924); in 1922 he won 17 games and his 3.01 ERA was the league's lowest; he won 16 games the next season, nine of those in relief; also pitched for the Boston Braves in 1925-26, the New York Yankees in 1928 and Brooklyn in 1933; after piloting Eau Claire (Northern) in 1941-42 and Minneapolis (American Association) in 1944-45, he moved into the general manager's chair at Minneapolis for 12 years, at Phoenix for 10 and at Tacoma for six.

Hal Sayles, 69, president of two minor leagues—the Longhorn and the West Texas-New Mexico—in the 1950s, at Abilene, Tex., April 10.

Andrew J. Schmitz, 83, purchaser with Walter O'Malley and Branch Rickey of stock in the Brooklyn Dodgers in 1944, at Huntington, N. Y., February 16.

James Robert (Bob) Shawkey, 90, a pitcher who spent most of his 15 years with the New York Yankees, at Syracuse, N.Y., December 31; pitched for the Philadelphia Athletics from 1913 until midseason of 1915 when he was sent to the Yankees, for whom he hurled through the 1927 season; in 488 games he won 198 and lost 150 with a 3.09 ERA; four times he won 20 or more games and in 1920 he led the American League with a 2.45 ERA; managed the Yankees in 1930, the Huggins-McCarthy interregnum, but had trouble maintaining discipline and the team finished 87-67 and in third place; he went on to manage in the minors, coach at Dartmouth College and serve as a scout for Pittsburgh and Detroit in the late 1940s.

Ernest Grady (Ernie) Shore, 89, pitcher of a controversial perfect game, at Winston-Salem, N. C., September 24; it was June 23, 1917, when the righthander relieved Boston Red Sox starting pitcher Babe Ruth after Babe had been ejected for protesting a called fourth ball to Ray Morgan, the first Washington batter of the afternoon; after Morgan was retired trying to steal, Shore retired the next 26 batters; made his major league debut in 1912, pitching one inning for the New York Giants; pitched for Boston from 1914-17 and for the New York Yankees in 1919-20; he had a record of 56-32 with Boston and was 63-42 lifetime with a 2.45 ERA.

Walter H. (Wally) Snell, 91, catcher in five games for the 1913 Boston Red Sox, at Providence, R. I., July 23.

Charles William (Charlie) Sproull, 61, pitcher in 34 games with a 4-10 record for the 1945 Philadelphia Phillies, at Rockford, Ill., January 13.

John Franklin (Stuffy) Stewart, 83, second baseman for the St. Louis Cardinals in 1916-17, Pittsburgh in 1922, Brooklyn in 1923 and Washington from 1925-27 and 1929, at Lake City, Fla., December 30; in those eight years, he played only 176 games, batting .238.

John C. Stiglmeier, 90, general manager at Buffalo beginning in 1941 and later the president of that International League club, at Cheektowaga, N. Y., February 11; in 1957 THE SPORTING NEWS named him Minor League Executive of the Year.

Charles Richard (Dick) Stone, 68, pitcher in three games for Washington in 1945, February 18.

Herbert Emil Strunk, 72, scout for the Philadelphia and Kansas City Athletics on a sporadic basis from 1926-45 and full time from 1945-59 and for the New York Yankees from 1961-63, at Royal Oak, Mich., April 2.

Alex C. Swails, 66, scout for the Philadelphia Phillies since 1958, at Kingstree, N. C., June 8; walked 32 batters in a 1938 Western Association game when he was pitching for Muskogee against Ponca City, which won the game, 16-7.

C. L. (Chink) Taylor, 82, outfielder in eight games for the 1925 Chicago Cubs, at Temple, Tex., July 7.

Danny Lee Thomas, 29, a troubled outfielder who played for Milwaukee in 1976-77, of suicide by hanging in a jail cell, at Mobile, Ala., June 12; the former Southern Illinois University-Carbondale athlete was a member of THE SPORTING NEWS College All-America team in 1972 and the Brewers' first pick in that year's June draft; he won the Triple Crown as the Eastern League's MVP in 1976 when he hit 29 homers for Pittsfield; the following year, he joined the World Wide Church of God and obeyed the church's injunction against working from sundown Friday until sundown Saturday; although he hit .276 in 32 games in 1976 and was hitting .271 in 22 games in 1977, the Brewers sent him back to the minors; eventually, he dropped out of the game only to try a comeback with Miami (Inter-American); at the time of his suicide, Thomas was being held on a rape charge.

Austin (Ben) Tincup, 89, pitcher for the Philadelphia Phillies in 1914-15 and 1918 and the Chicago Cubs in 1928, at Claremore, Okla., July 5; after managing and umpiring in the minors, he scouted for the Boston Braves from 1946-48, Pittsburgh from 1949-53 and the Philadelphia Phillies from 1956-58; he was a pitching coach for the New York Yankees in 1960-61.

Robert (Bob) Trowbridge, 49, pitcher for Milwaukee from 1956-59 and Kansas City in 1960, at Hudson, N. Y., April 3; in 116 games, 91 as a reliever, he was 13-13.

Arthur Patrick (Art) Veltman, 74, catcher for four major league teams in six seasons, at San Antonio, Tex., October 1; his sorties into the big leagues—for the Chicago White Sox in 1926, the New York Giants in 1928-29 and 1932, the Boston Braves in 1931 and Pittsburgh in 1934—were always brief; he played in only 23 games and hit .132 in 38 at-bats.

Henry Arthur (Ernie) Vick, 80, catcher in 57 games for the St. Louis Cardinals in 1922 and from 1924-26, at Ann Arbor, Mich., July 18; he was an All-America football center at the University of Michigan, a pro football player for three years in the late 1920s and a Big Ten football official for 23 years; umpired in the Piedmont League and managed at Scranton (New York-Pennsylvania) in 1931.

James Fred (Whale) Walters, 65, catcher for the Boston Red Sox in 1945, at Laurel, Miss., February 1; played and managed in the minors for more than 10 years but hit only .172 in 40 games with Boston; he was the hero for Mississippi State University in its 13-7 football upset of Army in 1935, catching a 65-yard pass for the winning touchdown.

John Clifford Watwood, 73, outfielder and first baseman for the Chicago White Sox from 1929-32, the Boston Red Sox in 1932-33 and the Philadelphia Phillies in 1939, at Goodwater, Ala., March 1; hit .283 in 469 games.

Winfield Scott Welch, scout for the Philadelphia Phillies from 1959-61 and player and manager in the Negro leagues for more than 20 years, at Pineville, La., March 2.

Albert Wickland, 90, outfielder for Cincinnati in 1913, the Boston Braves in 1918 and the New York Yankees in 1919, at Port Washington, Wisc., March 14; he hit .243 in 147 games; in two years of Federal League play, 1914-15, he batted .283 in 297 games for Chicago and Pittsburgh.

John Samuel Wilson, 75, pitcher in seven games for the Boston Red Sox in 1927-28, at Chattanooga, Tenn., August 27.

George Anthony Woodend, 62, pitcher in three games for the 1944 Boston Braves, at Hartford, Conn., February 6.

ELSTON HOWARD   EMMETT ASHFORD

Big Dealer Herzog Shuffled Cards Three Times at Dallas Meetings

By CARL CLARK

"I'm going to be amazing down there," promised St. Louis Cardinals Manager and General Manager Whitey Herzog before setting off for baseball's 1980 winter meetings at Dallas. And that he was, making three substantial trades involving 21 players.

Herzog, in his fourth month as general manager, set the stage for his machinations by reaching an agreement with free agent Darrell Porter, catcher for Herzog's American League West Division champions at Kansas City in 1977-78. Porter, who drove in 112 runs in 1979 but possessed only a .251 career batting average, signed a five-year contract worth an estimated $3.5 million.

The meetings opened the next day, December 8, and Herzog was ready. He began by sending seven players—infielder Mike Phillips, pitchers John Littlefield, John Urrea, Kim Seaman and Al Olmsted, and catchers Steve Swisher and Terry Kennedy, the latter a very promising 24-year-old—to San Diego for pitchers Rollie Fingers and Bob Shirley, catcher-first baseman Gene Tenace and minor league receiver Bob Geren.

Fingers, a standout reliever at Oakland for many years and THE SPORTING NEWS National League Fireman of the Year in three of his four seasons with the Padres, was seeking $2 million for a three-year extension of his pact that was to expire after 1981.

As it turned out, Herzog didn't have to wrestle with that particular problem because the deal he swung the following day made Fingers expendable. The Cardinals gave up third baseman Ken Reitz, minor league infielder Ty Waller and outfielder-first baseman Leon Durham, another of the game's top prospects, for Cubs reliever Bruce Sutter, the 1979 N.L. Cy Young winner who had saved 123 games in the last four years. Chicago had been eager to move Sutter ever since he stung them for $700,000 in his 1980 arbitration case, an amount twice as large as the Cubs' offer.

Herzog closed the week by trading Fingers, pitcher Pete Vuckovich and All-Star catcher Ted Simmons to Milwaukee for pitchers Lary Sorensen and Dave LaPoint and outfielders Sixto Lezcano and David Green, a 20-year-old with enormous potential and without whom the deal would have collapsed.

Most pundits thought that the Brewers had fleeced the Cardinals; Herzog disagreed and also pointed out that he had little choice after Simmons indicated a desire to leave St. Louis if he couldn't be behind the plate for at least 100 games. With a commitment made to Porter, Herzog could not honor that request.

Simmons initially said, "I would think I'll be playing a lot of first base and it'll be just fine for me," but he soon decided that adapting to a new position late in his career would be too trying—in part because St. Louisans were accustomed to the Gold Glove acrobatics of Keith Hernandez, who would have moved to left field in Herzog's scheme.

And so the deal was struck, but not before Simmons, who with ten years in the majors and five with the same club could have refused a trade, wrung an extra $750,000 from the Brewers. Give most of the credit for that concession to Simmons' attorney, Larue Harcourt, who laid the groundwork earlier in the week when he persuaded the Cubs and Cardinals to give Reitz $75,000 apiece to waive the final year of his no-trade clause.

Boston and California took advantage of Herzog's brief midweek cease-fire to step into the spotlight with a blockbuster of their own. The Red Sox swapped shortstop Rick Burleson and third baseman Butch Hobson to the Angels for third baseman Carney Lansford, relief pitcher Mark Clear and outfielder Rick Miller.

Again, contract problems forced a club's hand—in this case, Boston's, who figured to lose Burleson to free agency after the 1981 season. Even under the circumstances, the Red Sox got equal value. Lansford hit 42 home runs and knocked in 211 runs in his first three years, and Clear had 22 wins and 23 saves in two seasons.

Other noteworthy players changing uniforms in December included pitchers Bert Blyleven of Pittsburgh and Randy Jones of San Diego. Blyleven, who had won at least a dozen games in each of the past nine seasons before slipping to 8-13 in 1980, was traded to Cleveland after expressing his disapproval of Pirates Manager Chuck Tanner's quick hook. Jones, twice a 20-game winner and the N.L. Cy Young winner in 1976, went to the Mets for pitcher John Pacella, a hard-throwing youngster, and backup infielder Jose Moreno.

The major in-season trade was a one-for-one deal between Detroit and California. The Tigers gave up first baseman Jason Thompson for outfielder Al Cowens. Both men benefited from the change. Thompson, hitting .214 at the time, batted .317 with 17 homers and 70 RBIs in 102 games with the Angels. Cowens raised his .227 average to .268 by hitting .280 for the Tigers.

The Indians found the year's best bargain, plucking outfielder Miguel Dilone off the Cubs' Wichita (American Association) club in May for $35,000. A .214 lifetime hitter, Dilone wound up third in the league in batting (.341) and steals (61).

That pickup offset a mistake Cleveland made earlier. Prior to the season, the Indians traded outfielder Jerry Mumphrey to San Diego, where he hit .298 and stole 52 bases in 57 attempts. Bob Owchinko, the pitcher the Indians received in return, finished 2-9 with a 5.29 ERA and was one of the players later sent to Pittsburgh for Blyleven.

Another good find was the Angels' Andy Hassler. Purchased from the Pirates in June, Hassler had five wins and ten saves with a 2.49 ERA in 41 games with California.

A chronological listing of major league deals and free-agent signings in 1980 follows:

January 4—Indians traded pitcher David Clyde and outfielder Jim Norris to Rangers for pitcher Larry McCall, first baseman-outfielder Gary Gray and third baseman-outfielder Mike Bucci; Gray was assigned to Tacoma and Bucci was assigned from Tucson to Tacoma.

January 15—Royals traded outfielder Joe Zdeb, assigned from Omaha to Iowa, to White Sox for pitcher Eddie Bane, assigned to Omaha.

January 29—White Sox signed catcher Glenn Borgmann, a re-entry free agent formerly with the Twins.

January 30—Indians signed pitcher Roger Moret, a free agent.

January 31—Astros signed second baseman Joe Morgan, a re-entry free agent formerly with the Reds.

January 31—Phillies signed pitcher Lerrin LaGrow, a re-entry free agent formerly with the Dodgers.

February 8—Astros released pitcher Tom Dixon.

February 15—Padres traded pitcher Gaylord Perry, third baseman Tucker Ashford and pitcher Joe Carroll to Rangers for first baseman Willie Montanez; Carroll was assigned from Hawaii to Charleston, W.Va.

February 15—Padres traded pitcher Bob Owchinko and outfielder Jim Wilhelm to Cleveland for outfielder Jerry Mumphrey.

February 15—Braves traded pitcher Don Collins to Indians for pitcher Gary Melson.

February 15—Padres released second baseman Fernando Gonzalez.

February 19—White Sox re-signed outfielder Rusty Torres, a re-entry free agent.

February 20—Astros traded catcher Reggie Baldwin to Mets for outfielder Keith Bodie; Baldwin was assigned to Tidewater and Bodie was assigned from Jackson to Columbus, Ga.

February 20—A's re-signed pitcher Dave Hamilton, a re-entry free agent.

February 21—Astros released pitcher Frank Riccelli.

February 22—Mets signed second baseman Rob Andrews, a free agent, and assigned him to Tidewater.

February 26—Mets signed pitcher Tom Dixon, a free agent, and assigned him to Tidewater.

March 13—Cardinals signed pitcher Don Hood, a re-entry free agent formerly with the Yankees.

March 13—Giants signed infielder Rudy Meoli, a free agent, and assigned him to Phoenix; released him, April 3.

March 15—Expos traded catcher Duffy Dyer to Tigers for infielder Jerry Manuel, assigned to Denver.

March 15—Giants acquired infielder Joe Pettini from Expos to complete deal of June 13, 1979, in which Expos acquired catcher John Tamargo.

March 18—Expos released infielder Jim Mason.

March 20—Mariners signed third baseman Lenny Randle, a free agent, and assigned him to Spokane.

March 21—A's released outfielder Joe Wallis and pitcher Jim Todd.

March 27—Dodgers released pitcher Ken Brett and catcher Johnny Oates.

March 28—Braves traded pitcher Eddie Solomon to Pirates for a player to be named; pitcher Greg Field was assigned from Portland to Richmond to complete deal, April 25.

March 28—Indians released pitcher Roger Moret.

March 29—Blue Jays released designated hitter Rico Carty and pitcher Steve Luebber.

March 29—Mariners released pitcher Dan O'Brien.

March 29—Indians acquired pitcher Bud Anderson from Mariners and assigned him to Tacoma to complete deal of December 6, 1979, in which Indians traded third baseman-outfielder Ted Cox for pitchers Rob Pietroburgo and Rafael Vasquez.

March 29—Braves released pitcher Mickey Mahler.

March 29—Royals signed infielder Dave Chalk, a re-entry free agent formerly with the A's.

March 30—Phillies traded catcher Dave Rader to Red Sox for cash or a player to be named; Phillies acquired second baseman Stan Papi and assigned him to Oklahoma City to complete deal, May 12.

March 31—Rangers released pitcher David Clyde.

March 31—Expos traded first baseman-outfielder Rusty Staub to Rangers for infielder LaRue Washington, assigned to Denver, and third baseman Chris Smith, assigned from Charleston, W. Va., to Memphis.

March 31—Cardinals released pitchers Will McEnaney and Tom Bruno.

April 1—Mets released outfielder Bruce Boisclair.

April 1—Angels released first baseman-outfielder Ike Hampton, infielder Orlando Ramirez and pitcher Dave Freisleben.

April 1—Yankees signed pitcher Jim Kaat, a free agent.

April 1—Mariners traded pitcher Odell Jones to Pirates for cash and a player to be named; Jones was assigned to Portland, same club from which Mariners acquired pitcher Larry Anderson to complete deal, October 29.

April 1—Angels acquired pitcher Craig Eaton from Royals and assigned him to Salt Lake City to complete deal of December 6, 1979, in which Angels traded first baseman Willie Aikens and shortstop Rance Mulliniks for outfielder Al Cowens and shortstop Todd Cruz.

April 1—White Sox released outfielder Rusty Torres.

April 1—Giants reclaimed third baseman-shortstop Guy Sularz from Twins, who selected Sularz from Phoenix in the 1979 major league draft.

April 1—Yankees purchased first baseman Marshall Brant from Mets and assigned him to Columbus, O.

April 2—Mariners traded third baseman Lenny Randle to Cubs' Wichita affiliate for cash or a player to be named; Mariners later accepted cash settlement.

April 2—Reds released pitcher Manny Sarmiento.

April 2—Blue Jays released pitcher Butch Edge.

April 2—Cards released first baseman-outfielder Roger Freed.

April 3—White Sox released catcher Glenn Borgmann.

April 3—Giants released pitcher Pedro Borbon.

April 3—Orioles released second baseman Billy Smith.

April 3—Brewers released catcher Ray Fosse.

April 3—Twins released pitcher Paul Hartzell and second baseman Bobby Randall.

April 3—Twins purchased outfielder Greg Johnston from Giants and assigned him to Toledo.

April 4—A's signed infielder Dave McKay, a free agent.

April 4—Yankees signed catcher Johnny Oates, a free agent.

April 4—Phillies released shortstop Bud Harrelson and pitchers Doug Bird and Rawly Eastwick.

April 4—Dodgers released infielder Teddy Martinez.

April 5—Royals released pitcher Eduardo Rodriguez.

April 6—Red Sox traded pitcher Allen Ripley to Giants for cash or a player to be named; Red Sox later accepted cash settlement.

April 7—Cubs purchased pitcher Mark Lemongello from Blue Jays and assigned him to Wichita.

April 7—Phillies signed first baseman-outfielder Roger Freed, a free agent, and assigned him to Oklahoma City.

April 9—Mariners purchased pitcher Dave Heaverlo from A's.

April 12—Mets signed pitcher Dyar Miller, a free agent, and assigned him to Tidewater.

April 24—Mariners purchased pitcher Dave Roberts from Pirates.

April 30—Cardinals signed pitcher Pedro Borbon, a free agent; purchased pitcher Jim Kaat from Yankees; and released pitcher Darold Knowles.

May 5—Royals signed outfielder Rusty Torres, a free agent, and assigned him to Omaha.

May 7—Rangers signed shortstop Bud Harrelson, a free agent.

May 7—Indians purchased outfielder Miguel Dilone from Cubs' Wichita affiliate.

May 12—Tigers traded pitcher Jack Billingham to Red Sox for a player or players to be named. Deal originally called for outfielder Sam Bowen of Pawtucket to join Tigers, but an injury prevented that.

May 13—Angels purchased catcher Dave Skaggs from Orioles.

May 15—Twins activated coach Bobby Randall as second baseman; released him, June 3.

May 27—Cardinals released pitcher Pedro Borbon and outfielder Bernie Carbo.

May 27—Tigers traded first baseman Jason Thompson to Angels for outfielder Al Cowens.

May 28—Yankees signed outfielder Paul Blair, a free agent.

May 29—Tigers purchased second baseman Stan Papi from Phillies' Oklahoma City affiliate.

May 30—Red Sox released second baseman Ted Sizemore.

June 2—Cardinals traded outfielder Jim Lentine (on Springfield roster) to Tigers for pitcher John Martin and outfielder Al Greene, both assigned from Evansville to Springfield.

June 2—Royals released outfielder Steve Braun.

June 3—Blue Jays traded pitcher Dave Lemanczyk to Angels for a player to be named; Blue Jays acquired pitcher Ken Schrom from Angels' Salt Lake City affiliate and assigned him to Syracuse to complete deal, June 10.

June 6—Twins released pitcher Mike Marshall.

June 6—Angels released outfielder Ralph Garr.

June 7—White Sox traded outfielder Claudell Washington to Mets for pitcher Jesse Anderson, assigned from Lynchburg to Appleton.

June 10—Angels purchased pitcher Andy Hassler from Pirates.

June 12—Angels traded shortstop Todd Cruz to White Sox for pitcher Randy Scarbery, assigned from Iowa to Salt Lake City.

June 13—Reds signed catcher Joe Nolan, a free agent. Nolan, a three-year man, became a free agent when he refused his assignment by Braves to Richmond, June 12.

June 13—Indians traded catcher-outfielder Ron Pruitt to White Sox for utilityman Alan Bannister.

June 17—Mets traded pitcher Kevin Kobel to Royals' Omaha affiliate for a player to be named; pitcher Randy McGilberry was assigned to Tidewater to complete deal, June 23.

June 20—Indians purchased infielder Jack Brohamer from Red Sox.

June 20—Angels purchased pitcher Ed Halicki from Giants.

June 20—Mariners purchased catcher Marc Hill from Giants.

June 21—Blue Jays signed outfielder Steve Braun, a free agent, and assigned him to Syracuse.

June 21—Red Sox released pitcher Jack Billingham.

June 23—Indians traded catcher-first baseman Cliff Johnson to Cubs for two players to be named; first baseman-outfielder Karl Pagel was assigned from Wichita to Tacoma, June 30.

June 24—Angels released outfielder Merv Rettenmund.

June 24—Cubs released third baseman Steve Ontiveros.

July 1—Yankees released outfielder Paul Blair.

July 8—Dodgers signed outfielder Vic Davalillo, a free agent, and assigned him to Albuquerque.

July 11—Rangers purchased pitcher Charlie Hough from Dodgers.

July 11—Expos traded pitcher Ross Grimsley to Indians for infielder Dave Oliver, assigned from Tacoma to Memphis, and cash.

July 11—Mets signed shortstop Bill Almon, a free agent. Almon, a three-year man, became a free agent when he refused his assignment by Mets to Tidewater, July 7.

July 17—Phillies released pitcher Lerrin LaGrow.

July 19—Reds traded infielder Rick Auerbach to Rangers for a player to be named; Auerbach refused to report and was placed on disqualified list, July 23.

July 20—Cubs released outfielder Ken Henderson.

July 25—Phillies traded first baseman-outfielder Orlando Gonzalez (on Oklahoma City roster) to A's for cash or a player to be named; Phillies later accepted cash settlement.

July 28—Rangers purchased pitcher Ed Figueroa from Yankees.

August 4—Yankees purchased third baseman Aurelio Rodriguez from Padres.

August 5—Padres traded third baseman Kurt Bevacqua and a player to be named to Pirates for outfielder Rick Lancellotti, assigned from Buffalo to Amarillo, and third baseman-outfielder Luis Salazar, assigned from Portland to Hawaii; pitcher Mark Lee was assigned to Portland to complete deal, August 12.

August 8—Braves released shortstop Larvell Blanks.

August 8—Blue Jays released pitcher Tom Buskey.

August 8—Mariners released catcher Bob Stinson.

August 11—Padres traded pitcher John D'Acquisto to Expos for a player to be named; Padres purchased outfielder Randy Bass from Denver to complete deal, September 5.

August 11—Padres released outfielder Von Joshua and catcher Fred Kendall.

August 13—Mets released outfielder Jose Cardenal.

August 14—Rangers traded pitcher Gaylord Perry to Yankees for pitcher Ken Clay (on Columbus, O., roster) and a player to be named; outfielder Marvin Thompson was assigned from Columbus to Charleston, W. Va., to complete deal, October 1.

August 16—Giants released shortstop Roger Metzger.

August 20—Pirates released outfielder Alberto Lois.

August 21—Royals released pitcher Rawly Eastwick and signed outfielder Jose Cardenal, a free agent.

August 28—Expos released pitcher Dale Murray.

August 29—Royals released pitcher Steve Busby and outfielder Rusty Torres.

August 29—Dodgers activated coach Manny Mota as pinch-hitter; released him, October 8.

August 31—Padres traded first baseman Willie Montanez to Expos for infielder Tony Phillips (on Memphis roster) and cash.

September 1—Brewers purchased first baseman-outfielder John Poff from Phillies' Oklahoma City affiliate.

September 1—Phillies activated broadcaster Tim McCarver as catcher; released him, October 24.

September 1—Pirates signed outfielder Bernie Carbo, a free agent.

September 2—Reds released pitcher Dave Tomlin.

September 3—Blue Jays released pitcher Balor Moore.

September 11—Pirates purchased pitcher Jesse Jefferson from Blue Jays.

September 13—Rangers traded pitcher Sparky Lyle to Phillies for a player to be named; Rangers acquired pitcher Kevin Saucier to complete deal, November 19.

September 13—Rangers traded shortstop Pepe Frias to Dodgers for pitcher Dennis Lewallyn (on Albuquerque roster) and cash.

September 22—Brewers purchased pitcher Jamie Easterly from Expos' Denver affiliate.

October 3—White Sox activated coach Minnie Minoso as pinch-hitter; released him, October 6.

October 8—Pirates released outfielder Bernie Carbo.

October 10—Pirates released pitcher Jim Rooker.

October 16—Dodgers released outfielder Vic Davalillo.

October 17—Reds traded pitcher Jay Howell to Cubs for catcher Mike O'Berry.

October 21—Pirates released pitcher Gene Pentz.

October 24—White Sox purchased pitcher Hector Eduardo from Cardinals' Springfield affiliate on a conditional basis.

October 24—Yankees traded infielder Roger Holt to Rangers for cash and a player to be named; third baseman Tucker Ashford was assigned from Charleston, W. Va., to Columbus, O., to complete deal.

October 24—Yankees released pitcher Don Gullett.

October 24—Reds released catcher Vic Correll.

October 24—Angels released pitchers Ed Halicki and Dave Lemanczyk.

October 24—Phillies released outfielder Mike Anderson.

October 25—Cardinals released pitcher Don Hood.

November 3—Yankees traded shortstop Fred Stanley and a player to be named to A's for pitcher Mike Morgan; A's acquired shortstop Brian Doyle November 17, but transfer was nullified because Doyle was frozen on AAA roster. A's selected Doyle from Columbus in major league draft to complete deal, December 12.

November 4—Yankees released first baseman Marshall Brant.

November 15—Braves signed outfielder Claudell Washington, a re-entry free agent formerly with the Mets.

November 18—Mariners traded infielder Larry Milbourne to Yankees for catcher Brad Gulden and an estimated $150,000.

November 20—White Sox signed catcher Jim Essian, a re-entry free agent formerly with the A's.

November 26—White Sox signed outfielder Ron LeFlore, a re-entry free agent formerly with the Expos.

December 2—White Sox released third baseman Kevin Bell.

December 2—Angels signed pitcher Geoff Zahn, a re-entry free agent formerly with the Twins.

December 4—Astros signed pitcher Don Sutton, a re-entry free agent formerly with the Dodgers.

December 6—A's traded shortstop Mario Guerrero to Mariners for a player to be named.

December 6—Phillies re-signed Tug McGraw, a re-entry free agent.

December 7—Cardinals signed catcher Darrell Porter, a re-entry free agent formerly with the Royals.

December 8—Indians re-signed pitcher Dan Spillner, a re-entry free agent.

December 8—Astros released second baseman Joe Morgan.

December 8—Padres traded pitchers Rollie Fingers and Bob Shirley, catcher-first baseman Gene Tenace and a player to be named to Cardinals for catchers Terry Kennedy and Steve Swisher, infielder Mike Phillips and pitchers John Littlefield, John Urrea, Kim Seaman and Al Olmsted; catcher Bob Geren was assigned from Waco to Gastonia to complete deal, December 10.

December 8—Padres released third baseman-outfielder Paul Dade.

December 8—Giants traded pitcher Bob Knepper and outfielder Chris Bourjos to Astros for third baseman Enos Cabell and a player to be named.

December 8—Twins traded outfielder Dave Edwards to Padres for infielder Chuck Baker.

December 9—Cubs traded pitcher Bruce Sutter to Cardinals for outfielder-first baseman Leon Durham, third baseman Ken Reitz and a player to be named; Cubs acquired infielder Ty Waller to complete deal, December 22.

December 9—Royals signed first baseman-designated hitter Lee May, a re-entry free agent formerly with the Orioles.

December 9—Pirates traded pitcher Bert Blyleven and catcher Manny Sanguillen to Indians for catcher Gary Alexander and pitchers Victor Cruz, Rafael Vasquez and Bob Owchinko.

December 10—Astros signed utilityman Dave Roberts, a re-entry free agent formerly with the Rangers.

December 10—Tigers traded shortstop Mark Wagner to Rangers for pitcher Kevin Saucier.

December 10—Red Sox traded shortstop Rick Burleson and third baseman Butch Hobson to Angels for third baseman Carney Lansford, outfielder Rick Miller and pitcher Mark Clear.

December 11—Angels signed pitcher John D'Acquisto, a re-entry free agent formerly with the Expos.

December 11—Cubs traded catcher-first baseman Cliff Johnson and infielder Keith Drumright, assigned from Wichita to Tacoma, to A's for pitcher Michael King, assigned from Ogden to Midland.

December 12—Braves traded pitcher Doyle Alexander to Giants for pitcher John Montefusco and outfielder Craig Landis.

December 12—Twins traded outfielder Willie Norwood to Mariners for pitcher Byron McLaughlin.

December 12—Giants traded second baseman Joe Strain and pitcher Phil Nastu to Cubs for outfielders Jerry Martin and Jesus Figueroa and a player to be named.

December 12—Cardinals traded pitchers Pete Vuckovich and Rollie Fingers and catcher Ted Simmons to Brewers for outfielders Sixto Lezcano and David Green, the latter assigned from Holyoke to Arkansas, and pitchers Lary Sorensen and Dave LaPoint.

December 12—A's second baseman Mike Edwards, a three-year man, became a free agent when he refused his assignment to Tacoma.

December 12—Cubs traded outfielder Mike Vail to Reds for outfielder Hector Cruz.

December 12—A's released pitcher Dave Hamilton.

December 12—Expos re-signed first baseman Willie Montanez, a re-entry free agent.

December 12—Expos traded second baseman Tony Bernazard to White Sox for pitcher Rich Wortham.

December 12—Tigers traded outfielder Dave Stegman to Padres for pitcher Dennis Kinney; Stegman was assigned to Hawaii.

December 12—Blue Jays traded outfielder-third baseman Bob Bailor to Mets for pitcher Roy Lee Jackson.

December 12—Rangers traded outfielder Richie Zisk, infielder Rick Auerbach and pitchers Ken Clay, Jerry Don Gleaton, Brian Allard and Steve Finch to Mariners for pitcher Rick Honeycutt, shortstop Mario Mendoza, catcher Larry Cox, outfielder Leon Roberts and designated hitter Willie Horton.

December 15—Yankees signed outfielder Dave Winfield, a re-entry free agent formerly with the Padres.

December 15—Padres traded pitcher Randy Jones to Mets for pitcher John Pacella and infielder Jose Moreno, assigned to Hawaii.

December 15—Orioles released pitcher Paul Hartzell.

December 16—Mets signed first baseman-outfielder Rusty Staub, a re-entry free agent formerly with the Rangers.

December 17—Orioles signed catcher Jose Morales, a re-entry free agent formerly with the Twins.

December 17—Blue Jays released catcher Bob Davis.

December 19—Rangers signed third baseman Bill Stein, a re-entry free agent formerly with the Mariners.

December 19—White Sox released third baseman-outfielder Junior Moore.

December 19—Mets signed third baseman Mike Cubbage, a re-entry free agent formerly with the Twins, and released infielder Bill Almon.

December 19—Twins traded pitcher Mike Bacsik to Mariners for outfielder Steve Stroughter; Bacsik was assigned to Spokane and Stroughter was assigned from Spokane to Toledo.

December 19—Expos re-signed pitcher Stan Bahnsen, a re-entry free agent.

December 22—Phillies re-signed outfielder Del Unser, a re-entry free agent.

December 22—Dodgers released outfielder Gary Thomasson, but received a consideration when he subsequently joined the Tokyo Yomiuri Giants.

December 22—Cardinals released outfielder Bobby Bonds.

December 23—Mets signed pitcher Dave Roberts, a re-entry free agent formerly with the Mariners.

December 23—Orioles signed outfielder Jim Dwyer, a re-entry free agent formerly with the Red Sox.

December 23—Brewers signed third baseman Roy Howell, a re-entry free agent formerly with the Blue Jays.

December 24—Giants re-signed catcher Mike Sadek, a re-entry free agent.

December 29—Angels signed outfielder Juan Beniquez, a re-entry free agent formerly with the Mariners.

December 29—Indians signed outfielder Pat Kelly, a re-entry free agent formerly with the Orioles.

More Deals . . . Lynn, Fisk and Kingman

A clerical error which took place when Boston's Fred Lynn and Carlton Fisk were not tendered new contracts by December 20 threatened to cost the Red Sox both of their stars in early January of 1981.

According to the Basic Agreement, all players due a new contract must receive an offer in writing by December 20. Hence, the two players immediately filed for free agency.

On January 23, just prior to an arbitration hearing on the matter, Lynn agreed to a trade to the California Angels with pitcher Steve Renko for pitchers Frank Tanana and Jim Dorsey and outfielder Joe Rudi. Fisk was granted his free agency in the hearing and signed with the White Sox.

Dave Kingman was traded by the Cubs back to New York to the Mets for outfielder Steve Henderson and cash February 28. Joe Morgan, released by the Astros in December, signed on with the Giants February 9. And Jeff Burroughs, whose trade from Atlanta to Seattle during the winter meetings was delayed because of certain contractual problems, was finally sent to the Mariners March 7. The Braves got minor league pitcher Carlos Diaz in return.

Hotels of Major League Teams

AMERICAN LEAGUE

AT BALTIMORE: Baltimore Hilton–Detroit, Minnesota. **Cross Keys Inn**–All other clubs.

AT BOSTON: Sheraton-Boston–All clubs.

AT CALIFORNIA: Hyatt House Anaheim–All clubs.

AT CHICAGO: Continental Plaza–Baltimore, Detroit, Milwaukee, New York. **Executive House**–Cleveland, Minnesota, Oakland, Seattle. **Hyatt Regency**–California. **Marriott**–Boston. **Sheraton Plaza**–Kansas City, Texas (at Hyatt Regency July 27, 28, 29), Toronto.

AT CLEVELAND: Hollenden House–Boston, Milwaukee, New York. **Stouffer's Inn on the Square**–Chicago. **Bond Court**–All other clubs.

AT DETROIT: Ponchartrain–Chicago, Kansas City, Milwaukee, New York. **Detroit Plaza**–All other clubs.

AT KANSAS CITY: Sheraton Royal–Chicago, Cleveland, Milwaukee, Oakland. **Crown Center**–All other clubs.

AT MILWAUKEE: Haytt Regency–California, Chicago, Cleveland, Seattle, Toronto. **Pfister**–All other clubs.

AT MINNESOTA: Leamington–Cleveland. **Northstar Inn**–Boston. **Registry Hotel**–California, Detroit. **Marriott**–All other clubs.

AT NEW YORK: New York Sheraton–All clubs.

AT OAKLAND: Hyatt Oakland–All clubs.

AT SEATTLE: The David Denny Hotel–Minnesota, Toronto. **Doubletree Inn**–Baltimore, California, Chicago, Kansas City, Texas. **Park Hilton**–Boston, Detroit, New York, Oakland. **Downtown Hilton**–Cleveland, Milwaukee.

AT TEXAS: Doubletree Inn–Baltimore. **Hyatt Regency**–Boston, California, Milwaukee, Minnesota, Oakland, Toronto. **Rodeway Inn (Arlington)**–All other clubs.

AT TORONTO: Hotel Toronto–All clubs.

NATIONAL LEAGUE

AT ATLANTA: Hilton–Houston, Los Angeles, New York. **Marriott**–All other clubs.

AT CHICAGO: Continental Plaza–San Francisco. **Executive House**–Atlanta. **Hyatt Regency**–Houston, Los Angeles. **Marriott**–Cincinnati, Montreal, New York, St. Louis. **Sheraton Plaza**–Philadelphia, Pittsburgh (at Hyatt Regency September 15, 16).

AT CINCINNATI: Terrace Hilton–Chicago, Houston, Los Angeles, Montreal. **Stouffer's Inn**–All other clubs.

AT HOUSTON: Shamrock Hilton–Chicago, Los Angeles, Philadelphia, Pittsburgh, St. Louis. **Marriott**–All other clubs.

AT LOS ANGELES: Los Angeles Hilton–Cincinnati. **Wilshire Hyatt House**–Philadelphia. **Biltmore**–All other clubs.

AT MONTREAL: Hotel Parc-Regent–Atlanta, Chicago (at Regency Hyatt April 14, 15, 16 and June 26, 27, 28), Cincinnati, San Diego. **Regency Hyatt**–All other clubs.

AT NEW YORK: New York Sheraton–All clubs.

AT PHILADELPHIA: Franklin Plaza–Houston, Pittsburgh, San Francisco. **Hilton Hotel of Philadelphia (Penn Campus)**–Cincinnati, New York, St. Louis. **Marriott**–Los Angeles (at Franklin Plaza July 18, 19, 20). **Stadium Hilton**–Atlanta, San Diego. **University City Holiday Inn**–Chicago, Montreal.

AT PITTSBURGH: Hyatt House–Houston, Philadelphia. **Marriott**–Atlanta. **Pittsburgh Hilton**–All other clubs.

AT ST. LOUIS: Stouffer's Inn–Cincinnati, Philadelphia. **Marriott Pavilion**–All other clubs.

AT SAN DIEGO: Town & Country–Atlanta, Houston, Los Angeles, Philadelphia. **Sheraton Harbor Island**–All other clubs.

AT SAN FRANCISCO: Holiday Inn Union Square–Chicago. **San Francisco Hilton**–Cincinnati, Los Angeles (at Sheraton Fisherman's Wharf September 22, 23, 24), Pittsburgh. **San Francisco Hyatt**–Philadelphia. **Sheraton Palace**–Houston. **Sheraton Fisherman's Wharf**–All other clubs.

Brett Chased Coveted .400-Mark

By CARL CLARK

Ted Williams was safe. The most asked question of baseball's 1980 season—will George Brett hit .400?—had been answered in the negative.

The Kansas City Royals third baseman, who was at .400 as late as September 19, wound up at .390, the highest average by a major leaguer since Williams batted .406 for the Boston Red Sox in 1941.

"Coming into the past season, if I'd hit .305 or .302, I'd have been very happy," Brett said. "Now, I don't think I could live with that.

"If I hit .305 next season, I don't think that would be a very good year after what I did this year."

Brett cited the day-by-day attention in his chase of a .400 average as the most unforgettable experience.

"Every day there was a log in the paper in regard to where I stood and where (Ted) Williams stood on that date," Brett continued. "Every time I picked up the paper, I saw my name."

Brett had to overcome a slow start and several injuries to reach his lofty level. He was standing at only .267 through games of May 26. In his next 13 games, he rapped out 26 hits in 53 at-bats (.491), but damaged ligaments in his right ankle while stealing a base against Cleveland June 10.

The preliminary expectation was that Brett would miss perhaps a week. He did not return, however, until after the All-Star Game. George missed 26 games, of which the Royals won 13.

A week later, July 18, Brett launched a 30-game hitting streak that raised his average from .366 to .404. Minnesota's Ken Landreaux had the season's longest streak, 31 games, but it was not so destructive as Brett's. George batted .467 during the rampage, hit six home runs and drove in 42 runs, including seven game-winning RBIs. The streak ended when Texas lefthander Jon Matlack held Brett hitless in three trips August 19.

Brett peaked at .407 with a five-for-five night at Milwaukee August 26, but could manage only a .326 clip the rest of the way. It was one of 23 times that Brett had three or more hits in a game; he had four four-hit games and 18 three-hit games.

Brett was hitting .396 when tendinitis in his right wrist sidelined him for nine games from September 7 through September 16. Then, six hits in his next three games boosted him to .3995 before a 4-for-26 skid finished his chances.

In winning his second American League batting title, Brett, with 118 RBIs in 117 games, became the first player to drive in more than one run a game since Red Sox first baseman Walt Dropo knocked in 144 in 136 games in 1950.

Brett hit .391 at home and .388 on the road. He hit .318 against lefthanders, soft treatment compared with his .437 devastation of righthanders.

Cleveland and Oakland pitchers continued to be George's bugbear. Tribe hurlers limited him to five hits in 23 at-bats (.217), dropping his career average against the Indians to .223, 96 points below his lifetime average against the league as a whole. Of Brett's 578 career RBIs, only 20 of them had come against Cleveland. He hit .233 against Oakland, putting his career average against the A's at .264.

On the other hand, Brett enchanced his reputation as the bete noire of the Yankees. In 10 regular-season games against New York, he batted .425 and drove in 22 runs. Nine extra-base hits, including four homers, resulted in a slugging percentage of .900. Brett hit two more homers against the Yankees in the Championship Series. His three-run blast into the upper deck in right field off Goose Gossage in Game Three lifted the Royals to a 4-2 victory and a sweep of the series.

A complete breakdown of Brett's batting figures and a game-by-game account of his at-bats, hits and RBIs follow:

	Pct.	AB.	H.	2B.	3B.	HR.	RBI.
Totals	.390	449	175	33	9	24	118
Home	.391	235	92	18	6	13	63
Road	.388	214	83	15	3	11	55
vs. Lefthanders	.318	179	57	10	2	8	35
vs. Righthanders	.437	270	118	23	7	16	83
April	.259	54	14	3	3	2	11
May	.329	79	26	6	2	1	16
June	.472	36	17	3	0	5	14
July	.494	85	42	12	3	3	25
August	.430	121	52	6	1	6	30
September	.290	62	18	1	0	6	19
October	.500	12	6	2	0	1	3
Baltimore	.417	36	15	2	3	1	8
Boston	.514	35	18	3	2	1	8
California	.400	35	14	5	0	1	7
Chicago	.415	41	17	2	0	1	5
Cleveland	.217	23	5	1	0	2	2
Detroit	.333	45	15	5	0	3	10
Milwaukee	.524	21	11	1	0	2	6
Minnesota	.313	16	5	0	0	1	6
New York	.425	40	17	3	2	4	22
Oakland	.233	43	10	1	1	1	8
Seattle	.364	22	8	2	0	3	8
Texas	.426	47	20	3	0	3	10
Toronto	.444	45	20	5	1	1	18

Date	Opponent–Site	AB.	H.	RBI.	Date	Opponent–Site	AB.	H.	RBI.
4-10	Detroit	3	0	1	5-10	at Boston	6	2	1
4-11	Detroit	4	1	0	5-11	at Boston	2	1	0
4-12	Detroit	4	3	1	5-12*	at New York	0	0	0
4-13	Detroit	3	0	0	5-16	California	4	2	0
4-15	at Baltimore	4	1	1	5-17	California	4	0	0
4-16	at Baltimore	4	0	0	5-18	California	4	2	1
4-17	at Baltimore	3	2	2	5-19	Oakland	5	1	1
4-18	at Detroit	5	0	0	5-20	Oakland	3	0	0
4-19	at Detroit	3	1	0	5-21	Oakland	6	0	0
4-20	at Detroit	3	1	1	5-22	Oakland	5	2	1
4-21	Toronto	3	0	0	5-23	at California	6	2	2
4-22	Toronto	4	0	0	5-24	at California	4	1	1
4-23	Toronto	5	3	4	5-25	at California	5	3	3
4-25	Baltimore	1	1	1	5-26	at Oakland	3	0	0
4-26*	Baltimore	1	0	0	5-27	at Oakland	5	3	0
4-29	at Toronto	4	1	0	5-28	at Oakland	4	1	2
5- 6*	at Chicago	1	0	0	5-30	Chicago	4	2	0
5- 9	at Boston	4	1	3	5-31	Chicago	4	3	1

Date	Opponent–Site	AB.	H.	RBI.	Date	Opponent–Site	AB.	H.	RBI.
6- 1	Chicago	3	1	0	8-12	Baltimore	4	2	1
6- 2	New York	4	1	2	8-13	Baltimore	4	2	1
6- 3	New York	5	3	2	8-15	Toronto	4	1	3
6- 4	New York	5	3	4	8-16	Toronto	4	3	2
6- 5	at Texas	5	2	2	8-17	Toronto	4	4	5
6- 6	at Texas	4	3	1	8-18	at Texas	5	3	0
6- 7	at Texas	4	0	0	8-19	at Texas	3	0	0
6- 8	at Texas	5	3	2	8-20	at Texas	3	3	2
6-10	at Cleveland	1	1	1	8-21	Cleveland	4	1	1
					8-22	Cleveland	4	1	0
7-10	Detroit	4	2	0	8-23	Cleveland	3	0	0
7-11	Detroit	5	3	2	8-24	Cleveland	4	1	0
7-12	at Baltimore	3	1	0	8-25	at Milwaukee	4	2	1
7-13	at Baltimore	4	3	1	8-26	at Milwaukee	5	5	1
7-14	at Baltimore	4	2	1	8-27	at Milwaukee	3	1	0
7-15	at Boston	4	2	0	8-28	Texas	4	1	1
7-16	at Boston	5	4	1	8-29	Texas	5	2	1
7-17	at Boston	4	0	0	8-30	Texas	6	3	1
7-18	at New York	5	4	4	8-31	Texas	3	0	0
7-19	at New York	5	2	2					
7-20	at New York	4	1	3	9- 1	Milwaukee	4	1	1
7-21	Chicago	3	2	0	9- 3	Milwaukee	2	1	1
7-22	Chicago	4	1	0	9- 4	Milwaukee	3	1	2
7-23	Chicago	5	2	1	9- 5	at Cleveland	4	1	0
7-24	Chicago	4	2	2	9- 6	at Cleveland	3	0	0
7-25	New York	3	1	1	9-17	California	5	2	0
7-26	New York	4	1	2	9-18	California	3	2	0
7-27	New York	5	1	2	9-19	Oakland	4	2	2
7-29	Boston	5	4	1	9-20	Oakland	4	0	0
7-30	Boston	2	2	1	9-21	Oakland	4	1	2
7-31	Boston	3	2	1	9-22	at Seattle	4	1	1
					9-23	at Seattle	4	1	1
8- 1	at Chicago	4	1	1	9-24	at Seattle	3	0	0
8- 2	at Chicago	5	2	0	9-26	at Minnesota	4	1	0
8- 3	at Chicago	4	1	0	9-27	at Minnesota	4	0	1
8- 4	at Detroit	4	1	1	9-28*	at Minnesota	1	1	4
8- 5	at Detroit	3	1	3	9-30	Seattle	6	3	4
8- 6	at Detroit	4	2	1					
8- 8	at Toronto	4	2	2	10- 1	Seattle	3	3	1
8- 8	at Toronto	3	2	0	10- 2	Seattle	2	0	1
8- 9	at Toronto	5	1	1	10- 3	Minnesota	3	1	1
8-10	at Toronto	5	3	1	10- 4	Minnesota	4	2	0
8-11	Baltimore	4	1	0	*Pinch-hitter.				

Williams Made it With Six Points to Spare

Ted Williams' average stood at .3995 with two games remaining in the 1941 season. Technically, he was a .400-hitter already. But the Red Sox hitsmith went right out and stroked four hits in five at-bats in the first game of a doubleheader September 28 against the Philadelphia A's and came back with 2-for-3 in the nightcap to finish with a .406 average.

George Brett was seeking to equal that bit of nostalgia in 1980.

Williams' accomplishment put him in the .400-club with Nap Lajoie, Ty Cobb (three times), Joe Jackson, George Sisler (twice) and Harry Heilmann in the American League and Rogers Hornsby (three times) and Bill Terry in modern N.L. history.

A closer look at Williams' incredible season showed: he hit .389 (7-for-18) in April, .436 (44-for-101) in May, .372 (35-for-94) in June, .429 (27-for-63) in July, .402 (43-for-107) in August and 29-for-73 for a .397 mark in September.

Major League Farm Systems for 1981

AMERICAN LEAGUE

BALTIMORE (4): AAA—Rochester. AA—Charlotte. A—Miami. Rookie—Bluefield.

BOSTON (5): AAA—Pawtucket. AA—Bristol, Conn. A—Elmira, Winston-Salem, Winter Haven.

CALIFORNIA (5): AAA—Salt Lake City. AA—Holyoke. A—Redwood, Salem. Rookie—Idaho Falls.

CHICAGO (4): AAA—Edmonton. AA—Schenectady. A—Appleton. Rookie—Sarasota.

CLEVELAND (4): AAA—Charleston, W. Va. AA—Chattanooga. A—Batavia, Waterloo.

DETROIT (5): AAA—Evansville. AA—Birmingham. A—Lakeland, Macon. Rookie—Bristol, Va.

KANSAS CITY (6): AAA—Omaha. AA—Jacksonville. A—Fort Myers, Charleston, S. C. Rookie—Sarasota Blue and Sarasota Gold.

MILWAUKEE (5): AAA—Vancouver. AA—El Paso. A—Burlington, Ia., Stockton. Rookie—Butte.

MINNESOTA (5): AAA—Toledo. AA—Orlando. A—Visalia, Wisconsin Rapids. Rookie—Elizabethton.

NEW YORK (7): AAA—Columbus, O. AA—Nashville. A—Ft. Lauderdale, Greensboro, Oneonta. Rookie—Bradenton, Paintsville.

OAKLAND (4): AAA—Tacoma. AA—West Haven. A—Medford, Modesto.

SEATTLE (4): AAA—Spokane. AA—Lynn. A—Bellingham, Wausau.

TEXAS (4): AAA—Wichita. AA—Tulsa. A—Asheville. Rookie—Sarasota.

TORONTO (6): AAA—Syracuse. AA—Knoxville. A—Florence, Kinston. Rookie—Bradenton, Medicine Hat.

NATIONAL LEAGUE

ATLANTA (5): AAA—Richmond. AA—Savannah. A—Anderson, Durham. Rookie—Bradenton.

CHICAGO (5): AAA—Iowa. AA—Midland. A—Geneva, Quad Cities. Rookie—Sarasota.

CINCINNATI (6): AAA—Indianapolis. AA—Waterbury. A—Cedar Rapids, Eugene, Tampa. Rookie—Billings.

HOUSTON (5): AAA—Tucson. AA—Columbus, Ga. A—Daytona Beach. Rookie—Sarasota Orange and Sarasota Blue.

LOS ANGELES (5): AAA—Albuquerque. AA—San Antonio. A—Lodi, Vero Beach. Rookie—Lethbridge.

MONTREAL (5): AAA—Denver. AA—Memphis. A—Jamestown, West Palm Beach. Rookie—Calgary.

NEW YORK (6): AAA—Tidewater. AA—Jackson. A—Little Falls, Lynchburg, Shelby. Rookie—Kingsport.

PHILADELPHIA (6): AAA—Oklahoma City. AA—Reading. A—Bend, Peninsula, Spartanburg. Rookie—Helena.

PITTSBURGH (5): AAA—Portland. AA—Buffalo. A—Alexandria, Greenwood. Rookie—Bradenton.

ST. LOUIS (6): AAA—Springfield, Ill. AA—Arkansas. A—Erie, Gastonia, St. Petersburg. Rookie—Johnson City.

SAN DIEGO (6): AAA—Hawaii. AA—Amarillo. A—Reno, Salem, Walla Walla. Rookie—Bradenton.

SAN FRANCISCO (5): AAA—Phoenix. AA—Shreveport. A—Clinton, Fresno. Rookie—Great Falls.

Presidents of Minor Leagues for '81

CLASS AAA

American Association—Joe Ryan, P. O. Box 382, Wichita, Kan. 67201

International League—Harold Cooper, Box 608, Grove City, Ohio 43123

Mexican League—Lic. Antonio Ramirez (Muro), Angel Pola No. 16, Col. del Periodista, Mexico 10, D. F., Mexico

Pacific Coast League—Bill Cutler, 2101 E. Broadway Rd., Tempe, Ariz. 85282

CLASS AA

Eastern League—P. Patrick McKernan, Box 26267, Albuquerque, N.M. 87125

Southern League—Jimmy Bragan, 235 Main St., Suite 200, Trussville, Ala. 35173

Texas League—Carl Sawatski, 1501 N. University, Suite 412, Little Rock, Ark. 72207

CLASS A

California League—E. W. (Bill) Wickert, 677 Santa Barbara Road, Berkeley, Calif. 94707

Carolina League—Jim Mills, 910 Devonport Rd., Raleigh, N. C. 27610

Florida State League—George MacDonald, Jr., P. O. Box 414, Lakeland, Fla. 33802

Midwest League—William K. Walters, P. O. Box 444, Burlington, Ia. 52601

New York-Pennsylvania League—Vincent M. McNamara, 220 Brookside Drive, Buffalo, N. Y. 14220.

Northwest League—Bob Richmond, 66 Club Rd., Suite 130, Eugene, Ore. 97401

South Atlantic League—John H. Moss, P. O. Box 49, Kings Mountain, N. C. 28086

ROOKIE CLASSIFICATION

Appalachian League—Paul Fyffe, Box 1287-X, Paintsville, Ky. 41240

Gulf Coast League—Thomas J. Saffell, 420 Golden Gate Point, Apt. 18, Sarasota, Fla. 33577

Pioneer League—Ralph C. Nelles, P. O. Box 570, Billings, Mont. 59103

Official Minor League Averages

Official Averages Of All Triple A, Double A and A Leagues, Plus Rookie Leagues

JOHN JOHNSON—National Association President.

American Association

CLASS AAA

Leading Batter
TIM RAINES
Denver

League President
JOE RYAN

Leading Pitcher
AL OLMSTED
Springfield

CHAMPIONSHIP WINNERS IN PREVIOUS YEARS

1902—Indianapolis	.683
1903—St. Paul	.657
1904—St. Paul	.646
1905—Columbus	.658
1906—Columbus	.615
1907—Columbus	.584
1908—Indianapolis	.601
1909—Louisville	.554
1910—Minneapolis	.637
1911—Minneapolis	.600
1912—Minneapolis	.636
1913—Milwaukee	.599
1914—Milwaukee	.590
1915—Minneapolis	.597
1916—Louisville	.605
1917—Indianapolis	.588
1918—Kansas City	.589
1919—St. Paul	.610
1920—St. Paul	.701
1921—Louisville	.583
1922—St. Paul	.641
1923—Kansas City	.675
1924—St. Paul	.578
1925—Louisville	.635
1926—Louisville	.629
1927—Toledo	.601
1928—Indianapolis	.593
1929—Kansas City	.665
1930—Louisville	.608
1931—St. Paul	.623
1932—Minneapolis	.595
1933—Columbus*	.604
Minneapolis	.562
1934—Minneapolis	.570
Columbus*	.556

1935—Minneapolis	.591
1936—Milwaukee†	.584
1937—Columbus†	.584
1938—St. Paul	.596
Kansas City (2nd)‡	.556
1939—Kansas City	.695
Louisville (4th)‡	.490
1940—Kansas City	.625
Louisville (4th)‡	.500
1941—Columbus†	.621
1942—Kansas City	.549
Columbus (3rd)‡	.532
1943—Milwaukee	.596
Columbus (3rd)‡	.532
1944—Milwaukee	.667
Louisville (3rd)‡	.574
1945—Milwaukee	.604
Louisville (3rd)‡	.545
1946—Louisville†	601
1947—Kansas City	.608
Milwaukee (3rd)‡	.513
1948—Indianapolis	.649
St. Paul (3rd)‡	.558
1949—St. Paul	.608
Indianapolis (2nd)‡	.604
1950—Minneapolis	.584
Columbus (3rd)‡	549
1951—Milwaukee†	.623
1952—Milwaukee	.656
Kansas City (2nd)‡	.578
1953—Toledo	.584
Kansas City (2nd)‡	.571
1954—Indianapolis	.625
Louisville (2nd)‡	.556
1955—Minneapolis†	.597

1956—Indianapolis†	.597
1957—Wichita	.604
Denver (2nd)‡	.584
1958—Charleston	.589
Minneapolis (3rd)‡	.536
1959—Louisville§	.599
Omaha§	.516
Minneapolis (2nd)‡	.586
1960—Denver	.571
Louisville (2nd)‡	.556
1961—Indianapolis	.573
Louisville (2nd)‡	.533
1962—Indianapolis	.605
Louisville (4th)‡	.486
1963-1968—Did not operate.	
1969—Omaha	.607
1970—Omaha*	.529
Denver	.504
1971—Indianapolis	.604
Denver*	.521
1972—Wichita	.621
Evansville*	.593
1973—Iowa	.610
Tulsa*	.504
1974—Indianapolis	.578
Tulsa*	.567
1975—Evansville*	.566
Denver	.596
1976—Denver*	.632
Omaha	.574
1977—Omaha	.563
Denver*	.522
1978—Indianapolis	.578
Omaha*	.489
1979—Evansville*	.574
Oklahoma City	.533

*Won playoff (East vs. West). †Won championship and four-team playoff. ‡Won four-team playoff. §Respective Eastern and Western division winners.

— 397 —

STANDING OF CLUBS AT CLOSE OF SEASON, AUGUST 29

EAST DIVISION

Club	Spfd.	Evan.	Iowa	Ind.	Den.	O.C.	Oma.	Wich.	W.	L.	T.	Pct.	G.B.
Springfield (Cardinals)	....	15	13	14	5	9	10	9	75	61	0	.551	....
Evansville (Tigers)	9	....	13	13	7	7	7	5	61	74	0	.452	13½
Iowa (White Sox)	11	11	....	14	3	8	6	6	59	77	0	.434	16
Indianapolis (Reds)	10	11	10	....	4	4	10	9	58	77	0	.430	16½

WEST DIVISION

Denver (Expos)	11	9	13	12	....	15	15	17	92	44	0	.676	....
Oklahoma City (Phillies)	7	8	8	12	9	....	14	12	70	65	0	.519	21½
Omaha (Royals)	6	9	10	6	9	10	....	16	66	70	1	.485	26
Wichita (Cubs)	7	11	10	6	7	12	8	....	61	74	1	.452	30½

Iowa club represented Des Moines, Iowa.

Major league affiliations in parentheses.

Playoff—Springfield defeated Denver, four games to one.

Regular-Season Attendance—Denver, 565,214; Evansville, 106,849; Indianapolis, 180,483; Iowa, 126,981; Oklahoma City, 200,938; Omaha, 159,113; Springfield, 99,935; Wichita, 101,108. Total, 1,540,621. Playoffs, 24,129. No all-star game.

Managers: Denver—Billy Gardner; Evansville—Jim Leyland; Indianapolis—Jim Beauchamp; Iowa—Pete Ward, Sam Ewing; Oklahoma City—Jim Snyder; Omaha—Joe Sparks; Springfield—Hal Lanier; Wichita—Jack Hiatt.

All-Star Team: 1B—Phelps, Omaha; 2B—Raines, Denver; 3B—Wallach, Denver; SS—Manuel, Denver; OF—Briggs, Denver; Gardner, Denver; Gonzalez, Oklahoma City; Householder, Indianapolis; Utility—Ireland, Omaha; C—Borgmann, Iowa; McCormack, Oklahoma City; DH—Bass, Denver; P—Olmsted, Springfield; Ratzer, Denver; Manager—Gardner, Denver.

(Compiled by Ed Williams, League Statistician, Shawnee, Okla.)

CLUB BATTING

Club	G.	AB.	R.	OR.	H.	TB.	2B.	3B.	HR.	RBI.	SH.	SF.	Int. BB.	BB.	HP.	SO.	CS.	LOB.	Pct.
Denver	136	4669	865	575	1383	2146	231	47	146	806	20	49	567	59	36	647	143	53	995	.296
Okla. City	135	4611	697	684	1288	1903	202	67	93	633	42	48	520	38	21	653	114	59	1019	.279
Omaha	137	4648	628	634	1254	1794	193	46	85	581	59	48	549	33	25	602	116	52	1055	.270
Springfield	136	4383	618	558	1176	1677	189	35	80	558	46	37	507	41	40	676	157	61	970	.268
Evansville	135	4354	568	638	1134	1638	202	31	80	525	49	47	548	44	38	652	109	51	1005	.260
Wichita	136	4512	655	718	1172	1868	194	35	144	601	37	40	531	25	34	726	98	44	963	.260
Iowa	136	4381	581	687	1088	1582	195	13	91	524	59	36	548	41	20	714	123	58	951	.248
Indianapolis	135	4457	506	624	1099	1591	178	43	76	471	72	46	416	38	22	734	115	44	934	.247

INDIVIDUAL BATTING

(Leading Qualifiers for Batting Championship—367 or More Plate Appearances)

*Bats lefthanded. †Switch-hitter.

Player and Club	G.	AB.	R.	H.	TB.	2B.	3B.	HR.	RBI.	SH.	SF.	BB.	HP.	SO.	SB.	CS.	Pct.
Raines, Timothy, Denver†	108	429	105	152	215	23	11	6	64	0	2	61	5	42	77	13	.3543
Gonzalez, Orlando, Okla. City*	97	370	60	131	173	22	7	2	55	2	6	51	1	31	12	3	.3541
Bass, Randy, Denver*	123	450	106	150	290	25	2	37	143	0	9	85	5	64	3	2	.333
Garcia, Daniel, Omaha*	120	406	61	130	156	11	6	1	49	0	4	59	3	43	10	8	.320
Tracy, James, Wichita*	112	406	66	130	207	17	6	16	63	1	3	67	1	68	4	4	.320
Gardner, Arthur, Denver*	120	436	79	138	230	30	10	14	64	1	4	30	4	49	23	10	.317
Briggs, Dan, Denver*	110	427	59	135	205	25	3	13	74	0	4	32	3	68	2	3	.316
Rosinski, Brian, Wichita*	117	391	66	123	210	20	5	19	79	2	3	59	4	102	2	2	.315
Landrum, Terry, Springfield	93	350	55	106	177	23	6	12	46	2	4	18	3	65	18	7	.303
Fiala, Neil, Springfield*	126	385	58	114	145	17	4	2	40	6	1	63	0	42	11	3	.296
Ireland, Timothy, Omaha	126	450	70	133	205	32	2	12	63	9	8	81	6	59	22	14	.296

Departmental Leaders: G—Castillo, 137; AB—Castillo, 599; R—Bass, 106; H—Castillo, 173; TB—Wallach, 295; 2B—Ireland, 32; 3B—Bonaparte, Castillo, Raines, 11; HR—Bass, 37; RBI—Bass, 143; GWRBI—Wallach, 16; SH—DeJohn, Wolf, 14; SF—Bass, Wallach, 9; BB—Phelps, 128; HP—Roof, 11; SO—Hale, 133; SB—Raines, 77; CS—Ireland, 14.

(All Players—Listed Alphabetically)

Player and Club	G.	AB.	R.	H.	TB.	2B.	3B.	HR.	RBI.	SH.	SF.	BB.	HP.	SO.	SB.	CS.	Pct.
Aguayo, Luis, Okla. City	84	291	37	71	121	19	2	9	40	2	0	21	2	51	2	4	.244
Alfaro, Jesus, Wichita	69	239	43	60	102	12	3	8	27	1	1	34	0	40	1	0	.251
Allen, Roderick, Iowa	38	131	23	34	56	4	0	6	24	1	1	10	0	25	2	1	.260
Altamirano, Porfirio, Okla. City	38	1	0	0	0	0	0	0	0	0	0	0	0	0	0	0	.000
Anderson, Michael, Okla. City	84	248	44	81	121	12	2	8	41	1	1	39	0	45	1	3	.327
Angelini, John, Denver*	46	3	0	0	0	0	0	0	0	0	0	0	0	0	0	0	.000
Arroyo, Carlos, Okla. City*	46	1	0	0	0	0	0	0	0	0	0	1	0	1	0	0	.000
Atkinson, William, Iowa*	58	5	1	1	1	0	0	0	0	2	0	1	0	1	1	1	.200
Augustine, David, Omaha	75	304	33	70	98	10	3	4	28	1	0	14	1	39	4	1	.230
Aviles, Ramon, Okla. City	11	43	13	12	16	1	0	1	2	2	0	5	0	2	0	0	.279

Player and Club	G.	AB.	R.	H.	TB.	2B.	3B.	HR.	RBI.	SH.	SF.	BB.	HP.	SO.	SB.	CS.	Pct.
Barnes, Richard, Iowa	31	1	0	0	0	0	0	0	0	0	0	0	0	0	0	0	.000
Barranca, German, Omaha*	93	305	39	69	94	10	3	3	26	3	4	37	0	41	28	5	.226
Bass, Randy, Denver*	123	450	106	150	290	25	2	37	143	0	9	85	5	64	3	2	.333
Bazan, Pedro, Wichita*	24	86	9	20	31	3	1	2	9	0	0	2	0	12	1	0	.233
Beare, Gary, Okla. City	7	1	0	1	1	0	0	0	0	1	0	2	0	0	0	0	1.000
Berenyi, Bruce, Indianapolis	20	38	3	10	13	0	0	1	5	3	1	2	0	5	0	0	.263
Bialas, David, Springfield	43	139	15	42	55	6	2	1	18	0	1	16	0	22	1	3	.302
Bonaparte, Elijah, Ok. City*	116	407	62	114	164	16	11	4	44	6	1	37	5	73	22	13	.280
Borgmann, Glenn, Iowa	73	213	28	67	100	15	0	6	36	1	2	47	0	25	2	3	.315
Briggs, Dan, Denver*	110	427	59	135	205	25	3	13	74	0	4	32	3	68	2	3	.316
Brown, Darrell, Evansville	123	498	62	138	174	15	6	3	43	2	1	19	0	45	38	8	.277
Brown, Leon, Omaha	65	157	15	30	41	3	1	2	19	3	2	8	0	9	1	0	.191
Brown, Scott, Indianapolis	40	35	0	1	1	0	0	0	0	3	0	0	0	18	0	0	.029
Brummer, Glenn, Springfield	110	323	36	83	98	12	0	1	40	8	1	38	5	50	5	4	.257
Burnside, Sheldon, Indianapolis	51	8	1	1	1	0	0	0	0	3	0	0	0	3	0	0	.125
Bystrom, Martin, Okla. City	19	5	0	1	1	0	0	0	0	0	0	0	0	2	0	0	.200
Campbell, David, Denver	9	1	0	0	0	0	0	0	0	0	0	0	0	1	0	0	.000
Carrion, Leonel, Denver	45	129	23	31	57	4	2	6	18	2	0	18	1	17	1	3	.240
Castillo, E. Manuel, Omaha†	137	599	86	173	233	20	11	6	70	8	3	23	0	24	8	6	.289
Castillo, Martin, Evansville	132	455	59	114	186	28	4	12	62	3	5	41	5	118	14	4	.251
Chappas, Harry, Iowa†	76	248	33	51	64	7	0	2	22	2	5	32	1	50	15	6	.206
Chism, Thomas, Evansville*	33	103	18	33	48	9	0	2	14	2	2	16	2	9	0	0	.320
Churchill, Norman, Wichita*	9	1	0	0	0	0	0	0	0	0	0	0	0	0	0	0	.000
Colbern, Michael, Iowa	84	268	30	66	104	12	1	8	34	2	2	13	1	74	2	2	.246
Combe, Geoffrey, Indianapolis	60	12	0	2	2	0	0	0	0	1	0	0	0	4	0	0	.167
Concepcion, Onix, Omaha	58	210	22	59	86	9	3	4	34	3	3	10	1	20	10	0	.281
Cruz, Henry, 34 Iowa-10 Evan	44	142	11	28	40	5	2	1	11	0	1	19	1	21	7	3	.197
Dasen, Ted, Evansville*	21	67	8	8	17	2	2	1	5	0	0	7	0	18	1	0	.119
Davis, Jody, Springfield	13	36	3	6	7	1	0	0	2	0	1	3	0	9	0	0	.167
Dawley, William, Indianapolis	25	15	0	1	2	1	0	0	2	0	0	5	0	0	0	0	.067
Day, Charles, Evansville*	26	4	0	1	1	0	0	0	0	0	0	1	0	1	0	0	.250
DeJohn, Mark, Evansville†	122	383	35	91	115	14	2	2	35	14	5	35	0	52	5	1	.238
Dempsey, Peter, Okla. City	58	179	20	43	64	4	4	3	25	5	3	16	5	45	2	2	.240
De Sa, Joseph, Springfield	123	423	54	124	180	25	2	9	74	4	5	43	4	62	5	2	.293
Detherage, Robert, Omaha	87	284	29	69	99	10	4	4	29	4	1	25	1	67	4	3	.243
Dilone, Miguel, Wichita†	20	84	12	20	25	5	0	0	2	0	0	7	1	5	11	5	.238
Dimmel, Michael, Springfield	35	103	15	20	32	4	1	2	14	1	0	5	0	18	3	0	.194
Dotson, J. Eugene, Springfield	14	33	4	2	4	2	0	0	2	0	0	8	0	14	1	0	.061
Doyle, Blake, Indianapolis*	106	379	39	94	122	19	3	1	22	5	5	20	3	14	9	6	.248
Drumright, Keith, 68 Oma-22 Wich	90	332	42	95	112	7	2	2	19	8	2	11	1	18	8	3	.286
Dues, Hal, Denver	16	2	0	0	0	0	0	0	0	0	0	0	0	2	0	0	.000
Durham, Leon, Springfield*	32	128	20	33	63	5	5	5	23	0	0	15	0	27	10	3	.258
Earley, William, Wichita	21	4	2	2	2	0	0	0	0	0	0	0	0	0	0	0	.500
Easterly, James, Denver†	57	7	2	2	2	0	0	0	1	0	0	0	0	1	0	0	.286
Eduardo, Hector, Springfield	26	1	0	0	0	0	0	0	0	0	0	0	0	0	0	0	.000
Engle, Ricky, Denver	28	8	0	1	1	0	0	0	0	0	0	0	0	4	0	0	.125
Enright, George, Wichita	10	29	1	5	6	1	0	0	2	0	1	3	0	5	0	1	.172
Ewing, Samuel, Iowa*	30	92	9	31	44	7	0	2	19	0	0	6	1	13	1	0	.337
Farkas, Ronald, Springfield	96	263	33	69	81	5	2	1	29	7	3	45	0	44	5	1	.262
Ferrer M., Sergio, Indpls†	6	15	1	4	5	1	0	0	0	0	0	3	0	1	1	0	.267
Fiala, Neil S., Springfield*	126	385	58	114	145	17	4	2	40	6	1	63	0	42	11	3	.296
Fierro, Javier, Wichita	56	186	27	51	75	6	0	6	19	2	2	15	1	15	4	0	.274
Figueroa F., Jesus, Wichita*	11	39	5	4	7	0	0	1	3	0	0	4	2	6	2	2	.103
Filkins, Leslie, Evansville*	83	273	41	81	123	19	1	7	38	4	5	24	3	35	1	3	.297
Foley, Marvis, Iowa*	25	76	20	16	29	4	0	3	9	0	1	17	1	12	1	0	.211
Frazier, Frederic, Iowa	98	320	46	82	108	20	0	2	36	12	6	51	2	16	10	0	.256
Frazier, George, Springfield	35	1	0	0	0	0	0	0	0	0	0	0	1	0	0	0	.000
Freed, Roger, Okla. City	57	167	30	43	80	10	0	9	32	0	3	44	0	25	0	0	.257
Garcia, Daniel, Omaha*	120	406	61	130	156	11	6	1	49	0	4	59	3	43	10	8	.320
Gardner, Arthur, Denver*	120	436	79	138	230	30	10	14	64	1	4	30	4	49	23	10	.317
Gates, Joseph, Iowa*	58	213	21	49	73	9	0	5	20	2	0	22	0	28	0	2	.230
Gaudet, James, 18 Evan-71 Oma	89	296	35	77	107	16	1	4	31	6	5	22	1	40	1	0	.260
Gonzales, Daniel, Evansville*	15	49	7	10	20	2	1	2	5	0	0	6	0	7	0	0	.204
Gonzales, Orlando, Ok. City*	97	370	60	131	173	22	7	2	55	2	6	51	1	31	12	3	.354
Grace, Michael, Indianapolis	129	431	47	102	148	19	6	5	52	2	5	41	0	83	6	2	.237
Greene, Altar, 44 Evan-83 Spfld	127	391	66	98	174	15	5	17	61	0	4	92	7	94	5	2	.251
Gullickson, William, Denver	9	3	0	0	0	0	0	0	0	0	0	0	0	1	0	0	.000
Gulliver, Glenn, Evansville*	117	348	47	89	134	29	2	4	43	1	2	90	2	31	5	7	.256
Gustavson, Duane, Omaha	16	41	8	12	15	3	0	0	7	1	0	3	0	6	0	0	.293
Hale, John, Indianapolis*	122	412	62	113	223	21	4	27	77	0	4	62	3	133	13	4	.274
Hampton, Isaac, Evansville*	17	55	6	13	19	3	0	1	7	0	0	5	0	17	4	0	.236
Hart, J. Michael, Omaha†	49	155	30	52	77	5	4	4	30	0	4	38	0	30	3	4	.335
Hayes, William, Wichita	111	367	29	84	124	14	1	8	48	3	5	28	2	69	2	1	.229
Heath, Kelly, Omaha	56	182	22	46	67	10	1	3	22	8	1	14	1	25	2	0	.253
Herr, Thomas, Springfield†	37	141	29	44	57	6	2	1	16	0	0	14	2	10	19	3	.312

Player and Club	G.	AB.	R.	H.	TB.	2B.	3B.	HR.	RBI.	SH.	SF.	BB.	HP.	SO.	SB.	CS.	Pct.
Hoffman, Guy Alan, Iowa*	16	0	1	0	0	0	0	0	0	0	0	0	0	0	0	0	.000
Hogg, David, Omaha	40	108	10	21	28	5	1	0	17	1	2	22	0	25	0	0	.194
Holle, Gary, Iowa	25	88	10	22	34	3	0	3	8	0	0	4	0	21	1	1	.250
Hostetler, David, Denver	126	453	62	122	168	17	1	9	58	0	3	48	4	81	0	1	.269
Householder, Paul, Indpls†	125	464	74	137	200	26	5	9	50	1	6	44	1	88	30	5	.295
Howell, Jay, Indianapolis	25	27	1	2	3	1	0	0	0	4	0	0	0	7	0	0	.074
Hughes, Stephen, Indianapolis	30	77	8	13	15	2	0	0	9	0	1	8	0	22	0	0	.169
Hulett, Timothy, Iowa	3	8	1	2	2	0	0	0	0	0	0	1	0	1	0	0	.250
Ireland, Timothy, Omaha	126	450	70	133	205	32	2	12	63	9	8	81	6	59	22	14	.296
Isales P., Orlando, Ok. City	94	336	43	88	135	19	2	8	51	4	4	27	0	48	14	6	.262
James, Robert, Denver	17	3	0	0	0	0	0	0	0	0	0	0	0	1	0	0	.000
Javier, I. Alfredo, Wichita	120	418	57	106	167	16	3	13	53	1	4	34	8	55	10	1	.254
Johnson, Larry Doby, Evans	65	196	28	53	81	7	0	7	35	0	3	28	0	20	6	0	.270
Johnson, Randall, Iowa*	18	60	5	14	18	1	0	1	8	0	0	5	1	22	2	0	.233
Jones, Lynn, Evansville	34	121	10	33	37	4	0	0	11	2	0	14	2	18	2	2	.273
Kelly, William, Indianapolis	30	56	4	10	11	1	0	0	2	5	1	2	0	20	0	0	.179
Kuntz, Russell, Iowa	91	339	47	99	156	20	2	11	54	6	4	37	1	61	9	6	.292
Landrum, Terry, Springfield	93	350	55	106	177	23	6	12	46	2	4	18	3	65	18	7	.303
Larson, Daniel, Oklahoma City	11	3	2	1	1	0	0	0	0	0	0	0	0	0	0	0	.333
Lea, Charles, Denver	2	2	0	0	0	0	0	0	0	1	0	0	0	0	0	0	.000
Leach, Richard, Evansville*	126	430	69	117	148	14	1	5	58	4	7	76	6	37	9	10	.272
Lemengello, Mark, Wichita	29	14	2	1	1	0	0	0	0	0	0	0	0	7	0	1	.071
Lentine, James, Springfield	22	72	15	22	31	6	0	1	7	1	4	12	0	5	2	2	.306
Lezcano, Carlos, Wichita	77	293	46	68	148	9	7	19	56	2	2	28	1	62	10	2	.232
Little, Jeffrey, Springfield	23	1	1	1	1	0	0	0	0	0	0	0	0	0	0	0	1.000
Lopez, Juan, Evansville	52	160	18	36	48	5	2	1	9	2	1	11	1	24	1	0	.225
Lora, Ramon, Oklahoma City	56	135	8	31	42	3	1	2	24	1	4	5	0	21	1	1	.230
Loviglio, John, Oklahoma City	123	498	98	138	181	13	6	6	39	5	6	64	1	44	33	6	.277
Lucarelli, Vito, Iowa	4	5	0	1	1	0	0	0	0	0	0	1	0	2	0	0	.200
Lyle, Donald, Indianapolis	90	228	20	62	89	11	2	4	42	2	3	18	1	30	1	2	.272
Machemer, David, Evansville	45	167	23	50	60	6	2	0	11	4	1	22	2	11	5	4	.299
Macha, Michael, Evansville	88	278	42	70	113	8	1	11	41	4	5	55	3	66	8	4	.252
Macko, Steven, Wichita*	89	317	46	80	129	14	4	9	42	4	6	48	1	30	12	2	.252
Manuel, Jerry, Denver†	128	491	105	136	172	23	2	3	61	9	8	81	5	62	11	3	.277
Martin, Jared, Wichita*	18	52	5	10	10	0	0	0	1	0	4	4	0	6	0	0	.192
Martinez, Jose, Oklahoma City	33	7	0	0	0	0	0	0	0	1	0	0	0	4	0	0	.000
Martz, Randy, Wichita*	16	5	0	2	2	0	0	0	0	0	0	0	0	0	0	0	.400
Matuszek, Leonard, Okla. City*	67	256	38	78	125	16	5	7	35	0	1	24	0	31	3	3	.305
McCann, Francis, Omaha	44	120	13	27	36	1	1	2	16	2	1	19	0	28	2	0	.225
McCormack, Donald, Okla. City	121	411	55	108	172	16	3	14	64	5	1	47	1	60	2	2	.263
Mendon, Kevin, Denver	13	4	0	0	0	0	0	0	0	0	0	0	0	4	0	0	.000
Menees, Eugene, Indianapolis	129	456	62	119	165	15	8	5	36	12	3	32	3	43	5	6	.261
Miller, Mark, Indianapolis	15	39	1	6	8	0	1	0	6	0	0	2	0	15	0	0	.154
Miller, Randall, Denver	32	1	0	0	0	0	0	0	0	1	0	1	0	0	0	0	.000
Mills, Bradley, Denver*	52	201	43	58	80	10	3	2	27	0	2	27	3	16	0	2	.289
Milner, Eddie, Indianapolis*	130	468	63	118	158	11	7	5	37	5	3	45	3	42	24	10	.252
Moore, Alvin, Iowa	30	102	11	29	44	4	1	3	22	0	0	16	2	12	1	4	.284
Moore, Donnie, Springfield*	15	1	0	0	0	0	0	0	0	0	0	0	0	1	0	0	.000
Mullins, Francis, Iowa	53	201	25	51	83	12	1	6	35	0	2	18	2	37	5	1	.254
Mutz, Thomas, 49 Oma-42 Den*	91	267	36	68	107	20	2	5	46	2	2	40	0	43	1	1	.255
Myrick, Robert, Wichita*	42	2	0	0	0	0	0	0	0	0	0	0	0	1	0	0	.000
Naehring, Mark, Iowa	72	197	28	51	77	8	3	4	29	3	1	37	1	40	2	4	.259
Nandin, Robert, Evansville†	26	57	9	19	26	5	1	0	8	1	0	7	0	4	4	2	.333
Nyman, Christopher, Iowa	126	421	75	108	164	21	4	11	45	2	3	62	2	75	29	6	.257
O'Berry, Michael, Wichita	9	23	4	6	8	2	0	0	6	1	2	2	1	5	0	0	.261
O'Keeffe, Richard, Indianapolis*	14	22	0	6	7	1	0	0	3	2	1	0	0	6	0	0	.273
O'Neill, Paul, Indianapolis	29	70	6	13	17	1	0	1	9	0	1	9	2	9	2	1	.186
Otten, James, Springfield	8	1	0	1	2	1	0	0	0	0	0	0	0	0	0	0	1.000
Pagel, Karl, Wichita*	56	187	34	50	97	10	2	11	32	0	4	49	2	53	0	2	.267
Papi, Stanley, Oklahoma City	8	30	5	10	14	2	1	0	3	0	0	1	0	6	0	0	.333
Parker, Mark, Wichita*	28	7	0	1	1	0	0	0	0	0	0	0	0	4	0	0	.143
Pasillas, Joseph, Iowa	10	27	3	5	12	1	0	2	7	1	1	2	0	4	0	0	.185
Patchin, Steven, Evansville	91	285	34	71	112	14	0	9	45	1	3	25	1	46	1	3	.249
Pate, Robert, Denver	67	226	49	86	129	15	2	8	65	1	4	27	1	28	7	2	.323
Payne, James, Wichita	5	10	0	1	1	0	0	0	1	0	0	0	0	4	0	0	.100
Penniall, David, Springfield	50	165	32	49	101	13	0	13	39	0	1	20	6	31	9	1	.297
Perez, Julio, Iowa*	12	38	6	11	18	4	0	1	7	3	0	4	0	3	2	1	.289
Phelps, Kenneth, Omaha*	133	442	80	130	235	30	3	23	72	3	5	128	8	84	4	2	.294
Poff, John, Oklahoma City*	133	496	80	140	224	25	10	13	90	0	7	66	1	68	3	6	.282
Price, Joseph, Indianapolis	11	22	1	2	2	0	0	0	1	7	0	2	0	6	0	0	.091
Putman, Eddy, Evansville	41	125	13	27	43	4	0	4	12	3	3	16	3	27	0	2	.216
Quintana, Luis, Denver*	4	4	1	1	1	0	0	0	0	0	0	1	0	2	0	0	.250
Raines, Timothy, Denver†	108	429	105	152	215	23	11	6	64	0	2	61	5	42	77	13	.354
Ramos, Richard, Denver	23	9	0	1	1	0	0	0	0	0	0	0	0	2	0	0	.111
Ramos, Roberto, Denver	74	244	36	72	92	6	1	4	30	1	1	25	2	39	2	3	.295

Player and Club	G.	AB.	R.	H.	TB.	2B.	3B.	HR.	RBI.	SH.	SF.	BB.	HP.	SO.	SB.	CS.	Pct.
Ramsey, Michael, Springfield†	21	69	7	18	19	1	0	0	6	1	0	8	0	9	2	5	.261
Ratzer, Stephen, Denver	30	2	0	0	0	0	0	0	0	0	0	0	0	2	0	0	.000
Reece, Robert, Denver	34	92	11	23	26	3	0	0	9	0	0	5	0	7	1	0	.250
Reed, Jerry, Oklahoma City	37	4	1	1	2	1	0	0	0	0	0	0	0	1	0	0	.250
Riley, George, Wichita*	28	0	0	0	0	0	0	0	0	0	0	0	0	0	0	0	.000
Rodriguez, Luis, Oklahoma City	80	241	34	60	85	8	7	1	28	2	4	26	5	32	12	5	.249
Rohlfing, Wayne, Wichita*	4	8	0	0	0	0	0	0	0	0	0	0	0	3	0	0	.000
Rohn, Daniel, Wichita*	130	480	81	117	149	18	1	4	22	8	2	96	6	59	29	13	.244
Roof, Eugene, Springfield†	133	481	68	124	177	23	0	10	57	7	2	56	11	64	26	13	.258
Rosinski, Brian, Wichita*	117	391	66	123	210	20	5	19	79	2	3	59	4	102	2	2	.315
Rothschild, Lawrence, Indianapolis	41	45	2	12	12	0	0	0	4	4	1	3	0	4	0	0	.267
Rucker, David, Evansville*	53	1	0	1	1	0	0	0	0	0	0	0	0	0	0	0	1.000
Sanchez, Orlando, Oklahoma City	68	218	21	67	83	9	2	1	21	0	4	6	0	18	1	3	.307
Santo Domingo, Rafael, Indpls†	106	281	24	62	75	10	0	1	19	1	3	17	3	37	2	1	.221
Scanlon, Patrick, Iowa*	18	51	5	7	11	1	0	1	3	0	0	13	0	10	0	1	.137
Semall, Paul, Wichita	13	3	0	0	0	0	0	0	0	0	1	0	0	0	0	0	.000
Seoane, Manuel, Wichita	30	6	0	0	0	0	0	0	0	0	0	0	0	2	0	0	.000
Sherow, Dennis, Denver	25	59	5	14	17	3	0	0	5	0	1	3	0	9	3	2	.237
Silverio, Luis, Omaha	21	70	8	15	30	3	0	4	14	0	2	5	1	13	1	0	.214
Smith, Billy, Oklahoma City†	72	230	45	64	93	6	4	5	37	1	3	38	0	35	4	1	.278
Smith, Christopher, Denver†	9	25	3	5	8	0	0	1	3	0	0	3	0	4	0	0	.200
Smith, Keith, Springfield	69	271	39	80	109	10	2	5	32	0	2	19	2	16	22	6	.295
Smith, Lee, Wichita	52	4	0	0	0	0	0	0	0	0	0	0	0	1	0	0	.000
Smith, Ronald, Oklahoma City	5	13	1	1	1	0	0	0	1	1	0	1	0	2	2	1	.077
Stegman, David, Evansville	18	59	11	12	19	2	1	1	6	0	2	11	0	13	2	0	.203
Stockstill, David, Wichita*	17	58	7	17	26	3	0	2	7	0	2	1	5	0	1		.293
Suter, Burke, Oklahoma City	26	5	0	1	1	0	0	0	1	1	0	0	0	4	0	0	.200
Sutherland, Leonardo, Iowa*	96	365	56	95	115	10	2	2	23	6	0	41	0	46	29	8	.260
Terrell, Jerry, Omaha	41	163	25	47	59	6	0	2	21	2	3	14	2	16	4	5	.288
Thomas, Randall, Springfield	93	264	25	65	76	5	0	2	22	7	2	17	2	29	3	4	.246
Thormodsgard, Paul, Okla. City	35	5	0	0	0	0	0	0	0	0	0	0	0	1	0	0	.000
Torres, Angel, Indianapolis*	55	10	1	2	2	0	0	0	1	0	0	0	0	3	0	0	.200
Torres, A. Raymundo, Iowa	26	98	9	24	33	4	1	1	15	0	2	5	0	16	2	0	.245
Torres, Rosendo, Omaha†	8	25	8	9	22	1	0	4	11	0	1	7	0	4	0	1	.360
Tracy, James, Wichita*	112	406	66	130	207	17	6	16	63	1	3	67	1	68	4	4	.320
Turgeon, Michael, Wichita†	127	489	61	122	189	26	1	13	75	7	3	25	2	73	4	4	.249
Ujdur, Gerald, Evansville	30	1	0	1	1	0	0	0	2	0	0	0	0	0	0	0	1.000
Upton, Jack, Wichita	62	220	35	65	113	13	1	11	43	0	1	19	0	33	0	1	.295
Van Gorder, David, Indianapolis	71	253	11	57	80	12	1	3	26	2	3	22	1	38	1	1	.225
Viskas, Steven, Wichita	14	4	0	0	0	0	0	0	0	0	0	0	0	2	0	0	.000
Vuksan, Jeffrey, Iowa	2	5	1	1	4	0	0	1	0	0	0	1	0	1	0	0	.200
Walk, Robert, Oklahoma City	8	5	0	1	1	0	0	0	0	0	0	0	0	1	0	0	.200
Walker, Duane, Indianapolis*	109	351	41	87	129	16	4	6	30	3	1	54	0	62	18	6	.248
Wallach, Timothy, Denver	134	512	103	144	295	29	7	36	124	1	9	51	2	92	1	0	.281
Waller, Tyrone, Springfield	123	420	55	110	156	14	7	6	53	1	6	36	4	79	10	3	.262
Washington, LaRue, Denver	85	271	50	72	96	7	1	5	28	0	0	46	1	30	12	9	.266
Werner, Donald, Indianapolis	65	219	32	60	92	10	2	6	35	0	4	30	1	30	3	0	.274
Williams, Dan Clifton, Iowa*	87	304	44	71	109	17	0	7	40	2	2	46	2	56	0	1	.234
Winslow, Daniel, Springfield	41	73	10	12	13	1	0	0	3	1	0	9	0	15	0	0	.164
Wolf, Michael, Iowa	116	331	27	69	83	8	0	2	30	14	2	34	2	42	1	7	.208
Wright, James, Oklahoma City	24	5	0	2	2	0	0	0	0	0	2	0	0	2	0	0	.400
Young, Kip, Indianapolis	21	24	2	3	9	0	0	2	3	5	0	0	1	6	0	0	.125
Zdeb, Joseph, Iowa	19	66	7	13	16	1	1	0	2	0	1	8	0	11	0	0	.197

The following pitchers had no plate appearances primarily through use of designated hitters, listed alphabetically by club, games in parentheses:

DENVER—Lovins, Steven (15); Murray, Dale (16); O'Connor, Jack* (2).

EVANSVILLE—Anderson, Larry (20); Baker, Steven (9); Cappuzzello, George (3); Chris, Michael (28); Fidrych, Mark (24); Pashnick, Larry (6); Petry, Daniel (4); Presley, Billy* (18); Replogle, Andrew (25); Robbins, Bruce* (9); Steffen, David (4); Tobik, David (30); Treuel, Ralph (30); Viefhaus, Stephen (2); Weaver, Roger (10).

IOWA—Barnicle, Theodore (6); Barrios, Francisco (1); Bernard, Jeffrey (1); Bradley, Leonard (11); Contreras, Arnaldo† (20); Darcy, Patrick (3); Esser, Mark (11); Evans, Randy (2); Howard, Fred (19); Hoyt, Lamarr (18); Lukevics, Mitchell (41); Murillo, Ramon (18); Patterson, Reginald (14); Robinson, Dewey (40); Scarbery, Randy† (2).

OKLAHOMA CITY—DeMeo, Robert (1); Miscik, Dennis* (5); Munninghoff, Scott (20); Speck, Clifford (20).

OMAHA—Brett, Kenneth* (5); Busby, Steven (8); Chamberlain, Craig (27); Christenson, Gary* (25); Cram, Gerald (33); Cvejdlik, Kent (5); Dubee, Richard (15); Eastwick, Rawlins (17); Fischer, Daniel (22); Kobel, Kevin (17); Laskey, William (27); McGilberry, Randall (14); Morley, Michael† (7); Paschall, William (12); Schattinger, Jeffrey* (48); Twitty, Jeffrey* (31).

SPRINGFIELD—Chamberlain, Thomas (20); Davis, Christopher (36); Kittle, Hubert (1); Kurosaki, Ryan (4); Littlefield, John (17); Martin, John† (20–13 with Evansville); Olmsted, Alan (17); Schultz, Budd (5); Seaman, Kim* (22); Strelitz, Leonard (25); Thomas, Roy (20); Urrea, John (14).

WICHITA—Allen, Michael (10); Bane, Edward (28–14 with Omaha); Geisel, David* (9); Madden, Robert (11);

McClain, Joe (9); Valentini, Vincent (12).

GRAND SLAM HOME RUNS—Turgeon 2; Augustine, Bass, Briggs, E. M. Castillo, Colbern, Dimmel, Durham, Hale, Isales, Javier, R. Johnson, Lezcano, Milner, Moore, Mullins, Pate, Putman, A. R. Torres, Williams, 1 each.

AWARDED FIRST BASE ON INTERFERENCE—Aviles (Hogg), Cruz (Hogg), Dimmel (Foley), Doyle (Mutz), Drumright (Lora), Gardner (Patchin), Lucarelli (Hogg).

GAME-WINNING RBIs

DENVER (87)—Wallach 16, Bass 14, Manuel 11, Briggs 10, Pate 8, Raines 7, Gardner 6, Hostetler 4, Mills 3, Carrion 2, Mutz 2, Washington 2, Ramos 1, Reece 1.

EVANSVILLE (55)—Gulliver 7, Leach 7, Castillo 6, Filkins 6, Macha 5, Patchin 5, Brown 4, DeJohn 3, Johnson 3, Lopez 2, Chism 1, Cruz 1, Greene 1, Hampton 1, Jones 1, Machemer 1, Putman 1.

INDIANAPOLIS (54)—Hale 11, Householder 9, Grace 6, Menees 6, Lyle 5, Werner 5, Santo Domingo 4, Van Gorder 3, Doyle 2, Berenyi 1, Dawley 1, Young 1.

IOWA (53)—Nyman 6, Borgmann 5, Kuntz 5, Mullins 5, Frazier 4, Williams 4, Colbern 3, Gates 3, Allen 2, Ewing 2, Holle 2, Naehring 2, Torres 2, Chappas 1, Cruz 1, Foley 1, Johnson 1, Moore 1, Pasillas 1, Sutherland 1, Wolf 1.

OKLAHOMA CITY (64)—Poff 11, Anderson 6, Gonzalez 6, Isales 6, Aguayo 5, Freed 4, Loviglio 4, McCormack 4, Rodriguez 4, Bonaparte 3, Dempsey 3, Sanchez 3, Lora 2, Matuszek 2, Smith 1.

OMAHA (64)—Castillo 12, Phelps 11, Gaudet 8, Augustine 5, Garcia 4, Ireland 4, Barranca 2, Concepcion 2, Detherage 2, Hart 2, McCann 2, Mutz 2, Silverio 2, Torres 2, Brown 1, Heath 1, Hogg 1, Terrell 1.

SPRINGFIELD (59)—Roof 8, Smith 7, Brummer 6, De Sa 6, Greene 6, Fiala 4, Landrum 4, Farkas 3, Penniall 3, Bialas 2, Durham 2, Herr 2, Thomas 2, Waller 2, Davis 1, Dimmel 1.

WICHITA (60)—Turgeon 10, Rosinski 8, Macko 7, Lezcano 6, Rohn 6, Javier 5, Upton 5, Alfaro 3, Hayes 3, Bazan 2, Pagel 2, Tracy 2, Drumright 1.

CLUB FIELDING

Club	G.	PO.	A.	E.	DP.	PB.	Pct.
Springfield	136	3446	1403	111	127	16	.978
Denver	136	3560	1445	131	135	7	.974
Evansville	134	3441	1498	133	110	19	.974
Omaha	137	3635	1481	152	138	10	.971

Triple Play—Omaha.

Club	G.	PO.	A.	E.	DP.	PB.	Pct.
Indianapolis	135	3540	1299	147	101	9	.971
Wichita	136	3523	1599	160	153	8	.970
Iowa	136	3490	1493	158	129	11	.969
Oklahoma City	135	3534	1505	175	131	11	.966

INDIVIDUAL FIELDING

*Throws lefthanded.

FIRST BASEMEN

Player and Club	G.	PO.	A.	E.	DP.	Pct.
Putman, Evansville	12	79	12	0	4	1.000
Bass, Denver	10	81	3	0	9	1.000
Farkas, Springfield	13	50	6	0	4	1.000
De SA, Springfield*	118	1005	86	6	99	.995
Upton, Wichita	57	518	53	4	64	.993
Leach, Evansville*	79	690	56	6	59	.992
Pagel, Wichita*	47	448	37	4	47	.992
Chism, Evansville*	14	120	7	1	8	.992
Matuszek, Okla City	66	579	52	6	60	.991
Terrell, Omaha	12	102	6	1	9	.991
Phelps, Omaha*	122	1154	51	12	103	.990

Player and Club	G.	PO.	A.	E.	DP.	Pct.
Tracy, Wichita	37	354	27	4	35	.990
Nyman, Iowa	108	957	79	13	92	.988
Holle, Iowa*	17	148	6	2	12	.987
Hostetler, Denver	120	1039	63	16	96	.986
Hampton, Evansville	14	126	9	2	8	.985
Poff, Okla City*	63	560	58	10	44	.984
Lyle, Indianapolis	49	290	25	6	23	.981
Patchin, Evansville	11	91	8	2	5	.980
Hale, Indianapolis	86	655	30	15	50	.979
Santo Domingo, Ind	14	113	10	4	7	.969

Triple Play—Phelps.

(Fewer Than Ten Games)

Player and Club	G.	PO.	A.	E.	DP.	Pct.
Greene, Springfield	8	66	4	0	5	1.000
Freed, Okla City	8	57	4	0	3	1.000
Ewing, Iowa	6	51	3	0	3	1.000
Garcia, Omaha*	4	44	5	0	1	1.000
Williams, Iowa*	6	38	4	0	4	1.000
Naehring, Iowa	4	30	2	0	3	1.000
Briggs, Denver*	3	22	0	0	1	1.000
Billy Smith, Okla City	3	15	1	0	2	1.000
Lopez, Evansville	3	7	0	0	1	1.000
Marty Castillo, Evan	1	3	0	0	0	1.000
Bialas, Springfield	2	2	0	0	1	1.000

Player and Club	G.	PO.	A.	E.	DP.	Pct.
L. D. Johnson, Evans	1	2	0	0	0	1.000
Van Gorder, Ind	1	2	0	0	0	1.000
Day, Evansville*	1	1	0	0	0	1.000
Wallach, Denver	6	71	4	1	6	.987
Dasen, Evansville	8	68	3	1	5	.986
Durham, Springfield*	9	68	7	2	5	.974
O. Gonzalez, Okla C*	4	23	0	1	7	.958
Werner, Indianapolis	4	55	4	3	9	.952
Cruz, Iowa*	2	16	2	1	1	.947
J. Davis, Springfield	2	5	1	1	1	.857

SECOND BASEMEN

Player and Club	G.	PO.	A.	E.	DP.	Pct.
Menees, Indianapolis	51	101	125	1	23	.996
FIALA, Springfield	111	217	323	5	63	.991
Loviglio, Okla City	123	262	413	8	86	.988
Herr, Springfield	19	24	40	1	8	.985
Gates, Iowa	14	24	33	1	9	.983
Machemer, Evansville	29	60	83	3	14	.979
Ireland, Omaha	85	212	284	11	65	.978
Rohn, Wichita	130	295	434	19	104	.975
Raines, Denver	107	226	338	16	70	.972
Doyle, Indianapolis	96	189	259	14	48	.970

Player and Club	G.	PO.	A.	E.	DP.	Pct.
Gulliver, Evansville	65	117	189	10	31	.968
Wolf, Iowa	28	57	64	4	13	.968
Washington, Denver	32	66	78	5	14	.966
Nandin, Evansville	21	35	51	3	10	.966
Farkas, Springfield	23	31	48	3	9	.963
F. Frazier, Iowa	86	179	258	19	55	.958
Billy Smith, Okla C	12	15	29	2	5	.957
Drumright, Oma-Wch	56	114	180	14	31	.955
Lopez, Evansville	35	69	95	8	20	.953
Naehring, Iowa	10	13	16	2	2	.935

Triple Play—Ireland.

SECOND BASEMEN—Continued
(Fewer Than Ten Games)

Player and Club	G.	PO.	A.	E.	DP.	Pct.	Player and Club	G.	PO.	A.	E.	DP.	Pct.
Mills, Denver	6	5	12	0	1	1.000	Terrell, Omaha	6	13	9	1	3	.957
Ron Smith, Okla C	3	6	3	0	1	1.000	Mullins, Iowa	8	16	17	2	4	.943
Grace, Indianapolis	1	6	2	0	1	1.000	Macko, Wichita	3	6	10	1	2	.941
Fierro, Wichita	2	1	1	0	0	1.000	Rodriguez, Okla City	2	4	1	1	0	.833
Perez, Iowa	7	9	17	1	2	.963	Barranca, Omaha	1	1	3	1	0	.800

THIRD BASEMEN

Player and Club	G.	PO.	A.	E.	DP.	Pct.	Player and Club	G.	PO.	A.	E.	DP.	Pct.
O'Neill, Indianapolis	21	24	28	2	1	.963	Mills, Denver	50	37	101	9	15	.939
J. Moore, Iowa	10	7	18	1	2	.962	Grace, Indianapolis	113	91	177	18	18	.937
Fierro, Wichita	34	24	63	4	6	.956	Turgeon, Wichita	78	61	164	16	19	.934
MAN. CASTILLO, Om	137	139	272	20	27	.954	Waller, Springfield	121	81	215	22	16	.931
Alfaro, Wichita	30	30	80	6	9	.948	Naehring, Iowa	43	20	65	7	5	.924
Gates, Iowa	37	25	64	5	9	.947	Wallach, Denver	90	72	143	18	20	.923
Dempsey, Okla City	51	49	89	8	9	.945	Billy Smith, Okla City	46	27	86	10	5	.919
Mullins, Iowa	43	25	70	6	10	.941	Rodriguez, Okla City	50	44	62	10	8	.914
Marty Castillo, Evans	131	131	266	26	24	.939							

Triple Play—Manny Castillo.

(Fewer Than Ten Games)

Player and Club	G.	PO.	A.	E.	DP.	Pct.	Player and Club	G.	PO.	A.	E.	DP.	Pct.
Herr, Springfield	6	5	12	0	1	1.000	Farkas, Springfield	7	9	14	2	3	.920
Menees, Indianapolis	6	6	5	0	1	1.000	Drumright, Wichita	2	2	6	1	3	.889
Lopez, Evansville	4	2	9	0	0	1.000	Nyman, Iowa	4	3	3	1	0	.857
Wolf, Iowa	7	2	8	0	1	1.000	Tracy, Wichita	3	1	5	1	0	.857
F. Frazier, Iowa	1	1	4	0	0	1.000	Hughes, Indianapolis	5	6	1	2	0	.778
Scanlon, Iowa	5	2	2	0	1	1.000	Macha, Evansville	4	3	3	2	1	.750
Matuszek, Okla City	3	1	3	0	1	1.000	M. Anderson, Okla C	4	3	3	2	0	.750
Foley, Iowa	2	0	3	0	0	1.000	Washington, Denver	1	1	2	1	1	.750
Householder, Ind	2	2	0	0	0	1.000	Williams, Iowa*	1	0	3	1	0	.750
Roof, Springfield	1	0	1	0	1	1.000	Hulett, Iowa	2	0	6	3	0	.667
Werner, Indianapolis	1	0	1	0	0	1.000	Perez, Iowa	7	2	5	4	1	.636
Fiala, Springfield	7	6	11	1	1	.944	Gulliver, Evansville	6	0	3	3	0	.500

SHORTSTOPS

Player and Club	G.	PO.	A.	E.	DP.	Pct.	Player and Club	G.	PO.	A.	E.	DP.	Pct.
DeJOHN, Evansville	121	204	345	10	63	.982	Heath, Omaha	47	75	128	11	31	.949
Avilas, Oklahoma City	11	16	35	1	7	.981	Alfaro, Wichita	32	42	69	6	13	.949
Farkas, Springfield	50	80	140	8	34	.965	Fierro, Wichita	19	33	56	5	18	.947
Manuel, Denver	126	233	357	22	64	.964	Wolf, Iowa	86	141	249	24	44	.942
Macko, Wichita	85	161	303	18	72	.963	Ireland, Omaha	39	57	104	10	19	.942
Menees, Indianapolis	73	90	166	11	29	.959	Aguayo, Oklahoma City	84	154	268	28	55	.938
Chappas, Iowa	64	90	182	13	35	.954	Hughes, Indianapolis	21	20	55	5	10	.938
Randy Thomas, Spr	80	126	181	15	47	.953	Grace, Indianapolis	18	22	38	4	5	.938
Gulliver, Evansville	21	32	49	4	11	.953	Ramsey, Springfield	20	34	47	6	11	.931
Washington, Denver	13	18	43	3	12	.953	Santo Domingo, Ind	38	60	68	11	16	.921
Concepcion, Omaha	56	74	135	11	31	.950	Rodriguez, Okla C	25	53	63	10	10	.921

(Fewer Than Ten Games)

Player and Club	G.	PO.	A.	E.	DP.	Pct.	Player and Club	G.	PO.	A.	E.	DP.	Pct.
Dempsey, Okla C	4	4	14	0	4	1.000	Papi, Oklahoma City	7	12	18	2	8	.938
Drumright, Omaha	1	3	3	0	0	1.000	Billy Smith, Okla C	6	12	15	2	5	.931
Doyle, Indianapolis	3	3	2	0	1	1.000	Ferrer, Indianapolis	6	8	15	2	1	.920
Mullins, Iowa	1	0	1	0	0	1.000	Ron Smith, Okla C	2	2	6	1	2	.889
Payne, Wichita	1	0	1	0	0	1.000	Naehring, Iowa	5	3	4	2	2	.846
Terrell, Omaha	7	12	17	1	3	.967							

CATCHERS

Player and Club	G.	PO.	A.	E.	DP.	PB.	Pct.	Player and Club	G.	PO.	A.	E.	DP.	PB.	Pct.
Miller, Indianapolis	13	73	12	0	2	1	1.000	Reece, Denver	33	146	14	3	2	0	.982
VAN GORDER, Ind	70	440	45	4	3	6	.992	Brummer, Springfield	108	562	55	12	4	13	.981
Winslow, Springfield	39	112	14	1	0	3	.992	Colbern, Iowa	59	311	43	7	3	4	.981
Robert Ramos, Den	74	399	51	4	7	3	.991	Bazan, Wichita	21	87	13	2	0	1	.980
L. D. Johnson, Evan	48	237	31	3	5	5	.989	McCormack, Okla C	116	545	56	13	8	9	.979
Borgmann, Iowa	59	290	28	4	3	5	.988	Putman, Evansville	25	121	15	3	2	5	.978
Gaudet, Ev-Oma	84	427	45	7	5	1	.985	Hayes, Wichita	104	483	43	15	4	5	.972
Werner, Indianapolis	56	300	20	5	3	2	.985	Patchin, Evansville	56	282	25	11	1	9	.965
Mutz, Omaha-Denver	76	351	23	6	3	4	.984	Hogg, Omaha	38	139	27	7	2	7	.960
Gustavson, Omaha	14	57	6	1	1	2	.984	Lora, Oklahoma City	31	114	15	8	1	2	.942
Foley, Iowa	18	110	9	2	1	2	.983								

CATCHERS—Continued

(Fewer Than Ten Games)

Player and Club	G.	PO.	A.	E.	DP.	PB.	Pct.
J. Davis, Springfield	9	54	6	0	0	0	1.000
Enright, Wichita	8	51	2	0	0	0	1.000
Lucarelli, Iowa	3	4	2	0	0	0	1.000
Vuksan, Iowa	2	5	1	0	0	0	1.000
Marty Castillo, Evan	2	3	2	0	0	0	1.000
Macha, Evansville	1	4	0	0	0	0	1.000
DeMeo, Okla C	1	1	0	0	0	0	1.000
Pasillas, Iowa	7	32	2	1	0	0	.971
O'Berry, Wichita	7	26	5	2	1	2	.939

OUTFIELDERS

Player and Club	G.	PO.	A.	E.	DP.	Pct.
Hale, Indianapolis	46	70	7	0	1	1.000
Keith Smith, Springfield	42	72	0	0	0	1.000
Sherow, Denver	23	43	4	0	2	1.000
R. Allen, Iowa	27	42	0	0	0	1.000
Terrell, Omaha	19	36	2	0	0	1.000
Bialas, Springfield	23	36	1	0	0	1.000
Lyle, Indianapolis	24	34	1	0	0	1.000
Santo Domingo, Ind	21	32	1	0	0	1.000
Zdeb, Iowa	19	30	0	0	0	1.000
J. Moore, Iowa	13	23	2	0	1	1.000
D. Gonzales, Evansville	15	19	2	0	0	1.000
Gulliver, Evansville	12	9	0	0	0	1.000
ROOF, Springfield	122	226	7	1	1	.996
Macha, Evansville	82	136	4	1	2	.993
Hart, Omaha*	48	113	3	1	0	.991
Tracy, Wichita	60	73	1	1	1	.987
Carrion, Denver	36	71	0	1	0	.986
Penniall, Springfield	37	69	0	1	0	.986
Briggs, Denver*	107	192	10	3	3	.985
Pate, Denver	67	126	5	2	2	.985
L. Brown, Omaha	54	114	7	2	0	.984
Sutherland, Iowa*	95	223	6	4	0	.983
Williams, Iowa*	67	107	6	2	1	.983
Garcia, Omaha*	93	162	5	3	1	.982
Milner, Indianapolis*	129	363	6	7	1	.981
Landrum, Springfield	86	193	6	4	1	.980
Dilone, Wichita	19	48	0	1	1	.980
Bonaparte, Okla C*	104	237	9	6	2	.976
Filkins, Evansville*	71	110	8	3	2	.975
Wallach, Denver	41	79	0	2	0	.975
Rosinski, Wichita	71	110	4	3	0	.974
Stegman, Evansville	15	37	1	1	0	.974
D. Brown, Evansville	120	288	5	8	1	.973
Dimmell, Springfield	34	71	2	2	1	.973
Detherage, Omaha	86	241	5	7	1	.972
O. Gonzalez, Okla C	86	195	9	6	2	.971
Householder, Ind	125	247	10	8	2	.970
Barranca, Omaha	52	84	7	3	0	.968
Ray Torres, Iowa	26	57	3	2	1	.968
Figueroa, Wichita*	11	29	1	1	0	.968
Jones, Evansville	22	29	1	1	0	.968
Kuntz, Iowa	90	198	9	7	3	.967
Lezcano, Wichita	77	200	4	7	0	.967
Greene, Evans-Spr	65	114	4	4	1	.967
Poff, Oklahoma City*	59	113	6	4	1	.967
Gardner, Denver*	119	249	5	9	2	.966
Leach, Evansville*	48	77	6	3	0	.965
Lentine, Springfield	20	51	1	2	0	.963
M. Anderson, Okla C	66	98	3	4	0	.962
Stockstill, Wichita	11	23	2	1	1	.962
Augustine, Omaha	74	158	3	7	1	.958
Turgeon, Wichita	45	64	2	3	0	.957
Randy Johnson, Iowa	18	19	3	1	1	.957
Walker, Indianapolis*	96	169	14	9	1	.953
Isales, Oklahoma City	86	192	12	10	3	.953
Washington, Denver	34	77	2	4	0	.952
Javier, Wichita	119	211	15	12	4	.950
Gates, Iowa	17	16	2	1	0	.947
Cruz, Iowa-Evansville*	30	35	0	2	0	.946
Colbern, Iowa	21	33	1	2	0	.944
Chappas, Iowa	14	13	2	1	1	.938
Durham, Springfield*	18	28	1	2	0	.935
Sanchez, Oklahoma City	26	35	3	3	1	.927
Jared Martin, Wichita*	13	19	1	2	0	.909
McCann, Omaha	10	18	1	2	0	.905
Dotson, Springfield	11	20	1	3	0	.875

(Fewer Than Ten Games)

Player and Club	G.	PO.	A.	E.	DP.	Pct.
Rusty Torres, Omaha	7	9	0	0	0	1.000
Hampton, Evansville	2	7	1	0	0	1.000
Silverio, Omaha	3	4	0	0	0	1.000
Foley, Iowa	1	2	0	0	0	1.000
Ireland, Omaha	1	1	1	0	0	1.000
Lora, Oklahoma City	5	1	0	0	0	1.000
Rodriguez, Okla C	3	1	0	0	0	1.000
L.D. Johnson, Evansville	2	1	0	0	0	1.000
Enright, Wichita	1	1	0	0	0	1.000
Hayes, Wichita	1	1	0	0	0	1.000
Mutz, Omaha	1	1	0	0	0	1.000
Herr, Springfield	6	5	1	1	0	.857
Bazan, Wichita	2	3	0	1	0	.667

PITCHERS

Player and Club	G.	PO.	A.	E.	DP.	Pct.
RATZER, Denver	30	17	44	0	5	1.000
Parker, Wichita	28	15	37	0	2	1.000
Atkinson, Iowa	55	16	28	0	2	1.000
T. Chamberlain, Spr	20	16	22	0	1	1.000
Reed, Oklahoma City	33	7	27	0	3	1.000
Dues, Denver	16	8	25	0	2	1.000
Rothschild, Indpls	33	7	20	0	2	1.000
Urrea, Springfield	14	8	19	0	1	1.000
Lukevics, Iowa	41	11	15	0	2	1.000
Fidrych, Evansville	24	6	17	0	0	1.000
Engle, Denver*	28	10	11	0	0	1.000
Semall, Wichita	13	12	9	0	1	1.000
L. Anderson, Evansville	20	6	14	0	1	1.000
Schattinger, Omaha	48	2	15	0	0	1.000
O'Keeffe, Indianapolis*	12	4	13	0	0	1.000
Patterson, Iowa	13	6	10	0	1	1.000
Chris Davis, Springfield	36	8	7	0	1	1.000
G. Frazier, Springfield	35	3	11	0	2	1.000
Paschall, Omaha	12	2	12	0	1	1.000
Speck, Oklahoma City	20	5	8	0	1	1.000
Hoyt, Iowa	18	5	7	0	1	1.000
Esser, Iowa*	11	4	8	0	1	1.000
Presley, Evansville	18	2	9	0	1	1.000
Price, Indianapolis*	11	2	9	0	0	1.000
Day, Evansville*	24	2	8	0	0	1.000
Replogle, Evansville	25	3	6	0	0	1.000
Christenson, Omaha*	25	1	8	0	0	1.000
Kobel, Omaha	17	6	3	0	0	1.000
Littlefield, Springfield	17	2	5	0	0	1.000
Tobik, Evansville	30	3	3	0	0	1.000
John Martin, Evn-Spr	20	1	5	0	0	1.000
McGilberry, Omaha	14	0	6	0	0	1.000

PITCHERS—Continued

Player and Club	G.	PO.	A.	E.	DP.	Pct.
Randy Miller, Denver.....	32	2	3	0	1	1.000
Lovins, Denver................	15	2	3	0	1	1.000
Bradley, Iowa.................	11	1	3	0	0	1.000
Seaman, Springfield*.....	22	1	3	0	0	1.000
M. Allen, Wichita...........	10	0	3	0	2	1.000
Easterly, Denver*..........	56	8	33	1	2	.976
Strelitz, Springfield......	25	16	24	1	0	.976
Contreras, Iowa	20	7	24	1	1	.969
Robinson, Iowa	40	8	21	1	1	.967
Olmsted, Springfield*....	17	11	18	1	1	.967
Ujdur, Evansville...........	29	7	21	1	2	.966
Viskas, Wichita..............	14	13	15	1	0	.966
Berenyi, Indianapolis.....	20	7	19	1	1	.963
Cram, Omaha	33	5	19	1	0	.960
Earley, Wichita*............	21	7	16	1	3	.958
Altamirano, Okla City ...	38	8	14	1	2	.957
Murillo, Iowa.................	18	8	14	1	1	.957
Angelini, Denver*..........	46	8	12	1	1	.952
Martinez, Okla City	32	10	10	1	0	.952
C. Chamberlain, Omaha	27	4	16	1	2	.952
Chris, Evansville*..........	28	7	31	2	1	.950
Bystrom, Okla City	19	12	7	1	0	.950
A. Torres, Indpls*..........	55	5	13	1	2	.947
Rick Ramos, Denver	23	3	14	1	0	.944
Hoffman, Iowa*..............	15	1	16	1	0	.944
Arroyo, Okla City*.........	46	3	13	1	0	.941
Scott Brown, Indpls.......	40	8	8	1	1	.941
Eduardo, Springfield......	24	9	23	2	2	.941
Weaver, Evansville........	10	10	6	1	1	.941
Burnside, Indianapolis*.	51	4	11	1	1	.938
Fischer, Omaha	22	8	21	2	2	.935
Munninghoff, Okla City.	22	8	21	2	2	.935

Player and Club	G.	PO.	A.	E.	DP.	Pct.
Twitty, Omaha................	31	1	12	1	0	.929
Lemongello, Wichita	27	11	15	2	1	.929
Barnes, Iowa*................	26	12	26	3	2	.927
Myrick, Wichita*............	42	5	7	1	0	.923
Martz, Wichita	16	11	13	2	2	.923
Murray, Denver	16	1	11	1	1	.923
Combe, Indianapolis	60	0	11	1	0	.917
Rucker, Evansville*	52	5	28	3	1	.917
Riley, Wichita*	28	2	9	1	1	.917
Mendon, Denver..............	13	5	6	1	0	.917
Madden, Wichita	11	2	9	1	0	.917
Kelly, Indianapolis	29	13	29	4	0	.913
Howell, Indianapolis	25	5	16	2	0	.913
Thormodsgard, Okla C ...	35	8	12	2	0	.909
Laskey, Omaha	27	5	25	3	2	.909
Valentini, Wichita	12	7	2	1	0	.900
Dawley, Indianapolis	25	8	9	2	2	.895
Wright, Okla City...........	23	7	10	2	1	.895
James, Denver................	17	10	15	3	3	.893
Roy Thomas, Springfield	20	4	4	1	2	.889
L. Smith, Wichita	50	3	12	2	1	.882
Treuel, Evansville..........	30	6	8	2	0	.875
Young, Indianapolis	21	6	14	3	0	.870
Suter, Okla City.............	26	20	26	7	1	.868
Dubee, Omaha	15	1	12	2	0	.867
D. Moore, Springfield	14	9	10	3	0	.864
Bane, Omaha-Wichita	28	8	10	3	0	.857
Seoane, Wichita	30	14	21	6	1	.854
Eastwick, Omaha	17	1	7	2	2	.800
Little, Springfield	22	2	5	2	0	.778
Howard, Iowa	19	3	7	4	0	.714

(Fewer Than Ten Games)

Player and Club	G.	PO.	A.	E.	DP.	Pct.
Beare, Oklahoma City....	7	5	8	0	1	1.000
Petry, Evansville	4	4	9	0	0	1.000
Gullickson, Denver.........	9	2	6	0	0	1.000
Otten, Springfield	7	0	8	0	1	1.000
Morley, Omaha*	7	1	7	0	0	1.000
Cvejdlik, Denver.............	5	1	6	0	0	1.000
Brett, Omaha*	5	2	4	0	1	1.000
Quintana, Denver	4	2	3	0	1	1.000
Lea, Denver	2	1	4	0	0	1.000
Baker, Evansville	9	1	3	0	1	1.000
Barnicle, Iowa................	6	2	2	0	1	1.000
Schultz, Springfield*......	5	0	4	0	0	1.000
Miscik, Okla City............	5	0	3	0	0	1.000
Cappuzzello, Evansville*	3	0	3	0	0	1.000
Viefhaus, Evansville.......	2	0	3	0	0	1.000
Churchill, Wichita*	9	1	1	0	0	1.000

Player and Club	G.	PO.	A.	E.	DP.	Pct.
Geisel, Wichita*.............	9	1	1	0	0	1.000
Campbell, Denver	9	0	2	0	0	1.000
M. Anderson, Okla City .	5	1	1	0	0	1.000
Steffen, Evansville.........	4	1	1	0	0	1.000
O'Connor, Denver*.........	2	0	2	0	0	1.000
Scarbery, Iowa...............	2	1	1	0	0	1.000
Wolf, Iowa	5	0	1	0	1	1.000
Kurosaki, Springfield......	4	0	1	0	0	1.000
Farkas, Springfield	1	0	1	0	1	1.000
Winslow, Springfield	1	1	0	0	0	1.000
Walk, Oklahoma City	8	6	4	1	0	.909
Larson, Okla City	8	4	5	1	0	.900
Robbins, Evansville*......	9	0	15	2	0	.882
McClain, Wichita............	9	2	5	1	1	.875
Pashnick, Evansville.......	6	1	6	1	0	.875
Busby, Omaha................	8	2	10	4	0	.750

The following players had no recorded accepted chances at the positions indicated; therefore, are not listed in the fielding averages for those particular positions: Barnard, p; Barrios, p; Manny Castillo, p; Darcy, p; Dilone, 2b; Evans, p; Fiala, ss; F. Frazier, ss; Freed, 3b; Ireland, 3b; Kittle, p; Lora, 3b; Papi, 2b; Poff*, p; Roof, 2b; Scanlon, p; Waller, ss.

CLUB PITCHING

Club	G.	CG.	ShO.	Sv.	IP.	H.	R.	ER.	HR.	BB.	Int. BB.	HB.	SO.	WP.	Bk.	ERA.
Springfield	136	39	13	28	1149	1092	558	493	107	460	29	29	698	51	5	3.86
Denver............................	136	32	14	33	1187	1158	575	511	76	544	34	37	740	43	10	3.87
Omaha............................	137	23	9	24	1212	1247	634	542	113	497	27	25	610	40	19	4.03
Indianapolis	135	14	4	31	1180	1188	624	536	71	551	46	26	768	55	13	4.09
Evansville......................	135	24	8	21	1147	1168	638	552	85	530	53	24	682	63	11	4.33
Oklahoma City	135	16	5	36	1178	1243	684	583	90	522	50	33	594	60	15	4.45
Iowa...............................	136	20	5	27	1163	1209	687	599	114	533	44	26	710	59	14	4.64
Wichita...........................	136	12	7	32	1174	1289	718	627	139	549	36	36	602	78	10	4.81

PITCHERS' RECORDS

(Leading Qualifiers for Earned-Run Average Leadership—109 or More Innings)

*Throws lefthanded.

Pitcher–Club	G	GS	CG	ShO	W	L	Sv	Pct.	IP	H	R	ER	HR	BB	Int. BB	HB	SO	WP	ERA
Olmsted, Springfield*	17	17	8	3	10	5	0	.667	117	107	41	36	5	33	1	1	62	4	2.77
Thormodsgard, Okla C	35	8	2	1	5	9	5	.500	113	105	46	37	6	37	4	3	68	2	2.95
Ujdur, Evansville	29	13	7	3	9	4	3	.692	115	103	54	43	8	38	4	1	62	7	3.37
S. Brown, Indianapolis	40	11	1	0	6	7	2	.462	123	114	52	47	9	49	4	3	73	1	3.44
Fischer, Omaha	22	22	7	3	7	9	0	.438	141	131	64	55	6	42	2	5	92	3	3.51
Ratzer, Denver	30	18	6	2	15	4	2	.789	163	166	76	65	7	29	1	5	50	1	3.59
Easterly, Denver*	56	4	2	0	9	8	15	.529	134	118	64	54	5	56	5	2	105	7	3.63
Strelitz, Springfield	25	25	8	1	12	11	0	.522	175	182	80	71	13	43	1	2	76	5	3.65
Schattinger, Omaha	48	2	0	0	8	4	6	.667	111	122	55	48	3	53	5	4	48	6	3.89
Fidrych, Evansville	24	18	1	0	9	7	0	.462	117	123	56	51	4	54	4	4	62	13	3.92

Departmental Leaders: G—Combe, 60; GS—Engle, Parker, 28; CG—Olmsted, Strelitz, 8; ShO—Fischer, Olmsted, Ujdur, Urrea, 3; W—Ratzer, 15; L—Chris, 14; Sv—Combe, 23; Pct.—Ratzer, .789; IP—Kelly, 178; H—Kelly, 216; R—Parker, 107; ER—C. Chamberlain, 90; HR—C. Chamberlain, 23; BB—Berenyi, Eduardo, 100; IBB—Kelly, 12; SO—Berenyi, 121; HB—T. Chamberlain, Urrea, 7; WP—L. Smith, Munninghoff, 16.

(All Pitchers—Listed Alphabetically)

Pitcher–Club	G	GS	CG	ShO	W	L	Sv	Pct.	IP	H	R	ER	HR	BB	Int. BB	HB	SO	WP	ERA
Allen, Wichita	10	0	0	0	1	1	2	.500	11	14	11	11	2	9	0	0	6	1	9.00
Altamirano, Oklahoma	38	0	0	0	7	2	8	.778	89	67	51	48	9	27	4	4	39	3	4.85
L. Anderson, Evansville	20	14	3	0	5	6	1	.455	93	102	55	51	9	27	4	4	39	3	4.85
M. Anderson, Okla City	5	0	0	0	0	0	0	.000	8	6	1	1	0	3	0	0	4	0	1.13
Angelini, Denver*	46	0	0	0	9	5	8	.643	87	105	46	40	6	35	4	5	61	2	4.14
Arroyo, Oklahoma City*	46	1	0	0	8	6	13	.571	92	87	39	33	6	42	10	1	33	4	3.23
Atkinson, Iowa	55	2	0	0	3	5	6	.375	133	137	77	68	11	52	10	2	97	5	4.60
Baker, Evansville	9	5	1	0	1	3	0	.250	34	43	27	25	1	23	0	2	18	0	6.62
Bane, 14 Oma-14 Wch*	28	16	2	0	4	9	0	.308	134	181	94	79	29	48	0	4	60	0	5.31
Barnes, Iowa*	26	25	2	0	3	9	0	.250	123	131	73	63	7	93	1	2	59	13	4.61
Barnicle, Iowa*	6	5	1	0	5	0	0	1.000	37	37	26	14	1	24	1	0	34	0	3.41
Barrios, Iowa	1	1	0	0	0	0	0	.000	3	5	5	5	1	1	0	0	1	1	15.00
Beare, Oklahoma City	7	7	0	0	2	1	0	.667	30	41	22	20	2	11	1	1	18	0	6.00
Berenyi, Indianapolis	20	20	2	0	5	8	0	.385	123	111	66	59	5	100	3	1	121	14	4.32
Bernard, Iowa	1	1	0	0	0	1	0	.000	1	5	7	7	2	3	0	0	1	2	63.00
Bradley, Iowa	11	0	0	0	2	0	0	1.000	35	46	25	21	4	17	2	0	24	2	5.40
Brett, Omaha*	5	1	0	0	0	0	0	.000	9	11	5	4	0	4	0	1	2	0	4.00
S. Brown, Indianapolis	40	11	1	0	6	7	2	.462	123	114	52	47	9	49	4	3	73	1	3.44
Burnside, Indianapolis*	51	3	0	0	5	1	2	.833	80	89	30	27	4	31	1	3	46	4	3.04
Busby, Omaha	8	8	2	1	3	2	0	.600	58	45	19	16	4	28	3	3	29	5	2.48
Bystrom, Oklahoma City	14	14	4	1	6	5	0	.545	91	89	49	37	8	27	3	5	68	2	3.66
Campbell, Denver	9	0	0	0	0	1	1	.000	15	20	12	11	0	6	1	1	7	2	6.60
Cappuzzello, Evansville*	3	2	0	0	0	1	1	.000	14	17	8	7	1	3	0	0	9	0	4.50
Manny Castillo, Omaha	1	0	0	0	0	0	0	.000	1	0	3	3	0	6	0	0	1	0	27.00
C. Chamberlain, Omaha	27	27	3	0	11	10	0	.524	170	184	105	90	23	81	0	1	81	6	4.76
T. Chamberlain, Spr	20	20	3	0	7	5	0	.583	127	128	75	63	21	33	2	7	61	4	4.46
Chris, Evansville*	28	24	3	0	7	14	0	.333	140	148	82	71	8	90	2	6	85	6	4.56
Christenson, Omaha*	25	0	0	0	2	4	0	.333	41	29	18	11	4	21	1	0	37	2	2.41
Churchill, Wichita*	9	1	0	0	3	1	0	.750	24	33	13	12	3	10	0	0	15	2	4.50
Combe, Indianapolis	60	0	0	0	2	2	23	.500	77	50	20	19	4	35	6	2	72	6	2.22
Contreras, Iowa	20	20	1	1	9	7	0	.563	118	124	66	55	14	26	4	4	58	3	4.19
Cram, Omaha	33	2	0	0	6	5	3	.545	88	92	44	40	7	31	4	1	43	5	4.09
Cvejdik, Omaha	5	5	0	0	1	2	0	.333	33	40	19	18	5	12	0	0	11	0	4.91
Darcy, Iowa	3	2	0	0	1	1	0	.500	12	10	11	11	2	14	1	0	8	0	8.25
C. Davis, Springfield	36	2	1	1	7	5	4	.583	90	100	47	46	6	44	4	3	57	10	4.60
Dawley, Indianapolis	25	8	1	1	4	6	1	.400	77	90	46	39	5	31	3	3	28	1	4.56
Day, Evansville*	24	3	0	0	2	3	0	.400	43	48	31	30	8	31	0	0	26	6	6.27
Dubee, Omaha	15	9	1	0	2	4	0	.333	66	75	42	36	7	27	1	3	28	0	4.91
Dues, Omaha	16	16	4	2	7	4	0	.636	98	87	38	37	2	46	0	3	39	2	3.40
Earley, Wichita*	21	10	1	0	7	4	1	.636	98	103	44	42	7	37	0	4	51	6	3.86
Easterly, Denver*	56	4	2	0	9	8	15	.529	134	118	64	54	5	56	5	2	105	7	3.63
Eastwick, Omaha	17	0	0	0	2	2	0	.500	28	27	10	8	1	10	1	1	12	1	2.57
Eduardo, Springfield	25	24	7	1	8	13	0	.381	148	140	97	88	17	100	3	5	108	10	5.35
Engle, Denver*	28	28	5	1	12	7	0	.632	168	160	90	84	12	96	2	2	90	8	4.50
Esser, Iowa*	11	11	1	0	3	7	0	.300	63	60	38	31	10	52	0	1	41	6	4.43
Evans, Iowa	2	2	0	0	0	1	0	.000	8	15	9	8	2	5	1	0	4	0	9.00
Farkas, Springfield	1	0	0	0	0	0	0	.000	1	1	1	1	0	2	0	0	0	0	9.00
Fidrych, Evansville	24	18	1	0	9	7	0	.462	117	123	56	51	4	54	4	4	62	13	3.92
Fischer, Omaha	22	22	7	3	7	9	0	.438	141	131	64	55	6	42	2	5	92	3	3.51
Frazier, Springfield	35	0	0	0	1	3	11	.250	60	44	22	20	5	23	8	1	55	3	3.00
Geisel, Wichita*	9	0	0	0	1	0	4	1.000	15	14	12	11	1	13	0	2	17	2	6.60
Gullickson, Denver*	9	9	5	2	6	2	0	.750	66	47	14	14	3	29	0	1	64	1	1.91

Pitcher–Club	G	GS	CG	ShO	W	L	Sv	Pct.	IP	H	R	ER	HR	BB	Int. BB	HB	SO	WP	ERA
Hoffman, Iowa*	15	9	4	0	6	3	1	.667	75	59	31	30	5	34	1	0	56	6	3.60
Howard, Iowa	19	19	6	1	6	10	0	.375	113	121	69	63	13	32	5	1	49	6	5.02
Howell, Indianapolis	25	17	1	0	5	11	0	.313	98	95	70	55	5	71	7	3	73	9	5.05
Hoyt, Iowa	18	4	0	0	5	2	2	.714	62	61	22	20	2	22	2	2	36	0	2.90
James, Denver	17	17	2	0	9	2	0	.818	87	66	42	37	2	74	1	6	79	5	3.83
Kelly, Indianapolis	29	26	2	0	11	11	0	.500	178	216	88	80	10	55	12	3	72	4	4.04
Kittle, Springfield	1	1	0	0	0	0	0	.000	1	0	0	0	0	0	0	0	0	0	0.00
Kobel, Omaha*	17	8	2	1	2	1	0	.667	53	62	38	33	7	24	1	1	21	0	5.60
Kurosaki, Springfield	4	0	0	0	0	0	0	1.000	6	12	4	4	2	2	0	0	3	0	6.00
Larson, Oklahoma City	8	8	3	1	4	2	0	.667	48	41	24	21	1	20	2	4	35	1	3.94
Laskey, Omaha	27	22	3	1	5	8	0	.385	145	155	81	67	17	72	2	3	77	6	4.16
Lea, Denver	2	2	0	0	0	0	0	.000	12	8	2	2	1	5	0	1	9	3	1.50
Lemongello, Wichita	27	17	3	0	6	10	0	.375	128	158	85	73	18	34	7	4	42	2	5.13
Little, Springfield*	22	7	1	0	3	4	0	.429	62	60	32	31	6	28	3	0	46	4	4.50
Littlefield, Springfield	17	0	0	0	3	0	3	1.000	32	32	11	8	3	9	1	0	17	0	2.25
Lovins, Denver	15	0	0	0	0	0	0	.000	21	28	15	13	5	22	7	1	10	1	5.57
Lukevics, Iowa	41	8	0	0	2	10	1	.167	121	143	90	81	18	49	9	5	67	3	6.02
Madden, Wichita	11	9	1	0	1	4	0	.200	46	43	34	29	5	47	3	2	19	1	5.67
Martin, 13 Evn-7 Spr*	20	0	0	0	2	2	1	.500	38	39	25	25	9	22	3	1	31	0	5.92
Martinez, Oklahoma City	32	9	1	0	4	7	2	.364	111	123	72	64	14	57	5	1	63	5	5.19
Martz, Wichita	16	16	2	1	8	6	0	.571	107	98	41	37	9	29	0	2	53	5	3.11
McClain, Wichita	9	9	1	0	1	5	0	.167	44	54	41	37	4	31	2	1	32	4	7.57
McGilberry, Omaha	14	0	0	0	3	0	1	1.000	31	24	11	9	1	21	2	0	16	3	2.61
Mendon, Denver	13	12	3	0	7	1	0	.875	74	75	43	35	5	35	1	1	40	4	4.26
R. Miller, Denver	32	3	0	0	4	1	4	.800	72	89	47	43	9	47	4	4	59	4	5.38
Miscik, Oklahoma City*	5	2	1	0	0	2	0	.000	21	19	8	5	1	11	1	1	15	2	2.14
Moore, Springfield	14	13	7	1	6	5	0	.545	85	74	32	29	9	32	4	0	49	3	3.07
Morley, Omaha*	7	7	1	1	2	2	0	.500	38	43	16	13	2	17	2	0	14	1	3.08
Munninghoff, Okla City*	22	14	3	1	4	9	0	.308	92	112	63	52	3	54	4	3	30	16	5.09
Murillo, Iowa	18	15	2	0	5	8	0	.385	97	95	55	46	7	44	5	4	55	5	4.27
Murray, Denver	16	1	0	0	4	1	3	.800	44	31	13	8	0	17	4	3	25	1	1.64
Myrick, Wichita*	42	0	0	0	6	2	5	.750	73	63	23	21	5	35	3	2	45	4	2.59
O'Connor, Denver*	2	1	0	0	0	0	0	.000	5	3	1	1	1	6	0	0	7	0	1.80
O'Keeffe, Indianapolis*	12	10	0	0	3	4	0	.429	59	62	33	28	3	30	1	1	23	3	4.27
Olmsted, Springfield*	17	17	8	3	10	5	0	.667	117	107	41	36	5	33	1	1	62	4	2.77
Otten, Springfield	7	7	1	1	6	0	0	1.000	48	31	11	9	2	19	0	2	40	3	1.69
Parker, Wichita	28	28	3	2	7	11	0	.389	157	181	107	89	21	66	2	5	70	9	5.10
Paschall, Omaha	12	11	2	1	3	6	0	.333	70	72	37	35	10	19	0	0	40	0	4.50
Pashnick, Evansville	6	6	1	0	2	2	0	.500	38	44	24	21	2	12	1	0	13	2	4.97
Patterson, Iowa	13	12	3	1	4	8	0	.333	71	84	54	50	6	28	1	4	56	5	6.34
Petry, Evansville	4	4	1	0	2	0	0	1.000	30	21	11	9	0	12	0	0	16	1	2.70
Poff, Oklahoma City*	2	0	0	0	0	0	0	.000	9	4	4	4	0	5	0	0	4	2	12.00
Presley, Evansville	18	5	0	0	1	3	0	.250	48	44	27	20	2	17	4	0	36	3	3.75
Price, Indianapolis*	11	11	3	0	4	4	0	.500	79	64	36	34	5	30	1	0	83	2	3.87
Quintana, Denver*	4	4	1	0	2	0	0	1.000	27	30	7	6	1	6	0	1	18	0	2.00
Rick Ramos, Denver	23	21	4	2	7	5	0	.583	113	125	65	61	17	35	4	1	77	2	4.86
Ratzer, Denver	30	18	6	2	15	4	2	.789	163	166	76	65	7	29	1	5	50	1	3.59
Reed, Oklahoma City	33	7	0	0	6	5	4	.545	97	128	62	53	5	42	7	2	36	3	4.92
Replogle, Evansville	25	8	3	1	4	7	0	.364	82	90	42	37	9	31	5	0	50	3	4.06
Riley, Wichita*	28	0	0	0	3	3	4	.500	47	60	23	23	7	19	6	3	32	1	4.40
Robbins, Evansville*	9	9	1	0	2	6	0	.250	58	59	34	27	4	22	0	0	44	4	4.19
Robinson, Iowa	40	0	0	0	5	5	15	.500	73	60	26	23	8	30	3	0	58	2	2.84
Rothschild, Indianapolis	33	14	1	0	8	7	1	.533	113	111	60	53	11	44	3	1	74	4	4.22
Rucker, Evansville*	52	0	0	0	7	8	6	.467	92	94	53	35	3	52	10	6	53	5	3.42
Scanlon, Iowa	2	0	0	0	0	0	0	.000	4	3	1	1	0	4	0	0	2	0	2.25
Scarbery, Iowa	2	0	0	0	0	0	0	.000	5	5	0	0	0	1	1	0	4	1	0.00
Schattinger, Omaha	48	2	0	0	8	4	6	.667	111	122	55	48	3	53	5	4	48	6	3.89
Schultz, Springfield	5	5	0	0	0	2	0	.000	24	21	12	10	5	12	0	0	11	1	3.75
Seaman, Springfield*	22	1	0	0	2	3	3	.400	37	34	20	19	4	15	0	1	28	0	4.62
Semall, Wichita	13	8	1	0	1	7	0	.000	59	70	53	52	7	33	2	2	23	5	7.93
Seoane, Wichita	30	15	0	0	8	4	1	.667	113	128	66	54	14	50	5	4	58	8	4.30
L. Smith, Wichita	50	2	0	0	4	7	15	.364	90	70	49	37	4	56	4	2	63	16	3.70
Speck, Oklahoma City	20	9	0	0	1	5	0	.167	74	81	58	50	8	52	4	0	27	4	6.08
Steffen, Evansville	4	3	0	0	0	0	0	.000	7	11	13	13	3	9	0	0	3	0	16.71
Strelitz, Springfield	25	25	8	1	12	11	0	.522	175	182	80	71	13	43	1	2	76	5	3.65
Suter, Oklahoma City	26	25	2	0	9	6	0	.600	152	163	93	79	19	62	4	1	72	9	4.68
Roy Thomas, Springfield	19	0	0	0	5	1	6	.833	37	34	18	14	1	18	2	0	36	1	3.41
Thormodsgard, Okla City	35	8	2	1	5	5	9	.500	113	105	46	37	6	37	4	3	68	2	2.95
Tobik, Evansville	30	0	0	0	3	3	6	.500	48	35	22	21	3	26	2	0	49	2	3.94
A. Torres, Indianapolis*	55	1	0	0	2	7	1	.222	78	85	61	52	7	38	3	3	49	4	6.00
Treuel, Evansville	30	8	1	0	4	2	3	.667	97	103	50	46	11	35	4	2	38	4	4.27
Twitty, Omaha*	31	0	0	0	6	3	4	.667	48	34	16	10	3	9	3	0	24	1	1.88
Ujdur, Evansville	29	13	7	3	9	4	3	.692	115	103	54	43	8	38	4	1	62	7	3.37
Urrea, Springfield	14	14	3	3	5	4	0	.556	92	77	47	36	4	42	0	7	44	3	3.52
Valentini, Wichita	12	4	0	0	1	3	0	.250	31	40	27	27	5	18	2	0	20	4	7.84
Viefhaus, Evansville	2	2	0	0	0	0	0	1.000	8	8	6	6	0	6	0	0	4	0	6.75

Pitcher–Club	G.	GS.	CG.	ShO.	W.	L.	Sv.	Pct.	IP.	H.	R.	ER.	HR.	BB.	Int. BB.	HB.	SO.	WP.	ERA.
Viskas, Wichita	14	14	0	0	3	5	0	.375	78	84	46	42	11	34	0	1	30	8	4.85
Walk, Oklahoma City	8	8	0	0	5	1	0	.833	49	39	21	16	2	17	0	1	36	5	2.94
Weaver, Evansville	10	5	2	0	3	3	0	.500	37	29	16	13	3	17	4	0	21	2	3.16
Winslow, Springfield	1	0	0	0	0	0	0	.000	1	1	0	0	0	0	0	0	0	0	0.00
Wolf, Iowa	5	0	0	0	0	0	0	.000	8	6	2	2	1	2	0	0	1	0	2.25
Wright, Oklahoma City	23	23	0	0	9	9	0	.500	106	118	71	63	6	55	1	6	46	2	5.35
Young, Indianapolis	21	14	3	1	3	9	0	.250	95	101	62	45	3	38	2	3	54	3	4.26

BALKS—James 7; Fischer, Smith, 4 each; Barnes, Brown, Chris, Earley, Paschall, Reed, Rothschild, 3 each; Altamirano, Arroyo, Contreras, Cram, Dubee, Esser, Howell, Kelly, Laskey, McGilberry, O'Keeffe, Suter, Ujdur, Wright, 2 each; L. Anderson, Baker, Bane (Omaha), Barnicle, Barrios, Bradley, Busby, Bystrom, T. Chamberlain, Christenson, Dawley, Day, Dues, Frazier, Hoffman, Little, Lukevics, Martin (Springfield), Mendon, Miscik, Murillo, Myrick, Parker, Patterson, Presley, Ratzer, Schattinger, Seoane, Speck, Steffen, Strelitz, Thormodsgard, Weaver, Wolf, 1 each.

COMBINATION SHUTOUTS—Dues-Ratzer-Atkinson, James-Ratzer, Engle-Easterly, Lea-Angelini-Easterly, Miller-Easterly, Denver; Weaver-Martin, Fidrych-Rucker, Treuel-Rucker-Anderson, Chris-Tobik, Evansville; Howell-Combe 2, Indianapolis; Barnes-Atkinson, Murillo-Robinson, Iowa; Wright-Munninghoff-Arroyo, Oklahoma City; Laskey-Schattinger-Twitty-Cram, Omaha; Schultz-Seaman, Springfield; Viskas-Smith 2, Bane-Seoane, Earley-Smith, Wichita.

NO-HIT GAME—Madden (1⅔ inn.), Lemongello (7⅓ inn.), Wichita, defeated Iowa, 5-2, August 17.

Triplets Set Scoring Record

In the wildest one-inning scoring spree in American Association history, the Evansville Triplets erupted for 17 runs in the fourth inning on their way to a 20-3 romp over Iowa July 30.

The Triplets paraded 21 batters to the plate, collecting 10 hits, while the Oaks contributed two errors and six walks. The previous record of 15 runs was shared by St. Paul against Milwaukee July 27, 1930, and Minneapolis against Toledo May 18, 1936.

FOURTH INNING—Mike Macha singled in the hole at shortstop. Marty Castillo singled to left field. Both runners moved up on a wild pitch by Reggie Patterson. Larry Doby Johnson singled to center (2 runs). Mark DeJohn singled to center, Johnson going to third. Darrell Brown singled to center (3). Ted Barnicle replaced Patterson.

Glenn Gulliver walked to load the bases. Lynn Jones singled to center (4-5). Rick Leach walked to load the bases. Les Filkins bounced into a forceout at second base (6). Macha walked to load the bases. Castillo walked to force in a run (7). Johnson was safe when left fielder Dan Williams missed his line drive (8-9) for an error. Johnson was credited with a sacrifice fly. DeJohn was safe when third baseman Fran Mullins fielded his grounder and made a wild throw to first (10-11), DeJohn getting one RBI.

Brown singled to right. Gulliver singled to right (12). Jones walked to load the bases again. Leach walked, forcing in a run (13). Filkins singled to right (14). Macha hit a sacrifice fly to center (15). Castillo doubled off center-field wall (16-17). Bill Atkinson replaced Barnicle. Johnson flied out to right. 17 RUNS, 10 HITS, 2 ERRORS, 1 LEFT.

International League

CLASS AAA

Leading Batter
DAVE ENGLE
Toledo

League President
HAROLD COOPER

Leading Pitcher
KEN CLAY
Columbus

CHAMPIONSHIP WINNERS IN PREVIOUS YEARS

1884 – Trenton	.520	
1885 – Syracuse	.584	
1886 – Utica	.646	
1887 – Toronto	.644	
1888 – Syracuse	.723	
1889 – Detroit	.649	
1890 – Detroit	.617	
1891 – Buffalo (reg. season)	.727	
Buffalo (supplem'l)	.680	
1892 – Providence	.615	
Binghamton*	.667	
1893 – Erie	.606	
1894 – Providence	.696	
1895 – Springfield	.687	
1896 – Providence	.602	
1897 – Syracuse	.632	
1898 – Montreal	.586	
1899 – Rochester	.624	
1900 – Providence	.616	
1901 – Rochester	.642	
1902 – Toronto	.669	
1903 – Jersey City	.642	
1904 – Buffalo	.657	
1905 – Providence	.638	
1906 – Buffalo	.607	
1907 – Toronto	.619	
1908 – Baltimore	.593	
1909 – Rochester	.596	
1910 – Rochester	.601	
1911 – Rochester	.645	
1912 – Toronto	.595	
1913 – Newark	.625	
1914 – Providence	.617	
1915 – Buffalo	.632	
1916 – Buffalo	.586	
1917 – Toronto	.604	
1918 – Toronto	.693	
1919 – Baltimore	.671	
1920 – Baltimore	.719	
1921 – Baltimore	.717	
1922 – Baltimore	.689	
1923 – Baltimore	.677	

1924 – Baltimore	.709	
1925 – Baltimore	.633	
1926 – Toronto	.657	
1927 – Buffalo	.667	
1928 – Rochester	.549	
1929 – Rochester	.613	
1930 – Rochester	.629	
1931 – Rochester	.601	
1932 – Newark	.649	
1933 – Newark	.622	
Buffalo (4th)†	.494	
1934 – Newark	.608	
Toronto (3rd)†	.559	
1935 – Montreal	.597	
Syracuse (2nd)†	.565	
1936 – Buffalo‡	.610	
1937 – Newark‡	.717	
1938 – Newark‡	.684	
1939 – Jersey City	.582	
Rochester (2nd)†	.556	
1940 – Rochester	.611	
Newark (2nd)†	.594	
1941 – Newark	.649	
Montreal (2nd)†	.584	
1942 – Newark	.601	
Syracuse (3rd)†	.513	
1943 – Toronto	.625	
Syracuse (3rd)‡	.536	
1944 – Baltimore‡	.553	
1945 – Montreal	.621	
Newark (2nd)†	.582	
1946 – Montreal‡	.649	
1947 – Jersey City	.610	
Syracuse (3rd)†	.575	
1948 – Montreal‡	.614	
1949 – Buffalo	.584	
Montreal (3rd)†	.545	
1950 – Rochester	.609	
Baltimore (3rd)†	.556	
1951 – Montreal‡	.617	
1952 – Montreal	.629	
Rochester (3rd)†	.619	

1953 – Rochester	.630	
Montreal (2nd)†	.586	
1954 – Toronto	.630	
Syracuse (4th)§	.510	
1955 – Montreal	.617	
Rochester (4th)†	.497	
1956 – Toronto	.566	
Rochester (2nd)†	.553	
1957 – Toronto	.575	
Buffalo (2nd)†	.571	
1958 – Montreal‡	.588	
1959 – Buffalo	.582	
Havana (3rd)†	.523	
1960 – Toronto‡	.649	
1961 – Columbus	.597	
Buffalo (3rd)†	.559	
1962 – Jacksonville	.610	
Atlanta (3rd)†	.539	
1963 – Syracuse x	.533	
Indianapolis†	.562	
1964 – Jacksonville	.589	
Rochester (4th)†	.532	
1965 – Columbus	.582	
Toronto (3rd)†	.556	
1966 – Rochester	.565	
Toronto (2nd-tied)†	.558	
1967 – Richmond	.574	
Toledo (3rd)†	.525	
1968 – Toledo	.565	
Jacksonville (4th)†	.514	
1969 – Tidewater	.563	
Syracuse (3rd)†	.536	
1970 – Syracuse‡	.600	
1971 – Rochester‡	.614	
1972 – Louisville	.563	
Tidewater (3rd)†	.545	
1973 – Charleston	.586	
Pawtucket y†	.534	
1974 – Memphis	.613	
Rochester x‡	.611	
1975 – Tidewater‡	.610	

CHAMPIONSHIP WINNERS IN PREVIOUS YEARS—Continued

1976—Rochester	.638	1977—Pawtucket	.571	1978—Charleston	.607
Syracuse (2nd)†	.590	Charleston (2nd)†	.557	Richmond (4th)†	.511
				1979—Columbus‡	.612

*Won split-season playoff. †Won four-team playoff. ‡Won championsip and four-team playoff. §Defeated Havana in game to decide fourth place, then won four-team playoff. xLeague was divided into Northern, Southern divisions. yLeague divided into American, National divisions. (NOTE—Known as Eastern League in 1884, New York State League in 1885, International League in 1886-87, International Association in 1888, International League in 1889-90, Eastern Association in 1891, and Eastern League from 1892 until 1912.)

STANDING OF CLUBS AT CLOSE OF SEASON, SEPTEMBER 1

Club	Col.	Tol.	Roch.	Rich.	Char.	Tide.	Paw.	Syr.	W.	L.	T.	Pct.	G.B.
Columbus (Yankees)		16	9	11	12	10	12	13	83	57	0	.593	......
Toledo (Twins)	4		11	11	11	13	13	14	77	63	0	.550	6
Rochester (Orioles)	11	9	....	12	13	11	8	10	74	65	0	.532	8½
Richmond (Braves)	9	9	8	....	8	12	11	12	69	71	0	.493	14
Charleston (Rangers)	8	9	7	12	....	8	13	10	67	71	1	.486	15
Tidewater (Mets)	8	7	9	8	11	....	13	11	67	72	0	.482	15½
Pawtucket (Red Sox)	10	7	12	9	6	7	....	11	62	77	1	.446	20½
Syracuse (Blue Jays)	7	6	9	8	10	9	9	....	58	81	0	.417	24½

Tidewater club represented Norfolk and Portsmouth, Va.

Playoffs—Columbus defeated Richmond, three games to two; Toledo defeated Rochester, three games to one; Columbus defeated Toledo, four games to one (for Governor's Cup).

Regular-Season Attendance—Charleston, 118,881; Columbus, 546,074; Pawtucket, 163,283; Richmond, 187,462; Rochester, 292,667; Syracuse, 189,151; Tidewater, 116,756; Toledo, 199,602. Total, 1,813,876. Playoffs, 44,265. No all-star game.

Managers: Charleston—Tom Burgess; Columbus—Joe Altobelli; Pawtucket—Joe Morgan; Richmond—Fred Hatfield; Rochester—Doc Edwards; Syracuse—Harry Werner; Tidewater—Frank Verdi; Toledo—Cal Ermer.

All-Star Team: 1B—Brant, Columbus; 2B—Richardt, Charleston; 3B—Ashford, Charleston; SS—Bonner, Rochester; OF—Engle, Toledo; Johnston, Toledo; Wilson, Tidewater; C—Smith, Toledo; DH—Valle, Rochester; P—Babcock, Charleston; Kammeyer, Columbus; Manager—Altobelli, Columbus.

(Compiled by Leonard Alley, League Statistician, Richmond, Va.)

CLUB BATTING

Club	G.	AB.	R.	OR.	H.	TB.	2B.	3B.	HR.	RBI.	SH.	SF.	BB.	Int. BB.	HP.	SO.	SB.	CS.	LOB.	Pct.
Toledo	140	4603	612	542	1252	1730	202	33	70	564	96	58	396	52	39	637	156	62	954	.272
Tidewater	139	4424	535	577	1167	1569	191	41	43	486	98	40	479	35	31	630	117	51	996	.264
Pawtucket	140	4533	523	566	1149	1670	182	30	93	484	66	31	421	36	32	755	72	46	973	.253
Rochester	139	4495	588	579	1137	1633	204	17	86	538	68	34	448	52	28	635	89	66	928	.253
Richmond	140	4451	552	557	1110	1599	159	42	82	505	51	33	468	36	38	738	150	86	914	.249
Columbus	140	4421	590	477	1099	1622	190	33	89	537	77	40	509	45	29	650	50	31	937	.249
Syracuse	139	4662	558	591	1155	1685	171	55	83	508	65	35	480	40	30	693	104	52	981	.248
Charleston	139	4379	537	606	1067	1575	175	42	83	477	52	37	527	42	41	640	94	66	976	.244

INDIVIDUAL BATTING
(Leading Qualifiers for Batting Championship—378 or More Plate Appearances)

*Bats lefthanded. †Switch-hitter.

Player and Club	G.	AB.	R.	H.	TB.	2B.	3B.	HR.	RBI.	SH.	SF.	BB.	HP.	SO.	SB.	CS.	Pct.
Engle, R. David, Toledo	133	489	74	150	204	27	3	7	73	4	6	34	2	65	8	2	.307
Boggs, Wade, Pawtucket	129	418	51	128	152	21	0	1	45	1	3	64	0	25	3	2	.306
Vega, Jesus, Toledo	126	459	63	139	211	26	2	14	79	3	8	46	3	49	28	10	.303
Brooks, Hubert, Tidewater	113	417	50	124	161	18	5	3	50	4	4	36	1	56	14	5	.297
Johnston, Gregory, Toledo*	132	507	68	150	220	22	3	14	66	7	1	38	1	64	22	7	.296
Wilson, William, Tidewater†	132	515	92	152	203	11	14	4	44	9	4	44	4	86	50	14	.295
Backman, Walter, Tidewater†	125	400	53	117	145	15	5	1	51	7	4	87	0	67	11	7	.293
Brant, Marshall, Columbus	126	409	69	118	219	22	5	23	92	4	11	47	7	81	0	1	.289
Washington, Ronald, Toledo	114	407	62	117	167	31	5	3	36	14	6	18	5	81	19	5	.287
Ward, Gary, Toledo	128	496	82	140	217	22	8	13	66	2	8	41	5	76	26	6	.282

Departmental Leaders: G—Harper, 140; AB—Wells, 540; R—Wilson, 94; H—Wilson, 152; TB—Johnston, 220; 2B—Valle, 31; 3B—Wilson, 14; HR—Brant, 23; RBI—Brant, 92; SH—J. Walker, 24; SF—Brant, 11; BB—Backman, 87; HP—Gogener, E. Miller, 10; SO—K. Smith, 106; SB—E. Miller, 60; CS—Harper, 18.

(All Players—Listed Alphabetically)

Player and Club	G.	AB.	R.	H.	TB.	2B.	3B.	HR.	RBI.	SH.	SF.	BB.	HP.	SO.	SB.	CS.	Pct.
Ainge, Daniel, Syracuse	80	295	37	72	89	9	1	2	17	5	1	29	2	52	14	9	.244
Alberts, Francis, 54 Syr-12 Rich	66	202	24	44	75	5	4	6	21	3	1	26	2	43	1	0	.218
Aponte, Luis, Pawtucket	31	1	0	0	0	0	0	0	0	0	0	0	0	0	0	0	.000
Ashford, Thomas, Charleston	107	366	50	102	150	18	3	8	38	4	1	45	5	45	16	8	.279
Augustine, David, Charleston†	36	127	16	27	38	5	3	0	13	1	1	7	1	14	2	1	.213
Ault, Douglas, Syracuse	53	203	24	61	104	11	1	10	51	1	2	16	0	22	3	0	.300
Backman, Walter, Tidewater†	125	400	53	117	145	15	5	1	51	7	4	87	0	67	11	7	.293

Player and Club	G.	AB.	R.	H.	TB.	2B.	3B.	HR.	RBI.	SH.	SF.	BB.	HP.	SO.	SB.	CS.	Pct.
Baker, David, Syracuse*	34	101	9	18	27	2	2	1	11	1	2	14	4	23	0	0	.178
Baldwin, Reginald, Tidewater	96	311	34	85	120	20	0	5	43	9	3	15	5	12	0	0	.273
Beall, Robert, Richmond†	57	129	15	32	38	6	0	0	12	1	1	30	0	22	0	0	.248
Beamon, Charles, Syracuse*	62	201	13	44	60	4	0	4	23	0	1	11	1	23	5	3	.219
Benedict, Bruce, Richmond	3	10	0	3	3	0	0	0	0	0	0	0	0	1	0	0	.300
Benton, Alfred, Tidewater	67	240	36	63	97	15	2	5	34	8	3	6	5	36	3	6	.263
Berenguer, Juan, Tidewater	28	1	0	0	0	0	0	0	0	0	0	0	0	0	0	0	.000
Bogener, Terry, Charleston*	95	315	61	76	111	14	6	3	20	4	5	51	10	36	15	7	.241
Boggs, Wade, Pawtucket	129	418	51	128	152	21	0	1	45	1	3	64	0	25	3	2	.306
Bonner, Robert, Rochester	133	469	46	113	131	8	2	2	41	9	3	9	2	39	8	4	.241
Bowen, Samuel, Pawtucket	89	271	43	62	116	10	1	14	35	5	3	41	1	61	2	1	.229
Boyer, Raymond, Pawtucket	107	302	39	72	101	10	2	5	25	6	3	33	7	51	3	4	.238
Brant, Marshall, Columbus	126	409	69	118	219	22	5	23	92	4	11	47	7	81	0	1	.289
Braun, Stephen, Syracuse*	19	61	11	20	31	3	1	2	11	0	0	16	0	4	1	1	.328
Brizzolara, Anthony, Richmond	31	0	1	0	0	0	0	0	0	0	0	0	0	0	0	0	.000
Brooks, Hubert, Tidewater	113	417	50	124	161	18	5	3	50	4	4	36	1	56	14	5	.297
Bruhert, Michael, Charleston	30	1	0	0	0	0	0	0	0	0	0	0	0	0	0	0	.000
Bush, R. Randall, Toledo*	40	108	11	21	25	1	0	1	7	1	2	25	5	33	2	0	.194
Butera, Barry, Pawtucket*	46	120	10	28	39	5	0	2	15	0	2	18	0	18	2	3	.233
Chapman, Kelvin, Tidewater	81	232	30	49	63	6	1	2	19	5	3	21	4	25	4	3	.211
Chism, Thomas, 34 Tol-28 Roch*	62	218	33	56	92	12	0	8	29	1	2	31	0	20	2	2	.257
Cipot, Edwin, Tidewater*	109	326	30	75	113	19	2	5	40	1	2	58	1	52	2	0	.230
Coleman, David, Columbus	71	236	30	60	84	6	3	4	21	0	2	20	1	45	2	1	.254
Corey, Mark, Rochester	82	265	34	61	88	14	2	3	25	2	2	36	3	49	4	2	.230
Cowger, Tracy, Charleston	29	78	5	14	15	1	0	0	6	2	1	5	1	17	1	0	.179
Davis, Odie, Charleston	110	341	30	83	104	11	2	2	29	8	5	44	3	57	10	5	.243
Davis, Steven, Syracuse	126	438	36	100	139	18	3	5	33	11	4	53	2	90	23	5	.228
Derryberry, Timothy, Rochester*	13	41	4	4	10	0	0	2	5	1	0	6	0	11	0	0	.098
Douglas, Stephen, Toledo*	38	89	12	20	22	2	0	0	9	1	1	4	1	15	2	0	.225
Doyle, Brian, Columbus*	47	160	11	36	48	10	1	0	5	4	0	8	0	4	0	1	.225
Duran, Daniel, Charleston*	116	399	52	110	173	20	2	13	71	3	3	58	7	61	0	4	.276
Eden, E. Michael, Rochester†	65	187	37	48	74	10	2	4	31	5	5	43	2	14	4	1	.257
Engle, R. David, Toledo	133	489	74	150	204	27	3	7	73	4	6	34	2	65	8	2	.307
Ereu, William, Syracuse†	11	39	2	7	9	0	1	0	1	0	0	1	0	9	0	0	.179
Espino, Juan, Columbus	48	129	11	27	39	7	1	1	16	0	1	11	0	22	2	0	.209
Estes, Frank, Toledo*	41	128	11	41	52	9	1	0	20	2	3	17	1	7	5	1	.320
Felton, Terry, Toledo	25	0	0	0	0	0	0	0	0	0	0	0	0	0	0	0	.000
Ferrer, Sergio, Tidewater†	42	125	12	31	37	4	1	0	7	2	0	15	2	16	1	2	.248
Flores, Gilberto, Tidewater	99	306	53	84	108	13	4	1	16	11	3	47	4	39	21	7	.275
Freed, Roger, Syracuse	48	163	23	41	78	4	0	11	26	0	0	36	1	30	0	1	.252
Gedman, Richard, Pawtucket*	111	347	43	82	137	18	2	11	29	0	1	30	5	64	0	1	.236
Gonzales, Daniel, Rochester*	59	194	25	57	86	11	0	6	31	0	2	21	0	20	5	6	.294
Gooch, Ronald, Charleston	42	112	10	26	38	3	3	1	15	4	1	11	0	17	2	1	.232
Graham, Daniel, Rochester*	16	52	10	18	33	3	0	4	12	1	1	4	0	6	2	0	.346
Gulden, Bradley, Columbus*	14	51	6	8	16	2	0	2	10	0	1	8	0	9	0	0	.157
Hammond, Steven, Richmond*	130	445	45	107	144	18	5	3	59	4	6	31	2	35	8	6	.240
Hancock, R. Garry, Pawtucket*	60	216	24	52	80	6	2	6	19	6	1	13	0	22	1	1	.241
Harer, Wayne, Columbus†	116	432	51	110	135	16	3	1	35	12	1	59	0	35	5	5	.255
Harper, Terry, Richmond	140	512	66	143	217	19	8	13	72	3	4	54	3	82	34	18	.279
Hart, J. Michael, Charleston†	55	193	28	43	55	4	1	2	16	0	0	38	1	30	6	7	.223
Hernandez, Tobias, Syracuse*	7	12	0	1	1	0	0	0	0	0	0	3	0	6	0	0	.083
Herz, Steven, Toledo	51	149	14	32	42	4	0	2	18	8	3	9	2	17	1	0	.215
Holle, Gary, Charleston	26	81	8	17	28	3	1	2	9	0	0	11	1	16	0	0	.210
Holt, Roger, Columbus†	121	380	49	81	101	9	1	3	35	13	2	56	4	56	10	7	.213
Hubbard, Glenn, Richmond	38	143	23	45	66	11	2	2	25	5	1	24	0	22	4	4	.315
Huffman, Philip, Syracuse	19	0	1	0	0	0	0	0	0	0	0	0	0	0	0	0	.000
Iorg, Garth, Syracuse	32	134	17	40	55	6	3	1	14	3	1	7	1	17	7	4	.299
Johnson, Bobby, Charleston	12	34	5	5	7	2	0	0	3	0	0	3	0	8	0	0	.147
Johnson, Larry, Rochester	26	74	11	14	29	3	0	4	8	1	0	17	0	9	1	2	.189
Johnston, Gregory, Toledo*	132	507	68	150	220	22	3	14	66	7	1	38	1	64	22	7	.296
Jurak, Edward, Pawtucket	83	221	16	58	77	8	1	3	31	8	4	23	2	31	0	1	.262
Keller, Charles, Richmond	117	361	46	71	146	9	3	20	48	3	0	53	4	74	3	0	.197
Kelly, D. Patrick, Syracuse	72	236	24	49	69	10	2	2	12	5	5	15	2	61	0	1	.208
Kennedy, Kevin, Rochester	77	232	21	61	72	8	0	1	28	4	2	21	3	33	0	4	.263
Koza, David, Pawtucket	106	357	34	84	144	19	1	13	57	0	2	23	2	70	0	0	.235
Krenchicki, Wayne, Rochester*	87	311	42	82	107	13	3	2	39	6	1	49	0	38	7	4	.264
LaFrancois, Roger, Pawtucket*	62	158	14	39	59	7	2	3	16	3	0	10	1	27	0	0	.247
Lefebvre, Joseph, Columbus*	56	198	37	55	102	11	3	10	26	0	0	44	0	30	4	1	.278
Lewis, James, Columbus*	47	1	0	0	0	0	0	0	0	0	0	0	0	1	0	0	.000
Linares, Rufino, Richmond	63	234	31	77	106	12	4	3	41	1	4	6	0	28	3	3	.329
Lisi, Riccardo, Charleston	132	461	51	113	185	20	5	14	65	7	5	51	3	73	12	11	.245
Logan, H. Daniel, Rochester*	62	195	21	38	51	7	0	2	16	1	2	19	0	18	0	0	.195
MacDonald, Ronald, Tidewater	106	347	23	91	111	14	0	2	46	9	5	31	2	34	0	0	.262
Machemer, David, Toledo	53	162	15	35	39	4	0	0	14	2	0	17	2	17	1	3	.216
Mahlberg, Greg, Charleston	92	280	30	61	77	11	1	1	24	4	2	34	0	39	1	1	.218
Mankowski, Phil, Tidewater*	9	28	2	7	8	1	0	0	2	0	0	6	0	5	1	1	.250

Player and Club	G.	AB.	R.	H.	TB.	2B.	3B.	HR.	RBI.	SH.	SF.	BB.	HP.	SO.	SB.	CS.	Pct.
McDonald, James, Columbus*	91	290	32	76	102	16	2	2	40	1	4	28	2	20	2	3	.262
McDonald, Jerry, Richmond*	14	36	4	4	4	0	0	0	0	2	0	5	0	5	1	0	.111
Miller, Edward, Richmond†	110	411	57	86	99	11	1	0	22	8	0	31	10	67	60	13	.209
Moreno, Jose, Tidewater†	68	236	39	66	95	10	2	5	39	2	3	32	0	44	10	5	.280
Moseby, Lloyd, Syracuse*	37	146	28	47	76	8	6	3	19	0	1	17	1	20	9	2	.322
Nettles, James, Columbus*	115	353	47	90	131	9	4	8	37	8	1	46	0	58	6	5	.255
Nichols, T. Reid, Pawtucket	134	511	68	141	190	27	5	4	42	11	2	32	4	78	23	10	.276
Norman, Nelson, Charleston	28	99	7	24	26	2	0	0	5	1	0	14	0	6	4	4	.242
Norwood, Willie, Toledo	48	138	16	38	67	3	1	8	22	5	1	10	1	26	4	3	.275
O'Neill, Paul, Rochester	23	72	3	14	16	2	0	0	6	2	0	1	0	7	0	1	.194
Ongarato, Michael, Pawtucket	99	254	33	56	76	4	2	4	21	6	2	12	1	54	5	6	.220
Pasley, Kevin, Syracuse	86	303	16	75	94	7	3	2	34	7	1	13	0	17	0	1	.248
Pearsey, Leslie, Toledo	38	106	15	25	34	3	0	2	15	3	2	21	0	34	1	1	.236
Perez, Benjamin, Syracuse	6	4	3	1	1	0	0	0	0	0	0	0	0	0	0	0	.250
Pinkerton, Wayne, Charlestont	56	159	15	36	41	3	1	0	12	2	1	13	0	22	2	3	.226
Pisker, Donald, Syracuse*	93	303	27	68	108	16	6	4	29	0	3	29	0	70	0	3	.224
Putman, Eddy, Rochester	55	176	26	45	71	9	1	5	32	2	2	25	4	32	0	2	.256
Ramirez, Mario, Tidewater	71	208	17	42	53	7	2	0	15	9	1	14	0	45	0	0	.202
Ramirez, Rafael, Richmond	80	281	33	79	115	15	3	5	38	4	2	12	6	54	4	3	.281
Ramos, Domingo, Syracuse	84	319	45	80	108	8	4	4	27	4	4	30	2	29	8	4	.251
Randall, Robert, Toledo	52	146	17	32	46	5	0	3	14	6	4	14	2	12	2	1	.219
Rayford, Floyd, Rochester	107	387	51	89	138	22	0	9	46	3	3	24	3	87	5	2	.230
Reynolds, Michael, Richmond†	16	35	3	8	9	1	0	0	1	0	0	4	0	5	0	1	.229
Richardt, Michael, Charleston	124	487	74	136	219	21	13	12	46	4	4	32	2	51	22	6	.279
Robertson, Andre, Columbus	68	215	22	54	76	7	3	3	19	4	1	7	1	29	2	0	.251
Robinson, Bruce, Columbus*	104	334	40	80	132	14	1	12	48	2	2	33	3	40	2	1	.240
Rockett, Patrick, Syracuse	81	278	47	65	88	12	1	3	23	7	3	46	7	31	3	3	.234
Rosado, Luis, Tidewater	104	348	34	91	125	20	1	4	37	13	0	38	2	41	0	0	.261
Royster, Willie, Rochester	69	242	29	64	84	11	0	3	35	1	3	7	4	51	7	1	.264
Ruiz, Manuel, Richmond	85	258	26	67	84	7	2	2	23	8	4	30	3	41	5	5	.260
Russell, Joseph, Charleston	2	4	1	1	4	0	0	1	2	0	0	0	1	0	0	0	.250
Saferight, Harry, Richmond*	117	403	46	100	135	8	0	9	47	1	5	21	1	38	0	1	.248
Sakata, Lenn, Rochester	26	93	19	32	49	6	1	3	8	3	0	7	1	8	5	0	.344
Schmidt, David, Pawtucket	50	144	17	33	55	5	1	5	16	0	3	23	0	49	2	1	.229
Schmitz, Daniel, Columbus*	35	111	26	36	44	5	0	1	12	5	1	16	0	6	2	2	.324
Scott, Martin, Charleston	123	432	47	104	154	21	1	9	45	5	5	38	1	45	1	6	.241
Searage, Ray, Tidewater*	19	0	0	0	0	0	0	0	0	0	0	1	0	0	0	0	.000
Seibert, Kurt, Toledo†	74	207	35	52	61	5	2	0	17	6	2	38	4	32	2	2	.251
Sherrill, Dennis, Columbus	68	183	25	39	54	6	3	1	17	10	2	12	1	37	1	0	.213
Smith, Garry, Columbus	65	201	25	49	69	14	0	2	13	5	2	21	2	37	2	3	.244
Smith, James, 5 Roch-84 Tide.	89	290	23	71	105	17	1	5	34	3	4	17	1	57	0	2	.245
Smith, Kenneth, Richmond*	132	418	61	103	164	17	4	12	53	2	2	79	4	106	11	12	.246
Smith, Raymond, Toledo	115	398	36	109	131	14	4	0	46	6	4	18	1	32	5	3	.274
Smith, Thomas, Rochester†	10	30	4	6	6	0	0	0	1	0	0	3	0	5	1	1	.200
Smithson, B. Mike, Pawtucket	51	0	1	0	0	0	0	0	0	0	0	0	0	0	0	0	.000
Speed, Horace, Richmond	41	83	12	16	23	2	1	1	7	0	0	19	2	32	2	2	.193
Staiger, Roy, Columbus	90	269	35	63	99	12	3	6	40	5	4	29	4	64	0	0	.234
Stapleton, David, Pawtucket	37	150	25	51	65	3	1	3	19	0	3	10	1	13	2	2	.340
Stenholm, Richard, Columbus*	50	163	18	44	66	10	0	4	26	0	2	15	2	23	2	0	.270
Strawn, Cecil, Charleston	29	69	5	12	15	3	0	0	4	2	0	4	0	19	0	0	.174
Tevlin, Creighton, Syracuse*	50	196	21	58	71	7	3	0	19	7	2	14	0	15	5	3	.296
Thomas, Vernon, Rochester	113	397	53	103	125	17	1	1	35	10	1	63	2	65	19	14	.259
Thompson, Marvin, Columbus	90	215	40	53	71	9	0	3	30	4	3	28	1	27	8	0	.247
Tudor, John, Pawtucket*	12	1	0	0	0	0	0	0	0	0	0	0	0	0	0	0	.000
Upshaw, Willie, Syracuse*	100	358	55	91	145	13	7	9	52	3	5	65	2	62	11	7	.254
Valdez, Julio, Pawtucket†	101	279	22	61	89	10	3	4	27	13	1	12	6	58	7	2	.219
Valle, John, Rochester	126	443	70	115	206	31	3	18	70	6	5	53	1	77	4	3	.260
Vega, Jesus, Toledo	126	459	63	139	211	26	2	14	79	3	8	46	3	49	28	10	.303
Walker, Cleotha, Pawtucket†	139	536	59	146	202	18	7	8	52	6	0	41	1	91	21	10	.272
Walker, John, Toledo†	128	487	67	124	154	19	4	1	48	24	5	32	4	68	27	17	.255
Walton, Daniel, Charleston†	104	341	42	77	135	13	0	15	54	1	3	68	6	83	0	0	.226
Ward, Gary, Toledo	128	496	82	140	217	22	8	13	66	2	8	41	5	76	26	6	.282
Washington, Ronald, Toledo	114	407	62	117	167	31	5	3	36	14	6	18	5	81	19	5	.287
Webster, Mitchell, Syracuse†	49	161	23	35	46	4	2	1	12	4	1	8	0	18	4	4	.217
Wells, Gregory, Syracuse	139	540	54	142	218	24	5	14	76	4	3	31	3	56	10	1	.263
Werth, Dennis, Columbus	32	91	16	20	34	5	0	3	15	0	0	21	1	26	0	1	.220
Wessinger, James, Richmond	92	252	27	62	80	6	3	2	17	5	1	18	1	37	10	4	.246
Whisenton, Larry, Richmond*	109	409	54	103	159	17	6	9	67	1	3	51	2	83	5	14	.252
Williams, Dallas, Rochester*	137	529	63	143	201	21	2	11	54	11	4	22	3	53	16	17	.270
Wilson, William, Tidewater†	132	515	92	152	203	11	14	4	44	9	4	44	4	86	50	14	.295
Winterfeldt, Todd, Tidewater	6	15	0	2	2	0	0	0	1	0	0	0	0	2	0	0	.133
Wolfe, Lawrence, Pawtucket	78	247	24	56	68	7	0	7	35	1	1	36	1	43	1	2	.227
Zdeb, Joseph, Tidewater	36	94	7	18	25	2	1	1	9	5	1	12	0	15	0	0	.191

The following pitchers had no plate appearances primarily through use of designated hitters, listed alphabetically by club, games in parentheses:

CHARLESTON—Allard, Brian (22); Babcock, Robert (39); Butcher, John† (22); Carroll, Joseph (40); Crutcher, David (4); Farr, James (12); Finch, Steven (22); Jakubowski, Stanley (11); Johnson, John Henry (16); Kainer, Donald (22); Mercer, Mark* (39); Rajsich, David* (3); Umbarger, James* (2); Whitehouse, Leonard (19).

COLUMBUS— Bird, James (15); Clay, Kenneth (20); Cochran, Gregory (24); Cooper, Donald (12); Griffin, Michael (13); Kammeyer, Robert (25); Lollar, W. Timothy (11); Righetti, David (24); Slagle, Roger (5); Wehrmeister, David (39); Welsh, Christopher* (29).

PAWTUCKET—Faust, Alvin (34); Finch, Joel (16); Howard, Michael (9); Hurst, Bruce* (17); LaRose, H. John (34); MacWhorter, Keith (19); Ojeda, Robert (20); Parks, Daniel (28); Remmerswaal, Wilhelmus (24); Wright, James (22).

RICHMOND—Edge, Claude (26); Field, Gregory (13); Mahler, Richard (29); McLaughlin, Michael (7); Melson, Gary (28); Metzger, Clarence (38); Morogiello, Daniel* (29); O'Brien, Daniel (30); Shields, W. Michael (15); Skok, Craig (30).

ROCHESTER—Boddicker, Michael (25); Fierbaugh, N. Randy (14); Hartzell, Paul (16); Jones, Larry (28); Kerrigan, Joseph (39); Luebber, Stephen (27); Presley, Billy (9); Rineer, Jeffrey* (20); Rowe, Thomas (17); Schneider, Jeffrey* (45); Torrez, Pete (35); Wiley, Mark (35).

SYRACUSE—Baker, Steven (17); Barlow, Michael (20); Benson, V. Randall* (23); Brown, Thomas (23); Fore, Charles (19); Grilli, Stephen (33); Kucek, John (13); Leal, Luis (16); Mirabella, Paul (4); Moore, Balor (8); Robertson, Jay (43); Schrom, Kenneth (26); Thayer, Gregory (3); Todd, Jackson (22); Willis, Michael* (44).

TIDEWATER—Anderson, Richard (14); Dixon, Thomas (32); Harris, Greg† (39); Holman, R. Scott (11); Jackson, Roy Lee (22); Lynch, Edward (24); McGilberry, Randall (15); Mendoza, Michael (12); Miller, Dyar (29); Myrick, Robert (2); Scott, Michael (27); Von Ohlen, David* (45).

TOLEDO—Arroyo, Fernando (9); Bacsik, Michael (26); Brueggemann, Jeffrey (21); Kinnunen, Michael (14); MacPherson, Bruce (27); Mapel, Steven (19); Moore, David (23); Rogers, Charles (8); Sarmiento, Wilfredo (42); Serum, Gary (38); Veselic, Robert (27); Williams, Alberto (15).

GRAND SLAM HOME RUNS—Harper, Valle, Vega, 2 each; Ashford, Brant, Gulden, Johnston, Kennedy, Krenchicki, Nichols, Pearsey, Pisker, Rayford, Richardt, C. Walker, J. Walker, Werth, D. Williams, 1 each.

AWARDED FIRST BASE ON INTERFERENCE—Saferight, 8 (Baldwin, Graham, Herz, Kennedy, Mahlberg, Robinson, Rosado, R. Smith); Graham (Herz); Rockett (Royster); Ruiz (R. Smith), Valle (R. Smith); Whisenton (Russell).

GAME-WINNING RBIs

CHARLESTON (57)—Duran 9, Lisi 8, Scott 7, Ashford 6, Walton 5, Mahlberg 4, Richardt 4, Bogener 3, Davis 2, Gooch 2, Hart 2, Norman 2, Cowger 1, Holle 1, Strawn 1.

COLUMBUS (75)—Brant 9, Lefebvre 7, Nettles 7, Robinson 7, Espino 6, Coleman 5, McDonald 5, Harer 4, Stenholm 4, Thompson 4, Holt 3, Staiger 3, Werth 3, Robertson 2, Schmitz 2, Sherrill 2, Gulden 1, Smith 1.

PAWTUCKET (57)—Koza 9, Boggs 8, Jurak 8, Bowen 4, Hancock 4, Valdez 4, Boyer 3, Butera 3, LaFrancois 3, Nichols 3, Ongarato 3, Walker 3, Wolfe 3, Gedman 2, Stapleton 2, Schmidt 1.

RICHMOND (63)—Harper 9, Hammond 8, Keller 7, Miller 7, Hubbard 5, Linares 5, Smith 5, Ruiz 4, Saferight 4, Ramirez 3, Speed 2, Whisenton 2, Beall 1, Wessinger 1.

ROCHESTER (65)—Krenchicki 7, Williams 7, Royster 6, Thomas 6, Valle 6, Bonner 5, Corey 5, Rayford 5, Eden 3, Gonzales 3, Logan 3, Putman 3, Chism 2, Graham 2, Kennedy 2.

SYRACUSE (51)—Wells 11, Davis 7, Upshaw 7, Ault 4, Beamon 4, Pasley 4, Iorg 3, Ramos 3, Tevlin 3, Ainge 2, Braun 1, Freed 1, Pisker 1.

TIDEWATER (63)—Brooks 12, Backman 10, Wilson 9, Benton 7, Cipot 7, MacDonald 5, Baldwin 3, Smith 3, Moreno 2, Ramirez 2, Chapman 1, Ferrer 1, Flores 1.

TOLEDO (66)—Smith 11, Vega 11, Ward 8, Walker 7, Johnston 6, Washington 5, Engle 4, Randall 4, Bush 2, Herz 2, Norwood 2, Chism 1, Douglas 1, Estes 1, Machemer 1.

CLUB FIELDING

Club	G.	PO.	A.	E.	DP.	PB.	Pct.	Club	G.	PO.	A.	E.	DP.	PB.	Pct.
Charleston	139	3525	1641	135	127	13	.975	Toledo	140	3634	1612	147	132	10	.973
Columbus	140	3582	1645	138	116	13	.974	Richmond	140	3585	1593	154	117	8	.971
Rochester	139	3567	1647	146	119	10	.973	Pawtucket	140	3566	1633	155	122	10	.971
Syracuse	139	3705	1515	146	117	20	.973	Tidewater	139	3542	1359	168	102	22	.967

Triple Plays—Syracuse, Pawtucket.

INDIVIDUAL FIELDING

*Throws lefthanded.

FIRST BASEMEN

Player and Club	G.	PO.	A.	E.	DP.	Pct.	Player and Club	G.	PO.	A.	E.	DP.	Pct.
Rosado, Tidewater	18	163	15	0	13	1.000	Wells, Syracuse	121	1122	68	12	82	.990
Holle, Charleston	11	113	10	0	8	1.000	Valle, Rochester	20	186	15	2	11	.990
Harer, Columbus*	21	104	6	0	9	1.000	Bush, Toledo*	11	97	6	1	7	.990
Beall, Richmond*	12	68	8	0	2	1.000	K. Smith, Richmond	127	1158	84	15	95	.988
Chism, Tol-Rich*	32	297	19	1	22	.997	Logan, Rochester*	62	545	60	9	51	.985
Scott, Charleston	57	551	42	3	49	.995	Vega, Toledo	103	971	66	17	93	.984
Putman, Rochester	49	483	33	3	23	.994	Stapleton, Pawtucket	22	205	20	4	8	.983
BRANT, Columbus	117	1086	64	8	74	.993	Ongarato, Pawtucket	23	159	13	3	12	.983
MacDonald, Tidewater	100	774	59	7	58	.992	Baldwin, Tidewater	21	152	12	3	13	.982
Duran, Charleston*	75	696	76	6	63	.992	Coleman, Columbus	11	98	5	2	14	.981
Koza, Pawtucket*	92	864	56	8	40	.991	Upshaw, Syracuse*	17	141	13	4	10	.975

FIRST BASEMEN—Continued
(Fewer Than Ten Games)

Player and Club	G.	PO.	A.	E.	DP.	Pct.	Player and Club	G.	PO.	A.	E.	DP.	Pct.
McDonald, Columbus*	6	77	4	0	1	1.000	Beamon, Syracuse*	1	3	1	0	2	1.000
Estes, Toledo*	6	56	1	0	4	1.000	Keller, Richmond	2	2	2	0	0	1.000
Rayford, Rochester	3	26	0	0	1	1.000	Schmidt, Pawtucket	1	1	0	0	0	1.000
Krenchicki, Rochester	3	18	2	0	2	1.000	Boggs, Pawtucket	7	58	10	1	8	.986
Ault, Syracuse*	1	17	3	0	3	1.000	Alberts, Richmond	7	58	5	1	4	.984
LaFrancois, Pawtucket	5	16	1	0	0	1.000	Hancock, Pawtucket*	4	43	4	2	5	.959
Herz, Toledo	1	10	1	0	1	1.000	Saferight, Richmond	5	17	4	1	3	.955
Thompson, Columbus	1	7	1	0	0	1.000	Ward, Toledo	6	35	1	2	3	.947
Wessinger, Richmond	2	4	0	0	0	1.000	Benton, Tidewater	5	33	2	2	4	.946
Corey, Rochester	1	3	1	0	0	1.000							

Triple Plays—Koza, Wells.

SECOND BASEMEN

Player and Club	G.	PO.	A.	E.	DP.	Pct.	Player and Club	G.	PO.	A.	E.	DP.	Pct.
Stapleton, Pawtucket	10	27	20	0	6	1.000	Ferrer, Tidewater	10	26	21	1	7	.979
Seibert, Toledo	66	165	224	4	47	.990	Randall, Toledo	47	81	141	5	28	.978
Rockett, Syracuse	62	131	151	3	33	.989	Wessinger, Richmond	10	17	27	1	3	.978
Schmitz, Columbus	20	30	46	1	11	.987	Ruiz, Richmond	81	153	230	10	38	.975
RICHARDT, Charleston	124	262	385	10	74	.985	Iorg, Syracuse	29	58	87	4	21	.973
Doyle, Columbus	14	21	45	1	10	.985	Krenchicki, Rochester	59	117	185	9	28	.971
Holt, Columbus	115	207	332	9	53	.984	Sakata, Rochester	26	45	87	4	27	.971
S. Davis, Syracuse	59	132	180	5	32	.984	C. Walker, Pawtucket	135	252	394	21	74	.969
Eden, Rochester	39	63	110	3	15	.983	O'Neill, Rochester	16	21	42	2	9	.969
Hubbard, Richmond	38	89	127	4	30	.982	Backman, Tidewater	103	207	263	17	42	.965
Reynolds, Richmond	11	26	24	1	5	.980	Chapman, Tidewater	28	37	64	4	10	.962
Machemer, Rochester	21	36	56	2	9	.979	Washington, Toledo	18	24	46	8	4	.897

(Fewer Than Ten Games)

Player and Club	G.	PO.	A.	E.	DP.	Pct.	Player and Club	G.	PO.	A.	E.	DP.	Pct.
Bonner, Rochester	4	9	13	0	1	1.000	McDonald, Richmond	8	20	30	2	2	.962
Norman, Charleston	3	10	6	0	4	1.000	Moreno, Tidewater	5	9	13	1	5	.957
Gooch, Charleston	3	5	5	0	1	1.000	Pinkerton, Charleston	9	18	22	2	6	.952
Sherrill, Columbus	2	2	4	0	1	1.000	M. Ramirez, Tidewater	6	16	15	2	5	.939
Alberts, Richmond	1	2	1	0	0	1.000	Rayford, Rochester	3	7	8	1	1	.938
Perez, Syracuse	2	2	0	0	0	1.000	O. Davis, Charleston	4	8	9	2	3	.895
Staiger, Columbus	2	0	1	0	0	1.000							

Triple Play—S. Davis

THIRD BASEMEN

Player and Club	G.	PO.	A.	E.	DP.	Pct.	Player and Club	G.	PO.	A.	E.	DP.	Pct.
Machemer, Toledo	24	19	37	0	5	1.000	Ashford, Charleston	103	87	250	21	24	.941
Krenchicki, Rochester	21	15	31	0	5	1.000	Pearsey, Toledo	37	24	67	6	4	.938
Ereu, Richmond	11	10	23	0	2	1.000	Wolfe, Pawtucket	67	59	145	15	20	.932
Ainge, Syracuse	66	64	140	3	10	.986	Hammond, Richmond	118	79	232	23	17	.931
Schmitz, Columbus	15	10	31	1	3	.976	S. Davis, Syracuse	20	11	29	3	0	.930
Eden, Rochester	12	10	24	1	1	.971	Chapman, Tidewater	41	25	54	6	6	.929
Moreno, Tidewater	13	8	23	1	2	.969	Thompson, Columbus	12	5	19	2	0	.923
Ferrer, Tidewater	12	11	16	1	1	.964	Pinkerton, Charleston	19	12	45	5	2	.919
Staiger, Columbus	81	46	171	10	14	.956	J. Smith, Tidewater	36	31	53	8	5	.913
Baker, Syracuse	34	26	61	4	5	.956	Sherrill, Columbus	16	8	30	4	3	.905
Boggs, Pawtucket	71	50	146	11	9	.947	Wessinger, Richmond	22	13	31	5	0	.898
Coleman, Columbus	25	18	54	4	2	.947	Scott, Charleston	12	16	26	5	3	.894
Washington, Toledo	81	79	190	16	16	.944	Brooks, Tidewater	40	29	78	14	7	.884
RAYFORD, Rochester	96	75	200	17	19	.942	Rockett, Syracuse	11	7	15	5	3	.815

(Fewer Than Ten Games)

Player and Club	G.	PO.	A.	E.	DP.	Pct.	Player and Club	G.	PO.	A.	E.	DP.	Pct.
O. Davis, Charleston	8	8	19	0	1	1.000	Rosado, Tidewater	3	1	1	0	0	1.000
T. Smith, Rochester	9	4	19	0	1	1.000	Augustine, Charleston	1	0	1	0	0	1.000
Iorg, Syracuse	6	2	12	0	1	1.000	Keller, Richmond	1	0	1	0	0	1.000
Putman, Rochester	3	1	6	0	1	1.000	Doyle, Columbus	5	4	10	1	0	.933
Mankowski, Tidewater	2	3	3	0	0	1.000	O'Neill, Rochester	6	3	9	1	0	.923
Ruiz, Richmond	1	0	5	0	0	1.000	Werth, Columbus	3	2	6	2	0	.800
Reynolds, Richmond	1	0	3	0	0	1.000	Stapleton, Pawtucket	9	0	13	4	0	.765
Alberts, Syracuse	2	0	2	0	0	1.000	Jurak, Pawtucket	7	4	5	3	0	.750
Randall, Toledo	3	1	2	0	0	1.000	Winterfeldt, Tidewater	4	3	0	1	0	.750
Gooch, Charleston	1	0	2	0	0	1.000	Lefebvre, Columbus	1	0	0	1	0	.000

SHORTSTOPS

Player and Club	G.	PO.	A.	E.	DP.	Pct.	Player and Club	G.	PO.	A.	E.	DP.	Pct.
Norman, Charleston	24	40	75	3	15	.975	S. Davis, Syracuse	50	71	145	7	35	.969
J. Smith, Roch-Tide	59	80	139	7	18	.969	Pinkerton, Charleston	19	29	57	3	9	.966

SHORTSTOPS—Continued

Player and Club	G.	PO.	A.	E.	DP.	Pct.
Robertson, Columbus.....	68	88	222	13	30	.960
Rockett, Syracuse.........	11	18	29	2	5	.959
BONNER, Rochester....	129	221	454	31	73	.956
J. Walker, Toledo...........	127	224	368	30	69	.952
O. Davis, Charleston	94	128	312	22	58	.952
Wessinger, Richmond	59	80	167	13	28	.950
M. Ramirez, Tide	63	110	158	15	27	.947
R. Ramirez, Rich	80	117	294	23	45	.947
Valdez, Pawtucket	97	164	288	29	43	.940
Sherrill, Columbus	47	72	127	13	31	.939
Ramos, Syracuse	82	160	240	28	44	.935
Ferrer, Tidewater	18	31	56	6	13	.935
Backman, Tidewater	21	30	37	5	5	.931
Jurak, Pawtucket	54	68	125	16	20	.923
Washington, Toledo.......	14	28	32	6	10	.909
Doyle, Columbus	29	50	86	15	10	.901

(Fewer Than Ten Games)

Player and Club	G.	PO.	A.	E.	DP.	Pct.
Schmitz, Columbus	4	3	7	0	1	1.000
Seibert, Toledo............	2	2	0	0	1	1.000
Ainge, Syracuse	1	2	0	0	0	1.000
Hammond, Richmond....	1	0	2	0	0	1.000
Brooks, Tidewater	1	0	1	0	0	1.000
Randall, Toledo..............	1	0	1	0	0	1.000
Krenchicki, Roch...........	6	5	14	1	14	.950
Ashford, Charleston	5	10	12	2	4	.917
Ruiz, Richmond	6	9	11	2	3	.909
Rayford, Rochester	2	4	5	1	3	.900

Triple Plays—Valdez, Ramos.

OUTFIELDERS

Player and Club	G.	PO.	A.	E.	DP.	Pct.
HARER, Columbus*....	110	219	7	0	2	1.000
Boyer, Pawtucket	101	174	7	0	1	1.000
G. Smith, Columbus ...	63	110	6	0	1	1.000
Tevlin, Syracuse*	50	112	3	0	1	1.000
Beamon, Syracuse	53	91	4	0	1	1.000
Ongarato, Pawtucket ...	60	90	3	0	1	1.000
Linares, Richmond	34	56	5	0	2	1.000
Alberts, Syr-Rich.......	37	58	4	0	1	1.000
Ainge, Syracuse	18	45	0	0	0	1.000
Zdeb, Tidewater	25	33	1	0	0	1.000
Royster, Rochester	17	32	1	0	0	1.000
Butera, Pawtucket	20	30	2	0	1	1.000
Bush, Toledo*..........	15	15	0	0	0	1.000
Hart, Charleston	55	107	1	1	0	.991
Upshaw, Syracuse*	83	214	6	3	1	.987
Williams, Rochester*....	136	330	11	5	1	.986
Whisenton, Richmond*..	111	195	20	3	4	.986
Johnston, Toledo*.....	128	297	10	5	3	.984
Gonzales, Rochester ...	34	57	0	1	0	.983
Harper, Richmond	140	315	19	6	5	.982
Hancock, Pawtucket* ...	56	101	7	2	1	.982
Ault, Syracuse*	36	53	3	1	0	.982
Wilson, Tidewater	131	350	11	7	4	.981
Engle, Toledo	128	225	16	5	2	.980
Nichols, Pawtucket	133	250	12	6	2	.978
Bowen, Pawtucket	84	168	10	4	4	.978
Thompson, Columbus	65	88	3	2	0	.978
Cipot, Tidewater*	56	82	3	2	2	.977
Ward, Toledo	119	234	13	6	2	.976
Nettles, Columbus*	113	156	10	4	4	.976
Bogener, Charleston*.....	95	159	4	4	0	.976
Valle, Rochester	71	118	3	3	2	.976
Lisi, Charleston	132	278	16	8	4	.974
Corey, Rochester	76	146	4	4	0	.974
Brooks, Tidewater	74	123	11	4	0	.971
Pisker, Syracuse*	74	125	9	4	2	.971
Duran, Charleston*	36	63	3	2	1	.971
Miller, Richmond	108	218	9	7	1	.970
Scott, Charlotte	40	57	5	2	1	.969
Augustine, Charlotte	35	58	3	2	0	.968
Moseby, Syracuse	37	83	1	3	0	.966
Speed, Richmond	33	54	2	2	2	.966
Flores, Tidewater	93	147	4	6	0	.962
Webster, Syracuse*	48	112	3	5	0	.958
Lefebvre, Columbus	56	89	3	4	0	.958
Moreno, Tidewater.....	52	83	6	4	0	.957
Douglas, Toledo	30	36	0	2	0	.947
Gooch, Charleston	36	50	1	3	0	.944
Werth, Columbus	25	31	1	2	0	.941
Norwood, Toledo	25	43	3	3	1	.939
Thomas, Rochester	102	156	10	11	1	.938
Stenholm, Columbus	21	28	0	2	0	.933
Coleman, Columbus	18	22	0	2	0	.917

(Fewer Than Ten Games)

Player and Club	G.	PO.	A.	E.	DP.	Pct.
K. Smith, Richmond	7	9	2	0	0	1.000
Benton, Tidewater	8	6	1	0	0	1.000
Stapleton, Pawtucket ...	5	7	0	0	0	1.000
Machemer, Toledo	2	6	0	0	0	1.000
Beall, Richmond*	5	3	0	0	0	1.000
M. Ramirez, Tidewater...	4	3	0	0	0	1.000
Kelly, Syracuse	1	1	0	0	0	1.000
Koza, Pawtucket*	3	1	0	0	0	1.000
McDonald, Richmond ...	1	1	0	0	0	1.000
Schmidt, Pawtucket	1	0	1	0	0	1.000

CATCHERS

Player and Club	G.	PO.	A.	E.	DP.	PB.	Pct.
Cowger, Charleston	26	112	13	1	1	2	.992
ROSADO, Tidewater....	73	444	43	5	5	10	.990
Kennedy, Rochester	75	318	37	4	3	3	.989
Robinson, Columbus	93	532	56	8	5	7	.987
R. Smith, Toledo....	100	461	64	7	7	6	.987
Mahlberg, Charleston...	89	417	39	7	3	7	.985
Gedman, Pawtucket	84	367	65	7	13	6	.984
Keller, Richmond	57	277	24	5	4	3	.984
Schmidt, Pawtucket	37	154	21	3	2	3	.983
Pasley, Syracuse	80	450	51	9	7	8	.982
Espino, Columbus	48	238	29	5	2	5	.982
LaFrancois, Paw........	41	145	21	3	5	2	.982
Benton, Tidewater	39	220	23	5	4	8	.980
Saferight, Richmond ...	91	433	51	11	9	5	.978
Kelly, Syracuse	71	295	34	8	3	11	.976
B. Johnson, Charles....	12	36	1	1	1	1	.974
Herz, Toledo	45	214	35	8	2	4	.969
Royster, Rochester	42	182	20	7	2	5	.967
Graham, Rochester	13	60	7	3	1	1	.957
Baldwin, Tidewater ...	35	184	13	11	1	4	.947
Gulden, Columbus	12	54	13	4	0	1	.944

Triple Play—Pasley.

(Fewer Than Ten Games)

Player and Club	G.	PO.	A.	E.	DP.	PB.	Pct.
L. Johnson, Rochester ..	9	36	2	0	0	1	1.000
Benedict, Richmond	3	10	5	0	0	0	1.000
Putman, Rochester.....	1	1	0	0	0	0	1.000
Hernandez, Syracuse..	6	25	5	1	1	1	.968
Russell, Charleston....	2	9	0	1	0	0	.900
Rayford, Rochester.....	3	12	0	2	0	0	.857

PITCHERS

Player and Club	G.	PO.	A.	E.	DP.	Pct.
BUTCHER, Charleston .	22	19	24	0	0	1.000
Lynch, Tidewater	24	14	28	0	4	1.000
Cochran, Columbus	24	10	31	0	1	1.000
Hartzell, Rochester	16	12	20	0	3	1.000
Moore, Toledo	23	8	22	0	5	1.000
Serum, Toledo	38	7	20	0	1	1.000
Tudor, Pawtucket*	12	6	19	0	1	1.000
Fore, Syracuse	19	5	18	0	0	1.000
Jackson, Tidewater	22	12	10	0	3	1.000
Brown, Syracuse	23	5	16	0	0	1.000
Grilli, Syracuse	33	6	14	0	1	1.000
Mapel, Toledo	19	5	15	0	1	1.000
Hurst, Pawtucket*	17	5	14	0	0	1.000
Mercer, Charleston*	39	3	15	0	0	1.000
Lollar, Columbus*	21	6	11	0	1	1.000
Huffman, Syracuse	19	4	12	0	0	1.000
Williams, Toledo	15	4	10	0	1	1.000
Metzger, Richmond	38	7	6	0	0	1.000
Farr, Charleston	12	2	10	0	0	1.000
LaRose, Pawtucket*	34	6	5	0	1	1.000
Bacsik, Toledo	25	3	7	0	0	1.000
Mendoza, Tidewater	13	5	5	0	0	1.000
Kerrigan, Rochester	38	6	3	0	1	1.000
Schneider, Rochester*	45	0	8	0	0	1.000
Aponte, Pawtucket	31	3	5	0	1	1.000
Anderson, Tidewater	22	2	6	0	0	1.000
Remmerswaal, Paw	24	1	6	0	1	1.000
Bird, Columbus	15	4	3	0	0	1.000
Fierbaugh, Rochester	18	3	3	0	1	1.000
Shields, Richmond	15	0	5	0	0	1.000
Kinnunen, Toledo*	14	2	2	0	0	1.000
Jakubowski, Charleston	11	1	3	0	1	1.000
Kammeyer, Columbus	25	17	34	1	3	.981
Veselic, Toledo	27	7	40	1	0	.979
Faust, Pawtucket	34	17	24	1	1	.976
Morogiello, Richmond* .	29	4	29	1	1	.971
Benson, Syracuse*	23	9	21	1	3	.968
Wiley, Rochester	35	8	21	1	0	.967
Parks, Pawtucket	28	15	39	2	3	.964
Von Ohlen, Tidewater* .	45	6	19	1	0	.962
Allard, Charleston	22	17	29	2	3	.958
Wehrmeister, Columbus	39	5	18	1	1	.958
MacPherson, Toledo	27	23	44	3	5	.957
Jones, Rochester	28	23	19	2	0	.955
Boddicker, Rochester	25	33	50	4	4	.954
Barlow, Syracuse	20	3	17	1	1	.952
Holman, Tidewater	14	8	11	1	0	.950
Leal, Syracuse	16	4	15	1	2	.950
Smithson, Pawtucket	50	3	16	1	1	.950
Luebber, Rochester	27	25	31	3	4	.949
Mahler, Richmond	29	21	33	3	4	.947
Whitehouse, Charleston*	19	7	11	1	0	.947
Kucek, Syracuse	13	6	12	1	0	.947
Ojeda, Pawtucket*	20	4	32	2	2	.947
Finch, Pawtucket	16	10	24	2	0	.944
Griffin, Columbus	13	6	11	1	0	.944
Todd, Syracuse	22	7	26	2	0	.943
Brizzolara, Richmond	30	22	27	3	1	.942
Edge, Richmond	26	11	21	2	3	.941
Robertson, Syracuse	43	3	13	1	0	.941
Torrez, Rochester*	35	9	22	2	1	.939
O'Brien, Richmond	30	5	10	1	1	.938
MacWhorter, Pawtucket	19	12	18	2	2	.938
Finch, Charleston	24	9	20	2	0	.935
Felton, Toledo	25	8	19	2	1	.931
Babcock, Charleston	39	4	9	1	2	.929
Carroll, Charleston	40	4	9	1	0	.929
Skok, Richmond*	30	3	10	1	0	.929
Kainer, Charleston	22	15	23	3	2	.927
Lewis, Columbus	47	2	22	2	1	.923
Welsh, Columbus*	29	10	36	4	2	.920
Baker, Syracuse	17	11	11	2	0	.917
Johnson, Charleston*	16	4	17	2	0	.913
Clay, Columbus	20	13	27	4	0	.909
Sarmiento, Toledo	42	7	13	2	1	.909
Cooper, Columbus	12	1	9	1	2	.909
Willis, Syracuse*	44	0	10	1	0	.909
Scott, Tidewater	27	15	33	5	0	.906
Wright, Pawtucket	22	4	13	2	0	.895
Righetti, Columbus*	24	3	29	4	2	.889
Field, Richmond	13	8	8	2	1	.889
Searage, Tidewater*	19	3	5	1	0	.889
Harris, Tidewater	39	9	14	3	1	.885
Rineer, Rochester*	20	2	13	2	0	.882
Dixon, Tidewater	32	4	17	3	1	.875
Schrom, Syracuse	26	2	5	1	0	.875
Bruhert, Charleston	29	12	14	4	1	.867
Melson, Richmond	28	14	14	6	0	.824
Berenguer, Tidewater	27	8	6	3	0	.824
Rowe, Rochester	17	6	17	5	1	.821
McGilberry, Tidewater	15	6	8	4	0	.778
Miller, Tidewater	28	1	5	2	0	.750
Brueggemann, Toledo	21	0	6	2	1	.750

(Fewer Than Ten Games)

Player and Club	G.	PO.	A.	E.	DP.	Pct.
Howard, Pawtucket	9	7	8	0	1	1.000
McLaughlin, Richmond .	7	5	6	0	1	1.000
Rogers, Toledo	8	1	8	0	1	1.000
Slagle, Columbus	5	0	3	0	0	1.000
Scott, Charleston	4	1	1	0	0	1.000
McDonald, Columbus*	1	1	1	0	0	1.000
Beall, Richmond*	5	0	2	0	0	1.000
Mirabella, Syracuse*	4	0	2	0	0	1.000
Crutcher, Charleston	4	1	0	0	0	1.000
Rajsich, Charleston*	3	1	0	0	0	1.000
Umbarger, Charleston*.	2	0	1	0	0	1.000
Arroyo, Toledo	9	4	18	4	2	.846
Thayer, Syracuse	3	0	1	1	0	.500
Myrick, Tidewater*	2	0	1	1	0	.500

The following players do not have any recorded accepted chances at the position indicated; therefore, are not listed in the fielding averages for those particular positions: Cipot*, p; S. Davis, of; Estes*, of; Hammond, 2b; Johnston*, p; B. Moore*, p; Presley, p; K. Smith, 2b-3b; Valdez, 1b-of; Werth, 2b.

CLUB PITCHING

Club	G.	CG.	ShO.	Sv.	IP.	H.	R.	ER.	HR.	BB.	Int. BB.	HB.	SO.	WP.	Bk.	ERA.
Columbus	140	49	12	24	1194	1012	477	388	69	504	46	36	795	57	9	2.92
Toledo	140	44	12	20	1211	1140	542	458	75	449	26	35	619	38	6	3.40
Pawtucket	140	37	8	18	1189	1080	566	454	102	534	76	41	628	51	8	3.44
Richmond	140	48	7	28	1195	1183	557	469	69	422	19	22	660	66	6	3.53
Tidewater	139	36	6	26	1181	1152	577	470	70	473	50	30	788	46	8	3.58
Syracuse	139	38	10	18	1235	1192	591	519	79	503	46	34	718	48	8	3.78
Rochester	139	45	13	29	1189	1166	579	503	100	386	24	37	555	43	4	3.81
Charleston	139	40	12	28	1175	1211	606	517	65	457	51	33	615	50	3	3.96

PITCHERS' RECORDS

(Leading Qualifiers for Earned-Run Average Leadership—112 or More Innings)

*Throws lefthanded.

Pitcher—Club	G.	GS.	CG.	ShO.	W.	L.	Sv.	Pct.	IP.	H.	R.	ER.	HR.	BB.	Int. BB.	HB.	SO.	WP.	ERA.
Clay, Columbus	20	20	7	3	9	4	0	.692	138	106	40	30	9	50	0	6	78	8	1.96
Boddicker, Rochester	25	25	13	3	12	9	0	.571	190	149	67	46	12	35	1	4	109	3	2.18
Cochran, Columbus	24	24	7	1	12	7	0	.632	165	129	51	47	10	56	6	2	106	7	2.56
MacWhorter, Pawtucket..	19	18	7	2	7	6	0	.538	123	107	43	35	5	41	2	4	53	3	2.56
Mahler, Richmond	29	26	9	1	12	6	0	.667	188	172	68	54	5	80	2	3	101	7	2.59
Parks, Pawtucket	28	24	7	3	10	10	0	.500	174	141	62	50	11	96	11	7	89	13	2.59
Welsh, Columbus*	29	24	13	2	9	12	1	.429	158	134	78	48	7	68	4	5	84	4	2.73
Melson, Richmond	28	14	7	1	7	10	1	.412	139	117	53	44	3	64	2	2	110	13	2.85
Kainer, Charleston	22	22	6	3	9	7	0	.563	138	128	58	44	6	46	3	4	66	6	2.87
Kammeyer, Columbus	25	25	13	0	15	7	0	.682	176	176	70	57	6	61	5	3	72	4	2.91

Departmental Leaders: G—Smithson, 50; GS—Brizzolara, 30; CG—Butcher, 14; ShO—Veselic; 4; W—Kammeyer, 15; L—Berenguer, Brizzolara, 15; Sv—Babcock, Metzger, 14; Pct.—O'Brien, .800; IP—Brizzolara, 206; H—Morogiello, 206; R—Jones, 104; ER—Morogiello, 88; HR—Faust, Jones, 17; BB—Righetti, 101; IBB—Lewis, Smithson, 13; HB—Baker, Bruhert, 9; SO—Berenguer, 178; WP—Edge, 17.

(All Pitchers—Listed Alphabetically)

Pitcher—Club	G.	GS.	CG.	ShO.	W.	L.	Sv.	Pct.	IP.	H.	R.	ER.	HR.	BB.	Int. BB.	HB.	SO.	WP.	ERA.
Allard, Charleston	22	21	8	1	8	8	0	.500	152	146	62	53	5	43	8	1	68	4	3.14
Anderson, Tidewater	14	0	0	0	1	3	1	.250	40	36	18	17	4	15	2	0	25	0	3.83
Aponte, Pawtucket	31	0	0	0	6	2	9	.750	49	27	15	12	6	21	7	1	42	2	2.20
Arroyo, Toledo	9	8	4	2	6	1	0	.857	72	56	22	13	3	14	0	3	36	1	1.63
Babcock, Charleston	39	0	0	0	6	3	14	.667	65	38	13	11	1	26	4	2	59	3	1.52
Bacsik, Toledo	26	0	0	0	7	2	7	.778	45	45	19	18	3	29	6	2	30	4	3.60
S. Baker, Syracuse	17	17	5	0	6	5	0	.545	107	93	47	38	8	68	2	9	54	4	3.20
Barlow, Syracuse	20	0	0	0	3	2	1	.600	51	55	29	26	3	20	3	2	26	3	4.59
Beall, Richmond*	5	0	0	0	0	0	0	.000	14	21	16	16	3	7	0	0	7	0	10.29
Benson, Syracuse*	23	18	3	0	3	5	0	.375	117	120	69	63	10	33	3	3	77	0	4.85
Berenguer, Tidewater	27	24	7	2	9	15	2	.375	157	122	78	67	15	76	4	5	178	3	3.84
Bird, Columbus	15	4	0	0	6	0	2	1.000	48	33	15	12	4	13	1	0	36	3	2.25
Boddicker, Rochester	25	25	13	3	12	9	0	.571	190	149	67	46	12	35	1	4	109	3	2.18
Brizzolara, Richmond	30	30	13	1	10	15	0	.400	206	198	102	85	13	56	4	6	128	10	3.71
Brown, Syracuse	23	13	6	2	6	7	0	.462	114	111	41	39	7	31	3	2	51	4	3.08
Brueggemann, Toledo	21	0	0	0	1	0	1	1.000	32	35	26	22	2	20	1	1	11	2	6.19
Bruhert, Charleston	29	15	4	0	5	6	0	.455	123	168	91	80	11	56	4	9	45	6	5.85
Butcher, Charleston	22	21	14	3	10	7	1	.588	152	141	57	56	9	50	5	4	71	9	3.32
Carroll, Charleston	40	3	0	0	2	8	6	.200	86	94	60	52	6	59	5	6	43	8	5.44
Cipot, Tidewater*	1	0	0	0	0	0	0	.000	1	1	0	0	0	0	0	0	0	0	0.00
Clay, Columbus	20	20	7	3	9	4	0	.692	138	106	40	30	9	50	0	6	78	8	1.96
Cochran, Columbus	24	24	7	1	12	7	0	.632	165	129	51	47	10	56	6	2	106	7	2.56
Cooper, Columbus	12	4	0	0	3	2	0	.600	38	30	11	9	3	16	1	2	29	2	2.13
Crutcher, Charleston	4	0	0	0	0	0	0	.000	5	8	2	2	0	2	0	0	4	0	3.60
Dixon, Tidewater	32	19	6	1	8	12	3	.400	138	149	62	53	9	38	6	4	88	2	3.46
Edge, Richmond	26	18	5	2	7	7	2	.500	121	134	68	54	14	46	0	0	68	17	4.02
Farr, Charleston	12	9	1	1	4	3	1	.571	56	70	30	30	1	19	1	1	24	1	4.82
Faust, Pawtucket	34	16	2	0	4	9	1	.308	135	145	80	66	17	47	5	2	45	4	4.40
Felton, Toledo	25	23	6	0	7	8	0	.467	146	129	73	65	8	81	2	5	100	8	4.01
Field, Richmond	13	11	1	0	4	6	0	.400	65	79	38	33	5	29	2	0	28	4	4.57
Finch, Pawtucket	16	13	3	1	1	5	0	.167	84	74	41	36	6	35	7	7	29	1	3.54
Finch, Charleston	22	19	1	1	7	6	1	.538	116	125	59	54	4	30	2	2	52	4	4.19
Fierbaugh, Rochester	18	0	0	0	1	0	1	1.000	26	31	18	17	3	12	1	2	9	1	5.88
Fore, Syracuse	19	19	5	2	7	9	0	.438	104	110	51	45	7	36	1	1	40	2	3.89
Griffin, Columbus	13	13	5	2	7	2	0	.778	83	88	37	32	8	22	0	2	47	5	3.47
Grilli, Syracuse	33	3	0	0	1	7	0	.125	85	90	49	45	8	50	9	2	39	7	4.76
Harris, Tidewater	39	11	1	0	2	9	2	.182	110	95	53	33	7	40	4	4	92	7	2.70
Hartzell, Rochester	16	16	3	0	10	4	0	.714	104	112	42	37	3	20	0	7	43	5	3.20
Holman, Tidewater	11	11	1	0	3	3	0	.500	48	54	35	26	4	18	1	3	16	0	4.88
Howard, Pawtucket	9	9	3	0	1	5	0	.167	59	49	34	30	4	32	5	3	35	6	4.58
Huffman, Syracuse	16	15	4	0	3	9	0	.250	93	98	45	41	10	35	1	1	47	3	3.97
Hurst, Pawtucket*	17	17	4	1	8	6	0	.571	105	101	52	46	11	50	1	1	54	2	3.94
Jackson, Tidewater	22	7	1	0	3	5	3	.375	78	63	33	20	0	51	8	0	56	4	2.31
Jakubowski, Charleston	11	0	0	0	0	1	1	.000	21	20	10	8	1	10	1	0	12	0	3.43
J. H. Johnson, Char*	16	10	4	0	3	9	0	.250	77	84	49	33	6	35	6	1	55	2	3.86
Johnston, Toledo*	1	0	0	0	0	0	0	.000	2	1	0	0	0	1	0	0	0	0	0.00
Jones, Rochester	28	28	8	2	13	14	0	.481	180	168	104	87	17	81	2	0	88	7	4.35
Kainer, Charleston	22	22	6	3	9	7	0	.563	138	128	58	44	6	46	3	4	66	6	2.87
Kammeyer, Columbus	25	25	13	0	15	7	0	.682	176	176	70	57	6	61	5	3	72	4	2.91
Kerrigan, Rochester	39	0	0	0	3	3	12	.500	55	46	19	17	6	23	4	3	23	1	2.78
Kinnunen, Toledo*	15	0	0	0	2	2	3	.500	14	13	5	4	1	5	1	0	9	0	2.57
Kucek, Syracuse	13	9	4	2	3	0	0	.500	62	64	32	29	3	21	1	2	46	3	4.21
LaRose, Pawtucket*	34	0	0	0	1	0	1	1.000	39	38	15	12	2	16	5	2	13	3	2.77

Pitcher–Club	G	GS	CG	ShO	W	L	Sv	Pct	IP	H	R	ER	HR	BB	Int. BB	HB	SO	WP	ERA
Leal, Syracuse	16	16	2	0	6	5	0	.545	110	102	44	40	3	31	2	3	76	3	3.27
Lewis, Columbus	47	0	0	0	10	7	7	.588	93	73	34	24	5	45	13	0	76	6	2.32
Lollar, Columbus*	21	2	0	0	2	1	5	.667	49	29	15	14	1	27	4	3	50	5	2.57
Luebber, Rochester	27	27	10	1	13	8	0	.619	188	178	83	75	13	56	4	5	83	9	3.59
Lynch, Tidewater	24	24	11	0	13	6	0	.684	163	151	69	57	10	42	3	2	91	5	3.15
MacPherson, Toledo	27	26	11	2	11	7	1	.611	184	179	73	62	9	60	1	6	77	6	3.03
MacWhorter, Pawtucket..	19	18	7	2	7	6	0	.538	123	107	43	35	5	41	2	4	53	3	2.56
Mahler, Richmond	29	26	9	1	12	6	0	.667	188	172	68	54	5	80	2	3	101	7	2.59
Mapel, Toledo	19	11	1	1	3	5	0	.375	71	79	39	34	7	25	0	0	37	2	4.31
McDonald, Columbus*	2	0	0	0	0	0	0	.000	4	9	6	6	1	3	0	0	4	0	13.50
McGilberry, Tidewater	15	7	2	0	3	4	0	.429	59	69	48	41	4	38	2	3	29	7	6.25
McLaughlin, Richmond	7	6	0	0	1	1	0	.500	28	32	14	14	0	10	0	1	20	6	4.50
Melson, Richmond	28	14	7	1	7	10	1	.412	139	117	53	44	3	64	2	2	110	13	2.85
Mendoza, Tidewater	12	7	0	0	2	1	1	.667	41	47	20	19	1	17	2	1	23	1	4.17
Mercer, Charleston*	39	2	0	0	3	3	4	.500	70	63	46	42	8	37	7	3	46	5	5.40
Metzger, Richmond	38	2	0	0	3	6	14	.333	69	64	30	25	6	21	2	3	42	0	3.26
Mirabella, Syracuse*	4	4	1	0	1	2	0	.333	31	28	13	9	0	8	0	1	23	1	2.61
Miller, Tidewater	29	0	0	0	4	2	4	.667	52	66	33	27	4	23	3	1	35	3	4.67
Moore, Syracuse	8	0	0	0	0	3	1	.000	9	13	10	9	0	9	1	0	4	1	9.00
Moore, Toledo	23	21	6	0	9	10	0	.474	141	139	71	62	11	56	3	4	53	1	3.96
Morogiello, Richmond*	29	29	11	0	11	12	0	.478	196	206	102	88	14	50	1	2	71	2	4.04
Myrick, Tidewater	2	0	0	0	0	1	0	.000	6	7	3	1	1	4	2	0	3	0	1.50
O'Brien, Richmond	30	4	2	1	8	2	3	.800	106	95	38	35	3	33	0	5	44	5	2.97
Ojeda, Pawtucket*	19	18	4	0	6	7	0	.462	123	107	54	44	10	56	6	2	78	4	3.22
Parks, Pawtucket	28	24	7	3	10	10	0	.500	174	141	62	50	11	96	11	7	89	13	2.59
Presley, Rochester	9	0	0	0	0	1	0	.000	17	24	13	9	0	8	1	1	10	0	4.76
Rajsich, Charleston*	3	0	0	0	1	0	0	1.000	4	4	4	4	0	3	0	0	3	0	9.00
Remmerswaal, Pawtucket	24	0	0	0	5	5	3	.500	48	42	28	25	3	29	7	3	33	1	4.69
Righetti, Columbus*	24	23	4	1	6	10	0	.375	142	124	79	73	9	101	0	8	139	6	4.63
Rineer, Rochester*	20	10	2	1	4	4	1	.500	71	87	46	40	7	24	1	0	23	2	5.07
Robertson, Syracuse	43	3	0	0	5	5	4	.500	82	84	48	40	8	39	7	4	34	7	4.39
Rogers, Toledo	8	7	1	0	2	4	0	.333	48	58	29	26	2	9	0	3	15	0	4.88
Rowe, Rochester	17	17	4	2	6	7	0	.462	92	104	58	47	10	31	1	6	39	8	4.60
Sarmiento, Toledo*	42	1	0	0	6	6	6	.500	85	63	31	25	6	35	5	3	39	8	2.65
Schneider, Rochester*	45	0	0	0	2	4	8	.333	50	46	32	27	5	25	5	4	28	2	4.86
Schrom, Syracuse	26	0	0	0	0	2	7	.000	46	41	19	17	1	20	2	1	32	1	3.33
Scott, Charleston	4	0	0	0	0	0	0	.000	0	3	0	0	0	0	0	0	0	0	0.00
Scott, Tidewater*	27	25	7	0	13	7	0	.650	170	165	69	56	6	64	6	5	88	6	2.96
Searage, Tidewater*	19	0	0	0	1	0	2	1.000	30	35	24	23	4	20	3	1	20	2	6.90
Serum, Toledo	38	2	1	0	3	7	2	.300	91	96	47	37	10	27	3	3	48	2	3.66
Shields, Richmond	15	0	0	0	0	3	3	.000	21	30	13	11	1	10	1	0	12	2	4.71
Skok, Richmond*	30	0	0	0	6	3	5	.667	43	35	15	14	2	16	5	0	29	0	2.93
Slagle, Columbus	5	1	0	0	1	1	0	.500	15	15	11	9	2	6	3	1	7	1	5.40
Smithson, Pawtucket	50	2	1	0	5	9	4	.357	99	95	50	32	6	45	13	5	73	5	2.91
Thayer, Syracuse	3	0	0	0	0	0	0	.000	2	4	2	2	0	4	3	0	3	0	9.00
Todd, Syracuse	22	22	8	2	7	9	0	.438	153	135	68	58	7	63	6	3	118	5	3.41
Torrez, Rochester*	36	5	1	1	2	4	2	.333	88	98	46	43	9	32	2	4	43	1	4.40
Tudor, Pawtucket*	12	11	3	0	4	5	0	.444	74	67	36	30	10	33	2	0	51	4	3.65
Umbarger, Charleston*..	2	0	0	0	1	0	0	1.000	6	3	1	1	1	0	0		2	0	1.50
Veselic, Toledo	27	26	8	4	11	8	0	.579	174	162	73	65	9	55	2	4	105	3	3.36
Von Ohlen, Tidewater*	45	0	0	0	5	4	8	.556	87	88	40	31	1	27	4	1	44	1	3.21
Wehrmeister, Columbus	39	0	0	0	3	4	8	.429	86	66	30	27	4	36	9	4	67	6	2.83
Welsh, Columbus*	29	24	13	2	9	12	1	.429	158	134	78	48	7	68	4	5	84	4	2.73
Whitehouse, Charleston*.	18	17	2	1	8	9	0	.471	99	110	62	47	6	37	5	0	64	2	4.27
Wiley, Rochester	35	11	4	1	8	7	5	.533	129	123	61	58	15	39	2	1	57	4	4.05
Williams, Toledo	15	15	6	3	9	3	0	.750	107	85	34	25	4	32	2	1	59	2	2.10
Willis, Syracuse*	44	0	0	0	7	4	5	.636	69	44	24	19	4	35	2	0	48	1	2.48
Wright, Pawtucket	22	12	3	0	4	8	0	.333	75	90	50	43	11	33	5	4	33	5	5.16

BALKS—Edge, Ojeda, Schneider, Scott, 3 each; Berenguer, Cochran, J. Finch, Griffin, Hurst, Righetti, Robertson, Sarmiento, 2 each; Baker, Boddicker, Brizzolara, Butcher, Dixon, Felton, S. Finch, Fore, Harris, Huffman, Kammeyer, Leal, Lewis, MacPherson, MacWhorter, Mapel, McGilberry, Melson, Mercer, Moore, Morogiello, Thayer, Todd, Wehrmeister, 1 each.

COMBINATION SHUTOUTS—Mercer-Babcock, Kainer-Babcock, Charleston; Cochran-Lollar, Bird-Lewis, Cochran-Lewis, Columbus; Wright-Remmerswaal, Pawtucket; Field-Metzger, Richmond; Rineer-Kerrigan, Boddicker-Schneider, Rochester; Baker-Schrom, Leal-Schrom, Syracuse; Jackson-Berenguer, Harris-Miller, Scott-Berenguer, Tidewater.

NO-HIT GAMES—None.

Mexican League

CLASS AAA

Leading Batter
ROBERTO RODRIGUEZ
Union Laguna

League President
ANTONIO RAMIREZ, M.

Leading Pitcher
GILBERTO RONDON
Yucatan

CHAMPIONSHIP WINNERS IN PREVIOUS YEARS

1955—Mexico City Tigers* ..... .539	1966—Mexico City Tigers‡ ...... .614	1974—Jalisco............................ .627
1956—Mexico City Reds............ .692	Mexico City Reds............ .571	Mexico City Reds x........ .551
1957—Yucatan .... .567	1967—Jalisco............................ .607	1975—Tampico x .... .541
Mex. C. Reds (2nd)† ...... .550	1968—Mexico City Reds............ .586	Cordoba .... .649
1958—Nuevo Laredo................. .625	1969—Reynosa .... .591	1976—Mexico City Reds x........ .543
1959—Poza Rica....................... .575	1970—Aguila§ .... .580	Union Laguna .... .547
Mex. C. Reds (3rd)† .... .507	Mexico City Reds............ .607	1977—Mexico City Reds........... .623
1960—Mexico City Tigers .... .538	1971—Jalisco§.......................... .558	Nuevo Laredo x .... .507
1961—Veracruz........................ .575	Saltillo .... .593	1978—Aguascalientes x .... .589
1962—Monterrey...................... .592	1972—Saltillo .... .636	Union Laguna .... .523
1963—Puebla........................... .606	Cordoba§ .... .541	1979—Saltillo .... .704
1964—Mexico City Reds........... .586	1973—Saltillo .... .656	Puebla x .... .628
1965—Mexico City Tigers .... .590	Mexico City Reds x........ .590	

*Defeated Nuevo Laredo, two games to none, in playoff for pennant. †Won four-team playoff. ‡Won split-season playoff. §League divided into Northern, Southern divisions; won two-team playoff. xLeague divided into Northern. Southern zones; sub-divided into Eastern, Western divisions; won eight-team playoff.

NOTE: Players' strike caused halt to Mexican League season, July 3. Six clubs did not join in strike and finished season playing a new 40-game schedule.

20-Team Season

STANDING OF CLUBS AT CLOSE OF SEASON, JULY 3

NORTHERN ZONE
EASTERN DIVISION

Club	Ags.	Rey.	NL.	Leo.	Mon.	CJ.	Sal.	UL.	Chi.	Mva.	MT.	Agu.	Ctz.	Tab.	Tol.	W.	L.	T.	Pct.	G.B.
Aguascalientes.	..	5	6	7	5	1	6	4	4	6	3	5	3	3	3	61	33	0	.649	......
Reynosa	1	..	4	4	5	5	2	4	4	6	3	3	4	4	3	52	46	0	.531	11
N. Laredo..........	3	6	..	4	6	3	2	3	4	2	4	3	4	3	2	49	46	3	.516	12½
Leon	3	3	2	..	3	4	4	4	2	4	3	2	2	4	3	43	53	0	.448	19
Monterrey.........	1	3	3	3	..	2	3	2	4	2	3	2	3	4	2	37	56	0	.398	23½

WESTERN DIVISION

Club	Ags.	Rey.	NL.	Leo.	Mon.	CJ.	Sal.	UL.	Chi.	Mva.	Pue.	Yuc.	MR.	Cam.	PR.	W.	L.	T.	Pct.	G.B.
Ciudad Juarez..	5	3	4	3	5	..	9	3	5	6	1	3	2	4	4	57	37	1	.606	......
Saltillo	0	5	4	3	3	3	..	7	6	5	3	3	3	4	3	52	47	0	.525	7½
Union Laguna ..	3	5	3	6	7	3	3	..	3	3	2	1	1	2	4	46	51	1	.474	12½
Chihuahua	3	2	3	4	3	1	2	3	..	5	0	2	2	1	3	34	57	1	.374	21½
Monclova	2	1	5	3	3	2	3	3	7	..	0	1	4	1	2	36	61	0	.371	22½

SOUTHERN ZONE
EASTERN DIVISION

Club	Pue.	Yuc.	MR.	Cam.	PR.	MT.	Agu.	Ctz.	Tab.	Tol.	CJ.	Sal.	UL.	Chi.	Mva.	W.	L.	T.	Pct.	G.B.
Puebla	..	2	3	6	6	4	6	5	5	5	4	3	3	5	6	63	25	2	.716	......
Yucatan	3	..	3	3	5	2	4	5	6	3	3	5	4	5	4	57	41	0	.582	11
Mexico Reds	5	5	..	3	3	3	4	6	2	4	4	3	4	4	2	52	40	3	.565	13
Campeche	1	3	4	..	4	5	4	3	4	4	0	2	4	2	5	45	43	1	.511	18
Poza Rica	0	4	4	2	..	2	2	2	2	2	3	2	3	4	3	36	57	0	.387	29½

WESTERN DIVISION

Club	Pue.	Yuc.	MR.	Cam.	PR.	MT.	Agu.	Ctz.	Tab.	Tol.	Ags.	Rey.	NL.	Leo.	Mon.	W.	L.	T.	Pct.	G.B.
Mexico Tigers	2	6	4	5	4	..	4	5	3	4	3	3	2	3	3	51	47	0	.520	......
Aguila	2	3	2	2	7	5	..	4	4	4	1	3	3	4	4	48	47	0	.505	1½
Coatzacoalcos	1	5	3	3	4	2	2	..	6	8	2	2	2	4	3	47	48	0	.495	2½
Tabasco	4	3	3	2	3	4	4	1	..	5	3	3	2	1	2	39	54	3	.419	9½
Toluca	1	0	2	5	5	4	2	1	2	..	3	3	4	3	4	39	55	1	.415	10

Tabasco club represented Villahermosa.

Union Laguna club represented Gomez Palacio and Torreon.

Playoffs—None.

Regular-Season Attendance—Aguascalientes, 132,527; Aguila, 166,109; Campeche, 201,705; Chihuahua, 128,348; Ciudad Juarez, 144,450; Coatzacoalcos, 160,752; Leon, 119,427; Mexico Reds, 269,177; Mexico Tigers, 219,426; Monclova, 141,148; Monterrey, 95,621; Nuevo Laredo, 120,414; Poza Rica, 132,775; Puebla, 128,014; Reynosa, 151,766; Saltillo, 170,262; Tabasco, 209,885; Toluca, 68,689; Union Laguna, 156,403; Yucatan, 361,092. Total, 3,277,990. No all-star game.

Managers: Aguascalientes—Moises Camacho; Aguila—Miguel Sotelo, William Davis; Campeche—Jerry Hairston, Alfonso Pena; Chihuahua—Manuel Magallon; Ciudad Juarez—Jose Guerrero; Coatzacoalcos—Benjamin Cerda; Leon—Mario Saldana; Mexico Reds—Benjamin Reyes; Mexico Tigers—Fernando Remes Garza; Monclova—Victor Fabela; Monterrey—Hector Valle; Nuevo Laredo—Marte De Alejandro, Gerardo Gutierrez; Poza Rica—David Garcia; Puebla—Jorge Fitch, Rosendo Dominguez; Reynosa—Winston Llenas; Saltillo—Gregorio Luque; Tabasco—Raul Cano, Arnoldo Castro; Toluca—Carlos Trevino; Union Laguna—Jesus Diaz; Yucatan—Jaime Fabela.

All-Star Team—None.

(Compiled by Ana Luisa Perea de Silva, League Statistician, Mexico, D. F.)

CLUB BATTING

Club	G.	AB.	R.	OR.	H.	TB.	2B.	3B.	HR.	RBI.	SH.	SF.	Int. BB.	BB.	SO.	SB.	CS.	LOB.	Pct.
Aguascalientes	94	3146	452	350	943	1320	138	37	55	411	37	30	313	37	410	36	43	713	.300
Toluca	95	3286	500	617	970	1397	161	16	78	451	22	18	27	447	56	37	662	.295
Puebla	90	2986	421	229	854	1144	137	45	21	378	44	29	248	32	350	49	611	.286
Union Laguna	98	3222	424	420	918	1275	127	40	50	385	42	23	258	34	15	426	56	52	642	.285
Reynosa	98	3341	411	362	949	1291	126	36	48	366	42	25	349	30	41	417	36	53	815	.284
Saltillo	98	3179	412	428	894	1183	107	25	44	386	59	21	374	37	22	351	70	43	739	.281
Leon	96	3282	480	485	922	1369	134	35	81	433	24	19	303	19	42	578	53	52	685	.281
Mexico Reds	94	3205	422	366	899	1177	100	32	38	368	43	33	289	28	33	336	46	36	675	.280
Mexico Tigers	97	3254	402	383	909	1178	124	36	43	343	62	30	243	21	17	377	43	31	657	.279
C. Juarez	94	3146	418	339	877	1135	109	34	27	373	37	31	315	33	33	366	67	40	694	.279
Chihuahua	91	3121	362	458	859	1157	101	31	45	323	50	18	234	27	30	468	35	31	673	.275
Coatzacoalcos	94	3078	342	337	841	1093	121	25	27	297	51	21	257	18	23	363	49	42	634	.273
Monclova	96	3228	400	477	872	1215	118	12	67	353	38	18	362	37	22	449	35	28	731	.270
N. Laredo	98	3202	432	402	864	1178	112	29	48	381	49	30	365	37	39	491	71	49	717	.270
Tabasco	96	3211	313	368	857	1059	119	12	23	283	53	23	255	21	29	408	34	35	710	.267
Monterrey	93	3110	335	437	791	1073	93	30	43	303	70	24	253	26	23	412	39	27	654	.254
Aguila	95	3086	320	318	782	1026	121	15	31	283	34	20	223	18	34	365	28	34	606	.253
Yucatan	97	3158	350	297	789	1045	100	15	42	311	51	18	350	32	40	495	67	38	739	.250
Campeche	89	2904	299	318	705	937	99	11	37	258	46	23	293	28	31	391	48	31	649	.243
Poza Rica	93	2971	267	371	700	866	64	30	14	236	70	18	235	24	33	326	40	34	640	.236

INDIVIDUAL BATTING
(Leading Qualifiers for Batting Championship—257 or More Plate Appearances)

*Bats lefthanded.   †Switch-hitter.

Player and Club	G.	AB.	R.	H.	TB.	2B.	3B.	HR.	RBI.	SH.	SF.	BB.	HP.	SO.	SB.	CS.	Pct.
Rodriguez, Roberto, Laguna*	88	334	50	135	167	17	6	1	34	5	2	32	1	18	10	10	.404
Davalillo, Victor, Aguascalientes*	94	363	67	143	186	15	5	6	50	0	5	39	0	23	1	5	.394
Collins, James, Chihuahua*	91	346	62	131	188	19	13	4	52	1	2	47	5	34	19	7	.379
Lora, Luis, Puebla*	79	301	49	112	166	14	14	4	58	2	3	28	0	24	8	5	.372
Espino, Hector, 38 Lg-22 Mv-2 Sal .	62	230	27	84	128	12	1	10	33	0	1	35	3	12	0	1	.365
Monasterio, Juan, Toluca	90	355	64	129	173	3	7	59	2	6	24	2	30	15	9	.363
Obradovich, James, Aguas*	94	323	71	115	209	25	3	21	71	0	8	65	6	56	0	1	.356
Bernal, Arturo, Tabasco*	85	288	19	100	122	16	0	2	43	2	2	21	2	28	0	1	.347
Nettles, Morris, Puebla*	84	314	67	107	139	17	6	1	32	2	1	59	0	41	14	6	.341
Zamudio, Hector, Puebla	85	338	56	114	155	13	11	2	39	5	4	16	2	23	12	9	.337
Sanchez, Raul, Leon*	87	350	77	118	161	19	6	4	44	3	1	38	6	37	21	4	.337

Departmental Leaders: G—R. Batista, 98; AB—L. Alvarado, 391; R—R. Sanchez, 77; H—Davalillo, 143; TB—Murrell, 231; 2B—R. Robles, 29; 3B—Lora, 14; HR—Murrell, 32; RBI—Murrell, 91; GWRBI—DeFreites, Ruiz, 11;

SH—Leonides Sanchez, 19; SF—Obradovich, Pierce, 8; BB—Hairston, 77; HP—N. Alvarado, 12; SO—Murrell, 95; SB—Howard, 24; CS—L. Alvarado, Guerrero, 13.

(All Players—Listed Alphabetically)

Player and Club	G.	AB.	R.	H.	TB.	2B.	3B.	HR.	RBI.	SH.	SF.	BB.	HP.	SO.	SB.	CS.	Pct.
Acosta, Leonardo, Mex Reds	13	24	2	5	5	0	0	0	1	1	0	5	0	9	1	0	.208
Acosta, Marcos, Mex Tigers	6	4	0	1	1	0	0	0	0	0	0	0	0	1	0	0	.250
Acuna, Clemente, Puebla	15	37	3	8	9	1	0	0	6	1	1	0	0	4	3	0	.216
Aguilar, Enrique, Aguascalientes	93	350	53	103	159	21	1	11	62	3	3	27	3	37	15	7	.294
Aguilar, Jose, Puebla	59	189	16	53	66	11	1	0	21	1	0	24	0	14	2	2	.280
Alanis, Hector, 18 Agu-39 Tab	57	148	18	34	39	2	0	1	4	6	0	18	1	24	6	2	.230
Alcaraz, Luis, Leon	23	86	15	28	47	8	1	3	16	0	0	18	0	19	0	0	.326
Almeida, Reynaldo, Reynosa	12	22	2	2	3	1	0	0	0	1	0	1	1	10	2	0	.091
Alonso, Hermilo, Toluca	31	95	13	24	26	0	1	0	3	0	0	2	1	8	0	2	.253
Alou, Jesus, Coatzacoalcos	14	52	5	11	15	4	0	0	5	0	5	2	0	3	0	0	.212
Alvarado, Luis, Leon	93	391	56	117	171	17	8	7	57	2	3	29	3	36	7	13	.299
Alvarado, Natanael, Reynosa	93	352	48	111	147	17	5	3	30	6	2	33	12	57	8	7	.315
Alvarez, Jose, Monclova	2	4	0	1	1	0	0	0	0	0	0	0	0	1	1	0	.250
Alvarez, Juan, Aguascalientes	90	305	33	93	125	9	1	7	54	6	4	27	3	51	2	1	.305
Alvarez, Manuel, Reynosa*	68	197	32	58	83	9	2	4	32	1	4	30	1	29	0	3	.294
Aranda, Severo, Poza Rica	2	0	1	0	0	0	0	0	0	0	0	0	0	0	0	0	.000
Armbrister, Edson, Laredo	35	122	8	22	32	7	0	1	17	0	2	9	7	27	7	3	.180
Arvizu, Juan, Toluca	71	254	40	77	125	19	1	9	37	1	1	30	3	54	2	1	.303
Arzate, Martin, 7 Chi-38 Cam	45	113	7	25	29	2	1	0	11	2	1	6	1	20	1	3	.221
Avina, Franco, Monclova	65	164	18	33	40	5	1	0	10	5	0	5	0	32	3	4	.201
Baez, Jose, Puebla	14	50	3	14	18	2	1	0	7	0	2	1	0	5	1	1	.280
Balaz, John, Juarez	92	339	50	100	141	8	0	11	68	1	6	47	0	41	2	4	.295
Baldwin, William, Tabasco*	19	74	6	14	17	3	0	0	1	0	0	7	0	15	1	2	.189
Barajas, Franco, Aguascalientes	1	1	1	1	1	0	0	0	0	0	0	0	0	0	0	0	1.000
Barrera, Nelson, Mex. Reds	90	339	42	103	136	13	1	6	44	3	4	33	5	42	6	6	.304
Barren, Rafael, Mex. Reds	65	228	24	64	72	5	0	1	17	2	2	14	0	24	2	1	.281
Batista, Rafael, Laguna	98	343	59	112	205	23	5	20	83	0	6	51	1	45	2	1	.327
Bellacetin, Tomas, Leon	16	7	0	0	0	0	0	0	0	1	0	2	2	3	0	1	.000
Beltran, Miguel, Monclova	1	1	0	0	0	0	0	0	0	0	0	0	0	0	0	0	.000
Benitez, Jose, Leon	78	268	31	70	86	8	1	2	29	1	3	23	2	48	2	2	.261
Benitez, Julio, Laredo	25	43	7	8	13	2	0	1	7	0	0	5	0	9	0	0	.186
Bernal, Arturo, Tabasco*	85	288	19	100	122	16	0	2	43	2	2	21	2	28	0	1	.347
Bernhardt, Juan, Tabasco	96	380	51	125	170	25	1	6	50	3	5	14	6	24	0	4	.329
Biagini, Gregory, Monclova*	96	329	65	109	184	22	1	17	60	0	6	76	0	42	11	3	.331
Bobadilla, Manuel, Juarez	67	190	18	44	53	5	2	0	14	3	3	13	1	18	2	2	.232
Bojorquez, Jose, Monclova	51	168	18	51	76	7	0	6	25	0	2	17	1	24	0	0	.304
Borbon, Marcelo, Aguascalientes	42	139	18	38	44	4	1	0	9	3	0	7	0	19	0	3	.273
Briones, Antonio, Juarez	93	378	71	111	127	10	2	0	29	4	1	24	6	23	22	6	.294
Brown, Curtis, Poza Rica	92	338	41	84	114	3	3	7	31	4	2	37	1	20	5	1	.249
Camacho, Sergio, Aguascalientes	3	4	0	0	0	0	0	0	0	0	0	0	0	3	0	0	.000
Camargo, Fernando, Monterrey	85	316	49	83	145	16	2	14	55	5	5	30	2	42	1	0	.263
Cano, Ricardo, Saltillo	3	9	0	2	2	0	0	0	1	0	0	0	0	2	0	0	.222
Cantres, Angel, Monterrey	39	153	22	44	69	5	4	4	18	0	2	15	3	20	0	1	.288
Cardona, Candelario, Monclova	13	32	6	9	9	0	0	0	1	1	0	3	0	4	1	2	.281
Carreno, Luis, Puebla	77	268	33	75	107	19	2	3	35	3	4	34	7	6	6	.280
Castillo, Fernando, Campeche	1	1	0	0	0	0	0	0	0	0	0	0	0	1	0	0	.000
Castro, Antonio, Leon*	91	325	53	98	151	21	4	8	46	3	2	50	1	40	4	7	.302
Castro, Arnoldo, Mex Tigers	15	36	4	11	11	0	0	0	2	0	0	3	0	5	4	1	.306
Castro, David, Leon*	8	22	2	7	7	0	0	0	1	0	0	3	2	2	0	0	.318
Centeno, Jose, Toluca*	32	152	19	42	56	11	0	1	21	0	0	12	1	11	1	0	.276
Cerda, Benjamin, Coatzacoalcos	67	220	20	64	79	9	0	2	18	4	1	18	1	28	0	1	.291
Cervantes, Eduardo, Laredo	87	282	39	78	95	8	3	1	33	6	1	42	4	35	7	6	.277
Cervantes, Refugio, Aguila†	92	324	29	86	125	12	3	7	47	4	4	16	8	31	1	2	.265
Chavarria, Miguel, Laguna	91	281	36	70	93	6	4	3	21	5	0	14	1	39	5	5	.249
Chavarria, Roberto, Laguna	7	9	1	1	1	0	0	0	0	0	0	0	0	3	0	1	.111
Chavez, Carlos, Leon	5	1	1	0	0	0	0	0	0	0	0	0	0	0	0	0	.000
Chavez, Francisco, Mex Tigers	18	52	8	15	18	3	0	0	4	4	5	0	0	6	0	0	.288
Chavez, Guadalupe, Saltillo*	80	257	32	68	84	7	3	1	28	6	1	45	4	29	0	4	.265
Chavez, Hector, Aguascalientes	31	73	5	15	17	2	0	0	4	5	0	9	2	15	1	0	.205
Chavez, Jose, Laguna	28	58	8	16	21	1	2	0	9	3	0	3	0	13	1	1	.276
Chavez, Juan de Dios, Chihuahua	76	289	26	76	95	15	2	0	20	9	0	13	1	43	1	3	.263
Chavez, Marco, Puebla	24	43	3	11	11	0	0	0	2	1	0	1	0	5	3	0	.256
Christiansen, Dave, Poza Rica	52	174	18	38	50	4	1	2	15	1	2	16	4	15	0	0	.218
Collins, James, Chihuahua*	91	346	62	131	188	19	13	4	52	1	2	47	5	34	19	7	.379
Collins, Silvester, Coatzacoalcos	77	260	41	80	116	13	7	3	29	5	1	22	2	51	9	4	.308
Contreras, Juan C., Laguna	3	4	1	1	1	0	0	0	0	1	0	0	0	2	0	0	.250
Contreras, Juan V., Laguna	80	254	32	57	77	8	3	2	23	3	3	18	5	38	3	4	.224
Cosgaya, Ramon, Tabasco	9	1	1	0	0	0	0	0	0	0	0	1	0	1	0	0	.000
Cruz, Domingo, Coatzacoalcos	65	228	24	70	82	8	2	0	20	6	2	18	2	20	1	2	.307
Cuevas, Ricardo, Poza Rica	36	84	14	18	22	2	1	0	4	1	0	7	0	15	2	0	.214
Davalillo, Victor, Aguascalientes*	94	363	67	143	186	15	5	6	50	0	5	39	0	23	1	5	.394
Davila, Luis, Juarez	75	231	28	56	64	6	1	0	25	3	1	22	1	21	6	1	.242

Player and Club	G.	AB.	R.	H.	TB.	2B.	3B.	HR.	RBI.	SH.	SF.	BB.	HP.	SO.	SB.	CS.	Pct.
Davis, William, Aguila*	91	326	55	98	149	21	6	6	37	0	6	36	1	23	5	4	.301
DeFreites, Arturo, Reynosa	85	343	54	101	172	16	5	15	53	1	5	26	1	62	3	4	.294
De La Fuente, Jose, Tabasco	11	13	1	1	1	0	0	0	0	2	0	4	0	0	0	0	.077
De Hoyos, Arnoldo, Aguas*	80	273	21	71	78	7	0	0	15	2	0	24	2	27	4	7	.260
Delgado, Javier, Puebla	53	148	25	41	57	9	2	1	18	5	0	7	2	28	5	2	.277
Delgado, Luis, Saltillo	16	62	11	20	25	3	1	0	4	1	1	4	1	7	2	3	.323
Delgado, Manuel, Juarez*	50	148	25	44	56	6	3	0	24	1	5	20	0	15	6	2	.297
Deliza, Juan, Laguna	95	363	53	110	145	17	3	4	38	2	5	21	1	26	14	8	.303
De Los Santos, Jose, Toluca	5	13	0	2	2	0	0	0	0	0	0	0	0	5	0	0	.154
Diaz, Albino, 45 Mva-45 Lar	90	337	50	88	117	14	3	3	31	6	1	42	9	44	6	8	.261
Diaz, Arsenio, Monclova	95	344	55	106	175	12	0	19	70	0	3	51	4	51	4	2	.308
Diaz, Cesar, Puebla	2	0	2	0	0	0	0	0	0	0	0	0	0	0	0	0	.000
Diaz, Ernesto, Poza Rica	7	12	0	1	1	0	0	0	0	0	0	1	0	7	0	0	.083
Diaz, Gustavo, Yucatan	1	1	0	0	0	0	0	0	0	0	0	0	0	0	0	0	.000
Duran, Gerado, Chihuahua	49	143	15	33	51	4	1	4	11	2	0	12	1	49	1	0	.231
Duran, Roberto, Poza Rica*	33	97	11	33	43	5	1	1	13	0	2	9	7	6	0	1	.340
Elguezabal, Jose, Puebla	79	272	37	69	93	10	1	4	46	0	3	27	6	25	11	7	.254
Elizondo, Fernando, Aguila	92	301	26	52	63	11	0	0	17	3	3	18	1	52	1	2	.173
Enriquez, Graciano, Toluca	12	36	2	7	8	1	0	0	2	0	0	1	0	4	1	0	.194
Enriquez, Sergio, 10 Chi-4 Mva	14	45	1	7	7	0	0	0	2	1	0	3	0	20	0	0	.156
Esparza, Julio, 11 PR-49 Cam	60	171	7	39	41	2	0	0	8	4	1	21	0	18	1	3	.228
Espino, Hector, 38 Lg-22 Mv-2 Sl	62	230	27	84	128	12	1	10	33	0	1	35	3	12	0	1	.365
Espinosa de la Torre, Ernesto, Tol	93	353	48	90	123	14	2	5	41	5	5	14	5	34	2	2	.255
Espinosa Ramos, E., 8 Cm-21 Ch	29	48	5	7	9	0	1	0	0	2	0	6	1	14	0	0	.146
Esquedo, Carlos, Laguna	44	116	14	21	27	1	1	1	15	1	2	15	0	24	1	1	.181
Esquivias, Ruben, Mex Tigers	1	1	0	0	0	0	0	0	0	0	0	0	0	0	0	0	.000
Estrada, Francisco, Puebla	84	307	38	83	102	13	0	2	46	6	6	23	7	20	3	2	.270
Estrada, Pablo, Monclova*	1	0	1	0	0	0	0	0	0	0	0	0	0	0	0	0	.000
Faudoa, Victor, Mex Tigers*	64	181	18	50	56	6	0	0	16	3	3	27	0	21	2	1	.276
Felix, Claudio, Tabasco	6	6	2	1	1	0	0	0	0	0	0	0	0	3	0	0	.167
Felix, Fernando, Tabasco	85	311	19	82	92	5	1	1	31	3	3	19	1	49	4	3	.264
Felix, Victor, 29 Tab-54 Agu	83	269	45	63	81	13	1	1	10	5	1	56	6	32	8	6	.234
Figueroa, Baldemar, Tabasco	47	112	11	27	31	2	1	0	9	4	0	11	0	14	5	1	.241
Figueroa, Leobardo, Juarez	80	268	60	78	112	14	4	4	29	2	2	53	13	35	18	10	.291
Flores, Mario, Monterrey	41	107	9	27	32	3	1	0	8	3	1	6	0	18	1	2	.252
Flores, Ruben, Leon*	16	55	6	17	19	2	0	0	2	2	0	1	0	4	1	2	.309
Ford, Lambert, Tabasco*	22	78	11	24	31	3	2	0	5	1	1	8	0	6	1	2	.308
Ford, Theodore, Mex Reds	92	331	57	101	150	22	3	7	47	2	3	58	3	37	2	2	.305
Gamez, Sergio, Mex Reds	72	240	29	61	73	8	2	0	18	13	4	14	9	35	0	2	.254
Gamundi, Timoteo, Poza Rica	87	319	39	79	90	9	1	0	20	7	2	36	4	38	14	6	.248
Garcia, Bulmaro, Aguila	87	300	26	75	89	11	0	1	17	6	1	12	5	30	0	2	.250
Garcia, Humberto, Laguna	88	315	43	81	126	8	2	11	44	3	4	40	0	60	11	2	.257
Garica, Jesus, Campeche	7	24	1	5	5	0	0	0	2	0	0	1	0	10	0	1	.208
Garzon, Felix, Coatzacolcos	44	148	11	42	48	4	1	0	17	0	2	11	0	21	2	3	.284
Gaston, Clarence, Leon	48	185	16	44	61	5	0	4	27	0	0	11	0	26	0	3	.238
Gomez, Alejandro, Laredo	2	3	0	1	1	0	0	0	0	1	0	0	0	1	0	0	.333
Gomez, Graciano, Coatzacoalcos	59	149	18	35	42	5	1	0	19	5	1	5	3	16	5	1	.235
Gonzalez, Efrain, Laguna	42	100	5	23	28	2	0	1	10	2	0	5	3	14	1	2	.230
Gonzalez, Ernesto, Puebla	12	23	1	2	2	0	0	0	1	2	0	0	0	5	1	0	.087
Gonzalez, Jesus, Coatzacoalcos	74	211	17	59	68	9	0	0	14	5	1	6	0	29	2	1	.280
Gonzalez, Jose, Aguascalientes	67	251	33	61	86	9	5	2	24	3	2	24	3	49	7	6	.243
Gonzalez, Wenceslao, Chihuahua	71	249	28	59	118	8	0	17	44	1	3	32	8	69	0	2	.237
Guerra, Ricardo, Laredo	92	319	47	96	155	18	4	11	60	0	2	57	1	45	6	4	.301
Guerrero, Leobardo, Coatzacolcos	90	345	53	95	109	12	1	0	20	2	1	37	3	29	15	13	.275
Guillen, Norberto, Tabasco	51	126	8	27	28	1	0	0	10	2	2	9	1	18	0	1	.214
Guillermo, Leonardo, Campeche	15	23	2	4	5	1	0	0	1	1	0	4	0	6	0	0	.174
Gutierrez, Gerardo, Laredo	5	6	1	3	3	0	0	0	3	0	0	1	0	3	0	0	.500
Gutierrez, Porfirio, Juarez	2	0	1	0	0	0	0	0	0	0	0	0	0	0	0	0	.000
Guzman, Andres, Reynosa	89	317	27	89	110	10	4	1	20	1	0	22	4	46	1	6	.281
Guzman, Horacio, Campeche	78	299	33	56	80	9	3	3	17	4	2	17	7	53	7	4	.187
Guzman, Ramiro, Mex Tigers*	87	299	48	95	114	14	1	1	24	10	4	21	4	23	6	2	.318
Guzman, Ramon, Campeche	3	7	1	2	2	0	0	0	0	0	0	0	0	0	0	0	.286
Hairston, Jerry, Campeche*	77	235	50	74	114	15	2	7	28	3	4	77	2	27	15	4	.315
Heras, Roberto, Toluca	38	110	11	24	33	6	0	1	14	1	0	2	1	16	1	0	.218
Hernandez, Eduardo, Aguila	2	8	0	1	1	0	0	0	0	0	0	0	0	2	0	0	.125
Hernandez Morales, Javier, Mont	16	68	9	20	25	1	0	0	6	1	0	2	0	11	0	1	.294
Hernandez, Zamora, Javier, PR	45	156	9	33	38	3	1	0	13	4	0	4	4	13	2	3	.212
Hernandez, Jorge, Puebla	81	267	32	66	91	9	5	2	26	9	3	16	8	36	5	2	.247
Hernandez, Jose, Campeche	75	259	25	56	72	5	1	0	17	6	1	12	2	41	0	2	.216
Hernandez, Juan, Laguna	90	316	41	93	120	13	4	2	28	7	2	8	1	62	6	5	.294
Hernandez, Miguel, Coatzacoalcos	73	102	4	21	43	52	6	0	1	18	4	1	12	1	18	4	7	.205
Hernandez, Pedro, Juarez	49	129	14	45	61	8	4	0	16	2	1	7	2	15	1	0	.349
Hernandez, Ramon, Mex Reds	88	363	38	108	119	6	1	1	40	9	3	21	2	7	8	4	.298
Hernandez, Raul, Yucatan	15	17	3	3	3	0	0	0	1	0	0	0	0	2	0	1	.176
Hernandez, Rodolfo, Reynosa	92	332	43	101	149	16	1	10	47	2	5	46	6	36	4	4	.304
Hernandez, Salvador, Mex Tigers	41	129	17	29	34	5	0	0	12	4	2	14	0	10	1	3	.225

Player and Club	G.	AB.	R.	H.	TB.	2B.	3B.	HR.	RBI.	SH.	SF.	BB.	HP.	SO.	SB.	CS.	Pct.
Herrera, Crisanto, Tabasco	3	5	0	1	1	0	0	0	0	0	0	0	0	2	0	0	.200
Herrera, Ricardo, Campeche	7	24	4	4	4	0	0	0	0	0	0	2	0	3	0	0	.167
Howard, Wilbur, Yucatan*	90	376	36	118	142	11	5	1	31	2	2	19	0	30	24	10	.314
Ibarra, Humberto, Tabasco*	4	3	0	0	0	0	0	0	1	0	0	1	0	2	0	0	.000
Iglesias, Domingo, Aguila	13	24	2	4	6	2	0	0	1	1	0	4	0	7	0	0	.167
Iniguez, Roberto, 37 Mva-3 Tol	40	94	9	22	35	2	1	3	9	0	1	3	1	16	2	0	.234
Jackson, Alfonso, Laguna	4	7	1	1	2	1	0	0	0	0	0	1	0	1	0	0	.143
James, Arthur, Campeche*	84	316	39	100	125	11	1	4	26	1	3	26	0	28	4	2	.316
Jimenez, Alfonso, Puebla	75	254	29	62	75	8	1	1	24	6	2	20	3	20	10	6	.244
Johnson, Bart, Toluca	12	75	8	19	30	5	0	2	10	0	0	1	1	19	1	0	.253
Juarez, Marcelo, Saltillo	68	232	23	64	73	5	2	0	25	4	2	11	0	15	5	4	.276
Kekich, Mike, Juarez	1	2	1	1	1	0	0	0	0	0	0	1	0	0	0	0	.500
Krug, Gary, Tabasco	43	166	21	58	76	10	1	2	25	2	0	10	4	14	0	0	.349
Kurpiel, Edward, Mex Reds*	9	33	3	10	11	1	0	0	3	0	0	4	0	2	0	0	.303
Lara, Armando, Mex Tigers	89	316	31	78	110	15	1	5	34	3	1	20	0	32	0	1	.247
Lara, Cesar, Coatzacoalcos	62	112	9	22	22	0	0	0	7	3	1	8	1	17	4	1	.196
Lara, Francisco, 3 Lar-30 Sl-30 To	63	212	24	59	66	4	0	1	19	4	0	11	1	11	3	2	.278
Lara, Leopoldo, Aguila	3	9	3	0	0	0	0	0	0	0	0	1	0	2	0	0	.000
Lazaro, Alfredo, Monterrey	79	259	31	67	104	12	2	7	30	8	2	30	2	49	0	3	.259
Lazaro, Manuel, 60 Lar-7 Yuc	67	194	21	47	54	5	1	0	15	2	2	14	1	22	6	10	.242
Leal, Marco, Mex Tigers	73	283	36	76	92	11	1	1	18	5	1	27	0	27	8	7	.269
Leon, Maximino, Campeche	1	2	0	1	1	0	0	0	0	0	0	0	0	0	0	0	.500
Leon, Richard, Mex Tigers*	80	312	42	100	144	18	1	8	47	1	4	20	1	28	5	3	.321
Lizarraga, Alejandro, Mex Reds	83	317	47	97	131	11	7	3	31	3	2	13	2	23	7	6	.306
Lizarraga, Miguel, Yucatan	32	63	5	15	20	5	0	0	7	3	0	7	0	10	0	0	.238
Lizarraga, Raul, Leon	65	126	7	15	19	2	1	0	5	0	1	12	1	33	1	3	.119
Llenas, Winston, Reynosa	97	348	53	109	165	20	3	10	67	2	5	58	4	40	0	4	.313
Lopez, Baudel, 28 M Reds-49 Tol*	77	283	43	78	113	15	1	6	34	6	1	41	5	32	3	2	.276
Lopez, Carlos, 82 Tig-4 Rey	86	321	54	106	163	15	9	8	50	0	5	27	7	50	13	3	.330
Lopez, Jaime, Coatzacoalcos*	74	270	23	84	111	11	5	2	31	6	1	11	0	11	1	2	.311
Lopez, Leobardo, Poza Rica	32	118	7	21	24	1	1	0	7	3	0	3	2	15	0	2	.178
Lopez, Lorenzo, Toluca	78	270	26	69	100	8	1	7	35	1	1	17	1	46	0	3	.256
Lopez, Pablo, Saltillo*	8	22	1	3	3	0	0	0	0	2	0	2	0	6	0	0	.136
Lopez, Raul, Chihuahua*	11	25	4	5	5	0	0	0	1	0	1	0	0	4	1	1	.200
Lopez, Victor, Chihuahua	85	326	45	104	122	8	2	2	46	2	3	28	0	36	4	2	.319
Lora, Luis, Puebla*	79	301	49	112	166	14	14	4	58	2	3	28	0	24	8	5	.372
Lugo, Gabriel, 33 Ctz-16 Leo	49	167	18	42	51	4	1	1	21	2	3	11	1	17	0	1	.251
Lugo, Pedro, Poza Rica	22	57	3	12	13	1	0	0	6	3	1	0	0	8	0	0	.211
Luna, Jose, Monterrey	40	131	12	26	36	4	0	2	5	3	2	3	1	29	1	0	.198
Luque, Gregorio, Saltillo	3	4	0	0	0	0	0	0	1	1	0	0	0	0	0	0	.000
Maddox, Jerry, Laredo	55	195	33	56	84	9	2	5	31	1	2	21	1	29	3	3	.287
Mares, Hilario, Poza Rica	88	268	21	43	59	4	6	0	25	9	1	29	1	41	4	1	.160
Marquez, Francisco, Yucatan	93	302	34	88	119	10	0	7	43	2	1	36	10	59	2	2	.291
Marquez, Roberto, Coatzacoalcos	2	3	1	1	1	0	0	0	0	0	0	3	0	1	0	1	.333
Martin, Mike, Juarez	11	17	2	2	2	0	0	0	1	0	0	0	0	6	0	0	.118
Martinez, Juan, Monterrey	71	254	23	66	104	15	1	7	35	4	4	22	0	62	1	0	.260
Matina, Raymond, Laredo	26	84	12	24	28	1	0	1	10	1	0	10	1	8	2	3	.286
Mendez, Roberto, Campeche	82	315	33	86	102	13	0	1	21	3	2	32	8	34	5	4	.273
Mendoza, Luis, Juarez	31	286	37	83	95	9	0	1	23	7	2	24	2	18	2	1	.290
Mendoza, Margarito, 42 Mva-2 Sal	44	63	10	15	18	0	0	1	8	1	0	5	0	6	0	2	.238
Mendoza, Porfirio, 39 Yuc-29 Tig	68	213	27	50	63	9	2	0	23	6	1	21	2	23	0	5	.235
Mendoza, Saul, Yucatan	91	320	36	66	84	7	1	3	24	12	2	52	4	30	7	3	.206
Mojica, Baltasar, Laredo	3	2	0	1	1	0	0	0	0	0	0	0	0	1	0	0	.500
Mojica, Bartolo, Leon	36	83	7	23	29	4	1	0	7	3	0	6	2	16	1	0	.277
Molina, Jose, Aguila	44	133	7	35	47	6	0	2	16	0	0	7	2	28	0	0	.263
Monasterio, Juan, Toluca	90	355	64	129	173	17	3	7	59	2	6	24	2	30	15	9	.363
Monarrez, Jesus, Aguascalientes	14	25	2	3	4	1	0	0	1	2	0	2	0	6	0	0	.120
Montiel, Julio, 6 Sal-9 Lar	15	14	0	1	1	0	0	0	0	2	0	1	0	2	0	0	.071
Montoya, Raul, 9 Chi-81 Sal	90	330	38	84	95	1	5	0	20	6	0	33	1	28	20	9	.255
Mora, Andres, Saltillo	45	160	25	48	80	8	0	8	42	0	2	21	2	10	1	1	.300
Morales, Carlos, Aguascalientes	14	34	3	5	6	1	0	0	2	0	1	3	1	9	0	1	.147
Morales, Luis, Reynosa	36	57	9	13	18	3	1	0	3	2	0	2	1	21	1	3	.228
Munoz, Eduardo, 13 Lag-68 Rey	81	303	49	84	113	11	6	2	32	4	1	38	3	27	4	3	.277
Munoz, Jose Luis, Yucatan	53	136	22	30	41	5	0	2	14	0	3	18	3	29	3	2	.221
Munoz, Romulo, Leon	79	247	31	73	125	16	0	12	43	0	2	14	4	51	5	1	.296
Murrell, Ivan, Leon	96	380	67	117	231	14	2	32	91	0	2	31	5	95	5	4	.308
Naranjo, Jose, Monclova*	91	325	37	94	122	11	1	5	33	5	1	43	3	29	3	0	.289
Navarrete, Carlos, Coatzacoalcos	45	114	7	28	36	4	2	0	5	2	0	5	3	8	1	1	.246
Navarrete, Juan, Saltillo*	96	367	57	121	151	10	4	4	46	6	2	42	0	16	19	4	.330
Nettles, Morris, Puebla*	84	314	67	107	139	17	6	1	32	2	1	59	0	41	14	6	.341
Noriega, Franco, Chihuahua	3	5	1	1	2	0	0	0	1	0	1	0	1	0	0	0	.200
Nunez, Guadalupe, Puebla	5	12	1	1	1	0	0	0	0	1	0	0	0	2	1	0	.083
Obradovich, James, Ags*	94	323	71	115	209	25	3	21	71	0	8	65	6	56	0	1	.356
Ochoa, Julio, Campeche	1	3	0	0	0	0	0	0	0	0	0	0	0	0	0	0	.000
Olivares, Osvaldo, Tabasco	5	19	2	7	7	0	0	0	0	0	0	4	0	2	0	0	.368
Ornelas, Jesus, Tabasco	51	136	13	29	33	4	0	0	5	11	0	15	0	33	0	4	.213

Player and Club	G.	AB.	R.	H.	TB.	2B.	3B.	HR.	RBI.	SH.	SF.	BB.	HP.	SO.	SB.	CS.	Pct.
Ornelas, Rafael, Yucatan	93	288	28	61	89	5	1	7	26	11	1	48	2	75	5	6	.212
Ornelas, Roberto, Monclova	83	311	28	71	85	12	1	0	15	4	1	28	0	51	0	2	.228
Orozco, Arturo, Toluca	91	319	69	104	188	18	0	22	74	1	1	45	2	68	10	3	.326
Ortega, Angel, Mex Reds	54	169	13	38	45	3	2	0	19	3	2	8	3	18	2	3	.225
Ortiz, Alfredo, Tabasco*	18	26	3	7	10	3	0	0	5	0	0	2	0	2	0	0	.269
Ortiz, Armando, Yucatan	76	267	34	73	100	12	3	3	37	1	1	23	6	42	4	1	.273
Ortiz, Jose, Monterrey	50	173	12	38	52	3	1	3	19	6	1	7	1	15	3	1	.220
Osuna, Elpidio, Juarez	74	254	19	73	88	13	1	0	32	1	2	24	3	27	0	2	.287
Oviedo, Ismael, Saltillo	21	43	5	9	13	4	0	0	3	1	0	4	0	18	0	0	.209
Pacho, Juan Jose, Yucatan	2	2	0	0	0	0	0	0	0	0	0	0	0	0	0	0	.000
Padilla, Jose Luis, Monclova	43	64	9	17	17	0	0	0	5	1	0	5	0	9	2	1	.266
Paredes, Jesus, Laredo	87	349	56	107	130	12	1	3	40	2	5	13	8	53	15	4	.307
Paredes, Raul, 12 Pue-22 Tol	34	96	14	21	21	0	0	0	10	0	0	1	2	13	3	1	.219
Parra, Manuel, Juarez	60	202	16	54	75	12	0	3	29	2	2	10	0	24	0	1	.267
Parra, Salomon, Chihuahua	1	1	0	0	0	0	0	0	0	0	0	0	0	0	0	0	.000
Pedroza, Juan, Leon	71	177	30	35	44	3	3	0	12	3	1	29	4	58	0	5	.198
Peralta, Luis, Poza Rica	88	294	15	88	100	7	1	1	25	2	4	17	0	26	1	1	.299
Peralta, Vicente, Mex Tigers	33	90	9	19	20	1	0	0	6	5	1	3	0	8	0	0	.211
Perez, Alfredo, 11 Lar-74 Lag	85	262	34	68	89	8	5	1	24	3	0	31	1	24	3	5	.260
Perez, Carlos, Toluca	6	17	2	4	4	0	0	0	0	0	0	1	0	4	0	0	.235
Perez, Javier, Toluca	43	124	17	28	40	5	2	1	6	1	0	8	0	36	3	0	.226
Perez, Joel, Tabasco	96	357	41	95	135	10	3	8	32	5	1	24	2	45	5	3	.266
Perez, Jose, Aguascalientes*	86	290	41	91	129	16	5	4	36	2	1	28	4	42	1	2	.314
Pierce, Jack, 96 Sal-1 Ctz	97	331	50	88	160	21	0	17	75	1	8	59	5	75	2	0	.266
Plasencia, Rigoberto, Aguila	56	194	12	50	61	6	1	1	12	1	0	13	1	17	0	2	.258
Preciado, Mario, Laguna	23	64	2	14	19	3	1	0	6	2	0	2	0	9	0	0	.219
Prieto, Juvencio, Aguila	57	177	11	37	40	3	0	0	13	0	1	3	1	28	0	0	.209
Quintero, Frank, Laguna	1	2	0	2	3	1	0	0	2	0	0	0	0	0	0	1	1.000
Quintero, Guadalupe, Campeche	5	13	0	2	2	0	0	0	0	0	0	0	0	2	0	0	.154
Quintero, Victor, Saltillo	54	148	16	34	40	4	1	0	15	7	2	12	0	18	2	1	.230
Quinonez, Ventura, Juarez	16	9	5	1	1	0	0	0	0	1	0	2	0	1	0	0	.111
Ramirez, Manuel, Tabasco	95	361	43	99	116	10	2	1	21	4	4	34	3	29	7	6	.274
Ramirez, Orlando, Chihuahua	3	3	2	1	4	0	0	1	2	0	0	0	0	1	0	0	.333
Remes, Fernando, Mex Tigers	1	0	0	0	0	0	0	0	0	0	0	0	0	0	0	0	.000
Rey, Arturo, Aguila	60	169	10	32	38	6	0	0	12	2	2	19	3	17	0	2	.189
Reyes, Pedro, Aguascalientes	6	19	2	4	6	0	1	0	3	0	0	1	0	0	0	0	.211
Rios, Carlos, Campeche	71	259	23	56	74	7	1	3	30	4	2	14	1	33	7	4	.216
Rivera, Carlos, Mex Tigers	94	362	48	91	130	4	4	9	43	7	4	20	2	75	6	1	.251
Rivera, Eduardo, 48 Chi-13 Mva	61	194	19	46	54	4	2	0	18	2	0	20	0	17	0	0	.237
Rivera, Franco, Mex Tigers	2	6	1	1	1	0	0	0	1	0	0	0	0	5	0	0	.167
Rivero, Gener, Reynosa	90	314	37	78	91	5	4	0	27	9	2	45	4	21	4	7	.248
Robles, Alejandro, 52 Yuc-19 Lar*	71	239	23	58	64	6	0	0	11	6	1	15	3	20	1	1	.243
Robles, Humberto, Juarez	2	1	0	0	0	0	0	0	0	0	0	0	0	1	0	0	.000
Robles, Rigoberto, Toluca	94	389	64	130	187	29	2	8	42	2	3	33	1	39	2	5	.334
Robles, Sergio, Mex Reds	60	217	19	56	65	6	0	1	20	1	2	4	0	19	2	1	.258
Rodriguez, Arturo, Monterrey	66	229	16	58	64	4	1	0	24	9	1	18	2	20	5	0	.253
Rodriguez, Eliseo, Saltillo	16	50	9	13	19	3	0	1	7	1	0	12	2	6	0	0	.260
Rodriguez, Francisco, Ags	87	317	37	87	111	12	3	2	37	6	2	32	0	22	0	4	.274
Rodriguez, Jaime, Mex Tigers	5	10	0	1	0	0	0	0	0	0	0	0	0	0	0	0	.000
Rodriguez, Jose, Mex Tigers	63	213	17	64	76	12	0	0	22	6	3	17	1	22	0	2	.300
Rodriguez, Juan A., Toluca	8	7	2	3	3	0	0	0	3	0	0	2	1	3	0	1	.429
Rodriguez, Juan F., Reynosa	94	277	29	69	78	5	2	0	13	7	0	19	3	19	3	4	.249
Rodriguez, C. Leonardo, Mont†	89	325	35	80	113	7	4	6	35	2	2	48	2	43	6	5	.246
Rodriguez, M. Leonardo, Monterrey	69	192	15	40	46	2	2	0	12	6	1	21	3	10	0	3	.208
Rodriguez, Mario, Campeche	2	6	0	0	0	0	0	0	0	0	0	0	0	5	0	0	.000
Rodriguez, Roberto, Laguna*	88	334	50	135	167	17	6	1	34	5	2	32	1	18	10	12	.404
Rodriguez, Rodolfo, Saltillo*	86	298	42	94	113	7	3	2	25	7	1	54	3	30	6	7	.315
Rojas, Olegario, Campeche	51	165	10	42	59	8	3	1	16	6	4	10	2	15	5	1	.255
Roman, Dagoberto, Mex Reds*	54	191	34	56	72	5	4	1	20	2	2	20	1	31	2	2	.293
Romo, Jose, Coatzacoalcos	82	275	33	72	117	10	4	9	38	4	1	28	5	53	2	2	.262
Romo, Jesus, Mex Reds	23	46	4	13	14	1	0	0	1	2	0	4	0	5	0	1	.283
Rosales, Arturo, Juarez	57	138	15	36	60	4	4	4	22	4	4	5	1	28	2	1	.261
Rosario, Angel, Coatzacoalcos*	86	298	51	90	142	18	2	10	32	2	3	60	0	38	2	1	.302
Rosas, Clemente, Reynosa	65	200	10	53	61	5	0	1	25	1	1	16	0	27	2	2	.265
Rubio, Arturo, Tabasco	59	167	17	46	55	6	0	1	11	4	1	13	3	20	4	6	.275
Rubio, Jorge, Mex Reds	57	199	24	41	70	8	3	5	31	0	3	21	1	31	0	2	.206
Ruiz, Porfirio, Campeche	81	284	28	75	98	11	0	4	39	7	1	22	5	29	3	0	.264
Saiz, Francisco, Poza Rica*	79	279	26	70	89	7	6	0	19	10	3	26	1	27	1	3	.251
Salazar, Ronaldo, Aguascalientes	74	264	36	77	100	15	1	2	25	2	1	31	3	35	3	4	.292
Salinas, Manuel, Chihuahua	5	10	0	1	1	0	0	0	0	0	0	0	0	4	0	0	.100
Sanchez, Juan, Laguna	77	262	34	69	106	12	2	7	37	1	0	13	2	60	0	5	.263
Sanchez, Leonides, Poza Rica	88	329	26	84	102	6	3	2	24	19	0	12	6	24	8	7	.255
Sanchez, Oscar, Chihuahua	22	51	7	10	12	0	1	0	2	0	0	5	1	18	0	0	.196
Sanchez, Raul, Leon*	87	350	77	118	161	19	6	4	44	3	1	38	6	37	21	4	.337
Sandoval, Rodolfo, Laredo	4	3	0	0	0	0	0	0	0	0	0	1	0	1	0	0	.000
Santana, Blas, Aguila	95	381	42	110	151	16	2	7	50	1	2	11	2	30	5	4	.289

Player and Club	G.	AB.	R.	H.	TB.	2B.	3B.	HR.	RBI.	SH.	SF.	BB.	HP.	SO.	SB.	CS.	Pct.
Santos, Jose, Laredo*	84	273	44	72	98	5	6	3	24	10	4	30	5	51	4	6	.264
Sanudo, Ismael, 15 Sal-43 Mva	58	160	11	40	44	4	0	0	10	8	0	20	2	19	0	1	.250
Sauceda, Victor, Chihuahua	85	353	46	97	130	8	2	7	33	9	2	17	3	53	5	8	.275
Saucedo, Oscar, Chihuahua	1	0	1	0	0	0	0	0	0	0	0	0	0	0	0	0	.000
Scanlon, J. Patrick, Campeche*	31	99	11	24	36	6	0	2	10	1	1	25	0	17	0	0	.242
Scott, George, Yucatan	41	130	18	38	55	6	1	3	17	0	1	33	1	27	1	1	.292
Segui, Diego, Reynosa	1	1	0	0	0	0	0	0	0	0	0	0	0	0	0	0	.000
Serna, Joel, Monclova	93	368	55	106	167	3	11	45	7	2	38	3	70	2	1	.288
Serratos, Ramon, 6 Lar-55 Sal	61	161	18	41	47	1	1	1	13	3	0	16	0	22	5	3	.255
Silverio, Tomas 7 Tig-76 Sal-2 Lag*	85	302	41	86	135	18	5	7	40	4	0	31	0	39	4	3	.285
Sommers, Jesus, 46 Tol-47 Reds	93	350	59	108	162	12	6	10	65	0	3	41	1	39	3	4	.309
Sosa, Carlos, Laguna	1	1	0	0	0	0	0	0	0	0	0	0	0	1	0	0	.000
Sotelo, Emilio, Reynosa	16	21	1	2	2	0	0	0	0	0	0	1	0	6	0	0	.095
Soto, Carlos, 10 Lar-80 Sal	90	328	47	99	129	9	3	5	36	0	3	25	3	32	5	2	.302
Soto, Gregorio, Yucatan	81	282	31	56	64	6	1	0	10	6	1	11	2	55	10	3	.199
Stanton, Leroy, Puebla	37	141	20	32	48	11	1	1	16	0	0	12	0	38	2	1	.227
Stenholm, Richard, Mex Reds	69	246	49	74	126	7	6	11	42	0	3	31	5	21	10	4	.301
Suarez, Miguel, 74 Rey-3 Mex Tig*	77	293	22	84	101	8	3	1	20	5	0	23	1	21	3	6	.287
Tanaka, Alejandro, Monclova	15	32	3	7	7	0	0	0	2	0	0	3	1	8	0	0	.219
Tellez, Alonso, Monterrey	80	292	31	72	87	9	3	0	15	2	0	16	2	41	3	6	.247
Terrazas, Martin, Mex Tigers	74	224	19	54	60	6	0	0	19	7	1	11	2	27	1	1	.241
Thompson, Narciso, Leon	82	292	29	76	102	9	1	5	27	3	3	10	4	53	3	5	.260
Thompson, Robert, Poza Rica*	26	93	9	28	43	6	3	1	12	2	1	5	0	24	1	2	.301
Tiburcio, Zeferino, Poza Rica	11	34	2	6	6	0	0	0	2	0	0	1	0	8	0	2	.176
Torres, Nemesio, Monterrey	86	334	39	91	107	6	5	0	20	15	3	22	4	15	4	2	.272
Trevino, Juan, 3 Sal-82 Lar	85	270	24	61	73	8	2	0	16	9	1	25	3	27	2	1	.226
Tyrone, Wayne, Yucatan	93	336	44	98	146	14	2	10	51	3	3	46	1	59	5	2	.292
Uzcanga, Ali, Laredo	62	176	24	48	66	10	1	2	23	7	1	11	0	41	2	3	.273
Valdez, Baltasar, Chihuahua	90	326	30	78	108	13	4	3	29	7	2	15	5	67	2	1	.239
Valencia, Ignacio. Campeche	3	6	0	0	0	0	0	0	0	1	0	2	0	4	0	1	.000
Valenzuela, Carlos, 71 Mva-12 Chi.	83	255	12	62	67	5	0	0	16	3	0	32	0	36	2	2	.243
Valenzuela, Jose, Tabasco	69	200	2	41	46	3	1	0	11	4	1	12	2	42	0	0	.205
Valenzuela, Leonardo, Monterrey*	69	277	32	79	89	6	2	0	21	6	0	13	1	37	14	3	.285
Valle, Guadalupe, Juarez	92	285	26	69	97	6	11	0	28	4	1	26	1	64	1	5	.242
Vazquez, Efrain, Laredo†	70	251	38	81	120	10	4	7	40	1	4	44	2	31	2	3	.323
Vazquez, Nicolas, Yucatan	94	331	30	73	105	12	1	6	29	5	2	32	6	45	4	2	.221
Vega, Abelardo, Juarez	80	269	30	80	104	8	2	4	33	2	1	37	3	29	5	5	.297
Vega, Valenciano, 68 Mva-12 Lag	80	319	33	78	89	6	1	1	19	3	2	14	3	23	0	2	.245
Velarde, Roman, Campeche	42	117	10	24	34	4	0	2	9	1	0	12	0	15	0	0	.205
Villaescusa, Antonio, Toluca	37	155	25	54	57	3	0	0	19	3	0	13	2	16	13	6	.348
Villaflor, Franco, Poza Rica	26	54	4	3	3	0	0	0	1	1	0	5	0	11	0	3	.056
Villagomez, David, Aguila	74	251	40	78	110	10	2	6	38	3	1	23	4	39	4	3	.311
Villalobos, Gonzalo, Aguascalientes	92	388	50	107	137	8	11	0	33	5	5	20	0	43	6	9	.276
Villalobos, Lauro, Chihuahua	91	361	36	97	102	3	1	0	16	11	1	18	1	22	2	3	.269
Villela, Carlos, Laguna	69	252	27	58	73	6	3	1	29	6	2	9	0	33	9	1	.230
Villela, Rigoberto, Chihuahua	91	349	31	104	149	20	2	7	50	5	5	16	3	25	0	4	.298
Weeb, Marvin, Coatzacoalcos	21	72	7	21	26	5	0	0	8	2	0	3	1	11	1	1	.292
Williams, Earl, Campeche	47	175	18	35	59	6	0	6	22	0	1	12	3	30	0	2	.200
Yepez, Francisco, Poza Rica	82	247	18	53	60	5	1	0	17	4	0	22	3	27	2	2	.215
Zamora, Roberto, Mex Tigers	1	1	0	0	0	0	0	0	0	0	0	0	0	0	0	0	.000
Zamudio, Hector, Puebla	85	338	56	114	155	13	11	2	39	5	4	16	2	23	12	9	.337
Zavala, Alfredo, Mex Tigers	83	286	27	86	100	8	3	0	26	4	0	18	0	34	2	3	.301
Zavala, Marcos, Tabasco	60	181	15	29	35	3	0	1	16	2	2	11	1	31	1	0	.160
Zetina, Delio, Toluca	1	1	0	0	0	0	0	0	0	0	0	0	0	0	0	0	.000
Zuniga, Faustino, Laredo	28	47	4	6	7	1	0	0	2	0	0	9	0	12	1	0	.128
Zuniga, Rafael, Leon	74	229	40	66	92	5	6	3	20	2	1	23	6	49	6	2	.288

The following pitchers had no plate appearances primarily through use of designated hitters, listed alphabetically by club, games in parentheses):

AGUASCALIENTES—Abarca, David (18); Agundez, Victor (6); Cervantes, Lauro (17); Cisneros, Alfonso (5); Espinosa, Javier (3); Granillo, Carlos (4); Low, Gabriel (2); Martinez, Francisco (19); Moreno, Angel (19); Rodriguez, Manuel (22); Salomon, Porfirio (20); Valenzuela, Adan (4); Vallejano, Rodolfo (18).

AGUILA—Brunet, George (24); Cruz, Victor (13); Duran, David (1); Espinosa, Nestor (6); Franco, Pablo (15); Guzman, Jose (1); Limon, Jose (38); Lucero, Mike (1); Morales, Mario (13); Moreno, Jesus (5); Posadas, Calixto (2); Reynoso, Jesus (14); Sanchez, Luis (24); Valle, Urbano (15).

CAMPECHE—Duarte, Florentino (2); Gutierrez, Guillermo (20); Guzman, Luis (13); Marin, Jose (15); Valencia, Ignacio (24).

CHIHUAHUA—Alcala, Santo (15); Alvarez, Rigoberto (28); Anderson, Mike (7); Fabela, Wilfredo (25); Garcia, Francisco (1); Gaxiola, Fernando (8); Martinez, Gabriel (21); Mundo, Jesus (8); Veintidos, Juan (6); Vidana, Manuel (22).

CIUDAD JUAREZ—Dimas, Rodolfo (23); Durazo, Hector (8); Enriquez, Jorge (20); Garcia, Rafael (17); Higueras, Teodoro (19); Nieblas, Armando (13); Paul, Mike (20); Renteria, Hilario (26); Sanchez, Daniel (8).

COATZACOALCOS—Acosta, Cecilio (20); Carranza, Javier (7); Colorado, Salvador (23); Delfin, Justino (32); Henderson, Joseph (20); Lara, Gilberto (7); Miranda, Francisco (7); Rios, Rogelio (9); Rodriguez, Jose (20); Romo, Vicente (21); Uresti, Crisanto (1).

LEON—Armas, Tomas (23); Carrasco, Carlos (14); Cordova, Ernesto (24); Diaz, Hector (37); Garcia, Nicholas (25); Hernandez, Jaime (3); Lopez, Norberto (11); Montoya, Saul (28); Pineda, Ramon (25); Quinonez, Jorge (9); Urias, Filiberto (9).

MEXICO CITY REDS—Chavez, Rene (22); Cuen, Eleno (24); Division, Julio (5); Ferreira, Raul (23); Ibarra, Carlos (22); Mere, Luis (21); Ochoa, Domingo (25); Orea, Diacono (13); Orozco, Juan (3); Ortiz, Gilberto (2); Padrez, Guillermo (2); Preciado, Ignacio (9).

MEXICO CITY TIGERS—Castillejos, Jose (31); Chevez, Antonio (5); Contreras, Patricio (4); Cota, Francisco (1); Escalante, Sergio (2); Farias, Eloy (1); Garcia, David (5); Hughes, James (17); Lopez, Hector (25); Raygoza, German (1); Raygoza, Guillermo (1); Sanudo, Asuncion (1); Sauceda, Ramiro (26); Terlecky, Gregory (17); Thomas, Stan (18); Villanueva, Luis (24).

MONCLOVA—Alvarado, Francisco (1); Caballero, Guadalupe (3); Cisneros, Alfredo (1); Garcia, Rogelio (28); Martinez Alvarado, Francisco (5); Pruneda, Armando (2); Romero, Emigdio (7); Silva, Eduardo (25); Verdugo, Roberto (28).

MONTERREY—Aguilar, Rafael (23); Bernal, Andres (18); Butkus, Stanley (38); Cline, Steve (14); De La Torre, Adolfo (12); Esquer, Mercedes (23); Freisleben, Dave (1); Guerrero, Jose (3); Gutierrez, Eduardo (21); Longoria, Federico (4); Prieto, Adrian (14); Reyes, Armando (16); Tovar, Pedro (6).

NUEVO LAREDO—Burke, Steve (16); Decker, George (2); Franco, David (12); Garcia, Victor (20); Icedo, Enrique (16); Meza, Rigoberto (2); Salgado, Octavio (27); Solis, Jesus (36); Soto, Ciro (11); Valdivia, Miguel (16); Vargas, Fidel (2).

POZA RICA—Baruch, Matias (23); Bonfils, Peter (18); Fernandez, Victor (3); Franco, Francisco (14); Garcia, Alfredo (2); Garduza, Jose (21); Gonzalez, Marco (2); Hernandez, Rafael (13); Herrera, Juan (3); Lopez, Eduardo (19); Posadas, Rafael (3); Purata, Julio (3); Rodriguez, Ramon (3); Saldana, Eulogio (5); Sandate, Ricardo (10); Valenzuela, Hector (12).

PUEBLA—Escarrega, Ernesto (20); Esparza, Alfredo (4); Gutierrez, Pablo (21); Guzman, Gelasio (1); Lopez, Fernando (21); Luevano, Carlos (4); Munguia, Ramon (27); Pulido, Antonio (11); Soto, Francisco (15).

REYNOSA—Antunez, Martin (1); Arano, Ramon (21); Barbosa, Antonio (8); Barojas, Salome (29); Buentello, Israel (28); Pulido, Alfonso (26); Salinas, Guadalupe (23); Segui, Diego (21); Vazquez, Marco (3); Velazquez, Agustin (8); Vidana, Alejandro (11).

SALTILLO—Caballero, Juan (6); Camper, Cardell (17); Mauleon, Ignacio (31); Menendez, Rolando (31); Pollorena, Antonio (24); Retamoza, Rigoberto (2); Solis, Guillermo (24); Solis, Miguel (25); Soto, Alvaro (9); Torrealba, Jose (22); Urrea, Leonel (3).

TABASCO—Garcia, Jorge (30); Madrigal, Hector (26); Mariscal, Alfredo (24); Martinez, Javier (12); Ochoa, Roberto (16); Palacios, Raul (21); Perez, Cipriano (6); Ponce, Francisco (6); Rogers, Charles (26); Villegas, Roberto (12).

TOLUCA—Belman, Andres (18); Brandt, Randy (13); Hernandez, Guadalupe (10); Jiminez, Marco (1); Lugo, Manuel (33); Martinez, Raul (9); Morales, Roberto (7); Pereyra, Miguel (8); Perez, Candelario (20); Saucedo, Aristeo (15).

UNION LAGUNA—Arratia, Javier (20); Beltran, Eleazar (10); Delgado, Justino (3); Dominguez, Herminio (18); Garcia, Horacio (1); Maytorena, Francisco (28); Ontiveros, Francisco (9); Quintero, Frank (19); Torrealba, Pablo (13); Valdez, Humberto (32).

YUCATAN—Beltran, Margarito (24); Cazares, Sergio (20); Mota, Francisco (14); Nava, Victor (6); Pina, Horacio (21); Rivera, Abraham (23); Rodriguez, Pilar (25); Rondon, Gilberto (21).

TWO CLUBS—Abeytia, Manuel (6 Mexico City Tigers, 8 Chihuahua); Acosta, Eduardo (6 Chihuahua, 10 Monclova); Ahumada, Alejo (1 Saltillo, 22 Nuevo Laredo); De La Torre, Ernesto (15 Monclova, 8 Chihuahua); Hernandez, Angel (7 Poza Rica, 17 Monclova, 1 Saltillo); Huizar, Victor (8 Nuevo Laredo, 7 Monclova); Jiminez, Juan (9 Yucatan, 5 Union Laguna); Kuk Lee, Ernesto (7 Monclova, 12 Poza Rica); Lagunas, Crescencio (12 Mexico City Tigers, 8 Yucatan); Monteagudo, Aurelio (11 Monclova, 12 Toluca); Moreno, Cesar (15 Toluca, 3 Mexico City Tigers, 1 Monclova); Munoz, Adan (1 Campeche, 12 Mexico City Reds); Pena, Jose (6 Reynosa, 14 Coatzacoalcos); Pena, Manuel (4 Saltillo, 19 Chihuahua); Pena, Paulino (6 Aguascalientes, 1 Monclova); Reyes, Javier (15 Monclova, 1 Yucatan, 2 Union Laguna); Valdez, Jose (7 Aguila, 10 Tabasco); Valle, Reynaldo (1 Puebla, 19 Toluca); Williams, Gary (13 Aguascalientes, 7 Toluca).

GRAND SLAM HOME RUNS—Batista, Stenholm, 2 each; E. Aguilar, Juan Alvarez, Bernhardt, Bojorquez, Brown, Esqueda, Gaston, Llenas, B. Lopez, Lorenzo Lopez, Maddox, Obradovich, Orozco, Jose Romo, Scott, Tyrone, Uzcanga, 1 each.

AWARDED FIRST BASE ON INTERFERENCE—Biagini (Julio Benitez); F. Marquez (Guillen); P. Mendoza (L. Peralta); Ortega (Efrain Gonzalez); A. Rodriguez (L. Lara); Ruiz (L. Peralta).

GAME-WINNING RBIs

DeFreites, Ruiz, 11 each; Obradovich, 10; Aguilar, 9; J. C. Alvarez, Batista, Howard, Sommers, 9 each; L. Figueroa, Joel Perez, Tyrone, 8 each; Balaz, H. Garcia, Lora, Murrell, Pierce, Rosario, J. Sanchez, E. Vazquez, 7 each; L. Alvarado, M. Alvarez, Bernal, Carreno, R. Cervantes, Davalillo, Davila, Arsenio Diaz, F. Estrada, T. Ford, Guerra, Llenas, Monasterio, Nettles, Armando Ortiz, Jose Perez, Roberto Rodriguez, Santana, Serna, Zamudio, 6 each; Bernhardt, Briones, Camargo, Davis, De Hoyos, Elguezabal, Ramiro Guzman, Ramon Hernandez, Rodolfo Hernandez, Jimenez, A. Lazaro, J. Lopez, V. Lopez, G. Lugo, Maddox, F. Marquez, S. Mendoza, E. Munoz, J. Navarrete, Rafael Ornelas, Orozco, Osuna, Rios, E. Rivera, F. Rodriguez, C. L. Rodriguez, O. Rojas, Silverio, Villagomez, 5 each; Barrera, Bobadilla, Antonio Castro, Cerda, E. Cervantes, Cruz, Espino, Gamez, W. Gonzalez, R. Leon, C. Lopez, Mendez, Montoya, Mora, L. Peralta, A. Perez, C. Rivera, A. Rodriguez, Salazar, Stanton, Stenholm, N. Thompson, R. Thompson, N. Vazquez, A. Vega, R. Zuniga, 4 each; Acuna, J. Aguilar, Biagini, Bojorquez, Brown, G. Chavez, Christiansen, S. Collins, Deliza, J. Delgado, Albino Diaz, Elizondo, Esqueda, F. Felix, B. Garcia, Garzon, Gaston, H. Guzman, M. Hernandez, Juarez, Leal, A. Lizarraga, Molina, J. Munoz, R. Munoz, Naranjo, Padilla, J. Paredes, M. Ramirez, Rivero, R. Robles, Rodolfo Rodriguez, Rosas, Sauceda, C. Soto, Torres, Uzcanga, Valdez, L.

Valenzuela, L. Villalobos, C. Villela, R. Villela, Williams, 3 each; Alcaraz, N. Alvarado, Armbrister, Arvizu, Arzate, Barren, Cantres, Jose Chavez, J. Collins, J.V. Contreras, Espinosa de la Torre, M. Flores, Gamundi, G. Gomez, Jose Gonzalez, Guerrero, A. Guzman, Hairston, Heras, J. Hernandez Zamora, Jose Hernandez, P. Hernandez, Iniguez, James, Krug, M. Lazaro, B. Lopez, Lorenzo Lopez, Luna, Matina, C. Navarrete, Ortega, R. Paredes, M. Parra, Prieto, Jose Rodriguez, J. F. Rodriguez, Rosales, Saiz, L. Sanchez, Scott, Serratos, G. Soto, Tellez, V. Vega, Villaescusa, G. Villalobos, Yepez, A. Zavala, 2 each; Alanis, J. L. Benitez, Borbon, Centeno, H. Chavez, Juan Chavez, Cuevas, M. Delgado, G. Duran, Faudoa, L. Ford, J. Garcia, Efrain Gonzalez, Jesus Gonzalez, Guillen, Jorge Hernandez, Juan Hernandez, S. Hernandez, Johnson, A. Lara, F. Lara, M. Lizarraga, Leobardo Lopez, P. Lugo, Luque, Martinez, L. Mendoza, M. Mendoza, J. Ornelas, J. Ortiz, Plasencia, Preciado, O. Ramirez, Rey, Reyes, S. Robles, E. Rodriguez, M. L. Rodriguez, Jose Romo, R. Sanchez, Santos, Scanlon, Suarez, Tanaka, Terrazas, Trevino, J. Valenzuela, Valle, 1 each.

CLUB FIELDING

Club	G.	PO.	A.	E.	DP.	PB.	Pct.	Club	G.	PO.	A.	E.	DP.	PB.	Pct.
Mexico Reds	94	2508	974	64	64	6	.982	Mexico Tigers	97	2541	1124	106	91	5	.972
Aguila	95	2469	1059	75	66	3	.979	Union Laguna	98	2484	1118	118	87	19	.968
Ciudad Juarez	94	2487	1043	78	71	9	.978	Nuevo Laredo	98	2562	1098	122	102	6	.968
Saltillo	98	2505	1112	85	98	9	.977	Leon	96	2478	1085	123	88	8	.967
Campeche	89	2343	1007	88	61	10	.974	Chihuahua	91	2385	1111	122	102	8	.966
Puebla	90	2355	1104	91	100	4	.974	Monterrey	93	2475	1071	129	91	11	.965
Reynosa	98	2580	1019	99	82	7	.973	Monclova	96	2499	1116	132	102	23	.965
Coatzacoalcos	94	2433	1071	97	48	9	.973	Poza Rica	93	2412	1058	139	64	8	.961
Aguascalientes	94	2445	1055	97	98	6	.973	Tabasco	96	2526	1056	144	86	16	.961
Yucatan	97	2559	1172	106	73	11	.972	Toluca	95	2433	966	160	89	17	.955

Triple Plays—Poza Rica, Toluca, Union Laguna, 1 each.

INDIVIDUAL FIELDING

*Throws lefthanded.

FIRST BASEMEN

Player and Club	G.	PO.	A.	E.	DP.	Pct.	Player and Club	G.	PO.	A.	E.	DP.	Pct.
Sommers, Mex Reds	27	252	11	0	19	1.000	Carreno, Puebla	67	669	37	7	64	.990
Espino, Lag-Mva-Sal	20	185	14	0	16	1.000	Scott, Yucatan	36	358	21	4	21	.990
Parra, Juarez	13	106	3	0	7	1.000	Faudoa, Mex Tigers*	27	270	10	3	17	.989
Acosta, Mex Reds	11	54	5	0	2	1.000	Bernhardt, Tabasco	51	426	20	5	39	.989
A. Castro, Leon*	42	399	6	1	40	.998	Batista, Laguna	92	838	43	10	83	.989
LOPEZ, Coatzacoalcos*	70	664	27	2	28	.997	C. L. Rodriguez, Mon*	38	335	13	4	35	.989
Murrell, Leon	31	307	14	1	23	.997	Valdez, Chihuahua	88	792	33	11	85	.987
Scanlon, Campeche*	29	265	14	1	29	.996	DeFreites, Reynosa	31	265	15	4	20	.986
Rubio, Mex Reds	51	461	17	2	28	.996	Naranjo, Monclova*	78	659	32	10	63	.986
Hernandez, Poza Rica	39	364	17	2	22	.995	Delgado, Juarez*	15	118	0	2	7	.983
Lizarraga, Yucatan	23	141	5	1	5	.993	Cerda, Coatzacoalcos	18	168	8	3	4	.983
Cervantes, Aguila	89	826	43	6	56	.993	Krug, Tabasco	40	372	31	7	25	.983
Garcia, Laredo	87	824	42	6	88	.993	Robles, Yuc-Lar*	51	492	24	9	41	.983
Leon, Mex Tigers*	70	677	32	5	58	.993	Arvizu, Toluca	46	423	33	8	31	.983
Alvarez, Reynosa	55	395	22	3	32	.993	Tiburcio, Poza Rica	10	106	5	2	7	.982
Osuna, Juarez	66	571	28	5	50	.992	Centeno, Toluca	34	295	19	6	27	.981
Llenas, Reynosa	24	225	6	2	19	.991	Guerra, Laredo	11	93	2	2	8	.979
Obradovich, Ags*	94	881	39	8	81	.991	Gaston, Leon	14	126	3	3	6	.977
Baez, Puebla	12	100	7	1	12	.991	Munoz, Leon	12	111	1	3	13	.974
Williams, Campeche*	47	400	27	4	27	.991	Martinez, Monterrey	47	429	17	12	36	.974
Pierce, Sal-Ctz*	95	878	47	9	80	.990	Christiansen, Poza Rica	25	196	6	8	15	.962

Triple Plays—Christiansen, Orozco, Robles.

(Fewer Than Ten Games)

Player and Club	G.	PO.	A.	E.	DP.	Pct.	Player and Club	G.	PO.	A.	E.	DP.	Pct.
Ortiz, Monterrey	8	75	6	0	6	1.000	Gomez, Coatzacoalcos	1	4	0	0	0	1.000
Kurpiel, Mex Reds*	6	67	4	0	9	1.000	Hernandez, Juarez	1	3	0	0	0	1.000
De Hoyos, Aguila*	7	69	2	0	3	1.000	R. Chavarria, Laguna	1	2	0	0	1	1.000
Espinosa de la Torre, Tol	5	49	3	0	3	1.000	Iniguez, Monclova	1	2	0	0	0	1.000
Hernandez, Campeche	5	43	3	0	1	1.000	Delgado, Puebla	1	2	0	0	0	1.000
Saiz, Poza Rica*	6	41	5	0	2	1.000	Acosta, Mex Tigers	2	1	0	0	1	1.000
Brown, Poza Rica	5	44	1	0	2	1.000	Robles, Juarez	1	1	0	0	0	1.000
Rojas, Campeche	3	37	3	0	2	1.000	Guzman, Campeche	1	1	0	0	0	1.000
Arsenio Diaz, Monclova	4	32	1	0	2	1.000	Duran, Poza Rica*	9	97	3	1	9	.990
Lora, Yucatan*	4	26	1	0	2	1.000	Lugo, Coatzacoalcos	9	79	1	1	3	.988
Johnson, Toluca	3	27	0	0	2	1.000	Bobadilla, Juarez	9	68	4	1	7	.986
Camargo, Monterrey	3	22	1	0	1	1.000	Heras, Toluca	7	62	3	1	3	.985
Soto, Saltillo	2	18	0	0	2	1.000	Hairston, Campeche	5	49	3	1	1	.981
Castro, Mex Tigers	3	16	1	0	0	1.000	Barron, Mex Reds	4	45	3	1	0	.980
Sanchez, Poza Rica	3	17	0	0	1	1.000	Perez, Laguna	6	42	3	1	2	.978
Deliza, Laguna	2	6	3	0	0	1.000	Ortiz, Tabasco*	7	38	0	1	3	.974
Rodriguez, Campeche	2	8	0	0	1	1.000	R. Lopez, Chihuahua*	5	26	5	1	6	.969
Valencia, Campeche	2	8	0	0	1	1.000	Rosario, Coatzacoalcos	2	17	0	1	1	.944
Ibarra, Tabasco*	2	8	0	0	1	1.000	F. Felix, Tabasco	7	47	1	4	4	.923
Biagini, Monclova	1	8	0	0	1	1.000	Gonzalez, Chihuahua	1	12	0	1	2	.923
Luna, Monterrey	2	4	1	0	1	1.000	Stanton, Puebla	9	79	4	7	7	.922

FIRST BASEMEN—Continued

(Fewer Than Ten Games)

Player and Club	G.	PO.	A.	E.	DP.	Pct.	Player and Club	G.	PO.	A.	E.	DP.	Pct.
Aguilar, Puebla	3	9	2	1	2	.917	Orozco, Toluca	2	13	1	2	2	.875
Howard, Yucatan	2	11	0	1	0	.917	Garzon, Coatzacoalcos	4	8	4	2	1	.857
Peralta, Poza Rica	3	12	2	2	1	.875							

SECOND BASEMEN

Player and Club	G.	PO.	A.	E.	DP.	Pct.	Player and Club	G.	PO.	A.	E.	DP.	Pct.
Bernhardt, Tabasco	11	28	22	0	6	1.000	Maddox, Laredo	16	28	40	2	8	.971
Romo, Mex Reds	10	21	22	0	2	1.000	Lazaro, Lar-Yuc	59	130	188	10	45	.970
Ortiz, Yucatan	34	84	89	1	18	.994	Salazar, Aguascalientes	51	136	143	9	28	.969
MENDEZ, Campeche	80	261	198	3	41	.994	Elguezabal, Puebla	15	30	48	3	13	.963
Hernandez, Mex Tigers	33	85	79	2	18	.988	Avina, Monclova	52	120	108	9	29	.962
Briones, Juarez	93	274	280	7	58	.988	Esqueda, Laguna	24	55	70	5	17	.962
Deliza, Laguna	13	43	35	1	13	.987	Villela, Laguna	63	149	165	13	37	.960
Navarrete, Saltillo	96	231	267	7	63	.986	Cervantes, Laredo	14	30	39	3	8	.958
Garcia, Aguila	86	200	176	7	38	.982	Zavala, Mex Tigers	25	52	60	5	13	.957
Figueroa, Tabasco	21	48	58	2	11	.981	Borbon, Aguascalientes	41	101	99	9	22	.957
Sanchez, Poza Rica	74	204	145	7	37	.980	Uzcanga, Laredo	26	56	52	5	14	.956
Chavez, Chihuahua	76	219	216	9	62	.980	Gonzalez, Coatzacoalcos	10	21	22	2	5	.956
Alcaraz, Leon	22	66	78	3	25	.980	Robles, Toluca	94	260	251	24	75	.955
Rodriguez, Reynosa	89	213	218	9	49	.980	Alvarado, Reynosa	20	22	20	2	0	.955
Hernandez, Mex Reds	88	228	205	9	38	.980	Lugo, Ctz-Leon	19	52	52	5	10	.954
Hernandez, Puebla	68	168	218	9	53	.977	Munoz, Yucatan	44	112	115	11	30	.954
P. Mendoza, Yuc-Tig	48	107	150	6	24	.977	Sanchez, Chihuahua	11	33	28	3	10	.953
Guerrero, Coatzacoalcos	64	161	188	9	29	.975	Ortiz, Monterrey	25	70	47	6	21	.951
Lazaro, Monterrey	73	212	175	10	44	.975	Perez, Tabasco	72	175	189	19	42	.950
Serna, Monclova	59	144	152	8	41	.974	Cuevas, Poza Rica	24	59	49	6	17	.947
Chavez, Mex Tigers	18	52	54	3	11	.972	Zuniga, Leon	39	90	103	11	16	.946
Weeb, Coatzacoalcos	21	47	56	3	4	.972	Lizarraga, Leon	27	50	58	9	11	.923

Triple Plays—Cuevas, Munoz, Robles.

(Fewer Than Ten Games)

Player and Club	G.	PO.	A.	E.	DP.	Pct.	Player and Club	G.	PO.	A.	E.	DP.	Pct.
Rojas, Campeche	7	25	31	0	9	1.000	Arviru, Toluca	1	3	1	0	0	1.000
Almeuda, Reynosa	9	15	22	0	3	1.000	Figueroa, Juarez	1	1	3	0	0	1.000
Elizondo, Aguila	7	15	13	0	1	1.000	Hernandez, Campeche	1	0	3	0	0	1.000
Nunez, Puebla	5	16	10	0	4	1.000	Zamudio, Puebla	2	1	1	0	0	1.000
Montoya, Chihuahua	3	8	12	0	4	1.000	Rodriguez, Laguna	2	0	1	0	0	1.000
Quintero, Saltillo	3	6	8	0	2	1.000	Hernandez, Reynosa	2	0	1	0	0	1.000
Llenas, Reynosa	7	8	5	0	2	1.000	Garza, Mex Tigers	1	0	1	0	0	1.000
Baez, Puebla	2	6	7	0	2	1.000	Gomez, Laredo	1	0	1	0	0	1.000
Castro, Mex Tigers	4	6	6	0	2	1.000	Zavala, Tabasco	1	1	0	0	1	1.000
Carreno, Puebla	4	7	3	0	1	1.000	Iniguez, Monclova	1	1	0	0	1	1.000
Salinas, Chihuahua	1	1	7	0	1	1.000	Reyes, Aguascalientes	5	13	15	1	3	.966
Acuna, Puebla	2	5	2	0	1	1.000	Iglesias, Aguila	9	18	9	1	1	.964
Velarde, Campeche	1	0	6	0	0	1.000	Yepez, Poza Rica	6	7	11	1	0	.947
Lara, Coatzacoalcos	4	2	2	0	0	1.000	Serratos, Lar-Sal	2	6	3	1	3	.900
Delgado, Puebla	1	2	2	0	1	1.000	Bobadilla, Juarez	4	2	1	1	1	.750
Marquez, Coatzacoalcos	1	2	2	0	0	1.000	Hairston, Campeche	1	4	1	2	0	.714
Lara, Aguila	1	1	3	0	0	1.000							

THIRD BASEMEN

Player and Club	G.	PO.	A.	E.	DP.	Pct.	Player and Club	G.	PO.	A.	E.	DP.	Pct.
Acuna, Puebla	12	7	33	0	3	1.000	Vazquez, Laredo	62	58	116	13	18	.930
Delgado, Puebla	17	13	39	1	6	.981	Pedroza, Leon	67	42	140	14	9	.929
SANTANA, Aguila	95	114	243	10	12	.973	Elguezabal, Puebla	64	33	131	13	8	.927
Rodriguez, Ags.	85	77	157	7	20	.971	Maddox, Laredo	34	22	41	5	6	.926
Barrera, Mex Reds	75	78	144	7	10	.969	Zavala, Mex Tigers	19	15	45	5	2	.923
Bobadilla, Juarez	37	36	71	4	4	.964	Quintero, Saltillo	14	13	23	3	4	.923
Torres, Monterrey	86	101	209	12	17	.963	Preciado, Laguna	21	23	38	5	4	.922
Vega, Juarez	61	44	106	7	7	.955	Tyrone, Yucatan	91	71	222	25	13	.921
Rios, Campeche	55	67	125	9	10	.955	V. Lopez, Chihuahua	84	72	188	23	21	.919
Diaz, Monclova	35	41	84	6	9	.954	Bojorquez, Monclova	39	47	77	11	8	.919
Garzon, Coatzacoalcos	41	27	76	5	4	.954	Velarde, Campeche	20	14	41	5	5	.917
Rivera, Mex Tigers	78	80	178	14	15	.949	Lizarraga, Leon	14	12	20	3	1	.914
Guerrero, Coatzacoalcos	24	20	52	4	1	.947	Ramirez, Tabasco	92	92	202	28	16	.913
Cerda, Coatzacoalcos	31	23	66	5	2	.947	Sommers, Tol-Mex Reds	65	58	138	21	9	.903
Rojas, Campeche	10	15	33	3	3	.941	Llenas, Reynosa	14	6	12	2	0	.900
Montoya, Chi-Sal	81	53	184	15	21	.940	Mares, Poza Rica	88	64	219	33	13	.896
Deliza, Laguna	77	72	190	17	12	.939	Alonso, Toluca	23	14	35	6	3	.891
Zuniga, Leon	21	17	43	4	1	.938	Hernandez, Campeche	1	5	17	3	1	.880
Sanchez, Poza Rica	12	15	29	3	3	.936	Hernandez, Reynosa	83	58	113	24	11	.877
Sanudo, Sal-Mva	34	35	77	8	5	.933	Espinosa de la Torre, Tol	24	14	34	7	4	.873

THIRD BASEMEN—Continued
(Fewer Than Ten Games)

Player and Club	G.	PO.	A.	E.	DP.	Pct.	Player and Club	G.	PO.	A.	E.	DP.	Pct.
Ortiz, Monterrey	6	10	8	0	3	1.000	Arvizu, Toluca	4	3	11	1	0	.933
Gonzalez, Puebla	8	3	11	0	1	1.000	Zavala, Tabasco	8	8	15	2	2	.920
Barajas, Aguascalientes	1	1	4	0	1	1.000	Iniguez, Mva-Tol	5	4	9	2	0	.867
Hernandez, Puebla	1	2	2	0	1	1.000	Lugo, Coatzacoalcos	3	2	4	1	0	.857
Guzman, Reynosa	1	2	2	0	0	1.000	Valdez, Chihuahua	1	3	3	1	1	.857
J. V. Contreras, Laguna	2	1	2	0	1	1.000	Salazar, Aguascalientes	8	6	11	3	1	.850
Montiel, Sal-Lar	4	0	2	0	0	1.000	Ortiz, Yucatan	8	4	12	3	1	.842
Lazaro, Laredo	1	1	1	0	0	1.000	Sanchez, Chihuahua	4	1	3	1	0	.800
Pacho, Yucatan	2	1	1	0	0	1.000	Guerra, Laredo	5	1	3	2	0	.667
Lazaro, Monterrey	1	0	2	0	0	1.000	Cano, Saltillo	1	0	2	1	0	.667
Almeida, Reynosa	1	1	1	0	0	1.000	Bernhardt, Tabasco	1	1	1	1	1	.667
Romo, Mex Reds	1	0	1	0	0	1.000	De Los Santos, Toluca	1	1	0	1	0	.500
Murrell, Leon	5	7	9	1	2	.941	Figueroa, Tabasco	1	0	0	1	0	.000

Triple Plays—Mares, Ortiz.

SHORTSTOPS

Player and Club	G.	PO.	A.	E.	DP.	Pct.	Player and Club	G.	PO.	A.	E.	DP.	Pct.
Romo, Mex Reds	12	9	17	0	4	1.000	Villaescusa, Toluca	37	61	121	11	15	.943
S. MENDOZA, Yucatan	91	156	333	10	48	.980	Leal, Mex Tigers	71	117	263	23	42	.943
Barrera, Mex Reds	16	27	61	2	5	.978	Gonzalez, Coatzacoalcos	60	82	172	16	12	.941
Rivero, Reynosa	95	152	299	14	51	.970	Rivera, Mex Tigers	16	26	53	5	10	.940
Serna, Monclova	47	79	230	11	20	.966	Velarde, Campeche	15	14	48	4	6	.939
Elizondo, Aguila	86	136	278	15	40	.965	Esqueda, Laguna	18	26	51	5	6	.939
Chavez, Saltillo	78	118	287	15	46	.964	Perez, Tabasco	38	50	70	8	12	.938
Villalobos, Chihuahua	91	197	330	21	72	.962	Bobadilla, Juarez	10	4	11	1	1	.938
M. L. Rodriguez, Mon	66	115	235	15	36	.959	Cervantes, Laredo	69	142	236	26	56	.936
Alanis, Aguila-Tabasco	53	99	145	11	21	.957	Hernandez, Laguna	79	115	257	27	42	.932
Alvarado, Leon	93	165	333	23	59	.956	Vega, Monclova-Laguna	55	89	165	20	38	.927
Espinosa de la Torre, Tol	59	90	189	13	25	.955	Quintero, Saltillo	19	34	54	7	8	.926
Valle, Juarez	92	132	305	21	45	.954	Figueroa, Tabasco	11	16	21	3	1	.925
Esparza, Poza Rica-Cam	56	65	182	12	23	.954	Uzcanga, Laredo	37	46	112	13	15	.924
Jimenez, Puebla	73	139	263	20	50	.953	Yepez, Poza Rica	56	84	154	20	16	.922
Aguilar, Aguascalientes	92	167	348	26	57	.952	P. Mendoza, Yuc-Tig	12	18	48	6	9	.917
Tanaka, Monclova	15	18	41	3	5	.952	Flores, Monterrey	39	55	96	14	21	.915
Gamez, Mex Reds	72	115	244	19	31	.950	Zavala, Tabasco	21	24	71	12	12	.888
Lopez, Poza Rica	32	40	103	8	11	.947	Rios, Campeche	13	21	37	9	3	.866
Hernandez, Puebla	14	19	49	4	7	.944	Quinonez, Juarez	11	5	9	3	0	.824
Lara, Coatzacoalcos	54	66	135	12	17	.944							

Triple Play—Villaescusa.

(Fewer Than Ten Games)

Player and Club	G.	PO.	A.	E.	DP.	Pct.	Player and Club	G.	PO.	A.	E.	DP.	Pct.
Sanchez, Poza Rica	7	11	26	0	3	1.000	Ortiz, Monterrey	1	2	1	0	1	1.000
Lizarraga, Leon	5	8	12	0	2	1.000	Iglesias, Aguascalientes	1	0	1	0	0	1.000
Delgado, Puebla	3	4	10	0	2	1.000	Hernandez, Campeche	9	19	29	1	5	.980
R. Chavarria, Laguna	4	6	6	0	1	1.000	Rodriguez, Reynosa	5	8	14	1	2	.957
Zavala, Mex Tigers	2	4	8	0	1	1.000	Guerra, Laredo	5	6	11	1	1	.944
Hernandez, Reynosa	3	2	9	0	1	1.000	Ramirez, Tabasco	5	5	10	1	2	.938
Montoya, Saltillo	2	6	5	0	1	1.000	Guerrero, Coatzacoalcos	6	9	17	2	1	.929
Lazaro, Monterrey	9	5	7	0	2	1.000	F. Rivera, Mex Tigers	2	3	9	1	1	.923
Rodriguez, Ags	2	2	7	0	1	1.000	Herrera, Campeche	5	7	15	2	1	.917
Hernandez, Mex Tigers	2	1	3	0	0	1.000	Lazaro, Yucatan	1	5	3	1	0	.889
Mendez, Campeche	1	1	3	0	1	1.000	De La Fuente, Tabasco	7	9	13	7	2	.759

OUTFIELDERS

Player and Club	G.	PO.	A.	E.	DP.	Pct.	Player and Club	G.	PO.	A.	E.	DP.	Pct.
Ford, Tabasco*	21	59	1	0	0	1.000	Hairston, Campeche	56	140	8	2	0	.987
Cruz, Coatzacoalcos	40	52	1	0	0	1.000	Gamundi, Poza Rica	85	209	12	3	1	.987
Armbrister, Laredo	22	44	3	0	2	1.000	Howard, Yucatan*	90	216	4	3	0	.987
Zavala, Mex. Tigers	14	25	1	0	0	1.000	Ornelas, Tabasco	37	67	5	1	0	.986
B. LOPEZ, Reds-Toluca	76	143	7	1	1	.993	Santos, Laredo*	77	199	10	3	0	.986
Nettles, Puebla*	84	132	13	1	1	.993	Davila, Juarez	69	126	7	2	2	.985
Murrell, Leon	61	135	4	1	1	.993	James, Campeche	67	126	7	2	2	.985
Silverio, Tig-Sal-Lag*	83	215	11	2	3	.991	Davis, Aguila*	60	129	2	2	0	.985
Suarez, Rey-Tigers*	64	109	2	1	1	.991	V. Felix, Campeche-Aguila	79	176	12	3	4	.984
Lizarraga, Mex. Reds	83	197	5	2	1	.990	Thompson, Poza Rica*	26	59	3	1	1	.984
Roman, Mex. Reds*	50	94	3	1	0	.990	Zamudio, Puebla	84	214	15	4	3	.983
Ortega, Mex. Reds	53	86	4	1	0	.989	Hernandez, Campeche	29	52	3	1	1	.982
R. Rodriguez, Saltillo*	81	156	12	2	2	.988	Albino Diaz, Monc-Lar	87	209	10	4	2	.982
J. V. Contreras, Laguna	47	82	2	1	0	.988	Alvarado, Reynosa	88	199	9	4	4	.981
Balaz, Juarez	89	156	11	2	4	.988	Thompson, Leon	75	145	6	3	1	.981
Bernhardt, Tabasco	40	78	2	1	1	.988	Rodriguez, Laguna	88	134	8	3	1	.979
Rubio, Tabasco	41	72	5	1	0	.987	Sauceda, Chihuahua	85	221	9	5	1	.979
Collins, Chihuahua*	91	142	9	2	1	.987	Villagomez, Aguila	66	130	8	3	3	.979

OUTFIELDERS—Continued

Player and Club	G.	PO.	A.	E.	DP.	Pct.	Player and Club	G.	PO.	A.	E.	DP.	Pct.
Rosales, Juarez	46	90	2	2	0	.979	F. Felix, Tabasco	80	185	4	7	1	.964
Romo, Coatzacoalcos	64	86	4	2	0	.978	Zavala, Tabasco	21	50	4	2	2	.964
Serratos, Laredo-Saltillo	39	44	1	1	0	.978	Villela, Chihuahua	91	173	15	7	2	.964
Soto, Yucatan	78	126	8	3	0	.978	Ornelas, Yucatan	90	125	8	5	0	.964
Lora, Puebla*	77	212	8	5	2	.978	Brown, Poza Rica	84	150	7	6	0	.963
Barron, Mex. Reds	21	39	2	1	1	.976	Morales, Reynosa	24	25	1	1	0	.963
Arzate, Chi-Campeche	36	78	3	2	0	.976	Flores, Leon*	14	25	1	1	0	.963
Gonzalez, Aguascalientes	61	115	6	3	3	.976	Stenholm, Mex. Reds*	66	121	7	5	5	.962
Lara, Mex. Tigers	89	153	8	4	0	.976	Rosario, Coatzacoalcos	75	116	10	5	1	.962
Jose Rodriguez, M. Tig	52	115	5	3	1	.976	Juarez, Saltillo	33	66	6	3	0	.960
Vazquez, Yucatan	47	76	4	2	1	.976	A. Castro, Leon*	51	87	6	4	0	.959
Ornelas, Monclova	83	138	19	4	4	.975	Guzman, Reynosa	23	19	4	1	2	.958
Delgado, Saltillo	16	38	1	1	1	.975	Biagini, Monclova	86	171	12	8	2	.958
Tellez, Monterrey	78	143	9	4	2	.975	Guerra, Laredo	54	105	5	5	2	.957
Valenzuela, Monterrey*	67	177	10	5	3	.974	Chavez, Aguascalientes	17	19	3	1	0	.957
Prieto, Aguila	49	71	3	2	2	.974	Zuniga, Laredo	23	39	3	2	0	.955
H. Guzman, Campeche	77	175	8	5	2	.973	Delgado, Juarez*	23	38	3	2	0	.953
M. Chavarria, Laguna	90	206	9	6	2	.973	Guzman, Mex. Tigers*	80	135	6	7	0	.953
DeFreites, Reynosa	58	100	7	3	0	.973	Sanchez, Leon*	87	201	13	11	1	.951
Paredes, Laredo	86	133	5	4	2	.972	Arvizu, Toluca	14	17	2	1	0	.950
Munoz, Laguna-Reynosa	78	164	8	5	3	.972	Duran, Poza Rica*	10	18	1	1	0	.950
Villalobos, Aguas	92	196	10	6	4	.972	Lopez, Tigers-Reynosa	58	107	5	6	0	.949
Davalillo, Aguas*	44	66	2	2	0	.971	Cantres, Monterrey	39	53	3	3	1	.949
Delgado, Puebla	26	30	4	1	0	.971	Monasterio, Toluca	90	228	11	15	3	.941
Saiz, Poza Rica*	61	124	11	4	2	.971	A. Rodriguez, Monterrey	45	76	2	5	0	.940
De Hoyos, Aguila*	46	66	1	2	0	.971	Gomez, Coatzacoalcos	38	59	3	4	0	.939
Figueroa, Juarez	77	118	7	4	0	.969	L. Lopez, Toluca	18	29	1	2	0	.938
Mora, Saltillo	29	61	1	2	0	.969	Sotelo, Monclova	11	13	0	1	0	.929
Padilla, Monclova	29	58	1	2	0	.967	C. L. Rodriguez, Mont*	53	119	8	10	0	.927
Perez, Laredo-Laguna	75	132	11	5	2	.966	Lara, Lar-Sal-Tol	51	84	7	8	2	.919
Diaz, Monclova	49	107	6	4	3	.966	Paredes, Puebla-Toluca	28	38	1	4	0	.907
Collins, Coatzacoalcos	71	132	7	5	0	.965	Plasencia, Aguila	19	25	2	4	0	.871
Perez, Aguascalientes	79	158	7	6	2	.965	J. Perez, Toluca	29	46	3	8	0	.860
Baldwin, Tabasco*	19	50	5	2	3	.965	Villaflor, Poza Rica	12	11	0	3	0	.786

(Fewer Than Ten Games)

Player and Club	G.	PO.	A.	E.	DP.	Pct.	Player and Club	G.	PO.	A.	E.	DP.	Pct.
Olivares, Tabasco	5	14	1	0	0	1.000	De Los Santos, Toluca	3	2	0	0	0	1.000
Lopez, Saltillo*	8	13	1	0	0	1.000	Leon, Mex. Tigers*	1	2	0	0	0	1.000
Centeno, Toluca	5	13	1	0	0	1.000	Naranjo, Monclova*	2	1	1	0	0	1.000
Quintero, Saltillo	6	12	0	0	0	1.000	Hernandez, Laguna	2	2	0	0	0	1.000
Diaz, Poza Rica*	6	11	0	0	0	1.000	Castillo, Campeche	1	2	0	0	0	1.000
Alou, Coatzacoalcos	4	10	1	0	0	1.000	Faudoa, Mex. Tigers*	4	1	0	0	0	1.000
Esp. de la Torre, Tol	6	8	1	0	0	1.000	Navarrete, Coatzacoalcos	2	1	0	0	0	1.000
Cardona, Monclova	4	9	0	0	0	1.000	Bellacetin, Leon	2	1	0	0	0	1.000
Garcia, Campeche	7	6	2	0	0	1.000	Preciado, Laguna	2	1	0	0	0	1.000
C. Perez, Toluca	5	8	0	0	0	1.000	Ortiz, Tabasco*	1	1	0	0	0	1.000
Krug, Tabasco	3	7	1	0	1	1.000	Chavez, Puebla	1	1	0	0	0	1.000
Rodriguez, Toluca	5	7	0	0	0	1.000	Bojorquez, Monclova	5	13	1	1	0	.933
Ford, Mex. Reds	3	6	1	0	0	1.000	Alonso, Toluca	7	12	0	1	0	.923
Enriquez, Chi-Monc	5	5	1	0	0	1.000	Heras, Toluca	7	14	2	3	0	.842
Hernandez, Yucatan	6	5	0	0	0	1.000	Enriquez, Toluca	7	7	1	2	0	.800
Carreno, Puebla	3	5	0	0	0	1.000	Espinosa Ramos, Ca-Ch	8	3	0	1	0	.750
C. Felix, Tabasco*	3	5	0	0	0	1.000	Chavez, Laguna	5	2	1	1	1	.750
J. C. Contreras, Laguna	2	4	0	0	0	1.000	Guillermo, Campeche	6	2	0	1	0	.667
Rojas, Campeche	2	4	0	0	0	1.000	R. Lopez, Chihuahua*	3	2	0	1	0	.667
Valencia, Campeche	2	3	0	0	0	1.000	Llenas, Reynosa	1	2	0	1	0	.667
Gonzalez, Laguna	1	3	0	0	0	1.000	Herrera, Tabasco	1	2	0	1	0	.667
Bobadilla, Juarez	4	2	0	0	0	1.000	Cosagaya, Tabasco	2	1	0	1	0	.500

CATCHERS

Player and Club	G.	PO.	A.	E.	DP.	PB.	Pct.	Player and Club	G.	PO.	A.	E.	DP.	PB.	Pct.
Mojica, Leon	31	107	14	0	2	2	1.000	Navarrete, Coatz	34	147	10	2	0	4	.987
Lizarraga, Yucatan	11	29	6	0	0	1	1.000	Marquez, Yucatan	93	442	59	7	0	10	.986
Monarrez, Aguas	10	26	2	0	1	0	1.000	Mendoza, Juarez	85	482	52	8	2	5	.985
Molina, Aguila	42	224	21	1	3	3	.996	Ruiz, Campeche	75	347	41	6	4	8	.985
ROSAS, Reynosa	51	246	37	2	4	3	.993	E. Rodriguez, Saltillo	12	51	10	1	2	2	.984
Peralta, Mex. Tigers	31	119	13	1	2	1	.992	Valenzuela, Monc-Chi	83	339	57	7	5	12	.983
Peralta, Poza Rica	73	336	45	3	5	7	.992	Valenzuela, Tabasco	63	217	52	5	7	7	.982
Barron, Mex. Reds	40	223	22	2	3	1	.992	Orozco, Toluca	88	431	51	9	5	16	.982
Trevino, Saltillo-Lar	85	397	52	4	6	3	.991	Gonzalez, Laguna	34	137	21	3	1	8	.981
Guillen, Tabasco	50	193	20	2	1	9	.991	Sanchez, Laguna	70	299	65	7	8	11	.981
Robles, Mex. Reds	60	286	33	3	1	5	.991	Terrazas, Mex. Tigers	74	367	44	8	10	4	.981
Rey, Aguila	58	267	44	3	2	0	.990	Estrada, Puebla	82	355	50	8	4	4	.981
Hernandez, Coatz	73	385	50	5	1	5	.989	Soto, Laredo-Saltillo	79	359	43	8	9	5	.980

CATCHERS—Continued

Player and Club	G.	PO.	A.	E.	DP.	PB.	Pct.
Hernandez, Juarez	19	82	14	2	0	4	.980
Rivera, Chi-Monclova	56	258	43	7	3	3	.977
Guzman, Reynosa	58	323	35	9	3	4	.975
Chavez, Puebla	14	32	6	1	2	0	.974
Camargo, Monterrey	57	280	52	9	6	6	.974
Benitez, Leon	74	307	38	10	4	6	.972
Luna, Monterrey	38	166	28	6	5	5	.970
Beltran, Monc-Saltillo	39	102	19	4	5	11	.968
Lugo, Poza Rica	10	19	2	1	0	0	.955
Duran, Chihuahua	48	199	24	11	4	4	.953
Oviedo, Saltillo	20	71	10	4	0	3	.953
Heras, Toluca	14	59	1	4	1	1	.938
Hernandez, Cam	16	50	8	4	1	2	.935
Christiansen, PR	20	77	9	8	0	1	.915
Benitez, Laredo	13	28	3	3	1	2	.912

(Fewer Than Ten Games)

Player and Club	G.	PO.	A.	E.	DP.	PB.	Pct.
Jackson, Laredo	2	9	2	0	0	0	1.000
Guerra, Laredo	4	10	0	0	0	0	1.000
Quintero, Campeche	3	7	2	0	2	0	1.000
Luque, Saltillo	3	7	1	0	0	0	1.000
Alvarez, Monclova	2	6	2	0	0	1	1.000
Camacho, Aguas	3	6	1	0	0	0	1.000
Guzman, Reynosa	1	3	0	0	0	0	1.000
Gutierrez, Laredo	2	1	0	0	0	0	1.000
Ortega, Aguila	2	1	0	0	0	0	1.000
Arsenio Diaz, Monc	1	0	1	0	0	0	1.000
Yepez, Poza Rica	1	1	0	0	0	0	1.000
Lara, Aguascalientes	2	9	1	1	0	0	.909

PITCHERS

Player and Club	G.	PO.	A.	E.	DP.	Pct.
ESCARREGA, Puebla	20	7	38	0	1	1.000
Salomon, Aguascalientes	20	6	30	0	1	1.000
Garcia, Laredo	20	6	28	0	0	1.000
Villanueva, Mex Tigers*	24	5	24	0	5	1.000
Colorado, Coatzacoalcos	23	7	22	0	0	1.000
Williams, Ags-Tol*	20	4	24	0	1	1.000
Valdez, Agu-Tab	17	4	22	0	1	1.000
Garcia, Juarez	17	4	21	0	2	1.000
Chavez, Leon	19	1	23	0	4	1.000
Renteria, Juarez	26	2	21	0	0	1.000
Rogers, Tabasco	26	5	17	0	1	1.000
Higueras, Juarez*	19	1	17	0	1	1.000
Gutierrez, Juarez	14	4	14	0	1	1.000
Maytorena, Laguna	28	4	13	0	2	1.000
Hernandez, PR-Mva-Sal	25	4	13	0	1	1.000
Diaz, Puebla	18	3	14	0	3	1.000
Guzman, Campeche	13	2	15	0	1	1.000
Salgado, Laredo	27	3	13	0	0	1.000
Quintero, Laguna	19	8	8	0	3	1.000
Orea, Mex Reds	13	3	13	0	1	1.000
Ibarra, Mex Reds	22	5	10	0	1	1.000
Camper, Saltillo	17	5	10	0	0	1.000
Abeytia, Tig-Chi	14	4	11	0	1	1.000
Baltran, Laguna	10	5	10	0	2	1.000
Mauleon, Saltillo	31	0	14	0	1	1.000
Solis, Saltillo	24	3	11	0	0	1.000
Chavez, Laguna	18	2	12	0	0	1.000
Mota, Yucatan	14	2	12	0	0	1.000
Solis, Laredo	36	2	11	0	0	1.000
Valdez, Laguna	32	3	10	0	0	1.000
Alvarez, Chihuahua	28	0	13	0	0	1.000
Vidana, Chihuahua	22	1	12	0	2	1.000
Valenzuela, Poza Rica	12	3	10	0	0	1.000
Franco, Poza Rica	14	5	7	0	0	1.000
Ochoa, Mex Reds	25	2	9	0	1	1.000
Cervantes, Ags	17	1	10	0	3	1.000
Martinez, Ags*	17	0	11	0	0	1.000
Lugo, Toluca	33	3	7	0	0	1.000
Torrealba, Saltillo*	22	2	8	0	1	1.000
Marin, Campeche	15	1	9	0	0	1.000
Hernandez, Poza Rica	13	1	9	0	1	1.000
Dimas, Juarez	23	2	7	0	4	1.000
Pena, Sal-Chi*	23	1	8	0	0	1.000
Rodriguez, Campeche	17	0	9	0	1	1.000
Martinez, Tabasco	12	4	5	0	0	1.000
Sauceda, Mex Tigers	26	2	6	0	1	1.000
Munoz, Cam-Mex Reds	13	2	6	0	0	1.000
Castillejos, Mex Tigers	31	1	6	0	0	1.000
R. Guzman, Campeche	24	2	5	0	0	1.000
Fereira, Mex Reds	23	1	6	0	0	1.000
Rodriguez, Ags	22	1	6	0	2	1.000
Lopez, Mex Tigers	25	2	4	0	0	1.000
Valle, Pue-Tol*	20	1	5	0	1	1.000
Rodriguez, Ctz*	20	0	6	0	1	1.000
Prieto, Monterrey	14	1	5	0	0	1.000
Villegas, Tabasco	12	2	4	0	0	1.000
Vidana, Reynosa	11	0	6	0	0	1.000
Palacios, Tabasco	21	2	3	0	0	1.000
Lopez, Leon	11	2	3	0	0	1.000
Nieblas, Juarez	13	2	2	0	0	1.000
Pulido, Puebla	11	0	4	0	0	1.000
Hernandez, Toluca	10	1	2	0	0	1.000
Enriquez, Juarez	20	0	2	0	0	1.000
Zetina, Toluca*	17	1	1	0	0	1.000
Franco, Laredo	12	0	2	0	0	1.000
Belman, Toluca	18	0	1	0	0	1.000
Gutierrez, Puebla	23	8	41	1	4	.980
Rivera, Yucatan	23	9	36	1	2	.978
Ahumada, Sal-Lar	23	11	31	1	6	.977
Romo, Coatzacoalcos	21	7	32	1	1	.975
M. Solis, Saltillo	25	12	26	1	1	.974
Pollorena, Saltillo	24	8	27	1	1	.972
Valencia, Campeche	24	11	22	1	3	.971
Monteagudo, Mva-Tol	23	4	28	1	2	.970
Rondon, Yucatan	21	6	25	1	1	.969
Leon, Campeche	19	4	27	1	4	.969
Arano, Reynosa	21	7	23	1	1	.968
Lagunas, Tig-Yucatan	20	5	23	1	1	.966
Thomas, Mex Tigers	18	11	16	1	2	.964
Cline, Monterrey	14	4	23	1	0	.964
Menendez, Saltillo	31	5	21	1	1	.963
Garduza, Reynosa	21	2	23	1	1	.962
Ortiz, Tabasco*	19	1	24	1	1	.962
Hughes, Mex Tigers	17	17	31	2	3	.960
Pena, Rey-Ctz	20	5	19	1	1	.960
Acosta, Ctz	20	2	22	1	1	.960
Verdugo, Monclova	28	4	19	1	1	.958
Mere, Mex Reds	21	5	18	1	0	.958
Arratia, Laguna	20	3	20	1	0	.958
Segui, Reynosa	21	3	19	1	0	.957
Ochoa, Tabasco	16	6	16	1	0	.957
Diaz, Leon	37	4	17	1	1	.955
Franco, Aguascalientes	15	5	16	1	0	.955
Salinas, Reynosa	23	2	39	2	2	.953
Sanchez, Aguila	24	14	46	3	4	.952
Acosta, Chi-Mva	16	4	16	1	0	.952
Sosa, Laguna	22	2	17	1	1	.950
Estrada, Mva*	21	2	17	1	1	.950
Reynosa, Aguila	14	3	16	1	1	.950
Moreno, Aguascalientes*	19	10	27	2	3	.949
Saucedo, Chihuahua	21	5	30	2	1	.946
Cordova, Leon	24	4	13	1	0	.944
Martin, Juarez*	16	4	13	1	0	.944
Aguilar, Monterrey	23	3	13	1	2	.941
Butkus, Monterrey	38	3	12	1	2	.938
Buentello, Reynosa	28	4	11	1	2	.938
Silva, Monclova	25	11	33	3	4	.936
Cuen, Mex Reds	24	4	25	2	1	.935

PITCHERS—Continued

Player and Club	G.	PO.	A.	E.	DP.	Pct.
Gutierrez, Campeche*	20	2	27	2	2	.935
Barojas, Reynosa	29	5	38	3	2	.935
Henderson, Ctz	20	3	25	2	0	.933
Johnson, Toluca	22	8	19	2	0	.931
Abarca, Aguascalientes	18	6	21	2	2	.931
Garcia, Leon	25	2	24	2	2	.929
Burke, Laredo	16	0	26	2	2	.929
Garcia, Monclova	28	3	10	1	1	.929
Reyes, Monterrey*	16	2	11	1	1	.929
Soto, Laredo*	11	4	9	1	0	.929
Vallejano, Ags	18	3	22	2	1	.926
Martinez, Chihuahua	21	4	33	3	7	.925
Pina, Yucatan	21	9	27	3	4	.923
Armas, Leon*	23	1	23	2	1	.923
Alcala, Chihuahua	15	2	22	2	2	.923
Rodriguez, Yucatan	25	0	12	1	1	.923
Huizar, Lar-Mva*	15	1	11	1	2	.923
Kuk Lee, Mva-PR	19	8	38	4	1	.920
Esquer, Monterrey*	23	5	29	3	2	.919
Brunet, Aguascalientes*	24	2	42	4	2	.917
Fabela, Chihuahua	25	2	9	1	0	.917
Baruch, Poza Rica	23	1	10	1	0	.917
Perez, Toluca	20	2	9	1	1	.917
Soto, Puebla	15	3	8	1	0	.917
Jimenez, 9 Yuc-5 Lag	14	3	18	2	3	.913
Gutierrez, Monterrey	21	4	26	3	3	.909
Pulido, Reynosa*	26	3	17	2	1	.909
Manguia, Puebla	27	2	8	1	1	.909
Morales, Aguascalientes	13	1	9	1	0	.909
Paul, Juarez*	20	7	21	3	0	.903
Bernal, Monterrey	18	6	12	2	0	.900
Terlecky, Mex Tigers	17	3	15	2	3	.900
Carrasco, Leon	14	4	14	2	3	.900
Cazares, Yucatan*	20	1	8	1	0	.900
Chavez, Mex Reds	22	10	25	4	3	.897
Limon, Aguascalientes	38	3	14	2	0	.895
Lopez, Puebla	21	3	13	2	1	.889
Dominguez, Laguna	18	1	14	2	0	.882
Torrealba, Laguna*	13	4	11	2	2	.882
Sandate, Poza Rica*	10	2	20	3	2	.880
Madrigal, Tabasco	26	7	14	3	0	.875
Lopez, Poza Rica	19	6	15	3	1	.875
Cruz, Aguascalientes	13	4	10	2	0	.875
Delfin, Coatzacoalcos	32	1	6	1	0	.875
Ochoa, Campeche	26	3	11	2	0	.867
Valdivia, Laredo*	16	2	11	2	0	.867
Bonfils, Poza Rica*	18	9	35	7	2	.863
Moreno, Tol-Tig-Mva	19	5	7	2	0	.857
Montoya, Leon*	28	0	6	1	1	.857
Mariscal, Tabasco	24	1	5	1	0	.857
Icedo, Laredo*	16	0	5	1	1	.833
De La Torre, Mva-Chi	23	2	12	3	0	.824
Beltran, Yucatan	24	3	11	3	2	.824
Garcia, Tabasco	30	2	6	2	0	.800
Valle, Aguascalientes*	15	1	3	1	1	.800
Pineda, Leon	25	2	5	2	1	.778
Brandt, Toluca	13	0	3	1	1	.750
De La Torre, Monterrey	12	1	4	2	0	.714

(Fewer Than Ten Games)

Player and Club	G.	PO.	A.	E.	DP.	Pct.
Lara, Coatzacoalcos*	7	2	8	0	1	1.000
Purata, Poza Rica*	3	1	8	0	0	1.000
Moreno, Aguascalientes	5	2	6	0	0	1.000
Mundo, Chihuahua	8	0	7	0	1	1.000
Quinonez, Leon	9	2	4	0	1	1.000
Kekich, Juarez	3	1	5	0	0	1.000
Preciado, Mex Reds	9	2	3	0	1	1.000
Barbosa, Reynosa*	8	2	3	0	0	1.000
Durazo, Laredo	8	2	3	0	1	1.000
Rios, Coatzacoalcos	9	1	3	0	0	1.000
Ontiveros, Laguna	9	3	1	0	0	1.000
Sanchez, Juarez	8	1	3	0	0	1.000
Miranda, Coatzacoalcos	7	0	4	0	0	1.000
Tovar, Monterrey	6	0	4	0	0	1.000
Martinez, Mva*	5	2	2	0	0	1.000
Soto, Saltillo	9	2	1	0	0	1.000
Carranza, Coatz*	7	1	2	0	1	1.000
Morales, Toluca	7	0	3	0	0	1.000
Granillo, Aguascalientes	4	1	2	0	0	1.000
Raygoza, Mex Tigers	1	1	2	0	0	1.000
Velazquez, Reynosa	8	1	1	0	0	1.000
Pereyra, Toluca	8	0	2	0	0	1.000
Ponce, Tabasco	6	0	2	0	1	1.000
Contreras, Mex Tigers	4	1	1	0	0	1.000
Esparza, Puebla	4	0	2	0	0	1.000
Caballero, Monclova	3	1	1	0	0	1.000
Orozco, Mex Reds	3	0	2	0	0	1.000
Rodriguez, Poza Rica	3	0	2	0	0	1.000
Escalante, Mex Tigers	2	1	1	0	1	1.000
Reyes, Mva-Yuc-Lag*	8	0	1	0	0	1.000
Castillo, Campeche	7	1	0	0	0	1.000
Agundez, Aguascalientes	6	0	1	0	0	1.000
Perez, Tabasco	6	0	1	0	0	1.000
Divison, Mex Reds	5	0	1	0	0	1.000
Garcia, Mex Tigers	5	0	1	0	0	1.000
Saldana, Poza Rica	5	1	0	0	0	1.000
Longoria, Monterrey	4	0	1	0	0	1.000
Fernandez, Poza Rica	3	0	1	0	0	1.000
Posadas, Poza Rica	3	0	1	0	0	1.000
Garcia, Poza Rica	2	0	1	0	0	1.000
Duarte, Campeche	2	0	1	0	0	1.000
Garcia, Laguna	1	0	1	0	0	1.000
Garcia, Chihuahua	1	0	1	0	0	1.000
Freisleben, Monterrey	1	0	1	0	0	1.000
Guzman, Puebla	1	0	1	0	0	1.000
Duran, Aguascalientes	1	0	1	0	0	1.000
Lucero, Aguascalientes	1	0	1	0	0	1.000
Beltran, Monclova	8	0	8	1	2	.889
Urias, Leon*	9	1	4	1	0	.833
Veintidos, Chihuahua	6	3	6	2	1	.818
Anderson, Chihuahua	7	2	6	2	0	.800
Gaxiola, Chihuahua	8	0	3	1	0	.750
Myers, Aguascalientes	5	0	3	1	0	.750
Espinosa, Aguila	6	1	1	1	0	.667
Romero, Monclova	7	0	3	2	0	.600
Caballero, Saltillo	6	0	1	1	0	.500
Decker, Laredo	2	0	0	1	0	.000

CLUB PITCHING

Club	G.	CG.	ShO.	Sv.	IP.	H.	R.	ER.	HR.	BB.	Int. BB.	HB.	SO.	WP.	Bk.	ERA.
Puebla	90	47	16	10	785	732	229	197	22	204	10	19	328	16	0	2.26
Yucatan	97	42	19	8	853	739	297	232	28	212	17	34	430	24	4	2.45
Coatzacoalcos	94	43	15	14	811	763	337	244	28	246	18	35	491	25	1	2.71
Aguila	95	44	23	8	823	788	318	269	39	220	30	28	440	27	3	2.94
Campeche	89	27	8	16	781	762	318	260	28	256	29	17	343	31	3	3.00
Tabasco	96	34	10	12	842	858	368	298	32	244	23	26	353	21	0	3.19
Ciudad Juarez	94	36	11	8	829	818	339	296	38	318	20	35	515	32	3	3.21
Reynosa	98	52	11	7	860	877	362	311	33	294	20	13	529	35	4	3.25
Aguascalientes	94	44	6	14	815	835	350	297	30	277	21	25	428	46	1	3.28

CLUB PITCHING—Continued

Club	G.	CG.	ShO.	Sv.	IP.	H.	R.	ER.	HR.	BB.	Int. BB.	HB.	SO.	WP.	Bk.	ERA.
Mexico Reds	94	39	9	7	836	846	366	314	28	286	13	47	444	26	2	3.38
Poza Rica	93	56	11	2	804	878	371	305	44	236	28	17	351	30	3	3;41
Mexico Tigers	97	33	8	19	847	897	383	329	44	285	19	46	424	23	0	3.50
Nuevo Laredo	98	39	8	11	854	862	402	341	46	344	29	27	406	27	0	3.59
Union Laguna	98	35	4	9	828	876	420	339	49	359	31	28	382	26	1	3.68
Monterrey	93	20	1	13	825	928	437	351	51	274	38	30	376	38	1	3.83
Monclova	96	30	3	10	833	969	477	383	65	356	42	45	390	25	2	4.14
Saltillo	98	38	7	3	835	913	428	387	38	304	73	19	420	23	1	4.17
Chihuahua	91	32	6	8	795	892	458	384	46	409	68	44	408	32	2	4.35
Leon	96	22	7	18	826	944	485	402	76	296	11	17	361	27	2	4.38
Toluca	95	27	3	5	811	1018	617	508	86	356	17	41	407	37	1	5.64

PITCHERS' RECORDS
(Leading Qualifiers for Earned-Run Average Leadership—76 or More Innings)

*Throws lefthanded.

Pitcher—Club	G.	GS.	CG.	ShO.	W.	L.	Sv.	Pct.	IP.	H.	R.	ER.	HR.	BB.	Int. BB.	HB.	SO.	WP.	ERA.
Rondon, Yucatan	21	21	16	8	14	7	0	.667	169	123	35	27	2	33	3	3	124	2	1.44
Pina, Yucatan	21	18	10	4	9	8	0	.529	143	105	38	24	3	33	2	9	76	5	1.51
Gutierrez, Puebla	21	21	16	8	16	4	0	.800	176	156	37	30	3	27	1	4	62	1	1.53
Rogers, Tabasco	26	20	13	6	15	4	2	.789	167	122	33	31	3	23	1	6	81	1	1.67
Chavez, Mex Reds	22	20	14	5	15	3	1	.833	169	141	41	33	4	58	0	8	107	2	1.76
L. Guzman, Campeche	13	13	6	1	4	7	0	.364	98	80	29	20	3	23	2	3	47	2	1.84
Higueras, Juarez*	19	17	4	0	8	3	0	.727	117	111	30	24	0	59	1	3	76	6	1.85
Romo, Coatzacoalcos	21	21	12	3	10	8	0	.556	169	123	48	35	5	40	5	6	147	10	1.86
Acosta, 6 Chi-10 Mva	16	15	9	1	4	7	0	.364	116	116	35	25	5	43	5	7	48	6	1.94
Diaz, Puebla	18	18	7	2	10	4	0	.714	133	126	33	29	7	35	4	3	48	3	1.96
Escarrega, Puebla	20	20	15	4	16	4	0	.800	164	148	42	36	4	32	0	6	70	4	1.98
Alcala, Chihuahua	15	15	11	2	5	9	0	.357	113	95	33	25	4	29	6	3	74	1	1.99

Departmental Leaders: G—Butkus, Limon, 38; GS—Pollorena, Silva, 24; CG—Pablo Gutierrez, Rondon, Luis Sanchez, 16; ShO—Brunet, Pablo Gutierrez, Rondon, 8; W—Escarrega, Pablo Gutierrez, 16; L—Madrigal, 13; Sv—Butkus, Castillejos, 12; Pct.—P. Rodriguez, 1.000; IP—Brunet, 179; H—Monteagudo, 196; R—Monteagudo, 100; ER—Monteagudo, 80; HR—Cordova, Monteagudo, 15; BB—G. Martinez, 75; IBB—Menendez, 17; HB—C. Moreno, 14; SO—Luis Sanchez, 155; WP—Abarca, 12.

(All Pitchers—Listed Alphabetically)

Pitcher—Club	G.	GS.	CG.	ShO.	W.	L.	Sv.	Pct.	IP.	H.	R.	ER.	HR.	BB.	Int. BB.	HB.	SO.	WP.	ERA.
Abarca, Aguascalientes	18	18	8	1	9	5	0	.643	120	111	45	39	0	49	1	2	51	12	2.93
Abeytia, 6 Tig-8 Chi	14	13	5	2	6	5	1	.545	85	111	53	47	5	40	5	3	48	2	4.98
Acosta, Coatzacoalcos	20	20	10	2	10	7	0	.588	134	131	45	36	9	33	2	5	63	3	2.42
Acosta, 6 Chi-10 Mva	16	15	9	1	4	7	0	.364	116	116	35	25	5	43	5	7	48	6	1.94
Aguilar, Monterrey	23	7	2	0	2	6	0	.250	81	105	48	38	6	28	8	7	31	4	4.22
Agundez, Aguascalientes	6	0	0	0	0	0	0	.000	5	8	5	5	0	3	0	0	2	0	9.00
Ahumada, 1 Sal-22 Lar	23	18	14	1	12	6	3	.667	151	128	49	40	6	43	1	0	96	3	2.38
Alcala, Chihuahua	15	15	11	2	5	9	0	.357	113	95	33	25	4	29	6	3	74	1	1.99
Alvarado, Monclova	1	0	0	0	0	0	0	.000	1	3	2	2	0	1	0	0	0	0	18.00
Alvarez, Chihuahua	28	1	0	0	1	1	2	.500	59	54	37	34	2	44	7	4	28	2	5.19
Anderson, Chihuahua	7	5	0	0	1	4	0	.200	26	37	17	13	0	21	2	0	18	1	4.50
Antunez, Reynosa*	1	0	0	0	0	0	0	.000	1	0	0	0	0	0	0	0	0	0	0.00
Arano, Reynosa	21	21	15	1	12	9	0	.571	164	169	58	54	6	36	1	3	89	3	2.96
Armas, Leon*	23	22	6	2	9	12	1	.429	148	164	80	75	13	34	0	3	62	2	4.56
Arratia, Laguna	20	16	3	0	7	6	1	.538	105	121	66	56	12	32	3	4	46	1	4.80
Arzate, Campeche	2	0	0	0	0	0	0	.000	4	5	1	1	0	3	0	0	3	0	2.25
Barbosa, Reynosa*	8	1	0	0	0	1	0	.000	19	9	7	7	0	10	1	0	9	1	3.32
Barajas, Reynosa	29	13	8	1	9	5	1	.643	126	105	40	33	3	49	0	1	82	8	2.36
Baruch, Poza Rica	23	4	5	2	3	2	0	.600	92	81	35	28	2	34	4	2	36	3	2.74
Bellacetin, Leon	1	0	0	0	0	0	0	.000	5	10	10	5	3	1	0	0	5	1	9.00
Belman, Toluca	18	1	0	0	2	2	0	.500	31	21	19	16	0	3	1	3	17	3	4.89
Beltran, Laguna	10	10	3	0	4	4	0	.500	70	66	24	21	3	35	1	1	34	1	2.70
Beltran, Yucatan	24	1	0	0	3	0	2	1.000	68	67	29	21	2	31	2	3	24	3	2.78
Beltran, Monclova	8	1	0	0	1	1	0	.500	32	32	12	8	2	11	1	1	16	0	2.25
Bernal, Monterrey	18	15	2	0	5	6	0	.455	105	114	47	37	13	25	2	1	39	4	3.17
Bonfils, Poza Rica*	18	17	13	2	7	9	0	.438	147	129	40	35	3	32	6	0	92	9	2.14
Brandt, Toluca	13	11	3	1	4	7	0	.364	66	85	54	38	5	23	2	1	27	1	5.18
Brunet, Aguila*	24	24	15	8	11	10	0	.524	179	166	69	52	11	56	2	2	125	7	2.61
Buentello, Reynosa	28	0	0	0	1	3	5	.250	48	44	18	17	0	17	3	2	31	3	3.19
Burke, Laredo	16	14	6	1	8	6	0	.571	101	105	57	45	6	35	4	5	46	4	4.01
Butkus, Monterrey	38	0	0	0	6	7	12	.462	71	71	31	21	3	21	5	2	35	2	2.66
Caballero, Monclova	3	2	0	0	0	1	0	.000	10	15	13	13	1	6	0	1	6	0	11.70
Caballero, Saltillo	6	0	0	0	0	0	0	.000	7	16	8	6	0	9	4	0	2	0	7.71
Camper, Saltillo	17	15	9	0	11	4	1	.733	124	116	44	43	5	37	6	2	67	3	3.12

Pitcher–Club	G	GS	CG	ShO	W	L	Sv	Pct.	IP	H	R	ER	HR	BB	Int. BB	HB	SO	WP	ERA
Carranza, Coatzacoalcos*	7	1	0	0	1	2	0	.333	16	15	10	10	0	12	0	1	13	1	5.63
Carrasco, Leon	14	8	1	0	3	5	0	.375	58	66	40	33	8	15	2	2	11	0	5.12
Castillejos, Mex Tigers	31	0	0	0	4	3	12	.571	60	65	27	19	3	14	2	6	23	2	2.85
Castillo, Campeche	7	1	0	0	0	1	0	.000	16	25	18	15	2	7	2	0	4	0	8.44
Cazares, Yucatan*	20	11	0	0	2	4	1	.333	72	67	35	30	3	39	2	2	33	5	3.75
Cervantes, Aguascalientes	17	4	0	0	2	3	1	.400	58	66	28	26	0	25	4	3	27	5	4.03
Chavez, Leon	19	13	1	0	3	5	2	.375	77	85	42	40	8	46	0	1	25	2	4.68
Chavez, Laguna	18	7	2	0	3	2	0	.600	64	52	31	27	5	35	4	1	43	6	3.80
Chavez, Mex Reds	22	20	14	5	15	3	1	.833	169	141	41	33	4	58	0	8	107	5	1.76
Chevez, Mex Tigers	5	4	0	0	1	0	0	.000	21	35	15	15	3	8	1	0	12	0	6.43
Cisneros, Aguascalientes	5	0	0	0	2	0	1	0.000	11	8	1	1	0	3	1	1	7	0	0.82
Cisneros, Monclova	1	0	0	0	0	0	0	.000	0	0	0	0	0	0	0	0	0	0	....
Cline, Monterrey	14	12	3	0	4	5	0	.444	93	105	40	32	2	29	2	7	48	2	3.10
Colorado, Coatzacoalcos	23	13	7	0	6	10	4	.375	104	109	42	29	6	27	4	2	44	0	2.51
Contreras, Mex Tigers	4	0	0	0	0	0	0	.000	6	15	8	8	0	1	0	0	2	0	12.00
Cordova, Leon	24	22	5	0	9	11	0	.450	124	155	81	63	15	43	1	1	57	2	4.57
Cota, Mex Tigers	1	0	0	0	0	0	0	.000	1	3	3	3	1	2	0	0	2	1	27.00
Cruz, Aguila	13	10	3	1	4	5	0	.444	73	82	29	25	5	10	3	1	13	0	3.08
Cuen, Mex Reds	24	21	9	1	10	8	1	.556	152	157	73	63	7	58	2	9	97	3	3.73
Davalillo, Aguas*	1	0	0	0	0	0	0	.000	0	0	0	0	0	0	0	0	0	0	....
De La Torre, Monterrey	12	4	1	0	1	3	1	.250	46	50	21	14	2	5	1	0	12	0	2.74
De La Torre, 15 Mv-8 Ch..	23	14	3	2	5	8	1	.385	95	126	60	53	5	41	10	1	59	5	5.02
Decker, Laredo	2	0	0	0	0	1	0	.000	9	11	11	8	0	4	0	1	4	1	8.00
Delfin, Coatzacoalcos	32	0	0	0	3	4	7	.429	63	64	28	17	1	11	0	3	35	2	2.43
Delgado, Laguna	3	0	0	0	0	2	0	.000	2	6	2	2	0	2	0	0	1	0	9.00
Diaz, Puebla	18	18	7	2	10	4	0	.714	133	126	33	29	7	35	4	3	48	3	1.96
Diaz, Leon	37	7	3	0	5	5	9	.500	100	90	35	30	3	26	2	6	58	3	2.70
Dimas, Juarez	23	1	0	0	1	2	2	.333	37	46	25	19	2	19	4	7	18	4	4.62
Divison, Mex Reds	5	0	0	0	0	1	0	.000	14	10	3	3	0	6	1	1	4	0	1.93
Dominguez, Laguna*	18	18	8	2	10	3	0	.769	114	126	56	49	5	50	6	1	50	3	3.87
Duarte, Campeche	2	1	0	0	1	0	0	1.000	8	8	4	3	0	5	0	2	1	1	3.38
Duran, Aguila	1	0	0	0	0	0	0	.000	1	4	4	4	0	1	0	0	1	0	36.00
Durazo, Juarez	8	2	0	0	0	2	0	.000	11	15	13	13	1	10	1	3	3	2	10.64
Enriquez, Juarez	20	2	0	0	3	3	2	.500	34	51	28	28	5	16	3	2	19	1	7.41
Escalante, Mex Tigers*	2	0	0	0	0	0	0	.000	6	3	1	0	1	3	0	0	2	0	0.00
Escarrega, Puebla	20	20	15	4	16	4	0	.800	164	148	42	36	4	32	0	6	70	4	1.98
Esparza, Puebla	4	0	0	0	1	1	0	.500	13	13	6	4	0	3	1	0	7	0	2.77
Espinosa, Aguascalientes.	3	0	0	0	0	0	0	.000	0	5	1	1	0	0	0	0	0	0	....
Espinosa, Aguila	6	5	1	1	1	1	0	.500	28	26	13	12	2	12	1	1	7	0	3.86
Esquer, Monterrey*	23	20	8	0	9	7	0	.563	141	161	72	58	10	51	6	5	90	11	3.70
Estrada, Monclova*	21	20	2	0	8	8	0	.500	112	126	67	49	9	58	1	2	47	3	3.94
Fabela, Chihuahua	25	1	0	0	1	3	6	.250	41	54	37	30	5	20	4	5	20	1	6.59
Farias, Mex Tigers	1	0	0	0	0	0	0	.000	2	4	1	1	0	2	0	1	2	0	4.50
Fernandez, Poza Rica	3	0	0	0	0	0	0	.000	4	8	5	4	1	1	0	0	0	0	9.00
Ferreira, Mex Reds	23	0	0	0	3	4	0	.429	36	46	22	20	1	7	2	1	15	2	5.00
Franco, Laredo	12	1	0	0	3	2	0	.600	52	41	15	14	4	13	0	1	23	0	2.42
Franco, Poza Rica	14	6	0	0	4	4	0	.000	43	63	27	20	3	19	0	0	19	1	4.19
Franco, Aguila	15	14	3	1	4	6	0	.400	92	94	44	38	7	21	5	5	31	1	3.72
Freisleben, Monterrey	1	1	0	0	1	0	0	1.000	5	3	3	0	1	0	0	0	5	0	0.00
Garcia, Poza Rica	2	0	0	0	0	0	0	.000	6	12	5	4	1	1	0	2	0	0	6.00
Garcia, Mex Tigers	5	3	0	0	1	1	0	.500	20	20	12	11	1	12	1	1	10	3	4.95
Garcia, Chihuahua	1	0	0	0	0	0	0	.000	1	0	0	0	0	1	0	0	1	0	0.00
Garcia, Laguna	1	0	0	0	0	0	0	.000	4	3	3	3	0	0	0	2	1	0	6.75
Garcia, Tabasco	30	3	1	0	4	5	4	.444	69	65	40	29	2	36	4	3	41	3	3.78
Garcia, Leon	25	18	6	1	8	7	4	.533	127	174	90	63	12	25	1	2	43	6	4.46
Garcia, Juarez	17	15	10	2	10	3	0	.769	130	107	37	33	2	31	3	1	112	4	2.28
Garcia, Monclova	28	1	0	0	4	6	4	.400	56	45	25	20	3	29	8	7	32	4	3.21
Garcia, Laredo	20	20	8	2	12	5	0	.706	149	170	71	57	10	52	6	0	47	5	3.44
Garduza, Poza Rica	21	20	7	1	4	10	0	.286	131	139	62	45	12	25	1	5	53	2	3.09
Gaxiola, Chihuahua	8	0	0	0	0	0	0	.000	13	19	8	7	2	11	0	0	5	2	4.85
Gonzalez, Poza Rica	4	0	0	0	0	0	0	.000	3	4	0	0	0	1	0	0	0	0	0.00
Granillo, Aguascalientes..	4	0	0	0	0	0	0	.000	3	5	0	0	0	4	1	0	2	0	0.00
Guerra, Juarez	24	0	0	0	0	2	2	.000	35	33	9	8	1	13	0	0	8	1	2.03
Guerrero, Monterrey	3	1	0	0	0	2	0	.000	10	6	8	8	0	7	0	1	8	1	7.20
Gutierrez, Juarez	21	21	2	1	8	12	0	.400	140	148	75	58	5	57	4	3	63	5	3.73
Gutierrez, Campeche*	20	20	3	0	8	5	0	.615	140	131	46	38	8	46	3	2	69	6	2.44
Gutierrez, Puebla	21	21	16	8	16	4	0	.800	176	156	37	30	3	27	1	4	62	1	1.53
Gutierrez, Juarez	14	9	3	1	4	6	0	.400	73	90	33	30	1	40	2	6	36	1	3.70
Guzman, Puebla	1	1	0	0	1	0	0	1.000	7	4	1	1	0	5	0	0	4	1	1.29
H. Guzman, Campeche	1	0	0	0	0	0	0	.000	3	4	2	2	0	2	0	0	2	1	6.00
Guzman, Aguila	1	0	0	0	0	0	0	.000	3	2	0	0	0	0	0	0	2	2	0.00
L. Guzman, Campeche	13	13	6	1	4	7	0	.364	98	80	29	20	3	23	2	3	47	2	1.84
Guzman, Campeche	24	0	0	0	5	2	6	.714	41	34	16	16	1	21	6	1	24	0	3.51
Henderson, Coatzacoalcos	20	20	9	3	8	7	0	.533	136	114	55	41	2	42	3	5	94	2	2.71
Hernandez, 7PR-17Mv-1S	25	6	3	0	5	7	4	.417	81	107	53	43	7	18	5	3	48	1	4.78

Pitcher—Club	G.	GS.	CG.	ShO.	W.	L.	Sv.	Pct.	IP.	H.	R.	ER.	HR.	Int. BB.	BB.	HB.	SO.	WP.	ERA.
Hernandez, Toluca	10	5	0	0	1	1	0	.500	27	37	24	24	3	14	2	3	10	0	8.00
Hernandez, Leon	3	0	0	0	0	0	0	.000	3	7	2	1	0	1	0	0	0	1	3.00
Hernandez, Poza Rica	13	0	0	0	0	4	0	.000	32	39	16	16	3	17	5	0	17	1	4.50
Herrera, Poza Rica	3	0	0	0	0	0	0	.000	3	5	4	4	0	3	0	0	1	0	12.00
Higueras, Juarez*	19	17	4	0	8	3	0	.727	117	111	30	24	0	59	1	3	76	6	1.85
Hughes, Mex Tigers	17	17	12	3	10	7	0	.588	145	118	37	34	3	45	4	5	94	4	2.11
Huizar, 8 Lar-7 Mva	15	9	2	1	1	5	0	.167	44	51	32	29	4	36	0	0	18	4	5.93
Ibarra, Mex Reds	22	20	5	1	6	5	0	.545	129	126	53	47	5	63	1	4	74	2	3.28
Icedo, Laredo*	16	2	0	0	0	1	0	.000	21	31	20	18	1	19	2	0	13	1	7.71
James, Campeche*	1	0	0	0	0	0	0	.000	2	2	1	1	0	0	0	1	0	0	4.50
Jimenez, 9 Yuc-5 Lag	14	14	10	2	6	8	0	.429	105	106	40	31	3	10	2	1	34	0	2.66
Jimenez, Toluca	1	0	0	0	0	0	0	.000	2	2	2	2	0	0	0	0	0	0	....
Johnson, Toluca	22	22	10	2	7	9	0	.438	153	177	78	66	9	30	0	1	82	3	3.88
Kekich, Juarez	3	0	0	0	2	0	0	1.000	23	18	10	8	1	9	0	1	15	3	3.13
Kuk Lee, 7 Mva-12 PR	19	17	11	2	10	9	0	.526	138	157	67	52	2	56	6	3	48	3	3.39
Lagunas, 12 Tig-8 Yuc	20	20	4	1	7	12	0	.368	120	126	64	41	10	19	1	3	42	2	3.08
Lara, Coatzacoalcos*	7	4	0	0	0	2	0	.000	23	28	14	8	0	12	0	0	9	2	3.13
Leon, Campeche	19	19	5	1	9	9	0	.500	139	153	61	51	3	22	2	5	65	5	3.30
Limon, Aguila	38	0	0	0	5	5	8	.500	62	51	21	17	3	21	6	2	30	8	2.47
Longoria, Monterrey	4	0	0	0	0	0	0	.000	10	12	10	10	3	6	2	0	2	0	9.00
Lopez, Poza Rica	19	10	6	0	7	6	0	.538	74	96	39	32	4	16	4	5	17	0	3.89
Lopez, Puebla	21	20	8	2	10	6	1	.625	117	131	60	52	7	44	0	2	47	4	4.00
Lopez, Mex Tigers	25	0	0	0	4	1	4	.800	53	40	18	16	3	21	1	7	38	0	2.72
Lopez, Leon	11	0	0	0	1	0	1	1.000	24	19	15	13	1	13	0	1	13	2	4.88
Lopez, Saltillo*	2	0	0	0	0	0	0	.000	1	0	0	0	0	0	0	0	0	0	0.00
Low, Aguascalientes	2	0	0	0	0	0	0	.000	3	4	2	0	0	1	0	0	2	1	0.00
Lucero, Aguila	1	0	0	0	0	0	0	.000	1	2	1	1	0	0	0	0	1	0	0.00
Luevano, Puebla	4	0	0	0	0	0	0	.000	7	5	1	1	0	2	0	0	1	0	1.29
Lugo, Toluca	33	1	1	0	8	3	5	.727	63	80	55	50	8	24	6	5	31	2	7.14
Madrigal, Tabasco	26	20	9	1	7	13	0	.350	151	158	60	50	5	51	9	5	72	4	2.98
Marin, Campeche	15	9	2	0	2	4	0	.333	60	72	38	32	3	33	3	1	13	3	4.80
Mariscal, Tabasco*	24	1	0	0	2	2	9	.500	30	38	18	18	1	11	0	0	10	1	5.40
Martin, Juarez*	16	14	4	0	6	6	0	.500	90	89	45	40	5	54	1	0	53	3	4.00
Martinez, Aguascalientes*	17	4	4	0	4	4	3	.500	56	58	23	19	2	17	3	0	15	2	3.05
Martinez, Monclova*	5	0	0	0	0	0	0	.000	10	18	8	7	1	5	1	1	6	0	6.30
Martinez, Chihuahua	21	20	10	0	8	9	0	.471	146	152	67	54	8	75	11	10	68	6	3.33
Martinez, Tabasco	12	7	0	0	2	4	0	.333	42	50	22	19	1	10	0	0	6	0	4.07
Martinez, Toluca	9	0	0	0	1	1	0	.500	18	29	25	22	2	12	1	1	6	3	11.00
Mauleon, Saltillo	31	1	0	0	1	4	3	.200	71	70	50	45	4	31	8	1	29	2	5.70
Maytorena, Laguna	28	3	0	1	8	4	8	.667	75	66	23	15	1	19	5	3	36	0	1.80
Menendez, Saltillo	31	20	9	1	10	9	1	.526	156	175	85	75	7	65	17	3	76	5	4.33
Mere, Mex Reds	21	16	7	2	7	6	0	.538	118	125	52	46	4	27	1	5	61	1	3.51
Meza, Laredo	2	0	0	0	0	0	0	.000	1	1	2	2	0	2	1	0	0	0	18.00
Miranda, Coatzacoalcos	7	0	0	0	1	0	0	1.000	18	21	9	5	0	9	1	2	9	0	2.50
Monteagudo, 11 Mv-12 To	23	22	9	0	5	12	1	.294	151	196	100	80	15	51	5	7	75	11	4.77
Montoya, Leon*	28	3	0	0	2	4	1	.333	63	75	36	28	5	37	2	0	34	1	4.00
Morales, Aguila	13	0	0	0	0	1	0	.000	40	37	15	12	1	11	3	2	14	0	2.70
Morales, Toluca	7	5	0	0	0	1	0	.000	24	32	21	17	3	14	0	1	16	0	6.38
Moreno, Aguascalientes*	19	19	11	1	14	3	0	.824	147	127	42	34	1	39	0	6	101	5	2.08
Moreno, 15 To-3 Ti-1 Mv	19	18	4	0	3	10	0	.231	90	98	72	60	7	72	1	14	63	7	6.00
Moreno, Aguascalientes	5	1	1	1	2	0	0	1.000	23	20	6	4	1	9	5	0	8	1	1.57
Mota, Yucatan	14	7	1	1	1	3	0	.250	53	68	26	22	2	4	0	4	20	1	3.74
Mundo, Chihuahua	8	0	0	0	0	0	0	.000	25	30	15	13	3	13	1	4	10	0	4.68
Munguia, Puebla	27	0	0	0	4	4	7	.500	49	43	17	14	0	27	3	0	40	1	2.57
Munoz, 1 Cam-12 Mex	13	1	1	0	0	1	0	.000	40	56	35	28	4	14	1	0	15	2	6.30
Nava, Yucatan	6	0	0	0	1	0	1	1.000	14	9	4	3	1	3	1	0	7	0	1.93
Nieblas, Juarez	13	0	0	0	1	2	0	.333	33	43	23	21	4	13	0	2	7	5	5.73
Ochoa, Mex Reds	25	2	1	0	7	5	1	.583	77	69	29	27	1	24	5	8	22	4	3.16
Ochoa, Campeche	26	2	0	0	3	5	8	.375	54	57	22	18	3	20	6	0	17	2	3.00
Ochoa, Tabasco	16	16	4	1	3	7	0	.300	106	103	51	37	7	31	2	5	38	1	3.14
Ontiveros, Laguna	9	0	0	0	0	0	0	.000	17	21	11	8	2	10	1	0	8	0	4.24
Orea, Mex Reds	13	13	2	0	3	6	0	.333	69	76	40	29	2	19	0	7	38	6	3.78
Orozco, Mex Reds	3	0	0	0	0	1	0	.000	7	4	4	4	0	3	0	2	1	0	5.14
Ortiz, Tabasco*	19	19	5	0	3	10	0	.231	121	148	67	47	4	29	2	2	43	0	3.50
Ortiz, Mex Reds	2	1	0	0	0	0	0	.000	3	6	3	3	0	3	0	0	2	0	9.00
Padrez, Mex Reds	2	0	0	0	0	0	0	.000	0	3	1	1	0	0	0	0	1	0	....
Palacios, Tabasco*	21	0	0	0	1	3	1	.250	58	54	20	18	1	23	1	4	16	4	2.79
Paul, Juarez*	20	20	9	0	13	4	0	.765	158	140	48	42	5	29	3	2	105	2	2.39
Pena, 6 Rey-14 Ctz	20	20	5	0	6	10	0	.375	115	133	74	61	9	47	2	13	58	3	4.77
Pena, 4 Sal-19 Chi*	23	3	0	0	1	4	0	.200	52	71	45	42	5	29	4	1	31	8	7.27
Pena, 14 Ags-1 Mva	7	1	0	0	0	1	0	.000	20	24	14	13	1	7	1	0	8	3	5.85
Pereyra, Toluca	8	0	0	0	0	2	0	.000	10	19	9	8	2	3	0	0	4	1	7.20
Perez, Toluca	20	11	0	0	3	5	0	.375	90	117	76	55	10	56	2	6	36	2	5.50
Perez, Tabasco	6	0	0	0	1	0	0	1.000	14	18	10	10	1	3	0	0	11	2	6.43
Pineda, Leon	25	2	0	0	3	3	0	.500	57	61	39	33	2	35	2	1	32	7	5.21

Pitcher–Club	G	GS	CG	ShO	W	L	Sv	Pct.	IP	H	R	ER	HR	BB	Int. BB	HB	SO	WP	ERA.
Pina, Yucatan	21	19	10	4	9	8	0	.529	143	105	38	24	3	33	2	9	76	5	1.51
Pollorena, Saltillo	24	24	12	3	10	12	0	.455	172	189	67	60	4	43	15	2	109	4	3.14
Ponce, Tabasco	6	0	0	0	0	1	0	1.000	4	7	4	4	0	3	2	0	0	0	9.00
Posadas, Aguila	2	0	0	0	0	0	0	.000	5	5	4	4	2	2	0	0	2	0	7.20
Posadas, Poza Rica	3	2	1	1	1	2	0	.333	16	18	9	8	0	8	1	0	5	0	4.50
Preciado, Mex Reds	9	0	0	0	1	0	0	1.000	24	28	11	11	0	4	0	2	7	1	4.13
Prieto, Monterrey	14	1	0	0	0	2	0	.000	35	46	25	24	2	16	3	2	8	5	6.17
Pruneda, Monclova	2	0	0	0	0	1	0	.000	1	1	1	1	0	4	0	0	4	0	9.00
Pulido, Reynosa*	26	14	9	2	9	6	1	.600	132	142	58	52	9	39	7	2	69	2	3.55
Pulido, Puebla	11	0	0	0	4	0	1	1.000	38	28	5	5	0	6	0	0	14	0	1.18
Purata, Poza Rica*	3	3	2	1	1	2	0	.333	25	25	8	7	1	9	0	1	10	1	2.52
Quintero, Laguna	19	14	6	0	2	11	0	.154	87	98	56	49	6	52	3	2	28	6	5.07
Quinonez, Leon	9	1	0	0	0	1	0	1.000	18	12	8	8	2	9	1	0	13	0	4.00
Raygoza, German, Tigers	1	0	0	0	0	0	0	.000	1	2	3	2	1	1	0	0	1	0	18.00
Raygoza, Glrmo., Tigers ..	1	1	0	0	0	0	0	.000	10	6	1	0	0	2	0	0	6	0	0.00
Renteria, Juarez	26	11	6	4	7	6	3	.538	112	99	45	38	13	41	1	10	65	1	3.05
Retamoza, Saltillo	2	0	0	0	0	0	0	.000	2	2	1	1	0	0	0	0	0	0	4.50
Reyes, Monterrey	16	11	2	0	1	6	0	.143	71	88	47	41	3	26	5	2	33	4	5.20
Reyes, 5 Mv-1 Yu-2 Lag*.	8	0	0	0	1	0	0	.000	6	9	9	9	1	7	2	1	4	0	13.50
Reynoso, Aguila	14	12	5	1	6	4	0	.600	81	85	28	26	2	21	2	1	32	1	2.89
Rios, Campeche	1	0	0	0	0	0	0	.000	0	0	0	0	0	0	0	0	0	0	0.00
Rios, Coatzacoalcos	9	1	0	0	0	1	1	.000	15	21	17	13	0	8	0	1	4	0	7.80
Rivera, Yucatan	23	22	8	1	11	9	0	.550	159	146	60	51	5	46	0	8	65	5	2.89
Rodriguez, Coatz *	20	0	0	0	2	0	2	1.000	35	32	17	10	0	14	1	0	24	2	2.57
Rodriguez, Aguas	22	1	0	0	4	2	5	.667	49	58	29	24	5	15	3	2	13	0	4.41
Rodriguez, Campeche	17	1	0	0	2	1	0	.667	49	50	21	16	1	18	3	0	10	4	2.94
Rodriguez, Yucatan	25	0	0	0	9	0	5	1.000	58	44	17	11	1	14	5	4	36	3	1.71
Rodriguez, Poza Rica	3	0	0	0	0	0	0	.000	2	2	0	0	0	2	0	0	2	0	0.00
Rogers, Tabasco	26	20	13	6	15	4	2	.789	167	122	33	31	3	23	1	6	81	1	1.67
Romero, Monclova	7	0	0	0	0	0	0	.000	15	22	12	12	2	3	0	0	6	0	7.20
Romo, Coatzacoalcos	21	21	12	3	10	8	0	.556	169	123	48	35	5	40	5	6	147	10	1.86
Rondon, Yucatan	21	21	16	8	14	7	0	.667	169	123	35	27	2	33	3	3	124	5	1.44
Rosario, Coatzacoalcos ..	1	0	0	0	0	0	0	.000	2	5	2	2	0	2	0	0	0	0	9.00
Saldana, Poza Rica	5	0	0	0	0	0	0	.000	14	18	8	8	4	2	0	0	4	1	5.14
Salgado, Laredo	27	9	3	1	4	4	2	.500	96	103	39	34	2	24	6	3	50	1	3.19
Salinas, Reynosa	23	22	11	2	10	9	0	.526	154	175	76	63	5	61	3	0	80	6	3.68
Salomon, Aguascalientes .	20	18	11	2	13	4	1	.765	147	137	54	45	6	40	1	4	104	6	2.76
Sanchez, Juarez	8	2	0	0	1	2	0	.333	22	24	15	13	0	7	2	1	9	2	5.32
Sanchez, Aguila	24	22	16	7	14	9	0	.609	177	149	47	40	3	35	3	9	155	5	2.03
Sandate, Poza Rica	10	10	7	2	5	5	0	.500	77	65	31	21	5	24	2	1	62	7	2.45
Sanudo, Mex Tigers	1	0	0	0	0	0	0	.000	3	5	5	4	0	2	0	0	3	0	12.00
Sauceda, Toluca	15	0	0	0	0	2	0	.000	29	43	30	24	4	13	1	0	20	2	7.45
Sauceda, Mex Tigers	26	1	0	0	4	3	1	.571	66	70	31	28	6	22	2	1	31	1	3.82
Saucedo, Chihuahua	21	17	5	2	6	8	0	.429	107	129	73	60	7	58	11	8	49	2	5.05
Segui, Reynosa	21	21	9	3	9	9	0	.500	146	142	58	45	3	46	4	1	131	8	2.77
Serna, Monclova	1	0	0	0	0	0	0	.000	2	3	1	1	0	1	0	0	0	0	4.50
Silva, Monclova	25	24	5	0	4	12	0	.250	137	156	78	59	14	64	7	8	38	0	3.88
Silverio, Saltillo*	1	0	0	0	0	0	0	.000	2	4	2	2	0	2	0	0	1	0	9.00
G. Solis, Saltillo	24	12	4	0	6	4	0	.600	95	94	35	31	4	43	10	4	35	2	2.94
Solis, Laredo	36	8	4	0	4	6	6	.400	114	109	47	43	9	49	6	2	64	2	3.39
M. Solis, Saltillo	25	23	4	1	8	11	0	.421	140	180	92	83	11	30	7	5	55	2	5.34
Sosa, Laguna	22	16	3	0	6	8	0	.429	116	112	54	40	6	72	2	4	64	5	3.10
Soto, Saltillo	9	0	0	0	3	1	0	.750	14	7	3	3	0	2	0	2	8	2	1.93
Soto, Laredo*	11	8	0	0	1	7	0	.125	48	53	29	25	2	35	1	7	14	5	4.69
Soto, Puebla	15	10	1	0	1	2	1	.333	81	76	27	25	1	21	1	4	35	1	2.78
Terlecky, Mex Tigers	17	17	4	0	6	6	0	.500	115	125	46	32	4	34	2	6	49	2	2.50
Thomas, Mex Tigers	18	18	3	0	8	5	0	.615	110	125	54	47	5	39	3	3	42	5	3.85
Torrealba, Saltillo*	22	1	0	0	1	1	0	.500	33	32	21	19	1	31	4	0	20	3	5.18
Torrealba, Laguna*	13	8	2	0	2	7	0	.222	63	80	36	29	2	16	2	2	24	2	4.14
Tovar, Monterrey	6	0	0	0	0	0	0	.000	17	19	10	10	1	3	0	0	2	0	5.29
Uresti, Coatzacoalcos	1	0	0	0	0	0	0	.000	3	3	1	1	0	0	0	0	0	0	3.00
Urias, Leon*	9	0	0	0	0	0	0	.000	22	26	12	12	6	11	0	0	8	0	4.91
Urrea, Saltillo	3	0	0	0	0	0	0	.000	2	6	2	2	0	2	0	0	0	0	9.00
Valdez, 7 Agu-10 Tab	17	16	2	0	2	10	0	.167	91	93	45	40	6	26	2	1	42	2	3.96
Valdez, Laguna	32	1	0	0	2	1	0	.667	69	83	43	29	5	32	1	6	35	1	3.78
Valdivia, Laredo*	16	13	4	1	5	5	0	.500	86	81	39	32	4	43	2	6	38	2	3.35
Valencia, Campeche	24	23	11	4	12	7	0	.632	163	140	54	45	4	56	2	2	87	7	2.48
Valenzuela, Aguas	4	1	0	0	1	0	0	.000	15	18	7	4	1	3	1	0	7	3	2.40
Valenzuela, Poza Rica	12	10	0	0	0	6	1	.000	41	70	41	39	3	9	1	1	6	1	8.56
Valle, 1 Pue-19 Tol*	20	2	1	0	2	4	0	.333	54	65	42	36	5	28	2	3	31	3	6.00
Valle, Aguila*	15	0	0	0	1	0	0	1.000	21	30	20	20	1	8	0	1	4	2	8.57
Vallejano, Aguascalientes	18	10	4	0	5	6	3	.455	81	100	43	37	6	21	4	3	21	6	4.11
Vargas, Laredo	2	0	0	0	0	0	0	.000	1	4	2	2	6	1	0	1	1	0	18.00
Vazquez, Reynosa	3	0	0	0	0	0	0	.000	2	4	3	2	1	4	0	0	1	0	9.00
Veintidos, Chihuahua	6	6	1	0	1	3	0	.250	36	44	24	21	4	30	5	2	16	2	5.25

Pitcher—Club	G.	GS.	CG.	ShO.	W.	L.	Sv.	Pct.	IP.	H.	R.	ER.	HR.	Int. BB.	BB.	HB.	SO.	WP.	ERA.
Velazquez, Reynosa	8	0	0	0	0	0	0	.000	18	11	4	3	0	7	0	0	9	1	1.50
Verdugo, Monclova	28	2	0	0	3	2	1	.600	81	89	50	38	4	23	3	11	31	2	4.22
Vidana, Reynosa	11	0	0	0	1	1	0	.500	28	30	15	11	3	13	1	1	17	3	3.54
Vidana, Chihuahua	22	3	0	0	5	5	0	.500	62	68	41	35	5	24	5	2	39	3	5.08
Villanueva, Mex Tigers*	24	16	6	1	6	10	1	.375	116	126	55	53	6	33	2	9	59	1	4.11
Villegas, Tabasco	12	1	0	0	1	0	0	.000	26	37	15	10	2	11	0	1	9	3	3.46
Williams, 13 Ags-7 Tol*	20	20	9	1	11	4	0	.733	123	125	62	54	12	55	1	3	61	6	3.95
Zetina, Toluca	17	4	1	0	0	2	0	.000	43	59	42	39	8	30	1	3	15	3	8.16

BALKS—A. Garcia, M. Morales, P. Rodriguez, 2 each; Barojas, Buentello, Cazares, Cuen, E. De La Torre, Dimas, Enriquez, Estrada, Fabela, Garduza, G. Gutierrez, Longoria, Marin, R. Martinez, Maytorena, Orea, J. Pena, Alfonso Pulido, Quinonez, Renteria, A. Rivera, Manuel Rodriguez, M. Solis, Urias, J. Valdez, Valencia, R. Valle, Verdugo, Vidana, 1 each.

NO-HIT GAME—Henderson, Coatzacoalcos, defeated Monterrey, 3-0, May 20.

6-TEAM SEASON

STANDING OF CLUBS AT CLOSE OF SEASON

Club	Sal.	CJ.	Ctz.	UL.	Rey.	MT.	W.	L.	T.	Pct.	G.B.
Saltillo	..	5	5	8	4	6	28	11	0	.718	....
Ciudad Juarez	3	..	4	4	6	5	22	15	2	.595	5
Coatzacoalcos	3	4	..	1	7	3	18	18	0	.500	8½
Union Laguna	0	3	5	..	3	6	17	18	1	.486	9
Reynosa	3	1	1	3	..	6	14	22	1	.389	12½
Mexico City Tigers	2	2	3	2	2	..	11	26	0	.297	16

Union Laguna club represented Gomez Palacio and Torreon.

Playoffs—None.

MANAGERS: Ciudad Juarez—Jose Guerrero; Coatzacoalcos—Benjamin Cerda; Mexico City Tigers—Fernando Remes Garza; Reynosa—Winston Llenas; Saltillo—Gregorio Luque; Union Laguna—Jesus Diaz.

All-Star Team—None.

(Compiled by Ana Luisa Perea de Silva, League Statistician, Mexico, D.F.)

CLUB BATTING

Club	G.	AB.	R.	OR.	H.	TB.	2B.	3B.	HR.	RBI.	SH.	SF.	Int. BB.	BB.	HP.	SO.	SB.	CS.	LOB.	Pct.
Saltillo	39	1195	185	99	363	458	41	15	8	179	14	15	134	7	10	105	24	24	270	.304
Union Laguna	36	1144	121	117	299	369	43	6	5	95	14	9	84	7	7	187	37	13	239	.261
Mexico Tigers	37	1183	117	200	309	372	30	6	7	97	12	9	78	9	1	149	3	8	249	.261
Reynosa	37	1149	123	123	296	379	30	16	7	112	11	12	93	4	8	157	18	9	257	.258
Ciudad Juarez	39	1270	118	118	322	391	41	8	4	100	20	9	120	7	7	147	33	9	305	.254
Coatzacoalcos	36	1121	87	94	260	325	25	5	10	77	11	7	65	5	6	143	14	8	217	.232

INDIVIDUAL BATTING
(Leading Qualifiers for Batting Championship—108 or More Plate Appearances)

*Bats lefthanded.   †Switch-hitter.

Player and Club	G.	AB.	R.	H.	TB.	2B.	3B.	HR.	RBI.	SH.	SF.	BB.	HP.	SO.	SB.	CS.	Pct.
Collins, James, Saltillo*	39	137	25	52	72	8	3	2	31	0	1	15	1	12	5	4	.380
Soto, Carlos, Saltillo	34	112	15	41	57	4	3	2	20	0	2	9	2	7	0	3	.366
Navarrete, Juan, Saltillo*	37	142	22	51	58	1	3	0	17	1	1	8	0	11	7	5	.359
Silverio, Tomas, Laguna*	34	116	14	39	53	9	1	1	9	1	0	14	0	16	5	2	.336
Lopez, Carlos, Reynosa	30	105	14	35	50	6	0	3	15	0	3	5	2	13	2	2	.333
Espino, Hector, Saltillo	35	110	23	36	45	6	0	1	18	0	4	22	5	4	0	1	.327
Suarez, Miguel, Mex Tigers*	36	131	16	42	50	4	2	0	8	1	0	4	0	6	0	2	.321
Serna, Joel, Mex Tigers	29	97	9	31	40	6	0	1	11	0	2	10	1	16	0	2	.320
Alvarado, Natanael, Reynosa	36	132	18	42	57	5	2	2	12	1	1	14	1	14	3	3	.318
Biagini, Gregory, Mex Tigers†	31	99	17	31	43	3	0	3	12	0	1	24	0	14	0	1	.313

Departmental Leaders: G—Briones, J. Collins, Valle, 39; AB—Briones, 154; R—R. Rodriguez, 29; H—J. Collins, 52; TB—J. Collins, 72; 2B—Batista, 11; 3B—Alvarez, Briones, J. Collins, S. Collins, A. Guzman, J. Navarrete, Soto, 3; HR—Pierce, 9; RBI—J. Collins, 31; GWRBI—Bojorquez, Juarez, Soto, 4; SH—G. B. Chavez, 8; SF—Espino, A. Lara, 4; BB—R. Rodriguez, 30; HP—J. Navarrete, 5; SO—Batista, 29; SB—Briones, 18; CS—J. Navarrete, R. Rodriguez, 5.

(All Players—Listed Alphabetically)

Player and Club	G.	AB.	R.	H.	TB.	2B.	3B.	HR.	RBI.	SH.	SF.	BB.	HP.	SO.	SB.	CS.	Pct.
Aguilar, Jose, Mex Tigers	6	8	0	0	0	0	0	0	0	0	0	0	0	3	0	0	.000
Almeida, Reynaldo, Reynosa	15	16	1	2	4	0	1	0	0	0	0	6	0	0	0	1	.125
Alvarado, Natanael, Reynosa	36	132	18	42	57	5	2	2	12	1	1	14	1	14	3	3	.318
Alvarez, Manuel, Reynosa*	33	97	14	23	33	4	3	0	13	0	3	17	0	19	1	0	.237
Balaz, John, Juarez	28	97	11	23	33	4	0	2	10	1	1	11	0	14	2	0	.237
Batista, Rafael, Laguna*	32	112	13	34	54	11	0	3	20	0	2	13	1	29	1	0	.304
Biagini, Gregory, Mex Tigers†	31	99	17	31	43	3	0	3	12	0	1	24	0	14	0	1	.313
Bobadilla, Manuel, Juarez	28	88	5	21	24	3	0	0	7	3	1	6	0	14	1	1	.239
Bojorquez, Jose, Laguna	29	92	6	23	31	5	0	1	9	3	1	6	0	14	1	1	.250

Player and Club	G.	AB.	R.	H.	TB.	2B.	3B.	HR.	RBI.	SH.	SF.	BB.	HP.	SO.	SB.	CS.	Pct.
Briones, Antonio, Juarez	39	154	14	47	58	5	3	0	13	5	1	13	0	12	18	2	.305
Cabrera, Jorge, Coatzacoalcos	14	36	4	13	13	0	0	0	2	0	0	0	0	7	1	0	.361
Cerda, Benjamin, Coatzacoalcos	27	90	5	21	25	1	0	1	4	0	0	6	0	7	0	0	.233
Chavarria, Miguel, Laguna	36	122	17	33	37	2	1	0	7	2	2	12	2	18	5	1	.270
Chavez, Franco B., Mex Tigers	3	12	1	4	6	2	0	0	3	0	0	0	0	0	0	0	.333
Chavez, Guadalupe B., Saltillo*	37	117	13	24	29	3	1	0	9	8	2	11	0	18	1	0	.205
Chavez, Guadalupe G., Laguna	8	10	1	2	4	0	1	0	2	0	0	0	0	3	0	0	.200
Collins, James, Saltillo*	39	137	25	52	72	8	3	2	31	0	1	15	1	12	5	4	.380
Collins, Silvester, Coatzacoalcos	24	89	7	23	31	2	3	0	4	2	0	4	1	16	3	1	.258
Contreras, Juan C., Laguna	20	64	5	16	18	0	1	0	5	3	0	3	1	7	6	0	.250
Contreras, Juan V., Laguna	23	73	2	12	14	0	1	0	5	1	0	2	0	12	3	1	.164
Cruz, Domingo, Coatzacoalcos	27	78	5	19	24	2	0	1	5	2	1	4	3	6	1	3	.244
Davila, Luis, Juarez	37	126	13	31	39	6	1	0	9	3	2	19	0	15	1	0	.246
DeFreites, Arturo, Reynosa	37	123	9	32	35	1	1	0	16	0	2	9	1	25	1	0	.260
Delgado, Manuel, Juarez*	1	0	1	0	0	0	0	0	0	0	0	1	0	0	0	0	.000
Deliza, Juan, Laguna	30	115	12	35	35	1	0	0	8	1	1	6	0	13	6	4	.304
Espino, Hector, Saltillo	35	110	23	36	45	6	0	1	18	0	4	22	5	4	0	1	.327
Esqueda, Carlos, Laguna	14	31	2	8	8	0	0	0	1	0	0	2	0	9	1	0	.258
Faudoa, Victor, Mex Tigers*	26	80	5	26	32	4	1	0	2	3	0	5	0	8	0	0	.325
Felix, Victor, Laguna	33	99	22	26	32	6	0	0	6	1	1	17	1	4	2	2	.263
Figueroa, Leobardo, Juarez	32	106	10	27	34	3	2	0	7	3	1	23	2	10	4	0	.255
Garzon, Felix, Coatzacoalcos	11	33	3	6	6	0	0	0	5	2	1	1	0	6	1	0	.182
Gomez, Graciano, Coatzacoalcos	19	61	2	15	18	1	1	0	1	0	0	2	0	9	1	0	.246
Gonzalez, Efrain, Laguna	16	42	0	8	8	0	0	0	3	1	0	1	0	6	0	0	.190
Gonzalez, Jesus, Coatzacoalcos	31	96	6	21	22	1	0	0	4	1	2	2	0	14	0	2	.219
Guzman, Andres, Reynosa	27	87	6	23	32	3	3	0	6	0	2	3	0	17	1	0	.264
Guzman, Marco, Reynosa	20	46	6	15	19	2	1	0	3	0	0	5	0	6	0	0	.326
Heras, Roberto, Mex Tigers	29	100	5	20	24	1	0	1	12	0	0	0	0	20	1	0	.200
Hernandez, Juan, Laguna	28	94	9	27	31	4	0	0	7	1	1	3	0	12	4	1	.287
Hernandez, Miguel, Coatzacoalcos	24	65	4	8	9	0	0	1	1	0	1	2	8	0	0	1	.123
Hernandez, Pedro, Juarez	22	80	10	23	28	2	0	1	5	0	1	3	1	6	0	0	.288
Hernandez, Rodolfo, Reynosa	25	75	2	10	10	0	0	0	2	1	0	4	1	12	2	0	.133
Juarez, Marcelo, Saltillo	33	105	12	27	30	3	0	0	18	2	2	3	1	7	1	2	.257
Lara, Armando, Mex Tigers	37	125	13	24	28	1	0	1	15	3	4	7	0	6	1	0	.192
Lara, Cesar, Coatzacoalcos	30	82	2	10	10	0	0	0	3	2	0	0	0	14	1	1	.122
Lara, Franco, Mex Tigers	9	19	0	3	3	0	0	0	3	0	0	0	0	2	0	0	.158
Leon, Richard, Mex Tigers*	3	9	3	3	3	0	0	0	1	0	0	0	0	1	0	0	.333
Llenas, Winston, Reynosa	25	84	12	22	31	1	1	2	14	0	0	7	2	1	0	2	.262
Lopez, Carlos, Reynosa	30	105	14	35	50	6	0	3	15	0	3	5	2	13	2	2	.333
Lopez, Jaime, Coatzacoalcos*	32	115	8	28	29	1	0	0	7	0	0	9	0	6	1	0	.243
Luque, Gregorio, Saltillo	1	2	0	0	0	0	0	0	0	0	0	0	0	1	0	0	.000
Mendoza, Luis, Juarez	27	96	13	21	24	3	0	0	5	4	0	5	0	6	0	3	.219
Mendoza, Margarito, Saltillo	16	36	2	10	13	1	1	0	6	0	2	0	0	8	0	0	.278
Mendoza, Porfirio, Mex Tigers	34	133	16	31	35	2	0	0	2	2	0	6	0	10	1	0	.233
Montoya, Raul, Saltillo	28	88	9	18	20	2	0	0	7	2	0	6	0	3	3	2	.205
Mora, Andres, Saltillo	35	110	19	32	45	4	0	3	21	0	1	16	1	17	0	0	.291
Morales, Luis, Reynosa	14	21	2	3	7	0	2	0	3	0	0	1	0	7	0	0	.143
Munoz, Eduardo, Reynosa	36	121	16	37	41	4	0	0	6	4	0	18	1	10	3	0	.306
Navarrete, Carlos, Coatzacoalcos	18	55	4	15	15	0	0	0	4	1	0	3	0	5	0	0	.273
Navarrete, Juan, Saltillo*	37	142	22	51	58	5	1	3	17	1	1	8	0	11	7	5	.359
Osuna, Elpidio, Juarez	15	45	1	7	7	0	0	0	2	0	0	3	0	6	1	0	.156
Parra, Manuel, Juarez	39	144	10	40	47	4	0	1	15	0	0	8	1	19	0	1	.278
Pierce, Jack, Coatzacoalcos	36	128	18	31	57	5	0	7	18	0	0	14	0	25	1	0	.242
Quintero, Victor, Saltillo	31	78	13	24	28	2	1	0	13	1	1	8	0	7	3	1	.308
Quinonez, Ventura, Juarez	2	1	0	0	0	0	0	0	0	0	0	0	1	0	0	0	.000
Rivera, Carlos, Mex Tigers	34	119	6	35	43	6	1	0	11	2	1	5	0	18	0	2	.294
Rivera, Franco, Mex Tigers	16	39	3	5	5	0	0	0	1	0	0	3	0	13	0	0	.128
Rivero, Gener, Reynosa	36	101	11	20	22	2	0	0	5	1	0	9	1	7	2	2	.198
Robles, Humberto, Juarez	2	2	0	1	1	0	0	0	0	0	0	0	0	1	0	0	.500
Rodriguez, Guillermo, Coatz.	6	3	1	1	1	0	0	0	0	1	0	0	0	0	0	0	.333
Rodriguez, Jaime, Mex Tigers	18	54	8	16	20	1	0	1	5	0	0	2	0	8	0	0	.296
Rodriguez, Jose, Mex Tigers	31	102	10	26	26	0	0	0	5	0	1	7	0	6	0	1	.255
Rodriguez, Jose G., Mex Tigers	16	42	5	9	11	0	1	0	3	0	1	5	0	11	0	0	.214
Rodriguez, Juan, Reynosa	36	86	9	20	23	1	1	0	14	4	1	3	1	6	1	0	.233
Rodriguez, Rodolfo, Saltillo*	38	130	29	40	51	7	2	0	17	0	1	30	0	10	2	5	.308
Romo, Jose, Coatzacoalcos	26	79	5	21	28	5	1	0	8	1	3	0	9	2	0	.266
Rosales, Arturo, Juarez	28	82	10	23	27	4	0	0	9	0	0	4	1	10	2	0	.280
Rosario, Angel, Coatzacoalcos*	33	111	13	28	38	7	0	1	10	0	2	16	0	11	2	1	.252
Rosas, Clemente, Reynosa	17	34	2	8	11	1	1	0	2	0	0	2	0	4	0	0	.235
Sanchez, Juan, Laguna	30	89	12	24	29	3	1	0	8	0	0	5	2	26	1	1	.270
Serna, Joel, Mex Tigers	29	97	9	31	40	6	0	1	11	0	2	10	1	16	0	2	.320
Serratos, Ramon, Saltillo	21	28	3	8	10	0	1	0	2	0	0	1	0	4	0	0	.286
Silverio, Tomas, Laguna*	34	116	14	39	53	9	1	1	9	1	0	14	0	16	5	2	.336
Soto, Carlos, Saltillo	34	112	15	41	57	4	3	2	20	0	2	9	2	7	0	3	.366
Suarez, Miguel, Mex Tigers*	36	131	16	42	50	4	2	0	8	1	0	4	0	6	0	2	.321
Valenzuela, Guillermo, Reynosa	13	21	1	4	4	0	0	0	1	0	0	1	0	4	0	1	.190

Player and Club	G.	AB.	R.	H.	TB.	2B.	3B.	HR.	RBI.	SH.	SF.	BB.	HP.	SO.	SB.	CS.	Pct.
Valle, Guadalupe, Juarez	39	126	10	29	38	5	2	0	13	2	2	12	1	23	1	1	.230
Vega, Abelardo, Juarez	36	123	10	29	31	2	0	0	6	2	1	12	1	13	3	1	.236
Villela, Carlos, Laguna	26	85	6	12	14	2	0	0	5	0	0	0	0	18	2	0	.141
Zamora, Roberto, Mex Tigers	6	14	0	3	3	0	0	0	1	0	0	0	0	4	0	0	.214

The following pitchers had no plate appearances primarily through use of designated hitters, listed alphabetically by club, games in parentheses:

CIUDAD JUAREZ—Dimas, Rodolfo (4); Enriquez, Jorge (7); Garcia, Rafael (8); Gutierrez, Porfirio (4); Higueras, Teodoro (8); Kekich, Mike (8); Nieblas, Armando (1); Olguin, Salvador (1); Paul, Mike (8); Renteria, Hilario (5); Sanchez, Daniel (1).

COATZACOALCOS—Acosta, Cecilio (9); Brunet, George (7); Carranza, Javier (15); Colorado, Salvador (7); Delfin, Justino (7); Leyva, Jose (1); Pena, Jose (7); Quijada, Armando (1); Romo, Vicente (8); Uresti, Crisanto (4).

MEXICO CITY TIGERS—Burke, Steve (6); Castillejos, Jose (7); Hughes, James (3); Lopez, Hector (14); Ruiz, Miguel (7); Sauceda, Ramiro (17); Terlecky, Gregory (3); Thomas, Stan (1); Villanueva, Luis (6); Williams, Gary (3); Zaldivar, Arturo (7).

REYNOSA—Antunez, Martin (3); Arano, Ramon (9); Barbosa, Anthony (2); Barojas, Salome (7); Buentello, Israel (7); Pulido, Alfonso (7); Salinas, Guadalupe (6); Segui, Diego (6); Vazquez, Marco (5); Velazquez, Agustin (4); Fidana, Alejandro (4).

SALTILLO—Camper, Cardell (11); Hernandez, Angel (15); Mauleon, Ignacio (5); Menendez, Rolando (10); Pollorena, Antonio (6); Solis, Guillermo (7); Solis, Miguel (8); Torrealba, Alfredo (4); Urrea, Leonel (1).

UNION LAGUNA—Aguilar, Rafael (5); Arratia, Javier (6); Delgado, Justino (1); Elizalde, Efrain (1); Garcia, Horacio (1); Martinez, Javier (8); Mayorena, Franco (5); Quintero, Frank (9); Sosa, Carlos (8); Valdez, Humberto (8).

AWARDED FIRST BASE ON INTERFERENCE—C. Lopez (J. Sanchez); J. Navarrete (C. Navarrete).

GAME-WINNING RBIs

CIUDAD JUAREZ (19)—Briones 3, Rosales 3, Balaz 2, Davila 2, Figueroa 2, Valle 2, Bobadilla 1, Hernandez 1, Osuna 1, Parra 1, Vega 1.

COATZACOALCOS (17)—Pierce 3, Romo 3, Gonzalez 2, Lara 2, Lopez 2, Cerda 1, Cruz 1, Garzon 1, Navarrete 1, Rosario 1.

MEXICO CITY TIGERS (8)—Heras 2, A. Lara 2, C. Rivera 1, Jose Rodriguez 1, Jose G. Rodriguez 1, Serna 1.

REYNOSA (10)—Lopez 3, DeFreites 2, Alvarez 1, M. Guzman 1, Llenas 1, Munoz 1, Rivero 1.

SALTILLO (19)—Juarez 4, Soto 4, Mora 3, Collins 2, Montoya 2, Navarrete 2, Espino 1, Quintero 1.

UNION LAGUNA (16)—Bojorquez 4, Deliza 2, Hernandez 2, Sanchez 2, Villela 2, Chavarria 1, Chavez 1, J. C. Contreras 1, Gonzalez 1.

CLUB FIELDING

Club	G.	PO.	A.	E.	DP.	PB.	Pct.	Club	G.	PO.	A.	E.	DP.	PB.	Pct.
Saltillo	39	936	421	29	32	1	.979	Ciudad Juarez	39	1014	448	36	34	4	.976
Mexico Tigers	37	906	424	31	26	4	.977	Union Laguna	36	903	415	33	42	5	.976
Coatzacoalcos	36	897	391	31	20	3	.976	Reynosa	37	876	372	35	37	6	.973

Triple Plays—Reynosa 2; Mexico Tigers, Saltillo, 1 each.

INDIVIDUAL FIELDING

*Throws lefthanded.

FIRST BASEMEN

Player and Club	G.	PO.	A.	E.	DP.	Pct.	Player and Club	G.	PO.	A.	E.	DP.	Pct.
Soto, Saltillo	4	42	2	0	2	1.000	Rosas, Reynosa	2	2	0	0	1	1.000
DeFreites, Reynosa	3	35	2	0	2	1.000	BATISTA, Laguna*	31	256	13	1	32	.996
Rodriguez, Mex Tigers	5	32	1	0	3	1.000	Parra, Juarez	26	259	6	1	17	.996
Leon, Mex Tigers*	3	29	2	0	1	1.000	Pierce, Coatzacoalcos*	35	328	11	2	19	.994
Valenzuela, Reynosa	4	29	1	0	2	1.000	Espino, Saltillo	35	296	14	2	27	.994
Gonzalez, Laguna	2	18	0	0	1	1.000	Alvarez, Reynosa	30	241	10	2	22	.992
Juarez, Saltillo	2	17	1	0	1	1.000	Biagini, Mex Tigers	25	216	16	3	18	.987
Lopez, Coatzacoalcos*	1	15	0	0	0	1.000	Faudoa, Mex Tigers*	7	55	3	1	2	.983
Esqueda, Laguna	1	8	0	0	0	1.000	Contreras, Laguna	4	40	4	1	7	.978
Hernandez, Juarez	1	7	1	0	1	1.000	Osuna, Juarez	14	112	5	3	14	.975
Robles, Juarez	2	6	0	0	1	1.000	Hernandez, Reynosa	1	9	1	1	2	.909

Triples Plays—Espino, Leon.

SECOND BASEMEN

Player and Club	G.	PO.	A.	E.	DP.	Pct.	Player and Club	G.	PO.	A.	E.	DP.	Pct.
Alvaro, Reynosa	8	6	18	0	1	1.000	Deliza, Laguna	14	32	32	1	9	.985
Almeida, Reynosa	8	9	6	0	1	1.000	Rodriguez, Reynosa	31	81	85	3	20	.982
Quintero, Saltillo	2	3	6	0	0	1.000	Serna, Mex Tigers	28	63	87	3	16	.980
Alvarez, Reynosa	1	1	3	0	0	1.000	Villela, Laguna	25	67	74	4	24	.972
Mendoza, Mex Tigers	1	1	2	0	0	1.000	Gonzalez, Coatzacoalcos	21	38	60	4	8	.961
Contreras, Laguna	1	2	1	0	1	1.000	Chavez, Mex Tigers	3	11	12	1	3	.958
Hernandez, Ctz	1	0	1	0	0	1.000	Rosario, Coatzacoalcos	5	9	11	1	1	.952
NAVARRETE, Saltillo	37	85	99	1	25	.995	Cabrera, Coatzacoalcos	14	26	26	3	5	.945
Briones, Juarez	39	92	136	3	25	.987	Rivera, Mex Tigers	6	9	8	1	0	.944

Triple Play—F. Chavez.

THIRD BASEMEN

Player and Club	G.	PO.	A.	E.	DP.	Pct.	Player and Club	G.	PO.	A.	E.	DP.	Pct.
Deliza, Laguna	13	10	17	0	3	1.000	Vega, Juarez	23	16	43	3	4	.952
Esqueda, Laguna	3	2	5	0	3	1.000	Cerda, Coatzacoalcos	25	18	52	4	4	.946
Contreras, Laguna	5	2	5	0	0	1.000	Quintero, Saltillo	15	8	26	2	2	.944
DeFreites, Reynosa	1	1	1	0	0	1.000	Garzon, Coatzacoalcos	11	9	24	2	3	.943
J.G. Rodriguez, Tigers	1	0	1	0	0	1.000	Montoya, Saltillo	25	6	40	5	4	.902
Bojorquez, Laguna	24	21	42	1	2	.984	Almeida, Reynosa	5	4	5	1	0	.900
Alvarado, Reynosa	17	11	22	1	3	.971	Zamora, Mex Tigers	3	2	5	1	0	.875
RIVERA, Mex Tigers	34	28	59	3	4	.967	Hernandez, Reynosa	16	9	15	4	5	.857
Bobadilla, Juarez	17	14	37	2	4	.962							

Triple Play—Rivera.

SHORTSTOPS

Player and Club	G.	PO.	A.	E.	DP.	Pct.	Player and Club	G.	PO.	A.	E.	DP.	Pct.
F. Rivera, Mex Tigers	6	14	18	0	3	1.000	Valle, Juarez	39	62	132	7	28	.965
J.C. Rodriguez, Tigers	2	2	4	0	2	1.000	Mendoza, Mex Tigers	33	53	128	9	17	.953
Bobadilla, Juarez	1	1	1	0	0	1.000	Lara, Coatzacoalcos	30	39	95	8	8	.944
Almeida, Reynosa	2	0	2	0	0	1.000	Deliza, Laguna	9	18	30	3	6	.941
CHAVEZ, Saltillo	37	51	142	4	22	.980	Hernandez, Laguna	24	32	87	8	16	.937
Gonzalez, Coatzacoalcos	10	14	33	1	6	.979	Esqueda, Laguna	7	12	21	3	5	.917
Rivero, Reynosa	36	56	118	6	22	.967	Rodriguez, Reynosa	5	3	7	1	0	.909
Quintero, Saltillo	5	10	18	1	2	.966							

Triple Play—Quintero.

OUTFIELDERS

Player and Club	G.	PO.	A.	E.	DP.	Pct.	Player and Club	G.	PO.	A.	E.	DP.	Pct.
SILVERIO, Laguna*	34	89	4	0	3	1.000	Davila, Laguna	37	78	4	1	0	.988
Chavarria, Laguna	36	71	4	0	1	1.000	Juarez, Saltillo	31	77	1	1	1	.987
Rodriguez, Saltillo*	38	65	2	0	0	1.000	Jose Rodriguez, Mex Tig	30	70	4	1	2	.987
Collins, Coatzacoalcos	24	59	1	0	0	1.000	Collins, Saltillo*	39	62	2	1	0	.985
Rosario, Coatzacoalcos	27	47	0	0	0	1.000	Balaz, Juarez	26	41	2	1	0	.977
Felix, Laguna	27	46	0	0	0	1.000	Lopez, Reynosa	24	38	1	1	0	.975
Cruz, Coatzacoalcos	21	38	1	0	0	1.000	Suarez, Mex Tigers*	36	63	1	2	0	.970
Jaime Rodriguez, Tig	11	26	0	0	0	1.000	Alvarado, Reynosa	14	29	0	1	0	.967
Romo, Coatzacoalcos	21	17	1	0	1	1.000	Figueroa, Juarez	28	55	0	2	0	.965
Serratos, Saltillo	12	16	1	0	0	1.000	A. Lara, Mex Tigers	37	50	3	2	1	.964
A. Guzman, Reynosa	4	5	1	0	0	1.000	Gomez, Coatzacoalcos	16	42	0	2	0	.955
Contreras, Laguna	3	5	0	0	0	1.000	DeFreites, Reynosa	31	37	2	2	1	.951
Quintero, Saltillo	1	3	0	0	0	1.000	Contreras, Laguna	8	15	1	1	0	.941
Mora, Saltillo	2	1	0	0	0	1.000	Rosales, Juarez	26	39	1	3	0	.930
Rodriguez, Coatz.	1	1	0	0	0	1.000	Morales, Reynosa	11	11	2	1	0	.929
Munoz, Reynosa	35	84	4	1	1	.989	Bobadilla, Juarez	3	9	0	1	0	.900

CATCHERS

Player and Club	G.	PO.	A.	E.	DP.	PB.	Pct.	Player and Club	G.	PO.	A.	E.	DP.	PB.	Pct.
Hernandez, Coatz	22	123	11	0	2	2	1.000	F. Lara, Mex Tigers	9	41	3	1	0	0	.978
Hernandez, Juarez	12	67	12	0	1	1	1.000	Navarrete, Coatz	14	69	12	2	1	1	.976
Rosas, Reynosa	9	20	1	0	0	0	1.000	Soto, Saltillo	28	126	12	4	0	0	.972
Aguilar, Mex Tigers	2	6	3	0	0	0	1.000	Mendoza, Juarez	27	144	19	5	2	3	.970
HERAS, Mex Tig	29	121	14	1	2	4	.993	Gonzalez, Laguna	13	46	11	2	2	1	.966
A. Guzman, Reynosa	18	81	13	1	3	3	.989	Sanchez, Laguna	27	97	26	5	1	4	.961
M. Guzman, Reynosa	17	63	9	1	3	3	.986	Mendoza, Saltillo	16	56	2	4	1	1	.935

PITCHERS

Player and Club	G.	PO.	A.	E.	DP.	Pct.	Player and Club	G.	PO.	A.	E.	DP.	Pct.
ROMO, Coatzacoalcos	8	1	12	0	2	1.000	Hughes, Mex Tigers	3	1	4	0	0	1.000
VILLANUEVA, Tig*	6	3	10	0	1	1.000	Lopez, Mex Tigers	14	0	4	0	0	1.000
Acosta, Coatzacoalcos	9	2	10	0	0	1.000	Renteria, Juarez	5	1	3	0	0	1.000
Pollorena, Saltillo	6	5	7	0	0	1.000	Velazquez, Reynosa	4	2	1	0	0	1.000
Brunet, Coatzacoalcos*	7	0	11	0	0	1.000	Maytorena, Laguna	5	0	3	0	0	1.000
Camper, Saltillo	11	1	9	0	0	1.000	Castillejos, Mex Tigers	7	0	2	0	0	1.000
Burke, Mex Tigers	6	3	7	0	1	1.000	Delfin, Coatzacoalcos	7	0	2	0	0	1.000
Arratia, Laguna	6	4	6	0	0	1.000	Segui, Reynosa	6	1	1	0	0	1.000
Sauceda, Mex Tigers	17	3	6	0	0	1.000	Vazquez, Reynosa	5	0	2	0	1	1.000
M. Solis, Saltillo	8	3	5	0	0	1.000	Dimas, Juarez	4	1	1	0	0	1.000
Pulido, Reynosa*	7	1	7	0	0	1.000	Uresti, Coatzacoalcos	4	0	2	0	0	1.000
Aguilar, Laguna	5	1	6	0	0	1.000	Mauleon, Saltillo	5	0	1	0	0	1.000
Martinez, Laguna	8	3	3	0	0	1.000	Williams, Mex Tigers*	1	1	0	0	0	1.000
Higueras, Juarez*	8	2	4	0	0	1.000	Olguin, Juarez	1	1	0	0	0	1.000
Quintero, Laguna	9	1	4	0	0	1.000	Enriquez, Juarez	7	1	0	0	0	1.000
Valdez, Laguna	8	1	4	0	1	1.000	Paul, Juarez*	8	4	13	1	0	.944
Angel Ruiz, Mex Tigers..	7	2	3	0	0	1.000	Barojas, Reynosa	7	5	12	1	2	.944
Zaldivar, Mex Tigers*	7	0	5	0	0	1.000	G. Solis, Saltillo	7	4	10	1	0	.933
Gutierrez, Juarez	4	1	4	0	0	1.000	Menendez, Saltillo	10	2	10	1	0	.923

PITCHERS—Continued

Player and Club	G.	PO.	A.	E.	DP.	Pct.	Player and Club	G.	PO.	A.	E.	DP.	Pct.
Garcia, Juarez	8	1	9	1	1	.909	Terlecky, Mex Tigers	3	1	5	1	0	857
Pena, Coatzacoalcos	7	2	8	1	0	.909	Torrealba, Saltillo	4	0	5	1	0	.833
Sosa, Laguna	8	2	7	1	0	.900	Arano, Reynosa	9	0	8	2	1	.800
Kekich, Juarez	8	0	15	2	1	.882	Contreras, Mex Tigers	7	1	3	1	0	.800
Hernandez, Saltillo	15	1	6	1	1	.875	Buentello, Reynosa	7	0	2	1	0	.667
Colorado, Coatzacoalcos	7	0	7	1	0	.875	Delgado, Laguna	6	0	1	1	0	.500
Salinas, Reynosa	6	2	10	2	2	.857	Antunez, Reynosa*	3	0	0	1	0	.000
Chavez, Laguna	7	2	4	1	0	.857	Barbosa, Reynosa*	2	0	0	1	0	.000

Triple Play—Hernandez.

CLUB PITCHING

Club	G.	CG.	ShO.	IP.	H.	R.	ER.	HR.	BB.	Int. BB.	HB.	SO.	WP.	ERA.
Coatzacoalcos	36	22	8	299	256	94	71	12	80	3	5	170	3	2.14
Saltillo	39	15	8	312	304	99	83	7	63	7	6	160	6	2.39
Ciudad Juarez	39	27	4	338	323	118	97	1	89	5	7	187	2	2.58
Reynosa	37	23	1	292	326	123	100	7	79	12	3	142	5	3.08
Union Laguna	36	15	5	301	279	117	104	7	124	7	4	104	10	3.11
Mexico Tigers	37	5	0	302	361	200	167	7	139	5	14	125	18	4.98

PITCHERS' RECORDS
(Leading Qualifiers for Earned-Run Average Leadership—32 or More Innings)

*Throws lefthanded.

Pitcher—Club	G.	GS.	CG.	ShO.	W.	L.	Sv.	Pct.	IP.	H.	R.	ER.	HR.	BB.	Int. BB.	HB.	SO.	WP	ERA.
Hernandez, Saltillo	15	1	0	0	3	2	9	.600	32	25	8	4	0	4	1	1	27	0	1.13
Garcia, Juarez	8	8	7	1	6	0	0	1.000	75	59	14	10	0	11	1	4	47	0	1.20
Aguilar, Laguna	5	5	4	3	4	0	0	1.000	37	24	5	5	0	17	0	1	14	0	1.22
Romo, Coatzacoalcos	8	8	5	2	5	3	0	.625	59	40	12	8	1	15	1	1	47	1	1.22
Brunet, Coatzacoalcos*	7	7	5	1	3	3	0	.500	60	37	11	9	3	12	0	0	39	0	1.35
Camper, Saltillo	11	9	3	0	8	1	0	.889	57	48	15	11	0	16	0	0	30	0	1.74
M. Solis, Saltillo	8	7	5	2	7	1	0	.875	56	56	12	11	0	9	0	3	22	1	1.77
Menendez, Saltillo	10	9	3	2	6	1	0	.857	63	61	13	13	3	13	0	0	28	1	1.86
Sauceda, Mex Tigers	17	1	0	0	1	1	3	.500	37	32	10	9	1	9	1	2	15	3	2.19
Kekich, Juarez	8	8	7	0	3	4	0	.429	65	67	23	16	0	23	0	1	35	1	2.22

G—Sauceda, 17; GS—Acosta, Camper, Menendez, 9; CG—R. Garcia, Kekich, Paul, 7; ShO—Aguilar, Pena, 3; W—Camper, 8; L—Arano, 6; Sv—Hernandez, 9; Pct.—R. Garcia, 1.000; IP—R. Garcia, 75; H—Arano, 73; R—Arano, 33; ER—Zaldivar, 30; HR—Acosta, 5; BB—Zaldivar, 35; IBB—G. Solis, 4; HB—Burke, R. Garcia, 4; SO—G. Garcia, Romo, 47; WP—Burke, 5.

(All Pitchers—Listed Alphabetically)

Pitcher—Club	G.	GS.	CG.	ShO.	W.	L.	Sv.	Pct.	IP.	H.	R.	ER.	HR.	BB.	Int. BB.	HB.	SO.	WP	ERA.
Acosta, Coatzacoalcos	9	5	0	0	3	5	0	.375	61	62	25	22	5	17	0	2	27	1	3.25
Aguilar, Laguna	5	5	4	3	4	0	0	1.000	37	24	5	5	0	17	0	1	14	0	1.22
Antunez, Reynosa*	3	0	0	0	0	0	0	.000	2	6	3	3	0	3	0	0	1	0	13.50
Arano, Reynosa	9	8	6	0	2	6	1	.250	49	73	33	24	2	11	1	0	21	1	4.41
Arratia, Laguna	6	6	3	0	1	4	0	.200	44	45	17	17	2	12	1	0	8	1	3.48
Barbosa, Reynosa*	2	0	0	0	0	0	0	.000	3	6	4	4	0	3	0	0	5	0	12.00
Barojas, Reynosa	7	7	4	0	3	4	0	.429	53	52	20	18	1	15	2	0	30	3	3.06
Brunet, Coatzacoalcos*	7	7	5	1	3	3	0	.500	60	37	11	9	3	12	0	0	39	0	1.35
Buentello, Reynosa	7	0	0	0	0	1	0	.000	9	8	2	1	0	7	3	1	1	0	1.00
Burke, Mex Tigers	6	6	0	0	1	4	0	.200	35	41	24	20	0	15	0	4	7	5	5.14
Camper, Saltillo	11	9	3	0	8	1	0	.889	57	48	15	11	0	16	0	0	30	0	1.74
Carranza, Coatzacoalcos*	5	0	0	0	1	0	0	1.000	9	8	2	2	1	6	0	1	5	0	2.00
Castillejos, Mex Tigers	7	3	0	0	1	1	0	.500	28	39	25	20	1	9	0	2	9	1	6.43
Chavez, Laguna	7	5	0	0	1	2	0	.333	30	34	14	12	0	12	0	1	15	1	3.60
Colorado, Coatzacoalcos	7	5	4	0	2	3	1	.400	38	38	14	11	1	8	1	0	14	0	2.61
Contreras, Mex Tigers	7	0	0	0	0	0	0	.000	28	30	14	10	0	13	0	1	8	1	3.21
Delfin, Coatzacoalcos	7	0	0	0	1	1	0	.500	10	9	5	1	0	4	1	0	7	1	0.90
Delgado, Laguna	6	0	0	0	3	0	0	1.000	18	11	5	4	0	11	3	0	9	0	2.00
Dimas, Juarez	4	0	0	0	1	1	0	.500	6	9	3	3	0	3	0	0	1	0	4.50
Elizalde, Laguna	1	0	0	0	0	0	0	.000	1	2	3	3	0	1	0	0	0	1	27.00
Enriquez, Juarez	7	0	0	0	1	0	1	1.000	17	23	14	12	1	6	1	1	4	0	6.35
Garcia, Laguna	1	0	0	0	0	0	0	.000	0	1	0	0	0	0	0	0	0	0	0.00
Garcia, Juarez	8	8	7	1	6	0	0	1.000	75	59	14	10	0	11	1	4	47	0	1.20
Gutierrez, Juarez	4	3	1	0	0	3	0	.000	25	24	8	7	0	4	0	0	16	0	2.52
Hernandez, Saltillo	15	1	0	0	3	2	9	.600	32	25	8	4	0	4	1	1	27	0	1.13
Higueras, Juarez*	8	8	4	1	2	5	0	.286	49	44	22	20	0	17	0	0	29	0	3.67
Hughes, Mex Tigers	3	3	1	0	0	3	0	.000	23	25	18	12	1	11	1	2	20	2	4.70
Kekich, Juarez	8	8	7	0	3	4	0	.429	65	67	23	16	0	23	0	1	35	1	2.22
Leyva, Coatzacoalcos	1	0	0	0	0	0	0	.000	2	0	0	0	0	0	0	0	0	0	0.00
Lopez, Mex Tigers	14	0	0	0	1	3	4	.250	23	32	13	11	1	13	0	0	16	1	4.30
Martinez, Laguna	8	6	3	0	5	1	0	.000	33	38	21	17	2	11	1	0	6	0	4.64

Pitcher–Club	G.	GS.	CG.	ShO.	W.	L.	Sv.	Pct.	IP.	H.	R.	ER.	HR.	BB.	Int. BB.	HB.	SO.	WP.	ERA.
Maytorena, Laguna.........	5	1	0	0	1	2	0	.333	16	18	7	4	0	4	0	0	4	0	2.25
Mauleon, Saltillo.............	5	1	0	0	0	1	0	.000	13	22	7	7	2	0	0	0	6	0	4.85
Menendez, Saltillo............	10	9	3	2	6	1	0	.857	63	61	13	13	3	13	0	0	28	1	1.86
Nieblas, Juarez.................	1	0	0	0	0	0	0	.000	1	1	2	1	0	0	0	0	0	0	9.00
Olguin, Juarez..................	1	1	0	0	0	1	0	.000	7	6	3	3	0	4	0	0	6	0	3.86
Paul, Juarez*...................	8	8	7	1	7	1	0	.875	68	65	20	17	0	8	0	0	41	0	2.25
Pena, Coatzacoalcos	7	7	3	3	4	3	0	.571	51	46	16	11	1	16	0	1	23	0	1.94
Pollorena, Saltillo	6	6	4	1	2	2	0	.500	46	41	16	14	1	8	2	1	31	2	2.74
Pulido, Reynosa*	7	6	2	1	3	4	0	.429	47	59	18	12	2	13	2	0	19	0	2.30
Quijada, Coatzacoalcos ...	1	0	0	0	0	0	0	.000	2	2	0	0	0	0	0	0	0	0	0.00
Quintero, Laguna	9	4	2	1	2	2	0	.500	40	36	15	13	1	20	0	0	8	2	2.93
Renteria, Juarez...............	5	3	1	1	2	0	0	1.000	23	22	8	7	0	13	3	1	8	1	2.74
Romo, Coatzacoalcos	8	8	5	2	5	3	0	.625	59	40	12	8	1	15	1	1	47	1	1.22
Ruiz, Mex Tigers..............	7	6	0	0	1	5	0	.167	21	38	28	21	1	11	0	2	8	2	9.00
Salinas, Reynosa..............	6	6	4	0	3	2	0	.600	37	39	14	13	2	5	0	0	13	0	3.16
Sanchez, Juarez	1	0	0	0	0	0	0	.000	3	3	1	1	0	0	0	0	0	0	4.50
Sauceda, Mex Tigers	17	1	0	0	1	1	3	.500	37	32	10	9	1	9	1	2	15	3	2.19
Segui, Reynosa	6	6	5	0	1	4	0	.200	46	45	17	13	0	6	1	0	31	1	2.54
G. Solis, Saltillo..............	7	5	0	0	2	2	0	.500	32	40	23	19	1	7	4	1	7	2	5.34
M. Solis, Saltillo..............	8	7	5	2	7	1	0	.875	56	56	12	11	0	9	0	3	22	1	1.77
Sosa, Laguna....................	8	8	3	1	4	2	0	.667	55	42	23	22	2	28	0	1	31	2	3.60
Terlecky, Mex Tigers	3	3	2	0	2	1	0	.667	20	21	7	7	1	3	0	0	8	1	3.15
Thomas, Mex Tigers.........	1	1	0	0	0	1	0	.000	4	8	7	7	0	1	0	0	2	0	15.75
Torrealba, Saltillo............	4	1	0	0	0	1	0	.000	13	9	4	3	0	5	0	0	9	0	2.08
Uresti, Coatzacoalcos.......	4	0	0	0	0	0	0	.000	7	12	9	7	0	2	0	0	5	0	9.00
Urrea, Saltillo..................	1	0	0	0	0	0	0	.000	0	2	1	1	0	1	0	0	0	0	.....
Valdez, Laguna.................	8	1	0	0	1	1	1	.500	27	28	7	7	0	8	0	0	9	3	2.33
Vazquez, Reynosa	5	1	1	0	1	1	0	.500	22	15	4	4	0	7	1	0	8	0	1.64
Velazquez, Reynosa	4	2	1	0	1	0	0	1.000	14	10	3	3	0	5	1	0	7	0	1.93
Vidana, Reynosa...............	4	1	0	0	0	0	0	.000	10	13	5	5	0	4	1	2	6	0	4.50
Villanueva, Mex Tigers*....	6	5	2	0	1	3	0	.250	37	38	17	15	1	16	0	0	12	0	3.65
Williams, Mex Tigers*	3	2	0	0	1	1	0	.500	10	11	5	5	5	0	0	7	1	4.50
Zaldivar, Mex Tigers*	7	7	0	0	2	3	0	.400	36	46	32	30	0	35	0	1	13	1	7.50

COMBINATION SHUTOUTS–Camper-Hernandez, Menendez-Hernandez, M. Solis-Hernandez, Saltillo; Brunet-Deflin, Pena-Delfin, Coatzacoalcos.

NO-HIT GAMES–None.

New Union Forced Players Strike in Mexico

The newly formed Asocacion Nacional de Beisbol (National Association of Baseball) began a strike July 1 which halted the 20-club Mexican League. Six clubs which were not a part of the union—Juarez, Saltillo, Union Laguna, Reynosa, Coatzacoalcos and the Mexico City Tigers—played a new 40-game schedule.

The strike began after the Mexico City Reds refused to play against the Tigers and forfeited their game. Subsequently, 13 other clubs joined the Reds in the walkout and the league called off the regular season.

The players group asked for recognition by the owners and for reinstatement of second-string catcher Vicente Peralta of the Tigers, who was released by the club for his affiliation with the union. The owners refused to accede to the demands.

League rules allowed a maximum of three imported players on each established club and four on clubs added in recent expansions. Mexican-Americans, previously not counted against the imported player limit, were now included, thus causing players to form their union.

NOTES: Hector Espino set a league record for consecutive hits with 11 in a row April 22-24 in Union Laguna games against Leon. His streak was stopped by pitcher Victor Garcia. . . . Aguila outfielder Victor Manuel Felix tied a league record first established 19 years ago when he stroked four doubles in one game against Toluca. Felix was up five times and had one walk in addition to his two-baggers.

Pacific Coast League

CLASS AAA

Leading Batter
DANNY HEEP
Tucson

League President
BILL CUTLER

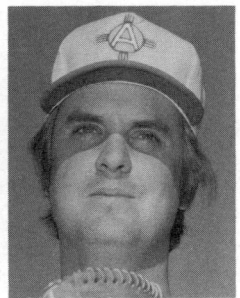

Leading Pitcher
DENNIS LEWALLYN
Albuquerque

CHAMPIONSHIP WINNERS IN PREVIOUS YEARS

1903 – Los Angeles		.630
1904 – Tacoma		.589
	Tacoma§	.571
	Los Angeles§	.571
1905 – Tacoma		.583
	Los Angeles*	.604
1906 – Portland		.657
1907 – Los Angeles		.608
1908 – Los Angeles		.585
1909 – San Francisco		.623
1910 – Portland		.567
1911 – Portland		.589
1912 – Oakland		.591
1913 – Portland		.559
1914 – Portland		.574
1915 – San Francisco		.570
1916 – Los Angeles		.601
1917 – San Francisco		.561
1918 – Vernon		.569
	Los Angeles (2nd) x	.548
1919 – Vernon		.613
1920 – Vernon		.556
1921 – Los Angeles		.574
1922 – San Francisco		.638
1923 – San Francisco		.617
1924 – Seattle		.545
1925 – San Francisco		.643
1926 – Los Angeles		.599
1927 – Oakland		.615
1928 – San Francisco*		.630
	Sacramento§§	.626
	San Francisco§§	.626
1929 – Mission		.643
	Hollywood*	.592
1930 – Los Angeles		.576
	Hollywood*	.650
1931 – Hollywood		.626
	San Francisco*	.608

1932 – Portland		.587
1933 – Los Angeles		.610
1934 – Los Angeles z		.786
	Los Angeles z	.689
1935 – Los Angeles		.648
	San Francisco*	.608
1936 – Portland‡		.549
1937 – Sacramento		.573
	San Diego (3rd)†	.545
1938 – Los Angeles		.590
	Sacramento (3rd)†	.537
1939 – Seattle		.580
	Sacramento (4th)†	.500
1940 – Seattle‡		.629
1941 – Seattle‡		.598
1942 – Sacramento		.590
	Seattle (3rd)†	.539
1943 – Los Angeles		.710
	S. Francisco (2nd)†	.574
1944 – Los Angeles		.586
	S. Francisco (3rd)†	.509
1945 – Portland		.622
	S. Francisco (4th)†	.525
1946 – San Francisco‡		.628
1947 – Los Angeles††		.567
1948 – Oakland‡		.606
1949 – Hollywood‡		.583
1950 – Oakland		.590
1951 – Seattle‡		.593
1952 – Hollywood		.606
1953 – Hollywood		.589
1954 – San Diego y		.604
1955 – Seattle		.552
1956 – Los Angeles		.637
1957 – San Francisco		.601
1958 – Phoenix		.578
1959 – Salt Lake City		.552
1960 – Spokane		.601

1961 – Tacoma		.630
1962 – San Diego		.604
1963 – Spokane		.620
	Oklahoma City a	.632
1964 – Arkansas		.609
	San Diego a	.576
1965 – Oklahoma City a		.628
	Portland	.547
1966 – Seattle a		.561
	Tulsa	.578
1967 – San Diego a		.574
	Spokane	.541
1968 – Tulsa a		.642
	Spokane	.586
1969 – Tacoma a		.589
	Eugene	.603
1970 – Spokane a		.644
	Hawaii	.671
1971 – Salt Lake City a		.534
	Tacoma	.545
1972 – Albuquerque		.622
	Eugene	.534
1973 – Tucson		.583
	Spokane a	.563
1974 – Spokane a		.549
	Albuquerque	.535
1975 – Salt Lake City		.556
	Hawaii a	.611
1976 – Salt Lake City		.625
	Hawaii a	.531
1977 – Phoenix a		.579
	Hawaii	.541
1978 – Tacoma b		.584
	Albuquerque b	.557
1979 – Albuquerque		.581
	Salt Lake City c	.541

*Won split-season playoff. †Won four-team playoff. ‡Won pennant and four-team playoff. §Tied for second-half title with Tacoma winning playoff. §§Tied for second-half title, with Sacramento winning playoff. ††Ended regular season in tie with San Francisco and won one-game playoff for pennant, then won four-club playoff. xWon playoff from first-place Vernon and awarded championship. yDefeated Hollywood in one-game playoff for pennant. zWon both halves, no playoff. aLeague was divided into Northern, Southern divisions in 1963, 1969-70-71, and Eastern, Western divisions in 1964 through 1968 and 1972 through 1977, won two-team playoff. bLeague divided into Eastern and Western divisions, Tacoma and Albuquerque declared co-champions following cancellation of four-team play-off due to continuing rain and wet grounds. cWon second-half title and defeated Hawaii in four-team playoff.

STANDINGS OF CLUBS AT CLOSE OF FIRST HALF, JUNE 21

NORTHERN DIVISION

Club	W.	L.	T.	Pct.	G.B.
Hawaii (Padres)	40	25	0	.615	......
Vancouver (Brewers)	37	30	0	.552	4
Tacoma (Indians)	39	34	0	.534	5
Portland (Pirates)	34	35	0	.493	8
Spokane (Mariners)	24	41	0	.369	16

SOUTHERN DIVISION

Club	W.	L.	T.	Pct.	G.B.
Tucson (Astros)	41	29	0	.586	......
Albuquerque (Dodgers)	39	33	0	.542	3
Salt Lake City (Angels)	34	34	0	.500	6
Ogden (A's)	30	38	0	.441	10
Phoenix (Giants)	28	47	0	.373	15½

STANDINGS OF CLUBS AT CLOSE OF SECOND HALF, SEPTEMBER 1

NORTHERN DIVISION

Club	W.	L.	T.	Pct.	G.B.
Vancouver (Brewers)	42	30	0	.583	......
Spokane (Mariners)	36	39	0	.480	7½
Hawaii (Padres)	36	40	0	.474	8
Tacoma (Indians)	35	40	0	.467	8½
Portland (Pirates)	35	41	0	.461	9

SOUTHERN DIVISION

Club	W.	L.	T.	Pct.	G.B.
Albuquerque (Dodgers)	46	29	0	.613	......
Tucson (Astros)	46	30	0	.605	½
Salt Lake City (Angels)	43	31	0	.581	2½
Ogden (A's)	29	45	0	.392	16½
Phoenix (Giants)	25	48	0	.342	20

COMPOSITE STANDING OF CLUBS AT CLOSE OF SEASON, SEPTEMBER 1

NORTHERN DIVISION

Club	Van.	Haw.	Tac.	Port.	Spo.	Tuc.	Alb.	SLC	Ogd.	Phx.	W.	L.	T.	Pct.	G.B.
Vancouver (Brewers)	....	13	13	12	9	7	6	5	7	7	79	60	0	.568	......
Hawaii (Padres)	9	....	13	16	9	6	6	4	6	7	76	65	0	.539	4
Tacoma (Indians)	9	9	....	13	12	4	7	5	4	11	74	74	0	.500	9½
Portland (Pirates)	10	5	9	....	13	8	5	4	7	8	69	76	0	.476	13
Spokane (Mariners)	12	7	10	9	....	4	5	4	4	5	60	80	0	.429	19½

SOUTHERN DIVISION

Club	Van.	Haw.	Tac.	Port.	Spo.	Tuc.	Alb.	SLC	Ogd.	Phx.	W.	L.	T.	Pct.	G.B.
Tucson (Astros)	5	6	8	4	8	....	11	10	16	19	87	59	0	.596	......
Albuquerque (Dodgers)	5	6	5	7	7	11	....	14	15	15	85	62	0	.578	2½
Salt Lake City (Angels)	4	8	7	6	8	11	8	....	14	11	77	65	0	.542	8
Ogden (A's)	1	6	8	5	7	5	7	8	....	12	59	83	0	.415	26
Phoenix (Giants)	5	5	1	4	7	3	7	11	10	....	53	95	0	.358	35

Hawaii club represented Honolulu, Hawaii.

Major league affiliations in parentheses.

Playoffs—Hawaii defeated Vancouver, two games to one; Albuquerque defeated Tucson, two games to none; Albuquerque defeated Hawaii, three games to two for championship.

Regular-Season Attendance—Albuquerque, 192,852; Hawaii, 137,077; Ogden, 76,336; Phoenix, 173,957; Portland, 129,814; Salt Lake City, 203,346; Spokane, 148,480; Tacoma, 191,738; Tucson, 207,591; Vancouver, 150,758. Total, 1,612,649. Playoffs, 21,081. No all-star game.

Managers: Albuquerque—Del Crandall; Hawaii—Doug Rader; Ogden—Jose Pagan; Phoenix—Rocky Bridges; Portland—Jim Mahoney; Salt Lake City—Larry (Moose) Stubing; Spokane—Rene Lachemann; Tacoma—Gene Dusan; Tucson—Jimmy Johnson; Vancouver—Bob Didier.

All-Star Team: 1B—Heep, Tucson; 2B—Perconte, Albuquerque; 3B—Edler, Spokane; SS—Baker, Hawaii; OF—Mitchell, Albuquerque; Rajsich, Tucson; Salazar, Portland-Hawaii; C—Pena, Portland; DH—Gray, Tacoma; P—Lewallyn, Albuquerque; Mahler, Portland; Manager—Johnson, Tucson.

(Compiled by William J. Weiss, League Statistician, San Mateo, Calif.)

CLUB BATTING

Club	G.	AB.	R.	OR.	H.	TB.	2B.	3B.	HR.	RBI.	SH.	SF.	BB.	Int. BB.	HP.	SO.	SB.	CS.	LOB.	Pct.
Tucson	146	4920	793	725	1455	2120	265	74	84	716	37	45	567	34	33	629	259	70	1112	.296
Ogden	142	4602	742	847	1320	1965	253	61	90	678	49	36	592	24	17	630	118	62	1037	.287
Salt Lake City	142	4595	736	728	1317	1961	264	52	92	678	42	53	571	35	31	711	84	44	1050	.287
Albuquerque	147	4704	787	696	1344	1864	210	53	68	689	74	64	704	32	28	580	194	88	1112	.286
Phoenix	148	4925	684	869	1388	1930	200	66	71	619	34	44	520	37	44	670	105	52	1115	.282
Vancouver	139	4444	621	587	1237	1735	199	61	59	569	68	47	493	37	26	612	196	95	945	.278
Tacoma	148	4753	725	717	1318	1934	244	48	92	656	48	37	579	42	41	757	147	78	1012	.277
Spokane	140	4458	628	691	1234	1765	226	46	71	591	49	44	482	22	33	598	252	104	955	.277
Portland	145	4653	693	613	1277	1902	259	60	82	627	43	40	564	26	25	613	134	45	1045	.274
Hawaii	141	4711	631	567	1281	1882	237	50	88	572	48	39	504	26	17	589	101	61	1057	.272

INDIVIDUAL BATTING
(Leading Qualifiers for Batting Championship—400 or More Plate Appearances)

*Bats lefthanded.   †Switch-hitter.

Player and Club	G.	AB.	R.	H.	TB.	2B.	3B.	HR.	RBI.	SH.	SF.	BB.	HP.	SO.	SB.	CS.	Pct.
Heep, Daniel, Tucson*	96	376	63	129	218	28	5	17	69	1	4	36	1	36	9	3	.343
Bryant, Derek, Ogden	119	398	71	136	189	22	11	3	68	1	2	49	1	33	7	8	.342
Gray, Gary, Tacoma	96	355	65	119	205	22	2	20	73	0	2	44	5	56	6	3	.335
Harris, John, Salt Lake City*	140	516	90	172	266	35	4	17	98	0	9	61	5	63	2	4	.333
Pena, Antonio, Portland	124	452	57	148	225	24	13	9	77	1	3	29	1	75	5	5	.327
Perconte, John, Albuquerque*	120	439	84	143	179	16	7	2	46	7	4	75	1	21	44	4	.326
Rajsich, Gary, Tucson*	134	445	94	143	256	22	14	21	99	1	5	87	6	41	12	10	.321
Mitchell, Robert, Albuquerque*	109	347	62	111	152	20	6	3	53	10	7	74	0	26	17	11	.320
Knicely, Alan, Tucson	133	468	69	149	241	18	4	22	105	4	4	61	2	76	3	0	.318
Dempsey, Patrick, Ogden	111	377	59	120	157	21	5	2	41	3	1	24	1	31	2	2	.318

Departmental Leaders: G—Littleton, 148; AB—Bourjos, 577; R—Wilson, 110; H—Harris, 172; TB—Harris, 266; 2B—Woods, 42; 3B—M. Edwards, 17; HR—Hosley, 26; RBI—Knicely, 105; SH—M. Edwards, 15; SF—Caughey, 12; BB—Cacek, 103; HP—Landis, 13; SO—Moore, 132; SB—Allen, 84; CS—Bucci, 26.

(All Players—Listed Alphabetically)

Player and Club	G.	AB.	R.	H.	TB.	2B.	3B.	HR.	RBI.	SH.	SF.	BB.	HP.	SO.	SB.	CS.	Pct.
Alcala, Santo, Portland	9	2	0	1	1	0	0	0	0	0	0	0	0	1	0	0	.500
Allen, Kim, Spokane	118	436	71	128	159	22	3	1	41	6	2	53	1	27	84	23	.294
Allietta, Robert, Tacoma	120	415	70	126	182	26	3	8	71	7	2	42	7	27	1	4	.304
Alston, Wendell, Tacoma*	69	241	43	53	81	11	4	3	29	1	2	45	1	22	36	9	.220
Ashby, Gary, Hawaii*	21	75	12	15	19	2	1	0	9	1	2	9	0	8	3	2	.200
Babitt, Mack, Ogden	93	312	49	73	97	11	5	1	25	10	1	43	1	36	12	8	.234
Baker, Charles, Hawaii	114	472	69	129	189	21	6	9	45	6	2	23	0	50	5	4	.273
Baker, Gregory, Phoenix	44	144	15	33	50	7	2	2	9	3	0	16	1	35	0	1	.229
Barrios, Jose, Phoenix	145	563	70	158	233	22	10	11	97	1	5	41	1	102	5	4	.281
Beall, Robert, Portland†	45	157	29	34	49	12	0	1	11	2	1	46	1	25	2	2	.217
Beamon, Charles, Spokane*	52	203	23	51	74	8	3	3	20	2	2	9	1	27	9	4	.251
Bertoni, Jeffery, Salt Lake C	90	296	48	85	128	19	6	4	43	4	2	34	3	51	6	5	.287
Beswick, James, Hawaii‡	128	443	67	118	160	25	4	3	54	6	4	54	1	96	10	5	.266
Bevington, Terry, Vancouver	33	86	13	29	37	5	0	1	8	2	0	14	0	7	6	4	.337
Bishop, Michael, Salt Lake City	9	32	8	11	21	1	3	1	7	1	0	7	1	4	0	0	.344
Bonilla, Juan, Tacoma	139	502	66	152	195	27	2	4	55	5	3	19	0	39	12	5	.303
Bordley, William, Phoenix	19	7	0	0	0	0	0	0	0	0	0	0	0	1	0	0	.000
Bourjos, Christopher, Phoenix	144	577	90	170	253	30	13	9	86	5	4	40	5	38	12	5	.295
Boyland, Dorian, Portland*	120	413	77	116	192	22	6	14	67	1	3	46	3	87	26	5	.281
Branch, Roy, Spokane	27	0	1	0	0	0	0	0	0	0	0	0	0	0	0	0	.000
Breining, Fred, Phoenix	54	1	0	0	0	0	0	0	0	0	0	0	0	1	0	0	.000
Brenly, Robert, Phoenix	84	287	34	74	116	9	6	7	45	0	1	24	1	51	2	0	.258
Brunansky, Thomas, S. L. City*	9	32	7	11	20	2	2	1	8	0	1	5	0	3	0	0	.344
Bryant, Derek, Ogden	119	398	71	136	189	22	11	3	68	1	2	49	1	33	7	8	.342
Bucci, Michael, Tacoma	123	413	63	123	151	18	2	2	48	11	6	59	5	38	31	26	.299
Budaske, Mark, Ogden†	103	340	64	104	162	25	3	9	41	3	5	56	1	60	6	6	.306
Bulling, Terry, Spokane	109	323	44	90	122	14	3	4	40	1	6	54	5	37	1	1	.279
Burke, Glenn, Ogden	25	84	7	19	30	3	1	2	12	2	1	7	0	15	2	3	.226
Cacek, Craig, Portland	140	477	86	136	216	41	3	11	76	2	5	103	4	36	4	0	.285
Cage, Wayne, Tacoma*	122	409	65	126	215	26	3	19	89	0	4	54	0	98	1	2	.308
Calvert, Mark, Phoenix	10	4	0	0	0	0	0	0	0	1	0	0	0	1	0	0	.000
Castillo, Anthony, Hawaii	60	182	13	46	72	14	0	4	27	4	1	9	0	29	0	0	.253
Caughey, Wayne, Albuquerque*	120	363	52	105	126	9	3	2	59	4	12	60	0	32	16	6	.289
Champion, R. Michael, Tacoma	142	533	83	150	180	18	3	2	55	3	5	54	1	89	9	5	.281
Chiles, Richard, Portland*	39	135	12	33	44	2	0	3	19	2	3	13	1	11	1	0	.244
Clark, Robert, Salt Lake City	33	113	18	39	65	6	4	4	21	0	1	14	1	21	4	1	.345
Cliburn, Stanley, Salt Lake City*	7	24	2	3	4	1	0	0	3	0	0	3	1	3	0	0	.125
Cliburn, Stewart, Portland	17	3	0	1	1	0	0	0	0	0	0	0	0	0	0	0	.333
Coleman, Joseph, Spokane	13	2	0	0	0	0	0	0	0	0	0	0	0	0	0	0	.000
Collins, Terry, Albuquerque*	11	14	1	2	2	0	0	0	1	0	0	3	0	4	1	1	.143
Cornutt, Terry, Phoenix	14	1	1	1	2	1	0	0	0	0	0	0	0	0	0	0	1.000
Cosey, D. Ray, Ogden*	95	331	52	98	146	17	5	7	52	2	5	23	2	35	2	3	.296
Cotes, Eugenio, Portland	32	100	12	23	30	2	1	1	9	1	1	12	1	19	6	2	.230
Cox, Jeffrey, Ogden	74	274	55	79	88	7	1	0	21	5	1	55	2	24	25	8	.288
Craig, Rodney, Spokane	36	131	19	39	57	5	5	1	15	2	0	10	1	19	14	4	.298
Cripe, David, Tucson	21	71	8	15	15	0	0	0	7	0	1	13	2	5	4	2	.211
Crow, Donald, Albuquerque	83	273	27	72	90	7	4	1	23	7	1	17	1	27	1	1	.264
Dade, L. Paul, Hawaii	4	14	1	5	5	0	0	0	2	0	1	2	0	1	2	0	.357
Davalillo, Victor, Albuquerque*	36	108	13	31	46	7	1	2	19	0	0	2	0	9	1	2	.287
Davis, Michael, Ogden*	19	69	14	21	35	7	2	1	14	2	0	9	1	13	9	1	.304
deLeon, Luis, Tacoma†	27	86	7	15	21	4	1	0	4	1	0	3	1	18	2	1	.174
Dempsey, Patrick, Ogden	111	377	59	120	157	21	5	2	41	3	1	24	1	31	2	2	.318
Djakonow, Paul, Portland	3	7	1	3	4	1	0	0	0	0	0	1	0	0	0	0	.429
Dorsey, James, Salt Lake City	27	1	0	0	0	0	0	0	0	0	0	0	0	0	0	0	.000
Dyes, Andrew, Hawaii	87	317	36	69	119	10	2	12	45	2	5	20	2	64	9	6	.218

Player and Club	G.	AB.	R.	H.	TB.	2B.	3B.	HR.	RBI.	SH.	SF.	BB.	HP.	SO.	SB.	CS.	Pct.
Eaton, Craig, Salt Lake City	34	0	1	0	0	0	0	0	0	0	0	0	0	0	0	0	.000
Edler, David, Spokane	140	458	79	132	199	25	6	10	72	5	3	82	4	84	9	14	.288
Edwards, Marshall, Vancouver*	134	478	70	139	193	14	17	2	68	15	2	38	7	28	68	13	.291
Elliott, Randy, Ogden	8	28	6	12	21	3	0	2	6	0	0	3	0	2	0	0	.429
Ellis, Robert, Portland	71	216	43	64	106	20	2	6	40	1	2	47	1	38	0	1	.296
Estrada, Manuel, Spokane	76	258	32	85	101	13	0	1	31	4	0	27	0	20	7	5	.329
Evans, Barry, Hawaii	28	104	13	26	42	8	1	2	15	1	2	10	0	18	0	0	.250
Ferris, Robert, Salt Lake City	26	2	0	1	1	0	0	0	1	0	0	0	0	1	0	0	.500
Firova, Daniel, Spokane	11	28	1	2	3	1	0	0	0	2	0	4	0	9	1	0	.071
Fischlin, Michael, Tucson	131	417	65	117	164	24	7	3	49	3	3	57	6	65	30	5	.281
Flannery, Timothy, Hawaii*	47	182	27	63	82	10	3	1	16	2	4	15	2	16	8	1	.346
Fleming, John, Tucson	48	147	17	47	63	14	1	0	18	0	0	3	0	15	1	0	.320
Foley, Rick, Salt Lake City	27	0	1	0	0	0	0	0	0	0	0	0	0	0	0	0	.000
Foley, William, Vancouver	100	277	29	74	100	14	0	4	38	3	5	24	7	50	1	3	.267
Fournier, Bruce, Ogden*	96	302	46	80	103	16	2	1	34	7	1	45	1	20	2	3	.265
Galasso, Robert, Vancouver*	29	6	1	2	2	0	0	0	0	0	0	0	0	1	0	0	.333
Garrison, Marvin, Tacoma	31	70	8	15	27	4	1	2	8	0	0	8	0	25	0	3	.214
Gilbreath, Rodney, Portland	108	351	52	95	132	12	5	5	47	4	4	46	4	55	7	5	.271
Gonzalez, J. Fernando, Salt Lake C	93	367	53	114	202	28	6	16	70	2	6	28	0	27	3	4	.311
Gonzalez, Julio, Tucson	38	149	21	44	63	9	2	2	25	1	1	4	1	15	1	3	.295
Grandas, Robert, Ogden	101	311	45	86	134	14	11	4	54	1	2	41	1	37	24	4	.277
Gray, Gary, Tacoma	96	355	65	119	205	22	2	20	73	0	2	44	5	56	6	3	.335
Gross, George, Tucson	108	370	49	97	136	23	5	2	44	5	2	45	3	51	12	6	.262
Hampton, Isaac, Vancouver	60	193	34	48	76	6	2	6	33	1	1	29	0	37	8	2	.249
Hargesheimer, Alan, Phoenix	2	3	0	1	1	0	0	0	0	0	0	0	0	1	0	0	.333
Hargis, Gary, Portland	84	316	36	88	130	21	3	5	43	2	3	7	1	26	4	1	.278
Harris, John, Salt Lake City*	140	516	90	172	266	35	4	17	98	0	9	61	5	63	2	4	.333
Harris, Victor, Vancouver†	69	238	29	65	90	12	2	3	37	2	4	35	0	26	13	4	.273
Hatcher, Michael, Albuquerque	43	181	28	65	97	7	2	7	40	0	3	5	1	11	4	2	.359
Heep, Daniel, Tucson*	96	376	63	129	218	28	5	17	69	1	4	36	1	36	9	3	.343
Henderson, David, Spokane†	109	341	48	95	144	26	1	7	50	1	3	49	0	62	16	10	.279
Henderson, Michael, Vancouver†	132	407	54	124	153	17	3	2	40	11	4	49	1	30	8	14	.305
Hilton, J. David, Portland	60	229	26	59	93	14	1	6	27	2	1	17	0	20	4	4	.258
Holle, Gary, Phoenix	60	226	28	86	124	11	3	7	43	0	1	24	3	25	1	5	.381
Hosley, Timothy, Ogden	139	491	94	148	255	25	2	26	102	0	4	93	2	83	11	8	.301
Jestadt, Garry, Phoenix	2	6	0	2	2	0	0	0	1	0	1	1	0	1	0	0	.333
Jones, T. Frederick, Portland*	28	5	0	1	1	0	0	0	1	0	0	2	0	0	0	0	.200
Kearney, Robert, Phoenix	92	298	42	68	88	8	3	2	24	4	2	26	3	44	5	1	.228
Keeton, Rickey, Vancouver	20	2	0	1	1	0	0	0	1	0	0	0	0	1	0	0	.500
Knicely, Alan, Tucson	133	468	69	149	241	18	4	22	105	4	4	61	2	76	3	0	.318
Kubski, Gilbert, Salt Lake City*	123	476	92	146	198	18	5	8	54	6	3	44	0	65	14	4	.307
Kusick, Craig, Hawaii	115	371	62	113	199	29	3	17	75	2	2	95	6	59	6	4	.305
Lancellotti, Richard, Portland*	61	199	25	44	73	8	0	7	29	1	1	20	0	18	1	2	.221
Landis, Craig, Phoenix	142	476	59	134	176	15	3	7	49	3	8	68	13	66	15	6	.282
Law, Vance, Portland	96	339	59	100	148	23	5	5	54	8	1	43	4	33	9	5	.295
Lee, Terry, Vancouver*	67	191	39	58	98	11	4	7	30	2	1	12	0	36	1	0	.304
Littlejohn, Dennis, Phoenix	53	169	32	54	79	5	1	6	26	0	2	45	0	32	4	1	.320
Littleton, Larry, Tacoma	148	501	79	136	233	30	8	17	80	6	2	69	7	108	6	5	.271
Long, Robert, Portland	35	6	0	2	2	0	0	0	0	0	0	0	0	0	0	0	.333
Lubratich, Steven, Salt Lake City	139	542	83	146	198	32	4	4	60	6	3	46	7	61	7	4	.269
Macauley, John, Portland	15	46	3	6	9	1	1	0	5	2	0	1	1	10	1	0	.130
Maler, James, Spokane	130	455	60	122	181	26	3	9	59	1	9	31	4	66	11	4	.268
Mangual, Jose, Salt Lake City	122	392	64	105	191	38	3	14	68	1	5	88	1	104	22	3	.268
Martinez, Teodoro, Albuquerque	86	252	32	59	75	6	2	2	35	8	5	9	4	21	6	6	.234
Matias, John, Hawaii*	12	43	4	8	9	1	0	0	2	0	0	2	0	6	0	0	.186
McDonald, Jerry, Portland*	79	311	43	75	101	15	4	1	26	3	3	39	1	30	19	4	.241
McHenry, Vance, Spokane	116	352	40	80	98	13	1	1	35	14	3	25	3	51	15	13	.227
Mendoza, Michael, Tucson	34	1	0	0	0	0	0	0	0	0	0	0	0	1	0	0	.000
Miller, Darrell, Salt Lake City	30	101	10	30	36	2	2	0	11	3	0	3	0	25	2	1	.297
Mitchell, Robert, Hawaii*	128	504	67	132	193	16	9	9	47	9	3	34	1	28	26	17	.262
Mitchell, Robert, Albuquerque*	109	347	62	111	152	20	6	3	53	10	7	74	0	26	17	11	.320
Mize, Paul, Ogden	22	63	6	13	16	1	1	0	3	4	0	10	1	14	2	2	.206
Moffitt, G. Scott, Salt Lake City	111	390	52	113	140	19	1	2	49	1	6	35	3	33	6	2	.290
Moore, Kelvin, Ogden	126	461	75	130	242	21	8	25	100	0	3	36	3	132	10	2	.282
Morgan, Michael, Ogden	21	1	0	0	0	0	0	0	0	0	0	0	0	0	0	0	.000
Murray, Larry, Ogden†	13	30	5	7	12	2	0	1	3	1	0	6	0	4	1	1	.233
Murray, Richard, Phoenix	49	168	22	44	73	6	1	7	31	0	1	22	1	35	1	1	.262
Narron, Jerry, Spokane*	67	233	40	66	111	14	2	9	39	0	3	20	6	35	1	0	.283
Nastu, Philip, Phoenix*	21	21	0	4	4	0	0	0	4	0	0	0	0	6	0	0	.190
Nocciolo, Mark, Salt Lake City	57	171	19	37	50	7	3	0	17	4	0	25	2	47	0	2	.216
Nordbrook, Timothy, Vancouver	84	217	24	44	53	6	0	1	18	11	2	28	2	34	4	2	.203
Norrid, Timothy, Tacoma*	103	286	26	58	85	8	2	5	32	7	4	37	4	52	3	0	.203
Oliver, David, 42 Tac-35 Port*	77	246	32	66	89	17	0	2	22	3	3	32	0	9	1	3	.268
Oliver, Richard, Salt Lake City	102	310	44	64	73	5	2	0	27	5	4	46	3	42	2	3	.206
Oquendo, Ismael, Vancouver*	20	68	10	13	23	3	2	1	4	0	0	8	1	11	2	0	.191

Player and Club	G.	AB.	R.	H.	TB.	2B.	3B.	HR.	RBI.	SH.	SF.	BB.	HP.	SO.	SB.	CS.	Pct.
O'Rear, John, Albuquerque	99	268	39	65	87	8	1	4	41	7	5	38	1	45	6	0	.243
Ortiz, Adalberto, Portland	8	27	1	3	5	0	1	0	3	0	0	3	0	3	0	0	.111
Pagel, Karl, Tacoma*	48	163	26	43	68	9	2	4	26	0	2	25	2	47	1	0	.264
Pankovits, James, Tucson	64	213	36	53	75	8	4	2	26	4	3	21	1	32	7	2	.249
Pape, Kenneth, Spokane	30	76	7	18	21	3	0	0	10	1	1	7	0	15	0	0	.237
Parsons, Casey, 65 Phx-66 Spo*	131	476	62	134	187	19	11	4	61	0	2	56	2	58	18	12	.282
Pastors, Gregory, Hawaii	20	69	10	20	30	7	0	1	10	0	1	10	0	10	0	1	.290
Patterson, Michael, Ogden*	17	56	10	17	28	4	2	1	5	0	0	7	0	12	1	1	.304
Pebley, Edward, Spokane*	13	37	3	8	10	0	1	0	6	2	1	4	0	2	1	1	.216
Pechek, Wayne, Phoenix*	27	98	20	33	38	3	1	0	9	2	2	15	0	11	4	3	.337
Peguero, Pablo, Albuquerque	9	11	0	1	1	0	0	0	2	0	0	0	0	1	0	0	.091
Pena, Antonio, Portland	124	452	57	148	225	24	13	9	77	1	3	29	1	75	5	5	.327
Perconte, John, Albuquerque*	120	439	84	143	179	16	7	2	46	7	4	75	1	21	44	4	.326
Perkins, Broderick, Hawaii*	118	436	53	136	197	29	7	6	65	0	3	66	0	46	6	4	.312
Peters, James, Salt Lake City*	130	396	73	119	204	29	4	16	78	1	7	79	1	86	5	4	.301
Pettini, Joseph, Phoenix	85	344	52	97	127	16	4	2	32	0	3	33	1	55	15	5	.282
Pittman, Joseph, Tucson	126	490	93	154	200	23	10	1	61	7	3	54	1	75	54	13	.314
Plank, Edward, Phoenix	38	4	0	0	0	0	0	0	0	0	0	0	0	2	0	0	.000
Rajsich, Gary, Tucson*	134	445	94	143	256	22	14	21	99	1	5	87	6	41	12	10	.321
Ramirez, Milton, Ogden	122	398	44	109	156	34	2	3	57	6	8	31	0	19	0	2	.274
Rende, Salvatore, Tacoma*	58	181	27	35	60	12	2	3	23	1	1	31	3	39	0	1	.193
Rex, Michael, Phoenix	136	471	74	137	182	23	2	6	61	8	3	61	6	33	10	6	.291
Reynolds, Donald, Hawaii	113	386	63	112	166	19	4	9	50	4	3	61	1	52	8	5	.290
Rhomberg, Kevin, Tacoma	142	477	80	137	188	20	14	1	51	5	3	71	5	94	37	14	.287
Rodriguez, Michael, Ogden	57	156	22	32	46	8	0	2	21	2	1	25	1	40	1	0	.205
Roenicke, Ronald, Albuquerque†..	77	270	60	80	124	18	3	7	47	0	2	62	0	37	16	4	.296
Romero, Edgardo, Vancouver	50	172	19	47	56	7	1	0	16	5	2	16	1	15	4	6	.273
Rosario, Simon, Tucson	25	103	14	30	40	3	2	1	19	0	1	6	0	8	0	1	.291
Rowland, Michael, Phoenix	23	3	1	0	0	0	0	0	0	1	0	0	0	3	0	0	.000
Runnells, Thomas, Portland†	37	149	21	45	49	4	0	0	10	3	0	9	0	11	2	0	.302
Rush, Lawrence, Vancouver	138	483	65	131	204	21	5	14	86	2	7	42	2	101	21	4	.271
Ryan, Craig, Vancouver*	137	456	61	131	207	27	5	13	64	3	5	77	0	97	7	12	.287
Salazar, Luis, 117 Port-10 Haw	127	497	91	157	237	23	15	9	64	4	5	52	2	83	43	6	.316
Sandt, Thomas, Portland	63	181	22	42	53	6	1	1	17	1	3	28	0	23	2	1	.232
Scarbery, Randy, Salt Lake City	22	1	1	0	0	0	0	0	0	0	0	0	0	0	0	0	.000
Schaefer, Douglas, Phoenix	33	17	2	5	6	1	0	0	0	0	0	2	0	5	0	0	.294
Schuler, David, Salt Lake City	45	2	0	0	0	0	0	0	0	0	0	0	0	2	0	0	.000
Scioscia, Michael, Albuquerque*..	52	160	33	53	75	11	1	3	33	2	4	36	0	13	3	4	.331
Severns, Billy, Vancouver*	131	443	54	108	141	16	7	1	54	3	10	59	3	28	12	9	.244
Sexton, Jimmy, Tucson	113	446	81	132	165	18	6	1	33	3	2	64	1	50	55	15	.296
Shoemaker, John, Albuquerque*..	8	26	2	5	5	0	0	0	2	0	0	1	0	4	0	1	.192
Smith, Bobby, Vancouver*	119	446	79	141	185	20	9	2	29	3	2	45	1	62	29	13	.316
Smith, Steven, Hawaii	93	308	27	60	75	10	1	1	16	4	1	31	1	26	4	3	.195
Snider, Kelly, Albuquerque*	102	346	58	105	154	25	0	8	77	3	8	48	2	32	4	2	.303
Soto, Thomas, Vancouver	9	22	1	4	4	0	0	0	2	0	0	1	0	4	0	1	.182
Spencer, H. Thomas, Tucson	71	239	31	65	103	12	7	4	34	0	2	11	0	23	7	2	.272
Sprowl, Bobby, Tucson*	27	1	0	0	0	0	0	0	0	0	0	1	0	0	0	0	.000
Stember, Jeffrey, Phoenix	8	10	1	2	2	0	0	0	0	0	0	0	0	5	0	0	.200
Stewart, David, Albuquerque	34	0	1	0	0	0	0	0	0	0	0	0	0	0	0	0	.000
Stillman, Royle, 42 Ogd-26 SLC*..	68	214	35	55	71	14	1	0	28	0	3	46	0	30	3	1	.257
Stimac, Craig, Hawaii	110	423	60	126	191	22	5	11	47	4	2	15	1	58	9	7	.298
Stokke, Douglas, Tucson	23	78	5	20	24	4	0	0	8	2	2	2	1	7	0	0	.256
Stroughter, Stephen, Spokane*...	123	423	58	130	201	26	6	11	75	4	6	38	3	58	15	5	.307
Sularz, Guy, Phoenix	88	306	44	84	107	17	0	2	26	1	4	32	5	34	5	4	.275
Sutton, Johnny, 32 Ogd-3 Haw	35	2	0	1	2	1	0	0	2	0	0	0	0	1	0	0	.500
Sweet, Ricky, Hawaii†	99	337	42	89	134	11	3	1	35	2	4	42	1	18	4	1	.261
Thon, Richard, Salt Lake City	40	155	28	61	85	14	2	2	28	2	2	12	1	14	9	5	.394
Todd, James, Phoenix*	11	4	0	0	0	0	0	0	0	0	0	0	0	1	0	0	.000
Tucker, Michael, Phoenix	19	5	0	1	1	0	0	0	1	0	0	1	0	2	0	0	.200
Tufts, Robert, Phoenix*	38	7	0	0	0	0	0	0	0	0	0	0	0	6	0	0	.000
Tyler, Michael, Portland*	40	99	8	22	27	5	0	0	12	3	1	4	0	10	1	0	.222
Venable, W. McKinley, Phoenix*..	78	312	52	89	134	10	10	5	40	2	4	34	2	30	15	5	.285
Walton, Reginald, Spokane	91	340	50	103	162	17	6	10	57	0	4	24	4	49	16	7	.303
Weiss, Gary, Albuquerque*	130	423	71	123	173	16	8	6	51	9	1	80	7	67	13	9	.291
Westmoreland, Claude, Alb	122	381	60	90	150	17	2	13	60	1	6	61	2	120	15	13	.236
Weston, Alfred, Spokane	38	112	12	15	20	2	0	1	9	4	1	16	0	6	6	2	.134
Wheelock, Gary, Spokane	18	4	0	1	1	0	0	0	0	0	0	0	0	1	0	0	.250
White, Myron, Albuquerque*	110	358	52	93	146	25	5	6	52	6	4	42	2	76	11	5	.260
Whitmer, Daniel, Salt Lake City..	59	183	24	41	56	6	0	3	27	5	3	24	2	46	0	1	.224
Wiedenbauer, Thomas, Tucson	108	384	45	98	115	15	1	0	33	4	2	25	2	47	28	5	.255
Wilkes, Gregory, Hawaii	25	3	0	1	1	0	0	0	0	1	0	0	0	0	0	0	.333
Williams, Michael, Phoenix†	39	4	0	1	1	0	0	0	1	0	0	0	0	3	0	0	.250
Wilson, Michael, Albuquerque	131	478	110	139	180	19	2	47	10	2	90	7	33	46	16	.291
Woods, Gary, Tucson	140	517	102	162	240	42	6	8	86	2	10	74	6	79	36	3	.313
Yost, Edgar, Vancouver	80	259	32	80	114	20	4	2	41	5	2	15	1	40	12	4	.309

The following pitchers had no plate appearances primarily through the use of designated hitters, listed alphabetically by club, games in parentheses:

ALBUQUERQUE—Bain, Paul† (3); Beckwith, T. Joseph* (7); Hannahs, Gerald* (28); Harrison, Douglas (30); Keefe, Kevin (28); Lewallyn, Dennis (55); Nipp, Mark (17); Patterson, David (44); Power, Ted (26); Rondon, Gilbert (4); Sanchez, Luis (5); Swiacki, William (22).

HAWAII—Armstrong, Michael (42); Beare, Gary (14); Blair, Dennis (23); Boone, Daniel* (8); Eichelberger, Juan (11); Kuhaulua, Fred* (26); Mustad, Eric (32); Stablein, George (23); Tellmann, Thomas (24); Yandle, John (31).

OGDEN—Abraham, Brian* (23); Beard, David* (16); Camacho, Ernie (33); Enyart, Terry (14); Green, C. Randall (27); Hamilton, David* (15); Harris, Frank (29); King, Michael* (6); Lysander, Richard (35); Minetto, Craig* (22); Souza, K. Mark* (41); Wirth, Alan (20).

PHOENIX—Denney, William (1); Prewitt, Larry† (10); Ripley, Allen (7).

PORTLAND—Andersen, Larry (52); Arias, Juan (2); Davey, Michael (21); Farr, Steven (2); Jones, Odell (19); Lee, Mark (43–39 with Hawaii); Mahler, Michael† (25); Pentz, Eugene (20); Perez, Pascual (25); Pole, Richard (5); Rhoden, Richard (10); Warthen, Daniel† (22).

SALT LAKE CITY—Botting, Ralph* (28); Eddy, Steven (27); Overy, H. Michael (21); Perez, Carlos (26); Phillips, Charles* (11); Schrom, Kenneth (14).

SPOKANE—Anderson, Richard (49); Biercevicz, Gregory (20); Clark, Bryan* (8); Diaz, Carlos (58); Harrison, Robert* (3); Lance, Gary† (30); McGee, Ronald† (7); Parrott, Michael (4); Sarmiento, Manuel (51); Smith, David (31); Stein, W. Randolph (24); Stoddard, Robert (21); Young, Kip (4).

TACOMA—Borchers, Rickey (27); Brennan, Thomas (25); Collins, Donald (25); Cuellar, Robert (51); Glaser, G. Gordon (8); Heimer, Todd* (6); Manos, Peter (19); McCall, Larry* (22); Paxton, Michael (23); Pietroburgo, Robert† (46); Vasquez, Rafael (32); Wihtol, Alexander (36); Wilkins, Eric (17).

TUCSON—Aponte, C. Ricardo (13); Ladd, Peter (18); Miggins, Mark (9); Miscik, Dennis* (27); Niemann, Randy* (9); Pladson, Gordon (17); Roberge, Bertrand (34); Smith, Billy L. (28); Strom, Brent (24); Williams, Richard (28); Wilson, Gary (26).

VANCOUVER—Bernard, Dwight (12); Boitano, Danny (44); DiPino, Frank* (24); Flinn, John (17); Holdsworth, Frederick (20); Jones, Douglas (8); LaPoint, David* (17); Mitchell, Paul (8); Mueller, Willard (57); Olsen, Richard (17); Quinones, Rene (43); Quiros, Gustavo (20); Rautzhan, Clarence (36); Reed, Steven (5); Replogle, Andrew (4).

GRAND SLAM HOME RUNS—R. D. Mitchell 2; C. Baker, Cage, Edler, Garrison, Gray, Hargis, J. Harris, Hosley, Knicely, Kusick, R. V. Mitchell, O'Rear, Peters, Rajsich, Roenicke, Ryan, Venable, Whitmer, 1 each.

AWARDED FIRST BASE ON INTERFERENCE—White 6 (Castillo 2, Dempsey, Littlejohn, Norrid, Whitmer); Bertoni 2 (Littlejohn 2); J. Harris (Dempsey, Westmoreland); R. V. Mitchell 2 (Knicely, Norrid); Bryant (Norrid); V. Harris (Littlejohn); Knicley (Crow); Sweet (Knicely).

GAME-WINNING RBIs

ALBUQUERQUE (74)—Hatcher 9, Perconte 8, Mitchell 7, Scioscia 6, White 6, Caughey 5, Roenicke 5, Snider 5, Wilson 5, Weiss 4, Crow 3, Martinez 3, O'Rear 3, Westmoreland 3, Davalillo 1, Shoemaker 1.

HAWAII (63)—Kusick 13, Perkins 7, Reynolds 7, Castillo 5, Dyes 5, Stimac 5, Baker 4, Beswick 3, Flannery 3, Evans 2, Mitchell 2, Smith 2, Sweet 2, Dade 1, Matias 1, Salazar 1.

OGDEN (46)—Moore 9, Hosley 8, Bryant 7, Ramirez 5, Cosey 4, Dempsey 4, Rodriguez 3, Fournier 2, Babitt 1, Cox 1, Davis 1, Grandas 1.

PHOENIX (40)—Barrios 6, Rex 5, Venable 5, Brenly 3, Landis 3, Murray 3, Parsons 3, Bourjos 2, Holle 2, Kearney 2, Pechek 2, Pettini 2, Littlejohn 1, Sularz 1.

PORTLAND (56)—Pena 10, Salazar 6, Boyland 5, Ellis 5, Cacek 4, Hargis 4, Law 4, Hilton 3, Lancellotti 3, McDonald 3, Gilbreath 2, Oliver 2, Beall 1, Cotes 1, Macauley 1, Ortiz 1, Sandt 1.

SALT LAKE CITY (64)—Gonzalez 11, Harris 11, Moffitt 8, Mangual 7, Peters 7, Whitmer 5, Bertoni 3, Kubski 3, Lubratich 3, Nocciolo 2, Brunansky 1, Miller 1, Oliver 1, Stillman 1.

SPOKANE (41)—Edler 7, Henderson 5, Maler 5, Stroughter 5, Estrada 4, Allen 3, McHenry 3, Parsons 3, Beamon 1, Bulling 1, Craig 1, Narron 1, Pape 1, Walton 1.

TACOMA (61)—Littleton 12, Gray 9, Bucci 8, Cage 7, Allietta 6, Champion 6, Rhomberg 5, Norrid 3, Bonilla 2, Alston 1, Pagel 1, Rende 1.

TUCSON (63)—Woods 10, Rajsich 9, Heep 8, Knicely 8, Fischlin 7, Pittman 6, Pankovits 5, Sexton 2, Spencer 2, Wiedenbauer 2, Cripe 1, Fleming 1, Gonzalez 1, Gross 1, Rosario 1, Stokke 1.

VANCOUVER (56)—Ryan 12, Rush 10, Edwards 6, Harris 4, Henderson 4, Smith 4, Hampton 3, Lee 3, Foley 2, Nordbrook 2, Yost 2, Bevington 1, Keeton 1, Romero 1, Severns 1.

CLUB FIELDING

Club	G.	PO.	A.	E.	DP.	PB.	Pct.	Club	G.	PO.	A.	E.	DP.	PB.	Pct.
Portland	145	3585	1549	133	109	16	.975	Tacoma	148	3715	1644	171	160	11	.969
Hawaii	141	3652	1638	140	125	11	.974	Phoenix	148	3724	1668	183	153	9	.967
Albuquerque	147	3709	1593	157	150	20	.971	Tucson	146	3734	1778	192	159	17	.966
Vancouver	139	3546	1610	153	143	22	.971	Spokane	143	3460	1519	182	139	15	.965
Salt Lake City	142	3531	1496	160	122	16	.969	Ogden	142	3475	1584	224	110	10	.958

Triple Plays—Tucson 2.

INDIVIDUAL FIELDING

FIRST BASEMEN

*Throws lefthanded.

Player and Club	G.	PO.	A.	E.	DP.	Pct.
SNIDER, Albuquerque*	100	828	56	2	93	.998
J. Harris, Salt Lake C*	134	1145	82	4	104	.997
O'Rear, Albuquerque	40	291	24	1	30	.997
Rende, Tacoma*	43	390	28	2	44	.995
Perkins, Hawaii*	115	1168	79	8	93	.994
Ryan, Vancouver	134	1191	110	10	111	.992
Beall, Portland*	14	119	10	1	9	.992
Holle, Phoenix*	14	115	4	1	13	.992
Heep, Tucson*	82	810	53	8	70	.991
Gray, Tacoma	48	405	24	4	40	.991
Boyland, Portland*	105	885	58	10	75	.990
Moore, Ogden*	122	1045	76	12	92	.989
Gross, Tucson	64	658	31	8	76	.989
Barrios, Phoenix	122	1072	76	14	105	.988
Cacek, Portland	25	228	18	3	9	.988
Maler, Spokane	126	1056	122	16	117	.987
Cage, Tacoma*	40	319	23	5	32	.986
Ashby, Hawaii*	17	155	13	3	16	.982
Budaska, Ogden*	18	148	9	4	9	.975
Alston, Tacoma	16	123	8	4	18	.970
Westmoreland, Alb	18	155	3	5	16	.969

Triple Plays—Heep, Gross.

(Fewer Than Ten Games)

Player and Club	G.	PO.	A.	E.	DP.	Pct.
Strougther, Spokane	5	51	3	0	3	1.000
Beamon, Spokane*	5	40	8	0	4	1.000
Hosley, Ogden	3	32	2	0	2	1.000
Sweet, Hawaii	4	30	3	0	2	1.000
Narron, Spokane	3	27	5	0	2	1.000
Severns, Vancouver*	3	27	1	0	4	1.000
Jestadt, Phoenix	2	20	1	0	3	1.000
Sandt, Portland	3	19	2	0	2	1.000
Pittman, Tucson	2	17	1	0	1	1.000
Landis, Phoenix	2	16	1	0	0	1.000
Rush, Vancouver	4	14	1	0	2	1.000
Stimac, Hawaii	2	11	0	0	0	1.000
Matias, Hawaii*	1	7	0	0	1	1.000
Yost, Vancouver	1	7	0	0	1	1.000
Bevington, Vancouver	1	6	1	0	1	1.000
Norrid, Tacoma	2	4	0	0	1	1.000
Ellis, Portland	1	4	0	0	0	1.000
Dempsey, Ogden	1	3	0	0	0	1.000
Stillman, Ogden*	1	3	0	0	0	1.000
Oquendo, Vancouver*	1	2	0	0	1	1.000
Parsons, Phx-Spo	8	57	8	1	3	.985
Moffitt, Salt Lake City	6	58	0	1	2	.983
Pagel, Tacoma*	8	79	14	2	15	.979
Littlejohn, Phoenix	4	29	2	1	8	.969
R. Murray, Phoenix	3	23	5	1	6	.966
Kusick, Hawaii	3	22	0	1	2	.957
Bishop, Salt Lake City	2	18	1	1	1	.950
Roenicke, Albuquerque*	2	16	0	1	0	.941
Hampton, Vancouver	3	13	1	1	1	.933

SECOND BASEMEN

Player and Club	G.	PO.	A.	E.	DP.	Pct.
D. Oliver, Tac-Port	41	65	105	0	23	1.000
O'Rear, Albuquerque	15	38	42	0	16	1.000
Gilbreath, Portland	11	18	30	0	7	1.000
Pittman, Tucson	12	19	27	0	6	1.000
Martinez, Albuquerque	14	21	23	0	5	1.000
Hargis, Portland	15	30	35	1	7	.985
M. Henderson, Van.	119	263	326	11	77	.982
Bonilla, Tacoma	138	366	422	15	110	.981
Estrada, Spokane	66	147	214	7	54	.981
Evans, Hawaii	26	57	95	3	17	.981
Flannery, Hawaii	47	102	146	5	32	.980
Sularz, Phoenix	20	37	59	2	12	.980
Ramirez, Ogden	15	30	19	1	8	.980
Rex, Phoenix	135	316	342	15	92	.978
Perconte, Albuquerque	116	291	320	15	85	.976
Allen, Spokane	41	81	117	5	25	.975
J. F. Gonzalez, SLC	32	73	82	4	20	.975
Cox, Ogden	53	122	137	7	24	.974
S. Smith, Hawaii	61	133	169	9	32	.971
R. Oliver, Salt Lake City	96	222	256	15	59	.970
Sexton, Tucson	96	213	338	20	76	.965
McDonald, Portland	77	171	189	13	44	.965
Thon, Salt Lake City	23	49	57	4	8	.964
Pankovits, Tucson	41	103	108	8	26	.963
Babitt, Ogden	86	209	244	19	50	.960
Weston, Spokane	37	70	98	7	23	.960
Sandt, Portland	17	29	43	3	4	.960
Lee, Vancouver	39	57	73	7	22	.949
R. D. Mitchell, Hawaii	10	22	30	3	7	.945

Triple Play—Sexton.

(Fewer Than Ten Games)

Player and Club	G.	PO.	A.	E.	DP.	Pct.
Soto, Vancouver	3	6	9	0	0	1.000
Nordbrook, Vancouver	2	8	6	0	2	1.000
Pape, Spokane	3	6	4	0	2	1.000
deLeon, Tacoma	3	4	5	0	2	1.000
Romero, Vancouver	1	2	4	0	1	1.000
Lubratich, Salt Lake C	1	3	1	0	1	1.000
Runnells, Phoenix	1	2	1	0	1	1.000
M. Wilson, Albuquerque	1	2	2	0	0	1.000
Pebley, Spokane	1	0	1	0	0	1.000
Shoemaker, Alb	8	16	26	1	7	.977
Stokke, Tucson	4	10	21	1	2	.969
T. Collins, Albuquerque	4	7	14	2	3	.913
Champion, Tacoma	4	10	7	2	2	.895

THIRD BASEMEN

Player and Club	G.	PO.	A.	E.	DP.	Pct.
Lee, Vancouver	11	7	17	0	0	1.000
Sandt, Portland	14	8	24	1	0	.970
Caughey, Albuquerque	74	43	137	6	20	.968
Stimac, Hawaii	86	78	181	11	13	.959
Gilbreath, Portland	63	41	115	7	4	.957
Rodriguez, Ogden	48	21	91	5	8	.957
Sularz, Phoenix	50	46	104	7	9	.955
Lubratich, Salt Lake C	96	71	154	11	15	.953
R. D. Mitchell, Hawaii	15	12	27	2	3	.951
Hilton, Portland	59	44	107	9	6	.944
RUSH, Vancouver	133	110	332	27	39	.942
Martinez, Albuquerque	26	12	46	4	5	.935
J. C. Gonzalez, Tucson	38	22	105	9	9	.934
Westmoreland, Alb	12	6	19	2	1	.926
Edler, Spokane	129	82	189	22	15	.925
Brenly, Phoenix	40	39	70	9	11	.924
Sweet, Hawaii	25	23	50	6	4	.924
Champion, Tacoma	130	102	273	32	33	.921

THIRD BASEMEN—Continued

Player and Club	G.	PO.	A.	E.	DP.	Pct.	Player and Club	G.	PO.	A.	E.	DP.	Pct.
S. Smith, Hawaii	18	11	34	4	2	.918	Fournier, Ogden	93	70	181	29	20	.896
Barrios, Phoenix	22	18	58	7	4	.916	Moffitt, Salt Lake City	12	6	15	3	1	.875
Pittman, Tucson	78	46	163	21	24	.909	O'Rear, Albuquerque	34	19	57	11	7	.874
Allen, Spokane	18	12	38	5	2	.909	R. Murray, Phoenix	46	30	82	18	7	.862
Cripe, Tucson	21	17	42	6	6	.908	Hatcher, Albuquerque	16	13	27	7	0	.851
Bucci, Tacoma	18	12	44	6	5	.903	Ramirez, Ogden	16	9	30	7	1	.848
J. F. Gonzalez, SLC	39	18	64	9	6	.901							

(Fewer Than Ten Games)

Player and Club	G.	PO.	A.	E.	DP.	Pct.	Player and Club	G.	PO.	A.	E.	DP.	Pct.
Soto, Vancouver	3	3	6	0	1	1.000	Grandas, Ogden	7	2	10	1	0	.923
Norrid, Tacoma	2	2	3	0	1	1.000	Cox, Ogden	4	3	10	2	1	.867
Nocciolo, Salt Lake City	2	0	4	0	0	1.000	Stokke, Tucson	7	3	15	3	3	.857
Pape, Spokane	4	1	2	0	0	1.000	Hargis, Portland	6	2	8	2	1	.833
Djakonow, Portland	2	0	2	0	0	1.000	Tyler, Portland	3	1	3	1	0	.800
Estrada, Spokane	1	1	1	0	0	1.000	Ellis, Portland	2	1	3	1	0	.800
T. Collins, Albuquerque	2	0	1	0	0	1.000	Ryan, Vancouver	1	0	4	2	1	.667
Bertoni, Salt Lake City	1	0	1	0	0	1.000	Dade, Hawaii	1	0	1	1	0	.500
Pankovits, Portland	7	4	16	1	2	.952							

SHORTSTOPS

Player and Club	G.	PO.	A.	E.	DP.	Pct.	Player and Club	G.	PO.	A.	E.	DP.	Pct.
Hargis, Portland	12	10	28	0	5	1.000	Mize, Ogden	21	32	74	6	9	.946
Runnells, Phoenix	36	49	119	4	21	.977	Macauley, Portland	15	22	48	4	10	.946
Pastors, Hawaii	19	31	52	2	10	.976	McHenry, Spokane	116	192	323	30	82	.945
Romero, Vancouver	49	70	149	6	28	.973	Martinez, Albuquerque	29	31	72	6	23	.945
Lubratich, SLC	46	66	145	6	30	.972	Edler, Spokane	16	19	31	3	6	.943
Law, Portland	96	169	295	14	52	.971	Fischlin, Tucson	127	200	437	40	88	.941
M. Henderson, Van.	28	35	61	3	14	.970	Pettini, Phoenix	85	157	284	29	50	.938
Sularz, Phoenix	24	46	71	4	16	.967	Bertoni, SLC	86	150	264	30	44	.932
Gilbreath, Portland	25	39	74	4	15	.966	Cox, Ogden	21	27	70	8	11	.924
C. BAKER, Hawaii	112	170	378	20	73	.965	Ramirez, Ogden	95	128	265	33	42	.923
Bucci, Tacoma	104	147	311	21	66	.956	Thon, Salt Lake City	16	32	50	8	9	.911
Weiss, Albuquerque	111	182	378	26	66	.956	deLeon, Tacoma	25	36	83	12	16	.908
S. Smith, Hawaii	13	20	44	3	7	.955	D. Oliver, Tacoma	31	33	75	13	12	.893
Sexton, Tucson	17	24	52	4	8	.950	Pebley, Spokane	12	21	37	8	5	.879
Nordbrook, Vancouver	80	80	213	16	48	.948	Triple Plays—Fischlin 2.						

(Fewer Than Ten Games)

Player and Club	G.	PO.	A.	E.	DP.	Pct.	Player and Club	G.	PO.	A.	E.	DP.	Pct.
Stokke, Tucson	8	9	19	0	5	1.000	Caughey, Albuquerque	5	4	10	2	2	.875
Sandt, Portland	3	5	10	0	0	1.000	Fournier, Ogden	7	5	13	3	1	.857
Pankovits, Tucson	2	3	4	0	1	1.000	Babitt, Ogden	7	5	22	5	4	.844
Grandas, Ogden	2	1	1	0	0	1.000	Brenly, Phoenix	5	2	14	4	0	.800
Estrada, Spokane	7	7	20	3	5	.900	Hampton, Vancouver	2	4	4	2	0	.800
O'Rear, Albuquerque	6	4	11	2	1	.882	Djakonow, Portland	1	1	2	1	0	.750
Rodriguez, Ogden	4	6	8	2	1	.875							

OUTFIELDERS

Player and Club	G.	PO.	A.	E.	DP.	Pct.	Player and Club	G.	PO.	A.	E.	DP.	Pct.
R.D. Mitchell, Hawaii	96	165	12	0	3	1.000	Craig, Spokane	28	58	1	1	0	.983
Chiles, Portland*	39	72	5	0	3	1.000	R. Clark, Salt Lake C	26	57	2	1	0	.983
Gilbreath, Portland	11	26	1	0	0	1.000	Kubski, Salt Lake City	117	309	13	6	4	.982
M. Patterson, Ogden	15	25	1	0	0	1.000	Woods, Tucson	133	264	13	5	1	.982
Garrison, Tacoma	12	16	1	0	0	1.000	Rhomberg, Tacoma	137	242	14	5	4	.981
Rosario, Tucson	11	13	1	0	0	1.000	Peters, Salt Lake C*	121	280	19	6	4	.980
LITTLETON, Tacoma	147	362	6	1	2	.997	Strougther, Spokane	83	143	4	3	3	.980
Rajsich, Tucson*	127	205	10	1	2	.995	Venable, Phoenix	75	179	7	4	1	.979
R.V. Mitchell, Alb*	105	292	11	2	4	.993	Alston, Tacoma	49	85	3	2	0	.978
B.G. Smith, Vancouver*	77	124	4	1	1	.992	Beswick, Hawaii	127	285	14	7	3	.977
Hargis, Portland	53	114	5	1	0	.992	Severns, Vancouver*	119	206	5	5	3	.977
Ellis, Portland	65	105	6	1	0	.991	White, Albuquerque	102	195	7	5	0	.976
M. Wilson, Alb	95	226	6	3	1	.987	Reynolds, Hawaii	107	154	8	4	1	.976
Allen, Spokane	47	74	4	1	1	.987	Salazar, Port-Haw	127	304	11	8	2	.975
Parsons, Phx-Spo	68	129	7	2	1	.986	V. Harris, Van	67	151	3	4	1	.975
Spencer, Tucson	49	72	0	1	0	.986	D. Henderson, Spo	107	258	9	7	0	.974
Hampton, Vancouver	43	64	5	1	1	.986	Cosey, Ogden*	78	144	4	4	0	.974
Cage, Tacoma*	41	67	1	1	0	.986	Mangual, Salt Lake C	66	106	3	3	1	.973
Lancellotti, Port*	36	62	3	1	2	.985	Davis, Ogden*	17	34	2	1	0	.973
Landis, Phoenix	138	293	10	5	5	.984	Edwards, Vancouver	130	234	13	7	0	.972
Pagel, Tacoma*	32	59	4	1	0	.984	G. Baker, Phoenix	44	99	3	3	0	.971

OUTFIELDERS—Continued

Player and Club	G.	PO.	A.	E.	DP.	Pct.	Player and Club	G.	PO.	A.	E.	DP.	Pct.
Stillman, Ogd-SLC*	41	59	4	2	0	.969	Grandas, Ogden	91	183	5	9	0	.954
Wiedenbauer, Tucson	107	264	6	9	1	.968	Bourjos, Phoenix	143	249	15	13	4	.953
Moffitt, Salt Lake C	90	164	11	6	1	.967	Pittman, Tucson	28	39	2	2	0	.953
Dyes, Hawaii	83	149	10	6	0	.964	Caughey, Albuquerque	18	18	2	1	0	.952
Budaska, Ogden*	79	144	10	6	1	.963	Burke, Ogden	23	35	0	2	0	.946
Bryant, Ogden	102	172	4	7	0	.962	L. Murray, Ogden	11	16	1	1	0	.944
Roenicke, Alb*	73	151	9	7	1	.958	Cotes, Portland	31	46	2	3	0	.941
Pechek, Phoenix*	27	44	1	2	0	.957	Cacek, Portland	83	88	4	7	1	.929
Hatcher, Albuquerque	24	39	5	2	2	.957	Westmoreland, Alb	31	48	4	4	0	.929
Norris, Tacoma	50	82	4	4	1	.956	Beamon, Spokane*	28	42	4	4	0	.920
Walton, Spokane	79	125	2	6	0	.955							

(Fewer Than Ten Games)

Player and Club	G.	PO.	A.	E.	DP.	Pct.	Player and Club	G.	PO.	A.	E.	DP.	Pct.
Brunansky, SLC	9	28	1	0	0	1.000	Holle, Phoenix*	2	1	0	0	0	1.000
Gray, Tacoma	5	10	0	0	0	1.000	Long, Portland	2	1	0	0	0	1.000
Barrios, Phoenix	4	9	0	0	0	1.000	Stimac, Hawaii	2	1	0	0	0	1.000
Elliott, Ogden	4	8	1	0	0	1.000	Babitt, Ogden	1	1	0	0	0	1.000
Schaefer, Phoenix	3	6	0	0	0	1.000	Fischlin, Tucson	1	1	0	0	0	1.000
Davalillo, Albuquerque*	6	5	0	0	0	1.000	Hosley, Ogden	1	1	0	0	0	1.000
Pape, Spokane	6	5	0	0	0	1.000	Wilkes, Hawaii	1	1	0	0	0	1.000
Beall, Portland*	3	5	0	0	0	1.000	Martinez, Albuquerque	7	12	0	1	0	.923
Yost, Vancouver	5	4	0	0	0	1.000	Ashby, Hawaii*	4	6	1	2	0	.778
Dade, Hawaii	3	4	0	0	0	1.000	Bucci, Tacoma ᶜ	4	3	0	1	0	.750
Brenly, Phoenix	2	2	0	0	0	1.000	T. Collins, Alb	2	1	0	1	0	.500
T.F. Jones, Port*	2	2	0	0	0	1.000	M. Henderson, Van	1	1	0	1	0	.500
Nastu, Phoenix*	1	2	0	0	0	1.000	Gross, Tucson	1	0	0	2	0	.000
Oquendo, Vancouver*	3	1	0	0	0	1.000							

CATCHERS

Player and Club	G.	PO.	A.	E.	DP.	PB.	Pct.	Player and Club	G.	PO.	A.	E.	DP.	PB.	Pct.
Fleming, Tucson	39	138	13	1	1	1	.993	Narron, Spokane	44	196	14	6	2	3	.972
Stimac, Hawaii	19	84	12	1	1	2	.990	Pena, Portland	116	639	85	23	6	9	.969
ALLIETTA, Tac	113	484	52	6	4	6	.989	Hosley, Ogden	43	199	20	7	1	6	.969
Crow, Albuquerque	74	312	58	6	1	4	.984	Bevington, Van	27	110	13	4	3	5	.969
Firova, Spokane	10	39	9	1	1	1	.980	Nocciolo, SLC	49	186	21	7	1	6	.967
Littlejohn, Phx	41	192	40	5	8	3	.979	Dempsey, Ogden	104	489	78	20	6	4	.966
Scioscia, Alb	40	207	19	5	3	5	.978	Whitmer, SLC	59	240	42	10	3	5	.966
Yost, Vancouver	71	305	34	8	3	9	.977	Bulling, Spokane	91	450	59	19	4	10	.964
Tyler, Portland	24	116	13	3	3	4	.977	Knicely, Tucson	124	511	93	23	8	16	.963
W. Foley, Van	67	292	39	8	2	8	.976	Brenly, Phoenix	39	140	26	7	1	2	.960
Kearney, Phoenix	75	358	68	11	7	4	.975	Miller, SLC	29	113	18	6	2	3	.956
Sweet, Hawaii	70	323	47	10	3	4	.974	Norrid, Tacoma	44	164	24	10	2	5	.949
Castillo, Hawaii	59	321	28	10	5	5	.972	Westmoreland, Alb	39	156	25	11	1	9	.943

(Fewer Than Ten Games)

Player and Club	G.	PO.	A.	E.	DP.	PB.	Pct.	Player and Club	G.	PO.	A.	E.	DP.	PB.	Pct.
Ortiz, Portland	8	42	10	0	1	1	1.000	Coleman, Spokane	1	3	0	0	0	0	1.000
Stan Cliburn, SLC	7	28	5	0	1	1	1.000	Hampton, Van	2	2	0	0	0	0	1.000
Peguero, Alb	8	23	3	0	1	2	1.000	Ellis, Portland	2	1	2	1	0	2	.750
Bishop, SLC	5	20	0	0	0	1	1.000	Walton, Spokane	1	0	0	0	0	1	.000

PITCHERS

Player and Club	G.	PO.	A.	E.	DP.	Pct.	Player and Club	G.	PO.	A.	E.	DP.	Pct.
ROWLAND, Phoenix	23	6	34	0	0	1.000	Sarmiento, Spokane	51	4	9	0	0	1.000
Morgan, Ogden	20	11	25	0	0	1.000	Camacho, Ogden	33	5	7	0	1	1.000
Stewart Cliburn, Port	17	10	22	0	1	1.000	Armstrong, Hawaii	42	3	9	0	0	1.000
Strom, Tucson*	24	5	25	0	2	1.000	Manos, Tacoma	19	7	4	0	0	1.000
R. Foley, Salt Lake City	25	11	18	0	0	1.000	Nipp, Albuquerque	17	4	7	0	0	1.000
Lewallyn, Albuquerque	55	6	22	0	6	1.000	Minetto, Ogden*	22	3	8	0	0	1.000
Pentz, Portland	20	8	15	0	1	1.000	Long, Portland	33	6	4	0	0	1.000
Plank, Phoenix	38	8	12	0	0	1.000	Tucker, Phoenix	18	3	7	0	2	1.000
O. Jones, Portland	19	7	11	0	1	1.000	Calvert, Phoenix	10	3	6	0	0	1.000
C. Perez, Salt Lake City	26	5	12	0	0	1.000	DiPino, Vancouver*	24	1	7	0	0	1.000
Beard, Ogden	16	5	12	0	1	1.000	Overy, Salt Lake City	21	1	6	0	1	1.000
Schuler, Salt Lake City*	45	3	13	0	1	1.000	Schrom, Salt Lake City	14	1	6	0	1	1.000
D. Patterson, Alb.	44	2	14	0	2	1.000	Flinn, Vancouver	17	3	3	0	0	1.000
Rhoden, Portland	10	2	14	0	1	1.000	Bernard, Vancouver	12	4	1	0	1	1.000
Miscik, Tucson*	27	3	12	0	2	1.000	Phillips, Salt Lake City*	11	2	2	0	1	1.000
Todd, Phoenix	11	6	7	0	0	1.000	Coleman, Spokane*	12	2	1	0	0	1.000

PITCHERS—Continued

Player and Club	G.	PO.	A.	E.	DP.	Pct.
Scarbery, Salt Lake City	20	0	3	0	0	1.000
P. Perez, Portland	24	11	34	1	2	.978
Tufts, Phoenix*	38	9	30	1	2	.975
Green, Ogden	27	9	29	1	2	.974
Stablein, Hawaii	23	9	26	1	2	.972
Lance, Spokane	30	12	21	1	0	.971
Sprowl, Tucson*	26	3	29	1	1	.970
McCall, Tacoma	22	18	12	1	1	.968
Rautzhan, Vancouver*	36	9	21	1	4	.968
Wheelock, Spokane	17	12	16	1	2	.966
T. F. Jones, Portland*	26	6	22	1	0	.966
D. Collins, Tacoma*	25	3	24	1	0	.964
B. L. Smith, Tucson	28	4	22	1	0	.963
Brennan, Tacoma	24	15	35	2	5	.962
Abraham, Ogden*	23	6	19	1	0	.962
M. Williams, Phoenix	39	5	19	1	1	.960
Botting, Salt Lake City*	28	4	19	1	3	.958
D. Smith, Spokane	31	8	14	1	1	.957
Borchers, Tacoma*	27	6	16	1	0	.957
Eaton, Salt Lake City	32	17	26	2	3	.956
Paxton, Tucson	23	15	27	2	2	.955
Eichelberger, Hawaii	11	6	15	1	3	.955
Swiacki, Albuquerque	22	5	16	1	0	.955
Tellmann, Hawaii	24	16	24	2	0	.952
Diaz, Spokane*	58	10	10	1	1	.952
Mahler, Portland*	25	7	30	2	0	.949
Kuhaulua, Hawaii*	26	4	33	2	3	.949
Warthen, Portland*	22	2	16	1	0	.947
LaPoint, Vancouver*	17	9	8	1	0	.944
Mueller, Vancouver	57	9	24	2	3	.943
Blair, Hawaii	23	10	22	2	3	.941
Anderson, Spokane	49	9	7	1	0	.941
Ferris, Salt Lake City	26	12	32	3	0	.936
Bordley, Phoenix*	19	3	22	2	1	.926
R. Williams, Tucson	28	12	36	4	4	.923
Wilkes, Hawaii	25	9	15	2	1	.923
Pietroburgo, Tacoma*	46	4	8	1	1	.923
Roberge, Tucson	34	4	8	1	0	.923
Cuellar, Tacoma	51	4	19	2	2	.920
Yandle, Hawaii*	31	3	20	2	0	.920
Power, Albuquerque	26	2	21	2	1	.920
Andersen, Portland	52	7	26	3	0	.917
Hannahs, Albuquerque*	28	6	27	3	2	.917
Olsen, Vancouver	17	9	13	2	1	.917
Biercevicz, Spokane	20	11	21	3	1	.914
Quiros, Vancouver	20	6	15	2	1	.913
G. Wilson, Tucson	26	11	30	4	3	.911
Wirth, Ogden	20	4	16	2	0	.909
Davey, Portland*	21	3	7	1	0	.909
Branch, Spokane	26	12	27	4	3	.907
F. Harris, Ogden	29	16	13	3	1	.906
Souza, Ogden*	41	4	25	3	0	.906
Breining, Phoenix	54	6	13	2	0	.905
D. Harrison, Alb.	30	5	23	3	0	.903
Pladson, Tucson	17	20	16	4	1	.900
Stewart, Albuquerque	31	8	19	3	1	.900
Keefe, Albuquerque	28	6	12	2	0	.900
Hamilton, Ogden*	15	1	8	1	0	.900
Loe, Haw-Port	43	5	12	2	0	.895
Wilkins, Tacoma	17	5	12	2	1	.895
Keeton, Vancouver	20	23	19	5	0	.894
Eddy, Salt Lake City	27	13	26	5	0	.886
Holdsworth, Vancouver	28	8	15	3	1	.885
Schaefer, Phoenix	28	14	16	4	1	.882
Mustad, Hawaii	30	5	10	2	0	.882
Beare, Hawaii	14	6	14	3	1	.870
Lysander, Ogden	35	5	15	3	1	.870
Wihtol, Tacoma	36	0	18	3	0	.857
Galasso, Vancouver	25	6	6	2	0	.857
Mendoza, Tucson	34	1	5	1	0	.857
Prewitt, Phoenix	10	1	5	1	0	.857
Boitano, Vancouver	44	4	13	3	2	.850
Nastu, Phoenix*	16	3	13	3	2	.842
Stoddard, Spokane	21	8	17	5	1	.833
Sutton, Ogden-Hawaii	35	5	18	5	2	.821
Stein, Spokane	24	14	21	8	1	.814
Aponte, Tucson	13	2	2	1	0	.800
Quinones, Vancouver	43	6	14	6	3	.769
Ladd, Tucson	18	1	2	1	0	.750
Dorsey, Salt Lake City	27	6	12	7	2	.720
Vasquez, Tacoma	32	4	14	7	0	.720
Cornutt, Phoenix	14	1	4	3	0	.625
Enyart, Ogden*	14	0	3	3	1	.500

Triple Play—Strom.

(Fewer Than Ten Games)

Player and Club	G.	PO.	A.	E.	DP.	Pct.
D. Jones, Vancouver	8	4	13	0	3	1.000
Niemann, Tucson*	9	2	15	0	1	1.000
B. Clark, Spokane*	8	3	13	0	0	1.000
Glaser, Tacoma	8	4	7	0	2	1.000
Stember, Phoenix	8	3	6	0	2	1.000
Ripley, Phoenix	7	5	4	0	1	1.000
Boone, Hawaii*	8	2	7	0	1	1.000
Heimer, Tacoma*	6	2	4	0	0	1.000
Farr, Portland	2	1	2	0	0	1.000
King, Ogden*	6	0	2	0	0	1.000
Davalillo, Albuquerque*	3	2	0	0	1	1.000
Sanchez, Albuquerque	5	1	0	0	0	1.000
Kusick, Hawaii	1	1	0	0	0	1.000
Arias, Portland	2	0	1	0	0	1.000
McGee, Spokane	7	7	5	1	0	.923
P. Mitchell, Vancouver*	8	5	5	1	0	.909
Parrott, Spokane	4	4	4	1	1	.889
Young, Spokane	4	3	3	1	0	.857
Miggins, Tucson*	9	1	5	1	0	.857
Beckwith, Albuquerque	7	1	2	1	2	.750
Pole, Portland	5	1	2	1	0	.750
Hargesheimer, Phoenix	2	1	2	1	0	.750
Alcala, Portland	9	1	1	1	0	.667
Reed, Vancouver	5	0	0	1	0	.000

The following players do not have any recorded accepted chances at the positions indicated; therefore, are not listed in the fielding averages for those particular positions: Bertoni, 2b; Bryant, 2b; Castillo, 3b; Cuellar, of; Denney, p; Edler, 1b; J. F. Gonzalez, of; V. Harris, 2b; R. Harrison, p; Heep, of; Nocciolo, of; Nordbrook, 3b; O'Rear, p; Ramirez, p; Replogle, p; Rodriguez, p; Rondon, p; Rush, of; Sandt, of; Scioscia, 3b; Tucker, 3b.

CLUB PITCHING

Club	G.	CG.	ShO.	Sv.	IP.	H.	R.	ER.	HR.	BB.	Int. BB.	HB.	SO.	WP.	Bk.	ERA.
Hawaii	141	31	13	31	1217	1169	567	479	69	476	11	37	666	68	8	3.54
Vancouver	139	20	11	33	1182	1142	587	493	61	592	39	27	672	71	8	3.75
Portland	145	38	8	24	1195	1228	613	529	73	469	23	35	733	54	4	3.98
Albuquerque	147	30	3	40	1236	1277	696	596	91	666	38	29	663	70	7	4.34
Tucson	146	47	7	32	1245	1432	725	600	69	523	26	45	612	45	6	4.34
Tacoma	148	27	6	32	1238	1405	717	602	90	509	47	32	598	65	4	4.38
Spokane	140	19	5	26	1153	1284	691	582	64	510	35	32	642	57	6	4.54
Salt Lake City	142	37	5	27	1177	1355	728	637	90	546	15	23	550	56	4	4.87
Ogden	142	26	1	19	1158	1405	847	697	102	584	46	19	638	61	12	5.42
Phoenix	148	31	5	16	1241	1474	869	760	88	700	38	36	616	88	5	5.51

PITCHERS' RECORDS
(Leading Qualifiers for Earned-Run Average Leadership—118 or More Innings)

*Throws lefthanded.

Pitcher–Club	G	GS	CG	ShO	W	L	Sv	Pct.	IP	H	R	ER	HR	BB	Int.BB	HB	SO	WP	ERA
Lewallyn, Albuquerque....	55	1	1	1	15	2	24	.882	127	110	33	30	5	40	7	5	58	1	2.13
Brennan, Tacoma	24	22	2	1	9	3	0	.750	152	167	48	42	4	29	5	7	77	2	2.49
Mahler, Portland*	25	24	14	3	14	8	0	.636	173	143	67	51	7	85	3	4	140	4	2.65
Holdsworth, Vancouver	20	15	3	1	5	5	0	.500	118	99	42	35	5	47	4	0	65	6	2.67
Hannahs, Albuquerque*..	28	28	6	1	15	9	0	.625	189	178	82	67	11	108	3	1	93	2	3.19
Tellmann, Hawaii	24	24	5	4	13	5	0	.722	170	155	74	61	1	58	1	4	83	3	3.23
Keeton, Vancouver	20	19	6	1	10	4	0	.714	136	131	58	50	8	54	4	2	51	5	3.31
G. Wilson, Tucson	26	26	7	1	12	9	0	.571	192	216	94	74	9	76	1	4	78	6	3.47
Pladson, Tucson	17	17	9	1	10	5	0	.667	128	121	62	51	4	44	2	1	66	3	3.59
Stewart, Albuquerque	31	29	11	0	15	10	1	.600	202	189	94	83	13	89	6	0	125	13	3.70

Departmental Leaders: G—Diaz, 58; GS—Stewart, 29; CG—Mahler, 14; ShO—Tellmann, 4; W—Botting, Hannahs, Lewallyn, Stewart, 15; L—Breining, 13; Sv—Lewallyn, 24; Pct.—Lewallyn, .882; IP—Stewart, 202; H—R. Williams, 240; R—R. Williams, 123; ER—Botting, 107; HR—Botting, 26; BB—Harrison, 123; IBB—Lysander, 13; HB—Branch, Plank, 9; SO—Mahler, 140; WP—Harrison, 19.

(All Pitchers—Listed Alphabetically)

Pitcher–Club	G	GS	CG	ShO	W	L	Sv	Pct.	IP	H	R	ER	HR	BB	Int.BB	HB	SO	WP	ERA
Abraham, Ogden*	23	21	4	0	2	8	1	.200	122	166	85	78	10	54	2	0	69	9	5.75
Alcala, Portland	9	7	0	0	2	4	0	.333	36	40	23	19	2	16	0	1	18	1	4.75
Andersen, Portland	52	0	0	0	5	7	15	.417	93	78	24	18	3	16	5	1	65	5	1.74
Anderson, Spokane	49	0	0	0	6	0	3	1.000	80	70	35	29	2	49	2	3	65	7	3.26
Aponte, Tucson	13	1	0	0	1	1	0	.500	28	27	16	12	1	17	2	0	11	1	3.86
Arias, Portland	2	0	0	0	0	0	0	.000	6	3	2	2	0	2	0	0	3	1	3.00
Armstrong, Hawaii	42	0	0	0	4	4	16	.500	74	48	18	16	3	26	2	4	67	3	1.95
Bain, Albuquerque	3	0	0	0	0	1	0	.000	7	9	7	7	1	1	3	0	9	0	9.00
Beard, Ogden	16	16	4	0	7	8	0	.467	97	110	76	69	15	44	1	1	70	6	6.40
Beare, Hawaii	14	12	3	2	5	3	0	.625	79	73	32	28	7	21	0	1	35	2	3.19
Beckwith, Albuquerque ...	7	0	0	0	2	1	1	.667	14	15	8	4	1	5	2	0	12	2	2.57
Bernard, Vancouver	12	0	0	0	0	0	0	.000	19	34	16	15	1	14	1	1	5	4	7.11
Biercevicz, Spokane........	20	20	7	1	10	9	0	.526	126	145	77	69	12	40	2	4	60	3	4.93
Blair, Hawaii	23	21	6	1	6	12	0	.333	146	137	78	69	8	52	0	7	82	8	4.25
Boitano, Vancouver	44	0	0	0	6	4	12	.600	54	52	31	26	4	34	4	1	33	4	4.33
Boone, Hawaii*	8	0	0	0	2	0	0	1.000	14	12	2	2	1	3	1	0	7	0	1.29
Borchers, Tacoma*	27	13	3	0	4	5	0	.444	104	133	67	54	3	56	5	3	44	8	4.67
Bordley, Phoenix*	19	18	4	0	4	8	0	.333	111	129	70	66	9	54	1	4	66	11	5.35
Botting, Salt Lake City* ..	28	27	8	0	15	8	0	.652	173	202	117	107	26	86	0	2	87	5	5.57
Branch, Spokane	26	24	6	0	3	12	0	.200	152	190	106	93	8	68	3	9	73	7	5.51
Breining, Phoenix	54	0	0	0	6	13	9	.316	100	106	57	46	4	56	4	3	84	13	4.14
Brennan, Tacoma	24	22	2	1	9	3	0	.750	152	167	48	42	4	29	5	7	77	2	2.49
Calvert, Phoenix	10	10	2	0	2	4	0	.333	54	63	43	38	5	34	1	0	26	6	6.33
Camacho, Ogden	33	1	0	0	5	3	6	.625	64	60	29	28	1	26	1	2	58	3	3.94
B. Clark, Spokane*	8	8	0	0	2	4	0	.286	41	43	35	24	2	37	2	2	19	7	5.27
Stewart Cliburn, Port......	17	12	1	0	2	9	0	.182	82	97	56	50	1	39	2	1	44	3	5.49
Coleman, Spokane	12	0	0	0	1	0	0	1.000	22	15	6	4	0	4	0	0	13	2	1.64
D. Collins, Tacoma*	25	25	6	2	10	8	0	.556	158	175	99	77	9	78	2	4	74	9	4.39
Cornutt, Phoenix	14	0	0	0	1	3	0	.250	33	35	29	28	2	12	2	1	16	2	7.64
Cuellar, Tacoma	51	0	0	0	8	3	15	.727	90	82	37	33	5	35	9	1	55	3	3.30
Davalillo, Albuquerque* .	3	0	0	0	0	0	0	.000	7	10	4	4	0	5	0	0	0	1	5.14
Davey, Portland*	21	1	0	0	1	0	0	1.000	52	71	31	29	9	11	2	2	21	2	5.02
Denney, Phoenix	1	1	0	0	0	0	0	.000	1	0	0	0	0	0	0	0	0	0	0.00
Diaz, Spokane*	58	0	0	0	3	5	9	.375	64	72	31	28	6	27	4	0	51	1	3.94
DiPino, Vancouver*	24	1	0	0	3	1	2	.750	28	24	10	7	1	14	0	0	32	1	2.25
Dorsey, Salt Lake City	27	27	8	2	14	7	0	.667	173	177	89	77	7	93	2	4	109	6	4.01
Eaton, Salt Lake City	32	13	1	0	4	12	5	.250	130	150	77	70	10	43	6	3	41	3	4.85
Eddy, Salt Lake City	27	27	6	2	8	12	0	.400	158	194	117	97	14	71	0	3	45	8	5.53
Eichelberger, Hawaii	11	11	2	0	7	3	0	.700	77	56	35	30	5	49	0	2	62	15	3.51
Enyart, Ogden*	14	6	0	0	2	2	0	.500	47	61	38	33	6	19	2	2	21	4	6.32
Farr, Portland	2	2	0	0	0	1	0	.000	7	10	9	9	2	2	0	0	0	1	10.29
Ferris, Salt Lake City	26	26	7	0	14	8	0	.636	167	196	89	76	7	68	4	4	88	5	4.10
Flinn, Vancouver	17	5	0	0	2	3	5	.400	43	46	24	21	1	15	1	4	28	1	4.40
R. Foley, Salt Lake City...	25	19	5	1	7	8	0	.467	144	176	95	80	9	55	1	2	61	5	5.00
Galasso, Vancouver	8	7	2	0	4	3	0	.571	50	72	39	36	3	22	2	2	44	1	6.48
Glaser, Tacoma	27	27	5	1	6	12	0	.333	138	190	114	90	15	43	3	0	56	3	5.87
Green, Ogden	15	1	0	0	0	0	0	.000	31	32	19	12	1	25				3	3.48
Hamilton, Ogden*	28	28	6	1	15	9	0	.625	189	178	82	67	11	108	3	1	93	2	3.19
Hannahs, Albuquerque*..	28	28	6	1	15	9	0	.625	189	178	82	67	11	108	3	1	93	2	3.19
Hargesheimer, Phoenix ..	2	2	1	1	0	1	0	.500	17	18	8	8	2	13	0	0	13	1	4.24
F. Harris, Ogden.........	29	17	6	0	5	11	0	.313	129	166	98	82	15	42	3	3	81	2	5.72
D. Harrison, Albuquerque	30	28	6	0	9	12	0	.429	161	160	99	86	12	123	3	7	81	19	4.81

Pitcher—Club	G	GS	CG	ShO	W	L	Sv	Pct.	IP	H	R	ER	HR	BB	Int. BB	HB	SO	WP	ERA
R. Harrison, Spokane	3	0	0	0	0	0	0	.000	4	6	3	1	0	0	0	0	2	0	2.25
Heimer, Tacoma*	6	3	0	0	1	2	0	.333	14	24	18	17	2	14	0	1	1	1	10.93
Holdsworth, Vancouver	20	15	3	1	5	5	0	.500	118	99	42	35	5	47	4	0	65	6	2.67
D. Jones, Vancouver	8	8	1	1	3	2	0	.600	53	52	19	19	2	15	2	1	28	0	3.23
O. Jones, Portland*	19	17	3	1	6	7	0	.462	98	96	49	45	4	46	0	2	89	12	4.13
T. F. Jones, Portland	26	25	5	0	10	11	0	.476	160	199	91	83	13	34	2	3	70	0	4.67
Keefe, Albuquerque	28	13	1	0	4	5	4	.444	122	118	80	62	7	60	7	3	66	0	4.57
Keeton, Vancouver	20	19	6	1	10	4	0	.714	136	131	58	50	8	54	4	2	51	5	3.31
King, Ogden*	6	5	0	0	0	4	0	.000	21	21	27	18	0	30	2	0	11	6	7.71
Kuhaulua, Hawaii*	26	26	8	3	10	10	0	.500	174	191	85	73	12	73	1	2	74	10	3.78
Kusick, Hawaii	1	0	0	0	0	0	0	.000	1	1	1	1	0	3	0	1	0	1	9.00
Ladd, Tucson	18	0	0	0	0	1	2	.333	21	18	7	6	1	4	0	0	24	5	2.57
Lance, Spokane	30	9	1	0	3	5	1	.375	78	101	63	51	7	41	3	4	49	4	5.88
LaPoint, Vancouver	17	17	1	0	7	4	0	.636	93	71	48	29	4	45	0	0	64	9	2.81
Lee, Haw-Port	43	1	0	0	6	6	15	.500	66	70	33	30	3	30	4	3	43	2	4.09
Lewallyn, Albuquerque	55	1	1	1	15	2	24	.882	127	110	33	30	5	40	7	5	58	1	2.13
Long, Portland	33	3	0	0	4	4	5	.500	93	86	48	44	5	41	3	8	54	2	4.26
Lysander, Ogden	35	1	0	0	4	5	1	.444	81	103	55	46	1	43	13	1	46	5	5.11
Mahler, Portland*	25	24	14	3	14	8	0	.636	173	143	67	51	7	85	3	4	140	8	2.65
Manos, Tacoma	19	0	0	0	0	4	2	.000	42	57	34	25	7	17	3	1	24	3	5.36
McCall, Tacoma	22	19	7	1	8	7	1	.500	126	142	82	73	13	26	1	1	44	3	5.21
McGee, Spokane	7	7	0	0	0	4	0	.000	34	43	28	25	1	22	1	1	9	2	6.62
Mendoza, Tucson	34	0	0	0	1	3	6	.250	59	83	50	45	4	33	3	3	47	7	6.86
Miggins, Tucson*	9	0	0	0	1	2	1	.333	9	10	8	5	0	7	0	0	3	1	5.00
Minetto, Ogden*	22	2	0	0	3	2	3	.600	41	50	34	21	8	24	1	0	35	2	4.61
Miscik, Tucson*	27	4	0	0	5	1	0	.833	60	72	46	36	3	40	3	3	32	4	5.40
P. Mitchell, Vancouver	8	8	3	0	5	3	0	.625	49	53	27	18	6	10	1	1	29	0	3.31
Morgan, Ogden	20	20	3	0	6	9	0	.400	115	135	79	69	7	77	4	3	46	7	5.40
Mueller, Vancouver	57	2	0	0	8	6	4	.571	112	105	60	50	6	48	8	3	43	6	4.02
Mustad, Hawaii	30	2	0	0	4	4	0	.500	74	57	26	19	3	34	1	6	53	6	2.31
Nastu, Phoenix*	16	16	5	0	4	8	0	.333	93	105	63	56	6	63	2	1	39	8	5.42
Niemann, Tucson*	9	8	3	1	4	1	1	.800	52	64	36	28	3	26	1	1	26	3	4.85
Nipp, Albuquerque	17	2	0	0	1	1	0	.500	54	79	42	40	4	41	1	0	28	3	6.67
Olsen, Vancouver	17	17	2	2	7	6	0	.538	91	93	46	40	6	42	2	2	64	4	3.96
O'Rear, Albuquerque	1	0	0	0	0	0	0	.000	1	0	0	0	0	0	0	0	0	0	0.00
Overy, Salt Lake City	21	1	0	0	0	1	0	.000	33	39	23	18	1	25	1	0	13	2	4.91
Parrott, Spokane	4	4	1	0	1	2	0	.333	22	13	3	2	0	9	0	0	13	2	0.82
D. Patterson, Albuquer	44	0	0	0	5	3	9	.625	73	88	46	39	4	25	4	3	39	5	4.81
Paxton, Tacoma	23	21	5	0	6	10	0	.375	135	155	82	75	10	53	3	3	46	4	5.00
Pentz, Portland	20	15	3	1	3	8	2	.273	102	109	67	59	4	52	0	3	58	8	5.21
C. Perez, Salt Lake City	26	1	0	0	1	2	3	.333	52	60	40	35	4	40	0	0	33	4	6.06
P. Perez, Portland	24	24	9	0	12	10	0	.545	160	172	76	72	10	48	1	4	105	3	4.05
Phillips, Salt Lake City*	11	0	0	0	0	1	0	.000	19	28	14	11	1	10	0	0	7	2	5.21
Pietroburgo, Tacoma*	46	0	0	0	5	5	3	.500	70	75	32	28	4	26	7	0	61	6	3.60
Pladson, Tucson	17	17	9	1	10	5	0	.667	128	121	62	51	4	44	2	1	66	3	3.59
Plank, Phoenix	38	9	1	0	3	8	2	.273	103	88	79	7	87	7	9	45	15	6.90
Pole, Portland	5	2	1	0	0	2	0	.000	17	19	14	10	1	13	0	2	6	1	5.29
Power, Albuquerque	26	26	3	0	13	7	0	.650	155	160	93	78	12	95	1	0	113	14	4.53
Prewitt, Phoenix	10	6	0	0	1	6	0	.143	29	32	38	31	2	38	3	1	20	6	9.62
Quinones, Vancouver	43	11	1	0	7	7	5	.500	103	92	47	40	4	90	5	1	74	8	3.50
Quiros, Vancouver	20	15	0	0	9	4	1	.692	106	115	55	52	8	38	3	7	52	7	4.42
Ramirez, Ogden	1	0	0	0	0	0	0	.000	2	3	4	2	1	2	0	0	0	0	9.00
Rautzhan, Vancouver*	36	11	0	0	2	4	1	.333	78	76	53	47	1	71	3	0	32	12	5.42
Reed, Vancouver	5	0	0	0	1	0	0	.000	8	12	8	7	0	6	1	1	2	1	7.88
Replogle, Vancouver	4	0	0	0	1	0	0	1.000	5	10	9	6	1	5	0	0	3	0	10.80
Rhoden, Portland	10	10	3	2	6	3	0	.667	52	47	22	17	4	21	0	1	24	3	2.94
Ripley, Phoenix	7	7	0	0	5	0	0	1.000	44	48	18	12	4	15	1	2	19	0	2.45
Roberge, Tucson	34	0	0	0	5	3	15	.625	49	44	28	26	2	28	4	1	47	1	4.78
Rodriguez, Ogden	1	0	0	0	0	0	0	.000	3	1	1	0	0	0	0	0	0	0	9.00
Rondon, Albuquerque	4	0	0	0	1	1	0	1.000	10	18	13	10	2	5	0	2	7	1	9.00
Rowland, Phoenix	23	21	5	0	5	11	0	.313	140	180	81	71	10	28	6	2	58	0	4.56
Sanchez, Albuquerque	5	5	0	0	2	1	0	.667	22	27	14	13	1	10	0	0	15	1	5.32
Sarmiento, Spokane	51	0	0	0	8	7	13	.533	63	57	27	21	5	20	8	1	66	3	3.00
Scarbery, Salt Lake City	20	1	0	0	3	1	1	.750	34	47	29	28	4	15	0	1	13	6	7.41
Schaefer, Phoenix	28	23	5	2	7	10	0	.412	137	171	117	102	15	82	1	1	67	8	6.70
Schrom, Salt Lake City	14	0	0	0	1	2	0	.000	23	32	25	20	1	17	1	2	11	5	7.83
Schuler, Salt Lake City*	45	0	0	0	11	4	16	.733	71	54	23	18	6	23	0	2	42	1	2.28
B. L. Smith, Tucson	28	15	7	2	12	4	1	.750	143	169	77	59	6	41	4	4	47	4	3.71
D. Smith, Spokane	31	4	0	0	2	4	0	.333	79	79	43	38	3	42	2	0	26	4	4.33
Souza, Ogden*	41	1	0	0	7	5	4	.583	86	89	44	32	4	42	3	0	47	4	3.35
Sprowl, Tucson*	26	25	9	0	10	11	0	.476	180	211	102	87	13	79	1	3	89	3	4.35
Stablein, Hawaii	23	23	5	0	12	7	0	.632	153	152	75	66	10	46	1	3	81	5	3.88
Stein, Spokane	24	24	1	0	12	8	0	.600	150	170	79	65	3	51	2	3	87	2	3.90
Stember, Phoenix	8	8	2	0	5	2	0	.714	55	48	22	21	3	29	0	4	29	1	3.44

Pitcher–Club	G.	GS.	CG.	ShO.	W.	L.	Sv.	Pct.	IP.	H.	R.	ER.	HR.	BB.	Int. BB.	HB.	SO.	WP.	ERA.
Stewart, Albuquerque	31	29	11	0	15	10	1	.600	202	189	94	83	13	89	6	0	125	13	3.70
Stoddard, Spokane	21	20	1	0	4	9	0	.308	124	147	84	68	9	53	4	1	84	6	4.94
Strom, Tucson*	24	22	4	2	11	6	0	.647	136	157	76	66	8	59	0	2	57	2	4.37
Sutton, Ogden-Hawaii	35	4	1	0	6	5	4	.545	79	99	57	46	6	47	7	4	30	3	5.24
Swiacki, Albuquerque	22	15	2	1	4	9	0	.308	94	116	81	73	16	53	3	7	23	8	6.99
Tellmann, Hawaii	24	24	5	13	5	0	.722	170	155	74	61	7	58	1	4	83	3	3.23
Todd, Phoenix	11	4	0	0	0	1	0	.000	36	35	19	17	2	15	3	0	6	5	4.37
Tucker, Phoenix	18	4	0	0	0	4	1	.000	42	69	36	33	2	17	3	1	18	1	7.07
Tufts, Phoenix*	38	10	2	1	4	7	3	.364	127	166	103	92	11	63	1	4	54	5	6.52
Vasquez, Tacoma	32	21	1	0	8	10	0	.444	139	170	99	83	21	67	2	5	55	7	5.37
Warthen, Portland*	22	3	0	0	3	1	1	.750	57	48	32	21	6	36	2	2	30	3	3.32
Wheelock, Spokane	17	17	1	1	4	9	0	.308	99	117	60	53	6	37	2	2	23	9	4.82
Wihtol, Tacoma	36	0	0	0	4	9	11	.308	58	52	28	23	1	30	7	1	38	6	3.57
Wilkes, Hawaii	25	17	2	1	6	9	0	.400	123	143	72	51	3	59	3	2	49	9	3.73
Wilkins, Tacoma	17	17	1	0	7	4	0	.636	101	108	59	44	8	66	1	5	72	9	3.92
M. Williams, Phoenix*	39	9	3	0	5	9	1	.357	121	134	77	61	5	94	3	3	56	6	4.54
R. Williams, Tucson	28	28	8	0	14	11	0	.560	188	240	123	105	14	69	5	3	85	6	5.03
G. Wilson, Tucson	26	26	7	1	12	9	0	.571	192	216	94	74	9	76	1	4	78	6	3.47
Wirth, Ogden	20	20	3	0	6	9	0	.400	111	129	95	78	12	73	2	1	45	5	6.32
Yandle, Hawaii*	31	4	0	0	2	2	1	.500	69	72	30	27	7	25	1	1	33	6	3.52
Young, Spokane	4	3	1	0	1	1	0	.500	14	16	11	11	0	12	0	1	4	0	7.07

BALKS—Beard, D. Harrison, 3 each; Blair, Bordley, Botting, Keeton, Lance, LaPoint, Quinones, Souza, 2 each; Abraham, Aponte, Armstrong, Boitano, Boone, Borchers, Brennan, Calvert, Camacho, Clark, Cliburn, Eddy, Eichelberger, Green, Hannahs, Harris, T. F. Jones, Keefe, King, Kuhaulua, Manos, McGee, Mendoza, Niemann, Olsen, C. Perez, P. Perez, Plank, Power, Sanchez, Schaefer, B. L. Smith, Sprowl, Stoddard, Sutton (Ogden), Tellmann, Warthen, Wheelock, Wihtol, R. Williams, Wirth, Yandle, 1 each.

COMBINATION SHUTOUTS—Blair-Armstrong, Eichelberger-Lee, Hawaii; Rowland-Plank, Phoenix; Long-Andersen, Portland; Clark-Diaz-Sarmiento, Stein-Sarmiento, Wheelock-Sarmiento, Spokane; Brennan-Pietroburgo-Cuellar, McCall-Vasquez-Cuellar, Tacoma; Galasso-DiPino-Quinones, Galasso-Mueller, LaPoint-Mueller-Boitano, Quinones-Rautzhan-Mueller, Quinones-Replogle, Rautzhan-Quinones, Vancouver.

NO-HIT GAMES—Rhoden, Portland, defeated Phoenix, 1-0, April 23, first game (seven innings); Keefe, Albuquerque, was defeated by Tucson, 1-0, July 3, first game (eight innings) after allowing one hit with two out in eighth inning. McCall, Tacoma, defeated Spokane, 1-0, August 24, second game (seven innings).

Allen Hit Safely in 35 Straight Games

For a guy who was out of a job and sent to Spokane as an afterthought, outfielder Kim Allen made the most of his opportunity.

Allen, a 27-year-old fly-chaser who had been unemployed since the dissolution of the ill-fated Inter-American League, connected for the Pacific Coast League's longest hitting streak in years (35 games) and set a modern record with his 84 stolen bases.

During his long hitting streak which ended on July 17 against Ogden's John Sutton, Allen batted .399 with 57 hits in 143 at-bats. He raised his average from .222 to .316 during the streak.

Eastern League

CLASS AA

Leading Batter
JUNIOR ORTIZ
Buffalo

League President
PAT McKERNAN

Leading Pitcher
MARK DAVIS
Reading

CHAMPIONSHIP WINNERS IN PREVIOUS YEARS

1923—Williamsport .661	1944—Hartford .723	Elmira (2nd)‡ .514
1924—Williamsport .654	Binghamton (4th)‡ .474	1963—Charleston .593
1925—York§ .583	1945—Utica .615	1964—Elmira .586
Williamsport§ .583	Albany (3rd)‡ .564	1965—Pittsfield .607
1926—Scranton .627	1946—Scranton† .691	1966—Elmira .633
1927—Harrisburg .630	1947—Utica† .652	1967—Binghamton z .586
1928—Harrisburg .603	1948—Scranton† .636	Elmira .532
1929—Binghamton .597	1949—Albany .664	1968—Pittsfield .604
1930—Wilkes-Barre .572	Binghamton (4th)‡ .500	Reading (2nd)‡ .579
1931—Harrisburg .597	1950—Wilkes-Barre‡ .652	1969—York .640
1932—Wilkes-Barre .561	1951—Wilkes-Barre .612	1970—Waterbury a .560
1933—Binghamton .690	Scranton (2nd)† .562	Reading a .553
1934—Binghamton .694	1952—Albany .603	1971—Three Rivers .569
Williamsport* .603	Binghamton (2nd)‡ .562	Elmira b .561
1935—Scranton .657	1953—Reading .682	1972—West Haven b .600
Binghamton* .580	Binghamton (2nd)‡ .636	Three Rivers .559
1936—Scranton* .609	1954—Wilkes-Barre .576	1973—Reading b .551
Elmira .629	Albany (3rd)‡ .540	Pittsfield .551
1937—Elmira† .622	1955—Reading .613	1974—Thetford Mines (2nd)c .536
1938—Binghamton .622	Allentown (2nd)‡ .565	Pittsfield (2nd) .496
Elmira (3rd)‡ .522	1956—Schenectady† .609	1975—Reading .613
1939—Scranton† .571	1957—Binghamton .607	Bristol* .587
1940—Scranton .568	Reading (3rd)‡ .529	1976—Three Rivers .601
Binghamton (2nd)‡ .554	1958—Lancaster x .568	West Haven d .576
1941—Wilkes-Barre .630	Binghamton (6th)‡ .493	1977—West Haven e .623
Elmira (3rd)‡ .514	1959—Springfield† .607	Three Rivers .551
1942—Albany .600	1960—Williamsport y .551	1978—Reading .642
Scranton (2nd)‡ .593	Springfield (3rd)y .496	Bristol* .580
1943—Scranton .630	1961—Springfield .612	1979—West Haven f .597
Elmira (2nd)‡ .568	1962—Williamsport .593	

*Won split-season playoff. †Won championship and four-team playoff. ‡Won four-team playoff. §Tied for pennant, York winning playoff. xLeague was divided into Northern, Southern divisions and played a split season; Lancaster over-all season leader. yPlayoff finals canceled after one game because of rain with Williamsport and Springfield declared playoff co-champions. zLeague was divided into Eastern, Western divisions; Binghamton won playoff. aTied for pennant, Waterbury winning playoff. bLeague was divided into American, National divisions; won playoff. cLeague was divided into American and National divisions; won four-team playoff. dLeague was divided into Northern, Southern divisions, won playoff. eLeague was divided into New England and Canadian-American divisions, won playoff. fWon both halves of split season (no playoffs). (NOTE—Known as New York-Pennsylvania League prior to 1938.)

STANDING OF CLUBS AT CLOSE OF FIRST HALF, JUNE 20

NORTHERN DIVISION

Club	W.	L.	T.	Pct.	G.B.
Buffalo (Pirates)	39	29	0	.574	......
Glens Falls (White Sox)	37	31	0	.544	2
Lynn (Mariners)	35	32	1	.522	3½
Holyoke (Brewers)	35	34	1	.507	4½

SOUTHERN DIVISION

Club	W.	L.	T.	Pct.	G.B.
Waterbury (Reds)	41	28	0	.594	......
Bristol (Red Sox)	32	37	0	.464	9
Reading (Phillies)	30	39	0	.435	11
West Haven (A's)	25	44	0	.362	16

STANDING OF CLUBS AT CLOSE OF SECOND HALF, AUGUST 30

NORTHERN DIVISION

Club	W.	L.	T.	Pct.	G.B.
Holyoke (Brewers)	43	27	0	.614	......
Lynn (Mariners)	31	39	0	.443	12
Buffalo (Pirates)	28	41	0	.406	14½
Glens Falls (White Sox)	26	43	0	.377	16½

SOUTHERN DIVISION

Club	W.	L.	T.	Pct.	G.B.
Reading (Phillies)	48	22	0	.686	......
Bristol (Red Sox)	47	23	0	.671	1
Waterbury (Reds)	34	36	0	.486	14
West Haven (A's)	22	48	0	.314	26

COMPOSITE STANDING OF CLUBS AT CLOSE OF SEASON, AUGUST 30

SOUTHERN DIVISION

Club	Bri.	Rea.	Wat.	W.H.	Holy.	Buff.	Lynn.	G.F.	W.	L.	T.	Pct.	G.B.
Bristol (Red Sox)	..	11	12	15	6	13	12	10	79	60	0	.568	......
Reading (Phillies)	9	..	8	15	9	12	11	14	78	61	0	.561	1
Waterbury (Reds)	8	12	..	14	5	13	10	13	75	64	0	.540	4
West Haven (A's)	5	5	6	..	8	9	8	6	47	92	0	.338	32

NORTHERN DIVISION

Club	Bri.	Rea.	Wat.	W.H.	Holy.	Buff.	Lynn.	G.F.	W.	L.	T.	Pct.	G.B.
Holyoke (Brewers)	14	11	15	12	..	9	6	11	78	61	0	.561	......
Buffalo (Pirates)	7	8	6	11	11	..	11	13	67	70	0	.489	10
Lynn (Mariners)	8	8	10	12	13	8	..	7	66	71	1	.482	11
Glens Falls (White Sox)	9	6	7	13	9	6	13	..	63	74	0	.460	14

Major league affiliations in parentheses.

Playoffs—Holyoke defeated Buffalo, two games to none; Waterbury defeated Reading, two games to none; Holyoke defeated Waterbury, two games to one for championship.

Regular-Season Attendance—Bristol, 65,991; Buffalo, 130,674; Glens Falls, 84,472; Holyoke, 65,036; Lynn, 50,786; Reading, 97,235; Waterbury, 54,807; West Haven, 30,112. Total, 579,113. Playoffs, 12,335. No all-star game.

Managers: Bristol—Tony Torchia; Buffalo—Steve Demeter; Glens Falls—Mike Pazik; Holyoke—Lee Sigman; Lynn—Bobby Floyd; Reading—Ron Clark; Waterbury—Mike Compton; West Haven—Ed Nottle.

All-Star Team: 1B—Vargas, Buffalo; 2B—Curry, Reading; 3B—Esasky, Waterbury; SS—Sandberg, Reading; OF—Bass, Holyoke; Dernier, Reading; Green, Holyoke; R. Johnson, Glens Falls; C—Ortiz, Buffalo; DH—Torres, Buffalo; Virgil, Reading; P—Davis, Reading; Manager—Sigman, Holyoke.

(Compiled by Howe News Bureau, Boston, Mass.)

CLUB BATTING

Club	G.	AB.	R.	OR.	H.	TB.	2B.	3B.	HR.	RBI.	SH.	SF.	BB.	Int. BB.	HP.	SO.	SB.	CS.	LOB.	Pct.
Reading	139	4579	781	615	1318	1898	205	57	87	683	59	58	583	21	34	622	159	69	1018	.288
Glens Falls	137	4506	732	773	1231	1870	209	35	120	651	42	28	526	27	56	705	134	77	914	.273
Buffalo	137	4524	745	674	1221	1906	212	25	141	652	35	39	569	22	46	752	110	56	956	.270
Holyoke	140	4379	585	527	1148	1593	181	60	48	512	51	55	510	31	35	606	177	129	896	.262
Bristol	139	4379	606	596	1143	1544	186	22	57	523	68	42	597	41	27	546	132	90	971	.261
Lynn	138	4376	598	685	1140	1634	201	52	63	518	55	26	526	27	30	644	126	80	968	.261
West Haven	139	4351	512	721	1085	1508	175	19	70	449	67	26	574	15	37	679	81	76	989	.249
Waterbury	139	4340	516	484	1049	1523	159	45	75	455	57	35	476	40	34	704	112	74	899	.242

INDIVIDUAL BATTING

(Leading Qualifiers for Batting Championship—378 or More Plate Appearances)

*Bats lefthanded.   †Switch-hitter.

Player and Club	G.	AB.	R.	H.	TB.	2B.	3B.	HR.	RBI.	SH.	SF.	BB.	HP.	SO.	SB.	CS.	Pct.
Ortiz, Adalberto, Buffalo	126	515	79	178	241	25	1	12	78	4	0	43	2	57	7	2	.346
Curry, Steven, Reading	129	434	83	138	226	26	1	20	81	5	4	71	5	74	8	6	.318
Sandberg, Ryne, Reading	129	490	95	152	230	21	12	11	79	10	3	73	5	72	32	11	.310
Castro, Jose, Reading	117	426	71	132	175	15	5	6	59	8	10	46	0	40	8	0	.310
McDonald, Manuel, Reading	136	502	73	155	185	16	4	2	56	2	3	21	1	31	20	12	.309
Kraus, Jeffrey, Reading	119	410	65	124	168	20	9	2	65	7	5	37	3	36	4	9	.302
Perez, Julio, Glens Falls	89	318	66	96	133	13	3	6	39	3	1	56	2	18	11	6	.302
Bass, Kevin, Holyoke	136	490	79	147	204	31	7	4	51	5	2	41	7	59	35	16	.300
Dernier, Robert, Reading	136	536	111	160	227	29	4	10	57	7	6	92	3	53	71	16	.299
Hart, Michael, Lynn	117	399	69	119	176	15	6	10	61	7	0	68	1	39	12	6	.298

Departmental Leaders: G—W. Barnes, Loman, 138; AB—Dernier, 536; R—Dernier, 111; H—Ortiz, 178; TB—Vargas, 242; 2B—Bass, 31; 3B—Green, 19; HR—Esasky, 30; RBI—Virgil, 104; GWRBI—Esasky, 14; SH—Barrett, 15; SF—Soto, 12; BB—M. Barnes, 122; HP—Gray, 15; SO—Sandberg, 131; SB—Dernier, 71; CS—Thomas, 26.

Player and Club	G.	AB.	R.	H.	TB.	2B.	3B.	HR.	RBI.	SH.	SF.	BB.	HP.	SO.	SB.	CS.	Pct.
Abreu, Armand, Reading*	29	0	0	0	0	0	0	0	0	1	0	0	0	0	0	0	.000
Aldrich, Russell, Waterbury*	127	409	37	95	131	17	2	5	43	6	1	44	6	50	3	6	.232
Allen, James, Lynn	120	446	60	128	184	24	7	6	56	2	3	40	1	53	5	3	.287
Allen, Roderick, Glens Falls	31	121	26	43	65	5	4	3	27	0	0	9	2	13	6	1	.355
Babitt, Mack, West Haven	29	107	10	31	43	7	1	1	15	0	0	17	0	12	2	3	.290
Barnes, Michael, Buffalo*	133	437	86	116	168	19	3	9	59	6	2	122	6	92	13	9	.265
Barnes, William, Waterbury	138	533	62	156	207	27	6	4	64	6	7	24	1	54	18	10	.293
Barrett, Martin, Bristol	128	475	72	130	154	17	2	1	41	15	6	56	5	17	22	12	.274
Bass, Kevin, Holyoke†	136	490	79	147	204	31	7	4	51	5	2	41	7	59	35	16	.300
Bell, Jorge, Reading	22	55	11	17	26	5	2	0	11	0	0	3	0	8	3	2	.309
Bienek, Vincent, Glens Falls	117	411	56	106	170	21	5	11	62	5	4	56	3	79	7	9	.258
Bisceglia, David, Waterbury	13	23	2	4	5	1	0	0	0	0	0	3	1	5	0	0	.174
Bradley, S. Bert, West Haven	30	1	0	1	1	0	0	0	0	0	0	0	0	0	0	0	1.000
Brito, Jose, Waterbury	25	59	9	11	12	1	0	0	1	4	0	2	0	26	0	0	.186
Brunson, Eddie, Holyoke	127	424	66	118	161	20	7	3	61	3	7	59	5	85	22	12	.278
Brunswick, Thomas, West Haven	44	138	14	32	36	4	0	0	8	2	0	20	0	25	3	3	.232
Bryant, Erwin, Bristol	58	137	14	34	34	0	0	0	12	4	2	28	0	16	3	1	.248
Buckle, Larry, Waterbury	4	6	1	0	0	0	0	0	0	0	0	5	0	3	0	0	.000
Buckner, James, Buffalo*	112	422	72	119	195	20	4	16	53	1	4	33	0	46	19	7	.282
Burroughs, Darren, Reading*	11	1	0	0	0	0	0	0	0	0	0	1	0	0	0	0	.000
Butera, Barry, Bristol*	9	34	8	10	21	2	0	3	8	0	0	3	0	3	0	1	.294
Castro, Jose, Reading	117	426	71	132	175	15	5	6	59	8	10	46	0	40	8	0	.310
Cato, J. Keefe, Waterbury	12	22	0	0	0	0	0	0	0	1	0	1	1	6	0	0	.000
Chauncey, Keathel, West Haven*	101	374	56	101	145	17	3	7	36	7	3	64	0	34	12	12	.270
Christmas, Stephen, Waterbury*	115	347	44	84	124	15	2	7	44	0	3	61	4	35	1	1	.242
Cias, Darryl, West Haven	91	310	36	74	113	13	1	8	33	5	5	23	1	64	0	1	.239
Clark, Roy, Lynn	132	470	75	138	170	18	7	0	44	10	2	51	3	43	19	12	.294
Comstock, Keith, West Haven†	32	8	0	0	0	0	0	0	0	0	0	1	0	3	0	0	.000
Conroy, Timothy, West Haven*	26	2	0	0	0	0	0	0	0	0	0	0	0	0	0	0	.000
Cotes, Eugenio, Buffalo	66	245	48	76	133	19	1	12	48	3	3	19	5	40	15	8	.310
Curry, Steven, Reading	129	434	83	138	226	26	1	20	81	5	4	71	5	74	8	6	.318
Davis, Mark, Reading	28	8	0	0	0	0	0	0	0	1	0	0	0	5	0	0	.000
Dawley, William, Waterbury	7	16	0	2	3	1	0	0	0	3	0	0	0	3	0	0	.125
DeVito, Frederick, West Haven	126	444	53	114	148	17	1	5	47	13	2	34	6	55	2	1	.257
Dempsey, Peter, Reading	56	210	29	54	80	13	2	3	31	2	4	19	3	35	3	1	.257
Dernier, Robert, Reading	136	536	111	160	227	29	4	10	57	7	6	92	3	53	71	16	.299
Dierberger, Bill, Glens Falls	18	52	8	11	13	2	0	0	4	1	0	8	1	7	0	0	.212
Djakonow, Powel, Buffalo	131	344	67	79	141	23	0	13	54	4	2	60	8	108	4	4	.230
Duval, Michael, Waterbury*	63	163	16	36	59	9	4	2	23	2	0	21	0	46	7	5	.221
Dye, Scott, Waterbury	48	18	1	2	5	0	0	1	3	2	0	1	0	8	0	0	.111
Esasky, Nicholas, Waterbury	135	425	79	115	231	18	4	30	79	0	6	83	9	131	2	6	.271
Estrada, Manuel, Lynn	41	131	23	32	50	12	0	2	20	4	4	29	2	13	2	2	.244
Federici, Richard, Buffalo*	120	411	46	90	115	12	2	3	39	3	3	33	4	33	17	4	.219
Fiorillo, Nicholas, Waterbury*	26	16	1	4	4	0	0	0	1	0	0	0	1	1	0	.250
Flannery, Kevin, Glens Falls	8	1	0	0	0	0	0	0	0	0	0	1	0	0	0	0	.000
Foley, Marvis, Glens Falls*	21	68	10	22	30	5	0	1	9	0	0	15	0	9	1	0	.324
Foley, Thomas, Waterbury*	131	477	49	119	155	16	4	4	41	5	3	47	2	50	3	8	.249
Foster, Otis, Bristol	96	309	42	83	135	20	1	10	60	1	5	57	1	28	1	2	.269
Fournier, Bruce, West Haven*	29	98	9	23	39	4	0	4	14	2	0	10	1	9	0	0	.235
Fowler, Don, Reading	28	7	2	1	1	0	0	0	2	1	2	0	2	0	0	.143
Fucci, Dominic, Glens Falls*	112	361	57	99	164	21	1	14	62	4	0	74	3	87	23	14	.274
Gause, Ernest, Reading*	57	3	0	0	0	0	0	0	1	0	0	1	0	0	0	0	.000
Gelfarb, Stephen, West Haven*	70	252	27	71	98	13	1	4	32	5	1	18	1	42	2	0	.282
Gentile, Gene, Bristol*	120	350	55	90	122	16	2	4	33	6	4	69	2	46	12	9	.257
Gilbert, Mark, Waterbury†	49	154	12	31	33	2	0	0	6	2	0	14	2	13	3	4	.201
Graham, Lee, Bristol*	132	463	70	128	142	11	0	1	37	6	1	74	4	45	40	16	.276
Gray, Lorenzo, Glens Falls	135	503	94	145	191	24	2	6	68	4	4	51	15	49	29	6	.288
Green, David, Holyoke	129	446	71	130	205	13	19	8	67	3	7	51	3	78	27	16	.291
Hamilton, Robert, Waterbury*	106	255	29	60	89	12	4	3	33	1	6	44	2	34	3	3	.235
Harrison, Mack, West Haven†	7	21	2	4	5	1	0	0	2	1	0	4	0	6	0	0	.190
Hart, Michael, Lynn*	117	399	69	119	176	15	6	10	61	7	0	68	1	39	12	6	.298
Herring, Paul, Waterbury	131	453	59	121	201	14	9	16	62	1	3	39	2	49	5	8	.267
Hickey, Kevin, Glens Falls*	27	4	1	1	1	0	0	0	0	0	0	0	0	3	0	0	.250
Hill, Anthony, Glens Falls	79	312	48	84	100	5	4	1	14	7	1	22	1	48	31	13	.269
Hobbs, Rodney, Lynn	125	412	57	89	142	16	5	9	40	3	3	52	1	92	16	15	.216
Hughes, Gregory, Waterbury	23	28	5	4	5	0	0	0	1	0	3	1	13	0	0	.143
Hulett, Timothy, Glens Falls	6	23	2	4	4	0	0	0	0	0	0	3	0	5	0	1	.174
Ibarra, Miguel, Reading	71	187	30	41	52	7	2	0	18	1	3	26	0	43	1	1	.219
Incaviglia, Tony, Buffalo	57	215	44	59	76	6	1	3	20	1	0	41	5	42	5	4	.274
Johnson, Randall, Glens Falls*	78	280	59	79	169	15	0	25	70	1	3	56	4	62	0	2	.282
Jones, Joe L., Reading	43	137	17	31	48	5	3	2	14	3	0	17	0	30	1	2	.226
Keating, Dennis, Glens Falls	21	64	8	15	21	3	0	1	2	0	0	2	0	15	0	1	.234
Kittle, Ron, Glens Falls	17	65	11	20	37	3	1	4	9	0	0	4	1	14	0	0	.308
Klebba, Robert, West Haven	70	230	27	51	64	8	1	1	14	7	2	37	2	51	0	2	.222
Koke, Kyle, Lynn	45	140	15	28	36	4	2	0	14	3	0	17	1	24	0	3	.200

Player and Club	G.	AB.	R.	H.	TB.	2B.	3B.	HR.	RBI.	SH.	SF.	BB.	HP.	SO.	SB.	CS.	Pct.
Kraus, Jeffrey, Reading	119	410	65	124	168	20	9	2	65	7	5	37	3	36	4	9	.302
La Francois, Roger, Bristol*	59	197	34	52	88	9	0	9	41	3	1	25	2	25	1	0	.264
Lahti, Jeffrey, Waterbury	55	17	1	4	6	0	1	0	5	2	0	1	0	5	0	0	.235
Lake, Steven, Holyoke	102	325	26	84	103	9	2	2	44	9	4	13	0	27	3	6	.258
Lancellotti, Richard, Buffalo*	30	107	19	28	59	1	0	10	21	0	0	13	2	17	3	1	.262
Laribee, Russell, Bristol*	109	321	62	97	163	21	3	13	66	1	4	48	1	53	16	6	.302
Lawless, Thomas, Waterbury	130	498	83	137	177	20	7	2	29	7	4	41	3	82	63	20	.275
Lee, Terry, Holyoke*	33	98	9	27	36	5	2	0	11	0	1	15	0	22	0	1	.276
Lickert, John, Bristol	124	436	47	112	150	27	1	3	52	5	5	30	6	46	4	4	.257
Lindsay, Charles, Lynn†	61	212	31	58	67	5	2	0	7	5	0	22	3	31	22	10	.274
Loman, Douglas, Holyoke*	138	471	78	123	185	20	9	8	62	5	6	81	7	71	14	12	.261
Lombarski, Thomas, Reading*	112	394	62	111	152	18	7	3	64	6	5	39	5	58	4	2	.282
Macauley, J. Andrew, Buffalo†	103	396	74	113	175	19	5	11	42	6	4	56	6	64	13	6	.285
Maitland, Michael, Glens Falls	13	5	0	0	0	0	0	0	0	0	0	0	0	1	0	0	.000
Markham, Robert, West Haven*	27	82	9	18	19	1	0	0	1	1	0	10	0	21	2	1	.220
Mayer, Robert, Waterbury†	11	13	0	1	1	0	0	0	0	2	0	1	0	6	0	0	.077
McDonald, Manuel, Reading	136	502	73	155	185	16	4	2	56	2	3	21	1	31	20	12	.309
McHenry, Vance, Lynn	14	45	5	10	12	2	0	0	4	0	0	2	1	5	4	3	.222
Mercado, Orlando, Lynn	117	396	55	101	171	25	6	11	71	5	3	43	1	65	3	1	.255
Mesa, Ivan, Glens Falls	46	160	26	30	41	11	0	0	17	3	1	24	5	25	6	5	.188
Meyer, Scott, West Haven	101	362	47	88	132	21	1	7	45	4	7	41	6	49	1	3	.243
Minker, Allan, West Haven	118	354	50	89	151	21	1	13	52	0	3	70	5	67	1	7	.251
Mitchell, Ronald, Buffalo	58	160	26	33	47	3	1	3	25	3	5	30	0	38	5	2	.206
Mize, Paul, West Haven	107	383	48	109	123	10	2	0	24	9	0	71	7	45	24	15	.285
Moore, Michael, Lynn*	122	405	42	89	130	19	2	6	51	1	2	41	6	95	5	3	.220
Morris, Donald, West Haven	117	416	36	105	132	12	3	3	46	2	1	34	3	56	13	9	.252
Morse, Michael, Glens Falls	8	32	5	6	11	2	0	1	4	0	0	4	0	7	0	0	.188
Mullins, Francis, Glens Falls	59	212	46	64	111	7	2	12	39	0	3	26	1	32	4	1	.302
Negron, Miguel, Lynn*	128	450	52	133	183	27	7	3	41	4	4	33	0	45	5	8	.296
Neuenschwander, Douglas, Water..	56	11	1	1	1	0	0	0	0	0	1	0	2	0	0	0	.091
Nottle, Edward, West Haven	5	10	1	0	0	0	0	0	0	0	0	0	0	5	0	0	.000
O'Keefe, Richard, Waterbury*	23	34	2	7	7	0	0	0	1	5	1	0	3	0	4	0	.206
Ortiz, Adalberto, Buffalo	126	515	79	178	241	25	1	12	78	4	0	43	2	57	7	2	.346
Pasillas, J. Andrew, Glens Falls	84	306	43	89	128	16	1	7	50	1	4	22	2	40	0	3	.291
Pastrovich, Steven, Glens Falls	21	1	1	0	0	0	0	0	0	0	0	2	0	0	0	0	.000
Patterson, Larry, Lynn	66	182	20	53	72	5	1	4	28	2	0	24	3	40	2	2	.291
Patterson, Michael, West Haven*	114	392	47	103	164	12	2	15	50	2	1	46	1	62	14	9	.263
Pellant, Gary, Lynn†	136	441	63	99	165	20	5	12	59	4	5	88	4	73	15	5	.224
Perez, Julio, Glens Falls*	89	318	66	96	133	13	3	6	39	3	1	56	2	18	11	6	.302
Perry, Ronald, Glens Falls	49	171	22	45	63	6	3	2	23	1	2	11	0	20	2	2	.263
Prior, Daniel, Reading	37	3	0	1	1	0	0	0	0	0	0	0	0	1	0	0	.333
Pruitt, Russell, Bristol*	27	55	6	14	21	4	0	1	5	1	1	10	0	15	0	0	.255
Quetti, Russell, Bristol	130	408	38	100	125	17	4	0	41	10	3	44	1	68	3	11	.245
Rasmussen, James, Reading	18	6	0	1	1	0	0	0	1	1	0	0	0	2	0	0	.167
Reed, Jerry, Reading	9	2	1	0	0	0	0	0	0	0	0	0	0	0	0	0	.000
Reelhorn, Jonathan, Reading	16	3	0	0	0	0	0	0	0	0	0	0	0	1	0	0	.000
Robbins, Leroy, West Haven	19	55	9	8	9	1	0	0	2	0	0	9	1	17	2	0	.145
Robinette, Gary, Glens Falls	23	80	10	15	17	2	0	0	2	0	1	4	1	17	2	1	.188
Rodriguez, Ivan, Holyoke	119	357	29	79	101	15	2	1	36	4	4	34	1	48	4	5	.221
Rodriguez, Michael, West Haven	8	25	3	10	13	3	0	0	3	1	0	6	1	7	0	2	.400
Rois, Luis, Glens Falls	123	420	53	110	162	18	5	8	60	9	1	9	8	63	5	8	.262
Rouse, Randy, Buffalo	45	142	14	23	33	7	0	1	18	0	2	17	2	18	2	0	.162
Sandberg, Ryne, Reading	129	490	95	152	230	21	12	11	79	10	3	73	5	72	32	11	.310
Sarrett, Daniel, Waterbury	37	98	7	17	18	1	0	0	4	2	1	12	0	27	1	2	.173
Sauer, Jack, Bristol	115	335	43	88	110	11	4	1	36	2	2	39	1	47	13	6	.263
Scherrer, William, Waterbury*	25	49	2	4	4	0	0	0	3	0	2	0	1	0	0	0	.082
Schoppee, David, Bristol	55	0	1	0	0	0	0	0	1	0	2	0	0	0	0	0	.000
Schuster, R. Mark, Holyoke*	137	467	62	115	197	27	2	17	66	2	4	58	3	76	11	9	.246
Seeger, Mark, Glens Falls	10	29	1	7	10	1	1	0	3	0	1	4	1	5	1	0	.241
Seilheimer, Ricky, Glens Falls*	67	231	35	60	104	11	3	9	46	1	0	25	1	45	4	2	.260
Shoebridge, Terence, Holyoke*	64	183	17	50	60	8	1	0	21	2	3	30	1	25	3	5	.273
Skorochocki, John, Holyoke*	107	381	51	94	131	13	6	4	31	4	1	33	3	44	21	12	.247
Smith, Jackie, Glens Falls	6	4	0	0	0	0	0	0	0	0	0	0	0	3	0	0	.000
Sohns, Thomas, Waterbury*	80	176	13	30	41	4	2	1	14	2	1	19	0	32	0	1	.170
Soto, Thomas, Holyoke	84	285	37	65	80	10	1	1	31	10	12	19	3	18	3	9	.228
Speck, R. Clifford, Reading	9	2	0	0	0	0	0	0	0	0	0	0	0	2	0	0	.000
Spillane, Paul, West Haven	34	108	10	21	32	5	0	2	13	0	1	17	0	19	0	0	.194
Stevens, Paul, West Haven†	42	112	9	18	23	3	1	0	7	2	0	28	2	12	2	5	.161
Stockley, Paul, West Haven	17	54	7	14	18	2	1	0	5	1	0	11	0	16	0	3	.259
Teutsch, Mark, Glens Falls	58	1	0	1	1	0	0	0	0	0	0	0	0	0	0	0	1.000
Thomas, Franklin, Holyoke	124	452	62	116	130	10	2	0	31	4	4	76	2	53	34	26	.257
Torres, Alfredo, Buffalo	122	455	72	129	226	24	2	23	93	1	6	54	2	72	2	2	.284
Torres, Raymundo, Glens Falls	40	134	17	32	44	6	0	2	10	2	0	12	3	20	1	2	.239
Town, Randall, Waterbury	34	40	0	4	4	0	0	0	1	3	0	3	0	10	2	0	.100
Vargas, Hediberto, Buffalo	133	509	78	138	242	28	2	24	87	0	6	36	4	107	2	5	.271

Player and Club	G.	AB.	R.	H.	TB.	2B.	3B.	HR.	RBI.	SH.	SF.	BB.	HP.	SO.	SB.	CS.	Pct.
Virgil, Osvaldo, Reading	135	456	92	123	226	15	2	28	104	1	9	100	6	81	3	2	.270
Waag, William, Buffalo	46	166	20	40	55	6	3	1	15	3	2	12	0	18	3	2	.241
Weston, Alfred, Lynn	69	254	34	66	83	10	2	1	25	5	0	23	3	26	16	7	.260
Wieters, Richard, Glens Falls	32	3	0	1	1	0	0	0	0	0	0	0	0	2	0	0	.333
Williams, Dan, Glens Falls*	39	134	33	46	79	12	0	7	29	0	2	26	2	16	1	0	.343
Williams, Wayne, Reading	96	307	38	77	100	15	4	0	40	1	5	35	3	48	2	5	.251
Wilson, James, Bristol	129	415	51	101	136	18	1	5	45	8	4	48	1	51	3	7	.243
Woodard, Michael, West Haven	6	13	2	0	0	0	0	0	0	3	0	3	0	2	1	0	.000
Wright, Jackie, Bristol	54	152	18	28	33	5	0	0	6	1	0	27	1	29	1	3	.184
Young, Kenneth, Bristol†	90	292	46	76	110	8	4	6	39	5	0	37	2	57	13	12	.260

The following pitchers had no plate appearances primarily through use of designated hitters, listed alphabetically by club, games in parentheses:

BRISTOL—Aponte, Luis (29); Baum, Mark (11); Birrell, Robert *(12); Burtt, Dennis (31); Crawford, Steve (24); Denman, Brian (10); Givens, Gary (16); Howard, Michael (19); Kane, Kevin (23); King, Jerome (28); Moloney, William *(16); Shields, Stephen (39).

BUFFALO—Allen, Michael (24); Arias, Juan (32); Britt, Douglas (8); Calderon, Jose (29); Cliburn, Stewart (1); Dravecky, David *(27); Evans, Ricky (13); Farr, Steven (23); Field, Gregory (2); Garrity, Peter (3); Martinez, Ignacio (11); Nicholson, Larry *(23); Notarino, Anthony (16); Rock, Robert (21); Thibodeaux, Keith (10); Weismiller, Robert (13); Williams, Donald *(4); Wiltbank, Benjamin (26).

GLENS FALLS—Agosto, Juan (48); Barnicle, Theodore *(20); Bradley, T. Leonard (7); Esser, Mark (9); Evans, Randall (23); Johnson, Charles (9); Johnson, Thomas (15); Patterson, Reginald (13); Platel, Mark (22).

HOLYOKE—Ako, Gerald (44); Bernard, Dwight (9); Carroll, Edgar *(16); Cort, Barry (5); Curran, David (3); DiPino, Frank *(16); Jones, Douglas (8); Kranitz, Richard (25); Meyer, Gregory *(23); Montgomery, Larry (28); Ogawa, Kunikazu (47); Porter, Charles (14); Reed, Steven (19); Swift, Weldon (28); Torres, Anthony (20).

LYNN—Adair, Michael *(30); Best, Karl (26); Cary, Jeff (22); Clark, Bryan *(16); Georger, Joseph (38); Harrison, Robert *(41); Hobbs, John D. *(11); Minnick, Donald *(15); Musselman, R. Ronald (53); Randolph, Robert (14); Simond, Robert *(28); Welborn, Sammye *(20).

READING—DeVincenzo, John (51); Faulk, M. Kelly (29); Hart, Thomas (5); Larson, Daniel (4).

WEST HAVEN—Atherton, Keith (27); Bordi, Richard (11); Gosse, M. John (30); Harris, D. Craig (21); Harris, Frank (2); Moore, Robert (5); Sealy, Randall (33); Tronerud, Ricky (25); Wyszynski, Dennis (34).

GRAND SLAM HOME RUNS—Rois 2; Aldrich, Butera, Dempsey, Djakanow, Fucci, Gray, R. Johnson, LaFrancois, Mercado, Pasillas, M. Patterson, Sandberg, Torres, Vargas, 1 each.

AWARDED FIRST BASE ON INTERFERENCE—Esasky 2 (M. Foley, Pasillas); Herring 2 (Ortiz, L. Patterson); Gray (Mercado); Nottle (Shoebridge); Soto (Mercado).

GAME-WINNING RBIs

BRISTOL (64)—Laribee 12, Lickert 9, Wilson 9, Foster 8, Gentile 5, Sauer 5, Barrett 4, Graham 4, Young 4, La Francois, 3, Quetti 1.

BUFFALO (35)—Federici 5, Vargas 5, Barnes 4, Buckner 3, Djakonow 3, Ortiz 3, Torres 3, Cotes 2, Macauley 2, Mitchell 2, Rouse 2, Lancellotti 1.

GLENS FALLS (47)—Gray 9, R. Johnson 7, Perez 7, Bienek 5, Fucci 5, Rois 4, Allen 3, Mullins 3, Pasillas 2, Hill 1, Williams 1.

HOLYOKE (63)—Brunson 11, Schuster 10, Bass 8, Green 6, Rodriguez 6, Lake 5, Loman 5, Soto 5, Shoebridge 3, Skorochocki 2, Lee 1, Thomas 1.

LYNN (57)—Pellant 11, Hart 9, Allen 8, Moore 6, Negron 5, Weston 5, R. Clark 3, R. Hobbs 3, Mercado 3, Estrada 2, Koke 1, McHenry 1.

READING (66)—Curry 11, Sandberg 9, Castro 7, Lombarski 7, McDonald 6, Virgil 6, Dernier 5, Kraus 5, Williams 4, Bell 3, Dempsey 2, Ibarra 1.

WATERBURY (62)—Esasky 14, Barnes 12, Herring 12, Foley 9, Christmas 4, Hamilton 4, Lawless 3, Duval 2, Aldrich 1, Sohns 1.

WEST HAVEN (35)—Minker 6, Morris 5, DeVito 4, Cias 3, Mize 3, Babitt 2, Chauncey 2, Gelfarb 2, Meyer 2, Patterson 2, Klebba 1, Markham 1, Spillane 1, Stevens 1.

CLUB FIELDING

Club	G.	PO.	A.	E.	DP.	PB.	Pct.	Club	G.	PO.	A.	E.	DP.	PB.	Pct.
Waterbury	139	3540	1406	142	100	15	.972	Buffalo	137	3513	1588	196	139	20	.963
Holyoke	140	3574	1619	167	134	18	.969	Bristol	139	3561	1533	210	128	11	.960
Reading	139	3536	1581	175	137	19	.967	Lynn	138	3414	1567	212	124	34	.959
West Haven	139	3494	1570	189	118	20	.964	Glens Falls	137	3488	1666	229	156	23	.957

Triple Play—Holyoke.

INDIVIDUAL FIELDING

*Throws lefthanded.

FIRST BASEMEN

Player and Club	G.	PO.	A.	E.	DP.	Pct.	Player and Club	G.	PO.	A.	E.	DP.	Pct.
Sohns, Waterbury	19	121	9	0	6	1.000	Federici, Buffalo*	3	36	2	0	3	1.000
Pruitt, Bristol	7	54	7	0	6	1.000	Mercado, Lynn	4	33	3	0	2	1.000
Skorochocki, Holyoke	7	48	5	0	3	1.000	Seeger, Glens Falls	4	33	0	0	1	1.000

FIRST BASEMEN—Continued

Player and Club	G.	PO.	A.	E.	DP.	Pct.	Player and Club	G.	PO.	A.	E.	DP.	Pct.
Virgil, Reading	2	24	1	0	2	1.000	Fucci, Glens Falls*	87	813	60	11	107	.988
Christmas, Waterbury	4	23	1	0	1	1.000	La Francois, Bristol	38	299	20	4	22	.988
Mitchell, Buffalo	1	12	1	0	1	1.000	Sauer, Bristol	28	155	15	2	18	.988
Brunson, Holyoke	1	3	1	0	2	1.000	Moore, Lynn*	120	1016	101	15	94	.987
ALDRICH, Waterbury	124	1001	72	2	81	.998	Foster, Bristol	84	668	73	10	67	.987
Minker, West Haven	109	1004	51	4	87	.996	De Vito, West Haven	7	53	10	1	6	.984
Jones, Reading	39	366	47	3	34	.993	Patterson, Lynn	16	137	8	4	8	.973
Schuster, Holyoke*	135	1188	106	11	109	.992	Robinette, Glens Falls	14	127	7	4	6	.971
Gelfarb, West Haven*	29	234	13	2	9	.992	Dempsey, Reading	6	64	4	3	4	.958
Lombarski, Reading	95	838	71	8	87	.991	Dierberger, Glens Falls	1	13	0	1	0	.929
Vargas, Buffalo	133	1268	85	15	115	.989	Triple Play—Skorochocki.						
Williams, Glens Falls*	34	333	21	4	30	.989							

SECOND BASEMEN

Player and Club	G.	PO.	A.	E.	DP.	Pct.	Player and Club	G.	PO.	A.	E.	DP.	Pct.
Skorochocki, Holyoke	20	39	60	0	12	1.000	Gray, Glens Falls	6	9	15	1	0	.960
Waag, Buffalo	8	16	18	0	6	1.000	Mesa, Glens Falls	43	101	112	9	33	.959
Bryant, Bristol	5	8	10	0	2	1.000	Brunswick, West Haven	36	73	115	8	17	.959
Djakonow, Buffalo	2	2	12	0	0	1.000	Incaviglia, Buffalo	9	20	27	2	9	.959
Seeger, Glens Falls	1	4	3	0	0	1.000	Weston, Lynn	66	131	186	14	35	.958
Stevens, West Haven	1	0	3	0	0	1.000	Estrada, Lynn	14	23	43	3	9	.957
Laribee, Bristol	1	0	1	0	0	1.000	Curry, Reading	87	180	242	21	66	.953
Sohns, Waterbury	16	29	40	1	8	.986	Castro, Reading	55	132	175	15	33	.953
BARRETT, Bristol	125	279	364	10	84	.985	Perez, Glens Falls	8	19	19	2	6	.950
Lawless, Waterbury	128	316	333	14	64	.979	Soto, Holyoke	4	7	10	1	2	.944
Mullins, Glens Falls	7	14	29	1	4	.977	Wilson, Bristol	14	24	26	3	1	.943
Barnes, Buffalo	120	292	408	21	88	.971	Lee, Holyoke	3	8	8	1	3	.941
Thomas, Holyoke	118	254	341	20	73	.967	Babitt, West Haven	29	61	73	9	15	.937
Mize, West Haven	40	91	116	7	25	.967	Harrison, West Haven	7	20	13	3	4	.917
Hill, Glens Falls	78	202	245	16	68	.965	Woodard, West Haven	6	8	9	2	0	.895
Klebba, West Haven	23	36	68	4	11	.963	Pellant, Lynn	2	0	3	1	1	.750
R. Clark, Lynn	61	132	162	12	41	.962	Triple Play—Thomas.						

THIRD BASEMEN

Player and Club	G.	PO.	A.	E.	DP.	Pct.	Player and Club	G.	PO.	A.	E.	DP.	Pct.
Waag, Buffalo	5	4	13	0	2	1.000	Pellant, Lynn	25	19	49	5	3	.932
Green, Holyoke	3	4	6	0	1	1.000	Wilson, Bristol	62	46	110	12	15	.929
Brunswick, West Haven	2	3	3	0	0	1.000	Gray, Glens Falls	128	101	287	31	26	.926
Lombarski, Reading	4	2	4	0	0	1.000	Skorochocki, Holyoke	62	55	133	15	9	.926
Patterson, Lynn	3	1	4	0	0	1.000	Djakonow, Buffalo	107	94	206	26	16	.920
Sandberg, Reading	4	3	2	0	0	1.000	Allen, Lynn	86	66	184	23	18	.916
Meyer, West Haven	2	0	4	0	1	1.000	R. Clark, Lynn	27	16	44	6	7	.909
Rodriguez, Holyoke	1	2	1	0	0	1.000	Thomas, Holyoke	3	3	6	1	3	.900
Spillane, West Haven	1	0	3	0	0	1.000	Perry, Glens Falls	4	2	7	1	1	.900
Hulett, Glens Falls	2	1	1	0	0	1.000	Butera, Bristol	8	9	17	3	1	.897
DE VITO, West Haven	110	89	232	11	13	.967	Fournier, West Haven	24	28	50	10	8	.886
Soto, Holyoke	60	63	98	6	12	.964	Bryant, Bristol	32	17	31	7	4	.873
Dempsey, Reading	51	25	114	6	7	.959	Wright, Bristol	53	39	76	18	7	.865
Sohns, Waterbury	10	7	14	1	1	.955	Barnes, Buffalo	1	3	3	1	1	.857
McDonald, Reading	39	19	82	6	8	.944	Incaviglia, Buffalo	15	10	31	7	8	.854
Robinette, Glens Falls	7	3	13	1	0	.941	Shoebridge, Holyoke	1	0	4	1	0	.800
Esasky, Waterbury	133	98	241	23	19	.936	Rouse, Buffalo	11	5	14	5	0	.792
Lee, Holyoke	20	15	27	3	3	.933	Morris, West Haven	1	0	2	1	1	.667
Castro, Reading	48	42	96	10	9	.932	Fucci, Glens Falls*	1	0	0	1	0	.000

SHORTSTOPS

Player and Club	G.	PO.	A.	E.	DP.	Pct.	Player and Club	G.	PO.	A.	E.	DP.	Pct.
Skorochocki, Holyoke	7	10	17	0	2	1.000	Allen, Lynn	12	29	30	4	9	.937
Barrett, Bristol	3	0	8	0	0	1.000	Quetti, Bristol	130	251	347	41	68	.936
Castro, Bristol	1	1	1	0	1	1.000	Stockley, West Haven	17	29	72	7	8	.935
Wilson, Bristol	2	0	1	0	0	1.000	McHenry, Lynn	14	22	36	4	4	.935
SANDBERG, Reading	120	153	386	20	81	.964	Mullins, Glens Falls	53	95	168	19	48	.933
Soto, Holyoke	17	33	65	4	10	.961	Sohns, Waterbury	14	19	35	4	1	.931
McDonald, Reading	21	27	63	4	11	.957	Hulett, Glens Falls	5	14	13	2	4	.931
Bryant, Bristol	12	18	25	2	9	.956	Koke, Lynn	45	71	127	15	17	.930
Rodriguez, Holyoke	117	188	335	25	61	.954	Perez, Glens Falls	44	79	125	17	24	.923
Pe'lant, Lynn	4	4	15	1	2	.950	Morse, Glens Falls	8	8	35	4	3	.915
Foley, Waterbury	128	222	329	31	49	.947	Estrada, Lynn	25	39	65	11	16	.904
Klebba, West Haven	31	43	98	8	16	.946	Macauley, Buffalo	103	186	299	54	69	.900
Waag, Buffalo	34	71	119	11	23	.945	Thomas, Holyoke	3	6	7	2	4	.867
Stevens, West Haven	26	38	79	7	19	.944	Fournier, West Haven	1	3	3	1	0	.857
Perry, Glens Falls	31	50	93	9	18	.941	Djakonow, Buffalo	2	1	5	1	0	.857
Mize, West Haven	70	110	237	23	37	.938	Mesa, Glens Falls	2	4	1	2	0	.714
R. Clark, Lynn	40	72	111	12	26	.938	Sauer, Bristol	1	0	0	1	0	.000

OUTFIELDERS

Player and Club	G.	PO.	A.	E.	DP.	Pct.
Hamilton, Waterbury*...	81	152	3	0	1	1.000
Mitchell, Buffalo	53	97	5	0	2	1.000
Allen, Glens Falls	21	29	1	0	1	1.000
Fucci, Glens Falls*	19	26	0	0	0	1.000
Perez, Glens Falls	14	23	2	0	0	1.000
Klebba, West Haven	9	23	0	0	0	1.000
Rouse, Buffalo	8	10	2	0	0	1.000
Skorochocki, Holyoke	4	10	1	0	0	1.000
Mercado, Lynn	5	10	0	0	0	1.000
Seeger, Glens Falls	5	8	1	0	0	1.000
Stevens, West Haven	6	5	1	0	1	1.000
Cias, West Haven	8	5	1	0	0	1.000
Perry, Glens Falls	1	5	0	0	0	1.000
Comstock, West Haven*	3	4	0	0	0	1.000
Patterson, Lynn	5	4	0	0	0	1.000
Lickert, Bristol	1	3	0	0	0	1.000
Estrada, Lynn	1	1	0	0	0	1.000
Butera, Bristol	2	1	0	0	0	1.000
Duval, Waterbury	53	132	3	2	2	.985
CHAUNCEY, W Haven*	101	241	7	4	1	.9841
Buckner, Buffalo*	107	177	4	3	0	.9836
Gilbert, Waterbury	43	108	5	2	1	.983
Federici, Buffalo*	116	285	13	6	2	.980
Dernier, Reading	136	325	9	9	0	.974
Morris, West Haven	114	239	11	7	1	.973
Kraus, Reading	120	234	12	7	3	.972
Hart, Lynn*	117	204	5	6	2	.972
Laribee, Bristol	70	98	4	3	0	.971
Torres, Glens Falls	38	86	7	3	3	.969
Brunson, Holyoke	27	52	4	2	1	.966
Incaviglia, Buffalo	19	25	1	1	1	.963
Bell, Reading	19	24	0	1	0	.960

Player and Club	G.	PO.	A.	E.	DP.	Pct.
Patterson, W Haven	111	200	9	9	1	.959
Loman, Holyoke*	135	271	16	13	0	.957
Torres, Buffalo	41	60	6	3	0	.957
Barnes, Waterbury	135	264	15	13	0	.955
Sauer, Bristol	97	102	3	5	2	.955
Lancellotti, Buff*	27	61	3	3	2	.955
Green, Holyoke	126	257	12	13	1	.954
Graham, Bristol*	131	253	14	13	1	.954
Gentile, Bristol*	118	207	17	11	3	.953
Lindsay, Lynn	56	130	4	7	0	.950
McDonald, Reading	81	118	14	7	4	.950
Gelfarb, West Haven*	22	37	1	2	0	.950
Bass, Holyoke	133	305	14	18	7	.947
Herring, Waterbury	122	208	5	12	2	.947
Keating, Glens Falls	19	34	2	2	0	.947
R. Hobbs, Lynn	126	265	18	16	5	.946
Rois, Glens Falls	120	231	12	15	3	.942
Cotes, Buffalo	57	90	9	7	1	.934
Bienek, Glens Falls*	100	164	14	13	1	.932
R. Johnson, G Falls*	75	108	10	9	6	.929
Negron, Lynn*	126	184	6	15	1	.927
Robbins, West Haven	18	24	1	2	1	.926
Dierberger, Glens Falls..	9	11	1	1	0	.923
Wilson, Bristol	65	86	8	10	1	.904
Williams, Reading	79	97	5	11	0	.903
Kittle, Glens Falls	16	24	4	3	0	.903
Markham, West Haven*	19	29	2	6	0	.838
Rodriguez, West Haven	8	10	0	2	0	.833
Spillane, West Haven	10	10	2	3	0	.800
DeVito, West Haven	2	3	0	1	0	.750
Lee, Holyoke	5	2	0	1	0	.667

CATCHERS

Player and Club	G.	PO.	A.	E.	DP.	PB.	Pct.
Pruitt, Bristol	11	51	2	0	0	1	1.000
Rouse, Buffalo	6	25	9	0	0	2	1.000
Dierberger, Glens F......	6	24	6	0	0	1	1.000
Foley, Glens Falls	13	59	10	1	0	3	.986
Torres, Buffalo	22	114	16	2	2	3	.985
CHRISTMAS, Water..	105	598	80	11	10	6	.984
Shoebridge, Holyoke ..	55	209	32	4	3	4	.984
Mercado, Lynn	106	574	75	11	8	23	.983
Lake, Holyoke	94	445	107	10	13	14	.982
Cias, West Haven	59	282	52	7	1	6	.979
Lickert, Bristol	120	660	127	20	14	7	.975

Player and Club	G.	PO.	A.	E.	DP.	PB.	Pct.
Virgil, Reading	102	568	61	16	7	13	.975
Ortiz, Buffalo	111	497	91	16	9	15	.974
Bisceglia, Waterbury .	3	33	4	1	0	0	.974
Meyer, West Haven	64	305	51	10	6	10	.973
Sarrett, Waterbury	35	153	26	5	2	9	.973
La Francois, Bristol...	23	126	21	5	0	3	.967
Ibarra, Reading	46	196	25	8	1	6	.965
Patterson, Lynn	36	172	20	7	1	11	.965
Seilheimer, Glens F...	60	269	30	12	5	13	.961
Pasillas, Glens Falls	63	287	56	17	5	6	.953
Spillane, West Haven .	19	90	9	8	1	4	.925

PITCHERS

Player and Club	G.	PO.	A.	E.	DP.	Pct.
HICKEY, Glens Falls*...	26	16	45	0	8	1.000
Georger, Lynn	38	8	29	0	4	1.000
Lahti, Waterbury	55	9	27	0	0	1.000
Wiltbank, Buffalo	26	10	24	0	2	1.000
De Vincenzo, Reading....	51	14	19	0	1	1.000
Gosse, West Haven*	30	9	17	0	1	1.000
Rock, Buffalo	21	7	17	0	1	1.000
Ako, Holyoke	44	5	16	0	0	1.000
Patterson, Glens Falls	13	6	12	0	0	1.000
Barnicle, Glens Falls*	20	3	15	0	1	1.000
Dye, Waterbury	48	4	12	0	1	1.000
Evans, Buffalo	13	1	13	0	0	1.000
Arias, Buffalo	32	3	10	0	0	1.000
J. Hobbs, Lynn*	11	2	9	0	0	1.000
Aponte, Bristol	29	4	7	0	0	1.000
Ogawa, Holyoke	46	3	8	0	2	1.000
Comstock, West Haven*	29	1	9	0	1	1.000
Cort, Holyoke	5	3	6	0	0	1.000
Agosto, Glens Falls*......	8	1	8	0	1	1.000
Allen, Buffalo	24	5	4	0	0	1.000
Wyszynski, West Haven	34	2	7	0	0	1.000
Moore, West Haven	5	1	7	0	0	1.000
Baum, Bristol	11	3	5	0	1	1.000

Player and Club	G.	PO.	A.	E.	DP.	Pct.
Faulk, Reading	29	7	1	0	0	1.000
Neuenschwander, Water	56	1	7	0	1	1.000
Maitland, Glens Falls*	12	1	6	0	0	1.000
Hart, Reading	5	5	1	0	1	1.000
Smith, Glens Falls*	5	1	4	0	0	1.000
Reed, Reading	8	1	4	0	1	1.000
Reed, Holyoke	19	0	5	0	0	1.000
Cliburn, Buffalo	1	0	4	0	0	1.000
Buckle, Waterbury	4	1	3	0	0	1.000
Weismiller, Buffalo	13	0	4	0	0	1.000
Bradley, Glens Falls	7	0	3	0	0	1.000
Williams, Glens Falls*	1	1	1	0	0	1.000
Moloney, Bristol*	16	1	1	0	0	1.000
Ibarra, Reading	1	0	1	0	0	1.000
Field, Buffalo	2	0	1	0	0	1.000
Curran, Holyoke	3	0	1	0	0	1.000
Larson, Reading	4	0	1	0	0	1.000
Williams, Buffalo*	4	0	1	0	1	1.000
Britt, Buffalo*	8	0	1	0	1	1.000
Simond, Lynn*	28	11	50	1	4	.984
Montgomery, Holyoke....	27	22	32	1	1	.982
Dravecky, Buffalo*	27	8	39	1	1	.979
B. Clark, Lynn*	16	7	31	1	0	.974

PITCHERS—Continued

Player and Club	G	PO	A	E	DP	Pct.
Harrison, Lynn	41	5	28	1		.971
Scherrer, Waterbury*	25	2	28	1	0	.968
Torres, Holyoke	20	12	17	1	2	.967
C. Harris, West Haven	21	9	20	1	4	.967
Best, Lynn	26	6	22	1	2	.966
T. Johnson, Glens Falls	15	3	22	1	3	.962
Gause, Reading*	57	4	21	1	1	.962
Hughes, Waterbury	21	9	15	1	1	.960
Crawford, Bristol	24	21	42	3	1	.955
DiPino, Holyoke*	16	4	15	1	0	.950
Fowler, Reading	28	26	26	3	4	.945
Swift, Holyoke	28	14	37	3	1	.944
Pastrovich, Glens Falls	21	4	13	1	1	.944
Evans, Glens Falls	23	5	28	2	1	.943
Denman, Bristol	10	10	6	1	0	.941
Farr, Buffalo	23	5	25	2	2	.938
Tronerud, West Haven	25	11	19	2	5	.938
Jones, Holyoke	8	5	10	1	1	.938
Wieters, Glens Falls	32	13	30	3	2	.935
Porter, Holyoke	14	11	17	2	3	.933
Burroughs, Reading*	11	1	13	1	1	.933
Howard, Bristol	19	10	17	2	1	.931
Rasmussen, Reading	18	11	15	2	0	.929
Brito, Waterbury	25	6	20	2	3	.929
Thibodeaux, Buffalo	10	4	9	1	1	.929
Atherton, West Haven	27	9	27	3	2	.923
Schoppee, Bristol	55	9	27	3	0	.923
Abreu, Reading*	29	2	10	1	1	.923
Teutsch, Glens Falls	58	10	34	4	1	.917
Randolph, Lynn	14	8	14	2	0	.917
Cato, Waterbury	12	3	8	1	0	.917
Kranitz, Holyoke	25	11	29	4	5	.909
King, Bristol	28	7	23	3	0	.909
Birrell, Bristol*	12	3	17	2	1	.909
Sealy, West Haven	33	4	6	1	0	.909
Burtt, Bristol	31	20	26	5	1	.902
Adair, Lynn*	30	2	35	4	1	.902
Nicholson, Buffalo*	23	2	16	2	2	.900
Meyer, Holyoke*	23	3	6	1	0	.900
Reelhorn, Reading	16	6	20	3	0	.897
Welborn, Lynn	20	9	17	3	0	.897
Davis, Reading*	28	8	18	3	0	.897
Platel, Glens Falls	22	2	15	2	2	.895
Musselman, Lynn	53	9	16	3	0	.893
Conroy, West Haven*	25	9	23	4	1	.889
O'Keefe, Waterbury*	18	6	18	3	1	.889
Esser, Glens Falls	9	1	7	1	1	.889
Calderon, Buffalo*	29	2	6	1	1	.889
C. Johnson, Glens Falls	9	4	10	2	0	.875
Mayer, Waterbury	11	3	11	2	2	.875
Carroll, Holyoke*	16	3	4	1	0	.875
Town, Waterbury	29	8	26	5	4	.872
Givens, Bristol	16	4	9	2	1	.867
Prior, Reading	37	9	15	4	0	.857
Bradley, West Haven	24	6	27	6	2	.846
Dawley, Waterbury	7	4	7	2	1	.846
Shields, Bristol	39	5	10	3	0	.833
Notarino, Buffalo	16	2	7	2	1	.818
Cary, Lynn	22	3	10	3	1	.813
Kane, Bristol	23	9	16	6	1	.806
Bordi, West Haven	11	2	6	2	0	.800
Fiorillo, Waterbury*	26	0	9	3	0	.750
Speck, Reading	9	4	2	2	0	.750
Garrity, Buffalo	3	1	2	1	1	.750
Flannery, Glens Falls	8	0	3	1	0	.750
Minnick, Lynn*	15	1	2	1	0	.750
Martinez, Buffalo	11	2	3	2	1	.714
Bernard, Holyoke	9	1	0	1	0	.500

The following players do not have any recorded accepted chances at the positions indicated; therefore, are not listed in the fielding averages for those particular positions: Brunswick, of; Foster, 3b; F. Harris, p; Lake, of; Laribee, 3b; Lombarski, of; Mitchell, p; Nottle, p; Pruitt, of; Sauer, 2b-3b; Sohns, of; Weston, ss.

CLUB PITCHING

Club	G	CG	ShO.	Sv.	IP.	H.	R.	ER.	HR.	BB.	Int. BB.	HB.	SO.	WP.	Bk.	ERA.
Waterbury	139	25	12	35	1182	1057	484	434	74	490	33	24	729	44	7	3.30
Holyoke	140	32	16	27	1194	1069	527	447	53	496	23	30	609	46	7	3.37
Bristol	139	30	9	30	1187	1188	597	491	65	610	58	45	774	73	11	3.72
Reading	139	35	16	26	1181	1120	615	530	75	532	23	42	707	58	8	4.04
Lynn	138	30	10	23	1151	1150	686	529	58	611	28	45	697	93	6	4.14
Buffalo	137	37	6	21	1172	1216	674	572	125	529	15	38	566	56	11	4.39
West Haven	139	50	4	17	1166	1231	731	613	97	494	22	33	602	60	12	4.73
Glens Falls	137	22	3	18	1163	1303	773	636	114	607	22	42	575	75	11	4.92

PITCHERS' RECORDS

(Leading Qualifiers for Earned-Run Average Leadership—112 or More Innings)

*Throws lefthanded.

Pitcher—Club	G	GS	CG	ShO	W	L	Sv	Pct.	IP	H	R	ER	HR	BB	Int. BB	HB	SO	WP	ERA
Davis, Reading*	28	28		4	19	6	0		193	140	63	53	11	75	0	4	185	6	2.47
Crawford, Bristol	24	23	10	2	9	7	0	.563	177	170	68	52	6	64	6	5	97	8	2.64
Montgomery, Holyoke	27	26	8	3	9	13	0	.409	195	190	75	57	8	38	4	2	82	2	2.93
Tronerud, West Haven	27	26	8	1	5	8	0	.385	151	143	76	52	12	47	1	4	66	6	3.10
B. Clark, Lynn*	16	16	8	1	9	5	0	.643	116	102	49	40	2	50	2	2	93	11	3.10
Brito, Waterbury	25	25	8	1	12	6	0	.667	172	125	66	60	11	75	1	8	175	3	3.14
Teutsch, Glens Falls	58	0	0	0	13	6	14	.684	119	113	53	43	5	55	9	4	67	4	3.25
Rasmussen, Reading	18	18	7	1	8	5	0	.615	120	106	50	44	4	43	2	3	64	9	3.30
Town, Waterbury	29	25	2	1	8	9	0	.471	147	142	62	54	12	43	5	4	50	4	3.31
Scherrer, Waterbury*	25	25	4	3	7	8	0	.467	151	139	58	56	10	58	2	0	84	2	3.34

Departmental Leaders: G—Teutsch, 58; GS—Davis, Fowler, 28; CG—Atherton, 13; ShO—Davis, Fowler, 4; W—Davis, 19; L—B. Bradley, 15; Sv—Schoppee, 19; Pct.—Davis, .760; IP—Davis, 193; H—Simond, 198; R—B. Bradley, 121; ER—B. Bradley, 105; HR—Hickey, 20; BB—Best, 106; IBB—Shields, 14; HB—Howard, Simond, 10; SO—Davis, 185; WP—Conroy, Rock, 16.

(All Pitchers—Listed Alphabetically)

Pitcher–Club	G	GS	CG	ShO	W	L	Sv	Pct.	IP	H	R	ER	HR	BB	Int. BB	HB	SO	WP	ERA
Abreu, Reading*	29	5	1	0	1	4	1	.200	64	58	44	37	6	49	1	7	32	5	5.20
Adair, Lynn*	30	15	2	0	7	6	1	.538	98	98	60	45	7	52	2	3	51	6	4.13
Agosto, Glens Falls*	8	0	0	0	1	0	1	1.000	22	26	18	17	2	18	0	2	8	2	6.95
Ako, Holyoke	44	5	0	0	6	4	5	.600	103	87	41	33	1	23	5	5	30	0	2.88
Allen, Buffalo	24	0	0	0	1	4	7	.200	36	29	20	14	1	17	2	0	33	3	3.50
Aponte, Bristol	29	0	0	0	9	1	4	.900	54	46	17	15	2	23	5	3	43	6	2.50
Arias, Buffalo	32	5	2	1	5	6	8	.455	72	80	39	37	8	33	0	1	40	2	4.63
Atherton, West Haven	27	27	13	2	11	12	0	.478	190	185	101	87	14	58	0	7	117	2	4.12
Barnicle, Glens Falls*	20	4	0	0	5	2	1	.714	70	75	37	33	5	47	2	2	42	5	4.24
Baum, Bristol	11	7	0	0	1	4	0	.200	35	44	28	24	5	28	2	3	20	3	6.17
Bernard, Holyoke	9	0	0	0	1	0	1	1.000	14	20	17	12	1	12	1	0	11	1	7.71
Best, Lynn	26	26	5	0	9	14	0	.391	154	144	116	95	10	106	0	4	92	8	5.55
Birrell, Bristol*	12	8	1	0	5	3	0	.625	61	52	21	21	1	19	1	0	30	6	3.10
Bordi, West Haven	11	9	6	0	4	6	0	.400	76	75	42	35	3	30	2	0	49	2	4.14
Bradley, West Haven	24	24	7	0	3	15	0	.167	146	190	121	105	16	51	4	5	56	5	6.47
Bradley, Glens Falls	7	0	0	0	2	0	0	1.000	18	17	6	6	0	7	0	2	19	5	3.00
Brito, Waterbury	25	25	8	1	12	6	0	.667	172	125	66	60	11	75	1	8	175	3	3.14
Britt, Buffalo*	8	0	0	0	1	0	1	1.000	11	11	5	4	1	11	0	0	5	1	3.27
Buckle, Waterbury	4	4	1	0	1	2	0	.333	26	27	13	11	0	10	2	0	12	4	3.81
Burroughs, Reading*	11	11	2	0	2	7	0	.222	57	70	46	39	4	27	1	2	33	2	6.16
Burtt, Bristol	31	22	8	3	11	8	1	.579	165	141	74	65	11	93	5	2	102	8	3.55
Calderon, Buffalo*	29	7	1	1	5	2	2	.714	64	64	47	38	8	40	0	2	31	0	5.34
Carroll, Holyoke*	16	1	0	0	1	2	1	.333	24	14	13	13	3	22	2	1	21	2	4.88
Cary, Lynn	22	2	0	0	1	1	1	.500	62	59	41	26	2	42	4	3	42	6	3.77
Cato, Waterbury	12	12	2	0	3	7	0	.300	73	75	36	31	2	28	3	2	25	0	3.82
B. Clark, Lynn*	16	16	8	1	9	5	0	.643	116	102	49	40	2	50	2	3	93	11	3.10
Cliburn, Buffalo	1	1	0	0	1	0	0	1.000	6	5	0	0	0	3	0	0	3	0	0.00
Comstock, West Haven*	29	3	2	0	2	4	1	.333	73	64	40	34	8	37	4	0	52	10	4.19
Conroy, West Haven	25	25	5	0	8	14	0	.364	147	160	119	101	8	93	3	8	72	16	6.18
Cort, Holyoke	5	5	0	0	1	4	0	.200	24	33	20	18	1	12	1	0	6	0	6.75
Crawford, Bristol	24	23	10	2	9	7	0	.563	177	170	68	52	6	64	6	5	97	2	2.64
Curran, Holyoke	3	2	0	0	0	0	0	.000	5	6	7	7	3	3	0	1	1	0	12.60
Davis, Reading*	28	28	8	4	19	6	0	.760	193	140	63	53	11	75	0	4	185	6	2.47
Dawley, Waterbury	7	7	1	0	2	2	0	.500	49	43	18	16	3	25	2	1	33	2	2.94
De Vincenzo, Reading	51	0	0	0	6	5	4	.545	99	104	51	47	9	40	3	0	32	5	4.27
Denman, Bristol	10	9	0	0	6	5	0	.545	78	71	26	20	4	12	2	2	35	5	3.10
DiPino, Holyoke*	16	8	1	1	7	0	0	1.000	76	46	13	11	0	27	0	0	58	5	1.30
Dravecky, Buffalo*	27	21	8	0	13	7	0	.650	161	165	76	60	14	60	3	2	64	2	3.35
Dye, Waterbury	48	3	1	0	9	7	11	.563	102	96	48	47	9	37	5	1	75	5	4.15
Esser, Glens Falls*	9	9	1	0	3	5	0	.375	49	51	31	28	5	31	0	2	26	1	5.14
Evans, Buffalo	13	8	1	0	3	5	0	.375	63	72	43	38	7	25	1	3	25	5	5.43
Evans, Glens Falls	23	23	3	0	8	10	0	.444	146	137	82	61	15	82	3	2	80	6	3.76
Farr, Buffalo	23	22	10	1	11	6	0	.647	161	158	84	71	18	64	0	7	71	4	3.97
Faulk, Reading	29	0	0	0	4	1	8	.800	40	45	27	22	0	19	3	0	24	5	4.95
Field, Buffalo	2	2	0	0	1	1	0	.500	12	13	11	3	1	6	1	0	6	1	2.25
Florillo, Waterbury*	26	4	0	0	4	3	0	.571	51	56	30	24	1	28	1	0	28	5	4.24
Flannery, Glens Falls	8	0	0	0	0	0	0	.000	16	27	15	9	2	6	1	1	7	1	5.06
Fowler, Reading	28	28	7	4	13	7	0	.650	179	182	95	80	10	65	0	9	71	3	4.02
Garrity, Buffalo	3	0	0	0	1	0	0	.000	9	13	10	8	1	8	0	0	4	2	8.00
Gause, Reading*	57	2	0	0	2	9	10	.182	82	84	57	51	7	45	6	7	61	6	5.60
Georger, Lynn	38	8	0	0	3	7	4	.300	89	78	45	34	4	44	1	2	51	6	3.44
Givens, Bristol	16	13	0	0	2	6	0	.250	59	73	51	44	4	46	3	3	29	3	6.71
Gosse, West Haven*	30	2	1	0	3	8	3	.273	62	66	37	29	5	24	1	2	25	2	4.21
C. Harris, West Haven	21	21	6	0	5	12	0	.294	142	134	80	64	10	70	3	2	56	5	4.06
F. Harris, West Haven	2	0	0	0	0	1	0	.000	3	3	0	0	2	2	1	0	1	0	0.00
Harrison, Lynn	41	3	1	0	4	7	3	.364	99	133	77	56	2	33	7	2	39	9	5.09
Hart, Reading	5	5	0	0	0	2	0	.000	25	23	15	13	2	14	0	0	17	1	4.68
Hickey, Glens Falls*	26	26	5	2	9	7	0	.563	169	184	92	81	20	73	2	4	80	6	4.31
J. Hobbs, Lynn*	11	6	1	1	2	4	0	.333	44	45	25	23	1	17	0	2	32	4	4.70
Howard, Bristol	19	16	7	2	10	5	0	.667	112	109	51	47	6	48	3	10	99	7	3.78
Hughes, Waterbury	21	17	2	0	5	7	0	.417	96	103	47	44	10	30	1	3	57	6	4.13
Ibarra, Reading	1	0	0	0	0	0	0	.000	1	4	3	3	0	0	0	0	0	0	0.00
C. Johnson, Glens Falls	9	9	1	0	3	3	0	.500	52	71	46	42	5	29	0	4	32	2	7.27
T. Johnson, Glens Falls	15	15	1	0	2	5	0	.286	65	86	58	48	9	22	1	2	28	4	6.65
Jones, Holyoke	8	8	4	0	5	3	0	.625	62	57	23	20	2	26	0	2	39	5	2.90
Kane, Bristol	23	18	2	0	6	9	0	.400	118	135	69	53	7	59	6	2	79	3	4.04
King, Bristol	28	16	3	0	6	6	0	.500	131	123	72	58	9	91	4	6	119	7	3.98
Kranitz, Holyoke	25	24	6	1	13	7	1	.650	168	139	81	68	7	105	2	8	78	9	3.64
Lahti, Waterbury	55	0	0	0	7	8	16	.467	91	75	34	28	7	40	4	1	78	7	2.77
Larson, Reading	4	0	0	0	3	0	0	1.000	14	13	5	5	2	9	0	2	11	0	3.21
Maitland, Glens Falls*	12	8	1	0	4	5	0	.444	51	66	47	36	6	26	1	1	20	6	6.35
Martinez, Buffalo	11	0	0	0	2	2	0	.500	30	35	20	20	6	14	1	3	24	2	6.00
Mayer, Waterbury*	11	8	0	0	4	3	0	.571	49	51	23	19	4	27	0	0	32	1	3.49

Pitcher–Club	G.	GS.	CG.	ShO.	W.	L.	Sv.	Pct.	IP.	H.	R.	ER.	HR.	BB.	Int. BB.	HB.	SO.	WP.	ERA.
Meyer, Holyoke*	23	3	0	0	2	2	1	.500	48	65	35	28	3	21	1	0	24	8	5.25
Minnick, Lynn*	15	0	0	0	1	0	0	1.000	19	29	29	19	1	18	1	3	20	9	9.00
Mitchell, Buffalo	2	0	0	0	0	0	0	.000	2	3	3	3	1	2	0	0	1	0	13.50
Moloney, Bristol*	16	0	0	0	1	3	4	.250	11	9	7	4	2	8	1	1	8	2	3.27
Montgomery, Holyoke	27	26	8	3	9	13	0	.409	175	190	75	57	8	38	4	2	82	2	2.93
Moore, West Haven	5	5	0	0	4	0	0	.000	23	32	25	23	3	15	0	2	7	4	9.00
Musselman, Lynn	53	1	0	0	6	6	15	.500	86	75	49	37	6	34	6	3	47	8	3.87
Neuenschwander, Water..	56	0	0	0	7	1	7	.875	89	60	25	22	5	41	5	4	48	2	2.22
Nicholson, Buffalo*	23	17	2	0	5	8	0	.385	109	139	84	72	13	53	1	2	59	5	5.94
Notarino, Buffalo	16	1	1	0	1	3	3	.250	42	39	15	15	5	9	1	1	17	1	3.21
Nottle, West Haven	1	0	0	0	0	0	0	.000	2	0	0	0	0	1	0	1	0	0	0.00
O'Keefe, Waterbury*	18	9	5	3	6	1	1	.857	86	65	24	22	0	48	2	0	32	3	2.30
Ogawa, Holyoke	47	0	0	0	6	2	16	.750	69	50	18	15	3	18	4	0	53	1	1.96
Pastrovich, Glens Falls	21	1	0	0	0	3	0	.000	61	76	52	41	8	26	1	3	26	10	6.05
Patterson, Glens Falls	13	13	4	0	6	3	0	.667	89	80	46	37	8	45	0	4	52	6	3.74
Platel, Glens Falls	22	11	2	0	2	9	1	.182	77	97	69	57	10	48	0	2	33	7	6.66
Porter, Holyoke	14	10	5	1	8	2	1	.800	90	84	32	29	1	16	0	4	30	2	2.90
Prior, Reading	37	17	4	0	6	8	1	.429	127	139	91	77	7	74	5	4	52	8	5.46
Randolph, Lynn	14	14	4	1	6	6	0	.500	85	83	44	33	4	43	1	4	40	5	3.49
Rasmussen, Reading	18	18	8	1	8	5	0	.615	120	106	50	44	4	43	2	3	64	9	3.30
Reed, Reading	8	1	1	1	1	2	2	.500	17	17	6	6	0	10	1	0	10	0	3.18
Reed, Holyoke	19	2	0	0	0	4	2	.000	31	28	18	18	1	26	0	0	15	1	5.23
Reelhorn, Reading	16	16	4	2	9	3	0	.750	111	102	40	34	7	37	0	3	72	8	2.76
Rock, Buffalo	21	20	5	0	8	8	0	.500	144	141	81	68	11	60	2	3	56	16	4.25
Scherrer, Waterbury*	25	25	4	3	7	8	0	.467	151	139	58	56	10	58	2	0	84	2	3.34
Schoppee, Bristol	55	0	0	0	8	2	19	.800	92	85	33	27	1	41	6	4	50	4	2.64
Sealy, West Haven	33	5	2	0	2	6	4	.250	94	120	63	57	14	37	1	1	61	5	5.46
Shields, Bristol	39	6	1	0	5	6	4	.455	113	128	79	61	7	77	14	4	63	11	4.86
Simond, Lynn*	28	27	6	1	10	11	0	.476	186	198	90	75	13	91	3	10	111	11	3.63
Smith, Glens Falls*	5	5	1	0	0	4	0	.000	26	37	21	18	3	11	1	0	12	0	6.23
Speck, Reading	9	8	1	0	4	3	0	.571	51	39	25	22	6	25	1	1	43	2	3.88
Swift, Holyoke	28	27	4	1	11	10	0	.524	179	148	76	67	9	97	2	6	92	5	3.37
Teutsch, Glens Falls	58	0	0	0	13	6	14	.684	119	113	53	43	5	55	9	4	67	4	3.25
Thibodeaux, Buffalo	10	10	2	0	3	4	0	.429	63	58	40	36	13	30	1	7	38	1	5.14
Torres, Holyoke	20	19	4	2	8	8	0	.500	123	102	58	52	10	50	1	1	69	5	3.80
Town, Waterbury	29	25	2	1	8	9	0	.471	147	142	62	54	12	43	5	4	50	4	3.31
Tronerud, West Haven	25	18	7	1	5	8	0	.385	151	143	76	52	12	47	1	4	66	6	3.10
Weismiller, Buffalo	13	0	0	0	0	2	0	.000	16	24	11	11	4	7	2	0	4	0	6.19
Welborn, Lynn	20	20	3	0	8	4	0	.667	111	106	60	50	6	81	1	7	79	10	4.05
Wieters, Glens Falls	32	13	3	0	5	12	1	.294	132	158	99	78	11	10	1	7	43	10	5.32
Williams, Buffalo*	4	0	0	0	0	0	0	.000	9	7	0	0	4	0	0	3	0	0.00
Williams, Glens Falls*	1	0	0	0	0	0	0	.000	1	2	1	1	0	1	0	0	0	0	9.00
Wiltbank, Buffalo	26	23	6	0	7	11	0	.389	163	160	85	74	13	83	0	7	86	11	4.09
Wyszynski, West Haven ..	34	1	1	0	4	3	8	.571	57	59	27	26	4	29	2	1	40	3	4.11

BALKS—Hickey 6; B. Bradley, King, Nicholson, 3 each; Atherton, Brito, Davis, Fowler, C. Harris, Kranitz, Randolph, Rock, Sealy, Shields, 2 each; Abreu, Allen, Aponte, Arias, Barnicle, Birrell, Burroughs, Burtt, Calderon, Carroll, Cato, Conroy, Cort, Crawford, DiPino, Dye, Field, Georger, Howard, T. Johnson, Lahti, Moore, Musselman, Neuenschwander, Notarino, O'Keefe, Patterson, Platel, Porter, Prior, Reelhorn, Simond, Smith, Welborn, Wiltbank, Wyszynski, 1 each.

COMBINATION SHUTOUTS—Birrell-Shields, Bristol; Cliburn-Arias, Rock-Calderon, Wiltbank-Allen, Buffalo; Evans-Teutsch, Glens Falls; DiPino-Ogawa 2, DiPino-Meyer-Ako, Porter-Ako, Ako-Ogawa, Swift-Kranitz, Torres-Meyer-Reed-Bernard, Holyoke; Simond-Adair-Musselman, B. Clark-Musselman, Simond-Musselman, Lynn; Speck-Abreu, Davis-Faulk, Reading; Scherrer-Dye 2, Mayer-Neuenschwander, Town-Lahti, Waterbury; Harris-Wyszynski-Comstock-Sealy, West Haven.

NO-HIT GAME—DiPino, Holyoke, defeated Reading, 6-0, June 8, second game, seven innings.

Southern League

CLASS AA

**Leading Batter
CHRIS BANDO
Charlotte**

**League President
JIMMY BRAGAN**

**Leading Pitcher
ANDY McGAFFIGAN
Nashville**

CHAMPIONSHIP WINNERS IN PREVIOUS YEARS

1904—Macon	.598	Macon	.643
1905—Macon	.625	1931-35—Did not operate.	
1906—Savannah	.637	1936—Jacksonville	.652
1907—Charleston	.620	Columbus*	.650
1908—Jacksonville	.694	1937—Columbus	.572
1909—Chattanooga*	.738	Savannah (3rd)†	.565
Augusta	.702	1938—Savannah	.574
1910—Columbus	.588	Macon (2nd)†	.570
1911—Columbus*	.681	1939—Columbus	.601
Columbia	.710	Augusta (2nd)†	.597
1912—Jacksonville*	.679	1940—Savannah	.627
Columbus	.632	Columbus (2nd)†	.583
1913—Savannah	.754	1941—Macon	.643
Savannah	.593	Columbia (2nd)†	.636
1914—Savannah*	.667	1942—Charleston	.620
Albany	.650	Macon (2nd)†	.585
1915—Macon	.588	1943-45—Did not operate.	
Columbus*	.686	1946—Columbus	.568
1916—Augusta*	.617	Augusta (4th)†	.547
Columbia	.631	1947—Columbus	.575
1917—Charleston	.741	Savannah (2nd)†	.563
Columbia*	.667	1948—Charleston	.572
1918—Did not operate.		Greenville (3rd)†	.549
1919—Columbia	.585	1949—Macon‡	.623
1920—Columbia	.633	1950—Macon‡	.588
1921—Columbia	.642	1951—Montgomery	.607
1922—Charleston	.625	1952—Columbia	.649
1923—Charlotte*	.653	Montgomery (3rd)†	.558
Macon	.580	1953—Jacksonville	.679
1924—Augusta	.612	Savannah (2nd)†	.571
1925—Spartanburg	.620	1954—Jacksonville	.593
1926—Greenville	.662	Savannah (2nd)†	.571
1927—Greenville	.622	1955—Columbia	.636
1928—Asheville	.664	Augusta (3rd)†	.543
1929—Greenville	.605	1956—Jacksonville‡	.621
Knoxville*	.634	1957—Augusta	.636
1930—Greenville	.620	Charlotte (2nd)†	.562

1958—Augusta	.550
Macon (3rd)†	.500
1959—Knoxville	.557
Gastonia (4th)†	.504
1960—Columbia	.597
Savannah (3rd)†	.561
1961—Asheville	.635
1962—Savannah	.662
Macon (3rd)†	.576
1963—Augusta*	.661
Lynchburg	.662
1964—Lynchburg	.579
1965—Columbus	.572
1966—Mobile	.629
1967—Birmingham	.604
1968—Asheville	.614
1969—Charlotte	.579
1970—Columbus	.569
1971—Did not operate as league—clubs were members of Dixie Association.	
1972—Asheville	.583
Montgomery§	.561
1973—Montgomery§	.580
Jacksonville	.559
1974—Jacksonville	.565
Knoxville§	.533
1975—Orlando	.587
Montgomery§	.545
1976—Montgomery x	.591
Orlando	.540
1977—Montgomery x	.628
Jacksonville	.522
1978—Knoxville x	.611
Savannah	.500
1979—Columbus	.587
Nashville x	.576

*Won split-season playoff. †Won four-club playoff. ‡Won championship and four-club playoff. §League was divided into Eastern and Western divisions; won playoff. xLeague was divided into Eastern and Western divisions and played split-season. Playoff winner.

— 466 —

STANDING OF CLUBS AT CLOSE OF FIRST HALF, JUNE 1

EASTERN DIVISION

Club	W.	L.	T.	Pct.	G.B.
Charlotte (Orioles)	38	33	0	.535	......
Columbus (Astros)	35	34	0	.507	2
Savannah (Braves)	35	34	0	.507	2
Jacksonville (Royals)	31	40	0	.437	7
Orlando (Twins)	29	41	0	.414	8½

WESTERN DIVISION

Club	W.	L.	T.	Pct.	G.B.
Memphis (Expos)	47	23	0	.671	......
Nashville (Yankees)	46	25	0	.648	1½
Montgomery (Tigers)	31	39	0	.443	16
Chattanooga (Indians)	31	39	0	.443	16
Knoxville (Blue Jays)	28	43	0	.394	19½

STANDING OF CLUBS AT CLOSE OF SECOND HALF, SEPTEMBER 1

EASTERN DIVISION

Club	W.	L.	T.	Pct.	G.B.
Savannah (Braves)	42	33	0	.560	......
Columbus (Astros)	41	34	0	.547	1
Orlando (Twins)	36	37	0	.493	5
Charlotte (Orioles)	34	39	0	.466	7
Jacksonville (Royals)	32	41	0	.438	9

WESTERN DIVISION

Club	W.	L.	T.	Pct.	G.B.
Nashville (Yankees)	51	21	0	.708	......
Montgomery (Tigers)	37	37	0	.500	15
Memphis (Expos)	36	38	0	.486	16
Chattanooga (Indians)	30	44	0	.405	22
Knoxville (Blue Jays)	29	44	0	.397	22½

COMPOSITE STANDING OF CLUBS AT CLOSE OF SEASON, SEPTEMBER 1

WESTERN DIVISION

Club	Nash.	Mem.	Mon.	Chat.	Knox.	Sav.	Col.	Char.	Orl.	Jax.	W.	L.	T.	Pct.	G.B.
Nashville (Yankees)	....	9	10	8	9	13	10	11	13	14	97	46	0	.678	......
Memphis (Expos)	7	....	8	14	13	9	8	7	8	9	83	61	0	.576	14½
Montgomery (Tigers)	6	8	....	8	10	5	7	7	11	6	68	76	0	.472	29½
Chattanooga (Indians)	8	2	8	....	7	5	9	7	9	6	61	83	0	.424	36½
Knoxville (Blue Jays)	7	3	6	9	....	8	4	9	5	6	57	87	0	.396	40½

EASTERN DIVISION

Club	Nash.	Mem.	Mon.	Chat.	Knox.	Sav.	Col.	Char.	Orl.	Jax.	W.	L.	T.	Pct.	G.B.
Savannah (Braves)	3	7	11	11	8	....	7	12	8	10	77	67	0	.535	......
Columbus (Astros)	6	8	9	7	12	9	....	8	7	10	76	68	0	.528	1
Charlotte (Orioles)	5	9	9	9	7	4	8	....	11	10	72	72	0	.500	5
Orlando (Twins)	2	8	5	7	11	8	9	5	....	10	65	78	0	.455	11½
Jacksonville (Royals)	2	7	10	10	10	4	6	6	6	....	63	81	0	.438	14

Major league affiliations in parentheses.

Playoffs—Charlotte, first half leader, defeated Savannah, second half leader, three games to none for Eastern Division championship. Memphis, first half leader, defeated Nashville, second half leader, three games to one for Western Division championship. Charlotte (Eastern Division Champion) defeated Memphis (Western Division Champion), three games to one for League Championship.

Regular-Season Attendance—Charlotte, 198,528; Chattanooga, 132,338; Columbus, 123,173; Jacksonville, 133,218; Knoxville, 56,927; Memphis, 322,037; Montgomery, 81,168; Nashville, 575,676; Orlando, 49,801; Savannah, 88,326. Total, 1,761,192. Playoffs, 30,909. No all-star game.

Managers: Charlotte—Jimmy Williams; Chattanooga—Woody Smith; Columbus—Matt Galante; Jacksonville—Gene Lamont; Knoxville—Duane Larson; Memphis—Larry Bearnarth; Montgomery—Roy Majtyka; Nashville—Carl Merrill; Orlando—Roy McMillan; Savannah—Eddie Haas.

All-Star Team: 1B—Balboni, Nashville; 2B—Tabler, Nashville; 3B—Ripken, Charlotte; SS—Concepcion, Jacksonville; OF—Hazewood, Charlotte; Rooney, Memphis; Showalter, Nashville; C—Bando, Chattanooga; DH—Gates, Montgomery; Utility—Ray, Columbus; Tolman, Columbus; P—McGaffigan, Nashville; Meredith, Columbus; Manager—Merrill, Nashville.

(Compiled by Howe News Bureau, Boston, Mass.)

CLUB BATTING

Club	G.	AB.	R.	OR.	H.	TB.	2B.	3B.	HR.	RBI.	SH.	SF.	BB.	Int. BB.	HP.	SO.	SB.	CS.	LOB.	Pct.
Nashville	143	4837	753	550	1345	1912	192	60	85	668	50	40	565	38	46	675	139	86	1087	.278
Columbus	144	4603	660	600	1230	1782	220	28	92	584	51	45	515	17	27	652	114	69	980	.267
Memphis	144	4706	728	613	1255	1865	228	35	104	663	31	54	634	24	42	682	187	85	1012	.267
Savannah	144	4613	596	576	1211	1737	188	37	88	523	30	41	455	19	39	773	131	62	978	.263
Chattanooga	144	4772	679	711	1243	1878	219	34	116	616	46	47	494	29	35	849	83	65	976	.260
Jacksonville	144	4724	664	715	1213	1778	201	47	90	582	43	44	558	16	35	701	169	66	1001	.257
Montgomery	144	4572	596	664	1173	1672	213	14	86	537	58	34	554	24	41	731	98	63	1041	.257
Knoxville	144	4644	565	711	1168	1634	160	42	74	505	41	29	462	19	42	699	59	39	986	.252
Charlotte	144	4641	605	608	1148	1765	190	44	113	537	30	33	516	17	32	877	176	84	963	.247
Orlando	143	4698	559	657	1104	1635	170	20	107	519	47	20	520	16	36	869	70	45	1038	.235

INDIVIDUAL BATTING

(Leading Qualifiers for Batting Championship—389 or More Plate Appearances)

*Bats lefthanded.   †Switch-hitter.

Player and Club	G.	AB.	R.	H.	TB.	2B.	3B.	HR.	RBI.	SH.	SF.	BB.	HP.	SO.	SB.	CS.	Pct.
Bando, Christopher, Chattanooga ..	121	404	78	141	214	31	3	12	73	0	4	68	1	49	1	3	.349
Showalter, W. Nathaniel, Nashville	142	550	84	178	206	19	3	1	82	5	2	53	5	23	6	9	.324
Ray, John, Columbus....................	138	497	86	161	235	32	6	10	72	0	5	43	1	45	2	2	.324
Barton, Kenneth, Chattanooga	112	405	77	124	184	22	4	10	59	2	3	65	2	57	4	6	.306
Sheridan, Patrick, Jacksonville......	97	367	63	112	158	17	7	5	42	4	1	31	0	62	14	4	.305
Rosario, Simon, Columbus	107	397	47	120	149	20	0	3	52	3	1	15	1	53	3	6	.302
Balboni, Stephen, Nashville	141	521	101	157	288	25	2	34	122	1	4	82	5	162	4	2	.301
Johnson, Anthony, Memphis	135	511	79	153	215	24	7	8	89	3	5	69	1	107	60	19	.299
Tabler, Patrick, Nashville..............	136	479	82	142	244	38	8	16	83	4	2	66	9	74	9	6	.296
Schmitz, Daniel, Nashville.............	101	365	58	108	140	14	3	4	41	4	4	48	2	28	9	5	.296

Departmental Leaders: G—Eaton, Ripken, 144; AB—Shelby, 560; R—Balboni, 101; H—Showalter, 178; TB—Balboni, 288; 2B—Ron Johnson, 40; 3B—Wilborn, 14; HR—Balboni, 34; RBI—Balboni, 122; GWRBI—Tabler, 13; SH—Harris, 12; SF—Gates, Ripken, 9; BB—Phillips, 98; IBB—Balboni, 15; HP—Gates, 12; SO—Hazewood, 177; SB—A. Johnson, 60; CS—Eaton, 22.

(All Players—Listed Alphabetically)

Player and Club	G.	AB.	R.	H.	TB.	2B.	3B.	HR.	RBI.	SH.	SF.	BB.	HP.	SO.	SB.	CS.	Pct.
Alvarez, Roberto, Chattanooga	30	103	11	26	31	5	0	0	5	1	0	7	0	14	0	1	.252
Anderson, Thomas, Chattanooga*..	22	79	9	14	22	3	1	1	9	0	1	10	0	15	1	0	.177
Armstrong, Gary, Montgomery*.....	129	402	56	101	113	8	2	0	41	8	2	86	1	39	7	12	.251
Atkinson, James, Jacksonville*......	20	69	9	20	31	5	0	2	9	1	1	6	0	9	2	1	.290
Baker, David, Knoxville*...............	98	341	44	82	142	16	4	12	56	3	1	38	8	90	0	1	.240
Baker, Kenneth, Nashville*............	78	252	43	72	92	12	1	2	26	1	3	36	0	22	2	2	.286
Balboni, Stephen, Nashville	141	521	101	157	288	25	2	34	122	1	4	82	5	162	4	2	.301
Ballard, Glenn, Orlando................	17	53	5	11	17	3	0	1	2	0	0	3	0	7	1	0	.208
Bando, Christopher, Chattanooga‡.	121	404	78	141	214	31	3	12	73	0	4	68	2	49	1	3	.349
Barfield, Jesse, Knoxville..............	124	433	63	104	174	12	8	14	65	1	7	57	6	113	11	2	.240
Barton, Kenneth, Chattanooga†	112	405	77	124	184	22	4	10	59	2	3	65	2	57	4	6	.306
Batter, Ronald, Jacksonville	36	109	7	17	19	2	0	0	6	1	0	17	0	22	5	1	.156
Belanger, Lee, Orlando*	18	2	0	1	1	0	0	0	0	0	0	0	0	1	0	0	.500
Benson, Steve, Orlando	53	208	30	43	53	8	1	0	18	6	1	18	3	29	9	7	.207
Bockhorn, Glen, Savannah	3	7	1	1	1	0	0	0	1	0	0	1	0	3	0	0	.143
Bodie, Keith, Columbus................	131	452	60	112	161	21	5	6	50	2	4	44	1	68	10	9	.248
Boelter, Tarry, Orlando	6	14	0	4	4	0	0	0	0	0	0	2	0	1	0	0	.286
Brett, Russell, Charlotte	11	30	3	3	3	0	0	0	5	0	1	7	0	4	0	2	.100
Buffamoyer, John, Charlotte	43	138	13	31	49	6	0	4	13	0	1	7	0	26	0	0	.225
Bush, R. Randall, Orlando*	51	175	32	41	66	2	1	7	26	0	0	30	4	46	1	2	.234
Cadahia, Aurelio, Orlando	101	342	35	83	118	12	1	7	44	2	3	32	2	27	3	1	.243
Callahan, Patrick, Nashville	75	206	20	56	63	7	0	0	22	4	3	28	2	24	4	1	.272
Carrion, Leonel, Memphis	43	133	26	38	61	6	1	5	20	0	1	26	0	19	4	2	.286
Chaney, Bruce, Chattanooga	46	145	20	34	49	8	2	1	14	2	3	15	0	40	1	2	.234
Chapman, Nathan, Nashville*	135	520	94	144	206	17	12	7	63	8	6	47	4	58	46	18	.277
Christopher, Scott, Charlotte........	8	26	4	1	1	0	0	0	1	1	1	3	0	7	2	1	.038
Concepcion, Onix, Jacksonville......	74	273	48	88	143	13	3	12	44	4	8	24	6	24	17	5	.322
Cooper, Gary, Savannah†	109	400	58	90	112	10	3	2	29	0	4	46	4	94	21	9	.225
Cripe, David, Columbus	41	127	17	33	45	3	0	3	20	3	3	18	2	19	4	2	.260
Crowley, Raymond, Memphis*	93	278	42	60	101	15	1	8	37	0	3	73	5	46	0	2	.216
Cypret, Gregory, Columbus...........	120	406	64	116	202	19	2	21	74	6	4	61	3	40	6	7	.286
Dahl, Gregory, Columbus..............	77	244	24	58	79	7	1	4	36	6	3	28	0	50	0	1	.238
Dasen, Ted, Montgomery*	83	252	30	65	83	11	2	1	22	1	1	44	1	59	6	3	.258
Dayette, Brian, Nashville	35	100	15	21	29	8	0	0	9	2	2	12	0	26	4	2	.210
De La Rosa, Jesus, Knoxville	17	58	6	13	21	2	0	2	4	1	0	3	0	15	0	0	.224
Denman, John, Charlotte...............	128	444	51	122	174	13	6	9	60	0	4	53	1	102	28	15	.275
Dennis, Eduardo, Knoxville	137	480	47	116	143	15	3	2	44	7	2	19	0	41	9	8	.242
Derryberry, Timothy, Charlotte*.....	6	20	3	4	4	0	0	0	2	0	0	1	2	5	1	1	.200
Douglas, Stephen, Orlando	37	140	12	30	37	2	1	1	12	1	0	11	0	17	7	1	.214
Duncan, Taylor, Knoxville	32	100	14	29	46	5	0	4	16	0	2	11	0	12	0	1	.290
Eaton, Tom, Charlotte	144	542	92	127	181	26	2	8	48	4	1	84	6	49	52	22	.234
Elliott, Clayton, Savannah	66	222	33	49	81	12	1	6	22	0	2	35	3	47	14	7	.221
Ervin, Todd, Montgomery*	16	44	2	9	11	2	0	0	3	1	2	7	0	2	1	0	.205
Eschen, James, Jacksonville†........	47	144	17	37	44	1	0	2	18	0	2	16	0	12	2	1	.257
Espino, Juan, Nashville	17	56	3	9	10	1	0	0	5	1	0	1	3	13	0	0	.161
Estes, Frank, Orlando*	88	333	62	94	134	16	3	6	48	1	4	46	1	33	8	6	.282
Fabrizio, Kurt, Charlotte*	84	292	30	66	95	11	3	4	28	2	1	29	2	41	3	2	.226
Faedo, Leonardo, Orlando	114	437	47	105	138	13	1	6	26	7	4	34	4	50	1	3	.240
Filkins, Leslie, Montgomery*	49	174	22	50	80	10	1	6	31	1	1	18	4	24	2	5	.287
Firova, Daniel, Jacksonville	3	9	0	5	7	2	0	0	1	0	0	1	0	3	0	0	.556
Followell, Vernon, Montgomery†	143	488	52	129	156	17	2	2	47	6	6	60	6	50	6	4	.264
Francona, Terry, Memphis*	60	210	20	63	83	13	2	1	23	2	1	10	1	20	1	4	.300
Franklin, Glen, Memphis*	124	426	61	118	177	27	4	8	52	4	2	42	4	55	20	13	.277
Fry, Jerry, Memphis	5	15	3	3	7	1	0	1	2	0	0	4	0	1	0	0	.200

Player and Club	G.	AB.	R.	H.	TB.	2B.	3B.	HR.	RBI.	SH.	SF.	BB.	HP.	SO.	SB.	CS.	Pct.
Funderburk, Mark, Orlando	139	525	70	131	234	21	2	26	87	0	3	46	7	150	8	5	.250
Garcia, Michael, Savannah	28	77	7	18	26	3	1	1	5	2	0	6	0	8	2	0	.234
Gardner, Vassie, Chattanooga	122	486	64	135	198	13	10	10	61	7	3	27	2	102	29	11	.278
Garrison, Marvin, Chattanooga	61	232	39	67	104	12	2	7	29	6	4	16	0	52	11	8	.239
Gates, Eddie, Montgomery	111	382	65	107	208	26	0	25	91	0	5	58	12	69	2	1	.280
Gates, Michael, Memphis*	143	538	87	137	182	18	6	5	67	5	9	77	3	50	23	11	.255
Gavillan, Pedro, Memphis†	10	25	1	2	2	0	0	0	0	0	0	1	0	7	0	1	.080
Glaser, G. Gordon, Chattanooga	25	0	1	0	0	0	0	0	0	0	0	0	0	0	0	0	.000
Goldetsky, Lawrence, Memphis	19	34	8	4	5	1	0	0	1	1	0	5	0	10	0	0	.118
Green, Steven, Orlando	33	1	0	0	0	0	0	0	0	0	0	0	0	1	0	0	.000
Grout, Ronald, 11 Orl-119 Sav	130	473	52	123	196	21	2	16	76	0	3	37	2	67	0	1	.260
Gulden, Bradley, Nashville*	85	295	34	70	113	13	6	6	46	1	4	48	2	43	3	7	.237
Gustavson, Duane, Jacksonville	54	165	25	39	52	10	0	1	19	2	2	34	2	29	1	1	.236
Haley, J. Michael, Jacksonville	78	266	26	57	85	12	2	4	27	1	1	24	1	31	6	5	.214
Hallberg, Lance, Orlando	30	94	13	15	21	3	0	1	10	1	0	13	2	16	1	1	.160
Hampton, Isaac, Knoxville	30	104	14	23	42	2	1	5	20	0	2	15	2	29	2	1	.221
Hampton, Raphael, Montgomery	112	356	63	89	112	16	2	1	28	9	2	65	3	62	34	10	.250
Hanggie, Daniel, Nashville†	75	237	34	60	69	4	1	1	18	4	1	28	2	25	4	2	.253
Harper, Arvis, Columbus*	28	84	11	16	26	7	0	1	4	0	1	6	1	9	1	2	.190
Harper, Daryl, Jacksonville†	56	136	10	23	26	1	1	0	3	2	1	22	0	22	1	1	.169
Harris, Lamart, Jacksonville†	132	479	74	117	155	10	8	4	39	12	3	48	9	96	53	10	.244
Haslerig, J. William, Savannah†	38	139	24	41	61	6	4	2	20	0	3	9	0	29	4	2	.295
Hazewood, Drungo, Charlotte	142	499	80	130	242	16	6	28	80	0	3	74	1	177	29	9	.261
Heath, Kelly, Jacksonville	55	205	26	63	92	10	2	5	27	1	2	12	1	25	2	3	.307
Hench, Ralph, Nashville	2	5	0	1	1	0	0	0	0	0	0	0	0	0	0	0	.200
Hernandez, Pedro, Knoxville	112	424	51	120	154	14	4	4	43	1	4	22	5	51	11	9	.283
Hodge, Eddie, Orlando*	27	3	0	0	0	0	0	0	0	0	0	0	0	2	0	0	.000
Hodgson, Paul, Knoxville	59	187	22	44	79	8	6	5	26	1	0	24	2	48	2	2	.235
Hogg, David, Jacksonville	43	136	16	30	36	6	0	0	18	1	1	27	1	27	1	1	.221
Hudgens, David, Chattanooga*	113	376	31	79	120	9	4	8	49	2	3	24	3	63	4	1	.210
Huppert, David, Charlotte	107	319	43	70	98	15	2	3	23	2	2	64	2	50	0	3	.219
Hurdle, Michael, Knoxville	15	53	3	14	15	1	0	0	5	0	0	5	0	13	1	1	.264
Ingle, Randy, Savannah	40	138	13	31	38	4	0	1	11	2	0	13	1	34	1	2	.225
Jacobs, Ronald, Columbus	72	214	22	45	55	10	0	0	22	2	1	34	2	26	1	2	.210
Jacoby, Brook, Savannah	3	8	0	1	1	0	0	0	0	0	0	0	0	4	0	0	.125
Jemison, Gregory, Nashville*	13	25	7	3	3	0	0	0	1	0	4	2	5	2	0	0	.120
Johnson, Craig, Montgomery	18	43	1	8	10	2	0	0	3	1	1	4	1	10	0	0	.186
Johnson, Randy, Savannah	54	167	18	53	69	10	0	2	11	5	1	15	5	19	2	3	.317
Johnson, Ronald D., Jacksonville	142	514	81	139	248	40	4	23	104	2	6	79	1	53	1	1	.270
Johnson, Anthony, Memphis	135	511	79	153	215	24	7	8	89	3	5	69	1	107	60	19	.299
Johnson, Wallace, Memphis†	4	13	1	1	2	1	0	0	1	0	0	1	0	2	0	0	.077
Johnston, J. Mark, Nashville*	33	72	15	18	36	4	1	4	13	0	0	11	3	6	0	0	.250
Keatley, Gregory, Montgomery	42	133	17	28	48	8	0	4	16	2	0	16	0	32	1	1	.211
Kenaga, Jeffrey, Montgomery*	124	450	58	118	178	27	0	11	56	2	3	21	2	55	2	6	.262
Laudner, Timothy, Orlando	17	61	7	14	25	5	0	2	5	0	0	7	0	14	0	1	.230
Lewis, J. Tod, Jacksonville	28	82	11	14	19	2	0	1	8	1	0	6	1	19	2	0	.171
Linares, Rufino, Savannah	51	200	37	85	121	18	6	2	38	0	2	16	0	13	8	1	.425
LoGrande, Angelo, Chattanooga*	125	469	71	137	243	31	0	25	81	0	4	24	2	95	2	4	.292
Logan, H. Daniel, Charlotte*	78	288	34	80	128	9	0	13	57	2	3	25	3	31	0	1	.278
Loucks, Scott, Columbus	137	515	90	125	180	13	6	10	45	6	6	75	2	109	53	13	.243
MacDonald, James, Columbus	29	1	0	0	0	0	0	0	0	0	0	0	0	0	0	0	.000
Madison, C. Scott, Orlando†	81	282	31	65	100	9	4	6	32	5	2	46	1	39	1	1	.230
Maher, Mark, Orlando	3	9	1	0	0	0	0	0	0	0	0	2	1	4	0	0	.000
Matthews, Jeffrey, Savannah	12	34	4	8	10	2	0	0	2	0	0	9	1	2	0	0	.235
McCann, Francis, Jacksonville	64	229	36	63	107	15	4	7	44	4	5	44	2	46	12	3	.275
McGee, Willie, Nashville	78	223	35	63	80	4	5	1	22	4	1	19	2	39	7	8	.283
McInerny, Daniel, Chattanooga*	6	12	1	0	0	0	0	0	0	0	0	1	0	3	0	0	.000
McManaman, Steven, Orlando	59	217	18	38	69	7	0	8	27	4	0	12	4	80	1	1	.175
McWhirter, Kevin, Orlando	81	305	43	69	120	11	2	12	38	1	0	30	1	70	6	3	.226
Meridith, Ronald, Columbus*	28	0	2	0	0	0	0	0	0	0	0	0	0	0	0	0	.000
Michael, Steven, Montgomery*	64	213	38	66	102	14	2	6	21	2	2	37	2	31	5	3	.310
Miller, Michael, Savannah†	116	365	33	89	105	11	1	1	28	6	2	29	0	76	6	6	.244
Mills, J. Bradley, Memphis*	55	190	32	56	96	18	2	6	44	0	2	28	4	18	1	1	.295
Mitchell, Weston, Chattanooga	67	211	34	55	71	14	1	0	20	2	2	19	4	32	2	4	.261
Morrison, Steven, Memphis*	19	51	6	10	14	4	0	0	4	1	1	2	1	9	1	0	.196
Motley, Darryl, Jacksonville	51	182	30	58	90	15	1	5	31	0	2	11	5	13	8	2	.319
Nandin, Robert, Montgomery†	82	243	37	57	66	9	0	0	15	7	2	34	1	33	16	6	.235
Neal, Edwin, Charlotte	11	38	6	7	13	1	1	1	2	0	0	3	1	9	1	0	.184
Oliver, David, Memphis*	5	14	5	4	6	2	0	0	1	0	0	3	0	2	0	0	.286
Owen, Lawrence, Savannah	76	228	27	48	76	8	1	6	20	3	0	41	1	31	2	0	.211
Parker, Darrell, Jacksonville	43	159	19	43	61	4	1	4	26	0	1	14	1	19	1	1	.270
Pearsey, Leslie, Orlando	62	218	17	40	56	4	0	4	14	1	0	18	1	62	3	4	.183
Peltz, Peter, Chattanooga	50	162	24	41	49	4	2	0	11	4	2	28	0	25	7	5	.253
Pena, Adalberto, Columbus†	124	386	47	97	144	20	0	9	49	11	3	24	2	69	2	0	.251
Petralli, Eugene, Knoxville†	116	382	42	109	142	20	2	3	38	3	3	54	1	30	0	1	.285
Phillips, K. Anthony, Memphis††	136	502	100	125	166	18	4	5	41	3	5	98	5	89	50	19	.249

Player and Club	G.	AB.	R.	H.	TB.	2B.	3B.	HR.	RBI.	SH.	SF.	BB.	HP.	SO.	SB.	CS.	Pct.
Poole, S. Walter, Montgomery	66	223	27	49	77	10	6	2	37	3	2	15	1	61	1	0	.220
Porter, Robert, Savannah*	135	500	78	146	229	28	5	15	80	0	7	35	9	62	7	4	.292
Primante, Valentino, Columbus†	2	4	1	0	0	0	0	0	0	0	0	1	0	3	0	0	.000
Quintana, Luis, Charlotte*	35	2	0	1	1	0	0	0	0	0	0	0	0	0	0	0	.500
Ramie, Vernon, Knoxville*	33	106	12	31	44	7	3	0	12	0	0	17	1	19	2	1	.292
Ramirez, Alexis, Orlando	90	289	36	72	77	3	1	0	13	11	1	24	1	26	0	2	.249
Rausch, Albert, Chattanooga	130	483	62	132	196	24	2	12	67	5	4	35	5	48	5	6	.273
Ray, John, Columbus†	138	497	86	161	235	32	6	10	72	3	3	59	6	38	13	10	.324
Rende, Salvatore, Chattanooga*	69	225	40	55	105	6	1	14	40	0	5	43	1	45	2	2	.244
Reynolds, Andre, Nashville*	78	240	23	49	64	6	3	1	16	2	2	31	0	41	4	3	.204
Richards, Kevin, Montgomery	28	0	0	0	0	0	0	0	0	0	0	2	0	0	0	0	.000
Ripken, Calvin, Charlotte	144	522	91	144	257	28	5	25	78	0	9	77	3	81	4	2	.276
Rivera, David, Chattanooga	118	402	45	79	120	15	1	8	39	6	4	38	3	108	11	4	.197
Robertson, Andre, Nashville	13	46	7	12	19	2	1	1	11	0	1	3	0	3	1	0	.261
Rodriguez, Victor, Charlotte	19	65	4	15	15	0	0	0	4	0	3	0	0	6	1	0	.231
Rooney, Patrick, Memphis	142	482	86	135	254	23	6	28	102	0	7	49	4	85	10	5	.280
Rosario, Simon, Columbus	107	397	47	120	149	20	0	3	52	3	1	15	1	53	3	6	.302
Rowe, Peter, Knoxville	99	336	46	93	136	8	1	11	40	2	0	29	2	21	0	0	.277
Royster, Willie, Charlotte	26	79	10	17	27	5	1	1	14	0	2	6	1	28	3	1	.215
Runge, Paul, Savannah	75	248	32	68	112	11	3	9	34	1	5	28	0	44	3	1	.274
Saavedra, Edwin, Chattanooga	62	174	19	36	46	10	0	0	11	5	2	15	1	34	3	2	.207
Santana, Rafael, Knoxville	45	1	0	0	0	0	0	0	0	1	0	0	0	0	0	0	.000
Santana, Rafael F., Nashville	86	275	33	64	74	4	3	0	20	5	3	23	2	23	7	1	.233
Schafer, Randall, Montgomery	9	30	1	3	4	1	0	0	1	0	1	0	0	1	0	0	.100
Schmitz, Daniel, Nashville*	101	365	58	108	140	14	3	4	41	4	4	48	2	28	9	5	.296
Schoeller, Michael, Montgomery*	111	369	45	99	131	14	0	6	44	4	3	32	4	45	6	2	.268
Sheets, Larry, Charlotte*	13	48	1	9	13	4	0	0	5	0	0	4	0	18	0	0	.188
Shelby, John, Charlotte	134	560	66	135	202	27	11	6	51	5	1	22	1	122	34	14	.241
Sheridan, Patrick, Jacksonville	97	367	63	112	158	17	7	5	42	4	1	31	0	62	14	4	.305
Sherow, Dennis, Memphis	13	41	9	11	15	4	0	0	3	1	0	3	2	9	4	0	.268
Showalter, W. Nathaniel, Nash*	142	550	84	178	205	19	3	1	82	5	2	53	5	23	6	9	.324
Silverman, Robert, Knoxville	138	475	59	107	134	11	5	2	42	3	4	57	3	59	16	7	.225
Simunic, Douglas, Memphis	102	322	46	88	140	16	0	12	46	1	4	49	3	65	0	3	.273
Sinatro, Matthew, Savannah	122	449	76	125	176	16	1	11	50	6	4	48	5	57	17	10	.278
Smith, Garry, Nashville	43	156	18	44	55	5	0	2	18	0	2	14	3	27	4	3	.282
Smith, Christopher, Memphis†	89	336	51	102	156	16	1	12	70	0	5	31	6	24	1	0	.304
Smith, Thomas, Charlotte	95	323	32	83	131	12	3	10	40	1	1	29	2	62	5	5	.257
Snitker, Brian, Savannah	18	68	5	11	16	2	0	1	6	0	1	4	2	11	0	0	.162
Speed, Horace, Savannah	10	37	1	5	6	1	0	0	2	0	1	3	0	9	0	0	.135
Stenhouse, Michael, Memphis*	1	3	0	0	0	0	0	0	0	0	0	1	0	1	0	0	.000
Stokke, Douglas, Columbus	69	280	45	81	115	11	1	7	37	2	5	16	2	22	6	2	.289
Tabler, Patrick, Nashville	136	479	82	142	244	38	4	16	83	4	2	66	7	74	9	6	.296
Teufel, Timothy, Orlando	86	287	38	76	130	15	3	11	47	3	2	49	0	61	3	1	.265
Tevlin, Creighton, Knoxville*	44	170	25	42	43	1	0	0	10	1	1	16	2	15	0	0	.247
Thompson, Milton, Savannah*	71	278	35	83	99	7	3	1	15	3	1	19	2	67	22	5	.299
Thompson, Timothy, Knoxville*	83	259	30	61	85	8	2	4	24	4	1	31	4	31	0	1	.236
Toal, Arthur, Montgomery	19	50	5	10	14	1	0	1	4	2	0	5	0	7	1	2	.200
Tobias, Grayling, 25 Mem-42 Mon†	67	248	27	66	82	14	1	0	21	3	1	14	0	15	6	5	.266
Tolman, Timothy, Columbus	139	481	67	142	208	37	4	7	73	2	8	80	1	50	4	6	.295
Tomski, Jeffrey, Chattanooga	74	193	25	33	54	3	6	0	24	3	3	47	9	42	0	3	.171
Tovar, Raul, Jacksonville	22	74	12	18	32	2	3	2	10	1	1	10	2	17	2	1	.243
Tyson, Terry, Chattanooga	61	211	28	55	72	9	1	2	24	1	0	12	1	25	0	3	.261
Ullger, Scott, Orlando	135	460	55	121	170	25	0	8	51	4	0	73	3	89	2	4	.263
Upshaw, John, Montgomery	88	278	21	59	99	10	0	10	32	5	2	25	1	84	2	1	.212
Valley, Charles, Columbus†	36	115	18	24	33	3	0	2	5	1	1	16	1	19	0	0	.209
Vargas, Leonel, Savannah	106	370	48	94	150	14	3	12	61	0	3	37	4	61	18	8	.254
Walker, W. Keith, Knoxville*	29	5	0	0	0	0	0	0	0	0	0	0	0	1	0	0	.000
Waller, Reginald, Columbus	120	400	59	100	150	17	3	9	45	4	2	38	3	77	11	9	.250
Weaver, James, Orlando*	58	208	19	44	53	9	0	0	15	0	0	21	1	38	15	2	.212
Webb, Dennis, Jacksonville*	130	501	81	129	150	9	6	0	32	4	3	57	1	58	36	18	.257
Westendorf, Philip, Jacksonville	102	360	40	92	151	16	2	13	49	0	4	36	2	75	0	2	.256
Wheeler, Ralph, Knoxville	119	419	50	111	142	16	3	3	31	9	0	36	4	60	3	3	.265
Whitfield, Robert, Charlotte	122	406	42	103	131	4	1	26	10	3	25	7	57	13	6		.254
Wieghaus, Thomas, Memphis	120	371	44	101	128	13	1	4	44	9	6	46	3	39	4	2	.272
Wieser, Daniel, Jacksonville†	93	264	32	49	77	9	0	7	24	2	0	38	0	39	3	5	.186
Wilborn, Thaddeus, Nashville	121	455	70	123	184	15	14	6	63	6	2	40	4	75	27	20	.270
Williams, Larry, Jacksonville	5	1	1	0	0	0	0	0	0	1	0	1	0	0	0	0	.000
Wilson, Glenn, Montgomery	77	284	36	75	116	16	2	7	31	2	0	14	2	52	3	2	.264
Wood, Andre, Savannah	94	311	37	69	92	14	0	3	29	4	2	28	2	51	2	3	.222
Wren, Frank, Memphis	38	117	14	26	33	4	0	1	10	0	2	12	0	16	5	3	.222

The following pitchers had no plate appearances primarily through use of designated hitters, listed alphabetically by club, games in parentheses:

CHARLOTTE—Anderson, Lawrence (6); Carey, Brooks *(25); Edwards, Allen (4); George, William *(28); Gonzalez, Julian *(16); McArthur, Gregory (6); Norris, Timothy (14); Pensiero, Russell (40); Peralta, Luis (7); Presley,

Billy *(2); Ramirez, Daniel (29); Rowe, Thomas (9); Smith, Mark *(3); Swaggerty, William (26); Welchel, Donald (28).

CHATTANOOGA—Anderson, Karl (20); Bullinger, Dominick *(11); Fuson, Robin (29); Gonzalez, Arturo (13); Heimer, Todd *(20); Holmstedt, Victor (27); Hrynko, Lawrence (7); Narleski, Steven (47); Nicholson, Carl (2); Nuismer, N. Jack (16); Owens, Thomas (12); Rambis, Randall (8); Teising, John *(37); Warnecke, David (6); Wilder, Troy *(18).

COLUMBUS—Aponte, C. Ricardo (9); Boxberger, Rodney (23); Cacciatore, Paul (5); Hessler, John (27); Ladd, Peter (33); Leatherwood, Delrick *(17); Leland, Stanley (28); Miggins, Mark (35); Quealey, Steven (33); Ross, Mark (14); Troedson, Thad (14); Welenc, Douglas (2).

JACKSONVILLE—Candiotti, Thomas (17); Cornell, Jeffery (43); Daly, Mark *(39); Dubee, Richard (12); Fischer, Daniel (6); Ganger, Robert (25); Grzybek, Benjamin (5); Hammaker, C. Atlee †(20); Hanslovan, Jeffrey *(14); Hendricks, Erik (41); Jones, Michael *(24); Skinner, John *(25)

KNOXVILLE—Cuellar, Miguel (33); Dejak, Thomas (26); Flores, Jesse (22); Fore, Charles (9); May, Davis (28); Morgan, Richard (9); Poloni, John *(28); Pulco, Charles (19); Stoeber, Mark (49); Thayer, Gregory (31).

MEMPHIS—Abone, Joseph (31); Anderson, Scott (7); Bargar, Gregory (16); Gorman, Thomas *(25); Hesketh, Joseph *(3); Josephson, Paul (5); Lea, Charles (9); Lovins, Steven (27); Mendon, D. Kevin (14); O'Connor, Jack *(7); Shimp, Tommy (25); Smith, Bryn (27); Tenenini, Robert (33); Williams, Richard *(18); Winfield, Steven (36); Yanus, Raymond (17).

MONTGOMERY—Bailey, Howard *(27); Blair, Theodore *(36); Cappuzzello, George *(27); Chretien, Gordon (24); Codiroli, Christopher (27); Enyart, Terry *(8); Lackey, John (8); Mathis, Ronald (1); Pashnick, Larry (21); Pole, Richard (43); Polvi, Michael (10); Simerly, James (4); Smith, Jack (26); Steffen, Karl *(18); Viefhaus, Stephen (12).

NASHVILLE—Boris, Paul (49); Cooper, Donald (32); Filer, Thomas (29); Gleckel, Scott *(3); Kaufman, Curt (11); Ledduke, Daniel (28); Lewis, Timothy *(9); McEnaney, William *(22); McGaffigan, Andrew (31); Ryder, Brian (28); Slagle, Roger (13); Taylor, Jeff (19); Taylor, Steve (6); Werly, James (16).

ORLANDO—Adamson, Wade (31); Biko, Thomas *(11); Brueggeman, Jeffrey (7); Mapel, Steven (12); Mulligan, Robert *(10); Reyes, Jose (16); Sheehan, Terrence *(31); Ungs, Michael (28); Wagner, Steven (9).

SAVANNAH—Acker, James (13); Alvarez, Jose (12); Bedrosian, Stephen (29); Cole, Timothy *(27); Cowley, Joe (4); Dayley, Kenneth *(16); Demery, Lawrence *(2); Field, Gregory (10); Gore, B. Lance *(23); Leach, Terry (22); Livingstone, Stuart (51); Lucia, Daniel (12); McMurtry, J. Craig (14); Pratt, Louis *(4); Rogers, James (21); Shields, W. Michael (22); Theiss, Duane (16).

TWO CLUBS—Barr, Timothy *(13 Orlando, 3 Savannah); Braun, Barton (3 Chattanooga, 11 Knoxville); Corr, Larry (19 Jacksonville, 10 Montgomery); Dooner, Glenn (14 Memphis, 32 Orlando); Graven, Timothy *(6 Charlotte, 5 Savannah).

GRAND SLAM HOME RUNS—Gates 3; Logan, Tyson, 2 each; Barton, Cadahia, Carrion, Estes, Funderburk, Hernandez, Hudgens, A. Johnson, R. Johnson, Lewis, Motley, Poole, D. Porter, Rausch, Rende, Rooney, Royster, G. Smith, T. Smith, Tabler, Vargas, Westendorf, Wheeler, 1 each.

AWARDED FIRST BASE ON INTERFERENCE—Chaney 4 (Callahan, Jacobs, Petralli, Wieghaus); Batter (Huppert); Chapman (Owen) Crowley (Keatley); Douglas (Bando); Gustavson (Petralli); Jacobs (Lewis); McCann (Huppert); Motley (Cadahia); Sheets (Callahan); Tabler (Knicely).

GAME-WINNING RBIs

CHARLOTTE (54)—Hazewood 10, T. Smith 8, Logan 7, Eaton 5, Ripken 5, Buffamoyer 3, Denman 3, Huppert 3, Shelby 3, Brett 2, Fabrizio 2, Whitfield 2, Royster 1.

CHATTANOOGA (46)—Bando 5, Gardner 5, Garrison 5, Rausch 5, Rende 5, Barton 3, LoGrande 3, Rivera 3, T. Anderson 2, Hudgens 2, Tomski 2, Tyson 2, Alvarez 1, Mitchell 1, Peltz 1, Saavedra 1.

COLUMBUS (54)—Cypret 6, Pena 6, Ray 6, Tolman 6, Rosario 5, Waller 5, Loucks 4, Bodie 3, Cripe 3, Dahl 3, Stokke 3, Jacobs 2, Harper 1, Valley 1.

JACKSONVILLE (37)—Johnson 8, Gustavson 3, Haley 3, Motley 3, Webb 3, Westendorf 3, Concepcion 2, Heath 2, McCann 2, Sheridan 2, Batter 1, Eschen 1, Harris 1, Hogg 1, Parker 1, Tovar 1.

KNOXVILLE (37)—Dennis 6, Silverman 6, Baker 5, Rowe 4, Barfield 3, Petralli 3, Wheeler 3, Duncan 2, Hernandez 2, Thompson 2, Ramie 1.

MEMPHIS (54)—Rooney 9, A. Johnson 6, Mills 6, C. Smith 6, Wieghaus 6, Franklin 4, Gates 4, Simunic 4, Crowley 3, Carrion 2, Phillips 2, Francona 1, Oliver 1.

MONTGOMERY (55)—Followell 9, Gates 7, Keatley 5, Armstrong 4, Hampton 4, Schoeller 4, Wilson 4, Dasen 3, Kenaga 3, Poole 3, Filkins 2, Michael 2, Nandin 2, Ervin 1, Toal 1, Tobias 1.

NASHVILLE (73)—Tabler 13, Chapman 12, Balboni 9, Wilborn 8, Showalter 5, Gulden 4, Schmitz 4, Baker 3, Hanggie 3, Robertson 3, Callahan 2, Dayette 2, McGee 2, Espino 1, Santana 1, Smith 1.

ORLANDO (61)—Funderburk 10, Cadahia 8, Estes 6, McWhirter 6, Madison 5, Teufel 5, Ullger 5, Bush 4, Benson 2, Douglas 2, McManaman 2, Pearsey 2, Faedo 1, Hallberg 1, Ramirez 1, Weaver 1.

SAVANNAH (53)—Sinatro 8, Grout 7, Porter 7, Cooper 4, Linares 4, Runge 4, Vargas 4, Garcia 3, Haslerig 3, Miller 3, Elliott 2, Johnson 2, Owen 1, Reynolds 1.

CLUB FIELDING

Club	G.	PO.	A.	E.	DP.	PB.	Pct.	Club	G.	PO.	A.	E.	DP.	PB.	Pct.
Columbus	143	3605	1623	158	159	21	.971	Nashville	143	3770	1520	187	136	18	.966
Montgomery	143	3606	1648	169	116	24	.969	Orlando	143	3713	1681	191	120	18	.966
Charlotte	144	3700	1566	186	130	11	.966	Savannah	144	3614	1526	188	127	21	.965
Jacksonville	144	3714	1548	185	120	27	.966	Chattanooga	144	3709	1685	212	149	23	.962
Memphis	144	3771	1557	189	118	16	.966	Knoxville	144	3623	1544	234	111	14	.957

INDIVIDUAL FIELDING

FIRST BASEMEN

*Throws lefthanded.

Player and Club	G.	PO.	A.	E.	DP.	Pct.
Rende, Chattanooga*	25	215	17	0	29	1.000
Ramie, Knoxville	10	63	1	0	7	1.000
Hudgens, Chattanooga*	9	49	3	0	4	1.000
Goldetsky, Memphis	2	30	0	0	2	1.000
Cypret, Columbus	2	22	1	0	1	1.000
Funderburk, Orlando	2	17	5	0	1	1.000
Madison, Orlando	1	15	2	0	1	1.000
Rausch, Chattanooga	2	14	0	0	0	1.000
Showalter, Nashville*	3	12	0	0	1	1.000
Cripe, Columbus	1	7	1	0	1	1.000
Hogg, Jacksonville	1	8	0	0	1	1.000
Brett, Charlotte	1	6	1	0	0	1.000
Atkinson, Jacksonville	3	6	0	0	0	1.000
Duncan, Knoxville	1	4	0	0	0	1.000
Batter, Jacksonville	1	2	0	0	0	1.000
Kenaga, Montgomery	1	2	0	0	0	1.000
Gates, Montgomery	1	1	0	0	0	1.000
Miller, Savannah	1	1	0	0	0	1.000
Wren, Memphis	1	1	0	0	0	1.000
Armstrong, Montgomery	2	0	1	0	0	1.000
McCann, Jacksonville	2	1	0	0	0	1.000
Upshaw, Montgomery	45	374	26	2	31	.995
Valley, Columbus*	36	334	30	2	35	.995
Dasen, Montgomery	26	203	17	1	16	.995
Logan, Charlotte*	78	671	51	5	74	.993
Rowe, Knoxville	15	136	13	1	10	.993
Schoeller, Montgomery	83	731	54	6	64	.992
Fabrizio, Charlotte*	50	486	28	4	38	.992
Bush, Orlando*	50	458	28	4	38	.992
Wheeler, Knoxville	13	108	9	1	10	.992
Johnson, Jacksonville	72	626	34	6	52	.991
Crowley, Memphis*	64	500	29	5	42	.991
T. Smith, Charlotte	18	113	3	1	13	.991
BALBONI, Nashville	140	1218	76	13	125	.990
Grout, Savannah	126	1100	39	14	95	.988
Tolman, Columbus	110	952	90	14	106	.987
LoGrande, Chattanooga	96	915	42	14	80	.986
Estes, Orlando*	58	595	35	10	42	.984
Westendorf, Jacksonville	74	648	48	12	55	.983
Thompson, Knoxville*	82	681	39	16	40	.978
Snitker, Savannah	14	129	7	3	8	.978
Simunic, Memphis	75	581	26	14	50	.977
C. Smith, Memphis	15	122	3	3	8	.977
T. Anderson, Chat*	21	186	14	5	19	.976
McManaman, Orlando	27	290	25	8	24	.975
Petralli, Knoxville	7	59	6	2	6	.970
Hampton, Nashville	24	202	23	8	25	.966
Elliott, Savannah	9	80	7	4	9	.956
Johnston, Nashville	4	17	1	1	3	.947
Buffamoyer, Charlotte	1	11	1	1	0	.923
Linares, Savannah	2	12	0	1	3	.923
Schafer, Montgomery	1	8	1	1	1	.900
Carrion, Memphis	1	8	0	1	0	.889

SECOND BASEMEN

Player and Club	G.	PO.	A.	E.	DP.	Pct.
Cripe, Columbus	7	16	23	0	3	1.000
Rausch, Chattanooga	6	12	20	0	4	1.000
Cypret, Columbus	5	12	17	0	3	1.000
W. Johnson, Memphis	4	5	12	0	0	1.000
Oliver, Memphis	1	7	3	0	2	1.000
Garcia, Savannah	3	3	5	0	0	1.000
Phillips, Memphis	1	2	3	0	2	1.000
Wieser, Jacksonville	1	3	0	0	0	1.000
Elliott, Savannah	1	0	2	0	0	1.000
Armstrong, Montgomery	66	155	190	2	45	.994
Miller, Savannah	45	89	152	4	20	.984
Matthews, Savannah	12	21	41	1	6	.984
Alvarez, Chattanooga	21	46	65	2	15	.982
Ingle, Savannah	40	87	134	5	33	.978
Barton, Chattanooga	76	170	232	10	49	.976
Benson, Orlando	62	111	174	7	31	.976
EATON, Charlotte	144	360	442	21	108	.9745
Webb, Jacksonville	127	291	347	17	80	.9740
Gates, Memphis	137	335	394	20	72	.973
Stokke, Columbus	65	155	188	10	53	.972
Dennis, Knoxville	79	184	218	12	47	.971
Toal, Montgomery	8	17	16	1	8	.971
Wood, Knoxville	59	126	163	10	27	.967
Nandin, Montgomery	74	145	160	11	37	.965
Teufel, Orlando	86	196	246	17	46	.963
Ray, Columbus	70	150	175	13	49	.962
Johnston, Nashville	7	8	16	1	4	.960
Reynolds, Savannah	47	120	114	10	27	.959
Tabler, Nashville	135	262	361	27	89	.958
Harper, Jacksonville	12	20	22	2	5	.955
Mitchell, Chattanooga	40	89	133	12	26	.949
Ramirez, Orlando	3	6	12	1	2	.947
Eschen, Jacksonville	9	18	17	2	3	.946
Tyson, Chattanooga	10	19	28	3	4	.940
Schmitz, Nashville	9	13	18	2	3	.939
Ervin, Montgomery	4	6	7	1	3	.929
Goldetsky, Memphis	3	6	5	1	0	.917
Wheeler, Knoxville	9	20	21	5	2	.891
Boelter, Orlando	4	7	9	2	2	.889
Franklin, Memphis	1	0	2	1	0	.667

THIRD BASEMEN

Player and Club	G.	PO.	A.	E.	DP.	Pct.
Eschen, Jacksonville	5	2	11	0	2	1.000
Toal, Montgomery	3	4	8	0	2	1.000
Gates, Memphis	3	2	6	0	0	1.000
Nandin, Montgomery	2	1	6	0	1	1.000
Miller, Savannah	1	2	1	0	0	1.000
Jacoby, Savannah	1	0	2	0	0	1.000
Buffamoyer, Charlotte	1	0	1	0	0	1.000
Owen, Savannah	1	0	1	0	0	1.000
Tomski, Chattanooga	1	0	1	0	0	1.000
Hench, Nashville	2	0	1	0	0	1.000
Bando, Chattanooga	20	17	40	2	4	.966
Rodriguez, Charlotte	17	14	37	2	1	.962
Ervin, Montgomery	8	4	18	1	2	.957
Cripe, Columbus	7	8	13	1	1	.955
Mills, Memphis	55	39	135	9	6	.951
Pearsey, Orlando	61	58	115	9	13	.951
Ray, Columbus	64	53	156	11	15	.950
Dennis, Knoxville	12	16	18	2	1	.944
Tyson, Chattanooga	7	3	12	1	2	.938
Motley, Jacksonville	51	43	100	10	6	.935
Atkinson, Jacksonville	19	11	47	4	3	.935
Schmitz, Nashville	51	31	72	6	6	.934
RIPKEN, Charlotte	120	119	268	28	34	.933
Reynolds, Savannah	17	14	42	4	5	.933
Wieser, Savannah	7	3	11	1	3	.933
T. Smith, Charlotte	8	6	8	1	0	.933
Hanggie, Nashville	73	60	144	15	13	.932
McCann, Jacksonville	62	52	127	13	12	.932
Ramirez, Orlando	56	46	131	13	10	.932
Franklin, Memphis	24	22	45	5	3	.931
Johnson, Savannah	54	46	111	12	11	.929
Johnston, Nashville	12	7	6	1	0	.929
Dayette, Nashville	32	16	60	6	7	.927
Armstrong, Montgomery	64	45	145	16	8	.922
Cypret, Columbus	78	59	149	18	20	.920
Harper, Jacksonville	8	6	15	2	2	.913

THIRD BASEMEN—Continued

Player and Club	G.	PO.	A.	E.	DP.	Pct.
Rausch, Chattanooga	79	43	163	20	5	.912
Elliott, Savannah	53	46	107	15	13	.911
C. Smith, Memphis	51	36	83	12	7	.908
Wheeler, Knoxville	21	25	37	7	4	.899
Baker, Knoxville	97	54	197	29	14	.896
Garcia, Savannah	23	22	27	6	4	.891
Wilson, Montgomery	77	56	189	33	20	.881
Peltz, Chattanooga	40	43	83	19	12	.869
Faedo, Orlando	2	2	4	1	0	.857
Hallberg, Orlando	28	21	69	19	8	.826
Alvarez, Chattanooga	7	4	15	4	2	.826
Hernandez, Knoxville	8	1	13	3	2	.824
Morrison, Memphis	14	7	17	6	1	.800
Dasen, Montgomery	1	1	2	1	1	.750
Wood, Knoxville	7	4	7	4	0	.733
Goldetsky, Memphis	4	0	2	1	0	.667

SHORTSTOPS

Player and Club	G.	PO.	A.	E.	DP.	Pct.
Stokke, Columbus	5	4	12	0	3	1.000
Boelter, Orlando	2	3	9	0	1	1.000
Johnston, Nashville	3	0	4	0	0	1.000
Gates, Memphis	1	1	2	0	0	1.000
Rausch, Chattanooga	36	58	113	6	22	.966
FOLLOWELL, Mon	143	226	469	25	69	.9653
Faedo, Orlando	111	185	361	20	49	.9647
Concepcion, Jacksonville	73	117	249	16	41	.958
Heath, Jacksonville	55	75	186	12	28	.956
Pena, Columbus	123	193	363	26	78	.955
Dennis, Savannah	45	77	147	11	22	.953
Runge, Savannah	75	115	196	17	33	.948
Mitchell, Chattanooga	25	32	79	7	6	.941
Chaney, Chattanooga	45	79	135	14	34	.939
Ripken, Charlotte	25	32	73	7	15	.938
Phillips, Memphis	132	224	405	42	68	.937
Santana, Nashville	86	125	247	25	54	.937
Schmitz, Nashville	53	74	133	14	29	.937
Whitfield, Charlotte	120	193	355	38	71	.935
Goldetsky, Memphis	5	7	7	1	1	.933
Robertson, Nashville	13	23	43	5	9	.930
Miller, Savannah	69	98	189	22	33	.929
Ramirez, Orlando	32	49	107	14	19	.918
Tyson, Chattanooga	43	63	134	18	24	.916
Cypret, Columbus	22	31	50	8	14	.910
Hernandez, Knoxville	86	119	220	39	35	.897
Harper, Jacksonville	24	24	63	10	6	.897
Wheeler, Knoxville	13	20	40	7	6	.896
Franklin, Memphis	11	14	35	6	4	.891
Toal, Montgomery	3	0	8	1	2	.889
Barton, Chattanooga	3	1	6	1	1	.875
Hanggie, Nashville	2	3	9	2	3	.857
Peltz, Chattanooga	2	4	4	2	1	.800
Reynolds, Savannah	3	2	1	1	0	.750

OUTFIELDERS

Player and Club	G.	PO.	A.	E.	DP.	Pct.
Wren, Memphis	32	79	3	0	0	1.000
Hudgens, Chattanooga*	48	75	4	0	2	1.000
Douglas, Orlando	36	67	4	0	0	1.000
Parker, Jacksonville	41	59	2	0	0	1.000
Gates, Montgomery	18	37	1	0	0	1.000
Harper, Columbus	22	37	1	0	1	1.000
Hurdle, Knoxville	15	27	1	0	1	1.000
Sherow, Memphis	10	25	0	0	0	1.000
McManaman, Orlando	15	23	0	0	1	1.000
Barton, Chattanooga	17	19	2	0	0	1.000
Neal, Charlotte	9	11	0	0	0	1.000
Wood, Knoxville	4	8	1	0	0	1.000
Harper, Jacksonville	5	7	1	0	0	1.000
Poole, Montgomery	1	6	0	0	0	1.000
Peltz, Chattanooga	3	5	0	0	0	1.000
Sheets, Charlotte	3	4	1	0	0	1.000
Oliver, Memphis	1	4	0	0	0	1.000
Fabrizio, Charlotte*	2	3	1	0	0	1.000
Schoeller, Montgomery	3	4	0	0	0	1.000
Morrison, Memphis	4	4	0	0	0	1.000
Bockhorn, Savannah	1	3	0	0	0	1.000
Gulden, Nashville	2	3	0	0	0	1.000
Nandin, Montgomery	3	3	0	0	0	1.000
Reynolds, Savannah	3	3	0	0	0	1.000
De La Rosa, Knoxville	1	2	0	0	0	1.000
C. Smith, Memphis	1	2	0	0	0	1.000
Stenhouse, Memphis	1	2	0	0	0	1.000
Ervin, Montgomery	2	2	0	0	0	1.000
Eschen, Jacksonville	3	2	0	0	0	1.000
Toal, Montgomery	1	1	0	0	0	1.000
Petralli, Knoxville	2	1	0	0	0	1.000
Michael, Montgomery*	67	104	4	1	0	.991
Hodgson, Knoxville	54	75	4	1	0	.988
ULLGER, Orlando	128	283	11	4	4	.987
Wieser, Jacksonville	84	114	7	2	1	.984
Showalter, Nashville*	31	59	2	1	0	.984
Gardner, Chattanooga	121	285	8	5	2	.983
Waller, Columbus	69	110	6	2	0	.983
Loucks, Columbus	117	264	12	6	3	.979
Rooney, Memphis	134	296	13	7	2	.978
Weaver, Orlando*	55	121	3	3	1	.976
Rosario, Columbus	86	117	4	3	1	.976
Haslerig, Savannah	23	40	1	1	0	.976
Tevlin, Knoxville	23	37	3	1	0	.976
Cooper, Savannah	108	235	14	7	2	.973
Funderburk, Orlando	124	206	10	6	0	.973
Smith, Nashville*	43	98	6	3	1	.972
Franklin, Memphis	38	66	4	2	0	.972
Silverman, Knoxville	138	245	22	8	4	.971
Dasen, Montgomery	47	62	4	2	0	.971
Wilborn, Nashville	112	210	7	7	1	.969
Tolman, Columbus	23	28	3	1	0	.969
Hampton, Montgomery	110	241	3	8	0	.968
Tobias, Montgomery*	69	142	3	5	0	.967
Porter, Savannah*	71	108	9	4	1	.967
Chapman, Nashville*	130	252	5	9	1	.966
McWhirter, Orlando	75	160	11	6	3	.966
Filkins, Montgomery*	49	82	4	3	0	.966
Baker, Nashville*	68	106	3	4	1	.965
Barfield, Knoxville	123	309	14	12	2	.964
Vargas, Savannah	104	175	12	7	3	.964
Saavedra, Chattanooga	61	99	7	4	1	.964
Harris, Jacksonville	129	255	18	11	2	.961
Hazewood, Charlotte	139	260	13	11	1	.961
Denman, Charlotte	128	213	11	9	0	.961
Shelby, Charlotte	134	361	21	16	0	.960
Thompson, Savannah	71	133	11	6	1	.960
Carrion, Memphis	38	94	1	4	0	.960
Sheridan, Jacksonville	95	201	7	9	0	.959
Garrison, Chattanooga	59	89	4	4	1	.959
McGee, Nashville	73	127	6	6	0	.957
Linares, Savannah	49	100	4	5	0	.954
A. Johnson, Memphis	127	224	19	12	3	.953
Rende, Chattanooga*	39	58	3	3	2	.953
T. Smith, Charlotte	19	38	2	2	0	.952
Wheeler, Knoxville	66	103	10	6	2	.950
Rivera, Chattanooga	115	175	8	10	0	.948
Johnson, Montgomery	13	17	0	1	0	.944
Haley, Jacksonville	81	154	7	10	1	.942
Kenaga, Montgomery	106	141	6	9	1	.942
Francona, Memphis	37	59	4	4	0	.940
Ramie, Knoxville	10	13	1	1	0	.933

OUTFIELDERS—Continued

Player and Club	G.	PO.	A.	E.	DP.	Pct.
Bodie, Columbus	132	181	15	15	3	.929
Tovar, Jacksonville	21	42	2	4	0	.917
McInerny, Chattanooga*	6	8	0	1	0	.889
Jemison, Nashville	5	7	0	1	0	.875
Speed, Savannah	6	8	0	2	0	.800
Duncan, Knoxville	11	7	0	2	0	.778
Hernandez, Knoxville	2	1	0	1	0	.500

CATCHERS

Player and Club	G.	PO.	A.	E.	DP.	PB.	Pct.
Firova, Jacksonville	3	22	2	0	0	1	1.000
Maher, Orlando	3	9	0	0	0	0	1.000
Hogg, Jacksonville	39	237	23	2	3	10	.992
Buffamoyer, Char.	24	106	13	1	1	3	.992
Upshaw, Montgomery	40	202	18	2	1	9	.991
Royster, Charlotte	17	104	12	1	1	0	.991
DAHL, Columbus	77	397	40	5	4	15	.989
Laudner, Orlando	17	81	10	1	0	0	.989
Wieghaus, Memphis	118	678	82	9	7	13	.988
Jacobs, Columbus	71	381	45	7	2	6	.984
Espino, Nashville	16	115	6	2	0	2	.984
Keatley, Montgomery	42	193	35	4	3	1	.983
Gavillan, Memphis	10	52	5	1	2	0	.983
Gulden, Nashville	84	540	80	12	9	10	.981
Bando, Chattanooga	87	463	57	10	4	9	.981
Poole, Montgomery	63	343	47	8	3	12	.980
Owen, Savannah	51	304	43	7	6	8	.980
Madison, Orlando	38	170	22	4	5	4	.980
Tomski, Chattanooga.	65	306	39	8	6	14	.977
Gustavson, J'ksonville	43	229	25	6	1	9	.977
Batter, Jacksonville	35	231	19	6	3	3	.977
Rowe, Knoxville	56	311	20	8	3	6	.976
Sinatro, Savannah	96	514	70	15	10	13	.975
Petralli, Savannah	94	509	76	16	4	8	.973
Simunic, Memphis	28	116	24	4	1	3	.972
Callahan, Nashville	55	324	30	11	1	6	.970
Lewis, Jacksonville	25	140	15	5	2	4	.969
Huppert, Charlotte	106	521	61	20	3	8	.967
Cadahia, Orlando	72	352	68	16	5	11	.963
Ballard, Orlando	16	59	11	5	2	3	.933
Schafer, Montgomery	5	19	2	2	0	2	.913

PITCHERS

Player and Club	G.	PO.	A.	E.	DP.	Pct.
Boxberger, Columbus	23	17	30	0	2	1.000
Ledduke, Nashville	28	14	21	0	0	1.000
J. Taylor, Nashville	19	6	25	0	3	1.000
MERIDITH, Col*	25	5	25	0	0	1.000
Shimp, Memphis	25	13	17	0	1	1.000
Slagle, Nashville	12	9	17	0	1	1.000
Acker, Savannah	13	6	18	0	2	1.000
Bargar, Memphis	14	6	18	0	4	1.000
Leach, Savannah	22	6	16	0	1	1.000
Daly, Jacksonville*	39	2	17	0	1	1.000
Gonzalez, Chattanooga	13	5	13	0	1	1.000
Ryder, Nashville	28	7	11	0	0	1.000
Stoeber, Knoxville	49	6	11	0	0	1.000
Dayley, Savannah*	16	5	11	0	0	1.000
Viefhaus, Montgomery	12	5	10	0	0	1.000
Norris, Charlotte	14	7	8	0	0	1.000
Boris, Nashville	49	8	7	0	0	1.000
Cooper, Nashville	32	4	9	0	2	1.000
Livingstone, Savannah	51	2	11	0	0	1.000
Thayer, Knoxville	31	3	9	0	0	1.000
Hanslovan, Jacks*	14	2	9	0	0	1.000
Cole, Savannah*	27	1	10	0	1	1.000
Lea, Memphis	9	4	6	0	0	1.000
Braun, Chattanooga	13	1	9	0	1	1.000
Shields, Savannah	22	3	7	0	1	1.000
Morgan, Knoxville	9	2	7	0	0	1.000
Simerly, Montgomery	4	2	6	0	0	1.000
Polvi, Montgomery	10	2	6	0	0	1.000
Rowe, Charlotte	9	3	4	0	0	1.000
Field, Savannah	10	2	5	0	2	1.000
Biko, Orlando	11	4	3	0	0	1.000
Troedson, Columbus	14	3	4	0	0	1.000
Grzybek, Jacksonville	5	3	3	0	0	1.000
Hesketh, Memphis*	3	0	5	0	0	1.000
Wagner, Orlando	9	0	5	0	0	1.000
Kaufman, Nashville	11	1	4	0	0	1.000
Gore, Savannah*	23	1	4	0	0	1.000
Lovins, Memphis	27	2	3	0	1	1.000
Hrynko, Chattanooga	7	1	3	0	0	1.000
Peralta, Charlotte	7	2	2	0	0	1.000
Lewis, Nashville*	9	0	4	0	1	1.000
Owens, Chattanooga	12	0	4	0	1	1.000
Ross, Columbus	14	2	2	0	0	1.000
Williams, Memphis*	18	2	2	0	0	1.000
McEnaney, Nashville*	22	1	3	0	1	1.000
Gleckel, Nashville*	3	0	3	0	0	1.000
M. Smith, Charlotte	3	1	2	0	0	1.000
Cacciatore, Columbus	5	1	2	0	0	1.000
Josephson, Memphis	5	1	2	0	0	1.000
Williams, Jacks	5	2	1	0	0	1.000
Warnecke, Chat	6	1	2	0	0	1.000
Enyart, Montgomery*	8	1	2	0	1	1.000
Codiroli, Montgomery	2	1	1	0	0	1.000
Presley, Charlotte	2	1	1	0	0	1.000
Welenc, Columbus	2	0	2	0	0	1.000
O'Connor, Memphis*	7	0	2	0	0	1.000
Rambis, Chattanooga	8	1	1	0	0	1.000
Graven, Charlotte*	11	1	1	0	1	1.000
Eschen, Jacksonville	1	1	0	0	0	1.000
Demery, Savannah	2	0	1	0	1	1.000
McArthur, Charlotte	6	0	1	0	0	1.000
Green, Orlando	32	21	24	1	1	.978
Leatherwood, Col*	17	7	34	1	1	.976
Cappuzzello, Mont*	27	4	32	1	2	.973
B. Smith, Memphis	27	7	27	1	5	.971
Pensiero, Charlotte	40	8	26	1	1	.971
Candiotti, Jacksonville	17	8	21	1	2	.967
Heimer, Chattanooga*	20	1	27	1	2	.966
Dubee, Jacksonville	12	10	17	1	4	.964
Miggins, Columbus*	35	5	21	1	1	.963
Mapel, Orlando	12	3	22	1	0	.962
McMurtry, Savannah	14	7	17	1	2	.960
Carey, Charlotte*	25	8	15	1	1	.958
Yanus, Memphis	17	5	17	1	2	.957
Puleo, Knoxville	19	5	14	1	0	.950
Glaser, Chattanooga	24	6	13	1	3	.950
Teising, Chattanooga*	37	1	18	1	1	.950
MacDonald, Columbus	29	19	36	3	6	.948
George, Charlotte*	28	3	15	1	1	.947
Ungs, Orlando	28	14	38	3	1	.945
Ramirez, Charlotte	29	5	29	2	1	.944
Pashnick, Montgomery	21	14	18	2	1	.941
Walker, Knoxville*	27	6	26	2	0	.941
Gonzalez, Charlotte*	16	4	12	1	0	.941
Hammaker, Jackson*	20	4	12	1	0	.941
Bailey, Montgomery*	27	7	40	3	2	.940
Filer, Nashville	27	14	33	3	2	.940
Poloni, Knoxville*	28	10	36	3	0	.939
Chretien, Montgomery	24	5	10	1	3	.938
Corr, Jacksonville	28	6	9	1	0	.938
May, Knoxville	28	10	32	3	2	.933
Fore, Knoxville	9	7	21	2	1	.933

PITCHERS—Continued

Player and Club	G.	PO.	A.	E.	DP.	Pct.	Player and Club	G.	PO.	A.	E.	DP.	Pct.
Barr, Orlando	16	4	10	1	0	.933	Ladd, Columbus	33	4	11	2	0	.882
Quealey, Columbus	32	5	9	1	0	.933	Fuson, Chattanooga	29	10	42	7	4	.881
Tenenini, Memphis	33	5	9	1	1	.933	Blair, Montgomery*	36	6	16	3	1	.880
Holmstedt, Chat	27	9	18	2	3	.931	S. Taylor, Nashville	6	3	4	1	0	.875
Abone, Memphis	31	7	33	3	0	.930	Nuismer, Chattanooga	16	8	18	4	1	.867
Hodge, Orlando*	27	2	24	2	2	.929	Sheehan, Orlando*	31	8	18	4	0	.867
Cuellar, Knoxville	33	15	23	3	2	.927	Cornell, Jacksonville	41	4	15	3	2	.864
Leland, Columbus	28	16	34	4	6	.926	Adamson, Orlando	31	3	15	3	1	.857
Wilder, Chattanooga*	18	7	18	2	2	.926	Quintana, Charlotte*	35	2	4	1	0	.857
Lucia, Savannah	12	6	6	1	0	.923	Mulligan, Orlando*	10	3	8	2	1	.846
Smith, Montgomery	26	5	7	1	1	.923	Dejak, Knoxville*	26	4	7	2	0	.846
Winfield, Memphis	36	2	10	1	1	.923	Mendon, Memphis	14	2	19	4	2	.840
Narleski, Chattanooga	47	5	18	2	0	.920	K. Anderson, Chat	20	10	16	5	2	.839
Bedrosian, Savannah	29	8	37	4	2	.918	Alvarez, Savannah	12	0	5	1	0	.833
Werly, Nashville	16	2	20	2	0	.917	Richards, Montgomery	28	7	27	7	0	.829
Lackey, Montgomery	8	4	6	1	0	.909	Skinner, Jacksonville	25	12	16	6	1	.824
Steffen, Montgomery*	18	2	8	1	0	.909	Flores, Knoxville	22	3	11	3	1	.824
Santana, Knoxville	45	4	15	2	0	.905	Hendricks, Jacks	41	3	11	3	1	.824
Rogers, Savannah	21	4	24	3	1	.903	McGaffigan, Nash	31	8	24	8	0	.800
Dooner, Orlando	46	4	24	3	1	.903	Aponte, Columbus	9	1	3	1	0	.800
Pole, Montgomery	43	9	9	2	2	.900	Jones, Jacksonville*	24	6	8	4	0	.778
Fischer, Jacksonville	6	4	5	1	1	.900	Swaggerty, Charlotte	26	3	7	3	0	.769
Reyes, Orlando	16	3	6	1	0	.900	Ganger, Jacksonville	25	1	5	2	0	.750
Welchel, Charlotte	28	18	35	6	2	.898	Cowley, Savannah	4	0	8	4	1	.667
Hessler, Columbus	27	9	16	3	1	.893	Anderson, Charlotte	6	1	1	1	0	.667
Gorman, Memphis*	25	6	10	2	2	.889	Bullinger, Chattanooga*	11	0	2	2	1	.500
Theiss, Savannah	15	4	4	1	0	.889	Edwards, Charlotte	4	1	0	1	0	.500
Belanger, Orlando*	18	1	7	1	0	.889	Anderson, Memphis	7	1	0	1	0	.500

The following players do not have any recorded chances at the positions indicated; therefore, are not listed in the fielding averages for those particular positions: Baker*, p; Ballard, of; Boris, 3b; Brett, 3b; Brueggeman, p; Cripe, p; Eschen, 1b; Madison, of; Mathis, p; Nandin, ss; Nicholson, p; Pratt*, p; Ray, of; Stenhouse, 1b; Ullger, 2b; Upshaw, 3b-of; Valley*, p.

CLUB PITCHING

Club	G.	CG.	ShO.	Sv.	IP.	H.	R.	ER.	HR.	BB.	Int. BB.	HB.	SO.	WP.	Bk.	ERA.
Nashville	143	43	15	25	1249	1094	544	432	72	525	30	27	922	60	7	3.11
Savannah	144	35	11	33	1206	1131	578	473	89	528	20	54	768	52	8	3.53
Memphis	144	46	11	19	1253	1268	613	505	100	447	19	41	795	39	11	3.63
Charlotte	144	44	5	24	1233	1251	607	502	96	472	5	24	669	47	8	3.66
Columbus	144	43	10	22	1202	1134	600	498	90	576	20	55	729	48	9	3.73
Orlando	143	42	12	23	1237	1294	656	541	90	447	7	19	638	53	8	3.94
Montgomery	144	47	16	15	1202	1157	664	553	105	538	22	24	760	76	13	4.14
Knoxville	144	32	7	17	1208	1267	713	569	94	513	28	60	715	75	13	4.24
Jacksonville	144	45	9	23	1239	1257	715	586	116	606	31	28	798	63	5	4.26
Chattanooga	144	42	10	15	1242	1229	711	599	94	624	26	31	724	60	8	4.34

PITCHERS' RECORDS

(Leading Qualifiers for Earned-Run Average Leadership—115 or More Innings)

*Throws lefthanded.

Pitcher–Club	G.	GS.	CG.	ShO.	W.	L.	Sv.	Pct.	IP.	H.	R.	ER.	HR.	Int. BB.	BB.	HB.	SO.	WP.	ERA.
McGaffigan, Nashville	31	20	6	2	15	5	0	.750	170	139	62	45	5	62	2	7	125	5	2.38
Meridith, Columbus*	25	17	7	2	9	5	0	.643	145	143	48	41	14	40	3	4	82	3	2.54
Pensiero, Charlotte	40	4	2	1	9	4	9	.692	118	134	44	35	9	35	0	1	61	8	2.67
Candiotti, Jacksonville	17	17	8	2	7	8	0	.467	117	98	45	36	6	40	4	1	93	7	2.77
B. Smith, Memphis	27	25	12	1	10	9	0	.526	181	179	75	56	10	54	1	2	110	4	2.78
Welchel, Charlotte	28	28	12	1	9	12	0	.429	202	210	86	65	9	47	2	3	56	6	2.90
Filer, Nashville	27	26	7	4	13	9	0	.591	187	168	94	61	10	86	4	4	112	6	2.94
Pashnick, Montgomery	21	21	12	3	13	4	0	.765	161	143	63	53	13	51	1	4	83	10	2.96
Ramirez, Charlotte	29	29	16	1	16	8	0	.667	196	151	73	65	11	92	0	3	160	6	2.98
Shimp, Memphis	25	18	7	1	11	5	2	.688	150	136	64	50	12	48	0	7	130	6	3.00

Departmental Leaders: G—Livingstone, 51; GS—Bedrosian, MacDonald, Ramirez, 29; CG—Cappuzzello, Pashnick, B. Smith, Welchel, 12; ShO—Cappuzzello, 6; W—MacDonald, 17; L—Ungs, 15; Sv—Livingstone, 17; Pct.—Pashnick, .764; IP—Bedrosian, 203; H—Welchel, 210; R—Ungs, 111; ER—Skinner, 90; HR—Skinner, 27; BB—Hessler, 135; IBB—Boris, 8; HB—Bailey, 22; SO—Bedrosian, 161; WP—Hessler, 17.

(All Pitchers—Listed Alphabetically)

Pitcher—Club	G	GS	CG	ShO	W	L	Sv	Pct.	IP	H	R	ER	HR	BB	Int. BB	HB	SO	WP	ERA.
Abone, Memphis	31	26	8	3	9	12	0	.429	170	193	89	73	14	43	0	11	94	0	3.86
Acker, Savannah	13	13	3	0	5	5	0	.500	95	84	33	28	6	29	1	5	47	4	2.65
Adamson, Orlando	31	15	5	3	3	11	3	.214	128	113	65	59	12	56	0	0	82	2	4.15
Alvarez, Savannah	12	1	0	0	2	2	2	.500	31	15	5	4	1	11	0	0	35	2	1.16
Anderson, Memphis	7	1	0	0	1	0	0	1.000	18	11	14	14	1	18	0	2	25	7	7.00
Anderson, Charlotte	6	0	0	0	4	0	1	1.000	19	9	9	9	1	9	0	0	10	1	4.26
K. Anderson, Chatt.	20	20	7	1	7	9	0	.438	128	116	68	59	8	50	1	4	98	2	4.15
Aponte, Columbus	9	0	0	0	1	1	0	.500	20	19	8	8	0	5	1	1	10	0	3.60
Bailey, Montgomery*	27	27	10	2	12	12	0	.500	186	174	84	71	15	55	1	22	132	14	3.44
Baker, Nashville*	1	0	0	0	0	0	0	.000	3	2	5	5	0	5	0	1	1	0	15.00
Bargar, Memphis	14	14	2	0	5	5	0	.500	86	95	52	48	10	48	2	2	54	4	5.02
Barr, Orlando	16	10	1	0	3	7	0	.300	85	88	49	31	3	36	1	3	58	4	3.28
Bedrosian, Savannah	29	29	9	2	14	10	0	.583	203	167	91	72	16	96	4	6	161	9	3.19
Belanger, Orlando*	18	0	0	0	2	1	1	.667	48	47	32	30	3	32	3	2	23	7	5.63
Biko, Orlando	11	1	0	0	0	1	0	.000	22	28	13	12	4	6	0	0	14	1	4.91
Blair, Montgomery*	36	6	1	0	1	7	1	.125	81	87	61	49	10	44	5	6	43	8	5.44
Boris, Nashville	49	2	0	0	7	0	9	1.000	94	74	35	26	4	40	8	0	83	2	2.49
Boxberger, Columbus	23	23	3	0	4	13	0	.235	117	118	83	73	6	97	2	13	57	4	5.62
Braun, Knoxville	13	1	0	0	1	3	1	.250	23	29	14	12	0	9	3	0	6	4	4.70
Brueggeman, Orlando*	7	0	0	0	0	0	4	.000	9	3	1	0	0	9	0	0	8	0	0.00
Bullinger, Chattanooga*	11	0	0	0	1	2	3	.333	20	30	19	18	2	18	0	2	10	0	8.10
Cacciatore, Columbus	5	4	1	0	2	0	0	1.000	20	29	13	12	3	9	0	1	10	2	5.40
Candiotti, Jacksonville	17	17	8	2	7	8	0	.467	117	98	45	36	6	40	4	3	93	7	2.77
Cappuzzello, Mont*	27	19	12	6	9	9	1	.500	152	114	65	55	9	70	7	3	121	5	3.26
Carey, Charlotte*	25	25	7	0	8	7	0	.533	163	158	74	67	15	39	0	7	78	6	3.70
Chretien, Montgomery	24	3	0	0	1	2	0	.333	62	78	41	38	10	19	1	1	33	3	5.52
Codiroli, Montgomery	2	2	0	0	0	0	0	.000	4	7	6	6	0	4	0	0	1	0	13.50
Cole, Savannah*	27	27	6	2	10	13	0	.435	154	145	98	80	12	105	1	8	108	12	4.68
Cooper, Nashville	32	0	0	0	9	5	8	.643	60	43	18	12	4	29	4	0	62	3	1.80
Cornell, Jacksonville	41	9	4	2	6	7	10	.462	135	137	80	61	16	66	1	1	111	9	4.07
Corr, Jacksonville	28	4	0	0	2	5	0	.286	73	100	59	51	6	27	3	6	32	5	6.29
Cowley, Savannah	4	4	0	0	1	3	0	.250	12	24	18	17	1	9	0	3	13	1	12.75
Cripe, Columbus	1	0	0	0	0	0	0	.000	1	2	1	1	0	0	0	0	0	0	9.00
Cuellar, Knoxville	33	19	3	1	4	13	0	.235	150	160	99	74	18	59	1	3	84	4	4.44
Daly, Jacksonville*	39	7	1	0	6	6	2	.500	98	96	48	42	6	70	6	3	66	5	3.86
Dayley, Savannah*	16	16	3	0	8	3	0	.727	105	86	38	30	8	54	1	6	104	4	2.57
Dejak, Knoxville*	26	4	0	3	0	0	1	1.000	58	69	37	33	5	27	2	0	32	7	5.12
Demery, Savannah	2	0	0	0	0	0	0	.000	3	1	0	0	0	3	0	0	1	0	0.00
Dooner, Orlando	46	0	0	0	7	7	15	.500	103	93	38	30	9	27	7	2	51	1	2.62
Dubee, Jacksonville	12	11	5	1	6	2	0	.750	78	77	34	26	6	20	0	0	32	0	3.00
Edwards, Charlotte	4	2	1	1	2	1	0	.667	21	29	21	20	6	13	2	0	16	0	2.05
Enyart, Montgomery*	8	1	0	0	0	0	0	.000	21	29	21	20	6	13	2	0	11	0	8.57
Eschen, Jacksonville	1	0	0	0	0	0	0	.000	1	2	1	1	0	0	0	0	0	0	9.00
Field, Savannah	10	10	2	1	6	2	0	.750	72	76	31	28	5	27	1	1	37	1	3.50
Filer, Nashville	27	26	7	4	13	9	0	.591	187	168	94	61	10	86	4	4	112	6	2.94
Fischer, Jacksonville	6	6	0	0	3	6	0	.333	51	43	20	13	1	18	2	1	30	1	2.29
Flores, Knoxville	22	11	0	0	3	8	0	.273	85	88	51	44	7	54	2	2	62	3	4.66
Fore, Knoxville	9	9	3	0	3	6	0	.333	58	59	40	30	7	23	0	1	37	3	4.66
Fuson, Chattanooga	29	28	7	1	10	11	0	.476	188	175	101	83	13	98	1	6	114	10	3.97
Ganger, Jacksonville	25	2	0	0	1	6	5	.143	44	54	29	27	4	22	5	2	25	3	5.52
George, Charlotte*	28	25	5	0	5	14	0	.263	170	188	101	81	22	71	0	3	84	5	4.29
Glaser, Chattanooga	24	9	3	0	6	4	0	.600	100	88	40	29	8	21	2	1	41	3	2.61
Gleckel, Nashville*	3	0	0	0	0	0	0	.000	7	6	4	4	0	2	0	0	3	0	5.14
Gonzalez, Charlotte*	16	16	3	0	5	5	0	.500	92	100	61	54	8	49	0	0	80	1	5.28
Gonzalez, Chattanooga	13	13	6	1	5	5	0	.500	82	66	33	24	1	31	0	0	44	5	2.63
Gore, Savannah*	23	0	0	0	1	1	4	.500	21	24	12	8	1	9	0	2	10	2	3.43
Gorman, Memphis*	25	5	1	0	6	4	2	.600	69	64	34	21	6	22	2	1	45	3	2.74
Graven, Savannah*	11	0	0	0	1	1	0	.500	16	20	8	8	1	7	1	0	2	1	4.50
Green, Orlando	32	19	5	0	9	11	1	.450	162	203	90	71	11	26	1	2	49	2	3.94
Grzybek, Jacksonville	5	5	1	0	0	4	0	.000	27	35	20	19	1	16	1	0	6	0	6.33
Hammaker, Jacksonville*	20	20	6	1	8	9	0	.471	137	131	64	51	16	37	1	2	88	2	3.35
Hanslovan, Jacksonville*	14	11	1	0	3	6	0	.333	68	85	61	50	4	42	2	2	42	4	6.62
Heimer, Chattanooga*	20	19	8	0	3	12	0	.200	130	115	79	69	13	96	2	5	81	15	4.78
Hendricks, Jacksonville	41	2	0	0	2	6	6	.250	92	88	74	60	10	82	3	7	63	14	5.87
Hesketh, Memphis*	3	3	0	0	1	0	0	1.000	20	20	13	9	0	7	0	0	20	2	4.05
Hessler, Columbus	27	27	7	2	9	7	0	.563	153	127	87	75	6	135	0	2	121	17	4.41
Hodge, Orlando*	27	27	9	2	14	9	0	.609	186	188	95	77	11	62	0	9	90	6	3.73
Holmstedt, Chattanooga	27	13	2	0	5	3	1	.625	107	130	65	55	11	51	3	2	28	7	4.63
Hrynko, Chattanooga	7	0	0	0	0	0	0	1.000	14	18	6	6	1	5	1	0	5	0	3.86
Jones, Jacksonville*	24	24	6	2	13	6	0	.684	158	152	79	68	15	83	2	1	116	3	3.87
Josephson, Memphis	5	0	0	0	0	0	0	.000	10	12	4	3	0	0	0	3	2	0	2.70
Kaufman, Nashville	11	7	2	1	6	2	0	.750	46	43	24	23	1	29	0	1	35	2	4.50
Lackey, Montgomery	8	4	1	5	1	0	0	.833	51	36	14	11	3	10	0	2	23	1	1.94
Ladd, Columbus	33	0	0	0	6	5	5	.545	55	47	27	21	8	29	2	3	38	4	3.44

Pitcher-Club	G	GS	CG	ShO	W	L	Sv	Pct.	IP	H	R	ER	HR	BB	Int. BB	HB	SO	WP	ERA
Lea, Memphis	9	9	7	3	9	0	0	1.000	75	34	10	7	0	21	0	1	54	2	0.84
Leach, Savannah	22	6	2	0	5	1	1	.833	87	83	36	31	8	17	2	4	58	1	3.21
Leatherwood, Columbus*	17	14	6	0	7	5	0	.583	107	98	48	36	9	38	1	5	60	0	3.03
Ledduke, Nashville	28	18	4	0	9	3	1	.750	122	133	70	62	10	60	2	2	84	16	4.57
Leland, Columbus	28	28	9	2	8	11	0	.421	201	186	99	78	17	76	1	10	95	7	3.49
Lewis, Nashville*	9	6	1	0	4	1	0	.800	49	46	29	24	3	22	1	0	31	4	4.41
Livingstone, Savannah	51	0	0	0	6	5	17	.545	81	92	34	23	4	20	2	0	43	1	2.56
Lovins, Memphis	27	0	0	0	3	4	7	.429	33	40	26	20	6	26	2	3	39	1	5.45
Lucia, Savannah	12	5	0	0	3	1	0	.750	48	34	22	16	5	24	1	3	27	1	3.00
MacDonald, Columbus	29	29	9	1	17	7	0	.708	200	209	98	81	16	54	1	5	126	4	3.65
Mapel, Orlando	12	11	5	1	7	3	0	.700	86	84	38	31	8	21	0	3	50	1	3.24
Mathis, Montgomery	1	1	0	0	0	1	0	.000	3	4	4	4	1	4	0	0	3	0	12.00
May, Knoxville	28	24	6	1	11	12	0	.478	149	146	85	64	11	63	1	3	95	9	3.87
McArthur, Charlotte	6	0	0	0	0	2	0	.000	6	12	12	9	0	10	0	0	6	4	13.50
McEnaney, Nashville*	22	0	0	0	4	0	6	1.000	25	22	4	4	1	6	1	1	13	0	1.44
McGaffigan, Nashville	31	20	6	2	15	5	0	.750	170	139	62	45	5	62	2	7	125	5	2.38
McMurtry, Savannah	14	13	5	1	7	4	0	.636	86	82	40	34	8	35	1	4	37	3	3.56
Mendon, Memphis	14	13	4	0	7	2	0	.778	95	91	35	29	6	23	2	4	59	1	2.75
Meridith, Columbus*	25	17	7	2	9	5	0	.643	145	143	48	41	14	40	3	4	82	3	2.54
Miggins, Columbus*	35	3	1	0	4	6	8	.400	68	50	28	24	5	42	3	4	48	1	3.18
Morgan, Knoxville	9	0	0	0	0	0	2	.000	20	23	11	11	3	5	0	2	14	2	4.95
Mulligan, Orlando*	10	3	2	0	0	3	0	.000	39	44	18	15	4	15	1	0	16	2	3.46
Narleski, Chattanooga	47	1	0	0	11	12	6	.478	102	102	52	45	9	42	5	1	68	0	3.97
Nicholson, Chattanooga	2	0	0	0	0	0	0	.000	3	6	5	5	0	1	0	0	2	0	15.00
Norris, Knoxville	14	5	2	0	2	3	1	.400	52	50	28	25	6	18	1	1	14	1	4.33
Nuismer, Chattanooga	16	14	4	1	3	7	0	.300	92	89	52	38	4	50	0	1	59	2	3.72
O'Connor, Memphis*	7	7	0	0	1	2	0	.333	29	30	27	25	5	20	0	0	17	3	7.76
Owens, Chattanooga	12	10	2	0	2	4	0	.333	51	65	44	41	6	32	1	1	40	1	7.24
Pashnick, Montgomery	21	21	12	3	13	4	0	.765	161	143	63	53	13	51	1	4	79	10	2.96
Pensiero, Charlotte	40	4	2	1	9	4	9	.692	118	134	44	35	9	35	0	1	61	8	2.67
Peralta, Charlotte	7	0	0	0	0	1	0	.000	11	15	25	18	4	12	0	1	4	0	14.73
Pole, Montgomery	43	0	0	0	7	4	10	.636	71	67	35	24	6	27	6	1	36	4	3.04
Poloni, Knoxville*	28	27	9	1	10	12	0	.455	172	204	101	81	12	51	0	3	105	13	4.24
Polvi, Montgomery	10	0	0	0	1	3	1	.250	15	12	13	5	0	6	0	3	10	1	3.00
Pratt, Savannah*	4	0	0	0	0	0	0	.000	3	0	0	0	0	2	0	1	0	0	0.00
Presley, Charlotte	2	0	0	0	0	0	2	.000	6	5	0	0	0	3	0	0	3	1	0.00
Puleo, Knoxville	19	19	3	1	8	7	0	.533	108	87	51	34	8	66	1	2	97	9	2.83
Quealey, Columbus	32	0	0	0	6	4	7	.600	61	50	22	19	5	25	3	5	56	2	2.80
Quintana, Charlotte*	35	0	0	0	3	5	8	.375	52	62	30	24	4	22	1	2	32	1	4.15
Rambis, Chattanooga	8	0	0	0	1	0	1	1.000	17	12	8	8	1	10	2	2	13	1	4.24
Ramirez, Charlotte	29	29	10	1	16	8	0	.667	196	151	73	65	11	92	0	3	160	6	2.98
Reyes, Orlando	16	5	0	0	2	2	0	.500	53	47	26	23	2	27	0	1	39	5	3.91
Richards, Montgomery	28	18	2	0	7	8	1	.467	115	124	81	62	11	66	0	7	45	8	4.85
Rogers, Savannah	21	20	5	1	4	10	0	.286	121	126	73	64	10	49	3	6	44	4	4.76
Ross, Columbus	14	0	0	0	2	2	2	.500	27	30	11	11	1	4	0	0	13	1	3.67
Rowe, Charlotte	9	8	2	1	4	2	0	.667	49	58	22	15	2	18	0	1	35	6	2.76
Ryder, Nashville	28	28	9	3	15	9	0	.625	201	170	83	68	16	83	4	5	134	2	3.04
Santana, Knoxville	45	1	0	0	0	8	4	.000	83	91	39	36	4	39	4	1	63	6	3.90
Sheehan, Orlando*	31	24	4	3	9	10	0	.474	157	174	96	80	16	74	1	8	87	7	4.59
Shields, Savannah	22	0	0	0	4	3	7	.571	32	34	13	11	1	12	1	3	13	4	3.09
Shimp, Memphis	25	18	7	1	11	5	2	.688	150	136	64	50	12	48	0	7	130	6	3.00
Simerly, Montgomery	4	3	0	0	2	1	0	.667	21	21	9	9	0	15	1	0	10	2	3.86
Skinner, Jacksonville	25	25	7	0	14	10	0	.333	160	170	108	90	27	84	4	1	92	10	5.06
Slagle, Nashville	12	11	8	0	5	4	0	.556	91	70	25	19	6	20	2	2	84	0	1.88
Smith, Montgomery	26	10	3	2	5	7	0	.417	102	91	54	51	3	39	3	4	63	3	4.50
B. Smith, Memphis	27	25	12	1	10	9	0	.526	181	179	75	56	10	54	1	3	110	4	2.78
M. Smith, Charlotte	3	2	0	0	1	1	0	.500	15	19	14	13	2	6	0	1	6	0	7.80
Steffen, Montgomery*	18	14	2	1	4	8	0	.333	83	81	51	42	10	48	0	2	63	9	4.55
Stoeber, Knoxville	49	0	0	0	7	2	8	.778	80	72	44	36	5	40	4	0	54	3	4.05
Swaggerty, Charlotte	26	0	0	0	3	6	3	.333	51	47	20	14	1	24	0	1	23	1	2.47
J. Taylor, Nashville	19	6	0	0	2	4	1	.333	71	79	36	31	4	21	2	1	42	5	3.93
S. Taylor, Nashville	6	3	0	0	2	1	0	.667	19	20	11	10	2	11	0	0	15	6	4.74
Teising, Montgomery*	37	2	0	0	1	5	3	.167	88	100	62	51	8	52	5	4	52	8	5.22
Tenenini, Memphis	33	2	0	0	5	4	4	.556	75	78	33	32	3	27	4	2	21	0	3.84
Thayer, Knoxville	31	3	2	0	4	4	1	.500	68	60	39	31	0	44	2	2	37	4	4.10
Theiss, Savannah	15	0	0	0	1	4	2	.200	29	27	15	11	2	16	2	2	19	0	3.41
Troedson, Columbus	14	0	0	0	1	2	0	.333	21	29	16	16	1	18	3	2	8	1	6.86
Ungs, Orlando	28	27	11	2	10	15	0	.400	180	206	111	89	17	61	0	0	74	2	4.45
Valley, Columbus*	1	0	0	0	0	0	0	.000	3	4	2	1	0	1	0	0	3	0	3.00
Viefhaus, Montgomery	12	8	1	0	0	4	1	.000	46	49	36	32	5	32	0	4	29	5	6.26
Wagner, Orlando	9	0	0	0	1	0	0	.000	22	26	16	14	2	4	1	1	12	0	5.73
Walker, Knoxville*	27	26	6	0	3	12	0	.200	157	183	103	84	14	59	2	5	76	13	4.82
Warnecke, Chattanooga	6	0	0	0	1	2	0	.333	13	13	13	12	1	10	2	0	3	0	8.31
Welchel, Charlotte	28	28	12	1	9	12	0	.429	202	210	86	65	9	47	2	3	56	6	2.90
Welenc, Columbus	2	0	0	0	0	0	0	.000	3	2	1	1	0	3	0	0	2	2	3.00

Pitcher—Club	G.	GS.	CG.	ShO.	W.	L.	Sv.	Pct.	IP.	H.	R.	ER.	HR.	BB.	Int. BB.	HB.	SO.	WP.	ERA.
Werly, Nashville	16	16	6	2	6	3	0	.667	113	87	50	43	7	53	1	4	104	9	3.42
Wilder, Chattanooga*	18	15	3	1	5	7	1	.417	103	100	63	55	8	56	1	2	64	6	4.81
Williams, Jacksonville	5	4	1	0	1	2	0	.333	29	30	18	12	1	9	0	0	15	3	3.72
Williams, Memphis*	18	3	0	0	1	2	1	.333	23	39	23	22	4	15	0	1	12	3	8.61
Winfield, Memphis	36	1	0	0	4	6	2	.400	73	81	45	39	9	38	5	4	30	4	4.81
Yanus, Memphis	17	17	5	1	9	2	0	.818	117	134	52	47	10	29	1	0	63	3	3.62

BALKS—Abone, J. Gonzalez, 4 each; Corr, Hodge, Leatherwood, Pashnick, Rogers, 3 each; Bailey, Bargar, Field, Fuson, George, Leland, McGaffigan, Richards, Teising, Ungs, 2 each; Adamson, L. Anderson, K. Anderson, Aponte, Barr, Belanger, Brueggeman, Cacciatore, Candiotti, Cuellar, Dayley, Dooner, Filer, Fore, Ganger, Hendricks, Hessler, Ledduke, Mapel, McMurtry, Mendon, Miggins, Nuismer, Owens, Pole, Ramirez, Reyes, Ryder, Shimp, Skinner, Slagle, J. Smith, Steffen, S. Taylor, Tenenini, Thayer, Viefhaus, Wilder, R. Williams, 1 each.

COMBINATION SHUTOUTS—Owens-Narleski, Gonzalez-Narleski, Glaser-Narleski, Chattanooga; Meridith-Ladd, Leatherwood-Quealey, Columbus; Puleo-Flores, Knoxville; Abone-Williams, Memphis; Ledduke-S. Taylor, Lewis-McEnaney, Kaufman-Boris, Nashville; Sheehan-Dooner, Barr-Dooner, Orlando; Cole-Livingstone, Dayley-Alvarez, Savannah.

NO-HIT GAMES—None.

Unlucky '13'

For the third time in Southern League history, 13 proved to be the unlucky number for a pitcher's string of victories.

William Edgerton of Mobile won 12 in a row in 1966, but was stopped when he tried for his 13th. The same thing happened to Bill Zepp of Charlotte in 1969.

In 1980, it was Andy McGaffigan of Nashville. The winner of 12 straight, the Sounds' righthander went after No. 13 against Chattanooga August 6 and was stopped by the Lookouts, 7-3.

History also repeated itself in another way in the game. Chattanooga's Robin Fuson, who had handed McGaffigan his last previous defeat on May 27, turned the trick again.

Rooney Clubbed 15 Homers in July

Prior to July 1, Pat Rooney of Memphis in the Southern League had a .218 average. However, during July he slugged 15 homers, drove in 35 runs and batted .344.

The 15 homers were the most hit in one month by any major or minor league player in the history of the Montreal Expos' organization. The major league record for homers in July is also 15, accomplished by Joe DiMaggio in 1937, Hank Greenberg in 1938 and Joe Adcock in 1956.

Texas League

CLASS AA

Leading Batter
DARYL SCONIERS
El Paso

League President
CARL SAWATSKI

Leading Pitcher
JOE EDELEN
Arkansas

CHAMPIONSHIP WINNERS IN PREVIOUS YEARS

1888—Dallas	.671	1919—Shreveport*	.677	1942—Beaumont	.605
1889—Houston	.551	Fort Worth	.651	Shreveport (2nd)§	.576
1890—Galveston	.705	1920—Fort Worth	.700	1943-44-45—Did not operate.	
1892—Fort Worth	.741	Fort Worth	.750	1946—Fort Worth	.656
Houston	.613	1921—Fort Worth	.691	Dallas (2nd)§	.591
1895—Dallas	.754	Fort Worth	.662	1947—Houston‡	.623
Fort Worth*	.750	1922—Fort Worth	.694	1948—Fort Worth‡	.601
1895—Fort Worth	.757	Fort Worth	.711	1949—Fort Worth	.649
Houston.*	.679	1923—Fort Worth	.632	Tulsa (2nd)§	.584
Galveston	.548	1924—Fort Worth	.689	1950—Beaumont	.595
1897—San Antonio†	.657	Fort Worth	.763	San Antonio (4th)§	.513
Galveston†	.717	1925—Fort Worth	.711	1951—Houston‡	.619
1898—League disbanded.		Fort Worth y	.653	1952—Dallas	.571
1899—Galveston	.622	1926—Dallas	.574	Shreveport (3rd)§	.522
Galveston	.762	1927—Wichita Falls	.654	1953—Dallas‡	.571
1900-01—Did not operate.		1928—Houston*	.679	1954—Shreveport	.559
1902—Corsicana	.866	Wichita Falls	.731	Houston (2nd)§	.553
Corsicana	.682	1929—Dallas*	.588	1955—Dallas	.581
1903—Paris-Waco	.615	Wichita Falls	.620	Shreveport (3rd)§	.540
Dallas*	.648	1930—Wichita Falls	.697	1956—Houston‡	.623
1904—Corsicana*	.615	Fort Worth*	.632	1957—Dallas	.662
Fort Worth	.800	1931—Houston**	.625	Houston (2nd)§	.630
1905—Fort Worth	.545	Houston	.734	1958—Fort Worth	.582
1906—Fort Worth	.677	1932—Beaumont*	.640	Cor. Christi (3rd)§	.507
Cleburne x	.609	Dallas	.727	1959—Victoria	.589
1907—Austin	.629	1933—Houston	.623	Austin (2nd)§	.548
1908—San Antonio	.664	San Antonio (4th)§	.523	1960—Rio Grande Valley	.590
1909—Houston	.601	1934—Galveston‡	.379	Tulsa (3rd)ʃ	.528
1910—Dallas†	.586	1935—Oklahoma City‡	.590	1961—Amarillo	.643
Houston†	.586	Tulsa (3rd)§	.519	San Antonio (3rd)§	.532
1911—Austin	.575	1936—Dallas	.604	1962—El Paso	.571
1912—Houston	.626	1937—Oklahoma City	.635	Tulsa (2nd)§	.550
1913—Houston	.620	Fort Worth (3rd)§	.535	1963—San Antonio	.564
1914—Houston†	.671	1938—Beaumont	.635	Tulsa (3rd)§	.529
Waco†	.671	1939—Houston	.606	1964—San Antonio†	.607
1915—Waco	.592	Fort Worth (4th)§	.540	1965—Tulsa	.574
1916—Waco	.587	1940—Houston‡	.652	Albuquerque xx	.550
1917—Dallas	.600	1941—Houston	.673	1966—Arkansas	.579
1918—Dallas	.584	Dallas (4th)§	.519	1967—Albuquerque	.557

CHAMPIONSHIP WINNERS IN PREVIOUS YEARS—Continued

1968—Arkansas .586	1972—Alexandria .600	1976—Amarillo xx .600
El Paso xx .562	El Paso xx .557	Shreveport .515
1969—Amarillo .593	1973—San Antonio .590	1977—El Paso .600
Memphis xx .504	Memphis xx .558	Arkansas a .485
1970—Albuquerque** .615	1974—Victoria xx .581	1978—El Paso a .593
Memphis .507	El Paso .555	Jackson .567
1971—Did not operate as league—clubs were members of Dixie Association.	1975—Lafayette xxx .558	1979—Arkansas a .571
	Midland xxx .604	Midland .563

*Won split-season playoff. †No playoff for title. ‡Finished first and won four-club playoff. §Won four-club playoff. xTitle to Cleburne by default. yTied with Dallas in second half and won playoff for championship. zFort Worth disbanded. **Tied with Beaumont at end of first half and won title in best-of-five series played as part of second half schedule. xxLeague divided into Eastern, Western divisions; won two-team playoff. xxxLeague divided into Eastern, Western divisions; declared co-champions when playoffs were not completed. aLeague divided into Eastern and Western divisions and played split-season; won playoffs. NOTE—Championship awarded to winner of four-team playoff, 1933-51; first-place team and playoff winner co-champions, 1952-64.

STANDING OF CLUBS AT CLOSE OF FIRST HALF, JUNE 22

EASTERN DIVISION

Club	W.	L.	T.	Pct.	G.B.
Arkansas (Cardinals)	46	22	0	.676	......
Tulsa (Rangers)	40	27	0	.597	5½
Jackson (Mets)	29	39	0	.426	17
Shreveport (Giants)	25	40	0	.385	19½

WESTERN DIVISION

Club	W.	L.	T.	Pct.	G.B.
San Antonio (Dodgers)	41	30	0	.577	......
Amarillo (Padres)	40	31	0	.563	1
Midland (Cubs)	28	43	0	.394	13
El Paso (Angels)	27	44	0	.380	14

STANDING OF CLUBS AT CLOSE OF SECOND HALF, AUGUST 30

EASTERN DIVISION

Club	W.	L.	T.	Pct.	G.B.
Jackson (Mets)	45	23	0	.662	......
Arkansas (Cardinals)	35	33	0	.515	10
Tulsa (Rangers)	35	34	0	.507	10½
Shreveport (Giants)	24	47	0	.338	22½

WESTERN DIVISION

Club	W.	L.	T.	Pct.	G.B.
Amarillo (Padres)	37	28	0	.569	......
Midland (Cubs)	36	29	0	.554	1
San Antonio (Dodgers)	33	32	0	.508	4
El Paso (Angels)	23	42	0	.354	14

COMPOSITE STANDING OF CLUBS AT CLOSE OF SEASON, AUGUST 30

EASTERN DIVISION

Club	Ark.	Tul.	Jack.	Shrv.	Amar.	S.A.	Mid.	ElP.	W.	L.	T.	Pct.	G.B.
Arkansas (Cardinals)	....	18	14	26	5	4	8	6	81	55	0	.596	......
Tulsa (Rangers)	14	....	19	19	5	6	7	5	75	61	0	.551	6
Jackson (Mets)	18	13	....	18	6	4	6	9	74	62	0	.544	7
Shreveport (Giants)	6	13	14	....	4	6	3	3	49	87	0	.360	32

WESTERN DIVISION

Club	Ark.	Tul.	Jack.	Shrv.	Amar.	S.A.	Mid.	ElP.	W.	L.	T.	Pct.	G.B.
Amarillo (Padres)	5	5	4	6	....	16	17	24	77	59	0	.566	......
San Antonio (Dodgers)	6	4	6	4	16	....	17	21	74	62	0	.544	3
Midland (Cubs)	2	3	4	7	15	15	....	18	64	72	0	.471	13
El Paso (Angels)	4	5	1	7	8	11	14	....	50	86	0	.368	27

Arkansas club represented Little Rock, Ark.

Major league affiliations in parentheses.

Playoffs—Arkansas defeated Jackson, two games to none; San Antonio defeated Amarillo, two games to none; Arkansas defeated San Antonio, three games to none for championship.

Regular-Season Attendance—Amarillo, 70,097; Arkansas, 216,592; El Paso, 265,062; Jackson, 98,833; Midland, 95,820; San Antonio, 153,355; Shreveport, 40,370; Tulsa, 58,020. Total, 998,149. Playoffs, 11,922. All-star game, 2,416.

Managers: Amarillo—Eddie Watt; Arkansas—Sonny Ruberto; El Paso—Jim Saul; Jackson—Bob Wellman; Midland—Randy Hundley, Les Moss, George Enright; San Antonio—Don LeJohn; Shreveport—Andy Gilbert; Tulsa—Wayne Terwilliger.

All-Star Team: 1B—Sconiers, El Paso; 2B—Fletcher, Midland; 3B—Riggleman, Arkansas; SS—Tolleson, Tulsa; OF—Barrow, Tulsa; Bishop, El Paso; Brunansky, El Paso; Utility—Klimas, Tulsa; C—Hunsaker, Arkansas; DH—George, Amarillo; P—Boone, Amarillo; DeLeon, Arkansas; Gleaton, Tulsa; Leary, Jackson; Manager—Wellman, Jackson.

(Compiled by Ed Williams, League Statistician, Shawnee, Okla.)

CLUB BATTING

Club	G.	AB.	R.	OR.	H.	TB.	2B.	3B.	HR.	RBI.	SH.	SF.	BB.	Int. BB.	HP.	SO.	SB.	CS.	LOB.	Pct.
El Paso	136	4713	740	910	1360	2112	261	31	143	673	25	29	523	21	43	759	86	40	1045	.289
Midland	136	4540	789	824	1304	1878	203	49	91	701	45	40	612	27	30	801	100	69	985	.287
San Antonio	136	4445	705	586	1245	1737	183	36	79	634	47	42	612	33	38	645	111	59	1038	.280
Amarillo	136	4426	686	692	1223	1769	201	36	91	614	55	45	601	31	26	816	107	68	1023	.276
Tulsa	136	4391	700	655	1206	1772	219	46	85	620	32	41	585	36	38	866	210	93	965	.275
Arkansas	136	4356	629	528	1192	1742	239	37	79	556	55	40	505	42	31	769	140	80	915	.274
Jackson	136	4402	626	545	1184	1736	196	55	82	555	45	29	466	37	43	675	101	81	952	.269
Shreveport	136	4354	452	587	1060	1454	184	30	50	388	48	36	441	35	27	742	84	63	950	.243

INDIVIDUAL BATTING

(Leading Qualifiers for Batting Championship—367 or More Plate Appearances)

*Bats lefthanded. †Switch-hitter.

Player and Club	G.	AB.	R.	H.	TB.	2B.	3B.	HR.	RBI.	SH.	SF.	BB.	HP.	SO.	SB.	CS.	Pct.
Sconiers, Daryl, El Paso*	136	506	95	187	296	48	8	15	87	2	2	80	7	78	17	6	.370
Holman, Q. Dale, San Antonio*	135	483	79	166	230	22	3	12	78	4	3	74	3	87	7	10	.344
Ashby, Gary, Amarillo*	109	412	69	141	180	22	4	3	56	5	4	42	2	73	20	5	.342
Barrow, Melvin, Tulsa	103	386	76	131	206	20	2	17	61	1	4	54	5	60	20	10	.339
Bhagwat, Thomas, El Paso	124	483	87	163	245	32	1	16	67	1	2	63	2	45	2	2	.337
George, Frankie, Amarillo	124	445	86	147	224	22	2	17	102	2	5	76	1	67	1	4	.330
Fletcher, Scott, Midland	130	501	111	164	220	16	11	6	65	3	4	82	9	65	20	8	.327
Bishop, Michael, El Paso	126	489	96	159	295	27	5	33	104	2	4	63	2	87	4	4	.325
Hunsaker, Frank, Arkansas	115	357	41	116	139	17	0	2	50	3	4	43	7	42	2	2	.325
Brunansky, Thomas, El Paso	128	495	103	160	272	24	8	24	97	0	4	75	3	96	23	7	.323

Departmental Leaders: G—Bradley, Sconiers, G. Wright, 136; AB—Beyers, 546; R—Fletcher, 111; H—Sconiers, 187; TB—Sconiers, 296; 2B—Sconiers, 48; 3B—Fletcher, 11; HR—Bishop, 33; RBI—Bishop, 104; GWRBI—Capra, Perry, 13; SH—DeSimone, 12; SF—Mitchell, Swoope, 8; BB—Bradley, 97; HP—Bradley, 12; SO—B. Johnson, 106; SB—Capra, 55; CS—M. Howard, 19.

(All Players—Listed Alphabetically)

Player and Club	G.	AB.	R.	H.	TB.	2B.	3B.	HR.	RBI.	SH.	SF.	BB.	HP.	SO.	SB.	CS.	Pct.
Adams, Ricky, El Paso	92	382	68	112	164	16	0	12	53	2	3	28	4	48	19	4	.293
Adams, Rollo, Shreveport†	18	50	7	10	14	1	0	1	3	1	1	1	1	14	0	0	.200
Alexander, Patrick, Shreveport	9	7	0	1	1	0	0	0	0	0	0	0	0	5	0	0	.143
Alfaro, Jesus, Midland	53	202	52	72	98	7	2	5	34	0	1	33	1	31	4	0	.356
Alvarez, John, Amarillo	129	456	58	124	196	22	4	14	70	1	4	53	2	79	4	4	.272
Amerson, Archie, Amarillo	103	381	57	107	162	18	2	11	64	0	1	34	3	63	8	8	.281
Anderson, Richard, Jackson	25	5	0	1	1	0	0	0	0	0	0	0	0	0	0	0	.200
Anthony, Tom, Shreveport†	86	240	29	51	74	13	2	2	21	4	2	22	1	39	3	3	.213
Aranzamendi, Jorge, Arkansas	103	269	33	73	88	7	1	2	22	10	0	29	1	43	4	5	.271
Ashby, Gary, Amarillo*	109	412	69	141	180	22	4	3	56	5	4	42	2	73	20	5	.342
Baez, Jesse, San Antonio	50	119	15	27	40	4	0	3	18	3	5	22	5	20	0	1	.227
Baldwin, Kenneth, San Antonio*	21	62	6	16	18	0	1	0	7	0	0	4	1	5	1	2	.258
Barrow, Melvin, Tulsa	103	386	76	131	206	20	2	17	61	1	4	54	5	60	20	10	.339
Bauman, Brad, Shreveport	17	54	5	10	13	0	0	1	3	1	0	11	0	13	0	0	.185
Belmonte, Phillip, Midland	1	3	0	0	0	0	0	0	0	0	0	1	0	1	0	1	.000
Beltre, Sergio, Jackson	45	148	17	46	67	8	2	3	19	2	0	18	3	30	5	5	.311
Beyers, Tom, San Antonio*	138	546	63	162	213	21	4	9	80	2	5	26	4	48	7	7	.297
Bhagwat, Thomas, El Paso	124	483	87	163	245	32	1	16	67	1	2	63	2	45	2	2	.337
Bialas, David, Arkansas	7	26	2	10	11	1	0	0	1	0	0	3	0	4	0	0	.385
Bishop, Michael, El Paso	126	489	96	159	295	27	5	33	104	2	4	63	2	87	4	4	.325
Bjorkman, George, Arkansas	70	196	20	47	75	14	1	4	18	1	1	27	3	48	7	2	.240
Bradley, Mark, San Antonio	136	469	95	117	184	19	6	12	76	3	3	97	12	103	28	13	.249
Brenly, Robert, Shreveport	2	10	2	3	6	0	0	1	3	0	0	0	1	0	0	0	.300
Brewster, Richard, El Paso*	29	113	20	28	35	5	1	0	4	2	0	17	1	8	4	1	.248
Brown, Randall, Jackson	9	8	1	0	0	0	0	0	0	0	0	3	0	2	0	0	.000
Brunansky, Thomas, El Paso	128	495	103	160	272	24	8	24	97	0	4	75	3	96	23	7	.323
Buckner, James, Jackson*	6	8	0	0	0	0	0	0	0	0	0	0	0	0	0	0	.000
Budner, Scott, Shreveport†	40	46	3	7	8	1	0	0	3	0	0	10	0	9	0	0	.152
Cacciatore, Paul, Jackson	14	13	0	1	1	0	0	0	0	0	0	0	0	4	0	0	.077
Calise, Michael, Arkansas	16	58	8	21	38	8	0	3	16	0	0	5	1	16	0	1	.362
Calvert, Mark, Shreveport	14	18	0	3	3	0	0	0	1	0	0	0	0	4	0	0	.167
Capra, Nick, Tulsa	117	440	90	127	188	25	4	6	53	2	3	57	4	69	55	14	.289
Cardwell, J. David, Shreveport	52	183	19	34	44	8	1	0	15	3	3	7	0	45	0	1	.186
Carnes, Scott, El Paso	103	399	44	87	110	12	1	3	22	3	4	51	6	66	8	7	.218
Carpenter, Willie, Tulsa	14	39	5	10	11	1	0	0	6	1	0	2	1	7	2	0	.256
Chamberlain, Thomas, Arkansas	3	5	0	0	0	0	0	0	0	0	1	0	0	1	0	0	.000
Clark, J. Randall, Midland	27	2	0	0	0	0	0	0	0	0	0	0	2	0	0	0	.000
Clark, Russell, Jackson	42	3	1	1	1	0	0	0	1	0	0	0	1	0	0	0	.333
Cowger, Tracy, Tulsa	72	255	32	65	91	11	3	3	41	1	3	24	1	41	3	7	.255
Crow, Donald, San Antonio	17	48	8	11	15	1	0	1	6	0	0	2	1	9	0	0	.229
Crutcher, David, Tulsa	40	0	0	0	0	0	0	0	0	0	0	0	0	0	0	0	.000
Cuervo, Edward, Jackson†	109	410	57	102	139	13	3	6	34	4	4	21	2	44	17	11	.249

Player and Club	G.	AB.	R.	H.	TB.	2B.	3B.	HR.	RBI.	SH.	SF.	BB.	HP.	SO.	SB.	CS.	Pct.
Davis, Charles, Shreveport†	129	442	50	130	204	30	4	12	67	3	7	52	3	94	19	18	.294
DeLeon, Luis, Arkansas	76	7	0	0	0	0	0	0	0	2	0	0	0	4	0	0	.000
Del Monte, John, Arkansas	4	9	1	2	4	0	1	0	1	0	0	1	0	1	0	0	.222
DeSimone, Gerald, Amarillo†	99	352	58	96	129	16	4	3	32	12	3	49	1	49	12	8	.273
Dimmel, Michael, Arkansas	90	359	59	100	137	19	9	0	28	2	3	37	4	41	16	11	.279
Donofrio, Larry, Tulsa*	23	56	3	9	16	4	0	1	4	0	0	7	0	19	1	0	.161
Doss, Richard, Shreveport	35	106	6	17	22	2	0	1	6	1	0	5	0	34	0	0	.160
Dotson, J. Eugene, Arkansas	102	345	59	95	166	20	3	15	50	0	3	45	3	83	16	7	.275
Duff, David, Jackson	6	16	3	6	10	2	1	0	2	0	0	1	0	2	0	0	.375
Dunn, James, Shreveport	68	213	16	35	43	4	2	0	9	4	2	17	3	27	2	3	.164
Edelen, Benny Joe, Arkansas	32	38	4	14	19	2	0	1	4	3	1	1	0	15	1	0	.368
Enright, George, Tulsa	23	72	6	18	19	1	0	0	7	0	0	8	0	14	0	1	.250
Fierro, Javier, Midland	33	106	20	29	49	5	0	5	29	0	1	19	0	16	7	2	.274
Fisher, Glenn, Shreveport	20	17	0	2	2	0	0	0	0	0	0	0	0	0	0	0	.118
Flannery, John, Amarillo	110	418	61	117	134	11	0	2	32	3	5	37	4	49	13	5	.280
Fletcher, Scott, Midland	130	501	111	164	220	16	11	6	65	3	4	82	9	65	20	8	.327
Fobbs, Larry, San Antonio	127	483	96	149	199	23	3	7	53	8	0	84	4	49	28	9	.308
Gaff, Brent, Jackson	25	24	0	1	1	0	0	0	0	1	0	1	0	5	0	0	.042
Garcia, Frank, Tulsa	36	115	15	27	35	2	0	2	13	0	2	15	1	30	3	1	.235
Garcia, Nelson, Arkansas	71	221	29	60	74	12	1	0	21	1	0	23	0	43	2	5	.271
Gardenhire, Ronald, Jackson	127	458	58	118	164	16	6	6	64	6	4	45	4	68	13	9	.258
George, Frankie, Amarillo	124	445	86	147	224	22	2	17	102	2	5	76	1	67	1	4	.330
Gilbert, Dennis, El Paso	30	103	13	25	45	5	0	5	16	0	0	13	0	16	0	0	.243
Giles, Brian, Jackson	132	448	76	128	204	30	8	10	57	0	6	51	8	80	9	13	.286
Gladden, C. Daniel, Shreveport	74	292	51	86	128	11	2	9	35	2	1	22	4	46	22	11	.295
Glinatsis, Michael, Shreveport	35	18	0	1	1	0	0	0	0	1	0	1	1	15	0	0	.056
Gonzalez, Luis, Tulsa*	95	343	57	104	173	27	3	12	66	1	3	38	1	75	1	3	.303
Gooch, Ronald, Tulsa	29	111	17	39	49	7	0	1	16	1	2	12	0	14	5	0	.351
Grant, Thomas, Midland*	135	523	99	161	241	38	6	10	92	3	4	67	3	104	5	8	.308
Greer, Brian, Amarillo	101	317	42	58	97	11	2	8	35	3	4	63	3	105	9	0	.183
Gutierrez, Julian, Arkansas	115	356	52	96	119	14	3	1	35	7	2	37	1	36	13	9	.270
Gwosdz, Douglas, Amarillo	97	286	40	70	113	18	2	7	43	9	5	37	2	73	7	6	.245
Hall, Melvin, Midland*	37	128	17	34	50	7	3	1	14	0	0	14	0	37	2	1	.266
Hamilton, James, El Paso	64	212	19	45	53	8	0	0	11	4	2	14	1	51	3	4	.212
Hargesheimer, Alan, Shreveport	12	17	1	1	1	0	0	0	0	1	0	0	0	9	0	0	.059
Harper, Brian, El Paso	105	400	61	114	179	23	3	12	66	1	2	38	5	46	3	2	.285
Haslerig, William, Jackson*	52	180	39	62	120	8	7	12	46	0	1	26	1	45	4	3	.344
Heimueller, Gorman, Shreveport*	32	15	2	2	3	1	0	0	2	1	0	2	0	1	0	0	.133
Heredia, Ubaldo, San Antonio	15	11	0	1	1	0	0	0	0	3	0	0	0	2	0	0	.091
Hernandez, Leonardo, San Ant	41	136	27	33	52	9	2	2	26	1	1	11	0	12	1	1	.243
Herschiser, Orel, San Antonio	49	4	1	1	2	1	0	0	0	0	0	0	0	2	0	0	.250
Hicks, Joseph, Amarillo	126	464	70	116	163	15	4	8	40	5	1	78	1	78	25	14	.250
Hicks, Joseph A., Midland	122	425	78	123	220	19	3	24	87	4	7	61	4	77	6	6	.289
Hinrichs, Phillip, Shreveport	23	4	0	0	0	0	0	0	0	0	0	1	0	1	0	0	.000
Holman, Q. Dale, San Antonio*	135	483	79	166	230	22	3	12	78	4	3	74	3	87	7	10	.344
Holton, Brian, San Antonio	29	13	0	0	0	0	0	0	0	2	0	0	0	5	0	0	.000
Hough, Stanley, Jackson	89	280	33	65	93	10	3	4	33	4	0	30	5	36	1	1	.232
Howard, David, Jackson	21	60	3	11	13	0	1	0	5	0	2	4	2	12	0	3	.183
Howard, Michael, Jackson	135	508	91	148	221	30	8	9	56	3	2	66	5	55	24	19	.291
Humphry, Brandt, El Paso	110	392	49	109	171	25	2	11	56	0	4	22	5	65	2	1	.278
Hunsaker, Frank, Arkansas	115	357	41	116	139	17	0	2	50	3	4	43	7	42	2	2	.325
Jirschele, Michael, Tulsa	91	235	36	49	58	3	0	2	27	6	2	36	3	46	6	1	.209
Johnson, Bobby, Tulsa	115	382	64	93	163	25	3	13	70	0	7	79	2	106	15	9	.243
Johnson, David, Arkansas*	37	18	5	4	6	0	1	0	1	2	0	1	0	8	1	0	.222
Johnson, Jerry, Amarillo	82	265	60	72	96	7	4	3	28	1	3	54	3	43	5	4	.272
Johnson, Randall, Jackson	28	72	9	22	22	0	0	0	5	2	1	8	1	6	1	0	.306
Jones, Donny, El Paso	95	352	40	86	119	15	0	6	43	3	0	22	6	65	1	1	.244
Jorn, David, Arkansas	22	13	2	4	6	2	0	0	0	1	0	0	2	0	0	0	.308
Keedy, C. Patrick, El Paso	26	98	11	14	20	3	0	1	10	1	0	5	0	31	0	1	.143
Kim, Wendell, Shreveport	2	0	1	0	0	0	0	0	0	0	0	0	0	0	0	0	.000
Klimas, Philip, Tulsa	126	442	79	139	219	32	3	14	84	1	7	75	2	71	5	2	.314
Korbe, Gregory, Jackson	68	187	20	50	70	5	3	3	21	0	2	19	0	32	1	1	.267
Krug, Gary, Midland*	67	259	50	89	134	16	1	9	51	1	3	16	1	37	1	3	.344
Kurosaki, Ryan, Arkansas	37	7	0	0	0	0	0	0	0	1	0	1	0	1	0	0	.000
Lancellotti, Richard, Amarillo*.	22	79	15	30	52	8	1	4	15	0	0	11	1	6	1	0	.380
Lane, Jerry, Shreveport	132	488	46	123	178	24	2	9	45	1	2	19	2	84	1	1	.252
Lane, Richard, Arkansas	64	188	24	45	57	8	2	0	18	3	0	19	1	16	0	1	.239
LaVigne, Randall, Midland	133	526	88	158	247	26	6	17	96	6	2	33	3	105	9	6	.300
Lazorko, Jack, Tulsa	56	1	1	0	0	0	0	0	0	0	0	0	0	1	0	0	.000
Leach, Terry, Jackson	8	12	0	1	1	0	0	0	0	0	0	0	0	6	0	0	.083
Leary, Timothy, Jackson	27	37	2	6	9	3	0	0	3	1	0	0	0	17	0	0	.162
Lewis, Amos, Tulsa	25	80	8	10	16	3	0	1	11	0	1	22	0	37	0	2	.125
Little, Donald, Arkansas	9	2	1	1	2	1	0	0	0	0	0	0	0	0	0	0	.500
Lowry, Michael, Jackson	15	17	2	0	0	0	0	0	0	0	0	3	0	9	0	0	.000
Marshall, Mike, San Antonio	134	470	95	151	232	21	6	16	82	1	5	86	1	97	6	2	.321
Martin, Jared, Midland*	66	256	34	61	76	7	4	0	26	6	1	30	3	31	10	8	.238

Player and Club	G.	AB.	R.	H.	TB.	2B.	3B.	HR.	RBI.	SH.	SF.	BB.	HP.	SO.	SB.	CS.	Pct.
Martin, John, Arkansas	5	4	0	0	0	0	0	0	0	0	0	0	0	2	0	0	.000
McCauley, Stanley, Arkansas	28	55	5	9	16	1	0	2	7	3	0	4	0	15	0	1	.164
McCrary, Arnold, Tulsa*	54	177	29	46	69	2	6	3	22	1	0	22	4	28	12	5	.260
McDonald, Russell, San Antonio	33	1	0	0	0	0	0	0	1	2	0	0	0	0	0	0	.000
McIntyre, James, Arkansas	10	29	3	5	6	1	0	0	1	0	0	1	0	11	0	0	.172
Miller, Richard, Jackson*	11	20	6	7	12	0	1	1	4	0	0	5	0	5	0	0	.350
Miller, Thomas, Jackson*	18	10	1	1	1	0	0	0	0	0	0	2	1	2	0	0	.100
Mitchell, James, Midland*	129	447	55	109	131	16	3	0	56	8	8	64	0	79	6	3	.244
Moyer, Gregory, Shreveport	4	3	0	0	0	0	0	0	0	0	0	0	0	1	0	0	.000
Murphy, John, Arkansas*	31	16	3	1	1	0	0	0	0	1	0	0	0	3	0	0	.063
Neufang, Gerald, Tulsa	11	30	3	9	10	1	0	0	2	0	1	3	1	4	2	2	.300
Nipp, Mark, San Antonio	6	1	0	1	1	0	0	0	0	0	0	0	0	0	0	0	1.000
Nobles, James, San Antonio	37	2	0	0	0	0	0	0	0	0	0	0	0	1	0	0	.000
O'Berry, P. Michael, Midland	57	173	31	42	60	9	3	1	23	1	2	37	0	41	2	4	.243
Ollar, C. Rick, San Antonio*	10	11	1	4	5	1	0	0	1	0	0	2	0	2	0	0	.364
Olmsted, Alan, Arkansas	8	7	0	0	0	0	0	0	0	0	0	0	0	2	0	0	.000
Orosco, Jesse, Jackson	37	6	2	4	7	1	1	0	1	0	0	0	0	0	0	0	.667
Owen, Dave, Midland†	78	257	45	74	91	8	0	3	31	6	4	58	2	52	16	8	.288
Ownbey, Richard, Jackson	2	2	0	0	0	0	0	0	0	0	0	0	0	0	0	0	.000
Paris, Kelly, Arkansas	116	399	63	120	166	28	3	4	49	1	6	38	2	59	17	11	.301
Pastors, Gregory, Amarillo	74	266	38	69	95	12	1	4	40	4	4	22	0	58	5	4	.259
Payne, James, Midland	28	64	5	15	19	1	0	1	12	0	0	2	0	20	0	0	.234
Pechek, Wayne, Shreveport*	57	198	23	61	82	10	4	1	16	3	1	30	6	20	18	10	.308
Penniall, David, Arkansas	47	180	39	53	81	16	0	4	23	2	0	27	2	22	12	5	.294
Perlman, Jonathon, Midland*	32	1	1	0	0	0	0	0	0	0	0	0	0	0	0	0	.000
Perry, Kenneth, Jackson	130	457	73	131	189	23	7	7	68	2	4	66	4	59	16	4	.287
Pinkerton, C. Wayne, Tulsa†	4	11	2	4	5	1	0	0	1	0	0	0	0	2	0	1	.364
Prewitt, Larry, Shreveport	16	7	0	0	0	0	0	0	1	0	0	0	0	3	0	0	.000
Ransom, Jeffrey, Shreveport†	124	394	38	104	122	14	2	0	39	3	6	48	1	49	3	1	.264
Reed, Curtis, Amarillo*	134	507	66	144	226	33	8	11	97	7	5	52	5	98	3	3	.284
Reynolds, Larry, Tulsa†	46	156	23	40	49	7	1	0	19	1	0	16	1	27	15	6	.256
Richards, David, San Antonio	85	274	37	67	73	6	0	0	22	4	2	18	1	26	0	1	.245
Richmond, Albert, Amarillo	8	19	1	4	8	1	0	1	4	0	0	1	0	2	1	0	.211
Riggleman, James, Arkansas	127	431	84	127	233	29	7	21	90	4	10	60	2	67	28	6	.295
Rincon, Andrew, Arkansas	26	29	3	5	9	1	0	1	1	2	0	0	0	8	0	0	.172
Rogers, Randall, Jackson	56	196	21	52	74	11	1	3	19	1	0	22	0	41	0	2	.265
Rothford, James, Shreveport	126	455	38	111	169	28	0	10	41	2	4	25	2	93	0	0	.244
Runnels, Thomas, Shreveport†	73	258	27	50	56	4	1	0	10	5	1	36	0	19	9	7	.194
Schultz, Greg, San Antonio	4	9	0	1	1	0	0	0	0	0	0	0	0	1	0	0	.111
Sconiers, Daryl, El Paso*	136	506	95	187	296	48	4	15	87	2	2	80	7	78	17	6	.370
Searage, Ray, Jackson*	14	8	0	0	0	0	0	0	0	2	0	0	0	2	0	0	.000
Shepston, Michael, Midland	70	208	32	47	61	7	2	1	18	6	0	25	2	36	3	3	.226
Shirley, Steven, San Antonio	18	11	0	0	0	0	0	0	0	1	0	0	0	2	0	0	.000
Shoemaker, John, San Antonio*	65	219	29	53	61	6	1	0	19	3	3	20	1	21	8	2	.242
Smith, Daniel, 19 Jcksn-11 ElP	30	11	1	3	3	0	0	0	2	5	0	0	0	1	0	0	.273
Snell, Nathaniel, Shreveport	35	4	0	3	5	1	0	2	0	0	0	0	0	0	0	1	.750
Springman, Bill, El Paso	49	187	22	49	69	12	1	2	23	4	1	20	0	30	0	0	.262
Stadler, Jeffrey, Shreveport	14	10	1	0	0	0	0	0	0	0	0	2	0	6	0	0	.000
Stember, Jeffrey, Shreveport	16	20	0	3	3	0	0	0	0	5	0	0	0	7	0	0	.150
Stockstill, David, Midland*	103	342	60	93	144	19	4	8	53	1	2	54	2	51	6	6	.272
Strawn, C. DeFla, Tulsa	18	61	13	17	30	3	0	3	13	0	0	5	1	23	1	0	.279
Stuper, John, Arkansas	25	14	0	1	1	0	0	0	1	1	1	1	0	5	0	0	.071
Swoope, C. William, San Antonio	98	327	29	75	99	13	1	3	46	2	8	37	1	49	1	4	.229
Szymarek, Paul, Shreveport	28	76	5	7	8	1	0	0	4	0	2	13	1	14	0	0	.092
Taveras, Alejandro, San Antonio	115	426	66	121	161	18	2	6	54	7	3	83	1	44	20	7	.284
Thomas, William, Arkansas	14	5	1	1	1	0	0	0	0	0	0	0	0	2	0	0	.200
Thorp, Bradley, San Antonio	26	8	0	0	0	0	0	0	0	0	0	0	0	4	0	0	.000
Thurberg, Thomas, Jackson	35	27	4	10	13	3	0	0	9	0	0	4	0	6	0	1	.370
Tinkler, Jack, Arkansas	18	29	1	2	2	0	0	0	0	0	0	1	2	8	1	2	.069
Tipa, Stephen, El Paso	30	102	12	22	39	6	1	3	14	0	1	12	0	27	0	0	.216
Tisdale, Freddie, Arkansas*	134	471	70	126	213	26	5	17	85	1	7	61	2	77	14	8	.268
Tjader, James, Tulsa	46	161	18	37	52	4	3	1	16	1	2	14	0	51	4	2	.230
Tolleson, J. Wayne, Tulsa†	131	452	69	124	160	19	7	1	30	7	2	68	6	82	46	18	.274
Troedson, Thad, Shreveport	15	3	0	1	1	0	0	0	0	0	0	0	0	2	0	0	.333
Tucker, Michael, Shreveport	19	7	1	0	0	0	0	0	0	1	2	0	3	0	0	0	.000
Valenzuela, Fernando, San Ant*	27	13	0	2	2	0	0	0	1	0	0	0	0	3	0	0	.154
Vessey, Thomas, Amarillo	51	140	22	35	56	3	0	6	20	3	2	26	1	36	1	1	.250
Wiggins, David, Shreveport*	125	407	42	110	148	17	6	3	42	1	3	75	1	47	3	5	.270
Wilson, James, Midland	2	1	0	0	0	0	0	0	0	0	0	0	0	0	0	0	.000
Winterfeldt, Todd, 14 Mid-60 Jck	74	243	30	69	98	10	2	5	31	3	3	28	3	42	5	1	.284
Wojcik, James, Shreveport*	78	295	39	95	116	15	3	0	21	1	1	40	1	33	3	3	.322
Wright, George, Tulsa	136	458	60	126	173	22	5	5	65	7	4	33	5	73	14	10	.275
Wright, J. Richard, San Ant*	28	14	5	3	4	1	0	0	3	0	0	1	0	1	0	0	.214
Zayas, Felipe, Arkansas	121	359	35	91	118	17	2	2	49	3	2	46	1	85	4	4	.253
Zouras, Michael, San Antonio	82	285	53	84	144	17	2	13	63	1	3	38	4	57	4	0	.295
Zunino, Gary, Arkansas	28	42	6	8	11	3	0	0	3	1	0	12	0	13	2	1	.190

The following pitchers had no plate appearances primarily through use of designated hitters, listed alphabetically by club, games in parentheses:

AMARILLO—Boone, Daniel* (46); Chiffer, Floyd (39); Church, Sydney* (5); Dixon, Troy (27); Fireovid, Stephen† (27); Hirschy, Francis (19); Jannusch, David (8); Miller, K. Randall (38); Pickert, Gary* (33); Ronnenbergh, J. Martin (15); Show, Eric (26); Thurmond, Mark* 26).

ARKANSAS—Fulgham, John (1); Williams, Ray (34).

EL PASO—Border, Robert (14); Brown, Steven (27); Chevolek, Thomas* (26); Conner, Jeffrey* (8); Crisler, Joel (22); Dugger, Lawrence (11); Duran, David (21); Miller, Mark* (9); Morrison, Perry (13); Phillips, Charles* (26); Rommel, Richard (42); Steirer, Ricky (29); Vallone, James† (4); Walters, Michael (29); Wardlow, Michael (11); Witt, Michael (12).

MIDLAND—Blyth, Robert (49); Churchill, Norman* (16); Earley, William (8); Gerlach, James (1); Hunziker, Kent (34); Mack, Henry (26); Moore, Edmund (16); Rogers, Charles* (4); Segelke, Herman (47); Semall, Paul (17); Spino, Thomas (16); Valentini, Vincent (18); Viskas, Steven (8); Wright, Michael (15).

SAN ANTONIO—Bain, Paul (3); Hayes, Brian* (1); Rau, Douglas* (4).

TULSA—Comer, Steven† (3); Davis, Ted (28); Farr, James (10); Gleaton, Jerry* (25); Hudson, Anthony (14); Jakubowski, Stanley (1); Lamson, Charles* (21); Nielsen, Steven (27); Roberts, Michael (28); Schmidt, David (12); Umbarger, James* (22); Vickers, Michael* (9); Whitehouse, Leonard((10).

GRAND SLAM HOME RUNS—Riggleman, 3; Beyers, Gardenhire, M. Howard, Winterfeldt((2 Jackson), 2 each; Calise, Cowger, Doss, Fletcher, Gonzalez, LaVigne, Marshall, Payne, Rothford, Sconiers, Tisdale, Zouras, 1 each.

AWARDED FIRST BASE ON INTERFERENCE—Bhagwat 6 (Gwosdz 2, Zunino, B. Johnson, Richards, Vessey); J. A. Hicks 3 (Harper, Cowger); Rothford 2 (Gwosdz, Jones); Tolleson 3 (Harper, Lane); Bjorkman (Lane); Carnes (Richards); M. Howard (Jones); Hunsaker (Jones); Owen (Jones); Tucker (Hough); Wojcik (Jones).

GAME-WINNING RBIs

AMARILLO (63)—George 11, Ashby 10, Gwosdz 8, Alvarez 7, Hicks 6, Reed 6, Greer 4, DeSimone 3, Flannery 2, Pastors 2, Vessey 2, Johnson 1, Lancellotti 1.

ARKANSAS (73)—Hunsaker 12, Riggleman 11, Tisdale 10, Dotson 8, Paris 8, Gutierrez 7, Zayas 7, Aranzamendi 2, Bjorkman 2, Garcia 2, McCauley 2, Calise 1, Dimmel 1.

EL PASO (43)—Brunansky 8, Adams 7, Bishop 7, Harper 6, Bhagwat 5, Humphry 4, Sconiers 3, Gilbert 1, Hamilton 1, Springman 1.

JACKSON (67)—Perry 13, Amerson 11, M. Howard 8, Giles 7, Gardenhire 5, Haslerig 5, Beltre 4, Cuervo 3, Hough 3, Johnson 2, Rogers 2, Winterfeldt 2, D. Howard 1, Korbe 1, Lowry 1.

MIDLAND (51)—Grant 7, Krug 6, Fletcher 5, Hicks 5, LaVigne 5, Mitchell 5, Alfaro 3, Stockstill 3, Hall 2, Martin 2, Winterfeldt 2, Enright 1, Fierro 1, O'Berry 1, Owen 1, Payne 1, Shepston 1.

SAN ANTONIO (64)—Marshall 11, Beyers 8, Holman 7, Zouras 7, Bradley 6, Taveras 6, Hernandez 4, Swoope 4, Fobbs 3, Shoemaker 3, Baez 2, Richards 2, Ollar 1.

SHREVEPORT (41)—Davis 8, Lane 5, Ransom 5, Wiggins 5, Gladden 4, Pechek 3, Anthony 2, Rothford 2, Runnels 2, Wojcik 2, Cardwell 1, Doss 1, Snell 1.

TULSA (60)—Capra 13, Klimas 11, Barrow 6, Johnson 6, Tolleson 4, Wright 4, Cowger 3, Gonzalez 3, Jirschele 3, Garcia 2, Reynolds 2, Donofrio 1, Gooch 1, McCrary 1.

CLUB FIELDING

Club	G.	PO.	A.	E.	DP.	PB.	Pct.
San Antonio	136	3459	1550	147	138	16	.971
Arkansas	136	3474	1466	176	135	14	.966
Amarillo	136	3461	1522	180	147	10	.965
Tulsa	136	3444	1546	184	131	20	.964
Midland	136	3500	1611	193	152	16	.964
Shreveport	136	3464	1602	193	146	25	.963
Jackson	136	3414	1572	196	127	15	.962
El Paso	136	3504	1540	210	119	39	.960

Triple Plays—Arkansas, Jackson, Midland.

INDIVIDUAL FIELDING

*Throws lefthanded.

FIRST BASEMEN

Player and Club	G.	PO.	A.	E.	DP.	Pct.
ROTHFORD, Shrvport.	126	1139	65	10	116	.992
Tisdale, Arkansas	125	1057	67	10	110	.991
Perry, Jackson	128	1134	95	13	102	.990
Ashby, Amarillo*	99	848	59	9	91	.990
Krug, Midland*	27	251	12	3	26	.989
J.A. Hicks, Midland	110	959	68	12	110	.988
Marshall, San Antonio	132	1157	64	16	120	.987
Klimas, Tulsa	62	484	35	7	49	.987
Sconiers, El Paso*	100	887	46	16	76	.983
Bishop, El Paso	34	305	17	7	20	.979
L. Gonzalez, Tulsa	74	632	46	15	54	.978
George, Amarillo	38	326	15	8	35	.977
Wiggins, Shreveport*	19	117	11	4	10	.970
Aranzamendi, Arkansas	12	43	1	2	5	.957

Triple Plays—Tisdale, Perry.

(Fewer Than Ten Games)

Player and Club	G.	PO.	A.	E.	DP.	Pct.
McCauley, Arkansas	9	64	4	0	3	1.000
Mike Howard, Jackson	6	48	0	0	4	1.000
Humphry, El Paso	2	21	2	0	3	1.000
Hough, Jackson	3	22	2	0	2	1.000
Bialas, Arkansas	1	7	0	0	0	1.000
Donofrio, Tulsa	1	6	0	0	1	1.000
Lewis, Tulsa	1	5	0	0	0	1.000
Randy Johnson, Jackson	1	5	0	0	1	1.000
Gutierrez, Arkansas	1	1	0	0	0	1.000
Stockstill, Midland	1	1	0	0	0	1.000
Jirschele, Tulsa	8	66	5	1	9	.986
Shoemaker, San Antonio	6	47	6	2	10	.964
Hunsaker, Arkansas	6	22	1	1	4	.958
Lancellotti, Amarillo*	1	10	2	1	2	.923
Barrow, Tulsa	2	6	1	1	0	.875

SECOND BASEMEN

Player and Club	G.	PO.	A.	E.	DP.	Pct.
Aranzamendi, Arkansas	40	89	106	0	29	1.000
Jirschele, Tulsa	20	33	39	0	7	1.000
Zouras, San Antonio	10	20	13	0	6	1.000
Carnes, El Paso	45	94	124	3	25	.986
FOBBS, San Antonio	105	209	292	11	76	.979
Tjader, Tulsa	12	25	22	1	4	.979
Capra, Tulsa	101	281	303	17	76	.972
Dunn, Shreveport	51	136	144	8	38	.972
Shoemaker, San Antonio	24	42	62	3	15	.972
Gooch, Tulsa	12	27	33	2	11	.968
Flannery, Amarillo	28	62	78	5	25	.966
Wojcik, Shreveport	50	139	121	10	35	.963
Fletcher, Midland	130	354	390	29	112	.962
Gutierrez, Arkansas	107	224	268	20	65	.961
Giles, Jackson	122	291	325	26	79	.960
DeSimone, Amarillo	75	158	206	18	57	.953
J. Johnson, Amarillo	41	75	95	9	27	.950
Lane, Shreveport	38	94	111	12	30	.945
Hamilton, El Paso	48	84	125	13	32	.941
Cuervo, Jackson	17	29	34	4	6	.940
Springman, El Paso	42	102	126	16	20	.934

Triple Plays—Fletcher, Giles.

(Fewer Than Ten Games)

Player and Club	G.	PO.	A.	E.	DP.	Pct.
Winterfeldt, Mid.-Jack.	3	10	12	0	3	1.000
Fierro, Midland	4	10	8	0	3	1.000
Pinkerton, Tulsa	2	2	7	0	1	1.000
Anthony, Shreveport	2	3	6	0	0	1.000
Payne, Midland	2	1	3	0	0	1.000
Randy Johnson, Jackson	1	1	2	0	0	1.000
M. Howard, Jackson	2	1	1	0	1	1.000
Tinkler, Arkansas	2	0	1	0	0	1.000
Wilson, Midland	1	1	0	0	0	1.000
Brewster, El Paso	8	27	22	1	5	.980
Baldwin, San Antonio	2	9	7	1	3	.941
Gardenhire, Jackson	1	1	5	1	0	.857
Kim, Shreveport	1	0	2	1	0	.667

THIRD BASEMEN

Player and Club	G.	PO.	A.	E.	DP.	Pct.
Randy Johnson, Jackson	10	4	20	0	2	1.000
Klimas, Tulsa	33	22	63	4	2	.955
Jirschele, Tulsa	51	32	106	8	9	.945
Carnes, El Paso	38	18	65	5	3	.943
Rogers, Jackson	56	36	109	9	9	.942
Zouras, San Antonio	69	45	158	13	8	.940
Aranzamendi, Arkansas	13	6	25	2	0	.939
Shoemaker, San Antonio	30	32	86	8	11	.937
MITCHELL, Midland	125	99	282	28	34	.932
Riggleman, Arkansas	109	98	243	26	27	.929
Lane, Shreveport	92	75	215	23	26	.927
Garcia, Tulsa	31	22	67	7	4	.927
Alvarez, Amarillo	127	113	260	30	28	.926
Anthony, Shreveport	14	10	26	3	4	.923
Winterfeldt, Mid.-Jac.	64	49	142	18	13	.914
Humphry, El Paso	95	69	188	27	13	.905
Calise, Arkansas	16	9	35	6	7	.880
Hernandez, San Antonio	33	23	77	14	5	.877
Doss, Shreveport	30	25	66	13	9	.875
Lewis, Tulsa	22	16	38	8	2	.871
Cuervo, Jackson	13	9	20	11	3	.725

Triple Plays—Calise, Rogers.

(Fewer Than Ten Games)

Player and Club	G.	PO.	A.	E.	DP.	Pct.
Brewster, El Paso	3	3	6	0	2	1.000
Schultz, San Antonio	4	1	6	0	1	1.000
Pinkerton, Tulsa	2	1	4	0	0	1.000
Brenly, Shreveport	2	1	2	0	1	1.000
Tinkler, Arkansas	2	1	1	0	0	1.000
Fierro, Midland	6	4	18	1	1	.957
Hamilton, El Paso	5	6	10	1	2	.941
Gooch, Tulsa	7	6	22	2	1	.933
J. Johnson, Amarillo	3	3	11	1	0	.933
McCauley, Arkansas	9	3	13	2	1	.889
Szymarek, Shreveport	2	1	6	1	0	.875
Payne, Midland	4	2	4	1	0	.857
Flannery, Amarillo	2	1	4	1	0	.833
Adams, El Paso	1	3	2	1	0	.833
L. Gonzalez, Tulsa	1	2	2	1	0	.800
M. Howard, Jackson	1	0	4	1	0	.800
Tjader, Tulsa	2	0	7	2	0	.778
Baldwin, San Antonio	3	4	1	2	0	.714
Keedy, El Paso	1	1	1	1	0	.667

SHORTSTOPS

Player and Club	G.	PO.	A.	E.	DP.	Pct.
Fobbs, San Antonio	23	32	62	3	15	.969
TAVERAS, San Antonio	115	202	368	26	80	.956
Adams, El Paso	91	180	286	23	47	.953
Runnells, Shreveport	117	240	188	18	45	.952
Pastors, Amarillo	56	84	189	14	41	.951
Alfaro, Midland	53	76	198	14	36	.951
Dunn, Shreveport	13	13	45	3	5	.951
Tolleson, Shreveport	130	161	395	31	62	.947
Gardenhire, Jackson	126	167	406	40	69	.935
Paris, Arkansas	116	181	349	38	68	.933
Cardwell, Shreveport	52	69	156	17	33	.930
Fierro, Midland	15	22	57	6	8	.929
Flannery, Amarillo	79	116	270	34	52	.919
Jirschele, Tulsa	12	18	27	4	7	.918
Aranzamendi, Arkansas	24	15	48	6	4	.913
Owen, Midland	69	96	213	32	49	.906
Keedy, El Paso	25	28	86	13	17	.898
Carnes, El Paso	22	27	62	11	14	.890

(Fewer Than Ten Games)

Player and Club	G.	PO.	A.	E.	DP.	Pct.
Tinkler, Arkansas	8	6	11	0	1	1.000
Zayas, Arkansas	1	0	1	0	0	1.000
M. Howard, Jackson	8	15	23	2	2	.950
DeSimone, Amarillo	7	5	15	2	4	.909
Tisdale, Arkansas	1	3	3	1	2	.857
Gladden, Shreveport	2	0	5	1	0	.833
Giles, Jackson	3	2	7	2	2	.818
Capra, Tulsa	1	2	0	1	0	.667

CATCHERS

Player and Club	G.	PO.	A.	E.	DP.	PB.	Pct.
Neufang, Tulsa	11	64	10	0	2	2	1.000
Crow, San Antonio	17	101	20	0	2	0	1.000
Brenly, Shreveport	1	9	1	0	0	0	1.000
Strawn, Tulsa	1	1	1	0	0	0	1.000
Adams, Shreveport	1	1	0	0	0	0	1.000
Shepston, Midland	67	329	38	2	3	8	.995
Baez, San Antonio	49	261	25	2	3	5	.993
HUNSAKER, Ark	90	493	57	8	7	3	.986

CATCHERS—Continued

Player and Club	G.	PO.	A.	E.	DP.	PB.	Pct.
Vessey, Amarillo	51	265	24	4	1	4	.986
Hough, Jackson	79	512	65	10	9	8	.983
Jones, El Paso	89	536	99	12	8	28	.981
Richards, San Ant	85	506	70	11	5	11	.981
Gwosdz, Amarillo	95	597	66	14	12	6	.979
Donofrio, Tulsa	12	45	2	1	0	3	.979
Lane, Jackson	59	330	42	9	3	7	.976
Ransom, Shreveport	113	618	90	18	13	19	.975
Johnson, Tulsa	92	520	70	16	10	13	.974
Enright, Midland	22	102	12	3	3	2	.974
O'Berry, Midland	55	337	39	11	6	6	.972
Harper, El Paso	36	214	30	7	2	9	.972
Bjorkman, Arkansas	50	278	30	10	6	6	.969
Bauman, Shreveport	17	75	17	3	0	6	.968
Bishop, El Paso	12	66	12	3	3	2	.963
Cowger, Tulsa	29	135	22	7	2	2	.957
Zunino, Arkansas	23	46	5	3	1	5	.944
Davis, Shreveport	6	32	8	3	2	0	.930
Duff, Jackson	6	25	1	2	1	0	.929

OUTFIELDERS

Player and Club	G.	PO.	A.	E.	DP.	Pct.
Stockstill, Midland	47	87	7	0	2	1.000
Cowger, Tulsa	27	25	1	0	0	1.000
Riggleman, Arkansas	15	25	0	0	0	1.000
Lancellotti, Amarillo*	15	24	0	0	0	1.000
Klimas, Tulsa	13	20	1	0	0	1.000
Bjorkman, Arkansas	13	20	0	0	0	1.000
GRANT, Midland	134	239	13	3	2	.988
Penniall, Arkansas	36	62	1	1	0	.984
Zayas, Arkansas	97	155	15	3	4	.983
Beyers, San Antonio	133	275	12	6	2	.980
Dotson, Arkansas	96	138	10	3	1	.980
Johnson, Amarillo	33	48	1	1	1	.980
Bhagwat, El Paso	106	183	10	4	2	.980
Gladden, Shreveport	70	169	9	4	4	.978
Wojcik, Shreveport	24	39	4	1	0	.977
Martin, Midland*	62	145	12	4	1	.975
Beltre, Jackson	40	65	4	2	1	.972
Dimmel, Arkansas	90	198	7	6	3	.972
Holman, San Antonio	134	193	8	6	1	.971
Wiggins, Shreveport*	101	158	10	5	0	.971
McCrary, Tulsa*	50	58	8	2	2	.971
Korbe, Jackson	24	29	5	1	0	.971
Bradley, San Antonio	134	241	17	8	1	.970
Wright, Tulsa	136	319	22	11	4	.969
Greer, Amarillo	101	213	9	7	2	.969
Tipa, El Paso	29	59	3	2	1	.969
M. Howard, Jackson	120	196	19	7	2	.968
Amerson, Jackson	98	162	19	6	4	.968
Hicks, Amarillo	126	223	16	8	4	.968
Reed, Amarillo	121	166	11	6	2	.967
Garcia, Arkansas	56	113	6	4	2	.967
Cuervo, Jackson	68	94	13	4	2	.964
Brunansky, El Paso	127	306	17	14	4	.958
Barrow, Tulsa	101	194	12	9	3	.958
Pechek, Shreveport*	57	111	0	5	0	.957
Hall, Midland*	35	58	3	3	0	.953
LaVigne, Midland	132	216	29	12	1	.953
Anthony, Shreveport	52	69	10	4	2	.952
Haslerig, Jackson	39	71	7	4	1	.951
Davis, Shreveport	93	152	12	9	2	.948
Carpenter, Tulsa	13	16	2	1	0	.947
Sconiers, El Paso*	33	62	4	4	0	.943
Gilbert, El Paso	30	54	7	4	1	.938
Tjader, Tulsa	32	39	4	3	0	.935
Szymarek, Shreveport	18	28	1	2	0	.935
Reynolds, Tulsa	44	75	7	6	2	.932
Bishop, El Paso	72	97	8	9	2	.921
D. Howard, Jackson	16	19	0	2	0	.905
Swoope, San Antonio	12	6	1	1	0	.875

(Fewer Than Ten Games)

Player and Club	G.	PO.	A.	E.	DP.	Pct.
Ashby, Amarillo*	9	19	1	0	1	1.000
George, Amarillo	9	19	0	0	0	1.000
Johnson, Jackson	8	10	0	0	0	1.000
Hough, Jackson	7	10	0	0	0	1.000
Brewster, Shreve	5	10	0	0	0	1.000
Gutierrez, Arkansas	5	9	0	0	0	1.000
McIntyre, Arkansas	8	8	0	0	0	1.000
Gooch, Tulsa	6	6	1	0	0	1.000
Del Monte, Arkansas	3	5	0	0	0	1.000
Payne, Midland	3	5	0	0	0	1.000
Richmond, Amarillo	5	4	0	0	0	1.000
Budner, Shreveport*	3	4	0	0	0	1.000
Zunino, Arkansas	3	3	0	0	0	1.000
Adams, Shreveport	4	2	1	0	0	1.000
R. Miller, Jackson	2	2	0	0	0	1.000
Aranzamendi, Arkansas	1	1	0	0	0	1.000
DeSimone, Amarillo	1	1	0	0	0	1.000
Fierro, Midland	1	1	0	0	0	1.000
Tisdale, Arkansas	9	10	3	1	0	.929
Bialas, Arkansas	5	12	1	1	1	.929
Humphry, El Paso	8	10	1	1	0	.917
Krug, Midland*	7	9	0	1	0	.900
Capra, Tulsa	7	5	0	1	0	.833
Donofrio, Tulsa	1	0	0	1	0	.000

PITCHERS

Player and Club	G.	PO.	A.	E.	DP.	Pct.
DIXON, Amarillo	27	18	24	0	2	1.000
S. Brown, El Paso	27	12	29	0	2	1.000
Boone, Amarillo*	46	7	21	0	0	1.000
Thurmond, Amarillo*	26	7	21	0	2	1.000
Anderson, Jackson	25	5	20	0	1	1.000
Hargesheimer, Shreve	12	6	21	0	1	1.000
R. Miller, Amarillo	38	4	16	0	2	1.000
Roberts, Tulsa	28	14	20	0	0	1.000
Ronnenbergh, Amarillo	15	3	17	0	1	1.000
Lazorko, Tulsa	55	8	19	0	4	1.000
Stember, Shreveport	16	4	19	0	1	1.000
Spino, Midland*	16	4	14	0	1	1.000
Lamson, Tulsa*	21	4	18	0	0	1.000
Jorn, Arkansas	20	5	13	0	1	1.000
Tucker, Shreveport	19	1	17	0	0	1.000
McDonald, San Antonio	33	2	16	0	2	1.000
Chevolek, El Paso	26	3	9	0	0	1.000
Glinatsis, Shreveport	35	8	11	0	1	1.000
Nobles, San Antonio*	37	1	10	0	1	1.000
Hinrichs, Shreveport	23	3	7	0	0	1.000
Witt, El Paso	12	2	8	0	2	1.000
Duran, El Paso	21	2	7	0	0	1.000
Troedson, Jackson	15	3	6	0	0	1.000
Chiffer, Amarillo	39	2	5	0	1	1.000
Wright, Midland	15	0	5	0	0	1.000
Dugger, El Paso	11	1	4	0	0	1.000
Whitehouse, Tulsa*	10	2	5	0	0	1.000
Morrison, El Paso	13	1	2	0	0	1.000
Phillips, El Paso	26	1	1	0	0	1.000
Holton, San Antonio	27	12	27	1	0	.975
Valenzuela, S. Ant*	27	6	33	1	1	.975
Steirer, El Paso	29	7	25	1	2	.970
Smith, Jack-ElP	30	9	22	1	2	.969
Perlman, Midland	30	23	36	2	3	.967
Budner, Shreveport*	29	5	24	1	3	.967
Thurberg, Jackson	31	7	20	1	0	.964

PITCHERS—Continued

Player and Club	G.	PO.	A.	E.	DP.	Pct.	Player and Club	G.	PO.	A.	E.	DP.	Pct.
Wright, San Antonio*	23	10	42	2	1	.963	Show, Amarillo	26	12	25	4	0	.902
Rincon, Arkansas	26	15	31	2	2	.958	Nielsen, Tulsa	27	8	10	2	0	.900
Walters, Jackson	29	2	20	1	1	.957	Border, El Paso	14	1	8	1	1	.900
Crutcher, Tulsa	40	6	16	1	1	.957	Mack, Midland	26	2	15	2	0	.895
DeLeon, Arkansas	76	6	14	1	0	.952	Edelen, Arkansas	26	16	26	5	1	.894
Pickert, Amarillo	33	4	16	1	1	.952	Gaff, Jackson	25	11	31	5	1	.894
Hirschy, Amarillo	19	7	12	1	1	.950	Randy Clark, Midland	27	8	25	4	1	.892
Crisler, El Paso	22	13	25	2	2	.950	Gleaton, Tulsa*	25	7	26	4	4	.892
Fireovid, Amarillo	27	13	24	2	4	.949	Prewitt, Shreveport	16	4	4	1	1	.889
Heredia, San Antonio	15	6	12	1	0	.947	Thomas, Arkansas	14	3	5	1	1	.889
Rommel, El Paso	41	4	12	1	0	.941	Rusty Clark, Jackson	42	0	15	2	2	.882
Leary, Jackson	26	12	35	3	4	.940	Thorp, San Antonio	28	5	10	2	0	.882
Blyth, Midland	49	3	12	1	0	.938	Davis, Tulsa	28	5	9	2	0	.875
Kurosaki, Arkansas	37	2	13	1	1	.938	Orosco, Jackson*	37	2	12	2	1	.875
Heimueller, Shreveport*	32	4	40	3	3	.936	Calvert, Shreveport	14	6	15	3	0	.875
Snell, Shreveport	33	3	11	1	1	.933	Segelke, Midland	47	9	24	5	3	.868
Stadler, Shreveport	14	4	10	1	0	.933	Herschiser, San Antonio	49	4	15	3	2	.864
Shirley, San Antonio*	18	6	20	2	3	.929	Fisher, Shreveport	20	5	17	4	1	.846
T. Miller, Jackson*	16	2	11	1	1	.929	Williams, Arkansas	34	6	9	3	1	.833
Churchill, Midland*	16	6	6	1	0	.923	Stuper, Arkansas	25	2	7	2	1	.818
Schmidt, Tulsa	12	2	10	1	0	.923	Hunziker, Midland	34	3	9	3	1	.800
Farr, Tulsa	10	3	9	1	1	.923	Umbarger, Tulsa*	22	1	3	1	0	.800
Lowry, Jackson	15	6	16	2	2	.917	Cacciatore, Jackson	14	5	5	3	0	.769
Johnson, Arkansas*	28	10	11	2	3	.913	Searage, Jackson*	14	5	5	3	0	.769
Semall, Midland	17	8	12	2	0	.909	Wardlow, El Paso	11	1	12	4	0	.765
Valentini, Midland	18	4	6	1	1	.909	Murphy, Arkansas*	29	1	8	3	0	.750
Hudson, Tulsa	14	8	11	2	1	.905	Moore, Midland	16	3	2	2	0	.714

Triple Play–Viskas.

(Fewer Than Ten Games)

Player and Club	G.	PO.	A.	E.	DP.	Pct.	Player and Club	G.	PO.	A.	E.	DP.	Pct.
Brown, Jackson	9	6	8	0	0	1.000	Chamberlain, Arkansas .	3	0	2	0	0	1.000
Jannusch, Amarillo	8	1	8	0	0	1.000	Fierro, Midland	1	0	2	0	0	1.000
Vickers, Tulsa*	9	3	4	0	0	1.000	Church, Amarillo*	5	1	0	0	0	1.000
Dunn, Shreveport	6	2	5	0	0	1.000	Shoemaker, San Antonio	4	0	1	0	0	1.000
Cowger, Tulsa	3	1	4	0	0	1.000	Alexander, Shreveport* .	9	3	14	1	0	.944
M. Miller, El Paso*	9	0	4	0	0	1.000	Viskas, Midland	8	4	8	1	0	.923
Nipp, San Antonio	6	1	3	0	1	1.000	Olmsted, Arkansas*	8	1	11	1	0	.923
Vallone, El Paso*	4	1	3	0	0	1.000	Leach, Jackson	8	9	12	2	1	.913
Little, Arkansas	9	1	2	0	0	1.000	Conner, El Paso*	8	0	6	1	0	.857
Moyer, Shreveport	4	0	3	0	0	1.000	Earley, Midland*	8	3	5	2	2	.800
Rau, San Antonio*	4	0	3	0	0	1.000	Martin, Arkansas*	5	1	2	1	0	.750
Pastors, Amarillo	1	2	1	0	0	1.000	Bain, San Antonio	3	0	3	2	0	.600
Rogers, Midland	4	0	2	0	0	1.000							

The following players do not have any recorded accepted chances at the positions indicated; therefore, are not listed in the fielding averages for those particular positions: Alvarez, p; Anthony, p; Barrow, p; Flannery, of; Fletcher, ss; Fulgham, p; Gerlach, p; Hamilton, of; Hayes, of; J. A. Hicks, c; Holman, 2b; McCauley, 2b-of; Ollar, of; Ownbey, p; Shepston, of; Tinkler, of; Tisdale, p; Zayas, 3b; Buckner* appeared as designated hitter/pinch-hitter only.

CLUB PITCHING

Club	G.	CG.	ShO.	Sv.	IP.	H.	R.	ER.	HR.	BB.	Int. BB.	HB.	SO.	WP.	Bk.	ERA.
Jackson	136	36	24	24	1138	1075	545	427	64	524	42	35	797	66	13	3.38
Arkansas	136	24	9	27	1158	1092	528	436	56	478	42	29	755	52	13	3.39
Shreveport	136	33	10	17	1155	1128	587	457	98	530	34	36	681	63	6	3.56
San Antonio	136	45	8	27	1153	1147	586	503	78	546	29	25	838	84	17	3.93
Tulsa	136	24	9	30	1148	1282	655	543	91	491	44	35	716	63	17	4.26
Amarillo	136	24	3	45	1154	1226	692	593	81	491	16	43	814	69	9	4.62
Midland	136	28	4	27	1167	1400	824	679	123	642	38	38	708	88	8	5.24
El Paso	136	31	2	14	1168	1424	910	721	109	643	17	34	764	89	12	5.56

PITCHERS' RECORDS
(Leading Qualifiers for Earned-Run Average Leadership—109 or More Innings)
*Throws lefthanded.

Pitcher–Club	G.	GS.	CG.	ShO.	W.	L.	Sv.	Pct.	IP.	H.	R.	ER.	HR.	BB.	Int. BB.	HB.	SO.	WP.	ERA.
Edelen, Arkansas	26	24	6	1	13	5	1	.722	161	150	64	47	6	53	5	0	100	5	2.63
Leary, Jackson	26	26	11	6	13	7	0	.650	173	150	67	53	5	62	4	8	138	10	2.76
Valenzuela, San Antonio*	27	25	11	4	13	9	0	.591	174	156	70	60	4	70	5	2	162	9	3.10
Rincon, Arkansas	26	26	8	1	10	7	0	.588	172	165	80	65	12	51	3	7	138	8	3.40
Heimueller, Shreveport*	32	11	3	2	7	8	2	.467	127	122	67	48	15	62	5	1	90	8	3.40
Holton, San Antonio	27	27	16	2	15	10	0	.600	207	204	93	79	16	65	2	2	139	11	3.43
Herschiser, San Antonio	49	3	1	0	5	9	14	.357	109	120	59	43	7	59	5	2	75	13	3.55
Gleaton, Tulsa*	25	25	6	1	13	7	0	.650	178	179	83	72	17	68	3	5	138	10	3.64

PITCHING LEADERS—Continued

Pitcher–Club	G	GS	CG	ShO	W	L	Sv	Pct.	IP	H	R	ER	HR	BB	Int. BB	HB	SO	WP	ERA
Brown, El Paso	27	27	16	0	14	12	0	.538	209	215	103	85	12	81	2	3	103	3	3.66
Show, Amarillo	26	26	6	0	12	6	0	.667	166	141	81	69	8	81	0	10	144	8	3.74

Departmental Leaders: G—DeLeon, 76; GS—Perlman, 30; CG—S. Brown, Holton, 16; ShO—Leary, 6; W—Holton, Leary, 15; L—S. Brown, Glinatsis, 12; Sv—Boone, 26; Pct.—Davis, .769; IP—S. Brown, 209; H—Perlman, 230; R—Mack, 125; ER—Dixon, 101; HR—Dixon, Gleaton, Mack, Valentini, 17; BB—Mack, 142; IBB—Lazorko, 12; HB—Show, 10; SO—Valenzuela, 162; WP—R. Wright, 17.

(All Pitchers—Listed Alphabetically)

Pitcher–Club	G	GS	CG	ShO	W	L	Sv	Pct.	IP	H	R	ER	HR	BB	Int. BB	HB	SO	WP	ERA
Alexander, Shreveport*	9	9	1	0	2	5	0	.286	55	59	33	21	5	27	2	1	27	2	3.44
Alvarez, Amarillo	1	0	0	0	0	0	0	.000	1	0	0	0	0	0	0	0	0	0	0.00
Anderson, Jackson	25	1	0	0	3	2	4	.600	64	57	24	23	7	17	4	1	48	1	3.23
Anthony, Shreveport	1	0	0	0	0	0	0	0.00	2	3	2	2	0	2	0	0	0	1	9.00
Bain, San Antonio	3	3	0	0	1	0	0	.000	14	23	13	13	1	13	0	1	9	5	8.36
Barrow, Tulsa	1	0	0	0	0	0	0	.000	2	6	3	3	0	0	0	0	1	0	13.50
Blyth, Midland	49	0	0	0	10	7	10	.588	81	87	41	37	10	40	11	2	53	6	4.11
Boone, Amarillo*	46	0	0	0	5	4	26	.556	73	68	27	24	3	16	2	3	62	1	2.96
Border, El Paso	14	12	0	0	2	8	0	.200	70	86	72	58	6	45	0	4	38	11	7.46
Brown, Jackson	9	8	1	1	1	5	0	.167	45	51	23	21	2	27	2	0	15	2	4.20
Brown, El Paso	27	27	16	0	14	12	0	.538	209	215	103	85	12	81	2	3	103	3	3.66
Budner, Shreveport*	29	11	3	0	4	11	1	.267	107	116	68	54	10	52	5	3	78	7	4.54
Cacciatore, Jackson	14	14	1	1	2	5	0	.286	73	89	56	41	4	41	3	4	35	7	5.05
Calvert, Shreveport	14	14	3	1	6	7	0	.462	88	79	38	29	7	40	3	3	56	6	2.97
Chamberlain, Arkansas	3	3	2	0	3	0	0	1.000	21	17	7	5	0	7	1	1	14	0	2.14
Chevolek, El Paso*	25	0	0	0	3	6	1	.333	48	66	47	43	10	41	1	1	22	2	8.06
Chiffer, Amarillo	39	0	0	0	4	5	9	.444	62	41	17	15	2	28	2	4	61	1	2.18
Church, Amarillo*	5	0	0	0	0	0	0	.000	5	5	5	5	1	3	0	0	4	1	9.00
Churchill, Midland*	16	6	0	0	3	2	1	.600	65	74	29	28	2	33	3	2	50	3	3.88
Clark, Midland	27	17	5	0	8	6	0	.571	103	150	97	83	12	69	4	2	31	12	7.25
Clark, Jackson	42	0	0	0	6	6	15	.500	64	65	30	24	6	28	5	0	51	4	3.38
Comer, Tulsa	3	3	0	0	1	2	0	.333	14	22	10	10	1	2	1	1	8	1	6.43
Conner, El Paso*	8	4	0	0	3	0	0	.000	30	46	45	32	4	26	1	1	18	1	9.60
Chisler, El Paso	22	20	3	0	4	9	0	.308	118	140	95	65	7	80	0	2	79	16	4.96
Crutcher, Tulsa	40	8	1	0	3	8	6	.273	108	115	65	53	5	60	4	3	76	8	4.42
Davis, Tulsa	28	0	3	0	10	3	2	.769	102	120	42	42	6	30	0	3	63	6	3.71
DeLeon, Arkansas	76	0	0	0	7	6	17	.538	107	85	46	39	4	49	10	5	92	2	3.28
Dixon, Amarillo	27	27	6	0	11	11	0	.500	160	189	113	101	17	73	0	7	72	7	5.68
Dugger, El Paso	11	10	2	0	0	9	0	.000	43	64	50	44	8	32	0	1	37	4	9.21
Dunn, Shreveport	6	0	0	0	2	2	0	.500	25	30	13	12	1	16	0	0	22	1	4.32
Duran, El Paso	21	0	0	0	1	1	1	.500	39	44	27	19	2	17	2	0	26	4	4.38
Earley, Midland*	8	1	0	0	0	2	0	.000	21	27	18	11	2	10	2	0	20	0	4.71
Edelen, Arkansas	26	24	6	1	13	5	1	.722	161	150	64	47	6	53	5	0	100	5	2.63
Farr, Tulsa	10	10	3	2	4	3	0	.571	66	56	30	15	4	22	4	0	29	3	2.05
Fierro, Midland	1	0	0	0	0	0	0	.000	2	1	1	1	0	2	0	0	0	0	4.50
Fireovid, Amarillo	27	27	4	0	12	6	0	.667	164	196	100	86	10	52	0	3	106	11	4.72
Fisher, Shreveport	20	20	6	1	6	9	0	.400	106	90	49	38	9	55	4	4	65	2	3.23
Fulgham, Arkansas	1	1	0	0	0	0	0	.000	5	1	0	0	0	1	0	0	5	1	0.00
Gaff, Jackson	25	25	6	1	8	10	0	.444	158	184	95	76	14	55	3	0	83	6	4.33
Gerlach, Midland	1	0	0	0	0	0	0	.000	2	1	0	0	0	0	0	0	3	0	0.00
Gleaton, Tulsa*	25	25	6	1	13	7	0	.650	178	179	83	72	17	68	3	5	138	10	3.64
Glinatsis, Shreveport	35	12	4	0	4	12	1	.250	126	125	72	65	12	68	3	8	61	7	4.64
Hargesheimer, Shreve.	12	12	3	1	2	6	0	.250	81	67	28	16	4	30	1	0	40	3	1.78
Hayes, San Antonio*	1	0	0	0	0	0	0	.000	2	1	0	0	0	1	0	0	1	0	0.00
Heimueller, Shreveport*	32	11	3	2	7	8	2	.467	127	122	67	48	15	62	5	1	90	8	3.40
Heredia, San Antonio	15	15	6	0	9	3	0	.750	97	93	41	31	5	31	0	0	63	5	2.88
Herschiser, San Antonio	49	3	1	0	5	9	14	.357	109	120	59	43	7	59	5	2	75	13	3.55
Hinrichs, Shreveport	23	0	0	0	1	4	7	.200	50	46	25	22	5	18	1	0	35	2	3.96
Hirschy, Amarillo	19	11	1	0	5	5	0	.500	77	100	57	46	7	19	0	5	32	3	5.38
Holton, San Antonio	27	27	16	2	15	10	0	.600	207	204	93	79	16	65	2	2	139	11	3.43
Hudson, Tulsa	14	13	0	0	5	4	0	.556	73	90	47	38	7	23	0	4	29	1	4.68
Hunziker, Midland	34	0	0	0	1	3	5	.250	82	103	71	55	13	39	4	4	57	4	6.04
Jakubowski, Tulsa	1	0	0	0	0	0	0	.000	5	9	5	5	1	0	0	0	7	1	9.00
Jannusch, Midland	8	7	0	0	1	3	0	.250	33	50	37	31	2	27	0	0	19	3	8.45
Johnson, Arkansas*	28	21	3	0	8	8	1	.500	125	137	74	60	12	58	2	1	61	3	4.32
Jorn, Arkansas	20	11	1	0	6	4	2	.600	84	81	47	43	7	25	2	2	49	6	4.61
Kurosaki, Arkansas	37	3	0	0	6	5	3	.545	92	85	34	29	4	21	5	2	64	0	2.84
Lamson, Tulsa*	21	20	4	1	6	8	0	.429	108	134	68	58	10	51	2	4	54	6	4.83
Lazorko, Tulsa	55	0	0	0	6	5	12	.545	82	78	50	34	7	53	12	5	47	2	3.73
Leach, Jackson	8	7	3	2	5	1	0	.833	54	50	16	9	1	15	3	0	30	0	1.50
Leary, Jackson	26	26	11	6	15	8	0	.652	173	150	67	53	5	62	4	8	138	10	2.76
Little, Arkansas*	9	0	0	0	3	3	0	.750	11	13	7	6	0	7	2	0	9	0	4.91
Lowry, Jackson	15	14	5	4	7	3	0	.700	88	83	36	32	6	42	3	1	50	7	3.27

Pitcher—Club	G	GS	CG	ShO	W	L	Sv	Pct.	IP	H	R	ER	HR	BB	Int. BB	HB	SO	WP	ERA
Mack, Midland	26	24	3	0	5	11	0	.313	142	176	125	99	17	142	2	7	115	13	6.27
Martin, Arkansas*	5	5	0	0	1	1	0	.500	27	23	7	5	1	7	2	1	19	1	1.67
McDonald, San Antonio	33	4	0	0	6	2	6	.750	77	75	36	31	8	40	2	2	60	4	3.62
Miller, El Paso*	9	1	0	0	0	0	0	.000	16	39	29	25	3	12	2	0	4	3	14.06
Miller, Amarillo	38	0	0	0	6	3	7	.667	82	79	49	45	9	43	6	2	58	7	4.94
T. Miller, Jackson*	16	8	2	1	1	6	0	.143	61	58	32	19	1	29	4	3	23	3	2.80
Moore, Midland	16	0	0	0	0	1	0	.000	24	25	12	9	3	12	2	2	16	1	3.38
Morrison, El Paso	13	0	0	0	0	1	2	.000	26	40	28	24	3	29	2	0	25	2	8.31
Moyer, Shreveport	4	4	0	0	0	1	0	.000	16	30	16	15	5	11	1	1	5	0	8.44
Murphy, Arkansas*	29	20	1	1	6	7	1	.462	106	96	56	48	2	75	2	1	58	4	4.08
Nipp, San Antonio	6	6	2	1	2	2	0	.500	42	48	21	19	5	16	0	2	25	2	4.07
Nielsen, Tulsa	27	9	2	1	9	5	0	.643	99	109	65	57	7	55	8	3	43	4	5.18
Nobles, San Antonio*	37	1	0	0	2	3	4	.400	75	62	52	48	9	64	5	4	77	6	5.76
Olmsted, Arkansas*	8	8	1	0	3	4	0	.429	55	51	23	20	3	17	1	0	41	5	3.27
Orosco, Jackson*	37	1	0	0	4	4	3	.500	71	52	36	29	3	62	4	2	85	3	3.68
Ownbey, Jackson	2	2	0	0	1	0	0	1.000	13	7	3	2	2	7	0	0	12	0	1.38
Perlman, Midland	30	30	9	2	13	7	0	.650	200	230	115	95	13	76	4	3	78	11	4.28
Phillips, El Paso*	26	0	0	0	2	1	4	.667	36	43	25	21	4	21	1	0	36	6	5.25
Pickert, Amarillo*	33	3	0	0	8	1	2	.889	98	98	69	57	11	59	2	4	89	10	5.23
Prewitt, Shreveport	16	4	0	0	0	3	0	.000	48	55	37	30	2	25	0	2	28	5	5.63
Rau, San Antonio*	4	4	0	0	0	1	0	.000	15	19	11	9	5	2	0	0	7	1	5.40
Rincon, Arkansas	26	26	8	1	10	7	0	.588	172	165	80	65	12	51	3	7	138	8	3.40
Roberts, Tulsa	28	15	5	0	7	5	1	.583	131	155	72	59	16	46	5	4	85	9	4.05
Rogers, Midland	4	1	1	0	1	0	0	1.000	8	10	6	5	0	1	0	3	0	0	5.63
Rommel, Midland	41	1	0	0	4	4	2	.500	90	93	53	40	4	51	3	2	60	4	4.00
Ronnenbergh, Amarillo	15	10	0	0	3	6	0	.333	76	95	57	47	2	29	1	3	42	9	5.57
Schmidt, Tulsa	12	12	1	0	4	6	0	.400	73	90	42	36	5	28	3	0	46	7	4.44
Searage, Jackson*	14	10	2	1	4	5	0	.444	70	54	32	26	5	26	3	4	71	4	3.34
Segelke, Midland	47	12	2	0	7	10	11	.412	129	155	92	68	11	63	3	5	88	12	4.74
Semall, Midland	17	15	5	1	9	5	0	.643	103	106	55	49	12	33	2	1	64	6	4.28
Shirley, San Antonio*	18	11	2	1	6	5	2	.545	84	85	36	35	5	40	3	4	51	2	3.75
Shoemaker, San Antonio	4	0	0	0	0	0	0	.000	4	7	7	7	2	0	0	0	2	2	15.75
Show, Amarillo	26	26	6	0	12	6	0	.667	166	141	81	69	8	81	0	10	144	8	3.74
Smith, Jackson-ElP.	30	15	5	1	8	9	0	.471	134	146	82	71	9	72	4	6	82	13	4.77
Snell, Shreveport	33	2	0	0	4	3	3	.500	77	77	38	32	6	18	4	3	44	5	4.50
Spino, Midland*	16	11	1	0	1	6	0	.143	59	77	52	43	6	40	1	4	34	5	6.56
Stadler, Shreveport	14	12	3	0	2	7	0	.222	85	88	45	27	7	43	1	4	41	6	2.86
Steirer, El Paso	29	23	2	0	5	11	1	.313	148	208	121	98	12	58	0	7	87	8	5.96
Stember, Shreveport	16	16	4	4	5	5	0	.500	102	78	39	30	6	47	1	4	61	5	2.65
Stuper, Arkansas	25	8	2	2	7	2	0	.778	88	77	28	24	0	40	1	2	57	2	2.45
Thomas, Arkansas	14	6	0	0	3	4	0	.429	50	55	27	26	3	29	1	0	25	5	4.68
Thorp, San Antonio	26	14	2	0	8	7	1	.533	102	110	62	57	6	58	1	2	40	7	5.03
Thurberg, Jackson	31	9	2	2	7	2	2	.778	92	64	39	28	4	59	0	7	84	11	2.74
Thurmond, Amarillo*	26	25	7	1	10	9	1	.526	156	164	80	67	9	61	3	2	125	8	3.87
Tisdale, Arkansas	2	0	0	0	0	0	0	.000	3	4	1	0	0	2	0	0	2	1	0.00
Troedson, Jackson	15	1	0	0	4	1	0	.800	34	34	12	7	0	12	1	0	21	3	1.85
Tucker, Shreveport	19	5	3	0	4	3	0	.571	73	63	17	16	4	16	3	2	28	3	1.97
Umbarger, Tulsa*	22	1	0	0	3	1	0	.750	32	25	19	9	2	12	1	0	33	0	2.53
Valentini, Midland	18	9	0	0	1	6	0	.143	62	89	57	47	17	32	0	3	30	5	6.82
Valenzuela, San Antonio*	27	25	11	4	13	9	0	.591	174	156	70	60	4	70	5	2	162	9	3.10
Vallone, El Paso*	2	0	0	0	0	0	0	.000	12	16	11	4	1	8	1	0	7	0	3.00
Vickers, Tulsa*	9	5	0	0	1	2	0	.333	26	42	28	27	0	19	0	1	19	5	9.35
Viskas, Midland	8	8	2	0	4	2	0	.667	55	58	30	27	4	15	0	2	36	1	4.42
Walters, El Paso	29	7	1	1	5	5	3	.500	96	116	59	46	12	33	1	6	46	4	4.31
Wardlow, El Paso	11	11	3	0	3	6	0	.333	62	64	55	38	5	50	0	2	57	9	5.52
Whitehouse, Tulsa*	10	7	1	0	3	2	0	.600	48	52	36	29	3	22	1	2	38	0	5.44
Williams, Arkansas	34	0	0	0	5	1	0	.833	51	52	27	20	2	36	5	7	21	5	3.53
Witt, El Paso	12	12	2	0	5	5	0	.500	70	72	53	45	11	39	0	4	64	5	5.79
Wright, Midland	15	2	0	0	1	4	0	.200	28	31	23	22	1	35	0	1	30	9	7.07
Wright, San Antonio*	23	23	5	8	8	10	0	.444	152	144	85	71	7	85	6	4	127	17	4.20

BALKS—Crutcher, Gaff, R. Wright, 4 each; Heredia, Holton, Murphy, Orosco, Rincon, Show, 3 each; Border, Duran, Gleaton, Hudson, Hunziker, Johnson, Lamson, Leary, McDonald, Moyer, Thorp, Valenzuela, Vickers, Witt, 2 each; Anderson, Blyth, Boone, Budner, Cacciatore, Randy Clark, Rusty Clark, Connor, Chisler, Davis, Edelen, Fireovid, Fisher, Heimueller, Herschiser, Hinrichs, Jannusch, Kurosaki, Mack, M. Miller, K. R. Miller, Moore, Nielsen, Perlman, Phillips, Roberts, Ronnenbergh, Searage, Smith (El Paso), Stuper, Thomas, Thurmond, Tisdale, Umbarger, Viskas, Walters, Whitehouse, 1 each.

COMBINATION SHUTOUTS—Show-Miller, Hirschy-Miller-Boone, Amarillo; Edelen-Williams-Stuper, Olmsted-Little, Stuper-Jorn, Arkansas; Brown-Steirer, El Paso; Leach-Orosco-Clark, Leary-Clark, Leary-Anderson, Gaff-Anderson, Jackson; Perlman-Segelke, Midland; Hargesheimer-Tucker, Shreveport; Farr-Lazorko, Hudson-Lazorko, Roberts-Lazorko, Davis-Umbarger, Tulsa.

NO-HIT GAMES—None.

California League

CLASS A

CHAMPIONSHIP WINNERS IN PREVIOUS YEARS

1914–Fresno .571	1958–Fresno* .639	1969–Stockton§ .600
1915–Modesto .857	Bakersfield .672	Visalia .614
1916-40–Did not operate.	1959–Bakersfield .592	1970–Bakersfield .667
1941–Fresno .643	Modesto§ .643	Bakersfield .671
S. Barbara (2nd)* .597	1960–Reno .614	1971–Visalia§ .583
1942–Santa Barbara† .642	Reno .657	Fresno .500
1943-44-45–Did not operate.	1961–Reno .743	1972–Modesto§ .547
1946–Stockton‡ .600	Reno .643	Bakersfield .629
1947–Stockton‡ .679	1962–San Jose§ .686	1973–Lodi§ .657
1948–Fresno .607	Reno .587	Bakersfield .571
S. Barbara (3rd)* .529	1963–Modesto .589	1974–Fresno§ .607
1949–Bakersfield .612	Stockton§ .687	San Jose .579
San Jose (4th)* .543	1964–Fresno .638	1975–Reno .614
1950–Ventura .607	Fresno .600	Reno .614
Modesto (2nd)* .586	1965–San Jose .586	1976–Salinas .650
1951–Santa Barbara‡ .599	Stockton§ .614	Reno§ .547
1952–Fresno† .629	1966–Modesto .577	1977–Salinas .564
1953–San Jose‡ .664	Modesto .671	Lodi§ .579
1954–Modesto‡ .623	1967–San Jose§ .676	1978–Visalia§ .698
1955–Stockton .733	Modesto .586	Lodi .607
Fresno§ .718	1968–San Jose§ .629	1979–San Jose§ .636
1956–Fresno† .650	Fresno§ .623	Reno .525
1957–Visalia x .622		
Salinas (4th)* .504		

*Won four-club playoff. †League disbanded June 28. ‡Won championship and four-club playoff. §Won split-season playoff. xWon both halves of split-seaon.

STANDING OF CLUBS AT CLOSE OF FIRST HALF, JUNE 19

NORTHERN DIVISION

Club	W.	L.	T.	Pct.	G.B.
Stockton (Brewers)	49	21	0	.700	......
Modesto (A's)	41	28	0	.594	7½
Reno (Padres)	35	35	0	.500	14
Lodi (Dodgers)	31	39	0	.443	18
Redwood (Co-op)	31	39	0	.443	18

SOUTHERN DIVISION

Club	W.	L.	T.	Pct.	G.B.
Fresno (Giants)	37	33	0	.529	......
San Jose (Mariners)	32	37	0	.464	4½
Salinas (Angels)	31	39	0	.443	6
Visalia (Twins)	27	43	0	.386	10

STANDING OF CLUBS AT CLOSE OF SECOND HALF, AUGUST 31

NORTHERN DIVISION

Club	W.	L.	T.	Pct.	G.B.
**Stockton (Brewers)	41	30	0	.577	......
Reno (Padres)	40	31	0	.563	1
Modesto (A's)	33	37	0	.471	7½
Lodi (Dodgers)	26	44	0	.371	14½
Redwood (Co-op)	24	46	0	.343	16½

SOUTHERN DIVISION

Club	W.	L.	T.	Pct.	G.B.
Visalia (Twins)	44	26	0	.629	......
San Jose (Mariners)	41	29	0	.586	3
Fresno (Giants)	37	33	0	.529	7
Salinas (Angels)	30	40	0	.429	14

**Stockton and Reno finished second half regular season tied for first place in the Northern Division. Stockton defeated Reno in a single-game tie-breaker.

COMPOSITE STANDING OF CLUBS AT CLOSE OF SEASON, AUGUST 31

NORTHERN DIVISION

Club	Sto.	Mod.	Reno	Lodi	Red.	Fr.	S.J.	Vis.	Sal.	W.	L.	T.	Pct.	G.B.
Stockton (Brewers)	....	13	15	14	17	7	9	6	9	90	51	0	.638	......
Modesto (A's)	14	....	14	14	13	6	4	5	4	74	65	0	.532	15
Reno (Padres)	10	9	....	12	14	7	7	9	7	75	66	0	.532	15
Lodi (Dodgers)	6	7	11	....	9	5	3	7	9	57	83	0	.407	32½
Redwood (Co-op)	4	9	10	15	....	3	6	3	5	55	85	0	.393	34½

SOUTHERN DIVISION

Club	Sto.	Mod.	Reno	Lodi	Red.	Fr.	S.J.	Vis.	Sal.	W.	L.	T.	Pct.	G.B.
Fresno (Giants)	6	6	3	6	8	....	15	11	19	74	66	0	.529	......
San Jose (Mariners)	1	9	5	11	9	12	....	16	10	73	66	0	.525	½
Visalia (Twins)	6	6	5	5	7	16	10	....	16	71	69	0	.507	3
Salinas (Angels)	4	6	3	6	8	10	12	12	....	61	79	0	.436	13

Major league affiliations in parentheses.

Playoffs—Visalia, second half leader, defeated Fresno, first half leader, two games to none for Southern Division championship. Stockton (Northern Division champion) defeated Visalia (Southern Division champion), three games to none for League Championship.

Regular-Season Attendance—Fresno, 85,929; Lodi, 49,570; Modesto, 65,614; Redwood, 55,686; Reno, 50,108; Salinas, 47,017; San Jose, 58,132; Stockton, 80,790; Visalia, 39,690. Total, 532,536. Playoffs, 7,903. No all-star game.

Managers: Fresno—Jack Mull; Lodi—Dick McLaughlin; Modesto—Keith Lieppman; Redwood—Barry Woodhead; Reno—Jack Maloof; Salinas—Tom Zimmer; San Jose—Bill Plummer; Stockton—Tony Muser; Visalia—Tom Kelly.

All-Star Team: 1B—Davis, Stockton; 2B—McMullen, Reno; 3B—Hanley, Redwood; SS—Stevenson, Reno; OF—Chambers, San Jose; Estepa, San Jose; Maldonado, Lodi; C—Durrman, Modesto; DH—Bennett, Modesto; P—Cocanower, Stockton; Hinrichs, Fresno; Koontz, Stockton; Stranski, San Jose; Managers—Kelly, Visalia; Mull, Fresno.

(Compiled by William J. Weiss, League Statistician, San Mateo, Calif.)

CLUB BATTING

Club	G.	AB.	R.	OR.	H.	TB.	2B.	3B.	HR.	RBI.	SH.	SF.	BB.	Int. BB.	HP.	SO.	SB.	CS.	LOB.	Pct.
Reno	141	4658	819	705	1312	1893	191	57	92	717	54	50	718	11	35	777	138	87	1148	.282
Modesto	139	4622	725	640	1274	1733	214	25	65	635	50	53	658	26	50	707	181	83	1111	.276
Lodi	140	4525	696	895	1246	1764	176	24	98	620	38	42	599	22	46	588	240	104	1024	.275
San Jose	139	4497	743	631	1237	1722	165	52	72	649	85	36	595	19	38	702	155	86	994	.275
Stockton	141	4572	705	551	1207	1732	192	36	87	605	44	52	670	36	34	917	217	88	1074	.264
Visalia	140	4435	629	689	1165	1567	152	35	60	538	57	57	629	19	38	733	149	81	1000	.263
Redwood	140	4390	682	826	1142	1699	177	19	114	600	41	42	712	16	40	853	135	69	1025	.260
Fresno	140	4317	688	581	1096	1560	186	43	64	599	51	46	655	8	54	735	109	51	1019	.254
Salinas	140	4332	540	708	1074	1436	157	35	45	453	54	33	542	17	48	902	183	86	995	.248

INDIVIDUAL BATTING
(Leading Qualifiers for Batting Championship—378 or More Plate Appearances)
*Bats lefthanded.   †Switch-hitter.

Player and Club	G.	AB.	R.	H.	TB.	2B.	3B.	HR.	RBI.	SH.	SF.	BB.	HP.	SO.	SB.	CS.	Pct.
Flammang, J. Christopher, SJ*	96	351	58	122	164	18	6	4	49	5	4	48	3	40	19	15	.348
Estepa, Ramon, San Jose	129	487	83	153	219	21	9	9	81	12	3	52	6	77	9	9	.314
Davis, Stanley, Stockton*	112	406	71	127	187	22	1	12	58	0	3	49	0	66	17	4	.313
Lanning, David, Lodi*	107	359	64	112	135	18	1	1	37	4	1	59	3	21	12	8	.312
Bennett, James, Modesto*	113	398	60	124	207	28	2	17	94	3	7	40	3	58	8	1	.312
Maldonado, Candido, Lodi	121	456	75	139	247	27	3	25	102	2	6	41	3	63	12	7	.305
Gausepohl, Daniel, Reno	136	522	102	158	229	23	9	10	92	3	9	79	8	68	29	7	.303
Durrman, James, Modesto*	112	391	57	118	169	33	0	6	72	6	5	55	3	43	5	3	.302
McMullen, Ricky, Reno	122	464	85	140	166	19	2	1	50	5	5	73	4	24	20	16	.302
Chambers, Albert, San Jose*	115	426	76	128	197	18	12	9	63	6	6	64	1	80	12	7	.300

Departmental Leaders: G—Irvine, 141; AB—Irvine, 605; R—B. Garrett, 117; H—Irvine, 177; TB—Maldonado, 247; 2B—Durrman, 33; 3B—Chambers, 12; HR—Brock, 29; RBI—Maldonado, 102; SH—Aponte, 13; SF—Schultz, 12; BB—Skube, 120; HP—Hatcher, Sheehy, 13; SO—Schroeder, 141; SB—Wiggins, 120; CS—B. Garrett, 30.

(All Players—Listed Alphabetically)

Player and Club	G.	AB.	R.	H.	TB.	2B.	3B.	HR.	RBI.	SH.	SF.	BB.	HP.	SO.	SB.	CS.	Pct.
Adams, Ricky, Salinas	15	56	5	14	16	2	0	0	4	0	0	4	1	6	4	3	.250
Adams, W. Craig, Redwood	115	381	71	98	160	12	4	14	51	1	3	67	2	110	32	12	.257
Alexander, Patrick, Fresno	11	1	0	0	0	0	0	0	0	0	0	0	0	0	0	0	.000
Alvarez, Roberto, Redwood	101	387	67	116	166	23	6	5	49	4	5	44	8	37	6	8	.300
Anderson, Thomas, 75 Red-36 Fr*	111	372	69	99	172	19	3	16	68	1	2	72	4	109	6	3	.266
Aponte, Edwin, San Jose	136	504	63	138	186	25	4	5	67	13	1	23	1	59	13	1	.274
Argee, Daniel, Redwood*	131	457	87	134	197	23	2	12	75	1	5	79	4	43	2	5	.293
Armstead, Vernon, Modesto	102	317	54	71	113	13	4	7	47	1	3	54	3	103	26	10	.224
Baez, Jesse, Lodi	8	23	2	5	8	0	0	1	1	0	0	7	2	4	0	1	.217
Bailey, Robert, Lodi	7	22	6	9	15	3	0	1	3	0	0	2	1	4	0	0	.409
Baker, Gregory, Fresno	83	271	43	80	114	10	3	6	37	2	0	43	4	43	6	7	.295
Baldwin, Kenneth, Lodi*	53	184	30	54	73	9	2	2	24	2	1	27	1	23	2	6	.293
Bauman, Brad, Fresno	18	41	7	7	8	1	0	0	3	0	0	8	1	10	0	0	.171
Bennett, James, Modesto*	113	398	60	124	207	28	2	17	94	3	7	40	3	58	8	1	.312
Benson, Steve, Visalia	22	75	10	19	24	0	1	1	17	1	2	14	1	7	3	2	.253
Bilardello, Dann, Lodi	41	117	22	36	58	4	0	6	15	3	0	11	1	12	4	2	.308
Black, Harry, San Jose*	33	4	0	1	1	0	0	0	0	0	0	0	0	2	0	0	.250
Booker, Roderick, Visalia*	69	242	45	68	81	5	4	0	26	1	3	37	4	35	9	4	.281
Brackenridge, Lyle, Visalia	60	197	32	57	69	9	0	1	17	4	2	35	0	43	17	2	.289
Brock, Gregory, Lodi*	121	418	72	125	237	19	3	29	95	0	6	62	1	50	3	0	.299
Brown, Michael, Salinas	47	152	24	40	62	7	0	5	15	1	5	19	5	32	3	3	.263
Brunswick, Thomas, Modesto	54	176	26	53	58	5	0	0	17	2	1	25	0	18	3	5	.301
Buckley, Brian, Salinas	30	1	0	1	2	1	0	0	0	0	0	0	0	0	0	0	1.000
Byrum, Terry, Modesto*	51	173	32	49	72	12	4	1	20	1	2	33	2	33	4	1	.283
Cain, Aaron, Redwood	43	94	12	19	29	1	0	3	11	2	0	19	2	14	7	5	.202
Cannon, Michael, 11 Red-67 Sal	78	220	22	47	65	9	0	3	19	0	0	15	3	66	2	1	.214

Player and Club	G.	AB.	R.	H.	TB.	2B.	3B.	HR.	RBI.	SH.	SF.	BB.	HP.	SO.	SB.	CS.	Pct.
Casarez, Frank, Fresno	12	3	0	0	0	0	0	0	0	0	0	0	0	2	0	0	.000
Celidonia, James, Salinas*	76	238	23	49	64	7	1	2	21	3	2	36	0	28	7	3	.206
Chambers, Albert, San Jose*	115	426	76	128	197	18	12	9	85	6	6	64	1	80	12	7	.300
Chelette, J. Mark, San Jose*	110	350	44	84	95	5	3	0	39	8	4	48	0	36	14	8	.240
Christianson, Alec, Redwood†	62	25	1	2	2	0	0	0	0	1	0	0	0	7	0	0	.080
Clark, Christopher, Salinas†	68	218	30	68	98	16	1	4	35	6	2	40	1	31	5	4	.312
Codiroli, Michael, San Jose	94	338	72	97	116	12	2	1	42	11	4	62	5	57	33	11	.287
Colby, Charles, Redwood	11	30	4	6	8	2	0	0	3	0	1	4	0	7	1	1	.200
Collins, Timothy, Salinas*	64	194	19	50	72	11	4	1	22	3	0	29	0	35	4	2	.258
Croft, Paul, Visalia	87	270	56	86	129	2	4	11	42	3	2	54	4	68	30	12	.319
Crone, William, San Jose	30	95	22	26	38	3	3	1	8	2	1	22	0	14	8	4	.274
Cyburt, Philip, Redwood*	30	1	0	0	0	0	0	0	0	0	0	0	0	1	0	0	.000
David, Andre, Visalia*	63	210	33	68	81	9	2	0	32	0	3	38	0	15	3	8	.324
Davis, Stanley, Stockton	112	406	71	127	187	22	1	12	58	0	3	49	0	66	17	4	.313
Dunn, James, Fresno	37	148	29	46	52	2	2	0	19	3	3	9	1	12	5	2	.311
Durrunder, James, Modesto*	112	391	57	118	169	33	0	6	72	6	5	55	3	43	5	3	.302
Eakin, Gordon, Modesto	100	358	62	100	130	13	1	5	39	3	4	46	2	64	2	1	.279
Eiler, Dale, San Jose	3	9	1	2	2	0	0	0	0	0	0	1	0	0	0	0	.222
Esau, Steven, Redwood	19	57	6	12	13	1	0	0	4	2	0	12	0	7	1	1	.211
Estepa, Ramon, San Jose	129	487	83	153	219	21	9	9	81	12	3	52	6	77	9	9	.314
Ferst, Larry, Lodi	31	0	1	0	0	0	0	0	0	0	0	0	0	0	1	0	.000
Firova, Daniel, San Jose	4	14	2	2	2	0	0	0	2	0	0	1	0	5	0	0	.143
Flammang, J. Christopher, SJ*	96	351	58	122	164	18	6	4	49	5	4	48	3	40	19	15	.348
Franjul, Miguel, Lodi	31	110	10	29	32	3	0	0	11	2	2	10	0	15	8	2	.264
Funk, David, Visalia*	34	82	8	14	20	1	1	1	8	2	0	19	0	25	1	0	.171
Gaffney, William, San Jose	37	103	14	13	14	1	0	0	5	0	0	21	1	25	2	3	.126
Gandy, Chris, Modesto	78	246	30	61	82	9	0	4	31	2	2	28	7	61	3	2	.248
Garrett, Bobby, Modesto	139	549	117	160	192	20	6	0	53	7	7	89	1	39	61	30	.291
Garrett, Lynn, Modesto	133	484	72	129	192	19	4	12	85	6	8	78	5	62	19	3	.267
Gauntlett, G. Todd, Lodi	39	119	7	21	24	3	0	0	7	1	0	17	6	16	3	2	.176
Gausepohl, Daniel, Reno	136	522	102	158	229	23	9	10	92	3	9	79	8	68	29	7	.303
Gelfarb, Stephen, Modesto*	64	223	28	70	91	16	1	1	28	1	3	30	4	26	2	2	.314
Geren, Robert, Reno	48	157	24	45	66	7	1	4	23	2	1	24	1	41	1	0	.287
Gladden, C. Daniel, Fresno†	62	237	46	72	113	10	2	9	41	2	3	11	8	36	15	8	.304
Gloyd, Timothy, Lodi	36	109	8	29	30	1	0	0	12	0	14	0	22	9	4		.266
Gonzalez, Filiberto, Salinas*	57	187	16	44	63	8	1	3	20	4	2	19	0	41	2	1	.235
Gundelfinger, Matthew, Salinas	36	113	15	22	37	4	1	3	9	0	0	15	0	31	6	1	.195
Guzman, Hector, Lodi†	37	127	10	27	31	4	0	0	10	2	0	5	1	30	3	4	.213
Hall, Rocky, Stockton*	60	104	13	15	18	3	0	0	13	3	0	8	0	14	2	5	.144
Hallberg, Lance, Visalia	84	296	52	99	136	9	2	8	60	1	6	41	2	45	5	4	.334
Hamilton, James, Salinas	32	126	12	27	34	7	0	0	11	1	0	7	1	17	6	1	.214
Hanley, John, Redwood	131	436	67	126	217	18	2	23	93	0	4	72	1	106	10	5	.289
Hansen, John, Stockton	123	432	60	96	162	25	4	11	49	1	2	39	5	107	20	4	.222
Harris, Tracy, San Jose	27	2	0	1	1	0	0	0	0	0	0	0	0	0	0	0	.500
Hatcher, Richard, 36 Mod-36 Red...	72	207	31	48	59	6	1	1	19	1	3	17	13	46	9	5	.232
Hernandez, Nicolas, Stockton	75	185	22	45	59	6	1	2	22	2	0	37	2	46	2	2	.243
Hood, Michael, San Jose	41	120	8	26	32	3	0	1	9	3	3	6	0	34	2	2	.217
Hudson, Rodney, Visalia	64	196	30	51	72	5	2	4	21	1	0	37	5	31	2	3	.260
Hunt, Ronald, Salinas	122	398	43	102	123	10	4	1	32	9	4	32	6	54	18	17	.256
Hunter, Marion, Salinas	10	21	1	3	3	0	0	0	0	1	0	3	1	9	1	1	.143
Huth, Kenneth, Salinas†	141	605	95	177	212	19	5	2	57	4	4	45	0	71	77	28	.293
Irvine, Edward, Stockton	126	431	63	111	165	22	1	10	57	5	3	76	4	63	3	4	.258
Jacobson, Kevin, Modesto	126	395	65	89	125	16	4	4	51	6	0	67	11	59	12	5	.225
Jamerson, Donald, Fresno*†	27	86	6	17	22	1	2	0	2	1	1	4	0	33	3	2	.198
Johnson, Steven, Reno	35	1	0	0	0	0	0	0	0	0	0	1	0	1	0	0	.000
Jones, Robert, Visalia*	42	118	16	26	42	4	0	4	17	0	2	13	1	44	1	1	.220
Keedy, C. Patrick, Salinas	105	331	57	83	114	16	0	5	47	5	2	54	3	48	3	3	.251
Kemp, Rodney, Lodi*	62	206	16	46	55	6	0	1	23	2	4	17	0	25	3	1	.223
Kneuer, Frank, Modesto	45	1	0	0	0	0	0	0	0	1	0	0	0	1	0	0	.000
Knight, Steven, San Jose	33	109	11	31	36	5	0	0	7	0	0	11	2	11	2	4	.284
Kniss, John, Salinas	132	487	81	125	159	16	3	4	64	6	9	83	2	87	8	5	.257
Koenigsfeld, Ronald, Stockton	4	11	1	5	5	0	0	0	1	0	0	0	1	0	0		.455
Koke, Kyle, San Jose	43	136	14	25	37	1	1	3	17	0	2	15	2	26	6	2	.184
Koval, Joseph, Visalia	46	1	0	0	0	0	0	0	0	0	0	1	0	0	0	0	.000
Krajewski, Christopher, SJ	30	1	0	0	0	0	0	0	0	0	0	0	0	0	0	0	.000
Kromy, Ted, Visalia	133	474	59	112	128	12	2	0	44	11	11	45	5	46	3	10	.236
Kyzer, Richard, Visalia	107	359	64	112	135	18	1	1	37	4	1	59	3	21	12	8	.312
Lanning, David, Lodi*	112	410	80	108	205	21	2	24	95	2	4	73	1	98	2	1	.263
Lansford, Joseph, Reno	56	186	23	42	85	13	0	10	29	1	4	29	1	39	0	5	.226
Laudner, Timothy, Visalia	127	399	63	108	128	8	3	2	40	10	2	45	8	59	44	15	.271
Lemon, Leo, Salinas	20	1	0	0	0	0	0	0	0	0	0	0	0	1	0	0	.000
Lohuis, Mark, Fresno	20	1	0	0	0	0	0	0	0	0	0	0	0	0	0	0	.000
Lopez, Antonio, Visalia	68	248	31	67	92	9	5	2	32	3	1	12	1	18	3	3	.270
Lozado, William, Stockton	134	459	59	112	155	16	6	5	58	6	9	57	3	74	22	7	.244
Lulay, Douglas, Reno	123	476	74	141	215	18	10	12	75	4	2	26	2	91	8	3	.296

Player and Club	G.	AB.	R.	H.	TB.	2B.	3B.	HR.	RBI.	SH.	SF.	BB.	HP.	SO.	SB.	CS.	Pct.
Maldonado, Candido, Lodi	121	456	75	139	247	27	3	25	102	2	6	41	3	63	12	7	.305
Manning, M. Allen, Stockton	138	432	56	97	118	14	2	1	31	7	5	84	5	114	17	10	.225
Marietta, Louis, Fresno	37	1	0	0	0	0	0	0	0	0	0	0	0	1	0	0	.000
Markham, Robert, Visalia*	32	92	7	26	32	4	1	0	19	0	2	6	3	15	0	4	.283
Martin, J. M., 81 Red-33 Reno*	114	363	48	97	133	13	1	7	47	7	5	64	1	56	2	3	.267
Martinez, Ronald, Visalia	118	427	67	127	186	24	4	9	66	6	5	39	4	60	23	4	.297
McInerny, Daniel, Redwood*	50	171	28	44	73	2	0	9	25	2	1	35	4	31	3	1	.257
McMullen, Ricky, Reno	122	464	85	140	166	19	2	1	50	5	5	73	4	24	20	16	.302
McMurray, Steven, Redwood	19	51	4	8	9	1	0	0	6	1	0	5	0	15	2	1	.157
McNealy, Robert, San Jose*	15	53	12	9	11	0	1	0	5	1	0	12	0	13	5	0	.170
McWhirter, Kevin, Visalia	39	148	23	37	66	8	3	5	20	1	1	16	0	28	4	1	.250
Miller, Darrell, Salinas	64	195	26	56	80	6	3	4	28	4	0	12	1	48	4	0	.287
Minnick, Donald, San Jose*	9	1	0	0	0	0	0	0	0	0	0	0	0	1	0	0	.000
Minor, David, Redwood	3	7	1	0	0	0	0	0	0	0	0	1	0	3	0	0	.000
Mobberley, Steven, Reno*	26	72	15	17	22	2	0	1	12	2	0	24	1	4	0	1	.236
Moon, Glen, Fresno*	35	115	19	25	34	5	2	0	12	1	0	17	3	33	7	2	.217
Morgan, William, Visalia	48	136	16	24	31	3	2	0	11	2	2	34	0	50	1	0	.176
Morrison, Perry, Salinas	30	2	2	1	1	0	0	0	0	0	0	0	0	1	0	0	.500
Morton, Stanley, Fresno*	13	31	2	5	5	0	0	0	0	0	0	7	0	10	0	3	.161
Murray, Jed, San Jose	34	2	0	0	0	0	0	0	0	0	0	0	0	2	0	0	.000
Nanni, Tito, San Jose*	57	191	25	38	57	6	2	3	23	3	2	26	0	53	8	6	.199
Nichols, Alfred, Lodi†	22	81	8	22	30	6	1	0	11	1	0	10	0	10	2	1	.272
Nocciolo, Mark, Salinas	5	10	2	0	0	0	0	0	0	0	0	7	0	3	3	0	.000
O'Connor, Daniel, Visalia	35	84	6	10	11	1	0	0	2	1	0	13	2	29	1	0	.119
Oliver, Bruce, Fresno	74	205	21	43	54	9	1	0	22	4	4	26	2	49	1	1	.210
O'Malley, Thomas, Fresno*	122	435	67	125	172	20	9	3	74	4	5	49	2	55	0	2	.287
Parent, Mark, Reno	30	99	8	20	23	3	0	0	12	3	2	4	1	16	0	0	.202
Peguero, Pablo, Lodi	3	6	0	0	0	0	0	0	0	0	0	1	0	1	0	0	.000
Pettis, Gary, Salinas†	118	393	71	94	121	15	3	2	31	1	2	79	11	128	43	13	.239
Pignotti, John, Redwood	11	33	4	6	7	1	0	0	3	2	0	7	0	4	0	0	.182
Pittman, John, San Jose	83	248	52	63	101	7	2	9	49	3	3	60	6	59	3	2	.254
Plinski, Paul, Fresno	116	365	60	78	99	16	1	1	28	4	5	55	2	55	15	7	.214
Purpura, Daniel, Reno	129	401	77	117	163	18	5	6	60	2	5	105	1	52	3	11	.292
Pyburn, Jeffrey, Reno	78	283	64	95	129	21	2	3	54	11	5	60	3	41	25	12	.336
Rabb, John, Fresno	128	395	69	96	178	21	2	19	80	0	9	80	9	89	11	4	.243
Randolph, John, San Jose*	126	458	71	114	145	17	4	2	54	10	1	56	2	43	19	7	.249
Rasmussen, Dennis, Salinas*	12	1	0	0	0	0	0	0	0	0	0	0	0	0	0	0	.000
Regier, Alan, Redwood†	37	116	10	20	25	5	0	0	13	1	1	20	1	21	3	2	.172
Reynolds, Robert, Lodi	86	299	33	84	108	6	3	4	31	3	1	16	0	48	9	9	.281
Richards, David, Lodi	2	5	0	1	1	0	0	0	0	0	0	0	0	1	0	0	.200
Richmond, Albert, Reno	71	240	40	52	100	8	5	10	45	0	3	52	3	73	14	13	.217
Riffel, J. Branner, Salinas	39	122	4	27	36	4	1	1	16	1	2	14	0	21	0	0	.221
Riley, Michael, Visalia	22	2	0	0	0	0	0	0	0	0	0	0	0	2	0	0	.000
Robbins, Johnny, Lodi*	56	114	19	27	32	3	1	0	8	0	0	34	0	28	7	4	.237
Robins, George, Stockton	40	109	9	30	35	3	1	0	3	1	1	11	0	22	2	4	.275
Roche, Timothy, Redwood*	81	276	59	87	139	22	0	10	51	0	2	52	0	60	5	4	.315
Rodriguez, Eduardo, Redwood	75	239	38	57	77	8	0	4	28	7	2	20	2	55	6	3	.238
Rosenberg, Brendan, Visalia	61	202	24	49	68	8	1	3	23	1	3	25	4	45	2	2	.243
Rowe, Harold, Fresno	73	188	26	41	56	9	0	2	27	6	3	40	2	47	5	0	.218
Saavedra, Edwin, Redwood	58	173	32	48	68	8	0	4	26	2	2	40	0	32	19	4	.277
Salcido, Ted, Lodi	1	2	2	1	1	0	0	0	0	0	0	2	0	0	0	0	.500
Sax, David, Lodi	43	123	9	21	27	3	0	1	11	2	2	24	0	20	1	1	.171
Schexnayder, Wade, Salinas	104	310	38	73	104	7	6	4	29	4	3	39	1	120	10	6	.235
Schields, Steven, Redwood	111	302	33	58	71	7	0	2	26	3	2	56	3	62	12	9	.192
Schroeder, A. William, Stockton	123	437	68	117	197	20	3	18	97	4	4	48	6	141	10	3	.268
Schultz, Greg, Lodi	113	366	62	104	168	17	4	13	73	2	12	69	2	37	14	9	.284
Sheeehy, Mark, Lodi	112	393	62	106	138	14	0	6	51	3	2	35	13	39	25	11	.270
Sijer, Daniel, Redwood*	42	2	0	0	0	0	0	0	0	0	0	0	0	0	0	0	.000
Skube, Robert, Stockton*	135	453	91	132	229	26	7	19	81	5	8	120	6	103	29	2	.291
Slembecker, George, Visalia	86	269	33	67	94	11	2	4	29	3	3	43	0	59	5	2	.249
Slettvet, Douglas, Reno	73	219	29	53	77	12	0	4	34	0	0	34	1	62	0	0	.242
Smith, Curtis, Redwood	58	3	0	2	2	0	0	0	0	0	0	2	0	1	1	0	.667
Spillane, Paul, Redwood	92	285	46	79	119	13	0	9	39	2	7	47	6	42	7	0	.277
Spurlin, Robert, Fresno	39	115	19	29	38	4	1	1	19	3	0	21	1	26	3	1	.252
Steels, James, Reno*	73	285	42	86	111	8	4	3	27	1	4	19	1	36	13	5	.302
Stevenson, John, Reno	117	436	86	122	177	14	10	7	53	7	6	60	1	65	15	11	.280
Stockley, Paul, Modesto	68	223	32	54	58	4	0	0	9	4	0	31	2	63	7	5	.242
Stone, Wayne, Salinas	122	409	53	102	124	12	5	0	36	5	2	52	1	64	16	6	.249
Stranski, H. Scott, San Jose	28	2	0	1	1	0	0	0	0	0	0	0	0	1	0	0	.500
Sua, Murphy, Salinas	58	185	24	47	69	8	1	4	27	0	3	12	3	33	1	1	.254
Sutton, Philip, Fresno	105	314	46	75	87	5	2	1	24	8	0	39	0	41	8	2	.239
Szymarek, Paul, Fresno	54	178	30	51	79	10	3	4	28	0	3	29	3	42	9	1	.287
Thys, Gregory, Reno	71	208	35	53	66	9	2	0	26	6	0	28	6	23	5	4	.255
Tingley, Ronald, Reno	65	204	37	61	79	3	3	4	35	4	2	33	0	35	1	0	.299
Tipa, Stephen, 18 Red-50 Sal	68	242	28	64	94	12	6	2	34	0	3	22	0	39	2	1	.264

Player and Club	G.	AB.	R.	H.	TB.	2B.	3B.	HR.	RBI.	SH.	SF.	BB.	HP.	SO.	SB.	CS.	Pct.
Valle, David, San Jose	119	430	81	126	176	14	0	12	70	5	2	50	11	54	6	7	.293
Villaescusa, Juan, Lodi*	22	63	4	16	18	2	0	0	8	0	0	5	0	9	2	4	.254
Wabeke, Douglas, Fresno	63	204	33	55	75	15	1	1	24	3	1	38	3	17	5	3	.270
Ward, Steven, Salinas*	36	1	0	1	2	1	0	0	0	0	0	0	0	0	0	0	1.000
White, Michael, San Jose	85	297	61	88	159	15	4	16	60	2	2	42	1	64	2	4	.296
Whiting, Don, Stockton*	136	458	79	132	198	21	3	13	73	3	6	88	4	73	9	4	.288
Wiggins, Alan, Lodi†	135	513	108	148	168	10	5	0	35	4	4	82	6	54	120	25	.288
Wilhelmy, Scott, Visalia*	18	20	3	3	4	1	0	0	0	0	0	3	0	6	0	0	.150
Wilkinson, Ronald, Visalia†	117	399	49	105	118	11	1	0	20	11	1	39	4	42	30	4	.263
Williams, Joseph, Redwood	34	113	10	23	32	3	0	2	6	2	0	20	0	25	2	1	.204
Wojcik, James, Fresno*	60	221	36	64	93	11	6	2	37	1	3	29	0	34	5	1	.290
Woodard, Michael, Modesto*	73	289	52	86	96	8	1	0	32	1	1	40	3	18	35	9	.298
Woodhead, Barry, Redwood	2	1	0	0	0	0	0	0	0	0	0	1	0	1	0	0	.000
Woods, Ronald, 14 Red-9 Lodi	23	6	0	1	1	0	0	0	0	0	0	2	0	3	0	0	.167
Ziccardi, John, Fresno*	116	329	46	82	119	14	4	5	47	4	6	62	0	37	2	1	.249
Zimmerer, George, Redwood†	2	1	0	1	1	0	0	0	1	0	0	0	0	0	0	0	1.000

The following pitchers had no plate appearances, primarily through use of designated hitters, listed alphabetically by club, games in parentheses:

FRESNO—Anderson, Kelly (79); Buice, DeWayne (37); Fowlkes, Alan (18); Gonsalves, Dennis †(1); Hinrichs, Phillip (25); Kittrell, Rickey *(25); Moyer, Gregory (12); Pisel, Ronald (24); Sensenbrenner, Davis *(16); Sutherland, Matthew *(20); Williams, Frank (21).

LODI—Alexander, Roberto (15); Bain, Paul †(16); Bullock, Kenneth (8); Cordova, Rocky (29); Goulding, Richard (5); Hayes, Brian *(19); Joyce, Kevin (8); Kenyon, Robert (12); Lindsey, Kenneth *(18); O'Neill, Timothy (46); Oroz, Felix †(26); Reeves, Mathew *(26); Sander, Richard (25); Terry, Glenn *(10); White, Robert (3).

MODESTO—Call, Keith (17); Corzel, Kennedy (22); Dougherty, Charles (27); Ferguson, Mark (24); Gosse, M. John (7); Holloway, Richard (23); Mantsch, Ronnie (46); Moore, Robert (18); Moretti, Roy (40); Retzer, Edwin (24); VanMarter, Donald (23); Wood, Robert (21).

REDWOOD—Aldrich, Lance (1); Andersen, Edward (1); Bigos, Walter (21); Blateric, Stephen (13); Brokop, Thomas (11); Froelich, David (9); Hoban, John (13); Kibbe, Jay (28); Lund, Frederick (24); Owens, Thomas (8); Peterson, Rodney (28–3 with Reno); Prevost, Eric (11); Regan, Francis (5); Walters, John (10); Walters, Michael (9); Wilder, Troy *(5).

RENO—Barber, Michael (44); Bryant, R. Neil (2); Church, Sydney *(42); Couchee, Michael (2); Danielson, Daniel (30); Hamm, Timothy (25); Hardwick, Willie †(23); Hawkins, M. Andrew (26); Jannusch, David (10); Johnson, Donald *(18); Patton, Gregory (8); Ronnenbergh, J. Martin (11); Wagner, Steven (17); White, John (2); Wilson, Philip (8); Wyrick, Courtney (49).

SALINAS—Border, Robert (21); Brown, Curtis (20); Conner, Jeffrey *(14); Dugger, Lawrence (14); Duran, David (20); Lindsey, Edward *(24); Mooneyham, William (12); Saatzer, Michael *(10); Skaggs, Jackie (9); Sylvia, Ronald (6); Turpin, Dwight (8); Venezia, Michael (21); Witt, Michael (13).

SAN JOSE—Batten, Mark (29); Graser, Richard *(1); Hallgren, Tim (14); Krueger, Steve *(8); McGee, Ronald †(2); Snyder, Brian *(25); Steger, Kevin *(7); Stottlemyre, Jeffrey *(12).

STOCKTON—Beene, R. Andrew (15); Cocanower, James (27); Cook, G. Timothy (27); Diaz, Roberto (35); Donovan, Micahel (13); Gibson, Robert (33); Jenkins, Jerry (27); Jones, Douglas (11); Koontz, James (39); Madden, Michael *(29); Meyer, Gregory (10); Park, Chel Sun (11); Schroeck, Robert *(16).

VISALIA—Angulo, Kenneth *(19); Arrieta, Albert (12); Arrington, Samuel (2); Biko, Thomas *(12); Bullinger, D. Matthews *(38); Fagely, Timothy *(4); Havens, Bradley *(28); Kelly, J. Thomas *(3); Olshane, Scott (40); Ramirez, Oscar †(15); Thomson, Douglas (12); Tirella, Michael *(19).

GRAND SLAM HOME RUNS—Maldonado, 3; Anderson (Redwood), Argee, Armstead, Benson, Hallberg, Hanley, Jamerson, Kemp, O'Malley, Reynolds, Richmond, Saavedra, Schroeder, Slembecker, Stevenson, Tipa, Valle, Wabeke, Whiting, 1 each.

AWARDED FIRST BASE ON INTERFERENCE—Plinski 10 (Durrman 2, Martin 2, Miller 2, Schroeder 2, Brown, Laudner); Bilardello 2 (Geren, Martin); Gausepohl 2 (McMurray, Valle); Gundelfinger 2 (Hernandez, Pignotti); Keedy (Sax); Maldonado (Slettvet); Pittman (Miller); Pyburn (Durrman); Spurlin (Kneuer); Whiting (Martin).

GAME-WINNING RBIs

FRESNO (34)—Baker 4, Jamerson 4, Rabb 4, Oliver 3, Wojcik 3, Dunn 2, Gladden 2, O'Malley 2, Rowe 2, Sutton 2, Szymarek 2, Ziccardi 2, Moon 1, Spurlin 1.

LODI (50)—Schultz 11, Sheehy 7, Maldonado 6, Brock 5, Kemp 5, Sua 5, Baldwin 2, Nichols 2, Reynolds 2, Bilardello 1, Franjul 1, Gauntlett 1, Sax 1, Wiggins 1.

MODESTO (54)—Durrman 9, B. Garrett 8, Armstead 7, Bennett 5, L. Garrett 5, Woodard 5, Jacobson 4, Eakin 3, Byrum 2, Gandy 1, Gelfarb 1, Hatcher 1, Kneuer 1, Markham 1, Stockley 1.

REDWOOD (45)—Hanley 7, Spillane 5, Anderson 4, Argee 4, Adams 3, Hatcher 3, Martin 3, Rodriguez 3, Schields 3, Alvarez 2, McInerny 2, Saavedra 2, Tipa 2, Colby 1, Roche 1.

RENO (61)—Gausepohl 12, Lulay 7, Pyburn 7, Lansford 5, Purpura 5, McMullen 4, Tingley 4, Martin 3, Richmond 3, Slettvet 3, Thys 3, Parent 2, Steels 2, Stevenson 1.

SALINAS (52)—Schexnayder 5, Stone 5, M. Brown 4, Cannon 4, Clark 4, Hunter 4, Lemon 4, Miller 4, Pettis 4, Keedy 3, Celidonia 2, Collins 2, Gonzalez 2, Hamilton 2, Gundelfinger 1, Hunt 1, Tipa 1.

SAN JOSE (45)—Chambers 10, Codiroli 6, Flammang 6, Estepa 5, White 5, Aponte 3, Pittman 2, Randolph 2, Valle 2, Chelette 1, Crone 1, Gaffney 1, Hood 1.

STOCKTON (54)—Schroeder 10, Koenigsfeld 9, Whiting 9, Davis 8, Lozado 6, Irvine 4, Skube 4, Hansen 2, Manning 2.

VISALIA (57)—Hallberg 11, Martinez 10, Croft 5, David 4, Laudner 4, Slembecker 4, Booker 3, Wilkinson 3, Brackenridge 2, Hudson 2, Kyzer 2, Morgan 2, Rosenberg 2, Benson 1, Funk 1, McWhirter 1.

CLUB FIELDING

Club	G.	PO.	A.	E.	DP.	PB.	Pct.	Club	G.	PO.	A.	E.	DP.	PB.	Pct.
Modesto	139	3606	1442	191	124	28	.964	San Jose	139	3539	1569	238	118	26	.955
Fresno	140	3448	1578	196	123	20	.962	Salinas	140	3440	1363	238	119	40	.953
Stockton	141	3644	1561	205	150	16	.962	Redwood	140	3473	1517	253	144	19	.952
Visalia	140	3587	1623	208	129	16	.962	Lodi	140	3499	1642	264	135	21	.951
Reno	141	3569	1693	220	140	32	.960								

Triple Plays—Reno, Stockton.

INDIVIDUAL FIELDING

*Throws lefthanded.

FIRST BASEMEN

Player and Club	G.	PO.	A.	E.	DP.	Pct.	Player and Club	G.	PO.	A.	E.	DP.	Pct.
BROCK, Fresno	106	906	79	5	81	.995	Anderson, Red-Fresno*	100	837	66	19	79	.979
Lansford, Reno	111	1067	73	10	101	.991	Davis, Stockton	93	819	51	19	76	.979
Gelfarb, Modesto*	62	471	27	6	44	.988	Skube, Stockton*	37	355	16	8	41	.979
Hunt, Salinas	61	445	29	6	43	.988	Wiggins, Lodi	21	175	13	4	23	.979
Ziccardi, Fresno*	45	371	32	5	36	.988	Slettvet, Reno	15	129	8	3	12	.979
Gandy, Modesto	69	484	32	7	43	.987	Riffel, Salinas	19	117	4	3	9	.976
Whiting, Stockton*	10	70	6	1	8	.987	Pittman, San Jose	49	364	25	10	28	.975
White, San Jose	73	661	39	11	60	.985	Flammang, San Jose*	13	111	6	3	7	.975
Oliver, Fresno	72	600	32	10	49	.984	Lulay, Reno	16	188	12	6	17	.971
Hallberg, Visalia	63	514	34	9	46	.984	Markham, Modesto*	14	93	3	3	11	.970
Gonzalez, Salinas*	46	334	34	6	34	.984	Kemp, Lodi	12	52	7	2	10	.967
Collins, Salinas	24	168	11	3	13	.984	Chelette, San Jose	10	99	4	4	10	.963
Lopez, Visalia	65	592	44	12	47	.981	Hudson, Visalia	15	113	8	5	16	.960
Argee, Redwood*	69	526	52	11	51	.981							

Triple Plays—Lansford, Davis.

(Fewer Than Ten Games)

Player and Club	G.	PO.	A.	E.	DP.	Pct.	Player and Club	G.	PO.	A.	E.	DP.	Pct.
Eakin, Modesto	6	60	6	0	6	1.000	Kneuer, Modesto	2	9	0	0	1	1.000
Hanley, Redwood	6	57	2	0	3	1.000	J. Williams, Redwood	1	6	0	0	1	1.000
Schultz, Lodi	5	51	4	0	3	1.000	Villaescusa, Lodi	2	3	0	0	0	1.000
Sax, Lodi	6	49	2	0	3	1.000	Cannon, Salinas	1	1	1	0	1	1.000
Slembecker, Visalia	6	20	1	0	1	1.000	Black, San Jose*	1	1	0	0	0	1.000
Schroeder, Stockton	1	12	1	0	0	1.000	Regier, Redwood*	9	41	5	1	3	.979

SECOND BASEMEN

Player and Club	G.	PO.	A.	E.	DP.	Pct.	Player and Club	G.	PO.	A.	E.	DP.	Pct.
Crone, San Jose	11	20	32	0	5	1.000	Sheehy, Lodi	108	280	293	23	71	.961
Schields, Redwood	11	11	13	0	2	1.000	Byrum, Modesto	46	120	136	11	33	.959
Eakin, Modesto	11	31	25	1	6	.982	Dunn, Fresno	14	31	37	3	7	.958
Brunswick, Modesto	14	24	26	1	3	.980	Alvarez, Redwood	99	226	249	24	65	.952
Wabeke, Fresno	54	112	149	8	32	.970	Hunter, Salinas	95	247	223	25	54	.949
RANDOLPH, San Jose	124	299	366	23	78	.967	Woodard, Modesto	72	177	165	19	48	.947
Esau, Redwood	19	41	43	3	8	.966	Hamilton, Salinas	23	63	42	6	9	.946
McMullen, Reno	117	251	377	23	78	.965	Baldwin, Lodi	20	43	52	6	10	.941
Koenigsfeld, Stockton	119	229	339	21	85	.964	Kniss, Salinas	25	43	55	7	11	.933
Plinski, Fresno	73	149	195	13	49	.964	Wiggins, Lodi	18	46	39	7	9	.924
Hall, Stockton	42	56	70	5	16	.962	Colby, Redwood	11	16	16	3	3	.914
Kyzer, Visalia	132	337	384	29	84	.961	Thys, Reno	21	49	63	11	20	.911

(Fewer Than Ten Games)

Player and Club	G.	PO.	A.	E.	DP.	Pct.	Player and Club	G.	PO.	A.	E.	DP.	Pct.
Wilkinson, Visalia	5	9	8	0	3	1.000	Chelette, San Jose	4	4	12	1	1	.941
Mobberley, Reno	4	6	9	0	0	1.000	Rowe, Fresno	7	14	15	2	6	.935
Purpura, Reno	2	3	8	0	1	1.000	J. Williams, Redwood	8	25	17	5	3	.894
Villaescusa, Lodi	2	4	6	0	2	1.000	Wojcik, Fresno	3	4	4	1	1	.889
Schultz, Lodi	2	4	2	0	1	1.000	Roche, Redwood	9	12	13	4	4	.862
Guzman, Lodi	2	3	2	0	0	1.000	B. Garrett, Modesto	1	3	0	1	0	.750
Brackenridge, Visalia	1	0	2	0	0	1.000	Slembecker, Visalia	2	2	0	1	0	.667
Aponte, San Jose	1	1	0	0	0	1.000	Zimmerer, Redwood	2	2	0	1	0	.667
Casarez, Fresno	1	1	0	0	1	1.000	Harris, San Jose	1	1	0	1	0	.500
Benson, Visalia	7	12	20	2	3	.941							

Triple Play—Koenigsfeld.

THIRD BASEMEN

Player and Club	G.	PO.	A.	E.	DP.	Pct.	Player and Club	G.	PO.	A.	E.	DP.	Pct.
Slembecker, Visalia	14	12	30	1	2	.977	O'MALLEY, Fresno	119	69	253	22	19	.936
Brunswick, Modesto	11	5	17	1	1	.957	Jacobson, Modesto	124	101	242	25	32	.932
Stone, Salinas	20	16	34	3	5	.943	Lanning, Lodi	91	58	187	18	21	.932

THIRD BASEMEN—Continued

Player and Club	G.	PO.	A.	E.	DP.	Pct.
Thys, Reno	38	26	81	8	5	.930
Purpura, Reno	104	82	199	24	18	.921
Wilkinson, Visalia	98	72	225	26	14	.920
Aponte, San Jose	135	120	299	43	23	.907
Manning, Stockton	138	101	270	40	32	.903
Spillane, Redwood	34	30	51	9	7	.900
Rowe, Fresno	28	8	54	7	3	.899
Collins, Salinas	11	14	10	3	4	.889
Schexnayder, Salinas	84	74	146	28	16	.887
Schultz, Lodi	36	31	83	15	9	.884
J. Williams, Redwood	23	18	41	8	4	.881
Funk, Visalia	24	15	48	9	4	.875
Roche, Redwood	46	31	78	16	11	.872
Benson, Redwood	14	13	19	6	2	.842
Hanley, Redwood	44	35	67	20	2	.836
Cannon, Salinas	25	21	27	13	0	.787

(Fewer Than Ten Games)

Player and Club	G.	PO.	A.	E.	DP.	Pct.
Eakin, Modesto	6	7	13	0	2	1.000
Alvarez, Redwood	5	1	4	0	0	1.000
Huth, Salinas	1	0	2	0	0	1.000
White, San Jose	1	0	1	0	0	1.000
Hunter, Salinas	5	4	10	1	0	.933
Christianson, Redwood	7	7	17	2	0	.923
Chelette, San Jose	5	1	11	1	1	.923
Kneuer, Modesto	3	2	7	1	1	.900
Sua, Lodi	8	8	13	3	2	.897
Hamilton, Salinas	4	5	10	2	2	.882
Koenigsfeld, Stockton	8	5	6	2	1	.846
Baldwin, Lodi	5	5	5	2	1	.833
Lulay, Reno	2	2	3	1	0	.833
Plinski, Fresno	3	2	2	1	0	.800
Keedy, Salinas	7	3	8	3	1	.786
Sax, Lodi	5	7	7	5	1	.737
Schields, Redwood	3	1	1	1	0	.667
C. Adams, Redwood	1	2	1	2	1	.600
Pettis, Salinas	2	0	1	1	0	.500

SHORTSTOPS

Player and Club	G.	PO.	A.	E.	DP.	Pct.
R. Adams, Salinas	15	33	44	2	11	.975
Wilkinson, Visalia	17	19	40	2	3	.967
Rowe, Fresno	22	23	47	3	7	.959
Koenigsfeld, Stockton	12	11	34	2	3	.957
Crone, San Jose	19	32	55	4	12	.956
LOZADO, Stockton	134	252	401	32	90	.953
Rodriguez, Redwood	74	134	213	19	50	.948
Eakin, Modesto	63	100	158	16	42	.942
Booker, Visalia	68	91	198	18	36	.941
Dunn, Fresno	25	36	76	7	16	.941
Stevenson, Reno	116	218	421	41	71	.940
Schields, Redwood	67	130	170	19	38	.940
Sutton, Fresno	103	144	297	30	48	.936
Gaffney, San Jose	34	45	94	10	17	.933
Stockley, Modesto	67	110	191	22	23	.932
Keedy, Salinas	31	29	81	8	11	.932
Purpura, Reno	23	35	79	9	17	.927
Slembecker, Visalia	67	65	200	23	36	.920
Lemon, Salinas	18	28	39	6	8	.918
Chelette, San Jose	89	144	258	37	39	.916
Schultz, Lodi	41	83	114	19	20	.912
Gloyd, Lodi	36	47	108	15	19	.912
Franjul, Lodi	30	37	103	14	21	.909
Stone, Salinas	49	50	116	17	19	.907
Brunswick, Modesto	15	22	32	6	8	.900
Guzman, Lodi	25	41	65	17	15	.862
Hunter, Salinas	17	34	40	12	8	.860
Pettis, Salinas	13	13	22	6	2	.854

Triple Plays—Lozado, Stevenson.

(Fewer Than Ten Games)

Player and Club	G.	PO.	A.	E.	DP.	Pct.
Jacobson, Modesto	3	6	4	0	1	1.000
Alvarez, Redwood	5	2	5	0	0	1.000
Hood, San Jose	2	1	4	0	0	1.000
Koke, San Jose	1	2	2	0	0	1.000
Hall, Stockton	2	1	2	0	0	1.000
Plinski, Fresno	1	1	1	0	0	1.000
Hamilton, Salinas	6	4	11	1	0	.938
Mobberley, Reno	7	11	10	2	2	.913
Baldwin, Lodi	1	3	5	1	1	.889
Wiggins, Lodi	6	18	19	5	4	.881
Villaescusa, Lodi	9	11	25	6	1	.857
Benson, Visalia	1	3	6	2	2	.818
Collins, Salinas	1	0	3	1	0	.750
Randolph, San Jose	2	4	2	3	0	.667

OUTFIELDERS

Player and Club	G.	PO.	A.	E.	DP.	Pct.
Flammang, San Jose*	72	114	5	0	1	1.000
Tipa, Redwood-Salinas	48	97	4	0	1	1.000
Rosenberg, Visalia	56	96	2	0	0	1.000
Gundelfinger, Salinas	21	22	0	0	0	1.000
Roche, Redwood	10	9	1	0	0	1.000
McWhirter, Visalia	33	98	5	1	3	.990
B. GARRETT, Modesto	138	352	8	4	2	.989
Argee, Redwood*	51	74	4	1	0	.987
Lemon, Salinas	101	198	6	3	1	.986
Gladden, Fresno	44	68	3	1	0	.986
Irvine, Stockton	141	297	14	5	3	.984
Moon, Fresno*	35	61	1	1	1	.984
Morgan, Visalia	47	101	7	2	0	.982
Codiroli, San Jose*	85	186	6	4	2	.980
Gausepohl, Reno	136	228	20	6	2	.976
Whiting, Stockton*	54	78	4	2	0	.976
Armstead, Modesto	76	149	6	4	2	.975
Bennett, Modesto*	63	109	8	3	1	.975
Estepa, San Jose	112	174	11	5	3	.974
David, Visalia*	49	99	10	3	0	.973
Pettis, Salinas	105	193	13	6	2	.972
Brackenridge, Visalia	56	60	10	2	2	.972
Kemp, Lodi	87	152	13	5	1	.971
Nanni, San Jose*	52	98	3	3	0	.971
Wojcik, Fresno	47	62	4	2	0	.971
L. Garrett, Modesto	133	246	15	8	2	.970
Szymarek, Fresno	33	57	3	2	2	.968
McInerny, Redwood*	49	80	9	3	4	.967
Collins, Salinas	21	29	0	1	0	.967
Hanley, Redwood	46	48	9	2	4	.966
Saavedra, Redwood	57	126	12	5	4	.965
Pyburn, Reno	78	132	1	5	1	.964
Baker, Fresno	80	149	5	6	0	.963
Skube, Stockton*	90	157	18	7	5	.962
Chambers, Mod-Red	82	122	3	5	0	.962
Hatcher, Mod-Red	47	95	3	4	1	.961
Martinez, Visalia	79	138	6	6	1	.960
Clark, Salinas*	59	93	4	4	2	.960
Hansen, Stockton	121	182	7	9	1	.955
Maldonado, Lodi	121	211	13	11	2	.953
Croft, Visalia	73	174	8	9	4	.953
Koval, Visalia	37	51	7	3	2	.951

OUTFIELDERS—Continued

Player and Club	G.	PO.	A.	E.	DP.	Pct.
Wiggins, Lodi	83	126	5	7	1	.949
Lulay, Reno	64	84	8	5	0	.948
Jamerson, Fresno	119	162	16	10	3	.947
Steels, Reno*	60	78	9	5	2	.946
C. Adams, Redwood	112	217	17	14	2	.944
Reynolds, Lodi	84	188	10	12	6	.943
Ziccardi, Fresno*	52	70	10	5	0	.941
Richmond, Reno	62	73	4	5	2	.939
S. Johnson, Reno	23	31	0	2	0	.939
Stone, Salinas	49	60	13	5	1	.936
Robins, Stockton	34	41	1	3	0	.933
Riffel, Salinas	16	25	2	2	1	.931
Cain, Redwood	37	49	4	4	1	.930
Robbins, Lodi	32	37	1	3	0	.927
Cannon, Red-Salinas	39	48	1	4	0	.925
Schields, Redwood	26	31	5	3	1	.923
Morton, Fresno*	12	22	1	2	0	.920
Plinski, Fresno	21	28	2	3	1	.909
McNealy, San Jose*	15	29	1	4	0	.882
Nichols, Lodi	15	24	2	4	0	.867

(Fewer Than Ten Games)

Player and Club	G.	PO.	A.	E.	DP.	Pct.
Regier, Redwood*	3	8	1	0	0	1.000
Sax, Lodi	6	6	1	0	0	1.000
Hallberg, Visalia	5	5	1	0	0	1.000
Spillane, Redwood	4	5	0	0	0	1.000
Schultz, Lodi	5	3	0	0	0	1.000
Minor, Redwood	3	3	0	0	0	1.000
Tingley, Reno	3	2	0	0	0	1.000
Hall, Stockton	1	1	1	0	0	1.000
M. Brown, Salinas	2	1	0	0	0	1.000
Gelfarb, Modesto*	2	1	0	0	0	1.000
Stranski, San Jose	1	1	0	0	0	1.000
Wilhelmy, Visalia	1	1	0	0	0	1.000
Sua, Lodi	8	14	1	1	0	.938
Huth, Salinas	8	13	1	1	0	.933
White, San Jose	5	11	0	1	0	.917
Markham, Modesto*	7	10	0	1	0	.909

CATCHERS

Player and Club	G.	PO.	A.	E.	DP.	PB.	Pct.
Wilhelmy, Visalia	14	26	4	0	1	0	1.000
Schexnayder, Salinas	17	103	14	1	0	7	.992
SCHROEDER, Stock.	111	657	95	7	10	10	.991
Spillane, Redwood	37	180	30	2	5	4	.991
Parent, Reno	29	128	23	2	2	9	.987
Rabb, Fresno	115	661	70	11	5	17	.985
Gauntlett, Lodi	39	196	43	4	1	7	.984
Laudner, Visalia	47	251	36	5	6	2	.983
O'Connor, Visalia	31	145	16	3	1	3	.982
Bauman, Fresno	18	84	10	2	0	2	.979
Durrman, Modesto	93	506	97	14	11	17	.977
Miller, Salinas	51	289	57	8	3	9	.977
Valle, San Jose	101	570	102	17	8	15	.975
Tingley, Reno	58	331	46	10	2	9	.974
Sax, Lodi	23	97	15	3	1	4	.974
Celidonia, Salinas	69	387	67	13	7	15	.972
Kneuer, Modesto	53	329	59	12	2	11	.970
Hudson, Visalia	72	386	45	14	3	11	.969
Hood, San Jose	37	186	26	7	1	5	.968
Hernandez, Stockton	48	251	15	9	3	6	.967
Geren, Reno	18	89	17	4	3	7	.964
Sua, Lodi	31	156	26	7	1	8	.963
Bilardello, Lodi	38	169	30	8	4	1	.961
Martin, Red-Reno	85	430	75	21	9	11	.960
Spurlin, Fresno	20	80	14	4	0	1	.959
Hanley, Redwood	27	157	26	8	1	5	.958
Slettvet, Reno	21	99	16	5	2	2	.958
Pignotti, Redwood	10	58	8	3	1	2	.957
McMurray, Redwood	16	62	12	4	0	2	.949
M. Brown, Salinas	13	71	4	5	0	6	.938

(Fewer Than Ten Games)

Player and Club	G.	PO.	A.	E.	DP.	PB.	Pct.
Baez, Lodi	8	47	4	0	1	0	1.000
Nocciolo, Salinas	4	32	4	0	1	3	1.000
Bailey, Lodi	6	29	6	0	0	1	1.000
Eiler, San Jose	2	20	6	0	1	3	1.000
Peguero, Lodi	3	8	4	0	0	0	1.000
Richards, Lodi	2	4	1	0	0	0	1.000
Cannon, Salina	1	4	1	0	0	0	1.000
Firova, San Jose	4	29	1	1	0	3	.968
Knight, San Jose	1	3	0	1	0	0	.750

PITCHERS

Player and Club	G.	PO.	A.	E.	DP.	Pct.
PETERSON, Red-Reno.	28	8	29	0	2	1.000
Jones, Visalia*	34	9	27	0	2	1.000
Venezia, Salinas	21	12	22	0	1	1.000
Alexander, Fresno*	11	4	29	0	1	1.000
Wood, Modesto	21	3	28	0	2	1.000
Riley, Visalia	22	6	17	0	4	1.000
Murray, San Jose	34	5	15	0	1	1.000
Gibson, Stockton	33	7	12	0	1	1.000
Biko, Visalia*	12	5	14	0	0	1.000
Lindsey, Salinas*	24	5	13	0	1	1.000
Fowlkes, Fresno	18	5	13	0	0	1.000
Knight, San Jose	44	3	15	0	1	1.000
Rasmussen, Salinas	11	0	18	0	1	1.000
Angulo, Visalia*	19	1	15	0	2	1.000
Brown, Salinas	20	7	7	0	0	1.000
Smith, Redwood	57	5	9	0	2	1.000
Diaz, Stockton	35	5	9	0	1	1.000
Wagner, Reno	17	3	10	0	0	1.000
Jannusch, Reno	10	5	7	0	0	1.000
VanMarter, Modesto	23	2	9	0	1	1.000
J. Walters, Redwood	10	2	9	0	1	1.000
Brokop, Redwood	11	3	4	0	0	1.000
Kenyon, Lodi	12	2	4	0	1	1.000
Tirella, Visalia*	19	2	3	0	0	1.000
Ramirez, Visalia	15	2	2	0	0	1.000
Park, Stockton	11	0	3	0	0	1.000
Blateric, Redwood	13	1	0	0	0	1.000
Olshane, Visalia	40	9	31	1	1	.976
Havens, Visalia*	28	6	24	1	0	.968
Schroeck, Stockton*	16	3	26	1	3	.967
Conner, Salinas*	14	8	19	1	1	.964
O'Neill, Lodi	46	5	20	1	2	.962
Bain, Lodi	16	6	17	1	1	.958
Witt, Salinas	13	6	15	1	2	.955
Ferst, Lodi	28	6	13	1	2	.950
Jenkins, Stockton	27	9	28	2	3	.949
Black, San Jose*	32	6	12	1	1	.947
Ronnenbergh, Reno	11	4	14	1	1	.947
Koontz, Stockton	39	3	14	1	2	.944
Wyrick, Reno	49	2	14	1	0	.941
Kittrell, Fresno	24	6	39	3	0	.938
Hawkins, Reno	26	12	32	3	4	.936
Sander, Lodi	25	8	21	2	1	.935
Jones, Stockton	11	6	8	1	1	.933

PITCHERS—Continued

Player and Club	G.	PO.	A.	E.	DP.	Pct.
Dugger, Salinas	13	5	9	1	0	.933
Cyburt, Redwood*	29	14	41	4	1	.932
Marietta, Fresno	37	8	19	2	2	.931
Mantsch, Modesto	46	7	20	2	1	.931
Pisel, Fresno	24	9	29	3	4	.927
Reeves, Lodi*	26	4	20	2	1	.923
Kromy, Visalia	28	10	37	4	3	.922
Beene, Stockton	15	3	8	1	0	.917
Sensenbrenner, Fresno*	16	3	18	2	1	.913
Stranski, San Jose	27	20	31	5	3	.911
Hamm, Reno	25	17	24	4	1	.911
Hoban, Redwood	13	6	14	2	1	.909
Batten, San Jose	29	3	17	2	1	.909
Woods, Red-Lodi	21	11	8	2	3	.905
Johnson, Reno*	18	12	16	3	1	.903
Buckley, Salinas	30	5	13	2	0	.900
Arrieta, Visalia	12	4	14	2	0	.900
Danielson, Reno	30	3	15	2	2	.900
Bigos, Redwood	21	0	9	1	0	.900
Krajewski, San Jose	46	9	8	2	0	.895
Moyer, Fresno	12	8	9	2	0	.895
Oroz, Lodi*	26	13	60	9	5	.890
Lindsey, Lodi*	18	4	20	3	0	.889
Madden, Stockton*	29	5	18	3	1	.885
Sijer, Redwood*	42	8	37	6	1	.882
Harris, San Jose	26	8	22	4	1	.882
Ferguson, Modesto	24	4	11	2	0	.882
Hayes, Lodi*	19	3	12	2	0	.882
Alexander, Lodi	15	1	14	2	1	.882
Sutherland, Fresno*	20	6	15	3	2	.875
Cordova, Lodi	29	4	10	2	1	.875
Border, Salinas	20	4	3	1	0	.875
Hinrichs, Fresno	25	1	6	1	1	.875
Dougherty, Modesto	27	8	26	5	2	.872
Buice, Fresno	36	7	20	4	0	.871
Christianson, Redwood	55	6	7	2	1	.867
Corzel, Modesto	22	3	10	2	0	.867
Call, Modesto	3	3	16	3	1	.864
Stottlemyre, San Jose	12	6	12	3	1	.857
Lohuis, Fresno	20	1	5	1	0	.857
Cocanower, Stockton	27	15	40	10	2	.846
Church, Reno*	42	2	9	2	2	.846
Retzer, Modesto	24	8	8	3	1	.842
Moore, Modesto	18	10	11	4	1	.840
Morrison, Salinas	26	3	7	2	0	.833
Moretti, Modesto	40	1	9	2	0	.833
Duran, Salinas	20	2	3	1	0	.833
Thomson, Visalia	12	7	7	3	1	.824
Williams, Fresno	21	7	16	5	3	.821
Cook, Stockton		8	37	10	4	.818
Holloway, Modesto	23	9	9	4	0	.818
Snyder, San Jose	25	9	22	7	1	.816
Bullinger, Visalia*	38	3	10	3	1	.813
Saatzer, Salinas	10	2	6	2	1	.800
Kibbe, Redwood	28	6	19	7	2	.781
Hardwick, Reno	23	9	15	7	1	.774
Ward, Salinas*	35	2	11	4	1	.765
Barba, Reno	44	3	13	5	0	.762
Mooneyham, Salinas	12	7	11	6	0	.750
Terry, Lodi*	10	0	3	1	1	.750
Casarez, Fresno	11	0	3	1	0	.750
Meyer, Stockton*	10	2	3	2	0	.714
Hallgren, San Jose	14	3	16	8	0	.704
Donovan, Stockton	13	0	1	2	0	.333

(Fewer Than Ten Games)

Player and Club	G.	PO.	A.	E.	DP.	Pct.
Owens, Redwood	8	2	11	0	2	1.000
M. Walters, Redwood	9	6	6	0	0	1.000
Froelich, Redwood	9	3	5	0	0	1.000
Regan, Redwood	5	2	6	0	0	1.000
Gosse, Modesto*	7	1	6	0	1	1.000
Anderson, Fresno	7	1	5	0	0	1.000
Goulding, Lodi	5	0	6	0	0	1.000
Wilder, Redwood*	5	1	4	0	0	1.000
Patton, Reno	8	0	5	0	0	1.000
Bullock, Lodi*	8	0	4	0	0	1.000
Kelly, Visalia*	2	0	4	0	0	1.000
Joyce, Lodi*	8	1	1	0	0	1.000
Bryant, Reno*	2	0	2	0	0	1.000
Turpin, Salinas	8	2	1	0	0	1.000
White, Reno	2	0	3	0	0	1.000
Wilson, Reno	8	1	2	0	0	1.000
Couchee, Reno	2	1	0	0	0	1.000
Skaggs, Salinas	9	0	1	0	0	1.000
Lund, Redwood	2	0	1	0	0	1.000
Andersen, Redwood	1	0	1	0	0	1.000
Sax, Lodi	1	0	1	0	1	1.000
Minnick, San Jose*	8	1	11	1	1	.923
Prevost, Redwood*	8	3	7	1	1	.909
Sylvia, Salinas	6	5	9	2	0	.875
Steger, San Jose	7	2	4	2	0	.750
McGee, San Jose	2	1	2	1	1	.750
Krueger, San Jose*	8	0	7	3	0	.700
White, Lodi*	3	1	0	1	0	.500
Arrington, Visalia	2	1	0	1	0	.500

The following players do not have any recorded accepted chances at the positions indicated; therefore, are not listed in the fielding averages for those particular positions: Aldrich, p; Argee*, p; Anderson*, of; Bailey, of; Benson, of; Chelette, of; Fagely*, p; Gonsalves, p; Graser*, p; Hernandez, of; Hood, 3b-p; Hudson, 3b; Krajewski, 3b-of; Kyzer, 3b; Lanning, p; Manning, ss; Martin, of; Miller, 1b-of; Minnick, p; O'Connor, p; Oliver, of; Rabb, 3b-of; Randolph, of-p; Robins, 3b; Slettvet, p; Spillane, 2b-p; Spurlin, of; Sutton, 3b; Thys, ss; Valle, p; Woodward, of; Woods, of.

CLUB PITCHING

Club	G.	CG.	ShO.	Sv.	IP.	H.	R.	ER.	HR.	BB.	Int. BB.	HB.	SO.	WP.	Bk.	ERA.
Stockton	141	34	10	15	1215	1044	551	429	58	632	14	47	837	69	19	3.18
Fresno	140	36	14	33	1149	1124	581	467	50	515	2	53	780	84	6	3.66
Modesto	139	38	6	15	1202	1151	641	491	86	721	36	39	797	62	6	3.68
San Jose	139	37	13	17	1180	1076	631	516	49	650	22	42	770	92	13	3.94
Visalia	140	39	7	28	1196	1278	689	548	80	560	16	31	756	76	5	4.12
Reno	141	38	8	23	1190	1261	705	550	100	599	45	35	774	97	5	4.16
Salinas	140	35	6	18	1147	1183	708	546	62	658	14	48	831	93	10	4.28
Redwood	140	21	3	8	1158	1286	826	653	111	722	12	42	690	71	8	5.08
Lodi	140	33	1	23	1166	1350	895	699	102	721	13	42	679	119	10	5.40

PITCHERS' RECORDS

(Leading Qualifiers for Earned-Run Average Leadership—112 or More Innings)

*Throws lefthanded.

Pitcher—Club	G.	GS.	CG.	ShO.	W.	L.	Sv.	Pct.	IP.	H.	R.	ER.	HR.	BB.	Int. BB.	HB.	SO.	WP.	ERA.
Madden, Stockton*	29	12	5	0	12	4	2	.750	134	88	46	29	4	63	0	3	92	5	1.95
Cocanower, Stockton	27	27	10	1	17	5	0	.773	198	143	74	48	6	105	0	11	132	11	2.18
Wood, Modesto	21	18	4	1	6	9	0	.400	118	96	55	35	9	78	1	3	45	2	2.67
Stranski, San Jose	27	27	10	4	18	5	0	.783	198	131	78	59	13	118	1	8	139	14	2.68
Holloway, Modesto	23	23	10	0	12	8	0	.600	165	138	79	57	9	105	5	7	141	10	3.11
Hamm, Reno	27	25	9	3	15	7	0	.682	179	203	82	62	9	42	8	3	122	4	3.12
Cook, Stockton	27	27	4	0	8	6	0	.571	166	161	84	58	12	96	1	7	97	14	3.14
Dougherty, Modesto	27	16	5	0	5	9	1	.357	142	150	75	52	10	54	5	1	78	2	3.30
Williams, Fresno	21	18	1	1	12	3	0	.800	114	105	53	42	3	70	1	18	80	9	3.32
Havens, Visalia*	28	28	12	3	14	9	0	.609	195	186	90	72	11	82	0	5	179	7	3.32

Departmental Leaders: G—Smith, 57; GS—Havens, Kromy, 28; CG—Havens, 12; ShO—Stranski, 4; W—Stranski, 18; L—Cyburt, Oroz, 13; Sv—Hinrichs, O'Neill, 15; Pct.—Call, .846; IP—Cocanower, Stranski, 198; H—Hamm, 203; R—Reeves, 111; ER—Reeves, 86; HR—Peterson, 19; BB—Stranski, 118; IBB—Wyrick, 10; HP—Williams, 18; SO—Havens, 179; WP—Hardwick, 27.

(All Pitchers—Listed Alphabetically)

Pitcher—Club	G.	GS.	CG.	ShO.	W.	L.	Sv.	Pct.	IP.	H.	R.	ER.	HR.	BB.	Int. BB.	HB.	SO.	WP.	ERA.
Aldrich, Redwood	1	0	0	0	0	0	0	.000	1	3	3	2	0	2	0	0	2	1	18.00
Alexander, Fresno*	11	11	5	1	7	3	0	.700	73	79	32	29	4	27	0	5	32	8	3.58
Alexander, Lodi	15	15	1	0	1	7	0	.125	81	115	81	64	5	55	0	3	49	9	7.11
Andersen, Redwood	1	1	0	0	0	0	0	.000	1	4	4	4	0	4	0	1	1	1	36.00
Anderson, Redwood	7	0	0	0	1	0	0	1.000	21	25	17	14	1	12	0	1	11	4	6.00
Angulo, Visalia*	19	9	1	0	4	2	0	.667	70	81	42	37	6	45	2	0	44	6	4.76
Argee, Redwood*	3	0	0	0	0	1	0	.000	3	2	1	1	0	1	0	0	1	2	3.00
Arrieta, Visalia	12	11	2	1	3	6	0	.333	71	87	50	40	10	18	1	1	43	4	5.07
Arrington, Visalia	2	1	0	0	0	0	0	.000	6	6	1	1	0	3	0	0	5	0	1.50
Bain, Lodi	16	16	7	0	4	7	0	.364	115	120	73	61	9	56	0	2	56	14	4.77
Barba, Reno	44	1	0	0	3	6	6	.333	77	83	56	37	4	61	2	2	69	9	4.32
Batten, San Jose	29	7	1	1	4	1	0	.800	98	87	39	25	3	29	0	2	65	0	2.30
Beene, Stockton	15	12	0	0	2	1	0	.667	58	46	34	28	3	43	0	2	53	9	4.34
Bigos, Redwood	21	4	0	0	0	5	0	.000	45	67	41	26	8	29	0	1	31	3	5.20
Biko, Visalia*	12	9	2	1	4	2	0	.667	68	62	22	16	2	40	3	0	38	3	2.12
Black, San Jose*	32	5	4	0	5	3	0	.625	86	67	34	33	4	49	2	2	73	5	3.45
Blateric, Redwood	13	1	0	0	2	0	0	1.000	26	16	12	7	0	20	2	0	23	0	4.15
Border, Salinas	20	2	0	0	1	2	0	.333	36	51	34	29	0	21	1	0	34	2	7.25
Brokop, Redwood	11	8	1	1	1	4	0	.200	48	55	31	29	4	34	0	1	14	2	5.44
Brown, Salinas	20	5	1	0	7	3	0	.700	73	80	32	24	3	19	2	2	28	4	2.96
Bryant, Reno*	2	1	0	0	0	0	0	.000	5	6	3	2	0	5	0	0	5	2	3.60
Buckley, Salinas	30	14	3	1	6	7	2	.462	117	119	99	79	6	85	0	8	101	14	6.08
Buice, Fresno	36	6	2	0	7	4	0	.636	100	101	42	37	6	38	0	2	88	7	3.33
Bullinger, Visalia*	38	0	0	0	8	5	10	.615	62	60	28	23	6	32	2	2	60	7	3.34
Bullock, Lodi*	8	0	0	0	0	0	0	.000	18	23	22	13	0	19	1	0	10	3	6.50
Call, Modesto	17	17	4	1	11	2	0	.846	115	113	52	46	13	59	0	5	71	8	3.60
Casarez, Fresno	11	2	0	0	1	2	0	.333	35	31	22	17	1	33	0	1	29	7	4.37
Christianson, Redwood	55	0	0	0	7	3	0	.700	87	107	54	47	7	46	2	4	53	3	4.86
Church, Reno*	42	0	0	0	3	5	5	.375	51	43	22	17	5	31	8	1	42	3	3.00
Cocanower, Stockton	27	27	10	1	17	5	0	.773	198	143	74	48	6	105	0	11	132	11	2.18
Conner, Salinas*	14	14	6	1	9	3	0	.750	95	93	42	31	1	43	1	2	55	13	2.94
Cook, Stockton	27	27	4	0	8	6	0	.571	166	161	84	58	12	96	1	7	97	14	3.14
Cordova, Lodi	29	0	0	0	3	6	0	.333	49	47	26	20	2	38	4	5	38	11	3.67
Corzel, Modesto	22	13	1	0	3	4	0	.429	90	121	73	60	15	50	2	3	43	10	6.00
Couchee, Reno	2	0	0	0	0	1	0	.000	2	2	3	2	0	1	0	0	2	0	9.00
Cyburt, Redwood*	29	20	6	1	6	13	0	.316	131	147	99	73	13	91	2	4	56	10	5.02
Danielson, Reno	30	8	2	1	5	6	2	.455	94	115	63	55	10	41	5	7	41	7	5.27
Diaz, Stockton	35	2	0	0	2	4	5	.333	81	93	52	44	8	31	6	5	35	3	4.89
Dugger, Salinas	13	13	5	2	5	7	0	.417	82	53	29	24	4	46	0	1	86	3	2.63
Donovan, Stockton	13	0	0	0	3	2	1	.600	25	28	14	14	1	10	2	1	18	3	5.04
Dougherty, Modesto*	27	16	5	0	5	9	1	.357	142	150	75	52	10	54	5	1	78	2	3.30
Duran, Salinas	20	0	0	0	4	2	9	.667	35	21	9	9	0	23	0	2	28	3	2.31
Fagely, Visalia*	4	0	0	0	2	0	0	.000	8	13	12	10	3	4	0	4	1	33	11.25
Ferguson, Modesto	24	24	7	3	10	10	0	.500	162	149	85	67	7	104	5	4	120	8	3.72
Ferst, Lodi	28	11	1	0	5	7	0	.417	103	142	102	69	10	58	2	3	50	16	6.03
Fowlkes, Fresno	18	9	7	2	5	5	0	.500	88	69	26	20	2	16	0	4	90	3	2.05
Froelich, Redwood	9	8	0	0	0	0	0	.000	32	40	24	18	3	14	0	1	20	3	5.06
Gibson, Stockton	33	1	0	0	6	3	1	.667	67	45	32	29	2	58	0	4	59	10	3.90
Gonsalves, Fresno	1	0	0	0	0	0	0	.000	1	1	0	0	0	1	0	0	0	0	0.00
Gosse, Modesto*	7	0	0	0	2	0	4	1.000	11	4	0	0	0	3	0	1	9	1	0.00
Goulding, Lodi	5	0	0	0	0	0	0	.000	16	19	12	11	2	10	0	7	0	6.19
Graser, San Jose*	1	1	0	0	0	1	0	.000	3	5	9	7	4	3	0	3	0	21.00
Hallgren, San Jose	14	13	2	1	4	6	0	.400	77	75	45	36	5	31	0	1	45	3	4.21

Pitcher–Club	G.	GS.	CG.	ShO.	W.	L.	Sv.	Pct.	IP.	H.	R.	ER.	HR.	BB.	Int. BB.	HB.	SO.	WP.	ERA.
Hamm, Reno	25	25	9	3	15	7	0	.682	179	203	82	62	9	42	8	3	122	4	3.12
Hardwick, Reno	23	23	1	0	6	7	0	.462	128	124	96	74	10	98	1	7	79	27	5.20
Harris, San Jose	26	18	7	1	10	5	0	.667	136	130	78	65	2	93	2	4	76	15	4.30
Havens, Visalia*	28	28	12	3	14	9	0	.609	195	186	90	72	11	82	0	5	179	7	3.32
Hawkins, Reno	26	26	10	2	13	10	0	.565	171	183	108	81	13	79	4	5	124	11	4.26
Hayes, Lodi*	19	6	2	0	4	3	1	.571	55	75	66	58	3	60	0	0	35	10	9.49
Hinrichs, Fresno	25	0	0	0	1	2	15	.333	47	29	15	7	2	13	0	1	39	1	1.34
Hoban, Redwood	13	9	2	0	1	8	0	.111	68	73	49	36	8	38	0	2	37	3	4.76
Holloway, Modesto	23	23	10	0	12	8	0	.600	165	138	79	57	9	105	5	7	141	10	3.11
Hood, San Jose	1	0	0	0	0	1	0	.000	1	2	3	3	0	3	0	0	0	2	27.00
Jannusch, Reno	10	10	4	0	4	5	0	.444	66	84	45	44	11	32	1	1	39	7	6.00
Jenkins, Stockton	27	27	8	2	15	10	0	.600	177	168	88	75	11	83	1	7	99	4	3.81
Johnson, Reno*	18	18	2	1	5	5	0	.500	110	114	61	45	9	39	2	3	58	4	3.68
Jones, Stockton	11	11	5	1	6	2	0	.750	76	63	32	24	2	31	1	3	54	0	2.84
Jones, Visalia*	34	17	3	0	7	7	4	.500	147	168	91	71	6	93	1	2	65	15	4.35
Joyce, Lodi*	8	3	0	0	2	0	0	.000	9	12	12	12	1	22	0	4	3	5	10.80
Kelly, Visalia*	2	1	0	0	0	0	0	.000	13	12	1	1	0	6	1	0	2	1	0.69
Kenyon, Lodi	12	4	0	0	0	5	1	.000	37	52	36	30	9	18	0	1	20	0	7.30
Kibbe, Redwood	28	20	2	0	5	9	2	.357	138	161	88	69	7	79	0	2	86	11	4.50
Kittrell, Fresno*	24	23	4	1	10	10	0	.500	146	162	89	68	10	47	0	4	81	7	4.19
Knight, San Jose	44	1	0	0	4	5	9	.444	73	74	37	31	4	26	5	5	43	5	3.82
Koontz, Stockton	39	0	0	0	12	3	4	.800	89	83	29	24	6	31	0	2	91	3	2.43
Krajewski, San Jose	46	0	0	0	4	6	4	.400	73	75	28	25	3	29	8	3	41	7	3.08
Kromy, Visalia	28	28	9	2	12	12	0	.500	196	200	108	75	9	68	1	5	113	13	3.44
Krueger, San Jose*	8	8	2	1	4	2	0	.667	52	52	30	28	3	17	1	1	43	1	4.85
Lanning, Lodi	1	0	0	0	0	0	0	.000	4	4	3	1	0	3	0	0	0	0	2.25
Lindsey, Salinas*	24	16	4	0	1	11	0	.083	105	123	84	54	15	61	0	8	50	5	4.63
Lindsey, Lodi*	18	12	6	0	6	5	1	.545	103	112	61	47	7	42	0	2	69	2	4.11
Lohuis, Fresno	20	0	0	0	1	3	6	.250	34	36	19	19	3	17	0	0	21	4	5.03
Lund, Redwood	2	2	0	0	0	1	0	.000	11	9	9	9	1	10	0	1	10	1	7.36
Madden, Stockton*	29	12	5	0	12	4	2	.750	134	88	46	29	4	63	0	3	92	5	1.95
Mantsch, Modesto	46	0	0	0	8	4	5	.667	73	67	24	20	5	27	9	2	33	1	2.47
Marietta, Fresno	37	1	0	0	4	4	5	.500	100	95	47	43	8	34	0	10	57	4	3.87
McGee, San Jose	2	2	0	0	0	0	0	.000	12	10	8	3	0	7	0	0	6	3	2.25
Meyer, Stockton*	10	0	0	0	1	1	2	.500	19	19	8	7	0	10	0	0	10	2	3.32
Minnick, San Jose*	8	8	2	0	3	4	0	.429	44	35	30	28	2	60	0	2	31	9	5.73
Mooneyham, Salinas	12	12	5	0	4	7	0	.364	74	66	44	31	3	64	1	3	88	7	3.77
Moore, Modesto	18	17	6	0	4	6	0	.400	109	107	72	56	9	84	2	7	72	7	4.62
Moretti, Modesto	40	0	0	0	4	9	3	.308	74	69	40	27	1	54	5	1	76	7	3.28
Morrison, Salinas	26	1	0	0	3	2	3	.600	66	51	23	13	2	20	1	2	76	4	1.77
Moyer, Fresno	12	12	5	2	4	7	0	.364	79	76	39	27	1	33	0	1	64	3	3.08
Murray, San Jose	34	8	4	2	7	10	4	.412	101	79	32	26	4	28	1	0	52	8	2.32
O'Connor, Visalia	1	0	0	0	0	0	0	.000	3	4	3	3	0	5	0	0	2	0	9.00
Oliver, Fresno	2	0	0	0	0	0	0	.000	1	0	0	0	0	2	0	0	1	0	0.00
Olshane, Visalia	40	12	5	0	9	10	8	.474	128	138	66	57	8	43	1	7	84	7	4.01
O'Neill, Lodi	46	0	0	0	5	4	15	.556	78	98	55	40	3	32	4	3	61	5	4.62
Oroz, Lodi*	26	25	10	1	6	13	0	.316	177	186	102	76	12	86	0	5	187	14	3.86
Owens, Redwood	8	8	4	1	5	3	0	.625	56	55	31	22	9	30	0	2	45	2	3.54
Park, Stockton	11	6	0	0	3	2	0	.600	35	26	10	9	0	9	1	0	32	1	2.31
Patton, Reno	8	4	0	0	1	3	0	.250	22	34	24	21	4	19	0	0	5	2	8.59
Peterson, Red-Reno	28	17	3	0	8	9	0	.471	132	132	87	79	19	84	1	4	93	9	5.39
Pisel, Fresno	24	24	5	1	13	8	0	.619	146	157	85	66	3	67	0	2	84	14	4.07
Prevost, Redwood*	8	7	0	0	2	3	0	.400	34	34	22	17	2	33	0	0	22	2	4.50
Ramirez, Visalia	15	0	0	0	0	1	0	.000	29	37	25	17	2	11	2	1	11	1	5.28
Randolph, San Jose	1	0	0	0	0	0	0	.000	1	1	1	1	0	1	0	1	0	0	9.00
Rasmussen, Salinas*	11	11	4	1	4	6	0	.400	76	69	51	46	6	52	0	4	63	8	5.45
Reeves, Lodi*	26	22	3	0	5	11	1	.313	117	130	111	96	17	76	0	5	86	11	6.62
Regan, Redwood	5	4	0	0	1	3	0	.250	24	25	19	14	6	11	0	0	22	0	5.25
Retzer, Modesto	24	10	3	0	4	4	1	.500	96	75	53	38	5	67	1	3	80	4	3.56
Riley, Visalia	22	13	2	0	5	7	1	.417	88	91	69	56	8	67	0	5	42	7	5.73
Ronnenbergh, Reno	11	11	6	1	5	4	0	.556	87	65	28	22	3	40	3	1	53	2	2.28
Saatzer, Salinas	10	10	2	0	4	8	0	.000	43	69	55	46	6	44	0	3	13	4	9.63
Sander, Lodi	25	21	3	0	13	7	0	.650	141	144	82	73	15	95	1	5	68	8	4.66
Sax, Lodi	1	0	0	0	0	0	0	.000	5	8	4	5	3	2	0	0	0	0	9.00
Schroeck, Stockton*	16	16	2	0	3	8	0	.273	90	80	48	40	3	62	2	2	65	4	4.00
Sensenbrenner, Fresno*	16	15	4	2	5	7	0	.417	77	66	30	22	2	46	0	2	49	5	2.57
Sijer, Redwood*	42	18	2	0	8	11	0	.421	139	152	99	72	8	76	4	13	74	10	4.66
Skaggs, Salinas	9	0	0	0	0	0	0	.000	17	21	19	11	2	20	0	0	11	0	5.82
Slettvet, Reno	2	0	0	0	0	0	0	.000	4	5	3	1	0	4	0	0	4	0	2.25
Smith, Redwood	57	1	0	0	5	5	1	.500	76	86	68	52	2	70	4	2	36	7	6.16
Snyder, San Jose*	25	23	3	2	7	5	0	.583	127	139	96	80	3	92	0	6	97	11	5.67
Spillane, Redwood	1	0	0	0	0	0	0	.000	⅓	2	1	1	0	1	0	0	0	0	27.00
Steger, San Jose	7	7	0	0	0	1	0	.000	32	40	42	33	1	26	0	3	19	3	9.28
Stottlemyre, San Jose	12	11	2	1	3	6	0	.333	66	73	41	34	1	31	2	3	35	6	4.64
Stranski, San Jose	27	27	10	4	18	5	0	.783	198	131	78	59	13	118	1	8	139	14	2.68

Pitcher–Club	G.	GS.	CG.	ShO.	W.	L.	Sv.	Pct.	IP.	H.	R.	ER.	HR.	BB.	Int. BB.	HB.	SO.	WP.	ERA.
Sutherland, Fresno*	20	19	4	1	3	8	0	.273	88	92	65	56	4	59	0	2	54	9	5.73
Sylvia, Salinas	6	6	2	0	3	2	0	.600	43	32	22	21	1	26	0	2	35	9	4.40
Terry, Lodi*	10	0	0	0	1	1	0	.500	19	29	21	14	1	17	0	1	14	4	6.63
Thomson, Visalia	12	9	3	0	1	6	1	.143	63	71	38	30	3	18	2	1	23	4	4.29
Tirella, Visalia*	19	2	1	0	4	0	0	1.000	47	62	43	39	6	25	0	2	41	1	7.47
Turpin, Salinas	8	0	0	0	0	1	0	.000	19	24	13	12	1	15	2	0	7	1	5.68
Valle, San Jose	1	0	0	0	0	0	0	.000	1	1	0	0	0	2	0	1	2	0	0.00
Van Marter, Modesto	23	1	0	0	5	0	1	1.000	48	62	33	31	3	36	0	3	29	2	5.81
Venezia, Salinas	21	18	3	0	3	10	0	.231	99	139	86	67	2	44	2	4	30	5	6.09
Wagner, Reno	17	8	0	0	6	3	1	.667	68	91	45	40	10	24	0	1	42	2	5.29
J. Walters, Redwood	10	4	0	0	0	4	2	.000	33	30	26	23	3	27	0	2	19	1	6.27
M. Walters, Redwood	9	7	1	0	2	2	0	.500	49	56	36	34	7	20	0	1	29	1	6.24
Ward, Salinas*	35	5	0	0	4	5	2	.444	77	87	51	32	4	51	1	5	45	8	3.74
White, Reno	2	2	1	0	2	0	0	1.000	14	14	8	7	1	2	0	0	11	3	4.50
White, Lodi*	3	2	0	0	0	2	0	.000	6	8	7	7	1	7	0	0	2	0	10.50
Wilder, Redwood*	5	3	2	0	2	1	0	.667	26	19	9	8	2	11	0	0	15	1	2.77
Williams, Fresno	21	18	1	1	12	3	0	.800	114	105	53	42	3	70	1	18	80	9	3.32
Wilson, Reno	8	2	0	0	1	0	1	1.000	20	24	26	19	6	19	0	0	12	0	8.55
Witt, Salinas	13	13	3	0	7	3	0	.700	90	85	30	21	6	35	0	3	76	4	2.10
Wood, Modesto	21	18	4	1	6	9	0	.400	118	96	55	35	9	78	1	3	45	2	2.67
Woods, Redwood-Lodi	21	3	1	0	5	2	2	.714	49	44	36	22	3	38	2	3	39	7	4.04
Wyrick, Reno	49	0	0	0	5	4	7	.556	73	53	28	17	3	53	10	4	54	10	2.10

BALKS—Cocanower, 6; Oroz, Snyder, 5 each; Madden, 4; R. Alexander, Havens, Mooneyham, Murray, Schroeck, 3 each; P. Alexander, Arrieta, Black, Danielson, Park, 2 each; Batten, Blateric, Brokop, C. Brown, Buckley, Buice, Bullock, Casarez, Cordova, Corzel, Cyburt, Diaz, Duran, Hallgren, Hawkins, Holloway, Jannusch, Kibbe, Kittrell, Lanning, Mantsch, Moore, Moyer, O'Neill, Peterson (Redwood), Prevost, Rasmussen, Retzer, Skaggs, Smith, Stottlemyre, Terry, Turpin, Wagner, J. Walters, Witt, Wood, 1 each.

COMBINATION SHUTOUTS—Marietta-Hinrichs, Pisel-Lohuis, Sensenbrenner-Hinrichs, Fresno; Wood-Dougherty, Modesto; Witt-Duran, Salinas; Cook-Meyer, Jenkins-Koontz, Madden-Beene, Park-Donovan, Park-Koontz, Schroeck-Koontz, Stockton.

NO-HIT GAME—Snyder, San Jose, defeated Modesto, 4-0, June 24.

Undisputed King of Thiefs

Alan Wiggins of Lodi became the undisputed base stealing king of professional baseball when he swiped 120 bases in 135 games, breaking the previous modern minor league mark of 116 set by Allan Lewis in the Florida State League in 1966, and the major league mark of 118 set by Lou Brock of the Cardinals in 1974.

Since 1900, only one man has stolen more bases in a single season. Jim Johnston of San Francisco recorded 124 steals in the Pacific Coast League in 1913, but he played in 65 more games than Wiggins did in 1980.

Stevenson's 7-for-7 Sparked Record

Reno of the California League defeated Visalia in a record-breaking 25-3 massacre July 1 without hitting a home run. Reno batters collected 21 singles to break the league record of 19, set by Visalia in 1951. The Silver Sox had 28 hits, tying their own league mark set in 1966. Every Reno player scored a run, got a base hit and drove in a run.

Shortstop John Stevenson became the first man in league history to get seven hits in one game. Stevenson, who drove in four runs and scored four more, raised his average from .269 to .289.

Carolina League

CLASS A

CHAMPIONSHIP WINNERS IN PREVIOUS YEARS

1945—Danville .... .681	1959—Raleigh .... .600	1969—Rocky M (East.).............. .569
1946—Greensboro.................... .599	Wilson (2nd)†................ .550	Salem (West.)................ .542
Raleigh (2nd)† .... .563	1960—Greensboro‡............... .636	Ral-Dur z (East.)........... .560
1947—Burlington..................... .613	Burlington..................... .586	1970—Winston-Salem‡......... .586
Raleigh (3rd)†............... .574	1961—Wilson....................... .594	Burlington.................... .597
1948—Raleigh .... .592	1962—Durham .... .636	1971—Peninsula‡................. .647
Martinsville (2nd)†....... .570	Wilson......................... .600	Kinston........................ .623
1949—Danville .... .601	Kinston (2nd)†.............. .593	1972—Salem‡..................... .657
Burlington (4th)† 500	1963—Kinston§ .... .538	Burlington.................... .632
1950—Winston-Salem* .... .693	Greensboro§................ .590	1973—Lynchburg............... .588
1951—Durham .... .600	Wilson (2nd)†................ .535	Winston-Salem‡.......... .557
Wins-Salem (2nd)†....... .583	1964—Kinston§ .... .572	1974—Salem..................... .671
1952—Raleigh .... .581	Winston-Salem§†......... .590	Salem........................ .582
Reidsville (4th)†........... .536	1965—Peninsula§............... .597	1975—Rocky Mount .... .667
1953—Raleigh .... .593	Durham§...................... .580	Rocky Mount .... .614
Danville (2nd)† .... .572	Tidewater†................... .528	1976—Winston-Salem .... .618
1954—Fayetteville* .... .628	1966—Kinston§ .... .547	Winston-Salem .... .551
1955—HP-Thomasville .... .580	Winston-Salem§............ .586	1977—Lynchburg‡.............. .5¢1
Danville (2nd)† .... .533	Rocky Mount†............... .533	Peninsula‡................... .556
1956—HP-Thomasville .... .591	1967—Durham x (West.)....... .536	1978—Peninsula................ .696
Fayetteville (4th)† .... .523	Raleigh (East.)............. .542	Lynchburg‡.................. .614
1957—Durham .... .632	1968—Salem (West.).......... .607	1979—Winston-Salem a.......... .607
HP-Thomasville .... .622	Ral-Dur (East.)............. .597	
1958—Danville .... .576	H P-Thom. y (W.)........... .493	
Burlington (4th)† .... .511		

*Won championship and four-club playoff. †Won four-club playoff. ‡Won split-season playoff. §League was divided into Eastern, Western divisions. xWon eight-club, two-division playoff.
yWon eight-club, two-division playoff against Raleigh-Durham.
zWon eight-club, two-division playoff against Burlington. aWon both halves of split-season (no playoffs).

STANDING OF CLUBS AT CLOSE OF FIRST HALF, JUNE 19

NORTH CAROLINA DIVISION						VIRGINIA DIVISION					
Club	W.	L.	T.	Pct.	G.B.	Club	W.	L.	T.	Pct.	G.B.
Durham (Braves).....................	42	28	0	.600	......	Peninsula (Phillies)	51	19	0	.729	......
Kinston (Blue Jays).................	38	32	0	.543	4	Lynchburg (Mets)	35	35	0	.500	16
Winston-Salem (Red Sox)	38	32	0	.543	4	Salem (Pirates)	33	36	1	.478	17½
Rocky Mount (Independent) ...	14	55	1	.203	27½	Alexandria (Co-op).................	28	42	0	.400	23

STANDING OF CLUBS AT CLOSE OF SECOND HALF, AUGUST 31

NORTH CAROLINA DIVISION						VIRGINIA DIVISION					
Club	W.	L.	T.	Pct.	G.B.	Club	W.	L.	T.	Pct.	G.B.
Durham (Braves).....................	42	28	0	.600	......	Peninsula (Phillies)	49	21	0	.700	......
Winston-Salem (Red Sox)	38	32	0	.543	4	Salem (Pirates)	46	24	0	.657	3
Kinston (Blue Jays)	31	37	1	.456	10	Lynchburg (Mets)	36	33	1	.522	12½
Rocky Mount (Independent)	10	59	0	.145	31½	Alexandria (Co-op).................	26	44	0	.371	23

COMPOSITE STANDING OF CLUBS AT CLOSE OF SEASON, AUGUST 31

Club	Pen.	Dur.	Sal.	W.-S.	Lyn.	Kin.	Alex.	R.M.	W.	L.	T.	Pct.	G.B.
Peninsula (Phillies)	..	11	13	13	13	15	17	18	100	40	0	.714	......
Durham (Braves)	9	..	11	11	12	12	11	18	84	56	0	.600	16
Salem (Pirates)	7	9	..	10	13	10	15	15	79	60	1	.568	20½
Winston-Salem (Red Sox)	7	9	10	..	13	9	13	15	76	64	0	.543	24
Lynchburg (Mets)...........	7	8	7	7	..	11	17	14	71	68	1	.511	28½
Kinston (Blue Jays)	5	8	10	11	8	..	10	17	69	69	1	.500	30
Alexandria (Co-op)	3	9	5	7	3	10	..	17	54	86	0	.386	46
Rocky Mount (Independent)	2	2	4	5	6	2	3	..	24	114	1	.174	75

Major League affiliations in parentheses.

Peninsula represented Hampton, Va.

Playoffs—Peninsula, Virginia Division, defeated Durham, North Carolina Division, three games to none for League Championship.

Regular-Season Attendance—Alexandria, 30,140; Durham, 175,963; Kinston, 38,822; Lynchburg, 66,207; Peninsula, 75,874; Rocky Mount, 26,702; Salem, 102,456; Winston-Salem, 84,645. Total, 600,809. Playoffs, 6,082. All-star game, 1,299.

Managers: Alexander—Mike Toomey; Durham—Al Gallagher; Kinston—Dennis Holmberg; Lynchburg—Jack Aker; Peninsula—Bill Dancy; Rocky Mount—Mal Fichman; Salem—John Lipon; Winston-Salem—Harold Hunter.

All-Star Team: 1B—Anicich, Lynchburg; 2B—Rittweger, Lynchburg; 3B—Borucki, Peninsula; SS—Franco, Peninsula; OF—Bruno, Peninsula; Culmer, Peninsula; Hall, Durham; C—Colbert, Winston-Salem; DH—Brooks, Winston-Salem; P—Fredlund, Winston-Salem; Goff, Peninsula; Smith, Peninsula; Manager—Lipon, Salem.

(Compiled by Montague Statistics, Winston-Salem, N.C.)

CLUB BATTING

Club	G.	AB.	R.	OR.	H.	TB.	2B.	3B.	HR.	RBI.	SH.	SF.	Int. BB.	BB.	HP.	SO.	SB.	CS.	LOB.	Pct.
Peninsula	140	4502	783	469	1242	1739	177	43	78	652	50	51	541	26	43	634	257	96	930	.276
Salem	140	4530	686	586	1213	1788	212	54	85	599	55	46	598	25	38	757	211	86	1010	.268
Kinston	139	4560	618	616	1211	1654	177	46	58	536	47	55	484	26	35	824	137	70	994	.266
Durham	140	4613	744	635	1213	1714	173	38	84	634	33	44	703	33	54	724	210	109	1099	.263
Lynchburg	140	4460	638	621	1132	1591	184	40	65	543	69	53	616	26	42	739	136	68	1018	.254
Winston-Salem	140	4521	691	599	1143	1639	166	30	90	608	22	37	712	33	53	963	156	35	1147	.253
Alexandria	140	4480	522	694	1060	1443	145	32	58	471	41	36	587	20	44	763	121	52	1101	.237
Rocky Mount	139	4446	375	837	962	1201	138	19	21	312	54	17	486	12	23	941	64	44	1004	.216

INDIVIDUAL BATTING

(Leading Qualifiers for Batting Championship—378 or More Plate Appearances)

*Bats lefthanded. †Switch-hitter.

Player and Club	G.	AB.	R.	H.	TB.	2B.	3B.	HR.	RBI.	SH.	SF.	BB.	HP.	SO.	SB.	CS.	Pct.
Culmer, Wilfred, Peninsula	139	498	112	184	276	28	5	18	93	0	3	64	6	72	26	14	.369
Brooks, Craig, Winston-Salem*	132	447	96	146	250	20	6	24	83	0	4	104	7	114	24	4	.327
Franco, Julio, Peninsula	140	555	105	178	248	25	6	11	99	3	10	33	8	66	44	12	.321
de la Rosa, Bienvenido, Salem*	108	382	60	122	176	12	15	4	39	5	1	32	4	63	29	12	.319
Tillman, Kerry, Lynchburg	135	526	94	166	239	27	11	8	79	3	4	46	1	90	43	8	.316
Bruno, Joseph, Peninsula*	132	492	102	150	204	17	11	5	61	6	13	81	2	21	53	17	.305
Ereu, William, Kinston	108	418	64	125	156	15	0	8	39	6	3	19	5	48	20	8	.299
Riemer, Mark, Salem	102	356	53	106	144	17	3	5	53	2	1	50	7	68	7	10	.298
Csefalvay, John, Lynchburg	132	481	90	139	201	30	7	6	54	5	4	102	3	73	22	15	.289
Rodriguez, Jose, Salem	126	459	68	132	219	24	12	13	75	3	6	47	8	90	31	11	.288

Departmental Leaders: G—Borucki, Culmer, Franco, 140; AB—Franco, 555; R—Culmer, 112; H—Culmer, 184; TB—Culmer, 276; 2B—Csefalvay, 30; 3B—de la Rosa, 15; HR—Brooks, 24; RBI—Franco, 99; GWRBI—Borucki, 17; SH—Oquendo, 13; SF—Anicich, Bruno, 13; BB—Brooks, 104; HP—Hall, 9; SO—Colbert, 132; SB—Hall, 104; CS—Hall, 27.

(All Players—Listed Alphabetically)

Player and Club	G.	AB.	R.	H.	TB.	2B.	3B.	HR.	RBI.	SH.	SF.	BB.	HP.	SO.	SB.	CS.	Pct.
Anicich, Michael, Lynchburg	130	447	74	119	205	20	0	22	73	4	13	69	6	77	1	1	.266
Bardin, Timothy, Rocky Mount*	22	55	2	9	10	1	0	0	2	2	0	8	1	11	1	0	.164
Behenna, Richard, Durham	27	1	0	0	0	0	0	0	0	0	0	0	0	1	0	0	.000
Berroa, Eduardo, Winston-Salem	60	140	14	20	23	3	0	0	5	2	0	6	2	35	2	0	.143
Bill, Robert, Rocky Mount	1	0	0	0	0	0	0	0	0	0	0	0	0	0	0	0	.000
Bockhorn, Glen, Durham	105	370	61	79	145	17	2	15	69	0	8	54	5	95	2	0	.214
Borucki, Raymond, Peninsula	140	511	91	137	195	20	4	10	86	3	2	71	2	39	23	13	.268
Bowman, Bruss, Alexandria*	55	201	22	46	66	6	1	4	18	2	1	15	3	43	0	1	.229
Bowman, Donald, Alexandria	15	53	8	12	24	1	1	3	10	0	1	6	2	12	0	0	.226
Boyce, Robert, Alexandria	107	337	26	71	84	11	1	0	26	8	4	41	6	55	3	1	.211
Bradley, Otis, Rocky Mount†	84	281	24	50	61	3	1	2	15	5	0	28	2	107	11	6	.178
Breeden, Joseph, Rocky Mount	95	246	9	47	52	5	0	0	11	5	2	23	0	78	0	1	.191
Bresnen, Robert, Rocky Mount†	12	1	0	0	0	0	0	0	0	0	0	0	0	0	0	0	.000
Brett, Russell, Alexandria	30	106	13	23	31	3	1	1	10	1	0	3	1	17	2	0	.217
Brooks, Craig, Winston-Salem*	132	447	96	146	250	20	6	24	83	0	4	104	7	114	24	4	.327
Brown, Michael, Winston-Salem	80	6	1	2	2	0	0	0	0	1	0	3	0	0	0	0	.333
Bruno, Joseph, Peninsula*	132	492	102	150	204	17	11	5	61	6	13	81	2	21	53	17	.305
Burtt, Gregory, Alexandria*	45	137	8	31	36	5	0	0	12	2	1	16	2	36	1	0	.226
Butler, Brett, Durham*	66	224	47	82	115	15	6	2	39	2	5	67	6	30	36	15	.366
Butler, William, Alexandria	22	91	12	25	27	2	0	0	3	0	0	7	2	16	3	1	.275
Caprio, Larry, Rocky Mount	119	395	41	87	107	17	0	1	32	0	2	61	4	85	3	1	.220
Carman, Donald, Peninsula*	28	1	0	0	0	0	0	0	0	0	0	0	0	0	0	0	.000
Carroll, Thomas, Alexandria*	11	8	0	2	2	0	0	0	0	0	0	0	0	3	0	0	.250
Carvajal, Crucito, Salem	41	0	0	0	0	0	0	0	0	0	0	0	0	0	0	0	.000
Castillo, Juan, Kinston	34	71	10	15	27	3	3	1	11	1	0	4	0	27	3	0	.211
Chamberlain, William, Lynchburg	52	171	25	53	72	8	1	3	24	0	0	30	3	34	4	1	.310
Cicatiello, Gary, Rocky Mount*	138	510	43	121	154	22	4	1	41	4	4	29	4	70	2	3	.237
Colbert, Richard, Winston-Salem	125	443	82	117	177	26	2	10	62	2	3	78	8	132	13	9	.264
Conley, Robert, Rocky Mount	44	105	5	21	24	3	0	0	5	2	1	0	15	0	23	4	.200
Connors, Edward, 32 WS-78 RM	110	330	32	74	108	16	3	4	33	4	2	39	2	95	4	2	.224
Crafort, Samuel, Kinston†	81	224	33	59	70	5	3	0	11	7	3	36	2	78	18	3	.263

Player and Club	G.	AB.	R.	H.	TB.	2B.	3B.	HR.	RBI.	SH.	SF.	BB.	HP.	SO.	SB.	CS.	Pct.
Cropper, L. William, Alexandria.....	26	15	3	3	3	0	0	0	0	1	0	1	0	0	0	0	.200
Csefalvay, John, Lynchburg*..........	132	481	90	139	201	30	7	6	54	5	4	102	3	73	22	15	.289
Culmer, Wilfred, Peninsula	139	498	112	184	276	28	5	18	93	0	3	64	6	72	26	14	.369
Daniels, Jessie, Rocky Mount*	10	33	7	9	14	1	2	0	3	1	0	4	1	5	1	0	.273
Dayett, Brian, Alexandria	13	48	12	21	37	5	1	3	17	0	0	7	0	2	1	0	.438
de la Rosa, Bienvenido, Salem*......	108	382	60	122	176	12	15	4	39	5	1	32	4	63	29	12	.319
Dennis, Roberto, Alexandria	124	487	49	134	183	17	7	6	52	2	2	9	4	63	14	7	.275
Donovan, Dan, Rocky Mount*	43	121	7	24	28	4	0	0	13	0	1	14	2	30	1	0	.198
Duff, David, Lynchburg	55	172	17	41	55	7	2	1	21	2	2	28	4	30	1	0	.238
Eddins, Glenn, Winston-Salem	103	389	52	102	143	14	3	7	64	1	0	40	0	44	1	4	.262
Ereu, William, Kinston	108	418	64	125	156	15	8	0	39	6	3	19	5	48	20	8	.299
Fernandez, Octavio, Kinston†	62	187	28	52	62	6	2	0	12	8	0	28	4	17	7	3	.278
Fitzgerald, Michael,'38 Alx-67 Lyn.	105	338	36	71	115	10	2	10	44	8	6	54	2	62	5	7	.210
Forbes, Andres, Durham	57	177	32	43	53	3	2	1	14	1	1	18	2	15	4	0	.243
Franco, Julio, Peninsula	140	555	105	178	248	25	6	11	99	3	10	33	8	66	44	12	.321
Frank, David, Winston-Salem	114	312	45	74	81	4	0	1	39	4	1	66	7	42	10	1	.237
Frash, Roger, Lynchburg*	23	88	7	16	20	1	0	1	12	0	1	6	1	20	1	0	.182
Frobel, Douglas, Salem*	40	144	21	34	65	8	1	7	18	1	1	16	1	33	3	3	.236
Gabella, James, Rocky Mount	117	371	36	85	107	9	2	3	24	10	2	42	2	60	5	3	.229
Gallagher, Alan, Durham	7	26	5	9	9	1	0	0	4	0	0	3	0	2	0	0	.346
Garcia, Michael, Durham	29	82	11	23	27	1	0	1	5	2	1	24	1	14	8	1	.280
Gibson, Scott, Rocky Mount	15	2	1	0	0	0	0	0	0	0	0	2	0	1	0	0	.000
Graves, Ron, Lynchburg	36	1	0	0	0	0	0	0	0	0	0	0	0	0	0	0	.000
Greer, Randy, Peninsula*..............	120	380	68	86	133	13	5	8	57	5	5	73	1	57	13	12	.226
Grubbs, Kevin, Rocky Mount	16	3	0	1	1	0	0	0	0	1	0	0	0	0	0	0	.333
Hair, Wesley, Rocky Mount*	49	139	14	29	36	4	0	1	5	1	0	13	0	41	2	2	.209
Hall, Albert, Durham†	125	491	95	139	181	16	7	4	41	3	2	77	9	52	100	27	.283
Hamner, J. Peter, Alexandria	48	16	3	4	5	1	0	0	3	0	0	4	0	7	1	0	.250
Hamric, Russell, Peninsula	76	255	33	57	70	10	0	1	22	1	1	20	3	35	14	6	.224
Hardie, Gary, Lynchburg	120	399	49	91	128	19	3	4	40	12	2	57	5	77	3	5	.228
Harris, R. Glenn, Alexandria	5	16	0	2	3	1	0	0	1	0	0	1	0	3	0	0	.125
Harris, D. Mark, Alexandria†	8	27	4	5	5	0	0	0	1	0	0	7	0	5	3	1	.185
Headford, Grant, Alexandria	34	91	4	10	14	2	1	0	4	0	0	6	5	31	2	0	.110
Henley, Douglas, Lynchburg	30	1	0	0	0	0	0	0	0	0	0	0	0	1	0	0	.000
Hernandez, Tobias, Kinston	7	9	1	2	4	2	0	0	1	0	0	0	0	2	0	0	.222
Hillenga, Brent, Salem*	75	214	35	50	77	9	0	6	36	1	2	68	1	52	10	4	.234
Hobbs, John, Alexandria*	19	1	0	0	0	0	0	0	0	0	0	0	0	1	0	0	.000
Hodgson, Paul, Kinston	60	219	39	77	115	17	0	7	39	0	2	28	0	45	7	2	.352
Holland, Elwood, Alexandria*	91	292	46	70	87	6	4	1	30	1	2	46	2	34	24	5	.240
Howard, David, Lynchburg	93	285	51	81	123	17	2	7	44	0	1	49	1	83	15	8	.284
Hudson, Christopher, Alexandria	93	318	40	74	102	7	0	7	35	3	2	55	2	66	6	3	.233
Hundley, John, Rocky Mount	36	1	0	0	0	0	0	0	0	0	0	0	0	1	0	0	.000
Incaviglia, Anthony, Salem	70	242	36	66	99	13	4	4	34	2	4	29	1	45	4	4	.273
Ivie, Lonnie, Alexandria	2	5	1	1	1	0	0	0	0	0	0	1	0	1	0	0	.200
Jablonski, Raymond, Rocky Mount	53	135	7	17	22	5	0	0	11	4	0	8	0	33	0	1	.126
Jackson, Ralph, Rocky Mount	41	2	0	1	1	0	0	0	0	0	0	0	0	0	0	0	.500
Jackson, Theodore, Alexandria	23	75	6	17	21	2	1	0	6	0	1	19	0	19	4	4	.227
Jemison, Gregory, Alexandria*........	39	149	27	36	57	7	1	4	16	1	1	35	0	26	18	2	.242
Johnston, J. Mark, Alexandria*	50	167	21	32	55	3	1	6	22	0	1	35	2	15	5	2	.192
Kiess, Paul, Peninsula*	102	303	34	66	93	17	2	2	34	7	2	24	1	102	8	2	.218
Kuvinka, M. Scott, Salem	114	385	56	83	150	22	3	13	56	2	3	27	4	92	17	8	.216
Lansford, Phillip, Kinston	119	422	74	116	146	13	4	3	47	6	3	29	2	79	7	3	.275
Lauer, James, Lynchburg†	94	261	35	63	75	6	3	0	23	2	3	35	2	28	15	7	.241
Leach, Don, Winston-Salem	6	12	1	1	1	0	0	0	1	0	0	3	0	5	1	0	.083
Lebo, Michael, Kinston*	97	282	27	65	115	17	3	9	42	1	2	40	3	76	1	0	.230
Lee, Eddie Joe, Winston-Salem	131	519	83	126	188	18	4	12	68	4	4	63	8	101	46	13	.243
Lee, John, Durham	47	169	16	32	34	2	0	0	8	2	1	12	0	27	2	1	.189
Leonard, Bernardo, Rocky Mount	5	17	1	4	5	1	0	0	2	0	0	2	0	4	1	0	.235
Linhart, Carl, Peninsula	23	68	13	19	22	1	1	0	13	2	1	15	0	10	3	1	.279
Littlefield, David, Rocky Mount.......	11	30	3	6	8	2	0	0	7	0	0	3	0	7	0	0	.200
Lohse, John, Rocky Mount	48	171	14	38	54	6	2	2	8	0	0	18	1	21	6	3	.222
Lucas, Mark, Durham*	3	9	0	2	2	0	0	0	0	0	0	1	0	2	0	0	.222
Manrique, Fred, Kinston	111	390	49	108	148	9	5	7	50	4	4	25	4	64	6	10	.277
Matamoros, Carlos, Alexandria	98	372	47	88	111	14	3	1	25	3	5	59	2	42	20	13	.237
Matthews, Jeffrey, Durham	87	285	40	84	95	8	0	1	32	8	1	46	0	35	0	4	.295
McCann, Joseph, Rocky Mount	113	404	37	90	102	6	3	0	19	6	1	49	2	54	17	10	.223
McDonald, Blane, Durham	81	260	34	68	92	9	0	5	33	1	1	26	3	36	1	0	.262
McQueen, Steven, Winston-Salem....	130	450	62	116	141	15	2	2	37	0	3	90	3	78	5	0	.258
Merulla, Tony, Salem*	107	351	41	97	134	19	0	6	56	0	4	55	1	42	5	2	.276
Milner, Brian, Kinston	124	452	57	116	158	18	3	6	71	1	6	54	3	83	9	3	.257
Moore, Alvin, Durham	106	314	54	76	116	14	1	8	51	0	3	55	4	44	8	5	.242
Morgal, Michael, Rocky Mount*......	44	3	0	0	0	0	0	0	0	0	0	1	0	2	0	0	.000
Morris, Ronald, Rocky Mount	1	1	0	0	0	0	0	0	0	0	0	0	0	1	0	0	.000
Neal, Earl, Alexandria	48	177	27	57	100	11	4	8	34	0	4	20	2	35	2	4	.322
Nelson, James, Lynchburg	25	65	10	15	21	3	0	1	8	2	1	10	1	11	1	1	.231
Neufang, Gerald, Alexandria	87	250	22	53	61	5	0	1	28	7	1	2	59	2	27	1	2	.212

Player and Club	G.	AB.	R.	H.	TB.	2B.	3B.	HR.	RBI.	SH.	SF.	BB.	HP.	SO.	SB.	CS.	Pct.
Nicely, Anthony, Salem	5	19	0	1	2	1	0	0	2	0	0	0	0	8	1	0	.053
Niggebrugge, Paul, 62 Lyn-45 WS.	107	303	41	58	83	11	1	4	36	4	2	66	4	73	4	4	.191
Noonan, James, Lynchburg	6	15	2	3	4	0	0	0	0	0	0	5	0	5	0	0	.200
Oleinik, Joel, Alexandria	32	126	10	39	53	9	1	1	21	1	1	7	0	17	1	1	.310
Oquendo, Jose, Lynchburg	109	301	38	51	67	10	3	0	26	13	2	47	0	59	14	6	.169
Orensky, Herbert, Peninsula*	108	360	42	83	135	13	3	11	68	6	4	44	8	63	6	5	.231
Ortiz, Luis, Alexandria	18	51	7	5	8	1	1	0	3	0	1	6	2	11	2	0	.098
Paula, Julio, Kinston†	121	430	45	95	113	10	4	0	29	1	7	37	2	52	11	8	.221
Pautt, Juan, Winston-Salem	126	465	71	119	159	19	3	5	71	1	6	67	3	89	12	5	.256
Pedrique, Alfredo, Lynchburg	105	321	37	79	86	3	2	0	24	8	6	19	8	28	6	3	.246
Perez, Benjamin, Kinston	113	412	59	116	144	19	3	1	43	5	10	29	3	27	19	12	.282
Perry, Gerald, Durham*	138	497	102	124	198	19	5	15	92	1	5	94	6	77	37	20	.249
Petryschuk, Edward, Kinston	61	158	14	38	58	8	0	4	21	0	3	17	1	32	1	1	.241
Pettaway, Felix, Durham	51	0	0	0	0	0	0	0	0	0	0	1	0	0	0	0	.000
Poff, James, Salem	101	261	30	55	79	14	2	2	27	6	3	24	1	47	0	2	.211
Pruitt, R. Lee, Winston-Salem*	64	219	29	49	72	8	0	5	29	0	1	35	0	50	1	0	.224
Pusterino, Frederick, Lynchburg†.	3	6	1	0	0	0	0	0	0	0	0	2	0	2	0	0	.000
Quade, G. Michael, Salem	131	417	75	115	136	12	3	1	34	5	3	90	0	67	27	8	.276
Ramie, Vernon, Kinston*	75	240	49	70	111	12	1	9	30	2	2	68	2	52	5	3	.292
Reynolds, Ronn, Lynchburg	36	105	14	21	30	3	0	2	17	2	2	13	2	17	0	2	.200
Riemer, Mark, Salem	102	356	53	106	144	17	3	5	53	2	1	50	7	68	7	10	.298
Rigby, Kevin, Durham*	5	22	5	6	14	2	0	2	5	0	0	4	0	1	1	0	.273
Rios, Carlos, Salem	130	402	63	103	127	14	5	0	42	11	6	58	1	39	35	10	.256
Rittweger, William, Lynchburg	119	437	49	120	145	19	3	0	45	8	7	41	1	32	6	2	.275
Rodriguez, Jose, Salem	126	459	68	132	219	24	12	13	75	3	6	47	8	90	31	11	.288
Rodriguez, Victor, Alexandria	33	130	20	39	53	4	2	2	15	0	1	13	2	17	5	0	.300
Rudd, Ronald, Durham*	99	373	52	103	135	9	4	5	56	3	3	31	0	54	33	10	.276
Rudolph, Jeffrey, Alexandria	72	207	29	39	53	6	1	2	23	3	4	39	0	70	2	1	.188
Runge, Paul, Durham	74	245	37	64	104	8	4	8	37	2	2	53	3	55	12	8	.261
Russell, Ronald, Alexandria	59	193	20	52	62	7	0	1	19	0	0	29	1	35	0	1	.269
Salazar, Terrell, Salem	115	414	75	118	201	21	4	18	83	5	6	37	0	55	7	1	.285
Samaniego, Arturo, Winston-Salem	57	170	18	35	40	2	0	1	19	3	3	7	2	26	0	0	.206
Schaive, John, Salem	55	178	31	46	74	10	0	6	25	2	5	24	6	28	7	5	.258
Shepherd, Ronald, Kinston	110	384	53	80	137	16	4	11	61	2	6	49	1	122	5	5	.208
Sinnen, Matthew, Alexandria	11	39	4	11	12	1	0	0	6	0	0	4	0	7	0	0	.282
Smith, H. Kevin, Rocky Mount	47	129	7	15	18	3	0	0	4	1	1	23	0	31	1	0	.116
Smith, Leroy, Peninsula	27	3	0	0	0	0	0	0	0	0	0	0	0	0	0	0	.000
Smith, Ronald, Peninsula†	25	58	8	15	15	0	0	0	8	0	0	9	0	5	1	1	.259
Snitker, Brian, Durham	3	10	0	2	4	0	1	0	3	0	0	0	1	0	0	0	.200
Sosa, Miguel, Durham	5	23	5	8	14	3	0	1	5	0	0	1	0	4	0	1	.348
Stemberger, Brian, Kinston	54	4	0	1	1	0	0	0	1	0	0	0	0	0	0	0	.250
Stieb, Steven, Durham	91	270	32	61	83	11	1	3	29	3	5	20	6	64	7	1	.226
Swain, Steven, Rocky Mount*	115	426	50	107	151	19	2	7	45	2	1	32	2	76	2	4	.251
Taylor, Jeffrey, Alexandria	8	5	1	0	0	0	0	0	0	0	0	2	0	2	0	0	.000
Teller, Jeems, Winston-Salem	61	188	28	44	63	7	0	4	26	1	2	33	7	56	14	0	.234
Thibodeaux, Keith, Salem	5	1	0	0	0	0	0	0	0	0	0	0	0	1	0	0	.000
Thomas, David, Rocky Mount	41	8	0	3	4	1	0	0	0	0	0	0	0	1	0	0	.375
Thompson, C. Len, Winston-Salem	16	37	4	10	12	0	1	0	8	0	2	6	0	5	0	0	.270
Thompson, Milton, Durham*	68	255	49	74	98	12	3	2	36	3	0	42	1	62	38	3	.290
Thompson, Tommy, Durham*	111	361	46	87	134	16	2	9	56	1	4	51	5	42	1	1	.241
Tillman, Kerry, Lynchburg	135	526	94	166	239	27	11	8	79	3	4	46	1	90	43	8	.316
Toomey, Michael, Alexandria*	2	4	0	0	0	0	0	0	0	0	0	0	0	0	0	0	.000
Tyson, Terry, Alexandria	45	167	20	35	55	5	0	5	20	4	1	12	1	23	1	1	.210
Ulrich, Jeffery, Peninsula	117	402	56	101	145	14	0	10	61	4	6	32	8	56	3	1	.251
Vazquez, Francisco, 30 WS-69 R.M.	99	360	25	66	74	6	1	0	15	3	2	36	0	83	5	2	.183
Violette, John, Lynchburg	30	1	0	0	0	0	0	0	0	0	0	0	1	0	0	0	.000
Waag, William, Salem	82	304	42	85	105	16	2	0	29	10	1	41	3	27	28	6	.280
Washington, Keith, Peninsula†	123	447	87	120	137	11	3	0	31	7	3	47	2	69	55	10	.268
Webster, Mitchell, Kinston†	65	258	43	76	89	7	3	0	28	3	4	21	3	21	16	9	.295
White, Alvin, Peninsula	72	169	32	46	66	8	3	2	19	5	1	28	2	37	8	2	.272
White, Harry, Rocky Mount*	113	335	31	88	105	11	0	2	36	5	1	52	1	68	1	4	.263
Whittemore, Reginald, Win.-Sal.	131	441	64	122	199	16	8	15	63	1	4	65	3	97	22	5	.277
Wojton, Walter, Salem	16	1	0	0	0	0	0	0	0	0	0	0	0	0	0	0	.000
Zuvella, Paul, Durham	48	149	21	47	60	7	0	2	19	1	2	23	2	12	3	4	.315

The following pitchers had no plate appearances primarily through use of designated hitters, listed alphabetically by club, games in parentheses:

ALEXANDRIA—Bottoroff, John (21); Cary, Jeff (27); Conroyd, Christopher (11–3 with Salem); DeMaria, George (20); Edwards, Allen (20); Johnson, Gary (2); Lewis, Timothy (20); Lysgaard, James (6); Norris, Timothy (13); Prohoniak, Paul (11); Rudiman, Paul (9); Salva, Elias (5); Sinopoli, Peter (12); Smith, Mark (8); Vorisek, Robert (5); Williams, Wesley (22).

DURHAM—Alduey, Juan (14); Alvarez, Jose L. (2); Castaigne, Arcilio (3); Chiti, H. Dominick (25); Coatney, Rick (26); Cowley, Joe (10); Edwards, Larry (15); Gore, B. Lance (11); Jones, Craig (13); Kerdolff, Russell (17); Lucia, Daniel (5); Pratt, L. Albert (18); Reiter, Gary (24); Ryan, Gil (39); Smith, Michael (22); Teixeira, Peter (4); Thiess, Duane (2).

KINSTON—Campbell, David (7); Dejak, Thomas (9); Eichhorn, Mark (26); Ford, Randy (34); Gill, John (28); Leal, Carlos (10); Lukish, Thomas (8); McLaughlin, Colin (18); Morgan, Richard (38); O'Dowd, Thomas (4); Phillips, Junior (28); Senteney, Steve (54); Tackitt, Robert (4); Wright, Terry (23).

LYNCHBURG—Anderson, Jesse (2); Brazzell, Donald (6); Buttles, David (26); Damiter, Theodore (39); Franklin, R. Jeffrey (19); Lowry, Michael (10); Miller, Thomas (11); Ownbey, Richard (12); Shockley, Preston (20); Semprini, John (18); Smith, David (29); Stelly, Kenneth (19).

PENINSULA—Acosta, Oscar (9); Adams, Daryl (36); Alicea, Miguel (37); Brusstar, Warren (7); Burroughs, Darren (16); Cabassa, Carlos (40); Faulk, M. Kelly (31); Goff, Wallace (27); Rasmussen, James (8); Teston, Philip (38); Warner, Fred (26); Wright, James (27).

ROCKY MOUNT—Baca, Richard (1); Baltz, W. Nickolas (23); Bryant, Franklin (2); Frandsen, Jack (5); Mayles, B. Allen (20); Smith, David (13); Wise, H. Michael (11).

SALEM—Barez, Angel (24); Garrity, Peter (29—2 with Alexandria); Gelinas, Mark (18); Guante, Cecilio (6); Huey, John (15); Jiminez, Luis (43); Labounty, David (1); Martinez, Ignacio (9); McAlarney, Patrick (11); Mohorcic, Dale (47); Notarino, Anthony (20); Parke, James (10); Peterson, Eric (4); Powell, Charles (24); Ray, Arthur (26); Rock, Robert (3); Taylor, Johnny (25); Zaske, L. Jeffrey (26).

WINSTON-SALEM—Cooke, Richard (40); Dale, Daniel (37); Fredlund, Jay (29); Gering, Scott (23); Hulbert, Alvin (20); McCarthy, Thomas (11); Mecerod, George (13); Pankratz, Carl (28); Pecka, Keith (14); Rivas, Martin (56); Tyler, David (23); Woody, Harley (13).

GRAND SLAM HOME RUNS—Eddins, 3; Franco, Kuvinka, Perry, 2 each; Anicich, Culmer, Duff, Gabella, Lebo, Lee, Orensky, Petryschuk, Pruitt, J. Rodriguez, Rudd, Salazar, Schaive, Shepherd, Swain, 1 each.

AWARDED FIRST BASE ON INTERFERENCE—Swain 6 (Colbert, Lebo, Merulla, Neufang, Reynolds); Jablonski 4 (Stieb 2, Lebo, Neufang); Bruno 2 (Colbert, Kuvinka); Hair (Colbert); Kuvinka (Colbert); Neufang (Kuvinka); Poff (Neufang); Salazar (Milner); R. Smith (Kuvinka); Stieb (Leach); Tillman (Kuvinka).

GAME-WINNING RBIs

ALEXANDRIA (50)—Dennis, 7, Rodriguez, 7, Hudson 5, Matamoros 5, Neufang 4, Tyson 4, Boyce 3, Johnston 3, Oleinik 3, Burtt 2, Dayett 2, Holland 2, Bowman 1, Brett 1, Jemison 1, Neal 1.

DURHAM (77)—Bockhorn 9, Perry 9, Rudd 9, Butler 8, Hall 7, Huang 6, M. Thompson 5, Matthews 4, Moore 4, Stieb 4, T. Thompson 3, Forbes 2, McDonald 2, Sosa 2, Garcia 1, Lee 1, Zuvella 1.

KINSTON (64)—Milner 8, Perez 7, Ramie 7, Shepherd 7, Ereu 5, Paula 5, Webster 5, Hodgson 4, Lebo 4, Manrique 4, Castillo 3, Lansford 2, Crafort 1, Fernandez 1, Petryschuk 1.

LYNCHBURG (62)—Tillman 12, Rittweger 7, Csefalvay 6, Anicich 5, Howard 5, Pedrique 5, Hardie 4, Chamberlain 3, Frash 3, Lauer 3, Duff 2, Niggebrugge 2, Oquendo 2, Fitzgerald 1, Nelson 1, Reynolds 1.

PENINSULA (80)—Borucki 17, Culmer 15, Franco 15, Orensky 11, Bruno 6, Ulrich 5, Linhart 3, Kiess 2, Washington 2, Greer 1, Hamric 1, R. Smith 1, White 1.

ROCKY MOUNT (21)—Swain 6, Cicatiello 4, Caprio 3, White 3, Conley 1, Donovan 1, Gabella 1, McCann 1, Smith 1.

SALEM (72)—Salazar 11, Merulla 10, Rodriguez 8, Kuvinka 7, Rios 7, Riemer 6, de la Rosa 4, Poff 4, Quade 4, Waag 4, Incaviglia 3, Schaive 2, Frobel 1, Hillenga 1.

WINSTON-SALEM (69)—Brooks 13, Lee 10, Eddins 8, Pautt 8, Whittemore 5, Colbert 4, McQueen 4, Teller 4, Pruitt 3, Samaniego 3, Connors 2, Frank 2, Vazquez 2, Niggebrugge 1.

CLUB FIELDING

Club	G.	PO.	A.	E.	DP.	PB.	Pct.	Club	G.	PO.	A.	E.	DP.	PB.	Pct.
Lynchburg	140	3590	1621	191	113	22	.965	Salem	139	3577	1642	237	133	34	.957
Salem	140	3603	1485	199	106	32	.962	Winston-Salem	140	3527	1543	241	106	28	.955
Durham	140	3636	1648	212	129	28	.961	Alexandria	140	3514	1508	255	122	22	.952
Peninsula	140	3561	1447	204	138	13	.961	Rocky Mount	139	3534	1522	273	126	44	.949

Triple Plays—Durham, Lynchburg, Rocky Mount, Winston-Salem.

INDIVIDUAL FIELDING

*Throws lefthanded.

FIRST BASEMEN

Player and Club	G.	PO.	A.	E.	DP.	Pct.	Player and Club	G.	PO.	A.	E.	DP.	Pct.
Petryschuk, Kinston	35	284	19	0	29	1.000	Anicich, Lynchburg	124	1110	98	22	88	.982
D. Bowman, Alexandria	15	117	10	0	10	1.000	Swain, Rocky Mount	113	985	50	19	88	.982
Hillenga, Salem*	74	647	35	4	41	.994	Frobel, Salem	39	294	29	8	28	.976
Lebo, Kinston	22	148	14	1	12	.994	Lauer, Lynchburg*	18	141	9	4	18	.974
LANSFORD, Kinston	99	885	66	7	72	.993	Pruitt, Winston-Salem	17	135	11	4	12	.973
Schaive, Salem	18	193	8	2	20	.990	Kiess, Peninsula*	101	794	37	24	78	.972
Perry, Durham	138	1296	93	16	109	.989	B. Bowman, Alexandria*	47	378	33	12	34	.972
Boyce, Alexandria	75	569	61	9	52	.986	Bardin, Rocky Mount*	20	165	11	5	15	.972
Whittemore, Win-Salem	127	1063	91	17	82	.985	White, Peninsula	54	377	18	14	42	.966
Cicatiello, Rocky Mt*	10	58	6	1	2	.985							

Triple Plays—Anicich, Perry, Swain, Whittemore.

(Fewer Than Ten Games)

Player and Club	G.	PO.	A.	E.	DP.	Pct.	Player and Club	G.	PO.	A.	E.	DP.	Pct.
Merulla, Salem	6	47	1	0	4	1.000	Kuvinka, Salem	3	23	0	0	3	1.000
Salazar, Salem	7	41	1	0	4	1.000	Smith, Rocky Mount	2	16	0	0	2	1.000
Fitzgerald, Alex-Lynch.	6	32	3	0	4	1.000	Hudson, Alexandria	1	11	0	0	0	1.000
Russell, Alexandria	4	26	1	0	4	1.000	Poff, Salem	2	10	0	0	0	1.000
Frash, Lynchburg*	3	20	4	0	1	1.000	McDonald, Durham	1	6	1	0	0	1.000
Bockhorn, Durham	3	22	1	0	1	1.000							

SECOND BASEMEN

Player and Club	G.	PO.	A.	E.	DP.	Pct.
T. Thompson, Durham...	10	23	24	0	6	1.000
Borucki, Peninsula	29	70	71	2	21	.986
Linhart, Peninsula	23	49	64	2	13	.983
Perez, Kinston	23	42	66	2	12	.982
Waag, Salem	77	141	215	7	27	.981
Conley, Rocky Mount	18	32	49	2	11	.976
FRANK, Winston-Salem	113	255	296	14	64	.975
Hamric, Peninsula	73	171	223	11	56	.973
Garcia, Durham	21	46	60	3	11	.972
Forbes, Durham	51	104	146	8	25	.969
Quade, Salem	25	42	51	3	14	.969
Rittweger, Lynchburg	115	249	351	20	71	.968
Rodriguez, Alexandria	33	62	94	6	19	.963
Poff, Salem	57	99	137	10	24	.959
Samaniego, Win-Salem	43	74	96	8	11	.955
Pedrique, Lynchburg	29	54	81	7	12	.951
Matthews, Durham	59	131	167	16	42	.949
McCann, Rocky Mount	107	250	253	28	55	.947
Matamoros, Alexandria	61	140	163	17	38	.947
Gabella, Rocky Mount	20	45	41	5	13	.945
Oleinik, Alexandria	31	80	71	9	20	.944
Paula, Kinston	119	269	357	40	73	.940
R. Smith, Peninsula	21	37	46	6	13	.933

Triple Plays—Matthews, McCann, Rittweger, Samaniego.

(Fewer Than Ten Games)

Player and Club	G.	PO.	A.	E.	DP.	Pct.
Tyson, Alexandria	3	5	13	0	1	1.000
Cropper, Alexandria	4	9	8	0	3	1.000
Dayett, Alexandria	2	2	2	0	0	1.000
Ereu, Kinston	1	1	0	0	0	1.000
McQueen, Win-Salem	1	0	1	0	0	1.000
Niggebrugge, W-Salem..	1	1	0	0	0	1.000
Teller, Winston-Salem	1	1	0	0	0	1.000
Rigby, Durham	4	14	17	2	3	.939
Johnston, Alexandria	2	6	7	1	2	.929
Lucas, Durham	2	4	5	1	1	.900
Boyce, Alexandria	7	22	21	5	6	.896
Noonan, Lynchburg	1	1	2	1	0	.750
Bockhorn, Durham	2	7	4	4	2	.733
Connors, Rocky Mount .	1	1	1	1	0	.667
Jackson, Alexandria	1	1	0	1	0	.500

THIRD BASEMEN

Player and Club	G.	PO.	A.	E.	DP.	Pct.
BORUCKI, Peninsula	112	92	229	12	25	.964
Perez, Kinston	81	59	159	12	10	.948
Brett, Alexandria	30	15	68	5	6	.943
Tyson, Alexandria	16	7	42	3	6	.942
Ereu, Kinston	48	34	92	8	7	.940
Matthews, Durham	19	11	32	3	1	.935
Incaviglia, Salem	67	60	120	14	8	.928
Hardie, Lynchburg	120	99	203	24	21	.926
T. Thompson, Durham..	72	55	153	17	19	.924
Poff, Salem	36	13	35	4	4	.923
Gabella, Rocky Mount ..	23	19	49	6	3	.919
Eddins, Winston-Salem .	99	76	193	24	21	.918
Schaive, Salem	35	28	60	8	6	.917
Connors, WS-RM	77	83	166	24	9	.912
Neufang, Alexandria ...	14	8	23	3	0	.912
McQueen, Win-Salem	21	19	42	6	5	.910
Hair, Rocky Mount	39	31	84	12	4	.906
Pedrique, Lynchburg	20	11	36	5	1	.904
Hudson, Alexandria	26	19	33	6	4	.897
Lee, Durham	47	33	84	18	8	.867
K. Smith, Rocky Mount .	24	14	35	8	6	.860
Quade, Salem	13	6	17	4	0	.852
Ortiz, Alexandria	14	10	25	7	2	.833
Culmer, Peninsula	30	13	48	17	6	.782
Bockhorn, Durham	10	5	9	4	0	.778
Lansford, Kinston	13	13	16	9	1	.763

Triple Plays—Eddins, Hair, T. Thompson.

(Fewer Than Ten Games)

Player and Club	G.	PO.	A.	E.	DP.	Pct.
Chamberlain, Lynch	8	2	27	0	0	1.000
Rudolph, Alexandria	5	2	11	0	1	1.000
Paula, Kinston	2	4	2	0	0	1.000
Boyce, Alexandria	2	4	1	0	0	1.000
Oleinik, Alexandria	3	1	4	0	1	1.000
M. Harris, Alexandria	2	1	0	0	0	1.000
Niggebrugge, Lyn-WS..	2	0	1	0	1	1.000
Taylor, Alexandria	1	1	0	0	0	1.000
Neal, Alexandria	5	0	11	1	0	.917
Garcia, Durham	6	2	8	1	1	.909
Matamoros, Alexandria	4	3	7	1	0	.909
McCann, Rocky Mount ..	4	4	6	1	1	.909
Samaniego, Win-Salem..	4	1	9	1	0	.909
Kuvinka, Salem	4	4	4	1	0	.889
Dayett, Alexandria	5	5	15	3	2	.870
Russell, Alexandria	6	2	4	1	0	.857
Hamner, Alexandria	6	2	12	3	1	.824
Noonan, Lynchburg	1	1	3	1	0	.800
Sinnen, Alexandria	6	5	9	4	1	.778
Salazar, Salem	6	4	6	3	0	.769
Dennis, Alexandria	3	1	3	2	0	.667
Breeden, Rocky Mount .	5	0	5	5	1	.500
Conley, Rocky Mount..	3	1	1	2	0	.500
Manrique, Kinston	1	0	1	1	0	.500

SHORTSTOPS

Player and Club	G.	PO.	A.	E.	DP.	Pct.
Tyson, Alexandria	26	44	76	4	11	.968
Zuvella, Durham	46	58	140	12	23	.943
OQUENDO, Lynchburg	107	126	358	31	59	.940
Runge, Durham	74	105	280	25	41	.939
Pedrique, Lynchburg	48	55	117	12	14	.935
Poff, Salem	10	9	34	3	5	.935
Waag, Salem	10	6	23	2	1	.935
Franco, Peninsula	140	179	412	42	73	.934
McQueen, Win.-Salem	109	137	322	35	45	.929
Rios, Salem	129	210	384	49	58	.924
Jackson, Alexandria	23	36	74	9	12	.924
Fernandez, Kinston	61	93	205	28	43	.914
Gabella, Rocky Mount	69	106	196	31	35	.907
Matamoros, Alexandria .	32	67	102	19	23	.899
Butler, Alexandria	22	39	68	12	15	.899
Rudolph, Alexandria	32	29	68	11	12	.898
Manrique, Kinston	66	103	190	34	40	.896
Vazquez, WS-Rocky M..	99	195	280	56	61	.895
Ereu, Kinston	17	32	58	11	14	.891
Matthews, Durham	11	7	26	5	8	.868

(Fewer Than Ten Games)

Player and Club	G.	PO.	A.	E.	DP.	Pct.
Schaive, Salem	4	4	2	0	2	1.000
Johnston, Alexandria	2	3	2	0	1	1.000
Garcia, Durham	1	1	1	0	1	1.000
Niggebrugge, Win.-Sal..	1	1	0	0	0	1.000

SHORTSTOPS—Continued

Player and Club	G.	PO.	A.	E.	DP.	Pct.
Pautt, Winston-Salem	2	1	0	0	0	1.000
Hair, Rocky Mount	8	13	10	2	6	.920
Sosa, Durham	5	15	15	3	4	.909
Hall, Durham	7	15	22	4	4	.902
M. Harris, Alexandria	6	13	13	3	3	.897
Conley, Rocky Mount	4	2	4	1	0	.857
Samaniego, Win.-Salem.	4	7	13	4	2	.833
Noonan, Lynchburg	1	0	4	1	0	.800
Hardie, Lynchburg	1	0	2	1	0	.667

OUTFIELDERS

Player and Club	G.	PO.	A.	E.	DP.	Pct.
Howard, Lynchburg	77	154	12	1	3	.994
Johnston, Alexandria	48	91	5	1	1	.990
Russell, Alexandria	40	72	3	1	0	.987
Lauer, Lynchburg*	68	134	3	2	0	.986
Niggebrugge, Lynch-WS	80	129	6	2	0	.985
Butler, Durham*	66	156	4	3	0	.982
Bradley, Rocky Mount	82	185	11	4	2	.980
Rudolph, Alexandria	29	40	6	1	1	.979
Hodgson, Kinston	55	86	4	2	1	.978
TILLMAN, Lynchburg	101	173	10	5	3	.9734
Bruno, Peninsula*	129	303	19	9	1	.9728
Quade, Salem	111	205	6	6	1	.972
Lee, Winston-Salem	114	261	7	8	2	.971
M. Thompson, Durham	66	159	8	5	1	.971
Ramie, Kinston	57	93	8	3	2	.971
Caprio, Rocky Mount	95	138	16	5	1	.969
Rodriguez, Salem	123	241	20	9	6	.967
Webster, Kinston*	62	129	8	5	2	.965
Connors, Rocky Mount	17	26	1	1	0	.964
Csefalvay, Lynchburg*	124	199	9	8	2	.963
Brooks, Winston-Salem	90	197	8	8	1	.962
Rudd, Durham	91	159	11	7	3	.960
Lohse, Rocky Mount	46	106	11	5	1	.959
Burtt, Alexandria	34	65	3	3	2	.958
Neal, Alexandria	40	61	5	3	1	.957
Cicatiello, Rocky M*	116	248	7	12	3	.955
Dennis, Alexandria	120	238	14	12	1	.955
Moore, Durham	70	96	11	5	1	.955
Pautt, Winston-Salem	122	209	15	11	6	.953
Bockhorn, Durham	29	39	1	2	0	.952
Shepherd, Kinston	109	239	7	13	2	.950
Riemer, Salem	91	142	4	8	1	.948
Salazar, Salem	19	16	2	1	0	.947
Washington, Peninsula	121	217	12	13	5	.946
Frash, Lynchburg*	19	33	2	2	0	.946
Holland, Alexandria	54	76	6	5	1	.943
Culmer, Peninsula	106	137	17	10	3	.939
Greer, Peninsula*	72	114	7	8	3	.938
Castillo, Kinston	33	38	6	3	3	.936
de la Rosa, Salem*	105	150	8	11	1	.935
Ereu, Kinston	43	39	3	3	0	.933
Hall, Durham	109	151	10	12	2	.931
Teller, Winston-Salem	56	69	1	6	0	.921
White, Rocky Mount	54	60	9	6	3	.920
Headford, Alexandria	32	40	1	4	0	.911
Jemison, Alexandria	39	54	4	6	1	.906
Crafort, Kinston	68	99	4	13	0	.888
Berroa, Winston-Salem.	35	48	1	7	0	.875
Manrique, Kinston	13	17	2	3	0	.864
White, Peninsula	10	5	1	1	0	.857

(Fewer Than Ten Games)

Player and Club	G.	PO.	A.	E.	DP.	Pct.
Breeden, Rocky Mount	6	16	1	0	1	1.000
Incaviglia, Salem	5	7	0	0	0	1.000
Conley, Rocky Mount	4	6	0	0	1	1.000
Sinnen, Alexandria	2	4	0	0	0	1.000
Brown, Rocky Mount	1	2	0	0	0	1.000
Gabella, Rocky Mount	3	2	0	0	0	1.000
G. Harris, Alexandria	2	2	0	0	0	1.000
Jablonski, Rocky Mount	3	2	0	0	0	1.000
Carroll, Alexandria	2	1	0	0	0	1.000
Fitzgerald, Alexandria	1	1	0	0	0	1.000
Gallagher, Durham	1	1	0	0	0	1.000
Hillenga, Salem*	1	1	0	0	0	1.000
Stieb, Durham	2	1	0	0	0	1.000
K. Smith, Rocky Mount.	9	13	1	1	0	.933
Leonard, Rocky Mount	5	19	1	2	0	.909
Nicely, Salem	5	7	0	1	0	.875
Chamberlain, Lynch.	7	3	1	1	0	.800
Hudson, Alexandria	5	4	0	1	0	.800
Perez, Kinston	2	1	3	1	0	.800
Thompson, Win.-Salem	1	0	0	1	0	.000

CATCHERS

Player and Club	G.	PO.	A.	E.	DP.	PB.	Pct.
Orensky, Peninsula	51	348	30	3	4	7	.992
Merulla, Salem	57	340	14	3	3	12	.992
Reynolds, Lynchburg	34	206	23	3	1	4	.987
Fitzgerald, Alex-Lyn.	66	405	42	7	1	11	.985
ULRICH, Peninsula	91	597	63	11	8	6	.984
McDonald, Durham	63	340	37	7	5	8	.982
Milner, Kinston	106	627	94	14	10	24	.981
Stieb, Durham	88	450	67	10	3	20	.981
Duff, Lynchburg	47	267	25	6	2	10	.980
Kuvinka, Salem	94	546	74	15	7	20	.976
Colbert, Win.-Salem	119	641	127	22	11	17	.972
Hudson, Alexandria	54	356	56	13	5	6	.969
Lebo, Kinston	29	166	21	6	4	10	.969
Thompson, Win.-Sal.	15	59	4	2	2	2	.969
Breeden, R.M.	80	317	67	13	5	20	.967
Neufang, Alexandria	57	390	50	15	6	6	.967
Nelson, Lynchburg	16	76	10	3	0	3	.966
Jablonski, Rocky M.	50	192	39	9	2	6	.963
Donovan, Rocky M.	31	126	6	6	0	15	.957

(Fewer Than Ten Games)

Player and Club	G.	PO.	A.	E.	DP.	PB.	Pct.
T. Thompson, Dur.	3	18	2	0	1	0	1.000
Bockhorn, Durham	1	10	1	0	0	0	1.000
Hernandez, Kinston	3	8	1	0	0	0	1.000
Ivie, Alexandria	2	6	1	0	0	0	1.000
K. Smith, Rocky M.	3	5	1	0	0	0	1.000
Russell, Alexandria	1	2	0	0	0	0	1.000
Littlefield, Rocky M.	9	58	6	1	0	3	.985
Pruitt, Win.-Salem	6	49	14	1	0	8	.981
Leach, Win.-Salem	5	30	3	1	0	0	.971
Rudolph, Alexandria	8	33	3	2	0	1	.947
Snitker, Durham	3	15	2	1	0	0	.944
G. Harris, Alexandria.	2	12	1	1	0	0	.929
Sinnen, Alexandria	3	19	5	2	1	2	.923
Niggebrugge, L-WS	4	5	2	1	0	2	.875
Pusterino, Lynchburg	3	7	0	1	0	0	.875

PITCHERS

Player and Club	G.	PO.	A.	E.	DP.	Pct.
Morgan, Kinston	38	8	23	0	4	1.000
Wright, Kinston	23	6	25	0	1	1.000
Violette, Lynchburg	30	8	18	0	1	1.000
Shockley, Lynchburg	20	9	15	0	1	1.000
Jiminez, Salem	43	8	15	0	0	1.000
Stemberger, Kinston	52	4	18	0	2	1.000
Mohorcic, Salem	47	3	18	0	1	1.000
Pratt, Durham*	18	2	19	0	1	1.000
Jackson, Rocky Mount	41	8	11	0	1	1.000
Cowley, Durham	10	2	17	0	1	1.000
Zaske, Salem	26	4	14	0	1	1.000
Coatney, Durham	26	5	11	0	1	1.000
Ownbey, Lynchburg	12	8	6	0	0	1.000
Garrity, Salem-Alex.	29	3	11	0	0	1.000
Anderson, Lynchburg	10	5	8	0	0	1.000
Adams, Peninsula	37	4	7	0	0	1.000
Faulk, Peninsula	31	4	5	0	0	1.000
Edwards, Durham*	15	2	6	0	1	1.000
Gelinas, Salem	17	4	3	0	0	1.000
Stelly, Lynchburg*	19	3	4	0	0	1.000
Cabassa, Peninsula*	40	0	6	0	0	1.000
DeMaria, Alexandria	10	0	6	0	0	1.000
Wise, Rocky Mount	11	1	5	0	1	1.000
Bottoroff, Alexandria	21	0	5	0	0	1.000
Wojton, Salem	16	0	5	0	0	1.000
Mecerod, Winston-Salem	13	1	2	0	0	1.000
Powell, Salem*	24	0	3	0	0	1.000
Semprini, Lynchburg	16	0	2	0	0	1.000
Leal, Kinston	10	1	1	0	0	1.000
Gore, Durham*	11	0	2	0	0	1.000
BALTZ, Rocky Mount	23	11	43	1	2	.982
Buttles, Lynchburg	26	16	24	1	0	.976
Gill, Kinston	28	11	27	1	4	.974
Lewis, Alexandria*	20	1	37	1	3	.974
Wright, Peninsula	27	11	21	1	1	.970
Eichhorn, Kinston	26	15	40	2	3	.965
Lowry, Lynchburg	10	8	16	1	0	.960
L. Smith, Peninsula	27	10	12	1	1	.957
Thomas, Rocky Mount	40	5	17	1	3	.957
Cropper, Alexandria	19	5	17	1	1	.957
Damiter, Lynchburg	39	4	18	1	2	.957
Mayles, Rocky Mount	20	5	16	1	0	.955
Alduey, Peninsula	14	7	13	1	0	.952
Notarino, Salem	20	5	14	1	0	.950
Carvajal, Salem	39	7	11	1	2	.947
Chiti, Durham*	25	5	13	1	1	.947
Ryan, Durham	29	14	21	2	1	.946
Hundley, Rocky Mount*	36	8	9	1	0	.944
Goff, Peninsula*	27	7	22	2	2	.935
Woody, Winston-Salem	13	3	11	1	0	.933
Gering, Winston-Salem	23	7	18	2	4	.926
Pecka, Winston-Salem*	14	6	18	2	0	.923
McAlarney, Salem*	11	3	9	1	1	.923
Rivas, Winston-Salem	56	9	14	2	1	.920
Behenna, Durham	27	12	33	4	2	.918
Jones, Durham	13	2	9	1	0	.917
Pankratz, Win.-Salem	28	10	11	2	2	.913
Cary, Alexandria	27	7	14	2	2	.913
Reiter, Durham*	22	7	14	2	0	.913
Dale, Winston-Salem	37	4	16	2	1	.909
Gibson, Rocky Mount	15	4	6	1	2	.909
Kerdolff, Durham	17	3	7	1	0	.909
Senteney, Kinston	54	4	15	2	1	.905
Hamner, Alexandria	44	4	24	3	3	.903
Hulbert, Winston-Salem	20	15	22	4	2	.902
Barez, Salem	24	3	34	4	1	.902
Fredlund, Win.-Salem	29	15	37	6	0	.897
Phillips, Kinston	28	5	21	3	0	.897
Tyler, Winston-Salem	23	7	17	3	1	.889
Pettaway, Durham	51	4	12	2	0	.889
Morgal, Rocky Mount*	44	3	20	3	0	.885
Grubbs, Winston-Salem	15	5	17	3	0	.880
Huey, Salem	15	1	6	1	1	.875
Ford, Kinston*	34	5	29	5	2	.872
Smith, Lynchburg	29	7	26	5	0	.868
Cooke, Winston-Salem*	40	3	23	4	2	.867
Norris, Alexandria	13	5	8	2	0	.867
Franklin, Lynchburg	19	2	11	2	2	.867
Hobbs, Alexandria	19	2	17	3	2	.864
Alicea, Peninsula	37	5	14	3	0	.864
Carman, Peninsula*	27	4	21	4	1	.862
Teston, Peninsula	38	3	9	2	1	.857
Taylor, Salem	25	9	20	5	0	.853
Smith, Durham	22	10	13	4	0	.852
Williams, Alexandria	22	5	6	2	0	.846
Brown, Rocky Mount	78	7	24	6	3	.838
McLaughlin, Kinston	18	5	15	4	1	.833
Burroughs, Peninsula*	16	2	13	3	0	.833
Miller, Lynchburg*	11	2	13	3	1	.833
Parke, Salem	10	3	2	1	0	.833
Henley, Lynchburg	28	20	28	10	0	.828
McCarthy, Win.-Salem	11	6	12	4	1	.818
Ray, Salem	26	9	22	7	3	.816
Conroyd, Salem-Alex.*	11	0	7	2	1	.778
Bresnen, Rocky Mount*	12	2	21	8	0	.742
Sinopoli, Alexandria	12	1	7	3	0	.727
D. Smith, Rocky Mount	13	2	3	2	0	.714
Warner, Peninsula	26	2	3	3	1	.625

Triple Play—Lowry.

(Fewer Than Ten Games)

Player and Club	G.	PO.	A.	E.	DP.	Pct.
Rasmussen, Peninsula	9	4	12	0	1	1.000
Lucia, Durham	5	4	9	0	0	1.000
Dejak, Kinston*	9	0	10	0	0	1.000
Taylor, Alexandria	5	3	7	0	0	1.000
Edwards, Alexandria	6	0	7	0	0	1.000
Alvarez, Durham	2	0	6	0	0	1.000
Rudolph, Alexandria	5	3	3	0	0	1.000
Smith, Alexandria	8	2	4	0	0	1.000
Tackitt, Kinston	4	1	4	0	0	1.000
Acosta, Peninsula	8	2	2	0	0	1.000
Lysgaard, Alexandria	6	1	3	0	0	1.000
Lukish, Kinston	8	1	3	0	0	1.000
Martinez, Salem	9	1	3	0	0	1.000
Brusstar, Peninsula	7	0	3	0	1	1.000
Guante, Salem	6	1	1	0	0	1.000
Rudiman, Alexandria	9	0	2	0	0	1.000
Teixeira, Durham	4	1	1	0	0	1.000
Baca, Rocky Mount*	1	0	1	0	0	1.000
Carroll, Alexandria	7	0	1	0	0	1.000
Frandsen, Rocky Mount	5	0	1	0	0	1.000
Labounty, Salem	1	1	0	0	0	1.000
O'Dowd, Kinston	4	0	1	0	0	1.000
Thibodeaux, Salem	4	0	1	0	0	1.000
Thiess, Durham	2	1	0	0	0	1.000
Campbell, Kinston	7	2	4	1	1	.857
Rock, Salem	3	2	4	2	0	.750
Prohoniak, Alexandria	9	2	3	2	0	.714
Salva, Alexandria	5	2	3	2	0	.714
Vorisek, Alexandria	4	0	1	1	0	.500

The following players had no recorded accepted chances at the positions indicated; therefore, are not listed in the fielding averages for those particular positions: Berroa, 2b; Bill, of; Borucki, ss; Brazzell, p; Bryant, p; Caprio, 2b-ss; Castaigne, p; Colbert, of; Conley, p; Connors, 1b-p; Cropper, 3b-of; Csefalvay*, p; Eddins, of; Frank, of; Frobel, 3b-of; Gaballa, p; Garcia, of; Gelinas, 1b; Hair, 2b-of; Hernandez, of; Hudson, ss; Johnson, p; Kuvinka, of; Lansford, of; McCann, of; Morris, of; Niggebrugge, 1b-p; Ortiz, c; Peterson*, p; Pettaway, 3b; Poff, p; Rios, of; Salazar, ss; Samaniego, of; Semprini, of; R. Smith, ss; Stieb, p; T. Thompson, of-p; Toomey*, 1b; White, p; Whittemore, of.

OFFICIAL BASEBALL GUIDE

CLUB PITCHING

Club	G.	CG.	ShO.	Sv.	IP.	H.	R.	ER.	HR.	BB.	Int. BB.	HB.	SO.	WP.	Bk.	ERA.
Peninsula	140	11	22	42	1187	996	469	373	57	503	15	35	917	50	11	2.83
Winston-Salem	140	29	10	27	1176	1153	599	442	56	564	39	34	734	61	16	3.38
Salem	140	12	6	41	1201	1049	586	469	66	656	18	57	818	111	21	3.51
Kinston	139	19	12	34	1192	1176	616	481	57	572	17	27	756	65	10	3.63
Lynchburg	140	36	8	28	1197	1162	621	508	70	511	35	43	798	60	12	3.82
Durham	140	26	10	31	1212	1208	635	517	88	549	16	52	789	60	11	3.84
Alexandria	140	41	4	15	1171	1136	694	552	74	651	24	40	898	96	18	4.24
Rocky Mount	139	20	4	9	1178	1296	837	655	71	721	37	44	635	97	22	5.00

PITCHERS' RECORDS

(Leading Qualifiers for Earned-Run Average Leadership—112 or More Innings)

*Throws lefthanded.

Pitcher—Club	G.	GS.	CG.	ShO.	W.	L.	Sv.	Pct.	IP.	H.	R.	ER.	HR.	BB.	Int. BB.	HB.	SO.	WP.	ERA.
Wright, Peninsula	27	17	3	1	13	1	1	.929	136	113	47	28	3	56	2	6	88	9	1.85
Tyler, Winston-Salem	23	16	2	0	9	6	0	.600	122	103	43	32	4	61	3	2	70	6	2.37
Smith, Peninsula	27	27	5	3	17	6	0	.739	163	101	54	47	7	63	0	5	134	6	2.60
Wright, Kinston	23	23	2	1	10	4	0	.714	132	109	51	38	6	75	0	0	79	6	2.60
Goff, Peninsula*	27	27	0	0	14	4	0	.778	145	126	68	46	10	75	0	0	136	3	2.86
Eichorn, Kinston	26	26	9	2	14	10	0	.583	183	158	72	59	5	56	3	3	119	8	2.90
Phillips, Kinston	28	14	1	0	10	4	0	.714	118	127	57	40	7	44	1	5	50	5	3.05
Thomas, Rocky Mount	40	1	0	0	2	6	2	.250	114	95	48	39	9	63	7	4	86	7	3.08
Smith, Lynchburg	29	10	3	0	8	7	1	.533	113	121	60	42	2	63	8	4	63	6	3.34
Taylor, Salem	25	25	1	0	13	6	0	.684	137	126	70	51	9	69	0	3	100	11	3.34

Departmental Leaders: G—Brown, 78; GS—Fredlund, 29; CG—Lewis, 10; ShO—L. Smith, M. Smith, 3; W—L. Smith, 17; L—Baltz, Behenna, Mayles, 13; Sv—Rivas, 21; Pct.—J. Wright, .929; IP—Fredlund, 192; H—Fredlund, 190; R—Morgal, 100; ER—Behenna, 83; HR—Buttles, 17; BB—Zaske, 116; IBB—Brown, 12; HB—Barez, 14; SO—Carman, 141; WP—Barez, 22.

(All Pitchers—Listed Alphabetically)

Pitcher—Club	G.	GS.	CG.	ShO.	W.	L.	Sv.	Pct.	IP.	H.	R.	ER.	HR.	BB.	Int. BB.	HB.	SO.	WP.	ERA.
Acosta, Peninsula	9	5	1	1	2	0	2	1.000	33	25	16	13	0	19	0	0	22	0	3.55
Adams, Peninsula	36	1	0	0	7	0	3	1.000	87	72	32	30	6	37	1	0	60	3	3.10
Alduey, Durham	14	13	2	1	4	5	0	.444	73	95	50	41	8	15	1	1	41	2	5.05
Alicea, Peninsula	37	13	1	1	10	6	9	.625	108	93	38	33	4	32	2	1	54	2	2.75
Alvarez, Durham	2	2	0	0	2	0	0	1.000	18	14	6	4	1	5	0	0	12	0	2.00
Anderson, Lynchburg*	10	10	3	0	2	6	0	.250	60	46	30	23	5	27	0	3	35	4	3.45
Baca, Rocky Mount*	1	0	0	0	0	1	0	.000	2	1	3	3	0	2	0	0	0	0	13.50
Baltz, Rocky Mount	23	23	9	1	8	13	0	.381	156	168	87	59	1	53	0	1	68	9	3.40
Barez, Salem	24	24	0	0	11	5	0	.688	126	126	75	58	8	78	0	14	67	22	4.14
Behenna, Durham	27	27	6	2	8	13	0	.381	180	181	97	83	16	81	1	10	107	9	4.15
Bottoroff, Alexandria	21	3	0	0	5	3	2	.625	67	47	29	25	3	39	2	6	68	3	3.36
Brazzell, Lynchburg	6	0	0	0	0	1	1	1.000	5	3	1	1	0	1	0	0	6	0	1.80
Bresnen, Rocky Mount*	12	9	0	0	1	8	0	.125	62	72	40	29	1	45	5	6	31	12	4.21
Brown, Rocky Mount	78	0	0	0	3	9	4	.250	157	140	92	71	8	113	12	1	102	19	4.07
Brusstar, Peninsula	2	2	0	0	1	0	0	.000	3	5	5	5	0	6	0	0	1	0	15.00
Bryant, Rocky Mount	7	0	0	0	1	0	0	.500	14	16	7	7	1	2	0	0	4	0	4.50
Burroughs, Peninsula*	16	10	1	0	6	3	0	.667	82	64	25	20	2	39	0	4	60	4	2.20
Buttles, Lynchburg	26	26	7	1	9	12	0	.429	145	169	97	82	17	46	2	10	63	12	5.09
Cabassa, Peninsula*	40	0	0	0	4	2	9	.667	55	37	14	12	2	28	3	4	43	1	1.96
Campbell, Kinston	7	1	0	0	1	0	0	1.000	15	13	9	5	0	15	0	2	12	4	3.00
Carman, Peninsula	27	27	0	0	14	5	0	.737	150	149	73	57	10	53	0	3	141	8	3.42
Carroll, Alexandria	7	4	0	0	0	4	0	.000	17	20	20	15	2	15	0	0	7	0	7.94
Carvajal, Salem	39	1	0	0	4	4	5	.500	83	76	29	23	4	37	2	2	51	6	2.49
Cary, Alexandria	27	6	0	1	9	4	2	.692	91	76	33	21	2	60	4	7	78	4	2.08
Castaigne, Durham	3	0	0	0	0	2	0	.000	5	4	4	2		5	0	0	2	1	7.20
Chiti, Durham*	25	3	0	0	1	3	0	.500	62	56	23	20	4	28	2	1	31	3	2.90
Coatney, Durham	26	12	0	0	9	2	0	.818	94	95	53	48	6	56	0	4	55	4	4.60
Conley, Rocky Mount	1	0	0	0	0	0	0	.000	1	1	0	0	0	0	0	0	1	0	0.00
Connors, Rocky Mount	1	1	0	0	0	0	0	.000	0	0	0	0	0	0	0	0	0	0	0.00
Conroyd, Salem-Alex*	11	3	0	0	0	1	0	.000	35	35	25	20	5	21	0	2	16	3	5.14
Cooke, Winston-Salem*	40	0	0	0	4	3	6	.429	79	75	35	20	3	33	8	0	59	9	2.28
Cowley, Durham	10	10	2	0	1	6	0	1.000	64	57	26	20	6	25	0	5	44	4	2.81
Cropper, Alexandria	19	2	1	0	3	3	0	.500	75	75	39	27	6	28	1	1	48	4	3.24
Csefalvay, Lynchburg*	1	0	0	0	0	0	0	.000	0	0	0	0	0	0	0	0	0	0	0.00
Dale, Winston-Salem	37	0	0	0	2	0	3	1.000	87	85	43	34	4	26	3	0	45	2	3.52
Damiter, Lynchburg	39	0	0	0	7	3	6	.700	60	67	39	31	7	22	2	2	41	4	4.65
Dejak, Kinston*	9	6	1	0	1	2	0	.333	33	39	18	17	3	17	0	0	19	2	4.64
DeMaria, Alexandria	10	9	1	0	1	6	0	.143	48	54	38	29	2	32	0	2	37	1	5.44
Edwards, Alexandria	6	6	2	0	3	1	0	.500	41	32	22	19	5	22	1	0	51	0	4.17
Edwards, Durham*	15	0	0	0	0	2	0	.714	26	30	18	12	0	10	0	0	14	0	4.15

Pitcher–Club	G.	GS.	CG.	ShO.	W.	L.	Sv.	Pct.	IP.	H.	R.	ER.	HR.	BB.	Int. BB.	HB.	SO.	WP.	ERA.
Eichhorn, Kinston	26	26	9	2	14	10	0	.583	183	158	72	59	5	56	3	3	119	8	2.90
Faulk, Peninsula	31	0	0	0	1	3	13	.250	43	37	12	11	1	19	3	0	31	2	2.30
Ford, Kinston*	34	22	2	1	4	12	0	.250	134	133	87	67	10	56	0	1	90	5	4.50
Frandsen, Rocky Mount ..	5	0	0	0	0	1	0	.000	5	11	11	9	1	8	1	0	2	1	16.20
Franklin, Lynchburg	19	7	1	0	3	4	1	.429	62	72	45	41	4	21	2	0	51	2	5.95
Fredlund, Winston-Salem	29	29	9	2	15	6	0	.714	192	190	96	72	14	67	6	9	101	6	3.38
Gabella, Rocky Mount	1	0	0	0	0	0	0	.000	1	3	2	2	0	1	0	0	1	0	18.00
Garrity, Salem-Alex	29	2	1	0	4	3	3	.571	71	61	35	25	3	34	1	7	42	8	3.17
Gelinas, Salem	17	1	0	0	2	0	0	.000	22	21	22	20	1	33	0	2	18	3	8.18
Gering, Winston-Salem	23	7	1	0	6	2	2	.750	76	77	30	21	8	32	1	1	48	2	2.49
Gibson, Rocky Mount .	15	15	1	0	12	0	0	.000	68	84	64	51	3	55	0	1	36	11	6.75
Gill, Kinston	28	27	2	1	7	7	0	.500	154	161	92	74	7	73	0	6	73	12	4.32
Goff, Peninsula*	27	27	0	0	14	4	0	.778	145	126	68	46	10	75	0	0	136	3	2.86
Gore, Durham*	11	0	0	0	1	2	1	.333	15	14	8	8	2	5	1	1	12	0	4.80
Graves, Lynchburg	36	1	0	0	4	2	4	.667	78	72	39	28	5	39	6	4	40	4	3.23
Grubbs, Rocky Mount	15	15	5	1	1	11	0	.083	91	102	63	49	7	39	2	4	18	4	4.85
Guante, Salem	6	0	0	0	0	0	2	.000	14	7	2	2	1	8	0	2	18	1	1.29
Hamner, Alexandria	44	3	2	0	6	5	10	.545	108	88	37	28	7	34	10	5	90	3	2.33
Henley, Lynchburg	28	27	2		10	11	0	.476	177	189	88	78	11	43	2	1	94	9	3.97
Hobbs, Alexandria*	19	17	9	0	7	10	0	.412	116	120	67	55	4	58	1	3	92	9	4.27
Huey, Salem	15	9	0	0	2	3	1	.400	53	51	34	29	4	33	1	0	28	7	4.92
Hulbert, Winston-Salem.	20	5	1		8	8	0	.500	129	115	69	54	7	71	1	5	91	4	3.77
Hundley, Rocky Mount*..	36	1	0	0	0	4	3	.000	73	71	47	39	5	53	3	7	52	4	4.81
Jackson, Rocky Mount ...	41	15	0	0	2	11	0	.154	123	132	97	80	8	91	3	1	85	8	5.85
Jiminez, Salem	43	2	0	0	8	0	6	1.000	80	60	39	34	7	45	3	7	75	5	3.83
Johnson, Alexandria	2	2	0	0	0	2	0	.000	6	9	6	4	1	7	0	0	4	0	6.00
Jones, Durham	13	13	3	2	6	5	0	.545	86	69	34	27	3	34	0	1	77	6	2.83
Kerdolff, Lynchburg	17	0	0	0	3	1	0	.000	40	48	24	19	5	10	3	4	22	0	4.28
Labounty, Salem	1	1	0	0	0	0	0	.000	3	3	3	0	3	0	1	0	3	0	9.00
Leal, Kinston	10	0	0	0	0	1	0	.000	16	25	14	14	1	8	0	0	13	2	7.88
Lewis, Alexandria*	20	19	10	1	8	9	1	.471	133	126	64	51	8	59	0	0	107	13	3.45
Lowry, Lynchburg	10	10	2	0	4	2	0	.667	75	51	25	22	2	27	1	4	59	3	2.64
Lucia, Durham	5	5	0		3	1	0	.750	31	31	14	10	2	12	0	0	14	0	2.90
Lukish, Kinston	8	0	0	0	1	2	2	.333	17	16	8	3	0	5	1	1	6	1	1.59
Lysgaard, Alexandria	6	6	0	0	1	3	0	.250	33	39	20	15	2	14	1	1	21	2	4.09
Martinez, Salem	9	2	1	0	1	3	1	.250	23	24	14	8	1	5	0	0	18	1	3.13
Mayles, Rocky Mount	20	20	3	0	3	13	0	.188	87	97	78	56	3	58	1	5	52	7	5.79
McAlarney, Salem*	11	8	1	0	4	1	0	.800	46	48	18	16	1	19	0	0	28	3	3.13
McCarthy, Win-Salem	11	11	1	0	4	4	0	.500	61	55	32	27	1	46	1	4	28	4	3.98
McLaughlin, Kinston	18	18	2	1	6	8	0	.429	102	97	58	46	1	70	0	3	90	6	4.06
Mecerod, Winston-Salem.	13	6	1	0	3	3	1	.500	45	50	25	19	0	25	0	4	28	7	3.80
Miller, Lynchburg*	11	10	1	0	4	4	0	.500	63	65	39	33	6	27	0	3	48	3	4.71
Mohorcic, Salem	47	0	0	0	7	5	17	.583	111	91	38	27	5	32	8	3	85	7	2.19
Morgal, Rocky Mount*	44	16	1	1	3	9	0	.250	138	189	100	78	16	62	3	3	44	2	5.09
Morgan, Kinston	38	2	0	0	5	4	7	.556	96	108	57	46	7	35	4	6	65	7	4.31
Niggebrugge, Win-Salem	1	0	0	0	0	0	0	.000	⅓	0	1	1	0	0	1	0	0	0	0.00
Norris, Alexandria	13	12	0	0	3	8	0	.273	76	83	49	42	8	38	2	2	54	7	4.97
Notarino, Alexandria	20	3	2	0	4	6	3	.400	59	48	26	15	3	10	1	2	37	1	2.29
O'Dowd, Kinston	4	0	0	0	1	0	0	.000	4	5	8	7	0	10	1	0	4	1	15.75
Ownbey, Lynchburg	12	12	6	2	8	1	0	.889	92	66	24	19	2	35	3	3	93	2	1.86
Pankratz, Winston-Salem	28	24	4	1	9	11	0	.450	136	158	99	73	2	79	4	2	80	8	4.83
Parke, Salem	10	1	0	0	2	1	1	.667	24	19	15	12	5	9	0	0	14	2	4.50
Pecka, Winston-Salem* ..	14	14	2	0	6	6	0	.500	73	82	45	33	5	48	3	3	54	6	4.07
Peterson, Salem*	4	0	0	0	0	0	0	.000	6	7	4	4	2	1	0	0	4	0	6.00
Pettaway, Durham	51	0	0	0	11	4	20	.733	91	65	32	21	2	48	4	6	95	8	2.08
Phillips, Kinston	28	14	1	0	10	4	0	.714	118	127	57	40	7	44	1	5	50	5	3.05
Poff, Salem	1	0	0	0	0	0	0	.000	1	0	1	0	0	1	0	0	0	0	0.00
Powell, Salem*	24	0	0	0	2	0	0	.000	25	20	19	17	4	15	0	1	19	2	6.12
Pratt, Durham*	18	14	2	0	8	4	0	.667	88	109	64	51	9	45	1	8	64	3	5.22
Prohoniak, Alexandria	9	3	1	0	1	1	0	.500	30	33	23	17	1	26	1	0	15	5	5.10
Rasmussen, Peninsula	8	8	0	0	6	1	0	.857	49	34	12	9	2	11	0	2	43	5	1.65
Ray, Salem	26	25	2	0	7	9	0	.438	138	115	65	53	4	82	2	4	74	10	3.46
Reiter, Durham*	22	12	1	0	3	4	0	.429	80	91	52	42	7	57	0	0	51	7	4.73
Rivas, Winston-Salem	56	0	0	0	6	10	21	.375	98	75	35	24	5	39	8	4	83	1	2.20
Rock, Salem	3	3	0	0	1	1	0	.500	17	17	6	6	0	10	0	4	14	2	3.18
Rudiman, Alexandria	9	0	0	0	0	0	0	.000	14	16	19	15	2	18	0	0	8	1	9.64
Rudolph, Alexandria	5	1	1	0	1	0	0	1.000	17	12	5	5	0	6	0	0	10	4	2.65
Ryan, Durham	29	8	3	0	5	6	2	.455	103	91	50	42	3	56	1	3	65	5	3.67
Salva, Alexandria	5	2	0	0	0	2	0	.000	9	13	12	10	2	7	1	0	6	0	10.00
Semprini, Lynchburg	16	0	0	0	1	1	4	.500	32	21	11	7	1	17	3	1	37	6	1.97
Senteney, Kinston	54	0	0	0	4	4	20	.500	85	71	31	20	4	48	5	0	66	4	2.12
Shockley, Lynchburg	20	20	5	1	5	10	0	.333	120	117	72	58	2	84	2	6	102	5	4.35
Sinopoli, Alexandria	12	10	2	0	2	6	0	.250	69	76	48	41	6	27	0	0	54	3	5.35
Smith, Rocky Mount	13	11	1	0	1	9	0	.100	52	66	53	46	3	38	0	7	38	7	7.96
Smith, Lynchburg	29	10	3	0	8	7	1	.533	113	121	60	42	2	63	8	4	63	6	3.35
Smith, Alexandria	8	5	1	0	0	2	0	.000	32	37	25	22	1	20	0	2	25	7	6.19

Pitcher–Club	G	GS	CG	ShO	W	L	Sv	Pct.	IP	H	R	ER	HR	BB	Int. BB	HB	SO	WP	ERA
Smith, Durham	22	21	5	3	11	3	0	.786	140	145	73	58	10	51	1	5	77	6	3.73
L. Smith, Peninsula	27	27	5	3	17	6	0	.739	163	101	54	47	7	63	0	5	134	6	2.60
Stelly, Lynchburg*	19	0	0	0	1	2	6	.333	21	24	14	13	1	16	2	0	13	0	5.57
Stemberger, Kinston	52	0	0	0	6	9	5	.400	98	103	45	38	4	56	2	0	66	2	3.49
Stieb, Durham	2	0	0	0	0	0	0	.000	4	1	0	0	0	0	0	1	3	1	0.00
Tackitt, Kinston	4	0	0	0	0	1	0	.000	6	11	9	7	2	4	0	0	4	0	10.50
Taylor, Alexandria	5	5	0	0	0	2	0	.000	26	32	22	15	1	9	0	1	18	1	5.19
Taylor, Salem	25	25	1	0	13	6	0	.684	137	126	70	51	9	69	0	3	100	11	3.35
Teixeira, Durham	4	0	0	0	1	1	1	.500	7	6	6	2	4	1		2	1		7.71
Teston, Peninsula	38	0	0	0	3	6	5	.333	62	62	24	21	3	25	3	4	46	4	3.05
Thibodeaux, Salem	4	4	0	0	2	1	0	.667	19	12	2	2	0	8	0	1	22	0	0.95
Thiess, Durham	2	0	0	0	0	0	0	.000	3	2	0	0	0	1	0	0	0	0	0.00
Thomas, Rocky Mount	40	1	0	0	2	6	2	.250	114	95	48	39	9	63	7	4	86	7	3.08
T. Thompson, Durham	1	0	0	0	0	0	0	.000	1	2	1	1	0	1	0	0	1	0	9.00
Tyler, Winston-Salem	23	16	2	0	9	6	0	.600	122	103	43	32	4	61	3	2	70	6	2.36
Violette, Lynchburg	30	7	2	1	5	2	5	.714	94	79	37	30	5	43	2	2	53	0	2.87
Vorisek, Alexandria*	5	2	0	0	0	2	0	.000	11	11	12	10	1	9	0	1	5	1	8.18
Warner, Peninsula*	26	5	0	0	2	2	0	.500	60	67	47	39	6	44	1	5	51	3	5.85
White, Rocky Mount	1	0	0	0	0	0	0	.000	3	1	0	0	3	0	1	0	1		0.00
Williams, Alexandria	22	18	3	0	4	9	0	.308	108	99	76	65	6	99	0	1	75	18	5.42
Wise, Rocky Mount	11	11	0	0	0	7	0	.000	42	59	43	39	5	32	0	3	16	4	8.36
Wojton, Salem	16	1	0	0	1	0	0	1.000	20	15	6	3	0	14	0	2	6	1	1.35
Woody, Winston-Salem*	13	13	4	0	5	4	0	.556	78	87	47	34	3	36	1	0	47	6	3.92
Wright, Peninsula	27	17	3	1	13	1	1	.929	136	113	47	28	3	56	2	6	88	9	1.85
Wright, Winston-Salem	23	23	2	1	10	4	0	.714	132	109	51	38	6	75	0	0	79	6	2.59
Zaske, Salem	26	26	4	1	8	10	0	.444	132	101	68	62	3	116	0	4	103	19	4.23

BALKS—Woody, 5; Burroughs, Eichhorn, Gibson, Hundley, Lewis, Ray, Taylor, 4 each; Alduey, Buttles, Cooke, Cropper, A. Edwards, Fredlund, Goff, Hobbs, Jones, Salva, 3 each; Anderson, Barez, Behenna, Bresnen, Brown, Carvajal, Hulbert, Mayles, McAlarney, McCarthy, Mohorcic, Morgal, D.W. Smith, Stemberger, Wise, J. Wright, Zaske, 2 each; Baltz, Coatney, Damiter, DeMaria, Ford, Frandsen, Garrity, Gill, Graves, Grubbs, Guante, Henley, Jackson, McLaughlin, Morgan, Ownbey, Pankratz, Pettaway, Powell, Rasmussen, Reiter, Rudolph, Shockley, L. Smith, 1 each.

COMBINATION SHUTOUTS—DeMaria-Hamner, Edwards-Hamner, Alexandria; Cowley-Gore, Cowley-Pettaway, Durham; Eichhorn-Senteney 2, Ford-Senteney, McLaughlin-Senteney, Wright-Senteney, Eichhorn-Stemberger, Kinston; Lowry-Damiter, Smith-Stelly-Semprini, Lynchburg; Goff-Cabassa 2, Alicea-Cabassa, Goff-Wright-Faulk, Smith-Adams-Cabassa-Faulk, Goff-Teston-Cabassa-Acosta, Smith-Teston, Carman-Faulk, Carman-Warner, Alicea-Faulk, Carman-Teston-Faulk, Smith-Alicea, Wright-Acosta, Carman-Alicea, Wright-Alicea, Burroughs-Alicea-Cabassa, Peninsula; Baltz-Thomas, Rocky Mount; Barez-Notarino-Jiminez, Ray-Garrity-Carvajal, Zaske-Mohorcic, Zaske-Jiminez, Ray-Parke, Salem; Pecka-Rivas 2, Fredlund-Gering 2, Hulbert-Rivas, Tyler-Rivas, Winston-Salem.

NO-HIT GAME—Behenna, Durham, defeated Rocky Mount, 8-0, August 29.

20 Strikeouts . . . But Hurler Was Out

Pitcher Tom Lewis of the Carolina League's Alexandria Dukes tied a league record for most strikeouts in a game June 18, but he still lost, 7-1, to the Winston-Salem Red Sox.

Lewis struck out 20 batters, fanning at least one batter in each inning and striking out the side four times. But the Sox tapped Lewis for 11 hits and took advantage of three Alexandria errors.

Charlie Timm of Raleigh had 20 strikeouts in 1945 and Wilson's Pete Cimino fanned 20 Burlington batters in 1962.

Back-to-Back One-Hitters

Roy Smith of Peninsula of the Carolina League tossed his second consecutive one-hitter May 26 as the Pilots nipped Alexandria, 2-1, in the first game of a doubleheader.

The Dukes' lone hit was a solo homer by Mike Fitzgerald. Smith and loser Jack Hobbs were locked in a 1-1 tie until the final inning when Joe Bruno's bases-loaded single made a winner of Smith.

Florida State League

CLASS A

CHAMPIONSHIP WINNERS IN PREVIOUS YEARS

1919—Sanford* ..... .605	1948—Orlando ..... .643	1964—Fort Lauderdale† ..... .629
Orlando* ..... .703	Daytona B'ch (2nd)‡ ..... .616	St. Petersburg ..... .594
1920—Tampa ..... .654	1949—Gainesville ..... .635	1965—Fort Lauderdale ..... .627
Tampa ..... .722	St. Augustine (3rd)‡ ..... .556	Fort Lauderdale ..... .634
1921—Orlando ..... .635	1950—Orlando ..... .629	1966—Leesburg† ..... .781
1922—St. Petersburg ..... .503	DeLand (3rd)‡ ..... .590	St. Petersburg ..... .700
St. Petersburg ..... .618	1951—DeLand§ ..... .643	1967—St. Petersburg y ..... .691
1923—Orlando ..... .667	1952—DeLand x ..... .704	Orlando ..... .638
Orlando ..... .678	Palatka (3rd)‡ ..... .569	1968—Miami ..... .613
1924—Lakeland ..... .695	1953—Daytona Beach† ..... .657	Orlando z ..... .579
Lakeland ..... .683	DeLand ..... .703	1969—Miami a ..... .606
1925—St. Petersburg ..... .667	1954—Jacksonville Beach ..... .629	Orlando ..... .606
Tampa† ..... .696	Lakeland† ..... .594	1970—Miami b ..... .662
1926—Sanford ..... .647	1955—Orlando ..... .671	St. Petersburg ..... .600
Sanford ..... .623	Orlando ..... .643	1971—Miami c ..... .667
1927—Orlando† ..... .600	1956—Cocoa ..... .614	Daytona Beach ..... .586
Miami ..... .661	Cocoa ..... .671	1972—Miami c ..... .562
1928-35—Did not operate.	1957—Palatka ..... .629	Daytona Beach ..... .606
1936—Gainesville ..... .542	Tampa† ..... .681	1973—St. Petersburg d ..... .575
St. Augustine (4th)† ..... .492	1958—St. Petersburg ..... .732	West Palm Beach d ..... .580
1937—Gainesville§ ..... .616	St. Petersburg ..... .681	1974—West Palm Beach d ..... .598
1938—Leesburg ..... .626	1959—Tampa ..... .591	Ft. Lauderdale ..... .626
Gainesville (2nd)‡ ..... .615	St. Petersburg† ..... .612	1975—St. Petersburg d ..... .652
1939—Sanford§ ..... .787	1960—Lakeland ..... .731	Miami ..... .581
1940—Daytona Beach ..... .619	Palatka‡ ..... .614	1976—Tampa ..... .559
Orlando (4th)‡ ..... .507	1961—Tampa† ..... .710	Lakeland d ..... .536
1941—St. Augustine ..... .659	Sarasota ..... .696	1977—Lakeland d ..... .616
Leesburg (4th)‡ ..... .488	1962—Sarasota ..... .689	West Palm Beach ..... .583
1942-45—Did not operate.	Fort Lauderdale† ..... .623	1978—Lakeland ..... .565
1946—Orlando§ ..... .681	1963—Sarasota ..... .645	Miami§ ..... .539
1947—St. Augustine ..... .625	Sarasota ..... .667	1979—Ft. Lauderdale ..... .643
Gainesville (2nd)‡ ..... .584		Winter Haven e ..... .577

*Split-season playoff abandoned after each team won three games. †Won split-season playoff. ‡Won four-club playoff. §Won championship and four-club playoff. xWon both halves of split season.

yLeague divided into Eastern and Western divisions with split season. St. Petersburg and Orlando won both halves of split season; St. Petersburg won playoff.

zLeague divided into Eastern and Western divisions. Miami won regular-season pennant on basis of highest won-lost percentage. Orlando won four-club playoff involving first two teams in each division.

aLeague divided into Southern and Central divisions. Miami won playoff between division leaders. (NOTE—Pennant awarded to playoff winner in 1936.)

bLeague divided into Eastern and Western divisions. Miami won regular-season pennant on basis of highest won-loss percentage, and also won four-club playoff involving first two teams in each division.

cLeague divided into Eastern and Western divisions. Won four-club playoff involving first two teams in each division.

dLeague divided into Northern and Southern divisions. Won four-club playoff involving first two teams in each division.

eLeague divided into Northern and Southern divisions. Same two clubs won both halves; won playoffs.

STANDING OF CLUBS AT CLOSE OF SEASON, AUGUST 31

NORTHERN DIVISION

Club	DB.	StP.	Tam.	WH.	Lak.	FtL.	VB.	FtM.	WPB.	Mia.	W.	L.	T.	Pct.	G.B.
Daytona Beach (Astros).....	..	17	10	20	25	2	3	4	2	3	86	51	0	.628	......
St. Petersburg (Cardinals)	7	..	17	17	16	3	2	3	1	4	70	66	0	.515	15½
Tampa (Reds)	18	11	..	17	9	1	4	2		3	64	67	0	.489	19
Winter Haven (Red Sox)..	7	11	15	..	14	1	2	4	4	2	60	80	0	.429	27½
Lakeland (Tigers)	3	10	18	14	..	4	3	2	1	1	56	77	0	.421	28

SOUTHERN DIVISION

Club	DB.	StP.	Tam.	WH.	Lak.	FtL.	VB.	FtM.	WPB.	Mia.	W.	L.	T.	Pct.	G.B.
Ft. Lauderdale (Yankees) .	4	3	2	5	2	..	14	15	17	21	83	54	0	.606	......
Vero Beach (Dodgers)	3	4	2	4	3	14	..	16	16	20	82	59	0	.582	3
Ft. Myers (Royals)..........	2	3	1	2	4	11	16	..	16	15	66	70	0	.485	16½
West Palm Beach (Expos)	4	5	1	2	2	11	12	12	..	15	64	73	0	.467	19
Miami (Orioles).............	3	2	1	3	2	7	8	12	13	..	51	85	0	.375	31½

Major league affiliations in parentheses.

Playoffs—Vero Beach defeated Daytona Beach, two games to none. Fort Lauderdale defeated St. Petersburg, two games to one. Fort Lauderdale defeated Vero Beach, three games to one, for League Championship.

Regular-Season Attendance—Daytona Beach, 50,162; Fort Lauderdale, 78,447; Fort Myers, 55,927; Lakeland, 46,001; Miami, 44,368; St. Petersburg, 124,350; Tampa, 87,660; Vero Beach, 80,063; West Palm Beach, 118,452; Winter Haven, 25,771. Total, 711,201. Playoffs, 7,813. No all-star game.

Managers: Daytona Beach—Carlos Alfonso; Fort Lauderdale—Doug Holmquist; Fort Myers—Brian Murphy; Lakeland—Eddie Brinkman; Miami—Lance Nichols; St. Petersburg—Tommy Thompson; Tampa—George Scherger; Vero Beach—Stan Wasiak; West Palm Beach—Bob Bailey; Winter Haven—Rac Slider.

All-Star Team: 1B—Craig, Vero Beach; Laga, Lakeland; 2B—Doyle, St. Petersburg; W. Johnson, West Palm Beach; 3B—Atkinson, Ft. Myers; Johnson, Lakeland; SS—Wellman, Ft. Myers; Wherry, Daytona Beach; OF—Brewer, Ft. Myers; Brewer, Vero Beach; Jordan, Ft. Lauderdale; L. Ray, Daytona Beach; Redus, Tampa; Watkins, Winter Haven; C—Buffamoyer, Ft. Lauderdale; Davis, St. Petersburg; Sobbe, Vero Beach; Sullivan, Winter Haven; DH—George, West Palm Beach; Sandberg, Winter Haven; P—Dowless, Tampa; Hesketh, West Palm Beach; Madden, Vero Beach; Nelson, Ft. Lauderdale; Paris, Daytona Beach; Perry, Daytona Beach; Riggins, St. Petersburg; Wickensheimer, Vero Beach; Managers—Alfonso, Daytona Beach; Murphy, Ft. Myers.

(Compiled by Howe News Bureau, Boston, Mass.)

CLUB BATTING

Club	G.	AB.	R.	OR.	H.	TB.	2B.	3B.	HR.	RBI.	SH.	SF.	BB.	Int. BB.	HP.	SO.	SB.	CS.	LOB.	Pct.
Vero Beach	141	4523	668	610	1195	1590	147	76	32	571	70	54	591	30	51	620	143	56	1046	.264
Ft. Myers	136	4329	592	577	1116	1445	147	37	36	492	43	45	582	26	32	691	114	44	1036	.258
Daytona Beach	137	4230	684	485	1085	1473	162	41	48	557	34	38	637	36	35	715	176	70	982	.257
Lakeland	133	4271	591	633	1095	1487	153	40	53	525	57	38	583	51	39	725	118	59	1018	.256
St. Petersburg	136	4302	531	558	1095	1394	148	26	33	470	65	46	517	34	26	602	102	73	988	.255
W. Palm Beach	137	4369	627	622	1113	1493	155	30	55	542	51	43	629	15	32	602	164	85	1011	.255
Ft. Lauderdale	137	4215	553	490	1026	1363	143	31	44	465	70	41	660	36	38	685	113	65	1046	.243
Winter Haven	140	4447	518	653	1077	1343	136	23	28	444	63	41	595	32	27	660	72	25	1111	.242
Miami	136	4256	525	651	995	1338	133	39	44	465	41	38	612	24	32	862	120	50	1016	.234
Tampa	131	4031	434	444	936	1239	122	38	35	368	93	30	475	28	39	797	121	46	927	.232

INDIVIDUAL BATTING

(Leading Qualifiers for Batting Championship—383 or More Plate Appearances)

*Bats lefthanded.   †Switch-hitter.

Player and Club	G.	AB.	R.	H.	TB.	2B.	3B.	HR.	RBI.	SH.	SF.	BB.	HP.	SO.	SB.	CS.	Pct.
Johnson, Wallace, W. Palm Beach†	126	488	86	163	199	17	5	3	49	5	3	60	0	22	58	22	.334
Wellman, Brad, Ft. Myers	105	390	67	130	162	15	7	1	39	2	4	38	1	30	11	5	.333
Redus, Gary, Tampa	128	452	78	136	220	18	9	16	68	5	2	66	4	78	50	12	.301
Ray, Larry, Daytona Beach*	125	386	64	115	165	24	4	6	67	1	6	73	3	95	17	5	.298
Doyle, Jeffrey, St. Petersburg†	130	484	65	142	174	20	6	0	52	10	4	53	3	37	22	9	.293
Johnson, Howard, Lakeland†	130	474	83	135	195	28	1	10	69	16	2	73	2	75	31	5	.285
Brewer, Anthony, Vero Beach	137	470	79	134	184	17	12	3	59	7	5	64	4	45	17	6	.285
Wherry, Clifton, Daytona Beach	121	369	62	105	130	9	8	0	39	5	5	49	2	62	12	4	.285
Watkins, James, Winter Haven	117	437	52	124	151	13	4	2	54	5	7	37	1	72	26	6	.284
Sax, Stephen, Vero Beach	139	530	78	150	193	18	8	3	61	11	5	51	5	26	33	10	.283

Departmental Leaders: G—Craig, S. Sax, 139; AB—Rivera, S. Sax, 530; R—Strucher, 88; H—W. Johnson, 163; TB—Redus, 220; 2B—H. Johnson, 28; 3B—Brewer, Craig, 12; HR—Strucher, 17; RBI—Rivera, 80; GWRBI—Stenhouse, 12; SH—H. Johnson, 16; SF—Auten, Rivera, 10; BB—Stenhouse, 123; HP—Walker, 15; SO—Strucher, 116; SB—W. Johnson, 58; CS—W. Johnson, 22.

(All Players—Listed Alphabetically)

Player and Club	G.	AB.	R.	H.	TB.	2B.	3B.	HR.	RBI.	SH.	SF.	BB.	HP.	SO.	SB.	CS.	Pct.
Adams, Jeffery, Tampa	26	54	4	14	17	0	0	1	7	0	1	11	0	13	0	0	.259
Adams, Kalvin, West Palm Beach	73	207	25	49	62	4	0	3	23	4	2	22	4	27	3	3	.237
Adduci, James, St. Petersburg*	37	118	29	32	42	4	0	2	13	0	0	24	2	24	2	1	.271
Anderson, Scott, West Palm Beach	27	0	1	0	0	0	0	0	0	0	0	0	0	0	0	0	.000
Atkinson, James J., W. Palm Beach	111	318	37	70	93	11	3	2	35	1	0	28	2	53	11	5	.220
Atkinson, James W., Ft. Myers*	117	408	59	108	157	16	9	5	54	5	5	67	3	53	15	2	.265
Auten, James, West Palm Beach	127	419	50	100	141	14	3	7	65	3	10	42	7	49	10	0	.239
Ayer, Jonathan, St. Petersburg	129	460	59	112	147	24	1	3	59	5	1	52	1	66	17	9	.243
Baskerville, Phillip, St. Pete.*	19	31	8	4	7	0	0	1	6	3	1	13	0	8	1	1	.129
Beltran, Julio, Daytona Beach	85	232	45	56	66	4	3	0	22	0	3	29	5	21	31	7	.241
Bessard, Lloyd, Winter Haven	90	290	31	54	80	10	2	4	28	0	3	32	3	70	1	0	.186
Biancalana, Roland, Ft. Myers†	92	258	30	44	53	5	2	0	28	6	4	40	4	54	4	4	.171
Boddy, William, Tampa	86	232	19	53	64	7	2	0	21	3	1	29	1	44	0	1	.228
Bonham, William, Tampa	3	4	0	1	1	0	0	0	1	0	0	1	0	0	0	0	.250
Bowman, Bruss, Miami*	17	47	6	11	13	2	0	0	3	0	0	9	0	16	0	1	.234
Bowman, Donald, Miami	105	367	41	92	139	10	2	11	56	2	2	40	5	82	6	0	.251
Boyce, Robert, Miami	11	32	5	6	7	0	0	0	1	0	1	6	2	8	1	0	.188
Bozich, Gary, Lakeland	119	433	85	113	134	9	3	2	29	4	2	83	6	46	26	11	.261
Bresnahan, Raymond, Ft. Myers	16	46	5	11	14	1	1	0	10	0	1	6	0	11	1	0	.239
Brewer, Anthony, Vero Beach	137	470	79	134	184	17	12	3	59	7	5	64	4	45	17	6	.285
Brewer, Michael, Ft. Myers	123	426	54	102	141	13	4	6	63	2	5	53	1	90	21	8	.239
Brummer, Thomas, Winter Haven*	77	221	24	51	57	4	1	0	16	3	2	32	2	30	1	0	.231

Player and Club	G.	AB.	R.	H.	TB.	2B.	3B.	HR.	RBI.	SH.	SF.	BB.	HP.	SO.	SB.	CS.	Pct.
Buchanan, Robert, Tampa*	28	29	3	3	3	0	0	0	0	2	0	7	0	8	0	0	.103
Buffamoyer, David, Ft. Lauderdale	60	154	27	41	55	9	1	1	20	1	0	47	4	28	2	2	.266
Burtt, Gregory, Miami*	40	110	11	24	30	1	1	1	9	0	2	21	0	27	2	2	.218
Bustabad, Juan, Winter Haven*	128	431	58	109	120	7	2	0	35	7	3	54	1	34	19	7	.253
Butler, William, Miami	12	41	7	6	8	0	1	0	3	0	0	0	1	2	2	1	.146
Butterfield, Brian, Ft. Lauderdale..	8	16	3	2	2	0	0	0	2	1	0	4	0	2	0	1	.125
Cajuso, A. Eduardo, Lakeland	23	61	6	11	13	2	0	0	2	1	0	4	0	2	0	1	.180
Campbell, Mark, Daytona Beach	70	188	29	52	61	9	0	0	9	2	0	2	0	17	0	0	.180
Carter, Howard, Lakeland	36	121	14	28	46	3	0	5	20	2	2	2	0	26	7	1	.277
Cato, J. Keefe, Tampa	11	23	2	2	2	0	0	0	0	4	0	3	0	8	0	0	.231
Clarkson, Michael, Miami*	49	147	15	30	34	2	1	0	14	2	1	20	1	22	8	3	.087
Clements, Wesley, Daytona Beach .	4	13	2	4	7	0	0	1	1	0	0	0	0	5	0	0	.204
Cochran, Michael, Lakeland	16	45	4	9	12	3	0	0	5	1	1	5	0	10	0	1	.308
Corbett, Raymond, Tampa	39	103	11	19	21	2	0	0	4	3	1	17	1	20	0	1	.200
Correll, Victor, Tampa	14	35	5	12	14	2	0	0	8	0	0	8	0	1	0	0	.184
Craig, Randall, Vero Beach†	139	481	72	133	175	15	12	1	62	0	4	94	6	76	7	3	.343
Cruz, Jose, West Palm Beach*	89	261	40	72	89	7	5	0	33	1	3	32	1	29	9	5	.277
Culbert, Aurdie, Lakeland	82	264	41	66	96	13	4	3	35	3	4	45	2	57	1	1	.276
Davis, Jody, St. Petersburg	45	155	27	43	65	4	0	6	27	0	5	18	1	36	1	0	.250
Dayette, Brian, Ft. Lauderdale	52	174	31	43	67	8	2	4	21	1	3	30	0	31	3	2	.277
Dees, Gregory, Miami*	80	257	17	52	70	11	2	1	21	3	2	28	2	72	1	0	.247
Del Monte, John, St. Petersburg*	60	166	16	32	38	3	0	1	15	1	1	30	0	28	6	5	.202
Delany, Dennis, St. Petersburg	103	324	28	68	81	10	0	1	28	10	6	45	2	27	2	6	.193
Derryberry, Timothy, Miami*	9	33	4	7	16	3	0	2	6	0	0	3	0	6	0	0	.210
Dewey, Duane, Ft. Myers	53	140	15	29	37	2	0	2	17	4	2	31	2	33	1	0	.212
Dieters, James, St. Petersburg*	10	27	2	3	3	0	0	0	3	2	1	5	1	4	0	0	.207
Dodd, Thomas, Ft. Lauderdale	103	269	45	68	105	10	3	7	29	3	1	50	6	57	3	3	.111
Dodson, Patrick, Winter Haven*	61	190	26	52	73	18	0	1	36	1	2	48	2	49	0	1	.253
Doran, William, Daytona Beach†	102	369	62	90	113	11	3	2	45	2	2	50	0	53	20	13	.274
Dowless, Michael, Tampa	29	52	4	8	11	0	0	1	4	4	0	7	0	23	0	0	.244
Doyle, Jeffrey, St. Petersburg†	130	484	65	142	174	20	6	0	52	10	4	53	3	37	22	9	.154
Dummar, George, Miami*	26	52	4	5	5	0	0	0	3	0	0	9	1	15	0	0	.293
Duval, Michael, Tampa*	39	119	20	33	45	3	3	1	14	2	0	9	0	19	5	3	.096
Ervin, Todd, Lakeland*	24	84	13	26	40	3	4	1	11	1	0	10	0	7	0	1	.277
Espinoza, Steven, Miami	113	303	42	64	89	11	4	2	38	10	2	57	3	54	8	7	.310
Feliz, Adolfo, Tampa	128	447	44	120	148	17	4	1	37	14	4	46	3	61	16	6	.211
Ferris, Robert, Ft. Myers	59	193	29	51	64	10	0	1	26	0	5	38	0	49	0	1	.268
Fick, Charles, West Palm Beach	16	39	5	3	4	1	0	0	5	0	0	9	0	1	1	1	.264
Fields, Bruce, Lakeland*	53	162	22	37	49	5	2	1	15	3	2	30	1	25	11	5	.077
Filson, W. Peter, Ft. Lauderdale*	23	0	0	0	0	0	0	0	0	1	0	0	0	0	0	0	.228
Fisher, Keith, Lakeland	82	253	21	52	76	11	2	3	28	2	1	32	4	51	1	0	.000
Gaglione, Matthew, Winter Haven*	39	133	5	25	31	6	0	0	11	0	2	7	2	38	0	0	.206
Gainey, Telmanch, Day. Beach*	5	12	3	1	1	0	0	0	0	0	0	0	0	3	1	0	.188
Garbey, Barbaro, Lakeland	26	88	15	32	39	4	0	1	16	1	1	10	2	5	1	1	.083
Garcia, Nelson, St. Petersburg†	18	41	3	8	11	1	1	0	5	1	2	5	0	7	1	1	.364
Gavillan, Pedro, West Palm Beach*	54	114	11	31	38	4	0	1	16	5	2	12	2	18	0	3	.195
George, Jerry, West Palm Beach*	93	279	54	74	104	15	0	5	38	3	4	73	4	64	3	3	.272
Gill, Frank, Winter Haven*	77	256	37	64	69	5	0	0	17	5	2	36	2	12	12	2	.265
Girata, Daniel, Ft. Lauderdale	26	65	8	12	17	3	1	0	7	1	1	11	0	10	0	0	.250
Glynn, Eugene, West Palm Beach .	109	291	50	63	78	10	1	1	23	3	2	64	2	49	17	12	.185
Good, James, Lakeland	33	93	5	21	27	3	0	1	8	1	2	8	1	34	0	0	.216
Guerra, Randall, Ft. Lauderdale	136	436	51	107	139	15	1	5	62	4	3	107	0	56	1	1	.226
Gutierrez, Joaquin, Winter Haven	111	368	46	94	103	4	1	1	40	10	1	39	2	34	2	2	.245
Guzman, Hector, Vero Beach*	39	114	17	26	29	3	0	0	11	2	2	9	0	24	8	2	.255
Hagemann, Kenneth, Win. Hav.*	87	233	26	52	59	7	0	0	19	3	1	49	0	51	4	1	.228
Haley, J. Michael, Ft. Myers	9	30	2	6	6	0	0	0	1	0	0	5	0	5	1	1	.223
Hardy, William, Lakeland	86	316	37	88	99	6	1	1	31	3	1	17	2	35	11	8	.200
Harper, Arvis, Daytona Beach†	82	257	45	75	111	18	0	6	47	1	2	50	2	29	7	4	.278
Harper, Daryl, Ft. Myers	16	62	9	23	23	0	0	0	13	0	0	11	0	2	0	0	.292
Harris, Michael, St. Petersburg	4	6	0	1	2	1	0	0	0	0	0	0	0	2	0	0	.371
Hawthorne, Kyle, Miami	48	164	19	40	56	8	1	2	22	0	1	30	1	31	0	2	.167
Hayes, Ben, Tampa	41	4	0	0	0	0	0	0	0	0	0	2	0	1	0	0	.244
Headford, Grant, Miami	16	48	6	7	9	0	1	0	3	0	0	2	0	1	0	0	.000
Hendrickson, Stanley, Miami*	17	48	7	10	12	2	0	0	3	0	1	0	1	19	2	0	.146
Hernandez, Leonardo, Vero Beach	82	307	53	95	144	13	3	10	46	1	3	30	1	37	10	2	.309
Herrick, Neal, Miami	59	168	21	35	42	2	1	1	13	1	0	24	2	43	5	1	.208
Hill, Elmore, Ft. Myers	18	44	9	16	26	2	1	2	6	0	1	5	0	5	0	0	.208
Holt, David, Winter Haven*	89	266	29	62	78	8	1	2	24	0	3	51	0	31	0	0	.364
Houlberg, Steven, Lakeland	67	212	26	55	80	8	4	3	21	2	2	25	3	51	9	4	.233
Hudler, A. Rex, Ft. Lauderdale	37	125	14	26	30	4	0	0	6	2	2	2	0	25	2	0	.259
Hughes, Joseph, Miami*	19	45	6	7	10	0	0	1	5	0	1	7	0	10	0	0	.208
Jabalera, Francisco, Day. Beach*	119	410	66	110	127	7	5	0	37	6	3	46	5	58	16	10	.156
Jackson, Larry, Tampa	23	33	3	4	5	1	0	0	2	0	5	0	19	0	0	1	.268
Johnson, Howard, Lakeland†	130	474	83	135	195	28	1	10	69	16	2	73	2	75	31	5	.121
Johnson, Rodney, Tampa	75	204	15	38	46	7	0	0	14	3	0	27	0	26	0	1	.285
Johnson, Roy, West Palm Beach*	24	85	11	19	28	4	1	1	12	1	1	8	0	16	1	0	.186
																	.224

Player and Club	G.	AB.	R.	H.	TB.	2B.	3B.	HR.	RBI.	SH.	SF.	BB.	HP.	SO.	SB.	CS.	Pct.
Johnson, Wallace, W. Palm Beach†	126	488	86	163	199	17	5	3	49	5	3	60	0	22	58	22	.334
Jones, Christopher, Day. Beach*	124	413	77	103	145	9	9	5	54	4	4	62	0	58	40	10	.249
Jones, Ross, Vero Beach	70	233	35	59	91	14	3	4	37	5	5	40	3	49	8	3	.253
Jordan, Timothy, Ft. Lauderdale	126	430	57	109	144	18	4	3	43	9	3	44	4	63	24	11	.253
Josephson, Paul, West Palm Beach	35	1	0	1	1	0	0	0	1	0	0	0	0	0	0	0	1.000
Kepshire, Kurt, Tampa*	29	5	0	1	1	0	0	0	0	2	0	0	0	4	0	0	.200
Khoury, Peter, Ft. Lauderdale	58	156	18	39	43	2	1	0	16	4	0	27	3	16	1	0	.250
Laga, Michael, Lakeland*	122	407	60	111	173	14	6	12	74	4	8	72	12	71	5	5	.273
Lais, John, Tampa*	73	225	22	59	73	5	3	1	26	5	2	25	2	36	1	3	.262
Layne, David, Vero Beach	4	6	1	2	2	0	0	0	0	0	0	2	1	0	0	0	.333
Lepel, Joel, West Palm Beach	45	137	12	36	47	5	0	2	26	1	1	15	0	21	1	1	.263
Lesley, Bradley, Tampa	37	19	0	1	1	0	0	0	1	1	0	0	0	3	0	0	.053
Lewis, J. Tod, Ft. Myers	61	178	25	39	55	8	1	2	21	6	2	30	5	46	1	0	.219
Liggins, Danny, St. Petersburg	61	216	22	58	62	2	1	0	10	5	0	2	5	34	6	5	.269
Lindberg, Ronald, Lakeland	25	64	12	9	10	1	0	0	8	1	1	12	0	9	0	0	.141
Little, R. Bryan, W. Palm Beach†	64	195	23	43	45	2	0	0	11	9	2	31	1	7	4	3	.221
Locascio, John, Tampa*	45	13	0	5	5	0	0	0	1	0	0	1	0	6	0	0	.385
Lowry, Dwight, Lakeland	45	142	18	28	33	5	0	0	16	0	3	21	0	22	0	0	.197
Malaspin, Gustavo, Winter Haven	112	368	46	84	104	5	0	5	35	5	4	60	3	34	3	1	.228
Malkin, John, Vero Beach	20	54	5	10	11	1	0	0	6	0	1	6	0	11	0	0	.185
Mann, Leo, Vero Beach†	87	276	51	72	87	6	3	1	20	6	1	48	4	34	21	3	.261
Maples, Stephen, Vero Beach	23	51	5	3	4	1	0	0	2	0	0	9	3	24	0	0	.059
Marin, Fernando, W. Palm Beach	15	35	6	9	10	1	0	0	1	0	0	5	0	9	0	0	.257
Marston, Anderson, Miami	45	127	14	26	30	4	0	0	20	0	0	24	0	19	0	0	.205
Martin, Jeffrey, Winter Haven	117	365	42	91	127	18	3	4	40	8	3	42	1	64	0	0	.249
Martin, Ruell, Vero Beach	4	10	0	1	1	0	0	0	1	0	2	0	3	0	0	.100
Martinez, M. Dean, Tampa	21	8	0	1	1	0	0	0	0	0	0	1	0	4	0	0	.125
May, Ted, Ft. Lauderdale*	46	114	15	24	41	2	0	5	16	1	1	35	0	46	0	1	.211
McCauley, Stanley, St. Petersburg	85	268	27	64	86	14	1	2	32	5	4	25	0	30	0	2	.239
McIntyre, James, St. Petersburg	95	301	37	79	111	12	4	4	45	1	2	44	1	64	7	6	.262
McKinney, Gregory, Tampa*	108	362	27	81	83	11	1	3	19	5	2	40	1	85	2	4	.223
McKnight, James, Daytona Beach	81	207	20	48	56	4	2	0	30	3	2	13	0	12	5	0	.232
Medina, Valintin, Daytona Beach	79	260	29	57	78	9	0	4	30	5	2	14	5	54	4	3	.219
Michael, Steven, Lakeland*	50	171	20	47	64	12	1	1	27	0	0	32	0	25	4	2	.275
Miklosi, Jerry, Winter Haven	65	233	26	59	70	5	3	0	16	7	2	19	1	30	1	1	.253
Mills, Rhadames, St. Petersburg	39	152	16	47	54	3	2	0	17	3	3	9	0	13	3	7	.309
Miserock, John, Daytona Beach	99	299	37	66	85	11	1	2	39	0	3	47	3	52	2	1	.221
Mohler, S. Keith, Vero Beach	81	204	19	36	53	4	5	1	21	5	1	19	5	45	1	4	.176
Moore, Donald, St. Petersburg†	89	312	39	94	138	11	3	9	52	0	3	31	2	46	4	3	.301
Morgan, John, Winter Haven	16	45	0	9	11	2	0	0	0	0	1	0	7	0	0	.200
Morrison, Steven, W. Palm Beach*	52	187	32	55	71	11	1	1	22	0	3	21	1	19	6	3	.294
Motley, Darryl, Ft. Myers	32	119	20	36	55	7	0	4	24	0	1	10	1	18	3	1	.303
Murelli, Donald, Miami	88	283	29	78	98	8	3	2	32	7	0	32	1	28	7	5	.276
Noble, Charles, Tampa*	15	7	0	0	0	0	0	0	0	2	0	0	0	3	0	0	.000
Palmer, Robert, Miami	77	209	18	44	57	8	1	1	20	3	2	31	3	57	2	2	.211
Patterson, S. Craig, Ft. Myers	121	415	67	110	127	13	2	0	35	3	3	79	2	57	9	3	.265
Paulino, Jose, Ft. Lauderdale	42	8	7	2	6	1	0	1	2	0	0	0	2	0	0	.250
Pavlik, John, Miami	113	409	54	99	118	6	5	1	29	6	1	60	3	84	36	11	.242
Phillips, Leonard, W. Palm Beach*	31	108	16	20	41	7	1	4	18	0	1	11	1	30	2	2	.185
Pierce, Walter, St. Petersburg	105	340	31	87	112	13	3	2	43	4	6	39	2	59	4	3	.256
Plante, Daniel, Ft. Lauderdale	88	232	17	53	61	5	0	1	25	8	5	28	1	36	1	1	.228
Primante, Valintino, Daytona Bch†	107	309	41	82	118	19	1	5	51	2	4	98	1	61	3	7	.265
Proulx, Patrick, St. Petersburg	52	144	16	41	44	3	0	0	15	6	1	22	3	24	1	2	.285
Pyle, Scot, Lakeland	30	76	8	16	16	0	0	0	7	0	1	21	1	12	0	1	.211
Raines, Ned, Miami	33	123	21	30	39	5	2	0	14	2	2	13	1	18	9	2	.244
Ramsey, Michael, Tampa	32	19	7	2	2	0	0	0	1	1	0	6	0	10	0	0	.105
Ray, Larry, Daytona Beach*	125	386	64	115	165	24	4	6	67	1	6	73	3	95	17	5	.298
Redus, Gary, Tampa	128	452	78	136	220	18	9	16	68	5	2	66	4	78	50	12	.301
Reyes, Mariano, Vero Beach†	3	3	0	0	0	0	0	0	0	0	0	1	0	0	0	0	.000
Reynolds, Jeffrey, Ft. Lauderdale	21	63	4	15	21	2	2	0	7	1	0	13	0	18	1	1	.238
Rincones, Hector, Tampa	125	419	41	93	105	10	1	0	24	12	3	31	6	34	10	5	.222
Rivas, Raymond, St. Petersburg*	102	359	50	89	109	11	3	1	24	7	3	49	2	31	10	4	.248
Rivera, D. German, Vero Beach	137	530	77	137	188	19	10	4	80	1	10	19	5	54	13	9	.258
Robbins, Wesley, Ft. Lauderdale	128	455	65	127	175	19	4	7	61	4	5	72	1	48	34	16	.279
Roberson, Ell, Lakeland	8	29	3	4	5	1	0	0	2	0	0	3	0	0	0	.138
Robertson, Andre, Ft. Lauderdale	63	233	30	58	73	7	4	0	22	7	2	17	2	41	10	3	.249
Robinson, Ronald, Tampa	13	25	2	6	9	0	0	1	6	3	0	1	0	9	0	0	.240
Rodriguez, Julio, Ft. Myers	47	111	14	19	22	1	1	0	6	3	0	15	0	33	3	0	.171
Rodriguez, Eduardo, Miami	15	36	1	7	8	1	0	0	4	0	1	5	0	5	2	1	.194
Rodriguez, R. Victor, Miami	50	184	21	60	80	10	2	2	21	1	3	18	0	16	1	2	.326
Roeder, Steven, West Palm Beach	11	27	2	3	3	0	0	0	2	0	0	5	0	8	0	0	.111
Rollin, Rondal, Lakeland	60	229	25	57	84	5	5	4	40	1	2	15	1	53	1	3	.249
Romero, Andres, Miami*	49	153	26	42	54	6	2	0	18	0	5	21	1	19	2	1	.275
Rossi, Joseph, Vero Beach	121	374	47	90	115	11	4	2	51	15	4	36	5	105	10	3	.241
Ruiz, August, Vero Beach*	41	1	0	1	1	0	0	0	0	0	0	0	0	0	0	0	1.000
Ryal, Mark, Ft. Myers*	123	440	60	117	159	21	3	5	51	1	3	29	1	70	6	4	.266

Player and Club	G.	AB.	R.	H.	TB.	2B.	3B.	HR.	RBI.	SH.	SF.	BB.	HP.	SO.	SB.	CS.	Pct.
Salazar, Roberto, Lakeland*	21	59	5	12	16	2	1	0	3	3	0	5	0	10	0	0	.203
Sandberg, Charles, Winter Haven*	57	176	24	43	70	10	1	5	32	1	4	37	0	41	1	0	.244
Santana, Rafael, Ft. Lauderdale	51	168	20	38	43	2	0	1	17	7	2	23	1	12	4	1	.226
Sax, David, Vero Beach	58	193	33	68	92	8	5	2	33	1	4	44	2	12	5	3	.352
Sax, Stephen, Vero Beach	139	530	78	150	193	18	8	3	61	11	5	51	5	26	33	10	.283
Sayler, Barry, St. Petersburg	4	5	0	0	0	0	0	0	0	0	0	2	0	3	0	0	.000
Scarpace, Kenneth, Tampa*	71	259	18	53	66	6	2	1	14	3	3	16	1	33	5	2	.205
Schrimsher, M. Keith, Tampa	10	7	0	1	1	0	0	0	0	0	0	0	0	3	0	0	.143
Sheridan, Patrick, Ft. Myers*	20	79	17	32	36	1	0	1	13	1	0	9	0	9	8	2	.405
Shines, Raymond, West Palm Bch†	73	267	27	64	99	15	1	6	40	1	0	26	2	30	5	5	.240
Silva, Ildemaro, St. Petersburg	8	12	3	4	4	0	0	0	1	0	0	2	0	4	0	0	.333
Simmons, D. Wayne, W. Palm Bch	62	192	30	53	56	3	0	0	16	3	0	22	0	27	7	2	.276
Simon, Mark, Tampa*	66	131	7	23	28	1	2	0	11	2	3	5	1	35	0	0	.176
Slaught, Donald, Ft. Myers	50	176	13	46	61	9	0	2	16	3	2	16	0	11	3	2	.261
Smith, Clay, Vero Beach*	91	284	43	75	108	10	10	1	42	5	4	38	4	40	2	3	.264
Sobbe, William, Vero Beach*	116	362	50	94	101	5	1	0	37	9	5	68	2	25	7	5	.260
Solomon, Neil, Miami	13	21	3	4	4	0	0	0	1	0	0	7	0	7	0	0	.190
Sorel, Michael, Tampa	36	71	5	13	15	0	1	0	6	2	0	2	1	9	0	2	.183
Sporrer, Gregory, Ft. Lauderdale	58	119	14	27	31	4	0	0	8	3	2	26	1	17	1	1	.227
Spreckles, Keith, St. Petersburg†	9	26	1	3	4	1	0	0	1	0	0	7	1	7	0	1	.115
Stefero, John, Miami*	101	307	32	66	98	9	4	5	30	0	4	36	1	73	1	1	.215
Stenhouse, Michael, W. Palm Bch*	133	439	77	120	190	17	7	13	71	10	6	123	3	70	17	13	.273
Strucher, Mark, Daytona Beach	128	422	88	99	186	26	5	17	71	3	1	71	6	116	7	4	.235
Sullivan, Marc, Winter Haven	94	293	32	66	92	8	3	4	30	4	2	42	3	51	2	1	.225
Sullivan, Michael, Tampa	18	29	3	5	5	0	0	0	2	0	4	0	0	10	0	0	.172
Swires, Glenn, Ft. Lauderdale	57	181	12	32	39	4	0	1	14	2	1	17	0	38	2	4	.177
Taylor, James, Tampa	63	203	15	44	62	9	3	27	3	0	14	3	45	3	0	.217
Teegarden, Robert, Ft. Lauderdale	118	360	55	79	114	8	3	7	54	6	9	71	8	72	1	5	.219
Thomas, Marc, Daytona Beach	34	84	14	22	24	2	0	0	4	2	0	9	1	14	4	1	.262
Tinkler, Jack, St. Petersburg	4	10	0	3	3	0	0	0	1	1	0	0	2	0	0	.300
Tirado, Julio, Tampa*	20	39	3	7	8	1	0	0	5	0	0	5	0	16	0	0	.179
Toal, Arthur, Lakeland	5	16	4	3	4	1	0	0	0	0	4	0	1	1	.188
Townley, Robin, Ft. Myers	122	413	47	97	119	13	3	1	28	4	2	69	5	53	11	8	.235
Turco, Steve, St. Petersburg*	99	315	51	78	94	11	1	1	21	1	2	33	0	41	15	7	.248
Turner, Ira, Ft. Myers	61	222	30	62	81	7	3	2	23	0	3	17	4	42	13	1	.279
Tyner, Matthew, Miami	54	149	18	38	63	10	0	5	23	1	5	27	1	32	6	3	.255
Upshaw, John, Lakeland	2	8	0	2	3	1	0	0	0	0	0	0	0	2	0	0	.250
Venger, Tad, Tampa*	44	101	9	18	25	2	1	1	7	1	1	10	0	41	1	1	.178
Villaescusa, Juan, Vero Beach*	13	35	2	9	11	2	0	0	5	1	0	3	0	3	1	0	.257
Villaman, Rafael, Ft. Lauderdale	124	457	59	124	157	20	5	1	33	4	3	36	5	67	23	12	.271
Walker, Tony, Tampa	127	397	65	100	153	20	9	5	43	5	7	75	15	90	28	5	.252
Wallace, Curtis, Ft. Myers†	68	179	21	38	47	3	0	2	15	2	1	15	0	22	3	1	.212
Watkins, James, Winter Haven	117	437	52	124	151	13	4	2	54	5	7	37	1	72	26	6	.284
Wellman, Brad, Ft. Myers	105	390	67	130	162	15	7	1	39	2	4	38	1	30	11	5	.333
Wells, John, Lakeland	74	231	30	59	73	6	1	2	27	5	1	42	2	38	9	5	.255
Wherry, Clifton, Daytona Beach	121	369	62	105	130	9	8	0	39	5	5	49	2	62	12	4	.285
Whitfield, N. Jerome, W. Palm Bch	22	63	6	10	11	0	0	1	4	0	1	0	1	18	0	1	.159
Winslow, Daniel, St. Petersburg	11	28	1	3	6	0	0	1	0	0	0	2	0	4	0	1	.107
Wren, Frank, West Palm Beach	62	217	23	55	81	7	2	5	31	1	2	25	1	35	9	1	.253
Wright, Jackie, Winter Haven	40	142	14	38	48	6	2	0	11	2	0	9	4	12	0	3	.268
Young, Michael, Miami*	115	393	72	105	149	13	8	5	52	2	3	73	2	91	18	6	.267
Younger, Stanley, Lakeland*	61	233	34	74	100	7	5	3	24	2	1	13	0	27	7	4	.318
Zunino, Gary, St. Petersburg	1	1	0	0	0	0	0	0	0	0	0	0	0	0	0	0	.000

The following pitchers had no plate appearances primarily through use of designated hitters, listed alphabetically by club, games in parentheses.

DAYTONA BEACH—Bonine, Eddie (15); Brown, Lawrence (24); Finch, Michael* (21); Houston, Kevin* (25); Meckes, Timothy (14); Morris, Jeffrey* (3); Paris, Sacarias (23); Perry, W. Patrick* (22); Petersen, Gregory (23); Quealey, Steven (21); Ray, William (6); Rice, Andrew* (27); Ross, Mark (30); Smith, K. Blaine (33); Welenc, Douglas (17).

FORT LAUDERDALE—Akchurin, Erol (16); Carlucci, Richard* (31); Ervey, Albert (4); Gaston, John (1); Gleckel, Scott* (24); Hernandez, Carlo* (1); Kaufman, Curt (27); Lein, Christopher (30); Nelson, R. Eugene (27); Nurthen, John (5); Olwine, Edward* (2); Pearson, Donald (11); Ricci, Frank (21); Toliver, Freddie (3); Wever, Stefan (15).

FORT MYERS—Candiotti, Thomas (7); Creel, S. Keith (6); DiLorenzo, Christopher (22); Ganger, Robert (13); Gladden, Jeffrey (4); Grzybek, Benjamin (14); Hanslovan, Jeffrey* (12); Miller, William (10); Pippin, Craig (45); Raine, Steve (24); Skinner, John (3); Smith, Ronald (17); Timlin, Timothy (24); Vanderbush, Walter (6); White, Peder (32—16 with Miami); Williams, Larry (20); Woodworth, Brian (19).

LAKELAND—Beecroft, Michael* (26); Camp, Michael (3); Chretien, Gordon (15); Clark, James (4); Codiroli, Christopher (9); Collyer, Richard* (3); Dacko, Mark* (5); Day, Charles* (5); Dunn, Steven* (19); Geiger, Burwell (48); Hensley, Charles* (28); Moller, John (29); Moncrief, Homer (13); Nail, Charles (13); Sanchez, Luis (10); Simerly, James (17); Smith, Jack (14); Warren, Michael (13); Wheeler, James (34).

MIAMI—Alvarez, Evelio (21); Brown, Mark* (10); Clark, Irvin* (12); Davis, George (25); Edwards, Allen (23); Franke, Thomas (16); Gonzalez, Julian* (8); Grant, Michael (21); Graven, Timothy (17); Hook, Edwin (8); Jordan,

Kenneth (1); Kreymborg, Michael (9); Maples, Timothy (11); Martinez, J. Dennis (2); Peralta, Luis (21); Smith, Freddie (22); Swaggerty, William (19); Villa, Tony† (9); Woodall, Lawrence* (17); Zedonek, Gary (4).

ST. PETERSBURG—Burchett, Kerry (27); Collins, Donald (2); Gotay, Ruben (16); Gott, James (25); Horton, Ricky* (6); Houser, Brett (10); Johnson, Jerry (27); Jones, David (7); Martinez, Silvio (2); Morton, Dennis* (10); Pimental, Rafael (36); Riggins, Mark (57); Russell, Robert (20); Stuper, John (24); Thomas, William (11); Vega, Axel (3); Weaver, Earl (4); Williams, Ray (10).

TAMPA—Mulholland, Kevin* (9).

VERO BEACH—Borbon, Ernesto (12); Daniel, David (33); Foster, Robert (8); Joyce, Kevin (21); Madden, Morris* (27); Malden, Christopher (25); Pena, Alejandro (35); Perry, Stephen (25); Sutcliffe, Terry (21); Tennant, Michael (19); Wickensheimer, C. Charles (26).

WEST PALM BEACH—Blows, Louis* (34); Caldwell, Ronnie (17); Cates, Timothy (11); Chapin, Peter (9); Fadhel, C. Antonio (11); Hesketh, Joseph* (11); Maher, R. James (4); O'Connor, Jack (17); Sattler, William (16); Schuler, Mark (13); St. John, William* (4); Staffon, Gregory (17); Taylor, Jeffrey* (17); Torres, Miguel (21); Wick, David* (25—11 with Miami); Williams, Richard* (4); Yanus, Raymond (10).

WINTER HAVEN—Baldwin, Oscar (31); Birrell, Robert* (19); Brown, Michael (17); Collins, Stephen (36); Davis, Gordon* (26); Davis, William (32); DeSanto, Thomas (19); Grubbs, Kevin (13); Hayford, Donald (29); Johnson, Clinton (29); Moloney, William* (30); Nipper, Albert (16); Schneck, Steven (13).

GRAND SLAM HOME RUNS—K. Adams, J. W. Atkinson, Auten, Ferris, A. Harper, McIntyre, Mizerock, Phillips, Sheridan, Stenhouse, Tyner, Walker, Young, 1 each.

AWARDED FIRST BASE ON INTERFERENCE—J. W. Atkinson 2 (Fick, Stefero), Watkins 2 (Fisher, Winslow), Doran (Shines), Doyle (Boddy), Mizerock (Sullivan), Simmons (Lewis), Wellman (Malkin).

GAME-WINNING RBIs

DAYTONA BEACH (59)—Jones 11, Mizerock 7, L. Ray 6, Doran 5, Medina 5, Strucher 5, Harper 4, Campbell 3, McKnight 3, Primante 3, Jabalera 2, Wherry 2, Beltran 1, Clements 1, Thomas 1.

FORT LAUDERDALE (56)—Jordan 7, Plante 7, Robbins 6, Dodd 5, Guerra 5, Teegarden 5, Villaman 5, Robertson 4, Buffamoyer 3, Dayette 2, Reynolds 2, Hudler 1, May 1, Santana 1, Sporrer 1, Swires 1.

FORT MYERS (43)—Atkinson 5, Brewer 5, Ryal 5, Townley 5, Wellman 4, Ferris 3, Biancalana 2, Bresnahan 2, Harper 2, Lewis 2, Wallace 2, Hill 1, Motley 1, Patterson 1, Rodriguez 1, Slaught 1, Turner 1.

LAKELAND (46)—Laga 7, Rollin 6, Hardy 5, Johnson 5, Michael 5, Good 4, Houlberg 4, Culbert 2, Fisher 2, Bozich 1, Cajuso 1, Ervin 1, Garbey 1, Pyle 1, Wells 1.

MIAMI (45)—D. Bowman 6, Espinoza 5, Palmer 4, Stefero 4, Young 4, Dees 3, Marston 3, Murelli 3, Derryberry 2, Pavlik 2, Boyce 1, Butler 1, Clarkson 1, Hawthorne 1, Herrick 1, Raines 1, V. Rodriguez 1, Romero 1, Tyner 1.

ST. PETERSBURG (36)—Doyle 5, McCauley 4, McIntyre 4, Ayer 3, Davis 3, Moore 3, Pierce 3, Turco 3, Adduci 2, Delaney 2, Liggins 2, Del Monte 1, Proulx 1.

TAMPA (48)—Redus 8, Taylor 7, Feliz 6, Rincones 5, Walker 5, Boddy 4, Lais 4, Scarpace 1, Bonham 1, Corbett 1, Dowless 1, Duval 1, Lesley 1, McKinney 1, Simon 1.

VERO BEACH (70)—Rivera 11, Craig 10, Sobbe 10, Brewer 9, S. Sax 9, D. Sax 5, Hernandez 3, Jones 3, Smith 3, Mann 2, Rossi 2, Malkin 1, Mohler 1, Villaescusa 1.

WEST PALM BEACH (51)—Stenhouse 12, Cruz 6, George 5, Glynn 4, Adams 3, Auten 3, Lepel 3, Shines 3, Gavillan 2, Little 2, Morrison 2, Atkinson 1, Fick 1, Marin 1, Roeder 1, Simmons 1, Wren 1.

WINTER HAVEN (47)—Watkins 6, Malespin 5, Martin 5, Dodson 4, Gutierrez 4, Hagemann 4, Holt 4, Bustabad 3, Sullivan 3, Gaglione 2, Miklosi 2, Bessard 1, Brummer 1, Gill 1, Sandberg 1, Wright 1.

CLUB FIELDING

Club	G.	PO.	A.	E.	DP.	PB.	Pct.	Club	G.	PO.	A.	E.	DP.	PB.	Pct.
Ft. Lauderdale	137	3459	1500	152	124	14	.970	Ft. Myers	136	3405	1335	177	125	21	.964
Lakeland	133	3348	1451	152	130	22	.969	St. Petersburg	136	3449	1462	182	107	14	.964
Winter Haven	140	3509	1543	163	153	30	.969	Daytona Beach	137	3329	1461	204	142	29	.959
Vero Beach	141	3612	1529	180	121	42	.966	West Palm Beach	137	3464	1487	209	127	29	.959
Tampa	131	3318	1306	166	86	20	.965	Miami	136	3365	1565	232	121	23	.955

Triple Play—Vero Beach.

INDIVIDUAL FIELDING

*Throws lefthanded.

FIRST BASEMEN

Player and Club	G.	PO.	A.	E.	DP.	Pct.	Player and Club	G.	PO.	A.	E.	DP.	Pct.
Sandberg, Win. Haven*	19	139	12	0	22	1.000	Culbert, Lakeland	18	158	13	1	18	.994
Whitfield, W. Palm Bch.	15	96	8	0	3	1.000	GUERRA, Ft. Laud*	134	1225	93	11	111	.992
Hill, Ft. Myers	5	26	0	0	2	1.000	Taylor, Tampa	56	448	29	4	26	.992
Sullivan, Winter Haven	4	12	4	0	1	1.000	Dummar, Miami*	14	116	10	1	8	.992
Simon, Tampa	4	14	0	0	0	1.000	Atkinson, Ft. Myers	66	528	46	5	52	.991
Carter, Lakeland	1	12	0	0	2	1.000	Primante, Day. Beach	49	370	24	4	43	.990
Hudler, Ft. Lauderdale	1	9	0	0	2	1.000	Turner, Ft. Myers	34	284	12	3	26	.990
D. Sax, Vero Beach	1	7	0	0	1	1.000	D. Bowman, Miami	101	933	54	11	85	.989
McKnight, Day. Beach	2	4	2	0	1	1.000	Craig, Vero Beach	138	1150	76	16	110	.987
Adams, W. Palm Beach	2	3	0	0	0	1.000	Stenhouse, W. Palm Bch	107	872	56	12	85	.987
Pierce, St. Petersburg	1	1	1	0	0	1.000	Strucher, Day. Beach	82	596	54	9	69	.986
Sorel, Tampa	1	1	0	0	0	1.000	Laga, Lakeland	118	1025	84	18	98	.984
Younger, Lakeland*	1	0	0	0	0	1.000	Lais, Tampa*	68	535	31	9	43	.984
Dodson, Winter Haven*	49	435	28	3	54	.994	Hagemann, Win. Hav*	66	540	48	9	57	.984

FIRST BASEMEN—Continued

Player and Club	G.	PO.	A.	E.	DP.	Pct.
McCauley, St. Pete	50	388	34	7	29	.984
Ferris, Ft. Myers	42	327	26	6	32	.983
Shines, W. Palm Beach	32	206	25	4	23	.983
Moore, St. Petersburg	86	690	52	15	62	.980
Campbell, Day. Beach	7	46	2	1	8	.980
Jordan, Ft. Lauderdale	11	40	2	1	3	.977
B. Bowman, Miami*	14	116	6	3	8	.976
Holt, Winter Haven	17	151	6	4	12	.975
Dieters, St. Petersburg	9	69	8	2	8	.975
Hernandez, Vero Beach	3	36	1	1	3	.974
Jones, Daytona Beach*	14	63	5	2	9	.971
Clements, Day. Beach	3	29	0	1	2	.967
Tirado, Tampa*	15	79	2	3	2	.964
Hawthorne, Miami	13	116	3	5	7	.960
Redus, Tampa	3	14	0	2	1	.875
Davis, St. Petersburg	2	12	1	2	2	.867

SECOND BASEMEN

Player and Club	G.	PO.	A.	E.	DP.	Pct.
Bresnahan, Ft. Myers	13	18	30	0	6	1.000
Toal, Lakeland	3	7	8	0	3	1.000
Harper, Ft. Myers	4	6	8	0	0	1.000
Mann, Vero Beach	2	4	8	0	1	1.000
Simon, Tampa	2	4	5	0	2	1.000
Cajuso, Lakeland	4	2	6	0	1	1.000
Lindberg, Lakeland	2	3	4	0	2	1.000
Pyle, Lakeland	1	3	0	0	0	1.000
Proulx, St. Petersburg	1	1	1	0	0	1.000
Boyce, Miami	1	1	0	0	0	1.000
Patterson, Ft. Myers	43	79	96	4	20	.978
Sporrer, Ft. Lauderdale	12	18	26	1	2	.978
S. SAX, Vero Beach	138	360	438	20	91	.976
McKnight, Day. Beach	20	35	40	2	7	.974
Doyle, St. Petersburg	84	188	229	12	47	.972
Bozich, Lakeland	116	280	320	20	74	.968
Miklosi, Winter Haven	65	141	191	11	49	.968
E. Rodriguez, Miami	15	21	39	2	4	.968
Sorel, Tampa	9	12	13	1	1	.962
Martin, Winter Haven	69	135	206	14	47	.961
Espinoza, Miami	42	88	105	8	20	.960
Gutierrez, Winter Haven	10	25	23	2	10	.960
Doran, Daytona Beach	100	232	258	21	73	.959
Campbell, Day. Beach	31	59	81	6	17	.959
Wallace, Ft. Myers	21	31	40	3	5	.959
Villaman, Ft. Laud	113	240	349	28	66	.955
W. Johnson, W. P. Bch.	120	294	350	31	84	.954
Robbins, Ft. Lauderdale	9	20	19	2	8	.951
Rivas, St. Petersburg	52	98	168	14	29	.950
V. Rodriguez, Miami	49	103	144	14	37	.946
Feliz, Tampa	127	227	328	32	45	.945
Raines, Miami	33	68	102	10	16	.944
Glynn, West Palm Beach	23	30	54	5	5	.944
Wellman, Ft. Myers	73	125	212	21	40	.941
Butterfield, Ft. Laud	3	6	10	1	4	.941
Ervin, Lakeland	14	31	32	4	10	.940
Morrison, W. Palm Bch.	2	6	8	1	2	.933
Hudler, Ft. Lauderdale	14	28	40	5	6	.932
Solomon, Miami	6	15	9	2	2	.923
Gill, Winter Haven	3	1	7	1	0	.889
Beltran, Daytona Beach	2	0	5	1	1	.833
Townley, Ft. Myers	1	2	0	1	0	.667
Marin, West Palm Beach	2	1	0	1	0	.500

THIRD BASEMEN

Player and Club	G.	PO.	A.	E.	DP.	Pct.
Hudler, Ft. Lauderdale	16	8	30	0	1	1.000
Malespin, Winter Haven	10	9	17	0	2	1.000
Wallace, Ft. Myers	10	6	9	0	2	1.000
Cajuso, Lakeland	2	1	7	0	2	1.000
Duval, Tampa	1	2	2	0	0	1.000
Simmons, W. Palm Bch.	1	0	4	0	0	1.000
Ervin, Lakeland	2	2	2	0	1	1.000
Bresnahan, Ft. Myers	1	0	2	0	0	1.000
Dodd, Ft. Lauderdale	1	0	1	0	0	1.000
Gavillan, W. Palm Bch	1	0	1	0	0	1.000
Mann, Vero Beach	3	0	1	0	0	1.000
Solomon, Miami	3	0	1	0	0	1.000
JOHNSON, Lakeland	130	110	264	13	21	.966
Hernandez, Vero Beach	46	44	98	7	11	.953
Patterson, Ft. Myers	56	51	90	7	11	.953
Swires, Ft. Lauderdale	57	43	96	7	8	.952
McKnight, Day. Beach	27	15	23	2	2	.950
Gutierrez, Winter Haven	59	46	89	8	11	.944
Sporrer, Ft. Lauderdale	12	8	23	2	0	.939
Espinoza, Miami	27	17	58	5	10	.938
Rivas, St. Petersburg	9	17	13	2	2	.938
Dayette, Ft. Lauderdale	50	51	103	11	8	.933
Wright, Winter Haven	40	33	79	8	8	.933
Johnson, Tampa	64	56	109	12	11	.932
Pierce, St. Petersburg	90	62	158	18	10	.924
Glynn, West Palm Beach	66	45	122	14	16	.923
Proulx, St. Petersburg	6	1	11	1	1	.923
Simon, Tampa	29	15	44	5	5	.922
Morrison, W. Palm Bch.	42	37	63	9	4	.917
McCauley, St. Pete	34	29	58	8	4	.916
Reynolds, Ft. Laud	9	2	19	2	2	.913
Atkinson, Ft. Myers	49	48	73	12	12	.910
Rivera, Vero Beach	96	81	203	29	20	.907
Motley, Ft. Myers	28	24	53	8	5	.906
Strucher, Day. Beach	54	36	66	12	6	.895
Boyce, Miami	11	11	23	4	1	.895
Redus, Tampa	51	44	81	15	6	.893
Doyle, St. Petersburg	7	2	14	2	1	.889
Medina, Daytona Beach	76	50	130	24	12	.882
Wren, West Palm Beach	17	11	34	6	4	.882
Hawthorne, Miami	36	19	91	15	8	.880
Adams, W. Palm Beach	16	5	16	3	0	.875
Harper, Ft. Myers	4	2	5	1	1	.875
Martin, Winter Haven	42	23	78	16	8	.863
Villaman, Ft. Laud	2	1	5	1	1	.857
Dees, Miami	62	49	113	29	10	.848
Campbell, Day. Beach	4	4	7	2	1	.846
Roeder, W. Palm Beach	10	5	12	4	1	.810
Butterfield, Ft. Laud	1	2	2	1	2	.800
Hughes, Miami	13	6	23	8	1	.784
Sorel, Tampa	10	5	8	4	3	.765
Toal, Lakeland	1	1	1	1	1	.667
Culbert, Lakeland	2	0	2	1	0	.667

Triple Play—Rivera.

SHORTSTOPS

Player and Club	G.	PO.	A.	E.	DP.	Pct.
Sorel, Tampa	6	5	10	0	0	1.000
Bozich, Lakeland	3	6	4	0	2	1.000
Johnson, Lakeland	2	0	5	0	0	1.000
Gill, Winter Haven	1	2	1	0	0	1.000
Atkinson, Ft. Myers	1	0	1	0	0	1.000
Malespin, W Haven	1	0	1	0	1	1.000
Doran, Daytona Beach	2	0	1	0	0	1.000
Robertson, Ft. Laud	63	109	184	10	34	.967
Houlberg, Lakeland	67	107	220	12	44	.965
Santana, Ft. Laud	51	81	158	9	30	.964
RINCONES, Tampa	121	205	323	21	53	.962
Little, WP Beach	64	95	212	12	37	.962

SHORTSTOPS—Continued

Player and Club	G.	PO.	A.	E.	DP.	Pct.	Player and Club	G.	PO.	A.	E.	DP.	Pct.
Wellman, Ft. Myers	37	50	89	6	18	.959	Butler, Miami	12	21	32	5	4	.914
Jones, Vero Beach	69	122	215	16	49	.955	Villaman, Ft. Laud	6	12	20	3	2	.914
Simon, Tampa	20	16	25	2	2	.953	Villaescusa, Vero B	8	5	16	2	1	.913
Turco, St. Pete	91	179	240	21	49	.952	Mann, Vero Beach	44	52	124	17	19	.912
Bustabad, W Haven	124	205	341	28	84	.951	Espinoza, Miami	44	72	111	18	17	.910
Pyle, Lakeland	30	51	86	7	24	.951	Cajuso, Lakeland	17	21	48	7	4	.908
Biancalana, Ft. Myers	91	189	232	23	58	.948	Tinkler, St. Pete	4	9	10	2	2	.905
Murelli, Miami	87	134	276	25	44	.943	Guzman, Vero Beach	18	33	41	9	3	.892
Wherry, Daytona B	120	185	397	38	96	.939	Sporrer, Ft. Laud	28	24	58	10	15	.891
Harper, Ft. Myers	9	19	25	3	4	.936	Glynn, WP Beach	22	28	38	9	8	.880
Lindberg, Lakeland	22	34	64	7	9	.933	McKnight, Daytona B	20	30	50	11	9	.879
Campbell, Daytona B	4	6	8	1	1	.933	Wallace, Ft. Myers	8	9	13	4	2	.846
Proulx, St. Pete	48	82	124	15	24	.932	Motley, Ft. Myers	1	1	3	1	0	.800
Simmons, WP Beach	60	109	170	23	26	.924	Martin, Vero Beach	4	6	8	4	0	.778
Gutierrez, W Haven	26	32	67	9	15	.917	Harris, St. Pete	4	5	5	3	2	.769

Triple Play—Mann.

OUTFIELDERS

Player and Club	G.	PO.	A.	E.	DP.	Pct.	Player and Club	G.	PO.	A.	E.	DP.	Pct.
Gutierrez, W Haven	22	44	5	0	0	1.000	Jabalera, Daytona B*	119	224	14	6	2	.975
Romero, Miami*	29	43	4	0	1	1.000	Auten, WP Beach	119	192	7	5	1	.975
Clarkson, Miami	31	41	0	0	0	1.000	Teegarden, Ft. Laud	118	186	11	5	2	.975
Stenhouse, WP Beach	39	40	0	0	0	1.000	George, WP Beach	32	37	0	1	0	.974
Mann, Vero Beach	24	31	6	0	1	1.000	Thomas, Daytona B	33	35	2	1	0	.974
Headford, Miami	14	22	1	0	1	1.000	Hardy, Lakeland	82	172	11	5	1	.973
Hill, Ft. Myers	8	13	0	0	0	1.000	Jones, Daytona B*	60	70	1	2	0	.973
Spreckles, St. Pete	8	13	0	0	0	1.000	L. Ray, Daytona B	120	172	1	5	1	.972
Garcia, St. Pete	10	12	1	0	1	1.000	Rossi, Vero Beach	121	263	8	8	0	.971
McKnight, Daytona B	16	12	1	0	0	1.000	Duval, Tampa	33	66	2	2	1	.971
Holt, W Haven	8	11	1	0	0	1.000	Young, Miami*	117	212	17	7	4	.970
Hudler, Ft. Laud	6	10	1	0	0	1.000	Adducci, St. Pete*	37	62	3	2	0	.970
Motley, Ft. Myers	3	8	0	0	0	1.000	Dodd, Miami	91	117	2	4	0	.967
Baskerville, St. Pete	7	8	0	0	0	1.000	Scarpace, Tampa*	71	106	9	4	4	.966
D. Bowman, Miami	3	7	0	0	0	1.000	Fields, Lakeland	53	113	1	4	0	.966
Reyes, Vero Beach	2	5	1	0	1	1.000	Younger, Lakeland*	43	56	1	2	0	.966
Gainey, Daytona B	4	4	0	0	0	1.000	Carter, Lakeland	29	47	8	2	2	.965
Gavillan, WPB	1	1	2	0	0	1.000	Michael, Lakeland*	50	78	2	3	3	.964
Layne, Vero Beach	2	3	0	0	0	1.000	Herrick, Miami	55	75	5	3	1	.964
Dodson, W Haven*	1	2	0	0	0	1.000	Gaglione, W Haven*	25	26	1	1	1	.964
Espinoza, Miami	1	1	0	0	0	1.000	Atkinson, WP Beach	103	169	12	7	4	.963
Glynn, WP Beach	2	1	0	0	0	1.000	Rodriguez, Ft. Myers	44	73	6	3	0	.963
Good, Lakeland	2	1	0	0	0	1.000	Pavlik, Miami	98	192	9	8	3	.962
Medina, Daytona B	2	1	0	0	0	1.000	Liggins, St. Pete	57	96	4	4	0	.962
Sorel, Tampa	4	1	0	0	0	1.000	Phillips, WP Beach*	28	46	2	2	0	.960
Paulino, Ft. Laud	6	1	0	0	0	1.000	Wells, Lakeland	73	133	5	6	1	.958
BREWER, Vero Beach	137	242	9	1	2	.996	Mohler, Vero Beach	83	103	9	5	1	.957
Malespin, W Haven	102	208	11	1	1	.995	Hernandez, Vero B	15	19	3	1	1	.957
Robbins, Ft. Laud	73	130	1	1	0	.992	Bessard, W Haven	71	101	6	5	0	.955
Gill, W Haven	71	105	7	1	1	.991	Garbey, Lakeland	26	60	4	3	0	.955
Ryal, Ft. Myers*	85	174	8	2	3	.989	Turner, Ft. Myers	15	42	0	2	0	.955
Khoury, Ft. Laud	46	82	2	1	0	.988	Brummer, W Haven	43	41	1	2	0	.955
Walker, Tampa	122	293	8	4	1	.987	Haley, Ft. Myers	9	21	0	1	0	.955
Ayer, St. Pete	127	220	12	3	2	.987	Brewer, Ft. Myers	121	199	8	11	1	.950
Watkins, W Haven	105	223	6	3	1	.987	Harper, Daytona B	44	86	9	5	2	.950
Jordan, Ft. Laud	119	255	6	4	1	.985	Hendrickson, Miami*	15	19	0	1	0	.950
Del Monte, St. Pete*	57	127	3	2	0	.985	McIntyre, St. Pete*	87	142	5	8	0	.948
Tyner, Miami	41	63	3	1	0	.985	Smith, Vero Beach	53	72	1	4	0	.948
Townley, Ft. Myers	121	284	14	5	4	.983	Salazar, Lakeland*	10	18	0	1	0	.947
McKinney, Tampa	82	160	6	3	1	.982	Marston, Miami	10	17	0	1	0	.944
Mills, St. Pete	39	92	5	2	0	.980	Hagemann, W Haven*	13	14	3	1	0	.944
Beltran, Daytona B	71	94	0	2	0	.979	Redus, Tampa	99	155	3	10	0	.944
R. Johnson, WPB	21	44	1	1	0	.978	Rollin, Lakeland	42	77	2	5	0	.940
Burtt, Miami	32	40	3	1	0	.977	Venger, Tampa	33	31	1	3	0	.914
D. Sax, Vero Beach	32	37	5	1	0	.977	Marin, WP Beach	6	8	0	1	0	.889
Wren, WP Beach	50	120	4	3	1	.976	Adams, WP Beach	16	22	1	4	0	.852
Cruz, WP Beach*	57	76	4	2	1	.976	Roberson, Lakeland	8	10	3	3	0	.813
Sheridan, Ft. Myers	18	37	4	1	1	.976							

Triple Play—Mohler.

CATCHERS

Player and Club	G.	PO.	A.	E.	DP.	PB.	Pct.	Player and Club	G.	PO.	A.	E.	DP.	PB.	Pct.
Maples, Vero Beach	15	77	10	0	1	6	1.000	May, Ft. Laud	9	33	1	0	0	0	1.000
Brummer, W Haven	25	76	10	0	0	5	1.000	Silva, St. Pete	8	25	4	0	0	0	1.000
Correll, Tampa	12	45	4	0	1	1	1.000	George, WP Beach	1	10	0	0	0	0	1.000

CATCHERS—Continued

Player and Club	G.	PO.	A.	E.	DP.	PB.	Pct.
Taylor, Tampa	2	3	0	0	0	0	1.000
Sayler, St. Pete	1	1	0	0	0	0	1.000
Corbett, Tampa	35	197	22	1	0	9	.995
PLANTE, Ft. Laud.	88	408	33	3	3	5	.993
D. Sax, Vero Beach	21	112	13	1	2	9	.992
Lepel, WP Beach	45	199	28	3	5	5	.987
Campbell, Daytona B.	14	64	8	1	1	4	.986
Mizerock, Daytona B.	95	532	52	9	8	17	.985
Sobbe, Vero Beach	112	654	81	13	6	26	.983
Delany, St. Pete	102	553	69	11	5	9	.983
Boddy, Tampa	81	412	55	8	8	8	.983
Davis, St. Pete	26	159	19	3	0	5	.983
Slaught, Ft. Myers	43	175	34	4	0	0	.981
Sullivan, W Haven	86	470	71	11	6	17	.980
Lowry, Lakeland	36	171	25	4	2	4	.980
Fisher, Lakeland	75	335	47	8	2	8	.979
Shines, WP Beach	53	300	39	8	3	17	.977
Holt, W Haven	38	160	12	4	1	7	.977
Buffamoyer, Ft. Laud	54	218	25	6	1	8	.976
Gavillan, WPB	54	214	27	6	4	3	.976
Primante, Daytona B.	45	207	21	6	2	8	.974
Palmer, Miami	68	314	56	11	7	5	.971
Good, Lakeland	17	86	8	3	0	4	.969
Morgan, W Haven	12	56	5	2	1	1	.968
Stefero, Miami	81	352	63	14	6	18	.967
Cochran, Lakeland	15	72	9	3	2	5	.964
Lewis, Ft. Myers	56	287	29	12	2	16	.963
Dewey, Ft. Myers	41	194	16	8	3	5	.963
Adams, Tampa	22	105	6	5	0	2	.957
Fick, WP Beach	15	77	6	4	0	4	.954
Winslow, St. Pete	8	33	6	2	0	0	.951
Malkin, Vero B.	7	34	1	3	0	1	.921
Girata, Ft. Laud	7	23	1	4	0	1	.857

Triple Play—Sobbe.

PITCHERS

Player and Club	G.	PO.	A.	E.	DP.	Pct.
BROWN, DAYTONA B.	24	9	29	0	1	1.000
Smith, Miami	22	10	24	0	4	1.000
Simerly, Lakeland	17	5	20	0	0	1.000
Baldwin, Winter Haven	31	7	18	0	1	1.000
Nipper, Winter Haven	16	6	18	0	2	1.000
Sullivan, Tampa	16	6	18	0	1	1.000
Locascio, Tampa*	45	4	16	0	1	1.000
Ramsey, Tampa*	20	5	13	0	0	1.000
Peralta, Miami	21	5	13	0	1	1.000
Ross, Daytona Beach	30	2	16	0	0	1.000
Geiger, Lakeland	48	7	11	0	0	1.000
Fadhel, W. Palm Beach	11	6	10	0	0	1.000
Taylor, W. Palm Beach*	17	2	14	0	0	1.000
Codiroli, Lakeland	9	4	11	0	0	1.000
Gotay, St. Petersburg	16	5	10	0	0	1.000
Josephson, W. Palm B.	35	7	8	0	0	1.000
Chretien, Lakeland	15	1	13	0	2	1.000
Tennant, Vero Beach	19	7	7	0	2	1.000
Grant, Miami	21	2	12	0	2	1.000
Grzybek, Ft. Myers	14	7	6	0	0	1.000
Horton, St. Petersburg*	6	10	2	0	1	1.000
Moloney, Win. Haven*	30	5	7	0	0	1.000
Pearson, Ft. Lauderdale	11	7	4	0	0	1.000
Woodall, Miami*	17	0	10	0	1	1.000
Vanderbush, Ft. Myers	6	1	8	0	2	1.000
Gonzalez, Miami*	8	1	8	0	0	1.000
Clark, Miami*	12	2	7	0	0	1.000
Smith, Lakeland	14	2	7	0	2	1.000
Paulino, Ft. Lauderdale	19	2	7	0	0	1.000
Creel, Ft. Myers	6	3	5	0	0	1.000
Yanus, W. Palm Beach	10	0	8	0	0	1.000
Akchurin, Ft. Laud.	15	3	5	0	2	1.000
Franke, Miami	16	1	7	0	1	1.000
Pimental, St. Petersburg	36	1	7	0	1	1.000
Morris, Daytona Beach*	3	1	6	0	1	1.000
Grubbs, Winter Haven	13	1	6	0	0	1.000
Torres, W. Palm Beach	21	2	5	0	0	1.000
Hensley, Lakeland*	28	3	4	0	0	1.000
Collins, St. Petersburg	2	2	4	0	0	1.000
Ervey, Ft. Lauderdale	4	3	3	0	1	1.000
Guerra, Ft. Lauderdale*	5	3	3	0	0	1.000
Houser, St. Petersburg	10	3	3	0	0	1.000
Collyer, Lakeland*	3	2	3	0	0	1.000
Mulholland, Tampa*	8	1	4	0	0	1.000
Ganger, Ft. Myers	13	2	3	0	0	1.000
Meckes, Daytona Beach	14	0	5	0	1	1.000
Graven, Miami*	17	1	4	0	0	1.000
Martinez, Miami	2	0	4	0	0	1.000
Clark, Lakeland	4	1	3	0	0	1.000
Zedonek, Miami	4	1	3	0	0	1.000
Foster, Vero Beach	9	0	4	0	1	1.000
Warren, Lakeland	13	3	1	0	0	1.000
Gladden, Ft. Myers	4	3	0	0	0	1.000
Dacko, Lakeland	5	1	2	0	0	1.000
Martinez, Tampa	20	0	3	0	0	1.000
Bonham, Tampa	3	0	2	0	0	1.000
Vega, St. Petersburg	3	1	1	0	0	1.000
Weaver, St. Petersburg	4	0	2	0	0	1.000
Vila, Miami	9	1	1	0	0	1.000
Borbon, Vero Beach*	12	1	1	0	0	1.000
Gaston, Ft. Lauderdale	1	0	1	0	0	1.000
Hernandez, Ft. Laud.*	1	0	1	0	0	1.000
Jordan, Miami	1	0	1	0	0	1.000
Medina, Daytona Beach	1	0	1	0	0	1.000
St. John, W. Palm B.*	4	0	1	0	0	1.000
Williams, W. Palm B.*	4	1	0	0	0	1.000
Williams, St. Petersburg	10	0	1	0	0	1.000
Johnson, West Haven	28	13	28	1	3	.976
Filson, Ft. Lauderdale*	23	3	32	1	0	.972
Dunn, Lakeland*	19	10	20	1	0	.968
Beecroft, Lakeland	26	9	19	1	1	.966
Houston, Daytona Bch*	25	5	19	1	0	.960
White, Miami-Ft. Myers	32	9	15	1	1	.960
Ruiz, Vero Beach*	41	7	15	1	0	.957
Caldwell, W. Palm Beach	17	9	11	1	0	.952
Lein, Ft. Lauderdale	30	15	22	2	4	.949
Burchett, St. Petersburg	27	11	43	3	1	.947
Pippin, Ft. Myers	45	5	13	1	0	.947
W. Davis, Winter Haven	32	11	21	2	2	.941
Robinson, Tampa	13	2	14	1	0	.941
Perry, Daytona Beach*	22	7	24	2	2	.939
Birrell, Winter Haven*	19	9	36	3	1	.938
Moncrief, Lakeland	13	5	10	1	0	.938
Moller, Lakeland*	29	2	13	1	0	.938
Alvarez, Miami	21	7	22	2	0	.935
Jackson, Tampa	22	8	21	2	1	.935
Dowless, Tampa	26	7	22	2	1	.935
Nelson, Ft. Lauderdale	27	9	20	2	0	.935
Russell, St. Petersburg	20	10	18	2	1	.933
Sutcliffe, Vero Beach	21	10	18	2	2	.933
Morton, St. Petersburg*	10	0	14	1	1	.933
G. Davis, Winter Haven*	27	3	11	1	0	.933
Carlucci, Ft. Lauderdale	31	3	11	1	2	.933
Johnson, St. Petersburg	27	11	42	4	3	.930
DiLorenzo, Ft. Myers	22	12	27	3	2	.929
Swaggerty, Miami	19	1	12	1	0	.929
Lesley, Tampa	37	3	10	1	1	.929
Edwards, Miami	19	9	16	2	1	.926
Petersen, Daytona Beach	23	17	32	4	6	.925
Brown, Winter Haven	17	5	19	2	3	.923
Chapin, West Palm B.	9	2	10	1	0	.923
Timlin, Ft. Myers	24	4	8	1	0	.923
Buchanan, Tampa*	27	5	18	2	1	.920
Wickensheimer, Vero B.	26	7	27	3	1	.919
Cato, Tampa	11	6	16	2	0	.917
Hesketh, W. Palm B.*	11	6	16	2	0	.917

PITCHERS—Continued

Player and Club	G.	PO.	A.	E.	DP.	Pct.
Candiotti, Ft. Myers	7	1	10	1	0	.917
Hanslovan, Ft. Myers*	12	2	9	1	0	.917
Nail, Lakeland	13	5	6	1	0	.917
Hook, Miami	8	4	6	1	0	.909
Stuper, St. Petersburg	24	3	7	1	2	.909
Davis, Miami	25	9	30	4	3	.907
Ricci, Ft. Lauderdale	21	5	14	2	0	.905
Williams, Ft. Myers	20	11	17	3	1	.903
Wever, Ft. Lauderdale	15	4	14	2	2	.900
Riggins, St. Petersburg*	57	14	14	2	1	.900
Nurthen, Ft. Lauderdale	5	4	5	1	2	.900
Miller, Ft. Myers	10	1	8	1	1	.900
Thomas, St. Petersburg	11	3	6	1	0	.900
Kaufman, Ft. Laud.	27	3	6	1	0	.900
Hayford, Winter Haven	29	9	17	3	2	.897
O'Connor, W. Palm B*	17	2	15	2	1	.895
Pena, Vero Beach	35	3	14	2	0	.895
Madden, Vero Beach*	27	8	16	3	0	.889
Noble, Tampa*	15	4	4	1	0	.889
Quealey, Daytona Beach	21	2	6	1	1	.889
Perry, Vero Beach	25	7	24	4	2	.886
Staffon, W. Palm Beach	17	7	15	3	1	.880
Malden, Vero Beach	25	4	17	3	1	.875
Kepshire, Tampa	29	7	7	2	0	.875
Day, Lakeland*	5	0	7	1	1	.875
Jones, St. Petersburg	7	5	2	1	1	.875
Cates, W. Palm Beach	11	1	6	1	0	.875
Bonine, Daytona Beach	15	4	3	1	1	.875
DeSanto, Winter Haven	18	1	6	1	0	.875
Paris, Daytona Beach	23	11	36	7	2	.870

Player and Club	G.	PO.	A.	E.	DP.	Pct.
Collins, Winter Haven	36	6	13	3	1	.864
Blows, W. Palm Beach*	34	6	18	4	0	.857
Sanchez, Lakeland	10	2	4	1	1	.857
Hayes, Tampa	41	1	5	1	0	.857
Gleckel, Ft. Lauderdale*	24	5	30	6	3	.854
Raine, Ft. Myers	24	8	14	4	1	.846
Daniel, Vero Beach	34	6	10	3	0	.842
Gott, St. Petersburg	25	10	16	5	0	.839
Wick, Mia.-W.P.B.*	25	4	11	3	2	.833
Woodworth, Ft. Myers	19	5	5	2	2	.833
Anderson, W. Palm B.	26	1	13	3	2	.824
Rice, Daytona Beach*	27	1	8	2	1	.818
Wheeler, Lakeland	34	2	7	2	0	.818
Sattler, W. Palm Beach	16	5	21	6	1	.813
Welenc, Daytona Beach	17	6	6	3	2	.800
Skinner, Ft. Myers	3	1	3	1	0	.800
Schuler, W. Palm Beach	13	2	2	1	0	.800
Finch, Daytona Beach*.	21	3	1	1	0	.800
Schrimsher, Tampa	10	0	7	2	0	.778
Maples, Miami	11	5	5	3	1	.769
Smith, Ft. Myers	17	0	5	2	0	.714
Schneck, Winter Haven	13	2	5	3	0	.700
Brown, Miami	10	2	6	4	0	.667
Smith, Daytona Beach	33	0	7	6	0	.538
Toliver, Ft. Lauderdale	3	0	1	1	0	.500
Kreymborg, Miami	9	0	1	2	0	.333
Martinez, St. Petersburg	2	0	0	1	0	.000
W. Ray, Daytona Beach	6	0	0	2	0	.000
Joyce, Vero Beach*	21	0	0	1	0	.000

The following players do not have any recorded accepted chances at the positions indicated; therefore, are not listed in the fielding averages for those particular positions: K. Adams, p; Ayer, ss; Beltran, 3b-ss; Bozich, p; Bresnahan, 1b-ss; Bustabad, 2b; Camp, p; Campbell, of; Dewey, of; Ferris, 3b; Guzman, 3b; Hagemann,* p; Harper, c; W. Johnson, of; Maher, p; Marston, 2b; Medina, 2b; Olwine,* p; Palmer, 1b; Pimental, of; Riggins, of; Rodriguez, p; S. Sax, of; Sheridan, c; Simmons, 2b; Simon, p; Sporrer, ss; Swires, 2b; Wallace, of.

CLUB PITCHING

Club	G.	CG.	ShO.	Sv.	IP.	H.	R.	ER.	HR.	BB.	Int. BB.	HB.	SO.	WP.	Bk.	ERA.
Tampa	131	34	23	21	1105	959	444	336	35	461	56	21	715	60	11	2.74
Fort Lauderdale	137	49	19	21	1156	986	490	393	47	523	17	24	647	46	20	3.06
Daytona Beach	137	36	13	18	1117	990	485	384	40	543	26	39	753	75	9	3.09
St. Petersburg	136	32	14	22	1153	1129	558	448	32	549	46	46	720	76	15	3.50
Vero Beach	141	45	8	20	1205	1064	610	487	29	766	21	32	831	73	17	3.64
Fort Myers	136	46	9	17	1134	1092	577	462	31	588	32	33	584	53	19	3.67
West Palm Beach	137	32	9	20	1163	1102	622	495	53	670	44	44	774	87	26	3.83
Miami	136	33	8	17	1123	1131	651	494	34	533	19	41	627	87	19	3.96
Winter Haven	140	31	13	26	1171	1192	653	532	55	617	23	42	703	78	16	4.09
Lakeland	133	15	9	13	1117	1086	633	538	52	625	30	29	610	69	19	4.33

PITCHERS' RECORDS

(Leading Qualifiers for Earned-Run Average Leadership—114 or More Innings)

*Throws lefthanded.

Pitcher—Club	G.	GS.	CG.	ShO.	W.	L.	Sv.	Pct.	IP.	H.	R.	ER.	HR.	Int. BB.	BB.	HB.	SO.	WP.	ERA.
Dowless, Tampa	26	23	8	3	12	8	1	.600	166	109	41	31	2	51	3	4	130	9	1.68
Nelson, Ft. Lauderdale	27	25	16	5	20	3	0	.870	196	146	51	43	4	70	1	1	130	4	1.97
Birrell, Winter Haven*	19	19	3	1	7	7	0	.500	122	96	49	29	5	51	2	4	114	6	2.14
Petersen, Daytona Beach.	24	24	13	3	12	10	0	.545	179	149	58	43	10	49	1	3	89	3	2.16
Wickensheimer, Vero B.	26	26	15	3	15	8	0	.652	200	167	57	49	2	93	2	4	162	8	2.21
O'Connor, WPB*	17	17	5	0	9	6	0	.600	139	105	46	37	4	70	3	1	93	3	2.40
Lein, Ft. Lauderdale	30	10	4	2	8	5	5	.615	126	111	43	35	4	23	5	1	40	3	2.50
Paris, Daytona Beach.	23	23	8	4	14	4	0	.778	154	119	57	44	5	66	2	10	119	1	2.57
Raine, Ft. Myers	24	23	10	1	8	10	0	.444	160	127	65	49	2	105	2	6	99	8	2.76
Brown, Daytona Beach	24	23	8	3	11	7	0	.611	165	122	63	52	6	73	1	7	101	9	2.84

Departmental Leaders: G—Riggins, 57; GS—J. Johnson, 27; CG—Nelson, 16; ShO—Nelson, 5; W—Nelson, . L—Edwards, 13; Sv—Riggins, 13; Pct.—Nelson, .870; IP—Wickensheimer, 200; H—Burchett, 186; R—S. Perry, 103; ER—Hayford, 87; HR—Caldwell, Petersen, 10; BB—Madden, 127; IBB—Riggins, 14; SO—Wickensheimer, 162; HB —J. Johnson, Paris, 10; WP—Houston, 21.

(All Pitchers—Listed Alphabetically)

Pitcher–Club	G.	GS.	CG.	ShO.	W.	L.	Sv.	Pct.	IP.	H.	R.	ER.	HR.	BB.	Int.BB.	HB.	SO.	WP.	ERA.
Adams, West Palm Beach	1	0	0	0	0	0	0	.000	1	3	4	4	0	2	0	1	0	1	36.00
Akchurin, Ft. Laud.	15	4	2	1	5	2	0	.714	54	39	23	16	2	25	1	2	24	3	2.67
Alvarez, Miami	21	10	4	0	3	8	2	.273	100	95	52	42	3	25	0	7	55	6	3.78
Anderson, WPB	26	6	0	0	3	7	7	.300	59	58	40	31	1	64	3	1	45	10	3.78
Baldwin, Winter Haven	31	11	3	1	5	7	2	.417	126	134	66	52	5	52	4	5	79	6	3.71
Beecroft, Lakeland	26	23	4	0	9	11	0	.450	157	131	70	50	3	104	4	5	85	8	2.87
Birrell, Winter Haven*	19	19	3	1	7	7	0	.500	122	96	49	29	5	51	2	4	114	6	2.14
Blows, West Palm Beach*	34	5	2	0	4	8	4	.333	82	78	30	28	3	36	4	3	62	3	3.07
Bonham, Tampa	3	3	0	0	1	0	0	1.000	16	7	3	1	0	5	0	1	14	0	0.56
Bonine, Daytona Beach	15	6	1	0	3	5	0	.375	53	47	24	17	2	17	0	1	55	6	2.89
Borbon, Vero Beach*	12	1	0	0	0	1	0	.000	18	22	15	13	1	13	0	0	12	3	6.50
Bozich, Lakeland	2	0	0	0	0	0	0	.000	1	0	0	0	1	0	0	0	4	0	0.00
Brown, Winter Haven	17	9	4	1	3	4	3	.429	71	79	37	34	2	32	0	4	50	1	4.31
Brown, Miami	10	2	0	3	5	0	0	.375	59	58	40	31	1	35	1	2	40	4	4.73
Brown, Daytona Beach	24	23	8	3	11	7	0	.611	165	122	63	52	6	73	1	7	101	9	2.84
Buchanan, Tampa*	27	18	3	2	7	7	2	.500	101	102	53	48	6	40	7	1	62	6	4.28
Burchett, St. Petersburg	27	25	11	2	16	7	0	.696	192	186	74	64	4	55	8	5	101	6	3.00
Caldwell, WPB	17	17	8	1	7	6	0	.538	110	96	56	46	10	62	0	4	80	9	3.76
Camp, Lakeland	3	0	0	0	0	0	0	.000	8	9	10	9	0	14	0	0	3	1	10.13
Candiotti, Ft. Myers	7	5	3	0	3	2	0	.600	44	32	16	11	0	9	1	2	31	1	2.25
Carlucci, Ft. Lauderdale	31	0	0	0	4	4	5	.500	51	53	22	18	2	35	3	2	30	6	3.18
Cates, West Palm Beach	11	7	1	0	1	5	0	.167	43	55	39	31	1	36	1	5	23	6	6.49
Cato, Tampa	11	11	3	2	6	3	0	.667	74	59	21	14	2	14	2	1	42	0	1.70
Chapin, West Palm Beach	9	0	0	0	2	4	1	.333	49	57	35	31	4	35	2	4	23	1	5.69
Chretien, Lakeland	15	3	1	0	2	3	2	.400	52	52	25	20	5	8	2	1	20	0	3.46
Clark, Miami*	12	3	0	0	2	1	2	.667	25	19	11	8	0	19	1	1	19	2	2.88
Clark, Lakeland	4	0	0	0	0	1	0	.000	11	5	6	6	0	12	1	0	5	1	4.91
Codiroli, Lakeland	9	9	0	0	1	1	0	.500	50	33	13	10	3	19	0	0	26	0	1.80
Collins, Winter Haven	36	11	2	0	5	7	3	.417	110	107	57	48	4	51	4	3	53	6	3.93
Collins, St. Petersburg	2	2	0	0	1	1	0	.500	13	9	1	1	0	4	1	0	6	1	0.69
Collyer, Lakeland*	3	0	0	0	0	0	0	.000	8	11	6	5	0	5	0	0	2	4	5.63
Creel, Ft. Myers	6	6	1	0	2	2	0	.500	26	48	29	24	0	16	0	0	5	2	8.31
Dacko, Lakeland	5	5	1	0	2	3	0	.400	31	33	17	15	2	14	0	0	11	2	4.35
Daniel, Vero Beach	33	0	0	0	6	2	5	.750	79	67	38	29	2	52	5	2	33	6	3.30
Davis, Miami	25	25	7	0	9	12	0	.429	151	157	85	59	3	55	0	4	90	13	3.52
G. Davis, Winter Haven*	26	3	0	0	1	5	0	.167	58	57	44	34	9	56	3	2	28	6	5.28
W. Davis, Winter Haven	32	19	4	1	10	11	4	.476	134	144	76	65	3	73	2	3	83	7	4.37
Day, Lakeland*	5	3	1	1	2	0	0	1.000	34	27	4	4	0	4	0	0	21	1	1.06
DeSanto, Winter Haven	18	10	1	0	0	7	0	.000	54	67	58	49	6	56	1	6	16	17	8.17
Dewey, Ft. Myers	1	0	0	0	0	0	0	.000	3	5	4	4	1	2	0	0	1	0	12.00
DiLorenzo, Ft. Myers	22	22	8	3	8	11	0	.421	148	132	60	52	4	65	3	2	102	9	3.16
Dowless, Tampa	26	23	8	3	12	8	1	.600	166	109	41	31	2	51	3	4	130	9	1.68
Dunn, Lakeland*	19	19	3	0	5	8	0	.385	96	95	68	58	4	70	0	4	33	4	5.44
Edwards, Miami	19	19	8	1	4	13	0	.235	112	109	65	53	2	45	0	6	66	7	4.26
Ervey, Ft. Lauderdale	4	3	0	0	2	1	0	.667	18	14	8	6	2	11	0	1	7	3	3.00
Fadhel, West Palm Beach	11	6	0	0	2	3	1	.400	49	45	35	30	2	34	6	2	33	3	5.51
Filson, Ft. Lauderdale*	23	20	7	3	10	9	0	.526	144	105	56	48	5	69	1	3	86	2	3.00
Finch, Daytona Beach*	21	0	0	0	1	1	0	.500	22	23	18	15	2	26	0	2	19	1	6.14
Foster, Vero Beach	8	0	0	0	0	1	0	.000	8	11	9	9	0	14	0	0	6	5	10.13
Franke, Miami	16	0	0	0	1	1	0	.500	27	40	28	27	1	24	5	0	9	9	9.00
Ganger, Ft. Myers	13	0	0	0	1	1	2	.500	32	25	10	9	1	7	0	0	15	0	2.53
Gaston, Ft. Lauderdale	1	1	0	0	0	0	0	.000	8	8	5	5	0	3	0	0	3	1	5.63
Geiger, Lakeland	48	0	0	0	5	7	7	.417	99	93	43	36	2	69	8	2	71	6	3.27
Gladden, Ft. Myers	4	2	1	0	1	1	0	.500	19	14	8	6	1	9	1	1	15	0	2.84
Gleckel, Ft. Lauderdale*.	24	20	7	1	8	11	1	.421	135	131	66	50	7	53	2	3	52	2	3.33
Gonzalez, Miami*	8	7	2	0	3	3	0	.500	46	40	24	19	4	29	1	2	48	4	3.72
Gotay, St. Petersburg	16	11	4	3	7	1	0	.875	92	65	26	25	3	51	2	3	77	4	2.45
Gott, St. Petersburg	25	21	4	1	5	11	0	.313	137	138	96	70	2	113	1	4	103	13	4.60
Grant, Miami	21	0	0	0	3	1	3	.750	35	27	14	10	1	15	1	3	15	3	2.57
Graven, Miami*	17	0	0	0	1	0	0	1.000	29	22	6	3	0	9	1	0	17	1	0.93
Grubbs, Winter Haven	13	2	0	0	3	0	0	.000	34	57	32	22	5	21	0	0	6	2	5.82
Grzybek, Ft. Myers	14	14	5	0	8	5	0	.615	97	89	45	39	1	56	1	0	40	5	3.62
Guerra, Ft. Lauderdale*	5	3	2	1	2	0	0	1.000	25	22	8	6	2	17	0	1	19	1	2.16
Hagemann, W Haven*	1	0	0	0	0	0	0	.000	2	1	0	0	0	0	0	0	0	0	0.00
Hanslovan, Ft. Myers*	12	4	2	0	3	2	1	.600	48	50	27	20	2	32	1	1	22	1	3.75
Hayes, Tampa	41	0	0	0	1	4	0	.200	61	49	33	26	3	42	6	1	59	5	3.84
Hayford, Winter Haven	29	23	2	0	9	12	0	.429	143	155	100	87	7	85	2	5	72	4	5.48
Hensley, Lakeland*	28	0	0	0	3	2	4	.600	59	67	27	22	2	27	2	1	42	2	3.36
Hernandez, Ft. Laud*	1	1	0	0	0	1	0	.000	2	2	4	4	0	4	0	1	1	2	18.00
Hesketh, WPB*	11	11	1	1	8	2	0	.800	75	71	30	16	4	32	1	0	43	6	1.92
Hook, Miami	8	8	1	0	2	5	0	.286	41	45	28	18	1	12	0	3	28	5	3.95
Horton, St. Petersburg*	6	5	0	0	0	2	0	.000	25	29	18	17	1	17	1	0	13	8	6.12
Houser, St. Petersburg	10	0	0	0	1	0	0	.000	20	17	13	12	2	19	0	3	9	5	5.40
Houston, Daytona Beach*	25	25	2	0	9	6	0	.600	135	135	85	77	2	107	2	4	120	21	5.13

Pitcher–Club	G	GS	CG	ShO	W	L	Sv	Pct	IP	H	R	ER	HR	BB	Int. BB	HB	SO	WP	ERA
Jackson, Tampa	22	19	1	0	7	6	0	.538	105	105	53	44	4	52	2	1	50	9	3.77
Johnson, Winter Haven	28	16	9	2	11	8	0	.579	157	153	63	53	7	43	2	4	92	5	3.04
Johnson, St. Petersburg	27	27	5	2	9	11	0	.450	179	178	89	63	5	62	6	10	100	7	3.17
Jones, St. Petersburg	7	4	0	0	3	2	0	.600	26	26	24	21	5	24	0	2	7	2	7.27
Jordan, Miami	1	1	0	0	0	1	0	.000	6	9	8	7	0	3	0	0	2	0	10.50
Josephson, W. P. Beach	35	4	2	1	3	1	5	.750	73	74	29	24	3	27	7	2	46	6	2.96
Joyce, Vero Beach*	21	0	0	0	0	2	1	1.000	29	20	19	13	0	29	0	2	37	1	4.03
Kaufman, Ft. Lauderdale	27	4	2	1	5	1	8	.833	65	41	10	7	1	18	0	2	63	4	0.97
Kepshire, Tampa	29	0	0	0	5	4	2	.556	54	48	35	33	4	35	4	1	26	2	2.00
Kreymborg, Miami	9	3	0	0	3	1	0	.750	31	33	28	21	4	18	0	1	17	6	6.10
Lein, Ft. Lauderdale	30	10	4	2	8	5	5	.615	126	111	43	35	4	23	5	1	40	3	2.50
Lesley, Tampa	37	0	0	0	4	2	5	.667	76	67	23	17	2	40	6	2	44	3	2.01
Locascio, Tampa*	45	3	1	0	3	5	5	.375	67	66	32	26	3	49	7	2	53	3	3.49
Madden, Vero Beach*	27	26	11	1	11	9	0	.550	171	129	79	64	4	127	2	2	141	16	3.37
Maher, West Palm Beach	4	0	0	0	0	1	0	.000	7	11	9	8	0	7	1	3	5	0	10.29
Malden, Vero Beach	25	25	6	2	10	11	0	.476	164	171	100	78	6	92	2	0	127	11	4.28
Maples, Miami	11	10	0	0	1	7	0	.125	48	63	45	35	0	37	0	4	36	6	6.56
Marston, Miami	4	0	0	0	0	1	0	.000	5	13	12	12	0	10	0	0	6	5	21.60
Martinez, Miami	2	2	0	0	0	0	0	.000	12	3	1	0	0	5	1	0	7	0	0.00
Martinez, Tampa	20	0	0	0	1	1	4	.500	39	28	11	11	2	22	3	2	27	7	2.54
Martinez, St. Petersburg	2	2	0	0	0	0	0	.000	6	7	1	1	0	6	0	0	1	0	1.50
Meckes, Daytona Beach	14	0	0	0	4	1	4	.800	19	21	7	7	1	7	1	1	15	3	3.32
Miller, Ft. Myers	10	9	2	0	1	6	0	.143	56	59	48	35	3	29	0	2	26	6	5.63
Moller, Lakeland*	29	15	0	0	4	7	1	.750	53	37	12	11	0	15	1	1	45	2	1.87
Moloney, Winter Haven*	30	0	0	0	3	1	7	.750	73	37	37	33	3	37	0	1	43	4	4.56
Moncrief, Lakeland	13	13	2	1	4	6	0	.400	73	70	38	37	3	37	0	0	11	1	4.56
Morris, Daytona Beach*	3	3	1	0	2	0	0	1.000	24	13	5	3	0	10	0	0	11	1	1.13
Morton, St. Petersburg*	10	9	1	0	2	5	0	.286	54	64	28	25	1	20	0	2	36	1	4.17
Mulholland, Tampa*	8	0	0	0	1	0	1	1.000	14	8	5	5	0	6	0	0	7	1	3.27
Nail, Lakeland	13	13	1	0	4	4	0	.400	53	66	52	43	2	37	1	2	30	10	7.30
Nelson, Ft. Lauderdale	27	25	16	5	20	3	0	.870	196	146	51	43	4	70	1	1	130	4	1.97
Nipper, Winter Haven	16	11	2	1	6	4	1	.600	85	82	29	24	1	49	0	0	48	6	2.54
Noble, Tampa*	15	3	0	0	2	3	0	.400	36	36	13	9	0	19	2	1	24	1	2.25
Nurthen, Ft. Lauderdale	5	1	0	0	2	1	0	.667	16	18	13	6	4	6	0	0	3	1	3.38
O'Connor, W. P. Beach*	17	17	5	0	9	6	0	.600	139	105	46	37	4	70	3	1	93	3	2.40
Olwine, Ft. Lauderdale*	2	0	0	0	0	0	0	.000	1	5	4	1	1	0	0	0	0	0	9.00
Paris, Daytona Beach	23	23	8	4	14	4	0	.778	154	119	57	44	5	66	2	10	119	1	2.57
Paulino, Ft. Lauderdale	18	4	0	0	0	0	0	.000	57	52	37	23	3	48	1	0	13	6	3.63
Pearson, Ft. Lauderdale	11	9	2	0	2	5	0	.286	55	54	31	29	0	36	0	0	33	0	4.75
Pena, Vero Beach	35	3	0	0	10	3	8	.769	73	57	32	26	0	41	1	6	46	3	3.21
Peralta, Miami	21	8	1	1	4	5	0	.444	71	59	41	34	3	50	1	2	35	3	4.31
Perry, Vero Beach	25	25	7	1	8	12	0	.400	155	149	103	75	1	104	4	7	97	8	4.35
Perry, Daytona Beach*	22	19	1	0	9	5	0	.643	115	121	51	38	4	46	3	2	54	7	2.97
Petersen, Daytona Beach	24	23	13	3	12	10	0	.545	179	149	58	43	10	49	1	3	89	3	2.16
Pimental, St. Petersburg	36	0	0	0	5	0	7	1.000	71	50	17	16	1	32	2	3	73	3	2.03
Pippin, Ft. Lauderdale	45	0	0	0	4	5	11	.444	82	66	25	22	2	37	11	4	48	10	2.41
Quealey, Daytona Beach	21	0	0	0	4	1	6	.800	31	19	3	3	0	13	2	0	35	3	0.87
Raine, Ft. Myers	24	23	10	1	8	10	0	.444	160	127	65	49	2	105	2	6	99	8	2.76
Ramsey, Tampa*	20	16	1	1	3	7	0	.300	79	37	27		1	40	4	2	67	7	2.79
W. Ray, Daytona Beach	6	1	0	0	1	2	0	.333	10	10	9	5	0	8	1	1	3	1	4.50
Ricci, Ft. Lauderdale	21	14	5	1	8	6	2	.571	101	98	47	42	6	39	3	1	70	4	3.74
Rice, Daytona Beach*	27	3	0	0	0	1	1	.000	36	53	25	15	2	28	1	3	21	6	3.75
Riggins, St. Petersburg*	57	1	0	0	7	3	13	.700	97	84	25	20	3	39	14	3	69	6	1.86
Robinson, Tampa	13	13	2	0	4	6	0	.400	76	76	32	28	8	16	3	1	44	0	3.32
Rodriguez, Ft. Myers	1	0	0	0	0	0	0	.000	1	1	0	0	0	3	2	0	0	0	0.00
Ross, Daytona Beach	30	1	0	0	5	3	4	.625	58	50	14	11	0	11	7	0	39	2	1.71
Ruiz, Vero Beach*	41	1	0	0	5	1	6	.833	89	71	30	23	3	49	3	3	59	1	2.33
Russell, St. Petersburg	20	20	4	0	10	9	0	.526	119	127	68	50	4	44	4	4	63	7	3.78
Sanchez, Lakeland	10	4	0	0	0	4	0	.000	36	35	34	30	8	35	2	1	19	5	7.50
Sattler, West Palm Beach	16	16	4	1	7	5	0	.583	113	93	46	34	4	45	5	5	67	6	2.71
Schneck, Winter Haven	13	4	0	0	0	4	2	.000	21	23	26	24	1	33	2	5	15	10	10.29
Schrimsher, Tampa	10	6	0	0	1	5	0	.167	33	30	22	18	1	19	1	1	12	3	4.91
Schuler, W. Palm Beach	13	0	0	0	1	2	0	.333	23	17	8	8	1	8	0	1	15	1	3.13
Simerly, Lakeland	17	14	1	1	6	5	0	.545	86	87	52	47	2	32	4	5	54	2	4.92
Simon, Tampa	1	0	0	0	0	0	0	.000	0	1	0	0	0	0	0	0	0	0	0.00
Skinner, Ft. Myers	3	3	2	1	2	0	0	1.000	19	7	7	7	0	5	1	0	10	0	3.15
Smith, Daytona Beach	33	3	0	0	5	3	3	.625	58	47	28	22	3	43	4	2	39	8	3.41
Smith, Lakeland	14	1	1	0	2	2	3	.500	42	37	19	13	1	9	1	2	19	0	2.79
Smith, Miami	22	21	2		8	11	0	.421	138	138	63	44	1	49	3	4	54	12	2.87
Smith, Ft. Myers	17	1	0	0	1	2	0	.500	33	34	24	20	0	31	1	0	17	5	5.45
Sporrer, Ft. Lauderdale	1	0	0	0	0	0	0	.000	2	3	3	3	0	2	0	0	2	0	13.50
St. John, W. Palm Beach*	1	0	0	0	0	0	0	.000	10	13	9	9	0	9	1	0	7	2	8.10
Staffon, West Palm Beach	17	12	2	0	3	6	0	.333	79	81	53	44	4	66	5	0	51	7	5.01
Stuper, St. Petersburg	24	0	0	0	1	4	2	.200	39	38	12	10	0	19	6	1	28	2	2.31
Sullivan, Tampa	16	16	5	1	6	6	0	.500	102	84	42	20	1	27	6	0	54	4	1.76

Pitcher–Club	G	GS	CG	ShO	W	L	Sv	Pct.	IP	H	R	ER	HR	BB	Int. BB	HB	SO	WP	ERA
Sutcliffe, Vero Beach	21	21	5	0	11	7	0	.611	138	128	73	57	3	76	0	5	73	8	3.72
Swaggerty, Miami	19	0	0	0	3	1	0	.750	43	39	16	11	0	22	2	0	25	4	2.30
Taylor, W. Palm Beach*	17	17	1	0	4	8	0	.333	94	84	66	50	6	76	1	7	98	10	4.79
Tennant, Vero Beach	19	13	1	0	4	4	0	.500	80	75	53	51	7	76	2	1	38	3	5.74
Thomas, St. Petersburg	11	5	1	1	2	5	0	.286	39	45	28	21	0	22	1	2	14	4	4.85
Timlin, Ft. Myers	24	11	4	2	7	5	0	.583	99	103	54	46	3	58	3	8	37	2	4.18
Toliver, Ft. Lauderdale	3	3	0	0	0	2	0	.000	8	14	15	13	0	10	0	1	4	2	14.63
Torres, West Palm Beach	21	6	4	1	5	4	1	.556	67	73	40	30	0	34	1	4	30	9	4.03
Vanderbush, Ft. Myers	6	6	1	0	3	2	0	.600	26	41	31	24	1	24	0	1	16	2	8.31
Vega, St. Petersburg	3	0	0	0	0	0	0	.000	4	6	3	3	0	4	0	2	1	1	6.75
Vila, Miami	9	0	0	0	0	1	1	.000	20	23	10	7	3	9	0	0	7	0	3.15
Warren, Lakeland	13	11	0	0	3	6	0	.333	52	60	45	41	5	48	0	2	33	4	7.10
Weaver, St. Petersburg	4	4	0	0	1	3	0	.250	18	26	17	11	1	9	0	1	8	1	5.50
Welenc, Daytona Beach	17	6	1	0	6	2	0	.750	58	61	38	32	3	39	1	3	33	3	4.97
Wever, Ft. Lauderdale	15	15	3	0	7	3	0	.700	94	70	44	38	4	54	0	5	67	2	3.64
Wheeler, Lakeland	34	0	0	0	4	4	4	.500	58	63	39	31	3	33	4	0	33	9	4.81
White, Ft. Myers	32	2	0	0	1	6	6	.143	88	97	38	32	6	34	4	3	38	2	3.27
Wick, West Palm Beach*	25	1	0	0	0	4	0	.000	44	53	34	24	1	27	5	1	16	3	4.91
Wickensheimer, Vero B	26	26	15	3	15	8	0	.652	200	167	57	49	2	93	2	4	162	8	2.21
Williams, St. Petersburg	10	0	0	0	1	1	0	.500	22	34	18	18	0	9	0	1	11	2	7.36
Williams, W. P. Beach*	4	0	0	0	0	0	0	.000	4	9	5	4	1	0	0	0	2	0	9.00
Williams, Ft. Myers	20	20	7	1	7	11	0	.389	135	120	65	46	3	58	3	3	69	7	3.07
Woodall, Miami*	17	8	1	1	1	6	1	.143	55	61	39	25	4	31	1	0	21	3	4.09
Woodworth, Ft. Myers	19	8	0	0	6	2	0	.750	64	79	40	30	3	29	1	1	15	1	4.22
Yanus, West Palm Beach	10	3	2	0	5	0	1	1.000	47	48	19	14	3	6	0	0	41	2	2.68
Zedonek, Miami	4	0	0	0	0	0	0	.000	9	18	8	8	1	6	0	1	2	1	8.00

BALKS—Wever, 7; Raine, 6; Beecroft, Pena, 5 each; Alvarez, Michael Brown, Filson, Sattler, Sutcliffe, Taylor, 4 each; Bonine, Dunn, Jackson, Nail, Ramsey, Russell, Woodworth, 3 each; Anderson, L. Brown, Burchett, Caldwell, Cates, George Davis, Gordon Davis, W. Davis, Fadhel, Gleckel, Grubbs, Horton, Houston, C. Johnson, J. Johnson, Kreymborg, Lesley, Nelson, Paulino, Sanchez, St. John, Torres, Warren, Wheeler, White (1 Mia.-1 FtM.), Wickensheimer, L. Williams, 2 each; Baldwin, Birrell, Borbon, Candiotti, Chapin, Chretien, I. Clark, D. Collins, Creel, Daniel, DiLorenzo, Foster, Franke, Gotay, Gott, Grant, Grzybek, Hanslovan, Hayford, Hesketh, Hook, Houser, Jordan, Kaufman, Kepshire, Locascio, Madden, Maher, Malden, Maples, Moloney, Nurthen, O'Connor, Paris, Pearson, Peralta, S. Perry, W. P. Perry, Pippin, Skinner, J. Smith, Staffon, Sullivan, Swaggerty, Thomas, Weaver, Wick (Mia.), Richard Williams, Zedonek, 1 each.

COMBINATION SHUTOUTS—Perry-Brown, Brown-Finch, Perry-Quealey, Daytona Beach; Nelson-Kaufman, Pearson-Kaufman, Ricci-Kaufman, Filson-Kaufman, Fort Lauderdale; Warren-Geiger, Simerly-Wheeler, Dunn-Wheeler, Codiroli-Beecroft, Beecroft-Hensley, Beecroft-Geiger, Lakeland; Clark-Grant, Miami; Gotay Riggins, Collins-Pimental, Gotay-Pimental, St. Petersburg; Ramsey-Noble, Jackson-Hayes, Bonham-Buchanan, Dowless-Martinez-Hayes, Tampa; Wickensheimer-Ruiz, Vero Beach, Taylor-Josephson, Anderson-Fadhel, O'Connor-Torres-Anderson, Caldwell-Anderson, West Palm Beach; Birrell-Johnson, W. Davis-Johnson, Baldwin-W. Davis, W. Davis-Moloney, Hayford-Moloney-Brown, DeSanto-Collins, Birrell-G. Davis-W. Davis, Winter Haven.

NO-HIT GAMES—Dowless, Tampa, defeated Fort Myers, 4-0, May 22, first game, (seven innings); Williams, Fort Myers, defeated West Palm Beach, 5-0, August 26.

23 Skiddoo

Jerry Johnson of St. Petersburg in the Florida State League blanked the Tampa Tarpons with no-hit pitching through the first five innings June 8, but he had to wait 23 days to find out whether he could complete the no-hitter because a power failure knocked out the lights down the third base line at Al Lopez Field.

Under league rules, the suspended game was completed July 2 with St. Pete taking its 4-0 lead and potential no-hitter into play.

However, when action continued Johnson was not the same unhittable hurler. He pitched three more innings, giving up seven hits and two runs while making 52 pitches. Mark Riggins hurled the final inning to pick up the save in the 4-2 victory.

Midwest League

CLASS A

CHAMPIONSHIP WINNERS IN PREVIOUS YEARS

1947—Belleville .667	1960—Waterloo .629	1970—Quincy z .691
Belleville .672	Waterloo .677	Quad Cities .581
1948—West Frankfort* .708	1961—Waterloo .613	1971—Appleton .642
1949—Centralia .627	Quincy z .594	Quad Cities a .548
Paducah (4th)† .454	1962—Dubuque z .667	1972—Appleton .598
1950—Centralia‡ .675	Waterloo .625	Danville a .584
1951—Paris§ .700	1963—Clinton .710	1973—Wisconsin Rapids a .562
Danville (4th)† .432	Clinton .629	Danville .537
1952—Danville x .685	1964—Clinton .667	1974—Appleton .593
Decatur (3rd)† .584	Fox Cities z .667	Danville a .517
1953—Decatur* .576	1965—Burlington .667	1975—Waterloo a .727
1954—Decatur .587	Burlington .677	Quad Cities .624
Danville (2nd)‡ .528	1966—Fox Cities z .689	1976—Waterloo a .600
1955—Dubuque* .587	Cedar Rapids .762	Cedar Rapids .595
1956—Paris y .656	1967—Wisconsin Rapids .685	1977—Waterloo .550
Dubuque .603	Appleton z .587	Burlington a .511
1957—Decatur y .683	1968—Decatur .656	1978—Appleton a .708
Clinton .623	Quad Cities z .648	Burlington .500
1958—Michigan City .623	1969—Appleton .648	1979—Waterloo a .600
Waterloo z .613	Appleton .690	Quad Cities a .579
1959—Waterloo .613		
Waterloo .613		

*Won championship and our-club playoff. †Won four-club playoff. ‡Playoff finals canceled because of bad weather. xWon first half of split-season and tied Paris for second-half title. yWon first-half title and four-team playoff. zWon split-season playoff. (NOTE—Known as Illinois State League in 1947-48 and Mississippi-Ohio Valley League from 1949 through 1955.)

aLeague divided into Northern and Southern divisions and played split-season. Playoff winner.

STANDING OF CLUBS AT CLOSE OF FIRST HALF, JUNE 20

NORTHERN DIVISION

Club	W.	L.	T.	Pct.	G.B.
Waterloo (Indians)	48	23	0	.676	....
Wausau (Co-op)	34	36	0	.486	13½
Appleton (White Sox)	34	37	0	.479	14
Wisconsin Rapids (Twins)	32	39	0	.451	16

SOUTHERN DIVISION

Club	W.	L.	T.	Pct.	G.B.
Quad Cities (Cubs)	39	32	0	.549	....
Cedar Rapids (Reds)	34	36	0	.486	4½
Burlington (Brewers)	32	39	0	.451	7
Clinton (Giants)	30	41	0	.423	9

STANDING OF CLUBS AT CLOSE OF SECOND HALF, SEPTEMBER 1

NORTHERN DIVISION

Club	W.	L.	T.	Pct.	G.B.
Wisconsin Rapids (Twins)	45	25	0	.643	....
Appleton (White Sox)	42	26	0	.618	2
Waterloo (Indians)	38	32	0	.543	7
Wausau (Co-op)	23	46	0	.333	21½

SOUTHERN DIVISION

Club	W.	L.	T.	Pct.	G.B.
Burlington (Brewers)	38	33	0	.535	....
Quad Cities (Cubs)	35	33	0	.515	1½
Clinton (Giants)	32	38	0	.457	5½
Cedar Rapids (Reds)	25	45	0	.357	12½

COMPOSITE STANDINGS OF CLUBS AT CLOSE OF SEASON, SEPTEMBER 1

NORTHERN DIVISION

Club	Wat.	Apl.	W.R.	Wau.	Q.C.	Bur.	Cln.	C.R.	W.	L.	T.	Pct.	G.B.
Waterloo (Indians)	..	13	14	19	5	9	14	12	86	55	0	.610	....
Appleton (White Sox)	13	..	11	10	7	11	11	13	76	63	0	.547	9
Wisconsin Rapids (Twins)	12	15	..	16	7	7	11	9	77	64	0	.546	9
Wausau (Co-op)	6	16	10	..	7	7	4	7	57	82	0	.410	28

SOUTHERN DIVISION

Club	Wat.	Apl.	W.R.	Wau.	Q.C.	Bur.	Cln.	C.R.	W.	L.	T.	Pct.	G.B.
Quad Cities (Cubs)	11	7	8	9	..	15	12	12	74	65	0	.532	....
Burlington (Brewers)	7	5	9	9	11	..	12	17	70	72	0	.493	5½
Clinton (Giants)	2	4	5	12	14	14	..	11	62	79	0	.440	13
Cedar Rapids (Reds)	4	3	7	7	14	9	15	..	59	81	0	.421	15½

Quad Cities represented Davenport and Bettendorf, Ia., and Moline and Rock Island, Ill.

Major League affiliations in parentheses.

Playoffs—Waterloo, first half leader, defeated Wisconsin Rapids, second half leader, two games to one for Northern Division championship. Quad Cities, first half leader, defeated Burlington, second half leader, two games to one for Southern Division championship. Waterloo (Northern Division Champion) defeated Quad Cities (Southern Division Champion), two games to one for League Championship.

Regular-Season Attendance—Appleton, 74,207; Burlington, 51,486; Cedar Rapids, 84,062; Clinton, 58,723; Quad Cities, 103,445; Waterloo, 72,606; Wausau, 37,175; Wisconsin Rapids, 47,899. Total, 529,603. Playoffs, 9,846. All-star game, 7,413.

Managers—Appleton—Gordy Lund; Burlington—Duane Espy; Cedar Rapids—Jim Lett; Clinton—Wayne Cato; Quad Cities—Jim Napier; Waterloo—Cal Emery; Wausau—Orlando Martinez; Wisconsin Rapids—Rich Stelmaszek.

All-Star Team: 1B—Walker, Appleton; 2B—Christensen, Wisconsin Rapids; 3B—Hayes, Waterloo; SS—Viltz, Cedar Rapids; OF—K. Brown, Appleton; Kubit, Wisconsin Rapids; Levi, Burlington; C—Cummings, Clinton; DH—Kittle, Appleton; P—Gil, Quad Cities; Konopa, Wisconsin Rapids; Thompson, Quad Cities; Vasquez, Appleton; Manager—Stelmaszek, Wisconsin Rapids.

(Compiled by Howe News Bureau, Boston, Mass.)

CLUB BATTING

Club	G.	AB.	R.	OR.	H.	TB.	2B.	3B.	HR.	RBI.	SH.	SF.	Int. BB.	BB.	HP.	SO.	SB.	CS.	LOB.	Pct.
Waterloo	141	4599	772	605	1212	1784	201	25	107	656	43	20	587	19	45	824	282	85	965	.264
Quad Cities	139	4573	645	546	1188	1629	186	36	61	540	41	37	592	21	38	756	196	83	1077	.260
Appleton	139	4555	691	580	1170	1707	203	47	80	598	38	41	539	17	47	806	133	39	984	.257
Wis Rapids	141	4654	701	619	1159	1668	178	20	97	599	54	37	636	16	53	769	139	39	1079	.249
Burlington	142	4465	620	650	1096	1474	164	26	54	518	27	31	591	13	44	777	319	101	957	.245
Clinton	141	4456	548	690	1080	1448	152	30	52	445	55	29	476	14	35	810	237	98	918	.242
Wausau	139	4437	623	787	1056	1577	146	15	115	548	27	32	536	15	49	924	201	87	864	.238
Cedar Rapids	140	4485	518	641	1014	1374	136	25	58	439	88	28	558	29	39	958	143	54	1025	.226

INDIVIDUAL BATTING

(Leading Qualifiers for Batting Championship—383 or More Plate Appearances)

*Bats lefthanded.   †Switch-hitter.

Player and Club	G.	AB.	R.	H.	TB.	2B.	3B.	HR.	RBI.	SH.	SF.	BB.	HP.	SO.	SB.	CS.	Pct.
Hayes, Von, Waterloo	134	492	105	162	246	33	3	15	90	1	7	66	1	63	51	8	.329
Brown, Keith, Appleton	126	455	78	139	179	23	1	5	64	8	6	58	0	60	12	3	.305
Levi, Stanley, Burlington	128	441	102	132	168	17	5	3	54	4	3	87	6	39	47	16	.299
Hall, Melvin, Quad Cities	97	347	54	102	142	14	4	6	42	2	3	51	5	65	21	10	.294
Diaz, Michael, Quad Cities	105	386	51	113	156	17	1	8	47	2	2	35	3	48	7	1	.293
Estepan, Rafael, Clinton	115	397	41	115	144	15	1	4	45	13	2	7	2	41	6	4	.290
Viltz, Escamillo, Cedar Rapids	124	488	60	140	181	16	5	5	54	4	4	22	10	68	15	8	.287
Kornfeld, Craig, Quad Cities	118	451	74	129	180	24	6	5	56	3	6	37	7	34	55	10	.286
Bohnet, Robert, Waterloo	127	405	70	116	191	28	1	15	91	0	7	92	6	67	8	5	.286
Cummings, Robert, Clinton	116	365	50	103	163	15	3	13	79	2	6	67	3	62	18	9	.282

Departmental Leaders: G—Christensen, 140; AB—Christensen, 567; R—Baker, 108; H—Hayes, 162; TB—Christensen, 248; 2B—Hayes, 33; 3B—J. Brown, Daniels, Kutcher, 8; HR—Gaetti, 22; RBI—G. Walker, 98; GWRBI—Christensen, 16; SH—Estepan, 13; SF—Christensen, 9; BB—Colletti, 122; HP—Presley, 12; SO—Higgins, 139; SB—Frierson, 90; CS—Frierson, 32.

(All Players—Listed Alphabetically)

Player and Club	G.	AB.	R.	H.	TB.	2B.	3B.	HR.	RBI.	SH.	SF.	BB.	HP.	SO.	SB.	CS.	Pct.
Albright, Gilbert, Clinton	23	63	6	12	13	1	0	0	4	1	0	6	1	14	0	1	.190
Anthony, Dane, Waterloo	26	1	0	0	0	0	0	0	0	0	0	0	0	0	0	0	.000
Austin, Richard, Wisconsin Rapids	104	320	46	69	109	18	2	6	42	4	5	40	9	56	11	4	.216
Baker, Ricky, Waterloo†	138	530	108	142	180	17	3	5	45	8	1	49	8	84	78	18	.268
Ballard, Glenn, Wisconsin Rapids	19	72	11	22	34	1	3	1	12	0	1	5	0	10	0	0	.306
Barbee, Andrew, Cedar Rapids	48	118	9	25	31	4	1	0	11	1	0	20	1	27	3	0	.212
Barron, Robert, Clinton*	58	193	25	48	67	6	2	3	21	0	4	18	0	31	6	3	.249
Bass, Ricki, Burlington	61	200	22	45	57	5	2	1	16	2	3	25	1	25	20	2	.225
Bazan, Pedro, Quad Cities*	39	116	9	30	39	6	0	1	12	1	0	11	0	15	1	6	.259
Belmonte, Philip, Quad Cities	81	231	19	44	48	4	0	0	17	5	0	33	0	32	6	6	.190
Bevington, Terry, Burlington	39	117	14	31	44	7	0	2	11	0	0	13	3	9	11	4	.265
Bohnet, John, Waterloo*	25	3	0	1	2	1	0	0	1	0	0	1	0	0	0	0	.333
Bohnet, Robert, Waterloo	127	405	70	116	191	28	1	15	91	0	7	92	6	67	8	5	.286
Boothe, Charles, Clinton*	12	27	1	3	3	0	0	0	1	0	1	5	1	8	0	1	.111
Box, Newton, Cedar Rapids*	54	25	2	4	6	2	0	0	3	0	0	4	0	9	0	0	.160
Brennan, Thomas, Wausau*	35	1	1	1	2	1	0	0	0	0	0	0	0	0	0	0	1.000
Brown, Christopher, Clinton	103	337	38	80	112	5	3	7	35	6	2	35	4	67	12	6	.237
Brown, Jeffrey M., Appleton	85	311	63	76	98	6	8	0	27	5	0	50	0	37	16	2	.244
Brown, Keith, Appleton*	126	455	78	139	179	23	1	5	64	8	6	58	0	60	12	3	.305
Buckle, Larry, Cedar Rapids	17	31	3	3	7	1	0	1	4	2	0	3	0	14	0	0	.097
Buckley, Michael, Quad Cities	26	74	10	15	16	1	0	0	1	1	0	9	0	18	3	0	.203
Carlson, Brad, Wisconsin Rapids	54	172	21	44	60	8	1	2	18	4	1	11	1	41	0	0	.256
Carroll, Timothy, Appleton	86	285	44	76	103	9	3	4	31	3	1	26	4	33	11	3	.267
Casarez, Frank, Clinton	11	3	0	0	0	0	0	0	0	0	0	0	0	2	0	0	.000
Castillo, Juan, Burlington†	30	103	12	22	22	0	0	0	6	0	0	6	1	30	5	3	.214
Castillo, M. Carmello, Waterbury	117	390	69	103	152	14	1	11	64	2	3	45	2	59	46	12	.264
Cato, Wayne, Clinton	2	1	1	1	3	0	1	0	0	0	0	0	0	0	0	0	1.000
Cecchetti, George, Waterbury*	123	405	60	107	172	22	2	13	72	2	2	51	11	84	16	5	.264

Player and Club	G.	AB.	R.	H.	TB.	2B.	3B.	HR.	RBI.	SH.	SF.	BB.	HP.	SO.	SB.	CS.	Pct.
Chandler, Kenneth, Wis Rapids......	33	107	10	21	29	5	0	1	8	1	0	12	0	37	0	1	.196
Chaney, Bruce, Waterbury...............	56	145	26	29	43	3	1	3	21	1	1	21	1	33	9	1	.200
Christensen, James, Wis Rapids	140	567	96	159	248	32	3	17	93	2	9	47	4	68	24	5	.280
Chue, Jose, Clinton......................	28	0	1	0	0	0	0	0	0	0	0	0	0	0	0	0	.000
Churchill, Norman, Quad Cities* ...	7	1	0	0	0	0	0	0	0	1	0	1	0	1	0	0	.000
Colletti, Manuel, Wis Rapids†	128	422	73	97	106	6	0	1	42	12	1	122	1	56	10	4	.230
Compton, Bruce, Quad Cities	7	16	1	3	4	1	0	0	3	0	0	2	0	3	0	0	.188
Corbett, Raymond, Cedar Rapids ...	57	188	19	39	51	6	0	2	12	2	0	22	1	42	3	3	.207
Coronell, Dairo, Wisconsin Rapids .	3	2	0	0	0	0	0	0	0	0	0	0	0	0	0	0	.000
Cotto, Enrique, Quad Cities	19	78	9	22	25	1	1	0	5	0	0	4	0	10	8	1	.282
Cummings, Robert, Clinton	116	365	50	103	163	15	3	13	79	2	6	67	3	62	18	9	.282
Daniels, David, Appleton	115	366	55	89	120	12	8	1	29	2	2	47	1	78	13	8	.243
Daniels, Stephen, Cedar Rapids.....	52	8	0	0	0	0	0	0	0	0	0	2	0	3	0	0	.000
DeJesus, Jorge, Burlington*..........	39	134	12	31	41	7	0	1	9	2	0	21	0	27	1	0	.231
DeJiulio, Frank, Cedar Rapids*.....	35	16	0	2	3	1	0	0	3	3	0	3	0	4	1	0	.125
DeLoach, Richard, Quad Cities*	107	305	38	68	96	11	1	5	25	2	0	50	1	56	12	1	.223
Deer, Robert, Clinton	127	434	60	114	194	31	5	13	58	3	4	34	4	115	20	7	.263
Diaz, Michael, Quad Cities	105	386	51	113	156	17	1	8	47	2	2	35	3	48	7	1	.293
Diaz, Enrique, Wausau	53	170	22	36	51	4	1	3	26	0	4	15	0	50	2	4	.212
Diaz, Mario, Wausau	110	349	28	63	77	5	0	3	21	4	2	19	1	37	5	6	.181
Doby, Larry, Appleton†	67	220	33	63	104	14	6	5	43	0	1	41	5	44	1	3	.286
Dotson, Lawrence, Waterloo*........	68	226	38	71	86	10	1	1	22	2	1	20	5	25	8	10	.314
Downs, Kirk, Burlington	125	403	44	94	109	9	3	0	26	6	0	30	3	84	36	9	.233
Drzayich, Emil, Cedar Rapids*.....	113	425	46	100	175	18	0	19	66	4	3	40	4	74	0	2	.235
Dugas, Shanie, Waterloo*............	66	204	30	48	82	11	4	5	27	1	2	23	0	69	4	0	.235
Eisenreich, James, Wis Rapids*.....	5	16	4	7	7	0	0	0	3	0	0	1	0	0	1	0	.438
English, James, Appleton	33	95	16	15	17	0	1	0	6	3	0	16	1	28	2	0	.158
Epping, Troy, Clinton	24	62	6	7	7	0	0	0	5	1	0	9	4	23	0	0	.113
Estepan, Rafael, Clinton	115	397	41	115	144	15	1	4	45	13	2	7	2	41	6	4	.290
Evans, Johnny, Burlington..........	110	370	49	98	161	25	1	12	68	0	2	62	8	50	3	3	.265
Favata, Salvatore, Burlington	80	285	55	75	113	14	3	6	34	8	1	31	1	38	43	5	.263
Fazzio, Daryl, 39 Wat-30 QC*	69	167	20	41	49	8	0	0	21	1	3	41	1	39	0	3	.246
Figueroa, Richard, Clinton	30	66	8	17	24	4	0	1	8	0	1	10	0	17	2	0	.258
Fiorillo, Nicholas, Cedar Rapids* ..	12	28	4	5	6	1	0	0	3	1	0	2	0	6	0	0	.179
Fonseca, Chris, Clinton	22	60	6	8	8	0	0	0	1	0	8	0	10	1	1	.133
Frierson, Michael, Wausau†	127	410	83	99	113	6	1	2	19	5	1	110	5	83	90	32	.241
Gaetti, Gary, Wisconsin Rapids	138	503	77	134	233	27	3	22	82	2	4	67	7	120	24	8	.266
Garrelts, Scott, Clinton	29	2	0	0	0	0	0	0	0	0	0	0	0	0	0	0	.000
Gibson, Paul, Cedar Rapids	28	47	2	14	16	2	0	0	4	4	0	3	0	8	0	0	.298
Gifford, Roger, Wausau	2	5	0	0	0	0	0	0	0	0	0	0	0	1	0	0	.000
Gil, Carlos, Quad Cities	27	5	0	0	0	0	0	0	0	0	0	0	0	4	0	0	.000
Gilmartin, Daniel, Burlington	4	8	1	1	2	1	0	0	0	0	0	2	0	2	0	0	.125
Glass, Timothy, Waterloo	96	236	43	59	124	15	1	16	33	1	1	44	0	71	1	2	.250
Gonzalez, Orlando, Burlington	70	219	28	53	70	5	3	2	15	1	1	14	4	33	6	4	.242
Graser, Richard, Wausau*	33	11	0	0	0	0	0	0	0	1	0	1	0	3	0	0	.000
Guinn, Wayne, Cedar Rapids	28	44	3	5	7	2	0	0	5	3	1	9	0	18	0	0	.114
Hall, Larry, Appleton	54	193	24	52	66	14	0	0	25	1	3	16	1	34	0	0	.269
Hall, Melvin, Quad Cities*	97	347	54	102	142	14	4	6	42	2	3	51	5	65	21	10	.294
Hansen, Gregory, Wis Rapids	9	43	5	12	16	1	0	1	4	0	1	4	2	8	3	0	.279
Hardy, Bryan, Quad Cities*	15	4	0	1	1	0	0	0	1	2	0	0	0	2	0	0	.250
Hayes, Von, Waterloo*	134	492	105	162	246	33	3	15	90	1	7	66	1	63	51	8	.329
Henderson, Matthew, Wis Rapids*..	36	107	12	16	20	1	0	1	7	0	1	23	0	29	0	1	.150
Henry, Chris, Wausau*..............	107	363	45	92	132	11	4	7	63	1	4	49	3	48	6	2	.253
Higgins, Mark, Burlington	120	378	32	62	81	7	3	2	25	1	3	38	6	139	14	4	.164
Hill, Anthony, Appleton	43	167	30	47	59	6	3	0	14	2	1	18	0	23	33	2	.281
Hinson, Gary, Waterloo	26	71	15	21	29	3	1	1	9	3	1	19	0	13	2	0	.296
Hodgson, Gordon, Quad Cities	35	123	23	30	39	6	0	1	18	0	0	18	2	27	5	2	.244
Hoenstine, David, Cedar Rapids ...	91	277	25	59	70	7	2	0	27	8	1	50	2	38	14	5	.213
Holbrook, Alan, Clinton	1	0	0	0	0	0	0	0	0	0	0	1	0	0	0	0	.000
Hood, Michael, Wausau	20	60	9	10	20	4	0	2	4	0	0	7	1	9	1	0	.167
Hrbek, Kent, Wisconsin Rapids* ...	115	419	74	112	185	16	0	19	76	3	1	61	3	54	1	0	.267
Hrynko, Lawrence, Waterloo	40	1	0	0	0	0	0	0	0	0	0	0	0	0	0	0	.000
Hughes, Steven, Cedar Rapids	51	144	8	30	35	3	1	0	14	1	2	18	1	34	2	2	.208
Hulett, Timothy, Appleton	79	278	49	72	124	11	1	13	47	0	3	34	3	56	5	4	.259
James, Dion, Burlington*	3	10	0	1	1	0	0	0	1	0	1	2	0	1	0	1	.100
Jendra, Richard, Cedar Rapids	53	181	26	39	50	5	0	2	17	3	1	26	0	38	1	2	.215
Jensen, Timothy, Wisconsin Rapids	2	6	0	1	1	0	0	0	0	0	0	1	0	1	0	0	.167
Johnson, Kevin, Clinton†	122	384	39	78	105	12	3	3	39	3	0	32	0	90	14	7	.203
Johnson, Rodney, Cedar Rapids ...	37	119	13	37	44	4	0	1	15	4	1	27	0	13	9	0	.311
Jones, Jeffery, Cedar Rapids	100	332	48	66	118	13	3	11	33	6	0	62	9	121	8	6	.199
Jones, Thomas, Clinton	10	39	7	15	17	2	0	0	6	0	0	2	0	1	2	0	.385
Keating, Dennis, Appleton	73	234	26	47	66	10	3	1	10	3	1	7	2	43	4	1	.201
Kelley, Michael, Quad Cities*	86	300	51	83	100	3	7	0	23	3	6	40	0	31	23	10	.277
King, Kevin, Wausau	109	377	71	97	174	16	2	19	62	0	4	54	2	138	11	6	.257
Kingsolver, Kurtis, Burlington	124	406	75	114	174	18	3	12	65	0	3	97	2	80	56	21	.281
Kittle, Ron, Appleton	61	209	31	66	123	15	3	12	56	0	4	20	8	47	0	2	.316

Player and Club	G.	AB.	R.	H.	TB.	2B.	3B.	HR.	RBI.	SH.	SF.	BB.	HP.	SO.	SB.	CS.	Pct.
Kornfeld, Craig, Quad Cities	118	451	74	129	180	24	6	5	56	3	6	37	7	34	55	10	.286
Kripner, Michael, Cedar Rapids†	52	170	22	44	54	7	0	1	20	4	2	24	1	44	7	3	.259
Kubit, Joseph, Wisconsin Rapids	135	523	67	145	201	19	5	9	79	4	2	42	3	93	9	2	.277
Kutcher, Randy, Clinton	138	525	72	133	175	17	8	3	46	5	5	50	3	74	65	16	.253
Lajszky, Werner, Wausau	120	399	64	92	148	17	0	13	48	1	0	51	3	131	6	5	.231
Lapple, Robert, Cedar Rapids	58	144	14	22	23	1	0	0	7	3	1	23	0	34	4	1	.153
Levi, Stanley, Burlington*	128	441	102	132	168	17	5	3	54	4	3	87	6	39	47	16	.299
Lucarelli, Vito, Appleton	30	84	8	14	18	4	0	0	9	3	1	7	0	27	0	0	.167
Lunar, Manuel, Wisconsin Rapids..	7	1	0	0	0	0	0	0	0	0	0	0	0	0	0	0	.000
Luzinski, William, Appleton	8	17	0	5	5	0	0	0	1	0	0	3	0	4	0	1	.294
Madden, Robert, Quad Cities	12	7	1	2	4	0	1	0	1	0	0	0	0	3	0	0	.286
Martinez, Carmelo, Quad Cities	128	460	65	118	177	23	0	12	64	1	4	54	2	68	8	7	.257
Martinez, Orlando, Wausau	4	5	0	2	2	0	0	0	0	0	0	0	0	1	0	0	.400
Martinez, Tommy, Waterloo	76	249	38	53	90	12	2	7	43	0	2	14	3	47	8	1	.213
Masone, Anthony, Cedar Rapids	129	449	56	101	155	16	4	10	58	8	7	50	5	117	12	4	.225
McCrary, Arnold, Wausau*	56	209	47	56	86	7	1	7	33	1	2	23	2	25	10	6	.268
McKay, Karl, Burlington	120	425	39	94	107	11	1	0	47	3	4	25	3	84	40	14	.221
McKinney, Charles, Cedar Rapids..	16	19	2	1	4	0	0	1	3	0	1	3	0	7	0	0	.053
McManaman, Steven, Wis Rapids ..	18	17	3	3	4	1	0	0	4	0	0	1	1	6	0	0	.176
Meier, Bryan, Waterloo	33	90	12	20	25	5	0	0	3	4	0	6	1	23	1	0	.222
Mesa, Ivan, Appleton	71	270	31	66	95	9	1	6	28	1	2	11	5	27	10	3	.244
Miller, Kevin, Wisconsin Rapids	129	477	53	112	148	15	0	7	51	2	4	58	7	82	3	0	.235
Miller, Mark, Cedar Rapids	122	346	61	87	103	5	4	1	23	10	2	81	2	53	24	6	.251
Millhauser, Glenn, Quad Cities	9	20	3	5	5	0	0	0	2	1	0	4	0	5	0	1	.250
Millner, Timothy, Quad Cities	25	7	1	1	2	1	0	0	1	0	0	1	0	2	0	0	.143
Mims, Gerry, Quad Cities	22	3	0	0	0	0	0	0	0	0	0	0	0	0	0	0	.000
Minium, Matthew, Waterloo*	44	114	18	32	34	2	0	0	17	1	2	20	0	11	3	4	.281
Mitchell, Weston, Waterloo	58	218	36	62	73	4	2	1	22	1	0	37	1	21	20	7	.284
Molina, Norberto, Wis Rapids†	11	28	1	3	3	0	0	0	1	0	1	0	0	9	0	0	.107
Monroe, Gary, Quad Cities	18	26	1	7	9	0	1	0	1	1	0	2	1	6	1	0	.269
Moon, Glenn, Clinton*	49	163	30	49	64	13	1	0	10	1	0	32	2	35	20	6	.301
Moore, Edmund, Quad Cities	21	2	0	0	0	0	0	0	0	0	0	0	0	0	0	0	.000
Moore, Mark, Cedar Rapids*	64	8	1	2	5	0	0	1	3	3	0	1	0	4	0	0	.250
Morgan, William, Quad Cities	60	187	14	39	48	7	1	0	13	2	1	24	3	48	5	4	.209
Mork, Dennis, Quad Cities*	107	323	49	79	130	16	7	7	51	2	2	43	4	65	10	8	.245
Morris, Thomas, Quad Cities*	32	2	0	0	0	0	0	0	0	0	0	0	0	1	0	0	.000
Morton, Stanley, Clinton*	67	205	23	37	42	5	0	0	12	2	1	28	1	41	6	6	.180
Mota, Jose, Cedar Rapids†	130	523	60	126	146	12	4	0	31	3	2	35	2	103	32	8	.241
Nanni, Tito, Wausau*	64	237	33	60	104	8	0	12	40	0	2	25	4	47	9	2	.253
Noble, Charles, Cedar Rapids*	3	7	0	0	0	0	0	0	0	0	0	0	0	4	0	0	.000
Norwood, Steven, Burlington	15	4	0	1	1	0	0	0	1	0	0	0	0	2	0	0	.250
Olson, Mitchell, Appleton	3	10	0	0	0	0	0	0	0	0	0	0	0	3	0	0	.000
Ortega, Kirk, Clinton	23	67	2	17	18	1	0	0	1	1	0	2	0	15	1	3	.254
Ortiz, Jorge, Waterloo	15	27	1	4	4	0	0	0	0	3	0	3	0	8	0	0	.148
Owen, Dave, Quad Cities	56	188	43	49	55	5	1	0	17	5	1	61	0	37	14	5	.261
Painton, Tim, Clinton*	126	412	38	84	105	9	0	4	33	1	3	57	2	64	15	10	.204
Payne, James, Quad Cities	24	78	12	19	24	2	0	1	12	0	1	7	0	22	2	2	.244
Peltz, Peter, Appleton	61	233	49	65	93	16	3	2	31	2	2	36	2	29	9	1	.279
Perdue, Doran, Clinton*	65	245	32	70	77	5	1	0	17	5	1	26	3	37	21	9	.286
Perodin, Ronald, Clinton*	47	125	18	25	30	1	2	0	6	4	0	16	2	23	7	4	.200
Peterson, Erik, Waterloo	30	92	6	17	22	5	0	0	10	2	0	10	2	10	2	1	.185
Pilla, Antonio, Wisconsin Rapids	35	102	23	25	32	4	0	1	6	2	1	22	6	21	7	1	.245
Porte, Carlos, Cedar Rapids	100	227	19	47	63	8	1	2	20	0	0	11	1	40	7	3	.207
Presley, James, Wausau	126	429	45	105	164	21	1	12	52	3	3	24	12	98	9	4	.245
Rathjen, Dennis, Clinton	50	12	0	2	3	1	0	0	1	0	1	0	0	4	0	0	.167
Renwick, Richard, Quad Cities	27	15	0	2	2	0	0	0	2	1	0	4	0	0	0	0	.133
Rey, Everett, Waterloo	80	225	30	56	83	4	1	7	37	3	1	15	1	45	6	1	.249
Robins, George, Burlington	3	10	1	1	1	0	0	0	1	0	0	1	1	0	0	0	.100
Rohlfing, Wayne, Quad Cities	66	204	25	60	89	14	0	5	30	1	3	24	2	68	2	2	.294
Schwab, Kenneth, Clinton	29	1	0	0	0	0	0	0	0	0	0	0	1	0	0	0	.000
Skaggs, Steven, Cedar Rapids	24	35	3	5	5	0	0	0	0	0	0	6	0	15	0	0	.143
Smith, Kelly, Clinton	63	214	42	56	67	8	0	1	16	3	0	30	1	30	18	4	.262
Spino, Thomas, Quad Cities*	5	3	0	0	0	0	0	0	0	0	0	0	0	1	0	0	.000
Steele, Walter, Burlington	46	132	10	31	43	6	0	2	17	0	0	28	0	34	4	3	.235
Stein, Raymond, Wis Rapids*	60	174	23	37	45	5	0	1	16	4	0	26	4	17	2	1	.213
Stewart, Gregory, Appleton	17	64	7	12	17	2	0	1	5	0	1	8	1	9	1	0	.188
Stocker, Bruce, Wisconsin Rapids†	101	331	63	80	97	7	2	2	29	9	2	59	4	49	23	10	.242
Stockstill, John, Quad Cities	82	244	35	59	77	7	1	3	33	0	3	23	6	38	3	0	.242
Stovall, Jerry, Clinton†	29	1	0	0	0	0	0	0	0	0	0	0	0	0	0	0	.000
Straker, Lester, Cedar Rapids	34	33	3	3	3	0	0	0	0	3	0	4	0	13	0	0	.091
Tanzi, Robert, Wausau	121	444	66	123	171	16	1	10	61	1	2	34	10	52	11	2	.277
Taylor, Michael, 56 Wat-57 Wau	113	376	53	81	128	11	3	10	54	3	5	32	1	74	22	5	.215
Thompson, Michael, Quad Cities* ..	35	5	2	1	3	0	1	0	2	1	0	1	0	1	0	0	.200
Thon, Frank, Clinton	17	53	2	6	7	1	0	0	3	2	0	1	0	3	3	1	.113
Trevino, A. Ted, 8 QC-67 Wau..	75	224	23	58	88	10	1	6	29	1	3	23	1	37	0	2	.259
Upshur, Takashi, Wausau	90	194	33	48	72	5	2	5	22	4	0	42	3	33	20	9	.247

Player and Club	G.	AB.	R.	H.	TB.	2B.	3B.	HR.	RBI.	SH.	SF.	BB.	HP.	SO.	SB.	CS.	Pct.
Upton, Jack, Quad Cities	63	223	38	73	117	17	3	7	48	1	2	28	1	21	7	3	.327
Valley, Charles, Burlington	96	339	49	90	137	18	1	9	60	0	7	35	2	51	17	2	.265
Vasquez, Jesse, Burlington	52	1	0	0	0	0	0	0	0	0	0	0	0	1	0	0	.000
Viltz, Escamillo, Cedar Rapids†	124	488	60	140	181	16	5	5	54	4	4	22	10	68	15	8	.287
Voigt, Paul, Wisconsin Rapids	24	1	0	0	0	0	0	0	0	0	0	0	0	1	0	0	.000
Vuksan, Jeffrey, Appleton	50	165	13	38	47	6	0	1	12	2	0	11	2	42	1	2	.230
Walker, Gregory, Appleton*	135	464	88	130	219	20	3	21	98	0	8	88	11	76	11	2	.280
Waller, Kevin, Cedar Rapids	29	53	7	8	13	2	0	1	3	0	0	7	0	7	1	1	.151
Watanabe, Curt, Burlington	135	480	75	120	142	14	1	2	67	0	3	75	3	47	16	10	.250
Whisler, Gary, Waterloo*	66	199	21	46	46	0	0	8		9	1	15	1	32	7	6	.231
White, David, Appleton	121	435	46	98	154	26	3	8	62	3	5	42	1	106	4	2	.225
White, Larry, Waterloo	26	1	0	0	0	0	0	0	0	0	0	0	0	0	0	0	.000
Williams, Kevin, Wisconsin Rapids	70	244	39	60	90	12	3	4	25	4	3	32	1	27	21	2	.246
Wilson, Michael, Quad Cities	14	24	6	7	8	1	0	0	2	1	1	8	0	6	3	3	.292
Wright, Michael, Quad Cities	15	6	0	0	0	0	0	0	0	0	0	0	0	5	0	0	.000
Young, Gary, Quad Cities	21	5	0	0	0	0	0	0	0	0	0	1	0	1	0	0	.000
Zisk, John, Wausau	120	380	37	82	128	13	0	11	47	3	3	42	3	96	11	4	.216

The following pitchers had no plate appearances primarily through use of designated hitters, listed alphabetically by club, games in parentheses:

APPLETON—Agosto, Juan *(23); Anderson, Jesse (13); Barrios, Francisco (2); Burger, Bradley (1); Esser, Mark (5); Estrada, Luis (25); Fallon, Robert *(22); Johnson, Charles (17); Maitland, Michael *(10); Melendez, Diego (9); Mills, William (10); Naumann, Richard *(27); Ortega, Daniel *(8); Pastrovich, Steven (14); Rodriguez, Nelson (3); Smith, Jackie *(6); Vasquez, Dennis (47); Wright, Larry (26).

BURLINGTON—Anderson, Michael *(34); Biggus, Bengie (21); Cicotte, Gregory (4); Coleman, Ty *(4); De-Hart, Gregory (14); Donovan, Michael (18); Grier, David (27); Lepson, Mark (14); Manderfield, Steven *(26); Matias, Luis (1); McCoy, Kevin (23); Meadows, Brian (16); Meyer, Randy (4); Pone, Vincent (8); Porter, Charles (7); Walker, Alan *(10).

CLINTON—Bangert, Gregory *(12); Bautista, Ramon (6); Felt, Jerald (10); Goodchild, Christopher (26); Hagemann, Timothy *(6); Maebe, Arthur (31); Matrisciano, Ronald (18); Wilhelmi, David (27); Wrobel, Ronald *(4).

QUAD CITIES—Soff, Raymond (40); Swaggerty, F. Glenn (11); Wilkins, Mark (6).

WATERLOO—Asbell, John (26); Barnhart, Richard (3); Gilbert, Angelo †(4); Hoban, John (10); Jeffcoat, J. Michael *(4); Leach, Ron *(14); Lintz, Rickey (7); Nuismer, N. Jack (13); Owens, Tom (5); Pope, Gregory (6); Regan, Francis (7); Richard, Todd (7); Romero, Ramon *(31); Willis, Alan (21).

WAUSAU—Bauman, Alan *(28); Burden, John (5—8 with Waterloo); Cahill, Mark (26); Jordan, Anthony (5); Little, Martin (13); McKenzie, Donald (7); Nunez, Edwin (22); Pettibone, H. Jay (9); Roche, Stephen (26—12 with Waterbury); Salva, Elias (12); Seymour, Ronald (14); Softy, Mark (23); Steger, Kevin (19).

WISCONSIN RAPIDS—Arrington, Samuel (10); Everett, Conrad *(36); Francingues, Kenneth (35); Gurholt, Jack (2); Jackson, Harold (10); Konopa, Robert †(28); Krueger, Kirby (5); Lamkey, William (17); May, Larry †(27); Mulligan, Robert *(18); Ruzek, Donald (24); Santos, Luis *(21); Thomas, Christopher *(7).

GRAND SLAM HOME RUNS—C. Castillo, Christensen, DeLoach, Drzayich, Favata, Hullett, Kubit, Mesa, Peltz, Rey, Stockstill, Taylor, 1 each.

AWARDED FIRST BASE ON INTERFERENCE—Higgins 2 (Hanson, Kingsolver); T. Martinez 2 (Boothe, White); J. Brown (Cummings); King (Diaz); Stein (Hood); Watanabe (Diaz).

GAME-WINNING RBIs

APPLETON (59)—Walker 13, White 8, K. Brown 7, Kittle 5, Doby 4, Daniels 3, Hulett 3, Peltz 3, J. Brown 2, Carroll 2, Hall 2, Lucarelli 2, Mesa 2, English 1, Hill 1, Stewart 1.

BURLINGTON (47)—Watanabe 11, Evans 9, Kingsolver 7, Valley 5, Downs 4, Levi 3, McKay 3, Favata 2, Higgins 2, DeJesus 1.

CEDAR RAPIDS (48)—Drzayich 8, Barbee 5, Hughes 4, Jones 4, Kripner 4, Masone 4, Viltz 4, Mota 3, Jendra 2, Johnson 2, Miller 2, Porte 2, Corbett 1, Fiorillo 1, Hoenstine 1, Lapple 1.

CLINTON (45)—Cummings 9, Estepan 8, Brown 5, Barron 3, Deer 3, Kutcher 3, Painton 3, Johnson 2, Jones 2, Morton 2, Smith 2, Figueroa 1, Moon 1, Perodin 1.

QUAD CITIES (52)—Martinez 14, Upton 7, Mork 5, Stockstill 4, Diaz 3, Fazzio 3, Hall 3, Kelley 3, Kornfeld 3, Rohlfing 3, DeLoach 1, Morgan 1, Owen 1, Payne 1.

WATERLOO (37)—Hayes 6, R. Bohnet 4, Cecchetti 4, Rey 4, Baker 3, Glass 3, Minium 3, Castillo 2, Martinez 2, Taylor 2, Dotson 1, Mitchell 1, Peterson 1, Whisler 1.

WAUSAU (49)—Henry 8, King 7, Tanzi 5, McCrary 4, Zisk 4, M. Diaz 3, Nanni 3, Presley 3, Trevino 3, E. Diaz 2, Frierson 2, Lajszky 2, Taylor 1.

WISCONSIN RAPIDS (62)—Christensen 16, Gaetti 10, Hrbek 8, Kubit 8, Austin 6, Miller 4, Stocker 2, Ballard 1, Carlson 1, Chandler 1, Colletti 1, Eisenreich 1, Henderson 1, Pilla 1, Williams 1.

CLUB FIELDING

Club	G.	PO.	A.	E.	DP.	PB.	Pct.	Club	G.	PO.	A.	E.	DP.	PB.	Pct.
Appleton	139	3556	1623	200	128	42	.963	Wisconsin Rapids	141	3674	1587	224	129	22	.959
Quad Cities	139	3571	1439	203	103	17	.961	Burlington	142	3584	1570	255	123	34	.953
Cedar Rapids	140	3625	1608	217	103	31	.960	Clinton	141	3547	1617	262	122	30	.952
Waterloo	141	3598	1712	220	111	39	.960	Wausau	139	3552	1547	258	113	16	.952

Triple Play—Appleton.

INDIVIDUAL FIELDING

FIRST BASEMEN

*Throws lefthanded.

Player and Club	G.	PO.	A.	E.	DP.	Pct.
De Loach, Quad Cities....	12	79	0	0	6	1.000
Lajszky, Wausau	8	62	8	0	10	1.000
Steele, Burlington	4	22	0	0	5	1.000
Cummings, Clinton	2	17	3	0	1	1.000
Hall, Appleton	2	17	1	0	1	1.000
Presley, Wausau	2	13	2	0	0	1.000
McManaman, Wis Rap	2	10	0	0	0	1.000
Stewart, Appleton	2	7	2	0	3	1.000
K. Brown, Appleton*	1	3	1	0	0	1.000
Stockstill, Quad Cities	1	4	0	0	0	1.000
Masone, Cedar Rapids..	1	1	0	0	0	1.000
Moon, Clinton*	1	1	0	0	0	1.000
Valley, Burlington*	91	825	71	3	71	.997
Upton, Quad Cities	51	418	45	2	31	.996
WALKER, Appleton	135	1298	88	10	108	.993
R. Bohnet, Waterloo	68	560	40	4	33	.993
Cecchetti, Waterloo*	94	780	46	7	51	.992
Brown, Clinton	35	305	19	3	15	.991
De Jesus, Burlington	13	88	19	1	9	.991
Drzayich, Cedar Rapids*	112	1050	43	12	65	.989
Evans, Burlington	38	346	23	5	23	.987
Hoenstine, Cedar Rapids	32	263	18	4	17	.986
Painton, Clinton*	100	939	58	15	69	.985
Martinez, Quad Cities	47	361	35	6	33	.985
Miller, Wisconsin Rapids	39	291	12	5	19	.984
Hrbek, Wisconsin Rap	107	1005	81	20	97	.982
Zisk, Wausau	90	786	38	15	53	.982
Rohlfing, Quad Cities	29	226	14	5	14	.980
E. Diaz, Wausau	45	363	15	8	32	.979
Fazzio, Quad Cities	13	108	3	3	13	.974
Glass, Waterloo	10	32	0	1	6	.970
Jones, Clinton	3	23	1	1	3	.960
Johnson, Clinton	10	53	4	3	7	.950
White, Appleton	1	8	0	1	1	.889
Meier, Waterloo	2	14	1	2	1	.882

Triple Play—Walker.

SECOND BASEMEN

Player and Club	G.	PO.	A.	E.	DP.	Pct.
Pilla, Wisconsin Rapids .	10	22	23	0	2	1.000
Martinez, Quad Cities	2	3	5	0	1	1.000
M. Diaz, Wausau	1	2	5	0	0	1.000
Tanzi, Wausau	1	2	4	0	2	1.000
Coronell, Wisconsin Rap	1	1	0	0	0	1.000
Mitchell, Waterloo	35	63	91	3	20	.981
Belmonte, Quad Cities ..	24	46	53	2	8	.980
Castillo, Burlington	26	60	72	3	8	.978
R. Bohnet, Waterloo	34	39	42	2	8	.976
Hinson, Waterloo	10	14	27	1	4	.976
CHRISTENSEN, W Rap	130	283	333	17	81	.973
Hulett, Appleton	64	148	203	12	42	.967
Porte, Cedar Rapids	57	102	139	9	19	.964
Kornfeld, Quad Cities	112	267	292	22	56	.962
Upshur, Wausau	58	107	149	10	32	.962
Perdue, Clinton	57	125	143	11	35	.961
English, Appleton	22	46	49	4	11	.960
Johnson, Clinton	54	112	137	11	24	.958
Miller, Cedar Rapids	90	187	257	22	50	.953
Peterson, Waterloo	24	35	63	5	4	.951
Favata, Burlington	79	144	196	18	48	.950
Gonzalez, Burlington	37	76	87	9	25	.948
J. Brown, Appleton	3	7	11	1	1	.947
Molina, Wisconsin Rap .	4	8	10	1	2	.947
Frierson, Wausau	77	167	224	23	40	.944
Whisler, Waterloo	65	119	187	19	38	.942
Kutcher, Clinton	13	22	42	4	3	.941
Hall, Appleton	17	30	42	5	9	.935
Hill, Appleton	40	91	98	14	27	.931
Presley, Wausau	14	39	37	6	5	.927
Thon, Clinton	17	26	33	7	5	.894
Wilson, Quad Cities	6	11	13	4	3	.857
Fonseca, Clinton	7	10	8	4	3	.818
Gilmartin, Burlington	2	2	2	2	0	.667

Triple Play—Hulett.

THIRD BASEMEN

Player and Club	G.	PO.	A.	E.	DP.	Pct.
Mitchell, Waterloo	2	1	5	0	0	1.000
Kutcher, Clinton	1	2	3	0	0	1.000
Chaney, Waterloo	1	0	2	0	0	1.000
Jones, Clinton	1	0	2	0	0	1.000
Martinez, Wausau	1	1	1	0	0	1.000
Ortiz, Waterloo	2	1	1	0	0	1.000
Wilson, Quad Cities	1	0	1	0	0	1.000
Miller, Cedar Rapids	14	6	34	1	2	.976
Johnson, Cedar Rapids ..	37	35	86	5	8	.960
J. Brown, Appleton	9	5	17	1	1	.957
Gonzalez, Burlington	10	7	15	1	1	.957
Hinson, Waterloo	6	6	14	1	0	.952
Peltz, Appleton	59	51	135	11	17	.944
Presley, Wausau	72	69	111	11	9	.942
Hulett, Appleton	12	9	32	3	1	.932
HAYES, Waterloo	111	86	262	26	12	.930
Martinez, Quad Cities	29	22	58	6	6	.930
Gaetti, Wisconsin Rap..	137	94	363	35	35	.929
Hughes, Cedar Rapids ..	22	17	47	5	5	.928
Hoenstine, Cedar Rapids	22	19	52	6	4	.922
Stockstill, Quad Cities..	58	26	91	10	8	.921
Estepan, Clinton	89	88	215	27	14	.918
Watanabe, Burlington ..	132	90	270	35	21	.911
Brown, Clinton	53	47	113	16	17	.909
Belmonte, Quad Cities ..	19	12	35	5	1	.904
Jendra, Cedar Rapids...	49	27	92	13	7	.902
Tanzi, Wausau	73	66	133	22	10	.900
Upshur, Wausau	8	2	7	1	0	.900
R. Bohnet, Waterloo	34	23	62	11	8	.885
White, Appleton	58	34	140	24	11	.879
De Loach, Quad Cities..	50	31	66	19	8	.836
Olson, Appleton	3	0	5	1	1	.833
Whisler, Waterloo	2	2	2	1	0	.800
Miller, Wisconsin Rapids	5	4	4	4	1	.667
Lajszky, Wausau	3	2	0	1	0	.667
Johnson, Clinton	7	3	5	7	0	.533
Robins, Burlington	2	0	1	1	0	.500

SHORTSTOPS

Player and Club	G.	PO.	A.	E.	DP.	Pct.
Jendra, Cedar Rapids...	4	4	8	0	0	1.000
Gilmartin, Burlington ..	1	1	4	0	1	1.000
Johnson, Clinton	3	2	2	0	0	1.000
Stockstill, Quad Cities..	1	0	1	0	0	1.000
Martinez, Quad Cities ..	2	1	0	0	0	1.000
Presley, Wausau	31	40	85	5	15	.962
Upshur, Wausau	10	14	32	2	2	.958
Mesa, Clinton	65	101	189	13	33	.957
Hughes, Cedar Rapids ..	22	34	74	5	9	.956
J. Brown, Appleton	40	46	127	9	16	.951
COLLETTI, Wis Rap	128	205	413	38	74	.942
Dugas, Waterloo	64	82	213	18	30	.942
Mitchell, Waterloo	21	19	59	5	4	.940
English, Appleton	10	13	18	2	3	.939

SHORTSTOPS—Continued

Player and Club	G.	PO.	A.	E.	DP.	Pct.
Kutcher, Clinton	123	202	362	39	62	.935
Owen, Quad Cities	56	88	155	17	30	.935
Chaney, Waterloo	54	78	147	16	25	.934
Hill, Appleton	2	2	12	1	3	.933
Fonseca, Clinton	14	23	39	5	5	.925
M. Diaz, Wausau	108	170	323	41	59	.923
Payne, Quad Cities	21	20	52	6	4	.923
Millhauser, Quad Cities	4	4	8	1	2	.923
Belmonte, Quad Cities	40	49	97	13	14	.918
Viltz, Cedar Rapids	121	177	368	53	52	.911
Perdue, Clinton	8	11	17	3	5	.903
Hayes, Waterloo	11	8	29	4	1	.902
Hulett, Appleton	3	5	13	2	4	.900
Gonzalez, Burlington	21	25	55	9	9	.899
Buckley, Quad Cities	26	34	58	11	10	.893
Downs, Burlington	125	195	354	70	55	.887
Hall, Appleton	22	22	52	11	11	.871
Pilla, Wisconsin Rapids	11	10	23	5	1	.868
Ortiz, Clinton	12	9	16	5	5	.833
R. Bohnet, Waterloo	1	2	1	1	0	.750
Molina, Wis Rapids	7	8	12	7	1	.741

Triple Play—Mesa.

OUTFIELDERS

Player and Club	G.	PO.	A.	E.	DP.	Pct.
Hodgson, Quad Cities	34	77	5	0	2	1.000
Kittle, Appleton	3	10	0	0	0	1.000
James, Burlington*	3	8	1	0	1	1.000
Jones, Clinton	4	7	0	0	0	1.000
Miller, Cedar Rapids	3	6	0	0	0	1.000
DeLoach, Quad Cities	3	5	0	0	0	1.000
Millhauser, Quad Cities	3	3	1	0	0	1.000
Ortega, Clinton	1	3	0	0	0	1.000
Gifford, Wausau	2	3	0	0	0	1.000
Compton, Quad Cities	6	2	1	0	0	1.000
Luzinski, Appleton	8	3	0	0	0	1.000
Henry, Wausau	1	2	0	0	0	1.000
Rathjen, Clinton	1	1	1	0	0	1.000
Evans, Burlington	1	1	0	0	0	1.000
Bazan, Quad Cities	2	1	0	0	0	1.000
Williams, Wis Rapids	70	168	10	3	2	.983
Painton, Clinton*	25	52	6	1	3	.983
Doby, Appleton	35	54	4	1	3	.983
Martinez, Quad Cities	48	46	1	1	0	.979
Cecchetti, Waterloo*	32	42	3	1	1	.978
Kelley, Quad Cities*	83	161	10	4	4	.977
DANIELS, Appleton	114	228	6	6	1	.975
Dotson, Waterloo	56	76	2	2	1	.975
Hall, Quad Cities*	91	171	9	5	1	.973
Mota, Cedar Rapids	124	307	11	9	2	.972
Morgan, Quad Cities	60	95	10	3	0	.972
Stocker, Wis Rapids	98	192	10	6	3	.971
Rohlfing, Quad Cities	17	29	4	1	0	.971
Barron, Clinton	58	89	9	3	1	.970
Smith, Clinton	63	132	17	5	2	.968
McCrary, Wausau*	50	91	1	3	0	.968
Hoenstine, Cedar Rapids	31	53	4	2	2	.966
Lajszky, Wausau	101	151	12	6	2	.964
Jones, Cedar Rapids	97	192	16	8	7	.963
Kubit, Wis Rapids	135	217	16	10	4	.959
Nanni, Wausau*	64	129	11	6	1	.959
Masone, Cedar Rapids	124	188	16	9	3	.958
Moon, Clinton*	34	65	1	3	1	.957
J. Brown, Appleton	18	20	2	1	0	.957
Baker, Waterloo	134	193	10	10	2	.953
Carroll, Appleton	81	114	4	6	0	.952
Barbee, Cedar Rapids	34	39	1	2	0	.952
Figueroa, Clinton	21	19	1	1	0	.952
Minium, Waterloo*	17	18	1	1	0	.950
Taylor, Wausau	102	141	9	8	1	.949
Deer, Clinton	125	184	17	11	3	.948
Keating, Appleton	73	136	3	8	1	.946
Johnson, Clinton	27	33	2	2	1	.946
Mork, Quad Cities*	74	117	3	7	1	.945
McKay, Burlington	120	206	10	13	3	.943
Carlson, Wis Rapids	48	63	2	4	0	.942
Bass, Burlington	60	107	5	7	4	.941
Perodin, Clinton	35	59	5	4	1	.941
K. Brown, Appleton*	121	136	12	10	1	.937
Stein, Wis Rapids*	58	103	1	7	1	.937
Martinez, Waterloo	63	90	8	7	1	.933
Levi, Burlington*	125	185	7	14	1	.932
Castillo, Waterloo	117	173	10	14	2	.929
Frierson, Wausau	45	70	5	6	1	.926
Higgins, Burlington	118	191	3	18	1	.915
Henderson, Wis Rapids	31	34	9	4	1	.915
Morton, Clinton*	60	95	9	10	2	.912
Kingsolver, Burlington	9	8	0	1	0	.889
Tanzi, Wausau	10	8	0	1	0	.889
Cotto, Quad Cities	19	27	2	4	0	.879
Zisk, Wausau	22	18	2	3	0	.870
King, Wausau*	87	113	13	20	1	.863
Waller, Cedar Rapids	12	21	2	4	1	.852
Monroe, Quad Cities	13	9	0	2	0	.818
Steele, Burlington	6	4	0	1	0	.800

CATCHERS

Player and Club	G.	PO.	A.	E.	DP.	PB.	Pct.
R. Bohnet, Waterloo	1	2	3	0	0	0	1.000
Cato, Clinton	2	2	0	0	0	0	1.000
Steele, Burlington	15	104	10	1	5	6	.991
Bazan, Quad Cities	33	209	31	3	1	3	.988
Rey, Waterloo	69	364	51	6	6	10	.986
Fazzio, Quad Cities	36	163	18	3	3	9	.984
Lucarelli, Appleton	29	161	18	3	5	5	.984
Corbett, Cedar Rapids	54	309	46	6	7	13	.983
HENRY, Wausau	72	456	49	9	4	11	.9824
Kingsolver, Burl	100	594	122	13	9	26	.9821
Lapple, Cedar Rapids	44	246	29	5	0	6	.982
Kittle, Appleton	10	46	9	1	2	6	.982
Trevino, Wausau	67	444	62	10	6	6	.981
Boothe, Clinton	8	42	6	1	0	1	.980
Cummings, Clinton	97	460	94	12	8	17	.979
Kripner, Cedar Rap	49	286	34	7	3	12	.979
Austin, Wis Rapids	87	513	68	13	8	15	.978
Diaz, Quad Cities	96	627	63	16	2	13	.977
White, Appleton	54	513	48	9	5	20	.976
Vuksan, Appleton	50	295	43	9	6	11	.974
Glass, Waterloo	49	262	17	8	4	8	.972
Epping, Clinton	22	97	20	4	1	7	.967
Chandler, Wis Rapids	33	199	25	8	2	5	.966
Meier, Waterloo	26	137	13	6	2	12	.962
Ballard, Wis Rapids	17	116	11	5	0	0	.962
Rohlfing, Quad Cities	8	23	2	1	1	0	.962
Bevington, Burl'ton	32	199	20	9	2	2	.961
Ortega, Clinton	17	81	14	5	3	4	.950
Jensen, Wis Rapids	2	16	0	1	0	1	.941
Hansen, Wis Rapids	8	41	4	3	1	1	.938
Albright, Clinton	12	40	5	3	0	1	.938
Hood, Wausau	16	67	17	7	0	0	.923

PITCHERS

Player and Club	G.	PO.	A.	E.	DP.	Pct.
ANTHONY, Waterloo	25	16	42	0	2	1.000
Johnson, Appleton	17	15	24	0	1	1.000
J. Bohnet, Waterloo*	23	6	29	0	1	1.000
Estrada, Appleton	25	8	24	0	1	1.000
Konopa, Wis Rapids*	28	9	17	0	1	1.000
Box, Cedar Rapids*	54	7	16	0	1	1.000

PITCHERS—Continued

Player and Club	G.	PO.	A.	E.	DP.	Pct.
DeJiulio, Cedar Rapids ...	35	7	3	0	1	1.000
Meadows, Burlington	16	8	10	0	0	1.000
Vasquez, Appleton	47	5	12	0	0	1.000
Nuismer, Waterloo	13	2	12	0	0	1.000
Hardy, Quad Cities*	15	1	13	0	1	1.000
Moore, Quad Cities	21	8	6	0	0	1.000
Donovan, Burlington	18	2	11	0	0	1.000
Smith, Appleton*	6	3	9	0	1	1.000
Jackson, Wis Rapids	10	2	10	0	0	1.000
Seymour, Wausau	14	4	7	0	0	1.000
Graser, Wausau*	28	1	10	0	0	1.000
Spino, Quad Cities*	5	2	6	0	0	1.000
Swaggerty, Quad Cities .	11	1	7	0	0	1.000
Burger, Appleton	12	0	7	0	0	1.000
Gilbert, Waterloo*	4	2	3	0	0	1.000
Wrobel, Clinton*	4	0	5	0	0	1.000
Anderson, Appleton	13	0	5	0	0	1.000
Esser, Appleton*	5	2	2	0	1	1.000
Wilkins, Quad Cities	6	1	3	0	0	1.000
Regan, Waterloo	7	4	0	0	0	1.000
McKenzie, Wausau	7	1	2	0	0	1.000
Barrios, Appleton	2	0	2	0	0	1.000
Coleman, Burlington*	4	1	1	0	0	1.000
Jeffcoat, Waterloo*	4	0	2	0	1	1.000
Bautista, Clinton	6	1	1	0	0	1.000
Pope, Waterloo	6	1	1	0	0	1.000
Lunar, Wis Rapids	7	1	1	0	0	1.000
Richard, Waterloo	7	0	2	0	0	1.000
Melendez, Appleton	9	0	2	0	0	1.000
Barnhart, Waterloo	3	0	1	0	0	1.000
Pone, Burlington	8	0	1	0	0	1.000
Pettibone, Wausau	9	0	1	0	0	1.000
Grier, Burlington	27	16	29	1	1	.978
Ruzek, Wis Rapids	23	13	28	1	4	.976
Hrynko, Waterloo	40	4	26	1	1	.968
Renwick, Quad Cities	27	12	41	2	0	.964
Morris, Quad Cities*	32	6	20	1	1	.963
Agosto, Appleton*	23	19	54	3	4	.961
Madden, Quad Cities	12	5	19	1	0	.960
McCoy, Burlington	23	5	19	1	1	.960
Vasquez, Burlington	52	9	14	1	1	.958
Mulligan, Wis Rapids*	18	5	14	1	1	.950
Skaggs, Cedar Rapids	24	11	25	2	2	.947
Manderfield, Burl*	26	7	29	2	2	.947
Rathjen, Clinton	46	8	10	1	0	.947
Millner, Quad Cities	25	12	23	2	3	.946
Anderson, Burlington*	34	16	36	3	3	.945
Chue, Clinton	27	5	12	1	1	.944
Casarez, Clinton	10	7	8	1	0	.938
Gil, Quad Cities	24	20	24	3	1	.936
Willis, Waterloo	21	4	25	2	2	.935
Daniels, Cedar Rapids	52	4	24	2	1	.933
Porter, Burlington	7	6	8	1	1	.933
Guinn, Cedar Rapids	28	6	35	3	0	.932
Moore, Cedar Rapids*	64	3	10	1	0	.929
Wright, Appleton	26	13	35	4	2	.923
Young, Quad Cities	21	3	9	1	0	.923
Biggus, Burlington	21	8	27	3	3	.921
Fallon, Appleton*	22	5	18	2	1	.920
Stovall, Clinton	29	4	19	2	0	.920
Wilhelmi, Clinton	27	21	45	6	2	.917
Burden, Waterloo	53	10	12	2	2	.917
Arrington, Wis Rapids ...	10	3	8	1	1	.917
Bangert, Clinton*	12	0	11	1	0	.917
Thompson, Quad Cities*	33	2	9	1	0	.917
Gibson, Cedar Rapids*	28	7	33	4	0	.909
Naumann, Appleton*	27	7	13	2	0	.909
Valley, Burlington*	3	4	6	1	0	.909
Maitland, Appleton*	10	3	7	1	0	.909
Maebe, Clinton	31	10	19	3	1	.906
Softy, Wausau	23	9	19	3	1	.903
Nunez, Wausau	22	10	26	4	2	.900
Cahill, Wausau	25	5	31	4	3	.900
Mims, Quad Cities*	22	4	5	1	1	.900
White, Waterloo	26	9	34	5	2	.896
Francingues, Wis Rap.....	35	7	17	3	0	.889
DeHart, Burlington	14	7	9	2	2	.889
Fiorillo, Cedar Rapids* ..	11	2	13	2	0	.882
Voigt, Wisconsin Rapids	24	7	22	4	2	.879
Roche, Waterloo	26	9	33	6	0	.875
Lepson, Burlington	14	3	11	2	2	.875
Norwood, Burlington	14	1	6	1	0	.875
Bauman, Wausau*	28	2	5	1	0	.875
Leach, Waterloo*	14	2	17	3	2	.864
Romero, Waterloo*	31	4	21	4	2	.862
Buckle, Cedar Rapids.....	17	3	21	4	2	.857
Steger, Wausau	19	4	25	5	3	.853
Churchill, Quad Cities*..	7	3	8	2	1	.846
Asbell, Waterloo	26	3	18	4	2	.840
May, Wisconsin Rapids..	27	10	16	5	1	.839
Goodchild, Clinton	26	11	14	5	0	.833
Noble, Cedar Rapids*...	3	0	5	1	0	.833
Little, Wausau	13	3	21	5	0	.828
Hoban, Waterloo	10	5	9	3	0	.824
Ortega, Appleton*	8	0	9	2	0	.818
Schwab, Clinton*	29	1	15	4	0	.800
McKinney, Cedar Rap...	16	3	9	3	0	.800
Matrisciano, Clinton	18	2	6	2	0	.800
Cicotte, Burlington	4	0	4	1	0	.800
Krueger, Wis Rapids	5	2	2	1	0	.800
Soff, Quad Cities	40	4	11	4	0	.789
Mills, Appleton	10	4	7	3	1	.786
Garrelts, Clinton	27	4	32	10	6	.783
Lamkey, Wis Rapids	17	2	5	2	0	.778
Brennan, Wausau*	35	3	16	6	0	.760
Straker, Cedar Rapids	34	1	24	8	0	.758
Santos, Wis Rapids*	21	3	6	3	0	.750
Owens, Waterloo	5	0	3	1	0	.750
Walker, Burlington	10	1	2	1	2	.750
Pastrovich, Appleton	14	1	7	3	0	.727
Felt, Clinton	10	1	4	2	0	.714
Thomas, Wis Rapids	7	1	6	3	0	.700
Everett, Wis Rapids	36	3	4	3	1	.700
Wright, Quad Cities*	15	2	6	4	0	.667
Rodriguez, Appleton	3	0	2	1	0	.667
Salva, Wausau	12	1	2	2	0	.600
Hagemann, Clinton*	6	0	3	3	0	.500
Meyer, Burlington	4	0	1	1	0	.500
Jordan, Wausau	5	0	1	1	0	.500
Lintz, Waterloo	7	1	0	1	0	.500

The following players do not have any recorded accepted chances at the positions indicated; therefore, are not listed in the fielding averages for those particular positions: Baker, 3b; J. Brown, c; Chaney, 2b; Coronell, ss; Dugas 2b-3b; Glass, p; Gurholt*, p; Holbrook, c; Lucarelli, p; O. Martinez, p; Matias, p; McManaman, p; M. Miller, ss; Tanzi, 1b; Whisler, ss.

CLUB PITCHING

Club	G.	CG.	ShO.	Sv.	IP.	H.	R.	ER.	HR.	BB.	Int. BB.	HB.	SO.	WP.	Bk.	ERA.
Appleton	139	30	11	32	1187	1022	580	444	49	611	26	52	815	100	9	3.37
Quad Cities	139	38	17	25	1196	1035	546	448	60	488	32	58	928	65	5	3.37
Waterloo	141	32	12	27	1205	1020	606	463	79	568	26	40	850	87	13	3.46
Wisconsin Rapids	141	45	13	20	1226	1154	620	477	129	449	3	25	834	67	15	3.50

CLUB PITCHING —Continued

Club	G	CG	ShO	Sv	IP	H	R	ER	HR	BB	Int. BB	HB	SO	WP	Bk	ERA
Burlington	142	47	15	22	1197	1145	650	495	63	538	15	27	880	89	12	3.72
Clinton	141	24	8	21	1186	1151	689	502	52	660	16	54	671	89	14	3.81
Cedar Rapids	140	17	11	31	1208	1175	641	515	78	511	20	39	803	75	10	3.84
Wausau	139	36	5	17	1184	1262	787	614	114	687	8	54	850	91	11	4.67

PITCHERS' RECORDS

(Leading Qualifiers for Earned-Run Average Leadership—114 or More Innings)

*Throws lefthanded.

Pitcher—Club	G	GS	CG	ShO	W	L	Sv	Pct.	IP	H	R	ER	HR	BB	Int. BB	HB	SO	WP	ERA
Biggus, Burlington	21	16	5	2	9	5	0	.643	115	98	41	29	1	38	0	1	84	11	2.27
Renwick, Quad Cities	27	27	14	6	14	8	0	.636	201	150	65	52	14	45	4	9	139	5	2.33
Millner, Quad Cities	25	24	9	4	12	8	1	.600	175	148	51	46	7	60	3	5	146	3	2.37
Johnson, Appleton	17	17	6	1	9	4	0	.692	137	100	45	40	7	52	2	0	103	9	2.63
Agosto, Appleton*	23	16	5	1	11	6	1	.647	144	118	60	43	1	52	1	11	93	10	2.69
Grier, Burlington	27	27	15	4	16	8	0	.667	197	177	73	60	12	42	0	1	128	4	2.74
Anderson, Burlington*	34	15	10	3	13	7	1	.650	164	139	65	50	13	69	1	2	132	14	2.74
May, Wisconsin Rapids	27	25	10	5	16	5	0	.762	200	161	82	64	17	63	0	2	152	12	2.88
Konopa, Wis Rapids*	28	27	8	1	17	6	0	.739	197	152	75	63	22	66	0	4	156	5	2.88
Box, Cedar Rapids*	54	2	1	0	5	5	3	.500	120	99	50	39	10	27	4	12	60	13	2.93

Departmental Leaders: G—M. Moore, 64; GS—Garretts, Grier, Konopa, Renwick, Wilhelmi, 27; CG—Grier, 15; ShO—Renwick, 6; W—Konopa, 17; L—Cahill, Gibson, Wilhelmi, 15; Sv—D. Vasquez, 16; Pct—Gil, .882; IP—Renwick, 201; H—Wilhelmi, 184; R—Roche, 122; ER—Roche, 87; HR—Konopa, 22; BB—Garretts, 149; IBB—M. Moore, 7; HB—Goodchild, 17; SO—Garretts, 159; WP—Wilhelmi, 19.

(All Pitchers—Listed Alphabetically)

Pitcher—Club	G	GS	CG	ShO	W	L	Sv	Pct.	IP	H	R	ER	HR	BB	Int. BB	HB	SO	WP	ERA
Agosto, Appleton*	23	16	5	1	11	6	1	.647	144	118	60	43	1	52	1	11	93	10	2.69
Anderson, Appleton	13	5	0	0	2	4	2	.333	41	43	31	22	1	27	2	3	31	8	4.83
Anderson, Burlington*	34	15	10	3	13	7	1	.650	164	139	65	50	13	69	1	2	132	14	2.74
Anthony, Waterloo	25	25	11	1	15	6	0	.714	164	150	75	62	14	49	4	2	105	9	3.40
Arrington, Wis Rapids*	10	8	1	0	0	7	0	.000	50	51	39	26	6	22	0	3	18	4	4.68
Asbell, Waterloo	26	5	0	0	5	7	4	.417	98	86	50	33	4	44	4	6	74	3	3.03
Bangert, Clinton*	12	12	1	0	3	8	0	.273	73	72	51	40	1	50	0	3	37	7	4.93
Barnhart, Waterloo	3	0	0	0	0	0	0	.000	5	6	4	4	2	5	0	0	3	0	7.20
Barrios, Appleton	2	2	0	0	2	0	0	1.000	13	5	2	1	1	4	0	0	5	0	0.69
Bauman, Wausau*	28	7	1	0	2	4	2	.333	72	71	43	38	6	38	0	1	61	7	4.75
Bautista, Clinton	6	0	0	0	0	0	0	.000	9	13	8	8	1	10	0	3	0	1	8.00
Biggus, Burlington	21	16	5	2	9	5	0	.643	115	98	41	29	1	38	0	1	84	11	2.27
J. Bohnet, Waterloo*	23	19	2	1	9	5	0	.643	116	86	60	41	7	64	1	1	99	8	3.18
Box, Cedar Rapids*	54	2	1	0	5	5	3	.500	120	99	50	39	10	27	4	12	60	13	2.93
Brennan, Wausau*	35	3	0	0	4	6	1	.400	100	92	65	49	15	41	2	5	77	6	4.41
Buckle, Cedar Rapids	17	17	3	1	5	9	0	.357	103	84	43	35	4	42	1	4	82	7	3.06
Burden, Waterloo	53	0	0	0	6	3	11	.667	110	89	41	35	12	39	1	8	113	2	2.86
Burger, Appleton	12	1	0	0	1	1	0	.500	32	21	8	5	0	14	1	0	16	5	1.41
Cahill, Wausau	25	25	8	1	9	15	0	.375	160	177	101	65	14	79	0	6	83	2	3.66
Casarez, Clinton	10	9	3	2	5	4	0	.556	69	63	32	27	5	38	1	2	43	5	3.52
Chue, Clinton	27	4	1	0	5	4	2	.556	83	90	35	28	5	23	3	0	45	1	3.04
Churchill, Quad Cities*	7	6	1	1	2	3	0	.400	36	29	18	9	0	13	1	0	29	2	2.25
Cicotte, Burlington	4	2	0	0	0	1	0	.000	15	9	5	5	1	17	1	2	7	1	3.00
Coleman, Burlington*	4	0	0	0	0	0	0	.000	6	8	5	5	1	11	0	0	3	4	7.50
Daniels, Cedar Rapids	52	0	0	0	4	9	6	.308	79	97	51	43	3	31	2	3	59	5	4.90
DeHart, Burlington	14	7	0	0	2	4	1	.333	39	34	34	25	1	34	1	3	26	1	5.77
DeJiulio, Cedar Rapids	35	4	0	0	5	3	9	.625	82	68	25	22	5	22	3	3	55	2	2.41
Donovan, Burlington	18	1	0	0	2	2	1	.500	41	51	34	29	3	27	2	1	49	7	6.37
Esser, Appleton*	5	5	3	1	4	0	0	1.000	37	23	11	5	0	14	0	3	34	2	1.22
Estrada, Appleton	25	23	7	2	7	9	2	.438	145	134	66	57	7	73	4	5	72	4	3.54
Everett, Wis Rapids	36	0	0	0	3	4	10	.429	61	56	19	14	8	11	1	0	71	6	2.07
Fallon, Appleton*	22	2	0	0	3	1	0	.750	32	23	12	10	1	24	0	1	11	2	2.81
Felt, Clinton	10	5	1	1	4	3	0	.571	74	73	40	35	7	27	1	1	67	1	4.26
Fiorillo, Cedar Rapids*	11	10	3	0	4	3	0	.571	84	84	37	24	3	33	1	1	57	3	2.59
Francingues, Wis Rapids	35	26	3	0	6	5	0	.545	165	159	91	74	6	82	1	6	118	11	4.04
Garretts, Clinton	27	27	3	0	11	11	0	.500	176	155	98	76	2	149	0	7	159	16	3.89
Gibson, Cedar Rapids*	28	26	2	2	6	15	1	.286	146	171	97	80	5	53	0	0	74	5	4.93
Gil, Quad Cities	24	20	6	1	15	2	2	.882	140	112	67	56	7	66	2	6	128	10	3.60
Gilbert, Waterloo*	4	1	0	0	0	1	0	.000	9	11	5	3	1	8	1	0	6	0	3.00
Glass, Appleton	2	0	0	0	0	0	0	.000	3	4	3	3	0	2	0	1	0	1	9.00
Goodchild, Clinton	26	26	5	2	8	11	0	.421	155	167	89	67	6	56	2	17	87	9	3.89
Graser, Wausau*	28	10	0	0	1	8	1	.111	89	94	70	62	8	75	1	4	73	15	6.27
Grier, Burlington	27	27	15	4	16	8	0	.667	197	177	73	60	12	42	0	1	128	4	2.74
Guinn, Cedar Rapids	28	26	4	1	9	10	1	.474	158	154	82	64	9	93	1	3	109	16	3.65
Gurholt, Wis Rapids*	2	2	0	0	0	1	0	.000	4	7	7	7	1	9	0	0	2	2	15.75

Pitcher–Club	G.	GS.	CG.	ShO.	W.	L.	Sv.	Pct.	IP.	H.	R.	ER.	HR.	BB.	Int. BB.	HB.	SO.	WP.	ERA.
Hagemann, Clinton*	6	6	0	0	0	5	0	.000	27	19	21	11	2	33	0	0	9	3	3.67
Hardy, Quad Cities*	15	13	4	1	4	6	2	.400	92	81	35	30	6	15	1	2	62	1	2.93
Hoban, Waterloo	10	9	1	1	4	4	0	.500	50	45	25	19	2	33	0	3	25	3	3.42
Hrynko, Waterloo	40	0	0	0	9	2	15	.818	79	58	22	8	2	15	1	1	52	1	0.91
Jackson, Wis Rapids	10	7	1	0	2	5	0	.286	59	75	41	31	8	12	0	2	29	1	4.73
Jeffcoat, Waterloo*	4	0	0	0	0	0	0	.000	6	12	12	4	2	3	0	0	7	1	6.00
Johnson, Appleton	17	17	6	1	9	4	0	.692	137	100	45	40	7	52	2	0	103	9	2.63
Jordan, Wausau	5	5	0	0	1	2	0	.333	17	10	24	21	1	34	0	1	12	2	11.12
Konopa, Wis Rapids	28	27	8	1	17	6	0	.739	197	152	75	63	22	66	0	4	156	5	2.88
Krueger, Wis Rapids	5	4	1	0	1	4	0	.200	25	28	20	16	5	13	0	1	13	0	5.76
Lamkey, Wis Rapids	17	0	0	0	1	2	0	.333	30	41	33	25	2	24	1	2	18	6	7.50
Leach, Waterloo*	14	12	0	0	4	6	0	.400	60	47	45	40	7	45	0	1	46	10	6.00
Lepson, Burlington	14	10	1	0	2	7	0	.222	58	74	56	42	3	33	0	1	33	8	6.52
Lintz, Waterloo	7	0	0	0	0	0	0	.000	9	10	5	5	0	3	0	0	8	0	5.00
Little, Wausau	13	13	3	0	5	6	0	.455	82	87	61	48	7	72	1	8	62	11	5.27
Lucarelli, Appleton	1	0	0	0	0	0	0	.000	1	0	0	0	0	3	0	0	2	1	0.00
Lunar, Wisconsin Rapids	7	1	0	0	0	1	0	.000	16	15	12	10	1	15	0	1	9	2	5.63
Madden, Quad Cities	12	8	2	0	2	4	0	.333	52	58	27	23	4	40	2	1	36	2	3.98
Maebe, Clinton	31	13	2	0	3	10	0	.231	116	116	86	51	10	62	1	2	73	4	3.96
Maitland, Appleton*	10	3	0	0	3	4	0	.429	46	36	28	17	3	22	0	1	40	3	3.33
Manderfield, Burl*	26	25	6	0	10	13	0	.435	154	165	98	75	7	72	1	5	117	3	4.38
Martinez, Wausau	2	0	0	0	0	0	0	.000	6	12	10	7	2	1	0	0	5	3	10.50
Matias, Burlington	1	0	0	0	0	0	0	.000	1	1	0	0	0	0	0	0	0	0	0.00
Matrisciano, Clinton	18	1	0	0	1	2	3	.333	32	31	32	20	0	32	0	1	18	2	5.63
May, Wisconsin Rapids	27	25	10	5	16	5	0	.762	200	161	82	64	17	63	0	2	152	12	2.88
McCoy, Burlington	23	23	6	2	10	6	0	.625	144	131	78	66	5	71	1	0	110	11	4.13
McKenzie, Wausau	7	1	0	0	0	1	0	.000	17	16	6	6	1	19	0	0	6	2	3.18
McKinney, Cedar Rapids	16	10	1	0	4	5	1	.444	70	58	34	28	3	35	0	2	51	3	3.60
McManaman, Wis Rapids	4	0	0	0	0	1	0	.000	5	4	3	1	0	8	0	0	7	1	1.80
Meadows, Burlington	16	1	0	0	2	2	2	.500	43	49	24	23	1	15	2	1	15	6	4.81
Melendez, Appleton	9	3	0	0	0	1	0	.000	13	18	31	21	1	26	0	4	11	4	14.54
Meyer, Burlington	4	0	0	0	0	0	0	.000	6	9	4	2	0	1	0	0	6	1	3.00
Millner, Quad Cities	25	24	9	4	12	8	1	.600	175	148	51	46	7	60	3	5	146	3	2.37
Mills, Appleton	10	10	2	0	0	7	0	.000	49	52	41	35	0	43	0	0	30	7	6.43
Mims, Quad Cities*	22	1	0	0	0	0	0	.000	46	54	37	34	1	31	0	2	27	7	6.65
Moore, Cedar Rapids*	64	0	0	0	4	6	8	.400	91	80	51	40	7	51	7	6	75	4	3.96
Moore, Quad Cities	21	0	0	0	2	3	6	.400	31	17	11	10	1	14	1	0	23	1	2.90
Morris, Quad Cities*	32	3	0	0	5	1	1	.833	54	51	26	20	1	23	4	1	36	3	3.33
Mulligan, Wis Rapids*	18	7	3	3	7	2	0	.778	89	70	34	20	6	20	0	2	62	1	2.02
Naumann, Appleton*	27	0	0	0	0	2	4	.000	64	66	35	28	4	39	2	3	37	8	3.94
Noble, Cedar Rapids*	3	3	1	1	2	1	0	.667	18	12	5	5	2	12	0	0	9	0	2.50
Norwood, Burlington	14	10	0	0	0	5	0	.000	48	53	42	26	4	33	0	5	32	5	4.88
Nuismer, Waterloo	13	2	1	1	1	1	2	.500	36	22	12	11	1	16	2	1	32	2	2.75
Nunez, Wausau	22	19	8	2	9	7	0	.563	138	145	71	57	9	58	1	7	91	3	3.72
Ortega, Waterloo*	8	2	0	0	2	3	0	.400	25	22	17	13	1	22	2	1	16	5	4.68
Owens, Waterloo	5	4	0	0	0	0	0	.000	21	28	17	15	1	9	0	1	12	2	6.43
Pastrovich, Appleton	14	0	0	0	2	2	4	.500	36	24	14	9	3	18	2	3	51	1	2.25
Pettibone, Wausau	9	0	0	0	1	2	0	.000	11	16	8	8	1	6	0	0	9	0	6.55
Pone, Burlington	8	0	0	0	0	0	0	.000	14	16	18	13	3	12	0	2	13	4	8.36
Pope, Waterloo	6	2	0	0	0	0	0	.000	16	9	7	6	2	9	0	0	12	3	3.38
Porter, Burlington	7	4	3	0	0	4	1	.000	38	40	25	14	3	5	0	1	22	0	3.32
Rathjen, Clinton	46	0	0	0	7	3	12	.700	77	54	27	18	3	22	2	2	36	7	2.10
Regan, Waterloo	7	1	0	0	2	1	0	.667	18	15	13	12	2	19	0	1	18	3	6.00
Renwick, Quad Cities	27	27	14	6	14	8	0	.636	201	150	65	52	14	45	4	9	139	5	2.33
Richard, Waterloo	7	0	0	0	1	0	0	1.000	13	5	2	0	0	9	0	0	18	2	0.00
Roche, Waterloo	26	26	8	0	12	11	0	.522	162	168	122	87	18	58	0	7	89	10	4.83
Rodriguez, Appleton	3	0	0	0	0	0	0	.000	6	8	8	6	1	7	0	1	3	1	9.00
Romero, Waterloo*	31	5	0	0	5	5	2	.500	98	78	53	40	9	62	5	2	87	11	3.67
Ruzek, Wisconsin Rapids	23	15	7	0	6	5	0	.545	121	124	55	43	9	23	0	2	61	5	3.20
Salva, Wausau	12	0	0	0	0	1	1	.000	28	28	20	17	4	10	1	1	17	1	7.65
Santos, Wis Rapids*	21	17	4	2	5	6	0	.455	96	97	60	50	14	43	0	2	46	10	4.69
Schwab, Clinton*	29	7	3	0	4	4	3	.500	89	101	54	43	5	45	1	2	53	8	4.35
Seymour, Wausau	14	5	1	0	4	2	0	.667	51	72	38	34	9	32	1	0	19	3	6.00
Skaggs, Cedar Rapids	24	22	1	0	5	13	1	.278	131	142	87	67	11	51	1	3	73	13	4.60
Smith, Appleton*	6	5	0	0	3	0	0	1.000	25	25	11	11	1	10	0	2	13	2	3.96
Soff, Quad Cities	40	2	0	0	1	8	7	.111	66	61	49	35	2	62	6	7	59	10	4.77
Softy, Wausau	23	18	5	0	6	10	0	.375	126	155	91	71	7	85	1	3	99	12	5.07
Spino, Quad Cities*	5	4	0	0	1	2	0	.333	28	24	13	9	0	10	0	1	16	4	2.89
Steger, Wausau	19	19	6	0	6	10	0	.375	118	114	64	48	7	71	0	6	84	16	3.66
Stovall, Clinton	29	4	2	1	5	1	2	.833	75	56	25	19	5	24	4	4	45	4	2.28
Straker, Cedar Rapids	34	20	1	0	6	5	1	.545	135	135	74	56	12	66	0	2	89	6	3.73
Swaggerty, Quad Cities	11	3	0	0	0	2	0	.000	21	29	23	21	5	16	1	0	13	4	9.00
Thomas, Wis Rapids	7	5	0	0	1	3	0	.250	29	39	22	21	1	17	0	1	27	2	6.52
Thompson, Quad Cities*	33	4	2	0	8	4	3	.667	85	77	34	29	5	23	4	2	68	1	3.07
Valley, Burlington*	3	1	1	0	1	0	0	.000	15	13	8	5	1	3	0	0	11	2	3.00

Pitcher–Club	G	GS	CG	ShO	W	L	Sv	Pct.	IP	H	R	ER	HR	BB	Int. BB	HB	SO	WP	ERA
Vasquez, Appleton	47	0	0	0	7	4	16	.636	76	58	24	16	3	36	5	6	63	5	1.89
Vasquez, Burlington	52	0	0	0	4	6	15	.400	87	64	31	25	4	43	6	2	81	6	2.59
Voigt, Wisconsin Rapids	24	22	10	0	12	8	0	.600	157	153	81	61	20	70	0	2	106	8	3.50
Walker, Burlington*	10	0	0	0	0	1	1	.000	14	16	4	1	0	8	0	0	9	1	0.64
White, Waterloo	26	25	9	1	15	7	0	.682	179	143	85	66	11	86	4	11	120	14	3.32
Wilhelmi, Clinton	27	27	5	0	7	15	0	.318	163	184	108	77	8	82	1	10	47	19	4.25
Wilkins, Quad Cities	6	2	0	0	0	2	1	.000	18	20	13	10	1	10	1	2	18	4	5.00
Willis, Waterloo	21	20	4	0	8	5	0	.615	129	123	63	52	5	56	3	6	76	10	3.63
Wright, Quad Cities*	15	14	0	0	5	5	0	.500	83	71	44	35	3	55	0	11	88	6	3.80
Wright, Appleton	26	25	5	0	12	11	0	.522	174	167	86	67	10	67	5	6	92	15	3.47
Wrobel, Clinton*	4	0	0	0	0	0	0	.000	10	7	7	7	0	10	1	0	8	1	6.30
Young, Quad Cities	21	8	0	0	3	7	1	.300	66	53	33	29	3	35	2	7	40	2	3.95

BALKS—Konopa 6; Asbell, Naumann, Schwab, 5 each; White, Wilhelmi, 4 each; McCoy, McKinney, Meadows, Ruzek, Straker, 3 each; Buckle, Garrelts, Grier, Jordan, Leach, Morris, Mulligan, Nunez, Roche, Romero, Santos, 2 each; Agosto, Box, Brennan, Donovan, Felt, Gil, Goodchild, Graser, Guinn, Hagemann, Hardy, Krueger, Lepson, Little, Lunar, Mills, Ortega, Renwick, Salva, Seymour, J. Vasquez, Walker, L. Wright, 1 each.

COMBINATION SHUTOUTS—Fallon-Naumann, Mills-Vasquez, Wright-Pastrovich, Maitland-Pastrovich, Appleton; Manderfield-Vasquez, McCoy-Porter, Burlington; Guinn-Daniels-Moore, DeJiulio-Skaggs, Buckle-DeJiulio, Guinn-Moore-DeJiulio, Cedar Rapids; Chue-Maebe, Stovall-Rathjen, Clinton; Milner-Churchill-Moore, Young-Soff, Gil-Thompson, Thompson-Soff, Quad Cities; Hoban-Hrynko, J. Bohnet-Hrynko, J. Bohnet-Nuismer, Leach-Asbell, Waterloo; Bauman-Burden, Wausau; Konopa-Francingues, May-Francingues, Wisconsin Rapids.

NO-HIT GAMES—Guinn-Daniels-Moore, Cedar Rapids, defeated Quad Cities, 2-0, April 16, second game (11 innings); Stovall, Clinton, defeated Wausau, 2-0, June 4, second game (seven innings); Anthony, Waterloo, defeated Appleton, 3-0, June 7, first game (seven innings).

No-Hitter, Two One-Hitters in Twinbill

The largest Waterloo Stadium crowd in several seasons—6,180—was treated to some stingy pitching as the Midwest League Indians swept a doubleheader June 7 from the Appleton Foxes, 3-0 and 1-0.

In the first game, Indians righthander Dane Anthony raised his record to 8-1 by unfurling a no-hitter. He allowed only three baserunners, all on walks. Earlier in the season, he had pitched a one-hitter and two-hitter.

In the nightcap, Appleton's Chuck Fox and Waterloo's Jack Nuismer each tossed a one-hitter. The lone safe blow off Fox decided the game. It was an eighth-inning single by Waterloo right fielder Carmen Castillo that scored first baseman Bob Bohnet from second. Bohnet had reached first base on an error and was sacrificed to second.

NY-Pennsylvania League

CLASS A
CHAMPIONSHIP WINNERS IN PREVIOUS YEARS

1939—Olean* .631	1953—Jamestown* .704	1966—Auburn x .620
1940—Olean* .625	1954—Corning* .621	Binghamton .646
1941—Jamestown .618	1955—Hamilton* .656	1967—Auburn .667
Bradford (2nd)† .549	1956—Wellsville* .617	1968—Auburn .645
1942—Jamestown* .672	1957—Wellsville .632	Oneonta (2nd)* .558
1943—Lockport .591	Erie (2nd)† .598	1969—Oneonta .662
Wellsville (3rd)† .532	1958—Wellsville .556	1970—Auburn .623
1944—Lockport .608	Geneva (2nd)† .548	1971—Oneonta .662
Jamestown (2nd)† .565	1959—Wellsville† .635	1972—Niagara Falls† .686
1945—Batavia* .677	1960—Erie .643	1973—Auburn .667
1946—Jamestown‡ .672	Wellsville (2nd)† .535	1974—Oneonta .768
Batavia‡ .672	1961—Jamestown .616	1975—Newark .698
1947—Jamestown .690	Olean (4th)† .512	Newark .714
1948—Lockport* .603	1962—Jamestown .580	1976—Elmira .727
1949—Bradford* .635	Auburn (3rd)† .521	Elmira .703
1950—Hornell .653	1963—Auburn .585	1977—Oneonta y .671
Olean (2nd)† .568	Batavia (3rd)† .485	Batavia .600
1951—Olean .622	1964—Auburn§ .622	1978—Oneonta .729
Hornell (3rd)† .568	1965—Binghamton .677	Geneva z .718
1952—Hamilton .659	Binghamton .607	1979—Geneva z .725
Jamestown (2nd)† .643		Oneonta z .618

*Won championship and four-club playoff. †Won four-club playoff. ‡Jamestown and Batavia declared co-champions; Batavia defeated Jamestown in final of four-club playoff. §Won championship and two-club playoff. xWon split-season playoff. yLeague divided into Eastern and Western Divisions; won playoff. zLeague divided into Wrigley and Yawkey Divisions; won playoff. (NOTE—Known as Pennsylvania-Ontario-New York League from 1939 through 1956.)

STANDING OF CLUBS AT CLOSE OF SEASON, AUGUST 28
EASTERN DIVISION

Club	Ont.	L.F.	Elm.	Utica	Gen.	Bat.	Jtn.	Aub.	W.	L.	T.	Pct.	G.B.
Oneonta (Yankees)	..	6	9	9	7	5	6	7	49	25	0	.662	......
Little Falls (Mets)	8	..	5	9	3	5	6	4	40	33	0	.548	8½
Elmira (Red Sox)	5	9	..	9	3	5	4	4	39	35	0	.527	10
Utica (Blue Jays)	5	5	5	..	3	3	4	2	27	44	0	.380	20½

WESTERN DIVISION

Club													
Geneva (Cubs)	1	5	5	5	..	10	10	12	48	26	0	.649	......
Batavia (Indians)	3	2	3	5	4	..	6	8	31	42	0	.425	16½
Jamestown (Expos)	2	2	4	1	4	8	..	8	29	42	0	.408	17½
Auburn (Co-op)	1	4	4	6	2	6	6	..	29	45	0	.392	19

Major league affiliations in parentheses.

Playoff—Oneonta defeated Geneva, two games to one.

Regular-Season Attendance—Auburn, 9,474; Batavia, 29,670; Elmira, 56,912; Geneva, 20,970; Jamestown, 48,078; Little Falls, 18,840; Oneonta, 35,500; Utica, 17,179. Total, 236,623. Playoffs, 2,567. No all-star game.

Managers: Auburn—Bill Julio; Batavia—Rick Colzie; Elmira—Dick Berardino; Geneva—Bob Hartsfield; Jamestown—Pat Daugherty; Little Falls—Danny Monzon; Oneonta—Art Mazmanian; Utica—Larry Hardy.

All-Star Team: 1B—Stevens, Elmira; 2B—Oddo, Elmira; 3B—Reynolds, Oneonta; SS—Hoeksema, Jamestown; OF—Ciampa, Elmira; Frash, Little Falls; Glenn, Elmira; Johnson, Jamestown; C—Shannon, Oneonta; Rohlfing, Geneva; DH—Poe, Little Falls; Utility—Guzman, Utica; P—Boyd, Elmira; Housey, Geneva; Lefferts, Geneva; Spicer, Little Falls; Manager—Hartsfield, Geneva.

(Compiled by Howe News Bureau, Boston, Mass.)

CLUB BATTING

Club	G.	AB.	R.	OR.	H.	TB.	2B.	3B.	HR.	RBI.	SH.	SF.	Int. BB.	BB.	HP.	SO.	SB.	CS.	LOB.	Pct.
Jamestown	71	2276	321	359	602	834	85	27	31	267	20	21	256	5	13	358	63	26	515	.264
Geneva	74	2369	408	270	605	895	114	10	52	343	19	25	370	10	26	441	69	25	555	.255
Elmira	74	2362	398	371	600	874	88	15	52	338	45	32	396	9	17	481	92	14	596	.254
Little Falls	73	2369	387	368	599	869	83	17	51	316	22	23	332	11	14	435	76	24	529	.253
Utica	71	2333	370	474	581	903	93	23	61	305	9	11	300	1	22	563	84	21	506	.249
Auburn	74	2404	330	406	593	879	91	21	51	288	7	12	320	9	24	472	73	11	567	.247
Oneonta	74	2297	366	263	568	778	78	21	30	306	38	33	426	20	35	445	117	41	577	.247
Batavia	73	2306	347	416	540	765	72	19	38	287	20	24	351	11	26	457	94	24	543	.234

INDIVIDUAL BATTING

(Leading Qualifiers for Batting Championship—200 or More Plate Appearances)

*Bats lefthanded.   †Switch-hitter.

Player and Club	G.	AB.	R.	H.	TB.	2B.	3B.	HR.	RBI.	SH.	SF.	BB.	HP.	SO.	SB.	CS.	Pct.
Frash, Roger, Little Falls	64	211	55	73	128	12	2	13	39	0	1	31	5	41	14	1	.346
Nealeigh, Rodney, Jamestown	68	221	38	73	89	9	2	1	23	2	1	32	2	12	7	4	.330
Piggott, Russell, Geneva	69	271	50	85	125	13	0	9	43	1	2	23	4	27	6	3	.314
Oddo, Ronald, Elmira	63	210	31	66	71	3	1	0	23	7	2	35	1	23	4	2	.314
Poe, Richard, Little Falls	61	198	38	62	81	9	2	2	27	0	3	20	1	15	4	3	.313
Ciampa, Michael, Elmira	71	241	59	75	100	8	1	5	38	4	4	61	5	26	35	6	.311
Glenn, James, Elmira	67	225	51	70	92	9	2	3	30	4	3	54	1	27	28	2	.311
Whitfield, N. Jerome, Jamestown	67	249	34	77	113	8	8	8	37	2	1	10	0	40	5	2	.309
Connally, Fritzie, Geneva	67	229	46	70	130	18	0	14	43	1	1	53	6	31	2	1	.306
Davis, Michael, Little Falls	68	239	44	72	108	15	3	5	36	1	4	31	0	33	2	0	.301

Departmental Leaders: G—Bailey, 73; AB—Piggott, 271; R—Ciampa, 59; H—Piggott, 85; TB—Stevens, 136; 2B—Connally, Guzman, 18; 3B—Hoeksema, 6; HR—Stevens, 15; RBI—J. Reynolds, 56; GWRBI—Stevens, 8; SH—K. Smith, 9; SF—Hall, Shannon 7; BB—Ciampa, 61; HP—Filkins, 7; SO—Allen, 65; SB—Ciampa, 35; CS—Ciampa, Eldridge, R. Johnson, McDaniel, 6.

(All Players—Listed Alphabetically)

Player and Club	G.	AB.	R.	H.	TB.	2B.	3B.	HR.	RBI.	SH.	SF.	BB.	HP.	SO.	SB.	CS.	Pct.
Ackley, John, Elmira	36	108	25	24	49	2	1	7	27	4	2	25	0	26	4	0	.222
Adams, Kalvin, Jamestown	30	115	21	35	43	3	1	1	17	0	2	12	1	7	2	0	.304
Allen, S. Shane, Geneva*	69	259	40	58	89	12	2	5	32	2	5	26	1	65	5	2	.224
Alvis, Andrew, Batavia*	13	25	4	3	3	0	0	0	2	0	0	6	0	12	0	0	.120
Andrews, Sheldon, Oneonta	17	2	0	0	0	0	0	0	0	0	0	0	0	0	0	0	.000
Austin, Terry, Geneva	56	229	32	49	59	5	1	1	22	1	1	25	0	50	9	2	.214
Bailey, David, Oneonta	73	246	32	65	81	9	2	1	32	2	3	35	2	34	6	3	.264
Banes, David, Oneonta	43	137	16	30	47	7	2	2	17	0	1	12	0	38	3	1	.219
Banes, N. Alan, Elmira	16	1	0	1	1	0	0	0	0	0	0	0	0	0	0	0	1.000
Beane, William, Little Falls	43	138	10	29	39	3	2	1	14	1	1	9	0	35	3	4	.210
Benedict, Scott, Oneonta	17	28	1	3	3	0	0	0	2	0	0	7	0	7	0	0	.107
Bennett, Bradley, Oneonta*	61	188	31	48	63	8	2	1	23	2	3	41	1	30	12	5	.255
Bittiger, Jeffrey, Little Falls	22	37	4	7	9	1	0	1	3	0	0	7	1	10	0	0	.189
Borges, George, Jamestown	41	143	18	39	51	6	3	0	16	0	1	4	3	18	3	1	.273
Brophy, Martin, Little Falls	17	28	4	5	8	0	0	1	2	0	0	4	0	11	0	0	.179
Bryan, A. Curt, Geneva†	6	4	2	1	1	0	0	0	1	0	0	2	0	2	0	0	.250
Bryant, Michael, Elmira	54	124	12	24	32	2	0	2	6	3	1	12	2	39	0	0	.194
Burgess, Gus, Elmira*	58	130	23	27	41	6	1	2	18	4	2	31	1	37	10	2	.208
Burton, Jeffrey, Geneva	65	212	34	52	74	11	1	3	38	2	6	33	1	46	5	2	.245
Butera, Brian, Auburn†	71	247	38	63	100	9	2	8	40	0	1	39	6	29	15	5	.255
Cabrera, Carlos, Utica	25	67	14	16	28	1	1	3	12	0	1	16	0	22	0	0	.239
Carroll, Michael, Jamestown	40	126	11	38	47	7	1	0	17	1	2	16	0	22	0	0	.302
Cartwright, Mark, Oneonta	12	2	0	0	0	0	0	0	0	0	0	0	0	2	0	0	.000
Castillo, Juan, Utica	55	194	26	43	66	7	2	4	19	0	0	13	5	61	9	1	.222
Castillo, J. Tomas, Utica	20	56	7	11	18	2	1	1	8	0	0	5	1	18	2	0	.196
Cates, Timothy, Jamestown	8	0	1	0	0	0	0	0	0	0	0	1	0	0	0	0	.000
Ciampa, Michael, Elmira*	71	241	59	75	100	8	1	5	38	4	4	61	5	26	35	6	.311
Cohron, D. Tracy, Jamestown*	40	117	5	29	43	3	1	3	12	1	0	10	0	26	0	0	.248
Connally, Fritzie, Geneva	67	229	46	70	130	18	0	14	43	1	1	53	6	31	2	1	.306
Davis, Michael, Little Falls	68	239	44	72	108	15	3	5	36	1	4	31	0	33	2	0	.301
DeLano, Alexander, Little Falls	16	37	11	11	15	1	0	1	6	0	0	17	0	6	2	0	.297
Denby, Darryl, Little Falls	63	216	34	54	80	7	2	5	22	3	1	18	1	40	14	4	.250
Despaux, C. Ric, Oneonta	46	157	28	43	66	6	1	5	18	4	1	17	5	37	12	4	.274
Duarte, Luis, Batavia	48	134	18	37	58	4	1	5	28	0	2	28	2	17	0	0	.276
Duncan, Timothy, Elmira	63	189	24	45	44	9	0	0	23	3	2	22	1	30	1	0	.238
Eldridge, Terry, Jamestown*	63	172	27	41	51	8	1	0	13	3	2	26	1	44	7	6	.238
Elkin, Ricky, 6 Bat-5 Aub	11	18	0	3	4	1	0	0	1	0	0	0	0	8	0	0	.167
Ellison, Darold, 11 Bat-58 Aub	69	257	31	68	104	12	0	8	37	1	3	15	5	57	0	0	.265
Engstler, Edward, Auburn	12	44	5	11	15	2	1	0	2	0	0	5	1	11	1	1	.250
Escobar, Jose, Utica	67	231	23	57	71	5	3	2	27	3	1	23	1	45	13	4	.246
Evans, Duane, Little Falls*	49	130	19	32	59	6	0	7	28	0	1	21	0	42	1	0	.246
Fauland, Herbert, Oneonta	30	1	0	0	0	0	0	0	0	0	0	0	0	0	0	0	.000
Fazio, Vincent, Auburn	6	16	3	1	1	0	0	0	1	0	0	2	0	10	0	0	.063
Fazzio, Daryl, Geneva*	4	7	0	3	4	1	0	0	2	0	0	2	0	1	0	0	.429
Figueroa, Luis, Oneonta	2	1	0	0	0	0	0	0	0	0	0	0	0	0	0	0	.000
Filkins, Randy, Oneonta	62	181	38	41	71	3	3	7	34	2	5	45	7	47	11	4	.227
Fimple, John, 1 Bat-60 Aub	61	215	27	52	74	7	0	5	24	0	2	37	0	58	7	1	.242
Forbes, Kirk, Jamestown†	64	232	42	54	84	12	3	4	33	0	3	35	0	35	6	2	.233
Frash, Roger, Little Falls*	64	211	55	73	128	12	2	13	39	0	1	31	5	41	14	1	.346
French, Ted, Auburn*	45	216	34	53	108	13	3	13	53	1	1	38	2	56	0	0	.245
Gallagher, David, Batavia	69	241	33	66	93	6	3	5	36	6	5	29	3	16	11	4	.274
Garcia, Michael, Little Falls	1	4	0	1	1	0	0	0	0	0	0	0	0	1	0	0	.250
Gilles, Robert, Geneva	29	58	12	11	17	3	0	1	8	1	0	20	1	19	1	0	.190
Gilmore, Anthony, Utica	59	197	35	45	69	3	3	5	24	1	1	27	1	55	11	3	.228
Glenn, James, Elmira	67	225	51	70	92	9	2	3	30	4	3	54	1	27	28	2	.311

Player and Club	G.	AB.	R.	H.	TB.	2B.	3B.	HR.	RBI.	SH.	SF.	BB.	HP.	SO.	SB.	CS.	Pct.
Goldberg, Douglas, Jamestown	27	68	9	8	17	3	0	2	6	2	2	13	0	15	0	0	.118
Grady, Patrick, Batavia*	21	51	7	13	13	0	0	0	10	0	0	16	0	13	6	1	.255
Gross, James, Oneonta	27	61	5	9	13	0	2	0	6	0	2	14	1	7	1	1	.148
Groves, Larry, Jamestown	30	47	4	8	9	1	0	0	3	0	0	4	0	11	0	0	.170
Gruber, Kelly, Batavia	61	212	27	46	59	3	2	2	19	3	2	15	3	46	6	3	.217
Guzman, Luis, Utica	68	268	51	79	131	18	5	8	34	1	3	11	1	42	10	1	.295
Hall, Jeffrey, Elmira	69	240	32	61	87	10	2	4	42	2	7	10	0	42	3	0	.254
Harris, Rafael, Utica†	16	27	4	8	12	4	0	0	6	0	0	9	0	8	0	0	.296
Helsom, Robert, Oneonta*	51	171	23	45	66	8	2	3	29	0	5	37	1	37	2	3	.263
Hennessy, Michael, Little Falls†	12	35	5	6	6	0	0	0	2	0	0	8	0	2	3	0	.171
Hernandez, Tobias, Utica	44	138	21	28	43	3	0	4	13	1	2	10	3	32	0	2	.203
Hilton, Gary, Little Falls	52	152	26	37	69	8	0	8	37	2	5	18	0	41	1	0	.243
Hoeksema, David, Jamestown	54	201	29	60	88	7	6	3	24	1	3	13	1	25	4	2	.299
Holden, Gary, Batavia	26	62	14	14	20	1	1	1	4	1	0	8	1	19	4	1	.226
Hunter, Jeffrey, Elmira*	57	166	20	37	55	9	0	3	14	4	1	22	0	23	0	0	.223
Hurdle, Michael, Utica	33	113	22	36	63	9	0	6	26	1	1	12	0	24	4	0	.319
Irwin, Robert, Auburn	48	150	27	32	44	3	3	1	14	0	0	20	1	34	2	1	.213
Johnson, Gregory, Jamestown	14	1	0	1	1	0	0	0	0	0	0	0	0	0	0	0	1.000
Johnson, Roy, Jamestown*	36	126	29	41	71	6	3	6	19	0	0	24	2	10	16	6	.325
Jones, Eric, Batavia	56	179	39	45	54	3	0	2	14	1	1	37	0	42	23	2	.251
Julio, Bill, Auburn	1	5	1	1	1	0	0	0	0	0	0	0	0	0	0	0	.200
Kaczor, Gary, Auburn	27	79	12	22	36	4	2	2	18	0	1	13	0	9	0	1	.278
Keenan, Kevin, Elmira	12	17	3	3	6	0	0	1	3	0	0	2	0	7	0	0	.176
Latrenta, Douglas, Oneonta*	68	218	56	64	87	9	4	2	25	5	1	52	4	27	19	5	.294
Leach, Don, Elmira	42	107	18	19	33	2	0	4	19	1	0	29	0	45	0	1	.178
Lepel, Joel, Jamestown*	17	47	6	10	11	1	0	0	7	0	2	10	0	5	1	0	.213
Lewis, Herman, Utica	36	115	23	18	21	3	0	0	7	1	0	25	1	28	6	1	.157
Little, R. Bryan, Jamestown†	7	27	6	8	8	0	0	0	3	0	0	6	0	1	2	0	.296
Littlefield, David, Oneonta	7	17	2	3	6	0	0	1	2	1	0	2	0	4	1	0	.176
Mackie, Bart, 2 Aub-44 Bat	46	121	18	22	29	3	2	0	12	0	3	40	2	41	2	2	.182
MacMillan, Jon, Geneva	30	80	13	10	17	1	0	2	8	0	0	14	0	14	2	1	.125
Malkin, John, Auburn	63	209	27	52	87	9	1	8	28	0	1	29	5	33	1	0	.249
Malone, Kevin, 22 Bat-1 Aub†	23	63	16	16	17	1	0	0	2	0	1	21	1	8	2	3	.254
Martinez, Ray, 14 Aub-48 Bat*	62	223	25	44	63	8	1	3	25	0	1	17	1	52	4	1	.197
McClendon, Lloyd, Little Falls	40	117	25	32	52	9	1	3	20	1	1	32	2	20	2	1	.274
McDaniel, J. Randy, Oneonta	62	173	22	40	44	4	0	0	7	1	0	25	1	27	22	6	.231
McKie, David, Auburn	17	44	5	10	14	2	1	0	6	1	0	6	2	3	0	0	.227
McNair, Robert, Utica*	68	238	35	68	113	11	2	10	36	0	0	33	0	45	2	0	.286
Meier, Brian, Batavia	5	5	1	1	1	0	0	0	0	0	0	4	0	2	0	0	.200
Melito, Charles, Batavia*	62	205	28	55	95	13	0	9	39	0	4	28	0	33	0	0	.268
Methven, Marlin, 29 Aub-40 Bat	69	254	39	74	101	13	4	2	31	3	3	37	4	40	17	3	.291
Michalek, James, Utica	21	61	8	14	19	3	1	0	5	0	0	15	1	13	0	0	.230
Minium, Matthew, Batavia*	13	37	13	9	16	1	0	2	7	0	2	13	1	4	1	1	.243
Montgomery, Allen, Utica	34	99	18	24	41	2	0	5	20	0	0	19	0	20	1	1	.242
Montpetit, David, Auburn	45	110	12	18	19	1	0	0	3	0	0	10	2	36	11	0	.164
Moore, Stephen, Little Falls†	63	205	43	55	72	5	3	2	25	4	4	33	2	32	21	4	.268
Moronko, Jeffrey, Batavia	63	231	29	56	88	10	2	6	35	0	2	19	1	55	15	2	.242
Nealeigh, Rodney, Jamestown*	68	221	38	73	89	9	2	1	23	2	1	32	2	12	7	4	.330
Nicolet, Donald, Batavia	1	2	0	0	0	0	0	0	0	0	0	2	0	0	0	0	.000
Nicolo, John, Auburn	42	154	25	40	43	3	0	0	6	1	0	27	1	11	14	3	.260
Norko, Thomas, Utica	56	176	35	51	96	14	2	9	30	0	2	41	4	52	9	4	.290
O'Brien, Kevin, Oneonta*	48	101	17	20	26	3	0	1	13	0	0	25	4	15	5	1	.198
Oddo, Ronald, Elmira*	63	210	31	66	71	3	1	0	23	7	2	35	1	23	4	2	.314
Oros, James, Auburn	22	68	16	18	34	2	1	4	11	0	0	15	0	8	1	0	.265
Ortiz, Jorge, Batavia	1	4	0	0	0	0	0	0	0	0	0	0	0	1	0	0	.000
Ortiz, Miguel, Utica	20	45	7	8	10	0	1	0	4	1	0	2	0	11	1	0	.178
Osmulski, Frank, Auburn	5	11	2	1	1	0	0	0	0	0	0	5	0	2	0	0	.091
Pagel, David, Geneva*	70	253	35	63	83	14	0	2	29	1	0	44	0	43	4	3	.249
Piggott, Russell, Geneva	69	271	50	85	125	13	0	9	43	1	2	23	4	27	6	3	.314
Poe, Richard, Little Falls*	61	198	38	62	81	9	2	2	27	0	3	20	1	15	4	3	.313
Pustorino, Frederick, Little Falls	39	80	10	14	17	3	0	0	7	0	0	21	0	19	1	1	.175
Quinones, Rene, Jamestown	21	63	4	15	16	1	0	0	6	0	1	0	0	10	0	0	.238
Ramos, Wolfgangh, Elmira	53	145	17	33	45	1	1	3	15	4	1	9	1	29	2	0	.228
Rehbaum, Christopher, Bat*	59	212	28	45	65	8	3	2	23	4	0	31	2	37	7	1	.212
Renfroe, Steven, Geneva	42	145	26	37	61	5	2	5	23	0	2	11	4	33	10	2	.255
Reynolds, Jeffrey, Oneonta	70	265	39	75	116	14	3	7	56	1	5	32	4	62	10	5	.283
Reynolds, Ronn, Little Falls	15	44	6	8	14	1	1	1	6	0	0	10	0	8	0	0	.182
Ricciardi, John, Little Falls†	46	128	15	27	27	0	0	0	5	5	0	21	0	19	4	1	.211
Rivas, Rafael, Utica†	21	39	4	8	11	0	0	1	4	0	0	4	1	15	1	1	.205
Rodriguez, Michael, Utica	32	98	12	23	25	2	0	0	7	0	0	4	0	15	1	1	.235
Roeder, Steven, Jamestown	32	78	11	14	17	1	1	0	9	1	1	4	0	28	1	1	.179
Rogers, Dane, Jamestown*	6	6	1	0	0	0	0	0	0	0	0	1	0	5	0	0	.000
Rohlfing, Wayne, Geneva	30	89	20	29	51	8	1	4	19	0	2	22	0	20	3	1	.326
Ruiz, Nelson, Batavia	21	40	7	9	11	2	0	0	3	0	5	0	4	22	2	0	.225
Saavedra, Justo, Batavia	9	12	0	0	0	0	0	0	0	0	0	0	0	6	0	0	.000
Schnoor, Charles, Little Falls	49	112	15	15	15	0	0	0	9	2	1	16	1	24	1	0	.134

Player and Club	G.	AB.	R.	H.	TB.	2B.	3B.	HR.	RBI.	SH.	SF.	BB.	HP.	SO.	SB.	CS.	Pct.
Scott, T. Kelly, Oneonta*	16	2	0	0	0	0	0	0	0	1	0	1	0	1	1	0	.000
Shannon, Kevin, Oneonta	60	152	24	35	40	5	0	0	26	4	7	56	3	23	3	1	.230
Simmons, D. Wayne, Geneva	39	138	26	42	54	10	1	0	18	2	0	32	0	17	8	3	.304
Sloan, James, Jamestown	21	55	4	11	14	3	0	0	3	0	0	3	0	17	0	1	.200
Smith, P. Keith, Oneonta	65	193	32	47	49	2	0	0	11	9	0	25	2	46	10	2	.244
Stanton, Mike, Auburn	5	11	1	3	3	0	0	0	2	0	0	3	0	4	1	0	.273
Stefani, Joseph, Oneonta	12	1	0	0	0	0	0	0	0	0	0	0	0	1	0	0	.000
Stevens, Anthony, Elmira	71	243	41	72	136	15	2	15	51	0	3	41	2	61	2	0	.296
Sullivan, Arthur, 1 Bat-44 Aub	45	145	17	32	45	6	2	1	13	1	0	22	0	44	8	2	.221
Sunderlage, Jeffrey, Little Falls*	14	1	0	0	0	0	0	0	0	0	0	0	0	0	0	0	.000
Sutton, L. Rico, Utica	50	171	25	47	66	6	2	3	23	0	1	33	1	42	13	0	.275
Tanner, Edwin, 1 Bat-27 Aub*	28	102	13	28	34	4	1	0	12	0	0	3	1	6	2	0	.275
Tillett, Charles, Auburn*	15	28	5	9	12	1	1	0	5	0	0	3	0	6	1	0	.321
Torres, Miguel, Jamestown	7	0	0	0	0	0	0	0	0	0	0	1	0	0	0	0	.000
Torres, Samuel, Auburn	10	40	5	6	6	0	0	0	0	1	0	10	0	10	1	1	.150
Triplett, Robert, Geneva	34	94	22	22	32	2	1	2	18	2	0	27	5	26	5	1	.234
Veith, Anthony, Geneva	52	151	28	37	54	5	0	4	26	3	3	32	0	21	3	2	.245
Walsh, James, Geneva	10	33	5	7	11	2	1	0	4	0	0	3	0	6	0	0	.212
Weislak, Kenneth, Jamestown	61	181	21	40	61	6	3	3	29	4	3	26	2	39	0	1	.221
Whitfield, N. Jerome, Jamestown	67	249	34	77	113	8	2	8	37	2	1	10	0	40	5	2	.309
Wilner, Kevin, Auburn*	34	122	6	29	39	4	0	2	14	0	1	10	1	22	2	0	.238
Wilson, J. Michael, Geneva	44	117	17	29	33	4	0	0	8	3	3	11	2	12	7	3	.248
Wilson, J. Parker, Elmira	49	148	27	35	59	7	4	3	24	2	3	26	2	42	3	0	.236
Woodward, James, Little Falls	68	257	23	59	69	4	0	2	26	4	1	16	1	36	3	5	.230
Wright, Mark, Batavia†	39	107	17	27	32	3	1	0	9	1	1	14	4	16	2	0	.252
Zell, Brian, Elmira*	37	68	15	18	23	5	0	0	5	2	1	17	1	24	0	1	.265

The following pitchers had no plate appearances primarily through use of designated hitters, listed alphabetically by club, games in parentheses:

AUBURN—Bajus, Mark *(12–5 with Batavia); Crowley, Michael *(5–2 with Batavia); Foster, Robert (30); Gnacinsky, Paul (14); Hundley, John *(12); Jakubowicz, Michael (1); Jenter, Steven (6–3 with Batavia); LaFranco, Mark *(8); Nay, Daniel *(7); Nero, Ronald (8); Nichols, Dale (5); Nicholson, Craig (4); Plunkett, Thomas (16); Salgado, Orlando *(7); Santana, Rodolfo *(7); Strother, James (5); Valdez, Miguel (12).

BATAVIA—Berenguer, Francisco *(8–2 with Auburn); Blackmon, Thomas (4); Burns, Thomas (17); Dixon, Michael *(15–6 with Auburn); Gebin, Richard *(4); Gilbert, Angelo *(10); Holland, W. Monte (6); Hollowell, Charles (12); Jeffcoat, Michael *(12); Jones, Kirk (3); Kolodny, Michael (15); Larison, Jerry (1); Lintz, Rickey (22); Moldes, Orestes (6); Norman, Terry *(18); Richard, Todd *(11); Roberts, Mark *(1); Saavedra, Richard (5); Schwarber, Michael *(16); Stibora, Thomas *(2); Thompson, Richard (7).

ELMIRA—Bolton, Thomas *(23); Bowlin, Allan *(10); Boyd, Dennis (12); Cote, Brice (19); Garrett, Steven (5); Gonzalez, Gilberto (18); Greco, George *(14); Herman, Tyrone (14); Hill, Ronnie *(13); Johnson, Mitchell (15); McCarthy, Thomas (3); Mecerod, George (2); Plainte, Brandon *(18); Sandling, Robert *(10); Weinbrecht, Mark *(16).

GENEVA—Alevizos, Robert (17); Banks, Darryl (12); Housey, Joseph (13); Kyles, Stanley (9); Lefferts, Craig *(12); Miglio, John *(22); Pryce, Kenneth (26); Roerden, Brian (5); Smith, Thomas (14); Swaggerty, F. Glenn (14).

JAMESTOWN—Byrket, Blake (4); Fadhel, Antonio (12); Glasscock, Larry (9); Grapenthin, Richard (7); Kellogg, Kerry (19); Littrell, Jack (3); Musum, Craig *(2); Oliver, Donald (12); Shuler, Mark (12); St. John, William *(3); Taylor, Jeffrey *(6); Westray, Kenneth *(16).

LITTLE FALLS—Bettendorf, Jeffrey (12); Bisot, Alfred (8); Cooperider, James *(13); Johnston, Jody (13); Kolbe, Brian (17); Rech, Edward *(11); Replogle, Mickey (15); Rockwell, E. Ted (17); Spicer, Kevin †(14); Stelly, Kenneth *(4); Turner, John *(6); Zwolinski, Mark (14).

ONEONTA—Campbell James (9); Christiansen, Clay (15); DeMaria, George (4); Ervey, Albert (6); Foster, R. Michael *(12); Kuhn, Lawrence (13); Mason, Martin (3); Mendez, Mark (14); Olwine, Edward *(6).

UTICA—Baker, James (13); Cerrud, Roberto (10); Feliciano, Felix (7); Holton, Mark (18); Howard, Dennis †(16); Langfield, Paul (17); Leal, Carlos (15); Lukish, Thomas (20); O'Dowd, Thomas (16); Patterson, Richard (4); Reade, William (19); Valdez, Silverio (10); White, P. Richard (15).

GRAND SLAM HOME RUNS—Malkin 2; Ciampa, French, Hurdle, Montgomery, Moronko, Oros, J. Reynolds, 1 each.

AWARDED FIRST BASE ON INTERFERENCE—Pustorino 3 (Malkin 2, Rivas); Piggott 2 (Borges, Hall); Poe 2 (Hernandez, Rodriguez); Beane (Malkin); Nicolo (Pagel); Rehbaum (McClendon); Sutton (Bailey); Wilner (McClendon).

GAME-WINNING RBIs

AUBURN (26)—Fimple 4, French 4, Butera 3, Malkin 3, Ellison 2, Methven 2, Oros 2, Wilner 2, Irwin 1, McKie 1, Sullivan 1, Tanner 1.

BATAVIA (29)—Melito 6, Gallagher 5, Rehbaum 4, Methven 3, Gruber 2, Moronko 2, Duarte 1, Ellison 1, Grady 1, E. Jones 1, Mackie 1, Ruiz 1, Wright 1.

ELMIRA (29)—Stevens 8, Ciampa 3, Hall 3, Leach 3, Oddo 2, Ramos 2, Ackley 1, Bryant 1, Burgess 1, Duncan 1, Glenn 1, Hunter 1, Zell 1.

GENEVA (42)—Connally 7, Pagel 6, Austin 5, Burton 4, Piggott 4, Triplett 4, Renfroe 3, Allen 2, Rohlfing 2, Simmons 2, Gilles 1, Veith 1, Wilson 1.

JAMESTOWN (23)—Borges 4, Whitfield 4, Forbes 2, Hoeksema 2, R. Johnson 2, Weislak 2, Adams 1, Cohron 1, Eldridge 1, Goldberg 1, Lepel 1, Nealeigh 1, Roeder 1.

LITTLE FALLS (28)—Frash 4, Hilton 4, Denby 3, Evans 3, Moore 3, Poe 3, McClendon 2, Beane 1, Davis 1, Hennessy 1, Reynolds 1, Ricciardi 1, Woodward 1.

ONEONTA (39)—Filkins 7, Reynolds 5, Shannon 4, Banes 3, Despaux 3, McDaniel 3, O'Brien 3, Smith 3, Bennett 2, Helsom 2, Latrenta 2, Bailey 1, Gross 1.

UTICA (25)—McNair 4, Gilmore 3, Lewis 3, Norko 3, J. T. Castillo 2, Hernandez 2, Hurdle 2, Montgomery 2, Cabrera 1, J. Castillo 1, Escobar 1, Sutton 1.

CLUB FIELDING

Club	G.	PO.	A.	E.	DP.	PB.	Pct.	Club	G.	PO.	A.	E.	DP.	PB.	Pct.
Jamestown	71	1724	791	98	65	18	.962	Batavia	73	1818	715	123	57	34	.954
Oneonta	74	1898	858	111	66	9	.961	Elmira	74	1864	775	135	75	12	.951
Geneva	74	1858	830	117	66	30	.958	Auburn	74	1856	764	151	54	12	.946
Little Falls	73	1857	738	119	54	22	.956	Utica	71	1747	758	175	53	18	.935

Triple Play—Oneonta.

INDIVIDUAL FIELDING

*Throws lefthanded.

FIRST BASEMEN

Player and Club	G.	PO.	A.	E.	DP.	Pct.	Player and Club	G.	PO.	A.	E.	DP.	Pct.
Piggott, Geneva	7	67	1	0	2	1.000	Rodriguez, Utica	8	51	5	1	5	.982
Malkin, Auburn	5	39	2	0	4	1.000	Hilton, Little Falls	39	280	32	6	23	.981
Evans, Little Falls*	3	29	1	0	0	1.000	Stevens, Elmira	64	508	31	11	61	.980
Carroll, Jamestown*	1	12	1	0	0	1.000	Martinez, Batavia*	61	503	29	11	43	.980
Oros, Auburn	1	5	0	0	0	1.000	Ellison, Auburn	46	328	17	7	24	.980
Cabrera, Utica	3	5	0	0	0	1.000	Melito, Batavia	12	83	6	2	10	.978
Nesleigh, Jamestown*	1	4	0	0	0	1.000	Cohron, Jamestown*	30	235	18	6	24	.977
CONNALLY, Geneva	67	674	46	1	56	.999	Hunter, Elmira	19	110	10	3	8	.976
Duarte, Batavia	11	86	6	1	5	.989	Alvis, Batavia	6	32	1	1	4	.971
McNair, Utica*	68	537	40	7	38	.988	Kaczor, Auburn	4	23	2	1	3	.962
Whitfield, Jamestown	47	369	30	5	37	.988	Despaux, Oneonta	3	18	0	1	0	.947
Poe, Little Falls*	42	259	29	4	22	.986	French, Auburn*	14	98	8	6	6	.946
Bailey, Oneonta	49	445	25	7	35	.985	Frash, Little Falls*	4	4	0	2	1	.667
O'Brien, Oneonta*	36	215	18	4	22	.983	Banes, Oneonta	1	0	0	0	1	.000

Triple Play—O'Brien.

SECOND BASEMEN

Player and Club	G.	PO.	A.	E.	DP.	Pct.	Player and Club	G.	PO.	A.	E.	DP.	Pct.
Davis, Little Falls	19	51	37	0	9	1.000	Methven, Batavia	68	177	166	11	33	.969
Quinones, Jamestown	6	15	14	0	5	1.000	Woodward, Little Falls	24	37	60	4	11	.960
Eldridge, Jamestown	2	8	6	0	2	1.000	Ricciardi, Little Falls	38	83	79	8	14	.953
Oros, Auburn	3	5	9	0	1	1.000	Banes, Oneonta	26	54	65	6	13	.952
Fazio, Auburn	2	8	4	0	2	1.000	Ortiz, Utica	14	8	31	2	0	.951
Gross, Oneonta	5	8	3	0	2	1.000	Little, Jamestown	4	6	13	1	3	.950
Butera, Auburn	3	3	4	0	0	1.000	Piggott, Geneva	57	99	161	15	38	.945
Wilson, Elmira	1	3	1	0	1	1.000	Forbes, Jamestown	63	141	198	20	36	.944
Escobar, Utica	1	0	1	0	0	1.000	Oddo, Elmira	61	114	152	17	41	.940
Roeder, Jamestown	1	0	1	0	0	1.000	Ramos, Elmira	20	28	51	5	12	.940
Malone, Auburn	22	44	69	1	14	.991	Fimple, Auburn	32	90	65	11	15	.934
Wright, Batavia	18	29	38	1	11	.985	Wilson, Geneva	21	40	40	6	6	.930
McDANIEL, Oneonta	58	116	153	8	28	.971	Guzman, Utica	67	144	148	28	33	.913
Nicolo, Auburn	9	12	21	1	3	.971							

THIRD BASEMEN

Player and Club	G.	PO.	A.	E.	DP.	Pct.	Player and Club	G.	PO.	A.	E.	DP.	Pct.
Gross, Oneonta	5	4	9	0	1	1.000	Piggott, Geneva	5	3	10	1	0	.929
Ortiz, Utica	3	2	6	0	0	1.000	Bailey, Jamestown	2	9	3	1	1	.923
Adams, Jamestown	3	1	4	0	0	1.000	Moronko, Batavia	58	57	144	17	10	.922
Alvis, Batavia	4	4	1	0	0	1.000	Woodward, Little Falls	8	8	12	2	4	.909
Reynolds, Little Falls	1	1	3	0	1	1.000	Davis, Little Falls	50	40	75	12	4	.906
Holden, Batavia	1	0	3	0	0	1.000	Reynolds, Oneonta	68	41	174	24	7	.900
Wright, Batavia	3	2	1	0	1	1.000	Wilson, Elmira	48	28	80	13	12	.893
Engstler, Auburn	1	0	2	0	0	1.000	Hunter, Elmira	35	21	51	10	4	.878
Banes, Oneonta	1	1	0	0	0	1.000	Butera, Auburn	26	22	48	11	5	.864
Despaux, Oneonta	1	1	0	0	0	1.000	Allen, Geneva	69	50	141	31	15	.860
Irwin, Auburn	1	1	0	0	0	1.000	Schnoor, Little Falls	12	3	8	2	2	.846
Simmons, Geneva	1	0	1	0	0	1.000	J. Castillo, Utica	42	39	94	26	7	.836
Fimple, Auburn	27	23	56	3	6	.963	Bittiger, Little Falls	14	9	21	6	2	.833
WEISLAK, Jamestown	55	48	92	7	11	.952	Ellison, Auburn	13	7	22	6	1	.829
Roeder, Jamestown	17	7	29	2	1	.947	Harris, Utica	9	1	8	2	0	.818
Ruiz, Batavia	8	4	12	1	1	.941	Ramos, Elmira	7	3	4	3	2	.700
Norko, Utica	25	18	43	4	1	.938	Fazio, Auburn	2	5	0	5	3	.583
Oros, Auburn	10	8	32	3	2	.930							

SHORTSTOPS

Player and Club	G.	PO.	A.	E.	DP.	Pct.	Player and Club	G.	PO.	A.	E.	DP.	Pct.
Ricciardi, Little Falls	7	9	8	0	1	1.000	Harris, Utica	1	0	1	0	0	1.000
Banes, Oneonta	3	4	2	0	2	1.000	Hurdle, Utica	1	0	1	0	0	1.000
Bryan, Geneva	5	1	1	0	0	1.000	Hoeksema, Jamestown	48	75	154	11	27	.954

SHORTSTOPS—Continued

Player and Club	G.	PO.	A.	E.	DP.	Pct.
Gross, Oneonta	14	11	41	3	5	.945
Nicolo, Jamestown	34	60	110	10	15	.944
Simmons, Geneva	39	63	130	12	23	.941
Quinones, Jamestown	13	18	26	3	7	.936
Woodward, Little Falls	42	54	115	12	17	.934
SMITH, Oneonta	64	104	186	21	32	.932
Little, Jamestown	2	5	8	1	3	.929
Duncan, Elmira	63	98	197	25	42	.922
Gruber, Batavia	60	87	155	21	27	.920
Escobar, Utica	66	90	181	24	27	.919
Pagel, Geneva	35	56	114	15	20	.919
Schnoor, Little Falls	36	43	77	12	13	.909
Norko, Utica	8	9	23	4	4	.889
Fimple, Auburn	4	5	11	2	3	.889
Roeder, Jamestown	4	5	11	2	0	.889
Tanner, Auburn	28	39	77	15	7	.885
Weislak, Jamestown	8	9	14	3	3	.885
Wright, Batavia	15	13	29	8	7	.840
Torres, Auburn	9	12	12	5	2	.828
Ramos, Elmira	22	16	38	12	9	.818
Oros, Auburn	2	4	6	3	1	.769
Ortiz, Batavia	1	1	1	2	0	.500

Triple Play—Smith.

OUTFIELDERS

Player and Club	G.	PO.	A.	E.	DP.	Pct.
Whitfield, Jamestown	16	17	1	0	0	1.000
Hennessy, Little Falls*	13	16	1	0	0	1.000
Minium, Batavia*	13	17	0	0	0	1.000
Kaczor, Auburn	12	16	0	0	0	1.000
Walsh, Geneva	10	9	0	0	0	1.000
J. Saavedra, Batavia	6	6	0	0	0	1.000
Borges, Batavia	3	4	1	0	0	1.000
Nicolet, Batavia	1	3	0	0	0	1.000
Adams, Jamestown	2	3	0	0	0	1.000
Tillett, Auburn*	2	3	0	0	0	1.000
Rohlfing, Geneva	1	2	0	0	0	1.000
LaFranco, Auburn*	1	1	0	0	0	1.000
Benedict, Geneva	2	1	0	0	0	1.000
CIAMPA, Elmira*	71	144	5	2	1	.987
Veith, Geneva	44	64	5	1	0	.986
Gallagher, Batavia	64	114	4	2	0	.983
Hall, Elmira	38	52	6	1	1	.983
Frash, Little Falls*	61	105	7	2	2	.982
Moore, Little Falls	43	49	4	1	1	.981
Austin, Geneva	56	93	4	2	2	.980
Carroll, Jamestown*	37	40	1	1	0	.976
Irwin, Auburn	47	102	6	3	1	.973
Burgess, Elmira*	55	66	3	2	1	.972
Beane, Little Falls	40	93	5	3	1	.970
Butera, Auburn	40	54	4	2	1	.967
Denby, Little Falls	62	110	5	4	1	.966
Sullivan, Auburn	32	51	5	2	0	.966
Renfroe, Geneva	21	25	3	1	0	.966
Poe, Little Falls*	17	27	0	1	0	.964
Bennett, Oneonta*	59	94	10	4	1	.963
Filkins, Oneonta	49	48	3	2	0	.962
Latrenta, Oneonta*	56	68	5	3	1	.961
R. Johnson, Jamestown*	36	63	1	3	0	.955
Montgomery, Utica	28	39	3	2	0	.955
Helsom, Oneonta	39	40	1	2	0	.953
Wilner, Auburn*	29	50	1	3	0	.944
Banes, Oneonta	9	15	2	1	0	.944
Eldridge, Jamestown	56	71	11	5	0	.943
Nealeigh, Jamestown*	68	89	8	6	1	.942
Norko, Utica	24	28	4	2	0	.941
Lewis, Utica	27	42	4	3	1	.939
Montpetit, Auburn	43	78	4	6	0	.932
Glenn, Elmira	36	46	6	4	1	.929
Despaux, Oneonta	28	37	2	3	0	.929
Rehbaum, Batavia*	59	94	6	8	1	.926
French, Auburn*	32	48	2	4	0	.926
Zell, Elmira	25	25	0	2	0	.926
MacMillan, Geneva	25	33	2	3	0	.921
Holden, Batavia	23	23	0	2	0	.920
Burton, Geneva	64	83	6	8	1	.918
Bryant, Elmira	49	50	5	5	0	.917
Grady, Batavia*	16	17	5	2	2	.917
Hurdle, Utica	32	61	4	6	0	.915
Sutton, Utica	48	89	7	9	0	.914
DeLano, Little Falls	15	18	2	2	1	.909
Roeder, Jamestown	6	10	0	1	0	.909
E. Jones, Batavia*	55	99	4	11	1	.904
Cabrera, Utica	6	6	0	1	0	.857
J. T. Castillo, Utica	9	10	1	2	0	.846
Gilmore, Utica	49	56	3	11	1	.843
Triplett, Geneva	12	9	0	2	0	.818
J. Castillo, Utica	12	6	2	3	0	.727
Engstler, Auburn	2	1	0	1	0	.500

Triple Play—Bennett.

CATCHERS

Player and Club	G.	PO.	A.	E.	DP.	PB.	Pct.
Lepel, Jamestown	16	79	10	0	1	4	1.000
Brophy, Little Falls	5	29	1	0	0	0	1.000
Sloan, Jamestown	5	25	1	0	0	1	1.000
Keenan, Elmira	8	22	2	0	0	0	1.000
Whitfield, Jamestown	3	16	6	0	0	1	1.000
Meier, Jamestown	5	12	1	0	1	1	1.000
Fazzio, Geneva	2	7	0	0	0	1	1.000
Ruiz, Batavia	2	5	1	0	0	0	1.000
Stanton, Auburn	3	5	0	0	0	0	1.000
Eldridge, Jamestown	1	3	0	0	0	0	1.000
Alvis, Batavia	1	2	0	0	0	0	1.000
Benedict, Oneonta	1	1	0	0	0	0	1.000
SHANNON, Oneonta	59	412	43	3	7	6	.993
Leach, Elmira	34	226	26	3	2	3	.988
Mackie, Batavia	44	282	28	4	1	21	.987
Goldberg, Jamestown	24	140	9	2	2	7	.987
Borges, Jamestown	30	163	15	3	1	5	.983
Pagel, Geneva	31	194	23	4	1	17	.982
Ackley, Elmira	26	187	14	4	2	4	.980
Rohlfing, Geneva	24	128	16	3	2	9	.980
Reynolds, Little Falls	14	85	3	2	1	1	.978
Gilles, Geneva	26	113	11	3	0	4	.976
Rodriguez, Utica	7	33	1	1	0	3	.971
Littlefield, Oneonta	5	31	2	1	0	1	.971
McClendon, L Falls	34	203	20	7	3	9	.970
Hall, Elmira	18	90	5	3	1	5	.969
Malkin, Auburn	52	322	37	12	5	9	.968
Pustorino, Little Falls	39	173	19	7	1	12	.965
Hernandez, Utica	41	224	39	10	6	10	.963
Duarte, Batavia	29	164	15	7	2	12	.962
Rivas, Utica	21	64	5	3	0	3	.958
Elkin, Auburn	11	33	1	2	0	1	.944
Bailey, Oneonta	15	81	7	6	0	2	.936
Michalek, Utica	21	141	19	12	2	2	.930
McKie, Auburn	14	64	6	7	1	1	.909
Osmulski, Auburn	4	22	3	3	1	1	.893
Engstler, Auburn	1	6	1	0	0	0	.875

PITCHERS

Player and Club	G.	PO.	A.	E.	DP.	Pct.
HOUSEY, Geneva	13	4	20	0	0	1.000
Bolton, Elmira*	23	5	14	0	4	1.000
Dixon, Batavia*	15	2	13	0	1	1.000
Alevizos, Geneva	17	6	7	0	0	1.000
Hundley, Auburn*	12	3	9	0	0	1.000
Jeffcoat, Batavia*	12	3	9	0	1	1.000
Herman, Elmira	15	2	9	0	0	1.000
Pryce, Geneva	25	1	10	0	0	1.000
McCarthy, Elmira	3	3	7	0	0	1.000
Johnson, Elmira	15	4	6	0	0	1.000
Rockwell, Little Falls	17	0	10	0	1	1.000
Kuhn, Oneonta	12	4	5	0	1	1.000
Shuler, Jamestown	12	2	7	0	2	1.000
Lukish, Utica	17	3	6	0	0	1.000
Ervey, Oneonta	6	4	4	0	0	1.000
Lintz, Batavia	22	3	5	0	0	1.000
Fauland, Oneonta	27	0	8	0	0	1.000
Nichols, Auburn	5	3	4	0	0	1.000
Hollowell, Batavia*	12	3	4	0	0	1.000
Schwarber, Batavia	16	3	4	0	0	1.000
Weinbrecht, Elmira*	16	0	7	0	0	1.000
Musum, Jamestown*	2	2	4	0	0	1.000
Campbell, Oneonta	8	1	5	0	0	1.000
Nero, Auburn	8	1	5	0	0	1.000
Miglio, Geneva	22	0	6	0	1	1.000
Demaria, Oneonta	4	2	3	0	0	1.000
Bisot, Little Falls	8	1	4	0	0	1.000
Cerrud, Utica	9	0	5	0	1	1.000
Bettendorf, Little Falls	12	2	3	0	1	1.000
Oliver, Jamestown	12	2	2	0	0	1.000
Holton, Utica	17	1	3	0	0	1.000
Kellogg, Jamestown	18	2	2	0	1	1.000
Plainte, Elmira*	18	1	3	0	0	1.000
St. John, Jamestown*	3	1	2	0	0	1.000
Blackmon, Batavia	4	0	3	0	0	1.000
Patterson, Utica	4	2	1	0	0	1.000
Olwine, Oneonta*	6	1	2	0	0	1.000
Repogle, Little Falls	15	1	2	0	0	1.000
Reade, Utica*	19	2	1	0	0	1.000
Littrell, Jamestown	3	2	0	0	0	1.000
Crowley, Auburn*	4	0	2	0	0	1.000
Roerden, Geneva	5	0	2	0	0	1.000
Strother, Auburn	5	1	1	0	0	1.000
Jenter, Auburn	6	0	2	0	0	1.000
Moldes, Batavia	6	1	1	0	1	1.000
Thompson, Batavia	7	1	1	0	0	1.000
Tillett, Auburn*	7	0	2	0	0	1.000
Roeder, Jamestown	1	0	1	0	0	1.000
Stibora, Batavia*	2	1	0	0	0	1.000
K. Jones, Batavia	3	0	1	0	0	1.000
Byrket, Jamestown	4	1	0	0	0	1.000
Stelly, Little Falls*	4	0	1	0	0	1.000
R. Saavedra, Batavia	5	0	1	0	0	1.000
Gilbert, Batavia*	10	0	1	0	0	1.000
Sandling, Elmira*	10	0	1	0	0	1.000
Gnacinsky, Auburn	14	6	19	1	0	.962
Smith, Geneva	14	8	17	1	2	.962
Mendez, Oneonta	14	7	17	1	3	.960
Baker, Utica	13	8	12	1	1	.952
Valdez, Auburn	11	8	8	1	1	.941
Cates, Jamestown	7	2	13	1	0	.938
Langfield, Utica	17	8	7	1	1	.938
Banks, Geneva	12	4	10	1	0	.933
Cooperider, Little Falls*	13	6	21	2	0	.931
Foster, Oneonta	12	1	12	1	0	.929
Johnston, Little Falls	13	5	8	1	0	.929
Greco, Elmira*	14	1	12	1	0	.929
Lefferts, Geneva*	12	7	17	2	1	.923
Torres, Jamestown	7	2	10	1	0	.923
O'Dowd, Elmira	15	3	9	1	2	.923
Stefani, Oneonta	12	5	6	1	0	.917
Christiansen, Oneonta	15	5	16	2	0	.913
Grapenthin, Jamestown	7	3	7	1	0	.909
Swaggerty, Geneva	14	8	19	3	0	.900
Glasscock, Jamestown	9	2	16	2	0	.900
White, Utica	15	5	13	2	2	.900
Banes, Elmira	16	1	8	1	1	.900
Groves, Jamestown	13	10	15	3	2	.893
Leal, Utica	15	5	11	2	0	.889
Boyd, Elmira	12	3	5	1	0	.889
Scott, Oneonta*	15	2	6	1	0	.889
Fadhel, Jamestown	12	9	12	3	1	.875
Kyles, Geneva	9	7	7	2	0	.875
Kolodny, Batavia	15	4	10	2	1	.875
Cartwright, Oneonta	11	1	6	1	1	.875
Howard, Utica	16	5	15	3	0	.870
Richard, Batavia*	11	4	9	2	0	.867
Sunderlage, Little F*	14	4	9	2	0	.867
Foster, Auburn	29	5	8	2	1	.867
Spicer, Little Falls*	14	5	26	5	0	.861
G. Johnson, Jamestown	13	1	5	1	0	.857
Burns, Batavia	17	1	10	2	1	.846
Cote, Elmira	19	3	8	2	1	.846
Westray, Jamestown*	16	1	9	2	0	.833
Gonzalez, Elmira	18	2	3	1	0	.833
Bajus, Auburn*	12	0	13	3	0	.813
Andrews, Oneonta	16	3	14	4	0	.810
Rech, Little Falls*	11	4	12	4	0	.800
La Franco, Auburn*	7	1	3	1	1	.800
Kolbe, Little Falls	17	6	12	5	0	.783
Nicholson, Auburn	3	3	0	1	0	.750
Gebin, Batavia*	4	0	3	1	0	.750
Taylor, Jamestown*	6	0	3	1	0	.750
Feliciano, Utica	7	2	1	1	0	.750
Nay, Auburn*	7	1	7	3	0	.727
Bittiger, Little Falls	7	2	3	2	0	.714
Berenguer, Batavia	8	1	4	2	0	.714
Plunkett, Auburn	16	0	5	2	0	.714
Norman, Batavia*	18	2	3	2	0	.714
Garrett, Elmira	5	1	3	2	1	.667
Santana, Auburn*	7	1	1	1	0	.667
Zwolinski, Little Falls*	14	0	2	1	0	.667
Bowlin, Elmira*	10	1	2	2	1	.600
Valdez, Utica	10	0	0	1	0	.000

The following players had no recorded accepted chances; therefore, are not listed in the fielding averages for those positions: Allen, ss; Alvis, of; Bailey, ss; Duarte, 3b; Escobar, of; Figueroa, p; Hall, p; Hill*, p; Hoeksema, 3b; Holland, p; Jakubowicz, p; Kellogg, of; Larison, p; Mason, p; McDaniel, of; Mecerod, p; Moore, 3b; O'Brien*, of; Quinones, 3b; Ricciardi, 3b; Roberts*, p; Rogers, of; Salgado, p; Schnoor, 2b; Scott*, of; Sloan, 1b; Sullivan, p; Turner*, p; Wilson, 3b.

CLUB PITCHING

Club	G.	CG.	ShO.	Sv.	IP.	H.	R.	ER.	HR.	BB.	Int. BB.	HB.	SO.	WP.	Bk.	ERA.
Oneonta	74	17	11	17	641	538	263	201	33	286	11	22	518	36	1	2.82
Geneva	74	23	8	16	626	532	270	222	36	262	9	27	434	42	1	3.19
Elmira	74	4	5	18	619	600	371	262	35	368	21	22	484	46	4	3.81
Little Falls	73	15	5	14	619	553	368	287	50	395	3	19	465	53	0	4.17
Auburn	74	18	4	5	616	595	406	310	37	368	1	27	416	53	4	4.53
Jamestown	71	23	1	7	578	597	359	299	40	323	12	22	405	45	1	4.66
Batavia	73	8	3	11	609	599	421	325	68	382	13	18	471	54	8	4.80
Utica	71	11	1	9	593	679	474	350	70	360	5	20	450	57	4	5.31

PITCHERS' RECORDS

(Leading Qualifiers for Earned-Run Average Leadership—59 or More Innings)

*Throws lefthanded.

Pitcher—Club	G.	GS.	CG.	ShO.	W.	L.	Sv.	Pct.	IP.	H.	R.	ER.	HR.	BB.	Int. BB.	HB.	SO.	WP.	ERA.
Housey, Geneva	13	13	7	1	10	2	0	.833	102	71	24	17	1	27	0	6	66	2	1.50
Foster, Auburn	30	2	1	0	3	5	7	.375	61	49	26	15	2	46	4	1	44	17	2.21
Fadhel, Jamestown	12	12	9	1	6	6	0	.500	88	73	30	22	5	38	3	3	59	4	2.25
Boyd, Elmira	12	12	8	1	7	1	0	.875	69	54	20	19	2	30	1	0	79	2	2.48
Mendez, Oneonta	14	14	7	4	9	3	0	.750	101	85	33	28	3	50	1	4	72	3	2.50
Christiansen, Oneonta	15	13	5	2	4	3	0	.571	92	89	43	26	9	24	0	3	62	4	2.54
Smith, Geneva	14	10	4	2	8	4	2	.667	81	80	25	23	6	25	0	1	53	2	2.56
Rech, Little Falls*	11	9	3	0	6	0	1	1.000	66	57	23	19	5	32	0	1	51	6	2.59
Johnson, Elmira	15	14	0	0	5	1	0	.625	69	69	32	20	5	35	3	2	28	5	2.61
Lefferts, Geneva*	12	12	5	1	9	1	0	.900	94	74	29	29	7	24	1	0	99	5	2.78

Departmental Leaders: G—Fauland, Foster, 30; GS—Dixon, Gnacinsky, Howard, M. Johnson, Leal, Mendez, Spicer, Swaggerty, 14; CG—Fadhel, 9; ShO—Mendez, 4; W—Housey, Spicer, 10; L—Kolbe, 8; Sv—Fauland, Pryce, 9; Pct.—Lefferts, .900; IP—Housey, 102; H—Howard, 106; R—Howard, 63; ER—Howard, 51; HR—Swaggerty, 14; BB—Spicer, 63; IBB—Kolodny, 6; HB—Banks, 7; SO—Lefferts, 99; WP—R. Foster, 17.

(All Pitchers—Listed Alphabetically)

Pitcher—Club	G.	GS.	CG.	ShO.	W.	L.	Sv.	Pct.	IP.	H.	R.	ER.	HR.	BB.	Int. BB.	HB.	SO.	WP.	ERA.
Alevizos, Geneva	17	1	1	0	4	1	1	.800	42	37	15	13	3	14	2	2	32	2	2.79
Andrews, Oneonta	16	12	2	1	6	3	0	.667	81	69	39	30	5	38	1	2	89	3	3.33
Bajus, Auburn*	12	7	3	1	2	6	0	.250	56	50	37	25	1	33	0	1	34	4	4.02
Baker, Utica	13	13	3	0	6	5	0	.545	83	86	50	31	7	35	0	3	59	5	3.36
Banes, Elmira	16	0	0	0	3	5	3	.250	38	32	18	9	3	14	2	1	26	3	2.13
Banks, Geneva	12	12	1	1	3	4	0	.429	64	49	44	36	0	60	1	7	37	16	5.06
Berenguer, Batavia	8	0	0	0	0	2	0	.000	14	14	9	6	0	9	2	2	8	0	3.86
Bettendorf, Little Falls	12	6	0	0	0	5	0	.000	40	47	49	43	4	41	0	1	29	8	9.68
Bisot, Little Falls	8	4	0	0	1	1	0	.500	16	22	16	12	1	19	0	2	10	3	6.75
Bittiger, Little Falls	7	2	0	0	0	1	1	.000	26	10	6	3	0	20	0	1	33	0	1.04
Blackmon, Batavia	4	1	0	0	0	1	0	.000	4	5	7	6	1	8	1	0	1	2	13.50
Bolton, Elmira*	23	1	1	0	6	2	0	.750	56	43	26	15	4	22	1	0	43	2	2.41
Bowlin, Elmira*	10	4	0	0	2	1	0	.667	31	26	12	8	1	16	0	1	10	1	2.32
Boyd, Elmira	12	12	8	1	7	1	0	.875	69	54	20	19	2	30	1	0	79	2	2.48
Boyd, Elmira	17	8	1	1	2	4	1	.333	56	54	48	32	7	37	1	1	37	8	5.14
Burns, Batavia	4	0	0	0	0	0	0	.000	7	9	6	6	0	7	0	1	5	1	7.71
Byrket, Jamestown	9	3	0	0	1	2	1	.333	27	20	15	13	0	19	0	2	21	4	4.33
Campbell, Oneonta	11	8	1	0	5	3	0	.625	54	43	24	21	3	29	0	3	38	2	3.50
Cartwright, Oneonta	7	7	1	0	3	3	0	.500	44	42	25	21	3	19	0	0	29	6	4.30
Cates, Jamestown	10	0	0	0	0	1	0	.000	14	25	16	14	2	13	0	3	6	8	9.00
Cerrud, Utica	13	5	2	4	3	0	0	.571	92	89	43	26	9	24	0	3	62	4	2.54
Christiansen, Oneonta	15	13	1	1	3	5	0	.375	68	76	61	44	4	48	0	5	43	9	5.82
Cooperider, L Falls*	13	13	3	0	5	2	0	.714	94	84	43	30	4	31	1	4	65	11	4.35
Cote, Elmira	19	6	0	0	4	4	0	.500	60	58	42	29	3	51	5	4	63	11	4.35
Crowley, Auburn*	5	2	0	0	0	2	0	.000	9	16	14	12	4	8	0	0	6	4	12.00
DeMaria, Oneonta	4	2	0	0	0	2	0	.000	13	12	12	8	2	11	1	1	9	1	5.54
Dixon, Batavia*	15	14	3	2	6	6	0	.500	82	77	45	40	2	48	1	5	87	6	4.39
Ervey, Oneonta	6	6	2	0	5	0	0	1.000	42	36	16	14	2	14	0	2	25	0	3.00
Fadhel, Jamestown	12	12	9	1	6	6	0	.500	88	73	30	22	5	38	3	3	59	4	2.25
Fauland, Oneonta	30	0	0	0	4	2	9	.667	44	34	20	14	4	19	3	1	46	2	2.86
Feliciano, Utica	7	0	0	0	0	0	0	.000	3	4	1	1	0	1	0	0	1	0	3.00
Figueroa, Oneonta	2	0	0	0	0	0	0	.000	9	16	14	12	1	9	1	0	5	1	11.25
Foster, Oneonta*	12	4	0	0	3	0	0	1.000	51	38	13	12	1	19	1	0	41	6	2.12
Foster, Auburn	30	2	1	0	3	5	7	.375	61	49	26	15	2	46	4	1	44	17	2.21
Garrett, Elmira	5	3	0	0	2	2	0	.500	19	15	10	7	1	8	0	2	13	0	3.32
Gebin, Batavia*	4	1	0	0	0	1	0	.000	12	6	9	6	1	17	0	0	7	3	4.50
Gilbert, Batavia*	10	2	0	0	0	5	0	.000	42	48	38	27	4	29	0	5	40	1	5.79
Glasscock, Jamestown	9	9	0	0	5	3	0	.615	102	83	51	40	2	60	0	3	74	4	3.53
Gnacinsky, Auburn	14	14	5	1	8	5	0	.615	102	83	51	40	2	60	0	3	74	4	3.53
Gonzalez, Elmira	18	2	0	0	1	2	1	.333	30	34	33	19	3	34	5	3	34	2	5.70
Grapenthin, Jamestown	7	2	0	0	2	2	0	.500	27	30	17	17	0	14	0	1	24	2	5.67
Greco, Elmira*	14	7	0	0	2	3	0	.400	39	55	34	23	1	23	0	1	23	6	5.31
Groves, Jamestown	13	13	7	0	7	5	0	.583	99	92	51	42	9	37	2	4	49	6	3.82
Hall, Elmira	1	0	0	0	0	0	0	.000	2	2	4	4	0	4	0	0	2	0	18.00
Herman, Elmira	14	13	0	0	3	4	0	.429	67	63	27	25	2	31	0	1	48	2	3.36
Hill, Elmira*	13	1	0	0	2	1	3	.667	22	35	25	20	3	14	0	0	10	3	8.18
Holland, Batavia	6	1	0	0	0	1	0	.000	10	13	13	3	0	8	0	0	7	2	2.70
Hollowell, Batavia*	12	6	0	0	4	3	0	.571	47	40	30	28	6	22	1	0	32	4	5.36
Holton, Utica	18	1	0	0	2	2	1	.500	34	52	36	28	5	22	1	0	37	8	7.41
Housey, Geneva	13	13	7	1	10	2	0	.833	102	71	24	17	1	27	0	6	66	2	1.50
Howard, Utica	16	14	4	1	4	8	0	.333	89	106	63	51	9	44	0	2	76	8	5.16
Hundley, Auburn*	12	5	0	0	3	4	0	.429	46	58	42	36	6	28	0	1	40	0	7.04
Jakubowicz, Auburn	1	1	0	0	0	1	0	.000	0	4	8	3	0	6	0	0	0	0	—
Jeffcoat, Batavia*	12	11	3	0	4	3	0	.571	68	65	40	30	9	45	1	0	71	6	3.97
Jenter, Auburn	6	0	0	0	5	0	1	1.000	10	19	8	6	1	5	0	1	2	1	5.40
Johnson, Elmira	15	14	0	0	5	1	0	.625	69	69	32	20	5	35	3	2	28	5	2.61

Pitcher–Club	G	GS	CG	ShO	W	L	Sv	Pct.	IP	H	R	ER	HR	BB	Int. BB	HB	SO	WP	ERA.
G. Johnson, Jamestown	13	2	0	0	0	2	0	.000	27	32	26	21	3	26	0	4	15	3	7.00
Johnston, Little Falls	13	13	2	0	7	2	0	.778	81	54	36	28	6	59	1	0	54	4	3.11
K. Jones, Batavia	3	0	0	0	0	0	0	.000	5	3	3	3	0	3	0	0	4	0	5.40
Kellogg, Jamestown	19	0	0	0	1	2	0	.333	32	33	18	15	1	18	0	0	24	5	4.22
Kolbe, Little Falls	17	9	5	2	3	8	1	.273	83	86	42	33	10	28	2	4	52	2	3.58
Kolodny, Batavia	15	12	0	0	1	7	1	.125	68	70	50	47	12	42	6	2	32	8	6.22
Kuhn, Oneonta	12	3	1	1	5	1	3	.833	36	26	9	6	2	21	1	0	29	2	1.50
Kyles, Geneva	9	9	2	2	5	0	0	.286	47	46	34	28	1	40	0	5	29	11	5.36
LaFranco, Auburn*	7	0	0	0	0	2	5	.000	11	18	14	11	0	3	0	1	4	3	9.00
Langfield, Utica	17	10	1	0	5	5	0	.500	67	69	59	41	7	49	0	2	50	9	5.51
Larison, Batavia	1	0	0	0	0	0	0	.000	2	3	3	3	0	2	0	0	1	0	13.50
Leal, Utica	15	14	1	0	1	7	0	.125	78	84	57	40	8	54	1	2	50	5	4.62
Lefferts, Geneva*	12	12	5	1	9	1	0	.900	94	74	35	29	7	24	1	0	99	2	2.78
Lintz, Batavia	22	0	0	0	2	1	6	.667	40	32	19	15	4	15	1	2	23	1	3.38
Littrell, Jamestown	3	0	0	0	1	0	0	1.000	5	7	4	4	1	5	0	0	4	1	7.20
Lukish, Utica	20	0	0	0	2	4	8	.333	31	27	9	6	3	7	0	0	36	0	1.74
Mason, Oneonta	3	0	0	0	1	0	0	1.000	5	4	1	1	0	2	0	1	7	0	1.80
McCarthy, Elmira	3	3	0	0	1	0	0	.667	20	10	7	7	2	13	0	1	14	1	3.15
Mecerod, Elmira	2	2	0	0	1	0	0	1.000	10	6	2	2	0	4	0	0	14	0	1.80
Mendez, Oneonta	14	14	7	4	9	3	0	.750	101	85	33	28	3	50	1	4	72	3	2.50
Miglio, Geneva	22	0	0	0	3	3	4	.500	44	33	15	12	1	22	3	3	28	3	2.45
Moldes, Batavia	6	0	0	0	1	1	0	.500	8	14	12	11	4	4	0	1	2	0	12.38
Musum, Jamestown*	2	1	0	0	0	1	0	.000	6	5	5	5	0	3	0	0	5	0	7.50
Nay, Auburn*	7	7	0	0	4	0	0	1.000	44	38	24	20	2	31	0	1	36	5	4.09
Nero, Auburn	8	6	4	1	2	4	0	.333	51	49	24	20	2	19	0	0	17	2	3.53
Nichols, Auburn	5	3	0	0	0	4	0	.000	13	18	25	20	4	15	0	2	8	2	13.85
Nicholson, Auburn	4	1	0	0	1	0	0	.000	13	10	9	6	1	7	0	2	6	0	4.15
Norman, Batavia	18	2	0	0	3	3	1	.500	44	42	21	19	5	21	1	1	37	1	3.89
O'Dowd, Utica	16	6	0	0	2	3	0	.400	51	52	43	30	5	38	1	4	43	5	5.29
Oliver, Jamestown	12	3	0	0	2	1	0	.667	26	31	20	17	5	16	0	0	15	3	5.88
Olwine, Oneonta*	6	0	0	0	2	1	2	.667	9	8	4	1	0	6	0	0	8	1	1.00
Patterson, Utica	4	4	0	0	0	2	0	.000	15	22	19	18	4	15	0	2	9	2	10.80
Plainte, Elmira*	18	0	0	0	2	3	0	.000	26	33	23	14	3	17	0	1	12	0	4.85
Plunkett, Auburn	16	4	0	0	0	6	0	.000	48	53	41	29	1	36	0	1	28	5	5.44
Pryce, Geneva	26	0	0	0	3	2	9	.600	48	42	20	16	2	16	1	0	42	0	3.00
Reade, Utica*	19	1	0	0	2	2	0	.500	43	48	36	27	5	29	1	0	41	5	5.65
Rech, Little Falls*	11	9	3	0	6	0	1	1.000	66	57	25	19	5	32	0	1	51	6	2.59
Replogle, Little Falls	15	0	0	0	1	3	3	.250	23	20	15	12	2	16	0	0	18	0	4.70
Richard, Batavia*	11	11	0	0	1	7	0	.125	58	58	33	23	4	36	0	3	47	1	3.57
Roberts, Batavia*	1	1	0	0	0	0	0	.000	3	3	2	2	1	3	0	0	2	1	6.00
Rockwell, Little Falls	17	0	0	0	4	2	5	.667	37	21	8	5	1	13	0	0	24	2	1.22
Roeder, Jamestown	1	0	0	0	0	0	0	.000	2	5	4	4	1	3	0	0	1	0	18.00
Roerden, Geneva	5	3	0	0	1	0	0	1.000	16	10	4	1	1	8	0	0	10	1	0.56
R. Saavedra, Batavia	5	0	0	0	1	0	1	1.000	8	7	1	1	0	4	0	0	11	1	1.13
Salgado, Auburn	1	0	0	0	0	0	0	.000	2	2	1	1	0	3	0	0	1	0	4.50
Sandling, Elmira*	10	1	0	0	0	1	0	.000	18	20	13	9	0	15	1	0	19	3	4.50
Santana, Auburn*	7	1	0	0	1	0	0	1.000	12	16	18	13	4	7	0	1	2	1	9.75
Schwarber, Batavia	16	9	2	0	5	3	0	.625	64	69	51	37	6	33	1	2	60	3	5.20
Scott, Oneonta*	15	1	0	0	4	4	0	.500	40	30	15	12	2	12	3	3	34	2	2.70
Shuler, Jamestown	12	0	0	0	1	3	3	.250	32	29	16	11	1	19	2	0	25	1	3.09
Smith, Geneva	14	10	4	2	8	4	2	.667	81	80	29	23	6	25	0	1	53	2	2.56
Spicer, Little Falls*	14	14	0	0	10	3	0	.769	94	73	40	33	7	63	0	3	93	7	3.16
St. John, Jamestown*	3	2	0	0	0	1	0	.000	8	7	10	10	1	10	0	0	3	1	11.25
Stefani, Oneonta	12	0	0	0	0	1	1	.000	44	40	18	14	0	21	0	0	36	6	2.86
Stelly, Little Falls*	4	0	0	0	1	0	1	1.000	7	2	2	0	0	4	0	0	9	1	0.00
Stibora, Batavia*	2	0	0	0	0	0	0	.000	2	7	2	2	0	4	0	0	1	1	3.60
Strother, Auburn	5	1	0	0	0	0	0	.000	13	13	10	7	0	8	0	0	6	0	4.85
Sullivan, Auburn	1	0	0	0	0	0	0	.000	1	3	4	4	1	1	0	1	0	0	36.00
Sunderlage, L Falls*	14	1	0	0	3	1	1	.750	40	38	26	19	5	17	0	0	29	2	4.28
Swaggerty, Geneva	14	14	3	0	5	4	0	.556	86	90	50	47	14	26	0	3	37	3	4.92
Taylor, Jamestown*	6	6	2	0	2	1	0	.667	40	30	17	15	1	25	1	0	42	3	3.38
Thompson, Batavia	7	0	0	0	0	0	0	.000	18	12	13	3	1	0	6	0	2	16	2	0.75
Tillett, Auburn*	7	2	1	0	1	0	0	1.000	18	12	3	1	0	6	0	2	16	2	0.75
Torres, Jamestown	7	7	3	0	3	4	0	.429	45	67	30	26	4	18	0	1	20	3	5.20
Turner, Little Falls*	6	0	0	0	0	0	0	.000	16	16	10	8	2	12	0	0	6	2	6.55
Valdez, Utica	10	0	0	0	0	0	1	.000	10	18	18	12	2	9	0	0	2	1	10.80
Valdez, Auburn	12	12	4	1	5	3	0	.625	81	64	37	30	8	38	0	4	55	5	3.33
Weinbrecht, Elmira*	16	9	0	0	1	5	3	.167	43	45	43	32	2	37	3	5	48	3	6.70
Westray, Jamestown*	16	7	0	0	2	7	0	.222	47	55	42	36	1	36	1	3	45	5	6.89
White, Utica	15	8	2	0	3	4	0	.429	65	74	50	37	11	37	1	0	42	1	5.12
Zwolinski, Little Falls*	14	2	0	0	1	2	1	.333	28	31	32	28	3	23	0	2	16	7	9.00

BALKS—Hollowell, 3; Bajus, Cerrud, Gonzalez, 2 each; Burns, Cartwright, Cote, Dixon, Feliciano, Gebin, M. Johnson, Kolodny, LaFranco, Leal, Lefferts, Lintz, Nichols, Taylor, 1 each.

COMBINATION SHUTOUTS—Garrett-Sandling, Elmira; Lefferts-Pryce, Smith-Miglio, Lefferts-Roerden, Geneva; Rech-Bittiger, Johnson-Replogle, Little Falls; Foster-Fauland, Scott-Fauland, Oneonta.

NO-HIT GAMES—None.

Northwest League

CLASS A

CHAMPIONSHIP WINNERS IN PREVIOUS YEARS

1901—Portland .... .675	1940—Spokane.................... .587	1962—Wenatchee*.................. .574
1902—Butte........................... .608	Tacoma (4th)†............ .500	Tri-City .... .580
1903—Butte........................... .578	1941—Spokane.................... .669	1963—Lewiston................... .594
1904—Boise........................... .625	1942—Vancouver .... .594	Yakima*...................... .613
1905—Vancouver .... .586	1943-45—Did not operate.	1964—Eugene .... .636
Everett*................. .667	1946—Wenatchee................ .622	Yakima*...................... .611
1906—Tacoma...................... .600	1947—Vancouver .... .566	1965—Lewiston................... .667
1907—Aberdeen................... .625	1948—Spokane.................... .614	Tri-City* .... .681
1908—Vancouver .... .578	1949—Yakima..................... .660	1966—Tri-City.................... .679
1909—Seattle....................... .653	Vancouver (2nd)†........ .615	1967—Medford................... .607
1910—Spokane..................... .596	1950—Yakima..................... .613	1968—Tri-City.................... .600
1911—Vancouver .... .628	1951—Spokane.................... .655	1969—Rogue Valley............ .633
1912—Seattle....................... .600	1952—Victoria.................... .631	1970—Lewiston a............... .538
1913—Vancouver .... .600	1953—Salem....................... .635	Coos Bay-No. Bend ...... .563
1914—Vancouver .... .632	Spokane*.................. .590	1971—Tri-City a .... .625
1915—Seattle....................... .564	1954—Vancouver *............. .636	Bend .... .538
1916—Spokane..................... .622	Lewiston.................. .629	1972—Lewiston a............... .675
1917—Great Falls .... .592	1955—Salem....................... .646	Walla Walla .... .513
1918—Seattle....................... .588	Eugene*..................... .639	1973—Walla Walla b......... .638
1919—Seattle....................... .590	1956—Yakima..................... .691	Portland .... .563
1920—Victoria..................... .600	Yakima .... .619	1974—Bellingham .... .619
1921—Yakima...................... .710	1957—Eugene .... .576	Eugene c.................. .571
Yakima.................. .660	Wenatchee*............... .647	1975—Portland .... .545
1922—Calgary§................... .600	1958—Lewiston................... .621	Eugene d.................. .684
1923-36—Did not operate.	Yakima*...................... .594	1976—Portland .... .556
1937—Wenatchee................ .603	1959—Salem....................... .623	Walla Walla d............ .639
Tacoma*.................. .627	Yakima*...................... .563	1977—Bellingham e............ .618
1938—Yakima...................... .583	1960—Yakima‡.................... .638	Portland .... .667
Bellingham (2nd)†.... .511	Yakima .... .562	1978—Grays Harbor f......... .671
1939—Wenatchee................ .601	1961—Lewiston*................. .621	Eugene .... .514
Tacoma (2nd)†........... .533	Yakima .... .600	1979—Central Oregon d .... .606
		Walla Walla .... .571

*Won split-season playoff. †Won four-club playoff. §League disbanded June 18. aLeague divided into Northern and Southern divisions, declared champion under league rules. (NOTE—Known as Pacific Northwest League 1901-02, Pacific National League 1903-04, Northwestern League 1905-18, Pacific Coast International League 1919-22 and Western International League 1937-54.) bLeague divided into Eastern and Western divisions, declared champion under league rules. cLeague divided into Eastern and Western divisions; won two-team playoff. dLeague divided into Northern and Southern divisions; won two-team playoff. eLeague divided into Affiliate and Independent divisions; won two-team playoff. fDeclared league champion after winning one-game playoff. Balance of playoff canceled due to rain and wet grounds.

STANDING OF CLUBS AT CLOSE OF SEASON, AUGUST 29

NORTHERN DIVISION

Club	Bell.	Vic.	W.W.	G.H.	Eug.	Sal.	C.O.	Med.	W.	L.	T.	Pct.	G.B.
Bellingham (Mariners)	...	4	6	8	7	6	5	9	45	25	0	.643	......
Victoria (Independent)................	6	...	4	7	6	6	7	6	42	28	0	.600	3
Walla Walla (Padres)	4	6	...	5	3	3	6	8	35	34	1	.507	9½
Grays Harbor (Mets)	2	3	4	...	4	6	4	6	33	36	0	.478	11½

SOUTHERN DIVISION

Eugene (Reds)	3	4	7	4	...	6	7	6	37	33	1	.529	......
Salem (Independent)	4	4	7	6	4	...	5	4	34	36	0	.486	3
Central Oregon (Phillies)	5	3	4	4	3	5	...	7	31	39	0	.443	6
Medford (A's)	1	4	2	2	4	6	3	...	22	48	0	.314	15

Central Oregon represented Bend, Ore.

Grays Harbor represented Aberdeen and Hoquiam, Wash.

Major league affiliations in parentheses.

Playoff—Bellingham and Eugene declared co-champions after winning one game apiece. Balance of playoff schedule canceled due to rain and wet ground.

Regular-Season Attendance—Bellingham, 42,292; Bend, 28,486; Eugene, 96,058; Grays Harbor, 20,020; Medford, 27,118; Salem, 35,268; Victoria, 11,127; Walla Walla, 15,118. Total, 275,487. Playoffs, 3,947. No all-star game.

Managers: Bellingham—Jeff Scott; Central Oregon—P. J. Carey; Eugene—Greg Riddoch; Grays Harbor—Bill Bryk; Medford—Bradley Fischer; Salem—Randolph Lamb; Victoria—Jim Gaddes; Walla Walla—Curt Daniels.

All-Star Team: 1B—McAbee, Medford; 2B—Samuel, Central Oregon; Serna, Bellingham; 3B—McGann, Bellingham; SS—Murphy, Victoria; OF—Little, Eugene; Perez, Walla Walla; Pratt, Eugene; C—Willard, Central Oregon; DH—Darkis, Central Oregon; P—Couchee, Grays Harbor; Johnson, Central Oregon; Klacza, Victoria; Stottlemyre, Bellingham; Vandeberg, Bellingham; Manager—Scott, Bellingham.

(Compiled by William J. Weiss, League Statistician, San Mateo, Calif.)

CLUB BATTING

Club	G.	AB.	R.	OR.	H.	TB.	2B.	3B.	HR.	RBI.	SH.	SF.	BB.	Int. BB.	HP.	SO.	SB.	CS.	LOB.	Pct.
Victoria	70	2315	445	391	650	900	122	19	30	365	18	35	414	10	24	281	128	54	570	.281
Bellingham	70	2388	451	335	667	945	99	25	43	386	29	25	349	9	18	354	81	32	538	.279
Eugene	71	2390	448	410	667	974	91	39	46	388	27	33	361	11	25	507	140	35	585	.279
Cent. Oregon	70	2440	418	436	652	1035	107	24	76	373	8	9	278	2	25	616	105	45	502	.267
Grays Harbor	69	2245	388	377	596	853	81	28	40	322	13	33	378	5	20	423	113	35	547	.265
Salem	70	2396	410	442	633	842	91	26	22	343	36	31	388	13	27	421	80	27	621	.264
Walla Walla	70	2385	407	435	629	912	93	23	48	358	25	22	391	21	34	397	54	35	569	.264
Medford	70	2301	377	518	582	829	110	10	39	322	37	27	370	5	23	356	98	46	535	.253

INDIVIDUAL BATTING

(Leading Qualifiers for Batting Championship—189 or More Plate Appearances)

*Bats lefthanded.   †Switch-hitter.

Player and Club	G.	AB.	R.	H.	TB.	2B.	3B.	HR.	RBI.	SH.	SF.	BB.	HP.	SO.	SB.	CS.	Pct.
Perez, George, Walla Walla*	63	247	46	93	129	12	6	4	35	3	0	38	3	40	11	5	.377
Pratt, Crestwell, Eugene	66	250	64	92	142	10	8	8	64	0	3	36	4	41	7	3	.368
Willard, Gerald, Cent Oregon*	65	231	53	85	123	21	1	5	59	2	3	51	2	27	2	2	.368
Scherger, Joseph, Grays Harbor	65	233	45	79	136	20	5	9	60	1	4	41	2	33	1	1	.339
Cain, Aaron, Grays Harbor	68	253	69	85	120	9	4	6	33	0	1	59	2	27	43	7	.336
Hyman, Donald, Eugene	66	233	48	78	122	27	1	5	48	0	2	26	6	24	4	4	.335
Hall, David, Eugene	60	214	38	71	112	11	6	6	51	1	4	40	1	33	12	2	.332
Serna, Paul, Bellingham	59	240	44	78	107	13	2	4	35	2	2	12	1	19	8	4	.325
Hinds, Kevin, Eugene	67	245	65	79	116	12	8	4	33	2	1	56	7	31	30	3	.322
Darkis, William, Cent Oregon	63	252	45	81	173	9	4	25	73	0	0	23	2	74	1	4	.321

Departmental Leaders: G—Little, 71; AB—Samuel, 298; R—Cain, 69; H—Perez, 93; TB—Darkis, 173; 2B—Hyman, 27; 3B—Calderon, 9; HR—Darkis, 25; RBI—Darkis, 73; GWRBI—Diaz, 9; SH—Crist, 10; SF—Gattis, 12; BB—Murphy, 73; HP—Thomas, 9; SO—Samuel, 87; SB—Cain, 43; CS—Samuel, 10.

(All Players—Listed Alphabetically)

Player and Club	G.	AB.	R.	H.	TB.	2B.	3B.	HR.	RBI.	SH.	SF.	BB.	HP.	SO.	SB.	CS.	Pct.
Adams, Norman, Eugene*	19	7	0	1	1	0	0	0	3	0	4	0	3	0	0	0	.143
Alderman, David, Salem	47	161	22	38	47	7	1	0	16	1	3	14	3	37	0	1	.236
Altobelli, Michael, Medford	36	101	18	24	34	4	3	0	9	1	2	13	0	4	4	5	.238
Arche, Richard, Victoria†	32	91	15	22	23	1	0	0	9	2	0	11	2	6	1	3	.242
Ayers, Jeffrey, Eugene	21	10	2	3	3	0	0	0	1	0	0	2	0	3	0	0	.300
Baugh, D. Dean, Cent. Oregon	13	47	7	11	16	2	0	1	7	0	0	4	0	3	2	3	.234
Bellamy, Rodney, Walla Walla	69	269	47	64	80	11	1	1	23	4	1	34	1	28	4	5	.238
Belmonte, Nicholas, Victoria	31	116	19	35	41	6	0	0	15	0	1	15	1	14	14	3	.302
Bertalot, Michael, Walla Walla*	51	194	23	45	63	8	2	2	24	2	3	10	2	14	2	4	.232
Blake, Angelo, Medford	62	196	43	48	70	14	1	2	29	6	1	59	0	34	12	5	.245
Blanche, Amos, Medford*	4	10	3	3	6	1	1	0	2	0	0	1	1	0	0	0	.300
Bloodsaw, Bobby, Salem†	25	78	10	15	18	3	0	0	7	1	0	10	0	18	6	1	.192
Blume, David, Bellingham*	49	159	29	46	72	8	3	4	32	0	2	41	1	17	1	0	.289
Burnett, Oscar, Medford	22	42	6	7	8	1	0	0	3	0	0	6	1	11	0	1	.167
Cain, Aaron, Grays Harbor	68	253	69	85	120	9	4	6	33	0	1	59	2	27	43	7	.336
Calderon, Ivan, Bellingham	57	195	44	62	99	7	9	4	32	0	3	15	1	41	7	2	.318
Calise, Daniel, Salem	27	82	4	20	23	1	1	0	10	1	0	7	0	14	0	0	.244
Cannon, Timothy, Grays Harbor†	52	149	21	29	40	0	4	1	6	0	1	30	0	49	10	4	.195
Casey, Patrick, Walla Walla	52	171	34	42	69	9	6	2	28	0	2	44	2	40	4	2	.246
Castro, Edgar, Grays Harbor*	52	148	18	28	34	6	0	0	20	4	5	38	2	30	1	0	.189
Christianson, David, W Walla*	48	158	26	36	72	4	1	10	37	0	4	37	0	43	0	0	.228
Coles, Darnell, Bellingham	35	117	23	25	36	3	1	2	12	2	1	22	1	24	1	3	.214
Crist, Clark, Bellingham	54	186	33	45	46	1	0	0	25	10	3	25	2	16	15	4	.242
Crone, William, Bellingham†	22	90	17	20	21	1	0	0	18	0	1	17	0	8	2	0	.222
Darkis, William, Cent Oregon	63	252	45	81	173	9	4	25	73	0	0	23	2	74	1	4	.321
Davis, Eric, Eugene	33	73	12	16	20	1	0	1	11	0	0	14	0	26	10	1	.219
Davis, Gerald, Walla Walla	54	197	39	60	90	4	1	8	50	0	3	46	3	26	5	2	.305
Diaz, Enrique, Bellingham	64	247	44	76	113	17	1	6	47	0	1	33	1	42	6	5	.308
Douglas, Lester, Salem*	56	165	20	49	63	11	0	1	34	3	4	33	2	32	2	0	.297
Ellenberg, K. Wayne, C Oregon	57	201	32	64	78	6	0	2	24	1	1	26	3	33	9	2	.318
Feliz, Rodolfo, Eugene	26	78	12	15	19	4	0	0	4	0	0	12	0	18	2	0	.192
Ferguson, Michael, Eugene	20	4	0	0	0	0	0	0	0	0	0	0	0	3	0	0	.000

Player and Club	G.	AB	R	H	TB	2B	3B	HR	RBI	SH	SF	BB	HP	SO	SB	CS	Pct.
Firova, Daniel, Bellingham	63	218	33	44	59	6	3	1	31	4	1	34	1	35	5	7	.202
Fitz, Timothy, Salem*	21	2	0	0	0	0	0	0	0	1	0	0	0	1	0	0	.000
Fonseca, C. David, Victoria	20	60	8	12	15	1	1	0	4	1	0	5	1	10	0	2	.200
Freeburg, Larry, Eugene	17	8	1	1	1	0	0	0	0	0	0	2	0	1	0	0	.125
Gattis, James, Victoria	62	223	41	68	102	15	2	5	43	2	12	16	1	13	6	3	.305
Geren, Robert, Walla Walla	51	177	19	45	61	8	1	2	28	5	1	24	1	33	0	1	.254
Gomez, Jose, Grays Harbor*	28	55	9	13	16	1	1	0	7	0	0	13	1	20	1	0	.236
Gonzalez, Robinson, Central Ore.	11	17	5	6	6	0	0	0	3	0	0	4	0	5	1	2	.353
Goodman, Kenneth, Victoria†	24	65	10	14	16	0	1	0	6	1	1	11	1	8	5	0	.215
Greb, Jay, Medford	37	131	14	33	41	5	0	1	18	4	2	21	1	31	3	2	.252
Guzman, Ruben, Eugene	41	134	23	37	54	2	3	3	21	0	3	15	5	35	5	3	.276
Hall, David, Eugene	60	214	38	71	112	11	6	6	51	1	4	40	1	33	12	2	.332
Hanson, Michael, Central Oregon	52	198	28	56	81	6	5	3	28	1	0	16	1	34	3	3	.283
Harper, Therron, Medford	64	223	33	63	84	9	0	4	38	1	3	34	1	21	4	2	.283
Harry, Whitney, Central Oregon	67	236	31	49	84	12	4	5	26	0	1	32	4	77	3	3	.208
Henley, William, Walla Walla*	23	36	4	5	5	0	0	0	1	0	0	5	0	6	0	2	.139
Hinds, Kevin, Eugene	67	245	65	79	116	12	8	3	33	2	1	56	7	31	30	3	.322
Hines, Bruce, Grays Harbor†	46	113	23	26	29	3	0	0	10	0	1	21	1	37	7	3	.230
Hinshaw, George, Walla Walla	63	230	46	66	93	10	4	3	29	1	1	33	2	43	12	4	.287
Humpston, Garry, Victoria†	41	136	25	36	48	8	1	6	22	0	0	26	2	26	3	1	.265
Hyman, Donald, Victoria	66	233	48	78	122	27	1	5	48	0	2	26	6	24	4	4	.335
Ireland, Billy, Grays Harbor	51	159	24	52	57	5	0	0	23	2	5	16	1	11	4	4	.327
Job, Scott, Medford	22	46	7	6	7	1	0	0	2	1	0	5	0	15	0	2	.130
Johnson, Daniel, Salem	70	285	56	82	146	12	8	12	62	1	3	33	1	72	5	0	.288
Johnson, Donald, Bellingham*	20	49	10	17	21	1	0	1	6	0	0	14	1	7	3	2	.347
Johnson, Kenneth, Medford	12	36	4	3	4	1	0	0	1	0	0	8	0	15	1	1	.083
Johnson, Steven, Grays Harbor	60	200	27	45	53	5	0	1	21	2	3	19	4	46	10	5	.225
Jones, Kenneth, Eugene	15	20	0	4	4	0	0	0	1	1	1	1	0	6	0	0	.200
Jones, Russell, Eugene	69	217	48	53	69	6	2	2	24	0	4	43	0	60	30	9	.244
Kepshire, Kurt, Eugene*	8	13	3	2	2	0	0	0	2	2	0	5	0	5	0	0	.154
King, J. Clay, Salem†	51	122	23	23	23	0	0	0	7	3	0	21	2	18	8	2	.189
Kirsch, Paul, Victoria*	43	175	31	65	93	11	1	5	43	0	3	7	0	6	12	5	.371
Klacza, Kenneth, Victoria	16	2	1	0	0	0	0	0	0	0	0	0	0	1	0	0	.000
Klosicki, Daniel, Eugene	17	29	3	7	7	0	0	0	5	4	0	1	0	10	0	0	.241
Krueger, William, Medford*	17	28	1	5	9	1	0	1	2	0	0	4	0	9	0	1	.179
Lamar, Daniel, Eugene	13	43	4	16	20	1	0	1	12	1	0	7	0	7	1	0	.372
LaSala, Leo, Victoria†	4	15	0	4	5	1	0	0	3	0	0	0	0	14	0	8	.267
Litchfield, Thomas, Victoria*	16	24	4	1	1	0	0	0	1	0	0	8	1	1	0	0	.042
Little, Ronald, Eugene	71	292	57	91	141	10	5	10	54	3	10	22	2	59	14	7	.312
Lorenz, Joe, Victoria	70	239	52	63	85	10	3	2	40	0	6	71	0	28	9	7	.264
Maggio, Douglas, Central Oregon	24	78	2	17	19	2	0	0	3	1	1	4	0	16	0	1	.218
Majam, Rosben, Salem†	55	174	37	43	60	9	4	0	24	3	3	50	0	32	11	3	.247
Marino, Thomas, Eugene	3	3	0	0	0	0	0	0	0	0	0	1	0	1	0	0	.000
Martin, William, Medford	18	60	8	11	16	2	0	1	5	1	0	4	0	22	0	0	.183
Mauch, Harry, Medford†	33	73	8	12	13	1	0	0	4	0	1	14	1	20	5	2	.164
Maynard, Ronny, Eugene	7	5	1	2	2	0	0	0	0	0	0	3	0	3	0	0	.400
McAbee, Monte, Medford*	70	242	45	72	121	10	0	13	58	3	3	49	5	36	4	4	.298
McGann, Kevin, Bellingham	62	219	43	66	90	10	1	4	32	1	3	44	1	23	6	2	.301
McNealy, Robert, Bellingham*	18	65	12	20	22	2	0	0	7	2	0	10	0	13	5	0	.308
Metil, William, Eugene*	48	171	27	51	59	4	2	0	20	1	0	21	0	14	18	4	.298
Mobberley, Steven, Grays Harbor*	26	84	23	30	38	3	1	1	12	0	0	20	2	7	10	3	.357
Moore, Jesse, Victoria	24	75	12	15	25	4	0	2	13	0	1	7	2	24	3	1	.200
Moses, John, Bellingham†	60	227	55	60	75	5	2	2	32	5	6	46	2	31	16	2	.264
Moss, Barry, Victoria†	58	221	42	68	86	10	1	2	29	4	3	35	2	27	16	8	.308
Mulholland, Kevin, Eugene*	11	1	0	0	0	0	0	0	0	0	0	0	0	0	0	0	.000
Murphy, Roderick, Victoria	69	225	47	58	70	7	1	1	26	4	1	73	2	30	24	4	.258
Murray, Steven, Walla Walla	55	176	41	38	55	5	3	2	27	3	2	46	6	48	9	4	.216
Musick, Craig, Central Oregon	23	65	6	9	10	1	0	0	3	0	0	10	0	22	3	0	.138
Nate, Jeffrey, Central Oregon	5	12	1	3	3	0	0	0	1	0	0	3	0	3	0	2	.250
Nigro, Anthony, Victoria	23	0	0	0	0	0	0	0	1	0	0	1	0	0	0	0	.000
O'Connor, Robert, Salem*	62	216	39	66	72	4	1	0	36	7	2	36	1	19	2	1	.306
Otto, Michael, Victoria	14	1	0	0	0	0	0	0	0	0	0	0	0	1	0	0	.000
Parent, Mark, Grays Harbor	66	239	29	55	91	11	2	7	32	2	6	17	0	30	1	0	.230
Perez, George, Walla Walla*	63	247	46	93	129	12	6	4	35	3	0	38	3	40	11	5	.377
Perone, Richard, Salem	1	1	0	0	0	0	0	0	0	0	0	0	0	0	0	0	.000
Pierce, Don, Bellingham†	37	88	15	22	29	5	1	0	12	3	0	11	0	20	4	1	.250
Pignotti, John, Medford	18	54	8	14	18	4	0	0	7	3	1	8	0	6	0	1	.259
Pratt, Crestwell, Eugene	66	250	64	92	142	10	8	8	64	0	3	36	4	41	7	3	.368
Purcell, Trent, Central Oregon*	39	122	15	21	32	3	1	2	17	1	0	25	0	34	2	2	.172
Pyle, John, Salem	66	264	44	83	115	8	6	4	43	1	4	33	2	38	12	4	.314
Quinones, Luis, Grays Harbor†	56	156	33	35	41	2	2	0	11	2	1	30	0	24	13	3	.224
Reynolds, L. Alfredo, Central Ore.	56	213	29	54	78	8	2	4	29	2	0	8	1	58	13	4	.254
Rogers, Dan, Victoria		0	0	0	0	0	0	0	0	0	0	0	0	0	0	0	.000
Rollins, Rip, Central Oregon	63	221	44	48	98	12	1	12	40	0	1	35	4	80	5	2	.217
Rothey, Mark, Eugene*	20	9	3	2	2	0	0	0	0	0	0	2	0	2	1	0	.222
Rudolph, Wayne, Medford†	63	257	55	73	87	14	0	0	25	8	2	34	0	17	41	7	.284

Player and Club	G.	AB.	R.	H.	TB.	2B.	3B.	HR.	RBI.	SH.	SF.	BB.	HP.	SO.	SB.	CS.	Pct.
Russell, Jeffrey, Eugene	17	34	6	6	9	3	0	0	1	1	0	4	0	10	0	0	.176
Rutan, Kenneth, Salem	39	89	16	16	20	4	0	0	12	3	1	14	0	19	9	1	.180
Salcido, Ted, Salem	34	110	12	24	27	1	1	0	10	0	2	12	1	29	5	4	.218
Samuel, Juan, Central Oregon	69	298	66	84	150	11	2	17	44	0	2	17	0	87	26	10	.282
Scherger, Joseph, Greys Harbor	65	233	45	79	136	20	5	9	60	1	4	41	2	33	1	1	.339
Seefried, John, Salem	67	243	49	73	108	16	2	5	46	0	6	58	4	32	2	1	.300
Serna, Paul, Bellingham	59	240	44	78	107	13	2	4	35	2	2	12	1	19	8	4	.325
Severns, Sean, Eugene	52	158	23	34	54	8	0	4	31	1	3	32	1	41	1	2	.215
Slavenski, C. Michael, Medford	32	77	13	15	18	3	0	0	6	1	1	18	4	11	8	3	.195
Soprano, Joseph, Medford	42	146	26	48	81	10	1	7	27	3	2	24	2	18	4	2	.329
Sorel, Michael, Eugene	40	147	22	34	46	9	0	1	15	2	0	14	2	25	3	1	.231
Stamper, Timothy, Eugene	15	2	0	0	0	0	0	0	0	0	0	1	0	0	0	0	.000
Stevens, Paul, Victoria†	50	177	41	48	74	12	4	2	32	3	3	49	1	16	11	7	.271
Stone, Jeffery, Central Oregon*	55	241	52	63	83	12	4	0	19	0	0	14	8	59	32	5	.261
Stowe, Dennis, Medford*	55	183	20	47	63	7	0	3	23	1	0	16	2	24	4	2	.257
Styons, Raymond, Grays Harbor	66	223	35	63	114	8	5	11	46	0	4	51	4	50	6	1	.283
Thomas, Jimmy, Walla Walla	59	195	31	59	92	6	3	7	40	1	3	43	9	30	1	3	.303
Tipton, Jeffery, Medford	53	166	20	35	54	7	3	2	30	1	5	24	1	37	1	3	.211
Tirado, Julio, Eugene*	13	36	7	9	12	0	0	1	6	0	0	3	0	12	0	0	.250
Uhey, Jackie, Victoria†	22	30	5	7	8	1	0	0	6	0	0	3	2	8	0	0	.233
Valdez, Angel, Walla Walla	33	100	4	18	20	2	0	0	8	4	0	2	0	15	4	0	.180
VandeBerg, Edward, Bellingham	14	3	0	0	0	0	0	0	0	0	0	0	0	3	0	0	.000
VanGytenbeek, J. Anthony, Salem	42	87	13	16	17	1	0	0	5	3	1	9	1	21	2	1	.184
Vestal, Johnny, Salem	66	255	57	70	86	12	2	0	24	8	2	52	4	31	16	8	.275
Walker, M. Glen, Bellingham	70	285	49	86	155	20	2	15	65	0	2	25	6	55	2	0	.302
Washington, Lozando, Victoria	57	204	44	55	69	8	0	2	24	1	2	40	1	29	17	6	.270
Weirum, Robert, Medford	47	177	33	48	69	13	1	2	23	3	3	18	3	21	3	3	.271
Weis, David, Victoria	17	2	0	1	1	0	0	0	0	0	0	1	0	1	0	0	.500
Wenzel, Lee Roy, Eugene	49	144	22	35	72	9	5	6	31	2	3	16	2	50	1	0	.243
Wilkerson, Harvey, Salem	22	62	7	15	17	2	0	0	7	0	0	5	8	0	0		.242
Willard, Gerald, Central Oregon*	65	231	53	85	123	21	1	5	59	2	3	51	2	27	2	2	.368
Williams, Joseph, Medford	15	53	12	15	26	2	0	3	10	0	1	10	1	4	4	1	.283
Williams, Raymond, Eugene†	14	43	5	6	7	1	0	0	1	0	1	3	1	10	0	0	.140
Witt, Richard, Walla Walla	42	154	37	45	67	11	1	3	23	1	2	24	3	17	1	2	.292
Wodrich, Daniel, Walla Walla	23	79	10	13	16	3	0	0	5	0	0	5	2	13	1	1	.165
Wood, Joseph, Grays Harbor*	60	233	32	56	84	8	4	4	41	0	2	23	1	59	6	4	.240
Ysambert, Sergio, Central Oregon	3	8	2	1	1	0	0	0	0	0	0	2	0	3	2	0	.125
Zerilla, James, Walla Walla*	1	2	0	0	0	0	0	0	0	0	0	0	0	1	0	0	.000

The following pitchers had no plate appearances primarily through the use of designated hitters, listed alphabetically by club, games in parentheses):

BELLINGHAM—Christiansen, John (18); Davila, Carlos (11); Hunger, Christopher (2); Krueger, Steve* (4); Mathews, Jon (9); McKenzie, Donald (9); Pederson, Mark (20); Salva, Elias (17); Stottlemyre, Jeffrey* (12); Verbon, Mark (19); Young, Matthew* (12).

CENTRAL OREGON—Acevedo, Julio (14); Barnett, Robert (12); Bennett, Herbert (8); Conti, Adam (6); Darnell, Jimmy (12); Dorin, Matthew (17); Drew, Dale (15); Johnson, William (27); Martinez, Randy* (23); Richardson, Ronald (13); Schiavo, Edward (14); Thoel, Ronald (11); Tillman, Rufus (16).

GRAYS HARBOR—Britt, Michael (15); Brokop, Thomas (11); Conroy, Steven* (15); Couchee, Michael (24); Duffy, Brian* (14); Figueroa, Ismael* (5); Hays, John (1); Krzanik, Andrew (6); Lovekamp, Scott (14); Rios, Hector (19); Stone, Steven (12).

MEDFORD—Arnold, Ricky (16); Bulleri, John (30); Carroll, Timothy* (8); Glass, Gregory (15); Horner, John* (5); Marlow, Stephen (4); Puckett, Brian (10); Schauer, Randall (17); Slattery, Peter (11); Soderman, John (11); Tolli, William (16); Vorisek, Robert* (13).

SALEM—Adams, Mark (3); Alexander, Roberto (9); Brown, Dale (15); Bullock, Kenneth (10); Gabriel, Michael* (3); Garcia, Richard (20); Lamb, Randolph† (8); Leyerle, Marc* (12); McLaughlin, Michael (28); Runyan, Mark (6); Saylor, Allen (4); Stearns, Anthony (14); White, Robert (14).

VICTORIA—Arrieta, Albert (15); Butler, S. Robert (10); Goff, James (2); Liber, Mark* (18); Peterson, Brian (3); Scott, Michael* (6); Snider, J. Eric (10); Vaulman, Paul† (11); Zeuch, Timothy (2).

WALLA WALLA—Blamey, Patrick (9); Bryant, R. Neil (13); Coffman, James (26); Collet, Jose (6); Daniels, Curtis† (11); Gerhardt, William (8); Kirk, David (2); Mahoski, Michael (17); Patton, Gregory (14); Smith, Michael† (20); White, John (14); Wilson, Philip (14).

GRAND-SLAM HOME RUNS—Casey, Hinshaw, Humpston, Pyle, Rollins, Walker, Willard, 1 each.

AWARDED FIRST BASE ON INTERFERENCE—Vestal 3 (Geren, Willard, Witt); Severns 2 (Geren, Willard); Blume (Tipton); Harry (Alderman); Ireland (Maggio); Majam (Lamar); Wilkerson (Willard).

GAME-WINNING RBIs

BELLINGHAM (31)—Diaz 9, Walker 4, Blume 3, Firova 3, Serna 3, Crist 2, Crone 2, McGann 2, Calderon 1, Coles 1, Johnson 1.

CENTRAL OREGON (29)—Darkis 8, Willard 7, Hanson 4, Reynolds 3, Samuel 2, Stone 2, Baugh 1, Harry 1, Purcell 1.

EUGENE (32)—Little 5, Pratt 5, R. Jones 4, Hall 3, Lamar 3, Hinds 2, Severns 2, Sorel 2, Wenzel 2, Ayers 1, Davis 1, Feliz 1, Guzman 1.

GRAYS HARBOR (22)—Scherger 7, Johnson 3, Styons 3, Parent 2, Cain 1, Cannon 1, Castro 1, Hines 1, Ireland 1, Quinones 1, Wood 1.

MEDFORD (17)—Blake 3, Tipton 3, Harper 2, Rudolph 2, Weirum 2, Greb 1, Martin 1, Soprano 1, Stowe 1, Williams 1.

SALEM (33)—O'Connor 7, Pyle 5, Seefried 4, Douglas 3, Johnson 3, Vestal 3, King 2, Majam 2, Salcido 2, Alderman 1, Calise 1.

VICTORIA (33)—Gattis 8, Hyman 5, Lorenz 4, Kirsch 3, Goodman 2, Humpston 2, Moss 2, Murphy 2, Arche 1, Belmonte 1, Stevens 1, Uhey 1, Washington 1.

WALLA WALLA (31)—Bellamy 6, Bertalot 4, Davis 4, Murray 3, Perez 3, Thomas 3, Casey 2, Hinshaw 2, Christianson 1, Geren 1, Witt 1, Wodrich 1.

CLUB FIELDING

Club	G.	PO.	A.	E.	DP.	PB.	Pct.	Club	G.	PO.	A.	E.	DP.	PB.	Pct.
Bellingham	70	1849	926	120	102	23	.959	Walla Walla	70	1878	768	151	57	28	.946
Victoria	70	1807	734	115	42	15	.957	Grays Harbor	69	1749	746	148	71	28	.944
Salem	70	1852	781	120	57	47	.956	Central Oregon	70	1835	758	161	59	30	.942
Eugene	71	1810	643	138	54	36	.947	Medford	70	1812	732	192	51	25	.930

Triple Plays—None.

INDIVIDUAL FIELDING

FIRST BASEMEN

*Throws lefthanded.

Player and Club	G.	PO.	A.	E.	DP.	Pct.	Player and Club	G.	PO.	A.	E.	DP.	Pct.
O'Connor, Salem	16	154	7	0	10	1.000	Witt, Walla Walla	24	223	9	4	13	.983
Kirsch, Victoria*	17	126	5	0	5	1.000	McAbee, Medford*	63	496	31	10	31	.981
DIAZ, Bellingham	61	593	35	4	75	.994	Castro, G Harbor*	49	400	15	8	48	.981
Humpston, Vic*	34	309	18	3	21	.991	Pyle, Salem	51	404	34	9	36	.980
Wenzel, Eugene	36	223	18	3	21	.988	Harry, Cent Oregon	65	591	33	15	51	.977
Tirado, Eugene*	10	72	3	1	4	.987	Parent, G Harbor	16	114	9	3	12	.976
Christianson, WW*	38	271	17	4	28	.986	Thomas, W Walla	11	95	6	3	8	.971
Moss, Victoria	15	129	6	2	9	.985	R. Jones, Eugene	32	269	9	10	26	.965

(Fewer Than Ten Games)

Player and Club	G.	PO.	A.	E.	DP.	Pct.	Player and Club	G.	PO.	A.	E.	DP.	Pct.
Rutan, Salem	6	47	4	0	4	1.000	D. Johnson, Bell*	8	45	2	1	5	.979
Lorenz, Victoria	4	30	1	0	0	1.000	Rollins, Cent Oregon	5	39	3	1	2	.977
Gattis, Victoria	3	21	2	0	3	1.000	Soprano, Medford	6	35	0	1	2	.972
Geren, Walla Walla	3	13	1	0	0	1.000	Styons, G Harbor	8	68	5	3	6	.961
Ireland, G Harbor	2	11	1	0	1	1.000	W. Krueger, Med*	2	18	2	1	2	.952
Belmonte, Victoria	2	10	1	0	0	1.000	J. Williams, Med	2	15	0	2	4	.882
Stowe, Medford	1	3	1	0	1	1.000	Goodman, Victoria*	2	10	0	2	1	.833
Blume, Bellingham	5	55	0	1	8	.982							

SECOND BASEMEN

Player and Club	G.	PO.	A.	E.	DP.	Pct.	Player and Club	G.	PO.	A.	E.	DP.	Pct.
Lorenz, Victoria	25	41	62	2	14	.981	Crist, Bellingham	10	27	23	3	8	.943
SERNA, Bellingham	57	180	193	8	71	.979	Mauch, Medicine Hat	12	26	23	3	6	.942
Vestal, Salem	66	192	197	9	37	.977	Hines, Grays Harbor	43	59	82	9	16	.940
Wodrich, W Walla	23	67	58	3	12	.977	Fonseca, Victoria	16	42	33	5	6	.938
Arche, Victoria	24	40	37	3	8	.963	Valdez, Walla Walla	30	61	73	9	14	.937
Bellamy, W Walla	65	121	168	16	35	.948	Blake, Medford	39	87	90	15	14	.922
Hinds, Eugene	23	54	68	7	18	.946	Samuel, Cent Oregon	66	162	188	30	38	.921
Mobberley, G Harbor	23	54	30	5	12	.943	Slavenski, Medford	25	72	53	15	14	.893
Cain, Grays Harbor	19	52	30	5	12	.943							

(Fewer Than Ten Games)

Player and Club	G.	PO.	A.	E.	DP.	Pct.	Player and Club	G.	PO.	A.	E.	DP.	Pct.
Walker, Bellingham	3	6	3	0	0	1.000	Gonzalez, Cent Oregon	8	7	9	1	1	.941
Moss, Victoria	3	4	4	0	1	1.000	Majam, Salem	5	7	5	1	0	.923
Crone, Bellingham	2	4	4	0	1	1.000	Stevens, Victoria	8	20	15	3	1	.921
Nate, Cent Oregon	1	2	2	0	1	1.000	LaSalle, Victoria	4	12	7	3	4	.864
Bertalot, W Walla	1	2	2	0	0	1.000	E. Davis, Eugene	3	3	7	2	3	.833
Gattis, Victoria	1	2	1	0	0	1.000	Perone (Pohle), Salem	1	1	0	1	0	.500
Metil, Eugene	8	8	19	1	2	.964							

THIRD BASEMEN

Player and Club	G.	PO.	A.	E.	DP.	Pct.	Player and Club	G.	PO.	A.	E.	DP.	Pct.
McGANN, Bellingham	61	45	174	11	25	.952	Gattis, Victoria	26	23	50	11	2	.869
Hanson, Cent Oregon	37	37	81	11	6	.915	G. Davis, WW	48	42	104	24	5	.859
Lorenz, Victoria	46	37	88	12	6	.912	Hall, Eugene	37	29	44	12	3	.859
Wood, Grays Harbor	48	38	99	14	16	.907	Ireland, G Harbor	30	26	50	14	6	.844
Ellenberg, C Oregon	34	37	62	11	9	.900	Martin, Medford	17	14	24	7	2	.844
Woirum, Medford	47	35	93	15	5	.895	Metil, Eugene	29	14	37	10	2	.836
Seefried, Salem	67	73	134	25	10	.892	Thomas, W Walla	20	14	36	10	2	.833

THIRD BASEMEN—Continued

(Fewer Than Ten Games)

Player and Club	G.	PO.	A.	E.	DP.	Pct.
Feliz, Eugene	3	1	5	0	0	1.000
Sorel, Eugene	2	0	6	0	0	1.000
Wenzel, Eugene	2	0	3	0	0	1.000
Uhey, Victoria	1	1	1	0	0	1.000
Washington, Victoria	1	0	1	0	0	1.000
Rutan, Salem	7	8	12	2	1	.909
J. Williams, Medford	8	5	20	3	1	.893
Crist, Bellingham	9	11	22	4	4	.892
Witt, Walla Walla	3	4	3	1	1	.875
Blake, Medford	2	0	4	1	0	.800
Hinds, Eugene	1	1	1	1	0	.667
Hines, Grays Harbor	2	2	0	3	0	.400

SHORTSTOPS

Player and Club	G.	PO.	A.	E.	DP.	Pct.
Crone, Bellingham	18	27	45	3	13	960
BELLAMY, W Walla	49	77	133	13	27	.942
Majam, Salem	31	61	98	10	10	.941
Crist, Bellingham	28	46	100	11	24	.930
K. Johnson, Medford	12	15	36	4	4	.927
Murphy, Victoria	69	109	207	26	29	.924
Wood, Grays Harbor	21	17	52	7	8	.908
Quinones, G Harbor	56	70	157	24	33	.904
Reynolds, Cent Oregon	53	78	158	26	33	.901
Musick, Cent Oregon	15	16	46	7	6	.899
Feliz, Eugene	23	16	66	10	10	.891
King, Salem	43	32	105	17	15	.890
Sorel, Eugene	39	54	97	19	23	.888
Greb, Medford	37	60	103	24	16	.872
Blake, Medford	17	28	42	12	6	.854
E. Davis, Eugene	18	21	28	9	6	.845
Hinshaw, W Walla	27	36	62	20	9	.831
Coles, Bellingham	27	37	80	28	15	.807

(Fewer Than Ten Games)

Player and Club	G.	PO.	A.	E.	DP.	Pct.
Mobberley, G Harbor	5	4	7	0	3	1.000
Fonseca, Victoria	3	4	2	0	0	1.000
Gonzalez, Cent Oregon	3	2	1	0	0	1.000
Nate, Cent Oregon	3	5	9	2	1	.875
Rutan, Salem	9	5	13	4	3	.818
G. Davis, W Walla	2	4	1	2	1	.714
Mauch, Medford	8	5	8	9	1	.591

OUTFIELDERS

Player and Club	G.	PO.	A.	E.	DP.	Pct.
R. Jones, Eugene	35	59	2	0	1	1.000
Hall, Eugene	16	36	3	0	0	1.000
Bloodsaw, Salem	24	62	2	1	1	.985
Moss, Victoria	38	58	2	1	0	.984
Casey, Walla Walla	35	44	6	1	2	.980
VanGytenbeek, Salem	41	42	5	1	1	.979
Hinshaw, W Walla	37	79	4	2	1	.976
Bertalot, W Walla	40	76	7	2	1	.976
Purcell, Cent Oregon	38	78	3	2	2	.976
RUDOLPH, Medford*	63	137	4	4	1	.972
McNealy, Bellingham*	18	32	3	1	0	.972
Moses, Bellingham*	59	92	6	3	2	.970
Darkis, Cent Oregon	55	90	7	3	1	.970
J. Stone, C Oregon	51	116	4	4	0	.968
Walker, Bellingham	67	103	14	4	6	.967
Salcido, Salem	34	78	2	3	1	.964
Baugh, Cent Oregon	13	48	4	2	0	.963
Little, Eugene*	71	200	4	8	0	.962
Goodman, Victoria*	18	24	0	1	0	.960
Murray, W Walla	46	111	5	5	1	.959
Stowe, Medford	49	83	3	4	0	.956
Perez, W Walla	52	92	13	5	1	.955
Job, Medford	15	21	0	1	0	.955
Washington, Victoria	46	102	2	5	0	.954
Altobelli, Medford	28	55	5	3	1	.952
Scherger, G Harbor	59	111	2	6	0	.950
Stevens, Victoria	43	55	2	3	0	.950
Pratt, Eugene	64	84	6	5	0	.947
Belmonte, Victoria	30	33	3	2	0	.947
Cannon, G Harbor	47	81	7	5	0	.946
D. Johnson, Salem	70	126	7	8	1	.943
Douglas, Salem	44	48	1	3	0	.942
Kirsch, Victoria*	28	47	2	3	1	.942
Pierce, Bellingham	35	40	3	3	1	.935
Alderman, Salem	14	29	0	2	0	.935
Cain, Grays Harbor	42	53	4	4	1	.934
S. Johnson, G Harbor	57	94	4	7	1	.933
Guzman, Eugene	37	68	2	5	0	.933
Soprano, Medford	39	64	6	5	1	.933
Henley, W Walla	15	14	0	1	0	.933
Rollins, Cent Oregon	49	74	7	6	0	.931
Rutan, Salem	11	11	0	1	0	.917
Calderon, Bellingham	47	56	4	7	1	.896
Gomez, Grays Harbor*	12	10	2	2	0	.857
Burnett, Medford	22	25	2	5	1	.844
Moore, Victoria	14	19	4	5	0	.821
Mauch, Medford	11	11	2	3	1	.813

(Fewer Than Ten Games)

Player and Club	G.	PO.	A.	E.	DP.	Pct.
Ysambert, Cent Oregon	3	11	0	0	0	1.000
O'Connor, Salem	5	4	3	0	0	1.000
E. Davis, Eugene	2	5	1	0	1	1.000
Ireland, G Harbor	7	5	0	0	0	1.000
Uhey, Victoria	6	4	0	0	0	1.000
Harper, Medford	2	2	0	0	0	1.000
Rothey, Eugene*	1	1	0	0	0	1.000
McAbee, Medford*	4	7	0	1	0	.875
Musick, Cent Oregon	8	6	0	1	0	.857
Litchfield, Victoria	1	1	0	1	0	.500

CATCHERS

Player and Club	G.	PO.	A.	E.	DP.	PB.	Pct.
Blume, Bellingham	12	60	5	0	1	6	1.000
Litchfield, Vic	11	45	3	0	0	2	1.000
Ireland, G Harbor	10	37	2	0	0	4	1.000
Gattis, Victoria	2	14	1	0	0	4	1.000
Maynard, Eugene	1	2	0	0	0	0	1.000
R. Williams, Eug	14	64	9	1	0	4	.986
Styons, G Harbor	19	151	17	3	2	10	.982
PARENT, G Harbor	45	267	29	6	3	14	.980
Calise, Salem	24	122	13	3	0	10	.978
Hyman, Victoria	63	416	48	11	0	9	.977
Firova, Bellingham	62	354	77	11	8	17	.975
Geren, W Walla	47	306	40	10	1	22	.972
Alderman, Salem	33	179	25	6	6	19	.971
O'Connor, Salem	6	28	6	1	0	7	.971
Severns, Eugene	52	334	22	11	4	27	.970
Wilkerson, Salem	22	102	15	4	1	11	.967

CATCHERS—Continued

Player and Club	G.	PO.	A.	E.	DP.	PB.	Pct.
Maggio, Cent Oregon .	21	115	15	5	2	10	.963
Thomas, W Walla	17	92	11	4	0	3	.963
Lamar, Eugene	12	66	6	3	0	1	.960
Tipton, Medford	38	233	43	14	9	6	.952
Harper, Medford	24	153	17	9	0	17	.950
Willard, C Oregon	51	283	37	18	5	20	.947
Witt, W Walla	10	53	7	4	1	3	.938
Pignotti, Medford	14	80	9	7	2	2	.927
Marino, Eugene	2	3	0	1	0	4	.750

PITCHERS

Player and Club	G.	PO.	A.	E.	DP.	Pct.
STOTTLEMYRE, Bell ...	12	8	19	0	2	1.000
Arnold, Medford	16	5	20	0	0	1.000
K. Jones, Eugene	15	6	17	0	0	1.000
Mahoski, Walla Walla ..	17	3	18	0	1	1.000
Nigro, Victoria	23	0	13	0	1	1.000
Christiansen, Bell.	18	2	9	0	0	1.000
Coffman, Walla Walla ..	26	6	4	0	1	1.000
Rios, Grays Harbor	19	3	7	0	1	1.000
Ferguson, Eugene	20	1	9	0	1	1.000
Darnell, Central Oregon	12	2	7	0	1	1.000
Davila, Bellingham	11	1	8	0	0	1.000
White, Salem*	14	3	5	0	2	1.000
Schauer, Medford*	17	2	6	0	1	1.000
Pederson, Bellingham	20	1	7	0	1	1.000
Butler, Victoria	10	1	7	0	0	1.000
McLaughlin, Salem	28	2	5	0	0	1.000
Drew, Central Oregon ..	15	2	4	0	0	1.000
Stamper, Eugene	15	2	4	0	0	1.000
Slattery, Medford	11	1	5	0	1	1.000
Leyerle, Salem*	12	1	4	0	0	1.000
Verbon, Bellingham	19	0	5	0	0	1.000
Mulholland, Eugene*	11	0	5	0	0	1.000
Soderman, Medford	11	1	2	0	0	1.000
Martinez, Cent. Oregon*	23	0	2	0	0	1.000
VandeBerg, Bell.*	14	5	32	1	0	.974
D. Brown, Salem	15	7	17	1	2	.960
White, Walla Walla	14	7	17	1	0	.960
Schiavo, Central Oregon	14	6	14	1	1	.952
Dorin, Central Oregon ..	17	3	15	1	1	.947
Russell, Eugene	13	6	10	1	0	.941
Couchee, Grays Harbor..	24	1	15	1	0	.941
Conroy, Grays Harbor*..	15	1	14	1	1	.938
Weis, Salem	17	3	25	2	1	.933
S. Stone, Grays Harbor ..	12	2	11	1	0	.929
Otto, Victoria	11	1	12	1	0	.929
Britt, Grays Harbor	15	8	16	2	2	.923
Glass, Medford	15	6	6	1	0	.923
Stearns, Salem	14	7	15	2	2	.917
Arrieta, Victoria	15	4	15	2	0	.905
Klacza, Victoria	16	7	21	3	0	.903
Ayers, Eugene	21	5	4	1	0	.900
Liber, Victoria*	18	1	8	1	0	.900
Rothey, Eugene*	17	0	9	1	0	.900
Lovekamp, Grays Har...	14	3	13	2	0	.889
Fitz, Salem*	21	1	15	2	0	.889
Tillman, Central Oregon	16	4	4	1	0	.889
Bullock, Salem*	10	2	6	1	0	.889
Puckett, Medford	10	1	7	1	0	.889
Acevedo, Central Oregon	14	9	14	3	0	.885
W. Johnson, Cent. Ore. ..	27	5	10	2	0	.882
Tolli, Medford	16	2	19	3	3	.875
Young, Bellingham*.....	12	7	13	3	3	.870
Wilson, Walla Walla	14	4	16	3	0	.870
Bryant, Walla Walla* ...	13	4	22	4	1	.867
Garcia, Salem*	20	4	8	2	0	.857
Thoel, Central Oregon*..	11	4	2	1	0	.857
Vaulman, Victoria*	11	0	6	1	0	.857
Patton, Walla Walla	14	2	19	4	0	.840
Bulleri, Medford	30	3	11	3	0	.824
Hunger, Bellingham	13	7	20	6	1	.818
Smith, Walla Walla*	20	3	9	3	0	.800
Duffy, Grays Harbor*	14	2	21	6	5	.793
Freeburg, Eugene	17	2	5	2	0	.778
Klosicki, Eugene	17	3	7	3	0	.769
Vorisek, Medford*	13	3	7	3	0	.769
Snider, Victoria	10	0	3	1	0	.750
Barnett, Central Oregon	12	2	3	2	0	.714
N. Adams, Eugene	19	1	4	2	0	.714
Richardson, Cent. Ore. ...	13	2	9	5	1	.688
Brokop, Grays Harbor ...	11	2	4	3	0	.667
Salva, Bellingham	17	2	5	4	0	.636

(Fewer Than Ten Games)

Player and Club	G.	PO.	A.	E.	DP.	Pct.
Uhey, Victoria	8	2	13	0	0	1.000
Altobelli, Medford	9	2	8	0	0	1.000
Kepshire, Eugene	8	3	3	0	1	1.000
Saylor, Salem	4	2	4	0	0	1.000
McKenzie, Bellingham ..	9	0	6	0	0	1.000
S. Krueger, Bellingham*	4	1	4	0	0	1.000
Lamb, Salem	8	3	1	0	0	1.000
Conti, Central Oregon ..	6	1	2	0	0	1.000
Gerhardt, Walla Walla ..	8	3	0	0	1	1.000
Kirk, Walla Walla	2	2	0	0	0	1.000
Runyan, Salem	6	1	1	0	0	1.000
Job, Medford	7	0	2	0	0	1.000
Scott, Victoria*	6	0	1	0	0	1.000
Daniels, Walla Walla	1	1	0	0	0	1.000
Zerilla, Walla Walla	1	1	0	0	0	1.000
Bennett, Central Oregon	8	0	1	0	0	1.000
Horner, Medford*	5	0	1	0	0	1.000
M. Adams, Salem	3	0	1	0	0	1.000
Peterson, Victoria	3	0	1	0	0	1.000
Alexander, Salem	9	4	11	1	0	.938
Carroll, Medford*	8	0	9	1	0	.900
W. Krueger, Medford*	9	1	7	1	0	.889
Krzanik, Grays Harbor..	6	2	2	1	0	.800
Blamey, Walla Walla	9	1	3	1	0	.800
Mathews, Bellingham ...	9	5	3	1	0	.700
Figueroa, Grays Har.* ..	5	1	1	1	0	.667
Collet, Walla Walla	6	0	2	2	0	.500
Marlow, Medford	4	0	1	1	0	.500

The following players do not have any recorded accepted chances at the positions indicated; therefore, are not listed in the fielding averages for those particular positions: Blanche*, of; Firova, of; Gabriel*, p; Goff, p; Hays*, p; Henley, p; Donald Johnson, of; King, of; LaSala, of; Litchfield, 3b; Lorenz, of; Majam, p; Nate, of; Valdez, ss; Wodrich, ss; Zeuch, p.

CLUB PITCHING

Club	G.	CG.	ShO.	Sv.	IP.	H.	R.	ER.	HR.	BB.	Int. BB.	HB.	SO.	WP.	Bk.	ERA.
Bellingham	70	22	7	10	616	576	335	277	39	407	14	32	392	51	11	4.05
Grays Harbor	69	24	4	6	583	565	377	277	33	351	8	30	427	55	5	4.28
Walla Walla	70	18	3	9	626	634	435	338	37	381	16	16	434	46	6	4.86

CLUB PITCHING—Continued

Club	G.	CG.	ShO.	Sv.	IP.	H.	R.	ER.	HR.	BB.	Int. BB.	HB.	SO.	WP.	Bk.	ERA.
Victoria	70	21	3	12	602	629	391	328	53	294	3	21	458	41	5	4.90
Central Oregon	70	11	1	15	611	615	436	335	52	379	10	20	353	42	8	4.93
Eugene	71	15	0	13	603	610	430	334	51	347	3	22	437	30	4	4.99
Salem	70	15	1	12	617	701	442	358	40	380	14	23	412	57	11	5.22
Medford	70	11	1	7	604	723	518	395	39	390	8	32	442	57	15	5.89

PITCHERS' RECORDS
(Leading Qualifiers for Earned-Run Average Leadership—56 or More Innings)

*Throws lefthanded.

Pitcher—Club	G.	GS.	CG.	ShO.	W.	L.	Sv.	Pct.	IP.	H.	R.	ER.	HR.	BB.	Int. BB.	HB.	SO.	WP.	ERA.
Bryant, Walla Walla*	13	13	5	1	6	5	0	.545	104	62	42	29	5	74	3	3	83	6	2.51
Hunger, Bellingham	13	13	3	1	5	4	0	.556	91	82	39	28	3	48	3	3	61	14	2.77
VandeBerg, Bellingham*	14	14	7	1	9	0	0	1.000	101	82	46	32	5	46	3	1	78	3	2.85
Russell, Eugene	13	13	3	0	6	5	0	.545	90	80	47	30	5	50	0	4	75	4	3.00
Arnold, Medford	16	11	6	0	7	4	0	.636	98	88	43	33	6	31	0	5	52	5	3.03
Klosicki, Eugene	17	9	3	0	6	2	3	.750	89	85	38	32	4	36	0	6	42	6	3.24
Stottlemyre, Bellingham	12	12	4	1	9	3	0	.750	87	76	44	31	7	35	0	6	60	1	3.21
Duffy, Grays Harbor*	14	14	8	0	6	4	0	.600	99	94	62	37	2	56	0	10	93	10	3.36
Smith, Walla Walla*	20	2	0	0	3	6	2	.333	70	65	38	27	0	24	5	2	47	4	3.47
Klacza, Victoria	16	13	6	1	11	4	0	.733	102	84	52	41	13	39	1	3	85	2	3.62

Departmental Leaders: G—Bulleri, 30; GS—Acevedo, Arrieta, Brown, Duffy, Lovekamp, Patton, Schiavo, Stearns, VandeBerg, Wilson, 14; CG—Duffy, 8; ShO—Britt, Krueger, Stone, 2; W—Klacza, 11; L—Glass, Patton, 9; Sv—W. Johnson, 8; Pct.—VandeBerg, 1.000; IP—Bryant, 104; H—Arrieta, 121; R—Patton, 85; ER—Patton, 67; HR—Klacza, 13; BB—Bryant, 74; IBB—Couchee, Smith, 5; HB—Duffy, 10; SO—Duffy, 93; WP—Hunger, 14.

(All Pitchers—Listed Alphabetically)

Pitcher—Club	G.	GS.	CG.	ShO.	W.	L.	Sv.	Pct.	IP.	H.	R.	ER.	HR.	BB.	Int. BB.	HB.	SO.	WP.	ERA.
Acevedo, Cent Oregon	14	14	3	0	3	7	0	.300	101	102	61	46	11	32	1	2	44	4	4.10
M. Adams, Salem	3	0	0	0	0	0	0	.000	2	6	7	7	1	6	0	0	2	0	31.50
N. Adams, Eugene	19	5	0	0	2	2	1	.500	47	62	39	33	5	21	1	2	30	0	6.32
Alexander, Salem	9	9	1	0	4	3	0	.571	55	72	46	43	6	29	0	0	31	3	7.04
Altobelli, Medford	9	7	2	0	2	5	0	.286	51	49	35	23	1	36	1	3	41	2	4.06
Arnold, Medford	16	11	6	0	7	4	0	.636	98	88	43	33	6	31	0	5	52	5	3.03
Arrieta, Victoria	15	14	6	0	7	3	0	.700	101	121	63	54	11	34	0	2	83	6	4.81
Ayers, Eugene	21	6	1	0	4	6	1	.400	58	69	45	43	5	32	0	0	41	2	6.67
Barnett, Central Oregon	12	4	0	0	0	2	1	.000	26	35	27	24	6	13	5	3	19	2	8.31
Bennett, Central Oregon	8	1	0	0	0	3	0	.000	26	27	34	26	1	38	0	4	13	6	9.00
Blamey, Walla Walla	9	2	0	0	0	2	0	.000	16	22	21	17	1	16	1	1	11	1	9.56
Britt, Grays Harbor	15	11	5	2	8	4	1	.667	94	100	57	41	8	30	1	5	61	7	3.93
Brokop, Grays Harbor	11	9	1	0	1	5	0	.167	42	62	48	35	3	32	0	1	16	8	7.50
Brown, Salem	15	14	3	0	5	6	0	.455	97	96	57	44	6	40	1	4	67	6	4.08
Bryant, Walla Walla*	13	13	5	1	6	5	0	.545	104	62	42	29	5	74	2	3	83	6	2.51
Bulleri, Medford	30	0	0	0	4	4	3	.500	50	57	33	18	1	18	2	4	38	0	3.24
Bullock, Salem*	10	10	2	0	5	2	0	.714	54	70	43	33	5	46	0	2	42	7	5.50
Butler, Victoria	10	1	1	0	2	1	5	.667	24	29	16	13	1	16	0	0	16	1	4.88
Carroll, Medford*	8	7	1	0	1	4	0	.200	43	62	45	41	3	25	0	0	28	6	8.58
Christiansen, Bell	18	1	0	0	1	2	1	.333	31	27	21	15	2	27	3	3	29	4	4.35
Coffman, Walla Walla	26	0	0	0	5	2	5	.714	34	27	15	11	1	21	1	0	28	3	2.91
Collet, Walla Walla	6	0	0	0	0	0	0	.000	14	18	13	9	1	7	0	1	12	2	5.79
Conroy, Grays Harbor*	15	2	0	0	0	0	0	.000	43	36	24	19	1	46	0	2	37	3	3.98
Conti, Central Oregon	6	0	0	0	0	0	0	.000	7	9	7	7	2	7	1	0	5	1	9.00
Couchee, Grays Harbor	24	0	0	0	4	4	0	.500	51	43	22	16	3	25	5	1	41	1	2.82
Daniels, Walla Walla	1	0	0	0	0	0	0	.000	2	0	0	0	0	0	0	0	0	0	0.00
Darnell, Central Oregon	12	9	1	0	2	4	0	.500	62	68	47	35	6	36	1	1	36	5	5.08
Davila, Bellingham	11	7	0	0	3	2	0	.600	39	40	35	33	4	32	1	1	20	4	7.62
Dorin, Central Oregon	17	10	0	0	8	2	0	.800	73	69	48	38	5	33	0	1	37	2	4.68
Drew, Central Oregon	15	0	0	0	1	0	0	1.000	28	31	21	21	2	25	1	0	14	1	6.75
Duffy, Grays Harbor*	14	14	8	0	6	4	0	.600	99	94	62	37	2	56	0	10	93	10	3.36
Ferguson, Eugene	20	5	1	0	1	2	2	.333	45	51	36	33	5	31	0	1	28	2	6.60
Figueroa, Grays Harbor*	5	1	0	0	1	0	0	1.000	10	5	9	2	0	11	0	0	7	1	1.80
Fitz, Salem*	21	4	0	0	5	3	1	.625	67	66	53	36	3	49	3	5	62	8	4.84
Freeburg, Eugene	17	3	0	0	1	1	1	.500	37	43	27	21	2	29	0	1	21	2	5.11
Gabriel, Salem*	3	0	0	0	0	0	0	.000	3	5	5	4	0	5	0	0	2	0	12.00
Garcia, Salem*	20	4	2	0	4	3	0	.571	66	74	39	29	4	33	3	1	33	7	3.95
Gerhardt, Walla Walla	8	0	0	0	0	0	0	.000	20	27	16	15	6	5	0	1	12	1	6.75
Glass, Medford	15	4	0	0	1	9	0	.100	45	64	50	41	3	33	3	4	35	5	8.20
Goff, Victoria	2	1	0	0	0	0	0	.000	2	6	9	9	0	7	0	0	1	2	40.50
Hays, Grays Harbor*	1	0	0	0	0	0	0	.000	2	5	5	5	1	0	0	0	2	0	13.50
Henley, Walla Walla	2	0	0	0	0	0	0	.000	2	2	4	4	0	6	0	0	0	0	18.00
Horner, Medford*	5	0	0	0	0	0	0	.000	6	7	4	4	2	7	0	0	3	1	6.00

Pitcher—Club	G.	GS.	CG.	ShO.	W.	L.	Sv.	Pct.	IP.	H.	R.	ER.	HR.	BB.	Int. BB.	HB.	SO.	WP.	ERA.
Hunger, Bellingham	13	13	3	1	5	4	0	.556	91	82	39	28	3	48	3	3	61	14	2.77
Job, Medford	7	0	0	0	4	8	.500	42	37	28	23	0	29	2	2	30	4	4.93
W. Johnson, Cent Oregon	27	0	0	0	7	4	2	.636	96	93	53	47	7	46	0	2	80	6	4.41
K. Jones, Eugene	15	13	5	0	7	7	0	.500	42	54	36	29	8	15	0	3	18	0	6.21
Kepshire, Eugene	8	7	2	0	3	0	0	.000	6	4	9	8	0	7	1	0	6	1	12.00
Kirk, Walla Walla	2	0	0	0	2	0	0	.733	102	84	52	41	13	39	1	3	85	2	3.62
Klacza, Victoria	16	13	6	1	11	4	0	.750	87	76	44	31	7	35	0	6	60	1	3.21
Klosicki, Eugene	17	9	3	0	6	2	3	0	1.000	26	31	4	0	13	0	0	24	0	1.38
S. Krueger, Bell*	4	3	2	2	3	0	0	1.000	44	54	38	25	2	29	2	48	5	5.11
W. Krueger, Medford*	9	7	1	0	0	4	0	.500	22	19	14	10	2	14	0	3	12	1	4.09
Krzanik, Grays Harbor	6	5	0	0	2	2	0	.500	23	26	18	14	2	9	0	1	10	5	5.48
Lamb, Salem	8	2	1	0	1	1	1	.500	23	29	26	22	1	30	4	1	12	4	8.61
Leyerle, Salem*	12	0	0	0	1	1	0	.286	49	56	49	40	6	39	0	1	43	7	7.35
Liber, Victoria*	18	6	1	0	2	5	2	.400	90	86	53	44	8	43	0	4	53	10	4.40
Lovekamp, Grays Harbor	14	14	5	0	4	6	0	.400	98	117	51	45	7	29	1	0	67	4	4.13
Mahoski, Walla Walla	17	12	7	0	8	4	2	.667	2	2	3	3	0	1	0	0	0	0	13.50
Majam, Salem	1	0	0	0	0	0	0	.000	2	2	3	3	0	1	0	0	6	3	14.40
Marlow, Medford	4	4	0	0	3	2	0	.000	10	14	20	16	1	14	0	0	6	3	3.71
Martinez, Cent Oregon*	23	0	0	0	2	1	4	.667	34	31	16	14	1	36	3	1	23	2	3.71
Mathews, Bellingham	9	4	2	0	2	1	0	.667	37	44	32	26	2	32	0	1	15	2	6.90
McKenzie, Bellingham	9	2	1	0	2	4	0	.333	30	33	26	23	5	32	0	1	35	4	4.71
McLaughlin, Salem	28	0	0	0	4	2	5	.667	42	36	23	28	20	15	1	17	0	0	21	4	5.87
Mulholland, Eugene*	11	3	0	0	1	1	1	.500	23	28	20	15	1	17	0	0	21	4	5.87
Nigro, Victoria	23	0	0	0	5	0	2	1.000	34	36	22	20	2	27	1	1	22	3	5.29
Otto, Victoria	11	6	1	1	4	1	0	.800	53	37	26	21	1	40	0	7	42	3	3.57
Patton, Walla Walla	14	14	2	1	2	9	0	.182	84	116	85	67	8	52	2	4	39	5	7.18
Pederson, Bellingham	20	1	0	0	2	2	6	.500	30	27	12	10	1	22	0	3	18	3	3.00
Peterson, Victoria	3	1	0	0	0	0	0	.000	7	4	1	1	0	1	0	0	4	0	1.29
Puckett, Medford	10	4	1	1	1	1	0	.500	36	38	26	20	1	19	1	4	30	1	5.00
Richardson, C Oregon	13	13	3	0	3	6	0	.333	82	78	48	35	8	42	0	6	61	5	3.84
Rios, Grays Harbor	19	1	0	0	3	3	1	.500	51	53	40	36	2	39	2	3	43	5	6.35
Rothey, Eugene*	17	7	0	0	3	4	1	.429	49	55	44	37	4	50	0	2	43	5	6.80
Runyan, Salem	6	0	0	0	0	1	0	.000	11	15	10	8	1	10	2	0	2	1	6.55
Russell, Eugene	13	13	3	0	6	5	0	.545	90	80	47	30	5	50	0	4	75	4	6.00
Salva, Bellingham	17	1	0	0	2	1	0	.667	38	36	29	25	5	41	1	8	22	7	5.92
Saylor, Salem	4	3	1	0	1	1	0	.500	18	21	12	10	2	15	0	0	8	0	5.00
Schauer, Medford*	17	0	0	0	0	1	0	.000	37	52	36	22	6	14	1	1	27	1	5.35
Schiavo, Cent Oregon	14	14	4	1	5	6	0	.455	90	82	49	37	11	35	0	1	49	6	3.70
Scott, Victoria*	6	0	0	0	0	0	0	.000	5	9	11	1	1	5	0	2	3	0	19.80
Slattery, Medford	11	3	0	0	1	1	1	.000	26	48	38	25	4	25	0	1	18	3	8.65
Smith, Walla Walla*	20	2	0	0	3	6	2	.333	70	72	33	27	0	24	5	2	47	4	3.47
Snider, Victoria	10	1	0	0	0	1	0	1.000	18	17	12	9	1	14	0	0	12	4	4.50
Soderman, Medford	11	3	0	0	0	1	0	.000	28	23	20	19	3	24	0	1	25	2	6.11
Stamper, Eugene	15	0	0	0	1	1	1	.500	29	22	19	15	0	21	1	1	20	4	4.66
Stearns, Salem	14	14	3	0	3	7	0	.300	88	104	55	44	3	34	0	3	44	11	4.50
S. Stone, Grays Harbor	12	12	5	2	5	5	0	.500	78	62	43	34	3	55	0	6	68	8	3.92
Stottlemyre, Bell	12	12	4	1	9	3	0	.750	89	85	38	32	4	36	0	6	42	6	3.24
Thoel, Central Oregon*	11	0	0	0	0	1	0	1.000	16	11	7	5	1	14	0	0	6	0	2.81
Tillman, Cent Oregon	16	5	0	0	2	2	0	.400	36	48	40	31	3	36	0	1	24	5	7.75
Tolli, Medford	16	5	0	0	2	2	1	.500	48	67	52	44	3	39	0	4	36	6	8.25
Uhey, Victoria	8	8	3	0	2	4	0	.333	53	68	38	29	6	11	0	2	28	0	4.92
VandeBerg, Bellingham*	14	14	7	1	9	0	0	1.000	101	82	40	32	5	46	3	1	78	3	2.85
Vaulman, Victoria*	11	7	1	1	4	2	0	.667	49	43	23	22	1	26	0	1	54	6	4.04
Verbon, Bellingham	19	0	0	0	3	1	0	.750	29	27	13	9	5	16	3	2	20	0	2.79
Vorisek, Medford*	13	13	0	0	4	6	0	.400	62	71	52	46	2	53	0	2	42	7	6.68
Weis, Victoria	17	11	2	0	5	5	0	.500	102	115	63	52	10	30	1	2	62	5	4.59
J. White, Walla Walla	14	13	4	0	7	1	0	.875	98	98	59	42	5	45	0	2	58	7	3.86
R. White, Salem*	14	10	2	0	1	6	0	.143	66	79	48	39	2	45	1	3	62	5	5.32
Wilson, Walla Walla	14	14	0	0	3	4	0	.429	73	76	64	52	2	69	1	2	60	3	6.41
Young, Bellingham*	12	12	3	1	4	5	0	.444	73	73	46	40	3	62	0	2	53	3	4.93
Zerilla, Walla Walla	1	0	0	0	1	0	0	1.000	9	3	1	1	0	6	3	2	7	0	1.00
Zeuch, Victoria	2	1	0	0	0	1	0	.000	14	7	5	5	2	3	0	0	3	2	13.50

BALKS—Fitz, McLaughlin, 4 each; Christiansen, Glass, W. Krueger, Vorisek, Wilson, 3 each; Acevedo, Arrieta, Britt, Carroll, Duffy, Jones, McKenzie, Schauer, Smith, Weis, 2 each; N. Adams, Bennett, Blamey, Bullock, Conroy, Conti, Darnell, Davila, Dorin, Hunger, Mathews, Otto, Puckett, Rothey, Saylor, Schiavo, Soderman, Stearns, Tillman, VandeBerg, Verbon, Young, 1 each.

COMBINATION SHUTOUTS—Hunger-Christiansen, Bellingham; Bullock-Garcia, Salem; Wilson-Mahoski, Walla Walla.

NO-HIT GAME—Otto, Victoria, defeated Grays Harbor, 3-0, August 21, second game, seven innings.

South Atlantic League

CLASS A

CHAMPIONSHIP WINNERS IN PREVIOUS YEARS

1948—Lincolnton*	.627
1949—Newton-Conover	.667
Ruth'ford Co. (2nd)†	.627
1950—Newton-Conover	.627
Lenoir (2nd)†	.626
1951—Morganton	.645
Shelby (2nd)†	.604
1952—Lincolnton	.649
Shelby (2nd)†	.645
1953-59—League inactive.	
1960—Lexington	.707
Salisbury (2nd)†	.650
1961—Salisbury	.627
Shelby (4th)†	.481
1962—Statesville	.563
Statesville	.700
1963—Greenville†	.576
Salisbury	.631

1964—Rock Hill	.672
Salisbury‡	.631
1965—Salisbury	.641
Rock Hill‡	.603
1966—Spartanburg	.682
Spartanburg	.767
1967—Spartanburg	.730
Spartanburg	.567
1968—Spartanburg	.597
Greenwood‡	.597
1969—Greenwood‡	.587
Shelby	.565
1970—Greenville	.576
Greenville	.619
1971—Greenwood	.631
Greenwood	.759

1972—Spartanburg‡	.788
Greenville	.652
1973—Spartanburg‡	.646
Gastonia	.619
1974—Gastonia	.606
Gastonia	.672
1975—Spartanburg	.543
Spartanburg	.614
1976—Asheville	.544
Greenwood‡	.600
1977—Greenwood	.557
Gastonia‡	.590
1978—Greenwood	.614
Greenwood	.565
1979—Greenwood‡	.565
Spartanburg	.525

*Won championship and four-club playoff. †Won four-club playoff. ‡Won split-season playoff. (NOTE—Known as Western Carolina League from 1948 through 1962 and known as Western Carolinas League through 1979.)

STANDING OF CLUBS AT CLOSE OF FIRST HALF, JUNE 22

NORTHERN DIVISION

Club	W.	L.	T.	Pct.	G.B.
Greensboro (Yankees)	45	25	0	.643	......
Asheville (Rangers)	39	29	0	.574	5
Gastonia (Cardinals)	37	33	0	.529	8
Shelby (Pirates)	29	41	0	.414	16

SOUTHERN DIVISION

Club	W.	L.	T.	Pct.	G.B.
Charleston (Royals)	38	32	0	.543	......
Spartanburg (Phillies)	35	33	0	.515	2
Anderson (Braves)	33	36	0	.478	4½
Macon (Co-op)	21	48	0	.304	16½

STANDING OF CLUBS AT CLOSE OF SECOND HALF, AUGUST 31

NORTHERN DIVISION

Club	W.	L.	T.	Pct.	G.B.
Greensboro (Yankees)	37	32	0	.536	......
Gastonia (Cardinals)	37	33	0	.529	½
Shelby (Pirates)	29	39	0	.426	7½
Asheville (Rangers)	30	42	0	.417	8½

SOUTHERN DIVISION

Club	W.	L.	T.	Pct.	G.B.
Charleston (Royals)	40	29	0	.580	......
Spartanburg (Phillies)	38	32	0	.543	2½
Macon (Co-op)	38	33	0	.535	3
Anderson (Braves)	31	40	0	.437	10

COMPOSITE STANDING OF CLUBS AT CLOSE OF SEASON, AUGUST 31

NORTHERN DIVISION

Club	Gbr.	Gas.	Ash.	Shel.	Char.	Spar.	And.	Mac.	W.	L.	T.	Pct.	G.B.
Greensboro (Yankees)	..	11	12	14	11	11	12	13	82	57	0	.590	......
Gastonia (Cardinals)	9	..	9	14	11	4	16	11	74	66	0	.529	8½
Asheville (Rangers)	8	11	..	11	8	8	14	9	69	71	0	.493	13½
Shelby (Pirates)	8	6	9	..	5	7	11	12	58	80	0	.420	23½

SOUTHERN DIVISION

Club	Gbr.	Gas.	Ash.	Shel.	Char.	Spar.	And.	Mac.	W.	L.	T.	Pct.	G.B.
Charleston (Royals)	8	9	12	15	..	14	8	12	78	61	0	.561	......
Spartanburg (Phillies)	9	16	12	11	6	..	8	11	73	65	0	.529	4½
Anderson (Braves)	8	4	6	9	12	12	..	13	64	76	0	.457	14½
Macon (Co-op)	7	9	11	8	8	9	7	..	59	81	0	.421	19½

Major league affiliations in parentheses.

Playoffs—Greensboro defeated Gastonia, two games to one for Northern Division championship. Charleston defeated Spartanburg, two games to one for Southern Division championship. Greensboro defeated Charleston, three games to none for League Championship.

Regular-Season Attendance—Anderson, 40,836; Asheville, 49,066; Charleston, 109,191; Gastonia, 90,198; Greensboro, 255,130; Macon, 56,671; Shelby, 15,393; Spartanburg, 35,480. Total, 651,965. Playoffs, 11,091. All-star game, 1,487.

Managers—Anderson, Sonny Jackson; Asheville, Tom Robson; Charleston, Ron Mihal; Gastonia, Nick Leyva; Greensboro, Bob Schaefer; Macon, Brock Pemberton, R. Brannon Bonifay, Ted Brazell; Shelby, Joe Frisina; Spartanburg, Tom Harmon.

All-Star Team: 1B—O'Brien, Asheville; 2B—Wolters, Gastonia; 3B—Nixon, Greensboro; SS—Lindsey, Spartanburg; Sosa, Anderson; Utility—Scranton, Charleston; OF—Jacoby, Anderson; Mattingly, Greensboro; Sanchez, Spartanburg; Wynne, Charleston; C—Scott, Asheville; DH—Winters, Greensboro; P—Arigoni, Gastonia; Ballard, Greensboro; Guante, Shelby; Murphy, Greensboro; Manager—Schaefer, Greensboro.

(Compiled by Howe News Bureau, Boston, Mass.)

CLUB BATTING

Club	G.	AB.	R.	OR.	H.	TB.	2B.	3B.	HR.	RBI.	SH.	SF.	BB.	Int. BB.	HP.	SO.	SB.	CS.	LOB.	Pct.
Greensboro	139	4534	765	626	1254	1804	194	34	96	675	18	56	592	21	53	706	179	81	999	.277
Charleston	139	4625	723	683	1238	1784	184	64	78	611	38	44	585	24	37	775	147	58	1011	.268
Macon	140	4628	673	736	1239	1708	196	27	73	588	47	39	577	12	36	729	138	38	1109	.268
Asheville	140	4626	735	752	1233	1829	225	28	105	656	34	55	653	18	30	850	136	44	1101	.267
Gastonia	140	4614	711	650	1202	1722	186	29	92	606	33	43	631	19	36	771	136	36	1070	.261
Spartanburg	138	4582	651	641	1197	1679	202	41	66	541	37	33	487	14	45	855	168	53	938	.261
Anderson	140	4566	726	744	1165	1699	210	45	73	617	49	47	602	19	54	751	196	70	1023	.255
Shelby	138	4363	617	769	1082	1637	190	22	107	535	39	37	448	15	35	881	131	86	819	.248

INDIVIDUAL BATTING

(Leading Qualifiers for Batting Championship—378 or More Plate Appearances)

*Bats lefthanded.   †Switch-hitter.

Player and Club	G.	AB.	R.	H.	TB.	2B.	3B.	HR.	RBI.	SH.	SF.	BB.	HP.	SO.	SB.	CS.	Pct.
Mattingly, Donald, Greensboro*	133	494	92	177	246	32	5	9	105	0	12	59	4	33	8	9	.358
Winters, Matthew, Greensboro*	112	363	72	116	195	15	2	20	92	2	3	58	4	62	10	6	.320
Arroyo, Hector, Charleston*	105	387	69	120	135	9	3	0	34	1	1	58	5	50	11	9	.310
Harvey, Steven, Spartanburg	116	437	71	132	179	16	8	5	43	3	5	43	1	64	18	5	.302
Jacoby, Brook, Anderson	132	496	82	147	252	40	4	19	108	2	5	53	6	95	4	4	.296
O'Brien, Peter, Asheville*	134	505	98	149	238	34	2	17	94	4	7	54	0	53	0	0	.295
Scott, Donald, Asheville	115	421	57	124	187	22	1	13	78	1	5	54	0	53	0	0	.295
Enos, David, Spartanburg†	123	405	64	119	143	16	1	2	45	5	2	71	2	81	12	4	.294
Hinson, Gary, Macon	88	324	59	95	134	17	2	6	51	1	2	61	2	31	10	2	.293
McGehee, C. Connor, Shelby*	115	397	67	115	169	16	1	12	36	0	4	66	1	104	25	16	.290

Departmental Leaders: G—Lindsey, 138; AB—Wynne, 547; R—Nixon, 124; H—Mattingly, 177; TB—Wynne, 256; 2B—Jacoby, 40; 3B—Wynne, 15; HR—Kable, 26; RBI—Jacoby, 108; GWRBI—Winters, 12; SH—Lindberg, 11; SF—Mattingly, 12; BB—Nixon, 113; HP—Harrigan, 11; SO—Demeter, 136; SB—Nixon, 67; CS—McGehee, 16.

(All Players—Listed Alphabetically)

Player and Club	G.	AB.	R.	H.	TB.	2B.	3B.	HR.	RBI.	SH.	SF.	BB.	HP.	SO.	SB.	CS.	Pct.
Aguayo, Carmelo, Asheville	39	144	18	41	51	7	0	1	14	1	3	20	1	9	0	1	.299
Akchurin, Erol, Greensboro	4	1	0	0	0	0	0	0	0	0	0	0	0	1	0	0	.000
Arroyo, Hector, Charleston*	105	387	69	120	135	9	3	0	34	1	1	58	5	50	11	9	.310
Ayala, Eric, Anderson	98	373	59	94	104	4	3	0	44	10	4	35	6	30	25	8	.252
Ball, Robert, Asheville	46	134	18	26	39	5	1	2	14	2	0	36	0	33	0	0	.194
Bailey, Welby, Anderson	111	423	78	110	145	18	7	1	26	8	5	68	6	66	64	14	.260
Baskerville, Phillip, Gastonia*	58	164	31	46	63	8	0	3	25	2	2	29	1	30	3	2	.280
Batter, Ronald, Charleston	13	46	1	8	12	1	0	1	5	1	1	0	0	6	1	0	.174
Baugh, Darrell, Spartanburg	59	224	34	62	96	10	3	6	28	3	0	12	3	27	7	4	.277
Belliard, Rafael, Shelby	8	24	1	3	3	0	0	0	2	0	1	1	0	3	0	2	.125
Benedict, Scott, Greensboro	19	61	6	13	16	1	1	0	12	0	0	10	0	10	0	2	.213
Bresnahan, Raymond, 45Mac-34Ch	79	240	35	61	77	7	3	1	22	2	7	40	2	47	9	4	.254
Butler, Brett, Anderson*	70	255	73	76	103	12	6	1	26	4	4	67	4	29	44	9	.298
Butterfield, Brian, Greensboro	22	81	14	25	42	8	0	3	17	0	1	11	0	22	1	0	.309
Calise, Michael, Gastonia	22	81	14	25	42	8	0	3	17	0	1	11	0	22	1	0	.309
Campbell, Robert, Macon	19	52	2	13	13	0	0	0	3	1	1	3	0	5	1	0	.250
Caraballo, Jose, Gastonia	12	19	6	6	8	2	0	0	0	0	0	1	0	1	1	0	.316
Carney, Ronald, Asheville*	31	1	0	0	0	0	0	0	0	0	0	1	0	0	0	0	.000
Castaigne, Arcilio, Anderson	35	1	0	0	0	0	0	0	0	0	0	0	0	1	0	0	.000
Cazares, Jose, Gastonia	119	353	31	86	99	11	1	0	28	7	3	25	2	42	2	5	.244
Chamberlain, William, Macon	75	259	45	73	115	11	2	9	42	4	2	29	5	59	2	2	.282
Cochran, Michael, Macon	8	14	3	4	5	1	0	0	0	0	0	2	0	0	0	0	.286
Cohron, D. Tracy, Macon*	50	177	26	37	59	7	3	3	19	0	2	14	0	43	0	0	.209
Cooper, Junior, Charleston	24	62	11	14	20	1	1	1	9	0	0	7	0	16	0	0	.226
Coyne, Michael, Shelby	10	24	5	7	8	1	0	0	4	0	3	4	2	6	1	1	.292
Crawford, J. David, Spartanburg*	32	102	15	22	30	3	1	1	3	4	4	16	0	25	0	1	.216
Curbelo, Jorge, Macon	47	148	17	39	58	10	0	3	26	4	4	10	0	21	1	0	.264
Darkis, William, Spartanburg	17	47	6	9	16	5	1	0	5	0	0	2	0	0	0	0	.191
DeAza, Manny, Charleston	51	159	28	53	64	5	3	0	18	0	0	14	1	29	9	8	.333
Del Monte, John, Gastonia*	5	14	0	1	1	0	0	0	1	0	0	3	0	0	0	0	.071
Demeter, Todd, Greensboro	123	395	63	94	153	12	4	13	59	0	7	62	10	136	3	4	.238
Doak, Leon, Charleston	72	202	23	36	59	10	2	3	27	6	1	28	2	59	6	2	.178
Donofrio, Larry, Asheville*	66	222	36	56	91	5	0	10	41	0	2	31	0	57	1	0	.252
Dunbar, Thomas, Asheville*	75	262	39	79	103	9	6	1	39	2	1	27	0	45	14	3	.302
Duncan, Lindon, Asheville	23	84	11	21	25	4	0	0	5	0	0	13	0	11	3	1	.250
Dusquesne, Roman, Macon*	11	34	3	9	12	0	0	2	0	2	0	0	0	8	0	0	.265
Echstenkamper, Thomas, Greens.	96	307	40	71	133	14	0	16	61	1	4	21	7	48	3	3	.231
Enos, David, Spartanburg†	123	405	64	119	143	16	1	2	45	5	2	71	2	81	12	4	.294

Player and Club	G.	AB.	R.	H.	TB.	2B.	3B.	HR.	RBI.	SH.	SF.	BB.	HP.	SO.	SB.	CS.	Pct.
Felt, James, Shelby	135	455	69	120	200	25	2	17	62	2	5	60	4	93	9	8	.264
Felt, William, Macon	3	4	0	1	1	0	0	0	0	0	0	2	0	1	0	0	.250
Fields, Bruce, Macon*	67	240	40	71	86	7	1	2	27	0	2	37	3	38	24	5	.296
Fiori, Joseph, Shelby	67	215	29	47	61	10	2	0	16	3	5	22	2	23	11	4	.219
Flores, Ricardo, Macon*	7	25	1	3	4	1	0	0	0	0	0	0	0	4	0	0	.120
Ford, Kenneth, Shelby	122	430	66	114	180	17	2	15	75	0	3	39	4	81	13	5	.265
Foussianes, George, Macon	72	261	32	76	119	20	1	7	47	3	2	35	0	41	0	1	.291
Freedman, Kerry, Macon	49	0	1	0	0	0	0	0	0	0	0	0	0	0	0	0	.000
Frobel, Douglas, Shelby*	67	246	42	80	135	14	1	13	41	0	1	19	2	65	11	3	.325
Fryer, Paul, Spartanburg	129	462	68	120	193	23	4	14	71	4	5	35	4	106	16	4	.260
Gagne, Gregory, Greensboro	98	337	39	91	130	20	5	3	32	1	4	22	2	46	8	7	.270
Gambrell, P. Gregory, Anderson	11	3	0	0	0	0	0	0	0	0	0	1	0	0	0	0	.000
Garcia, Frank, Asheville	86	299	56	77	124	20	0	9	56	4	7	51	5	62	1	2	.258
Garcia, Michael, Anderson	70	267	49	85	116	17	4	2	41	3	1	30	1	23	17	4	.318
Garnett, Bradley, Shelby*	103	294	45	68	118	15	1	11	42	2	1	47	4	104	7	6	.231
Garray, Allen, Charleston	101	312	25	71	108	14	1	7	42	4	4	37	4	77	2	0	.228
Gayden, Huey, Greensboro*	106	370	81	105	140	10	8	3	50	2	5	41	6	32	23	5	.284
George, Jerry, Macon*	28	92	16	18	33	4	1	3	15	1	2	13	3	15	1	0	.196
Girata, Daniel, Greensboro	33	105	16	31	58	9	0	6	23	0	1	9	0	17	0	0	.295
Gleissner, James, Charleston	1	1	0	0	0	0	0	0	0	0	0	0	0	1	0	0	.000
Gomez, George, Asheville	109	368	53	104	174	28	3	12	63	2	6	57	1	60	3	3	.283
Good, James, Macon	41	148	14	35	55	8	0	4	13	0	1	6	0	44	1	1	.236
Goodman, William, Asheville	64	182	22	40	44	4	0	0	13	1	0	42	0	31	8	3	.220
Grahek, Lawrence, Charleston*	112	341	64	97	149	15	11	5	64	1	5	67	2	65	8	3	.284
Green, Christopher, Shelby*	19	1	0	0	0	0	0	0	0	0	0	0	0	0	0	0	.000
Grossini, Leroy, Gastonia	125	434	70	104	141	13	3	6	44	5	3	70	2	75	16	3	.240
Hagman, Keith, Anderson*	62	215	36	61	81	11	3	1	24	1	3	29	0	12	2	1	.284
Haley, J. Michael, Charleston	18	62	14	16	25	1	1	2	9	0	1	6	1	17	7	0	.258
Haro, Samuel, Shelby	51	155	14	29	36	4	0	1	7	3	0	10	1	32	6	4	.187
Harrigan, David, Spartanburg	124	411	54	90	149	25	5	8	54	3	6	55	11	108	14	5	.219
Harvey, Steven, Spartanburg	116	437	71	132	179	16	8	5	43	3	5	43	1	64	18	5	.302
Hayes, Thomas, Anderson	70	240	33	52	74	11	1	3	29	1	4	36	3	45	4	1	.217
Hearn, Edward, Spartanburg	66	217	25	65	90	12	2	3	32	3	2	20	2	44	1	1	.300
Hibner, David, Asheville	89	256	34	49	80	7	0	8	36	0	4	43	4	101	14	8	.191
Hicks, Robert, Gastonia	131	499	62	133	194	23	1	12	55	1	3	23	3	113	7	3	.267
Hinson, Gary, Macon	88	324	59	95	134	17	2	6	51	1	2	61	2	31	10	2	.293
Holland, John, Macon	80	255	40	71	111	17	1	7	45	3	2	24	4	36	1	0	.278
Howser, Thomas, Greensboro	76	215	48	64	71	7	0	0	19	2	1	49	3	18	21	8	.298
Hudler, A. Rex, Greensboro	20	75	7	17	28	3	1	2	9	0	0	4	0	14	1	2	.227
Infante, Ulises, Charleston	53	137	23	32	40	3	1	1	16	3	1	29	1	30	8	0	.234
Isbell, Mark, Shelby	12	31	2	7	8	1	0	0	1	2	0	8	2	11	2	0	.226
Jackman, Mark, Charleston*	24	1	0	0	0	0	0	0	0	0	0	0	0	1	0	0	.000
Jacoby, Brook, Anderson	132	496	82	147	252	40	4	19	108	2	5	53	6	95	4	4	.296
Jeltz, L. Steven, Spartanburg†	31	107	19	31	35	2	1	0	8	0	0	24	0	20	8	4	.290
Jirschele, Michael, Asheville	12	41	6	7	9	2	0	0	6	2	0	6	3	7	4	0	.171
Kable, David, Gastonia*	134	437	86	106	207	19	2	26	99	2	6	93	7	103	9	0	.243
King, John, Greensboro	77	247	35	51	90	10	1	9	46	0	5	29	0	48	4	2	.206
Komminsk, Brad, Anderson	121	425	86	111	198	17	5	20	67	3	5	74	7	102	27	9	.261
Lewis, Amos, Asheville	84	273	52	76	121	10	1	11	33	2	1	57	1	102	1	1	.278
Liggins, Danny, Gastonia	36	136	21	39	48	6	0	1	9	0	1	6	0	21	3	1	.287
Lindberg, Ronald, Macon	72	213	33	50	59	7	1	0	17	11	1	39	1	37	4	1	.235
Lindsey, Jon, Spartanburg*	138	534	72	137	186	29	4	4	53	1	3	60	4	71	23	9	.257
Linhart, Carl, Spartanburg	46	127	16	30	33	3	0	0	17	5	2	17	1	12	1	0	.236
Littlefield, David, Spartanburg	7	19	2	3	4	1	0	0	0	0	0	0	0	5	0	0	.158
Lockwood, William, Shelby	109	394	65	112	169	18	6	9	70	5	3	24	4	47	12	9	.284
Luethy, David, Charleston	102	341	59	88	130	22	4	4	32	6	8	54	1	68	8	3	.258
Luzon, Robert, Anderson	71	280	37	60	75	9	3	0	26	5	1	30	3	47	11	8	.214
Marin, Fernando, Macon	44	134	17	25	38	7	0	2	10	1	0	15	3	45	0	3	.187
Martinez, Anardy, Shelby	73	185	12	33	38	5	0	0	11	3	0	10	0	34	2	1	.178
Martinez, Randy, Spartanburg*	5	1	0	0	0	0	0	0	0	0	0	0	0	0	0	0	.000
Martinson, Kenneth, Spartanburg	69	198	30	49	64	15	0	0	18	3	0	40	3	2	2	2	.247
Mastro, Steven, Macon*	133	487	56	133	171	15	4	5	62	3	3	50	6	53	11	3	.273
Mata, Victor, Greensboro	101	346	43	96	126	11	2	5	47	0	4	23	6	47	8	7	.277
Matos, Carlos, Gastonia	8	10	1	1	1	0	0	0	0	1	0	2	0	5	0	0	.100
Mattingly, Donald, Greensboro*	133	494	92	177	246	32	5	9	105	0	12	59	4	33	8	9	.358
Maxwell, James, Asheville	91	277	38	76	109	23	2	2	29	3	1	34	3	62	4	2	.274
McEvilly, Michael, Macon*	19	57	8	10	15	2	0	1	5	0	0	12	0	7	3	0	.175
McGehee, C. Connor, Shelby*	115	397	67	115	169	16	1	12	36	0	4	66	1	104	25	16	.290
McGill, Anthony, Charleston	55	224	29	49	59	3	2	1	17	1	1	15	3	49	15	7	.219
McMath, Shelton, Asheville	58	196	22	44	56	6	0	2	27	1	3	24	2	39	0	1	.224
Miller, William, Macon	14	0	1	0	0	0	0	0	0	0	0	0	0	0	0	0	.000
Mills, Rhadames, Gastonia	73	285	46	83	123	16	6	4	37	2	4	24	0	32	31	4	.291
Miscik, Robert, Shelby	61	214	37	53	89	10	1	8	25	3	2	30	0	27	8	9	.248
Mitchell, David, Spartanburg	24	0	1	0	0	0	0	0	0	0	0	0	0	0	0	0	.000
Moore, Donald, Gastonia†	20	53	13	16	18	2	0	0	5	0	0	6	1	8	0	0	.302
Moriarity, Dermot, Charleston*	128	441	50	114	147	22	1	3	59	1	8	66	3	52	2	2	.259

Player and Club	G.	AB.	R.	H.	TB.	2B.	3B.	HR.	RBI.	SH.	SF.	BB.	HP.	SO.	SB.	CS.	Pct.
Mueller, Timothy, Gastonia	29	91	12	19	27	2	0	2	15	0	0	17	1	17	0	0	.209
Nixon, Otis, Greensboro	136	493	124	137	168	12	5	3	48	5	2	113	1	88	67	13	.278
North, Roy, Anderson	28	3	1	0	0	0	0	0	1	0	0	0	0	1	0	0	.000
O'Brien, Peter, Asheville*	134	505	98	149	238	34	2	17	94	4	7	68	1	67	6	0	.295
Ojeda, Luis, Gastonia	14	26	1	3	3	0	0	0	1	0	1	4	0	6	0	0	.115
Owings, Mark, Spartanburg†	50	193	20	42	47	2	0	1	19	0	0	20	2	22	7	1	.218
Palmer, Michael, Charleston†	114	398	64	110	183	17	4	16	54	1	0	46	2	73	9	2	.276
Pardo, Braulio, Macon	32	114	18	26	30	2	1	0	15	0	0	15	0	22	0	0	.228
Patterson, Scott, Anderson	29	4	1	1	1	0	0	0	0	0	0	0	0	1	0	0	.250
Payano, Vidal, Anderson	6	19	1	4	5	1	0	0	1	1	0	1	0	5	1	1	.211
Pellack, James, Macon*	91	290	44	92	140	15	3	9	51	0	2	42	3	44	3	5	.317
Pemberton, Brock, Macon*	47	162	21	47	66	7	0	4	28	0	4	27	1	11	1	1	.290
Poldberg, Brian, Greensboro	95	308	39	90	120	19	1	3	43	1	5	32	4	33	9	6	.292
Porter, Denny, Charleston*	82	255	45	75	138	9	6	14	58	0	0	51	1	38	1	2	.294
Quezada, Rafael, Anderson	38	122	13	26	34	5	0	1	10	1	1	15	1	33	5	1	.213
Reeder, Michael, Macon	44	127	16	28	42	3	1	3	13	1	0	14	1	35	3	3	.220
Rigby, Kevin, Anderson	56	183	22	56	77	11	5	0	21	1	0	17	3	14	0	1	.306
Rodriguez, Angel, Shelby	98	311	37	77	112	14	0	7	46	4	5	15	4	56	3	4	.248
Roman, Luis, Gastonia*	116	432	55	121	145	15	3	1	38	3	2	41	5	41	6	7	.280
Rudolph, Jeffrey, Greensboro	25	60	9	19	26	4	0	1	7	1	1	10	0	9	1	0	.317
Sagedahl, Steven, Greensboro	34	1	0	0	0	0	0	0	0	0	0	0	0	1	0	0	.000
Salas, Mark, Gastonia*	98	267	42	67	108	8	3	9	46	3	5	23	5	22	3	0	.251
Sanchez, Alejandro, Spartanburg	127	490	84	140	227	26	8	15	76	2	4	30	7	88	25	3	.286
Sayler, Barry, Gastonia	10	32	2	5	9	1	0	1	2	0	0	3	0	11	0	0	.156
Scanlon, Kenneth, Anderson	95	323	40	77	90	13	0	0	35	8	2	31	4	32	12	5	.238
Schaefer, James, Asheville*	97	360	60	90	132	9	3	9	41	6	4	36	2	29	11	3	.250
Scott, Donald, Asheville†	115	421	57	124	187	22	1	13	78	1	5	54	0	53	0	0	.295
Scranton, James, Charleston	121	450	69	114	142	16	3	2	33	8	3	24	3	51	18	5	.253
Silva, Ildemaro, Gastonia	4	6	1	0	0	0	0	0	0	0	0	0	0	0	0	0	.000
Sinnen, Matthew, Shelby	19	57	4	13	15	2	0	0	8	1	0	6	0	10	1	3	.228
Skinner, Joel, Shelby	100	324	36	73	113	15	2	7	27	3	0	25	3	77	0	4	.225
Smith, Jeffrey, Macon	62	228	38	69	94	10	0	5	35	1	4	30	1	39	4	0	.303
Smith, P. Keith, Greensboro	21	63	10	12	15	3	0	0	1	0	0	5	0	17	4	2	.190
Snaith, Andrew, Shelby	108	374	55	80	120	16	3	6	41	5	2	38	0	79	9	2	.214
Sosa, Miguel, Anderson	125	511	81	137	220	23	3	18	92	0	8	34	3	84	27	7	.268
Soto, Julio, Macon	16	55	2	16	17	1	0	0	9	1	0	3	0	12	2	1	.291
Spreckels, Keith, Gastonia†	95	280	66	73	112	13	4	6	46	1	5	74	2	57	15	2	.261
St. Clair, Daniel, Charleston	38	1	0	0	0	0	0	0	0	0	0	0	0	0	0	0	.000
Stephans, Russell, Charleston	8	21	2	3	3	0	0	0	1	1	0	2	0	0	0	0	.143
Swires, Glenn, Greensboro	36	108	12	28	42	8	0	2	8	0	1	15	3	22	2	0	.259
Tapia, Santiago, Shelby†	24	74	12	15	18	0	0	1	2	1	0	9	0	15	3	2	.203
Tinkler, Jackson, Gastonia	9	6	0	1	1	0	0	0	1	2	0	0	0	1	0	0	.167
Tjader, James, Asheville	68	271	51	80	122	15	3	7	44	1	5	19	1	42	2	2	.295
Tobias, Grayling, Macon†	37	149	31	49	55	3	0	1	11	2	2	14	0	6	18	4	.329
Tovar, Raul, Charleston	97	326	48	102	129	15	6	0	43	4	1	28	7	39	18	6	.313
Uvodich, John, Macon	1	4	0	2	3	1	0	0	0	0	0	0	0	0	0	0	.500
Van Slyke, Andrew, Gastonia*	126	426	62	115	162	15	4	8	59	2	1	70	2	68	19	1	.270
Venner, W. Gary, Asheville*	15	48	4	10	18	2	0	2	7	0	1	3	0	7	0	0	.208
Vranesh, Keith, Charleston	16	35	7	6	10	1	0	1	3	0	0	7	1	15	2	0	.171
Warner, Harold, Spartanburg*	120	383	41	97	134	15	2	6	47	3	2	35	2	72	15	4	.253
Weaver, Dale, Anderson*	9	34	2	10	12	0	1	0	1	1	0	4	0	5	2	1	.294
Whistler, Randall, Anderson	96	310	41	63	79	12	2	0	19	3	2	44	3	62	3	3	.203
Williams, Harold, Anderson	127	420	76	94	170	20	4	16	80	2	7	83	10	105	20	7	.224
Winters, Matthew, Greensboro*	112	363	72	116	195	15	2	20	92	2	3	58	4	62	16	1	.320
Wolters, Michael, Gastonia	138	498	82	136	193	23	2	10	69	0	5	95	4	76	21	8	.273
Woodard, Darrell, Macon	125	497	85	137	165	18	5	0	41	5	0	54	2	53	47	5	.276
Wotus, Ronald, Shelby	45	158	19	36	45	7	1	0	19	2	2	15	2	14	8	3	.228
Wynne, Marvel, Charleston*	137	547	106	152	256	20	15	18	98	1	2	48	2	71	29	14	.278
Zunino, Gary, Gastonia	29	74	9	19	23	4	0	0	7	2	1	11	0	13	0	0	.257

The following pitchers had no plate appearances primarily through use of designated hitters, listed alphabetically by club, games in parentheses:

ANDERSON—Ames, Kenneth (36); Arroyo, Felipe (12); Church, Daniel (10); Coghill, David* (26); Dedmon, Jeffrey* (2); Edwards, Larry (11); Fuller, Timothy (16); Germer, Glen (22); Moses, Mark (10); Nice, Williams* (32); Payne, Michael (21); Rymer, Carlos (5); Theiss, Duane (4).

ASHEVILLE—Burdette, Ricky* (19); Cliburn, Perry (18); Eason, W. Gregory* (28); Fossas, E. Anthony* (30); Gilliam, Melvin* (27); Henke, Thomas (5); Henry, Timothy* (7); Keenan, Kerry (47); Long, Dennis (23); Mosby, Linvel (21); Pettibone, H. Jay (36); Schmidt, David (12); Smith, Daryl† (22); Taylor, William* (6); Terrell, C. Walter* (3); Vickers, Michael* (6).

CHARLESTON—Albright, David* (6); Begue, Roger (44—20 with Macon); Hergott, Scott (15); Krauss, Ronald* (26); Laughton, James (11); Porter, Cleveland* (25); Potestio, Douglas (9); Ryan, Frank (27); Sanford, Edmund (14); Vanderbush, Walter (28); Voyles, Curtis (27); Wills, Frank (9); Yuhas, Vincent (24).

GASTONIA—Arigoni, Scott (28); Brooks, Robert (11); Citarella, Ralph (51); Clark, Terry (49); David, Mark (7); Davis, Russell (13); Gadowski, Dennis† (31); Gonzalez, Jesus (14); Hagen, Kevin (29); Horton, Ricky* (14); Jones,

David (7); Martin, John (12); Pimental, Rafael (6); Pittman, Michael* (2); Rhodes, Michael* (15); Silva, Freddie (21); Vazquez, Raphael (10); Vega, Axel (10—4 with Macon); Weaver, Earl (16).

GREENSBORO—Ballard, Byron (26); Campbell, James (8); Collins, Joseph (9); DeMaria, George (7); Filson, W. Peter* (4); Fontenot, Silton* (11); Free, David (46); Hernandez, Carlo* (17); Irot, Kevin (18); Murphy, Brian* (35); Nurthen, John (44); Ricci, Frank (4); Toliver, Freddie (20); Vanderplas, B. Jeffrey* (22).

MACON—Bresnen, Robert (21); Dodd, Lance (30); Duleski, J. Michael (28); Doud, James (2); Feola, Lawrence (7); Gorey, Richard (25—9 with Anderson); Kirby, Dennis (4); Koziol, Edward (7); Leggatt, Richard* (33); Leisure, G. Philip* (15); Mathis, Ronald (12); Montgomery, Thomas* (26); Perry, Jerry (6); Ruffus, Robert* (12); Santin, Lazaro* (6); Semprini, John (7); Staffon, Gregory (5); West, Herman (2).

SHELBY—Acker, Larry* (12); Adkins, Robert (13); Archisoh, Iimo (7); Bastian, Bernie (5); Bielecki, Michael (29); DeLeon, Jose (26); Dexter, Charles (7); Fiepke, Scott* (15); Gelinas, Marc (10); Goff, James (14); Guante, Cecilio (39); Huey, John (4); Johnson, Michael (24); McCulloch, Alec (22); Palmer, Bradley* (11); Peralta, Sergio (15); Siebert, Thomas (13); Styles, Lawrence (10); Williams, Donald* (25).

SPARTANBURG—Baller, Jay (26); Cepeda, Rafael (40); Downs, Kelly (14); Dunnegan, Steven (27); Espinosa, Arnulfo (3); Guardia, Oscar (26); Gums, Russell (30); Lenaburg, B. Paul (34); Marshall, Charles (19); Money, J. Kyle (27); Palmieri, John* (25); Redmond, Roger (16); Thomas, Dennis (39).

GRAND SLAM HOME RUNS—Winters, 3; Donofrio, Jacoby, Komminsk, H. Williams, 2 each; Chamberlain, Echstenkamper, J. Felt, Ford, F. Garcia, Kable, Lewis, Lockwood, McGill, McMath, Mueller, O'Brien, Palmer, D. Porter, Salas, Scott, Spreckles, Wynne, 1 each.

AWARDED FIRST BASE ON INTERFERENCE—Winters 4 (Scott 2, Silva, Skinner); Hinson (Rodriguez); Lindberg (Harrigan); Mattingly (Holland); Mills (Harrigan); Scranton (Poldberg).

GAME-WINNING RBIs

ANDERSON (45)—Jacoby 11, Williams 7, Ayala 6, Sosa 6, Hayes 3, Komminsk 3, Scanlon 3, Butler 2, Luzon 2, Quezada 1, Rigby 1.

ASHEVILLE (35)—O'Brien 5, Scott 5, Dunbar 4, Garcia 4, Ball 3, Lewis 3, Maxwell 3, Tjader 2, Venner 2, Donofrio 1, Gomez 1, Hibner 1, Schaeffer 1.

CHARLESTON (59)—Wynne 8, Palmer 7, Tovar 7, Arroyo 6, Grahek 6, D. Porter 6, Garray 4, Scranton 4, Moriarity 3, DeAza 2, Luethy 2, Batter 1, Bresnahan 1, Cooper 1, Haley 1.

GASTONIA (30)—Kable 7, Van Slyke 5, Wolters 5, Hicks 4, Mills 3, Salas 3, Spreckels 2, Liggins 1.

GREENSBORO (53)—Winters 12, Mattingly 11, Poldberg 6, Mata 4, Echstenkamper 3, Gayden 3, King 3, Nixon 3, Demeter 2, Gagne 2, Benedict 1, Girata 1, Howser 1, Hudler 1.

MACON (44)—Foussianes 8, Holland 7, Hinson 6, Smith 6, Pellack 4, Pemberton 3, Woodard 3, Fields 2, Mastro 2, Campbell 1, Chamberlain 1, Tobias 1.

SHELBY (35)—Ford 7, Lockwood 6, Rodriguez 4, Frobel 3, Miscik 3, Felt 2, Fiori 2, Skinner 2, Snaith 2, Wotus 2, Garnett 1, Sinnen 1.

SPARTANBURG (54)—Fryer 10, Harvey 9, Lindsey 6, Baugh 5, Harrigan 5, Warner 5, Owings 3, Sanchez 3, Enos 2, Hearn 2, McGill 2, Linhart 1, Martinson 1.

CLUB FIELDING

Club	G.	PO.	A.	E.	DP.	PB.	Pct.	Club	G.	PO.	A.	E.	DP.	PB.	Pct.
Gastonia	140	3583	1530	161	113	33	.969	Charleston	139	3558	1403	237	115	37	.954
Anderson	140	3511	1438	206	136	24	.960	Macon	140	3503	1466	241	112	41	.954
Asheville	140	3448	1547	228	98	54	.957	Shelby	138	3445	1257	230	97	31	.953
Greensboro	139	3525	1353	219	106	47	.957	Spartanburg	138	3610	1368	250	105	28	.952

Triple Plays—Asheville, Charleston.

INDIVIDUAL FIELDING

*Throws lefthanded.

FIRST BASEMEN

Player and Club	G.	PO.	A.	E.	DP.	Pct.	Player and Club	G.	PO.	A.	E.	DP.	Pct.
Donofrio, Asheville	5	35	2	0	2	1.000	Poldberg, Greensboro*	16	124	10	2	15	.985
Lewis, Asheville	5	34	1	0	1	1.000	Moore, Gastonia	8	65	2	1	6	.985
Spreckels, Gastonia	1	12	0	0	1	1.000	Williams, Anderson	120	1044	61	18	103	.984
Felt, Macon	2	7	0	0	1	1.000	Pemberton, Macon*	20	170	11	3	11	.984
Girata, Greensboro	2	6	1	0	1	1.000	Winters, Greensboro	15	109	7	2	8	.983
Baugh, Spartanburg	1	4	0	0	1	1.000	Enos, Spartanburg	86	777	56	16	55	.981
Doak, Charleston	1	1	0	0	0	1.000	Demeter, Greensboro	109	819	55	19	67	.979
KABLE, Gastonia	133	1199	67	7	94	.995	D. Porter, Charleston	5	44	2	1	3	.979
Mattingly, Greensboro*	14	111	6	1	9	.992	Smith, Macon	4	40	3	1	4	.977
O'Brien, Asheville*	131	1227	96	14	93	.990	Rodriguez, Shelby	38	298	15	8	26	.975
Foussianes, Macon	70	636	32	7	69	.990	Garnett, Shelby*	78	581	32	17	48	.973
Hearn, Spartanburg	9	68	7	1	5	.987	Martinson, Spartanburg	51	412	22	12	32	.973
Dusquesne, Macon	9	72	2	1	4	.987	Frobel, Shelby	28	190	24	7	10	.968
Moriarity, Charleston*	115	941	41	14	79	.986	Cohron, Macon*	36	273	29	12	19	.962
Grahek, Charleston*	28	184	10	3	14	.985	Pellack, Macon*	4	36	0	2	1	.947
Hagman, Anderson*	22	181	12	3	23	.985							

Triple Plays—Moriarity, O'Brien.

SECOND BASEMEN

Player and Club	G.	PO.	A.	E.	DP.	Pct.	Player and Club	G.	PO.	A.	E.	DP.	Pct.
Reeder, Macon	6	9	12	0	1	1.000	Gomez, Asheville	38	98	105	8	30	.962
Hinson, Macon	3	8	12	0	4	1.000	Jirschele, Asheville	11	28	23	2	6	.962
Cazares, Gastonia	7	7	12	0	3	1.000	Owings, Spartanburg	37	73	97	7	18	.960
Lindsey, Spartanburg	1	8	4	0	0	1.000	Rigby, Anderson	51	124	127	11	34	.958
Wynne, Charleston*	1	2	2	0	0	1.000	Ayala, Anderson	25	39	53	4	10	.958
Flores, Macon	1	2	1	0	0	1.000	Martinez, Anderson	64	95	129	10	13	.957
Lindberg, Macon	1	2	1	0	0	1.000	Hudler, Greensboro	19	51	52	5	16	.954
Grossini, Gastonia	1	1	0	0	0	1.000	Goodman, Asheville	45	78	115	11	22	.946
Woodard, Macon	69	146	213	6	45	.984	Crawford, Spartanburg	30	60	94	9	16	.945
Fiori, Shelby	53	130	131	6	23	.978	Scanlon, Anderson	76	166	197	22	46	.943
WOLTERS, Gastonia	136	327	427	21	85	.973	Soto, Macon	13	20	28	3	7	.941
Scranton, Charleston	7	16	18	1	3	.971	Howser, Greensboro	45	67	111	12	12	.937
Linhart, Spartanburg	42	114	126	8	27	.968	Gagne, Greensboro	20	37	54	7	14	.929
Enos, Spartanburg	6	19	11	1	1	.968	Luethy, Charleston	31	63	80	12	14	.923
Snaith, Shelby	23	56	56	4	21	.966	Arroyo, Charleston	89	154	214	32	36	.920
Jeltz, Spartanburg	28	51	61	4	9	.966	Infante, Charleston	3	3	8	1	0	.917
Tjader, Asheville	55	107	150	10	30	.963	Marin, Macon	13	16	30	5	4	.902
Butterfield, Greensboro	71	127	150	11	32	.962	Hard, Shelby	16	27	23	6	9	.893
Bresnahan, Charleston	58	95	133	9	30	.962	Rodriguez, Shelby	1	1	5	2	0	.750

Triple Play—Tjader.

THIRD BASEMEN

Player and Club	G.	PO.	A.	E.	DP.	Pct.	Player and Club	G.	PO.	A.	E.	DP.	Pct.
Doak, Charleston	4	3	7	0	1	1.000	Frobel, Shelby	27	30	32	6	1	.912
Stephans, Charleston	3	1	6	0	0	1.000	Maxwell, Asheville	20	1	10	4	0	.911
Linhart, Spartanburg	1	3	3	0	0	1.000	Hinson, Macon	85	85	167	25	21	.910
Tjader, Asheville	1	0	5	0	0	1.000	Garcia, Asheville	77	52	182	24	14	.907
Wolters, Gastonia	1	0	5	0	0	1.000	DeAza, Charleston	43	42	65	11	3	.907
Lindberg, Macon	1	0	4	0	0	1.000	Fryer, Spartanburg	128	142	358	44	16	.901
Haley, Charleston	2	0	2	0	0	1.000	Gagne, Greensboro	22	18	36	6	8	.900
Vranesh, Charleston	2	0	2	0	1	1.000	Haro, Shelby	37	25	62	10	4	.897
Arroyo, Charleston	1	0	1	0	0	1.000	Swires, Greensboro	36	18	82	13	8	.885
Moore, Gastonia	1	0	1	0	0	1.000	Infante, Charleston	47	48	95	19	5	.883
Poldberg, Greensboro	1	1	0	0	0	1.000	Nixon, Greensboro	71	69	132	27	11	.882
Rigby, Anderson	1	1	0	0	0	1.000	Hayes, Anderson	53	55	100	21	15	.881
Wynne, Charleston*	1	1	0	0	0	1.000	Lewis, Asheville	39	24	79	16	8	.866
Tinkler, Gastonia	2	5	1	0	0	1.000	Mastro, Macon	55	48	100	23	5	.865
Jacoby, Anderson	10	5	21	1	4	.963	Rudolph, Greensboro	5	5	14	3	2	.864
Ojeda, Gastonia	13	5	18	1	0	.958	Cooper, Charleston	18	17	19	6	0	.857
Wotus, Shelby	22	22	42	3	1	.955	Howser, Greensboro	10	6	16	4	1	.846
CAZARES, Gastonia	93	87	158	12	14	.953	King, Greensboro	2	4	1	1	0	.833
Enos, Spartanburg	11	27	28	3	5	.948	Bresnahan, Charleston	9	7	15	5	1	.815
Scanlon, Anderson	9	9	23	2	2	.941	Goodman, Asheville	6	1	15	4	0	.800
Spreckels, Gastonia	57	49	109	12	9	.929	Mills, Gastonia	1	1	3	1	0	.800
Miscik, Shelby	7	3	10	1	2	.929	Rodriguez, Shelby	6	9	5	4	0	.778
Garcia, Anderson	64	41	127	13	13	.928	Echstenkamper, Grnb..	1	0	2	1	1	.667
Luethy, Charleston	34	23	52	6	2	.926	Payano, Anderson	6	1	4	3	0	.625
Fiori, Shelby	14	5	20	2	1	.926	Jirschele, Asheville	1	1	0	1	0	.500
Snaith, Shelby	38	36	60	8	4	.923							

Triple Plays—Cooper, Lewis.

SHORTSTOPS

Player and Club	G.	PO.	A.	E.	DP.	Pct.	Player and Club	G.	PO.	A.	E.	DP.	Pct.
Tinkler, Gastonia	7	2	11	0	0	1.000	Smith, Greensboro	20	23	47	5	6	.933
Scanlon, Anderson	4	2	6	0	0	1.000	Cazares, Gastonia	23	31	67	8	12	.925
Crawford, Spartanburg	1	2	3	0	1	1.000	Foussianes, Macon	2	5	7	1	0	.923
Liggins, Gastonia	1	2	2	0	0	1.000	Sosa, Anderson	125	186	397	49	78	.922
Goodman, Asheville	1	0	1	0	0	1.000	Miscik, Shelby	54	78	123	17	27	.922
Mills, Gastonia	1	0	1	0	0	1.000	Duncan, Asheville	19	38	57	8	8	.922
Nixon, Greensboro	66	95	176	9	29	.968	Luethy, Charlotte	32	53	68	11	9	.917
Hayes, Anderson	15	24	50	3	14	.961	Lindsey, Spartanburg	137	234	374	58	70	.913
Wotus, Shelby	25	39	63	5	18	.953	Gagne, Greensboro	58	78	143	22	26	.909
SCRANTON, Charlotte..	112	209	323	27	65	.952	Gomez, Asheville	70	76	205	34	30	.892
Woodard, Macon	36	67	108	9	22	.951	Belliard, Shelby	8	10	27	5	5	.881
Lindberg, Macon	68	99	199	18	39	.943	Rigby, Anderson	1	2	5	1	0	.875
Grossini, Gastonia	122	175	369	35	58	.940	Martinez, Shelby	9	11	11	4	1	.846
Maxwell, Asheville	53	60	157	15	19	.935	Uvodich, Macon	1	3	2	1	0	.833
Snaith, Shelby	56	91	121	15	15	.934	Flores, Macon	6	8	14	6	1	.786
Reeder, Macon	32	52	101	11	14	.933	Spreckels, Gastonia	1	1	2	1	2	.750

Triple Play—Gomez.

OUTFIELDERS

Player and Club	G.	PO.	A.	E.	DP.	Pct.	Player and Club	G.	PO.	A.	E.	DP.	Pct.
Quezada, Anderson	37	68	4	0	1	1.000	Mata, Greensboro	90	164	9	6	5	.966
McEvilly, Macon*	18	23	2	0	0	1.000	Echstenkamper, Green..	80	125	5	5	2	.963
Isbell, Shelby	9	24	0	0	0	1.000	Grahek, Charleston*	59	74	5	3	2	.963
Coyne, Shelby	9	17	0	0	0	1.000	Tobias, Macon	36	74	2	3	0	.962
Hagman, Anderson*	11	11	1	0	0	1.000	Jacoby, Anderson	113	214	9	9	2	.961
Weaver, Anderson	7	10	1	0	0	1.000	Hicks, Gastonia	128	187	10	8	2	.961
Haley, Charleston	6	10	0	0	0	1.000	Wynne, Charleston*	133	278	17	13	2	.958
Matos, Gastonia	6	7	3	0	1	1.000	Palmer, Charleston	111	192	13	9	1	.958
Del Monte, Gastonia*	4	7	0	0	0	1.000	Baugh, Spartanburg	55	106	4	5	1	.957
Bresnahan, Charleston	1	3	2	0	0	1.000	Tovar, Charleston	79	109	8	6	1	.951
Luethy, Charleston	1	5	0	0	0	1.000	McMath, Asheville	56	69	7	4	2	.950
Tjader, Asheville	4	4	1	0	0	1.000	Komminsk, Anderson	120	217	5	12	1	.949
Cohron, Macon*	1	4	0	0	0	1.000	Smith, Macon	52	70	5	4	1	.949
Grossini, Gastonia	1	3	0	0	0	1.000	Liggins, Gastonia	34	52	3	3	0	.948
Jeltz, Spartanburg	1	2	1	0	1	1.000	Chamberlain, Macon	72	105	8	7	1	.942
Scranton, Charleston	1	2	0	0	0	1.000	Mastro, Macon	78	113	11	8	2	.939
Howser, Greensboro	3	2	0	0	0	1.000	Doak, Charleston	50	70	7	5	2	.939
Spreckels, Gastonia	3	2	0	0	0	1.000	Enos, Spartanburg	12	26	4	2	2	.938
Butterfield, Greensboro..	1	1	0	0	0	1.000	Sanchez, Spartanburg..	125	223	15	16	4	.937
Garnett, Shelby*	1	1	0	0	0	1.000	McGehee, Shelby*	110	213	9	15	1	.937
Moore, Gastonia	1	1	0	0	0	1.000	Hibner, Asheville	83	120	13	9	2	.937
King, Greensboro	2	1	0	0	0	1.000	Warner, Spartanburg*	63	105	7	8	2	.933
Martinez, Shelby	2	1	0	0	0	1.000	Pemberton, Macon*	12	12	1	1	0	.929
Poldberg, Greensboro	2	1	0	0	0	1.000	Van Slyke, Charleston	105	177	16	16	4	.923
Butler, Anderson*	70	190	5	1	0	.995	Winters, Greensboro	45	56	3	5	1	.922
McGill, Spartanburg	54	118	6	2	1	.984	Ford, Shelby	37	63	4	6	1	.918
Fields, Macon	63	118	2	2	0	.984	Dunbar, Asheville*	72	101	9	11	2	.909
Mills, Gastonia	67	129	3	3	0	.978	Good, Macon	9	10	0	1	0	.909
Baskerville, Gastonia	27	41	1	1	0	.977	Lewis, Asheville	20	26	3	3	0	.906
Luzon, Anderson	72	152	8	4	2	.976	Tapia, Shelby*	20	35	1	4	0	.900
SCHAEFER, Asheville*	97	153	4	4	0	.975	Demeter, Greensboro	22	30	2	4	0	.889
Ball, Asheville	111	253	8	7	2	.974	Marin, Macon	32	53	7	8	3	.882
Harvey, Spartanburg	113	179	11	5	1	.974	George, Macon	27	36	3	6	0	.867
Roman, Gastonia*	73	147	5	4	2	.974	DeAza, Charleston	7	11	1	2	1	.857
Felt, Shelby	135	305	15	9	8	.973	Darkis, Spartanburg	8	11	1	2	0	.857
Gayden, Greensboro*	99	211	4	6	0	.973	Pellack, Macon*	19	23	3	5	1	.839
Lockwood, Shelby	110	186	12	6	3	.971	Vranesh, Charleston	8	13	0	4	0	.765
Woodard, Macon	19	30	0	1	0	.968	Campbell, Macon	3	4	0	2	0	.667
Mattingly, Greensboro*	112	194	10	7	2	.967							

CATCHERS

Player and Club	G.	PO.	A.	E.	DP.	PB.	Pct.	Player and Club	G.	PO.	A.	E.	DP.	PB.	Pct.
Benedict, Greensboro .	15	104	8	0	2	7	1.000	Venner, Asheville	7	42	2	1	0	2	.978
Batter, Charleston	11	89	9	0	1	5	1.000	Bailey, Anderson	47	237	17	6	5	5	.977
Tovar, Charleston	10	73	10	0	1	6	1.000	Rodriguez, Shelby	36	184	24	5	1	7	.977
Campbell, Macon	12	66	6	0	1	1	1.000	Mueller, Gastonia	29	144	17	4	2	5	.976
Sayler, Gastonia	8	36	4	0	0	3	1.000	Scott, Asheville	92	593	81	17	7	41	.975
Caraballo, Gastonia	11	29	5	0	0	2	1.000	Poldberg, Greensboro	56	325	26	10	3	12	.972
Cochran, Macon	6	24	2	0	0	2	1.000	Donofrio, Asheville	21	124	14	4	1	6	.972
Sinnen, Shelby	3	12	2	0	1	3	1.000	Skinner, Shelby	96	536	63	18	7	18	.971
Bresnahan, Char	3	12	1	0	0	1	1.000	Garray, Charleston	90	525	63	18	7	17	.970
Hudler, Greensboro	1	7	0	0	0	0	1.000	Harrigan, Spartan..	122	692	61	24	4	21	.969
Cazares, Gastonia	1	3	0	0	0	0	1.000	Pardo, Macon	19	134	13	5	1	12	.967
Gleissner, Charleston .	1	1	0	0	0	0	1.000	Ford, Shelby	11	74	4	3	1	3	.963
SALAS, Gastonia	88	452	41	5	6	17	.990	Stephans, Charleston .	4	22	4	1	2	0	.963
Rudolph, Greensboro	13	80	6	1	0	3	.989	Aguayo, Asheville......	23	130	11	6	1	5	.959
D. Porter, Charleston	31	190	29	3	4	7	.986	Good, Macon	22	123	15	6	1	3	.958
Girata, Greensboro	21	118	7	2	1	13	.984	Curbelo, Macon	28	194	26	11	1	8	.952
Zunino, Gastonia	27	137	16	3	1	6	.981	Martinson, Spartan ..	10	36	2	2	0	1	.950
Holland, Macon	68	385	52	9	6	14	.980	Littlefiel, Spartan ...	7	33	4	2	0	2	.949
King, Greensboro	45	262	20	6	2	12	.979	Enos, Spartanburg	7	29	1	2	0	3	.938
Whistler, Anderson	96	500	73	13	5	21	.978	I. Silva, Gastonia	3	7	0	1	0	0	.875

PITCHERS

Player and Club	G.	PO.	A.	E.	DP.	Pct.	Player and Club	G.	PO.	A.	E.	DP.	Pct.
Freedman, Macon	47	10	23	0	2	1.000	Fuller, Anderson	16	2	13	0	2	1.000
Hernandez, Greensboro*	17	5	22	0	0	1.000	Eason, Asheville*	28	4	11	0	0	1.000
NORTH, Anderson	28	14	12	0	1	1.000	Pettibone, Asheville	36	2	12	0	0	1.000
F. Silva, Gastonia	21	8	17	0	1	1.000	Martin, Gastonia	11	5	8	0	0	1.000
Schmidt, Asheville	12	8	16	0	0	1.000	Sanford, Charleston	14	2	11	0	1	1.000
Begue, Macon	44	3	21	0	1	1.000	Edwards, Anderson	11	0	11	0	0	1.000
Smith, Asheville	22	7	15	0	1	1.000	Gonzalez, Gastonia	14	2	9	0	0	1.000
Murphy, Greensboro*	35	5	12	0	0	1.000	Gadowski, Gastonia	31	3	7	0	1	1.000
Rhodes, Gastonia*	15	2	13	0	2	1.000	Ames, Anderson	36	1	9	0	0	1.000

PITCHERS—Continued

Player and Club	G.	PO.	A.	E.	DP.	Pct.
Vickers, Asheville*	6	3	6	0	0	1.000
DeMaria, Greensboro	7	4	5	0	0	1.000
Miller, Macon	12	2	7	0	0	1.000
Goff, Shelby	14	2	7	0	0	1.000
Vanderplas, Greensboro*	22	4	5	0	0	1.000
Long, Asheville	23	3	6	0	0	1.000
Castaigne, Anderson	35	2	7	0	0	1.000
Guante, Shelby	39	4	5	0	0	1.000
Semprini, Macon	7	4	4	0	0	1.000
Brooks, Gastonia	11	3	5	0	0	1.000
Adkins, Shelby	13	1	7	0	1	1.000
Marshall, Spartanburg	19	0	8	0	1	1.000
Staffon, Macon	5	4	3	0	2	1.000
Jones, Gastonia	7	3	4	0	0	1.000
Campbell, Greensboro	8	1	6	0	0	1.000
McCullock, Shelby	22	2	5	0	0	1.000
Jackman, Charleston*	24	2	5	0	0	1.000
Feola, Macon*	7	3	3	0	0	1.000
Koziol, Macon	7	2	4	0	0	1.000
Arroyo, Anderson	12	1	5	0	1	1.000
Mathis, Anderson	12	3	3	0	0	1.000
Burdette, Asheville*	19	1	5	0	0	1.000
Gambrell, Anderson*	10	2	3	0	0	1.000
Acker, Shelby	12	1	4	0	0	1.000
St. Clair, Charleston	38	0	5	0	0	1.000
Rymer, Anderson	5	3	1	0	0	1.000
David, Gastonia	7	1	3	0	0	1.000
Kirby, Macon	4	1	2	0	0	1.000
Henke, Asheville	5	1	2	0	0	1.000
Moses, Anderson	10	0	3	0	0	1.000
Vega, Macon	10	0	3	0	0	1.000
Akchurin, Greensboro	3	0	2	0	0	1.000
Bastian, Shelby	5	0	2	0	0	1.000
Taylor, Asheville	6	2	0	0	0	1.000
Archisoh, Shelby	7	1	1	0	0	1.000
Styles, Shelby	10	0	2	0	0	1.000
Cazares, Gastonia	2	0	1	0	0	1.000
West, Macon	2	0	1	0	0	1.000
Filson, Greensboro*	4	0	1	0	0	1.000
Huey, Shelby	4	0	1	0	0	1.000
Martinez, Spartanburg*	4	0	1	0	0	1.000
Theiss, Anderson	4	0	1	0	0	1.000
Albright, Charleston*	6	1	0	0	0	1.000
Santin, Macon*	6	0	1	0	0	1.000
Redmond, Spartanburg	16	0	1	0	0	1.000
Patterson, Anderson	29	7	27	1	3	.971
Toliver, Greensboro	20	9	24	1	2	.971
Vanderbush, Charleston	28	6	22	1	0	.966
Sagedahl, Greensboro	33	11	17	1	1	.966
Hagen, Gastonia	29	6	21	1	1	.964
Leggatt, Macon	34	4	20	1	1	.960
Clark, Gastonia	49	5	17	1	1	.957
Voyles, Charleston	27	2	19	1	2	.955
Dunnegan, Spartanburg	27	9	11	1	4	.952
Fossas, Asheville*	30	9	29	2	1	.950
Carney, Asheville*	31	4	15	1	3	.950
Money, Spartanburg	28	9	8	1	0	.944
Cliburn, Asheville	18	5	11	1	0	.941
Potestio, Charleston	9	3	12	1	1	.938
Wills, Charleston	9	5	9	1	2	.933
Thomas, Spartanburg	39	8	6	1	1	.933
Palmieri, Spartanburg*	25	3	23	2	0	.929
Palmer, Shelby*	11	2	11	1	0	.929
Mitchell, Spartanburg	22	2	11	1	1	.929
Free, Greensboro	46	6	7	1	0	.929
Payne, Anderson	21	11	13	2	3	.923
Gelinas, Shelby	10	4	8	1	0	.923
Ballard, Greensboro	26	14	19	3	1	.917
Collins, Greensboro	9	4	7	1	1	.917
Lenaburg, Spartanburg	35	12	16	3	0	.903
Keenan, Asheville	47	7	10	2	2	.895
Gilliam, Asheville*	27	3	21	3	0	.889
Church, Anderson	10	3	5	1	3	.889
Siebert, Shelby	13	4	4	1	0	.889
Peralta, Shelby	15	4	4	1	0	.889
Irot, Greensboro	18	2	6	1	1	.889
Cepeda, Spartanburg	40	3	5	1	1	.889
Mosby, Asheville	21	4	11	2	1	.882
Johnson, Shelby	24	3	12	2	1	.882
Williams, Shelby*	25	3	12	2	1	.882
DeLeon, Shelby	26	17	18	5	1	.875
Horton, Gastonia*	14	2	12	2	2	.875
Gorey, Anderson	25	6	20	4	0	.867
Ryan, Charleston	27	6	13	3	2	.864
Yuhas, Charleston	24	7	17	4	5	.857
Montgomery, Macon*	26	7	11	3	0	.857
Coghill, Anderson*	26	5	7	2	1	.857
Downs, Spartanburg	14	2	4	1	0	.857
Germer, Anderson	22	1	5	1	0	.857
Citarella, Gastonia	51	6	37	7	3	.850
Bresnen, Macon	21	6	16	4	1	.846
Arigoni, Gastonia*	28	4	12	3	0	.842
Nice, Anderson*	32	5	10	3	0	.833
Nurthen, Greensboro	44	5	10	3	1	.833
Ruffus, Macon*	12	2	8	2	1	.833
Ricci, Greensboro	4	2	3	1	0	.833
Laughton, Charleston	11	0	5	1	0	.833
Bielecki, Shelby	29	4	10	3	0	.824
Doleski, Macon	28	4	14	4	1	.818
Gums, Spartanburg	31	4	5	2	0	.818
Fontenot, Greensboro	11	3	9	3	1	.800
Weaver, Gastonia	16	3	5	2	1	.800
Krauss, Charleston*	26	2	13	4	0	.789
Fiepke, Shelby*	15	2	5	2	0	.778
C. Porter, Charleston	27	2	16	6	0	.750
Green, Shelby*	19	0	15	5	2	.750
Baller, Spartanburg	26	3	6	3	0	.750
Guardia, Spartanburg	26	1	2	1	0	.750
Dodd, Macon	30	3	6	4	0	.692
Rudolph, Greensboro	7	1	3	2	1	.667
Hergott, Charleston	15	2	0	1	0	.667
Pimental, Gastonia	6	1	0	1	0	.500
Dexter, Shelby	7	1	0	1	0	.500
Vazquez, Gastonia	10	0	1	1	0	.500
Leisure, Macon*	15	0	1	1	0	.500
Doud, Macon	2	0	0	1	0	.000

Triple Play—Voyles.

The following players do not have any recorded accepted chances at the positions indicated; therefore, are not listed in the fielding averages for those particular positions: Arroyo, ss; Benedict, 1b; Curbelo, of; Davis, p; Dedmon, p; Espinosa, p; Frobel, 2b; F. Garcia, of; Garray, 3b; Grahek*, 2b-3b; Harrigan, of; Henry*, p; Hicks, 1b; Kable, of; Lockwood, 3b; Martin, 3b; A. Martinez, 3b; Maxwell, 2b-of-p; Pardo, of; Pellack*, p; Perry, p; Pittman*, p; D. Porter, of; Salas, of; Terrell, p.

CLUB PITCHING

Club	G.	CG.	ShO.	Sv.	IP.	H.	R.	ER.	HR.	BB.	Int. BB.	HB.	SO.	WP.	Bk.	ERA.
Spartanburg	138	24	11	19	1204	1234	639	479	84	518	20	39	705	1	19	3.58
Greensboro	139	34	8	25	1178	1040	626	501	96	606	21	34	830	83	26	3.83
Charleston	139	30	15	20	1213	1261	686	551	75	571	12	42	877	94	24	4.09
Gastonia	140		7	23	1202	1167	658	553	92	552	21	52	764	88	9	4.14
Anderson	140	31	9	23	1204	1301	742	588	89	564	17	39	678	67	11	4.40
Macon	140	25	5	18	1194	1220	770	602	78	606	16	31	902	82	34	4.54
Asheville	140	24	4	17	1200	1267	761	616	96	551	6	46	845	9	22	4.62
Shelby	138	18	4	27	1153	1189	762	615	98	599	26	46	765	1	32	4.80

PITCHERS' RECORDS

(Leading Qualifiers for Earned-Run Average Leadership—112 or More Innings)

*Throws lefthanded.

Pitcher–Club	G.	GS.	CG.	ShO.	W.	L.	Sv.	Pct.	IP.	H.	R.	ER.	HR.	BB.	Int. BB.	HB.	SO.	WP.	ERA.
Citarella, Gastonia...........	51	6	1	0	11	4	8	.733	126	87	35	23	6	49	2	5	113	6	1.64
Toliver, Greensboro.........	20	20	4	0	6	8	0	.429	126	98	60	40	10	89	0	2	96	15	2.86
Dunnegan, Spartanburg ..	27	26	6	0	11	8	0	.579	165	152	72	57	6	69	1	2	94	11	3.11
Ballard, Greensboro	26	25	15	3	17	6	0	.739	192	167	86	67	14	50	1	5	125	12	3.14
Fossas, Asheville*............	30	27	8	2	12	8	2	.600	197	187	84	69	11	69	0	5	140	14	3.15
Baller, Spartanburg	26	25	2	1	10	5	0	.667	139	132	69	55	11	72	0	10	95	18	3.56
Money, Spartanburg	27	27	6	4	8	7	0	.533	149	160	76	62	12	48	1	5	93	6	3.74
Palmieri, Spartanburg*	25	25	4	1	6	10	0	.375	138	140	80	58	10	60	0	7	83	13	3.78
Vanderbush, Charleston ..	28	12	5	0	11	5	3	.688	121	115	64	51	5	80	6	3	106	17	3.79
Krauss, Charleston*.........	26	26	5	1	10	5	0	.667	161	153	77	68	10	73	0	5	150	10	3.80

Departmental Leaders: G–Citarella, 51; GS–Arigoni, Fossas, Gilliam, Money, C. Porter, 27; CG–Ballard, 15; ShO–Money, 4; W–Ballard, 17; L–Gorey, 16; Sv–Guante, 19; Pct.–Begue, .909; IP–Fossas, 197; H–Fossas, 187; R–Gilliam, 113; ER–DeLeon, 90; HR–DeLeon, Gilliam, 19; BB–C. Porter, 94; IBB–Begue, Cepeda, Sagedahl, Vanderbush, 6; HB–Baller, 10; SO–Krauss, 150; WP–Arigoni, 19.

(All Pitchers—Listed Alphabetically)

Pitcher–Club	G.	GS.	CG.	ShO.	W.	L.	Sv.	Pct.	IP.	H.	R.	ER.	HR.	BB.	Int. BB.	HB.	SO.	WP.	ERA.
Acker, Shelby.................	12	5	0	0	1	3	0	.250	43	50	32	27	4	17	1	1	20	0	5.65
Adkins, Shelby...............	13	13	3	0	3	2	0	.600	89	92	49	39	8	35	0	2	57	1	3.94
Akchurin, Shelby	3	0	0	0	0	0	0	.000	9	4	3	1	0	4	0	0	8	0	1.00
Albright, Charleston*......	6	1	0	0	0	1	0	.000	4	6	15	15	0	12	0	0	0	1	33.75
Ames, Anderson..............	36	0	0	0	2	9	6	.182	70	74	39	25	4	37	4	3	40	4	3.21
Archisoh, Shelby	7	0	0	0	0	0	0	.000	14	16	12	5	0	10	0	1	5	0	3.21
Arigoni, Gastonia*..........	28	27	2	1	8	6	0	.571	151	154	92	78	17	83	2	3	103	19	4.65
Arroyo, Anderson	12	0	0	0	2	0	1	1.000	27	24	16	13	5	14	0	0	13	3	4.33
Ballard, Greensboro	26	25	15	3	17	6	0	.739	192	167	86	67	14	50	1	5	125	12	3.14
Baller, Spartanburg	26	25	2	1	10	5	0	.667	139	132	69	55	11	72	0	10	95	18	3.56
Bastian, Shelby	5	0	0	0	1	1	0	.500	8	5	2	2	0	5	1	0	5	0	2.25
Begue, 24 Char-20 Mac....	44	1	0	0	10	1	3	.909	98	109	55	44	7	40	6	0	63	16	4.04
Bielecki, Shelby	29	6	1	0	3	5	3	.375	99	106	60	50	8	58	4	2	78	5	4.55
Bresnen, Macon	21	6	0	0	2	4	1	.333	70	84	53	39	6	44	0	3	52	6	5.01
Brooks, Gastonia	11	9	2	0	3	3	0	.500	52	74	45	41	8	17	0	1	22	5	7.10
Burdette, Asheville*	19	0	0	0	1	1	1	.500	31	41	26	18	3	14	1	2	22	2	5.23
Campbell, Greensboro	8	7	0	0	2	4	0	.333	41	44	26	25	3	15	1	1	27	3	5.49
Carney, Asheville*..........	31	7	1	0	3	5	2	.375	77	62	43	37	7	65	0	2	64	10	4.32
Castaigne, Anderson	35	0	0	0	3	6	6	.333	61	58	21	15	2	28	5	2	53	3	2.21
Cazares, Gastonia	2	0	0	0	0	0	0	.000	3	3	1	1	0	3	0	2	3	1	3.00
Cepeda, Spartanburg	40	0	0	0	8	8	9	.500	56	64	37	29	6	25	6	3	24	3	4.66
Church, Anderson	10	5	0	0	2	1	0	.000	37	42	28	20	4	33	0	0	24	3	4.86
Citarella, Gastonia..........	51	6	1	0	11	4	8	.733	126	87	35	23	6	49	2	5	113	6	1.64
Clark, Gastonia...............	49	0	0	0	4	7	10	.364	88	82	34	31	8	22	4	5	50	3	3.17
Cliburn, Asheville...........	18	6	0	0	3	9	0	.250	72	91	44	38	4	13	0	2	37	5	4.75
Coghill, Anderson*..........	26	17	4	2	10	7	1	.588	128	138	79	71	11	54	0	1	48	3	4.99
Collins, Greensboro	9	9	3	1	4	3	0	.571	51	47	27	26	6	21	0	2	29	5	4.59
David, Gastonia	7	0	0	0	1	1	1	.500	8	9	13	13	1	16	0	1	3	1	14.63
Davis, Gastonia	13	1	0	0	0	2	0	.000	29	23	17	15	5	23	1	2	24	2	4.66
DeLeon, Shelby	26	26	7	0	10	15	0	.400	168	160	108	90	19	69	3	9	118	8	4.82
DeMaria, Greensboro	7	5	1	1	2	1	0	.667	37	34	22	17	3	13	0	2	34	0	4.14
Dedmon, Anderson	2	1	1	0	1	0	0	1.000	11	10	3	1	0	3	0	1	8	3	0.82
Dexter, Shelby	7	0	0	0	0	1	0	.000	22	23	12	11	2	7	1	1	10	2	4.50
Dodd, Macon	30	17	1	1	4	8	6	.333	96	86	62	52	4	80	2	3	103	16	4.88
Doleski, Asheville	28	16	4	0	4	11	1	.267	120	121	83	60	8	53	1	0	65	8	4.50
Doud, Macon	2	1	0	0	0	0	0	.000	5	5	8	4	0	9	0	1	7	1	7.20
Downs, Spartanburg	14	12	4	1	5	7	0	.417	90	85	41	26	5	17	2	0	40	8	2.60
Dunnegan, Spartanburg ..	27	26	6	0	11	8	0	.579	165	152	72	57	6	69	1	2	94	11	3.11
Eason, Asheville*............	28	11	3	0	6	6	0	.500	95	139	79	62	9	31	0	3	74	7	5.87
Edwards, Anderson	11	6	2	0	2	3	1	.400	58	73	41	36	7	22	1	3	28	1	5.59
Espinosa, Spartanburg	3	3	1	0	1	1	0	.500	17	15	6	5	1	2	0	1	11	0	2.65
Feola, Macon*.................	7	7	1	0	0	5	0	.000	28	45	40	33	4	28	0	1	10	3	10.61
Fiepke, Shelby*	15	15	1	0	3	10	0	.231	65	80	66	52	10	49	0	3	38	15	7.20
Filson, Greensboro*........	4	4	1	1	3	0	0	1.000	27	13	5	5	0	14	0	3	34	0	1.67
Fontenot, Greensboro*	11	6	2	1	2	2	1	.500	49	41	27	20	4	19	0	1	50	1	3.67
Fossas, Asheville*...........	30	27	8	2	12	8	2	.600	197	187	84	69	11	69	0	5	140	14	3.15
Free, Greensboro	46	2	0	0	7	5	9	.583	75	60	40	33	4	48	4	1	49	3	3.96
Freedman, Macon	47	1	0	0	4	5	2	.444	91	85	50	38	4	38	5	6	94	5	3.76
Fuller, Anderson	16	13	3	2	5	4	0	.556	90	87	45	40	8	25	1	1	33	3	4.00
Gadowski, Gastonia	31	2	0	0	6	2	1	.750	82	79	48	39	9	29	1	5	38	1	4.28
Gambrell, Anderson*	10	1	0	0	0	0	0	.000	24	19	8	8	2	13	0	1	16	1	3.00
Gelinas, Shelby	10	10	2	1	5	0	0	1.000	58	36	23	17	2	47	0	3	37	3	2.64
Germer, Anderson	22	2	0	0	1	2	6	.333	43	45	18	14	2	9	0	3	36	2	2.93

Pitcher—Club	G.	GS.	CG.	ShO.	W.	L.	Sv.	Pct.	IP.	H.	R.	ER.	HR.	BB.	Int. BB.	HB.	SO.	WP.	ERA.
Gilliam, Asheville*	27	27	5	0	8	11	0	.421	155	167	113	88	19	84	2	7	119	14	5.11
Goff, Shelby	14	0	0	0	1	0	0	.000	24	33	30	25	1	25	1	5	7	5	9.38
Gonzalez, Gastonia	14	5	0	0	0	5	1	.000	43	43	38	32	4	44	1	4	23	5	6.70
Gorey, 16 Mac-9 And	25	23	6	0	4	16	0	.200	143	177	115	77	10	67	1	0	111	6	4.85
Green, Shelby	19	15	1	1	6	7	0	.462	95	103	57	45	13	28	2	1	57	5	4.26
Guante, Shelby	39	0	0	0	6	6	19	.500	90	58	32	29	3	25	2	4	114	7	2.90
Guardia, Spartanburg	26	1	0	0	2	1	1	.667	44	52	29	24	3	32	0	0	26	6	4.91
Gums, Spartanburg	30	0	0	0	5	2	2	.714	42	30	21	14	3	32	4	0	28	2	3.00
Hagen, Gastonia	29	27	6	0	14	8	0	.636	177	171	91	78	12	71	2	6	104	10	3.97
Henke, Asheville	5	5	0	0	0	2	0	.000	23	25	21	20	5	20	0	3	19	11	7.83
Henry, Asheville*	7	6	0	0	0	2	0	.000	17	17	17	15	2	22	0	1	8	5	7.94
Hergott, Charleston	15	2	0	0	2	3	1	.400	37	41	24	16	4	18	1	1	20	2	3.89
Hernandez, Greensboro*	17	14	1	0	4	6	0	.400	73	64	58	50	3	73	1	5	57	1	6.16
Horton, Gastonia*	14	3	0	0	2	4	1	.333	42	30	21	17	3	25	0	0	30	1	3.64
Huey, Shelby	4	1	0	0	1	1	0	.500	8	10	8	8	1	5	0	1	6	3	9.00
Irot, Greensboro	18	2	0	0	1	1	1	.500	41	38	22	18	5	27	1	2	30	2	3.95
Jackman, Charleston*	24	2	0	0	3	3	3	.500	46	39	25	24	4	23	0	0	33	2	4.70
Johnson, Shelby	24	23	2	0	6	10	0	.375	125	139	89	79	13	69	3	3	67	12	5.69
Jones, Gastonia	7	1	0	0	2	2	0	.500	14	16	10	8	0	6	0	0	6	0	5.14
Keenan, Asheville	47	0	0	0	9	4	7	.692	82	82	53	44	5	34	1	2	70	6	4.83
Kirby, Macon*	4	2	0	0	1	1	0	.500	12	15	8	7	1	8	0	0	8	3	5.25
Koziol, Macon	7	7	2	0	1	4	0	.200	28	42	42	35	9	23	0	0	18	1	11.25
Krauss, Charleston*	26	26	5	1	10	5	0	.667	161	153	77	68	10	73	0	5	150	10	3.80
Laughton, Charleston	11	10	1	1	2	3	1	.400	48	60	38	31	4	27	0	6	29	6	5.81
Leggatt, Macon	33	11	1	0	6	8	1	.429	144	134	78	65	12	70	1	4	100	8	4.06
Leisure, Macon*	15	0	0	0	2	1	3	.667	33	23	13	13	1	20	0	0	26	2	3.55
Lenaburg, Spartanburg	34	9	1	0	5	6	3	.455	100	114	61	47	8	38	4	3	47	12	4.23
Long, Asheville	23	1	0	0	3	2	0	.600	45	55	27	17	2	11	2	2	19	3	3.40
Marshall, Spartanburg	19	0	0	0	3	5	0	.375	44	56	34	27	2	17	2	4	19	2	5.52
Martin, Gastonia	11	6	0	0	3	5	0	.375	44	56	34	27	2	17	2	4	19	2	5.52
Martinez, Spartanburg*	4	0	0	0	1	0	0	1.000	5	1	0	0	0	1	0	0	0	0	0.00
Mathis, Macon	12	12	3	1	9	2	0	.818	86	60	25	20	4	38	0	1	78	1	2.09
Maxwell, Asheville	1	0	0	0	0	0	0	.000	2	4	2	2	1	0	0	0	3	1	9.00
McCullock, Shelby	22	0	0	0	2	1	2	.667	34	37	23	16	1	18	2	0	23	8	4.24
Miller, Macon	12	10	3	1	6	3	0	.667	69	56	30	26	1	36	3	1	36	2	3.39
Mitchell, Spartanburg	22	9	1	0	3	4	1	.429	88	96	52	36	7	49	1	4	59	11	3.68
Money, Spartanburg	27	27	6	4	8	7	0	.533	149	160	76	62	12	48	1	5	93	6	3.74
Montgomery, Macon*	26	10	0	0	4	5	2	.444	88	100	60	48	3	42	0	3	64	5	4.91
Mosby, Asheville*	21	18	1	0	5	7	0	.417	97	95	80	67	8	70	0	4	73	11	6.22
Moses, Anderson	10	1	0	0	2	2	1	.500	26	30	29	26	7	25	0	2	9	1	9.00
Murphy, Greensboro*	35	9	1	0	6	4	2	.600	108	98	56	43	10	58	1	2	59	9	3.58
Nice, Anderson	32	20	1	0	7	9	0	.438	117	147	84	67	17	58	2	3	58	11	5.15
North, Anderson	28	20	4	1	9	8	0	.529	156	167	101	72	6	71	2	6	77	10	4.15
Nurthen, Greensboro	44	0	0	0	8	4	11	.667	72	64	24	22	4	40	4	1	64	11	2.75
Palmer, Shelby*	11	11	1	0	3	4	0	.429	55	66	42	29	5	27	1	0	38	4	4.75
Palmieri, Spartanburg*	25	25	4	1	6	10	0	.375	138	140	80	58	10	60	0	7	83	13	3.78
Patterson, Anderson	28	22	8	3	7	10	0	.412	165	185	99	82	4	64	1	6	120	7	4.47
Payne, Anderson	21	21	7	0	12	6	0	.667	126	129	76	61	5	73	0	5	70	8	4.36
Pellack, Macon*	2	0	0	0	0	0	0	.000	3	9	6	6	0	3	0	2	1	1	18.00
Peralta, Shelby	15	0	0	0	1	3	2	.250	22	32	12	8	1	11	1	0	13	1	3.27
Perry, Macon	6	0	0	0	1	0	0	1.000	8	10	4	4	0	8	0	6	1	1	4.50
Pettibone, Asheville	36	4	0	0	1	5	0	.167	73	75	54	45	6	29	0	6	61	3	5.55
Pimental, Gastonia	6	0	0	0	1	0	1	1.000	11	10	5	5	1	4	1	0	12	0	4.09
Pittman, Gastonia*	2	0	0	0	1	0	0	1.000	5	5	2	2	0	0	1	0	4	0	3.60
C. Porter, Charleston	27	27	2	1	4	7	0	.364	148	166	97	85	12	94	0	5	74	8	5.17
Potestio, Charleston	9	9	3	2	7	1	0	.875	67	43	14	6	0	13	0	2	77	4	0.81
Redmond, Spartanburg	16	0	0	0	2	0	0	1.000	29	39	18	12	0	15	0	1	13	3	3.72
Rhodes, Gastonia	15	15	5	2	4	4	0	.500	98	87	39	31	1	38	1	3	61	7	2.85
Ricci, Greensboro	4	3	1	0	4	0	0	1.000	27	16	11	7	1	9	0	0	33	1	2.33
Rudolph, Greensboro	7	2	1	0	2	1	0	.667	26	29	16	15	3	11	0	0	7	0	5.19
Ruffus, Macon*	12	12	2	0	4	5	0	.444	77	77	37	28	5	41	0	5	52	3	3.27
Ryan, Charleston	27	10	5	1	7	7	0	.500	117	145	71	51	7	30	0	2	60	4	3.92
Rymer, Anderson	5	3	0	0	1	2	0	.333	11	11	16	14	0	16	0	1	6	3	11.45
Sagedahl, Greensboro	33	9	2	0	5	6	1	.455	118	125	78	57	17	33	6	4	62	9	4.35
Sanford, Charleston	14	6	1	0	1	4	2	.200	51	64	39	32	1	21	0	1	25	6	5.65
Santin, Macon*	6	0	0	0	0	1	0	.000	13	11	11	6	0	19	0	0	12	2	4.15
Schmidt, Asheville	12	11	5	1	8	1	0	.889	91	76	32	20	5	13	0	3	67	3	1.98
Semprini, Macon	7	6	2	0	0	5	0	.000	41	37	23	12	1	15	0	0	34	4	2.63
Siebert, Charleston	13	3	1	0	1	4	0	.200	35	44	38	28	2	30	4	4	14	11	7.20
F. Silva, Gastonia	21	19	1	1	9	5	0	.643	97	106	52	45	9	54	1	6	42	8	4.18
Smith, Asheville	22	7	0	0	5	3	0	.625	66	72	40	35	4	41	0	1	30	7	4.77
St. Clair, Charleston	38	0	0	0	6	4	7	.600	66	58	33	26	7	27	2	2	70	1	3.55
Staffon, Macon	5	5	1	0	2	1	0	.667	30	27	14	10	3	14	0	0	27	0	3.00
Styles, Shelby	10	1	0	0	0	1	0	1.000	14	14	14	12	0	17	0	2	15	4	9.82
Taylor, Asheville	6	2	0	0	0	2	0	.000	14	24	24	17	3	9	0	1	12	1	10.93

Pitcher—Club	G.	GS.	CG.	ShO.	W.	L.	Sv.	Pct.	IP.	H.	R.	ER.	HR.	BB.	Int. BB.	HB.	SO.	WP.	ERA.
Terrell, Asheville	3	2	0	0	1	1	0	.500	8	11	9	6	0	8	0	0	5	1	6.75
Theiss, Anderson	4	0	0	0	0	0	1	.000	5	4	2	1	0	1	0	1	3	0	1.80
Thomas, Spartanburg	39	1	0	0	5	4	3	.556	102	93	47	35	9	42	1	2	77	4	3.09
Toliver, Greensboro	20	20	4	0	6	8	0	.429	126	98	60	40	10	89	1	2	96	15	2.86
Vanderbush, Charleston ..	28	12	5	0	11	5	3	.688	121	115	64	51	5	80	6	3	106	17	3.79
Vanderplas, Greensboro*.	22	22	2	0	10	6	0	.625	106	98	65	55	9	82	1	3	66	11	4.67
Vazquez, Gastonia	10	6	0	0	1	2	0	.333	20	19	19	18	3	17	1	0	25	2	8.10
Vega, 6 Gas-4 Mac	10	1	0	0	0	1	0	.000	24	36	25	24	0	19	1	2	19	4	9.00
Vickers, Asheville*	6	6	1	0	4	2	0	.667	43	36	17	14	2	14	0	0	20	4	2.93
Voyles, Charleston	27	1	0	0	11	3	1	.786	83	74	40	31	5	60	0	3	73	7	3.36
Weaver, Gastonia	16	13	4	0	4	5	0	.444	96	95	52	39	3	20	1	3	67	10	3.66
West, Macon......................	2	0	0	0	0	1	0	.000	2	3	2	1	0	1	0	0	2	1	4.50
Williams, Shelby*	25	9	0	0	6	6	0	.500	89	85	53	43	5	47	0	4	43	7	4.35
Wills, Charleston	9	9	3	0	2	5	0	.286	57	59	33	23	1	32	0	5	48	6	3.63
Yuhas, Charleston	24	24	5	0	7	9	0	.438	139	169	82	67	12	39	1	7	73	7	4.34

BALKS—Bresnen, Green, 8 each; Fossas, 7; Guante, 5; Begue, Cliburn, DeLeon, Hernandez, Jackman, Krauss, Laughton, Nice, Porter, Toliver, Vanderplas, 4 each; DeMaria, Filson, Lenaburg, Mathis, Palmer, Staffon, Williams, 3 each; Baller, Cepeda, Doleski, Dunnegan, Horton, Keenan, Laughton, Leisure, Lenaburg, Mitchell, Payne, Peralta, Ryan, Semprini, Thomas, Wills, 2 each; Adkins, Arroyo, Ballard, Bielecki, Burdette, Castaigne, Citarella, Coghill, Collins, Dexter, Dodd, Doud, Downs, Eason, Feola, Fiepke, Fontenot, Free, Freedman, Gadowski, Gilliam, Goff, Gonzalez, Gorey, Gums, Irot, Johnson, Kirby, Koziol, Marshall, Martin, Money, Montgomery, Murphy, North, Palmieri, Pellack, Pettibone, Pimental, Redmond, Rhodes, Ricci, Sagedahl, Sanford, Schmidt, Smith, Styles, Vazquez, Vega, Voyles, West, 1 each.

COMBINATION SHUTOUTS—Payne-Edwards, Anderson; Fossas-Keenan, Asheville; Laughton-St. Clair, Porter-St. Clair, Krauss-Voyles, Wills-Voyles, Krauss-Jackman, Potestio-Jackman, Charleston; Silva-Clark, Vazquez-Horton, Davis-Citarella, Gastonia; Filson-Sagedahl, Greensboro; Johnson-Guante, Palmer-Guante, Shelby; Baller-Cepeda, Dunnegan-Redmond, Baller-Cepeda, Spartanburg.

NO-HIT GAMES—Filson, Greensboro, defeated Gastonia, 4-0, April 25 (first game, seven innings); Vazquez (⅔ inn.)-Horton (6⅓ inn.), Gastonia, defeated Charleston, 4-0, July 28 (second game, seven innings).

No-Hitter With Asterisk

Lefthander Rick Horton of the Gastonia Cardinals in the South Atlantic League had an 0-2 record and had been yanked from the starting rotation.

On July 28, the 21-year-old Horton entered the second game of a twi-night doubleheader at Charleston when starter Rafael Vasquez was forced to leave with a sore arm after two outs in the first inning.

Horton posted his first professional victory by tossing 6⅓ innings of hitless ball in the seven-inning game as the Cardinals topped the Royals, 4-0.

Appalachian League

SUMMER CLASS A CLASSIFICATION

CHAMPIONSHIP WINNERS IN PREVIOUS YEARS

1921—Greenville	.608
Johnson City*	.627
1922—Bristol	.557
1923—Knoxville	.635
1924—Knoxville*	.642
Bristol	.607
1925—Greenville	.667
1926-36—Did not operate.	
1937—Elizabethton	.559
Pennington Gap*	.580
1938—Elizabethton	.664
Greenville (3rd)†	.571
1939—Elizabethton‡	.597
1940—Johnson City§	.726
Elizabethton	.750
1941—Johnson City	.614
Elizabethton*	.661
1942—Bristol	.667
Bristol x	.660
1943—Bristol	.755
Bristol y	.617
1944—Kingsport‡	.575

1945—Kingsport‡	.670
1946—New River‡	.675
1947—Pulaski	.648
New River (3rd)†	.516
1948—Pulaski‡	.680
1949—Bluefield‡	.721
1950—Bluefield	.600
Bluefield z	.745
1951—Kingsport‡	.659
1952—Johnson City	.595
Welch (3rd)†	.509
1953—Welch*	.705
Johnson City	.672
1954—Bluefield‡	.619
1955—Salem**	.689
1956—Did not operate.	
1957—Bluefield	.701
1958—Johnson City	.662
1959—Morristown	.603
1960—Wytheville	.614
1961—Middlesboro	.591
1962—Bluefield	.671

1963—Bluefield	.652
1964—Johnson City	.662
1965—Salem	.614
1966—Marion	.623
1967—Bluefield	.627
1968—Marion	.583
1969—Pulaski a	.576
Johnson City	.544
1970—Bluefield	.638
1971—Bluefield a	.609
Kingsport	.559
1972—Bristol a	.588
Covington	.586
1973—Kingsport	.757
1974—Bristol a	.754
Bluefield	.536
1975—Marion	.515
Johnson City a	.603
1976—Johnson City a	.714
Bluefield	.600
1977—Kingsport	.623
1978—Elizabethton	.594
1979—Paintsville	.800

*Won split-season playoff. †Won four-team playoff. ‡Won championship and four-team playoff. §Johnson City, first-half winner, won playoff involving six clubs. xWon both halves and defeated second-place Elizabethton in playoff. yWon both halves, but Erwin won four-team playoff. zWon both halves, but Bristol won two-club playoff. **Salem and Johnson City declared playoff co-champions when weather forced cancellation of final series. aLeague was divided into Northern, Southern divisions; declared league champion, based on highest won-lost percentage.

STANDING OF CLUBS AT CLOSE OF SEASON, AUGUST 28

Club	Pvl.	Bri.	Kpt.	Eliz.	Blu.	J.C.	W.	L.	T.	Pct.	G.B.
Paintsville (Yankees)	..	9	11	8	10	8	46	24	0	.657	......
Bristol (Tigers)	5	..	7	7	6	11	36	33	0	.522	9½
Kingsport (Mets)	3	7	..	9	8	8	35	35	1	.500	11
Elizabethton (Twins)	6	7	5	..	8	6	32	36	0	.471	13
Bluefield (Orioles)	4	8	6	4	..	7	29	39	0	.426	16
Johnson City (Cardinals)	6	2	6	8	7	..	29	40	1	.420	16½

Major league affiliations in parentheses.

Playoffs—None.

Regular-Season Attendance—Bluefield, 24,413; Bristol, 12,300; Elizabethton, 10,974; Johnson City, 26,887; Kingsport, 35,730; Paintsville, 17,404. Total, 127,708. No playoffs or all-star game.

Managers: Bluefield—Grady Little; Bristol—Tom Kotchman; Elizabethton—Fred Waters; Johnson City—Johnny Lewis; Kingsport—Chuck Hiller; Paintsville—Mike Easom.

All-Star Team: 1B—Foster, Elizabethton; 2B—Millholland, Paintsville; 3B—Ojeda, Johnson City; SS—Harris, Johnson City; OF—Eisenreich, Elizabethton; Heller, Kingsport; Vejar, Paintsville; J. Williams, Bluefield; C—Carrasquel, Bristol; Utility-Pittman, Kingsport; DH—Peterson, Paintsville; P—Gaston, Paintsville; Johnson, Bluefield; Manager—Kotchman, Bristol.

(Compiled by Howe News Bureau, Boston, Mass.)

CLUB BATTING

Club	G.	AB.	R.	OR.	H.	TB.	2B.	3B.	HR.	RBI.	SH.	SF.	Int. BB.	BB.	HP.	SO.	SB.	CS.	LOB.	Pct.
Paintsville	70	2277	459	314	665	1012	118	11	69	386	31	34	363	18	28	306	42	17	517	.292
Bluefield	68	2236	361	373	615	902	95	24	48	312	8	22	246	10	11	379	59	23	482	.275
Elizabethton	68	2206	378	371	588	811	102	11	33	309	16	14	335	7	32	344	56	11	547	.267
Johnson City	70	2281	332	418	609	867	95	17	43	278	19	20	232	2	18	428	60	19	519	.267
Kingsport	71	2230	356	370	591	841	84	20	42	299	18	26	268	8	26	370	46	19	468	.265
Bristol	69	2184	312	352	494	729	90	11	41	270	29	14	314	12	22	432	31	13	510	.226

INDIVIDUAL BATTING

(Leading Qualifiers for Batting Championship—189 or More Plate Appearances)

*Bats lefthanded.   †Switch-hitter.

Player and Club	G.	AB.	R.	H.	TB.	2B.	3B.	HR.	RBI.	SH.	SF.	BB.	HP.	SO.	SB.	CS.	Pct.
Peterson, Erik, Paintsville	59	224	47	85	136	12	0	13	40	3	5	12	3	19	2	1	.379
Foster, Kenneth, Elizabethton	66	243	41	86	130	20	0	8	55	1	6	28	3	18	0	1	.354
Williams, Jeffrey, Bluefield*	58	214	34	74	91	10	2	1	28	2	0	23	0	29	7	4	.346
Vejar, Matthew, Paintsville	69	268	59	91	134	17	1	8	50	3	5	37	3	17	14	4	.340
Robertson, Glenn, Paintsville	64	193	44	62	100	15	1	7	44	2	4	47	3	14	1	1	.321
Wirkus, Paul, Johnson City	69	252	40	78	124	19	0	9	46	0	4	27	0	43	2	0	.310
Knight, Timothy, Paintsville*	70	240	53	74	104	11	2	5	39	2	2	47	2	42	6	3	.308
Hamilton, Larry, Paintsville	47	154	31	47	76	9	1	6	37	0	1	37	3	29	0	1	.305
Brown, Tim, Kingsport	45	162	30	49	58	4	1	1	12	5	1	14	7	10	1	2	.302
Ojeda, Luis, Johnson City	63	209	33	63	94	14	4	3	35	1	2	26	1	20	3	2	.301

Departmental Leaders: G—Knight, 70; AB—Vejar, 268; R—Vejar, 59; H—Vejar, 91; TB—Peterson, 136; 2B—Foster, 20; 3B—Eisenreich, Heller, J. Jackson, Ojeda, 4; HR—Sheets, 14; RBI—Foster, 55; GWRBI—Heller, 8; SH—Millholland, 7; SF—Foster, Perna, 6; BB—Knight, Robertson, 47; HP—T. Brown, Gibbons, 7; SO—L. Pittman, 53; SB—Dillard, 24; CS—Thrower, 7.

(All Players—Listed Alphabetically)

Player and Club	G.	AB.	R.	H.	TB.	2B.	3B.	HR.	RBI.	SH.	SF.	BB.	HP.	SO.	SB.	CS.	Pct.
Adduci, James, Johnson City*	17	63	15	21	40	4	0	5	16	0	0	12	0	13	0	1	.333
Baker, Brad, Elizabethton	41	127	24	32	43	8	0	1	26	5	0	23	2	16	1	0	.252
Baker, Christopher, Bristol	13	44	4	9	13	1	0	1	6	2	0	1	0	5	0	0	.205
Batista, Francisco, Johnson City	37	93	10	23	29	3	0	1	10	0	1	4	0	16	2	0	.247
Beswick, Rick, Elizabethton†	55	168	27	37	43	3	0	1	18	1	1	29	2	48	1	0	.220
Brandt, Kevin, Elizabethton	2	5	1	0	0	0	0	0	0	0	0	1	1	3	0	0	.000
Brigante, Steven, Kingsport	54	177	23	42	55	6	2	1	23	2	0	23	0	25	7	0	.237
Brown, Tim, Kingsport	45	162	30	49	58	4	1	1	12	5	1	14	7	10	1	2	.302
Burns, Carl, Bristol	25	64	5	9	12	0	0	1	2	0	0	2	0	19	0	0	.141
Butler, William, Bluefield	19	54	9	14	17	3	0	0	5	0	1	6	1	0	1	2	.259
Callahan, Benjamin, Paintsville	23	21	1	3	3	0	0	0	2	1	0	7	0	8	0	0	.143
Carrasquel, Emilio, Bristol	58	198	30	59	90	14	1	5	34	0	1	32	0	23	2	1	.298
Cashore, Ronald, Bluefield	55	170	25	39	60	9	0	4	22	1	4	13	0	36	4	3	.229
Cassanovas, Roberto, Bristol*	55	176	29	36	65	6	1	7	23	1	0	35	3	47	4	3	.205
Cole, Michael, Elizabethton*	54	212	41	61	69	6	1	0	20	0	0	34	4	21	14	2	.288
D'Aloia, James, Paintsville	35	66	17	13	14	1	0	0	2	0	0	11	0	3	2	1	.197
Dacko, Mark, Bristol*	10	1	0	0	0	0	0	0	0	0	0	0	0	0	0	0	.000
DeLeon, John, Bluefield	43	113	19	31	50	4	0	5	23	0	1	25	4	42	0	2	.274
Del Monte, John, Johnson City*	36	119	26	37	64	6	0	7	18	1	1	16	2	25	6	0	.311
Dillard, Ronald, Bluefield	61	229	51	60	79	10	3	1	18	1	2	30	0	44	24	4	.262
Driver, Jon, Bristol	25	72	9	13	17	4	0	0	8	0	2	4	0	12	0	0	.181
Duhon, Guy, Elizabethton	36	118	23	28	56	2	1	8	20	1	0	10	2	27	3	1	.237
Dummar, George, Bluefield*	38	109	9	25	34	5	2	0	12	0	0	9	0	20	0	0	.229
Dunbar, Bryan, Kingsport	21	46	10	11	16	2	0	1	4	1	1	7	1	13	0	0	.239
Echenique, Orlando, Kingsport	10	27	5	9	12	3	0	0	5	0	2	3	0	4	0	0	.333
Eisenreich, James, Elizabethton*	67	258	47	77	106	12	4	3	41	0	2	35	3	32	12	3	.298
Elliot, Mark, Kingsport*	34	80	12	19	24	5	0	0	8	3	3	12	1	6	3	2	.238
Fink, Bill, Johnson City*	22	45	6	9	13	1	0	1	4	0	0	5	1	12	0	0	.200
Foster, Kenneth, Elizabethton	66	243	41	86	130	20	0	8	55	1	6	28	3	18	0	1	.354
Fuller, Leo, Kingsport*	42	127	20	35	43	3	1	1	15	0	1	13	1	14	4	0	.276
Gambeski, Michael, Johnson City	14	34	3	4	4	0	0	0	1	0	0	3	0	6	0	0	.118
Garcia, Jose, Johnson City	32	75	11	14	19	0	1	1	4	0	0	8	2	17	1	1	.187
Gibbons, John, Kingsport	53	181	28	50	80	7	1	7	34	0	4	18	7	39	1	3	.276
Gilmore, Lawrence, Bristol*	47	126	20	31	55	7	1	5	25	2	1	31	0	18	2	1	.246
Gjesdal, Brent, Paintsville	12	32	3	5	6	1	0	0	2	0	0	5	1	9	0	0	.156
Glenn, Casey, Elizabethton*	11	28	3	1	1	0	0	0	2	0	0	3	0	8	0	0	.036
Gohde, George, Paintsville	33	108	13	23	33	5	1	1	14	4	1	10	2	13	1	1	.213
Gonzales, James, Johnson City	39	99	9	21	36	4	1	3	11	0	0	7	0	33	1	0	.212
Greenfield, Richard, Kingsport	56	145	11	27	31	4	0	0	14	2	2	25	1	34	1	2	.186
Gross, James, Paintsville	18	54	6	12	17	5	0	0	5	1	3	5	1	6	0	0	.222
Hamilton, Larry, Paintsville	47	154	31	47	76	9	1	6	37	0	1	37	3	29	0	1	.305
Hanson, Gregory, Elizabethton	10	24	2	5	5	0	0	0	1	0	0	0	0	7	0	0	.208
Harris, Michael, Johnson City	62	206	29	48	56	5	0	1	20	3	3	14	3	38	5	1	.233
Harvey, Nelson, Bluefield	7	25	1	4	5	1	0	0	1	0	0	0	0	9	0	0	.160
Harvey, Randall, Bristol*	57	176	21	41	58	8	0	3	21	2	0	23	0	36	1	2	.233
Heller, John, Kingsport*	68	241	41	66	101	6	4	7	41	0	4	18	0	40	2	2	.274
Hench, R. William, Paintsville	54	180	38	46	74	9	2	5	25	3	4	28	2	21	0	1	.256
Hennesey, Michael, Kingsport†	56	181	37	40	50	2	1	2	20	1	2	35	2	21	10	0	.221
Hughes, Donald K., Johnson City	18	1	0	0	0	0	0	0	0	0	0	0	0	0	0	0	.000
Ivie, Lonnie, Bluefield	31	81	12	19	35	6	2	2	12	0	1	7	0	17	0	0	.235
Jackson, John, Kingsport	54	190	32	57	82	11	4	2	27	1	2	17	3	14	5	5	.300
Jackson, Harold, Elizabethton	8	0	0	0	0	0	0	0	0	0	0	0	0	0	0	0	.000
Jones, Michael, Bristol*	31	66	7	14	15	1	0	0	7	2	0	17	0	21	1	0	.212
Jones, Richard, Bluefield	59	199	27	55	88	9	3	6	33	1	2	19	0	22	4	2	.276
Knight, Timothy, Paintsville*	70	240	53	74	104	11	2	5	39	2	2	47	2	42	6	3	.308

Player and Club	G.	AB.	R.	H.	TB.	2B.	3B.	HR.	RBI.	SH.	SF.	BB.	HP.	SO.	SB.	CS.	Pct.
Lanum, Michael, Elizabethton	19	55	11	14	18	2	1	0	7	1	0	10	0	9	0	0	.255
Littlefield, David, Paintsville	17	45	6	11	18	1	0	2	7	1	0	6	1	11	0	0	.244
Lundgren, Richard, Paintsville	5	10	2	4	4	0	0	0	1	0	0	2	0	4	0	0	.400
Manning, Mark, Kingsport	44	133	21	32	44	7	1	1	14	2	0	18	2	26	5	1	.241
Mariano, Bob, Paintsville	6	18	5	6	7	1	0	0	1	0	0	2	0	3	0	0	.333
Marshall, Richard, Bluefield*	46	121	16	25	43	2	2	4	21	0	1	11	1	32	3	0	.207
Martin, Jeffery, Elizabethton*	21	60	5	11	13	2	0	0	4	0	0	2	2	13	0	0	.183
Martinez, Luis, Bluefield*	40	95	20	23	33	3	2	1	13	0	1	8	0	15	2	2	.242
Martinez, Wilfredo, Johnson City	8	7	2	1	1	0	0	0	1	0	0	2	0	3	0	0	.143
Matos, Carlos, Johnson City	15	40	3	10	17	2	1	1	7	0	1	1	0	12	0	0	.250
McCauley, Jeffery, Bluefield*	14	11	1	1	1	0	0	0	0	0	0	1	0	3	0	0	.091
McClenden, Lloyd, Kingsport	14	46	7	15	20	2	0	1	9	0	0	5	0	7	0	1	.326
McEvilly, Michael, Bristol	19	61	10	15	23	2	0	2	12	0	0	9	3	6	2	0	.246
Mendez, Luis, Bristol	16	46	6	9	12	3	0	0	5	2	0	4	0	5	1	0	.196
Merkle, Thomas, Bristol	51	138	14	23	28	5	0	0	8	2	0	25	1	43	0	1	.167
Millholland, John, Paintsville	65	253	56	74	109	10	2	7	33	7	0	34	6	24	12	5	.292
Moore, Alan, Johnson City*	13	22	1	3	4	1	0	0	0	0	0	4	0	4	0	0	.136
Nash, William, Bristol*	19	33	3	6	6	0	0	0	3	0	0	3	2	10	3	0	.182
Nichols, Carl, Bluefield	37	85	24	18	24	2	0	0	10	0	1	18	3	12	4	1	.212
Nunez, Domingo, Elizabethton	43	133	32	34	59	7	0	6	27	3	0	30	0	37	8	1	.256
Ojeda, Luis, Johnson City	63	209	33	63	94	14	4	3	35	1	2	26	1	20	3	2	.301
Palica, John, Elizabethton	25	206	34	53	75	6	2	4	33	0	1	22	3	23	7	0	.257
Pardo, Alberto, Bluefield†	48	151	26	52	71	6	2	3	23	0	2	17	0	16	1	0	.344
Pardo, Braulio, Bluefield†	23	45	4	13	17	1	0	1	3	1	0	5	0	6	0	0	.289
Perkins, Davy, Bristol*	10	16	1	2	2	0	0	0	1	2	0	4	0	9	0	0	.125
Perna, Joe, Paintsville*	58	186	38	47	79	5	0	9	41	2	6	37	1	47	3	0	.253
Perrett, Kevin, Bristol	9	8	2	2	4	2	0	0	0	0	0	7	2	0	0	0	.250
Peterson, Erik, Paintsville	59	224	47	85	136	12	0	13	40	3	5	12	3	19	2	1	.379
Pittman, Larry, Kingsport	68	238	41	68	118	13	2	11	44	0	1	35	0	53	0	0	.286
Pittman, Michael, Johnson City*	18	1	0	0	0	0	0	0	0	0	0	0	0	1	0	0	.000
Price, William, Elizabethton	29	74	10	17	26	4	1	1	10	1	0	11	3	18	1	1	.230
Pyle, Scot, Bristol	14	39	9	7	9	2	0	0	5	1	0	11	1	10	2	1	.179
Ramppen, Frank, Elizabethton	50	165	22	40	49	9	0	0	11	0	1	22	2	27	4	0	.242
Redmond, Perry, Johnson City	15	29	2	2	2	0	0	0	0	0	0	1	0	15	0	0	.069
Reed, Jeff, Elizabethton*	65	225	39	64	84	15	1	1	20	2	2	51	4	23	2	2	.284
Reeder, Michael, Bristol	63	211	31	44	67	5	3	4	25	3	3	35	0	51	0	1	.209
Robertson, Glenn, Paintsville	64	193	44	62	100	15	1	7	44	2	4	47	3	14	1	1	.321
Rodriguez, Jose R., Johnson City	7	11	0	1	1	0	0	0	0	0	0	0	0	2	0	0	.091
Russell, Ronald, Paintsville	66	225	40	62	98	16	1	6	43	2	3	36	0	36	1	0	.276
Sadey, Richard, Bluefield	29	75	8	20	33	3	2	2	8	1	1	3	0	18	3	1	.267
Sanchez, Jose, Johnson City	35	64	7	17	19	2	0	0	4	3	1	5	0	8	0	2	.266
Schriner, Terry, Bluefield	6	14	4	4	8	1	0	1	1	0	0	5	0	7	0	0	.286
Sheets, Larry, Bluefield*	37	124	29	47	100	9	1	14	47	0	3	17	1	14	0	0	.379
Silber, Michael, Bristol	45	120	15	24	30	6	0	0	12	5	2	17	0	22	3	0	.200
Simononis, David, Bristol	41	92	16	27	44	8	0	3	14	2	3	6	3	12	0	1	.293
Smith, Mark S., Bristol	63	241	36	62	86	5	2	5	31	1	1	8	3	34	4	1	.257
Snell, Thomas, Bluefield	3	6	0	1	1	0	0	0	0	0	1	1	0	2	0	0	.167
Southern, Mitchell, Johnson City*	50	140	18	32	57	8	1	5	26	1	2	14	2	46	1	1	.229
Spears, Kenneth, Johnson City*	65	232	38	69	89	5	3	3	26	3	2	26	1	40	11	2	.297
Spencer, Jeff, Bluefield	49	155	21	40	54	6	1	2	18	0	1	11	1	19	1	1	.258
Stevens, James, Johnson City	4	6	1	1	1	0	0	0	0	0	0	0	1	3	0	0	.167
Stone, David, Kingsport	35	99	11	29	41	4	1	2	9	1	1	5	0	25	2	0	.293
Strawberry, Darryl, Kingsport*	44	157	27	42	66	5	2	5	20	0	2	20	1	39	5	1	.268
Stryffeler, Daniel, Johnson City*	52	170	20	50	67	8	3	1	14	2	1	17	0	23	6	1	.294
Suarez, Nelson, Elizabethton	33	103	16	28	34	6	0	0	14	1	1	23	1	13	3	0	.272
Thrower, Arnold, Johnson City†	54	207	31	62	72	7	0	1	22	3	1	21	4	23	17	7	.300
Timko, Andrew, Bluefield*	40	148	20	49	57	5	0	1	12	1	0	15	0	10	5	1	.331
Vaughn, R. Scott, Bristol	3	1	0	0	0	0	0	0	0	0	0	0	0	0	0	0	.000
Vejar, Matthew, Paintsville*	69	268	59	91	134	17	1	8	50	3	5	37	3	17	14	4	.340
Walsh, Thomas, Bristol	7	20	4	3	4	1	0	0	2	0	0	4	1	1	1	0	.150
Ward, Willie, Bristol	24	60	7	20	28	5	0	1	8	0	0	2	0	11	0	0	.333
Weems, C. Richard, Johnson City	49	128	24	37	52	6	3	1	9	2	1	17	0	19	3	1	.289
Williams, Ray, Johnson City	15	28	3	6	6	0	0	0	4	0	0	5	1	6	2	0	.214
Williams, Charles, Bluefield*	4	12	1	1	1	0	0	0	0	0	0	2	0	6	0	0	.083
Williams, Jeffrey, Bluefield*	58	214	34	74	91	10	2	1	28	2	0	23	0	29	7	4	.346
Wirkus, Paul, Johnson City	69	252	40	78	124	19	0	9	46	0	4	27	0	43	2	0	.310
Yett, Richard, Elizabethton	11	2	0	0	0	0	0	0	0	0	0	0	0	1	0	0	.000
Young, Kevin, Bristol*	55	175	33	38	61	5	3	4	18	2	1	34	3	37	5	1	.217

The following pitchers had no plate appearances primarily through use of designated hitters, listed alphabetically by club, games in parentheses:

BLUEFIELD—Brown, Mark* (6); Carcella, Kevin (11); Clark, Irvin* (4); Conradi, Fred* (3); Cratch, Richard (11); Dixon, Kenneth (13); Gessell, Steven (11); Hoke, Leon* (22); Johnson, Scott* (11); Jordan, Kenneth (9); Kreymborg, Michael (5); Maples, Timothy (10); Marston, Anderson* (12); Richmond, Richard (23); Usher, Kevin (6); Willsher, Christopher (10).

BRISTOL—Camp, Michael (2); Clark, James (12); Collyer, Richard* (13); Fellows, Mark (13); Gonzalski, Thomas (11); Jensen, Christoffer (2); Mathis, Ronald (3); Michaud, Norman* (11); Nutter, Gary (10); O'Connor, Nicholas (15); Ruffus, Robert (2); Sanchez, Luis (7); Snyder, Carl (5); Untisz, Michael (13); Vavrock, Robert (19); Warren, Michael (12).

ELIZABETHTON—Arrington, Samuel (10); Blumenschein, Mark* (15); Christensen, Harry (13); Galvez, Roberto (1); Govero, Barry (1); Harris, Larry (10); Jackson, David (12); Moll, Michael (14); Orosco, Boyce (9); Palica, Wayne (18); Parreira, Francis (8); Pfautsch, Michael* (2); Silva, Keith* (1); Thomas, Christopher (10); Wilson, David* (14).

JOHNSON CITY—Bretz, Michael (9); Brooks, Robert (15); Collins, Donald (11); Dozier, Thomas (11); Epple, Thomas† (6); Fehr, Kevin (20); Fish, Timothy* (9); Gonzalez, Jesus (6); Martin, John (2); Milligan, Brent (12); Mohler, Kenneth (13); North, Jay (14); Ramos, Mario (4); Taveras, Luis (14); Taylor, Jeffery* (14); Warburton, Jeffrey (11).

KINGSPORT—Alba, Fernando (13); Barton, David (1); Faust, Clifford* (25); Foust, Algernan (7); Ibarguen, Stephen (13); Kuntz, Eric (9); Magdziuk, Donald (14); Merlack, Scott* (18); Pina, Elvin* (7); Robinson, Lowrey (14); Sisk, Douglas (15); Teate, E. Kevin (14); Tibbs, Jay (12).

PAINTSVILLE—Bottoroff, John (6); Collins, Joseph (13); DeWitt, H. Donald (11); Fincher, Steve* (8); Gaston, John (13); Kennedy, Gerald (13); Kuhn, Laurence (4); Livesey, Michael* (12); Martin, Kenneth (2); Mitchell, Richard (6); Olwine, Edward* (13); Quirk, Kevin (16); Raftice, Robert* (1); Smith, Kenneth (18); Szymczak, David (13).

GRAND SLAM HOME RUNS—Fuller, Millholland, L. Pittman, Robertson, Sheets, 1 each.

AWARDED FIRST BASE ON INTERFERENCE—Gilmore 3 (Gibbons, Reed, Russell); Ramppen 2 (Driver, Littlefield); Young 2 (Dunbar, Martin); Gonzales (Martin); Mendez (Gibbons).

GAME-WINNING RBIs

BLUEFIELD (22)—Cashore 4, Sheets 4, Dillard 2, Ivie 2, Jones 2, DeLeon 1, Dummar 1, Marshall 1, Nichols 1, A. Pardo 1, Sadey 1, Spencer 1, J. Williams 1.

BRISTOL (23)—Carrasqual 4, Cassanovas 4, Gilmore 2, Jones 2, McEvilly 2, Reeder 2, Smith 2, Harvey 1, Pyle 1, Silber 1, Simononis 1, Young 1.

ELIZABETHTON (13)—Beswick 3, Duhon 2, Foster 2, Reed 2, Eisenreich 1, Nunez 1, Ramppen 1, Suarez 1.

JOHNSON CITY (19)—Spears 6, Batista 3, Thrower 3, Harris 2, Gonzales 1, Matos 1, Ojeda 1, Southern 1, Weems 1.

KINGSPORT (21)—Heller 8, Pittman 3, Hennesey 2, Jackson 2, Brigante 1, Echenique 1, Gibbons 1, Greenfield 1, McClenden 1, Strawberry 1.

PAINTSVILLE (33)—Hamilton 6, Robertson 6, Vejar 4, Perna 3, Peterson 3, Russell 3, Gohde 2, Hench 2, Knight 2, Littlefield 1, Lundgren 1.

CLUB FIELDING

Club	G.	PO.	A.	E.	DP.	PB.	Pct.	Club	G.	PO.	A.	E.	DP.	PB.	Pct.
Paintsville	70	1737	782	104	60	18	.960	Bristol	69	1714	727	128	46	9	.950
Elizabethton	68	1691	696	105	83	18	.958	Kingsport	71	1738	767	135	72	22	.949
Johnson City	69	1707	743	107	64	14	.958	Bluefield	68	1614	626	123	58	13	.948

Triple Plays—None.

INDIVIDUAL FIELDING

*Throws lefthanded.

FIRST BASEMEN

Player and Club	G.	PO.	A.	E.	DP.	Pct.	Player and Club	G.	PO.	A.	E.	DP.	Pct.
Nunez, Elizabethton	7	50	4	0	5	1.000	Wirkus, Johnson C	70	612	32	11	56	.983
Elliot, Kingsport	5	34	0	0	4	1.000	Callahan, Paintsville	6	37	3	1	1	.976
Nichols, Bluefield	4	27	1	0	5	1.000	Pittman, Kingsport	65	570	58	16	58	.975
Echenique, Kingsport	1	10	1	0	2	1.000	Dummar, Bluefield*	30	191	11	6	14	.971
D'Aloia, Paintsville	1	9	0	0	1	1.000	DeLeon, Bluefield	43	276	18	10	30	.967
Hamilton, Paintsville	1	9	0	0	1	1.000	Gilmore, Bristol	21	201	6	7	10	.967
A. Pardo, Bluefield	1	2	1	0	0	1.000	Ward, Bristol	14	75	3	3	5	.963
Harvey, Bristol*	44	338	26	3	22	.992	Mariano, Paintsville	3	20	3	1	2	.958
FOSTER, Elizabethton	63	552	37	7	68	.988	Stevens, Johnson C	4	17	0	1	1	.944
Russell, Paintsville	38	313	31	5	23	.986	Brigante, Kingsport	2	17	0	2	2	.895
Peterson, Paintsville	29	256	20	4	28	.986							

SECOND BASEMEN

Player and Club	G.	PO.	A.	E.	DP.	Pct.	Player and Club	G.	PO.	A.	E.	DP.	Pct.
Price, Elizabethton	18	36	61	0	16	1.000	Millholland, Paints	65	141	188	18	35	.948
D'Aloia, Paintsville	11	11	13	0	1	1.000	Brigante, Kingsport	27	67	94	9	11	.947
Timko, Bluefield	5	14	5	0	1	1.000	Pyle, Bristol	8	16	20	2	1	.947
Manning, Kingsport	1	1	1	0	0	1.000	Sanchez, Johnson C	10	9	27	2	2	.947
Ramppen, Elizabethton	1	1	1	0	1	1.000	Thrower, Johnson C	53	121	161	17	30	.943
Baker, Elizabethton	1	0	1	0	0	1.000	C. Williams, Bluefield	2	6	8	1	3	.933
Peterson, Paintsville	2	0	1	0	0	1.000	Jones, Bristol	27	36	44	6	10	.930
COLE, Elizabethton	51	123	144	5	37	.982	Spencer, Bluefield	3	9	3	1	1	.923
Brown, Kingsport	43	80	130	6	35	.972	Greenfield, Kingsport	1	1	5	1	0	.857
Silber, Bristol	38	74	105	8	21	.957	Butler, Bluefield	2	1	4	1	0	.833
Garcia, Johnson C	13	23	39	3	11	.954	Walsh, Bristol	7	10	12	5	1	.815
Dillard, Bluefield	56	152	152	16	27	.950	McCauley, Bluefield*	7	3	1	0	.800

THIRD BASEMEN

Player and Club	G.	PO.	A.	E.	DP.	Pct.	Player and Club	G.	PO.	A.	E.	DP.	Pct.
Dillard, Bluefield	4	6	3	0	0	1.000	Baker, Elizabethton	3	5	4	1	1	.900
Greenfield, Kingsport	1	1	3	0	0	1.000	Nunez, Elizabethton	19	17	24	5	6	.891
B. Pardo, Bluefield	1	0	1	0	1	1.000	Brigante, Kingsport	22	24	46	9	6	.886
Redmond, Johnson C	1	1	0	0	0	1.000	Gambeski, Johnson C.	10	8	15	3	1	.885
OJEDA, Johnson City	54	55	96	6	10	.962	Manning, Kingsport	23	18	43	8	5	.884
Gross, Paintsville	18	12	30	2	1	.955	Harvey, Bluefield	7	3	10	2	1	.867
Cassanovas, Bristol	14	14	22	2	1	.947	Heller, Kingsport	7	1	9	2	0	.833
Batista, Johnson C	13	12	18	2	4	.938	Fuller, Kingsport	27	13	51	13	3	.831
Hench, Paintsville	53	39	78	8	8	.929	Burns, Bristol	21	22	28	11	2	.820
Spencer, Bluefield	39	25	67	7	5	.929	Butler, Bluefield	9	3	10	3	0	.813
Merkle, Bristol	42	32	85	11	6	.914	Sadey, Bluefield	15	13	14	7	2	.794
Ramppen, Elizabethton	45	34	65	10	7	.908	Lanum, Elizabethton	1	0	0	1	0	.000

SHORTSTOPS

Player and Club	G.	PO.	A.	E.	DP.	Pct.	Player and Club	G.	PO.	A.	E.	DP.	Pct.
Butler, Bluefield	9	11	16	0	1	1.000	Silber, Bristol	4	8	13	2	5	.913
Pyle, Bristol	4	9	11	0	1	1.000	Jones, Bluefield	28	35	67	12	5	.895
Hench, Paintsville	1	2	1	0	0	1.000	Peterson, Paintsville	2	2	6	1	0	.889
Suarez, Elizabethton	13	16	38	3	9	.947	Price, Elizabethton	3	3	11	2	3	.875
REEDER, Bristol	61	78	169	16	19	.939	Baker, Elizabethton	37	51	104	23	29	.871
Robertson, Paintsville	62	99	209	21	39	.936	Garcia, Johnson C	17	26	32	9	7	.866
Harris, Johnson C	61	107	168	22	34	.926	C. Williams, Bluefield	2	0	6	1	2	.857
D'Aloia, Paintsville	8	6	17	2	3	.920	Jones, Bristol	1	2	3	1	0	.833
Timko, Bluefield	34	65	83	13	18	.919	Nunez, Elizabethton	1	3	5	4	1	.667
Manning, Kingsport	23	33	57	8	18	.918	Sanchez, Johnson C	2	0	1	1	0	.500
Greenfield, Kingsport	54	72	128	18	33	.917	Sadey, Bluefield	4	1	3	5	2	.444
Lanum, Elizabethton	18	29	48	7	10	.917							

OUTFIELDERS

Player and Club	G.	PO.	A.	E.	DP.	Pct.	Player and Club	G.	PO.	A.	E.	DP.	Pct.
Jones, Bluefield	29	43	1	0	1	1.000	Hennesey, Kings*	54	91	5	3	2	.970
McEvilly, Bristol*	18	37	5	0	0	1.000	Adduci, Johnson C*	14	27	2	1	0	.967
Williams, Johnson C	11	19	1	0	0	1.000	Southern, Johnson C*	28	24	4	1	0	.966
Mendez, Bristol	13	18	0	0	0	1.000	Knight, Paintsville*	70	139	10	6	3	.961
Redmond, Johnson C	10	15	0	0	0	1.000	Sheets, Bluefield	23	40	3	2	0	.956
Batista, Johnson C	8	12	2	0	0	1.000	Young, Bristol	54	110	11	6	1	.953
Fink, Johnson C	13	12	1	0	0	1.000	Smith, Bristol	66	93	8	5	3	.953
Glenn, Elizabethton	6	6	0	0	0	1.000	J. Palica, Eliz	49	77	2	4	1	.952
Peterson, Paintsville	6	4	2	0	0	1.000	Strawberry, Kings*	39	55	4	3	0	.952
Gjesdal, Paintsville	3	3	2	0	0	1.000	Del Monte, Johnson C*	33	50	1	3	0	.944
Fuller, Kingsport	4	5	0	0	0	1.000	Duhon, Elizabethton	25	34	0	2	0	.944
Echenique, Kingsport	5	4	1	0	0	1.000	Cassanovas, Bristol	40	60	6	4	0	.943
Schriner, Bluefield	5	5	0	0	0	1.000	Cashore, Bluefield	52	76	5	5	3	.942
Cole, Elizabethton	2	3	0	0	0	1.000	Suarez, Elizabethton	14	15	1	1	0	.941
Nichols, Bluefield	2	2	1	0	0	1.000	Stryffeler, Johnson C	42	41	5	3	1	.939
Littlefield, Paints.	1	2	0	0	0	1.000	Baker, Bristol	9	14	0	1	0	.933
Brandt, Elizabethton	2	2	0	0	0	1.000	Nash, Bristol	12	14	0	1	0	.933
Gonzales, Johnson C	1	1	0	0	0	1.000	Simononis, Bristol	11	13	0	1	0	.929
Moore, Johnson C	1	1	0	0	0	1.000	Matos, Johnson C	12	12	1	1	1	.929
Snell, Bluefield	1	1	0	0	0	1.000	Perna, Paintsville*	53	69	7	6	1	.927
Spencer, Bluefield	1	1	0	0	0	1.000	J. Williams, Bluefield*	57	115	3	10	0	.922
BESWICK, Eliz	49	69	2	1	2	.986	Hamilton, Paintsville	13	22	0	2	0	.917
Eisenreich, Eliz*	66	151	7	3	2	.981	Heller, Kingsport	46	64	6	7	1	.909
Martinez, Bluefield*	36	49	3	1	0	.981	Marshall, Bluefield	26	25	1	3	0	.897
Elliot, Kingsport	28	50	1	1	1	.981	Merkle, Bristol	4	6	1	1	0	.875
Jackson, Kingsport	52	75	4	2	0	.975	Perkins, Bristol	8	6	1	2	0	.778
Vejar, Paintsville	68	97	4	3	1	.971	Rodriguez, Johnson C	5	3	0	1	0	.750
Spears, Johnson C*	64	153	6	5	3	.970							

CATCHERS

Player and Club	G.	PO.	A.	E.	DP.	PB.	Pct.	Player and Club	G.	PO.	A.	E.	DP.	PB.	Pct.
A. Pardo, Bluefield	13	64	7	0	2	3	1.000	Dunbar, Kingsport	20	105	8	3	0	3	.974
Heller, Kingsport	5	38	4	0	1	0	1.000	Reed, Elizabethton	52	269	41	9	7	10	.972
Perrett, Bristol	6	11	1	0	0	1	1.000	Carrasquel, Bristol	52	297	40	11	1	4	.968
Merkle, Bristol	1	4	1	0	0	1	1.000	Gonzales, Johnson C.	32	113	8	4	1	5	.968
Sanchez, Johnson C.	1	2	0	0	0	0	1.000	Stone, Kingsport	14	53	3	2	0	6	.966
Littlefield, Paintsville	15	87	8	1	0	2	.990	Gibbons, Kingsport	34	177	11	7	3	11	.964
Ivie, Bluefield	30	151	19	2	2	3	.988	Martin, Elizabethton	18	88	9	6	1	6	.942
B. Pardo, Bluefield	20	70	14	1	0	0	.988	Driver, Bristol	19	80	9	7	4	3	.927
WEEMS, Johnson C.	43	188	18	3	3	8	.986	Hanson, Elizabethton	3	17	1	2	0	0	.900
Nichols, Bluefield	22	100	11	2	4	7	.982	Moore, Johnson City	9	15	3	2	0	1	.900
Gohde, Paintsville	32	178	28	4	4	11	.981	McClenden, King	8	19	5	3	0	2	.889
Russell, Paintsville	26	145	9	3	4	5	.981								

PITCHERS

Player and Club	G.	PO.	A.	E.	DP.	Pct.
COLLINS, Johnson City	11	6	21	0	0	1.000
Tibbs, Kingsport	12	6	20	0	1	1.000
Wilson, Elizabethton	14	4	14	0	0	1.000
Harris, Elizabethton	10	5	10	0	1	1.000
Milligan, Johnson City*	12	1	13	0	1	1.000
Vavrock, Bristol	19	4	10	0	1	1.000
Nutter, Bristol	10	3	10	0	0	1.000
Johnson, Bluefield*	11	1	12	0	2	1.000
Teate, Kingsport	14	5	7	0	0	1.000
Merlack, Kingsport*	18	4	7	0	0	1.000
Maples, Bluefield	10	0	10	0	0	1.000
Dixon, Bluefield	13	4	6	0	2	1.000
Dacko, Bristol	9	3	6	0	1	1.000
Untisz, Bristol	13	0	9	0	0	1.000
Brooks, Johnson City	15	4	5	0	1	1.000
Smith, Paintsville	18	2	7	0	0	1.000
Collins, Paintsville	3	0	8	0	1	1.000
Mitchell, Paintsville	6	2	6	0	1	1.000
D. Jackson, Elizabethton	12	4	4	0	0	1.000
Collyer, Bristol*	13	1	7	0	0	1.000
Taylor, Johnson City*	14	3	5	0	2	1.000
H. Jackson, Elizabethton	8	1	6	0	0	1.000
Usher, Bluefield	6	4	2	0	0	1.000
Marston, Bluefield	12	2	4	0	0	1.000
O'Connor, Bristol	15	1	5	0	0	1.000
Fehr, Johnson City	20	1	5	0	0	1.000
Martin, Johnson City	2	2	3	0	0	1.000
Epple, Johnson City*	6	0	5	0	0	1.000
Yett, Elizabethton	10	2	3	0	0	1.000
Cratch, Bluefield	11	1	4	0	1	1.000
Vaughn, Bristol	2	4	0	0	0	1.000
Parreira, Elizabethton	8	0	4	0	0	1.000
Jordan, Bluefield	9	2	2	0	0	1.000
Mohler, Johnson City*	13	1	3	0	0	1.000
Olwine, Paintsville*	13	0	4	0	1	1.000
Bottoroff, Paintsville	6	0	3	0	0	1.000
Gessell, Bluefield	11	1	2	0	0	1.000
Christensen, Eliz.	13	2	1	0	0	1.000
Conradi, Bluefield*	3	0	2	0	1	1.000
Hanson, Elizabethton	4	2	0	0	0	1.000
Ramos, Johnson City	4	0	2	0	0	1.000
Kreymborg, Bluefield	5	0	2	0	0	1.000
Gonzalez, Johnson City	6	2	0	0	0	1.000
Warburton, Johnson C.*	11	1	1	0	0	1.000
Barton, Kingsport	1	0	1	0	0	1.000
Galvez, Elizabethton	1	0	1	0	0	1.000
Raftice, Paintsville*	1	1	0	0	0	1.000
Jensen, Bristol*	2	0	1	0	0	1.000
Ruffus, Bristol	2	1	0	0	0	1.000
Bretz, Johnson City	9	0	1	0	1	1.000
Fish, Johnson City*	9	0	1	0	0	1.000
Foust, Kingsport	7	0	1	0	1	1.000
Kuntz, Kingsport	9	13	11	1	1	.960
Sisk, Kingsport	15	9	15	1	0	.960
North, Johnson City	14	3	16	1	0	.950
Arrington, Elizabethton	10	4	11	1	2	.938
Michaud, Bristol*	11	2	12	1	0	.933
Szymczak, Paintsville	13	7	17	2	0	.923
DeWitt, Paintsville	11	4	8	1	0	.923
Orosco, Elizabethton	9	3	7	1	0	.909
Clark, Bristol	12	1	8	1	1	.900
W. Palica, Elizabethton	18	1	8	1	0	.900
Faust, Kingsport*	25	2	7	1	0	.900
Livesey, Paintsville	12	5	20	3	1	.893
Gaston, Paintsville	13	4	12	2	0	.889
Dozier, Johnson City	11	4	4	1	0	.889
Warren, Bristol	12	2	6	1	0	.889
Blumenschein, Eliza.*	15	2	6	1	2	.889
Callahan, Paintsville	13	5	9	2	0	.875
Fellows, Bristol	13	4	10	2	1	.875
Thomas, Elizabethton	10	3	4	1	0	.875
Gunzalski, Bristol	11	2	4	1	0	.857
Alba, Kingsport	13	3	3	1	0	.857
Clark, Bluefield*	4	0	5	1	0	.833
Magdziuk, Kingsport	14	1	4	1	0	.833
Pittman, Johnson City*	18	0	5	1	0	.833
Hoke, Bluefield	22	0	5	1	0	.833
Ibarguen, Kingsport	13	6	8	3	1	.824
Moll, Elizabethton	14	7	7	3	0	.824
Sanchez, Bristol	7	1	8	2	1	.818
Willsher, Bluefield	10	6	3	2	0	.818
Quirk, Paintsville	16	3	10	3	1	.813
Robinson, Kingsport	14	3	5	2	3	.800
Fincher, Paintsville*	8	1	3	1	0	.800
Taveras, Johnson City	14	0	4	1	0	.800
Kennedy, Paintsville	13	1	5	2	0	.750
Hughes, Johnson City	18	0	6	2	0	.750
Richmond, Bluefield*	23	2	4	2	0	.750
Carcella, Bluefield	11	3	5	3	1	.727
Brown, Bluefield	6	1	4	2	0	.714
Pina, Kingsport	7	4	1	2	0	.714
Mathis, Bristol	3	2	0	1	0	.571
Camp, Bristol	2	0	1	1		.500
Snyder, Bristol	5	1	0	1	0	.500

The following players do not have any recorded accepted chances at the positions indicated; therefore, are not listed in the fielding averages for those particular positions: Brigante, of; Garcia, 3b-of; Gjesdal, 3b; Govero, p; Hanson, of; Hennesey*, 1b; Kuhn, p; Mariano, 3b; K. Martin, p; W. Martinez, of-c; McCauley*, 3b-p; Millholland, ss; Pfautsch*, p; Reeder, 3b; Sadey, of-p; Silber, of; Silva*, p; Stone, 1b; Vaughn, of.

CLUB PITCHING

Club	G.	CG.	ShO.	Sv.	IP.	H.	R.	ER.	HR.	BB.	Int. BB.	HB.	SO.	WP.	Bk.	ERA.
Paintsville	70	25	9	10	583	594	314	249	35	239	4	20	383	41	9	3.84
Bristol	69	12	5	13	586	601	348	283	34	280	3	24	397	64	4	4.35
Kingsport	71	15	3	11	586	581	370	286	50	295	4	20	384	40	8	4.39
Elizabethton	68	17	2	9	562	580	370	296	52	314	6	14	353	40	8	4.74
Bluefield	68	8	2	5	562	561	373	300	38	332	13	34	425	39	6	4.80
Johnson City	70	4	0	9	571	631	404	337	62	311	28	25	310	47	8	5.31

PITCHERS' RECORDS
(Leading Qualifiers for Earned-Run Average Leadership—56 or More Innings)
*Throws lefthanded.

Pitcher–Club	G.	GS.	CG.	ShO.	W.	L.	Sv.	Pct.	IP.	H.	R.	ER.	HR.	BB.	Int. BB.	HB.	SO.	WP.	ERA.
Callahan, Paintsville	13	7	5	0	6	1	1	.857	68	55	22	18	3	23	1	1	53	0	2.38
Gaston, Paintsville	13	11	6	2	8	1	0	.889	80	74	28	23	6	16	0	1	47	0	2.59
Sisk, Kingsport	15	15	4	0	8	5	0	.615	98	91	46	29	5	45	1	0	41	7	2.66
Fellows, Bristol	13	9	4	0	8	2	0	.800	73	81	34	26	2	24	0	1	63	10	3.21
Ibarguen, Kingsport	13	13	4	2	7	4	0	.636	78	87	52	31	3	37	0	2	57	5	3.58
Arrington, Elizabethton	10	9	4	1	5	1	0	.833	63	65	36	27	3	36	0	1	36	6	3.85

PITCHERS' RECORDS—Continued

Pitcher–Club	G.	GS.	CG.	ShO.	W.	L.	Sv.	Pct.	IP.	H.	R.	ER.	HR.	BB.	Int.BB.	HB.	SO.	WP.	ERA.
Milligan, Johnson City*	12	12	0	0	2	7	0	.222	67	82	38	29	8	25	4	3	36	2	3.90
Thomas, Elizabethton	10	8	2	1	2	3	0	.400	58	50	30	27	5	25	0	1	41	3	4.19
Johnson, Bluefield*	11	11	2	0	6	4	0	.600	70	64	37	33	4	32	0	2	43	5	4.24
Szymczak, Paintsville	13	12	6	1	5	4	0	.556	76	84	36	36	5	23	0	2	45	3	4.26

Departmental Leaders: G—Faust, 25; GS—Sisk, 15; CG—Gaston, Szymczak, 6; ShO—Dacko, Gaston, Ibarguen, Livesey, 2; W—Fellows, Gaston, Sisk, 8; L—Milligan, Tibbs, Warren, 7; Sv—Faust, K. Smith, 5; Pct.—Gaston, .889; IP—Sisk, 98; H—Sisk, 91; R—Teate, 56; ER—Teate, 48; HR—W. Palica, Teate, 10; BB—Dixon, 48; IBB—Cratch, Milligan, 4; HB—Dixon, Gessell, Maples, Merlack, Quirk, Snyder, 5; SO—Fellows, 63; WP—Collyer, 12.

(All Pitchers—Listed Alphabetically)

Pitcher–Club	G.	GS.	CG.	ShO.	W.	L.	Sv.	Pct.	IP.	H.	R.	ER.	HR.	BB.	Int.BB.	HB.	SO.	WP.	ERA.
Alba, Kingsport	13	0	0	0	2	1	2	.667	11	15	14	11	1	11	0	3	15	1	5.82
Arrington, Elizabethton	10	9	5	0	5	1	0	.833	63	65	36	27	3	36	0	1	36	6	3.86
Barton, Kingsport	1	0	0	0	0	0	0	.000	1	2	3	2	0	2	0	0	0	0	18.00
Blumenschein, Eliz*	15	0	0	0	3	3	2	.500	23	22	13	12	1	17	1	1	24	0	4.70
Bottoroff, Paintsville	6	3	0	0	3	0		1.000	25	31	17	9	1	11	0	0	19	1	3.24
Bretz, Johnson City	9	1	0	0	0	1	0	.000	11	12	12	11	2	18	1	2	5	3	9.00
Brooks, Johnson City	15	5	0	0	3	2	2	.600	45	61	30	30	5	10	2	3	13	4	6.00
Brown, Bluefield	6	1	0	0	1	0	1	1.000	19	11	5	2	0	8	0	2	16	1	0.95
Callahan, Paintsville	13	7	5	0	6	1	1	.857	68	55	22	18	3	23	1	1	53	0	2.38
Camp, Bristol	2	2	0	0	0	2	0	.000	5	14	15	13	0	6	0	0	4	2	23.40
Carcella, Bluefield	11	8	0	0	1	5	0	.167	47	47	35	30	3	40	2	2	36	2	5.74
Christensen, Elizabethton	11	0	0	0	1	1	2	.500	31	38	19	13	5	16	1	1	17	3	3.77
Clark, Bluefield*	4	3	0	0	2	2	0	.500	15	18	12	7	0	12	1	1	18	0	4.20
Clark, Bristol	12	0	0	0	1	1	2	.500	23	27	14	12	2	6	0	0	14	1	4.70
Collins, Johnson City	11	11	3	0	7	4	0	.636	76	76	38	37	6	24	0	2	38	9	4.38
Collins, Paintsville	3	3	1	1	2	0	0	1.000	16	11	5	4	1	4	0	0	5	1	2.25
Collyer, Bristol*	13	13	1	0	5	6	0	.455	70	83	44	34	4	31	0	1	39	12	4.37
Conradi, Bluefield*	3	0	0	0	2	0	0	.000	6	9	3	2	0	1	0	1	8	1	3.00
Cratch, Bluefield	11	0	0	0	2	2	0	.500	31	24	10	9	2	20	4	0	18	1	2.61
Dacko, Bristol	9	5	3	2	3	2	1	.600	46	33	12	6	2	7	1	0	35	2	1.17
DeWitt, Paintsville	11	6	3	0	4	1	0	.800	43	36	29	19	5	18	0	1	22	6	3.98
Dixon, Bluefield	13	13	3	1	4	5	0	.444	78	69	46	40	5	48	1	5	62	5	4.62
Dozier, Johnson City	11	8	1	0	3	2	0	.600	40	38	25	22	8	14	2	0	19	4	4.95
Epple, Johnson City*	6	1	0	0	0	1	0	.000	12	8	10	8	3	9	1	2	12	2	6.00
Faust, Kingsport*	25	0	0	0	2	1	5	.667	42	37	15	12	4	12	2	0	37	1	2.57
Fehr, Johnson City	20	0	0	0	3	3	0	.500	37	40	17	15	5	20	3	1	24	2	3.65
Fellows, Bristol	13	9	4	0	8	2	0	.800	73	81	34	26	2	24	0	1	63	10	3.21
Fincher, Paintsville*	8	6	0	0	1	2	0	.333	22	28	19	19	1	22	1	2	13	1	7.77
Fish, Johnson City*	9	5	0	0	0	4	0	.000	13	15	12	11	2	16	0	0	7	1	7.62
Foust, Kingsport	7	1	0	0	0	1	0	.000	3	4	3	3	0	1	0	0	2	0	9.00
Galvez, Elizabethton	1	0	0	0	0	0	0	.000	2	4	3	2	0	1	0	0	0	0	9.00
Gaston, Paintsville	13	11	6	2	8	1	0	.889	80	74	28	23	6	16	0	1	47	0	2.59
Gessell, Bluefield	11	3	0	0	0	1	0	.000	25	23	29	21	1	30	0	5	18	6	7.56
Gonzalez, Johnson City	6	6	1	0	2	4	0	.333	26	31	25	20	1	16	0	2	7	2	6.92
Gonzalski, Bristol	11	6	0	0	1	3	0	.250	27	23	23	21	2	31	0	3	18	6	7.00
Govero, Elizabethton	1	0	0	0	0	0	0	.000	2	7	7	3	0	3	0	0	3	0	13.50
Hanson, Elizabethton	4	0	0	0	0	0	0	.000	7	13	11	10	1	7	0	0	5	1	12.86
Harris, Elizabethton	10	9	3	0	1	3	0	.250	54	57	30	25	8	26	0	0	48	5	4.17
Hoke, Bluefield	22	0	0	0	3	1	2	.750	34	41	22	11	1	14	1	2	22	4	2.91
Hughes, Johnson City	18	0	0	0	2	0	11	1.000	35	37	28	22	6	18	2	2	28	0	5.66
Ibarguen, Kingsport	13	13	4	2	7	4	0	.636	78	87	52	31	3	37	0	2	57	5	3.58
D. Jackson, Elizabethton	12	2	0	0	1	1	1	.500	21	30	23	18	2	19	1	1	12	3	7.71
H. Jackson, Elizabethton	8	1	0	0	4	3	0	.571	18	19	11	10	2	9	0	1	19	0	5.00
Jensen, Bristol*	2	0	0	0	0	0	0	.000	3	6	8	6	0	3	0	0	1	0	18.00
Johnson, Bluefield*	11	11	2	0	6	4	0	.600	70	64	37	33	4	32	0	2	43	5	4.24
Jordan, Bluefield	9	5	0	0	1	3	0	.250	35	46	40	35	5	22	0	3	24	3	9.00
Kennedy, Paintsville	13	2	0	0	5	1	1	.833	42	57	29	25	1	15	0	1	31	7	5.36
Kreymborg, Bluefield	5	4	0	0	0	3	0	.000	18	30	22	20	4	8	0	0	5	1	10.00
Kuhn, Paintsville	4	0	0	0	0	0	0	.000	4	11	5	5	1	2	0	0	3	1	11.25
Kuntz, Kingsport	9	5	3	0	5	1	0	.833	48	31	12	11	0	12	0	3	30	2	2.06
Livesey, Paintsville*	12	11	2	2	5	2	0	.714	59	57	37	28	6	33	0	4	30	4	4.27
Magdziuk, Kingsport	14	3	0	0	2	2	2	.500	40	41	26	23	7	30	1	2	31	2	5.18
Maples, Bluefield	10	10	2	0	4	4	0	.500	55	70	41	38	8	24	0	5	50	2	6.22
Marston, Bluefield	12	0	0	0	1	1	0	.500	24	16	14	12	0	29	3	3	25	3	4.50
Martin, Paintsville	2	0	0	0	0	1	0	.000	3	5	4	4	0	3	0	0	2	0	12.00
Martin, Johnson City	2	2	0	0	0	0	0	.000	9	15	11	11	2	4	0	0	6	0	11.00
Mathis, Bristol	3	3	0	0	1	2	0	.333	16	19	11	11	2	5	0	1	18	1	6.19
McCauley, Bluefield*	2	0	0	0	0	0	0	.000	3	2	1	1	1	0	0	0	0	0	3.00
Merlack, Kingsport*	18	7	1	0	2	5	0	.286	58	63	41	35	3	29	0	5	41	6	5.43
Michaud, Bristol*	11	5	1	0	3	2	0	.600	44	40	26	21	3	33	1	4	35	3	4.30
Milligan, Johnson City*	12	12	0	0	2	7	0	.222	67	82	38	29	8	25	4	3	36	2	3.90

Pitcher–Club	G.	GS.	CG.	ShO.	W.	L.	Sv.	Pct.	IP.	H.	R.	ER.	HR.	BB.	Int. BB.	HB.	SO.	WP.	ERA.
Mitchell, Paintsville	6	4	0	0	1	1	0	.500	26	32	18	15	2	14	0	1	9	2	5.19
Mohler, Johnson City*	13	4	0	0	3	0	0	.000	30	29	24	20	3	25	3	0	17	2	6.00
Moll, Elizabethton	14	6	0	0	3	3	2	.500	47	55	37	33	7	31	1	1	18	5	6.32
North, Johnson City	14	13	1	0	2	6	0	.250	72	84	44	41	6	36	2	3	34	6	5.13
Nutter, Bristol	10	6	2	1	5	1	0	.833	54	40	14	11	2	12	0	1	40	1	1.83
O'Connor, Bristol	15	0	0	0	0	0	2	.000	35	32	22	21	3	22	0	2	23	2	5.40
Olwine, Paintsville*	13	0	0	0	5	2	2	.714	35	32	11	10	2	11	0	3	47	3	2.57
Orosco, Elizabethton*	9	8	2	0	4	1	0	.800	51	40	18	12	1	8	0	1	23	2	2.12
W. Palica, Elizabethton	18	4	0	0	4	5	2	.444	50	58	38	28	10	29	1	1	18	1	5.04
Parreira, Elizabethton	8	0	0	0	1	0	0	.000	14	16	12	12	2	9	0	1	11	1	7.71
Pfautsch, Elizabethton*	2	0	0	0	1	0	0	.000	1	5	3	2	0	2	0	0	1	0	18.00
Pina, Kingsport	7	1	0	0	0	1	0	.000	12	14	17	15	2	11	0	0	6	0	11.25
Pittman, Johnson City*	18	0	0	0	0	0	4	.000	19	11	10	7	2	18	1	1	17	1	3.32
Quirk, Paintsville	16	2	1	1	2	1	1	.667	39	34	19	16	0	27	2	5	25	1	3.69
Raftice, Paintsville*	1	1	0	0	1	0	0	.000	5	5	5	4	1	3	0	1	3	0	7.20
Ramos, Johnson City	4	0	0	0	0	0	0	.000	8	11	10	6	0	6	0	0	6	2	6.75
Richmond, Bluefield*	23	0	0	0	1	4	2	.200	34	29	18	11	1	9	0	0	29	0	2.91
Robinson, Kingsport	14	3	0	0	1	2	0	.333	32	35	22	21	5	13	0	0	22	5	5.91
Ruffus, Bristol	2	1	0	0	0	0	0	.000	7	12	10	7	0	6	0	0	5	0	9.00
Sadey, Bluefield	1	0	0	0	0	0	0	.000	1	2	1	0	0	2	0	0	1	0	0.00
Sanchez, Bristol	7	4	0	0	0	2	1	.000	23	36	23	21	2	14	0	2	13	6	8.22
Silva, Elizabethton*	1	0	0	0	0	0	0	.000	2	4	3	3	1	3	0	0	0	0	13.50
Sisk, Kingsport	15	15	4	0	8	5	0	.615	98	91	46	29	5	45	1	0	41	7	2.66
Smith, Paintsville	18	1	1	0	2	2	5	.500	34	36	19	16	1	14	1	0	26	4	4.24
Snyder, Bristol	5	1	0	0	0	0	0	.000	9	14	11	7	0	5	0	5	2	4	7.00
Szymczak, Paintsville	13	12	6	1	5	4	0	.556	76	84	42	36	5	23	0	2	45	3	4.26
Taveras, Johnson City	14	1	0	0	1	1	2	.500	14	23	21	17	3	16	1	1	7	2	10.93
Taylor, Johnson City*	13	1	0	0	4	1	0	.800	35	32	17	13	1	12	3	1	21	2	2.57
Teate, Kingsport	14	11	1	0	3	5	0	.375	72	62	56	48	10	45	0	4	52	5	6.00
Thomas, Elizabethton	10	8	2	1	2	3	0	.400	58	50	30	27	5	25	0	1	41	3	4.19
Tibbs, Kingsport	12	12	0	0	3	7	0	.300	76	88	54	37	8	32	0	1	45	5	4.38
Untisz, Bristol	13	1	1	0	3	2	2	.600	37	31	15	13	2	14	1	3	18	4	3.16
Usher, Bluefield	6	1	0	0	0	0	0	.000	11	17	19	16	0	14	0	3	1	2	13.09
Vaughn, Bristol	2	0	0	0	0	0	0	.000	6	11	6	3	0	4	0	0	3	2	4.50
Vavrock, Bristol	19	1	0	0	3	1	3	.750	41	33	13	11	2	12	0	0	21	1	2.41
Warburton, Johnson C*	11	0	0	0	0	0	0	.000	12	13	15	12	1	14	2	0	7	3	9.00
Warren, Bristol	12	12	0	0	2	7	0	.222	68	68	51	40	7	39	0	2	45	8	5.29
Willsher, Bluefield	10	9	2	1	3	3	0	.500	55	43	18	12	3	18	1	0	49	3	1.96
Wilson, Elizabethton	14	12	3	0	1	6	0	.143	65	51	46	34	2	44	1	4	36	10	4.71
Yett, Elizabethton	10	8	2	0	3	4	0	.429	52	46	30	25	2	19	0	0	35	0	4.33

BALKS—Livesey, 4; Dixon, 3; Arrington, Blumenschein, D. Collins, Epple, Ibarguen, Kuhn, Maples, Ramos, 2 each; Bottoroff, Christensen, Faust, Fehr, Gonzalski, Marston, Mathis, Merlack, Michaud, Mitchell, Moll, North, Pina, Raftice, Robinson, Ruffus, Sisk, Teate, Wilson, Yett, 1 each.

COMBINATION SHUTOUTS—Nutter-Clark, Bristol; Palica-Wilson, Elizabethton; Sisk-Kuntz, Kingsport; Collins-Quirk-Smith-Callahan, Paintsville.

NO-HIT GAMES—Willsher, Bluefield, defeated Johnson City, 13-0, July 29, seven innings.

Strawberry Festival

If you presented a strawberry at the gate July 20, you were admitted free to welcome the New York Mets' No. 1 draft pick Darryl Strawberry to Paintsville.

The Appalachian League club concessions stands sold nothing except strawberry-flavored soda and strawberry ice cream sundaes. Strawberry shortcake was served to fans between innings. Before the game, a helicopter dropped strawberries on home plate and the Mets' bonus baby was presented with a pint of strawberries before the game.

Two bottles of strawberry shampoo were raffled off to lucky ticket-holders.

The league-leading Yankees, however, played poor hosts when they spoiled Darryl's welcome by beating the Kingsport Mets, 17-6.

Gulf Coast League

SUMMER CLASS A CLASSIFICATION

CHAMPIONSHIP WINNERS IN PREVIOUS YEARS

1964—Sarasota Braves .... .610	1970—Chicago A.L. .... .600	1975—Texas .... .774
1965—Bradenton Astros .... .632	1971—Kansas City .... .755	1976—Texas .... .704
1966—New York A.L. .... .667	1972—Chicago N.L. a .... .651	1977—Chicago-AL .... .731
1967—Kansas City .... .614	Kansas City a .... .651	1978—Texas .... .600
1968—Oakland .... .650	1973—Texas .... .732	1979—Houston .... .635
1969—Montreal .... .585	1974—Chicago N.L. .... .702	

(Note—Known as Sarasota Rookie League in 1964 and Florida Rookie League in 1965.) aDeclared co-champions; no playoff.

STANDING OF CLUBS AT CLOSE OF SEASON, SEPTEMBER 1

Club	K.C. Blue	Hous. Blue	Atl.	Tex.	Hous. Org.	Chi. NL	N.Y. AL	Pitt.	K.C. Gold	Chi. AL	W.	L.	T.	Pct.	G.B.
Kansas City-Blue	..	3	4	5	2	6	2	6	6	6	40	23	0	.635	......
Houston-Blue	4	..	4	3	5	5	5	4	3	5	38	24	0	.613	1½
Atlanta	3	3	..	4	4	3	5	4	6	3	35	28	0	.556	5
Texas	2	4	3	..	3	5	3	6	3	5	34	28	0	.548	5½
Houston-Orange	5	1	3	4	..	2	5	4	5	3	33	29	1	.532	6½
Chicago-NL	1	2	4	2	5	..	5	4	4	5	27	35	0	.435	12½
New York-AL	5	2	1	4	2	2	..	2	4	3	24	39	0	.381	16
Pittsburgh	1	3	3	1	3	3	5	..	2	3	22	40	1	.355	17½
Kansas City-Gold	1	4	1	1	2	3	5	5	..	3	22	40	1	.355	17½
Chicago-AL	1	2	2	4	2	1	2	4	..	..	22	41	0	.349	18

Kansas City-Blue declared league champion on basis of highest won-lost percentage.

Club names indicate major league connections.

Games played at Bradenton and Sarasota, Fla.

Regular-Season Attendance—At Payne Park, Sarasota, 10,680; no admission charged at other parks. No playoffs. All-star game, 1,200.

Managers: Atlanta—Pedro Gonzalez; Chicago-NL—Rich Morales; Chicago-AL—Duane Shaffer; Houston-Blue—Eric Swanson; Houston-Orange—Fernando Tatis; Kansas City-Blue—Joe Jones; Kansas City-Gold—Roy Tanner; New York-AL—Carlos Tosca; Pittsburgh—Elwood (Woody) Huyke; Texas—Andy Hancock.

All-Star Team: 1B—Barclift, KC-G; Clements, Hou-O; 2B—McKinney, KC-G; Weems, Hou-B; 3B—Stokes, Tex.; Cleveland, Hou-B; SS—D'Onofrio, Hou-B; Morse, Chi-AL; OF—Bonner, Atl; Davis, KC-B; DeSena, Hou-O; Espy, Chi-AL; O'Regan, NY-AL; M. Thomas, Hou-B; C—Colburn, Tex; Sullivan, Hou-B; Utility—Medina, NY-AL; Weaver, Atl; P—Cooper, KC-B; Yan, Hou-O; Managers-Jones, KC-B; Swanson, Hou-B.

(Compiled by Howe News Bureau, Boston, Mass.)

CLUB BATTING

Club	G.	AB.	R.	OR.	H.	TB.	2B.	3B.	HR.	RBI.	SH.	SF.	BB.	Int. BB.	HP.	SO.	SB.	CS.	LOB.	Pct.
KC-Blue	63	2062	349	247	569	744	87	29	10	286	38	28	289	14	18	251	115	34	502	.276
Hous.-Blue	62	1970	311	242	523	673	83	17	11	241	27	20	265	11	14	190	84	38	430	.265
Hous.-Orange	62	2035	290	251	507	651	77	17	11	238	17	24	209	9	30	343	90	30	433	.249
Texas	63	2100	310	247	522	667	69	17	14	251	20	18	321	5	21	314	64	13	526	.249
Pittsburgh	63	2087	245	332	506	646	50	28	11	196	11	14	179	4	20	341	102	42	407	.242
Chicago-NL	63	2092	290	303	502	632	45	26	11	233	30	21	303	10	17	413	95	35	471	.240
Chicago-AL	63	2010	277	356	472	583	66	15	5	204	14	13	272	6	32	408	76	30	493	.235
Atlanta	62	1977	261	254	463	630	69	19	20	219	27	21	243	7	23	269	81	32	421	.234
KC-Gold	63	2059	241	301	477	626	77	21	10	203	8	21	211	6	16	352	46	33	436	.232
New York-AL	62	2005	248	289	439	541	48	15	8	191	51	20	254	16	13	334	97	29	469	.219

INDIVIDUAL BATTING

(Leading Qualifiers for Batting Championship—170 or More Plate Appearances)

*Bats lefthanded.   †Switch-hitter.

Player and Club	G.	AB.	R.	H.	TB.	2B.	3B.	HR.	RBI.	SH.	SF.	BB.	HP.	SO.	SB.	CS.	Pct.
Thomas, Marc, Hou-Blue	53	204	41	69	83	12	1	0	33	1	3	14	2	6	23	7	.338
Stokes, David, Texas	45	169	30	56	77	10	1	3	29	0	0	12	9	23	2	1	.331
Davis, Wallace, KC-Blue	61	235	46	74	105	17	4	2	35	0	5	29	1	36	31	4	.315

INDIVIDUAL BATTING—Continued

Player and Club	G.	AB.	R.	H.	TB.	2B.	3B.	HR.	RBI.	SH.	SF.	BB.	HP.	SO.	SB.	CS.	Pct.
Weems, William, Hou-Blue*	60	206	52	64	79	9	3	0	7	3	1	35	3	8	15	4	.311
Hatcher, Harold, KC-Gold	45	168	22	52	72	9	1	3	19	0	0	13	1	14	0	2	.310
Best, William, KC-Blue*	46	158	35	49	57	4	2	0	19	4	4	36	0	10	9	4	.310
Crum, George, Texas	47	146	27	45	51	1	1	1	22	1	2	28	0	27	8	3	.308
Seid, Bruce, Chicago-NL	55	192	28	59	68	2	2	1	19	4	5	22	0	12	6	3	.307
Smith, Mark, KC-Blue	59	203	24	62	71	7	1	0	34	3	2	17	3	21	17	3	.305
Owen, Carl, KC-Blue	51	142	29	43	57	9	1	1	24	1	1	30	0	23	4	0	.303

Departmental Leaders: G—R. Johnson, 63; AB—R. Johnson, 266; R—Weems, 52; H—W. Davis, 74; TB—W. Davis, 105; 2B—W. Davis, 17; 3B—O'Leath, 7; HR—Gjesdal, 7; RBI—T. Johnson, 42; GWRBI—Barclift, 8; SH—D'Onofrio, 11; SF—Bonner, 6; BB—Schoendienst, 58; HP—Stokes, 9; SO—Vranesh, 65; SB—W. Davis, 31; CS—R. Johnson, McKinney, 10.

(All Players—Listed Alphabetically)

Player and Club	G.	AB.	R.	H.	TB.	2B.	3B.	HR.	RBI.	SH.	SF.	BB.	HP.	SO.	SB.	CS.	Pct.
Abraham, Miguel, Pittsburgh	39	115	13	26	28	2	0	0	5	0	1	7	1	20	9	1	.226
Acosta, Eduarto, Pittsburgh	32	108	12	27	28	1	0	0	11	1	1	4	1	18	5	5	.250
Alcala, Jesus, New York-AL	46	131	18	21	23	2	0	0	9	5	1	27	0	21	4	1	.160
Angulo, Hector, New York-AL	6	15	1	3	5	2	0	0	1	1	0	1	5	0	1	0	.200
Antonetty, Elliot, Hou-Org	31	84	9	10	10	0	0	0	5	0	0	16	1	27	3	1	.119
Atkins, R. David, New York-AL	50	183	16	45	54	4	0	0	14	2	2	9	3	21	2	0	.224
Austin, Terry, Chicago-NL	4	14	5	4	6	0	1	0	5	0	0	3	0	3	1	0	.286
Babcock, Kenneth, Hou-Blue*	14	1	1	1	1	0	0	0	0	0	0	0	0	0	0	0	1.000
Barclift, Charles, KC-Gold	60	221	28	60	80	15	1	1	35	1	3	24	1	35	4	4	.271
Batter, Ronald, KC-Gold	6	6	2	1	1	0	0	0	2	0	0	3	0	3	1	0	.167
Belliard, Rafael, Pittsburgh	12	42	6	9	10	1	0	0	2	0	0	0	1	3	1	0	.214
Benjamin, Julio, Hou-Blue	46	150	11	23	32	3	3	0	18	1	3	19	0	25	1	2	.153
Benza, Bret, Texas	40	110	20	31	37	4	1	0	9	1	0	32	2	14	9	1	.282
Berger, Michael, Pittsburgh	5	13	1	5	7	0	1	0	2	0	0	1	1	3	0	0	.385
Best, William, KC-Blue*	46	158	35	49	57	4	2	0	19	4	4	36	0	10	9	4	.310
Betancourt, Juan, Chicago-AL*	24	74	12	13	17	4	0	0	6	0	0	15	0	23	0	1	.176
Bonner, Mark, Atlanta	62	214	35	55	79	16	1	2	24	1	6	30	0	18	6	3	.257
Buckley, Christopher, Hou-Blue	53	168	22	42	49	7	0	0	13	2	0	13	1	18	5	2	.250
Buckley, Michael, Chicago-NL	22	84	14	14	19	1	2	0	6	3	0	11	3	18	1	2	.167
Burgin, Russell, KC-Gold	34	109	11	27	30	3	0	0	10	1	1	13	0	14	1	0	.248
Caballero, Jose, Pittsburgh	1	4	1	1	1	0	0	0	1	0	0	0	0	1	0	0	.250
Cadahia, C. Benito, KC-Blue	52	149	21	31	49	8	2	2	20	9	2	21	1	16	1	1	.208
Carpenter, Willie, Texas	29	109	18	33	39	1	1	1	8	2	2	14	0	13	12	3	.303
Carter, Randall, Texas	29	107	17	26	35	5	2	0	16	1	1	15	1	11	1	0	.243
Castaneda, Nick, Pittsburgh*	16	45	2	5	5	0	0	0	1	0	0	3	0	9	0	1	.111
Cataline, Daniel, Chicago-NL	57	210	27	58	75	5	3	2	32	0	4	22	0	52	11	5	.276
Cheesman, Barry, New York-AL	15	4	0	0	0	0	0	0	0	0	0	0	0	2	0	0	.000
Clack, Marvin, Pittsburgh	41	150	15	38	49	5	3	0	8	1	1	9	1	27	10	2	.253
Clases, Ramon, New York-AL†	32	76	7	9	14	3	1	0	9	5	0	10	1	17	1	1	.118
Clements, Wesley, Hou-Orange	54	193	37	58	91	15	0	6	34	0	3	29	2	30	7	4	.301
Cleveland, Dennis, Hou-Blue	59	203	33	61	81	11	3	1	38	1	5	23	1	14	6	2	.300
Colburn, Thomas, Texas†	44	142	14	36	49	11	1	0	18	1	0	27	0	23	0	0	.254
Cooper, Junior, KC-Blue	15	3	1	0	0	0	0	0	0	0	0	0	0	0	0	0	.000
Cordova, Antonio, Chicago-NL	59	200	19	53	72	5	4	2	30	3	1	22	3	32	2	2	.265
Corry, Kevin, Chicago-AL	7	17	2	2	2	0	0	0	2	2	1	6	0	9	0	0	.118
Cotto, Henry, Chicago-NL	43	166	24	47	64	7	5	0	30	1	4	12	1	15	12	0	.283
Coyne, Michael, Pittsburgh	4	14	1	6	8	2	0	0	3	0	0	1	0	1	1	0	.429
Crum, George, Texas	47	146	27	45	51	1	1	1	22	1	2	28	0	27	8	3	.308
D'Onofrio, Gary, Hou-Blue	61	218	34	60	79	14	1	1	30	11	2	26	1	23	8	2	.275
Davis, Trench, Pittsburgh*	43	142	16	39	51	3	3	1	12	0	2	7	0	23	12	4	.275
Davis, Wallace, KC-Blue	61	235	46	74	105	17	4	2	35	0	5	29	1	36	31	4	.315
DeLaRosa, Nelson, Pittsburgh*	57	222	32	42	54	6	3	0	14	1	1	27	0	33	22	3	.189
DeSena, Sergio, Hou-Orange	61	238	30	66	82	10	3	0	23	1	4	16	2	32	10	4	.277
Diaz, Darwin, Pittsburgh*	1	5	0	0	0	0	0	0	0	0	0	0	0	0	0	0	.000
Diaz, Eduardo, New York-AL	18	40	3	8	8	0	0	0	1	2	0	7	0	3	0	0	.200
Dierberger, Bill, Chicago-AL	6	16	2	6	6	0	0	0	1	0	0	0	0	2	0	0	.375
Dippel, Gary, Chicago-NL	41	102	10	28	28	0	0	0	10	1	0	14	0	16	1	0	.275
Duncan, Lindon, Texas	7	25	6	9	12	1	1	0	4	0	0	4	0	2	1	0	.360
Eagle, Russell, Atlanta*	20	59	7	8	12	1	0	1	3	0	0	8	0	8	0	1	.136
Espinoza, Alvaro, Hou-Orange	59	200	24	43	48	5	0	0	14	2	1	15	5	18	6	1	.215
Espinoza, Ernesto, Hou-Blue	12	1	0	0	0	0	0	0	0	0	0	0	0	0	0	0	.000
Espy, Cecil, Chicago-AL†	58	212	33	58	71	7	3	0	26	2	3	26	0	38	23	6	.274
Flenoir, Keith, Chicago-NL	36	115	10	26	35	5	2	0	12	2	0	10	2	29	4	1	.226
Flores, Edison, Chicago-AL†	32	92	12	26	30	4	0	0	9	2	0	2	2	15	1	0	.283
Gainey, Telmanch, Hou-Orange*	47	167	41	47	61	4	2	2	26	3	0	34	2	39	17	5	.281
Gallo, Jack, New York-AL	14	32	4	7	7	0	0	0	2	0	0	3	0	1	0	0	.219
Garcia, A. Leonardo, Chi-AL*	32	108	8	26	26	0	0	0	7	1	0	9	0	12	3	0	.241
Garcia, Anthony, Texas	24	64	4	13	14	1	0	0	8	1	1	8	0	3	1	0	.203
Garcia, Ramon, Hou-Blue	29	80	8	17	20	3	0	0	8	3	0	5	1	19	1	0	.213
Giansanti, Ralph, Atlanta	31	88	13	14	20	3	0	1	6	0	1	10	3	10	3	0	.159

Player and Club	G.	AB.	R.	H.	TB.	2B.	3B.	HR.	RBI.	SH.	SF.	BB.	HP.	SO.	SB.	CS.	Pct.
Gjesdal, Brent, New York-AL	49	179	29	44	79	6	4	7	40	0	5	27	2	40	9	2	.246
Gonzalez, Joaquin, New York-AL	47	138	13	23	30	3	2	0	11	6	0	24	2	27	3	1	.167
Goodin, Craig, Texas	28	73	10	17	17	0	0	0	3	0	2	13	0	17	2	0	.233
Graham, Daniel, KC-Blue	26	50	11	13	17	2	1	0	5	2	0	14	0	12	0	1	.260
Guerrero, Inocencio, Atlanta	41	118	7	23	28	3	1	0	14	0	2	18	3	32	1	1	.195
Haas, Stanley, Texas	32	107	6	18	21	1	1	0	9	1	0	11	2	21	1	0	.168
Haddock, Donald, Atlanta	57	215	28	51	86	9	4	6	39	0	1	20	1	45	5	3	.237
Hagman, Keith, Atlanta*	1	4	0	1	2	1	0	0	1	0	0	1	0	0	0	0	.250
Hall, Michael, Chicago-NL	18	47	1	9	11	2	0	0	1	2	0	6	0	7	0	1	.191
Hansen, Roger, KC-Blue	55	167	28	38	45	3	2	0	15	0	2	33	5	28	3	0	.228
Haro, Samuel, Pittsburgh	38	149	18	43	49	4	1	0	10	0	0	13	1	20	12	7	.289
Hatcher, Harold, KC-Gold	45	168	22	52	72	9	1	3	19	0	0	13	1	14	0	2	.310
Hawk, Thomas, Hou-Blue	12	3	1	1	1	0	0	0	1	0	0	0	0	1	0	0	.333
Hayes, Thomas, Atlanta	1	4	1	2	4	0	1	0	1	0	0	1	0	1	1	0	.500
Hegman, Robert, KC-Gold	54	212	30	49	59	6	2	0	13	1	3	18	1	23	1	1	.231
Hench, Ralph, New York-AL	11	43	4	10	11	1	0	0	3	0	0	5	0	6	0	0	.233
Hernandez, Gustavo, Atlanta	40	104	15	19	23	1	0	1	8	6	0	19	3	20	12	3	.183
Herrera, Francisco, NY-AL	13	40	6	7	9	2	0	0	4	1	1	1	0	10	3	0	.175
Hill, George, Atlanta	4	6	1	2	2	0	0	0	1	0	0	1	0	1	0	0	.333
Holder, Robert, KC-Blue	19	53	7	15	23	4	2	0	10	0	0	6	0	8	3	2	.283
Holt, Darren, New York-AL*	50	122	16	25	31	4	1	0	11	0	1	21	1	25	6	3	.205
Howell, Timothy, Pittsburgh	32	90	4	12	12	0	0	0	3	0	1	10	0	16	0	1	.133
Huismann, Mark, KC-Blue	28	1	0	0	0	0	0	0	0	0	0	0	0	0	0	0	.000
Irizarry, Jose, Chicago-AL	25	77	5	14	14	0	0	0	4	0	0	4	2	15	0	1	.182
Irvin, Otis, KC-Gold	38	126	10	24	35	7	2	0	6	1	2	7	2	18	1	3	.190
Isbel, Mark, Pittsburgh	6	18	1	3	3	0	0	0	0	0	0	1	0	3	0	0	.167
Johnson, Thomas, Chicago-NL	59	218	30	64	91	11	2	4	42	2	1	35	2	45	12	3	.294
Johnson, Aubrey, KC-Gold	27	91	7	16	16	0	0	0	6	0	1	1	0	13	1	0	.176
Johnson, Ronald, KC-Blue*	63	266	43	70	79	5	2	0	21	5	2	29	0	37	24	10	.263
Jonson, Gregory, KC-Blue*	58	210	36	56	68	8	2	0	23	5	1	26	6	16	5	3	.267
King, Phillip, Atlanta*	9	21	4	5	5	0	0	0	0	0	0	6	0	6	2	1	.238
Kingery, Michael, KC-Gold*	44	143	12	32	41	3	3	0	13	0	0	21	0	23	4	0	.224
Likely, Albert, Chicago-AL	47	165	12	31	49	7	1	3	18	1	1	11	4	50	0	0	.188
Lloyd, Quinton, Atlanta	62	220	28	56	83	10	1	5	29	1	5	17	2	33	4	1	.255
Luzinski, William, Chicago-AL	40	115	20	30	33	1	0	0	13	1	0	28	7	37	0	4	.261
Made, Rafael, Pittsburgh	1	3	1	1	1	0	0	0	1	0	0	1	0	0	0	0	.333
Mariano, Bob, New York-AL*	4	18	4	5	9	0	2	0	3	0	0	3	0	2	1	1	.278
Martin, Mark, Atlanta	12	1	0	0	0	0	0	0	0	0	0	0	0	0	0	0	.000
Mason, Michael, Texas*	14	2	1	2	2	0	0	0	0	0	0	0	0	0	0	1	1.000
McKinney, F. Wade, KC-Gold	61	245	35	63	87	13	4	1	18	0	3	20	7	26	7	10	.257
McNealy, Darryl, New York-AL*	8	14	1	2	2	0	0	0	1	0	1	0	1	4	0	1	.143
McNealy, Derwin, New York-AL*	62	200	31	52	61	7	1	0	14	8	1	30	1	51	13	5	.260
Medina, Pedro, New York-AL	53	193	22	38	43	1	2	0	15	5	3	10	0	27	7	2	.197
Miscik, Robert, Pittsburgh	7	28	6	10	13	1	1	0	3	0	0	2	0	3	3	2	.357
Monroe, Gary, Chicago-NL	17	42	5	6	8	0	1	0	3	0	2	2	0	5	2	0	.143
Morse, Michael, Chicago-AL	54	191	39	53	80	7	4	4	34	0	1	36	1	19	15	2	.277
Murphy, Daniel, Texas*	18	55	10	11	14	1	1	0	5	0	0	16	0	12	5	3	.200
Naclerio, Ronald, Chicago-AL*	18	55	10	11	14	1	1	0	5	0	0	16	0	12	5	3	.200
Nataupsky, Harold, KC-Blue	8	14	2	2	3	1	0	0	3	1	1	2	1	5	0	0	.143
Neal, Willie, KC-Gold	57	211	29	53	61	6	1	0	26	0	3	22	1	32	12	4	.251
Nivar, Felix, Atlanta†	19	24	3	2	3	1	0	0	2	0	1	0	0	9	2	0	.083
Nolasco, Leonidas, Pittsburgh	39	145	17	42	55	4	3	1	19	1	0	17	0	20	6	6	.290
Notaroberto, Anthony, KC-Gold	50	153	17	36	44	4	2	0	20	2	1	34	1	30	9	6	.235
O'Leath, Robert, Pittsburgh*	40	135	15	32	55	3	7	2	9	0	0	19	1	33	1	0	.237
O'Regan, Daniel, New York-AL*	61	236	29	63	70	7	0	0	18	2	1	33	0	24	20	4	.267
Olson, Mitchell, Chicago-AL	42	128	19	24	30	3	0	1	11	0	3	29	0	20	7	1	.188
Ondo, Paul, Texas*	33	116	16	31	39	6	1	0	12	1	1	17	1	17	3	2	.267
Ortega, Daniel, Chicago-AL*	15	0	0	0	0	0	0	0	0	0	0	0	0	0	0	0	.000
Otersen, David, New York-AL*	35	105	13	26	28	2	0	0	13	0	2	6	1	25	7	0	.248
Owen, Carl, KC-Blue	51	142	29	43	57	9	1	1	24	1	1	30	0	23	4	0	.303
Ozoria, Ramon, Atlanta	40	129	11	23	38	6	3	1	8	3	0	10	0	17	4	4	.178
Pastornicky, Cliff, KC-Blue	62	206	28	57	74	5	6	0	32	5	5	22	0	12	5	3	.277
Payano, Vidal, Atlanta	33	96	20	21	26	2	0	1	5	5	0	12	1	11	3	2	.219
Pena, Ramon, Pittsburgh	22	52	5	9	11	0	1	0	7	0	1	12	1	11	3	2	.173
Peterson, Scott, Chicago-NL	17	37	4	5	7	2	0	0	1	2	0	2	0	9	0	0	.135
Powers, Mac, Chicago-NL†	24	61	9	15	15	0	0	0	4	0	0	10	0	16	8	2	.246
Ramirez, Francisco, Hou-Orange	45	141	15	35	46	5	3	0	14	3	0	21	5	32	4	4	.248
Reasonover, Larry, Texas	12	39	4	8	10	2	0	0	4	1	0	5	0	8	0	0	.205
Remo, Jeffrey, Chicago-NL	38	112	12	16	20	2	1	0	8	1	0	23	0	34	0	1	.143
Renteria, Richard, Pittsburgh	46	176	19	40	54	6	1	2	23	3	3	9	2	15	4	2	.227
Rice, Arlanda, Pittsburgh	46	150	19	37	53	8	1	2	19	0	1	16	4	51	3	1	.247
Rivera, Luis A., Chicago-AL†	40	125	20	31	37	6	0	0	17	1	0	22	1	13	3	2	.248
Rivera, Luis, Chicago-AL	19	42	2	5	5	0	0	0	0	0	0	7	0	13	4	0	.119
Rivera, Ricardo, Hou-Orange†	53	170	20	34	37	1	1	0	15	1	1	16	1	35	7	5	.200
Roberts, Joe, Texas	28	90	14	23	30	1	0	2	13	1	1	13	1	16	1	0	.256
Robinette, Gary, Chicago-AL	21	75	10	20	27	3	2	0	11	0	0	5	1	9	2	0	.267

Player and Club	G.	AB.	R.	H.	TB.	2B.	3B.	HR.	RBI.	SH.	SF.	BB.	HP.	SO.	SB.	CS.	Pct.
Robles, Ruben, Hou-Orange	57	219	27	48	72	9	6	1	34	1	1	8	6	55	9	2	.219
Rodriguez, Edwin, New York-AL	47	157	22	39	50	4	2	1	16	8	2	24	1	18	17	5	.248
Romano, Thomas, KC-Blue	58	186	32	48	78	10	4	4	37	3	5	23	1	26	10	3	.258
Romero, Ramon, Chicago-AL†	31	104	16	25	31	4	1	0	9	0	0	14	0	19	4	1	.240
Ronshausen, Ted, Chicago-AL*	34	104	5	22	25	3	0	0	7	0	0	5	2	22	0	0	.212
Roomes, A. Rolando, Chicago-NL	19	48	11	7	14	1	0	2	3	0	0	10	1	27	9	5	.146
Rosette, John, KC-Gold	26	76	5	7	8	1	0	0	0	2	0	1	6	24	1	1	.092
Schaive, John, Pittsburgh	6	23	3	6	9	0	0	1	3	0	0	5	0	5	0	0	.261
Schlosser, Randall, Hou-Blue	50	137	20	32	34	2	0	0	13	1	0	33	2	9	11	6	.234
Schmid, Jerry, Atlanta*	42	141	23	37	45	6	1	0	11	0	1	16	2	13	6	4	.262
Schoendienst, Kevin, Chicago-NL*	61	208	43	48	62	4	5	0	26	4	1	58	3	48	22	4	.231
Schumacher, Roy, Chicago-AL	18	2	0	0	0	0	0	0	0	0	0	0	0	2	0	0	.000
Seeger, Mark, Chicago-AL	33	109	20	32	45	6	2	1	19	1	1	14	1	21	0	2	.294
Seid, Bruce, Chicago-NL	55	192	28	59	68	7	2	1	19	1	5	22	1	19	3	1	.307
Serdar, Marc, Hou-Orange	46	170	30	50	67	7	2	2	25	2	5	20	0	10	6	2	.294
Shepard, Roderick, Hou-Orange	33	113	20	34	40	6	0	0	17	1	3	13	0	18	1	0	.301
Sheppard, Michael, Hou-Orange	55	200	25	51	60	9	0	0	21	3	5	18	2	29	9	1	.255
Shuck, Larry, New York-AL	26	79	9	16	16	0	0	0	6	1	1	13	0	5	4	2	.203
Simons, Neil, Hou-Blue*	62	212	34	57	83	8	3	4	23	0	2	46	1	11	10	5	.269
Sinnen, Matthew, Pittsburgh	5	14	2	4	7	0	0	1	4	0	0	0	0	4	0	0	.286
Siriano, Rick, Atlanta*	61	200	31	50	67	5	3	2	26	3	3	39	2	26	26	5	.250
Smith, Mark, KC-Blue	59	203	24	62	71	7	1	0	34	3	2	17	3	21	17	3	.305
Smith, Ronald, KC-Gold	11	0	1	0	0	0	0	0	0	0	0	0	0	0	0	0	.000
Smith, Sidney, Chicago-NL	37	66	11	9	9	0	0	0	3	2	0	13	0	23	2	0	.136
Squilla, Joseph, Hou-Blue	41	131	12	33	49	5	1	3	17	1	3	12	0	21	0	1	.252
Stefanski, James, Atlanta	51	183	23	52	67	6	3	1	25	2	1	19	2	7	1	2	.284
Stokes, David, Texas	45	169	30	56	77	10	1	3	29	0	0	12	9	23	2	1	.331
Strode, J. Lester, KC-Blue*	10	0	2	0	0	0	0	0	0	0	0	0	0	0	0	0	.000
Sullivan, David, Hou-Blue	56	189	36	51	67	6	2	2	36	0	3	27	1	19	4	5	.270
Talley, Jackie, KC-Gold	31	103	13	20	33	4	3	1	12	1	1	10	1	32	2	1	.194
Tapia, Santiago, Pittsburgh†	1	4	1	3	3	0	0	0	0	0	0	0	0	0	0	0	.750
Tappe, Anthony, Chicago-NL	1	1	0	0	0	0	0	0	0	0	0	0	0	0	0	0	.000
Tarnow, Greg, Chicago-NL	27	50	6	5	5	0	0	0	2	0	5	1	17	0	1		.100
Tenney, Mickey, Chicago-NL	55	153	26	37	39	2	0	0	10	3	3	27	1	15	6	6	.242
Thomas, Marc, Hou-Blue	53	204	41	69	83	12	1	0	33	1	3	14	2	6	23	7	.338
Tiamo, Jesus, Pittsburgh	33	99	12	30	36	2	2	0	19	1	0	3	0	3	1	0	.303
Turner, Ira, KC-Blue	4	19	4	11	18	4	0	1	8	0	0	1	0	1	3	0	.579
Valdez, Ramon, Pittsburgh	44	131	22	32	37	2	0	1	13	2	1	12	5	20	8	4	.244
Vasquez, Carl, Pittsburgh	2	8	1	3	3	0	0	0	2	0	0	1	0	1	0	0	.375
Venner, W. Gary, Texas*	13	43	5	12	13	1	0	0	5	0	0	7	0	4	0	0	.279
Villa, Manny, Texas	40	136	19	24	25	1	0	0	12	4	1	16	1	10	1	1	.176
Vranesh, Keith, KC-Gold	53	195	19	37	59	6	2	4	21	1	2	19	0	65	2	1	.190
Wallace, Brooks, Texas	40	116	18	21	24	1	1	0	7	1	1	21	2	18	4	0	.181
Wayne, Gary, Chicago-NL	23	41	3	4	4	0	0	0	0	0	0	5	0	13	0	0	.098
Weaver, Dale, Atlanta*	42	142	11	41	44	3	0	0	15	3	1	21	2	11	3	0	.289
Weems, William, Hou-Blue*	60	206	52	64	79	9	3	0	7	3	1	35	3	8	15	4	.311
Wiesler, Mark, Chicago-AL	45	162	33	36	40	2	1	0	11	1	0	29	6	26	22	3	.222
Wilkerson, Curtis, Texas	37	105	15	20	22	2	0	0	8	3	1	8	1	26	1	0	.190
Wilkinson, Richard, Texas*	52	174	23	41	64	12	1	3	27	1	2	31	0	32	1	0	.236
Williams, Jaime, Hou-Orange	44	165	16	38	47	9	0	0	14	1	1	8	3	21	7	3	.230
Wright, Andrew, Texas	20	36	4	3	6	0	0	1	3	1	1	3	0	10	1	0	.083
Zuvella, Paul, Atlanta	2	8	0	1	1	0	0	0	1	0	0	0	0	0	0	0	.125
Zuzuaregui, Roberto, Chicago-AL	11	33	5	8	11	1	1	0	5	0	1	5	0	9	1	1	.242

The following pitchers had no plate appearances primarily through use of designated hitters, listed alphabetically by club, games in parentheses.

ATLANTA—Acker, James (1); Alvarez, Jose (4); Ayers, J. Lynn (23); Church, Daniel (4); Dedmon, Jeffrey* (10); Figueroa, Luis (2); Fisher, Brian (12); Germer, Glen (1); Kennedy, Robert (14); Lawrence, Stephen (6); Matos, Alexander (8); Moses, Mark (9); Robles, Juan (10); Rymer, Carlos (5); Treadway, W. Andre (11); Valdez, Juan* (12); Wex, Gary (16).

CHICAGO-AL—Davis, Keefe (12); Flannery, Kevin (8); Heath, Allan* (11); Keating, Thomas (9); Korbas, Dean* (10); McAnnally, Terry (13); Mills, William (8); Mullen, Tom (14); Ortega, Daniel* (15); Samuel, Jay (4); Schuckert, Wayne* (11); Shoemaker, Martin (14).

CHICAGO-NL—Bair, Jeffrey (9); Buonantony, Richard (12); Chestnut, Troy (11); Eichholz, Scott (13); Geisel, John* (14); Gerlach, James (19); Landrum, T. William (11); Martz, Randy (2); Reilly, Francis (12); Schiewe, Mark (14); Schulze, Donald (12); Shulleeta, Mike (11); Weissmann, Craig (14).

HOUSTON-BLUE—Castro, Guillermo* (20); Elsee, Kenneth* (14); Hernandez, Manuel (11); Meckes, Timothy (10); Morris, Jeffrey* (9); Penate, A. Miguel (30); Ruiz, Quico (10); Thomas, Guillermo (12); Turner, Mark (14).

HOUSTON-ORANGE—Bossicy, Larry* (17); Calhoun, Jeffrey* (8); Cerefin, Michael* (7); DePaula, Elvido (15); Gardner, K. Scott (12); Kolacki, John* (9); Malinoski, Gary (16); Perez, Silvio* (14); Perez, Virgilio* (10); Regaldo, J. Uvaldo (1); Solano, Julio (18); Yan, Roberto (12).

KANSAS CITY-BLUE—Creel, S. Keith (9); Cutty, Francis (14); Johnson, Bert* (13); Lettrich, Stephen (1); Odekirk, Richard* (18); Swank, Kenneth* (12); Villalba, Libardo (14); Wills, Frank (4); Wong, David (24).

KANSAS CITY-GOLD—Albright, David* (7); Cecil, Timothy (13); Cook, Douglas (8); Gladden, Jeffrey (9); Johnson, Abner (19); King, Olice* (9); McMichael, Charles (21); Potestio, Douglas (2); Pour, Kenneth (9); Rankin, Martin (2); Schuchmann, Keith (1); Shaw, Robert* (13); Shaw, Theodore (13); Sparks, Randy (9); Vercoe, John (12).

NEW YORK-AL—Bratton, Reggie (17); Cano, Jose (3); Caraballo, Nelson (2); Collins, Joseph* (3); Despaux, C. Frederick (3); Diaz, Gumercindo (17); Doblitz, Kevin (2); Fincher, Steve* (3); Flores, Wilfredo* (15); Herrera, Henry (12); Marks, Jeffrey* (9); Martin, Kenneth (11); Patterson, Gilbert (8); Raftice, Robert (10); Rodriguez, Nelson (3); Rosario, Maximo* (11); Sarante, Agustin* (5); Scott, Thomas (1); Toporek, Steven (7).

PITTSBURGH—Acker, Larry* (2); Almanzar, Domingo (5); Bastian, Bernie (10); Bradshaw, David* (1); Clemente, Enrique (5); Conroyd, Christopher (2); Edwards, Christopher (13); Estiven, Bernardo (9); Gonzales, Fernando (12); Horne, Jeffrey (11); Howard, Don* (4); Kirby, Dennis (2); LaBounty, David (11); McAlarney, Patrick* (2); McCullock, Alec (2); Pena, Arturo (13); Peterson, Eric* (3); Storm, Luis (6); Styles, Lawrence (9); Tingler, Meredith (11); Wheeler, Timothy (12); White, Jeffery (12).

TEXAS—Arrieta, George† (14); Courtney, Matthew* (11); Gammage, Mark† (10); Hartman, Albert (13); Henke, Thomas (8); Henry, Dwayne (11); Henry, Timothy* (7); Long, Dennis (2); Maki, Timothy (12); Mayfield, Montye (10); Mengswasser, Bradley (16); Simmons, Jeffrey (2); Smith, Daryl† (14); Taylor, Willam* (14); Terrell, C. Walter* (7); Thomas, Joe (20).

GRAND SLAM HOME RUNS—Cjesdal 2, Murphy, T. Johnson, Roberts, Sinnen, 1 each.

AWARDED FRIST BASE ON INTERFERENCE—Talley (Garcia).

GAME-WINNING RBIs

ATLANTA (29)—Lloyd 5, Bonner 4, Haddock 4, Stefanski 4, Hernandez 3, Ozoria 3, Guerrero 2, Schmid 2, Eagle 1, Hayes 1.

CHICAGO-AL (14)—Espy 2, Flores 2, Likely 2, Seeger 2, Corry 1, Flenoir 1, Garcia 1, Luzinski 1, Olson 1, Robinette 1.

CHICAGO-NL (28)—Johnson 7, Dippel 4, Seid 4, Cordova 3, Cataline 2, Powers 2, Schoendienst 2, Cotto 1, Monroe 1, Smith 1, Tenney 1.

HOUSTON-BLUE (28)—Simons 6, Sullivan 6, Cleveland 5, M. Thomas 4, Buckley 2, Garcia 2, Benjamin 1, D'Onofrio 1, Weems 1.

HOUSTON-ORANGE (29)—Clements 7, Robles 6, Ramirez 3, Serdar 3, Antonetty 2, Espinoza 2, Shepard 2, Sheppard 2, Gainey 1, Williams 1.

KANSAS CITY-BLUE (31)—Davis 4, Pastornicky 4, Romano 4, Smith 4, Cadahia 3, R. Johnson 3, Jonson 3, Best 2, Owen 2, Hansen 1, Turner 1.

KANSAS CITY-GOLD (17)—Barclift 8, McKinney 2, Neal 2, Hatcher 1, Hegman 1, Irvin 1, Kingery 1, Vranesh 1.

NEW YORK-AL (23)—Gjesdal 6, Atkins 3, Gonzalez 3, Holt 3, Clases 2, O'Regan 2, Otersen 2, Alcala 1, Hench 1.

PITTSBURGH (17)—Acosta 2, Nolasco 2, Renteria 2, Rice 2, Coyne 1, Davis 1, DeLaRosa 1, Haro 1, Miscik 1, R. Pena 1, Schaive 1, Tiamo 1, Valdez 1.

TEXAS (18)—Murphy 5, Stokes 4, Crum 2, Ondo 2, Wilkinson 2, Haas 1, Roberts 1, Villa 1.

CLUB FIELDING

Club	G.	PO.	A.	E.	DP.	PB.	Pct.	Club	G.	PO.	A.	E.	DP.	PB.	Pct.
Kan City-Blue	63	1611	706	102	49	13	.958	Hou-Orange	62	1662	822	127	52	17	.950
Texas	63	1642	795	107	48	24	.958	Kan City-Gold	63	1613	756	132	62	20	.947
Hou-Blue	62	1576	806	108	56	12	.957	Pittsburgh	63	1633	720	141	52	12	.943
Atlanta	63	1627	796	114	60	16	.955	New York-AL	62	1618	746	150	63	15	.940
Chicago-NL	63	1679	821	120	49	22	.954	Chicago-AL	63	1550	637	163	44	38	.931

INDIVIDUAL FIELDING

FIRST BASEMEN

*Throws lefthanded.

Player and Club	G.	PO.	A.	E.	DP.	Pct.	Player and Club	G.	PO.	A.	E.	DP.	Pct.
Hatcher, KC-Gold	4	39	1	0	4	1.000	Jonson, KC-Blue	17	119	11	3	10	.977
Stokes, Texas	4	32	2	0	3	1.000	Holder, KC-Blue	15	122	4	3	4	.977
Stefanski, Atlanta	4	27	1	0	2	1.000	Benjamin, Hou-Blue	34	343	19	9	34	.976
Bonner, Atlanta	3	13	4	0	1	1.000	Da. McNealy, NY-AL*	4	38	0	1	2	.974
Made, Pittsburgh	1	16	0	0	1	1.000	Ramirez, Hou-Orange	20	208	7	6	12	.973
Mariano, New York-AL.	2	14	2	0	1	1.000	E. Rodriguez, NY-AL	20	172	4	5	18	.972
Hagman, Atlanta*	1	10	0	0	0	1.000	Ondo, Texas*	4	34	1	1	3	.972
Serdar, Hou-Orange	1	9	0	0	1	1.000	Likely, Chicago-AL*	39	322	18	12	22	.966
Clases, New York-AL	1	2	0	0	1	1.000	Herrera, N York-AL	11	104	7	4	8	.965
Schlosser, Hou-Blue	1	1	1	0	0	1.000	Turner, KC-Blue	4	46	2	2	5	.960
Hansen, KC-Blue	2	1	0	0	0	1.000	Gonzalez, N York-AL	9	64	4	3	8	.958
Squilla, Hou-Blue*	24	242	10	1	16	.996	Berger, Pittsburgh	3	22	0	1	1	.957
WILKINSON, Texas	48	435	32	4	36	.992	Owen, KC-Blue	36	258	12	13	22	.954
Garcia, Texas	15	99	12	1	11	.991	Davis, Pittsburgh*	21	184	15	10	10	.952
Schmid, Atlanta*	40	350	22	5	31	.987	Guerrero, Atlanta	15	125	8	7	12	.950
Atkins, New York-AL	19	182	12	3	16	.985	Talley, KC-Gold	2	19	0	1	2	.950
Schaive, Pittsburgh	4	48	1	1	5	.980	Irizarry, Chi-AL	5	44	3	3	2	.940
Barclift, KC-Gold	57	537	30	12	46	.979	Schoendienst, Chi-NL	7	54	5	4	3	.937
O'Leath, Pittsburgh	36	322	11	7	26	.979	Olson, Chicago-AL	3	7	0	1	0	.875
King, Atlanta	8	91	2	2	6	.979	Valdez, Pittsburgh	3	7	0	1	0	.875
Johnson, Chicago-NL	59	584	44	14	46	.978	Wayne, Chicago-NL	1	4	0	1	0	.800
Clements, Hou-Orange ..	51	516	28	12	39	.978							

SECOND BASEMEN

Player and Club	G.	PO.	A.	E.	DP.	Pct.
D'Onofrio, Hou-Blue	10	25	28	0	9	1.000
Tenny, Chicago-NL	10	16	15	0	5	1.000
Belliard, Pittsburgh	3	5	9	0	3	1.000
Wallace, Texas	2	4	9	0	1	1.000
Hegman, KC-Gold	1	6	5	0	0	1.000
Morse, Chicago-AL	1	2	2	0	1	1.000
Wilkerson, Texas	3	0	3	0	1	1.000
Gallo, N York-AL	1	2	0	0	0	1.000
Schlosser, Hou-Blue	16	32	36	1	8	.986
Alcala, N York-AL	11	21	26	1	6	.979
Villa, Texas	39	85	122	7	22	.967
Shuck, N York-AL	22	47	41	3	10	.967
R. JOHNSON, KC-B...	63	154	183	12	36	.966
Irvin, KC-Gold	3	12	15	1	3	.964
Dippel, Chicago-NL	27	67	70	6	10	.958
Romero, Chi-AL	6	9	14	1	0	.958
Carter, Texas	25	63	69	6	17	.957
Haro, Pittsburgh	12	35	30	3	9	.956
R. Rivera, Hou-Orange..	46	87	144	11	26	.955
Ozoria, Atlanta	35	69	102	8	25	.955
Nolasco, Pittsburgh	21	42	64	5	9	.955
Holt, N York-AL	5	8	13	1	3	.955
McKinney, KC-Gold	60	166	178	18	44	.950
Giansanti, Atlanta	20	50	63	6	14	.950
Serdar, Hou-Orange..	8	19	16	2	3	.946
Seeger, Chi-AL	17	31	34	4	10	.942
Weems, Hou-Blue	43	99	117	14	26	.939
Medina, N York-AL.	30	72	69	10	23	.934
Payano, Atlanta	16	37	39	6	8	.927
Seid, Chicago-NL	34	69	88	13	19	.924
E. Rodriguez, NY-AL..	3	7	5	1	0	.923
Wiesler, Chi-AL	44	98	87	16	16	.920
Acosta, Pittsburgh	29	58	62	13	16	.902
Schoendienst, Chi-NL..	6	18	16	4	2	.895
L. Rivera, Hou-Orange ..	15	21	33	10	5	.844

THIRD BASEMEN

Player and Club	G.	PO.	A.	E.	DP.	Pct.
Dippel, Chicago-NL	5	5	10	0	0	1.000
Tenney, Chicago-NL	4	0	13	0	0	1.000
Mariano, New York-AL .	1	1	5	0	0	1.000
Flenoir, Chicago-AL	1	2	3	0	0	1.000
Belliard, Pittsburgh	2	2	3	0	0	1.000
Owen, KC-Blue	1	0	2	0	1	1.000
Espinoza, Hou-Orange..	3	0	2	0	0	1.000
Hayes, Atlanta	1	0	1	0	0	1.000
Monroe, Chicago-NL	2	0	1	0	0	1.000
Tiamo, Pittsburgh	4	7	16	1	0	.958
Jonson, KC-Blue	38	30	94	7	12	.947
Talley, KC-Gold	22	26	43	4	6	.945
Nolasco, Pittsburgh	5	6	11	1	2	.944
Stokes, Texas	29	19	61	5	4	.941
Robinette, Chicago-AL .	16	14	32	3	6	.939
Wallace, Texas	28	9	64	5	4	.936
SCHOEND'ST, Chi-NL.	46	41	115	14	12	.918
Cleveland, Hou-Blue	56	33	150	17	12	.915
Hench, New York-AL..	11	6	36	4	5	.913
Schlosser, Hou-Blue	12	5	16	2	1	.913
Haddock, Texas	56	63	145	20	16	.912
Serdar, Hou-Orange..	18	11	51	6	7	.912
Sheppard, Hou-Orange..	45	28	104	14	6	.904
Haro, Pittsburgh	13	15	32	5	4	.904
Rivera, Chicago-AL...	19	17	27	5	3	.898
Hall, Chicago-NL	14	15	20	4	0	.897
Renteria, Pittsburgh	38	30	84	15	8	.884
Zuzuaregui, Chi-AL..	8	8	14	3	2	.880
Garcia, Texas	8	8	20	4	2	.875
Hansen, KC-Blue	30	25	55	13	4	.860
Olson, Chicago-AL	15	18	30	8	4	.857
Irvin, KC-Gold	20	15	34	9	6	.845
Gjesdal, N York-AL	46	51	88	28	13	.832
Au. Johnson, KC-G	23	17	41	12	5	.829
Romero, Chicago-AL..	3	1	8	2	0	.818
Weaver, Atlanta	4	5	8	3	2	.813
Reasonover, Texas	7	2	13	4	1	.789
E. Rodriguez, NY-AL...	4	3	8	3	0	.786
Benjamin, Hou-Blue	1	0	3	1	0	.750
Zuvella, Atlanta	1	0	3	1	1	.750
Acosta, Pittsburgh	2	1	4	2	0	.714
Seeger, Chicago-AL	5	2	3	0	0	.700
Valdez, Pittsburgh	1	2	0	1	0	.667
Schaive, Pittsburgh	1	0	1	2	0	.333
Ramirez, Hou-Orange..	1	0	1	3	0	.250

SHORTSTOPS

Player and Club	G.	PO.	A.	E.	DP.	Pct.
Jonson, KC-Blue	4	3	6	0	2	1.000
Cleveland, Hou-Blue	2	1	5	0	0	1.000
Howell, Pittsburgh	1	2	3	0	0	1.000
Acosta, Pittsburgh	1	0	1	0	0	1.000
Belliard, Pittsburgh	8	17	27	1	5	.978
D'ONOFRIO, Hou-Blue	52	88	201	16	28	.947
Tenney, Chicago-NL	41	66	142	13	21	.941
Wallace, Texas	9	13	33	3	2	.939
Hegman, KC-Gold	52	85	174	18	24	.935
Miscik, Pittsburgh	7	8	34	3	5	.933
Holt, New York-AL	10	8	20	2	1	.933
Espinoza, Hou-Orange..	58	114	217	25	33	.930
Zuvella, Atlanta	1	4	9	1	2	.929
Buckley, Chicago-NL..	22	40	86	10	14	.926
Haro, Pittsburgh	10	11	25	3	5	.923
Pastornicky, KC-Blue ..	62	83	183	24	24	.917
Hernandez, Atlanta	39	62	123	17	16	.916
Duncan, Texas	7	9	32	4	3	.911
Rivera, Chicago-AL...	17	23	57	8	6	.909
Medina, New York-AL..	22	36	70	12	10	.898
Alcala, New York-AL..	35	54	112	19	21	.897
Weaver, Atlanta	29	35	70	12	15	.897
Irvin, KC-Gold	14	21	43	8	8	.889
Clack, Pittsburgh	39	52	106	22	14	.878
Wilkerson, Texas	31	38	83	17	23	.877
Morse, Chicago-AL..	32	40	74	18	6	.864
R. Rivera, Hou-Orange..	8	7	23	5	2	.857
Gallo, New York-AL..	3	4	13	3	1	.850
Goodin, Texas	22	29	45	14	9	.841
Renteria, Pittsburgh	1	2	3	1	0	.833
Romero, Chicago-AL..	19	25	61	18	7	.827
Schlosser, Hou-Blue	15	14	41	13	8	.809
Dippel, Chicago-NL..	2	1	3	1	0	.800
Giansanti, Atlanta	1	1	0	1	0	.500

OUTFIELDERS

Player and Club	G.	PO.	A.	E.	DP.	Pct.
Flenoir, Chicago-AL..	34	52	3	0	1	1.000
Crum, Texas	34	48	3	0	0	1.000
Smith, Chicago-AL	35	32	3	0	0	1.000
Naclerio, Chicago-AL*..	17	31	2	0	0	1.000
Weems, Hou-Blue	20	28	4	0	0	1.000
Nivar, Atlanta	12	14	0	0	0	1.000
Monroe, Chicago-NL....	10	9	2	0	0	1.000
E. Rodriguez, N. Y.-AL..	4	8	2	0	0	1.000
Coyne, Pittsburgh	4	8	1	0	1	1.000
Isbel, Pittsburgh	5	9	0	0	0	1.000
Angulo, New York-AL ...	4	7	1	0	0	1.000
Atkins, New York-AL	2	6	1	0	0	1.000

OUTFIELDERS—Continued

Player and Club	G.	PO.	A.	E.	DP.	Pct.
Schlosser, Hou-Blue	6	4	2	0	0	1.000
Olson, Chicago-AL	1	5	0	0	0	1.000
Austin, Chicago-NL	3	5	0	0	0	1.000
Holder, KC-Blue	4	4	0	0	0	1.000
Seeger, Chicago-AL	1	3	0	0	0	1.000
Caballero, Pittsburgh	1	2	0	0	0	1.000
Talley, KC-Gold	1	2	0	0	0	1.000
O'Leath, Pittsburgh	2	2	0	0	0	1.000
Hill, Atlanta	4	2	0	0	0	1.000
Castaneda, Pittsburgh	1	1	0	0	0	1.000
Garcia, Texas	1	1	0	0	0	1.000
Ramirez, Hou-Orange	1	1	0	0	0	1.000
ROBLES, Hou-Orange	57	118	9	1	2	.992
Simons, Hou-Blue*	64	105	6	1	1	.991
Murphy, Texas*	52	77	7	1	1	.988
M. Thomas, Hou-Blue	49	71	4	1	0	.987
Benza, Texas	39	57	2	1	0	.983
De. McNealy, N. Y.-AL*	62	156	4	3	2	.982
Best, KC-Blue	46	95	3	2	0	.980
Siriano, Atlanta*	61	133	4	3	0	.979
Haas, Texas	32	45	2	1	0	.979
DeLaRosa, Pittsburgh*	56	157	10	4	2	.977
Davis, KC-Blue	60	117	5	3	1	.976
Kingery, KC-Gold*	38	78	5	2	1	.976
Carpenter, Texas	26	36	3	1	2	.975
Bonner, Atlanta	63	106	8	3	0	.974
Vranesh, KC-Gold	36	69	6	2	2	.974
Lloyd, Atlanta	60	117	15	4	5	.971
Cotto, Chicago-NL	42	93	6	3	0	.971
Smith, KC-Blue	35	61	4	2	0	.970
Garcia, Chicago-AL*	32	60	3	2	1	.969
O'Regan, New York-AL	61	122	6	5	3	.962
DeSena, Hou-Orange	62	88	6	4	2	.959
Romano, KC-Blue	55	104	8	5	1	.957
Espy, Chicago-AL	58	138	4	7	0	.953
Cordova, Chicago-NL	51	82	16	5	2	.951
Notaroberto, KC-Gold	37	54	3	3	1	.950
Buckley, Hou-Blue	51	53	2	3	0	.948
Abraham, Pittsburgh	35	50	4	3	1	.947
Rice, Pittsburgh	44	67	1	4	0	.944
Gainey, Hou-Orange	43	48	2	3	0	.943
Clases, New York-AL	30	46	2	3	1	.941
Luzinski, Chicago-AL	35	41	1	3	0	.933
R. Pena, Pittsburgh	20	27	0	2	0	.931
Neal, KC-Gold	54	95	4	8	0	.925
Cataline, Chicago-NL	48	59	3	5	2	.925
Ondo, Texas*	26	45	1	4	0	.920
Valdez, Pittsburgh	36	64	3	6	0	.918
Burgin, KC-Gold	26	40	7	5	0	.904
Betancourt, Chi.-AL*	22	35	2	4	1	.902
Squilla, Hou-Blue*	6	8	1	1	0	.900
Otersen, New York-AL*	30	43	1	5	0	.898
Powers, Chicago-NL	14	12	3	2	0	.882
Nolasco, Pittsburgh	2	7	0	1	0	.875
Antonetty, Hou-Orange	26	21	4	4	0	.862
Serdar, Hou-Orange	10	6	0	1	0	.857
Roomes, Chicago-NL	12	19	1	4	0	.833
Holt, New York-AL	8	7	0	2	0	.778
Medina, New York-AL	1	4	1	2	0	.714

CATCHERS

Player and Club	G.	PO.	A.	E.	DP.	PB.	Pct.
Sinnen, Pittsburgh	5	21	3	0	1	0	1.000
Nataupsky, KC-Blue	5	14	2	0	0	0	1.000
Batter, KC-Gold	6	11	0	0	0	0	1.000
Cleveland, Hou-Blue	1	5	0	0	0	1	1.000
Cheesman, N. Y.-AL	2	4	0	0	0	0	1.000
Berger, Pittsburgh	2	3	0	0	0	1	1.000
Clack, Pittsburgh	1	2	0	0	0	0	1.000
CADAHIA, KC-Blue	49	252	35	3	4	11	.990
Stefanski, Atlanta	34	159	28	2	3	8	.989
Eagle, Atlanta	19	78	13	1	3	3	.989
Howell, Pittsburgh	31	142	23	2	2	6	.988
Gonzalez, N. York-AL	38	174	40	3	5	11	.986
Williams, Hou-O.	38	202	48	4	6	11	.984
Graham, KC-Blue	23	93	15	2	0	2	.982
Wright, Texas	14	45	6	1	0	8	.981
Colburn, Texas	24	162	22	4	1	5	.979
Dierberger, Chi.-AL	6	34	7	1	1	2	.976
Sullivan, Hou-Blue	47	247	28	7	1	7	.975
Tarnow, Chicago-NL	26	91	23	3	0	9	.974
Peterson, Chicago-NL	17	60	12	2	0	4	.973
Ronshausen, Chi.-AL.	27	129	12	4	1	8	.972
Roberts, Texas	24	144	25	5	1	7	.971
Hatcher, KC-Gold	41	200	44	8	5	14	.968
Remo, Chicago-NL	33	184	23	7	1	6	.967
Shepard, Hou-Orange	25	139	24	6	1	6	.964
Venner, Texas	12	67	10	3	1	4	.963
Wayne, Chicago-NL	7	23	3	1	0	3	.963
Atkins, New York-AL	18	78	22	4	1	2	.962
Flores, Chicago-AL	30	117	23	6	2	20	.959
Rosette, KC-Gold	23	105	16	6	2	6	.953
Guerrero, Atlanta	14	48	10	3	0	5	.951
Garcia, Hou-Blue	25	91	14	6	1	4	.946
Tiamo, Pittsburgh	23	95	20	7	3	1	.943
Castaneda, Pitt	13	54	10	4	1	4	.941
E. Diaz, N. York-AL	13	35	9	3	1	2	.936
Corry, Chicago-AL	7	45	5	4	0	2	.926
Irizarry, Chicago-AL..	3	16	1	2	0	6	.895

PITCHERS

Player and Club	G.	PO.	A.	E.	DP.	Pct.
Morris, Hou-Blue*	9	5	18	0	1	1.000
Schiewe, Chicago-NL	14	7	16	0	0	1.000
Calhoun, Hou-Orange*	8	3	19	0	1	1.000
Martin, New York-AL	10	4	14	0	0	1.000
COOPER, KC-Blue	14	4	12	0	0	1.000
Martin, Atlanta	11	4	11	0	0	1.000
Eichholz, Chicago-NL	13	3	12	0	0	1.000
Malinoski, Hou-Orange	16	3	12	0	1	1.000
LaBounty, Pittsburgh	11	5	9	0	0	1.000
T. Shaw, KC-Gold	13	4	10	0	1	1.000
Weissmann, Chicago-NL	14	3	11	0	1	1.000
Schumacher, Chi-AL	18	3	11	0	0	1.000
D. Henry, Texas	11	1	12	0	1	1.000
Kennedy, Atlanta	14	4	9	0	0	1.000
Schuckert, Chicago-AL*	11	2	10	0	2	1.000
Babcock, Hou-Blue*	13	1	11	0	0	1.000
G. Diaz, New York-AL	17	3	9	0	2	1.000
Lawrence, Atlanta	6	3	8	0	0	1.000
Bair, Chicago-NL	9	2	9	0	0	1.000
Shulleeta, Chicago-NL	11	1	10	0	0	1.000
B. Johnson, KC-Blue*	13	3	8	0	0	1.000
McAnnally, Chicago-AL	13	4	7	0	0	1.000
Mengwasser, Texas	16	2	9	0	1	1.000
Bratton, New York-AL	17	5	6	0	1	1.000
Penate, Hou-Blue	30	2	9	0	1	1.000
Cecil, KC-Gold	13	2	8	0	0	1.000
Wex, Atlanta	16	2	8	0	1	1.000
Marks, New York-AL*	9	0	9	0	0	1.000
Taylor, Texas	14	2	7	0	0	1.000
Flores, New York-AL*	15	0	9	0	1	1.000
Toporek, New York-AL.	7	1	7	0	0	1.000
Creel, KC-Blue	9	2	6	0	0	1.000
Korbas, Chicago-AL*	10	3	5	0	1	1.000
Shoemaker, Chicago-AL	10	0	8	0	0	1.000
Landrum, Chicago-NL	11	2	6	0	0	1.000
Treadway, Atlanta	11	0	8	0	0	1.000
Espinoza, Hou-Blue	12	1	7	0	3	1.000
Thomas, Texas	20	0	8	0	0	1.000

PITCHERS—Continued

Player and Club	G.	PO.	A.	E.	DP.	Pct.
Cook, KC-Gold	8	0	7	0	0	1.000
Keating, Chicago-AL	9	0	7	0	1	1.000
Smith, KC-Gold	11	0	7	0	0	1.000
Tingler, Pittsburgh	11	2	5	0	1	1.000
Swank, KC-Blue*	12	1	6	0	0	1.000
Castro, Hou-Blue*	20	0	7	0	0	1.000
T. Henry, Texas*	7	0	6	0	1	1.000
Gladden, KC-Gold	9	1	5	0	0	1.000
Reilly, Chicago-NL	12	1	5	0	0	1.000
A. Pena, Pittsburgh	13	3	3	0	0	1.000
McAlarney, Pittsburgh*	2	0	5	0	0	1.000
Gammage, Texas	10	1	4	0	0	1.000
Geisel, Chicago-NL*	12	2	3	0	0	1.000
Gonzales, Pittsburgh	12	0	5	0	1	1.000
Valdez, Atlanta*	12	1	4	0	0	1.000
Alvarez, Atlanta	4	1	3	0	0	1.000
Church, Atlanta	4	1	3	0	0	1.000
Courtney, Texas*	11	0	4	0	0	1.000
Gerlach, Chicago-NL	19	2	2	0	0	1.000
Acker, Pittsburgh*	2	0	3	0	0	1.000
Martz, Chicago-AL	2	1	2	0	0	1.000
Rankin, KC-Gold	2	0	3	0	0	1.000
Almanzar, Pittsburgh	5	1	2	0	1	1.000
Flannery, Chicago-AL	8	0	3	0	0	1.000
Moses, Atlanta	9	0	3	0	0	1.000
Styles, Pittsburgh	9	0	3	0	0	1.000
Robles, Atlanta	10	0	3	0	0	1.000
Villaiba, KC-Blue	14	0	3	0	0	1.000
Bossidy, Hou-Orange*	17	2	1	0	0	1.000
Long, Texas	2	1	1	0	0	1.000
Cano, New York-AL	3	1	1	0	0	1.000
Peterson, Pittsburgh*	3	2	0	0	0	1.000
Howard, Pittsburgh	4	1	1	0	0	1.000
Samuel, Chicago-AL	4	1	1	0	0	1.000
V. Perez, Hou-Orange*	10	1	1	0	0	1.000
Acker, Atlanta	1	1	0	0	0	1.000
Lettrich, KC-Blue	1	0	1	0	0	1.000
Rosette, KC-Gold	1	0	1	0	0	1.000
Despaux, New York-AL	2	0	1	0	0	1.000
Doblitz, New York-AL	2	0	1	0	0	1.000
Kirby, Pittsburgh	2	0	1	0	0	1.000
Potestio, KC-Gold	2	1	0	0	0	1.000
Clemente, Pittsburgh	5	0	1	0	0	1.000
Sarante, New York-AL*	5	0	1	0	0	1.000
Kolacki, Hou-Orange*	9	0	1	0	0	1.000
Sparks, KC-Blue	9	1	0	0	0	1.000
Gardner, Hou-Orange	14	2	25	1	2	.964
Mason, Texas*	12	8	15	1	2	.958
Elsee, Hou-Blue	14	6	14	1	0	.952
Fisher, Atlanta	12	7	11	1	0	.947
Wong, KC-Blue	24	6	11	1	1	.944
Henke, Texas	8	4	11	1	0	.938
Cheesman, NY-AL	12	8	20	2	1	.933
White, Pittsburgh*	12	1	13	1	0	.933
R. Shaw, KC-Gold	13	1	12	1	1	.929
Turner, Hou-Blue*	14	1	12	1	1	.929
Dedmon, Atlanta	10	4	32	3	1	.923
Chestnut, Chicago-NL	11	5	6	1	0	.917
Davis, Chicago-AL	12	6	5	1	0	.917
Huismann, KC-Blue	28	8	3	1	0	.917
Horne, Pittsburgh	11	4	16	2	0	.909
Mayfield, Texas	10	1	9	1	0	.909
Cutty, KC-Blue	14	3	16	2	1	.905
Schulze, Chicago-NL	12	6	12	2	1	.900
Bastian, Pittsburgh	10	1	8	1	1	.900
Meckes, Hou-Blue	10	2	7	1	0	.900
Odekirk, KC-Blue*	18	3	6	1	0	.900
Solano, Hou-Orange	18	1	8	1	0	.900
Ab. Johnson, KC-Gold	19	1	8	1	0	.900
Ayers, Atlanta	23	0	9	1	1	.900
Hawk, Hou-Blue	12	3	14	2	3	.895
Edwards, Pittsburgh	13	2	14	2	0	.889
Ortega, Chicago-AL*	15	4	12	2	0	.889
Rosario, New York-AL*	11	1	7	1	3	.889
Arrieta, Texas	14	4	4	1	0	.889
Vercoe, KC-Gold*	12	1	22	3	2	.885
Terrell, Texas	7	3	4	1	0	.875
Regaldo, Hou-Orange	13	3	21	4	0	.857
Wheeler, Pittsburgh	12	3	9	2	0	.857
Albright, KC-Gold*	7	2	4	1	0	.857
Maki, Texas	12	4	12	3	0	.842
Herrara, New York-AL	11	5	5	2	0	.833
Buonantony, Chi-NL	12	4	6	2	2	.833
DePaula, Hou-Orange	15	1	4	1	0	.833
Hartman, Texas	13	1	8	2	0	.818
Patterson, New York-AL	8	1	16	4	2	.810
Mullen, Chicago-AL	14	5	11	4	1	.800
Matos, Atlanta	8	1	3	1	0	.800
Yan, Hou-Orange	12	3	8	3	2	.786
McMichael, KC-Gold*	21	0	11	3	0	.786
Wills, KC-Blue	4	0	7	2	0	.778
Raftice, New York-AL*	10	2	8	3	1	.769
Cerefin, Hou-Orange	7	1	5	2	0	.750
Strode, KC-Blue*	6	0	3	1	0	.750
Estiven, Pittsburgh	9	1	2	1	0	.750
S. Perez, Hou-Orange*	14	0	3	1	0	.750
Hernandez, Hou-Blue	11	1	10	4	0	.733
Mills, Chicago-AL	8	1	9	4	0	.714
Heath, Chicago-AL*	11	2	10	5	0	.706
Pour, KC-Gold	9	1	3	2	0	.667
Ruiz, Hou-Blue	10	0	4	2	1	.667
McCullock, Pittsburgh	2	0	2	1	0	.667
Collins, New York-AL*	3	0	2	1	0	.667
Smith, Texas	4	0	2	1	0	.667
King, KC-Gold	9	2	5	4	0	.636
Fincher, New York-AL*	3	1	2	2	0	.600
N. Rodriguez, NY-AL	3	0	2	2	0	.500
Rymer, Atlanta	5	0	2	2	0	.500
Bradshaw, Pittsburgh*	1	0	0	0	0	.000
Germer, Atlanta	1	0	0	0	0	.000
Figueroa, Atlanta	2	0	0	1	0	.000
G. Thomas, Hou-Blue	12	0	0	1	0	.000

The following players do not have any recorded accepted chances at the positions indicated, therefore, are not listed in the fielding averages for those particular positions: Babcock, of*; Bradshaw, p*; Caraballo, p; Conroyd, p; Cordova, 3b; T. Davis, of*; Despaux, of; Germer, p; Payano, 3b; Remo, of; Roberts, of; Schmid, of*; Schuchmann, p; Scott, p; Seid, 3b; Simmons, p; M. Smith, 3b; S. Smith, 3b; Storm, p; Tapia, of*; Vranesh, 3b; Williams, of; Wright, of.

CLUB PITCHING

Club	G.	CG.	ShO.	Sv.	IP.	H.	R.	ER.	HR.	BB.	Int. BB.	HB.	SO.	WP.	Bk.	ERA.
Texas	63	4	6	10	549	450	246	170	7	291	0	37	392	60	5	2.79
Houston-Orange	62	4	6	9	532	471	251	166	6	216	11	15	329	29	4	2.81
Houston-Blue	62	5	5	13	520	477	242	171	6	231	12	19	347	28	12	2.96
Kansas City-Blue	63	6	8	12	537	487	247	186	14	197	11	20	339	32	4	3.12
Atlanta	62	6	3	15	541	481	254	190	12	236	13	14	268	45	7	3.16
New York-AL	62	6	6	6	543	492	289	203	7	305	16	21	275	30	12	3.36
Chicago-NL	63	6	1	11	558	513	302	211	13	252	13	24	345	38	7	3.40
Kansas City-Gold	63	3	2	7	538	535	301	222	17	254	8	13	299	22	3	3.71
Pittsburgh	63	5	5	5	539	513	327	234	11	277	3	29	296	38	8	3.91
Chicago-AL	63	2	4	13	517	545	356	241	12	281	4	22	314	53	11	4.20

PITCHERS' RECORDS

(Leading Qualifiers for Earned-Run Average Leadership—50 or More Innings)

*Throws lefthanded.

Pitcher—Club	G.	GS.	CG.	ShO.	W.	L.	Sv.	Pct.	IP.	H.	R.	ER.	HR.	BB.	Int. BB.	HB.	SO.	WP.	ERA.
Eichholz, Chicago-NL	13	3	1	1	3	2	1	.600	55	36	10	7	2	8	2	1	32	1	1.15
Morris, Hou-Blue*	9	9	2	0	6	2	0	.750	56	41	17	8	0	7	0	3	31	1	1.29
Regaldo, Hou-Orange	13	13	1	0	7	3	0	.700	82	67	31	14	0	23	0	5	34	2	1.54
Patterson, New York-AL	8	8	1	1	5	2	0	.714	57	40	20	10	0	18	1	4	20	1	1.58
Cheesman, New York-AL	12	4	1	0	2	5	2	.286	59	46	19	11	0	28	3	0	24	2	1.68
Cooper, KC-Blue	14	11	2	1	8	2	0	.800	78	64	23	15	1	18	2	5	38	3	1.73
Martin, Atlanta	11	11	1	0	4	1	0	.800	59	53	17	12	0	26	0	2	28	3	1.83
Elsee, Hou-Blue	14	12	2	1	7	3	0	.700	78	44	19	16	2	39	3	2	52	3	1.85
Wong, KC-Blue	24	0	0	0	2	2	5	.500	52	30	13	11	1	28	3	4	40	0	1.90
Mullen, Chicago-AL	14	5	0	0	3	4	0	.400	60	54	28	13	0	16	0	1	40	4	1.95

Departmental Leaders: G—Penate, 30; GS—Gardner, 14; CG—Schulze, 3; ShO—LaBounty, 2; W—Cooper, B. Johnson, 8; L. Bounantony, 8; Sv—Ayers, 8; Pct.—Cooper, .750; IP—Gardner, 83; H—Gardner, 82; R—Edwards, 47; ER—Edwards, Horne, 34; HR—Treadway, 5; BB—Fisher, 53; IBB—Bossidy, 4; HB—Hartman, Mengwasser, 7; SO—Mason, 55; WP—Maki, 14.

(All Pitchers—Listed Alphabetically)

Pitcher—Club	G.	GS.	CG.	ShO.	W.	L.	Sv.	Pct.	IP.	H.	R.	ER.	HR.	BB.	Int. BB.	HB.	SO.	WP.	ERA.
Acker, Pittsburgh*	2	0	0	0	0	0	0	.000	4	5	2	2	0	1	0	0	2	0	4.50
Acker, Atlanta	1	1	0	0	1	0	0	1.000	5	1	0	0	0	0	0	0	5	0	0.00
Albright, KC-Gold*	7	2	0	0	0	2	1	.000	21	18	11	6	1	8	0	0	12	1	2.57
Almanzar, Pittsburgh	5	0	0	0	0	0	0	.000	8	6	7	5	0	5	0	0	2	0	5.63
Alvarez, Atlanta	4	3	1	1	0	0	0	1.000	21	16	4	3	0	7	0	0	16	0	1.29
Arrieta, Texas	14	0	0	0	5	0	0	1.000	27	22	8	6	0	12	0	3	12	2	2.00
Ayers, Atlanta	23	0	0	0	2	2	8	.500	37	31	11	7	0	8	3	1	21	1	1.70
Babcock, Hou-Blue*	13	2	0	0	1	1	0	.000	34	42	23	17	0	11	1	1	11	0	4.50
Bair, Chicago-NL	9	1	0	0	2	0	1	1.000	23	24	17	9	0	13	0	0	13	5	3.52
Bastian, Pittsburgh	10	1	0	0	4	3	1	.571	30	27	11	10	1	16	0	0	16	4	3.00
Bossidy, Hou-Orange*	17	0	0	0	2	1	5	.667	33	23	11	5	0	26	4	0	32	5	1.36
Bradshaw, Pittsburgh*	1	0	0	0	0	0	0	.000	1	0	2	2	0	4	0	1	1	0	18.00
Bratton, New York-AL	17	0	0	0	3	5	3	.375	50	56	29	28	2	20	3	0	30	0	5.04
Buonantony, Chicago-NL	12	12	1	0	3	8	0	.273	63	66	40	28	1	26	0	5	37	4	4.00
Calhoun, Hou-Orange*	8	8	1	0	2	2	0	.500	50	38	18	10	0	21	1	1	41	0	1.80
Cano, New York-AL	3	0	0	0	0	0	0	.000	3	8	7	6	0	3	0	1	2	1	18.00
Caraballo, New York-AL.	2	0	0	0	0	1	0	.000	3	4	3	3	0	2	0	0	0	1	9.00
Castro, Hou-Blue*	20	2	0	0	2	2	1	.500	43	36	20	14	2	21	0	1	35	1	2.93
Cecil, KC-Gold	13	0	0	0	2	0	1	.000	36	29	9	9	4	9	0	1	16	1	2.25
Cerefin, Hou-Orange	7	2	0	0	1	2	0	.333	17	16	15	6	0	13	1	1	7	3	3.18
Cheesman, New York-AL	12	4	1	0	2	5	2	.286	59	46	19	11	0	28	3	0	24	2	1.68
Chestnut, Chicago-NL	11	11	1	0	3	2	0	.600	59	54	30	19	3	23	0	1	24	2	2.90
Church, Atlanta	4	4	0	0	2	2	0	.500	24	17	5	2	0	12	1	0	8	1	0.75
Clemente, Pittsburgh	5	0	0	0	0	0	0	.000	11	12	7	4	0	2	0	1	2	1	3.27
Collins, New York-AL*	3	1	0	0	1	0	0	1.000	10	9	2	1	0	7	0	0	6	0	0.90
Conroyd, Pittsburgh*	2	2	0	0	0	1	0	.000	6	8	2	1	0	1	0	0	5	0	1.50
Cook, KC-Gold	8	7	0	0	0	4	0	.000	34	36	16	12	0	28	0	0	27	1	3.18
Cooper, KC-Blue	14	11	2	1	8	2	0	.800	78	64	23	15	1	18	2	5	38	3	1.73
Courtney, Texas*	11	2	0	0	1	0	0	1.000	30	31	17	10	0	14	0	0	21	2	3.00
Creel, KC—Blue	9	9	1	1	6	2	0	.750	54	47	21	13	1	9	0	1	39	2	2.17
Cutty, KC-Blue	14	12	1	0	5	5	0	.500	74	60	33	22	2	32	2	2	41	4	2.68
Davis, Chicago-AL	12	9	1	0	2	4	0	.333	65	67	35	19	2	22	0	3	29	4	2.63
DePaula, Hou-Orange	15	0	0	0	0	2	1	.000	24	26	18	12	1	13	2	1	13	3	4.50
Dedmon, Atlanta	10	9	2	0	3	4	0	.429	64	55	26	21	1	11	2	2	28	4	2.95
Despaux, New York-AL.	2	0	0	0	0	0	0	.000	4	5	9	4	0	5	1	0	5	1	9.00
Diaz, New York-AL	17	0	0	0	2	2	0	.500	47	36	13	12	0	20	3	0	12	3	2.30
Doblitz, New York-AL...	2	1	0	0	0	1	0	.000	3	6	4	4	0	3	0	0	2	1	12.00
Edwards, Pittsburgh	13	11	2	1	3	4	0	.429	74	76	47	34	2	33	0	1	30	5	4.14
Eichholz, Chicago-NL	13	3	1	1	3	2	1	.600	55	36	10	7	2	8	2	1	32	1	1.15
Elsee, Hou-Blue	14	12	2	1	7	3	0	.700	78	44	19	16	2	39	3	2	52	3	1.85
Espinoza, Hou-Blue	12	8	0	0	4	4	0	.500	38	42	32	27	2	41	0	2	18	8	6.39
Estiven, Pittsburgh	9	0	0	0	0	1	0	.000	15	20	17	10	0	11	1	4	6	0	6.00
Figueroa, Atlanta	2	0	0	0	0	0	0	.000	3	6	3	3	0	4	0	0	1	0	9.00
Fincher, New York-AL*	3	3	0	0	1	1	0	.500	14	10	6	6	0	13	0	0	13	1	3.86
Fisher, Atlanta	12	12	0	0	5	3	0	.625	61	55	34	26	0	53	1	2	48	10	3.81
Flannery, Chicago-AL	8	0	0	0	1	2	2	.500	10	5	5	5	1	5	1	0	13	2	3.75
Flores, New York-AL*	15	1	0	0	2	0	1	1.000	26	22	13	11	1	19	1	2	19	1	3.81
Gammage, Texas	10	6	0	0	2	4	0	.333	32	31	28	21	1	30	0	2	25	6	5.91
Gardner, Hou-Orange	14	14	2	0	7	4	0	.636	83	82	32	24	1	15	0	0	49	3	2.60
Geisel, Chicago-NL*	12	0	0	0	4	0	1	1.000	35	20	15	8	0	27	2	1	32	1	2.06
Gerlach, Chicago-NL	19	0	0	0	4	3	4	.571	36	33	12	10	0	8	2	0	26	0	2.50
Germer, Atlanta	1	0	0	0	0	0	0	.000	3	3	2	2	0	0	0	0	4	0	6.00
Gladden, KC-Gold	9	3	0	0	4	3	0	.571	34	35	13	7	0	5	1	1	23	0	1.85

Pitcher–Club	G.	GS.	CG.	ShO.	W.	L.	Sv.	Pct.	IP.	H.	R.	ER.	HR.	BB.	Int. BB.	HB.	SO.	WP.	ERA.
Gonzales, Pittsburgh	12	4	0	0	1	3	1	.250	35	30	22	14	0	16	0	1	26	1	3.60
Hartman, Texas	13	3	0	0	4	0	0	.000	35	30	21	17	0	15	0	7	16	0	4.37
Hawk, Hou-Blue	12	11	1	1	3	4	0	.429	66	59	38	22	1	28	1	5	54	4	3.00
Heath, Chicago-AL*	11	9	0	0	1	4	0	.200	45	36	43	27	2	47	0	5	36	7	5.40
Henke, Texas	8	4	1	1	3	3	0	.500	38	33	11	4	0	12	0	4	34	2	0.95
D. Henry, Texas	11	11	1	1	5	1	0	.833	54	36	23	16	2	28	0	1	47	6	2.67
T. Henry, Texas*	7	2	0	0	1	1	0	.500	22	16	7	7	1	11	0	1	13	2	2.86
Hernandez, Hou-Blue	11	11	0	0	5	2	0	.714	62	65	26	21	2	15	1	2	37	1	3.05
Herrara, New York-AL	11	9	0	0	4	5	0	.444	57	53	28	18	0	28	0	3	36	1	2.84
Horne, Pittsburgh	11	11	1	0	1	7	0	.125	64	67	38	34	4	31	0	4	34	2	4.78
Howard, Pittsburgh*	4	4	0	0	1	2	0	.333	17	14	12	5	0	17	0	0	9	1	2.65
Huismann, KC-Blue	28	0	0	0	1	2	7	.333	59	50	20	16	1	14	1	1	46	5	2.44
Ab. Johnson, KC-Gold	19	0	0	0	2	0	1	1.000	31	14	8	4	0	20	1	2	16	1	1.16
B. Johnson, KC-Blue*	13	13	0	0	8	3	0	.727	57	61	35	28	3	26	0	2	26	8	4.42
Keating, Chicago-AL	9	4	0	0	0	3	0	.000	25	38	29	25	1	19	0	1	7	10	9.00
Kennedy, Atlanta	14	6	1	0	5	1	0	.833	58	53	32	22	1	30	1	3	34	4	3.41
King, KC-Gold*	9	5	0	0	1	2	1	.333	33	29	15	10	1	25	1	0	11	2	2.73
Kirby, Pittsburgh	2	0	0	0	1	0	0	1.000	4	1	0	0	0	4	0	0	3	0	2.25
Kolacki, Hou-Orange*	9	0	0	0	0	1	0	.000	14	14	10	7	0	6	0	2	10	2	4.50
Korbas, Chicago-AL*	10	2	0	0	1	1	0	.500	30	24	9	9	1	24	0	0	13	2	2.70
LaBounty, Pittsburgh	11	9	2	2	4	2	0	.667	60	45	33	14	1	23	0	2	36	5	2.10
Landrum, Chicago-NL	11	0	0	0	2	0	0	1.000	37	37	21	17	1	11	1	0	27	1	4.14
Lawrence, Atlanta	6	2	0	0	2	1	0	.667	17	23	9	7	1	4	0	0	8	0	3.71
Lettrich, KC-Blue	1	0	0	0	0	0	0	.000	1	2	3	3	0	2	0	0	0	0	27.00
Long, Texas	2	0	0	0	0	0	0	.000	6	4	1	1	0	0	0	0	4	1	1.50
Maki, Texas	12	12	1	0	2	7	0	.222	57	58	36	28	0	44	0	4	41	14	4.42
Malinoski, Hou-Orange	16	6	0	0	2	2	1	.500	58	48	30	19	1	16	0	0	40	1	2.95
Marks, New York-AL*	9	9	1	0	3	5	0	.375	44	44	25	17	1	17	1	0	27	0	3.48
Martin, New York-AL	10	10	0	0	1	5	0	.167	46	47	40	29	1	49	1	0	15	3	5.67
Martin, Atlanta	11	11	1	0	4	1	0	.800	59	53	17	12	0	26	0	2	28	3	1.83
Martz, Chicago-NL	2	2	0	0	0	0	0	.000	7	5	4	2	1	1	0	0	2	1	2.57
Mason, Texas*	12	10	0	0	6	1	0	.857	61	40	17	14	1	46	0	2	55	4	2.07
Matos, Atlanta	8	1	0	0	2	1	1	.667	21	19	7	6	0	4	0	0	6	3	2.57
Mayfield, Texas	10	3	0	0	2	0	2	1.000	26	16	9	6	0	12	0	3	16	3	2.08
McAlarney, Pittsburgh*	2	2	0	0	1	0	0	1.000	8	4	1	1	0	2	0	1	7	0	1.13
McAnnally, Chicago-AL	13	5	0	0	4	3	1	.571	46	49	31	21	1	17	1	1	23	2	4.11
McCulloch, Pittsburgh	2	0	0	0	0	0	0	.000	4	10	7	6	0	2	0	0	2	3	13.50
McMichael, KC-Gold*	21	2	0	0	1	4	1	.200	59	65	39	21	1	25	1	1	49	4	3.20
Meckes, Hou-Blue	10	0	0	0	0	0	4	.000	16	10	3	3	0	7	0	1	15	0	1.69
Mengwasser, Texas	16	1	0	0	1	3	1	.250	37	30	25	14	1	25	0	7	34	9	3.41
Mills, Chicago-AL	8	7	0	0	1	4	0	.200	31	40	43	29	0	27	0	3	18	9	8.42
Morris, Hou-Blue*	9	9	2	0	6	2	0	.750	56	41	17	8	0	7	0	3	31	1	1.29
Moses, Atlanta	9	0	0	0	2	0	0	1.000	23	23	20	16	1	10	2	0	9	2	6.26
Mullen, Chicago-AL	14	5	0	0	2	3	4	.400	60	54	28	13	0	16	0	1	40	4	1.95
Odekirk, KC-Blue*	18	0	0	0	4	0	0	1.000	46	44	18	15	1	14	1	1	12	1	2.93
Ortega, Chicago-AL*	15	8	1	0	2	5	1	.286	58	62	33	22	2	28	1	3	45	2	3.41
Patterson, New York-AL	8	8	2	1	5	2	0	.714	57	40	20	10	0	18	1	4	20	1	1.58
A. Pena, Pittsburgh	3	0	0	0	0	2	2	.000	25	23	12	9	1	9	0	0	11	0	3.24
Penate, Hou-Blue	30	1	0	0	4	3	7	.571	47	47	14	9	2	7	3	0	33	4	1.72
S. Perez, Hou-Orange*	14	2	0	0	1	1	0	.500	27	32	26	18	2	12	0	0	16	4	6.00
V. Perez, Hou-Orange*	10	5	0	0	0	4	0	.000	32	29	20	18	1	22	0	2	20	1	5.06
Peterson, Pittsburgh*	3	0	0	0	0	0	0	.000	6	1	0	0	0	1	0	0	6	0	0.00
Potestio, KC-Gold	2	2	0	0	1	1	0	.500	10	12	9	7	0	2	0	1	10	2	6.30
Pour, KC-Gold	9	6	1	0	1	5	0	.167	31	38	36	33	1	24	0	1	10	2	9.58
Raftice, New York-AL*	10	9	2	1	3	1	0	.750	47	37	21	13	0	30	0	5	30	2	2.49
Rankin, KC-Gold	2	2	0	0	1	1	0	.500	12	8	2	2	1	3	0	0	5	1	1.50
Regaldo, Hou-Orange	13	13	1	0	7	3	0	.700	82	67	31	14	0	23	0	5	34	2	1.54
Reilly, Chicago-NL	12	0	0	0	3	0	1	1.000	33	26	9	8	0	13	2	0	28	0	2.18
Robles, Atlanta	10	0	0	0	0	1	0	.000	18	17	10	7	0	12	0	1	4	3	3.50
N. Rodriguez, NY-AL	3	0	0	0	1	0	0	1.000	9	8	6	2	1	5	0	1	5	0	2.00
Rosario, New York-AL*	11	0	0	0	1	0	0	.000	29	27	16	9	0	15	2	0	8	1	2.79
Rosette, KC-Gold	1	1	0	0	0	0	0	.000	4	6	6	4	0	5	0	0	1	1	9.00
Ruiz, Hou-Blue	10	0	0	0	0	0	0	.000	14	25	23	15	0	17	0	0	10	4	9.64
Rymer, Atlanta	5	1	0	0	2	0	0	1.000	16	11	12	10	0	19	0	0	6	3	5.63
Samuel, Chicago-AL	4	0	0	0	0	1	0	.000	6	11	8	7	0	8	0	0	5	0	10.50
Sarante, New York-AL*	5	2	0	0	0	0	0	.000	12	13	12	9	1	9	1	7	0	0	6.75
Schiewe, Chicago-NL	14	7	1	0	3	2	2	.600	58	60	40	29	2	26	2	5	31	2	4.50
Schuchmann, KC-Gold	1	0	0	0	0	0	0	.000	2	5	7	7	1	2	0	0	0	0	31.50
Schuckert, Chicago-AL*	11	6	0	0	4	3	0	.571	48	49	29	22	0	32	0	0	30	3	4.13
Schulze, Chicago-NL	12	12	3	0	2	7	0	.222	66	58	38	30	0	36	0	3	30	4	4.09
Schumacher, Chicago-AL	18	1	0	0	3	4	4	.429	55	68	29	23	2	11	1	4	40	4	3.76
Scott, New York-AL	1	1	0	0	0	0	0	.000	2	3	1	0	0	0	0	0	4	0	0.00
R. Shaw, KC-Gold*	13	10	1	0	2	3	0	.400	70	71	35	30	3	31	0	0	35	2	3.86
T. Shaw, KC-Gold	13	10	1	0	5	7	0	.417	61	61	34	23	2	24	1	1	29	2	3.39
Shoemaker, Chicago-AL	10	6	0	0	1	6	0	.143	38	41	34	19	0	25	0	4	15	4	4.50

Pitcher—Club	G.	GS.	CG.	ShO.	W.	L.	Sv.	Pct.	IP.	H.	R.	ER.	HR.	BB.	Int. BB.	HB.	SO.	WP.	ERA.
Shulleeta, Chicago-NL	11	3	0	0	2	2	1	.500	30	37	27	16	1	22	2	2	11	8	4.80
Simmons, Texas	2	0	0	0	0	0	0	.000	3	2	1	1	0	2	0	0	1	0	3.00
Smith, Texas	4	2	0	0	1	1	0	.500	12	13	9	6	0	4	0	0	4	2	4.50
Smith, KC-Gold	11	1	0	0	1	2	0	.000	20	15	9	7	0	13	2	0	15	1	3.15
Solano, Hou-Orange	18	0	0	0	5	2	2	.714	38	31	16	11	0	23	1	1	29	1	2.61
Sparks, KC-Gold	9	0	0	0	0	0	0	.000	28	33	17	16	2	8	0	1	12	0	5.14
Storm, Pittsburgh	6	1	0	0	0	1	0	.000	15	22	18	14	0	11	0	1	5	5	8.40
Strode, KC-Blue*	6	5	1	0	0	1	0	.000	20	13	5	4	1	10	0	1	27	1	1.80
Styles, Pittsburgh	9	0	0	0	1	3	0	.250	11	9	13	12	0	20	0	3	8	2	9.82
Swank, KC-Blue*	12	9	1	1	4	5	0	.444	44	55	40	30	1	24	1	0	26	2	6.14
Taylor, Texas	14	2	0	0	0	0	0	.000	35	36	14	9	0	16	0	2	22	3	2.31
Terrell, Texas	7	5	1	0	3	2	0	.600	38	20	11	6	1	12	0	0	23	0	1.42
Thomas, Texas	20	0	0	0	3	1	6	.750	37	32	8	4	0	8	0	1	24	4	0.97
G. Thomas, Hou-Blue	12	0	0	0	1	0	0	.000	16	15	9	6	0	15	1	1	11	2	3.38
Tingler, Pittsburgh	11	1	0	0	3	1	0	.750	30	28	15	15	0	15	1	0	14	4	4.50
Toporek, New York-AL	7	4	0	0	0	0	0	.000	19	16	11	10	0	16	0	5	12	0	4.74
Treadway, Atlanta	11	11	1	0	4	6	0	.400	56	56	38	29	5	14	0	3	22	5	4.66
Turner, Hou-Blue*	14	6	0	0	7	2	0	.778	57	51	18	13	1	23	2	1	40	0	2.05
Valdez, Atlanta*	12	1	0	0	0	2	1	.000	33	36	14	12	1	9	2	0	13	2	3.27
Vercoe, KC-Gold*	12	12	0	0	2	5	0	.286	53	60	35	24	0	22	1	4	28	2	4.08
Villalba, KC-Blue	14	0	0	0	1	0	0	.000	30	44	29	24	2	12	1	0	24	3	7.20
Weissmann, Chicago-NL	14	12	0	0	2	1	5	.667	23	9	7	5	2	13	1	0	7	4	1.96
Wex, Atlanta	16	0	0	0	2	2	1	.500	54	52	24	15	1	18	0	0	48	5	2.50
Wheeler, Pittsburgh	12	6	0	0	2	6	0	.250	63	57	41	27	1	37	1	0	29	2	3.86
White, Pittsburgh*	12	11	1	0	2	6	0	.250	63	57	41	27	1	37	1	0	29	2	3.86
Wills, KC-Blue	4	4	0	0	2	0	0	1.000	23	18	7	5	0	8	0	3	20	3	1.96
Wong, KC-Blue	24	0	0	0	2	5	5	.500	52	30	13	11	1	28	3	4	40	0	1.90
Yan, Hou-Orange	12	12	0	0	7	4	0	.636	75	65	24	22	0	26	2	2	38	4	2.64

BALKS—Hawk, 4; Espinoza, A. Pena, Rosario, 3 each; Babcock, Bratton, G. Diaz, Gonzales, Mills, Robles, Schulze, Schumacher, Taylor, Tingler, Toporek, Weissmann, Wills, 2 each; Arrieta, Buonantony, Castro, Cook, Cooper, Davis, DePaula, Dedmon, Edwards, Figueroa, Gardner, Hartman, Heath, Herrera, Keating, King, Kolacki, Korbas, LaBounty, Landrum, Marks, McAnnally, Mengwasser, Morris, Moses, Mullen, Odekirk, Reilly, Sarante, Shoemaker, Solano, Treadway, Turner, Valdez, 1 each.

COMBINATION SHUTOUTS—Church-Valdez, Martin-Rymer, Atlanta; Mullen-McAnnally, Heath-Korbas-Schumacher, McAnnally-Mullen, Korbas-Mullen, Chicago-AL; Hernandez-Penate, Gardner-Cerefin-DePaula, Castro-Penate, Elsee-Espinoza-Thomas-Penate, Houston-Blue; Yan-Solano, Regaldo-Malinoski-Bossidy, Regaldo-Solano, Malinoski-V. Perez, Houston-Orange; Cutty-Huisman, Cooper-Oderkirk, Cooper-Wong, Creel-Huismann 2, Kansas City-Blue; Marks-Cheesman, Marks-G. Diaz, Herrera-G. Diaz, New York-AL; Horne-Wheeler-Gonzales, Pittsburgh; Hartman-Mayfield-Mason-Mengwasser, Gammage-Mengwasser, Terrell-Mayfield, Henke-Mengwasser, Texas.

NO-HIT GAMES—Cutty (7⅔ inn.), Huisman (1⅓ inn.), Kansas City-Blue, defeated Houston-Blue, 4-0, July 10; LaBounty, Pittsburgh, defeated Chicago-NL, 2-0, July 16.

Pioneer League

SUMMER CLASS A CLASSIFICATION

CHAMPIONSHIP WINNERS IN PREVIOUS YEARS

1939—Twin Falls* .... .581	1952—Pocatello .... .595	1963—Idaho Falls .... .702
1940—Salt Lake City .... .608	Idaho Falls (2nd)* .... .573	Magic Valley† .... .643
Ogden (4th)* .... .492	1953—Ogden .... .679	1964—Treasure Valley .... .615
1941—Boise .... .623	Salt Lake C. (4th)* ...... .527	1965—Treasure Valley .... .530
Ogden (2nd)* .... .598	1954—Salt Lake City .... .595	1966—Ogden .... .591
1942—Pocatello† .... .690	Great Falls (4th)* .... .530	1967—Ogden .... .621
Boise .... .683	1955—Boise .... .588	1968—Ogden .... .609
1943-44-45—Did not operate.	Magic Valley (4th)* ..... .489	1969—Ogden .... .620
1946—Twin Falls‡ .... .585	1956—Boise .... .561	1970—Idaho Falls .... .629
Salt Lake City† .... .585	1957—Salt Lake City .... .650	1971—Great Falls .... .643
1947—Salt Lake City .... .618	Billings‡ .... .582	1972—Billings .... .694
Twin Falls† .... .600	1958—Great Falls .... .582	1973—Billings .... .629
1948—Pocatello .... .611	Boise† .... .615	1974—Idaho Falls .... .569
Twin Falls (2nd)* .... .595	1959—Boise .... .633	1975—Great Falls .... .577
1949—Twin Falls .... .624	Billings (2nd)* .... .523	1976—Great Falls .... .577
Pocatello (3rd)* .... .595	1960—Boise† .... .686	1977—Lethbridge .... .629
1950—Pocatello .... .635	Idaho Falls .... .650	1978—Billings x .... .735
Billings (3rd)* .... .571	1961—Boise .... .638	1979—Helena .... .623
1951—Salt Lake City .... .618	Great Falls* .... .571	Lethbridge y .... .559
Great Falls (3rd)* .... .559	1962—Boise§ .... .565	
	Billings† .... .706	

*Won four-club playoff. †Won split-season playoff. ‡Ended first half in tie with Salt Lake City and won one-game playoff. §Ended first half in tie with Billings and Great Falls and won playoff. xBillings (first place) defeated Idaho Falls (second place) in First Place-Second Place playoff. yLeague divided in Northern and Southern divisions; won two-club playoff.

STANDING OF CLUBS AT CLOSE OF SEASON, AUGUST 31

NORTHERN DIVISION

Club	Leth.	G.F.	Cal.	M.H.	Bil.	I.F.	Hel.	But.	W.	L.	T.	Pct.	G.B.
Lethbridge (Dodgers)	...	6	7	10	6	6	7	10	52	18	0	.743	....
Great Falls (Giants)	4	...	9	8	5	7	7	9	49	21	0	.700	3
Calgary (Expos)	3	1	...	8	3	5	3	0	23	46	0	.333	28½
Medicine Hat (Blue Jays)	0	2	2	...	0	3	3	6	16	54	0	.229	36

SOUTHERN DIVISION

Club									W.	L.	T.	Pct.	G.B.
Billings (Reds)	4	5	7	10	...	6	6	6	44	26	1	.629	....
Idaho Falls (Angels)	4	3	5	7	4	...	6	5	34	36	0	.486	10
Helena (Phillies)	3	3	7	7	4	4	...	4	32	38	0	.457	12
Butte (Brewers)	0	1	9	4	4	5	6	...	29	40	1	.420	14½

Major league affiliations in parentheses.

Playoff—Lethbridge defeated Billings, two games to one.

Regular-Season Attendance—Billings, 58,464; Butte, 29,410; Calgary, 26,317; Great Falls, 68,003; Helena, 18,888; Idaho Falls, 37,646; Lethbridge, 27,044; Medicine Hat, 15,700. Total, 281,472. Playoffs, 2,816. No all-star game.

Managers: Billings—Jim Hoff; Butte—Ken Richardson; Calgary—Steve Boros; Great Falls—Ernie Rodriguez; Helena—Rollie DeArmas; Idaho Falls—Reuben Rodriguez; Lethbridge—Gail Henley; Medicine Hat—John McLaren.

All-Star Team: 1B—Smith, Lethbridge; 2B—Ready, Butte; 3B—Tartabull, Billings; SS—Foote, Billings; OF—James, Butte; McGaffey, Idaho Falls; Reid, Great Falls; C—Gomez, Great Falls; DH—Cole, Lethbridge; P—Dempsey, Great Falls; Layton, Billings; Reade, Lethbridge; Manager—Henley, Lethbridge.

(Compiled by William J. Weiss, League Statistician, San Mateo, Calif.)

CLUB BATTING

Club	G.	AB.	R.	OR.	H.	TB.	2B.	3B.	HR.	RBI.	SH.	SF.	BB.	Int. BB.	HP.	SO.	SB.	CS.	LOB.	Pct.
Lethbridge........	70	2479	537	315	775	1084	127	34	38	457	15	21	370	9	29	417	101	38	620	.313
Butte................	70	2416	498	507	729	1066	133	42	40	414	21	22	376	6	24	482	83	43	581	.302
Great Falls	70	2453	510	354	721	1006	117	30	36	413	23	33	360	14	17	437	119	26	579	.294
Billings	71	2406	455	344	641	822	105	11	18	368	38	21	389	9	16	582	99	20	616	.266

CLUB BATTING—Continued

Club	G.	AB.	R.	OR.	H.	TB.	2B.	3B.	HR.	RBI.	SH.	SF.	Int. BB.	BB.	HP.	SO.	SB.	CS.	LOB.	Pct.
Calgary	69	2394	324	422	627	860	104	18	31	266	20	8	238	14	16	490	114	27	549	.262
Idaho Falls	70	2346	382	440	597	815	95	27	23	305	43	19	357	10	27	505	45	33	578	.254
Helena	70	2346	335	413	596	794	82	10	32	280	43	18	330	10	12	585	79	44	557	.254
Medicine Hat	70	2275	264	510	496	642	66	22	12	202	15	18	302	8	21	596	95	14	550	.218

INDIVIDUAL BATTING

(Leading Qualifiers for Batting Championship—189 or More Plate Appearances)

*Bats lefthanded. †Switch-hitter.

Player and Club	G.	AB.	R.	H.	TB.	2B.	3B.	HR.	RBI.	SH.	SF.	BB.	HP.	SO.	SB.	CS.	Pct.
Ready, Randy, Butte	61	226	65	85	140	23	4	8	50	0	4	57	1	32	2	2	.376
Reid, Jessie, Great Falls*	59	227	57	83	125	15	6	5	48	0	2	38	2	24	14	4	.366
Smith, Gregory, Lethbridge*	69	272	63	99	139	18	2	6	58	0	4	26	5	39	10	5	.364
Gomez, Randall, Great Falls	66	241	63	87	122	19	2	4	44	1	0	38	2	29	3	2	.345
Ponce, Carlos, Butte	69	259	48	90	143	18	7	7	55	2	3	19	2	44	3	3	.347
See, R. Laurence, Lethbridge	68	252	41	87	122	19	2	4	44	1	0	38	2	29	3	2	.345
Cole, W. Audie, Lethbridge	60	227	51	76	114	14	3	6	52	1	6	31	4	23	1	1	.335
Debus, Jon, Lethbridge	62	246	49	82	128	16	3	8	58	1	2	31	2	59	3	1	.333
Freeney, Delano, Helena*	58	202	27	67	86	16	0	1	29	0	3	32	2	25	1	2	.332
Miller, Gerard, Butte	67	233	55	77	130	18	4	9	67	0	5	39	5	55	5	3	.330

Departmental Leaders: G—Wesley, 71; AB—Wesley, 279; R—Ready, 65; H—G. Smith, 99; TB—Ponce, 143; 2B—Ready, 23; 3B—Harris, 8; HR—Miller, 9; RBI—Miller, 67; GWRBI—Debus, McGaffey, G. Smith, 8; SH—Estep, Krauss, Leppert, Walker, 6; SF—Everton, Krauss, 7; BB—Krauss, 61; HP—Miller, 7; SO—Kinnard, 93; SB—Lachowetz, 36; CS—Lachowetz, 10.

(All Players—Listed Alphabetically)

Player and Club	G.	AB.	R.	H.	TB.	2B.	3B.	HR.	RBI.	SH.	SF.	BB.	HP.	SO.	SB.	CS.	Pct.
Adams, Jeffrey, Billings	2	6	1	2	2	0	0	0	0	0	0	0	0	1	0	0	.333
Adams, Manuel, Great Falls†	35	118	23	40	52	6	0	2	23	1	0	14	2	20	1	1	.339
Albright, Henry, Great Falls	55	164	30	42	56	10	2	0	21	1	0	14	0	29	18	4	.256
Allen, Robert, Lethbridge	43	166	38	53	77	7	4	3	26	1	1	38	1	18	7	2	.319
Alonzo, Raymond, Butte*	29	107	21	44	67	10	2	3	26	0	2	10	2	12	4	1	.411
Amoros, Andres, Medicine Hat	20	40	7	10	10	0	0	0	2	1	0	10	1	11	2	0	.250
Bagiotti, Aldo, Idaho Falls	42	126	19	25	35	4	0	2	12	4	0	20	3	22	2	1	.198
Bailey, Robert, Lethbridge	41	149	27	53	66	10	0	1	26	0	1	18	2	21	0	1	.356
Barba, Douglas, Billings	15	2	0	0	0	0	0	0	0	0	0	0	0	2	0	0	.000
Barbee, Andrew, Billings	4	9	4	3	3	0	0	0	1	0	0	5	0	2	1	0	.333
Bard, Paul, Lethbridge	22	82	17	19	24	2	0	1	19	0	0	9	4	15	0	2	.232
Bowden, Mark, Billings*	15	25	8	7	11	1	0	1	6	1	0	5	0	6	0	0	.280
Brock, Joseph, Idaho Falls	47	157	20	39	47	6	1	0	20	1	1	23	5	44	1	2	.248
Brodeur, Claude, Calgary	29	40	3	3	4	1	0	0	3	2	0	10	0	12	0	0	.075
Burroughs, David W., Idaho Falls*	36	74	16	21	26	2	0	1	11	0	0	11	0	18	0	0	.284
Camacho, Julio, Medicine Hat	16	21	3	4	4	0	0	0	0	0	0	2	0	10	0	0	.190
Canavan, James, Billings*	20	10	0	1	1	0	0	0	1	0	0	1	0	6	0	0	.100
Cardwell, J. David, Great Falls	4	13	4	4	8	2	1	0	7	0	0	1	0	1	0	0	.308
Castillo, Juan, Butte†	59	183	28	53	68	9	3	0	20	3	0	10	3	30	6	7	.290
Castillo, U. Rafael, Idaho Falls	23	34	4	6	9	1	1	0	2	3	0	4	0	16	0	0	.176
Christopher, James, Idaho Falls	35	78	11	14	16	2	0	0	5	3	0	17	1	31	0	2	.179
Cole, W. Audie, Lethbridge	60	227	51	76	114	14	3	6	52	1	6	31	4	23	1	1	.335
Cosby, John, Medicine Hat	33	83	13	18	21	1	0	1	9	7	2	12	5	10	5	1	.217
Crawford, J. David, Helena	31	124	28	38	56	3	3	3	14	0	2	20	0	23	4	4	.306
Daulton, Darren, Helena*	37	100	13	20	27	2	1	1	10	0	2	23	0	29	5	0	.200
Dawes, Stephen, Calgary	67	254	35	73	87	11	0	1	31	2	0	24	0	34	8	0	.287
Debus, Jon, Lethbridge	62	246	49	82	128	16	3	8	58	1	2	31	2	59	3	1	.333
Delancey, Anthony, Billings	39	72	9	16	17	1	0	0	9	0	0	7	1	12	1	0	.222
Dowell, Kenneth, Helena	47	154	17	35	39	1	0	1	24	2	1	26	0	28	5	1	.227
Ender, Scot, Billings	15	15	1	1	1	0	0	0	0	1	2	0	4	0	0	0	.067
Erickson, Donald, Great Falls*	55	171	30	46	68	6	2	4	24	0	1	21	0	52	1	1	.269
Estep, Perry, Billings*	57	173	39	45	57	7	1	1	25	6	5	33	0	33	4	0	.260
Everton, Sean, Medicine Hat	65	223	29	61	80	9	5	0	26	2	7	33	1	27	13	3	.274
Figueroa, Richard, Great Falls	36	121	22	33	50	6	4	1	12	1	0	13	0	23	8	2	.273
Foote, Michael, Billings	67	253	55	77	98	14	2	1	28	1	3	51	1	50	19	3	.304
Francis, Harry, Idaho Falls	63	239	43	64	87	10	5	1	28	2	2	40	1	41	6	3	.268
Frazier, Kenneth, Great Falls	34	94	22	31	43	9	0	1	20	2	4	13	3	12	2	0	.330
Freeney, Delano, Helena*	58	202	27	67	86	16	0	1	29	0	3	32	2	25	1	2	.332
Galarraga, Andres, Calgary	59	190	27	50	81	11	4	4	22	0	0	7	5	55	3	0	.263
Garcia, Paulino, Billings	22	32	3	7	7	0	0	0	1	0	0	0	0	13	0	1	.219
Gauntlett, G. Todd, Lethbridge	9	33	4	7	14	2	1	1	7	0	1	4	0	5	0	0	.212
Gaynor, Richard, Helena	57	211	33	54	83	14	3	3	29	1	1	33	1	71	10	5	.256
Ghelfi, Anthony, Helena	13	0	1	0	0	0	0	0	0	0	0	0	0	0	0	0	.000
Gomez, Marcos, Butte†	44	78	9	15	21	1	1	1	12	2	1	11	1	19	0	2	.192
Gomez, Randall, Great Falls	66	241	63	87	133	14	4	8	53	1	5	40	1	17	2	1	.361
Hancock, Boris, Medicine Hat	58	200	26	42	52	6	0	2	12	2	2	20	0	28	12	1	.210
Harper, Ronald, Medicine Hat	25	49	11	7	9	0	1	0	5	0	0	9	0	16	10	0	.143

Player and Club	G.	AB.	R.	H.	TB.	2B.	3B.	HR.	RBI.	SH.	SF.	BB.	HP.	SO.	SB.	CS.	Pct.
Harris, Garry, Medicine Hat	66	268	38	73	105	10	8	2	28	1	0	27	1	46	14	2	.272
Heimach, William, Great Falls†	65	246	51	76	95	15	2	0	39	4	2	38	2	23	12	5	.309
Henderson, Joseph, Great Falls†	57	193	37	53	75	5	1	5	50	2	5	41	0	54	1	1	.275
Henley, Craig, Idaho Falls†	5	11	1	0	0	0	0	0	1	0	0	3	0	4	0	0	.000
Henry, Mark, Calgary	47	137	17	34	58	6	0	6	24	4	1	12	1	36	0	0	.248
Hoppie, Bryan, Helena	47	165	22	33	36	1	1	0	14	1	1	20	1	44	5	0	.200
Houston, John, Lethbridge	28	81	19	21	30	2	2	1	20	0	0	25	0	17	2	1	.259
Howard, Bernardo, Helena†	38	129	18	38	49	5	0	2	17	0	0	29	0	44	7	5	.295
Hume, Timothy, Billings	30	32	9	4	5	1	0	0	2	1	0	17	0	24	0	0	.125
Huth, Kenneth, Idaho Falls†	48	166	32	35	55	7	2	3	16	5	2	24	1	36	2	2	.211
Hysaw, Willie, Great Falls	14	1	0	0	0	0	0	0	0	0	0	0	0	1	0	0	.000
James, Dion, Butte*	59	224	57	71	87	14	1	0	27	3	2	42	0	11	15	8	.317
Javier, Ramon, Medicine Hat	46	107	10	22	27	3	1	0	6	1	1	7	2	35	2	0	.206
Johnson, James, Great Falls	65	247	58	71	88	10	2	1	26	1	4	42	1	47	34	1	.287
Johnson, Robert, Helena	42	148	25	29	44	3	0	4	20	0	0	17	0	57	3	2	.196
Jones, Harry, Calgary*	57	166	20	50	62	7	1	1	22	0	0	16	3	33	3	2	.301
Jones, Ronnie, Butte†	62	249	56	64	78	3	4	1	23	2	0	27	2	53	15	7	.257
Jordan, J. Steven, Butte	32	94	12	26	31	3	1	0	11	0	2	6	0	8	0	0	.277
Junker, Lance, Great Falls	57	197	41	55	86	8	1	7	45	1	4	26	3	35	12	4	.279
Kinnard, Kenneth, Medicine Hat	60	223	22	41	61	4	2	4	27	0	2	18	0	93	4	0	.184
Kirby, Charles, Butte	44	134	26	30	41	3	4	0	19	2	0	22	0	37	6	2	.224
Kovar, Jerome, Helena	5	18	3	8	14	3	0	1	2	0	0	1	0	3	1	0	.444
Krauss, Timothy, Idaho Falls*	68	241	56	65	80	9	3	0	30	6	7	61	0	20	3	3	.270
Kwiecinski, Michael, Calgary	51	155	18	35	52	6	1	3	18	2	1	12	2	39	3	0	.226
Lachowetz, Anthony, Lethbridge	62	212	62	68	115	15	7	6	52	2	5	47	3	52	36	10	.321
Lauziere, Michael, Calgary*	58	173	23	42	75	15	3	4	23	1	2	20	1	41	3	1	.243
Layton, Thomas, Billings*	18	15	1	1	1	0	0	0	1	4	0	5	1	9	0	0	.067
Leclerc, Raymond, Calgary†	41	90	16	26	32	3	0	1	7	0	0	22	1	13	12	6	.289
Lenti, Michael, Great Falls	22	30	6	8	11	1	1	0	5	0	0	8	0	5	1	1	.267
Leppert, Stephen, Billings†	65	242	50	70	88	10	4	0	36	6	3	48	2	46	18	5	.289
Littmann, Jerome, Great Falls*	38	78	15	20	29	4	1	1	12	1	0	17	2	16	5	0	.256
Lochner, David, Billings*	23	23	4	5	7	2	0	0	2	0	0	4	0	7	0	0	.217
Lyons, William, Butte	36	92	22	29	45	6	5	0	15	2	0	21	1	20	7	1	.315
Mallet, Andre, Helena	39	123	12	33	35	2	0	0	10	2	2	9	0	19	3	8	.268
Marchand, Rene, Calgary	43	139	16	33	44	3	1	2	17	1	2	5	0	32	0	0	.237
Marino, Thomas, Billings	12	34	3	12	19	4	0	1	11	0	0	5	0	7	0	1	.353
Maroney, Kevin, Billings	37	109	32	28	35	4	0	1	8	1	0	16	2	30	4	1	.257
Martin, R. Hollis, Lethbridge	36	130	23	27	31	2	1	0	17	3	0	8	0	26	0	2	.208
McDonald, Mark, Great Falls	18	1	1	0	0	0	0	0	0	0	0	1	0	0	0	0	.000
McGaffey, John, Idaho Falls	61	226	37	63	103	15	2	7	43	3	2	36	3	68	9	3	.279
Metts, Leonard, Billings	22	47	7	12	15	3	0	0	8	0	1	5	0	17	2	0	.255
Mieses, J. Rafael, Medicine Hat	46	118	9	19	24	5	0	0	8	0	1	13	1	42	0	1	.161
Miley, David, Billings*	58	194	33	56	70	8	0	2	38	0	2	35	1	21	10	3	.289
Miller, Gerard, Butte	67	233	55	77	130	18	4	9	67	0	5	52	7	48	9	5	.330
Molina, Hilton, Billings	18	13	3	5	6	1	0	0	3	3	0	2	0	2	0	0	.385
Montero, Danny, Helena	40	143	20	35	52	5	0	4	12	4	0	19	1	42	14	5	.245
Morillo, Rufino, Idaho Falls	34	109	14	36	47	7	2	0	14	2	0	4	0	17	0	3	.330
Morris, Angel, Butte	31	58	7	11	13	2	0	0	1	1	0	3	1	17	0	0	.190
Moscat, Fernando, Medicine Hat†..	38	102	9	17	18	1	0	0	7	3	0	16	0	34	4	3	.167
Murray, Michael, Billings	65	174	34	44	53	9	0	0	25	0	1	32	0	25	9	1	.253
Musick, Craig, Helena	1	3	0	1	1	0	0	0	0	0	0	1	0	0	0	0	.333
Musselwhite, Roman, Helena	29	108	12	21	28	4	0	1	13	1	0	11	1	23	1	0	.194
Musser, Jeffrey, Billings	5	2	0	0	0	0	0	0	0	0	0	0	0	0	0	0	.000
Myles, Rickey, Billings*	11	4	0	0	0	0	0	0	0	0	0	1	0	3	0	0	.000
Nay, Leonard, Calgary*	42	124	26	38	56	6	3	2	15	0	0	27	0	41	16	3	.306
Nocera, Terrence, Idaho Falls	36	82	11	19	27	3	1	1	11	0	1	17	1	32	2	1	.232
Olivas, Joe, Great Falls	12	4	2	0	0	0	0	0	0	0	0	2	0	4	0	0	.000
Ornest, Maury, Butte†	46	146	36	47	74	7	4	4	28	0	0	36	0	41	6	1	.322
Perez, Onesimo, Medicine Hat*....	43	104	4	25	26	1	0	0	7	1	0	6	0	34	1	0	.240
Pettibone, James, Billings	14	17	3	3	3	0	0	0	1	0	0	2	0	5	0	0	.176
Ponce, Carlos, Butte	69	259	48	90	143	18	7	7	55	2	3	19	2	44	3	3	.347
Powell, Henry, Helena	46	149	21	37	58	6	0	5	27	0	1	21	0	33	2	2	.248
Priessman, Kevin, Calgary	18	5	1	1	1	0	0	0	0	0	0	2	0	2	0	0	.200
Quinones, Rene, Calgary†	13	42	3	11	13	2	0	0	3	0	0	3	0	5	0	0	.262
Ragan, Terry, Butte*	19	37	8	8	8	0	0	0	5	0	1	6	0	13	3	0	.216
Raimondo, Pasquale, Lethbridge	38	162	47	52	68	5	4	1	16	1	0	21	3	18	12	2	.321
Raines, Michael, Billings	23	5	1	1	1	0	0	0	2	1	0	0	0	2	0	0	.200
Ramos, Carlos, Billings	16	15	1	3	5	2	0	0	2	0	0	0	0	10	0	0	.200
Rasmussen, Eric, Idaho Falls	30	105	15	25	45	5	0	5	22	1	0	14	5	19	0	0	.238
Ready, Randy, Butte	61	226	65	85	140	23	4	8	50	0	4	57	1	32	2	2	.376
Reid, Jessie, Great Falls*	59	227	57	83	125	15	6	5	48	0	2	38	2	24	14	4	.366
Reyes, Gilberto, Lethbridge	6	11	0	2	2	0	0	0	1	0	0	2	0	5	0	0	.182
Richmond, Kirk, Medicine Hat	34	72	7	8	9	1	0	0	2	0	0	21	0	32	1	0	.111
Ridling, Ronald, Helena	33	104	14	22	32	4	0	2	9	0	3	10	0	28	1	1	.212
Rivera, Hector, Calgary	46	144	14	45	63	7	1	3	21	0	1	11	0	31	0	0	.313
Robinson, Thomas, Lethbridge*	41	161	38	51	60	7	1	0	17	4	1	26	1	13	10	3	.317

Player and Club	G.	AB.	R.	H.	TB.	2B.	3B.	HR.	RBI.	SH.	SF.	BB.	HP.	SO.	SB.	CS.	Pct.
Rogers, Dane, Calgary*	47	145	18	34	53	4	3	3	20	0	0	13	0	34	10	3	.234
Rosenlund, William, Medicine Hat.	13	1	1	0	0	0	0	0	0	0	0	0	0	0	0	0	.000
Ryan, Duffy, Idaho Falls	36	124	23	37	52	5	2	2	22	2	1	24	1	15	4	0	.298
Ryan, Pedro, Medicine Hat	41	118	9	24	29	5	0	0	5	0	0	5	3	17	2	0	.203
Salava, Randy, Helena*	65	242	43	72	90	7	1	3	31	0	1	41	2	63	4	4	.298
Salazar, Angel, Calgary	51	169	29	41	43	2	0	0	11	3	0	12	0	14	19	3	.243
Salgueiro, Miguel, Billings	14	10	2	1	2	1	0	0	5	0	1	3	0	4	0	1	.100
Santiago, Edgar, Idaho Falls	32	82	12	19	20	1	0	0	2	1	0	5	1	16	0	0	.232
Schroeder, Jay, Medicine Hat	52	171	27	40	56	6	2	2	21	0	1	45	4	60	8	1	.234
See, R. Laurence, Lethbridge	68	252	41	87	122	19	2	4	44	1	0	38	2	29	3	2	.345
Smith, Charles, Billings	37	74	14	19	21	2	0	0	8	1	0	10	1	29	3	1	.257
Smith, Gregory, Lethbridge*	69	272	63	99	139	18	2	6	58	0	4	26	5	39	10	5	.364
Smith, Kelly, Great Falls	3	11	4	3	3	0	0	0	1	1	0	3	0	4	3	0	.273
Springs, David, Calgary	58	186	27	45	57	7	1	1	6	3	0	20	1	40	20	7	.242
Sproesser, Mark, Idaho Falls	28	105	18	33	43	3	2	1	12	2	1	17	1	12	5	3	.314
Steele, Walter, Butte	33	90	20	25	44	6	2	3	21	1	0	26	2	22	5	1	.278
Strawberry, Michael, Lethbridge	32	73	12	21	22	1	0	0	12	1	0	9	0	28	5	0	.288
Talbert, George, Butte	45	126	17	26	38	6	0	2	18	1	0	21	2	51	1	2	.206
Tartabull, Daniel, Billings	59	157	33	47	63	10	0	2	27	0	0	37	1	24	7	1	.299
Terry, Glenn, Lethbridge*	13	0	1	0	0	0	0	0	0	0	0	0	0	0	0	0	.000
Terry, Scott, Billings	67	251	39	65	92	9	3	4	45	2	2	27	3	75	7	0	.259
Thomas, W. Richard, Lethbridge.	52	181	41	48	62	6	4	0	29	0	0	36	1	35	11	4	.265
Threatt, Anthony, Billings	20	13	5	3	3	0	0	0	0	0	0	0	0	5	1	0	.231
Tillman, Kenneth, Idaho Falls	54	181	23	46	63	9	4	0	29	5	1	16	3	38	7	7	.254
Trimble, David, Medicine Hat	63	224	22	51	72	7	1	4	28	0	1	39	2	67	14	1	.228
Vaiana, James, 17 Cal-46 MH	63	198	20	41	49	8	0	0	11	2	1	24	1	45	3	1	.207
Valdes, Dennis, Idaho Falls	26	77	12	17	20	3	0	0	6	1	0	14	0	18	1	1	.221
Walker, Broderick, Billings	50	99	23	28	28	0	0	0	13	6	0	15	0	19	8	1	.283
Wallace, Michael, Great Falls	35	110	16	24	33	3	3	0	11	2	2	14	0	25	1	1	.218
Webber, Phillip, Lethbridge	13	41	4	9	10	1	0	0	3	0	0	1	1	14	1	2	.220
Wesley, Thomas, Billings	71	279	38	75	108	16	1	5	60	1	5	16	3	91	5	2	.269
Whelan, Jeffrey, Calgary	58	188	28	59	69	10	0	0	21	1	1	19	2	19	17	2	.314
Wilson, David, Great Falls	62	186	28	45	51	3	0	1	16	5	3	16	1	49	3	0	.242
Wood, Johnson, Butte*	44	80	11	28	38	4	0	2	16	2	2	8	0	25	1	1	.350
Wright, Paul, Idaho Falls	40	129	15	33	40	3	2	0	19	2	1	7	1	38	3	2	.256
Yraguen, Richard, Helena	50	193	24	46	55	4	1	1	15	2	1	13	3	43	11	4	.238
Ysambert, Sergio, Helena	8	30	2	7	9	2	0	0	4	0	0	4	1	9	2	1	.233

The following pitchers had no plate appearances, primarily through the use of designated hitters, listed alphabetically by club, games in parentheses:

BUTTE—Cavner, Elmer (25); Cicotte, Gregory (21); Coleman, Ty (17); Effrig, R. Mark (8); Elliott, Robert (14); Gallo, Raymond (9); Haggerty, James* (3); Herberholz, Craig (10); Jensen, David (16); Kollmann, Ronald* (15); Lepson, Mark (14); Matias, Luis (14); Meyer, Randy (2); Morris, David (12); Orlich, M. Scott (10); Pallas, P. Theodore (1); Parrott, Stephen (12); Pone, Vincent (17).

CALGARY—Baederick, Robert* (13); Boger, Larry (5); Emery, Joseph (8); Finch, Guy* (17); Gray, Chester (8); Huber, Randolph (17); Powers, Michael* (6); Rehmert, Rodney L.* (6); Roeder, Steven H. (1); Roy, Jacques G.* (13); St. Claire, Randy A.* (21); St. John, William* (9); Stubberfield, Ian (15); Valliant, Robert† (1); Vega, Randolph (12).

GREAT FALLS—Banach, Joseph* (9); Bashian, Denis† (7); Bautista, Ramon (8); Buckmier, James (9); Dempsey, Mark (15); Fowlkes, Alan (4); Gallo, Bernard* (21); McDonald, David (10); McLaughlin, Thomas (14); Trax, Jeffrey (15).

HELENA—Befort, Michael (15); Chaney, Anthony (12); Childress, Rodney (15); Cook, Dale (20); Decker, D. Martin (25); Griffin, Frankie* (15); Hutchinson, E. DeWayne (9); Knight, Larry (11); McAnally, John* (12); Money, Gregory (15); Rodriguez, Yonis (13); Stevenson, Timothy (1); True, Steven* (13).

IDAHO FALLS—Bankowski, Kris* (11); Bastian, Robert (13); Culbert, Michael† (21); Hammond, Gregory (12); McMahon, John (13); Pangborn, Mark (17); Ray, Christopher (8); Robins, Gary (9); Roen, Thomas* (14); Saatzer, Michael* (12); Schneider, Thomas* (24); Skaggs, Jackie (3); Steinbach, Drew* (9); Sylvia, Ronald (7).

LETHBRIDGE—DeLeon, Orlando (15); Dente, Frank (17); Felt, Richard (4); Jones, Charles (14); Kenyon, Robert (4); Klawitter, Thomas (13); Lesch, David (5); Lloyd, Richard (10); Marsden, Stephen (15); McQuade, Francis† (14); Montalvo, Rafael (14); Reade, Curtis (19); Wise, Brett (14).

MEDICINE HAT—Aponte, Juan (4); Campbell, David (16); Frank, Gray* (23); Goffena, W. David (10); Hawkins, Stanley* (23); Nawrocki, Matthew (19); Patterson, Richard (8); Pierce, Donald* (27); Rahmer, Daniel F.† (18); Rooks, Steven* (16); Seiber, John (13); Shipanoff, David (8); Smith, Steve (15); Tackitt, Robert (13).

GRAND-SLAM HOME RUNS—Estep, Gaynor, Henderson, Junker, Kinnard, Miley, Miller, Ornest, 1 each.

AWARDED FIRST BASE ON INTERFERENCE—See 3 (Bagiotti, Frazier, Jordan); Harris 2 (Frazier, Morris); Huth (Morris); Murray (Vaiana); Spriggs (Frazier); Whelan (Talbert).

GAME-WINNING RBIs

BILLINGS (34)—Terry 7, Miley 6, Wesley 5, Estep 4, Foote 3, Leppert 2, Tartabull 2, Delancey 1, Ender 1, Marino 1, Metts 1, Walker 1.

BUTTE (24)—James 4, Miller 4, Ornest 3, Ponce 3, Alonzo 2, Talbert 2, Castillo 1, Gomez 1, Jordan 1, Kirby 1, Ready 1, Steele 1.

CALGARY (20)—Jones 3, Galarraga 3, Dawes 2, Kwiecinski 2, Marchand 2, Brodeur 1, Herny 1, Lauziere 1, Leclerc 1, Quinones 1, Rivera 1, Rogers 1, Salazar 1.

GREAT FALLS (36)—Gomez 7, Henderson 5, Reid 5, Adams 3, Albright 3, Erickson 3, Heimach 3, Johnson 2, Junker 2, Cardwell 1, Frazier 1, Wilson 1.

HELENA (23)—Freeney 3, Musselwhite 3, Powell 3, Dowell 2, Gaynor 2, Mallet 2, Ridling 2, Hoppie 1, Howard 1, Johnson 1, Montero 1, Salava 1, Yraguen 1.

IDAHO FALLS (25)—McGaffey 8, Wright 3, Bagiotti 2, Burroughs 2, Huth 2, Krauss 2, Morillo 2, Ryan 2, Brock 1, Francis 1.

LETHBRIDGE (46)—Debus 8, Smith 8, Lachowetz 6, Cole 4, Houston 4, Thomas 4, Bailey 2, Gauntlett 2, Raimondo 2, See 2, Allen 1, Bard 1, Martin 1, Robinson 1.

MEDICINE HAT (11)—Trimble 3, Kinnard 2, Vaiana 2, Cosby 1, Everton 1, Harper 1, Schroeder 1.

CLUB FIELDING

Club	G.	PO.	A.	E.	DP.	PB.	Pct.	Club	G.	PO.	A.	E.	DP.	PB.	Pct.
Billings	71	1822	746	138	58	27	.949	Helena	70	1818	767	159	64	39	.942
Idaho Falls	70	1835	768	147	77	24	.947	Great Falls	70	1841	708	157	61	27	.942
Lethbridge	70	1809	737	149	60	31	.945	Butte	70	1764	719	187	41	45	.930
Calgary	69	1769	733	151	47	23	.943	Medicine Hat	70	1763	736	209	50	35	.923

Triple Play—Idaho Falls.

INDIVIDUAL FIELDING

*Throws lefthanded.

FIRST BASEMEN

Player and Club	G.	PO.	A.	E.	DP.	Pct.	Player and Club	G.	PO.	A.	E.	DP.	Pct.
Brodeur, Calgary*	19	125	3	1	9	.992	Ponce, Butte	43	348	21	12	18	.969
Marchand, Calgary	23	179	10	2	11	.990	Nocera, Idaho Falls*	10	61	2	2	7	.969
Reid, Great Falls*	11	74	6	1	8	.988	Richmond, Medicine Hat	23	134	12	5	12	.967
Brock, Idaho Falls	46	372	18	5	46	.987	R. Johnson, Helena	15	111	6	4	13	.967
G. SMITH, Lethbridge	68	552	48	8	46	.987	Galarraga, Calgary	33	212	13	9	14	.962
Alonzo, Butte*	15	131	1	2	12	.985	Everton, Medicine Hat	45	318	16	17	21	.952
Wesley, Billings	71	557	35	15	47	.975	Lauziere, Calgary	13	81	4	5	7	.944
J. Johnson, Great Falls	59	470	30	14	46	.973	Talbert, Butte	12	86	0	6	3	.935
Burroughs, Idaho Falls*	15	101	6	3	9	.973	Mieses, Medicine Hat	12	81	6	7	11	.926
Freeney, Helena*	46	392	27	12	36	.972							

(Fewer Than Ten Games)

Player and Club	G.	PO.	A.	E.	DP.	Pct.	Player and Club	G.	PO.	A.	E.	DP.	Pct.
Ridling, Helena	6	47	0	0	3	1.000	James, Butte*	2	5	0	0	1	1.000
Wallace, Great Falls	7	44	0	0	6	1.000	Salazar, Calgary	2	3	0	0	0	1.000
Henley, Idaho Falls	24	24	2	0	2	1.000	Lochner, Billings*	2	2	0	0	1	1.000
Cole, Lethbridge	4	22	1	0	1	1.000	Musselwhite, Helena	7	57	2	1	5	.983
Wood, Butte	3	12	1	0	0	1.000	Rasmussen, Idaho Falls	5	34	3	2	3	.949
Murray, Billings	5	12	0	0	3	1.000	Ornest, Butte	2	10	1	1	1	.917
Kwiecinski, Calgary	2	8	0	0	1	1.000	Reyes, Lethbridge	4	16	0	2	3	.889
Miley, Billings	2	7	0	0	1	1.000							

SECOND BASEMEN

Player and Club	G.	PO.	A.	E.	DP.	Pct.	Player and Club	G.	PO.	A.	E.	DP.	Pct.
Quinones, Calgary	12	35	26	1	6	.984	Leclerc, Calgary	25	36	44	4	5	.952
Albright, Great Falls	11	24	23	1	10	.979	Hoppie, Helena	35	82	91	9	14	.951
Crawford, Helena	27	73	75	5	19	.967	Robinson, Lethbridge	33	99	82	10	16	.948
Yraguen, Helena	12	24	30	2	6	.964	Moscat, Medicine Hat	36	86	88	11	19	.941
HEIMACH, Great Falls	63	123	147	11	39	.961	Hancock, Medicine Hat	43	108	111	19	16	.920
Ready, Butte	21	35	58	4	7	.959	J. Castillo, Butte	55	87	99	18	16	.912
Raimondo, Lethbridge	37	74	102	8	24	.957	Dawes, Calgary	22	28	44	7	4	.911
Krauss, Idaho Falls	68	156	206	17	47	.955	Hume, Billings	19	12	21	4	1	.892
Lappert, Billings	62	134	136	13	29	.954	Whelan, Calgary	19	31	22	8	4	.869

Triple Play—Krauss.

(Fewer Than Ten Games)

Player and Club	G.	PO.	A.	E.	DP.	Pct.	Player and Club	G.	PO.	A.	E.	DP.	Pct.
Wood, Butte	2	1	0	0	0	1.000	Amoros, Medicine Hat	2	6	4	1	2	.909
Kwiecinski, Calgary	1	1	0	0	0	1.000	Salazar, Calgary	8	19	23	5	8	.894
Sproesser, Idaho Falls	4	8	8	1	3	.941	Littmann, Great Falls	3	3	2	1	0	.833
Foote, Billings	4	4	11	1	0	.938	Lenti, Great Falls	1	3	3	1	1	.857
Kirby, Butte	8	11	20	3	2	.912	Tartabull, Billings	1	1	2	1	0	.750

THIRD BASEMEN

Player and Club	G.	PO.	A.	E.	DP.	Pct.	Player and Club	G.	PO.	A.	E.	DP.	Pct.
Santiago, Idaho Falls	12	10	16	2	4	.929	Sproesser, Idaho Falls	22	23	38	7	5	.897
Marchand, Calgary	10	5	7	1	0	.923	Tartabull, Billings	34	15	52	8	4	.893
Kwiecinski, Calgary	40	24	83	11	3	.907	SEE, Lethbridge	68	55	119	22	10	.888
Murray, Billings	59	39	97	15	7	.901	Dawes, Calgary	14	7	22	4	1	.879

THIRD BASEMEN—Continued

Player and Club	G.	PO.	A.	E.	DP.	Pct.	Player and Club	G.	PO.	A.	E.	DP.	Pct.
Henderson, Great Falls ..	54	43	110	23	10	.869	Ornest, Butte	36	16	60	14	3	.844
Everton, Medicine Hat ...	21	9	30	6	3	.867	Ready, Butte	20	8	13	4	1	.840
Francis, Idaho Falls	23	17	34	8	5	.864	Galarraga, Calgary	18	10	31	9	1	.820
Trimble, Medicine Hat ..	45	39	75	19	5	.857	Howard, Helena	38	33	69	24	8	.810
Yraguen, Helena	29	28	70	17	4	.852	Kirby, Butte	18	9	29	10	1	.792
Christopher, Idaho Falls	20	7	27	6	3	.850	Wallace, Great Falls	16	10	29	14	2	.736

(Fewer Than Ten Games)

Player and Club	G.	PO.	A.	E.	DP.	Pct.	Player and Club	G.	PO.	A.	E.	DP.	Pct.
Albright, Great Falls	2	1	3	0	0	1.000	Wilson, Great Falls	2	3	2	1	0	.833
R. Castillo, Idaho Falls ..	3	0	4	0	0	1.000	Huth, Idaho Falls	3	2	1	1	0	.750
Leppert, Billings	1	2	1	0	0	1.000	Lyons, Butte	1	1	2	1	0	.750
Allen, Lethbridge	2	0	2	0	0	1.000	Steele, Butte	6	2	6	4	0	.667
Wood, Butte	2	0	1	0	0	1.000	Bagiotti, Idaho Falls	3	0	4	2	0	.667
Montero, Helena	6	3	5	1	1	.889	Martin, Lethbridge	2	0	2	1	1	.667
Hancock, Medicine Hat..	9	1	21	3	3	.880	Hume, Billings	1	0	1	1	0	.500
Littmann, Great Falls	3	3	2	1	0	.833	Leclerc, Calgary	5	1	4	6	0	.455

Triple Play—Huth.

SHORTSTOPS

Player and Club	G.	PO.	A.	E.	DP.	Pct.	Player and Club	G.	PO.	A.	E.	DP.	Pct.
Lyons, Butte	31	37	97	8	11	.944	Martin, Lethbridge	33	43	88	15	16	.897
Dawes, Billings	39	51	131	11	24	.943	Garcia, Billings	14	5	12	2	2	.895
Yraguen, Helena	12	19	30	3	5	.942	Wilson, Great Falls	60	67	152	27	32	.890
FOOTE, Billings	65	101	204	20	32	.938	Kirby, Butte	14	29	37	9	3	.880
Dowell, Helena	47	74	163	17	32	.933	Allen, Lethbridge	42	61	120	27	17	.870
Salazar, Calgary	32	37	103	12	12	.921	Santiago, Idaho Falls	20	18	47	10	9	.867
Francis, Idaho Falls	42	58	118	16	27	.917	Harris, Medicine Hat	60	102	153	54	25	.825
Ready, Butte	32	46	103	14	8	.914	Amoros, Medicine Hat	14	10	29	9	4	.813
R. Castillo, Idaho Falls ..	20	12	38	5	2	.909	Hoppie, Helena	12	14	35	15	8	.766
Littmann, Great Falls	19	23	30	6	5	.898							

(Fewer Than Ten Games)

Player and Club	G.	PO.	A.	E.	DP.	Pct.	Player and Club	G.	PO.	A.	E.	DP.	Pct.
Cardwell, Great Falls	3	3	8	0	2	1.000	Leclerc, Calgary	6	4	9	1	0	.929
Lauziere, Calgary	1	1	5	0	1	1.000	Albright, Great Falls	7	7	9	2	1	.889
Musick, Helena	1	2	3	0	1	1.000	Hancock, Medicine Hat..	4	2	8	2	2	.833
Quinones, Calgary	2	1	3	0	0	1.000	Hume, Billings	7	5	11	4	1	.800
Sproesser, Idaho Falls	4	5	14	1	4	.950	Kwiecinski, Calgary	2	1	3	1	0	.800

OUTFIELDERS

Player and Club	G.	PO.	A.	E.	DP.	Pct.	Player and Club	G.	PO.	A.	E.	DP.	Pct.
Ponce, Butte	13	12	3	0	1	1.000	Thomas, Lethbridge	48	69	6	5	1	.938
Trimble, Medicine Hat ..	13	12	3	0	0	1.000	Montero, Helena	32	42	3	3	1	.938
JUNKER, Great Falls	56	92	4	1	0	.990	Lachowetz, Lethbridge..	61	88	10	8	1	.925
Maroney, Billings	35	56	3	1	0	.983	P. Ryan, Medicine Hat ...	34	44	3	4	0	.922
Javier, Medicine Hat	43	52	5	1	0	.983	Miller, Butte	66	109	6	10	0	.920
Walker, Billings	42	43	3	1	1	.979	James, Butte●	57	75	4	7	0	.919
Cole, Lethbridge	31	40	3	1	0	.977	C. Smith, Billings	27	22	0	2	0	.917
Gaynor, Helena	55	101	9	4	1	.965	Figueroa, Great Falls	33	46	8	5	1	.915
S. Terry, Billings	66	104	10	5	1	.958	Valdes, Idaho Falls	21	26	3	3	0	.906
M. Gomez, Butte	23	22	1	1	0	.958	Christopher, Idaho Falls	13	14	5	2	2	.905
Tillman, Idaho Falls	53	83	5	4	0	.957	Strawberry, Lethbridge .	30	32	5	4	2	.902
Mallet, Helena	36	42	2	2	1	.957	Debus, Lethbridge	62	77	5	9	0	.901
Rogers, Calgary	32	42	1	2	0	.956	Perez, Medicine Hat	22	25	1	3	0	.897
Reid, Great Falls●	49	63	1	3	0	.955	M. Adams, Great Falls	26	26	0	3	0	.897
Kinnard, Medicine Hat ..	60	98	2	5	1	.952	Albright, Great Falls	34	31	3	4	0	.895
Schroeder, Medicine Hat	52	93	6	5	1	.952	Huth, Idaho Falls	46	58	8	8	2	.892
Lauziere, Calgary	44	78	1	4	0	.952	Wright, Idaho Falls	33	38	2	5	1	.889
Henry, Calgary	35	37	2	2	0	.951	Delancey, Billings	22	8	0	1	0	.889
Erickson, Great Falls● ..	28	36	2	2	0	.950	Whelan, Calgary	45	40	5	6	1	.882
Salava, Helena	65	126	8	8	2	.944	Ragan, Butte	11	15	0	2	0	.882
R. Jones, Butte	60	106	7	7	0	.942	McCaffey, Idaho Falls	52	79	2	12	0	.870
Estep, Billings	56	93	5	6	1	.942	Ridling, Helena	24	24	2	4	0	.867
Nay, Calgary	36	47	1	3	0	.941	Tartabull, Billings	22	18	0	5	0	.783
Spriggs, Calgary●	54	87	5	6	1	.939	Camacho, Medicine Hat .	12	4	0	2	0	.667

(Fewer Than Ten Games)

Player and Club	G.	PO.	A.	E.	DP.	Pct.	Player and Club	G.	PO.	A.	E.	DP.	Pct.
Harper, Medicine Hat	8	13	0	0	0	1.000	Littmann, Great Falls	6	9	0	0	0	1.000
J. Johnson, Great Falls ..	5	13	0	0	0	1.000	Ysambert, Helena	8	8	1	0	1	1.000
K. Smith, Great Falls	3	10	1	0	0	1.000	Rivera, Calgary	9	5	0	0	0	1.000

OUTFIELDERS—Continued
(Fewer Than Ten Games)

Player and Club	G.	PO.	A.	E.	DP.	Pct.
Wallace, Great Falls	9	3	0	0	0	1.000
Webber, Lethbridge	2	3	0	0	0	1.000
Nocera, Idaho Falls	4	2	0	0	0	1.000
Barbee, Billings	3	2	0	0	0	1.000
Galarraga, Calgary	3	2	0	0	0	1.000
Priessman, Calgary	1	2	0	0	0	1.000
Mieses, Medicine Hat	2	1	0	0	0	1.000
Henderson, Great Falls	1	1	0	0	0	1.000
Murray, Billings	1	1	0	0	0	1.000
Morillo, Idaho Falls	9	11	0	1	0	.917
Marchand, Calgary	6	5	0	1	0	.833
R. Gomez, Great Falls	6	6	0	3	0	.667
Frazier, Great Falls	2	1	0	1	0	.500

CATCHERS

Player and Club	G.	PO.	A.	E.	DP.	PB.	Pct.
Metts, Billings	19	102	11	1	2	11	.991
MILEY, Billings	55	361	39	4	8	9	.990
Bagiotti, Idaho Falls	31	245	17	3	1	13	.989
Rivera, Calgary	28	154	9	2	0	8	.988
R. Gomez, Great Falls	63	447	42	8	2	19	.984
Daulton, Helena	37	224	17	4	0	13	.984
Cosby, Medicine Hat	33	217	23	4	3	14	.984
D. Ryan, Idaho Falls	27	208	25	4	6	6	.983
Steele, Butte	24	175	19	4	2	12	.980
Vaiana, Calgary-MH	59	366	39	12	3	19	.971
Bard, Lethbridge	22	180	24	6	2	11	.971
Rasmussen, Ida. Falls	14	93	9	3	1	3	.971
Bailey, Lethbridge	40	297	27	10	4	15	.970
H. Jones, Calgary	31	148	12	5	1	4	.970
Talbert, Butte	10	50	0	2	1	9	.962
Galarraga, Calgary	15	63	8	3	0	5	.959
Powell, Helena	41	241	30	12	3	24	.958
Jordan, Butte	32	181	26	9	2	7	.958
Ramos, Billings	14	45	1	3	0	7	.939
Frazier, Great Falls	11	74	12	8	1	5	.915
Morris, Butte	30	110	10	13	1	17	.902

(Fewer Than Ten Games)

Player and Club	G.	PO.	A.	E.	DP.	PB.	Pct.
Gauntlett, Lethbridge	9	66	5	0	0	5	1.000
Henderson, G. Falls	1	4	0	0	0	0	1.000
Houston, Lethbridge	1	4	0	0	0	0	1.000
Musselwhite, Helena	2	3	0	0	0	0	1.000
Salazar, Calgary	1	1	0	0	0	0	1.000
McGaffey, Ida. Falls	5	38	1	1	0	2	.975
M. Adams, G. Falls	6	47	4	2	0	2	.962
Kovar, Helena	2	23	2	1	0	1	.962
J. Adams, Billings	2	20	2	1	0	0	.957
Marino, Billings	5	29	1	2	0	0	.938
Henry, Calgary	5	28	3	3	0	4	.912
Richmond, Med. Hat	3	7	0	1	0	4	.875

PITCHERS

Player and Club	G.	PO.	A.	E.	DP.	Pct.
C. JONES, Lethbridge	14	6	11	0	1	1.000
Stubberfield, Calgary	15	5	10	0	0	1.000
Schneider, Idaho Falls	24	4	9	0	1	1.000
Childress, Helena	15	3	9	0	0	1.000
McLaughlin, G Falls	13	4	7	0	0	1.000
True, Helena*	13	2	9	0	0	1.000
Priessman, Calgary	16	4	6	0	0	1.000
Kollmann, Butte	15	3	7	0	1	1.000
Orlich, Butte	10	3	7	0	1	1.000
Burroughs, I Falls*	10	3	5	0	0	1.000
Rosenlund, Med Hat	13	2	5	0	1	1.000
Cook, Helena	20	3	3	0	0	1.000
Matias, Butte	14	2	4	0	0	1.000
B. Gallo, G Falls*	21	1	5	0	0	1.000
Reade, Lethbridge	19	0	5	0	0	1.000
M. McDonald, GF	18	2	2	0	0	1.000
Jensen, Butte	16	2	2	0	2	1.000
Steverson, Helena	12	1	3	0	0	1.000
Chaney, Helena	12	0	4	0	0	1.000
Montalvo, Leth.	14	0	4	0	0	1.000
G. Terry, Leth*	12	0	4	0	0	1.000
Decker, Helena	25	1	2	0	0	1.000
Hammond, I Falls	12	0	3	0	0	1.000
Goffena, Med Hat	10	0	2	0	0	1.000
Myles, Billings*	10	0	2	0	0	1.000
Barba, Billings	15	0	1	0	0	1.000
Roen, Idaho Falls*	14	6	14	1	0	.952
Tackitt, Med Hat	13	2	16	1	0	.947
Dempsey, Great Falls	15	9	8	1	1	.944
Ghelfi, Helena	12	3	14	1	0	.944
St. Claire, Calgary	21	4	12	1	2	.941
Griffin, Helena*	14	3	13	1	2	.941
Klawitter, Leth*	13	3	13	1	1	.941
Hawkins, Med Hat*	23	3	11	1	0	.933
Trax, Great Falls	15	3	11	1	3	.933
Ender, Billings	15	1	13	1	0	.933
Cicotte, Butte	21	6	7	1	1	.929
McQuade, Leth	14	3	10	1	0	.929
Morris, Butte	12	1	12	1	0	.929
Huber, Calgary	17	6	6	1	0	.923
Saatzer, Idaho Falls	12	4	8	1	1	.923
Pierce, Med Hat*	27	1	11	1	0	.923
Money, Helena	12	2	8	1	0	.909
Lloyd, Lethbridge	10	2	8	1	0	.909
Herberholz, Butte	10	4	5	1	2	.900
Molina, Billings	18	3	6	1	0	.900
Wise, Lethbridge	14	1	8	1	1	.900
Baldrick, Calgary*	13	0	9	1	1	.900
McMahon, I Falls	13	2	14	2	2	.889
Rahmer, Med Hat*	18	1	7	1	0	.889
Bowden, Billings*	13	3	20	3	2	.885
Elliott, Butte	13	4	10	2	1	.875
S. Smith, Med Hat	15	3	11	2	3	.875
Parrott, Butte	12	2	11	2	2	.867
Bankowski, I Falls*	11	2	4	1	0	.857
Brodeur, Calgary*	16	1	5	1	0	.857
Layton, Billings	18	4	7	2	1	.846
Lochner, Billings*	11	2	9	2	0	.846
Raines, Billings	23	1	10	2	0	.846
Roy, Calgary	13	2	14	3	2	.842
Marsden, Leth	15	7	13	4	1	.833
Rodriguez, Helena	13	4	6	2	0	.833
DeLeon, Lethbridge	15	2	3	1	1	.833
Bastian, Idaho Falls	13	3	11	3	0	.824
Cavner, Calgary*	25	2	7	2	1	.818
Seiber, Med Hat	13	6	10	4	0	.800
Nawrocki, Med Hat	19	5	11	4	2	.800
Olivas, Great Falls	11	0	4	1	0	.800
Dente, Lethbridge	17	3	4	2	0	.778
Rooks, Med Hat*	16	2	5	2	1	.778
McAnally, Helena*	12	1	6	2	1	.778
Canavan, Billings*	20	0	7	2	0	.778
Salgueiro, Billings	14	5	5	3	1	.769
Hysaw, Great Falls	14	4	9	4	2	.765
Vega, Calgary	12	3	10	4	0	.765
Campbell, Med Hat	16	1	8	3	0	.750
Befort, Helena	15	2	4	2	0	.750
Finch, Calgary*	17	0	3	1	0	.750

PITCHERS—Continued

Player and Club	G.	PO.	A.	E.	DP.	Pct.	Player and Club	G.	PO.	A.	E.	DP.	Pct.
Frank, Med Hat	23	4	4	3	0	.727	Threatt, Billings	18	2	4	3	0	.667
Pone, Butte	17	2	6	3	0	.727	Pangborn, I Falls	17	2	4	3	1	.667
Knight, Helena	11	0	5	2	0	.714	D. McDonald, GF*	10	0	3	2	0	.600
Coleman, Butte*	17	2	7	4	0	.692	Pettibone, Billings	14	1	3	3	0	.571

(Fewer Than Ten Games)

Player and Club	G.	PO.	A.	E.	DP.	Pct.	Player and Club	G.	PO.	A.	E.	DP.	Pct.
Robins, Idaho Falls	9	0	13	0	0	1.000	Hutchinson, Helena	9	0	1	0	0	1.000
Ray, Idaho Falls	8	2	4	0	0	1.000	Powers, Calgary	6	0	1	0	0	1.000
Felt, Lethbridge*	4	3	2	0	0	1.000	Musser, Billings	5	0	1	0	0	1.000
Gray, Calgary*	8	2	3	0	0	1.000	Culbert, Idaho Falls	2	0	1	0	1	1.000
Rehmert, Calgary*	6	2	3	0	0	1.000	Roeder, Calgary	1	0	1	0	0	1.000
St. John, Calgary*	9	1	4	0	0	1.000	Banach, G Falls*	9	1	7	1	0	.889
Steinbach, I Falls*	9	0	5	0	0	1.000	Sylvia, Idaho Falls	7	4	9	2	0	.867
R. Gallo, Butte*	9	1	2	0	0	1.000	Patterson, Med Hat	8	1	4	1	0	.833
Bashian, G Falls*	9	1	2	0	0	1.000	Buckmier, G Falls	9	5	8	3	0	.813
Emery, Calgary	8	1	2	0	0	1.000	Kenyon, Lethbridge	4	1	2	1	0	.750
Shipanoff, Med Hat	8	1	2	0	0	1.000	Erickson, G Falls*	7	0	2	1	0	.667
Boger, Calgary	5	1	2	0	0	1.000	Meyer, Butte	2	0	2	1	0	.667
Fowlkes, G Falls	4	0	3	0	0	1.000	Effrig, Butte	8	1	3	3	0	.571
Skaggs, Idaho Falls	3	1	1	0	0	1.000	Lesch, Lethbridge	5	0	1	1	0	.500
Bautista, G Falls	8	0	2	0	0	1.000	Lepson, Butte	4	0	0	2	0	.000
Haggerty, Butte*	3	0	2	0	0	1.000							

The following players do not have any recorded accepted chances at the positions indicated; therefore, are not listed in the fielding averages for those particular positions: Aponte, p; Garcia, of; Henley, of; J. Johnson, 2b; Leclerc, of; Lenti, of; Leppert, ss-of; Marino, 1b; Nay, p; Olivas, of; Pallas, p; Ramos, 3b; Threatt, of; Valliant, p.

CLUB PITCHING

Club	G.	CG.	ShO.	Sv.	IP.	H.	R.	ER.	HR.	BB.	Int. BB.	HB.	SO.	WP.	Bk.	ERA.
Lethbridge	70	14	4	16	603	613	315	223	20	288	3	28	537	39	3	3.33
Great Falls	70	21	6	12	614	591	354	240	13	326	7	16	554	46	7	3.52
Billings	71	7	6	17	607	589	344	279	21	324	13	24	543	52	9	4.14
Helena	70	4	4	16	606	643	413	292	33	338	3	18	470	57	5	4.34
Idaho Falls	70	18	4	11	612	686	440	325	26	350	13	24	558	61	8	4.78
Calgary	69	3	3	13	590	654	422	326	45	314	4	9	465	42	10	4.97
Medicine Hat	70	4	1	7	588	721	510	349	45	368	19	20	460	51	2	5.34
Butte	70	2	2	11	588	685	507	370	27	414	18	23	507	108	9	5.66

PITCHERS' RECORDS
(Leading Qualifiers for Earned-Run Average Leadership—56 or More Innings)

*Throws lefthanded.

Pitcher–Club	G.	GS.	CG.	ShO.	W.	L.	Sv.	Pct.	IP.	H.	R.	ER.	HR.	BB.	Int. BB.	HB.	SO.	WP.	ERA.
Dempsey, Great Falls	15	14	9	2	14	1	0	.933	114	96	33	20	2	27	0	1	109	1	1.58
C. Jones, Lethbridge	14	13	6	3	8	2	1	.800	96	72	26	20	4	33	0	1	115	3	1.88
Ender, Billings	15	9	0	0	6	1	0	.857	75	71	26	20	1	31	2	2	60	4	2.40
Marsden, Lethbridge	15	10	4	0	7	0	1	1.000	82	82	33	22	0	16	1	0	81	6	2.41
Childress, Helena	15	8	0	0	3	4	0	.429	68	79	32	19	1	20	0	0	43	7	2.51
Bastian, Idaho Falls	13	13	4	2	8	4	0	.667	88	97	42	26	1	29	0	1	88	3	2.66
Trax, Great Falls	15	12	6	3	7	3	1	.700	99	82	43	30	2	41	1	2	88	3	2.73
McLaughlin, Great Falls	13	12	4	0	5	5	0	.500	79	80	48	25	1	38	0	1	71	9	2.85
Molina, Billings	18	6	1	1	5	5	4	.500	69	61	28	22	3	23	0	4	51	2	2.87
Layton, Billings	18	8	2	0	5	3	3	.625	76	78	37	28	3	31	0	1	55	4	3.32

Departmental Leaders: G–Pierce, 27; GS–Dempsey, Griffin, 14; CG–Dempsey, 9; ShO–Jones, Trax, 3; W–Dempsey, 14; L–Seiber, Tackitt, 9; Sv–Decker, 9; Pct.–Marsden, 1.000; IP–Dempsey, 114; H–Smith, 116; R–Coleman, 67; ER–McMahon, 53; HR–Smith, 8; BB–McMahon, 65; IBB–Raines, 6; HP–Klawitter, 10; SO–Jones, 115; WP–Pone, 19.

(All Pitchers—Listed Alphabetically)

Pitcher–Club	G.	GS.	CG.	ShO.	W.	L.	Sv.	Pct.	IP.	H.	R.	ER.	HR.	BB.	Int. BB.	HB.	SO.	WP.	ERA.
Aponte, Medicine Hat	4	0	0	0	0	0	0	.000	3	8	10	10	0	4	0	1	2	3	30.00
Baldrick, Calgary*	13	12	2	1	5	2	0	.714	74	95	55	46	7	36	0	0	52	2	5.59
Banach, Great Falls*	9	8	0	0	0	0	0	.000	45	53	34	26	1	24	0	0	32	1	5.20
Bankowski, Idaho Falls*	11	1	0	0	3	1	1	.750	34	36	23	15	1	16	0	2	30	3	3.97
Barba, Billings	15	2	0	0	0	3	0	.000	23	21	20	10	1	21	0	1	16	5	3.91
Bashian, Great Falls*	9	0	0	0	3	0	0	1.000	19	11	5	6	0	10	0	0	23	5	2.84
Bastian, Idaho Falls	13	13	4	2	8	4	0	.667	88	97	42	26	1	29	0	1	88	3	2.66
Bautista, Great Falls	8	2	0	0	1	0	0	.000	11	20	17	16	0	14	0	1	4	2	13.09
Befort, Helena	15	4	0	0	1	2	0	.333	45	54	27	15	1	16	0	2	34	6	3.00
Boger, Calgary	5	1	0	0	1	0	0	.500	15	17	14	9	0	9	0	1	8	1	5.40

Pitcher–Club	G.	GS.	CG.	ShO.	W.	L.	Sv.	Pct.	IP.	H.	R.	ER.	HR.	BB.	Int. BB.	HB.	SO.	WP.	ERA.
Bowden, Billings*	13	12	2	0	8	3	0	.727	72	72	35	27	6	20	0	1	48	0	3.38
Brodeur, Calgary*	16	0	0	0	1	4	0	.000	29	16	8	7	1	19	0	1	34	3	2.17
Buckmier, Great Falls	9	9	1	0	5	1	0	.833	54	51	25	21	0	19	0	4	42	4	3.50
Burroughs, Idaho Falls*	10	0	0	0	0	0	0	.000	30	31	23	18	2	21	3	2	23	8	5.40
Campbell, Medicine Hat	16	8	0	0	0	7	0	.000	36	63	47	35	2	32	0	1	25	4	8.75
Canavan, Billings*	20	0	0	0	3	0	0	1.000	36	41	29	25	0	31	1	2	30	6	6.25
Cavner, Butte*	25	0	0	0	4	2	4	.667	37	41	19	10	0	20	2	0	30	5	2.43
Chaney, Helena	12	0	0	0	0	1	0	.000	32	29	16	10	2	22	0	2	18	5	2.81
Childress, Helena	15	8	0	3	4	0	0	.429	68	79	32	19	1	20	0	0	43	7	2.51
Cicotte, Butte	21	4	0	0	2	0	0	.000	43	46	43	32	1	48	0	1	43	13	6.70
Coleman, Butte*	17	3	0	0	1	3	1	.250	55	79	67	44	2	45	2	2	55	12	7.20
Cook, Helena	20	0	0	0	1	0	1	1.000	27	28	15	11	2	16	0	0	21	5	3.67
Culbert, Idaho Falls	2	0	0	0	0	0	0	.000	6	14	8	4	1	2	0	0	4	0	6.00
Decker, Helena	25	0	0	0	4	1	9	.800	42	23	10	10	2	12	1	0	68	4	2.14
DeLeon, Lethbridge	15	0	0	0	1	2	4	.333	29	28	10	8	0	9	0	0	26	0	2.48
Dempsey, Great Falls	15	14	9	2	14	1	0	.933	114	96	33	20	2	27	0	1	109	1	1.58
Dente, Lethbridge	17	1	0	0	3	1	1	.750	33	35	19	11	0	17	1	2	29	2	3.00
Effrig, Butte	8	4	0	0	2	1	1	.667	32	27	24	18	3	20	1	1	33	10	5.06
Elliott, Butte	13	7	0	0	4	3	2	.571	48	42	19	13	0	18	1	0	52	6	2.44
Emery, Calgary	8	4	0	0	1	2	0	.333	31	38	28	24	2	17	0	0	23	2	6.97
Ender, Billings	15	9	0	0	6	1	0	.857	75	71	26	20	1	31	2	2	60	4	2.40
Erickson, Great Falls*	7	7	0	0	3	1	0	.750	29	22	28	13	1	37	0	1	23	5	4.03
Felt, Lethbridge*	4	3	0	0	1	0	0	1.000	13	18	10	9	1	8	0	0	16	1	6.23
Finch, Calgary*	17	0	0	0	1	2	4	.333	35	42	28	15	3	16	0	0	27	4	3.34
Fowlkes, Great Falls	4	2	1	1	2	0	0	1.000	19	18	5	5	0	5	0	1	22	0	2.37
Frank, Medicine Hat	23	1	0	0	1	3	1	.250	40	43	35	27	4	30	1	1	29	2	6.08
B. Gallo, Great Falls*	21	1	0	0	4	2	1	.667	34	30	33	18	2	39	2	0	37	7	4.76
R. Gallo, Butte*	9	0	0	0	1	2	2	.333	15	15	8	4	0	9	0	0	17	4	2.40
Ghelfi, Helena	12	11	2	1	3	2	0	.600	61	74	41	31	5	17	0	5	43	3	4.57
Goffena, Medicine Hat	10	0	0	0	0	0	0	.000	8	12	15	7	0	11	0	1	3	1	7.88
Gray, Calgary*	8	0	0	0	0	1	0	.000	14	20	11	8	1	7	1	0	13	0	5.14
Griffin, Helena*	14	14	0	0	6	7	0	.462	74	70	50	46	3	44	0	4	53	4	5.59
Haggerty, Butte*	3	0	0	0	0	0	0	.000	3	6	7	1	1	5	0	0	1	3	3.00
Hammond, Idaho Falls	12	1	0	0	0	2	1	1.000	30	40	24	20	3	19	0	1	19	2	6.00
Hawkins, Medicine Hat*	23	1	0	0	2	2	1	.500	42	54	28	22	4	8	0	1	37	1	4.71
Herberholz, Butte	10	8	2	0	3	4	0	.429	55	64	48	37	4	26	0	4	42	7	6.05
Huber, Calgary	17	7	0	0	2	3	1	.400	60	70	43	33	2	27	0	0	49	2	4.95
Hutchinson, Helena	9	5	0	0	1	4	0	.200	19	20	32	24	4	40	0	0	9	6	11.37
Hysaw, Great Falls	14	2	0	0	3	1	0	.750	38	35	29	22	1	34	1	2	31	6	5.21
Jensen, Butte	16	1	0	0	1	2	0	.333	26	27	25	18	1	19	3	0	23	5	6.23
C. Jones, Lethbridge	14	13	6	3	8	2	1	.800	96	72	26	20	4	33	0	1	115	3	1.88
Kenyon, Lethbridge	4	4	2	0	4	0	0	1.000	29	29	8	6	1	8	0	0	19	0	1.86
Klawitter, Lethbridge*	13	12	0	0	5	4	0	.556	66	69	50	30	4	47	0	10	61	6	4.09
Knight, Helena	11	6	0	0	1	2	0	.333	31	39	35	22	0	26	0	2	25	1	6.39
Kollmann, Butte	15	1	0	0	1	1	1	.500	25	35	27	21	3	10	1	2	15	3	7.56
Layton, Billings	18	8	2	0	5	3	3	.625	76	78	37	28	3	31	0	1	55	4	3.32
Lepson, Butte	4	4	0	0	0	2	0	.000	13	31	28	24	2	16	1	2	4	0	16.62
Lesch, Lethbridge	5	1	0	0	1	0	1	1.000	10	8	11	6	2	10	0	1	8	1	5.40
Lloyd, Lethbridge	10	8	0	0	5	1	0	.833	53	58	31	24	2	18	0	2	42	2	4.08
Lochner, Billings*	11	8	1	1	4	1	0	.800	45	45	28	26	4	20	1	1	58	1	5.20
Marsden, Lethbridge	15	10	4	0	7	0	2	1.000	82	82	33	22	0	16	1	0	81	6	2.41
Matias, Butte	14	0	0	0	1	1	0	.500	17	28	22	17	1	6	2	0	20	0	9.00
McAnally, Helena*	12	4	0	0	1	2	0	.333	35	31	35	23	1	41	0	1	28	4	5.91
D. McDonald, G. Falls*	10	0	0	0	1	0	0	.000	21	29	22	19	2	12	1	0	19	1	8.14
M. McDonald, Great Falls	18	0	0	0	1	2	3	.333	27	38	20	14	0	18	1	1	32	2	4.67
McLaughlin, Great Falls	13	12	4	0	5	5	0	.500	79	80	48	25	1	38	0	1	71	9	2.85
McMahon, Idaho Falls*	13	13	4	0	3	5	0	.375	72	71	60	53	4	65	1	3	77	7	6.63
McQuade, Lethbridge	14	10	1	0	8	1	0	.889	67	84	45	32	2	41	0	5	39	4	4.30
Meyer, Butte	2	1	0	0	0	2	0	.000	9	6	10	5	0	10	1	1	6	3	5.00
Molina, Billings	18	6	1	1	5	5	4	.500	69	61	28	22	3	23	0	4	51	2	2.87
Money, Helena	15	0	0	0	3	6	1	.333	48	70	48	39	7	23	1	2	25	1	7.31
Montalvo, Lethbridge	14	0	0	0	4	2	0	.667	31	37	21	17	0	16	0	3	18	4	4.94
D. Morris, Butte	12	12	0	0	4	3	0	.571	67	78	42	36	2	52	3	0	39	12	4.84
Musser, Billings	5	0	0	0	0	0	0	.000	7	4	3	3	0	6	0	0	10	2	3.86
Myles, Billings*	10	1	0	0	2	0	1	1.000	16	18	18	15	0	20	0	1	23	7	8.44
Nawrocki, Medicine Hat	19	1	1	1	1	6	0	.143	64	66	44	29	4	42	2	1	56	5	4.08
Nay, Calgary	1	0	0	0	0	0	0	.000	3	3	2	1	0	0	0	0	1	0	9.00
Olivas, Great Falls	11	1	0	0	2	1	2	.667	26	26	8	5	1	8	1	2	21	0	1.73
Orlich, Butte	10	9	1	0	1	2	0	.333	40	52	36	26	3	21	0	1	30	4	5.85
Pallas, Butte	1	0	0	0	0	0	0	.000	0	1	1	1	0	1	0	0	1	0	.....
Pangborn, Idaho Falls	17	1	0	0	2	2	1	.500	41	45	20	13	3	20	2	0	33	3	2.85
Parrott, Butte	12	9	0	0	4	3	0	.571	53	61	29	24	2	29	1	2	40	4	4.08
Patterson, Medicine Hat	8	5	0	0	0	4	0	.000	24	36	32	20	1	18	0	2	16	5	7.50
Pettibone, Billings	14	11	1	1	2	6	0	.250	57	56	42	37	1	39	1	4	42	9	5.84
Pierce, Medicine Hat*	27	0	0	0	3	2	3	.600	38	50	29	22	3	16	2	1	44	5	5.21

Pitcher—Club	G.	GS.	CG.	ShO.	W.	L.	Sv.	Pct.	IP.	H.	R.	ER.	HR.	Int. BB.	BB.	HB.	SO.	WP.	ERA.
Pone, Butte	17	7	0	0	2	7	0	.222	47	46	52	39	2	59	0	6	57	19	7.47
Powers, Calgary	6	2	0	0	0	0	0	.000	15	11	8	3	0	5	0	0	15	0	1.80
Priessman, Calgary	16	3	0	0	1	4	1	.200	43	39	25	22	3	21	1	2	28	3	4.60
Rahmer, Medicine Hat*	18	0	0	0	1	0	0	1.000	27	20	25	13	0	45	1	3	31	11	4.33
Raines, Billings	23	0	0	0	2	2	3	.500	41	38	23	20	0	25	6	1	44	5	4.39
Ray, Idaho Falls	8	3	0	0	3	1	0	.750	19	29	30	18	1	16	0	0	9	4	8.53
Reade, Lethbridge	19	0	0	0	3	2	7	.600	29	20	15	7	1	27	1	1	36	1	2.17
Rehmert, Calgary*	6	0	0	0	0	1	1	.000	11	11	9	9	2	7	0	1	4	0	7.36
Robins, Idaho Falls	9	4	0	0	1	0	0	1.000	34	36	24	17	0	13	2	1	25	8	4.50
Rodriguez, Helena	13	2	2	0	4	2	0	.667	51	47	19	12	0	19	1	0	47	2	2.12
Roeder, Calgary	1	1	0	0	0	0	0	.000	4	5	4	4	1	5	0	0	2	0	9.00
Roen, Idaho Falls*	14	12	4	1	6	4	1	.600	82	65	44	36	2	46	2	1	77	9	3.95
Rooks, Medicine Hat*	16	0	0	0	0	2	2	.000	30	30	20	15	0	11	4	0	20	1	4.50
Rosenlund, Medicine Hat	13	0	0	0	0	0	0	.000	20	25	16	10	2	13	0	1	13	3	4.50
Roy, Calgary	13	7	0	0	1	8	1	.111	49	62	43	32	7	17	1	0	39	5	5.88
Saatzer, Idaho Falls	12	10	2	0	2	8	0	.200	48	67	52	44	1	40	0	3	33	1	8.25
St. Claire, Calgary	21	4	0	0	5	7	0	.417	57	65	36	27	2	23	0	0	51	3	4.26
St. John, Calgary*	9	8	0	0	3	2	0	.600	34	39	34	27	2	36	0	1	31	8	7.15
Salgueiro, Billings	14	8	0	0	2	1	1	.667	43	40	24	17	3	34	2	2	27	5	7.12
Schneider, Idaho Falls	24	3	1	0	3	6	7	.333	62	71	33	25	3	31	2	2	73	7	3.63
Seiber, Medicine Hat	13	12	1	0	3	9	0	.250	69	72	53	33	5	47	5	0	65	7	4.30
Shipanoff, Medicine Hat	8	8	0	0	1	4	0	.200	36	49	37	31	6	23	0	1	19	0	7.75
Skaggs, Idaho Falls	3	1	0	0	0	2	0	.000	4	7	7	7	1	4	1	0	1	0	15.75
S. Smith, Medicine Hat	15	13	2	0	4	6	0	.400	86	116	63	44	8	24	2	5	64	0	4.60
Steinbach, Idaho Falls*	9	1	0	0	0	1	0	.000	10	22	19	11	2	8	0	2	9	1	9.90
Steverson, Helena	12	0	0	0	2	0	0	1.000	26	34	13	8	3	10	0	0	21	2	2.77
Stubberfield, Calgary	15	11	1	0	3	6	1	.333	71	73	38	32	7	35	1	1	45	5	4.06
Sylvia, Idaho Falls	7	7	3	0	3	0	0	1.000	53	55	31	18	1	20	0	6	57	5	3.06
Tackitt, Medicine Hat	13	12	0	0	0	9	0	.000	66	77	56	31	6	44	2	1	36	3	4.23
G. Terry, Lethbridge*	12	4	0	0	0	1	1	.000	22	29	17	15	2	24	0	0	21	7	6.14
Threatt, Billings	18	4	0	0	5	1	5	.833	47	24	15	12	0	25	1	5	79	2	2.30
Trax, Great Falls	15	12	6	3	7	3	1	.700	99	82	43	30	2	41	1	2	88	3	2.73
True, Helena*	13	8	0	0	2	6	0	.250	48	45	40	22	2	32	0	0	35	7	4.13
Valliant, Calgary	1	1	0	0	0	0	0	.000	2	4	4	4	1	4	0	0	1	0	18.00
Vega, Calgary	12	8	0	0	0	6	0	.000	44	44	33	25	4	30	0	2	42	4	5.11
Wise, Lethbridge	14	4	0	0	2	2	0	.500	42	44	19	16	1	14	0	3	26	2	3.43

BALKS—Coleman, Hysaw, Pone, Saatzer, 3 each; Bowden, Morris, Priessman, Raines, Rodriguez, Schneider, Stubberfield, Vega, 2 each; Baldrick, Barba, Bashian, Buckmier, Childress, Effrig, Ender, Erickson, Felt, Finch, B. Gallo, Ghelfi, Griffin, Hammond, McMahon, McQuade, Molina, Rahmer, Ray, Reade, Rooks, St. Claire, St. John, Salgueiro, Threatt, 1 each.

COMBINATION SHUTOUTS—Layton-Lochner, Salgueiro-Canavan-Layton, Threatt-Molina, Billings; Elliott-Gallo, Elliott-Kollmann-Pone, Butte; Powers-St. Claire-Brodeur, Stubberfield-St. Claire, Calgary; Befort-Decker, Childress-Steverson, Hutchinson-Money, Helena; Bastian-Schneider, Idaho Falls; Klawitter-Marsden, Lethbridge.

NO-HIT GAMES—None.

Futility Record for Medicine Hat

The Medicine Hat Blue Jays set a Pioneer League record for futility when they lost their 19th consecutive game August 26.

Earlier in the season, the Lethbridge Dodgers won 19 in a row, also a league record.

How to Win a Batting Title . . . Or Lose One

Toledo's Dave Engle and Pawtucket's Wade Boggs were almost dead even in their battle for the International League batting title. And their teams squared off in the season's Labor Day finale.

Both batters went 1-for-4, with Engle winning the batting title by a .3067 to .3062 margin. But it wasn't that simple.

With Toledo ahead 6-1 after 8½ innings and Boggs due to bat fourth in the bottom of the ninth, the Pawtucket hitsmith could have stayed in the dugout and won the crown.

Knowing the only way their teammate Engle could win the title, the Toledo players had reliever Wally Sarmiento purposely walk light-hitting Ray Boyer with two out and Boggs on deck.

Turnabout being fair play, Boyer took off for second base in an attempt to be thrown out to end the game. No throw came from catcher Ray Smith. Another attempt by Boyer to be retired followed and again there was no throw. When Boyer raced for home, Sarmiento sent a throw to the screen.

Boggs then grounded out to first base to end the game and Engle had won the batting title by the slimmest of margins.

Tulsa Scored Three Runs on a Fly

It may not have been the strangest play of the season, but at least it was close when Tulsa stole three runs on a fly in its 7-1 decision over Jackson in a Texas League contest July 3.

With the bases loaded, Ron Gooch lofted a fly to right fielder Archie Amerson. Mike Jirschele raced home from third, colliding with catcher Stan Hough. Amerson's throw was off line and he was charged with an error when the ball bounced away, and George Wright scored from second. Pitcher Tom Thurberg had been backing up Hough and, after picking up the ball on Amerson's throw, he threw wildly, hitting on-deck batter Phil Klimas. That allowed Mel Barrow, who had started on first base, to trot home with the third run.

Pitching Instructor Shows by Example

Walla Walla of the Northwest League was so short of pitchers in 1980 that San Diego's organizational pitching coach Jim Zerilla was placed on the active list.

Zerilla, who figured he would be used only in short relief, entered a game against Salem in the ninth inning and worked nine frames to earn the 17-inning victory. The last time Zerilla, 36, had appeared in a professional game was with Mankato (Northern League) in 1967.

Brunansky Hit Four Homers in Row

El Paso center fielder Tom Brunansky slammed four consecutive homers and drove in nine runs to lead the Diablos to a 19-9 romp past Midland June 18. The four straight homers tied several Texas League and club records.

Brunansky connected for a two-run homer in the first inning, a solo shot in the second and three-run smashes in the fourth and fifth.

1981 N. L. Eastern Division Slate ...

1981	EAST					
	AT CHICAGO	**AT MONTREAL**	**AT NEW YORK**	**AT PHILADELPHIA**	**AT PITTSBURGH**	**AT ST. LOUIS**
CHICAGO		April 14, 15, 16 June 26*, 27*, **28** Sept. 18*, 19, **20**	May 29*, 30, **31** June 29*, 30* July 1*, 2 Sept. 30*, Oct.1*	April 17*, 18*, **19** Aug. 4*, 5*, 6* Oct. 2*, 3*, **4**	June 2*, 3*, 4* July 10*, 11*, **12-12** Sept. 28*, 29*	April 20, 21, 22 Aug. 7*, 8*, **9** Sept. 7*, 8*, 9*
MONTREAL	May 22, 23, **24** July 7, 8, 9 Sept. 11, 12, **13**		April 18, **19-19** Aug. 4*, 5*, 6 Oct. 2*, 3, **4**	April 27*, 28*, 29* July 3*, 4*, **5** Sept. 7*, 8*, 9*	April 9, 11, **12** June 29*, 30* Aug. 12*, 13* Sept. 30*, Oct. 1*	June 1*, 2*, 3*, 4 July 10*, 11*, **12** Sept. 28*, 29*
NEW YORK	April 9, 11, **12** Aug. 10, 11, 12, 13 Sept. 23, 24	April 24, 25, **26** June 23*, 24*, 25* Sept. 25*, 26, **27**		June 1*, 2*, 3* July 10*, 11 (Tn), **12** Sept. 28*, 29*	April 22*, 23 July 3*, 4, **5-5** Sept. 7*, 8*, 9*	May 22*, 23*, **24** July 7*, 8*, 9* Sept. 11*, 12*, **13**
PHILADELPHIA	April 24, 25, **26** June 23, 24, 25 Sept. 25, 26, **27**	April 20, 21, 22 Aug. 7*, 8, **9-9** Sept. 21*, 22*	May 25, 26*, 27* Aug. 14*, 15, **16** Sept. 15*, 16*, 17*		May 22*, 23*, **24** July 7*, 8*, 9* Sept. 11*, 12*, **13**	April 11, **12** June 29*, 30 (Tn) July 1*, 2 Sept. 23*, 24*
PITTSBURGH	May 25, 26, 27, 28 Aug. 14, 15, **16** Sept. 15, 16	May 29*, 30, **31** July 1*, 2* Aug. 10*, 11* Sept. 23*, 24*	April 28*, 29*, 30* Aug. 7*, 8, **9-9** Sept. 21*, 22*	April 13*, 15*, 16* June 26*, 27, **28** Sept. 18*, 19*, **20**		May 8*, 9*, **10** July 16*, 17*, 18 Sept. 25*, 26, **27**
ST. LOUIS	April 28, 29 July 3, 4-4, **5**, 6 Sept. 21, 22	May 25*, 26*, 27* Aug. 14*, 15*, **16** Sept. 15*, 16*, 17*	April 14, 15, 16 June 26*, 27*, **28** Sept. 18*, 19, **20**	May 29*, 30*, **31** Aug. 10*, 11*, 12*, 13 Sept. 30*, Oct. 1*	April 24*, 25, **26** Aug. 3*, 4*, 5* Oct. 2*, 3*, **4**	
ATLANTA	May 1, 2, **3** July 16, 17, 18	June 9*, 10*, 11* Aug. 28*, 29*, **30**	June 15 (Tn), 16* Sept. 4*, 5, **6**	June 12*, 13*, **14** Aug. 24*, 25*, 26*	May 19*, 20* July 31* Aug. 1*, **2-2**	May 4*, 5*, 6*, 7 July **19**, 20*
CINCINNATI	May 19, 20, 21 July 31 Aug. 1, **2**	June 12*, 13, **14** Aug. 25*, 26*, 27*	June 9*, 10*, 11* Aug. 28*, 29*, **30**	June 15*, 16* Sept. 3*, 4*, 5*, **6**	May 15*, 16, **17** July 27*, 28*, 29*	May 1*, 2, **3** July 21*, 22*, 23*
HOUSTON	May 4, 5, 6, 7 July **19**, 20	June 15*, 16* Sept. 3*, 4*, **5**, 6	June 12*, 13*, **14** Aug. 25*, 26*, 27	June 8*, 9*, 10* Aug. 21*, 22, **23***	May 1*, 2*, **3** June 23*, 24*, 25*	May 19*, 20*, 21 July 31* Aug. 1*, **2**
LOS ANGELES	June 5, 6, **7** Aug. 17, 18, 19	May 1*, 2, 3, 4* July 16*, 17*	May 8*, 9, **10** July 21*, 22*, 23	May 5*, 6*, 7* July 18*, **19**, 20*	June 12*, 13, **14** Aug. 24*, 25*, 26	June 9*, 10*, 11* July 21*, 22*, **23**
SAN DIEGO	June 12, 13, **14** Aug. 24, 25, 26	May 5*, 6*, 7* July 18*, **19**, 20*	May 1*, 2, **3-3** July 16, 17*	May 8*, 9*, **10** July 21*, 22*, 23	June 8*, 9*, 10* Aug. 21*, 22*, **23**	June 5*, 6*, **7** Aug. 17*, 18*, 19*
SAN FRANCISCO	June 9, 10, 11 Aug. 21, 22, **23**	May 8*, 9, **10-10** July 21*, 22*	May 5*, 6*, 7* July 18*, **19**, 20*	May 1*, 2*, **3**, 4* July 16*, 17*	June 5*, 6*, **7** Aug. 17*, 18*, 19*	June 12*, 13*, **14** Aug. 24*, 25*, 26
	13 SUNDAYS 0 NIGHT GAMES 2 HOLIDAYS (Memorial Day) (July 4)	**13 SUNDAYS** 50 NIGHT GAMES 2 HOLIDAYS (St. John de Baptiste) (Dominion Day)	**13 SUNDAYS** 47 NIGHT GAMES 1 HOLIDAY (Memorial Day)	**13 SUNDAYS** 66 NIGHT GAMES 2 HOLIDAYS (July 4) (Labor Day)	**13 SUNDAYS** 56 NIGHT GAMES 2 HOLIDAYS (July 4) (Labor Day)	**13 SUNDAYS** 55 NIGHT GAMES 1 HOLIDAY (Labor Day)

* NIGHT GAME

HEAVY BLACK FIGURES DENOTE SUNDAY
NIGHT GAME: Any game starting after 5:00 p.m.

And Complete Western Schedules

1981	WEST					
	AT ATLANTA	AT CINCINNATI	AT HOUSTON	AT LOS ANGELES	AT SAN DIEGO	AT SAN FRANCISCO
CHICAGO	May 8*, 9*, **10** July 21*, 22*, 23*	May 12*, 13*, 14* July 24*, 25*, **26**	May 15*, 16*, **17** July 27*, 28*, 29*	June 15*, 16* Aug. 27*, 28*, 29*, **30**	June 19*, 20*, **21** Aug. 31* Sept. 1*, 2*	June 17, 18 Sept. 3, 4*, 5, **6**
MONTREAL	June 17*, 18* Aug. 21*, 22 (Tn), **23**	June 5*, 6*, **7** Aug. 31* Sept. 1*, 2*	June 19*, 20*, **21** Aug. 17*, 18*, 19*	May 12*, 13*, 14* July 24*, 25*, **26**	May 18*, 19*, 20* July 31* Aug. 1*, **2**	May 15*, 16, **17** July 28*, 29, 30
NEW YORK	June 19*, 20*, **21** Aug. 18*, 19*, 20*	Aug. 17*, 18* Aug. 21*, 22*, **23**, 24*	June 5*, 6*, **7*** Aug. 31* Sept. 1*, 2*	May 15*, 16*, **17** July 27*, 28*, 29*	May 12*, 13*, 14 July 24*, 25*, **26**	May 18*, 19*, 20 July 31* Aug. 1, **2**
PHILADELPHIA....	June 5*, 6, **7** Aug. 31* Sept. 1*, 2*	April 8 June 19*, 20*, **21** Aug. 18*, 19*	June 17*, 18* Aug. 28*, 29 (Tn), **30***	May 18*, 19*, 20* July 31* Aug. 1, **2**	May 15*, 16*, **17** July 27*, 28*, 29*	May 12*, 13, 14 July 24*, 25, **26**
PITTSBURGH	May 11*, 12*, 13* July 24*, 25*, **26**	May 5*, 6*, 7* July **19-19**, 20*	April 17*, 18, **19** July 21*, 22*, 23*	June 19*, 20*, **21** Aug. 31* Sept. 1*, 2*	June 17*, 18 Sept. 3, 4*, 5*, **6**	June 15*, 16* Aug. 27*, 28*, 29, **30**
ST. LOUIS	May 15*, 16*, **17** July 27*, 28*, 29*	April 17*, 18, **19** June 23*, 24, 25*	May 12*, 13*, 14* July 24*, 25*, **26***	June 17*, 18* Sept. 3*, 4*, 5*, **6**	June 15*, 16* Aug. 27*, 29 (Tn), **30**	June 19*, 20, **21-21** Sept. 1*, 2
ATLANTA		April 21*, 22 June 26 (Tn), 27*, **28** Oct. 2*, 3, **4**	April 13*, 14*, 15* July 10*, 11*, **12*** Sept. 22*, 23*, 24*	June 1*, 2*, 3* Aug. 13*, 14*, 15*, **16** Sept. 16*, 17*	May 29*, 30*, **31** Aug. 10*, 11*, 12* Sept. 18*, 19, **20**	April 23, 24*, 25, **26-26** June 23*, 24 Sept. 14*, 15*
CINCINNATI	April 10*, 11*, **12** July 7*, 8*, 9* Sept. 25*, 26*, **27**		April 23*, 24*, 25, **26** June 29*, 30* July 1* Sept. 14*, 15	May 29*, 30, **31** Aug. 10*, 11*, 12* Sept. 18*, 19*, **20**	April 13*, 14*, 15* July 3*, 4*, **5** Sept. 21*, 22*, 23*	June 1*, 2*, 3* Aug. 7*, 8, **9-9** Sept. 16*, 17*
HOUSTON	April 28*, 29*, 30* July 3*, 4*, **5** Sept. 7*, 8*, 9*	May 8*, 9, **10**, 11* July 16*, 17*, 18 Sept. 30*, Oct. 1		April 9, 11, **12** July 7*, 8*, 9 Oct. 2*, 3, **4**	June 2*, 3*, 4 Aug. 13, 14*, 15*, **16** Sept. 16*, 17*	May 29*, 30, **31** Aug. 10*, 11*, 12 Sept. 18*, 19, **20**
LOS ANGELES.....	May 25*, 26*, 27*, 28* Aug. 7*, 8*, **9** Sept. 28*, 29*	May 22*, 23, **24-24** Aug. 4*, 5* Sept. 11*, 12*, **13**	April 20*, 21*, 22* June 26*, 27*, **28** Sept. 25*, 26, **27**		April 17*, 18*, **19** June 29*, 30* July 1*, **2** Sept. 14*, 15*	April 13*, 14*, 15* July 3*, 4, **5** Sept. 22*, 23*, 24*
SAN DIEGO........	May 22*, 23*, **24** Aug. 4*, 5*, 6* Sept. 11*, 12*, **13**	April 28*, 29*, 30* July 10*, 11*, **12** Sept. 7*, 8*, 9	May 25*, 26*, 27* Aug. 7*, 8 (Tn), **9** Sept. 28*, 29*	April 23*, 24*, 25*, **26** June 22*, 23*, 24* Sept. 30*, Oct. 1*		April 9, 10*, 11, **12** July 7*, 8 Oct. 2*, 3, **4**
SAN FRANCISCO.	April 17*, 18*, **19** June 30 (Tn) July 1*, 2* Sept. 30*, Oct. 1*	May 25*, 26*, 27*, 28 Aug. 14*, 15*, **16** Sept. 28*, 29*	May 22*, 23*, **24*** Aug. 3*, 4*, 5* Sept. 11*, 12*, **13**	April 27*, 28*, 29* July 7*, 8*, 9* Sept. 7*, 8*, 9*	April 20*, 21*, 22* June 26*, 27*, **28** Sept. 25*, 26*, **27**	
	13 SUNDAYS **67 NIGHT GAMES** **3 HOLIDAYS** (Memorial Day) (July 4, Labor Day)	**13 SUNDAYS** **55 NIGHT GAMES** **2 HOLIDAYS** (Memorial Day) (Labor Day)	**13 SUNDAYS** **70 NIGHT GAMES** **1 HOLIDAY** (Memorial Day)	**13 SUNDAYS** **63 NIGHT GAMES** **1 HOLIDAY** (Labor Day)	**13 SUNDAYS** **62 NIGHT GAMES** **1 HOLIDAY** (July 4)	**13 SUNDAYS** **38 NIGHT GAMES** **1 HOLIDAY** (July 4)

JULY 14—ALL STAR GAME AT CLEVELAND

AUGUST 3—HALL OF FAME GAME AT COOPERSTOWN, NY (Cincinnati vs. Oakland)

1981 A. L. Eastern Division Slate . . .

1981	AT MILWAUKEE	AT DETROIT	AT CLEVELAND	AT TORONTO	AT BALTIMORE	AT NEW YORK	AT BOSTON
SEATTLE	June 15*, 16*, 17 / July 24*, 25, **26**	May 12*, 13*, 14* / July 31* / Aug. 1, **2**	May 20*, 21* / Aug. 27*, 28*, 29*, **30**	June 30* / July 1 (Tn) / Sept. 10*, 11*, 12	June 19*, 20*, **21** / Aug. 31* / Sept. 1*	May 15*, 16*, **17** / July 27*, 28*, 29	May 18*, 19* / Sept. 3*, 4*, 5, **6**
OAKLAND	May 15*, 16*, **17** / July 27*, 28*, 29*	June 16*, 17*, 18* / July 24*, 25, **26**	June 19*, 20*, **21** / Aug. 31* / Sept. 1*, 2*	May 29*, 30, **31** / Sept. 21*, 22*, 23*	May 18*, 19* / Sept. 3*, 4*, 5*, **6**	May 12*, 13*, 14* / July 31* / Aug. 1, **2**	May 20*, 21* / Aug. 27*, 28*, 29, **30**
CALIFORNIA	May 12*, 13*, 14 / July 31* / Aug. 1*, **2**	May 15*, 16, **17** / July 27*, 28*, 29*	May 18*, 19* / Sept. 3*, 4*, 5, **6**	June 1*, 2*, 3* / Sept. 18*, 19, **20**	May 20*, 21* / Aug. 27*, 28*, 29*, **30**	June 16*, 17*, 18* / July 24*, 25*, **26**	June 19*, 20, **21** / Aug. 31* / Sept. 1*, 2*
TEXAS	June 10*, 11* / Aug. 27*, 28*, 29, **30**	May 18*, 19*, 20* / Aug. 21*, 22, **23**	April 24*, 25, **26** / July 7*, 8*, 9*	June 12*, 13, **14**, 15* / Aug. 24, 25	June 16*, 17*, 18* / July 31* / Aug. 1*, **2**	April 9, 11, **12** / Aug. 10*, 11*, 12	April 20, 21, 22 / July 10*, 11, **12**
KANSAS CITY	April 24*, 25, **26** / July 6*, 7*, 8	June 12*, 13, **14** / Aug. 24*, 25*, 26*	April 28*, 29* / Aug. 14*, 15, **16-16**	June 10*, 11* / Aug. 27, 28, 29, **30**	April 10, **12** / July 10*, 11*, 12*, 13*	May 18*, 19*, 20* / July 21*, 22, **23**	May 15*, 16, **17** / July 27*, 28*, 29*
MINNESOTA	May 19*, 20*, 21 / Aug. 21*, 22*, **23**	May 5*, 6, **7** / July 18*, 19*	June 16*, 17*, 18* / July 31* / Aug. 1*, 2*	June 26*, 27, **28** / Sept. 14*, 15*, 16*	May 4*, 5*, 6* / July 18*, 19**, 20*	May 19*, 20*, **21** / Aug. 24*, 25*, 26*	April 30* / May 1*, 2, **3** / July 16*, 17*
CHICAGO	June 12*, 13*, **14** / Aug. 24*, 25*, 26*	April 24, 25, **26** / July 6*, 8*, 9*	April 30* / May 1*, 2, **3** / July 16*, 17*	May 18, 19*, 20* / July 21, 22, 23	April 27*, 28*, 29* / Aug. 14*, 15*, **16**	May 5*, 6*, **7** / Aug. 17*, 18*, 19*	April 30* / May 1*, 2, **3** / July 16*, 17*
MILWAUKEE		June 1*, 2*, 3* / Sept. 25*, 26, **27**	April 11, **12** / Aug. 10*, 11 (Tn), 12*, 13*	April 20, 21*, 22* / Aug. 14*, 15, **16-16**	June 22*, 23*, 24*, 25* / Sept. 18*, 19*, **20**	July 3*, 4*, **5** / Sept. 7, 8, 9*	May 29*, 30, **31** / Sept. 21*, 22*, 23*
DETROIT	May 25, 26*, 27*, 28 / Oct. 2*, 3, **4**		June 29*, 30* / July 1* / Sept. 18*, 19, **20**	April 16*, 17, 18, **19** / Aug. 3, 4*, 5*	May 29*, 30*, **31** / Sept. 21*, 22*, 23*	April 20*, 21*, 22* / July 10*, 11, **12**	June 26*, 27, **28** / Sept. 14*, 15*, 16*, 17*
CLEVELAND	April 16, 18, **19** / Aug. 3*, 4*, 5	June 22*, 23*, 24 (Tn) / Sept. 11*, 12, **13**		May 5*, 6*, 7* / July 18, **19**, 20*	July 10*, 11*, **12** / Sept. 7*, 8*, 9*, 10*	May 22*, 23*, **24** / Sept. 21*, 22*, 23*	May 25*, 26*, 27* / Sept. 24*, 25*, 26, **27**
TORONTO	April 27, 28, 29 / July 10*, 11*, **12**	April 9, 11, **12** / Aug. 10*, 11*, 12*	May 15*, 16, **17-17** / July 27*, 28*, 29*		April 30* / May 1*, 2, **3** / July 16 (Tn), 17*	April 23*, 24*, 25, **26** / July 7*, 8*, 9*	June 16*, 17*, 18* / July 31* / Aug. 1, **2**
BALTIMORE	June 30* / July 1*, 2* / Sept. 11*, 12*, **13**	May 22*, 23, **24-24** / Sept. 28*, 29*, 30*	July 3*, 4, **5-5** / Sept. 15*, 16*	May 12*, 13*, 14* / July 24*, 25, **26**		June 2*, 3*, 4* / July 24*, 25*, 26*, **27**	April 13, 14, 15 / Aug. 6*, 7*, 8, **9**
NEW YORK	June 26*, 27*, **28**, 29* / Sept. 14*, 15*, 16*	April 27*, 28* 29 / Aug. 13*, 14* 15*, **16**	May 29*, 30, **31** / June 1* / Sept. 28*, 29*, 30*	April 13, 15* / Aug. 6*, 7*, 8, **9**	May 25*, 26*, 27* / Oct. 2*, 3*, **4**		June 30* / July 1*, 2* / Sept. 18*, 19, **20**
BOSTON	May 22*, 23, **24-24** / Sept. 28*, 29*, 30*	July 3*, 4*, **5** / Sept. 7*, 8*, 9*	June 2*, 3*, 4* / Oct. 2*, 3, **4**	May 8*, 9, **10**, 11* / July 21*, 22*, 23*	April 25, **26** / July 6*, 7*, 8*, 9*	June 22*, 23*, 24*, 25* / Sept. 11*, 12, **13**	
	80 HOME DATES **50 NIGHTS**	**79 HOME DATES** **53 NIGHTS**	**77 HOME DATES** **55 NIGHTS**	**79 HOME DATES** **45 NIGHTS**	**80 HOME DATES** **67 NIGHTS**	**81 HOME DATES** **59 NIGHTS**	**81 HOME DATES** **48 NIGHTS**

JULY 14—ALL STAR GAME AT CLEVELAND

AUGUST 3—HALL OF FAME GAME AT COOPERSTOWN, NY (Cincinnati vs. Oakland)

And Complete Western Schedules

1981	AT SEATTLE	AT OAKLAND	AT CALIFORNIA	AT TEXAS	AT KANSAS CITY	AT MINNESOTA	AT CHICAGO
WEST							
SEATTLE		April 17*, 18, **19-19** Aug. 4*, 5	April 20*, 21*, 22* June 26*, 27*, **28**	May 29*, 30*, **31*** Sept. 21*, 22*, 23*, 24*	June 1*, 2*, 3* Sept. 25*, 26*, **27**	April 27, 28, 29 Aug. 13*, 14*, 15*, **16**	July 10*, 11, **12-12** Sept. 7, 8*, 9*
OAKLAND	April 24*, 25*, **26** July 6*, 7*, 8*, 9		April 13*, 14*, 15*, 16* Aug. 7*, 8*, **9**	July 3*, 4*, **5** Sept. 14*, 15*, 16*	June 22*, 23*, 24* Oct. 2*, 3*, **4**	April 9, 10, 11, **12** Aug. 10*, 11*, 12*	June 2*, 3*, 4* Sept. 18*, 19, **20**
CALIFORNIA	April 9*, 10*, 11*, **12** Aug. 10*, 11*, 12	April 27*, 28*, 29 Aug. 14*, 15, **16**		June 23*, 24*, 25* Oct. 2*, 3*, **4**	July 9*, 10*, 11, **12** Sept. 7*, 8*, 9*	April 24, 25, **26-26** July 6*, 7*, 8*	May 29*, 30, **31-31** Sept. 29*, 30*
TEXAS	May 22*, 23*, **24** Sept. 28*, 29*, 30*	June 26*, 27, **28-28** Sept. 7, 8*, 9*	June 29*, 30* July 1*, 2* Sept. 11*, 12*, **13**		May 11*, 12*, 13*, 14* July 24*, 25*, **26**	June 2*, 3*, 4 Sept. 25*, 26, **27**	May 15*, 16*, **17** July 27*, 28*, 29*
KANSAS CITY	May 25 (Tn), 26*, 27* Sept. 18*, 19*, **20**	June 29*, 30* July 1*, 2 Sept. 11*, 12, **13**	July 3*, 4*, **5** Sept. 14*, 15*, 16*	April 30* May 1*, 2*, **3** July 16*, 17*		May 29*, 30*, **31** Sept. 28, 29, 30	May 8*, 9*, **10** July 21*, 22 (Tn), 23*
MINNESOTA	April 14*, 15* Aug. 6*, 7*, 8*, **9**	April 20*, 21*, 22 July 10*, 11, **12**	April 17*, 18*, **19** Aug. 3*, 4*, 5*	May 25*, 26*, 27*, 28 Sept. 18*, 19*, **20***	May 22*, 23*, **24** Sept. 21*, 22*, 23*, 24*		June 29*, 30* July 1*, 2 Oct. 2*, 3, **4**
CHICAGO	July 3*, 4*, **5*** Sept. 14*, 15*, 16*	May 25, 26*, 27 Sept. 25*, 26, **27-27**	May 22*, 23*, **24** Sept. 21*, 22*, 23*, 24*	May 5*, 6*, 7* July 18 (Tn), **19*, 20***	June 15*, 16*, 17* July 31* Aug. 1*, **2**	June 23*, 24*, 25 Sept. 11*, 12*, **13**	
MILWAUKEE	May 4*, 5*, 6*, 7* July 18*, **19***	May 8*, 9, **10** July 20*, 21*, 22	April 30* May 1*, 2*, **3** July 16*, 17*	June 19*, 20*, **21** Aug. 17*, 18*, 19*	June 5*, 6*, **7** Aug. 31* Sept. 1*, 2*	June 8*, 9* Sept. 3, 4*, 5, **6**	April 14, 15 Aug. 6*, 7*, 8*, **9**
DETROIT	April 30* May 1*, 2*, **3** July 16*, 17	May 5*, 6*, 7 July 18, **19-19**	May 8*, 9*, **10** July 20*, 21*, 22*	June 8*, 9* Sept. 3*, 4*, 5*, **6**	April 13*, 15* Aug. 6*, 7*, 8*, **9**	June 10*, 11* Aug. 27*, 28*, 29*, **30**	June 19*, 20, **21** Aug. 31* Sept. 1*, 2*
CLEVELAND	June 5*, 6*, **7** Aug. 18*, 19*, 20*	June 12*, 13, **14-14** Aug. 24*, 25	June 8*, 9* 10* Aug. 21*, 22*, **23**	April 14*, 15 Aug. 6*, 7*, 8*, **9***	April 20*, 21*, 22* June 26*, 27*, **28**	May 8*, 9, **10** July 21*, 22*, 23	May 11*, 12*, 13* July 24*, 25*, **26**
TORONTO	June 22*, 23*, 24* Oct. 2*, 3*, **4**	June 22*, 23, **24-24** Sept. 29, 30	May 25*, 26*, 27* Sept. 25, 26, **27**	June 5*, 6*, **7*** Aug. 31* Sept. 1*, 2*	June 19*, 20*, **21** Aug. 17*, 18*, 19*	July 3*, 4*, **5** Sept. 7, 8*, 9*	June 8*, 9* Sept. 3*, 4*, 5*, **6**
BALTIMORE	June 11*, 12*, 13*, **14*** Aug. 24*, 25*	June 9 (Tn), 10 Aug. 21*, 22, **23**	June 5*, 6*, **7** Aug. 18*, 19*, 20*	May 8*, 9*, **10** July 21*, 22*, 23*	April 17*, 18, **19** Aug. 3*, 4*, 5*	May 15*, 16, **17** July 27*, 28*, 29*	April 20*, 21*, 22* June 26*, 27*, **28**
NEW YORK	May 8*, 9*, **10*** July 20*, 21*, 22*	May 1*, 2, **3-3** July 16*, 17*	May 4*, 5*, 6*, 7* July 18*, **19**	April 17*, 18, **19** Aug. 3*, 4*, 5*	June 8*, 9* Sept. 3*, 4*, 5, **6**	June 12*, 13, **14** Aug. 31* Sept. 1*, 2*	June 10*, 11* Aug. 27*, 28*, 29*, **30**
BOSTON	June 8*, 9*, 10* Aug. 21*, 22*, **23***	June 5*, 6, **7** Aug. 18*, 19*, 20*	June 11*, 12*, 13*, **14** Aug. 24*, 25*	April 27*, 28*, 29* Aug. 14*, 15*, **16***	May 4*, 5*, 6* July 18*, **19**, 20*	May 12*, 13*, 14 July 24*, 25, **26**	April 17, 18, **19** Aug. 3*, 4*, 5*
	80 HOME DATES 70 NIGHTS	73 HOME DATES 35 NIGHTS	81 HOME DATES 67 NIGHTS	80 HOME DATES 74 NIGHTS	81 HOME DATES 65 NIGHTS	80 HOME DATES 44 NIGHTS	78 HOME DATES 55 NIGHTS

* NIGHT GAME
NIGHT GAME: Any game starting after 5:00 p.m.
HEAVY BLACK FIGURES DENOTE SUNDAY

Index to Contents

AMERICAN LEAGUE

NATIONAL LEAGUE

1980 Game Scores

1980 Game Scores

NATIONAL ASSOCIATION (MINOR LEAGUE) AVERAGES

Index to Minor League Clubs, Cities

NOTES

NOTES

NOTES

NOTES

NOTES

NOTES

NOTES